WOMEN IN AMERICAN MUSIC

WOMEN IN AMERICAN MUSIC

A Bibliography of Music and Literature

Compiled and Edited by Adrienne Fried Block and Carol Neuls-Bates

Greenwood Press • Westport, Connecticut • London, England

Library of Congress Cataloging in Publication Data

Block, Adrienne Fried.
 Women in American music.

 Includes index.
 1. Women musicians, American—Bibliography.
 2. Music, American—Bibliography. I. Neuls-Bates,
 Carol. II. Title.
 ML128.W7B6   780'.92'2 [B]   79-7722
 ISBN 0-313-21410-7

Library of Congress Catalog Card Number: 79-7722
ISBN: 0-313-21410-7

First published in 1979

Greenwood Press, Inc.
51 Riverside Avenue, Westport, Connecticut 06880

Printed in the United States of America

10 9 8 7 6 5 4 3 2 1

Contents

CONTENTS

Acknowledgments

This bibliography has been compiled under a grant from the National Endowment for the Humanities, with supplementary funding from the Ford Foundation and a donation from Mrs. Roberta Rymer Balfe. We gratefully acknowledge their support. We also wish to thank the administrators of the Graduate Center of the City University of New York, where the project has been housed, for its support and for the use of its computer facilities. Still another organization that has contributed to this project is the College Music Society, first in its support of our application for funding, and second in donating mailing labels.

We also wish to thank our staff, particularly the assistant editors, Joan Deaderisk, who has also been our computer expert, and Ruth Julius, who combined research with editing. They have both worked on the project staff from the beginning and have been not only skillful but resourceful as well. M. Beverly Morse, who compiled the Author-Subject Index to Literature, thereby made an important contribution to the book. Others who have helped are Laurice Jackson, Jo-Ellen Beder, and Elizabeth Wood.

Members of our Advisory Board also have been helpful. Barry S. Brook, Executive Officer of the Ph.D Program in Music at the Graduate Center of the City University of New York, gave the project both support and advice on bibliographic matters. He also gave permission to adapt the computer programs and abstract forms of *RILM abstracts of music literature*, of which he is Editor-in-Chief. Indeed, our use of the *RILM* system accounts for the resemblance between our book and *RILM abstracts*. H. Wiley Hitchcock, Director of the Institute for Studies in American Music at Brooklyn College, also offered useful advice. Other members of the Advisory Board, Vivian Perlis, Eileen Southern, and Judith Tick, have contributed to the book, and participated in a conference held by this project on sources and resources for studies about women in American music. Nancy Van de Vate aided us by identifying contemporary composers, and publicized our bibliography in the newsletter of the League of Women Composers, which she heads. Jean Bowen, Assistant Chief of the Music Division of the New York Public Library, has been especially valuable because she combines her concern for the advancement of women with expert knowledge of music bibliography. Julia Smith, a composer active in the National Federation of Music Clubs, has not only contributed abstracts of music and literature to the bibliography, but has inspired enthusiastic support for the bibliography from other members of the federation.

Many people in addition to those directly associated with the bibliography have aided us. Our neighbors at the Graduate Center, the members of the staff of *RILM abstracts*, have been on hand with advice about everything from computer programs to copy editing. We particularly wish to express our gratitude to Howard Accurso and Dorothy Curzon of the *RILM* staff.

The staffs of many public libraries have generously

assisted us, particularly that of the Music Division of the New York Public Library. In addition to Jean Bowen, we wish to thank Frank C. Campbell, Richard Jackson, Neil M. Ratliff, and Susan T. Sommer, along with the entire staff. Our thanks, too, to Barbara Henry, Wayne Shirley, and the other members of the staff of the Library of Congress's Music Division, to the librarians of the Boston and Chicago public libraries, and to Sam Dennison and the staff of the Fleisher Collection of the Free Library of Philadelphia. We also are grateful to the staffs of the American Music Center, and the American Composers Alliance, both of New York, and to Geraldine Ostrove, head of the library of the New England Conservatory of Music in Boston, for their assistance.

Finally, we wish to thank our contributors, among them composers and their families, librarians, and musicologists. Our particular thanks to major contributors, among whom we number Laurine Elkins-Marlow, Joan Meggett, and Judith Tick, as well as to the compilers of checklists of source materials. Their names can be found at the bottom right-hand corner of the abstracts they contributed.

Guide to the Use of the Bibliography

EXPLANATION OF THE ABSTRACT NUMBER

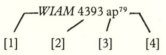

$$WIAM\ 4393\ ap^{79}$$

[1]   [2]   [3]   [4]

[1] Acronym for *Women in American music: a bibliography of music and literature*

[2] The first number is the consecutive abstract number of the entry.

[3] The two letters describe the item abstracted. The first letter places the item in one of five main categories: a (article), b (book), d (dissertation), m (music), and r (review). The second letter indicates the nature of the source. The complete list follows:

articles

ac	article in a collection
ad	article in a dictionary
af	article in a facsimile or reprinted article
an	article in a newspaper
ap	article in a periodical or yearbook
as	article in a symposium or congress report

books

bc	book of collected essays, letters, or documents
bd	book division or chapter
bf	book in facsimile or reprint
bm	book, checklist, monograph, or pamphlet
bp	book, periodical as a whole
bs	book of symposium proceedings or congress report

dissertations

dd	dissertation, doctoral
dm	dissertation, master's or other non-doctoral thesis

music

ma	anthology of music
mc	music in a collection
md	music division, excerpt, or part of an opus
mm	complete musical work, or complete opus
mp	music in a periodical

reviews

rb	review of a book, monograph, or reprint
rf	review of a facsimile or reprint
rm	review of a musical composition
ro	review of an opera or concert
rr	review of a recording

[4] The superscript is the *WIAM* classification number as outlined in the Table of Contents on pp. v-vi. The bibliography is in two large sections: Reference Materials, Collected Works, and General Literature

(categories 01-25), and Music and Literature grouped within 5 time periods (categories 30-79).

USES OF THE ABSTRACT NUMBER

a. Two parts of the complete abstract number can be found in the upper left-hand corner of each entry: the consecutive abstract number [2]; and directly below the abstract number, the 2-letter descriptor [3],

e.g., 4393
      mm

b. The acronym *WIAM* and the consecutive abstract number [2] are enclosed in parentheses and used together in the body of an abstract as a cross-reference, e.g., *(WIAM 4728)*.

c. In *see* references, which are preceded by an arrow, and in the indices, the consecutive number [2] is followed by the 2-letter descriptor [3], and by the superscript [4], e.g., 4393ap[79].

EXPLANATION OF SYMBOLS USED IN MUSIC ABSTRACTS*

3492	consecutive number of abstract
mm	complete musical work or complete opus
Dn	duration of musical work
At	author of text
Tr	translator of text
St	source of text
Lt	language(s) of text
Pf	performing forces (for chamber music)
Ct	contents of work (characteristic titles only)
Rg	recording
Da	date of completion of autograph
La	location of autograph
Li	librettist
Pf	performing forces (for orchestra)
md	music division, excerpt, or part of an opus
Tm	title of musical work from which selection is taken

3492 GIDEON, Miriam. **Rhymes from the hill** (Hillsdale, N.Y.: mm Mobart, 1976) 13 p. (score, parts).
Song cycle. *Dn* 8'. *At* Christian Morgenstern. *Tr* Max Knight. *St* Galgenlieder. *Lt* German, English. *Pf* solo M, cla, mba, vcl. *Ct* Bundeslied der Galgenlieder (Chorus of the gallows gang), Galgenkindes Wiegenlied (Gallows child's lullaby), Die korfsche Uhr (Korf's clock), Palmström's Uhr (Palmstroem's clock), Der Seufzer (The sigh). Also for solo M, pno (*WIAM* 4919). *Rg* Composers Recordings, CRI SD 286.

4793 DU PAGE, Florence. **New world for Nellie** (facsimile of MS on mm rental; Atlanta: Porter, 1965) 117 p. (score).
Ballad chamber opera. *Dn* 60'. *Da* 1960. *La* composer. *At* Rowland Emett. *Li* composer. *Pf* solo TB; choral SATB; 1-1-2-1; 2-1-1-0; tim; per including vib, xyl. *(Composer)*

2601 BAUER, Marion. **Indian pipes, op. 12, no. 2a**. Arr. by Martin md BERNSTEIN (facsimile of autograph at PPFleisher, 1927-28) 25 p. (score, parts).
Dn 3'. *Pf* 2-2enh-2-2, 4-2-3-0, hrp, str. First performed in 1928 by the Chautauqua Symphony Orchestra under the direction of Albert Stoessel. Originally for pno (*WIAM* 2661). *Tm From the New Hampshire woods, op. 12* (*WIAM* 2659).

---

*For a complete list of abbreviations, see pp. xv-xvi; for a list of two-letter descriptors in the abstract number, see p. ix.

ORGANIZATION OF THE MUSIC ENTRIES

Chronological Organization

Music entries are organized, along with literature, in chronological periods (i.e., COLONIAL TIMES TO 1820, 1820 TO 1870, 1870 TO 1920, 1920 TO 1950, 1950 TO 1978).

Organization by Genre

vernacular music

Works listed in categories 31, 41, and 51 (to 1920) include unison or solo hymns, dialect minstrel, temperance, abolition, and suffrage songs, instrumental marches, and dances. By the 1890s, the popular music field was well established, and the publishers, the formats, the covers for pop music had become distinct from either art or parlor music. Therefore, category 51 includes, as well, rags, marches, and songs, among them show tunes and blues.

art music

Music intended for the concert stage, as well as household or parlor music, is included in the category of art music. These distinctions have been made despite the occasional parlor song that became a popular favorite, such as Carrie Jacobs-Bond's *A perfect day* (*WIAM* 1743), because such songs were originally intended as parlor songs and for the concert rather than the popular stage.

Organization by Medium

Within each music category, works are organized by medium of performance, and then listed alphabetically by composer and title of work. The media of performance are defined below:

chamber music

a. Includes works for two or more instruments, or for one or more solo voices plus one or more solo instruments exclusive of accompanying instruments (e.g., piano, organ, or guitar).

b. Performing forces *(Pf)* for chamber music are listed with solo voice(s) first, followed by instruments in score order, each listed separately with a 3-letter abbreviation: *Pf* solo STB, flu, obo, bsn, vln, vla, vel (i.e., soprano, tenor, and bass solo voices, flute, oboe, bassoon, violin, viola, and violoncello).

choral music

a. Includes all works—except stage works—that employ choruses, whether accompanied or unaccompanied.

b. Voice parts for choruses are listed in order from the highest to the lowest voices (e.g., choral SSATTB); if more than two parts are required for any voice

type, numbers are used as well as capital letters (e.g., choral 3S-A-2T-2Bar-B). If vocal soloists also perform, these are listed before the choral forces required. Abbreviations for voices are found on pp. xv-xvi.

c. Accompanying instruments are listed last. If the accompanying instruments are a chamber ensemble, the instruments are listed as described above under chamber music. If a band or orchestra is required, the instruments are listed as described below under orchestral and band music.

electronic music

Includes works employing only electronically produced sound.

mixed media

Includes works requiring a combination of acoustic and non-acoustic sound sources, along with dance movement, or film projections, or other visual elements.

orchestral and band music

a. Includes all works for orchestra or band exclusive of stage and choral works accompanied by orchestra or band.

b. The symbols for orchestral and band music are in score order: woodwinds, brass, timpani, percussion, harp, keyboard, and strings. Solo instruments are identified as such and listed last.

Examples:

2-2-2-2, 4-2-3-1, tim, per, hrp, str. This means: 2 flutes, 2 oboes, 2 clarinets, 2 bassoons, 4 horns, 2 trumpets, 3 trombones, 1 tuba, timpani, percussion, harp and full string section including 1st and 2nd violins, violas, violoncelli, and double basses.

3pic-2-3bcl-2; 0-2-0-0; per including xxyl, cel; str; solo cla. This means: 3 flutes (3rd flute doubling on piccolo), 2 oboes, 2 clarinets, 1 bass clarinet, 2 bassoons, no horns, 2 trumpets, no trombones, no tubas, percussion including xylophone and celeste, strings, and solo clarinet.

pno (cel). This means that one performer plays piano and celeste in alternation.

c. Scoring for band is indicated by the same symbols as for orchestra, except that instruments specific to bands are inserted in the proper choirs using the 3-letter abbreviations also used for chamber music, described above. See also the List of Abbreviations, pp. xv-xvi.

stage works

a. Includes all works for the musical theater: opera, operetta, ballad opera, musical comedy, minstrel and variety shows, dance, incidental music, and film music.

b. Librettists *(Li)* are listed as well as authors of text *(At)*, translators *(Tr)*, source(s) of texts *(St)*, and language(s) of texts *(Lt)*. Where more than one language appears in the score, the original language is listed first.

solo instrumental music

Includes works for a single instrument.

vocal music

a. Includes works for one or more solo voices with or without an accompanying instrument (e.g., piano, organ, or guitar). If the score calls for additional optional instruments, the work is included in this category as well, and optional instruments are listed last under performing forces *(Pf)*.

b. Vocal music published before 1950 frequently appeared in the original key as well as in one or more transpositions to allow for performance by as many singers as possible. Therefore, voice ranges are not specified in music published before 1950, but are designated as solo vocal works under performing forces *(Pf)*, followed by the accompanying instrument.

c. Vocal music published after 1950 was more often intended for a specific voice and less frequently appeared in transposition. Therefore, for later works, the voice type is specified under performing forces *(Pf)*.

EDITORIAL POLICIES

Literature

a. One standard form has been adopted for each woman's name, based on the woman's own usage. However, in the case of a woman who for reasons of status used her husband's name (the most famous being Mrs. H.H.A. Beach), we have supplied the woman's own name (e.g., Amy Cheney Beach). Alternate forms can be found in the indices with cross-references to our standard form.

b. The chronological placement of each subject depends not only upon her life span, but also on the time of greatest activity. If a subject's active life spans two periods or more, all relevant information is placed in the period of greatest activity, or of productivity in the case of a composer. There are, however, a few women who are listed in two time periods because of mid-career changes in activities. For example, Ethel Leginska (1886-1970) is entered as a pianist in the period from 1870 to 1920 and as a conductor in the period from 1920 to 1950.

c. Names of organizations are treated like names of subjects.

d. When articles are signed only by initials, our staff has supplied full names wherever possible.

e. The most recent edition of a literary work is entered into the bibliography. Early editions are cited in the body of the abstract.

f. Individual items have been coordinated to eliminate repetition of data wherever possible. As a result, many abstracts stress material unique to that source.

g. Punctuation in titles of literary entries has been altered to conform to the style of this book.

h. In order to conserve space, gaps in quotations have not been signaled by the standard ellipses. Therefore, quoted material is not necessarily consecutive.

i. Contributors' names are in parentheses at the end of an abstract. Entries without contributors' names are the work of the project staff, i.e., the two editors and their assistants.

Music

a. Subtitles are separated from titles by a period. Translations following titles are in parenthesis if they appear on the title page of the work and in brackets if editorially supplied.

b. If a work is available in full score, the pagination given refers to the full score even if the work is also available in other forms (e.g., piano-vocal scores).

c. Music that is privately or self-published is located by city.

CRITERIA FOR THE SELECTION OF ENTRIES

Literature

a. The bibliography includes selected entries documenting women's activities as composers, educators, patrons, and performers in American music from colonial times to the present. However, women who have recorded the activities of others, among them American critics and musicologists, are not listed unless the subjects of their works are also women.

b. Subjects must be native-born or have spent ten years or more in the United States during which time they were active in music. An exception has been made in regard to Jenny Lind, whose impact on the United States' musical history is far greater than her two short stays would indicate.

c. Literary items include information about women in the vernacular music tradition from colonial times to 1920, and about women in the art music tradition from colonial times to the present.

d. Reviews of literature are included and follow directly after the work that is reviewed. Reviews of musical compositions are listed as independent entries with cross-references to the works themselves if the works are also listed in the bibliography. Reviews of performances by groups composed largely or entirely of women are included. However, reviews of an individual's performances are omitted unless the reviews offer information of significance other than the performance itself, e.g., debuts, farewell performances, or items of sociological interest.

Music

a. Works listed in the bibliography are composed by American women or by women who have spent ten or more years of their active lives in the United States.

b. Contemporary composers who have six or more published works are included in the bibliography. A work is considered published if it has been issued by a commercial publisher, is in facsimile, or is self-published, and if it is located in a place accessible to the public. In most cases the composer has chosen works she wishes included.

c. If the composer is deceased, our staff has located her works or, on occasion, has relied on independent researchers for information. Such entries have been made selectively in order to include works by the most important composers of the past, subject to limitations of time and space.

d. The earliest editions of music found by our staff are entered into the bibliography. Later editions are referred to in the body of the abstract.

e. The names of contributors are in parentheses at the end of abstracts. Where contributors' names are lacking, abstracts have been prepared by project staff.

LIBRARY LOCATIONS OF LITERATURE AND MUSIC

The reader who wishes to locate materials in this book will find many listed in issues of the *National union catalogue,* the *Union list of serials,* and the *New serial titles,* all published periodically under the auspices of the United States' Library of Congress. Much of the music and literature is listed in these references. Addresses for most music publishers are in the annual issues of the *Billboard international buyer's guide,* and in *The American music handbook* (New York: The Free Press, 1974) compiled by Christopher Pavlakis. Music that is self-published can be obtained through the composer.

The staff of the bibliography has been fortunate in having easy access to the rich holdings of musical Americana at the New York Public Library, where the major part of the research took place. Other libraries consulted were, in order of importance to the book: the Library of Congress, Washington, D.C., the American Music Center and the American Composers Alliance, both of New York, the Boston Public Library, the Free Library of Philadelphia, the New England Conservatory of Music in Boston, the Chicago Public Library, the Newberry Library, also of Chicago, and the libraries of Harvard University in Cambridge, Mass., and of Columbia University of New York.

A few contributors have used other libraries, including the New York Historical Society, the Long Island Historical Society of Brooklyn, N.Y., the Los Angeles Public Library, and the music libraries of Yale University in New Haven, Conn., and the University of Southern California and the University of California, both in Los Angles, Calif.

AUTHOR-SUBJECT INDEX TO LITERATURE

Typography

An AUTHOR appears with surname in capital letters.
A **subject heading** appears in bold face.
A *title* appears in italics.

Alphabetization

a. The arrangement is word-by-word. Hyphenated words and names are alphabetized as one word; compound names and names beginning with a separated prefix are alphabetized as two words. Diacritical marks and punctuation are ignored except for the first comma.

    Examples: De Cisneros, Eleanora
             De Lussan, Zelie
             Decca, Marie
             Delaborde, Elie Miriam

b. Abbreviations are alphabetized as though the abbreviated spelling were a word.
    Examples: New York (city)
             N.J.

c. Numbers (hence dates) follow the letter Z.

Abbreviations

See List of Abbreviations, pp. xv-xvi.

States are abbreviated except when they appear as subject headings. New York State appears as **New York** when used as a headword and as N.Y. elsewhere. New York City always appears as New York and never as a subject heading.

    Examples:
    New York, musical life, 1920s   (state)
      New York, musical life   (state, city)
    societies, associations, and clubs
      N.Y., League of Composers   (state)
      N.Y., Metropolitan Opera Guild   (state)
      _____, New York Opera Guild   (state, city in name)

Geographical Entries

All geographical subdivisions (cities, counties) appear under the names of their respective states.

Structured Subject Headings

academic institutions

Schools, conservatories, colleges, and universities are entered by state, and then by name; if foreign, they are entered by country and then by name.

auditoriums and concert halls

Entered by state, city and name of hall, followed by works about the hall itself, e.g., history, structure. An organization bearing the same name as a concert hall is entered under performing organizations.

composers, conductors, educators, musicologists, patrons, and performers

Below each of these occupations in alphabetical order are:

a. persons entered by last name and initials. These persons are also entered by their own names listed in **bold face.**

b. terms selected from the list of descriptors below:

aesthetics, bibliography, catalogues, collections, correspondence, discographies, festivals and conferences, influence on, influenced by, interviews, life, life and activities, life and works (composers only), literary works, manuscripts, performances, relation to, style, tribute, viewed by, views about, works.

Example: BEACH, Amy Cheney, life and works, to 1906

festivals

Entered by state, name of festival or city.

folk

The index distinguishes between "art", "folk", and "popular" music. Only material relating to art music appears under genre headings. Entries about folk music are gathered under the subdivided folk headings: folk dance, folk music, folk song, folklore.

instruments

The heading **instruments** is reserved for general works only. Families of instruments appear as subject headings, e.g., string instruments, as do individual instruments, e.g., violin. Four kinds of structured subheadings are available:

piano	(history)
piano building	(manufacture, builders)
piano music	
piano playing	(pedagogy and technique)

Players of instruments are listed under **performers.**

libraries, museums, collections

Entered by state, city, and name whenever possible.

manuscripts

Entered under the appropriate subdivisions: **manuscripts—collections** (by collector or genre), **manuscripts—individual author** (by author), **manuscripts—location or title** (by city repository or title).

performers

Individual performers appear in the appropriate subdivision (by instrument), entered by last name, with first initials. A performer is also listed as a subject heading under her own name.

performing organizations

Entered by state, name.

periodicals

Entered by title.

popular music

Popular music does not include folk materials.

publishers and printers

Entered by name.

religious music

All sects and denominations may appear as subject headings under their own names. Everything to do with churches, synagogues, etc., as institutions is entered under the name of the sect or denomination. Everything to do with church or synagogue music appears under **religious music,** under subdivisions of this category, or under specific genres or services.

Example: **religious music—Moravian,** 1741-1871

reviews

In an author entry, an asterisk (*) before the abstract number indicates that the item is a review of one of the author's works. For example, ALDA, Frances, 862bm[58], *863rb[58]: the first number refers to the book by Frances Alda; the second entry (with asterisk) refers to a review of the book by Alda.

societies, associations, and clubs

Entered by state, name. This includes organizations other than those belonging under different headings, such as **academic institutions.**

COMPOSER-AUTHOR INDEX TO MUSIC

Types of Entries

composers

The composer's name appears as the main entry, last name first. Below the name, the music is listed by medium of performance (e.g., chamber music, choral music), followed by the abstract numbers of works for that medium. No titles of works appear in the music index.

authors

Authors of texts, translators, and librettists are listed with last name first. On the same line, and *without* indication of performing medium, are the abstract numbers of works using texts by the author. If the author is also a composer, her name appears twice, first as an author, and second as a composer.

alternate names

Main entries are under the standard forms of the composers' or authors' names. Other forms of names appear in the index with cross-references to the standard form.

INDEX TO RECORDINGS

a. Main entries include the standard forms of composers' names, followed on a separate line by the medium and the appropriate abstract numbers of works in that medium. No titles of works appear in the index.

b. Alternate forms of composers' names are listed, with cross-references to the standard forms of names for this bibliography.

LIST OF ABBREVIATIONS

A	alto
Ala.	Alabama
anon.	anonymous
Apr.	April
Ark.	Arkansas
ArU	U. of Arkansas, Fayetteville, Ark.
Assoc.	Association
At	author of text
Aug.	August
b.	born
B	bass
Bar	baritone
bar	baritone horn
bcl	bass clarinet
bsn	bassoon
btn	bass trombone
c.	century, centuries
ca.	circa
Calif.	California
cbc	contrabass clarinet
cbn	contra bassoon
cbs	double bass
cla	clarinet
CLSU	U. of Southern California, Los Angeles, Calif.
CLU	U. of California at Los Angeles, Calif.
Co.	Company
Col.	College
Colo.	Colorado
comp.	compiler
Conn.	Connecticut
crn	cornet
Ct	counter-tenor
Ct	contents of musical work (characteristic titles only)
CU	U. of California at Berkeley, Calif.
Da	date of autograph
DAU	American U., Washington, D.C.
D.C.	District of Columbia
Dec.	December
diss.	dissertation
DLC	Library of Congress, Washington, D.C.
DME	Doctor of Music Education
Dn	duration of musical work
ebs	electric double bass
ed.	editor, edited by, edition
egr	electric guitar
enh	English horn
epm	euphonium
Feb.	February
Fla.	Florida
flu	flute
Ga.	Georgia
glk	glockenspiel
gtr	guitar
Haw.	Hawaii
hps	harpsichord
hrn	French horn
hrp	harp
IC	Chicago Public Library, Chicago, Ill.
ICN	Newberry Library, Chicago, Ill.
Ill.	Illinois
Inc.	Incorporated
Ind.	Indiana
Inst.	Institute
intro.	introduction
Jan.	January
Kan.	Kansas
Ky.	Kentucky
La.	Louisiana
La	location of autograph
Li	librettist
Lt	language of text
M	mezzo-soprano
M.A.	Master of Arts
Mar.	March
Mass.	Massachusetts
MB	Boston Public Library, Boston, Mass.
mba	marimba
MBNe	New England Conservatory, Boston, Mass.
Md.	Maryland

MH	Harvard U., Cambridge, Mass.	PP	Free Library of Philadelphia, Philadelphia, Penn.
Mich.	Michigan		
Minn.	Minnesota	PPFleisher	Fleisher Collection of Orchestral Music, Free Library of Philadelphia, Philadelphia, Penn.
Miss.	Mississippi		
M.M.	Master of Music		
Mo.	Missouri	Ps	Psalm(s)
MoKU	U. of Missouri at Kansas City, Mo.	rec	recorder (the instrument)
Mont.	Montana	rev.	revised
MS(S)	manuscript(s)	*Rg*	recording
N.C.	North Carolina	R.I.	Rhode Island
n.d.	no date (of publication)	S	soprano
Nev.	Nevada	sax	saxophone
N.H.	New Hampshire	S.C.	South Carolina
NIC	Cornell U., Ithaca, N.Y.	Sept.	September
N.J.	New Jersey	Soc.	Society
N.M.	New Mexico	Sr.	Sister, member of religious order
NmU	U. of New Mexico, Albuquerque, N.M.	*St*	source of text for musical composition
n.n.	no name (of publisher)	T	tenor
NN	New York Public Library, New York, N.Y.	tba	tuba
NNACA	American Composers Alliance, New York, N.Y.	tbn	trombone
		Tenn.	Tennessee
NNAMC	American Music Center, New York, N.Y.	Tex.	Texas
NNC	Columbia U., New York, N.Y.	tim	timpani
NNCU-G	Graduate Center of City U. of New York, New York, N.Y.	*Tm*	title of musical work from which selection is taken
no.	number	*Tr*	translator
Nov.	November	tpt	trumpet
n.p.	no place (of publication)	U.	University
NPU	Vassar Col., Poughkeepsie, N.Y.	U.S.A.	United States of America
NRU	U. of Rochester, Rochester, N.Y.	Va.	Virginia
N.Y.	New York State	vcl	violoncello
obo	oboe	vib	vibraphone
Oct.	October	vla	viola
op.	opus	vln	violin
Oreg.	Oregon	vol.	volume
org	organ	Vt.	Vermont
p.	page(s)	Wash.	Washington
Penn.	Pennsylvania	*WIAM*	*Women in American music: a bibliography of music and literature*
per	percussion		
Pf	performing forces	Wis.	Wisconsin
Ph.D.	Doctor of Philosophy	W. Va.	West Virginia
pno	piano	xyl	xylophone

Historical Introduction

This bibliography about women in American music from colonial times to the present was compiled for several purposes. The first is to encourage the performance of compositions by women. The second is to stimulate further research about women, not only as composers but also as performers, conductors, educators, and patrons. Third, by encouraging the discovery of women's music and their activities in the field, the bibliography aims both to restore women to their rightful place in American music history and, as a result, to enhance the status of contemporary women in music.

As the entries in the bibliography indicate, women have contributed in important ways to musical life in the United States. Yet many people today are unable to name more than one or two contemporary women composers, and do little better in naming women in other areas, with the exception, of course, of opera. Regarding women in the past, most people recall only the stereotypes, for example, women as eternal amateurs at the piano, or as badly trained private music teachers. In the past it was commonly believed that women were incapable of playing certain instruments or of composing in large forms. Such attitudes, although less prevalent today, have acted as brakes on women's activities, and continue to obscure women's actual achievements in music.

Therefore, a fourth purpose of the bibliography is to isolate information about the social context in which women's activities should be viewed. A number of literary sources in the book indicate the extent to which the stereotypes of "properly feminine" behavior reflected accurately and in turn influenced women's lives, and how conditions have changed over the years.

Because the study of women in American music is a relatively new field, a wide variety of source materials appears in the bibliography: articles from newspapers and from "ladies'" and music magazines; a small but growing body of scholarly articles and dissertations; and checklists of source materials such as music manuscripts, correspondence, scrapbooks, and clipping files. Book-length studies unfortunately are few. However, there is a surprisingly large number of biographies—primarily of singers, but also of women active in other areas of music. In addition, regional histories are listed for information about women active at local as well as national levels.

Although general histories have been examined, only those with more than brief references to women have been included. Frequently, earlier histories of American music give fuller coverage to women than more recent ones, suggesting that it was easier for women to achieve recognition before American music and musical life had come of age, and also that women's past achievements tend to be overlooked with the passage of time. Louis Charles Elson, in *The history of American music* of 1904, devoted an entire chapter to women composers working at the turn of the century.[1] Twenty-five years later, John

Tasker Howard, in *Our American music, three hundred years of it*, presented an extended discussion of the life and works of only one female composer, Amy Cheney Beach; although he mentioned many women composers, he allotted to them only thumbnail sketches.[2] More recent histories of music in the United States devote little or no space to women. Our bibliography seeks to reverse this trend and to focus on women's work in a variety of pursuits in American musical life.

The focus of this book is on the contributions of women. We do not wish to deny the significance of men's role in music, nor to suggest that women functioned in an all-female world. But we hope that this record of women's activities, in combination with other historical studies, will allow a more complete picture to emerge. Indeed, the reader will note the many inter-relationships between men and women as teachers, professional colleagues, and supportive family members. On the other hand, there is some truth to the picture that emerges of women in the past making music in a world apart from men: in the parlor, at female seminaries and colleges, in the mainly female music clubs as well as in women's clubs, and in all-female performing groups. The reader will also note that, with the exception of a relatively few highly visible and successful women, this segregation—a result of social and historical forces—has limited women's access to professional careers in music.

COLONIAL TIMES TO 1820

Beginning with the rise of idiomatic instrumental music in 16th-century Europe, women were encouraged to make music as amateurs. Harpsichords, virginals, and clavichords were the favorite domestic instruments because women could play them at home while appearing graceful and ladylike.

In colonial America only a limited number of families had the means to import instruments and provide women with the leisure time to study music. With the Federal era, however, increasing numbers of women took up the newly introduced pianoforte and also the study of voice. Journals and newspapers from the 18th through the middle of the 19th century championed music as an "accomplishment" for women, to be studied along with needlework, drawing, and dancing. Among the lady amateurs who played and sang at home were Washington's step-granddaughter, Eleanor Custis Parke, and Jefferson's wife, Martha Skelton Jefferson, and the Jeffersons' two daughters, Martha and Mary.

The published compositions of the first women composers in the United States bear the stamp of amateur music making: easy keyboard pieces and simple songs written on two rather than three staves for one person to both play and sing. Many early pieces by women were published anonymously, e.g., by "A Lady of Philadelphia". One major figure who did sign her name was Mary Ann Pownall, a composer as well as a singer active in ballad opera in cities along the eastern seaboard.

Another professional musician, Elizabeth Von Hagen, came to America from Amsterdam with her husband and son, both of whom were also musicians. She was active as a composer, singer, pianist, and teacher of keyboard and voice in New York, Boston, and Salem, Mass., from the 1790s to the 1810s. Other professional singers active in early American concert and theater life include Miss Broadhurst, Catherine Hillier Graupner, Arabella Brett Hodgkinson, Georgina Oldmixon, and Elizabeth Arnold Poe. Although women probably did not compose sacred music within the singing school tradition, in the middle of the 18th century at the Ephrata Cloister in Pennsylvania, women functioned as singers, writers of hymn texts, copyists, illuminators, and possibly as composers.

1820 TO 1870

A major development in the period 1820-70 was the emergence of native American women opera singers, beginning approximately ten years after the first performances of Italian opera in New York by Manuel Garcia's company in 1825. Despite the Puritan belief that life in the theater was immoral, particularly for women, a number of pioneering women did enter the profession. As a result of Jenny Lind's highly publicized American tour in the early 1850s, still more women began to train for opera. Lind also helped women in specific ways. For example, after hearing the young Adelaide Phillips sing, Lind became one of her patrons, enabling Phillips to study with Garcia in London. Thus Phillipps began a practice continued by ever-increasing numbers of ambitious American male and female musicians who finished their training in Europe, and remained there for performing experience. Following her return to the United States in 1855, Phillipps sang major roles with Philadelphia and New York opera companies, and appeared as soloist with the Handel and Haydn Society and at the National Peace Jubilee held in Boston in 1869.

Other singers who were important in this period were Ann Childe Séguin, Euphrosyne Parepa-Rosa, Caroline Richings, Elizabeth Taylor Greenfield, Anna Bishop, and Eliza Biscaccianti. The English-born Séguin worked in New York in opera and as a voice teacher for many years. Parepa-Rosa and Richings headed and sang in their own touring opera companies. A singer known as the "Black Swan", Elizabeth Taylor Greenfield, was born in slavery, but later gained her freedom to pursue singing. Greenfield's European successes paved the way for her acceptance in the United States. Anna Bishop, who with Eliza Biscaccianti performed in California during the Gold Rush, gave concerts throughout the United States and Europe, Central and South America, Hawaii, Australia and New Zealand, China, India, and South Africa.

Among the few instrumentalists active during the period was Sophia Hewitt Ostinelli, the daughter of James Hewitt and the mother of Eliza Biscaccianti. Ostinelli worked as a pianist and organist in Boston with the Handel and Haydn Society, and after 1822 in Portland, Maine, where she was employed by the First Parish Church. Jane Sloman, another pianist active during this period, was a composer as well. Camilla Urso, violinist, and Teresa Carreño, pianist, made their debuts as children during the 1850s and 1860s, respectively; their adult careers, however, flourished during the period after the Civil War.

Accompanying the modest increase in the number of women who functioned as professional musicians was a large increase in the number of women amateurs, particularly as the piano became a fixture of the middle- and upper-class parlor. In addition to piano and voice, women also studied harp and guitar. Women's seminaries, which increased rapidly in number beginning in the 1830s, typically fostered music as an accomplishment—often as a means of attracting suitors. Among the early music schools in the United States was the Music Vale Seminary in Salem, Connecticut, founded in 1835 by Oramel Whittlesey, whose daughters also served on the faculty.

Some schools cultivated the "monster concert" as a way of allowing many students to perform during one program, featuring most frequently women amateurs at multiple pianos. Monster concerts became a fad during the mid-century period. As part of his American concert tours in 1846-51, pianist-composer Henri Herz oversaw programs for sixteen female pianists at eight pianos. Herz's manager called these events "financial music" because they drew large crowds. Among others who exploited the monster concert was Louis Moreau Gottschalk.

The number of women composers also increased between 1820 and 1870, their products being the musical counterparts of quilts and watercolors: solo songs with or without chorus, piano pieces modeled on dance forms such as marches, waltzes, polkas, and quick-steps, and an occasional set of variations. Beginning in the 1850s, the first generation of professional composers included Augusta Browne, Jane Sloman, Marion Dix Sullivan, Faustina Hasse Hodges, and Susan Parkhurst.[3] Of this group, Augusta Browne was the most prominent and was, in addition, an outspoken advocate of professionalism for women. Hodges, the daughter of organist and composer Edward Hodges, wrote church music and songs. Her two best-known songs were *Dreams* and *The rose bush*,[4] the latter popularized by Adelaide Phillipps.

Not all female composers and performers functioned within the genteel tradition, however. Susan Parkhurst, for example, specialized in temperance, abolition, and comic songs, as well as sentimental ballads. A number of women wrote hymns, among them Mary S.B. Dana and Julia Ward Howe. Women were active in the Shaker movement as musicians and receivers of "gift" songs. And singing families such as the Swiss Raniers and the Hutchinsons included several women. Finally, one of the earliest American ethnomusicologists, Lucy McKim Garrison, notated and later published songs and spirituals she heard in 1862 on a trip to the colony of freed men and women on the Sea Islands, South Carolina.

Women were among the earliest proponents of music education in the public schools. Sarah Josepha Hale, editor for forty years of *Godey's Lady's Book*, contributed verses for Lowell Mason's school music collections and worked for the cultivation of music in Boston. At the same time in Cleveland, Mary Cushing Webster campaigned for the acceptance of public school music and introduced Pestalozzi's methods in her teaching a few years after Lowell Mason had done the same in Boston.

1870 TO 1920

In the years between the Civil War and World War I, women became increasingly active in the country's growing musical life. The largest number of women continued to be active as amateurs, particularly in the home where by means of music they sought to instill a love for culture and to mold the "unformed" personalities of their children. Women flocked to private, conservatory, and college music teachers, becoming in many cases the majority of students. Banding together in women's and music clubs, they sought to encourage an appreciation for art music among widening segments of the population. In the process they also developed their own administrative and leadership skills.

The women's club movement which arose in the latter half of the 19th century was an unprecedented phenomenon that provided middle- and upper-class women with an opportunity for self-development and the betterment of their communities, as well as a means of overcoming their isolation at home. The first amateur music club, the Rossini Club of Portland, Maine, was organized in 1867, and the club movement mushroomed after Fanny Raymond Ritter, in her address to the Association for the Advancement of Women at the Centennial Congress in Philadelphia in 1876, challenged women to assume the role of music patrons.[5] By the end of the century, music clubs were active in countless cities and towns throughout the country.

Rose Fay Thomas, at a meeting in Chicago that coincided with the Columbian Exposition of 1893, tried unsuccessfully to form a federation of music clubs; four years later, the dedicated organizer of women, Florence Edith Sutro, succeeded in the formation of the National Federation of Music Clubs. In addition, the General Federation of Women's Clubs, established in 1890, later included music committees in most of its chapters. Women in the clubs worked to raise the level of audience appreciation in their communities by organizing festivals and sponsoring artists on tour, thereby helping to establish national concert networks. Clubwomen performed regularly as instrumentalists and as solo and choral singers at club concerts designed to encourage women to "keep their music up" after marriage and motherhood. Many clubs sponsored study courses and organized circulating libraries of scores and music books.

Choral music was one of the important ways that amateurs made music together, and women's choral singing was both stimulated by and a contributor to the club movement. Three main choral traditions were carried over into American musical life: those of England, of Germany, and of Scandinavia. With the exception of the Handel and Haydn Society, most singing societies began as male groups, but parallel women's choirs later joined the men in performance of large choral works. Toward the end of the century, women's choral groups also began to perform independently, both within and outside of the clubs. Two significant results of the activities of women's choruses were the opportunities they offered to women as choral directors and the demand they created for music for women's voices, some of that demand filled by women composers.

Out of the fertile soil of such widespread amateur musical activity sprang an equally unprecedented group of professional musicians, many of them driven by economic need as well as emboldened by women's political activity on their own behalf. Never before or since have so many women worked so visibly as professional musicians: as solo instrumental performers, as orchestral musicians, as singers and entertainers, and as educators. In addition, women were being educated in music not only in large numbers, but to a higher level than ever before. The musical training women received in seminaries and colleges included not only vocal and instrumental lessons, but also theory, harmony, counterpoint, music history, and ensemble playing and singing. At the same time, the quality of teaching improved as more musicians came from Europe, while many Americans continued to go to Europe for advanced training.

This period witnessed the rise of women as concert artists, who shared with opera stars the role of culture heroines, among them the pianists Amy Fay, Julie Rivé-King, Teresa Carreño, and Fannie Bloomfield-Zeisler, and the violinists Camilla Urso and Maud Powell. Fay, after graduating from the New England Conservatory,

went to Germany in 1869 to complete her studies, a sojourn she vividly describes in her *Music-study in Germany*.[6] She worked there with a number of teachers, including Liszt. Julie Rivé-King, a native of Cincinnati, first studied with William Mason in New York, and then also with Liszt. After her return to the United States, Rivé-King was able, in the late 1870s and the 1880s, both to establish herself as a favorite performer and to raise the level of taste among concert-goers through performance of works of high artistic merit. Theodore Thomas, the leading orchestra conductor of the period, also had as his goal the education of American audiences, and it was probably no accident that Thomas and Rivé-King often performed together. Teresa Carreño came to New York from her native Caracas, and then went to Paris for further study. Known as the "Brünnhilde of the pianoforte", Carreño was an international artist from the 1890s until her death in 1917. Fannie Bloomfield-Zeisler, the fourth and youngest of this group, finished her training with Leschetizky in Vienna. In addition to playing on concert tours in the United States, she also performed in Europe, where she convinced European audiences that an artist of the highest calibre could come from the culturally backward United States.

Because these leading female concert artists demonstrated by their success the rewards of intensive study, they became role models for the serious amateur—who by this time had replaced the "accomplished" amateur of earlier generations. *Étude* magazine recorded and reinforced this change with numerous articles in the 1880s and 1890s advocating "achievement"—or meaningful study for only the talented female. By 1902 critic James Huneker reported the official demise of the "piano girl", replaced now by the new girl, who "is too busy to play the piano unless she has the gift; then she plays it with consuming interest". Huneker concludes that when the contemporary woman is not musical she is far happier playing tennis than the piano.[7]

The emergence of women as concert violinists also sprang out of a fertile soil, for after 1870 more women were playing instruments other than the piano. Thanks especially to Julius Eichberg of the Boston Conservatory, a large number of women now played the violin, an instrument formerly considered ungraceful and unladylike. Leading violinists Camilla Urso and Maud Powell also functioned as models for other women. Urso began her adult career in 1863, and by her performance of outstanding works such as the Beethoven violin concerto in D major, op. 61, and the Mendelssohn violin concerto in E minor, op. 64, helped to raise the level of public taste. Powell also contributed to the musical education of the public through her introduction of contemporary works such as concerti by Bruch and Sibelius.

Soon women played not only all stringed instruments,

but also the flute. However, lower winds and brass were declared inappropriate for women, who were told that they lacked the strength to play these instruments, and that if they persisted, they would spoil their looks. Nevertheless, by the turn of the century, women were playing all orchestral and band instruments, and "in most cases with marked success", according to an 1893 report in *Sewanee Review*.[8] This success, however, did not make women acceptable as orchestral players. Despite the fact that women such as Urso or Rivé-King brilliantly withstood the pressures of public performance, the reason given for the exclusion of women from orchestras was lack of endurance. An 1895 source, for instance, notes that whereas a soloist can increase her repertory by degrees, "the grinding tax of rehearsals with an orchestra which undertakes the production of several weighty novelties each season together with keeping in the best order a long list of standard works, would send her [woman's] physical forces to the wall".[9] In fact, the only women generally accepted in men's orchestras prior to the 1920s were harpists.

Because of the barriers to employment by established groups, beginning in the 1870s and 1880s in New York and Boston women banded together to form their own "lady orchestras". The typical early lady orchestra played popular music in a beer garden or theater, and was promoted as a curiosity because of its all-female composition. Such employment offered only modest pay along with crucial performing experience. By 1900, some orchestras were also playing light classical and classical works, among them the Woman's Orchestra of Los Angeles, the Women's String Orchestra of New York, and the Boston Fadette Lady Orchestra. Several offered opportunities to women as conductors. Caroline B. Nichols, a pupil of Julius Eichberg, not only founded the Boston Fadettes but was also its conductor for over thirty years, during which time she trained 600 young women for professional careers as orchestral musicians. In addition to orchestral musicians, a number of all-female chamber groups were active around the turn of the century. The most important was the Olive Mead Quartet, organized and headed by Mead, a violin pupil of Franz Kneisel. The pianist Carolyn Beebe, with the violinist Édouard Déthier, helped to popularize the violin and piano sonata recital, and in 1916 Beebe founded the long-lived New York Chamber Music Society.

Vocal music, especially opera, was a favorite among women, not only for the attendant glamour, but also because success brought with it financial rewards not usually possible in other areas of music. Indeed it is likely that women talented in two or more areas of music often chose voice for economic reasons; as a result opera was an overcrowded as well as a competitive field. The biographies of singers attest to their long and intensive training, their hard work, and the ample rewards for the favored few.

Many who chose opera as a career had to overcome financial problems as well as family and societal resistance to a career on the stage. Like Louise Homer, some worked at white-collar jobs, as well as working as church singers, vocal teachers, and accompanists in order to earn their passage to Europe and support themselves there while studying. Nevertheless, such a trip was often impossible without the support of patrons. American singers' destinations were Italy in the earlier years of the 19th century, France in the 1880s (particularly to study with Mathilde Marchesi in Paris), and later Germany, a pattern that reflects the changing fashions in opera repertory at home.

Many who went abroad to study remained to perform for a number of years in order to gain experience and a record of successes necessary to establish their reputations at home. Despite the numbers of women who gained reputations abroad, when the Metropolitan Opera opened in 1883, major singers engaged by the company were European, including Marcella Sembrich, Johanna Gadski, Ernestine Schumann-Heink, Frances Alda, Margaret Matzenauer, and Frieda Hempel, attracted at least in part by the large fees. However, ten years later the Metropolitan began to include native-born women on its roster, among them Lillian Nordica, Louise Homer, Geraldine Farrar, and Alma Gluck. Chicago's resident opera company, established in 1909, listed among its singers the Americans Jane Osborn-Hannah, Edyth Walker, and Mary Garden, who came to the United States as a child. From the 1870s on, touring opera companies were a regular feature of American musical life, and a number of women, including Emma Abbott, Minnie Hauk, and Clara Louise Kellogg, ran opera companies in which they were also the leading singers. Native-born singers prominent in concert and recital work include Emma Cecilia Thursby, Corinne Rider-Kelsey, Florence Hinkle, Clara Clemens, and Sissieretta Jones, also known as "Black Patti".

Educational opportunities for women increased significantly during this period, when midwestern universities opened their doors to women, and when liberal arts colleges for women were established in the East as equivalents of leading male institutions. In the new women's colleges such as Vassar and Wellesley, music became an important part of the curriculum; indeed, these colleges led in the development of music as an academic discipline. As a result of new educational opportunities, women were qualified to enter into a number of professions, among them, music education. Between 1870 and 1910 the percentage of women in music and music teaching rose from 36% to 61%.[10] Small numbers of women became public school music supervisors; most women, however, became private teachers of piano and voice. The latter was a poorly paid and precarious source of income, and one in which women found themselves at a disadvantage compared to men, who commanded higher fees and attracted more advanced students.

A number of women founded music schools and were active in other facets of music education. In Potsdam, New York, Julia Ettie Crane founded the Crane Normal School of Music, and in Detroit, Emma A. Thomas founded the Thomas Normal Training School. Both were for the training of public music school teachers. Clara Baur, a singer who emigrated from Germany, founded the Cincinnati Conservatory in 1867; in New York, Jeanette Thurber organized and subsidized the National Conservatory. Others like Carrie Louise Dunning and Evelyn Fletcher-Copp developed and trained teachers in the application of their own music education methods for children. Frances Elliott Clark, who organized the education department of the Victor Talking Machine Company, pioneered in the production of music education records for children.

Perhaps the most striking change of the period was the emergence of women as composers of art music in the 1880s and 90s, amid a heated debate in the contemporary press as to whether women could indeed compose, and if they could, whether they could achieve greatness as composers, or, instead, should confine themselves to small forms. As long as American women wrote only parlor and popular music, their activity was acceptable— or so the lack of comment in the literature suggests. Women's entrance into the ranks of art music composers, however, was not deemed suitable by many in the field. Critic George P. Upton opened the debate on women composers when he claimed in his book of 1880, *Woman in music*, that women could not compose music because they lacked the ability to think logically or abstractly.[11] Anton Rubinstein added to the list of supposed female failings when he stated in 1892 that women as composers were deficient in concentration, powers of thought and feeling, and freedom of imagination.[12] Two years later Edith Brower asked if the musical idea was masculine and answered with an emphatic "yes", because women, according to Brower, were emotionally deficient and could not handle abstractions.[13] In defense of women, Adolph Willhartitz noted that women who studied harmony and composition often were given inferior training,[14] while Helen A. Clarke, in reply to Brower, wrote that if women were given the same educational and professional opportunities as men, they would do as well.[15] An example of the double bind in which women composers were placed by this controversy is the comment by Alexander McArthur of 1902 that what women lacked was confidence, without which they could not be original.[16]

Nevertheless, large numbers of women were active as composers of art music, much of which was published by leading firms. Outstanding among these women are:

Amy Cheney Beach, Helen Hopekirk, Margaret Ruthven Lang, and Clara Kathleen Rogers in Boston; Eleanor Everest Freer and Carrie Jacobs-Bond in Chicago; and Fannie Charles Dillon and Mary Carr Moore on the West Coast. All eight composers wrote a large number of solo songs to satisfy the demands of the many singers active at the time. In addition, Beach, Dillon, Hopekirk, and Lang composed orchestral and other large-scale works, while Freer and Moore specialized in opera. Beach, Dillon, and Hopekirk were also active as pianists, whereas Freer and Rogers began as singers before turning to composition. Beach, who came to be known as the dean of American women composers, achieved levels of professional success hitherto unheard of for a woman. Most of her compositions were performed, many by outstanding orchestras and concert artists. Among her compositions were several written on commission: the *Festival jubilate, op. 14* for soloists, chorus, and orchestra, for the dedication of the Women's Building at the Columbian Exposition of 1893,[17] as well as pieces for the opening of the Trans-Mississippi Exposition in 1898 and the Panama Exposition of 1915.

Not only were women active as composers of art music, but they wrote vernacular music as well, including hymns, popular songs, and instrumental pieces. Women hymnodists created a tremendous body of hymn texts and tunes. Indeed, a single publication, *Woman in sacred song* of 1885, has over 2000 hymn texts and 130 four-part hymn settings by fifty women composers.[18] Because evangelical religion, like music, was largely the province of middle- and upper-class women during the 19th century, their activity as hymnodists was a logical outcome of this association.

The emergence of what we still know as popular music occurred during the 1890s. Often in a developing field the opportunities for women are greater than after the field is established and its commercial aspects apparent to all. This was the case for women composers in the popular field who, beginning in the 1890s through the early years of the century, wrote and published popular songs including show tunes and dialect songs, piano rags and marches, as well as other dances. Several women made considerable amounts of money on pieces such as *Shine on, harvest moon, Sweet Rosie O'Grady,* and *The sunshine of your smile.*[19] Prominent black singers in the early blues tradition were Gertrude ("Ma") Rainey and Bessie Smith, while the white singer Aunt Molly Jackson wrote and performed her own songs in support of union activity in her home state of Kentucky. The black concert singer Sissieretta Jones spent several years in vaudeville after her novelty as a concert singer no longer attracted white audiences. A number of women were of course active on the musical stage, performing in operettas and light opera. Of these Lillian Russell was one of the most famous.

Women were members of the Jubilee Singers of Fisk University, who sang black songs and spirituals on tour beginning in 1871. And Emma Azalia Hackley was an educator and promoter of black performers and composers in both the art and vernacular traditions. Hackley, who graduated from a Denver music school in 1899, helped to bring about the Harlem Renaissance, a movement in which she was active until her death in 1922. Others interested in recording and preserving ethnic music were the early ethnomusicologists Alice Cunninghan Fletcher and Frances Densmore, both collectors of the music of American Indians. Natalie Curtis-Burlin compiled two books of black folk music as well as music of American Indians, and Josephine McGill gathered Anglo-American folk songs in Kentucky in the 1910s. Like the female popular composers, these women seem to have flourished because ethnological studies constituted a new area, open to those who would try it.

The topic of women in music received increasing attention in books and periodicals beginning in the 1890s, reflecting the growing participation of women in clubs, and as composers, performers, and teachers, all influenced by the gathering momentum of the women's movement. One monument of the time is Frances Willard and Mary A. Livermore's biographical dictionary of 1893 entitled *A woman of the century*, which reviews the contributions of hundreds of leading figures in all fields in the post-Civil War era, almost 100 of them in music.[20] As a reflection of all this activity, in 1897 *Etude* introduced the "woman's page", and two years later *Musician* did the same.[21] *Etude* published three women's issues between 1901 and 1918,[22] while in 1909-10 *Musical America* printed a year-long series of profiles of women composers by Stella Reid Crothers.[23] Thus the literature about music between 1890 and 1920 reflects women's activism as they came to assume greater importance in public life than ever before in this country.

Another expression of women's significance in music, as well as a contribution to the cause of women musicians, was the performance of works by women during the Columbian Exposition in Chicago in 1893. Also meeting in Chicago at the same time, the Woman's Musical Congress was part of a larger meeting of the Music Teachers National Association and the American College of Musicians. The meeting of the Woman's Congress, the largest assembly of amateur and professional musicians to date, featured papers by leading performers and teachers about their work, discussions of the status of women as professional musicians, and recitals of music by women performed by women.

During World War I community singing of patriotic and popular songs was fostered to raise morale of civilians and soldiers alike. Women were encouraged to utilize their musical backgrounds and become song leaders through special courses held during the war years. In addition to supporting the war, music had an important part in the meetings and marches of the suffrage movement.

1920 TO 1950

Following the passage of the Nineteenth Amendment guaranteeing women the right to vote, activism among women in many areas of public and professional life decreased. This was not the case, however, for women instrumentalists intent on orchestral careers, who between 1925 and World War II pressed for acceptance by standard all-male symphony orchestras. During World War I women were able to find employment in restaurant and hotel orchestras, and subsequently during the 1920s and 1930s they set out to turn symphonies and all other orchestras into "mixed" institutions, made up of men and women chosen on the basis of ability. Paradoxically, women moved toward the realization of this aim through an alternate institution, the all-female symphony orchestra, which they organized to provide experience and employment.

Although orchestras of women were a feature of musical life beginning in the 1870s, a full complement of approximately eighty players performing standard symphonic repertory was a new phenomenon. Close to thirty women's symphonies flourished between 1925 and 1945, in Philadelphia, Chicago, New York, Los Angeles and adjacent Long Beach, Boston, St. Louis, and elsewhere. In their early years, several such groups included men as trombone and tuba players, for example, until the number of women playing such instruments increased. Some of the women's symphonies were short-lived; others, however, lasted through World War II and longer. Whatever their life span, these orchestras proved that women instrumentalists could handle the symphonic repertory.

In support of the activities of women in orchestras, the conductor Frederique Petrides published a newsletter from 1935 to 1940 entitled *Women in music*, which, despite its all-embracing title, focused solely on the orchestral field, tracing women's progress and advancing arguments for the mixed orchestra.[24] In 1938 in both New York and Chicago, orchestral musicians established committees for the recognition of women musicians, in order to press for better professional opportunities for women in all areas of orchestral work. The drafting of men during World War II opened the ranks of major orchestras to a limited number of women. As a result, the need for all-female groups diminished, and most women's symphonies did not survive the war years.

Women's symphonies were important not only in providing experience and employment for players, but also for female conductors. Notable women orchestral conductors during the period were Eva Anderson, Antonia Brico, Ruth Haroldson, Ann Kullmer, Ethel Leginska, Frederique Petrides, and Ebba Sundstrom, most of whom conducted all-female groups almost exclusively. Ethel Leginska, a distinguished pianist who eventually chose conducting rather than piano as her main pursuit, was the first woman to declare herself a professional symphonic conductor, a role for which she carefully prepared. Initially she conducted male orchestras, later all-female orchestras. She headed the Woman's Symphony Orchestra of Chicago from 1927 to 1929, the Boston Woman's Symphony Orchestra from 1926 to 1930, and the National Women's Symphony Orchestra in New York in 1932. The tours throughout the East and Midwest that Leginska undertook with the Boston orchestra in 1928 and 1929 probably attracted attention because of the orchestra's all-female composition; nevertheless, they did feature women in professional roles and thereby encouraged other women to play orchestral instruments. Leginska, like other female conductors, was an effective champion of women as orchestral musicians. Ironically, opportunities for female conductors diminished greatly with the demise of the women's symphonies.

In the field of solo instrumental performance none achieved the stature of their earlier counterparts such as Teresa Carreño and Maud Powell. Possible causes for this decline are the increased activity of male concert artists who came to the United States from Europe during the boom years of the 1920s and, following that, the effects of the Depression and World War II. It is also possible that women performers faced increased hardships because the women's movement, in decline since 1920, no longer provided the support that had been a significant factor in women's successes of the previous period.

Nevertheless there were major figures: the pianists included Myra Hess, Ray Lev, Hortense Monath, who organized the New Friends of Music series in New York, Ruth Slenczynska, and Rosalyn Tureck; the violinists Lea Luboshutz, and Marianne Kneisel, who appeared both as a soloist and as the leader of her own string quartet; cellist Phyllis Kraeuter; harpsichordists Yella Pessl and Wanda Landowska; and harpist Mildred Dilling. Olga Samaroff Stokowski combined in her career the roles of concert pianist, teacher, critic, and pioneer in music appreciation courses. The wide diversity of instruments apparent among orchestral players is lacking here; most women concert artists played piano, violin, or harp, or sang.

By 1920 a sojourn in Europe to finish one's studies and to accumulate early performing experience was no longer considered necessary for Americans. Although many musicians continued to journey abroad, New York became the main destination for serious students, reflecting its leadership as a musical center, a development accelerated by World War I and the many European musicians who settled in New York at that time. Students who looked to New York as the mecca for musicians, however, were advised by the press to exhaust local resources before making such a move and thereby to avoid the fate of earlier generations which in some instances had gone abroad too soon. In the early 1920s three prestigious conservatories were founded: the Eastman School (1921), the Curtis Institute (1924), and the Juilliard School (1924), further reducing the need to go to Europe to complete one's education. To fill the need for proper housing, resident hotels and clubs were established, some exclusively for women.

During this period, many leading concert and opera singers were entirely American-trained and also received their initial performing experience at home, as another proof of America's musical life coming of age. These included Rosa Ponselle and Eleanora De Cisneros, who made their debuts with the Metropolitan Opera, as well as Dusolina Giannini and Helen Traubel. In contrast, because she was black, Marion Anderson had to go to Europe to win initial acceptance, and upon her return she continued to battle racial discrimination. European singers who enriched the operatic life in New York, Chicago, and other cities include Lucrezia Bori, Julia Clausen, Amelita Galli-Curci, Marjorie Lawrence, Lotte Lehmann, Claudia Muzio, Lily Pons, and Elisabeth Rethberg. Leading concert singers were the American-born Sophie Braslau, the Canadian Eva Gauthier, and the Danish Povla Frijsh, all artists known for the variety of their repertory and for introducing new works.

Indeed, in addition to Frijsh and Gauthier, a number of other women were pioneers in the introduction of old or unfamiliar repertory. Margarete Dessoff, a choral conductor who emigrated from Germany, founded and conducted several choirs, raised standards of choral performance, and introduced choral music of the Renaissance and early Baroque that was not usually a part of the choral repertory at the time. Wanda Landowska was an early champion of the harpsichord who in the 1920s introduced long-forgotten Baroque keyboard works. Vera Brodsky Lawrence, with duo-pianist Harold Triggs, featured American music during the 1930s and 1940s. In a second career in music beginning in the late 1960s, Lawrence edited the complete piano works of Louis Moreau Gottschalk and Scott Joplin, and as a result, helped to revive their works.

The women who emerged as composers around 1920 tended to pursue composition alone, rather than after or in conjunction with a career in performance. This change mirrored the separation of composer from performer that had taken place in the music world as a whole, as well as the decline in the importance of the piano; but perhaps even more, it reflected women's increased confidence about entering the field of composition. Women were active in a large number of geographical centers: Gena Branscombe, Marion Bauer, and Ethel Glenn Hier in New York; Mabel Daniels in Boston; Mary Howe in Washington, D. C.; Ruth Crawford Seeger (in her early career), Florence Price, and Florence G. Galajikian in Chicago; and Frances Marion Ralston and Catherine Urner in California. Florence Price, who was born in Little Rock, Arkansas and studied at the New England Conservatory, was the first major black woman composer of art music. She in turn taught composition to Margaret Bonds.

Following a trend begun in the late 19th century, women turned increasingly to large-scale orchestral and chamber music forms, whereas earlier, art songs far outnumber other types of work composed by women. Yet even while women successfully cultivated large forms, some contemporary literature reported that creativity lay beyond women. José Iturbi's categorical statement made in 1938 that women could not achieve greatness in music because of physical and temperamental limitations was considered offensive by women musicians.[25] The editors of the *New York Times* agreed with Iturbi.[26]

Although not all female musicians were as militant as the orchestral players, composers also felt the need for an organization. The Society of American Women Composers, formed for the "production and advancement of compositions by American women", was active from 1924 to 1929.[27] Amy Cheney Beach and Gena Branscombe served as presidents of the society, which sponsored concerts of women's music until forced by the Depression to disband.[28] Other organizations that supported music by women were the National Federation of Music Clubs and the National League of American Pen Women, both of which featured works by women at their conventions.

Several women composers of this period won prizes and awards for their works. Ruth Crawford Seeger, for instance, received a Guggenheim Fellowship in 1930; Rebecca Clarke was twice a winner in the chamber music competition sponsored by Elizabeth Sprague Coolidge; and Florence Galajikian took a prize for her *Symphonic intermezzo* in the 1932 orchestral contest held by the National Broadcasting Company.[29] Gena Branscombe's *Pilgrims of destiny,* a choral drama about the early settlers at Plymouth, in Massachusetts, was hailed as an important advance for American music of the 1920s.[30]

Individual patrons made important contributions to music in this period, especially Elizabeth Sprague Coolidge, Marian MacDowell, Sophie Drinker, and Claire Reis. Through her organization of the Berkshire Festival of Chamber Music in 1918 and her gift of an auditorium to the Library of Congress together with an endowment fund, Coolidge played a crucial role in the support and encouragement of chamber music in the United States. Marian MacDowell, who founded the MacDowell Colony in Peterborough, New Hampshire, as a memorial to her husband Edward, remained active for decades directing the colony and concertizing as a pianist on its behalf. The MacDowell Colony supported through its resident fellowships a large number of women composers. Indeed, in the summer of 1939, among the residents were composers Marion Bauer, Amy Beach, Radie Britain, Mabel Daniels, Fannie Charles Dillon, Ethel Glenn Hier, Mary Howe, and Frances Marion Ralston. A number of these composers returned to Peterborough for many summers. Among contemporary women who have had fellowships are Miriam Gideon and Louise Talma.

Claire Reis founded in 1923 and directed for twenty-five years the League of Composers, an organization that was the leading supporter of contemporary composers in this country. She was also active in several other music organizations and wrote on music. Sophie Drinker supported choral music, especially women's choruses, during a period when choral singing was popular for working women and housewives. Drinker's book *Music and women,* written in 1948, is the earliest investigation of the history of women in music throughout Western civilization. Among her many insights into the special problems facing women, Drinker noted the profound importance of the exclusion of women from music making and leadership in the church.[31]

During this period, in the music clubs, in women's committees for operas and symphony orchestras, and as volunteers connected with many music organizations and festivals, women continued to exercise a collective form of patronage that was indispensable precisely because of its volunteer nature. The National Federation of Music Clubs continued its role as collective patron and music educator of the American people. The national organization provided leadership for constituent clubs by fostering American music and especially American opera, by supporting music education in the public schools, and by collecting instruments and recordings for the armed forces during wartime. Women's experience in club work, and specifically in managing concert artists on tour during the early years of the century, led to the emergence of significant numbers of female professional concert managers after World War I.

Among educators, the achievements of Mother Georgia Stevens, founder of the Pius X School of Sacred Music at Manhattanville College of the Sacred Heart, are outstanding, as are those of pianist Rosina Lhevinne, singer Estelle Liebling, and administrator Grace Spofford. Dorothy Lawton, music librarian at the New York Public Library, and Mary Cardwell Dawson, founder not only of the National Negro Opera in 1941 but also of a music school in Pittsburgh, are also important. Finally, Angela Diller and Elizabeth Quaile compiled and composed the Diller-Quaile instructional series for children, and founded and directed the Diller-Quaile School in New York.

1950 TO 1978

It is striking that a period that began with women retreating to the home should draw to a close with a new feminist movement that both recalls and transcends that of the late 19th and early 20th centuries. Those women who continued in paid employment during the 1950s and early 1960s found little societal support for their labors outside the home. Contemporary periodicals about women in music emphasized their domestic lives or at least stressed their dual role. For example, women orchestral players, to one orchestra manager, were considered important because they could "bridge the gap between the orchestra and the public" by means of discussing their roles as mothers, or by modeling in a fashion show, or by baking for cake sales.[32]

Regardless of their image, in the postwar years women orchestral musicians retained many of their gains, despite the return of veterans.[33] And slowly in the course of the last three decades, changes in hiring practices have taken place. One of the first such changes occurred in 1952 when the flutist Doriot Anthony Dwyer joined the Boston Symphony Orchestra, where she became the first woman principal in a major orchestra. In 1966, the New York Philharmonic hired the bass player Orin O'Brien as its first regularly employed female member. By 1975 women constituted 21.8% of players in major orchestras, 39.7% of players in metropolitan orchestras, and 47.4% of players in community orchestras. It is hardly accidental that those orchestras which hold blind auditions often have the largest female populations.[34] Although the relatively low percentage of women in major orchestras remains a serious problem, women have nevertheless made progress as professional orchestral musicians.

Among performers other than orchestral musicians, the most notable changes have been those affecting black women. The integration of the Metropolitan Opera stage, begun by Marian Anderson in her 1955 debut as Ulrica in *Un ballo in maschera,* opened the doors for a number of other black women, among them Martina Arroyo, Shirley Verrett, Grace Bumbry, and Leontyne Price. In 1961 Bumbry became the first black woman to sing at Bayreuth; five years later Leontyne Price, already an international opera star, sang Cleopatra at the opening of the new Metropolitan. The pianist Philippa Duke Schuyler, in her tragically short life, opened new doors for blacks as concert artists, and in this decade, Natalie Hinderas has given several solo performances with major orchestras. Few blacks are now in symphony orchestras, and those who pursue careers in classical rather than jazz or popular

music continue to have difficulties finding employment.

Conductors constitute another group that has made outstanding progress in the last few years. Whereas in earlier periods women were most often found conducting all-female orchestras, a new group of women conductors has moved into the leadership of mixed orchestras and occasionally major orchestras and opera companies. Antonia Brico has become the symbol for this change. During her early professional career in the 1930s, Brico was the first woman to conduct the Berlin and New York philharmonic orchestras, among other leading groups. Subsequently she headed the New York Women's Symphony Orchestra from 1935 until its demise in 1939 and, since the 1940s, has directed a community orchestra in Denver. However, in 1974, the film *Antonia: a portrait of the woman,* with its portrayals of her frustrations as well as her early achievements, was responsible, along with the women's movement, for a new career for Brico. Other conductors now active include Victoria Bond, Beatrice Brown, Elaine Browne, Sarah Caldwell, Iva Dee Hiatt, Margaret Hillis, Eve Queler, Judith Somogi, and Margaret Harris, the last named a conductor in the musical theater.

More women are now active as composers of art music than ever before. Works composed in the period from 1950 to 1978 and entered in this bibliography include over 200 for orchestra and band, a large number of stage works and works for mixed media and non-acoustic sound sources, as well as chamber and choral pieces. This distribution reflects women's widening choices as well as recent changes in the field of composition as a whole. Women, like men, have to contend with the neglect of contemporary music by performers and audiences, compounded by the neglect of American music. Many women, however, feel that they suffer greater disadvantages than men because they do not have equal access to commissions, grants, recordings, academic posts, and major performances, particularly by orchestras and opera companies.

Nevertheless, support for women has grown considerably in recent years as a result of women's activities on their own behalf in music as well as in society as a whole. One of the first of the recent expressions of this change was the publication in 1970 by the National Federation of Music Clubs of Julia Smith's *Directory of American women composers,*[35] the first such book since Edwin Barnes's biographical dictionary published in 1936.[36] Another example is a series of thirteen radio broadcasts of recorded music that Smith prepared in 1972, and that was broadcast by stations throughout the country. A major concert by the New York Philharmonic in 1975 conducted by Sarah Caldwell presented the works of five women, among them Ruth Crawford Seeger, Pozzi Escot, and Thea Musgrave. In 1976 a series of eleven concerts entitled *Meet the woman composer* was held at the New School for Social Research, also in New York, and subsequently festivals have been held in cities and on university campuses all over the country. Two new organizations, the League of Women Composers and the American Women Composers, Inc., are also promoting works by women.

Renewed interest in women's contributions to music in the United States is also apparent in the recent increase in the number of articles about women. Indeed, several journals have devoted issues or parts of issues to women in music, reminiscent of the earlier "women's issues" of *Étude*. Women's studies courses in music, although late starters compared to other disciplines, are increasing; it is anticipated that this book will further encourage such studies. In addition, women on college campuses have joined together to investigate their status in matters of salary, hiring, and promotion.

The editors hope that *Women in American music: a bibliography of music and literature* will serve to retrieve for women their own rich heritage as musicians and confirm their creativity today within the mainstream of American music.

NOTES

1. *WIAM* 668.
2. *WIAM* 144. The first edition was published in 1931.
3. *WIAM* 285, 68.
4. *WIAM* 377, 384.
5. *WIAM* 621.
6. *WIAM* 970.
7. *WIAM* 1028.
8. *WIAM* 595.
9. *WIAM* 1139.
10. *Census reports, Bureau of the Census* (Washington, D.C.: Department of Commerce and Labor, 1870-1910).
11. *WIAM* 177.
12. *WIAM* 1168.
13. *WIAM* 654.
14. *WIAM* 178.
15. *WIAM* 659.
16. *WIAM* 707.
17. *WIAM* 1305.
18. *WIAM* 91.
19. *WIAM* 506, 533, and 539.
20. *WIAM* 66.
21. *WIAM* 644-45.
22. *WIAM* 74-76.
23. *WIAM* 665.
24. *WIAM* 70.
25. *WIAM* 2142.
26. *WIAM* 1991.
27. After the bibliography was completed, Laurine Elkins-Marlow shared with the editors copies of the society's by-laws and concert programs, which she had recently discovered. These materials are now on file at the Music Division of the New York Public Library.
28. *WIAM* 2064 describes a festival that most likely was organized by the society, even though *Musical Courier* failed to take note of the organization's existence. The women composers represented on the festival's programs closely match a membership list of the society.
29. *WIAM* 2622.
30. *WIAM* 2517.
31. *WIAM* 126.
32, *WIAM* 3229.
33. *Ibid.*
34. *WIAM* 3355.
35. *WIAM* 64.
36. *WIAM* 49.

Carol Neuls-Bates
Brooklyn College of the City University of New York

Adrienne Fried Block
College of Staten Island of the City University of New York

Adelaide Phillipps. Courtesy New York Public Library.

Jenny Lind at the opening of her American tour, 1850. Courtesy New York Public Library.

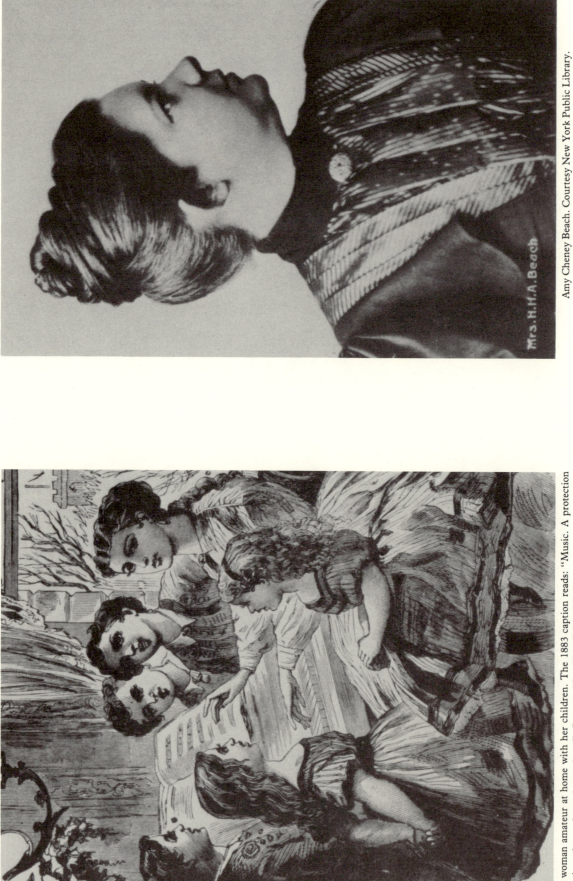

Amy Cheney Beach. Courtesy New York Public Library.

Mrs. H. H. A. Beach

A woman amateur at home with her children. The 1883 caption reads: "Music. A protection against vice, an incentive to virtue". Courtesy New York Public Library.

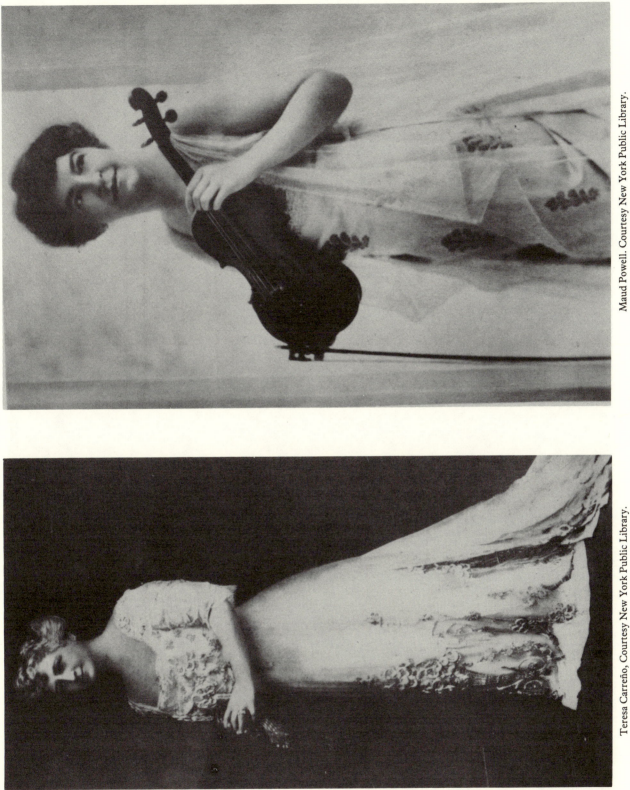

Maud Powell. Courtesy New York Public Library.

Teresa Carreño, Courtesy New York Public Library.

Brass and percussion players of the Boston Fadette Lady Orchestra, 1909. Courtesy New York Public Library.

Elizabeth Sprague Coolidge. Courtesy New York Public Library.

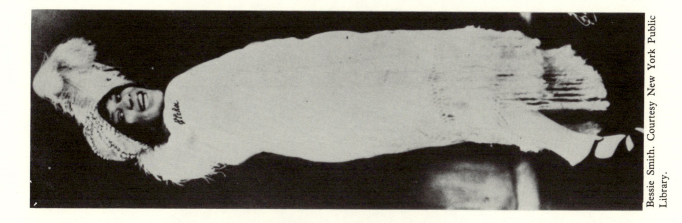

Bessie Smith. Courtesy New York Public Library.

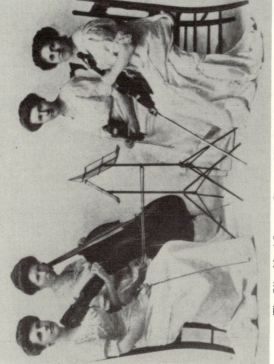

The Olive Mead Quartet. Courtesy New York Public Library.

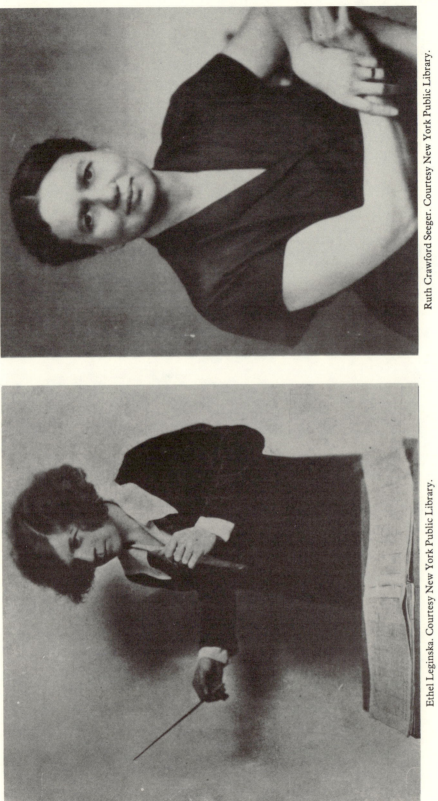

Ruth Crawford Seeger. Courtesy New York Public Library.

Ethel Leginska. Courtesy New York Public Library.

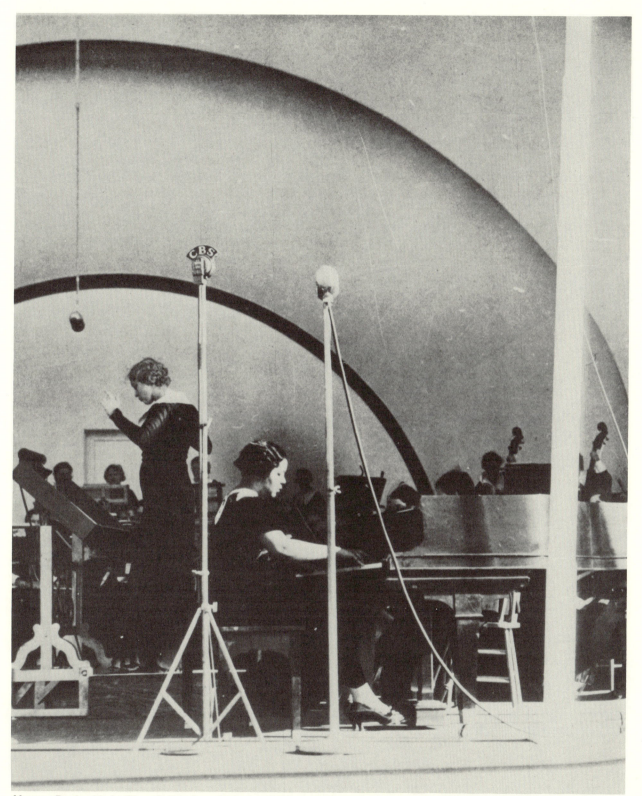

Margaret Bonds with the Woman's Symphony Orchestra of Chicago under the direction of Ebba Sundstrom, 1934. Bonds played Florence Price's piano concerto. From Lindsay Patterson, *The Negro in music and art* (New York Publishers Co., 1969). Courtesy of the author.

WOMEN IN AMERICAN MUSIC

REFERENCE MATERIALS

01   Bibliographies, catalogues, checklists, and discographies

1
bm
Albuquerque, New Mexico, University of New Mexico, Fine Arts Library. A checklist of music in manuscript by Eunice Lea Kettering. Comp. by Eunice Lea KETTERING (1977) 53 p.
The Fine Arts Library at the U. of New Mexico holds 53 compositions in autograph MSS by Eunice Lea Kettering: namely, 3 orchestral, 3 chamber, 2 solo instrumental, 24 choral, 13 solo vocal, and 8 dramatic works. This checklist includes descriptive information about the individual compositions and is available in photocopy from the library.

→   ASHLEY, Patricia. **Here they are--one plastic platter**, *see* **2996rr**[76].

2
ap
Available recordings of works by women composers, *High Fidelity/Musical America* XXIII/2 (Feb 1973) 53.
Lists recordings available commercially in 1973 of works by about 30 composers, chiefly contemporary American women.

→   BAKER, David; BELT, Lida. **Undine Smith Moore**, *see* **2997bd**[76].

→   BARNES, JR., Harold. **Claudia Muzio. A biographical sketch and discography,** *see* 2147bm[68].

→   BARNES, JR., Harold. **Mary Garden on records,** *see* 891ap[58].

3
bm
Bloomington, Indiana, Indiana University School of Music Library. A checklist of source materials by and about women in American music. Comp. by Kathryn M. TALALAY (1977) 51 p.
The Indiana U. School of Music Library holds the following items by and about women in American music: 1) clippings for cellist Zara Nelsova, composers Peggy Glanville-Hicks, Ruth Crawford Seeger, and Mana Zucca, harpist Mildred Dilling, pianists Ruth Laredo and Philippa Duke Schuyler, and singers Rose Bampton, Anne Bollinger, Grace Bumbry, Anna Case, Nadine Conner, Phyllis Curtin, Ella Fitzgerald, Maureen Forrester, Lena Horne, Marilyn Horne, Irene Jordan, Dorothy Kirsten, Mabel Mercer, Beverly Sills, Joan Sutherland, Helen Traubel, and Shirley Verrett; 2) 4 articles in typescript about women in music in the Paul Nettl Collection; 3) a typescript draft of names and sources of information for women in composition by Dominique-René de Lerma; 4) theses and dissertations in composition by Louise Bottorff, Catherine Carolyne Carl, Margaret Sisson Erickson, Carol Ann Giffels, Leslie Livengood Gilkey, Julia Marie Good, Ruby Lois Guilliams, Judith Kalivas, Marlene Langosch, Charlotte Reeves, and Alice Margaret Menninger Stempel; and 5) theses and dissertations about Amy Cheney Beach, Ruth Crawford Seeger, and Lily Strickland, composers, Suzanne Langer, philosopher, and Frances Elliott Clark and Mabelle Glenn, educators. A photocopy of the checklist is available from the library.

4
bm
Boston, Boston Public Library, Department of Rare Books and Manuscripts and the Music Division. A checklist of source materials by and about women in American music (1977) 6 p.
The Department of Rare Books and Manuscripts and the Music Division of the Boston Public Library include the following source materials by and about women in American music: 1) clipping files for composers Amy Cheney Beach, Helen Hopekirk, and Margaret Ruthven Lang, conductor Antonia Brico, singer Louise Homer, and the Boston Women's Symphony Orchestra; 2) correspondence of composers Mabel Wheeler Daniels, Annie Audios Hawley, Helen Hopekirk, Mana Zucca, Margaret C. Mason, and Clara Kathleen Rogers, educator Renée Longy Miquelle, patrons Margaret Starr McLain and Fanny Raymond Ritter, pianists Teresa Carreño and Amy Fay, singers Emma Abbott, Lillian Carlsmith, Elizabeth Mason, Louise Rollwagon, and Harriet Avery Strakosch, and violinist Teresa Liebe; 3) music in MSS by Mabel Wheeler Daniels and Clara Kathleen Rogers; 4) scrapbooks for conductor Ethel Leginska, singers Marian Anderson, Clara Clemens, Mary Garden, Adelina Patti, and Ernestine Schumann-Heink, the Apollo Soc. of Boston, the Boston Orchestral Club, the Boston Women's Symphony Orchestra and the Women's Symphony Orchestra Soc. from 1939-42, and the Massachusetts Federation of Music Clubs. A photocopy of the checklist is available from the library.

5
bm
Boston, Massachusetts, Isabella Stewart Gardner Museum. A checklist of source materials by and about women in American music. Comp. by Ralph P. LOCKE (1978) 12 p.

The Isabella Stewart Gardner Museum holds correspondence of patron Marian MacDowell, pianist Amy Fay, composer Margaret Ruthven Lang, and singers Susan Metcalfe Casals, Milka Ternina, and Yvonne Guilbert. The museum also holds scrapbooks and concert programs collected by Gardner. A photocopy of the checklist is available from the museum.

6
bm
Boston, New England Conservatory of Music, Spaulding Library. A checklist of source materials by and about women in American music (1977) 6 p.
The Spaulding Library at the New England Conservatory contains the following source materials by and about women in American music: 1) concert programs for pianists Teresa Carreño, Amy Fay, and Julie Rivé-King, and singer Amelita Galli-Curci; 2) correspondence of composers Amy Cheney Beach, Helen Hopekirk, and Isidora Martinez, patrons Elizabeth Sprague Coolidge and Marian MacDowell, and singer Eleanor Steber; and 3) music MSS by Amy Cheney Beach, Mabel Wheeler Daniels, Helen Hopekirk, Rosalie Housman, Anita Hough, Margaret Ruthven Lang, and Ethel Leginska. A photocopy of the checklist is available from the library.

→   BOWERS, Jane. **Recent researches on women in music,** *see* 101as[20].

→   **California's brilliant composer-pianist, Fannie Dillon,** *see* 658ap[56].

7
bm
Cambridge, Massachusetts, Harvard University, Schlesinger Library on the History of Women in America. A checklist of correspondence by Amy Fay. Comp. by Sylvia MITARACHI (1978) 9 p.
The Schlesinger Library on the History of Women in America at Harvard U. holds 2 collections of letters by Amy Fay: 1) letters from the pianist between 1859 and 1916 arranged alphabetically by addressee, and 2) letters written by the pianist in Germany from 1869-75, arranged chronologically. This checklist includes identifications for the addressees and topics mentioned in the letters. A photocopy of the checklist is available from the library.

8
bm
Catalogue of contemporary American women composers. Harold Branch Publishing, Inc.; Jelsor Music Co. (West Babylon, N.Y.: H. Branch, [1977]) 24 p. *Illus., list of works.*
Presents a list of compositions that have been recently published by Harold Branch, together with biographical information for the following women composers: Harriet Bolz, Radie Britain, Pauline Cruickshank, Helen Eastes, Wen-ying Hsu, Hulda Kreiss, Amy Miller Levine, Adabelle Gross Marcus, Leigh Scruggs, Jeanne Singer, Tui St. George Tucker, Vally Weigl, and Ruth Shaw Wylie.
(Jeanne Singer)

9
bm
Claremont, California, Scripps College Music Library. A checklist of compositions in manuscript by American women composers. Comp. by Joan MEGGETT (1977) [2] p.
The Music Library of Scripps Col. holds MSS by Fannie Charles Dillon and Frances Marion Ralston. A photocopy of the checklist is available from the library.

10
ap
DANIEL, Oliver. **New festival, The,** *Bulletin. American Composers Alliance* V/1 (1955) 3-9, 14-23.
This annotated discography of works by 44 composers includes the following works by women: Marion Bauer, *Prelude and fugue for flute and string orchestra, op. 43* (*WIAM* 2604) and *Symphonic suite for string orchestra, op. 33* (*WIAM* 2605); Esther Williamson Ballou, *Prelude and allegro for string orchestra and piano* (*WIAM* 4370); Miriam Gideon, *Fantasy on a Javanese motive* (*WIAM* 3485); and Peggy Glanville-Hicks, *Concertino da camera* (*WIAM* 3500), *Choral suite for female chorus, oboe, and string orchestra* (*WIAM* 3951), *Sonata for harp* (*WIAM* 4639), *Sonata for piano and percussion* (*WIAM* 3501), *Three gymnopédies* (*WIAM* 3503), and *The transposed heads* (*WIAM* 4804).

→   DENNIS, James. **Olive Fremstad,** *see* 948ap[58].

11
bm
Denver, Colorado, Denver Public Library, Music Division. A checklist of materials by and about women in American music. Comp. by Eleanor M. GEHRES (1977) 2 p.
The Music Division of the Denver Public Library includes miscellaneous papers, notebooks, programs, and scrapbooks pertaining to women in American music in the following collections: 1) May Arno, composer and founder of the May Arno School of Drama and Music in Denver, 1911-65; 2) Colorado Federation of Music Clubs, 1939-47; 3) Denver Businessmen's Orchestra (founded and conducted by Antonia Brico), 1948 to the present; 4) Denver Music Teachers' Assoc., 1958-72; 5) Denver Symphony Soc., 1960-63; 6) Musicians' Soc. of Denver; 7) Veda Reynolds, violinist, 1930-58; 8) Alice Roeschlaub, 1884-1950; 9) Alice Lytle Weber, singer, 1891-1931; and 10) Lillian Spencer White, lyricist. A photocopy of the checklist is available from the library.

12
bm **Detroit, Michigan, Detroit Public Library, Music and Performing Arts Division. A checklist of source materials by and about women in American music.** Comp. by Agatha Pfeiffer KALKANIS (1977) 1 p.
The Music and Performing Arts Division of the Detroit Public Library includes scrapbooks for the Tuesday Musicale and the Madrigal Soc.--both of which were women's organizations--and miscellaneous materials for Emma Azalia Hackley, educator, and Nellie Watts, patron. A photocopy of the checklist is available from the library.

13
bm **Durham, New Hampshire, University of New Hampshire Library, Special Collections. A checklist of source materials by and about Amy Cheney Beach.** Comp. by Barbara A. WHITE (1977) 1 p.
The Special Collections division of the U. of New Hampshire Library holds correspondence, diaries, music MSS, and scrapbooks of composer Amy Cheney Beach. A photocopy of the checklist is available from the library.

→ EAMES, Emma. **Some memories and reflections,** *see* 954bf[58].

14
ap ELKINS-MARLOW, Laurine. **Have women in this country written for full orchestra?,** *Symphony News* XXVII/2 (Apr 1976) 15-19.
A list of 250 works for full orchestra by 93 American women composers--mainly contemporary and arranged alphabetically by composer. Each entry includes title, date of composition, required instrumentation, duration, publication information, and/or the location of the score and parts.   *(Author)*

→ ELSON, James. **Practical aspects of our art. Music selection and program building for the women's chorus,** *see* 3231ap[78].

15
bm **Evanston, Illinois, Northwestern University Library, The Women's Collection. A checklist of source materials by and about women in American music.** Comp. by Sarah SHERMAN (1978) 1 p.
The Women's Collection at Northwestern U. houses a comprehensive collection of about 800 periodicals--i.e., journals, newsletters, and newspapers--generated by the contemporary women's movement. Clipping files in music include the following subject headings: music notices, women in music (general), woman-identified music, lyrics, song books, special issues of periodicals devoted to women in music, Anna Crusis Choir, College Music Soc., Decade of Women Concert, National Women's Music Festival, and Olivia Records. A photocopy of the checklist and related information about the collection are available from the library.

16
bm **Fayetteville, Arkansas, University of Arkansas Library, Special Collections Division. A checklist of source materials by and about Florence B. Price.** Comp. by Sam SIZER (1977) 18 p.
The Special Collections Division of the U. of Arkansas Library contains the following materials pertaining to composer Florence B. Price: 81 published and unpublished scores, 31 items of correspondence, 20 concert programs, and 30 miscellaneous items including photographs, clippings, and notebooks. A photocopy of the checklist is available from the library.

→ GALATOPOULOS, Stelios. **Callas: La divina,** *see* 3249bm[78].

17
bd GALT, Martha Caroline. **To the ladies,** *Know your American music* (Ithaca, N.Y.: National Federation of Music Clubs, 1943) 51-54.
This handbook includes a list of works by women composers who were active in the 1940s, arranged by genre.

→ GAUME, Mary Matilda. **Ruth Crawford Seeger: her life and works,** *see* 2020dd[66].

→ GOETSCHIUS, Percy. **Mrs. H.H.A. Beach,** *see* 681bm[56].

→ GOSS, Madeline. **Modern music makers,** *see* 2023bf[66].

→ GREENFIELD, Edward. **Joan Sutherland,** *see* 3254bm[78].

18
bm HIXON, Don L.; HENNESSEE, Don, comps. **Women in music: a biobibliography** (Metuchen, N.J.: Scarecrow, 1975) xiii, 347 p. *Index.*
A dictionary listing close to 7000 women musicians, both European and American, who were active in history or are active at the present time. Each entry consists of 1) the musician's name, including appropriate pseudonyms, maiden name, stage name, and variant forms and spellings, 2) place and date

of birth, 3) field(s) of musical activity or specialization, and 4) a coded list of sources in which biographies may be found. Approximately 50 standard sources were culled for biographies. A classified list of women musicians by activity and instrument is included. R. by Dominique-René de LERMA, *Notes,* XXXIII/2 (Dec 1976) 295-96.

→ JOHNSON, Christopher. **Rebecca Clarke. A catalogue of her works,** *see* 2034bm[66].

→ LASSIMONNE, Denise. **Myra Hess by her friends,** *see* 2245bm[68].

→ LAWTON, Mary. **Schumann-Heink. The last of the titans,** *see* 1055bf[58].

→ LE MASSENA, C.E. **Galli-Curci's life of song,** *see* 2249bm[68].

→ LERNER, Ellen. **Music of selected contemporary American women composers, The: a stylistic anaylsis,** *see* 3083dm[76].

19
bm **Los Angeles, University of California Music Library. A checklist of materials by and about women in American music.** Comp. by Stephen M. FRY (1977) [2] p.
The Music Library of the U. of California at Los Angeles includes music MSS by Fannie Charles Dillon, Kathleen Lockhart Manning, Mary Carr Moore, Frances Marion Ralston, and Helen Louise Shaffer. The library also holds clipping files for Dillon and numerous published works by the 5 composers. A photocopy of the checklist is available from the library.

20
bm **Los Angeles, University of Southern California Music Library. A checklist of compositions in manuscript by Mary Carr Moore.** Comp. by Joan MEGGETT (1977) [1] p.
The Music Library of the U. of Southern California holds 4 MSS by Mary Carr Moore. A photocopy of the checklist is available from the library.

21
ap LOVE, William G. **Ma Rainey. Discography,** *Jazz Information* II/4 (6 Sept 1940) 9-14.
Lists more than 90 numbers recorded for Paramount Records by Gertrude ("Ma") Rainey--the blues singer--together with information about accompanying instruments. Rainey's various instrumental groups were called the Georgia Jazz Band and the Tub-Jug-Washboard Band.

22
bm LOWENS, Irving. **Bibliography of songsters printed in America before 1821, A** (Worcester, Mass.: American Antiquarian Soc., 1976) 229 p. *List of works, index.*
Defines a songster as a collection of 3 or more secular poems intended to be sung, and lists 649 songsters. The rapid growth and strong influence of Free Masonry in the United States created a widespread demand for songsters prepared for male consumption exclusively. Even though women were excluded from Masonic rituals, nonetheless many of the songsters prepared for women include a selection of Masonic ditties. Songsters to 1821 were compiled by the following women: Miss Ashmore, Margaret Finch, and Nurse Lovechild. Mary Ann Pownall was the author of a songster.

→ LYON, Hugh Lee. **Leontyne Price: highlights of a prima donna,** *see* 3285bm[78].

23
bm **Mary Flagler Cary Music Collection, The** (New York: Pierpont Morgan Library, 1970) 108 p. *Facsim., music, bibliog.*
The Cary Music Collection was donated to the Pierpont Morgan Library in New York by the trustees of the Mary Flagler Cary Charitable Trust, following Cary's death in 1967. An introduction to this catalogue of the collection notes that Cary and her parents--Henry Harkness Flagler and Anne Lamont Flagler--were leaders in musical life in New York, although Cary and her father were modest about their benefactions and collecting. The Cary Music Collection contains music MSS (including more than 150 autographs), autograph letters of composers and musicians, printed books, portraits, and memorabilia, and represents one of the most important collections--public or private--in the United States.

→ MCKENNA, Marian. **Myra Hess. A portrait,** *see* 2284bm[68].

24
bm MCRAE, Lynn T., comp. **Computer catalogue of 19th-century American-imprint sheet music, A** (Charlottesville, Va.:

U. of Virginia Library, 1977) 13 fiche, $15. (microfiche). *List of works, index.*

A rich source of our American heritage is found in popular sheet music published in the 19th c., yet the status of early American-imprint music in our libraries is a sorry one at best. Needed is an economical method of bibliographic control, which will respond to the diverse interests of a widening group of scholars, bibliophiles, and performers. The cataloguing code devised here defines 32 data fields that can be retrieved and manipulated. The fields include title, composer, lyricist, detailed imprint, first line of chorus text, engraver, plate number, etc. This method of cataloguing has been applied to 8000 titles of 19th-c. American-imprint sheet music in the U. of Virginia Music Collection, resulting in a computer-generated catalogue and 11 indices. In the collection there are 2 or more works by each of the following American women: Frances Allitsen, Augusta Browne, Mary S.B. Dana, Jessie L. Gaynor, Faustina Hasse Hodges, Adele Hohnstock, Helen Hood, Frances Isabella King, Margaret Ruthven Lang, Maude Nugent, Mrs. A.V. Pendleton, Clara Kathleen Rogers, Miss M.B. Scott, Sue Ingersoll Scott, M.R. Siegling, Jane Sloman, Penelope Smith, Hattie Starr, Florence Vane, and Kate Vannah. *(Jean M. Bonin)*

25 MEAD, Janet Cutler. **Catalog of Composers Library** (rev. ed.;
bm Cincinnati: Delta Omicron Music Composers Library, 1974) 31 p.
The Delta Omicron International Music Fraternity was founded in 1909 to further the work of women composers and to promote American music, among other aims. Chapters or clubs are located in cities and on college campuses throughout the United States. The Delta Omicron Music Composers Library is located in the Public Library of Cincinnati and Hamilton County and houses works by 20th-c. American composers, more than one-half of whom are male. The women represented in the collection are as follows: Gladys Bell, Martha Binde, Gena Branscombe, Grace Bush, Mary Janet Cutler, Anne Shannon Demarest, Fannie Charles Dillon, Lois Myers Emig, Olive P. Endres, Lorraine Noel Finley, Edna Frankl, Elizabeth A.H. Green, Frances Wright Hausenfluck, Ethel Glenn Hier, Jeanellen McKee, Janet Cutler Mead, Grace Hamilton Morrey, Marion Morrey (Richter), Elizabeth Oldenburg, Bessie Whittington Pfohl, Claire Polin, Frances Marion Ralston, Helen Sears, Jeannette Sexton, Margaret Vance Shelley, Louise Harrison Snodgrass, Margaret McClure Stitt, and Marion Lehne Strickling. *(Gena Phenix)*

26 **Memphis, Tennessee, Memphis/Shelby County Library and**
bm **Information Center. A checklist of works by Naomi Carroll**
  Haimsohn. Comp. by Charlene BATSON (1978) 1 p.
The Memphis/Shelby County Library and Information Center holds music MSS by Naomi Carroll Haimsohn as well as published scores. A photocopy of the checklist is available from the library.

→ MERRILL, E. **Mrs. H.H.A. Beach. Her life and music,** *see* 709dd[56].

27 MITCHELL, Charles, comp. **Discography of works by**
bm **women composers** (Paterson, N.J.: Paterson Free Public Library, 1975) 9 p.
Lists recordings of works by both European and American women composers that were available commercially as of Mar. 1975 and in the record collection of the Paterson Free Public Library in New Jersey. This pamphlet is an outgrowth of a series of concerts at the library featuring compositions by women, sponsored by the library and the New Jersey State Council of the Arts.

28 MURDOCK, Mary Elizabeth. **Catalog of the Sophia Smith**
bm **Collection. Women's history archive** (2nd ed.; Northampton, Mass.: Smith Col., 1976) 78 p.
The archive contains extensive papers and memorabilia for music educators Grace Spofford and Eleanor W. Thayer, musicologist and conductor Sophie Drinker, and singers Zelie de Lussan and Risë Stevens. Also in the collection are occasional items including selected sheet music by Amy Cheney Beach; papers for impresario Sarah Caldwell, and singers Marian Anderson, Geraldine Farrar, and Jenny Lind. A scrapbook assembled by Effie Douglas Putnam has letters, notes, and photographs of eminent European artists and musicians from the 1880s to the 1920s.

→ **Netty Simons,** *see* 3108ap[76].

29 **New Haven, Connecticut, New Haven Historical Society. A**
bm **checklist of source materials by and about women in**
  American music. Comp. by Elizabeth R. HARKINS (1977) 1 p.
The library of the New Haven Historical Soc. includes 2 music books--dated 1798 and 1799--that belonged to Lucretia Champion, musical amateur. These MSS contain a description of the rudiments of music and songs with one-line accompaniments. The library also includes 1700 records about the Women's Choral Soc. of New Haven from 1927-59. A photocopy of the checklist is available from the library.

30 **New Haven, Connecticut, Yale University Music Library. A**
bm

checklist of source materials by and about women in American music. Comp. by Elizabeth R. HARKINS (1977) [2] p.
The Yale U. Music Library contains the following materials by and about women in American music: 1) clippings, correspondence, and photographs from 1907-54 for Madeline Wright, a piano student of Teresa Carreño and Myra Hess; 2) correspondence, diaries, and programs from 1886-93 for Emma Waleska Schneelock and her sister Emilie A. Schneelock, singers, who toured the United States with Patrick S. Gilmore's quartet; and 3) correspondence by the Love family, which includes 1400 letters and cards written between 1888 and 1960 to Helen Douglas Love Scranton and to her mother, Lucy Cleveland Prindle Love. Scranton was secretary to Franz Kneisel and was also active with the Friends of Music Soc. and the Beethoven Assoc. in New York. A collection of tapes on file with the project Oral History: American Music at Yale includes interviews with composers Eleanor Cory, Pozzi Escot, Vivian Fine, Jean Eichelberger Ivey, Ursula Mamlok, Marga Richter, Kay Swift, Louise Talma, Joan Tower, and Vally Weigl; educator Nadia Boulanger; music librarian Eva J. O'Meara; musicologist Eileen Southern; patron and administrator Claire Reis; keyboard players Myra Hess and Wanda Landowska; singers Lotte Lehmann, Esther Phillips, Maxine Sullivan, and Big Mama Thornton; and musicians' wives Ella Grainger, Olga Naoumoff Koussevitzky, Nuria Schönberg Nono, and Lois Porter. A photocopy of the checklist is available from the library.

31 **New York, Graduate Center of the City University of New**
bm **York, Project for the Oral History of Music in America. A**
  checklist of oral history materials about women in American
  music. Comp. by Ruth JULIUS (1977) 1 p.
The Project for the Oral History of Music in America at the Graduate Center of the City U. of New York holds tapes and transcripts of interviews conducted by Elizabeth Wood and Ruth Julius with the following contemporary composers: Ruth Anderson, Peggy Stuart Coolidge, Vivian Fine, Miriam Gideon, Doris Hays, Alison Knowles, Annea Lockwood, Ursula Mamlok, Dorothy Rudd Moore, Dika Newlin, Marga Richter, Jeanne Singer, Dhyani Thorner, Vally Weigl, Judith Lang Zaimont, and Ellen Taaffe Zwilich. A photocopy of the checklist is available from the project.

32 **New York, New York Public Library, Music Division. A**
bm **checklist of music in manuscript composed by women in**
  American music. Comp. by Jean BOWEN (1978) 11 p.
The Music Division of the New York Public Library includes music MSS by Alice Barnett, Marion Bauer, Amy Cheney Beach, Gena Branscombe, Ruth Braun, Lillian Brinsley, Elizabeth Sprague Coolidge, Helen Crane, Vivian Fine, Charlotte Fox, Eleanor Everest Freer, Katherine Heyman, Ethel Glenn Hier, Rosalie Housman, Carrie Jacobs-Bond, Berta Kalich, Hazel Kinscella, Mary Knight Wood, Fannie Snow Knowlton, Barbara Kolb, Jeannette Kremer, Margaret Ruthven Lang, Ethel Leginska, Sara Liventhan, Marguerite Merington, Letitia Radcliffe, Marthe Servine, Fanny M. Spencer, Lily Strickland, Alba Vietor, Harriet Ware, Caroline Webb, Florence Wickham, and Mabel Wood-Hill. A photocopy of the checklist is available from the library. The New York Public Library also holds an 18th-c. music MS from the Ephrata Cloister in Pennsylvania.

33 **New York, New York Public Library, Music Division. A**
bm **checklist of source materials by and about women in**
  American music. Comp. by Jean BOWEN (1977) 8 p.
The Music Division of the New York Public Library holds correspondence for the following women active in American music: 1) Isadora Bennett, administrator; 2) Marion Bauer, Amy Cheney Beach, Mabel Wheeler Daniels, Vivian Fine, Peggy Glanville-Hicks, Mary Howe, Ruth Crawford Seeger, Louise Talma, and Caroline Unger, composers; 3) Antonia Brico, conductor; 4) Juliette A. Graves Adams and Nadia Boulanger, educators; 5) Suzanne Bloch, lutenist; 6) Catherine Crozier, organist; 7) Fannie Bloomfield-Zeisler, Teresa Carreño, Myra Hess, Wanda Landowska, Rosina Lhevinne, Julie Rivé-King, and Olga Samaroff Stokowski, pianists; 8) Emma Abbott, Suzanne Adams, Sally Frothingham Akers, Frances Alda, Elsa Alsen, Marian Anderson, Anna Bishop, Lucrezia Bori, Sophie Braslau, Zelie De Lussan, Emma Eames, Olive Fremstad, Povla Frijsh, Johanna Gadski, Amelita Galli-Curci, Mary Garden, Eva Gauthier, Alma Gluck, Minnie Hauk, Frieda Hempel, Emma Juch, Clara Louise Kellogg, Jenny Lind, Grace Moore, Christine Nilsson, Lillian Nordica, Rosa Olitzka, Sigrid Onégin, Eugenie Pappenheim, Adelina Patti, Radiana Pazmor, Lily Pons, Rosa Ponselle, Marie Rappold, Clementine de Vere Sapio, Ernestine Schumann-Heink, Zelda Harrison Séguin, Marcella Sembrich, Antoinette Sterling, Joan Sutherland, Gladys Swarthout, Emma Cecilia Thursby, and Ellen Beach Yaw, singers; and 9) Carroll Glenn and Maud Powell, violinists. The collection also includes the papers of hymnist Fanny Crosby, patron Claire Reis, and singer Eva Gauthier, as well as scrapbooks for the following: 1) Gena Branscombe and Mary Howe, composers; 2) Stella Mark Cushing and Rosalyn Tureck, pianists; 3) Stell Anderson, Rosalyn Tureck, and Sylvia Zaremba, pianists; 4) Sophie Braslau, Dorothy Jardon, Elsa Oehme-Foerster, Lina Pagliughi, and Florence Quartararo, singers; and 5) Maud Powell, violinist. Extensive clipping files are available for large numbers of women. A photocopy of the checklist is available from the library.

34 **New York, New York Public Library, Theater Division. A**
bm

checklist of scrapbooks about women in American music (1978) 1 p.
The Robinson Locke Collection of Dramatic Scrapbooks in the Theater Division of the New York Public Library includes materials for the following women in American music: Lucille Crews, composer; Nora Bayes and May Irwin, composers and singers; Fannie Bloomfield-Zeisler, pianist; Frances Alda, Sophie Braslau, Emma Eames, Geraldine Farrar, Olive Fremstad, Amelita Galli-Curci, Mary Garden, Alma Gluck, Frieda Hempel, Louise Homer, Alice Nielsen, Lillian Nordica, Adelina Patti, Corinne Rider-Kelsey, Lillian Russell, Ernestine Schumann-Heink, and Marcella Sembrich, singers; and Maud Powell, violinist. A photocopy of the checklist is available from the library.

→ OLIVEROS, Pauline. **And don't call them lady composers**, *see* 3111an[76].

→ PANEKY, Claire. **American composer in Germany, An**, *see* 3114ap[76].

→ **Peggy Glanville-Hicks**, *see* 3117ap[76].

→ PERLE, George. **Music of Miriam Gideon, The**, *see* 3119ap[76].

35 **Philadelphia, Free Library of Philadelphia, Fleisher Collec-**
bm **tion. A checklist of source materials by and about women in American music.** Comp. by Laurine ELKINS-MARLOW (1977) 6 p.
The Fleisher Collection of the Free Library of Philadelphia includes music MSS and instrumental parts of works by the following American women composers: Martha Alter, Florence Anderson (Du Page), Esther Williamson Ballou, Elaine Barkin, Joyce Barthelson, Marion Bauer, Amy Cheney Beach, Norma Beecroft, Jeanne Behrend, Johanna Beyer, Jeanne Boyd, Elizabeth Clark, Pozzi Escot, Bella Fenstock, Dora Flick-Flood, Vivian Fine, Mary Howe, Minuetta Kessler, Beatrice Laufer, Helen Lipscomb, Joan Panetti, Dorothy M. Priesing, Eda Rapoport, Elna Sherman, Gitta Steiner, Lily Strickland, Elinor Remick Warren, and Grace Williams. The collection also holds correspondence of Mary Howe and Frances McCollin. A photocopy of the checklist is available from the library.

36 **Philadelphia, Free Library of Philadelphia, Music Depart-**
bm **ment. A checklist of source materials by and about Frances McCollin** (1977) card file.
The Music Department of the Free Library of Philadelphia holds music MSS for about 200 works by Frances McCollin, including songs, solo instrumental music, chamber music--chiefly for violin and cello--and a few orchestral pieces. The McCollin collection also includes 87 items of her published sheet music, correspondence, scrapbooks, and other memorabilia. A photocopy of the checklist is available from the library.

37 **POOL, Jeannie G. Women in music history: a research guide**
bm (New York: author, 1977) iv, 42 p. $3. *Bibliog., list of works, discog.*
An introductory guide to research about women in music, intended especially for undergraduate students in music and women's studies. Contains 1) an essay about the issues confronting the researcher in women's studies in music, e.g., the position of women in society, and the relationship between genius and gender, 2) a bibliography of literature including books and articles on the work of individual composers as well as women in composition in general, bibliographies, lists of women composers, and writings that deny women's creative abilities in music, 3) information on organizations, publishers, recording companies, and periodicals that are relevant to women's studies in music, 4) a list of 270 women composers (European and American) active to 1900 together with information about the types of works they composed, 5) a discography of recordings available as of Sept. 1977, and 6) a list of possible research topics. *(Author)*

38 **Poughkeepsie, New York, Vassar College, George Sherman**
bm **Dickinson Music Library. A checklist of source materials by and about women in American music.** Comp. by Virginia GIFFORD (1977) [4] p.
The George Sherman Dickinson Music Library at Vassar Col. contains the following source materials by and about women in American music: 1) correspondence by composers Esther Williamson Ballou, Amy Cheney Beach, Miriam Gideon, Netty Simons, and Louise Talma, educator Nadia Boulanger, patron Louise Dyer, singer Ernestine Schumann-Heink, and Harmony Twichell Ives and Frances MacDowell, relatives of composers; 2) music MSS by Martha Alter, Jean Slater Appel, and Miriam Gideon; 3) scrapbooks, correspondence, and diary of pianist Teresa Carreño; and 4) 8 tapes of music by Netty Simons and 2 tapes of Louise Talma's *The Alcestiad* (*WIAM* 4846). A photocopy of the checklist is available from the library.

→ **Pozzi Escot**, *see* 3121ap[76].

39 RALSTON, Jack L., comp. **Treasures from the collection of**
bm **the Institute for Studies in American Music** (Kansas City: U. of Missouri, 1972) 20 p. (typescript).
The library of the Inst. for Studies in American Music at the U. of Missouri contains the following autograph MSS by Amy Cheney Beach: 1) *Mama's waltz, Menuetto, Petit valse*, and *Air and variations*--all juvenalia for piano, 2) *The rainy day* (*WIAM* 1587), 3) *Cabildo, op. 149*, an opera in one act, 4) *Caprice for flute, cello, and piano*, 5) a full score of *The chambered nautilus, op. 66* (*WIAM* 1295), 6) the Graduale from the Mass in E-flat major, op. 5 (*WIAM* 1316), and 7) the piano quintet in F-sharp minor, op. 67 (*WIAM* 1268).

40 REED, Peter Hugh. **Recorded art of Frieda Hempel, The,**
ap *Record Collector* X/3 (Aug 1955) 53-71. *Illus., discog.*
A review of Hempel's discography, together with biographical notes by George T. Keating. Her recording output is divided into 7 groups: 1) Odeon records, 1906-09, 2) His Master's Voice, 1909-17, 3) Thomas A. Edison records, 4) His Master's Voice acoustic records, 1923-25, 5) His Master's Voice electrical records, 6) other records, and 7) records which were made from a WNYC radio broadcast in New York in 1943.

41 RICHARDS, J.B. **Recordings of Lucrezia Bori, The,** *Record*
ap *Collector* IX/5 (Oct 1954) 100-23. *Illus.*
Presents an annotated discography of Lucrezia Bori's recordings, organized in the following categories: selections from Italian, French, and Russian operas, excerpts from *zarazuelas* and Spanish operas together with Spanish art and folk songs, and Italian, English, and French art songs. A chronology of Bori's activity in recording from 1910-37 is included.

→ RIDLEY, N.A. **Johanna Gadski**, *see* 1162ap[58].

→ RIEGGER, Wallingford. **Music of Vivian Fine, The,** *see* 3125ap[76].

→ RINGENWALD, Richard. **Music of Esther Williamson Ballou, The: an analytical study,** *see* 3126dm[76].

42 **Rochester, New York, Eastman School of Music, Sibley**
bm **Music Library. A checklist of source materials by and about women in American music.** Comp. by Michael W. RECHEL (1977) [9] p.
The Sibley Library of the Eastman School holds the following materials for women in American music: 1) clippings from New York and Rochester, N.Y., newspapers arranged by subject from 1920 to the present; 2) clippings from a newspaper series entitled "Women in music" that appeared in the *Rochester Time-Union* in the 1950s; 3) concert programs for the Festival of American Music from 1925-71--which included many premières of works by women composers; 4) correspondence by composers Jeanne Boyd, Iris Brussels, Fay Foster, and Carrie Jacobs-Bond, music librarians Barbara Duncan and Ruth Watanabe, musicologist Ruth Hannas, singers Emma Eames and Jean Woolford, and violinist Maud Powell; 5) music MSS by Esther Williamson Ballou, Marion Bauer, Priscilla A. Beach, Evelyn Berckman, Jeanne Boyd, Gertrude M. Brown, Elizabeth Clark, Rosemary Clark, Julia Howell, Alma Lissow, Margaret Midelfart, Edythe Beth Miller, Blythe Owen, Stella Pauline Roberts, and Daria Semegen; 6) M.M. theses in composition by Martha Alter, Jean Mary Anderson, Virginia Brosius, Gertrude M. Brown, Elizabeth Anne Butz, Elizabeth Clark, Jewel Dawn Dirks, Adele Drill, Anne E. Eggleston, Jean Eichelberger (Ivey), Maryana Sue Garza, Joan Charlene Groom, Bernice Hensler, Beverly Elizabeth Holmes, Adelaide Ferry Hooker, Julia Howell, Mary Elizabeth Jones, Mary Ellen Kapp, Alma Lissow, Evelyn McCann, Arthede McFaul, Janet Gunn McLean, Edythe Beth Miller, Janice Overmiller, Ruth Marguerite Palmer, Gloria Pullen Penico, Nona Jean Reed, Josephine Lorraine Restelle, Natalie Claire Rhoden, Mary Scott Riesland, Phyllis Jean Saffran, Nancy Selinger, Annabelle Shrago, Betsy Finck Stevens, Margaret Vardell, Norma Ruth Wendelburg, Elizabeth Windham, and Miriam Workman; and 7) Ph.D. dissertations in composition by Rosemary Clark, Emma Lou Diemer, Joan Charlene Groom, Elizabeth Holloway, Sister Mary Theophane Hytrek, Tosca Berger Kramer, Annette LeSeige, Margarita L. Merriman, Alice Proctor, Norma Ruth Wendelburg, Gloria Agnes Wilson, and Ruth Shaw Wylie. A photocopy of the checklist is available from the library.

43 **Santa Barbara, California, University of California Library,**
bm **Lotte Lehmann Archive. A checklist of source materials by and about Lotte Lehmann.** Comp. by Martin SILVER (1977) 1 p.
The Lotte Lehmann Archive in the Library of the U. of California at Santa Barbara includes the following materials for the singer: 1) business and personal correspondence, 2) films, tapes, and transcripts of radio broadcasts and interviews, 3) 26 scrapbooks of press clippings, 4) manuscripts and proofs of her books, and 5) paintings and other art works by Lehmann. A photocopy of the checklist is available from the library.

44 **Scores and parts presented to the Music Library by the**
bm **Center of the Creative and Performing Arts, State University**

of New York, Buffalo (Buffalo: Music Library, State U. of New York, Buffalo, 1976) 30 p.
The collection includes facsimiles of autographs for Louise Talma's cantata *All the days of my life* (*WIAM* 3751) and Beatrice Witkin's *Interludes for solo flute.*
(Carol Bradley)

→   SEROFF, Victor. **Renata Tebaldi. The woman and the diva,** *see* 3329bm[78].

45   SKOWRONSKI, Jo Ann. **Women in American music: a**
bm   **bibliography** (Metuchen, N.J.: Scarecrow, 1978) 191 p. $8. *Index.*
Lists 1305 books and pertinent articles from major periodicals about women in American music from 1776-1976, with annotations for most of the entries. All areas of music are included, from religious to popular. Coverage is divided into 4 time periods, based on significant events in the history of women as demarcation points. There are 2 additional divisions: 1) general history, and 2) bibliographies, dictionaries, and indexes.   *(Publisher, abridged)*

→   SUTRO, Florence Edith. **Women in music and law,** *see* 729bc[56].

→   TUTHILL, Burnet. **Mrs. H.H.A. Beach,** *see* 733ap[56].

→   VAN DE VATE, Nancy. **American woman composer, The: some sour notes,** *see* 3164ap[76].

→   VAN DE VATE, Nancy. **Every good boy (composer) does fine,** *see* 3165ap[76].

→   WAGENKNECHT, Edward. **Geraldine Farrar. An authorized record,** *see* 1235bm[58].

46   **Washington, D.C., Library of Congress, Music Division. A**
bm   **checklist of music in manuscript composed by women in American music** (1978) 22 p.
The Music Division of the Library of Congress includes works by Juliette A. Graves Adams, Isabel Anderson, Marion Bauer, Amy Cheney Beach, Jeanne Boyd, Ruth Bradley, Gena Branscombe, Radie Britain, Mary Helen Brown, Rebecca Clarke, Ulric Cole, Elizabeth Sprague Coolidge, Natalie Curtis-Burlin, Mabel Wheeler Daniels, Fannie Charles Dillon, Theodora Dutton, Susan Dyer, Phyllis Fergus, Fay Foster, Eleanor Everest Freer, Jessie L. Gaynor, Miriam Gideon, Blanche Goode, Janet Harding, Faustina Hasse Hodges, Helen Hood, Helen Hopekirk, Mary Howe, Mary Knight-Wood, Margaret Ruthven Lang, Evangeline Lehman, Luella Lockwood Moore, Mary Carr Moore, Frances McCollin, Clara Kathleen Rogers, Mary Turner Salter, Ruth Crawford Seeger, Patty Stair, Lily Strickland, Anice Terhune, Frances Terry, Harriet Ware, Elinor Remick Warren, Mabel Wood-Hill, and Louise Drake Wright. A photocopy of the checklist is available from the Music Division. The Library of Congress also holds 18th-c. music MSS from the Ephrata Cloister in Pennsylvania and 19th-c. music MSS for the Shakers.

47   **Washington, D.C., Library of Congress, Music Division. A**
bm   **checklist of source materials by and about women in American music** (1978) 4 p.
The Music Division of the Library of Congress includes correspondence by women active in American music. The list consists of the following names: 1) Adella Prentiss Hughes, Marian MacDowell, Antonia Sawyer Miner (Sawyer), and Claire Reis, administrators and managers; 2) Marion Bauer, Amy Cheney Beach, Gena Branscombe, Radie Britain, Augusta Browne, Effie I. Canning, Rebecca Clarke, Ulric Cole, Mabel Wheeler Daniels, Fannie Charles Dillon, Dorothy Radde Emery, Phyllis Fergus, Fay Foster, Eleanor Everest Freer, Elizabeth Gyring, Ethel Glenn Hier, Helen Hopekirk, Rosalie Housman, Mary Howe, Margaret Ruthven Lang, Frances McCollin, Mana Zucca, Mary Carr Moore, Clara Kathleen Rogers, Ruth Crawford Seeger, Lily Strickland, Kay Swift, Louise Talma, and Mabel Wood-Hill, composers; 3) Antonia Brico, Margarete Dessoff, and Ethel Leginska, conductors; 4) Juliette A. Graves Adams, Frances Elliott Clark, Angela Diller, Clara Damrosch Mannes, Elizabeth Quaile, and Grace Spofford, educators; 5) Natalie Curtis-Burlin and Frances Densmore, ethnomusicologists; 6) Doriot Anthony Dwyer, flutist; 7) Wanda Landowska, Yella Pessl, and Rosalyn Tureck, harpsichordists; 8) Suzanne Bloch, lutenist; 9) Dika Newlin, musicologist; 10) Mary Curtis Bok (Zimbalist), Elizabeth Sprague Coolidge, Isabella Stewart Gardner, and Rose Fay Thomas, patrons; 11) Fannie Bloomfield-Zeisler, Teresa Carreño, Ruth Deyo, Maud Cuney-Hare, Katherine Heyman, Anne Hull, Guiomar Novaes, Nadia Reisenberg, Julie Rivé-King, Ann Schein, Olga Samaroff Stokowski, Ottilie Sutro, Rose Sutro, and Isabella Vengerova as pianists; 12) Merle Alcock, Lucrezia Bori, Sophie Braslau, Sarah Jane Cahier, Clara Clemens, Marcella Craft, Jessica Dragonette, Emma Eames, Geraldine Farrar, Olive Fremstad, Johanna Gadski, Amelita Galli-Curci, Mary Garden, Eva Gauthier, Alma Gluck, Minnie Hauk, Louise Homer, Emma Juch, Nina Koshetz, Marjorie Lawrence, Lotte Lehmann, Florence Macbeth, Margaret Matzenauer, Claudia Muzio, Emma Nevada, Alice Nielsen, Lillian Nordica, Adelina Patti, Roberta

Peters, Lily Pons, Rosa Ponselle, Rosa Raisa, Helen Rice, Sibyl Sanderson, Ernestine Schumann-Heink, Elisabeth Schwarzkopf, Marcella Sembrich, Mabel Garrison Siemann, Marguerite Sylva, and Emma Cecilia Thursby, singers; 13) Marianne Kneisel, Maud Powell, and Camilla Urso, violinists; 14) Alma Mahler Werfel, wife of the composer; and 15) Emilie Frances Bauer, Catherine Drinker Bowen, Margaret Chanler, and Minna Lederman, writers. The Music Division also holds the papers of writer Marcia Davenport, scrapbooks for educator Rebekah Crawford, and an unpublished biography of Fannie Bloomfield-Zeisler written by the pianist's husband. A photocopy of the checklist is available from the library.

→   WILLIAMS, Ora. **American black women in the arts and social sciences: a bibliographic survey,** *see* 180bm[25].

05   Dictionaries and encyclopedias

48   ANDERSON, E. Ruth, comp. **Contemporary American**
bm   **composers: a biographical dictionary** (Boston: G.K. Hall, 1976) 513 p. *Index.*
Presents biographies for 4000 Americans in composition, together with lists of their works. The data was supplied by the composers themselves in answer to a questionnaire developed by Anderson. The criteria for inclusion were: 1) a birth date no earlier than 1870, 2) United States citizenship or extended residence in the country, and 3) the publication, commercial recording, or performance in an urban area of at least one original composition. A separate index of women composers indicates that more than 400 women are represented in the dictionary.

49   BARNES, Edwin N.C. **American women in creative music**
bm   (Washington, D.C.: Music Education Publications, 1936) 44 p.
"Although 50 years have passed since George P. Upton (*Woman in music,* *WIAM* 177) denied women a place in creative music, many still see the woman composer 'through a veil darkly' ". Bio-bibliographical information for over 70 composers active in the 1930s is provided together with partial listings for about 100 additional women.

→   BOLDREY, Richard. **Women song composers,** *see* 115bm[25].

50   EBEL, Otto. **Women composers. A biographical handbook of**
bm   **women's work in music** (Brooklyn: F.H. Chandler, 1902) 151 p.
Contains biographical entries for more than 900 women composers of both American and European origins, active at the time of publication and in the recent past. Ebel contends that "woman has accomplished comparatively more in the field of music than is generally known", despite the fact that "scarcely 50 years ago music, with very few exceptions, was never seriously attempted as a study by women".

51   EWEN, David. **Composers since 1900** (New York: H.W.
bm   Wilson, 1969) 639 p. *Illus., bibliog., list of works.*
This compilation of biographical sketches and lists of works for 220 composers active since 1900 in western art music includes 3 women, each of whom has been prominent in American music: Marion Bauer, Miriam Gideon, and Peggy Glanville-Hicks.

52   FFRENCH, Florence, comp. **Music and musicians in Chi-**
bm   **cago** (Chicago: compiler, 1899) 236 p. *Illus., index.*
Contains articles on various aspects of musical life in Chicago and local music organizations and institutions in the middle and latter part of the 19th c., together with more than 150 biographical sketches of musicians active in the city in the 1890s. The leading women include Jessie L. Gaynor and Carrie Jacobs-Bond, composers; Juliette A. Graves Adams and Mary Chase Wood, educators; and Fannie Bloomfield-Zeisler and Birdice Blye, pianists. The history of the Amateur Musical Club, a women's organization in Chicago, is also considered.

53   HANAFORD, Phebe A. **Women of the century** (Boston: B.B.
bm   Russell, 1877) 648 p. *Port., index.*
A collection of biographical sketches of women in America to 1873, organized by sphere of activity. Among the musicians are: singers Abby, Elizabeth (wife of Asa), and Viola Hutchinson, active as advocates of abolition and temperance; professor Charlotte V. Winterburn, a music teacher at the Normal Col. of New York; Addie Ryan Coolidge, a Boston church singer; and Charlotte Cushman, a singer and actress in Boston. Information is also presented for singer Clara Louise Kellogg, and for Ellen M. Cartwright, who served 20 years as organist and chorister at the Methodist church in Nantucket, Mass., before giving up professional work in favor of child-rearing.

55   **I am woman. A tribute to women in music,** *BMI: The Many*
bp   *Worlds of Music* 4 (1977) 54. *Illus.*
Presents biographical sketches for about 200 women active in the 1970s and

earlier in classical, jazz, and popular music as composers and performers. The composers are all affiliated with Broadcast Music, Inc. (BMI).   *(Barbara Petersen)*

56 JAMES, Edward T.; JAMES, Janet Wilson; BOYER, Paul S.,
bc   eds. **Notable American women 1607-1950. A biographical dictionary**. With an introduction by Janet Wilson JAMES (Cambridge, Mass.: Belknap, 1971) 3 v. 687, 659, 729 p. *Bibliog., index.*
Prepared under the auspices of Radcliffe Col., this major resource for the history of women in the United States from 1607-1950 contains biographies for the following women in music: composers Amy Cheney Beach and Carrie Jacobs-Bond; music educators and patrons Emma Azalia Hackley, Adella Prentiss Hughes, Clara Damrosch Mannes, Georgia Stevens, Ellen Battell Stoeckel, Maria Longworth Nichols Storer, and Jeanette Thurber; performing musicians Emma Abbott, Anna Bishop, Fannie Bloomfield-Zeisler, Sophie Braslau, Teresa Carreño, Annie Louise Cary, Eleanora De Cisneros, Zelie De Lussan, Amy Fay, Della Fox, Elizabeth Taylor Greenfield, Alma Gluck, Minnie Hauk, Louise Homer, Helen Hopekirk, Sissieretta Jones, Emma Juch, Clara Louise Kellogg, Selma Kronold, Grace Moore, Helen Morgan, Emma Nevada, Alice Nielsen, Lillian Nordica, Adelina Patti, Adelaide Phillipps, Maud Powell, Gertrude ("Ma") Rainey, Corinne Rider-Kelsey, Julie Rivé-King, Olga Samaroff Stokowski, Ernestine Schumann-Heink, Sibyl Sanderson, Marcella Sembrich, Bessie Smith, Emma Cecilia Thursby, Camilla Urso, Marie Van Zandt, Edyth Walker, and Ellen Beach Yaw.

57 JONES, F.O., ed. **Handbook of American music and musi-**
bm   **cians** (Canaseraga, N.Y.: author, 1886) 182 p.
Presents brief histories of the leading musical institutions in the United States to 1886--including publishing firms, societies, and educational institutions--and biographies of American musicians active to the same date. The following women singers are represented: Emma Abbott, Eliza Biscaccianti, Anna Bishop, Clara M. Brinkerhoff, Annie Louise Cary, Emma Cranch, Hope Glenn, Minnie Hauk, Grace Heltz-Gleason, Clara Louise Kellogg, Marie Litta (Marie Eugenia Von Elsner), Ella Montejo, Emma Nevada, Christine Nielson-Rounsville, Lillian Norton-Gower (Nordica), Emma Aline Osgood, Adelaide Phillipps, Caroline Richings, Caroline Rivé, Erminia Rudersdorff, Ann Childe Séguin, Emma Seiler, Antoinette Sterling, Marie Van Zandt, and Emily Winant. Biographies for the hymn writer Lydia Baxter and the following pianists are also included: Teresa Carreño, Julie Rivé-King, Mary Nielson Fay Sherwood, and Anna Steiniger-Clark.

→   KING, Mrs. A.T. **Women as composers**, *see* 695ap[56].

58 MANGLER, Joyce Ellen. **Rhode Island music and musicians**
bm   **1733-1850** (Detroit: Information Services, 1965) 90 p. *Bibliog.*
This directory lists numerous women, active chiefly as teachers of voice and instruments.

→   MATHEWS, William S.B. **Hundred years of music in America, A**, *see* 602bf[55].

59 MOORE, John Weeks. **Appendix to *Encyclopaedia of music***
bm   **containing events and information occurring since the main work was issued** (Boston: O. Ditson, 1875) 45 p.
An appendix to Moore's *Complete encyclopaedia of music, elementary, technical, historical, biographical, vocal, and instrumental* (Boston: J.P. Jewett, 1854). Includes biographical entries for the following women in American music: composer Augusta Browne, pianist Teresa Carreño, and singers Anna Bishop, Annie Louise Cary, Clara Louise Kellogg, Euphrosyne Parepa-Rosa, Adelina and Carlotta Patti, Adelaide Phillipps, and Mary Paton Wood.

60 MOORE, John Weeks. **Dictionary of musical information**
bm   **1640-1875, A** (Boston: O. Ditson, 1876) 211 p.
A biographical dictionary with brief entries describing over 80 women active in American music during the 19th c., as well as a few active during the 18th c. Presents a "List of modern musical works published in the United States" that includes compositions by Mrs. M.E. Bailey, Octavia Hensel, Phoebe Knapp, Mrs. J.B. Paige, Elise Polko, Marie C. Rives, Mary S.B. Dana, Emma Seiler, Sisters of Notre Dame, Jane Sloman, and Sara Tyxler.

→   **More women composers**, *see* 711ap[56].

61 OSBURN, Mary Hubbell. **Ohio composers and musical**
bm   **authors** (Columbus, Ohio: privately published, 1942) 238 p. *Illus., bibliog., list of works, index.*
Presents a historical sketch of the development of musical life in Ohio, together with brief biographies for about 900 women and men who were active in composition to 1942, and who were either native-born or lived and worked in Ohio. When appropriate, additional areas of activity in music are noted, and in many cases the musician's major contribution was in an area other than composition. The following women figure most prominently: Florence Ellinwood Allen, Isabella Beaton, Josephine Forsyth, Ethel Glenn Hier, Mary Hubbell Osburn, Caroline Rivé, Julie Rivé-King, Ruth Crawford Seeger, and

Ella May Smith. Lists of educators, performers, and important events in the history of the Ohio Federation of Music Clubs are included.

62 REDWAY, Virginia, comp. **Music directory of early New**
bm   **York City. A file of musicians, music publishers, and musical instrument-makers listed in New York directories from 1786 through 1825, together with the most important New York music publishers from 1836 through 1875** (New York: New York Public Library, 1941) 102 p.
The names of about 50 women appear in all areas covered by the directory--mostly as musicians and publishers, and to a lesser extent as instrument makers and dancing teachers. Often a woman is listed as a widow, carrying on a business that formerly had been in her husband's name.

63 REIS, Claire **Composers in America** (New York: Da Capo,
bf   1977) 399 p. $19.50.
A reprint of the 1947 edition (New York: Macmillan). Presents biographical sketches for composers active in the 1940s, together with lists of their works and publication information. Composers were selected on the basis of 1) having written orchestral works and/or chamber music, and 2) having received at least one major performance. The following women are represented: Marion Bauer, Amy Cheney Beach, Jeanne Behrend, Evelyn Berckman, Gena Branscombe, Radie Britain, Ulric Cole, Ruth Crawford (Seeger), Mabel Wheeler Daniels, Vivian Fine, Florence G. Galajikian, Miriam Gideon, Mary Howe, Dorothy James, Beatrice Laufer, Eda Rapoport, Louise Talma, and Mabel Wood-Hill.

64 SMITH, Julia, ed. **Directory of American women composers**
bm   (Chicago: National Federation of Music Clubs, 1970) iv, 51 p.
A directory listing more than 600 American women composers--both contemporary and from the recent past--together with types of music composed and publishers.

65 TOWERS, John. **Woman in music** (Winchester, Va.: author,
bm   1897) 30 p.
A directory of more than 1000 European and American women in music, dedicated to Florence Edith Sutro, president of the Woman's Department of the Music Teachers National Assoc. The majority of women listed are contemporary composers of vocal music, although singers and instrumentalists are also included. Towers states that he has compiled the list to refute those who assert that woman is incapable of "creative musical productiveness".

→   TROTTER, James. **Music and some highly musical people**, *see* 1227bf[58].

66 WILLARD, Frances; LIVERMORE, Mary A. **Woman of the**
bm   **century, A** (Buffalo: n.n., 1893) 811 p. *Illus.*
A biographical dictionary tracing the "vast array of women's achievements in every branch", chiefly during the last decades of the 19th c. This "record of American women is offered at the close of 3 centuries in the New World, to the consideration of those who would know what the 19th c. of Christian civilization has here brought forth, and what are the vast outlook and the marvellous promise of the 20th c.". Biographies for the following women in music are included: composers Alice Andrews, Amy Cheney Beach, Sibylla Bailey Crane, Emma Hahr, Charlotte W. Hawes, Phoebe Knapp, Laura Emeline Newell, Constance Faunt Le Roy Runcie, Maria Staub, and Louise Brewster Williams; music educators (including critics, lecturers, and writers) Kate Brainard, Helen Louise Bullock, Abbey Perkins Cheney, Fanny Crosby, Eugenie Dussuchal, Sara Hershey Eddy, Mary Alice Fonda, Miriam Chase Ford, Nellie Hibler, Mary M. Howard, Josephine Keating, Clara Smart Millar, Aubertine Woodward Moore, and Annie Fillmore Sheardown; performers Emma Abbott, Ethel Atwood, Clara Bagg, Blanche Hermine Barbot, Flora Elizabeth Barry, Lillie Berg, Ella Augusta Bigelow, Anna Bishop, Fannie De Grasse Black, Aline Reed Blonder, Fannie Bloomfield-Zeisler, Birdice Blye, Clara M. Brinkerhoff, Luisa Cappiani, Abbie Carrington, Florence Andrews Clayton, Laura Sedgwick Collins, May Cook, Mrs. Ogden Crane, Jessie Bartlett Davis, Marie Decca, Mrs. A. Litsner DeFere, Christine Nielson Drier, Emma Eames, Alice May Esty, Amy Fay, Gertrude Franklin, Lillian Norton Gower (Nordica), Pauline Hall, Mrs. Francis R. Haswin, Minnie Hauk, Lillian Bailey Henschel, Agnes Huntington, Emma Juch, Clara Louise Kellogg, Adele Lewing, Maud Morgan, Emma Nevada, Celestina Joslin Northrop, Marion G. Osgood, Philippin E. von Overstolz, Eugenie Pappenheim, Adelina Patti, Abby Hutchinson Patton, Maud Powell, Annie Louise Cary Raymond, Emma Marcy Raymond, Caroline Keating Reed, Laura Andrews Rhodes, Alice May Bates Rice, Julie Rivé-King, Lillian Russell, Florence Eleanor Sage, Sibyl Sanderson, Florence E. Searing, Emelia Benic Serrano, Marrietta R. Sherman, Emma Roberto Steiner, Antoinette Sterling, Armanda Carlson Swenson, Emma Cecilia Thursby, Geraldine Ulmar, Maria Van Zandt, Bertha Webb, Julia E. Houston West, and Katherine Willard.

→   WILLHARTITZ, Adolph. **Some facts about women in music**, *see* 178bm[25].

COLLECTED WORKS

10 Literature

67 **Focus on women: composers, musicians--a not so silent**
bp **minority.** Ed. by Shirley FLEMING, *High Fidelity/Musical America*
XXV/6 (June 1975) MA 40.
Examines the work and the roles of contemporary women in music. The
authors, titles, and *WIAM* numbers under which abstracts of their articles
appear are as follows: Tom Johnson, *Lucia Dlugoszewski* (3074), Nancy Van de
Vate, *The American woman composer: some sour notes* (3164), *Women
composers: en route* (3171), and Elinor Kefalas, *Pauline Oliveros: an interview*
(3077). Adrienne Fried Block's *The woman musician on campus: hiring and
promotion patterns*, is a summary of the session on the status of women in
college music teaching that was held at the annual meeting of the College
Music Soc. in 1975. An abstract for Block's article appears in connection with
the published proceedings of the CMS session (*WIAM* 73, 98).

68 NEULS-BATES, Carol. **Sources and resources for women's**
ap **studies in American music: a report**, *Notes. Music Library
Association* XXXV/2 (Dec 1978) 269-83.
At a conference at the City U. of New York in May 1977 sponsored by *Women
in American music: a bibliography of music and literature*, 4 researchers reported
on their current areas of interest in women's studies in American music. 1)
Judith Tick discussed her research about women composers before the Civil
War and reviewed her methodology for isolating prominent composers: i.e.,
Augusta Browne, Faustina Hasse Hodges, Susan A. Parkhurst, Jane Sloman,
and Marion Dix Sullivan, who were chief among the first generation of
professional women composers that emerged in the 1850s. 2) Eileen Southern
presented a selected bibliography for the activities of black women and
discussed her reconstruction of the career of the concert singer Sissieretta
Jones. 3) Vivian Perlis reported about her oral history project with Claire Reis and
Reis's work in New York with the People's Music League from 1912 to 1922
and with the League of Composers from 1923-48. 4) Carol Neuls-Bates
discussed her source materials and methods for tracing the activity of women as
orchestral musicians ca. 1925-45 and earlier. Adrienne Fried Block chaired the
session. Comments from the general discussion following the papers are
included, and the status of women's studies within the field of music is
reviewed.

69 **Paid my dues. Journal of women and music** (Chicago: Calliope,
bp 1977) 40 p.
Vol. II, no. 1 of the newly-reorganized, quarterly journal devoted to music
composed and/or performed by women. To date the coverage has been chiefly
of the popular music field; however the editors are intent on including articles
on all kinds of music from as many different perspectives as possible. This issue
includes a discussion of Sophie Drinker's *Women in music* (*WIAM* 126) by Kay
Gardner, articles on the 4th National Women's Music Festival in Illinois by
Ronnie L. Scheier and the 2nd Michigan Women's Music Festival by Lori
Schroeder, Lisa Garrison's interview with instrument-maker Jennifer Crocker in
New York, songs with guitar accompaniment, and reviews of records,
periodicals, and other publications. The 6 issues of vol. I are available from
Women's Soul Publishing (Milwaukee).

70 PETRIDES, Frederique Joanne, ed. **Women in music I-VI**
bp (New York: Orchestrette Classique, 1935-40).
A one-page newsletter reporting on the activity of women as orchestral players
and conductors in the 1930s, issued at monthly and bi-monthly intervals under
the auspices of Petrides's all-female orchestra. News items about contemporary
women's orchestras throughout the United States as well as short articles on
past activity of women in the orchestral field in both Europe and the United
States are included. Petrides's chief objective was the support of women's
efforts to gain employment in the traditionally all-male orchestra.

71 **Report of the nineteenth annual meeting. Joint sessions**
ap **CMS-AMS: II. Women's studies in music.** Ed. by Henry
WOODWARD, *College Music Symposium* XVII/1 (spring 1977) 180-
91.
Presents abstracts for the 3 papers given at a women's studies session jointly
sponsored by the College Music Soc. and the American Musicological Soc. at
their national conventions in Washington, D.C. in Nov. 1976: 1) "Women as
orchestral players and conductors in the United States, ca. 1925-50", Carol
Neuls-Bates, 2) "Women as orchestral composers, ca. 1925-50", Laurine Elkins-
Marlow as the second paper in a pair, and 3) "The pathos of Barbara Strozzi",
Ellen Rosand. Adrienne Fried Block chaired the session and elicited replies
from respondents as follows: 1) Jane Bernstein regarding methodologies for
approaching the history of women in music, 2) Judith Tick on the progression
of women from amateur to professional status as performers and composers in
the United States during the 19th c., and 3) Pamela Susskind concerning
society's encouragement--and lack of encouragement--of women as composers
in the past, e.g., Clara Schumann and Fanny Mendelssohn Hensel.

72 **Report of the twentieth annual meeting. CMS interest**
ap **session on women's studies.** Ed. by Barbara English MARIS,
College Music Symposium XVIII/1 (spring 1978) 219-22.
Presents abstracts for the 3 papers given at a women's studies session during
the annual convention of the College Music Soc. in Evanston, Ill. in Nov. 1977:
1) "Corona Schröter 1751-1802: singer, actress, composer", Marcia J. Citron, 2)
"A critical study of the musical career of Amy Fay in America", Sr. Margaret
W. McCarthy, and 3) "By women and for women: choral music for women's
voices composed by American women, ca. 1890-1920", Adrienne Fried Block.
Donald M. McCorkle chaired the session. Nancy B. Reich, Carol Neuls-Bates,
and Laurine Elkins-Marlow were respondents.

73 **Status of women in college music, The: preliminary studies.**
bs Ed. by Carol NEULS-BATES. *College Music Society report number 1*
(Binghamton, N.Y.: College Music Soc., 1976) ix, 34 p.
Contains the texts of papers presented at the Meeting on Women in the
Profession at the annual meeting of the College Music Soc. (CMS) in Iowa
City, Iowa in Feb. 1975. The authors, titles, and *WIAM* numbers under which
abstracts of their papers appear are as follows: Adrienne Fried Block,
Introduction. The woman musician on campus: hiring and promotion patterns
(98), Elizabeth L. Elrod, *Women in music: results of the CMS questionnaire*
(104), Jane M. Bowers, *Recent research on women in music* (101), Carol Neuls-
Bates, *Foundation support for women in music* (2983), Judith Tick, *Women in
musicology* (110), Barbara B. Smith, *Women in ethnomusicology* (107), Eileen
Southern, *A partial report on black women in college music teaching* (108),
Adrienne Fried Block, *Women in composition* (99), and Anne Mayer, *Women in
applied music teaching* (106).

→ SUTRO, Florence Edith. **Women in music and law**, *see*
729bc[56].

74 **Woman's work in music number [I]**, *Etude* XIX/9 (Sept 1901)
bp 310-49. *Illus., music.*
An *Etude* issue devoted to women in music. The authors, titles, and *WIAM*
numbers for selected articles with abstracts are as follows: Fanny Morris Smith,
The record of woman in music (630), Daniel Batchelor, *Women's sphere in music
teaching* (743), Mary Chappell Fischer, *Women as concert organists* (976),
Everett E. Truette, *Women as organists* (1228), and George Lehman, *Woman's
position in the violin world* (1058). An editorial statement notes: "The aim has
not been to rhapsodize over what woman has done, and will do, but to make a
record of fact, of the many things that have been done for music by noble,
devoted women. If numbers are to count for anything it is fair to say that the
future of music is in the hands of women". Songs and piano music by women
composers are also included.

75 **Woman's work in music number [II]**, *Etude* XXVII/7 (July
bp 1909) 433-504. *Illus., music.*
An issue of *Etude* dedicated to women in music. The authors, titles, and *WIAM*
numbers for selected articles with abstracts are as follows: *Women's opportunity
in music* (854), *Music after marriage and motherhood* (1114), Lorna Gill, *The
American woman pianist of today and yesterday* (994), Corinne Rider-Kelsey,
Why American girls succeed in opera (1161), Maud Powell, *The American girl
and her violin* (1152), and Fanny Morris Smith, *The work of our women's music
clubs* (837). Two articles are continued in *Etude* XXVII/8 (Aug. 1909). An
editorial discusses the phenomenal success of American women as performers
both at home and abroad and the prominence of women as composers in the
United States. Songs and piano music by women are also included.

76 **Woman's work in music number [III]**, *Etude* XXXVI/11 (Nov
bp 1918) 689-746.
In this "women's issue", Arthur Elson discusses famous musical women of the
past, Olga Samaroff Stokowski considers the life of the performer, and Amy
Cheney Beach gives advice to the young woman contemplating a career in
composition. Frances Elliott Clark considers music as a vocation for women
with an emphasis on supervisory work in the public schools and selling sheet
music and records. Ernestine Schumann-Heink discusses the mother's role in
her child's musical training. The lead editorial salutes women for their work in
the music clubs as being responsible for "the country's musical progress" in the
previous 50 years. Programs of works by women composers, a list of well-
known contemporary women composers, and piano music by women are
included.

77 **Woman's work in music number [IV]**, *Etude* XLVII/11 (Nov
bp 1929) 789-872. *Illus., music.*
The 4th and final issue of *Etude* dedicated to women in music. James Francis
Cooke discusses the lives of the children of Robert and Clara Schumann, Carl
Engel considers woman as inspiration for the male composer, Theodora
Truendle relates how Fannie Bloomfield-Zeisler taught, and Rosa Ponselle
assesses the young American woman's opportunities in opera. Hope Stoddard
considers the mothers of great musicians, and Tod Buchanan Galloway
discusses women in music history as wives, composers, and performers. Edgar
A. Barrell presents a list of 350 notable women in music--both European and
American and chiefly contemporary--which continued in *Etude* through XLIX/
4 (Apr. 1930). The lead editorial discusses the fact that modern appliances, e.g.,

vacuum cleaners, electric washers, and refrigerators, have allowed the "woman of the house" to become the "lady of the house", with greater leisure time to devote to music.

15   Music

Solo instrumental music

78   MORATH, Max, ed. **One hundred ragtime classics** (Denver:
ma   Donn, 1963) 360 p.
Pf pno. A collection of reprints of the original sheet music. Includes Adeline Shepherd's *Pickles and peppers* (*WIAM* 496) and Muriel Pollock's *Rooster rag* (*WIAM* 491). *Rg Pickles and peppers*: *The ragtime women*, Vanguard, VSD 79402.

Vocal music

79   ALLOY, Evelyn, ed. **Working women's music. The songs and**
ma   **struggles of women in the cotton mills, textile plants, and**
         needle trades (Somerville, Mass.: New England Free Press, 1976)
44 p. $2.50. *Illus., music, bibliog.*
Presents 28 songs and ballads from the 19th and 20th c. that celebrate the work of women in the United States labor movement and illustrate how women have been part of the American tradition of using songs to voice opinions and grievances about workaday life. Each song has a melody line with instrumental chord indications. A historical overview of women's participation in the labor force in cotton mills, textile plants, and the needle trades is included. *(Richard K. Burns)*

80   BISSELL, T., ed. **American musical class book, designed for**
ma   **the use of female colleges, institutes, seminaries, and normal**
         and high schools, The (Boston: O. Ditson, [1859]) 232 p.
Contains instructions for reading music, solfège and other vocal exercises, and a collection of simple vocal pieces--chiefly duets and trios.

81   CHAPPLE, Joseph Mitchell, ed. **Heart songs. Dear to the**
ma   **American people** (Boston: Chapple, 1910) 512 p.
Pf solo voc, duos, trios, quartets, pno. This collection resulted from a campaign by the *National Magazine* to identify the "treasured songs" of the American people. 25,000 respondents indicated their selections, and the collection is a miscellany of operatic excerpts and folk, patriotic, devotional, and sentimental solo and part-songs. The following women composers and songs are represented: Hope Temple, *'Tis all that I can say*, Emma Olive Osgood, *Call me pet names*, and Marion Dix Sullivan, *The blue Juniata* (*WIAM* 258).

82   CHARTERS, Ann, ed. **Ragtime song book, The** (New York:
ma   Oak, 1965) 112 p.
Pf solo voc, pno. Includes 2 songs by women, Sadie Koninsky's *Eli Green's cakewalk* (*WIAM* 523), and Ida Emerson and Joseph E. Howard's *Hello! ma baby* (*WIAM* 513).

83   DANA, Mary S.B., ed. **Northern harp, The; consisting of**
ma   **original sacred and moral songs adapted to the most popular**
         melodies (New York: Dayton & Saxton, 1842) 99 p.
A collection of 33 sacred songs. *At* Mary Dana Shindler. *Pf* solo voc, duos, trios, pno. Includes *Flee as a bird to your mountain* (*WIAM* 368). The preface notes that this repertory is appropriate for the Christian home for morning and evening prayer, and for social occasions.   *(Judith Tick)*

84   DANA, Mary S.B., ed. **Southern harp, The; consisting of**
ma   **original sacred and moral songs adapted to the most popular**
         melodies (Boston: Parker & Ditson, [1841]) 99 p.
A collection of 43 sacred songs. *At* Mary Dana Shindler. *Pf* solo voc, duos, and trios with pno.   *(Judith Tick)*

86   HOPEKIRK, Helen, ed. **Seventy Scottish songs** (937/1006;
ma   Boston: O. Ditson, 1905) 189 p.
A collection of more than 70 Lowland Scottish and Celtic songs, with piano accompaniments and a historical introduction by Hopekirk. *Pf* solo voc, pno.

→   KNAPP, Phoebe, ed. **Notes of joy**, *see* 460ma[51].

87   LOMAX, John A.; LOMAX, Alan, eds. **Best loved American**
ma   **folk songs** (New York: Grosset & Dunlap, 1947) 407 p.
Pf solo voc, pno. Piano arrangements by Charles and Ruth Crawford Seeger

are provided so that the songs can be performed without singers. More than 100 representative American folk songs are included.

88   LOMAX, John A.; LOMAX, Alan, eds. **Our singing country**
ma   (New York: Macmillan, 1941) 416 p.
Pf solo voc, pno. Ruth Crawford Seeger transcribed 300 tunes from phonographic field recordings in the Archive of American Folk Song Research at the Library of Congress. 190 tunes were selected for inclusion and are grouped as follows: religious songs, social songs, men at work, outlaws, hollers and blues, and Negro gang songs.

89   MCGILL, Josephine, ed. **Folksongs of the Kentucky moun-**
ma   **tains** (1783; New York: Boosey, 1917) 106 p.
A collection of 20 traditional ballads and other English folk songs gathered by Josephine McGill during the fall of 1914 in Knott and Letcher counties, Kentucky. McGill provided the piano accompaniments.

90   SEEGER, Ruth Crawford, ed. **American folk songs for**
ma   **children** (New York: Doubleday, 1948) 190 p.
Pf solo voc, pno. Contains more than 100 folk songs, with simple piano accompaniments, which were selected for their appropriateness for performance by young children. Seeger made the collection in 1941 for the Silver Spring Cooperative Nursery School in Maryland. She worked from folk lore journals and field recordings.

→   SLOMAN, Jane, ed. **Melodist, The. Selected gems and**
         celebrated composers, arranged for the use of female
         seminaries, *see* 328ma[49].

91   SMITH, Eva Munson, ed. **Woman in sacred song. A library**
ma   **of hymns, religious poems, and sacred music by woman**.
         Foreword by Frances E. WILLARD (Boston: D. Lothrop, 1885)
xxviii, 883 p. *Port., index, music.*
Includes 130 4-part hymn settings by about 50 women composers, together with more than 2000 religious texts in 4 sections: the devotional department, the missionary department, the temperance department, and miscellaneous. Brief biographical sketches are presented for some of the contributors. The editor states that she has been advised to reject all songs and poems treating the themes of temperance or suffrage for women, but that to do so would be an injustice to the aspirations of womankind: "The triumph of woman in sacred song is but the prelude to the triumph that awaits her".

92   TICHENOR, Trebor Jay, ed. **Ragtime rarities** (New York:
ma   Dover, 1975) 305 p.
Pf pno. The collection includes, among other pieces, 5 rags by women: May Aufderheide's *Dusty rag* (*WIAM* 468), her *Thriller* (originally published in Indianapolis, 1909), Grace M. Bolen's *The smoky topaz* (originally published in St. Louis, 1901), Sadie Koninsky's *Eli Green's cakewalk* (originally published as a song, *WIAM* 523), and Ethyl B. Smith and Frank Wooster's *Black cat rag* (*WIAM* 498). *Rg Thriller*: *The ragtime women*, Vanguard, VSD 79402.

17   Song texts

93   **Christian Science hymnal** (Boston: Christian Science Publishing
bc   Soc., 1932) 628 p.
Contains 7 hymn texts by founder Mary Baker Eddy and 1 by Harriet Beecher Stowe, all written in the late 19th c.

94   CLARK, George Washington. **Liberty minstrel, The** (New
bm   York: Leavitt & Alden, 1844) 182 p. *Music, index.*
A collection of abolition song texts with music--both original and arranged by George Washington Clark and others. In the preface, Clark argues for "music for righteous causes" to voice the injustices of slavery. A great number of these freedom texts are by women, with several each by Mrs. Bailey, Miss E.M. Chandler, Eliza Lee Follen, Lydia Huntley-Sigourney, Jessie Hutchinson, and Mary H. Maxwell.

95   GILMAN, Charlotte Perkins, ed. **Suffrage songs and verses**
bc   (New York: Charlton, 1911) 24 p.
A collection of song texts from the suffrage movement of the late 19th and early 20th c. that were intended to be sung to well-known tunes.

→   LOWENS, Irving. **Bibliography of songsters printed in**
         America before 1821, A, *see* 22bm[01].

96   RAYE-SMITH, Eugénie M., ed. **Equal suffrage songsheaf**
bc   (New York: author, 1912) 20 p.

A collection of song texts about women's suffrage from the turn of the century. The texts were intended for popular tunes.

→ SILBER, Irwin. **Singing suffragettes sang for women's votes, equal rights**, *see* 449ap[50].

HISTORICAL STUDIES

20 Historiography: women's studies and the status of women

97 BARNES, Nancy; NEULS-BATES, Carol. **Women in music:**
ap **a preliminary report**, *College Music Symposium* XIV (fall 1974) 67-70.
This preliminary report is based on recent studies (1969-72) about the status of women at 5 colleges and universities that contained information on the activity of women as faculty and students in the discipline of music. Stressing that their investigation was necessarily limited to the 5 available and pertinent studies, the authors conclude that "while women constituted the majority of undergraduates in music and a lesser, but still significant percentage of graduate students in the field, women were poorly represented on music faculties, especially as rank increased. Women had not attained status in the profession commensurate with their qualifications".

98 BLOCK, Adrienne Fried. **Introduction. The woman musician**
as **on campus: hiring and promotion patterns**, *The status of women in college music: preliminary studies*. Ed. by Carol NEULS-BATES (*WIAM* 73) vi-ix.
The Committee on the Status of Women was established by the College Music Soc. in 1972, and in Feb. 1975 at the annual meeting a session dealing with women in college music teaching was held. This article--which originally appeared in *High Fidelity/Musical America* (*WIAM* 67)--summarizes the data collected to date, including statistics for women on music education faculties.

99 BLOCK, Adrienne Fried. **Women in composition**, *The status*
as *of women in college music: preliminary studies*. Ed. by Carol NEULS-BATES (*WIAM* 73) 26-29.
Women constituted only 5.8% of a total of approximately 1160 composition teachers on college and university faculties in the United States and Canada for 1972-74. The present-day cycle is a vicious one. The composer whose works are performed and recorded achieves the faculty position, while in turn the prestige of a faculty appointment can lead to greater visibility and more performances. A list of works by women composers performed by the New York Philharmonic from its formation in 1842 through the 1970-71 season is included.

100 BOWEN, Jean. **Women in music: their fair share?**, *High*
ap *Fidelity/Musical America* XXIV/8 (Aug 1974) MA 20.
Summarizes a colloquium on the status of women in the profession of music at the Graduate Center of the City U. of New York on 4 May 1974. Members of the panel were Adrienne Fried Block, Jean Bowen, Eleanor Cory, Susan Kedgley, Katherine Linville, Judith Tick, and Henrietta Yurchenko. The discussion covered the fields of music management, criticism, publishing, performance, and college teaching. In all of these fields, considerable discrimination against women was reported. Corrective actions suggested by the panel and from the floor included political action, publicity, support of the United Nations' International Women's Year, and the collection and dissemination of information about the role of women in the field of music. *(Author)*

101 BOWERS, Jane M. **Recent researches on women in music**,
as *The status of women in college music: preliminary studies*. Ed. by Carol NEULS-BATES (*WIAM* 73) 4-9. *Bibliog.*
Reviews the current state of women's studies in music as of 1975, suggests fruitful areas for future research, and presents a bibliography for women as composers and performers. The bibliography includes selected books and articles appearing in print between 1962 and 1975, dissertations completed after 1963, and work in progress. Most of the items listed concern women who lived in western Europe or North America between the late Middle Ages and the present, but a few deal with women musicians active in other locations and periods. A small number of items concern women as folk or popular musicians. *(Author)*

102 BOWERS, Jane M. **Teaching about the history of women in**
ap **western music**, *Women's Studies Newsletter* V/3 (summer 1977) 11-15. *Bibliog., discog.*
Describes a course entitled "Women musicians and composers in western Europe and the United States between 1100 and the present", which was taught by the author at Portland State U. in Oregon during the summer of 1976. The main objective of the course was to study the contributions of women particularly--but not exclusively--in relation to the professional music world. The lives of women composers, the obstacles they have faced in obtaining education and developing careers in music, the types of works they have written, and the relationship between their access to professional (or semiprofessional) positions as musicians and their compositional activities were considered. Women as amateur and professional singers and instrumentalists, women as teachers and conductors, and women as participants in institutions that women themselves have established, e.g., convents, were discussed. The author also describes the sense of community that developed among students in the course and reviews the necessity for integrating the study of women's compositions with a feminist historical perspective. *(Author, abridged)*

103 **Committee on the Status of Women**, *CMS Newsletter. College*
ap *Music Society* May 1976, 1.
Announces a regular column for the society's newsletter sponsored by the Committee on the Status of Women, to be devoted to the activities of and research about women in music. Includes information about publications, recordings, and employment. The newsletter is published 3 times annually.

104 ELROD, Elizabeth L. **Women in music: result of the CMS**
as **questionnaire**, *The status of women in college music: preliminary studies*. Ed. by Carol NEULS-BATES (*WIAM* 73) 1-3.
Reports on the questionnaire distributed by the Committee on the Status of Women of the College Music Soc. to all women listed in the *Directory of music faculties in colleges and universities, U.S. and Canada, 1972-74*. The return was slightly over 10%. The average respondent held a Master's degree, had 17 years of teaching experience--11 of which were at the college level--and was positioned at the rank of assistant professor or lower. Only 1 in 5 women was teaching at the highest level for which she had prepared.

105 FULLER, Sarah. **Report of the Committee on the Status of**
ap **Women**, *Newsletter. American Musicological Society* VIII/1 (Jan 1978) 1.
The Committee on the Status of Women of the American Musicological Soc. (AMS) received a 37% response to its questionnaire addressed to women members of the society. Interviewing and hiring practices were the primary concerns of the respondents, e.g., sex-biased questions in interviews and the failure of departments to advertise job openings sufficiently or at all. The committee recommends that local chapters of the AMS form their own individual committees on the status of women in order to engage the cooperation of local institutions in carrying out fair practices in interviewing and job posting. Future activities for the national committee are suggested and recent successful efforts of the AMS--during the tenure of Janet Knapp as president--to increase the formal participation of women in the society are commended.

106 MAYER, Anne. **Women in applied music teaching**, *The status*
as *of women in college music: preliminary studies*. Ed. by Carol NEULS-BATES (*WIAM* 73) 30-33.
While women represent a significant percentage of the applied music teachers in colleges and universities in the United States, the majority of women are concentrated at the lowest rank or are part-time instructors with little chance for advancement or salary commensurate with their ability or years of service. Figures for the following areas in 1972-74 are included: 1) ranks of women teachers of voice, violin, piano, and flute, and 2) numbers of women in applied music teaching by instrument.

→ NEULS-BATES, Carol. **Foundation support for women**, *see* 2983as[75].

→ NEULS-BATES, Carol. **Sources and resources for women's studies in American music: a report**, *see* 68ap[10].

→ POOL, Jeannie. **Women in music history: a research guide**, *see* 37bm[01].

→ **Report of the nineteenth annual meeting. Joint sessions CMS-AMS: II. Women's studies in music**, *see* 71ap[10].

→ **Report of the twentieth annual meeting. CMS interest session on women's studies**, *see* 72ap[10].

→ SKOWRONSKI, Jo Ann. **Women in American music: a bibliography**, *see* 45bm[01].

107 SMITH, Barbara B. **Women in ethnomusicology**, *The status of*
as *women in college music: preliminary studies*. Ed. by Carol NEULS-BATES (*WIAM* 73) 19-21.

In spite of evidence of some imbalance in the treatment of women ethnomusicologists as compared to men, the outlook for women in ethnomusicology--both in the discipline and in academic institutions in the United States--is encouraging. 1) Because of the relatively recent acceptance of ethnomusicology by academia, there is no huge backlog of tenured positions. 2) There is a need and a place for women to conduct research in situations where women can establish rapport more easily than men and in societies where music performance is sex-segregated. 3) Since ethnomusicologists accept all people as people--without artificial differentiations--women are accepted in the field on the basis of their abilities and contributions.

108 SOUTHERN, Eileen. **Partial report on black women in**
as **college music teaching, A**, *The status of women in college music: preliminary studies.* Ed. by Carol NEULS-BATES (*WIAM* 73) 22-25.
1) About 90% or more of black college music teachers in the United States are employed by predominantly black colleges. 2) Women constitute 23.1% of the music faculties at predominantly black institutions in the South and are concentrated at the ranks of instructor and assistant professor. 3) Only in the last 5 years have white colleges begun to employ black music teachers, and most frequently these black teachers are male.

109 **Statistics in music**, *School Musician* XLV/10 (June-July 1974) 56.
ap
56% of the 31,500,000 amateur musicians in the United States are women. Women constitute 77% of all pianists, but only 14% of the nation's percussionists and 11% of the trumpet players. Women represent 80% of all elementary school music teachers, but only 27% of the secondary-school music teachers.

110 TICK, Judith. **Women in musicology**, *The status of women in*
as *college music: preliminary studies.* Ed. by Carol NEULS-BATES (*WIAM* 73) 16-18.
Statistics indicate that the academic institutions producing the greatest proportion of female doctorates in musicology in the United States also discriminate against women most severely in their hiring practices. The percentage of women faculty teaching music history and musicology at "all schools" was 24% for 1972-74, while at the "selected schools"--the 34 chief Ph.D.-producing institutions--the percentage was 10%. Surely if women are good enough to train, they are good enough to hire.

111 WRIGHT, Gladys. **Career opportunities for the young**
ap **woman graduate**, *School Musician* XLVI/10 (June-July 1975) 41, 49.
Discusses the Women Band Directors National Assoc., which was formed in 1969 to "give women directors a voice and to help their professional adjustment". Presents the following statistics: 1) of 50,000 band directors in the United States, 5000 are women, 2) of 960 members in the American School Band Directors Assoc., 18 are women, 3) no women are included in the 275-member American Bandmasters Assoc., 4) 65% of women instrumental teachers teach in elementary or junior high schools, 33% in high school, and 2% in college, and 5) 80% of general music teachers are women.

25   General history

→   ALLOY, Evelyn, ed. **Working women's music. The songs and struggles of women in the cotton mills, textile plants, and needle trades**, *see* 79ma[15].

112 BEAN, Helen J. **Women in the music house**, *American Music*
ap *Teacher* VI/4 (Mar-Apr 1957) 4-5, 23.
Discusses contributions of leading American women to musical life in the late 19th and 20th c. to 1957 as follows: 1) teaching of voice, Clara E. Munger and Sara Hershey Eddy, 2) public school music, Jeannette Hall, Julia Ettie Crane, and Helen Place, 3) concert performance and opera, Julie Rivé-King and Clara Louise Kellogg, 4) music criticism and other journalism, Olga Samaroff Stokowski, Marion Bauer, and Angela Diller, 5) composition, Amy Cheney Beach, 6) folk song research, Laura Boulton and Helen Hartness Flanders, and 7) patronage, Marian MacDowell and Elizabeth Sprague Coolidge. In addition the collective activities of women as orchestral musicians and women in concert management in the 20th c. are discussed.

113 BLANTON, Carol Valerie. **Outstanding women pianists of**
md **the nineteenth and twentieth centuries** (M.S. thesis, Music: Inst. of Musical Art, Juilliard School of Music, 1939) 150 p. (typescript). *Bibliog.*
Considers the accomplishments of some outstanding women pianists of the 19th and 20th c.: the Europeans, Clara Schumann, Sophie Menter, Annette Essipoff, Mary Krebs, Anna Mehlig, Clotilda Kleeberg, and Elly Ney; and 6 women in American music, Katherine Bacon, Fannie Bloomfield-Zeisler, Teresa

Carreño, Myra Hess, Wanda Landowska, and Guiomar Novaes. The background, training, careers, and characteristic styles of playing of the various artists are discussed.   *(Janet Somers)*

114 BLITZ, Rudolph C. **Women in the professions**, *Monthly Labor*
ap *Review* XCVI/5 (May 1974) 53-58.
While the proportion of women in the labor force has grown steadily for many decades, the proportion of women in the professions reached a peak in 1930 and declined thereafter. Changes in occupational structure have also occurred. While in 1890 music and music teaching ranked 5th among the top 5 professions for women--ranking after elementary school teaching, medicine, social and religious work, and law--in 1970 music and music teaching no longer constituted a major work area for women.

115 BOLDREY, Richard L. **Women song composers** (Chicago:
bm author, 1978) 19 p. (typescript, xerox). *List of works.*
Surveys European and American women composers of art songs beginning with the 17th c. Entries for individual composers include dates, alternate names, brief biographical information, and lists of songs.   *(Author, abridged)*

116 BORROFF, Edith. **Women composers: reminiscence and**
ap **history**, *College Music Symposium* XV (spring 1975) 26-33.
A survey of the creative life of women in western music history from the Middle Ages to the present time, with reference to the work of individual composers in Europe and the United States. 1) Numerous surviving documents support the claim for the place of women in medieval musical life in religious orders and as troubadours and minstrels. 2) The Renaissance proved a step backwards, however, and in the 1600s-1800s creative musicianship for women depended upon 3 factors: monastic life, birth into a family of professional musicians active in the apprenticeship system, and nobility of birth--which ensured good private tutoring. 3) While the Romantic era was essentially another heady, self-conscious time for men, growing numbers of women emerged as composers and attempted to enter the male bastion. 4) Semi-popular music and the genre of children's song have traditionally been open to women. The author recalls that because of discriminatory practices she was forced to switch from composition as a major to piano in order to maintain her scholarship at the Oberlin Conservatory in 1944. She concludes that the climate for women in composition has been changing since the late 1960s.

→   BOWERS, Jane. **Teaching about the history of women in western music**, *see* 102ap[20].

117 BRITAIN, Radie. **Musical composition--a new world for**
ap **women**, *Instrumentalist* XXV/4 (Nov 1970) 55-56.
Reviews briefly the history of women's exclusion from composition. Welcomes the changing climate, while also calling for the continued performance of works by women. Ethel Leginska conducted Britain's first orchestral composition--*Symphonic intermezzo*--with the Woman's Symphony Orchestra of Chicago.

118 BURNS, Don. **Distaffed composers, The**, *Music Journal* [New
ap York] XXXII/3 (Mar 1974) 16-17, 32-37. *Illus.*
A survey of women composers from Greek and Roman times to the present. Amy Cheney Beach and Margaret Ruthven Lang are considered, among other American women composers. Antonia Brico, Ethel Leginska, and Nadia Boulanger are cited for their work as conductors.

119 CAROSSO, Vincent P. **Music and musicians in the White**
ap **House**, *New York Historical Society Quarterly* XLVIII/2 (Apr 1964) 101-29. *Illus.*
The selection of musicians for performances at the White House has typically rested with the First Family, and usually with the First Lady. Dolly Madison introduced numerous visiting artists, who played on the newly-acquired piano at the White House. Harriet Lane, the musical niece of James Buchanan, staged a memorable musicale in 1860 in honor of the Prince of Wales's visit, and in general the support of music during Buchanan's term was impressive. Edith Carow Roosevelt was an accomplished musician and invited many distinguished performers to the White House during her husband's presidency. Eleanor Roosevelt used musicales to draw attention to deserving, native musicians--regardless of race or creed. Musical programs at the White House under the direction of Jacqueline Kennedy attracted national attention. The following children and relatives of presidents and their musical interests are discussed: Eleanor Parke Custis, Martha and Mary Jefferson, Margaret Wilson, and Margaret Truman. Jenny Lind sang at the White House in 1850, Adelina Patti in the 1880s. In 1883 Minnie Hauk tried to interest President Arthur in establishing an American national opera company.

120 CREWS, Emma Katherine. **History of music in Knoxville,**
dd **Tennessee, 1791-1910** (DME diss., Music Education: Florida State U., 1962) ii, 246 p. (typescript, microfilm). *Bibliog.*
Includes information about the activity of women in music in Knoxville, Tenn., chiefly regarding educational institutions for women. The Knoxville Female Academy included music in the curriculum from its founding in 1827. By 1836

all students at the academy received instruction in voice, while piano lessons were available at an additional charge of $20 per school session. Music at Knoxville Female Seminary, founded in 1847, and the Daughter's Collegiate Inst., founded in 1860, is also discussed. Between 1891 and 1910 Knoxville became a cosmopolitan city, and women's music clubs sponsored concerts by major artists on tour.

121 CUNEY-HARE, Maud. **Negro musicians and their music**
bf (New York: Da Capo, 1974) 439 p. $27.50. *Illus., bibliog., index.*
A reprint of the 1936 edition (Washington, D.C.: Associated). Discusses African influence on songs in colonial America, and musical comedy and art music in the 19th and early 20th c. Among the pioneers as performers of art music were Elizabeth Taylor Greenfield, Abbie Mitchell, Nellie F. Brown, and Flora Batson, singers. The greatest of Negro prima donnas were Marie Selika, who concertized in both the United States and Europe, and Sissieretta Jones, the dramatic soprano who was known as the "Black Patti". Rachel Walker, a lyric soprano who won praise from Saint-Saëns and Massenet, and singers Anita Patti-Brown and Mayme Calloway-Byron of Chicago are also considered. Margaret Bonds, a graduate of Northwestern U., and Florence B. Price, a graduate of the New England Conservatory of Music, are cited as leading Negro women composers.

122 DAVIS, Ronald L. **History of opera in the American West**
bm (Englewood Cliffs, N.J.: Prentice-Hall, 1965) xii, 178 p. *Illus., index.*
Considers the growth of opera in New Orleans, Chicago, San Francisco, and Dallas. Discusses summer festivals of opera in Central City, Colo. and Santa Fe, N.M., in the 20th c. Women, of course, are central to this history as singers.

123 DAVIS, Ronald L. **Opera in Chicago** (New York: Appleton-
bm Century, 1966) 393 p. *Illus., index.*
Traces the history of opera in Chicago from the first operatic performance in 1850 at Rice's Theater of *La sonnambula* by a visiting troupe, through the establishment of a resident company in 1909, the Chicago Grand Opera. Discusses the activity of the Chicago Grand Opera from 1909-14 and the activity of a succession of resident companies. Women singers naturally figure importantly in this history, chief among them Mary Garden, Edith Barnes Mason, Claudia Muzio, and Rosa Raisa before 1940, and Maria Callas and Renata Tebaldi after 1940. Patrons of opera in Chicago have included Edith Rockefeller McCormick, who--with her husband Harold F. McCormick--underwrote the losses of the resident companies from 1909-22. Directors have included Mary Garden, who headed the Chicago Opera in 1921-22, and Carol Fox, who became director of the Chicago Lyric Opera in 1954.

124 DICKINSON, Edward. **Music in America fifty years ago**.
ac *Studies in musical education, history, and aesthetics* 23 (Hartford: Music Teachers National Assoc., 1929) 9-26.
Discusses musical life in the 1870s and traces developments throughout the 19th and early 20th c. The major social factors influencing growth have been immigration, emancipation of the Negro, and the entrance of women into public affairs. The movement of people to cities disrupted the earlier close-knit musical communities in towns; however, the educational functions of these communities were shifted to the schools as a result of the development of music education programs. The best proof of a national craving for music is the legendary welcome given to Jenny Lind in the 1850s--an example that has been many times repeated.

125 DINNEEN, William. **Music at the meeting house, 1775-**
bm **1958** (Providence: R. Williams, 1958) 64 p.
Presents an account of musical activities at the First Baptist Church in America, in Providence, R.I., which employed at various times 3 women as organists: Margaret A. Gardner, Emma J. Williams, and Mabel Woolsey.

126 DRINKER, Sophie. **Music and women** (Washington, D.C.:
bf Zenger, 1977) xv, 323 p. *Illus.*
A reprint of the 1948 edition (New York: Coward-McCann). Traces the history of women in music in western civilization, including women in primitive societies. 1) The music of western culture was originally bound to organized religion, and since women were disbarred from official participation in the religious ceremony, they were automatically cut off from the opportunity to create music. 2) Once music was used apart from ritual and liturgy, women were theoretically able to function again as musicians; however, musical training was still centered in the church, and since the supply of male musicians was sufficient, women were not in demand. 3) Even when the power formerly wielded by the church began to pass to the university system, the universities adopted the organization of the church to further their scholarly, social, and political aims. Women had no corresponding institutions until late in the 19th c. 4) The only field in which woman's opportunity and recognized function in music has been equal to that of man's is in the solo performance of the prima donna.

127 rb --
R. by Jacques BARZUN, *New York Herald Tribune* 22 Feb 1948, VII-4.

128 rb --
R. by James LYONS, *New York Times* 4 July 1948, VII-6.

129 rb --
R. by Doris SIEBERT, *Musical Quarterly* XXXIV/2 (Apr 1948) 285-88.

130 DRINKER, Sophie. **Participation of women in music, The,**
ap *Music Clubs Magazine* XIV/2 (Nov-Dec 1934) 11-13.
1) The participation of women in music is a rich area of potential research for musicologists and feminists alike. 2) While women as composers and virtuoso performers have received some attention, the activity of women in folk music and choral singing has been almost totally neglected. Drinker examines the role of women in music in ancient Greece and Rome, women as musicians in convents in the Middle Ages, women and the troubadour tradition, women as madrigal singers in homes in England during the late 16th-17th c., the acceptance of women in choruses for oratorios in 18th-c. England, and the widespread inclusion of women in secular choruses in Europe and the United States in the 19th c.

131 EATON, Quaintance. **Miracle of the Met, The. An informal**
bf **history of the Metropolitan Opera 1883-1967** (Westport, Conn.: Greenwood, 1976) xiii, 490 p. $29. *Illus., index.*
A reprint of the 1968 edition (New York: Meredith). Considers the careers of many women singers at the Metropolitan Opera and the role of women as patrons, beginning with Caroline Astor--who was active from 1883-1906. The social side of opera that was predominant when the Metropolitan opened in 1883 declined thereafter--slowly but steadily--until in 1940 a "shifting of gears" brought democracy to the Diamond Horseshoe.

132 EATON, Quaintance, ed. **Musical U.S.A.** (New York: Allen,
bm Towne, and Heath, 1949) 206 p. *Illus.*
Discusses musical centers and presents profiles of leading performers, teachers, and managers. In Baltimore, Olga Samaroff Stokowski taught the city's first music appreciation courses in the 1930s, at which time Lillian Powell Bonney headed a concert bureau. In Charleston, S.C., the first-known song recital in the United States was given by a Mrs. Cook in 1773. In Chicago, Rosa de Vries was influential in the presentation of opera in the city after 1850, while Mary Garden was prominent in operatic life for 20 years beginning in 1910. In Cincinnati, Maria Longworth Nichols Storer was the initiator of the May Festival in 1873, and members of the Ladies Musical Club were instrumental in establishing the Cincinnati Symphony Orchestra in the 1890s. In Los Angeles, Mrs. Lynden Ellsworth Behymer carries on the work of her late husband as the leading concert manager in the city since 1886. In Massachusetts, Mary Aspinwall Tappan and her niece Mrs. Andrew H. Hepburn donated land in Tanglewood as the site for the Berkshire Music Center and Festival in 1937. In Minneapolis, Anna Eugénie Schoen-René became a "musical czarina" in the 1890s--as an eminent voice teacher and the organizer of a concert series, and Verna Golden Scott worked both in concert management and as manager of the Minneapolis Symphony Orchestra between 1918 and 1945. In New Orleans, Mrs. H. Moylan Field was an early patron of the New Orleans Symphony Orchestra, beginning in 1917. In Seattle, the Ladies Musical Club has been a vital force for good music in the Northwest since its founding in 1891, while Cecilia Schultz has been a leading manager since 1922. This monograph is an outgrowth of a series of articles that originally appeared in *Musical America*.

133 EATON, Quaintance. **Opera caravan. Adventures of the**
bm **Metropolitan on tour 1883-1956** (New York: Farrar, Straus, and Cudahy, 1957) 400 p. *Illus., index.*
Includes information about numerous women singers who traveled with the Metropolitan Opera on its annual tours. The first tour occurred early in 1884, following directly upon the opening of the house in the fall of 1883. Henry Eugene Abbey, the director, had unfulfilled contracts with expensive artists, and feeling that he had exhausted audience potential in New York, he set out on tour with his company to Boston, Chicago, St. Louis, and Cincinnati. One of the more eventful Metropolitan tours took place in 1906 when the company was in San Francisco during the earthquake in April. In response to the plight of local musicians, Marcella Sembrich gave one of her famous benefits in which she sang and played both the violin and the piano.

134 EDWARDS, George Thornton. **Music and musicians of**
bm **Maine** (Portland, Me.: Southworth, 1928) 542 p. *Illus., index.*
Discusses the work of Sophia Hewitt Ostinelli, who became associated with music in Maine beginning in 1822, when she assumed the position of organist at the First Parish Church in Portland. Presents biographical sketches for Annie Louise Cary, Lillian Nordica, and Emma Eames--all natives of Maine and singers--and a brief history of the Rossini Club in Portland, which was founded during the winter of 1867-68 and is generally considered the oldest music club in the United States. Among the brief biographies of more than 1800 Maine musicians active at the time of publication are entries for Antonia Sawyer, singer, and Kate Vannah, composer. Information about many other women of less prominent stature is included.

135 ELLINWOOD, Leonard. **History of American church**
bf   **music, The** (New York: Da Capo, 1970) 274 p. $15. *Illus., bibliog.,*
     index.
A reprint of the 1953 edition (New York: Morehouse-Gorham). Discusses
briefly the development of the mixed choir in the 19th c. as an outgrowth of the
singing school tradition. Considers the question of appropriate dress for women
as choir members in the past. The section presenting biographies of church
musicians includes the following 4 women: Caroline Lattin Beardsley, organist
of the 2nd United Congregational Church of Bridgeport, Conn. from 1883-
1938; and Mary Cherubim Schaefer, Georgia Stevens, and Justine Ward, all of
whom were associated with the Pius X School of Liturgical Music at
Manhattanville Col. of the Sacred Heart, New York. Information about Helen
Adell Dickinson, a founder of the School of Sacred Music at Union Theological
Seminary, is also included.

136 ELSON, Arthur; TRUETTE, Everett Ellsworth. **Woman's**
bm   **work in music**. With a new intro. by Everett Ellsworth TRUETTE
     (rev. ed.; Boston: L.C. Page, 1931) 301 p.
A revised edition of Elson's 1903 book (*WIAM* 137), including coverage of the
years 1904-31.

137 ELSON, Arthur. **Woman's work in music** (Portland, Me.:
bf   Longwood, 1976) 268 p. *Illus., port.*
A reprint of the 1903 edition (Boston: L.C. Page). Traces women's role in music
in antiquity through the Middle Ages, with an emphasis on the connections of
women with the troubadour tradition. Considers women as composers in the
16th and 17th c., chiefly in Italy, and as wives of composers from Bach through
Schumann. Single chapters are devoted to women composers in England,
Germany, France, and the United States during the 18th and 19th c. The
American chapter discusses the following women, among others: Amy Cheney
Beach, Helen Hopekirk, Margaret Ruthven Lang, Julie Rivé-King, Clara
Kathleen Rogers, and Emma Roberto Steiner. Elson concludes that 1) while
music may be regarded as a female "accomplishment", there is no reason why
more earnest women should be discounted as viable composers, and 2) "even in
the larger forms, women's work in music will always show more of a delicate
grace and refinement than man's, and will be to some extent lacking in the
broader effects of strong feeling".

138 ELSON, Louis Charles. **Woman in music** (New York: Gordon,
bf   1976) 99 p. *Illus.*
A reprint of the 1918 edition (New York: U. Soc.). Discusses 1) woman as
inspiration to male composers beginning with the troubadours through the 19th
c. in Europe, and 2) women as composers in Europe beginning in the 16th c.,
with an emphasis on Fanny Mendelssohn Hensel and Clara Schumann. The
chapter on American women considers the work of the following composers:
Amy Cheney Beach, Gena Branscombe, Mabel Wheeler Daniels, Helen
Hopekirk, and Margaret Ruthven Lang. "Given the freedom that is accorded to
the woman composer in America, with numerous leading conservatories
opening wide their doors to women and offering them the most thorough
instruction, the United States may yet bring forth a woman composer of the
magnitude of Mozart, Chopin, or Haydn".

139 GAUL, Harvey. **Three hundred years of music in Pennsyl-**
ac   **vania**, *Music and musicians of Pennsylvania.* Ed. by Gertrude M.
     ROHRER (Philadelphia: T. Presser, 1940) 46-90, 121. *Illus., bibliog.*
This general account of music in Pennsylvania, beginning with the Moravian
settlement of 1741, includes information on women's activities in the Sister
House at Bezlem and among the Sisters at the Ephrata Cloister, and as early
members of the Musical Fund Soc. in Philadelphia in the 1820s and
philanthropic clubs in the 1880s. 31 women--active in the late 19th and the
20th c.--are listed among notable musicians and are provided with brief
biographies as follows: Eleanor Everest Freer, Marianne Genet, Celeste D.
Heckscher, Kate Ockleston Lippa, Frances McCollin, Alice Nevin, Ada Richter,
Anna Priscilla Risher, and Gertrude Martin Rohrer, composers; Marian
Anderson, Florence Hinkle, Louise Homer, Marie Stone Langston, Jeanette
MacDonald, Mary and Olive Nevin, Emma Seiler, and Florence Wickham,
singers.

140   **Golden Horseshoe, The. The life and times of the Metro-**
bm   **politan Opera**. Ed. by Frank MERKLING, John W. FREEMAN,
     and Arthur SOLIN. With a prologue by Eleanor R. BELMONT (New
     York: Viking, 1966) 319 p. *Illus.*
A pictorial history of the Metropolitan Opera from 1883-1966 in the house on
Broadway and 39th Street in New York. Numerous women singers are
featured.

141 GOOD, Marian Bigler. **Some musical backgrounds of Penn-**
bm   **sylvania** (Carrolltown, Penn.: Carrolltown News, 1932) 101 p.
Includes information on the family of Ethelbert Nevin, whose mother,
Elizabeth Duncan Nevin, was a musician. Discusses the activity of Sister
Anastasia and the female singing school at the Ephrata Cloister in the 18th c.,
as well as concert appearances in the state by Jenny Lind and Adelina Patti in
the 19th c.

142 GREEN, Miriam Stewart. **Consider these creators**, *American*
ap   *Music Teacher* XXV/3 (Jan 1976) 9-12.
An introduction to vocal music by American women composers from the
Revolution to the present in a variety of genres, e.g., art and popular song,
oratorio, and opera. The careers of over 50 composers are considered briefly,
and contemporary women are broadly categorized according to stylistic
approach. The work of women in transcribing many kinds of ethnic music in
the United States is also discussed.   *(Judith L. Zaimont)*

143 HILL, Tremont. **Siren serenade**, *Family Circle* 30 Apr 1937, 10-
ap   11, 20.
A survey of women's activity as composers and conductors in both Europe and
the United States up to the mid-1930s.

144 HOWARD, John Tasker. **Our American music, three hun-**
bm   **dred years of it** (3rd rev. ed.; New York: T. Crowell, 1954) 841 p.
     Illus., bibliog., list of works, index.
This history of American music focuses particularly on the work of late 19th
and 20th-c. composers. Among the women, the life and works of Amy Cheney
Beach receive the lengthiest consideration, while biographical sketches are
presented for the following: Gena Branscombe, Ulric Cole, Ruth Crawford
(Seeger), Pearl Curran, Fannie Charles Dillon, Fay Foster, Jessie L. Gaynor,
Miriam Gideon, Maria Grever, Peggy Glanville-Hicks, Mary Howe, Mana
Zucca, Anna Priscilla Risher, Mary Turner Salter, Lily Strickland, Harriet
Ware, and Mabel Wood-Hill. Less extensive information is included for
approximately 100 additional women throughout American history.

145 HUTTON, Edna Rait. **Sigma Alpha Iota's 65 years**, *Music*
ap   *Journal* [New York] XXVIII/3 (Mar 1970) 54, 76.
During its 65-year history, Sigma Alpha Iota--an international professional
fraternity for women musicians--has sponsored the following causes: 1)
recognition of alumnae for their achievements, 2) the International Music Fund
for the rehabilitation of music libraries after World War II, 3) music therapy
programs in veteran's hospitals, also after the war, 4) the People-to-People
program, which has provided instruments, records, music, and books to
numerous foreign countries, 5) the Orchestra Overseas Project, which has aided
struggling orchestras, and 6) other programs such as the Braille Music Project.
Sigma Alpha Iota has also funded the construction and maintenance of a
cottage at the MacDowell Colony in Peterborough, N.H., and a lodge at the
Interlochen Arts Center in Interlochen, Mich.

146 JACKSON, Irene V. **Black women and Afro-American song**
ap   **tradition**, *Sing-Out!* XXV/2 (July-Aug 1976) 10-13. *Illus., music.*
From traditional slave society to contemporary black society, Afro-American
women have created, nurtured, and sustained vital song traditions. The Afro-
American woman is singularly important in the merging of African and
European cultures. In the slave community, particularly in the role as "mammy"
or nurse, the black woman was the principal agent for cultural exchange. The
mammy was an integral part of early America, and her cradle songs or lullabies
comprise the most important part of black feminine song tradition. Apart from
lullabies, there is a great body of traditional songs that rose out of the patterns
and rhythm of the work of slave women. These women sang as they cooked,
sewed, cleaned, wove, washed, farmed, etc. There is a body of songs of black
women who functioned as folk doctors; their songs were used for healing and
for lifting "fixes", conjures, or voodoos. Traditionally, black women have been
important in burial and funeral ceremonies; it was the responsibility of women
to compose burial songs. Probably the best known music with which black
women are associated is the "classic blues". The blues are the black woman's
love songs; the singing style recalls the field holler or cry, the moaned lullaby, or
the death lament. The religious counterpart to the classic blues is gospel, and
the popularity and growth of gospel was largely a result of the efforts of Afro-
American women.   *(Author)*

→   JAMES, Edward. **Notable American women. 1607-1950. A**
     biographical dictionary, *see* 56bc[05].

→   JEPSON, Barbara. **American women in conducting**, *see*
     3274ap[78].

147 JOHNSON, H. Earle. **Operas on American subjects** (New
bm   York: Coleman-Ross, 1964) 125 p. *Bibliog., discog.*
Lists operas by European composers and composers from North, Central, and
South America based on subjects dealing with the 3 Americas. Includes
information about plot material, performances, and publication of scores. The
following women composers in the United States, active from the 1880s-1950s,
are represented: Lois Albright, Adeline Carola Appleton, Eleanor Everest Freer,
Abbie Gerrish Jones, Clara Anna Korn, Mary Carr Moore, Mrs. F.G. Tanner,
and Harriet Ware.

148 KAUFMANN, Helen; HANSL, E.E. von B. **From Jehovah**
bf   **to jazz, music in America from psalmody to the present day**
     (Port Washington, N.Y.: Kennikat, 1969) 303 p. *Illus.*
A reprint of the 1937 edition (New York: Dodd, Mead). Surveys 300 years of

music from the first Pilgrim psalter of 1620 to jazz and vaudeville in the 1920s, with an emphasis on East Coast activities. Early singers included Georgina Oldmixon, who made her Philadelphia debut in 1794 as Clorinda in *Robin Hood*. Mercy Warren published her *Liberty song* in 1768. Miss Ball was the first-known music and needlework teacher in Philadelphia in 1730. Women's music in the home, their compositions in the early 19th c.--which typically were sentimental ballads and amorous parlor songs--and notable 19th and 20th-c. musicians such as Amy Cheney Beach, Christine Nilsson, and Adelina Patti are discussed. Several women opera librettists of the 20th c. are considered, including Alice Neal Pollock and her work with Henry Hadley, Nelle Richmond Eberhart with Charles Wakefield Cadman, Edna St. Vincent Millay and Constance Collier, both with Deems Taylor, and Gertrude Stein with Virgil Thomson.

149 KEEFER, Lubov. **Baltimore's music. The haven of the**
bm **American composer** (Baltimore: author, 1962) 343 p.
This history of musical life in Baltimore from colonial times to ca. 1960 includes brief references to hundreds of women active both in Baltimore and on the national scene as composers, performers, lyricists, educators, and patrons. Information about performances includes dates, places, and occasionally the works performed. Women active at the Peabody Conservatory, in church, synagogue, and temperance music, and in music education are considered.

150 KERR, Phillip. **Music in evangelism** (3rd ed.; Glendale, Calif.:
bm Gospel Music, 1950) 241 p. *Index*.
Among American hymn writers of texts, the following women active in the 19th and 20th c. are cited: Mary A. Baker, Katharine L. Bates, Lydia Baxter, Ada Blenhorn, Mrs. Frank A. Breck, Harriet E. Buell, Lizzie De Armand, Ellen M.H. Gates, Elvian Mabel Hall, Annie Hawks, Annie Herbert, Eliza Edmunds Hewitt, Julia Ward Howe, Jennie Hussey, Mrs. M.A. Kidder, Mary A. Lathbury, Lida Shivers Leech, Jemima Thompson Luke, Ina D. Ogdon, Priscilla J. Owens, Jessie B. Pounds, Ida L. Reed, Fannie Edna Stafford, Anna Warner, and Susan Warner. Composers of hymn tunes include Flora H. Cassel, Fanny Crosby, Phoebe Knapp, May Whittle Moody, and Carrie E. Rounsefell. Women who wrote both the text and music are Phoebe Cary, Helen Howarth Lemmel, Mrs. C.H. Morris, Mrs. Will H. Murphy, and Mrs. F. W. Suffield.

→ KING, Mrs. A.T. **Women as composers**, *see 695ap[56]*.

151 KLINZING, Ernestine M. **Music in Rochester: a century of**
bm **musical progress, 1825-1925**, *Rochester History* XXIX/1 (Jan 1967) 1-24.
1) Anna Bishop and Jenny Lind were among the first artists of international stature to appear in Rochester, N.Y. in 1851. 2) Organized ca. 1890, the Tuesday Musicale was an important organization in the city for over 30 years, presenting local members in recitals and acting as a concert agency for prominent performers on tour. 3) Together with Herman Dossenbach, Mrs. Alf Klingenberg was primarily responsible for interesting George Eastman in establishing a music school in the 1920s--endowed and connected with the U. of Rochester. Mrs. Klingenberg came to Rochester from Norway in 1912 with her husband, a pianist, who joined the faculty of an early conservatory in the city.

152 KOLODIN, Irving. **Metropolitan Opera, The. 1883-1966**
bm (New York: A.A. Knopf, 1966) xxi, 762, xlvii p. *Illus., list of works, index.*
A history of the Metropolitan Opera at 1423 Broadway in New York. In addition to women singers, the work of women as patrons is considered--among them Eleanor R. Belmont. In the mid-1930s Belmont developed the idea of the Metropolitan Opera Guild as a means of support on an annual, recurrent basis. Early in the 1950s she designed the National Council of the Metropolitan as a type of "super guild" with higher entrance fees. Belmont was also active in planning benefits at the Metropolitan.

153 KUPFERBERG, Herbert. **Those fabulous Philadelphians**
bm (New York: C. Scribner's Sons, 1969) 256 p. *Illus., index.*
Discusses the valuable work of the Women's Committee of the Philadelphia Orchestra, the gradual inclusion of women in the orchestra's ranks, and the problems inherent in being the wife of an orchestral musician.

154 LAHEE, Henry Charles. **Annals of music in America. A**
bm **chronological record of significant musical events from 1640 to the present day** (Boston: M. Jones, 1922) 298 p. *Index.*
A chronology of dates, musicians, first performances, and major musical events organized into 8 time periods between 1640 and 1921. A checklist of early events includes the debuts in Chestnut Street Theater, Philadelphia, of Miss Broadhurst in 1793 and Georgina Oldmixon in 1794, as well as a performance in 1796 by Mary Ann Pownall in Charleston, S.C.

→ LAHEE, Henry. **Famous singers of today and yesterday**, *see* 1050bm[58].

155 LOESSER, Arthur. **United States of America**, *Men, women,*
bd *and pianos. A social history* (New York: Simon & Schuster, 1954) 434-613.
Discusses the following developments affecting women both as amateur and professional pianists in American music history to 1954: 1) the rise in piano manufacturing in the United States after the Revolution, 2) the arrival of European piano virtuosi in the mid-1840s, i.e., Leopold de Meyer, Henri Herz, and Bernard Ullmann, 3) the domestic triumph of the American-made piano in the 1850s, e.g., the Chickering and American Steinway pianos, 4) the emergence of the piano as a household staple and the expansion of the market for pianos in the West between 1890 and 1910, and 5) the decline in the piano business after World War I. Sophia Hewitt Ostinelli was one of the few women professional pianists active before the Civil War, while Amy Fay, Julie Rivé-King, and Fannie Bloomfield-Zeisler were highly popular artists among the first generation of major American pianists that became established after the Civil War.

156 MACKIN, Tom. **Women song writers**, *Music Journal* [New
ap York] X/3 (Mar 1952) 30-31, 74-79. *Illus.*
An overview of women's contributions as composers of art songs and popular songs--including Tin Pan Alley repertory--beginning with the early 19th c.

157 MERZ, Karl. **Woman in music**, *Music and culture* (Philadelphia:
ac T. Presser, 1890) 157-67.
Discusses the contributions of women to music throughout history in Europe, and concludes that a great woman composer might emerge in the United States because of the educational opportunities available to American women in general and the fact that American women have begun to study music seriously in recent years. Even if women cannot achieve greatness in composition, they are well-suited to teaching, and women are now making teaching a "life-calling" rather than a "pin-money pastime".

158 MÖLLER, Dr. Heinrich. **Can women compose?**, *Musical
ap Observer* XV/5-6 (May-June 1917) 11-12; 11-12. *Illus.*
"The most that can be said of existing music by women composers [in the United States] is that it shows a primitive, natural gift for a light flow of melody which seldom rises above the level of the merely pleasing. Women composers are perhaps more numerous in proportion to their male rivals than elsewhere, which is not surprising since woman in the New World has always enjoyed more leisure than her sisters in the Old. Moreover, not so very long ago, love of music was confined almost entirely to the women in American families". The work of numerous 18th and 19th-c. female composers--both European and American, arranged by nationality--is briefly discussed.

159 MORINI, Erica. **Women as musicians**, *Who is who in music*
ac (Chicago: L. Stern, 1940-41) 576-77.
Considers high points in the history of women as performers in the United States, and focuses on the activity of women as violinists.

160 **Musical Alabama.** Comp. by Margaret F. THOMAS (Montgom-
bm ery, Ala.: Alabama Federation of Music Clubs, 1925) 177 p. *Illus., music, list of works.*
A detailed history of the Alabama Federation of Music Clubs with information about music in Mobile beginning in the 18th c., Auburn since 1840, and Enfaula from 1860. The following women's colleges with strong music offerings were established early in the state's history: Judson Col. in Marion (1838), Masonic Female Col. in Auburn (1840s), and Union Female Col. in Enfaula (1860). In the 2nd half of the 19th c. there were many women's study clubs and choruses active in Alabama. Lists of works by women composers in the state--for the most part active in 1925--are included.

161 **Negro in music and art, The.** Ed. and with an introduction by
bm Lindsay PATTERSON (New York: Publishers, 1967) 304 p. *Illus., index.*
Reviews the contributions of black musicians to jazz, popular, and classical music as well as the visual arts throughout the history of the United States. In the field of classical music, Margaret Bonds discusses her background as a composer, including her studies with Florence B. Price in Chicago. Maud Cuney-Hare considers black pioneers in performance: (in chronological order) the singers Elizabeth Taylor Greenfield, Anna Madah Hyers and Emma Louise Hyers, Nellie F. Brown, Flora Batson, and Marie Selika. Phil Petries discusses the problems faced by black opera singers in the past--e.g., Lillian Evanti and Caterina Jarboro in the 1920s-30s--in gaining employment with major performing institutions. David Ewen reviews the career of Marian Anderson, singer; George Hoefer the career of the blues singer Bessie Smith.

→ NEULS-BATES, Carol. **Sources and resources for women's studies in American music: a report**, *see* 68ap[10].

→ OGDEN, Gertrude. **Growth of violin playing by women**, *see* 1131ap[58].

→   OSBURN, Mary. **Ohio composers and musical authors**, *see* 61bm[05].

162   OVERMYER, Grace. **Famous American composers** (New
bm   York: T.Y. Crowell, 1944) 202 p. *Illus., music, index.*
Devotes a chapter to singer Louise Homer, née Beatty in 1872, who--while not a composer--was an inspiration for the creative work of her husband Sidney Homer, as well as an outstanding musical personality in her own right. Includes less extensive information about Lillian Nordica's collaboration with Charles Wakefield Cadman and Cadman's concert tour with Tsianine Redfeather--a Cherokee singer and in large part the inspiration for Cadman's opera *Shanewis*. Brief biographies of Teresa Carreño, Elizabeth Hopkinson, President Jefferson's daughters Martha and Mary, and Marian MacDowell are presented.

163   PETRIDES, Frederique Joanne. **Outline of a prejudice**,
ap   *Musical Review* [Brooklyn] IV/6 (Sept-Oct 1935) 3, 7.
An overview of women's progress as performers in western Europe and the United States to ca. 1900. "Freed from the shackles and tatters of the old tradition and prejudices, American and European women in music are now universally hailed as important factors in the concert and teaching fields, and at the same time as promising and fast-developing assets in the creative sphere of the profession".

→   PETRIDES, Frederique. **Women in orchestras**, *see* 2327ap[68].

→   **Report of the nineteenth annual meeting. Joint sessions CMS-AMS: II. Women's studies in music**, *see* 71ap[10].

→   **Report of the twentieth annual meeting. CMS interest session on women's studies**, *see* 72ap[10].

→   RITTER, Fanny Raymond. **Woman as a musician. An art-historical study**, *see* 621bm[55].

164   RITTER, Frédéric Louis. **Music in America** (New York: C.
bm   Scribner, 1890) 521 p. *Index.*
Traces the development of musical life in the United States from 1620 to the mid-19th c. Includes brief mentions of the following singers: Miss Brett, Miss Broadhurst, and Georgina Oldmixon in the 18th c., and Mrs. Austin, Anna Bishop, Catherine Hillier Graupner, Mrs. Horn, Jenny Lind, Euphrosyne Parepa-Rosa, Adelaide Phillips, Zelda Harrison Séguin, and Mrs. Wood in the 19th c. Also cites Fanny Raymond Ritter's series of recitals of vocal and piano music in 1869-70. A list of vocal soloists--including many women--with the New York Philharmonic is presented.

165   ROACH, Hildred Elizabeth. **Black American music: past and
bm   present** (Boston: Crescendo, 1973) 200 p. $7.50. *Illus., port., music, bibliog., list of works, discog., index.*
A comprehensive survey of Afro-American composers and their music from colonial times to the present. Discusses the influence of black music on the forms, styles, and content of all American music. Considers notable women composers such as Margaret Bonds, Undine Smith Moore, Florence B. Price, and Mary Lou Williams, whose styles range from neo-romanticism to jazz. While black women performers have been more widely publicized in the past, black women composers have been solid pioneers and have made significant contributions.   *(Author, abridged)*

166   ROREM, Ned. **Ladies' music**, *Critical affairs. A composer's
bd   journal* (New York: G. Braziller, 1970) 95-110.
The few women that have been active as composers are of recent vintage because 1) until modern times, music in western civilization was chiefly a religious expression, while the Christian church was male-dominated, 2) music is an interpretive craft, and women make better interpreters than they do creators, and 3) the orchestra is a man's world, which treats the living composer--in general--with contempt and the female composer as an object of derision. It is difficult for a woman to achieve proficiency in the creation of a large-scale work while raising a family.

167   ROTH, Henry. **Women and the violin**, *Strad* LXXXIII (Mar
ap   1973) 551-63.
Surveys the role of women in the history of violin playing in Europe and the United States beginning in the 18th c., and concludes that after 3 centuries of "evolutionary struggle" women violinists are finally coming into their own. Erica Morini and Maud Powell are chief among the Americans discussed.

168   SCRUGGS, Leigh. **Creative women in music**, *Music Clubs
ap   Magazine* LV/2 (winter 1976) 98-99.
An overview of woman's contribution in the field of composition from biblical times to the present day. The author has used this material in a number of lecture-recitals at music clubs and colleges.   *(Author)*

169   SHANET, Howard. **Philharmonic. A history of New York's
bm   orchestra** (New York: Doubleday, 1975) xxi, 788 p. *Illus., bibliog., list of works, index.*
Founded in 1842, the New York Philharmonic Soc. admitted women beginning in 1847, with the immediate result that men decided to refrain from smoking cigars at open rehearsals. The inclusion of women as players in the Philharmonic Orchestra, other than harpists and keyboard players, occurred only in the mid-1960s. Helen M. Thompson served as the Philharmonic's manager from 1970 until her mandatory retirement in 1973. In 1909 Mrs. George R. Sheldon spearheaded the effort to organize a group of Guarantors of the Fund for the Permanent Orchestra of the Philharmonic Soc. of New York. Since 1909 women have been active as fund raisers and as committee members working on a variety of educational activities. Key women include Mrs. Bartlett Arkell, Brooke Astor, Ruth D. Draper, Mrs. Newbold LeRoy Edgar, Minnie Guggenheimer, Mrs. E.H. Harriman, Mrs. Charles E. Mitchell, Mrs. Arthur Sachs, Mrs. Francis G. Shaw, and Sophie Guggenheimer Untermeyer.

170   SOUTHERN, Eileen. **Music of black Americans, The: a
bm   history** (New York: W.W. Norton, 1971) 552 p. *Illus., music, list of works, discog.*
Presents biographical sketches for the composer Julia Perry, the conductor Eva Jessye, and the singer Marian Anderson. Less extensive information is included about the following women: Hazel Harrison, pianist; Flora Batson, Lillian Evanti, Anna Madah Hyers, Emma Louise Hyers, Caterina Jarboro, Sissieretta Jones, Dorothy Maynor, Leontyne Price, and Marie Selika, singers. In addition, the careers of numerous black women active since 1950 are briefly considered.

171   SPEARY, Nellie Best. **Music and life in Marietta, Ohio**
bm   (Marietta, Ohio: MacDonald, 1939) 74 p. *Illus.*
An account of early settlers and their music with special attention to immigrant families from Europe, whose women pioneered music-making in Ohio. Some came from England, e.g., the Blennerhassetts who arrived in 1797, the Ewings who settled in 1792, and the first organist in Marietta, Elizabeth Creel. Other immigrants were of German stock, including the Manatt, Wehrs, Becker, and Mueller families in the mid-19th c. Marietta women were mainly responsible for introducing early music societies, music schools, and elegant parlor musicales as well as for the installation of the first church organ in 1846. Two flourishing institutions with female vocal and instrumental teachers were the Ladies Seminary, established in 1826 (later part of the Inst. of Education) and Elizabeth Col., founded in 1890 (later a part of Marietta Col.).

172   STEANE, J.B. **Grand tradition, The** (New York: C. Scribner's
bm   Sons, 1974) 628 p. *Illus., bibliog., index.*
Discusses major recordings by the following women singers active in American music in 3 time periods. 1900-25: Frances Alda, Lucrezia Bori, Emma Eames, Geraldine Farrar, Johanna Gadski, Amelita Galli-Curci, Alma Gluck, Frieda Hempel, Adelina Patti, Ernestine Schumann-Heink, and Marcella Sembrich. 1925-50: Marian Anderson, Dusolina Giannini, Lotte Lehmann, Claudia Muzio, Sigrid Onégin, Lily Pons, Rosa Ponselle, Elisabeth Rethberg, Elisabeth Schumann, and Helen Traubel. 1950-70: Martina Arroyo, Grace Bumbry, Montserrat Caballé, Maria Callas, Victoria de los Angeles, Marilyn Horne, Christa Ludwig, Anna Moffo, Birgit Nilsson, Leontyne Price, Elisabeth Schwarzkopf, Beverly Sills, Joan Sutherland, Renata Tebaldi, and Shirley Verrett.

173   SWAN, Howard. **Music in the Southwest 1825-1950** (New
bf   York: Da Capo, 1977) 316 p. $22.50. *Illus., index.*
A reprint of the 1952 edition (San Marino, Calif.: Huntington Library). Traces the development of musical life in the southwestern United States at various locations and among various groups of people. 1) Emma Smith--the wife of Joseph Smith, the founder of the Church of the Latter Day Saints--selected 90 hymn texts for the first Mormon hymnal, published in 1835. This event took place prior to the Mormons' westward migration that eventually led them to Utah. 2) Women performed in the theaters of Virginia City and Tombstone, Nev.--towns which became established with the discovery of silver in 1859. 3) In early California during the 1830s-40s, women on *ranchos* typically played the guitar, while men played the violin. 4) Concert life was slow to develop in Los Angeles, but when Anna Bishop successfully presented an unprecedented total of 4 concerts there in 1873, other artists were encouraged to travel to the city. 5) Between 1879 and ca. 1905 Mamie Perry was a leading figure in Los Angeles music. Perry sang with her husband in light opera and founded the Monday Musical Club. 6) After 1885 Los Angeles experienced considerable growth, mainly due to the price war between railroads that brought an influx of settlers. One new settler was Lynden Ellsworth ("Bee") Behymer, who became a purveyor of culture in southern California for more than 50 years beginning in 1886. Mrs. "Bee" was his assistant.

174   THOMPSON, Oscar. **American singer, The** (New York: John-
bf   son Reprint, 1969) 429 p. *Index.*
A reprint of the 1939 edition (New York: Dial). America's first noteworthy opera singers were women, who emerged 10 years after the performances of Manuel Garcia's opera company in New York in 1825. These included Eliza Biscaccianti, Charlotte Cushman, Lucy Eastcott, Elise Hensler, Juliana May, Adelaide Phillipps, Genevieve Ward, Julia Wheatley, Cora de Wilhorst, and

Jennie Van Zandt. Clara Louise Kellogg was the first American singer to achieve fame in Europe as well as in the United States; Kellogg made her first appearances abroad in 1867. In addition to these early singers, Thompson also considers the work of nearly 40 women who rose to prominence later in the 19th and 20th c.

175 THRASHER, Herbert Chandler. **250 years of music in**
bm   **Providence, Rhode Island, 1636-1886** ([Providence]: Rhode Island Federation of Music Clubs, 1942) 31 p.
Oliver and Sarah Jencks Shaw were prominent in musical life in Providence in the first half of the 19th c., and their home became a veritable music conservatory with boarding students. Emma Greene was the organist at the South Baptist Church for more than 60 years before her death in 1937. Early appearances by artists of national stature are noted, and a list of Rhode Island composers beginning in the 19th c. is included. Dorothy J. Pearce compiled the list of composers.

176 TICK, Judith. **Why have there been no great women com-**
ap   **posers?**, *International Musician* LXXIV/1 (July 1975) 3-6.
Discusses the traditional prejudices against women as composers and the major areas of discrimination they have faced in the past and continue to face in the present.   (Author)

→   TOWERS, John. **Woman in music**, *see* 65bm[05].

177 UPTON, George P. **Woman in music** (Boston: J.R. Osgood,
bm   1880) 145 p. *Port., list of works.*
In Part I Upton argues that woman has not succeeded in composition because she lacks "mastery of the theoretical intricacies, the logical sequences, and the mathematical problems which are the foundation principles of music. She will always be the recipient and interpreter, but there is little hope she will be the creator". In Part II the influence of woman upon the male composer is considered, with reference to leading composers, e.g., J.S. Bach, Mozart, Beethoven, etc. Part III discusses woman as interpreter, with an emphasis on the work of women as singers. Lists of women composers active in Europe in the 17th-19th c. and works dedicated to women by men are included in an appendix.

178 WILLHARTITZ, Adolph. **Some facts about women in music**
bm   (Los Angeles: Out West, 1902) 16 p.
"It is a comparatively short time that women were allowed to even sing in churches, or that a teacher could be found who would condescend to listen to the appeals of his female pupils who desired to be taught harmony and composition. And even when they did receive instruction in the mathematics of music, it was given more for the purpose of satisfying a whim than to earnestly and systematically teach them the intricate rules of composition". Lists of European and American women as singers, instrumentalists, and composers from both the past and contemporary life are included. The list of composers is devoted solely to women composers of 150 operas and other dramatic works.

179 WILLHARTITZ, Adolph. **Woman in music**, *Musical Courier*
ap   XXXVII/9 (31 Aug 1898) 29.
Willhartitz recalls how he came to write *Some facts about women in music* (*WIAM* 178)--tracing past and present activity by women as composers and performers--in order to counter the negative judgments of Anton Rubinstein (*A conversation in music*, *WIAM* 1168) and George P. Upton (*Woman in music*, *WIAM* 177). Willhartitz believes that his book encouraged many young women to study music in earnest. He regrets, however, that other persons--mostly women--are appropriating his research without giving him credit.

180 WILLIAMS, Ora. **American black women in the arts and**
bm   **social sciences: a bibliographic survey** (rev. ed.; Metuchen, N.J.: Scarecrow, 1978) 197 p. $8. *Illus., bibliog., list of works, discog., index.*
A survey of American black women's contributions to the arts and social sciences. Presents an extensive bibliography, biographies of selected individuals, a chronology of significant dates in the history of American black women, and a list of ideas and achievements of selected women. Information about musical compositions and recordings is included.

181 **Women of music, The.** Ed. by THE AMERICAN MUSIC
ap   CONFERENCE, *Music Journal* [New York] XXX/1 (Jan 1972) 9-24, 55, 58-59. *Illus.*
Reviews the role of women in amateur and professional music making through the ages, discusses musical taboos and conventions, and assesses the current climate for women as performers in the United States. "The problem with women in music has nothing to do with ability. In fact, studies by music educators have suggested that girls are, if anything, quicker and more adept than boys in learning some musical skills--perhaps because girls are less inhibited in using their singing voices".

→   WURM, Marie. **Women's struggle for recognition in music**, *see* 2069ap[66].

COLONIAL TIMES TO 1820

30   Literature about women in vernacular music

→   ANDREWS, Edward. **Gift to be simple, The. Songs, dances, and rituals of the American Shakers**, *see* 232bf[40].

182 BLAKELY, Lloyd C. **Johann Conrad Beissel and music of**
ap   **the Ephrata Cloister**, *Journal of Research in Music Education* XV/2 (summer 1967) 120-38.
Discusses the predominance of women as singers at Ephrata in Pennsylvania and whether falsetto singing was the actual practice or not. Includes a translation of Beissel's preface to *Das Gesäng der einsamen und verlassenen Turtel Taube* [The song of the solitary and deserted turtle dove]. Despite the crudeness of the efforts by Beissel and his associates, the music of the Ephrata Cloister belongs among the first attempts made on American soil to compose sacred music. MSS of music from the cloister are extant at the Library of Congress, the Historical Soc. of Philadelphia, the Free Library of Philadelphia, and the 7th Day Baptist Historical Soc. in Plainfield, N.J.

183 EPSTEIN, Dena J. **Sinful tunes and spirituals: black folk**
bm   **music to the Civil War.** *Music in American life* (Urbana, Ill.: U. of Illinois, 1977) 433 p. $16.50. *Illus., port., facsim., music, bibliog., index.*
A history of black folk music in the United States from the 17th c. up to the appearance of the first published collection, *Slave songs of the United States* in 1867. Part I, "Development of black folk music to 1800", includes early reports of African music in British and French America, with contemporary descriptions of dancing and instruments: drums, musical bow, banjo, quills (panpipes), bones and balafo, and xylophone. The acculturation of this folk music into Afro-American music, and the conversion of blacks to Christianity are also considered. Part II, "Secular and sacred black folk music, 1800-1867" discusses African survivals, dancing, work songs, and the development of the spiritual, including the role played by women, e.g., Charity Bowery and Clarinda, a fiddler. Part III, "The emergence of black folk music during the Civil War", describes the gathering of *Slave songs of the United States*, to which many women contributed: Annie M. Bowen, Eliza Dodge, Charlotte L. Forten, Lucy McKim Garrison (1 of the 3 editors), Caroline Howard Gilman, Laura H. Towne, Ellen Murray, and Harriet Ware. The sources on which Part III is based are primarily unpublished correspondence.   (Author)

184 HOWARD, John Tasker. **Music of George Washington's**
bm   **time, The** (Washington, D.C.: Washington Bicentennial Commission, 1931) 96 p. *Illus., music, list of works.*
Describes 18th-c. popular songs, dances, band music, and concert life. Considers early singers in Philadelphia--e.g., Maria Storer and Arabella Brett Hodgkinson--women and girls as musical participants in welcoming festivities during Washington's inaugural year of 1789, and compositions written by women in tribute to Washington, among them Mary Ann Pownall's *Washington* of 1794 and *Washington and liberty* of 1796. Jane Rowson Crowe composed and published a song, *Truxton's victory*, in Boston in 1799 in commemoration of Capt. Truxton's defeat of the French on the frigate Constellation. Washington's step-grandchildren were musical; the household at Mount Vernon contained a flute, guitar, and harpsichord that were purchased for his step-granddaughter, Eleanor Parke Custis.

→   JOHNSON, H. **Musical interludes in Boston 1795-1830**, *see* 198bm[35].

→   LOWENS, Irving. **Bibliography of songsters printed in America before 1821, A**, *see* 22bm[01].

185 **New convent for the Sisters is built, A; the singing schools**
bd   **come into vogue.** Trans. from German by J. Max HARK, *Chronicon Ephratense: a history of the community of Seventh Day Baptists* (Lancaster, Penn.: S.H. Zahm, 1899) 157-69.
The choir at the Ephrata Cloister in Pennsylvania was formed by gathering 70 Brothers and Sisters who had talent into a singing school; these were instructed by a house Father, who was a master singer. Eventually the Sisters asked Conrad Beissel, the head of the community, to be their singing master, but they found they had to teach Beissel--a violinist--everything they had learned from their first teacher. In time, deciding Beissel was too strict a teacher, the Sisters

stopped attending the singing school. A reconciliation was eventually effected by Sister Anastasia, who became Beissel's assistant. Among Beissel's beliefs were that fruit, milk, and meat were injurious to the voice, and that celibacy was beneficial to it. The choirs sang antiphonally "to make manifest the wonderful harmony of eternity in a country which, but lately, wild savages had inhabited".

→   REDWAY, Virginia. **Music directory of early New York City. A file of musicians, music publishers, and musical instrument-makers listed in New York directories from 1786 through 1825, together with the most important New York music publishers from 1836 through 1875**, see 62bm[05].

186   SACHSE, Julius Friedrich. **Music of the cloister, The**, *German*
bd   *sectarians of Pennsylvania, 1708-1800, The. A critical and legendary history of the Ephrata Cloister and the Dunkers* (Philadelphia: author, 1900) II, 128-60. *Illus., music.*
Women were active as singers, writers of hymn texts, and possibly as composers at the Ephrata Cloister in Pennsylvania, which was settled in 1720 under the leadership of Conrad Beissel. Men also belonged to the community, but in music the Sisters appear to have been predominant. In 1747 the cloister printed a new hymnbook, *Das Gesäng der einsamen and verlassenen Turtel Taube* [The song of the solitary and deserted turtle dove], made up of hymns by the members. Beissel was the chief contributor with ca. 275 hymns, but 21 women and 16 men are represented with 96 pieces--those by women being more numerous. It is not clear whether the authors of the hymn texts also provided the musical settings. Rhythm in the Ephrata music follows the words, the accented syllables receiving the longer notes, the unaccented syllables, the shorter notes. Beissel's chord tables in all the keys facilitated composition. Women sang the tenor parts, men only the bass; falsetto voice was used exclusively. A singing school of the Sisterhood flourished under Beissel's direction, and women hand-copied and illuminated hymnbooks.

187   SACHSE, Julius Friedrich. **Music of the Ephrata Cloister,**
bf   **The** (New York: AMS, 1971) 108 p. *Illus., facsim., music.*
A reprint of the 1903 edition. Includes supplementary information to Sachse's *The music of the cloister* (*WIAM* 186) and presents Conrad Beissel's treatise on music, which was published as a preface to *Das Gesäng der einsamen und verlassenen Turtel Taube* [The song of the solitary and deserted turtle dove], in translation.

→   SONNECK, Oscar. **Early opera in America**, see 220bf[38].

188   STEVENSON, Robert. **Pennsylvania Germans**, *Protestant*
bd   *church music in America* (New York: W.W. Norton, 1966) 32-45. *Index.*
Discusses music at the Ephrata Cloister in Pennsylvania. Three years after director Conrad Beissel's death in 1728, a minister of Christ's Church, Philadelphia, described musical activity at Ephrata in the following way: when the sisters sang in chapel, the counter, treble, tenor, and bass were all sung by women who "sat with their heads reclined--their countenances solemn and dejected, their faces pale and emaciated from their manner of living, their clothing exceedingly white and quite picturesque, and their music such as thrilled to the very soul".

→   STOUTAMIRE, Albert. **Music of the old South: colony to Confederacy**, see 277bm[45].

31   Vernacular music by women

Vocal music

189   LADY, A. **Jerusalem. A hymn**, *Carr's Musical Miscellany* 53
mm   ([1818-19]) 3 p..
Sacred song. Dn 1'. Pf solo voc, org.   (*Judith Tick*)

34   Literature about women in related arts and disciplines

→   LOWENS, Irving. **Bibliography of songsters printed in America before 1821, A**, see 22bm[01].

→   MATES, Julian. **American musical stage before 1800, The**, see 212bm[38].

35   General literature about women in art music

190   BENNET, John. **Letters to a young lady. Letter VII: on**
ap   **female accomplishments**, *American Museum or Universal Magazine* XI/3 (Mar 1792) 91-92.
Instructs young women on suitable and beneficial pursuits. "The accomplishments of a woman may be comprised under some, or all of the following articles: needlework, embroidery, drawing, music, dancing, dress, politeness, etc.". It is desirable that any woman with sufficient time and money study an instrument or singing because music will provide entertainment for others and relaxation for the woman. Because of the immoral texts of some music, women should study sacred music, particularly works such as *Judas Maccabaeus* and *Messiah*.

191   BENSON, Mary Sumner. **Women in 18th-century America.**
bm   **A study of opinion and social usage** (Port Washington, N.Y.: Kennikat, 1935) 343 p. *Bibliog., index.*
Discusses 18th-c. views on women's social roles and education. 1) Music is mentioned by a number of sources as a usual part of female education and cultivation. 2) Cotton Mather in his *Ornaments for the daughters of Zion or The character and happiness of a vertuous woman* (1692) advises: "If she [the virtuous woman] had time she might study music and language but would not take pride in her skill in them". 3) In the late 18th c. women at Andrew Brown's school in Philadelphia studied vocal music under Andrew Adgate.

192   BROWN, Francis. **Address on music delivered before the**
bm   **Handel Society, Dartmouth College, August 1809, An** (Hanover, N.H.: C. & W. Spear, 1810) 23 p.
A lecture on the nature and influence of music, which is the universal language of "strong emotions of the pleasurable kind". Music begins with Nature's inspiration in a mother's soothing lullaby or, conversely, in the talent incited by the powerful stimulus of an infant's cries. The following contemporary developments are deplored: the preference for William Billings over Händel, a decline in sacred psalmody in New England, the use of unsuitable instruments in church services, and the lamentable attitude of upper-class women who have "considered it humiliating to bear a part in the music of the sanctuary", and thus have abandoned "its solemn devotional tradition to the noisy rhapsodies and frivolities of the young".

193   DINNEEN, William. **Early American manuscript music-**
ap   **books**, *Musical Quarterly* XXX/1 (Jan 1944) 50-62. *Illus., facsim., list of works.*
After 1790, peace and relative prosperity made it possible for Americans to indulge in a long-delayed desire for entertainment, and they turned rapidly to secular song as cultivated in Europe, in opposition to the traditions of the psalmodists. The contents of 4 MSS copied in the 1790s by 3 female amateurs in different locales indicate that secular song was widely accepted by amateurs at the time and that musical life was much more active than studies of professional programs and music editions would indicate. The women were Eunice Crew of Norwich, Conn., Maria Byrne of Philadelphia, and Susanna Mueller--who copied music for 2 MSS, one with German and the other with English texts. She signed the English MS Susan Miller.

194   EARLE, Alice Morse. **Colonial dames and good wives** (Boston: Houghton, Mifflin, 1895) 315 p.
bm
A history of colonial women: their activities, interests, and manners. Advertisements indicate that by the early 18th c. there were spinets in Boston, Philadelphia, and perhaps Virginia. By the late 18th c. fortepianos were being imported. Contemporary reports indicate that keyboard instruments were bought for and played by women as much as or more than by men.

195   EARLE, Alice Morse. **Women teachers and girl scholars**,
bd   *Child life in colonial days* (New York: Macmillan, 1899) 90-116. *Illus., index.*
Describes the upbringing and activities of children in colonial times and includes information on music. 1) Abigail Adams, wife of John Adams, is quoted on her New England background: "Female education, in the best families, went no further than writing and arithmetic; in some few and rare instances music and dancing". 2) Dr. John Earle, a contemporary writer, noted that the Puritan woman did not let her daughters learn to play virginals "because of their affinity with the organs", but that evidence shows that there were virginals owned by Puritan women. Printed music for harpsichord and spinet in use at the time was very simple.

196   ELLET, Elizabeth Fries Lummis. **Queens of American soci-**
bm   **ety** (Philadelphia: H.T. Coates, 1867) 464 p. *Index.*
Discusses the intellectual, cultural, and social activities of American society women from colonial times to the 1860s. During their courtship, Martha Skelton Jefferson is reported to have played harpsichord and sung to Thomas Jefferson's violin. Their daughter Martha was encouraged to devote much time to music. Eleanor Parke Custis of Virginia was required to practice harpsichord

4 to 5 hours a day in addition to her other studies. Margaret Shellman Hills, a Georgia woman who became part of New York society, composed and improvised at the piano; her daughter, Mrs. John Schermerhorn, was a gifted pianist who was praised by Louis Moreau Gottschalk, and her granddaughther, Minnie Parker, sang and played piano. Although not professional musicians, these women were well-known as performers within their social circles.

197   ELSON, Louis Charles. **National music of America and its**
bm   **sources, The** (Boston: L.C. Page, 1899) 338 p. *Illus., music, index.*
Traces the development of American music from its beginnings in the 17th c. through the growth of choral music in the mid-19th c. Considers the rise of secular music and various types of songs, e.g., national, sea, and Civil War songs. Women's contributions have included singer Catherine Hillier Graupner's concerts in Salem, Mass. in 1798, Sophia Hewitt Ostinelli's organ playing in Boston in the early 19th c., Eliza Clayland Tomlinson's nurturing of her son Stephen Foster in the traditions of her cultivated Maryland family, and new settings of the tune of *John Brown's body* by Julia Ward Howe and Edna Dean Proctor in the mid-19th c.

→   FRANK, Leonie. **Musical life in early Cincinnati and the origin of the May Festival**, *see* 269bm[45].

→   HOWARD, John. **Music of George Washington's time, The**, *see* 184bm[30].

198   JOHNSON, H. Earle. **Musical interludes in Boston 1795-**
bm   **1830** (New York: Columbia U., 1943) 366 p. *Illus., index.*
This history of Boston's musical life between 1795 and 1830 includes discussion of the activity of Elizabeth Von Hagen as keyboard player and teacher, Catherine Hillier Graupner as singer, and Sophia Hewitt Ostinelli as pianist and teacher. Von Hagen settled in Boston in 1796 with her husband and son--Peter Sr. and Peter Jr.--with whom she regularly gave concerts. She was organist at King's Chapel and was generally active until 1806--the date of her last recital. Catherine Hillier Graupner, the wife and working associate of Gottlieb Graupner, was a popular singing-actress at the Federal Theater beginning in 1800 and later a soloist at concerts of the Handel and Haydn Soc. Sophia Hewitt Ostinelli, the daughter of James Hewitt, made her adult debut in 1814 and subsequently became an important pianist and teacher in Boston until 1822, at which time she relocated in Maine. The work of the following women is also considered briefly: Mrs. Burke, Mrs. French, Arabella Brett Hodgkinson, Georgina Oldmixon, Elizabeth Arnold Poe, and Mary Ann Pownall as singers; Miss Mallet and Miss Eustaphieve as pianists; Catherine Graupner Cushing as pianist and the first organist for the Handel and Haydn Soc.; and Mrs. Powell, theater manager.

199   MCCORKLE, Donald M. **Moravian contribution to Ameri-**
bm   **can music, The.** *Moravian Music Foundation publications* 1 (Winston-Salem, N.C.: Moravian Music Foundation, 1956) 10 p.
Discusses the contributions to early American music of Moravian settlements in the United States--beginning in 1740--through their collections of music instruments and their *collegia musica*. Presents a letter dated 1787 from a 12-year old girl attending the Bethlehem Seminary, about the curriculum and the schedule for a typical day. The school enjoyed an excellent reputation and accorded the study of music an important status, in keeping with Moravian traditions.

→   MOORE, John. **Dictionary of musical information 1640-1875, A**, *see* 60bm[05].

→   **New Haven, Connecticut, New Haven Historical Society. A checklist of source materials by and about women in American music**, *see* 29bm[01].

200   RAU, Albert G.; DAVID, Hans T. **Critical catalogue of**
bm   **music by American Moravians 1742-1842, A; from the archives of the Moravian church at Bethlehem, Pennsylvania** (Bethlehem, Penn.: Moravian Seminary and Col. for Women, 1938) 118 p. *Illus., facsim., music, list of works.*
The introduction describes Moravian missionary and musical work before examining composers and sources. Hannah Weber, an organist and music copyist with the church, is mentioned.

→   REDWAY, Virginia. **Music directory of early New York City. A file of musicians, music publishers, and musical instrument-makers listed in New York directories from 1786 through 1825, together with the most important New York music publishers from 1836 through 1875**, *see* 62bm[05].

201   RUSH, Benjamin M.D. **Thoughts upon female education,**
ap   **accommodated to the present state of society, manners, and**

government, in the United States of America, *Universal Asylum and Columbia Magazine* IV (Apr-May 1790) 209-13; 288-92.
A revised version of an address to visitors at the Young Ladies Academy in Philadelphia, 28 July 1787, describing the manner in which a young woman ought to be educated. "Vocal music should never be neglected, in the education of a young lady, in this country. Besides preparing her to join in that part of publick worship which consists in psalmody, it will enable her to soothe the cares of domestick life". Singing is also recommended as a preventative and cure for consumption. Study of instrumental music--only guitar and harpsichord are mentioned--is not recommended except for a woman of means with a strong inclination. In addition to the expense, such study involves a quantity of time better spent in studying history, philosophy, and other subjects more useful to a lady in the eyes of her husband and society.

202   SPRUILL, Julia Cherry. **Women's life and work in the**
bf   **southern colonies.** With a new intro. by Anne Firor SCOTT (New York: W.W. Norton, 1972) 426 p. *Bibliog., index.*
A reprint of the 1938 edition (Chapel Hill, N.C.: U. of North Carolina). Considers women's roles and social life in the southern colonies. Information from contemporary journals, letters, and advertisements indicates that music studies were normally part of a woman's education. Although this usually meant study of the harpsichord or spinet, piano or guitar, other instruments more commonly played by men--e.g., flute, violin, and cello--were also studied by women. Vocal music was somewhat less common in the home than instrumental music. An extensive bibliography of primary sources is included.

→   STOUTAMIRE, Albert. **Music of the old South: colony to Confederacy**, *see* 277bm[45].

203   WOODY, Thomas. **History of women's education in the**
bm   **United States, A.** *Science and education* IV (New York: Science, 1929) 2 v. xvi, 608; 646 p. *Illus., bibliog., index.*
Includes information about music in the education of women during the colonial period through articles, journals, advertisements, etc. In colonial New England instructors advertised music lessons for both sexes, and instruction on "treble violin", flute, and spinet were part of the curriculum in a small private school for women in Boston. A tutor to a family in Virginia wrote of the girls studying piano, guitar, flute, harpsichord, and singing; violin and cello were also studied by women in the South. Quotations from Benjamin Rush's essay on women's education are included.

36   Literature about women as composers of art music

→   TICK, Judith. **History of American women composers before 1870, A**, *see* 285dd[46].

37   Literature about women as patrons and educators in art music

204   BROOKS, Henry M. **Olden-time music. A compilation from**
bf   **newspapers and books** (New York: AMS, 1973) 283 p.
A reprint of the 1888 edition (Boston: Ticknor). Documents musical life in Boston and Salem, Mass., and other places in New England to 1830. Among the items pertaining to women are advertisements by teachers (some female) and by schools seeking female students of voice, harpsichord, and piano. Also included are concert announcements of female singers and reports on the activities of female organists. One concert advertisement notes that a sonata for pianoforte and a song, both composed by "a lady or young lady", will be included on a Boston concert program, 21 Nov. 1792.

→   DEXTER, Elisabeth. **Career women of America 1776-1840**, *see* 206bm[38].

→   HEHR, Milton. **Musical activities in Salem, Massachusetts: 1783-1823**, *see* 209dd[38].

38   Literature about women as performers of art music

205   BERMAN, Eleanor Davidson. **Thomas Jefferson among the**
bm   **arts** (New York: Philosophical Library, 1947) 305 p. *Bibliog., index.*

Discusses Jefferson's attitudes toward and involvement with the arts, based on his letters and other documents. When Martha Skelton Jefferson, who played harpsichord and sang, married Jefferson in 1772 he had a piano imported from London for her. In 1783 Jefferson wrote to his elder daughter Martha, who was in school in Philadelphia, "With respect to the distribution of time, the following is what I should approve: from 8 to 10 a.m., practice music; from 4 to 5 p.m., exercise yourself in music". In a letter of 1787 he encouraged her to pursue music, drawing, and reading so that she might never be overcome with ennui.

206   DEXTER, Elisabeth Anthony. **Career women of America**
bm   **1776-1840** (Francestown, N.H.: Jones, Marshall, 1950) 262 p. *Index.*
Women's careers in the early United States are discussed by discipline, with the section on music including singers and teachers. "Music was usually taught by men, even in schools where most of the teachers were women". Elizabeth Von Hagen, a professional musician from Amsterdam active in New York in 1792, advertised herself as a vocal and instrumental music teacher, emphasizing that it was advantageous to have a girl study singing with someone who sings in the same vocal range. However, men continued to dominate the field of music education.

207   GILMAN, Samuel. **Memoirs of a New England village choir**
bm   **with occasional reflections** (Boston: S.G. Goodrich, 1829) 149 p.
A *roman à clef* based on the author's experiences as a member of a church choir in New England ca. 1800 and dedicated to the Handel and Haydn Soc. Satirizes prevalent customs and attitudes, and presents a lively picture of musical practices, rehearsals, the use of instruments in church, standard hymnals in use, the structure of choirs, and contrasting conducting techniques. Discusses the role of women choristers--who were seated separately and according to social class. One woman, a successful dairy farm manager, became choirleader, but male members hated her "mortifying domination". Similarly, the women were recalcitrant before a young, untried male conductor. The strongest voices took the tenor air regardless of sex or range, frequently with unhappy results.

208   GRIDER, Rufus A. **Historical notes on music in Bethlehem,**
bf   **Pennsylvania from 1741-1871**. *Moravian Music Foundation publications* 4 (Winston-Salem, N.C.: Moravian Music Foundation, 1957) 41 p.
A reprint of the 1873 edition (Philadelphia: J.L. Pile). Discusses the various music organizations within the Moravian community in Bethlehem and church music for specific occasions. Reports that until the building of the new church in 1803-06 men and women were separated during church services, with the result that the opportunities for a variety of choral music were limited. Also, women were excluded from performances in the "concert room". With the advent of the new church, however, men and women combined in one choir for "the better controlled and more effective renderment of music", and women (at first married, and then single) were allowed to sing in the concert room. Under the old order the unmarried sisters for many years had their own string quartet and choir.

209   HEHR, Milton Gerald. **Musical activities in Salem, Massa-**
dd   **chusetts: 1783-1823** (PhD diss., Musicology: Boston U., 1963) 424 p.
Traces the development of music in Salem, Mass. from psalm singing in churches through the rise of public concert life. Women appeared publicly in theater troupes ca. 1820. Among them were the singers Mrs. Brown, Catherine Hillier Graupner, Miss Harrison, Mrs. Hatch, Mrs. Jones, Mrs. Mills, Miss Solomon, and Mrs. Solomon. Two women active as music teachers ca. 1820 were Mehitabel Harris, who opened a singing school in that year, and Sophia Hewitt Ostinelli, who taught piano, organ, harp, and guitar. A Miss Turner maintained a dancing school prior to 1823; even earlier a dancing studio advertised in 1809 and 1810. Singers who traveled from Boston to Salem included Catherine Hillier Graupner, Mrs. Holman, Mrs. Jones, Mrs. Mallett, and Elizabeth Von Hagen.

210   HOWARD, John Tasker. **Hewitt family in American music,**
ap   **The**, *Musical Quarterly* XVII/1 (Jan 1931) 25-39.
A description of the musical activities of James Hewitt and his offspring. His older daughter Sophia Hewitt Ostinelli, who married violinist Louis Ostinelli, began performing on the piano at age 7, served as organist for the Handel and Haydn Soc. from 1820-29, and sang in New York concerts. Her younger sister Eliza Hewitt was a music teacher in Boston and in Burlington, N.J. Eliza Biscaccianti, daughter of Sophia, studied in Naples and became a well-known opera singer. Carrie W. Hewitt, great-granddaughter of James, and whose grandfather and father were also musicians, currently teaches music in Baltimore.

211   MAGUIRE, Helena M. **When the colonial girl took music**
ap   **lessons**, *Musician* XII/12 (Dec 1907) 581-82. *Illus.*
1) Music was first introduced into colonial society under the cover of "moral lectures, fashionable Thursdays, and afternoon teas". 2) Fathers returning from trips to England in the 18th c. typically brought their daughters music and

music books. 3) There were relatively few harpsichords in the United States in the 18th c., and these, of course, were confined to wealthy families. For instance, there were only 50 harpsichords in Boston at a time when the population numbered 6000 families. 4) Music teachers often advertised that pupils could practice upon the teacher's harpsichord while waiting for an instrument to arrive from England or to be made in America. Many young women must have taken advantage of this offer since music was considered a necessary part of their education.

212   MATES, Julian. **American musical stage before 1800, The**
bm   (New Brunswick, N.J.: Rutgers U., 1962) ix, 331 p. *Bibliog., index.*
This study of ballad opera in the United States in the 18th c. focuses on William Dunlap and Benjamin Carr's *The archers* of 1796. Information is included about the activity of Susannah Haswell Rowson and Anne Julia Hatton as librettists and the following women as singers: Elizabeth Arnold Poe, Miss Broadhurst, Arabella Brett Hodgkinson, Georgina Oldmixon, and Mary Ann Pownall. Women actresses, dancers, and women as audience members are also considered.

213   PICHIERRI, Louis. **Music in New Hampshire 1623-1800**
bm   (New York: Columbia U., 1960) 297 p. *Bibliog., index.*
This history of early musical life in New Hampshire reports that until the 1830s men with high voices typically sang the treble part in congregational singing in New England, because it was prominent. Women sang the tenor part, while men performed the alto part an octave higher as countertenors. However, since few men could handle the tessitura of such countertenor parts, the counter was seldom sung. Men with low voices sang the bass. Andrew Law of Connecticut was influential in the movement to give women the treble part--a change which provoked a great deal of controversy. Information on the following individual women active in early musical life in New Hampshire is included: Martha Wentworth as patron; Elizabeth Von Hagen as pianist; and Mrs. Arnold, her daughter Elizabeth (Elizabeth Arnold Poe), and Catherine Hillier Graupner as singers.

214   QUINN, Arthur Hobson. **Edgar Allan Poe** (New York: Cooper
bf   Square, 1969) 804 p. *Index.*
A reprint of the 1941 edition (New York: D. Appleton-Century). This biography of Edgar Allan Poe includes information about his mother, Elizabeth Arnold Poe, who came to America with her actress-mother and in 1796 at age 9 sang on the Boston stage. Because the religious climate in Massachusetts was hostile to the theater, mother and daughter moved to Charleston, S.C. Elizabeth Arnold Poe made stage appearances in Charleston, Richmond, Philadelphia, and Baltimore as a singer, dancer, and actress from 1797-1806. After her marriage to David Poe in 1806 she moved first to Boston and then to New York, where she died in 1811.

215   RANDOLPH, Sarah N. **Domestic life of Thomas Jefferson**
bm   (New York: Harper, 1871) 432 p.
A history of Thomas Jefferson's non-political life, including the musical activities of Jefferson and members of his family. His sister, Jane Jefferson, with whom he was close until her death in 1765, was devoted to music, particularly the singing of sacred songs. His wife, Martha Skelton Jefferson, was a gifted singer and harpsichordist, and his daughters Mary and Martha both studied harpsichord as part of the education Jefferson designed for them.

216   S.E. **Original thoughts on education**, *Columbian Magazine* I
ap   (Sept 1787) 642-46.
A gentleman's advice to a young woman on suitable areas for her education. French language and instrumental music are both considered charming ornaments, but of secondary importance compared with reading, writing, arithmetic, and other more serious studies. They are also time-consuming studies, and while they "are baits to catch admirers", they will not serve to keep them. Vocal music, more easily learned and more useful, should be studied by all young women.

217   SEWALL, Maud G. **Washington and its musical history**.
ac   *Studies in musical education, history, and aesthetics* 27 (Oberlin, Ohio: Music Teachers National Assoc., 1932) 35-44. *Index.*
In the "lean early years of public musical entertainment" in Washington, D.C., singers and dancers included Mme. Celeste, Jenny Lind, and Adelina Patti. The first public song recital in the city was given in June 1803 by Georgina Oldmixon.

218   SEYBOLT, Robert Francis. **Private schools of colonial**
bm   **Boston, The** (Cambridge, Mass.: Harvard U., 1935) 106 p.
A brief history of Boston private schools to 1776, based chiefly on announcements and advertisements culled from 18th-c. periodicals. Some of the announcements of instruction for girls or for both girls and boys mention music studies--violin, flute, spinet and harpsichord, fortepiano, bass viol, guitar, and psalmody. None of the music teachers mentioned was a woman.

219   SONNECK, Oscar George. **Early concert life in America**
bm   **1731-1800** (Leipzig: Breitkopf & Härtel, 1907) 338 p. *Index.*

Presents data on concerts given in Charleston, S.C., Philadelphia, New York, Boston, and other places in New England, 1731-1800. While the activity of numerous women--chiefly singers--is discussed only briefly, more substantial information is presented about concert appearances by the following 5 women: Catherine Hillier Graupner, Arabella Brett Hodgkinson, and Maria Storer, singers; Mary Ann Pownall, singer and composer; and Elizabeth Von Hagen, pianist and composer.

220 SONNECK, Oscar George. **Early opera in America** (New
bf York: B. Blom, 1963) 230 p. *Illus., index.*
A reprint of the 1915 edition (New York: G. Schirmer). Studies ballad opera in the United States to 1800 in New York, Philadelphia, Boston, Baltimore, Charleston, S.C., and the South. Includes information on the following women singers who were active in the period: Margaret Cheer, Arabella Brett Hodgkinson, Mary Ann Pownall, and Maria Storer.

221 STANARD, Mary Newton. **Music,** *Colonial Virginia. Its people*
bd *and customs* (Philadelphia: J.B. Lippincott, 1917) 308-13.
In this chapter on music the author notes that women in Virginia played the virginals in the 17th c., the spinet and harpsichord in the 18th c., and also sang for amusement. A woman advertised herself as a guitar teacher in Williamsburg in 1775. Although women's involvement with music generally took place at home, a Miss Davies gave a public performance on the armonica (Franklin's musical glasses) ca. 1770.

222 SUNDERMAN, Lloyd Frederick. **Beginning of singing in**
bm **America, The,** *Journal of Musicology* III/2 (fall 1941) 101-19.
A brief survey of choral singing (1600-1830), tracing early Catholic and Protestant church music, singing schools, early societies, hymnodists, and the growth of secular music in the early 19th c. The single reference to women is to the founding of an Ursuline convent in Louisiana in 1727, where Spanish Franciscans taught young women vocal and instrumental music.

223 WOLVERTON, Byron Adams. **Keyboard music and musi-**
dd **cians in the colonies and the United States of America** (PhD
diss., Musicology: Indiana U., 1966) vi, 495 p. (typescript, microfilm). *Music, bibliog.*
Selected women figure in this history as follows: 1) Mrs. Sewall of colonial Boston, the owner of the first keyboard instrument in New England; 2) Mary Margaret Zimmerman, the probable owner of a virginal brought to Pennsylvania in 1694; 3) Miss Ball of Philadelphia (the sister of Thomas Ball and possible teacher of Francis Hopkinson),who was teaching harpsichord in 1730 and later in 1754; 4) Mrs. Windsor of Charleston, S.C., who served as temporary organist at St. Michael's Church in the early 1770s; and 5) Mrs. D'Hemard, harpist, and her daughter, Marianne, a piano prodigy, who numbered among the immigrants to Baltimore who fled the aftermath of the French Revolution.

39 Art music by women (including concert and parlor music)

Solo instrumental music

224 VON HAGEN, Elizabeth. **Country maid, The, or L'amour**
mm **est un enfant trompeur. With variations for the pianoforte or**
harpsichord (n.p.: n.n., 180-?) 4 p.
Dn 2′. *Pf* hps or pno. Listed as no. 3287 by Richard J. Wolfe, *Secular music in America, 1801-25* (New York: New York Public Library, 1969) with biographical information about the composer.   *(Judith Tick)*

Vocal music

225 LADY OF PHILADELPHIA, A. **Asteria's field,** [*Moller &*
mp *Capron's monthly numbers*] *3* ([Philadelphia]: Moller & Capron, [1793]) 21-22.
Dn 1′. *Pf* solo voc, hps or pno.   *(Judith Tick)*

226 LADY OF PHILADELPHIA. **Cheerful spring begins today,**
mc **The,** *Early American imprints.* Ed. by Clifford K. SHIPTON (Evans 25831; Worcester, Mass.: American Antiquarian Soc., 1960) 7. (microprint).
Dn 1′. *Pf* solo voc, hps or pno. A reprint of the song as previously published in 1793 (Philadelphia: J.C. Moller & H. Capron).   *(Judith Tick)*

227 POWNALL, Mary Ann. **Jemmy of the glen** (New York: I.C.
mm Moller, 1798) 2 p.

Dn 2′. *At* composer. *Pf* solo voc, hps or pno.   *(Judith Tick)*

228 POWNALL, Mary Ann. **Kisses sued for** (New York: G.
mm Gilfert, [1795]) [2] p.
Dn 2′. *At* Shakespeare. *Pf* solo voc, hps or pno.   *(Judith Tick)*

229 POWNALL, Mary Ann. **Lavinia,** *Six songs, by Mrs. Pownall and*
mc *J. Hewitt* (New York: M. Carey, [1794]) 15.
Dn 2′. *Pf* solo voc, hps or pno.   *(Judith Tick)*

230 POWNALL, Mary Ann. **Straw bonnet, The,** *The bicentennial*
mc *collection of American music.* Ed. by Elwood Arthur WIENANDT (Carol Stream, Ill.: Hope, 1974) 159-62.
Dn 2′. *Pf* solo voc, hps or pno. Previously published in 1794 in *Six songs, composed by Mrs. Pownall and J. Hewitt* (New York: M. Carey).   *(Judith Tick)*

231 RICHARDS, Grace. **Orphan nosegay girl** (45; Boston: Graup-
mm ner, [180-]) 1 p.
Dn 2′. *At* Mrs. Rowson. *Pf* solo voc, hps or pno. Listed as nos. 7466-67 by Richard J. Wolfe, *Secular music in America, 1801-25* (New York: New York Public Library, 1969) with biographical information about the composer.
          (Judith Tick)

1820 TO 1870

40 Literature about women in vernacular music

232 ANDREWS, Edward Deming. **Gift to be simple, The.**
bf **Songs, dances, and rituals of the American Shakers** (New York: Dover, 1962) ix, 170 p. *Illus., bibliog., index.*
A reprint of the 1940 edition (n.p.: J.S. Augustin). Although Mother Ann Lee came to the United States in 1774 with only 9 followers, membership in the society of American Shakers grew to number around 6000 members in the 2nd quarter of the 19th c. Basic tenets in the Shaker faith concerned chastity and the community of goods; women had full equality with men in religious dogma, work, and leadership responsibilities. At their frequent meetings Shakers sang and danced far into the night, and their music is genuine folk art. Their early hymns include only a few borrowings from other separatist sects; rather the major share were deliberately composed by a few persons and were either printed or memorized. With the beginning of the revival movement in the early 19th c., many Shakers engaged in the writing of hymns, and numerous hymnals were printed. Typically these hymns were notated by a 2nd person and were ascribed to visionary sources, e.g., Mother Ann Lee, Mother Lucy Wright (a successor who assumed leadership in 1796), George Washington, William Penn, Thomas Jefferson, and Christopher Columbus. A collection of texts illustrating the various types of Shaker songs and 73 tunes with text are included.

233 BRINK, Carol. **Harps in the wind. The story of the singing**
bm **Hutchinsons** (New York: Macmillan, 1947) v, 312 p.
Considers the singing Hutchinson family from New England, among them Abby Hutchinson who formed the Aeolian Vocalists with 3 of her brothers. Modeled on the Swiss Rainer family, the group toured through much of the United States as well as England, always associated with the anti-slavery, women's suffrage, and temperance movements. Abby left the group in 1849 when she married, although she rejoined it for special occasions in line with her sense of patriotism. While never the composer of the quartet, in later life Abby Hutchinson did write some songs and texts. She also probably accompanied on the guitar. Dispersed by the 1870s, the Hutchinson family nonetheless produced 2nd and 3rd generation vocal quartets, usually consisting of one woman and 3 men.

→   BROWNE, C. **Story of** *The battle hymn of the republic,* *see*
260ap[44].

→   CHASE, Gilbert. **Note on Negro spirituals, A,** *see* 266ap[45].

→   EPSTEIN, Dena. **Lucy McKim Garrison, American musi-**
cian, *see* 267ap[45].

→   EPSTEIN, Dena. **Sinful tunes and spirituals: black folk**
music to the Civil War, *see* 183bm[30].

→ HANAFORD, Phebe. **Women of the century**, see 53bm[05].

235 HUTCHINSON, John Wallace. **Story of the Hutchinsons**.
bf With an intro. by Frederick DOUGLASS (New York: Da Capo, 1977) 2 v. xviii, 495; 416 p. $49.50.
A reprint of the 1896 edition (Boston: Lee and Shepard). Traces the history of the musical Hutchinson family beginning with the first generation in New England that included Asa, Judson, John (the author) and sister Abby, and the 2nd generation in Minnesota that also included singers of both sexes. Abby started singing with her brothers as the Aeolian Vocalists at age 11, touring New England, New York, and Pennsylvania. The group's association with the abolitionist movement led to a friendship with Frederick Douglass, who accompanied the Hutchinsons on their tour of England in 1845-46. Although Abby left the group when she married Ludlow Patton in 1849, she made some appearances to support the Civil War effort and sang at the Equal Rights Convention held in New York in 1869.

236 LEINBACH, Julius. **Regiment band of the twenty-sixth**
ap **North Carolina**. Ed. by Donald M. MCCORKLE, *Civil War History (Civil War Music issue)* IV/3 (Sept 1958) 225-36. *List of works.*
An eyewitness account of the Battle of Gettysburg in June 1863 by a member of a band from North Carolina. After the battle, the band regrouped to return to Salem, N.C., played to soldiers and the wounded, serenaded officers' wives en route, and eagerly received boxes from home with supplies--including new music written expressly for the band by Amelia A. Van Vleck of Salem. Van Vleck's military music includes a *Salem Band waltz, Serenade waltz,* and *Carolina march,* and is preserved in the library of the Salem Band at the Moravian Music Foundation in Winston-Salem, N.C. Her brother, Edward W. Lineback--also a composer in the Salem Moravian community--scored the parts for the band.

→ MCRAE, Lynn T. **Computer catalogue of 19th-century American-imprint sheet music, A**, see 24bm[01].

→ **Music of the Gold Rush era**, see 312bm[48].

237 NATHAN, Hans. **Tyrolese family Rainer, and the vogue of**
ap **singing mountain-troupes in Europe and America, The**, *Musical Quarterly* XXXII/1 (Jan 1946) 63-79. *Illus.*
The 3 most popular musical entertainments in the 1840s were Italian opera, blackfaced minstrel troupes, and singing families. The prototype for the singing families was the Tyrolean Rainer family, who arrived in Boston in 1839 and toured throughout the country until 1843. The Rainer family established the group arrangement of 2 women flanked by 4 men (or 1 woman flanked by 2 men), the popular informal concert, and a freely-harmonized yodelling style for humorous and sentimental songs. Later American family troupes modeled on the Rainer family include the Hutchinson and Baker families of New Hampshire and the Cheney troupe of Vermont. John Hutchinson heard the Rainers in 1841 and taught Judson, Abby, and Asa to dress and perform in the same style. Later, however, the Hutchinsons abandoned their imitation of the Rainer's Tyrolean guise in favor of progressive social causes, e.g., temperance. In 1843 the Rainer family disbanded upon the marriage of one of the members, but their songs in sheet music continued to sell well in Boston.

→ REDWAY, Virginia. **Music directory of early New York City. A file of musicians, music publishers, and musical instrument-makers listed in New York directories from 1786 through 1825, together with the most important New York music publishers from 1836 through 1875** , see 62bm[05].

→ STOUTAMIRE, Albert. **Music of the old South: colony to Confederacy**, see 277bm[45].

41   Vernacular music by women

Choral music

238 WILLARD, Frances E. **Prohibition round**, *Encore for male*
mc *chorus.* Ed. by Ralph HUNTER (New York: E.B. Marks, 1973) 5.
Dn variable. *At* composer. *Pf* solo TB, choral TTBB, pno.   *(Judith Tick)*

Solo instrumental music

239 PARKHURST, Emily A. **Sanitary fair polka** (New York: H.
mm Waters, 1864) 3 p.

Dn 2'. Pf pno.   *(Judith Tick)*

Vocal music

240 ARMSTRONG, Miss. **Poor Juna**. Arr. by James G. CLARK
mm (Boston: H. Tolman, 1856) 4 p.
Song with chorus. *Dn 2'. Pf* solo S, choral SATB, pno. "Sung by Ossian's Bards".   *(Judith Tick)*

→ BISSELL, J. **American musical class book designed for the use of female colleges, institutes, seminaries, and normal and high schools, The**, see 80ma[15].

→ DANA, Mary S.B. **Northern harp, The; consisting of original sacred and moral songs adapted to the most popular melodies**, see 83ma[15].

→ DANA, Mary S.B. **Southern harp, The; consisting of original sacred and moral songs adapted to the most popular melodies**, see 84ma[15].

241 DURHAM, Miss M.T. **Promised land, The**, *The southern*
mc *harmony songbook.* Ed. by William WALKER (New York: Hastings House, 1939) 51.
Pf solo voc, pno. This collection is a reprint of the 1847 edition, with an introduction by members of the Federal Writers' Project of Kentucky, Works Progress Administration.   *(Judith Tick)*

242 HILL, Martha. **Ghost of Uncle Tom, The** (New York: H.
mm Waters, 1854) 5 p.
Song with chorus. *Dn 3'. Pf* solo S, choral SATB, pno. "Sung by the Hutchinson family".   *(Judith Tick)*

243 HUTCHINSON, Abby. **Kind words can never die** (Boston: O.
mm Ditson, 1855) 5 p.
Dn 2'. At composer. *Pf* solo voc, pno.   *(Judith Tick)*

244 LADY OF RICHMOND. **God will defend the right** (New
mm Orleans: A.E. Blackmar, 1861) 5 p.
Dn 3'. At composer. *Pf* solo voc, pno.   *(Judith Tick)*

245 LANE, Alice. **Stars of our banner, The** (New Orleans: A.E.
mm Blackmar, 1861) 5 p.
Song with chorus. *Dn 2'. At* M.F. Bigney. *Pf* solo T, choral SATB, pno. *(Judith Tick)*

246 LIVINGSTON, Hattie. **Young folks at home** (New York: T.S.
mm Berry, 1852) 5 p.
Song with chorus. *Dn 1'. At* Frank Spencer. *Pf* solo T, choral SATB, pno. "Written and composed expressly for Wood's Minstrels".   *(Judith Tick)*

247 PARKHURST, Susan. **Come rally, freemen, rally** (1037;
mm New York: H. Waters, 1864) 5 p.
Song with chorus. *Dn 3'. At* John Adams. *Pf* solo S, choral SATB, pno. A campaign song for Lincoln's re-election in 1864.   *(Judith Tick)*

248 PARKHURST, Susan. **Dey said we wouldn't fight** (1028;
mm New York: H. Waters, 1864) 5 p.
Song with chorus. *Dn 3'. At* Mrs. M.A. Kidder. *Pf* solo S, choral SATB, pno.
                                                        (Judith Tick)

249 PARKHURST, Susan. **Don't marry a man if he drinks**
mm (1268; New York: C.M. Tremaine, 1866) 7 p.
Song with chorus. *Dn 5'. At* Mrs. M.A. Kidder. *Pf* solo voc, choral SATB, pno.
                                                        (Judith Tick)

250 PARKHURST, Susan. **Father's a drunkard and mother is**
mm **dead** (114; Washington, D.C.: J.F. Ellis, 1868) 5 p.
Song with chorus. *Dn 3'. At* Stella of the Good Samaritan Division, Washington, D.C. *Pf* solo S, choral SATB, pno.   *(Judith Tick)*

251 PARKHURST, Susan. **Girls, wait for a temperance man**
mm (1371; New York: C.W. Harris, 1867) 5 p.
Song with chorus. *Dn 3'. At* Mrs. M.A. Kidder. *Pf* solo S, choral SATB, pno. Sung by "little Effie Parkhurst at the great temperance meetings in New York".
                                                        (Judith Tick)

252 PARKHURST, Susan. **I'll marry no man if he drinks** (1290;
mm   New York: C.M. Tremaine, 1866) 5 p.
Dn 3'. *At* Dexter Smith. *Pf* solo voc, pno. "Sung by Effie Parkhurst at the
temperance meetings".   *(Judith Tick)*

253 PARKHURST, Susan. **I'm willing to wait** (1006; New York:
mm   H. Waters, 1864) 5 p.
Dn 2'. *At* Mrs. M.A. Kidder. *Pf* solo voc, pno.   *(Judith Tick)*

254 PARKHURST, Susan. **New emancipation song, The**, *The*
mc   *Civil War songbook*. Ed. by Richard CRAWFORD (New York:
Dover, 1977) 137.
Song with chorus. *Dn* 3'. *At* R.A.T. *Pf* solo S, choral SATB, pno.   *(Judith Tick)*

255 PARKHURST, Susan. **Sweet Evelina** (New York: H. Waters,
mm   1863) 5 p.
Song with chorus. Melody by T.; arrangement by Parkhurst. *Dn* 3'. *At* M. *Pf*
solo S, choral SATB, pno.   *(Judith Tick)*

256 PARKHURST, Susan. **Union medley, The. A selection of**
mm   **ballads, songs, solos, duetts, and chorusses of the most**
popular melodies of the day (New York: H. Waters, 1863) 11 p.
Song with chorus. *Dn* 6'. *Pf* solo ST, choral SATB, pno.   *(Judith Tick)*

257 SULLIVAN, Marion Dix. **Bible songs** (Boston: N. Richardson,
ma   1856) 52 p.
A collection of 26 sacred songs. *Dn* 60'. *Pf* solo voc, pno.   *(Judith Tick)*

258 SULLIVAN, Marion Dix. **Blue Juniata, The** (Boston: O.
mm   Ditson, 1844) 2 p.
Dn 3'. *At* composer, adapted by E.L. White. *Pf* solo voc, pno. Also in *Heart
songs* (*WIAM* 81).

44   Literature about women in related
arts and disciplines

259 **America's momentous contribution to public school music**,
ap   *Etude* L/4 (Apr 1932) 237-38.
Discusses the work of Lowell Mason in music in the public schools of Boston,
beginning in 1833, and his association with Sarah Josepha Hale, an early
champion of the advancement of women and the first woman editor in the
United States. For 40 years Hale presided over the destinies of *Godey's Lady's
Book*. Hale met Mason in 1828, and they became life-long friends. She wrote
the verses for many of his most successful school music books. Hale was an
active propagandist for music--in everyday life as well as the schools.

260 BROWNE, C. A. **Story of** *The battle hymn of the republic*,
ap   *Musician* XIII/10 (Oct 1908) 443, 466. *Illus.*
At the age of 89, Julia Ward Howe recalls how she came to write the poem, *The
battle hymn of the republic*, in the fall of 1861. Howe was born in 1819 in New
York to privileged circumstances, and she was able to obtain an unusually
strong education for a young woman at that time. She became fluent in French,
Italian, and German; she also studied piano and voice. In 1843 she married
Samuel Gridley Howe, a noted philanthropist.

→   CLARK, George. **Liberty minstrel, The**, *see* 94bm[17].

261 FOOTE, Henry Wilder. **Three centuries of American hym-**
bm   **nody** (Cambridge, Mass.: Harvard U., 1940) 418 p. *Index.*
A history of American psalmody and hymnody, beginning with the publication
of the *Bay psalm book* in 1640. Discusses the work of Julia Ward Howe, Eliza
Scudder, and Caroline A. Mason as women writers among the Unitarians
during the mid-19th c. when hymnodists became increasingly active. Considers
the contributions of Fanny Crosby to popular hymnody and Mary A. Lathbury
as a Methodist writer in the post-Civil War era.

262 **Royal wedding hymn work of American; lines written in 1864**
an   **put to new music**, *New York Times* 1 Dec 1934, 16.
Reports that a hymn text written by Love Marie Whitcomb Willis, *Father, hear
the prayer we offer*, was selected for use as an anthem at a royal wedding in
Westminster Abbey.

→   SANDERSON, Lydia. **Contribution of women to the hym-**
nody of this century, The, *see* 560ap[54].

263 STUTLER, Boyd B. *John Brown's body*, Civil War History (Civil
ap   *War Music issue*) IV/3 (Sept 1958) 251-60.
Discusses the confusing origins of the song *John Brown's body* and its
transformation by Julia Ward Howe into *The battle hymn of the republic*.
Although Howe interjected a note of mysticism into the narrative accounts she
often gave about her inspiration for the text, it seems she had a deliberate
purpose: namely to write a lyric that would give dignity, strength, and patriotic
fervor to the then most popular song. The tune itself has worn well for parodies
and extemporized songs throughout other wars. During World War I the
Americans sang *All we do is sign the payroll*, while during World War II the tune
became a Nazi marching song as *Lora, Lora*.

45   General literature about women in
art music

264 **Biographical sketch of Jane Sloman, the celebrated pianiste,**
bm   **A** (Boston: Dutton and Wentworth, 1844) 23 p.
An appreciation of Jane Sloman, written following her Boston debut. Sloman
was born in England in 1824. Her father, a singer and actor, and her mother, a
distinguished tragedienne, educated her at home in music, literature, and
languages. At age 5 she was able to play opera overtures on the piano and was
a "remarkable sight-reader". She began the study of voice and of composition
including thoroughbass at age 10. Following a trip to the United States, Sloman
at age 14 composed and performed in concert her *Remembrances of America*,
which incorporates *Hail Columbia* and *Yankee doodle*. Later she was taken
under the protection of the English royal family and received high praise from
Thalberg. In 1839 Sloman returned to the United States and began teaching
piano. Her New York debut in 1843 in Niblo's Garden created a "violent
sensation". For the performance she also wrote the orchestration for ca. 18-20
players. Sloman is well-informed and a brilliant conversationalist.

265 BROWNE, Augusta. **Woman on women, with reflections on**
ap   **the other sex, A**, *Knickerbocker* LXI/1 (Jan 1863) 10-20.
An attack on male attitudes toward women by the composer-pianist Augusta
Browne, who cites statements by philosophers, theologians, and writers which
impugn women's intellectual, moral, and creative qualities. While treating
women with contempt, men have traditionally at the same time exploited
women's abilities and arrogated to themselves the results of women's labors.
The works of outstanding women such as the biblical Miriam and Deborah,
and Elizabeth I of England among others are cited as evidence of women's
ability to achieve greatness. Although this article is not about music, Browne
does state that a woman can be feminine and also write a fugue. Concerning
the many barriers to women's progress, she notes: "every step of the rugged
way up the hill of Parnassus is disputed by some envious brother, who
ingeniously thrusts in her path some stumbling stone or deals her sly shoves. If
man could but warble soprano, the sum of her tribulations would be full". The
article is signed Augusta Browne Garrett.

266 CHASE, Gilbert. **Note on Negro spirituals, A**, *Civil War
ap   History (Civil War Music issue)* IV/3 (Sept 1958) 261-67.
Discusses 2 early writings by women about Negro singing in the South: *Journal
of a residence* by the English actress-singer, Frances Anne Kemble, about life
on a Georgia plantation in 1838; and an 1862 letter by Charlotte L. Forten,
who taught emancipated blacks at St. Helen's Island, S.C. The first spiritual to
appear in print--*Roll, Jordan roll* published in 1862--was notated by Lucy
McKim Garrison.

→   ELLET, Elizabeth Fries. **Queens of American society**, *see*
196bm[35].

→   ELSON, Louis. **National music of America and its sources,**
The, *see* 197bm[35].

267 EPSTEIN, Dena J. **Lucy McKim Garrison, American musi-**
ap   **cian**, *New York Public Library Bulletin* LXVI/8 (Oct 1963) 529-46.
Port.
Lucy McKim Garrison was the daughter of James Miller McKim, a noted
abolitionist, and Sarah Allibone Speakman McKim, whose father's home was a
regular stop on the Underground Railroad for fugitive slaves. Garrison studied
piano with Benjamin Carr Cross and Carl Wolfsohn in Philadelphia, and violin
with Friedrich Mollenhauer at the Eaglesswood School in Perth Amboy, N.J.
Subsequently she worked as a pianist and a teacher of piano. In 1862 Garrison
accompanied her father on a trip to the colony of freedmen in the Sea Islands,
S.C., where she first heard the songs and spirituals of southern blacks. Among
the northerners who gathered slave songs in this period, Garrison was the only
professional musician. Upon her return from South Carolina, Garrison notated
and published 2 spirituals, which were among the earliest to appear in print,
and she wrote about the slave-song repertory in *Dwight's Journal of Music*. She
married Wendell Phillips Garrison, editor of *The Nation*, in 1865. In 1867 she

collaborated with William Francis Allen and Charles Pickward Ware in publishing *Slave songs of the United States*, the first collection of its kind. Garrison died at the age of 34.   *(Author, abridged)*

→   EPSTEIN, Dena. **Sinful tunes and spirituals: black folk music to the Civil War**, *see* 183bm[30].

268   FATOUT, Paul. **Threnodies of the ladies' books**, *Musical*
ap   *Quarterly* XXXI/4 (Oct 1945) 464-78.
Discusses songs published during the 1840s-50s in magazines intended chiefly for female consumption, e.g., *The Ladies Garland, Godey's Lady's Book, The Ladies Pearl and Literary Gleaner*, etc. The texts are generally melancholy in nature: days-of-yore, desolation at the death of a loved one, and musing at eventide are frequent themes.

→   FFRENCH, Florence. **Music and musicians in Chicago**, *see* 52bm[05].

269   FRANK, Leonie C. **Musical life in early Cincinnati and the**
bm   **origin of the May Festival** (Cincinnati: author, 1932) 25 p.
Traces musical life in Cincinnati beginning in 1799 with the activity of French and German bands, through 1873 and the 3rd May Festival, by which time German music and musicians had shaped musical life in Ohio. Includes some information about early music societies in 1814, visiting artists--e.g., the singer Mrs. Knight in 1828, and the observations on music in Cincinnati by visitor Harriet Martineau in 1835. A Female Academy of Music was established in the early 1830s under the direction of Joseph Tosso, who had trained in Paris. Women singers were first admitted to male choruses in Cincinnati in 1860.

→   HAST, Lisette. **Classical music in early Kentucky, 1850-89**, *see* 587bm[55].

270   *History of music*, **being criticism upon the issue of the first**
ap   **three annual reports of the Boston Academy of Music for the years 1833-35**, *North American Review* XLIII/92 (July 1836) 53-85.
Argues that the taste for music is rooted in Nature as an expression of emotions. Uses female sexual imagery, biblical citations of women as dancers, and Greek mythology--e.g., Sappho's incitement of men to action--to stress the emotive as well as the refining aspects of music. Considers the newly-established Boston Academy of Music and the Handel and Haydn Soc. as agents for raising standards in American music.

271   HOLCOMB, Chauncey Pinney. **Lecture on music and its**
bm   **effects upon society and the expediency of having it taught in our common schools, delivered before the Academy of Science, of Montgomery County at Norristown, Pennsylvania** (Philadelphia: S.C. Atkinson, 1838) 21 p.
Commends contemporary efforts in Boston to improve moral, intellectual, and patriotic standards in American society through music education. Despite old assumptions that music produces effeminate character, it can both refine and ornament the nation. American women, being naturally endowed with "lobe of lung and organs of voice", need only training to equal the expressive powers of a Maria Malibran. Americans are destined for musical greatness if they forsake "the intoxicating bowl, dyspepsy, and excessive interest in fighting, wealth, and animal gratifications" for music.

272   JOHNSON, Frances Hall. **Music Vale Seminary, 1835-1876**.
bm   *Committee on historical publications* 27 (New Haven, Conn.: Yale U., 1934) 24 p. *Illus.*
One of the earliest music schools in the United States was the Music Vale Seminary, founded in 1835 in Salem, Conn. by Oramel Whittlesey of the Whittlesey family of piano makers and musicians. Hundreds of women from all over the country were educated at the school until Whittlesey's death in 1876. Students at the Music Vale Seminary studied voice, organ, harp, guitar, and piano, as well as fugue and counterpoint. The school was the first authorized institution to grant normal degrees in the United States in music. Four of Oramel Whittlesey's daughters were musical, and several taught at the school. Letters and memoirs of students comment upon the rigorous daily routine at the school, practice schedules, school instruments, and concert programs.

→   JONES, F.O. **Handbook of American music and musicians**, *see* 57bm[05].

→   MANGLER, Joyce. **Rhode Island music and musicians 1733-1850**, *see* 58bm[05].

→   MATHEWS, William S.B. **Hundred years of music in America, A**, *see* 602bf[55].

→   MOORE, John. **Appendix to *Encyclopaedia of music* containing events and information occurring since the main work was issued**, *see* 59bm[05].

→   MOORE, John. **Dictionary of musical information 1640-1875, A**, *see* 60bm[05].

273   **Musical education down south**, *Dwight's Journal of Music* I/14
ap   (10 July 1852) 111.
Reports on the commencement exercises at Georgia Female Col., which included the following musical selections performed by students: *Montezuma grand march, Lee Rigg: variations, Florida grand march: duet, Hyacinth gallop,* and *Air Swiss*, all played on from 3 to 7 pianos. "We were specially surprised at the perfect time--whether 1 or 21 women played". This article is reprinted from the *Augusta Chronicle*.

→   REDWAY, Virginia. **Music directory of early New York City. A file of musicians, music publishers, and musical instrument-makers listed in New York directories from 1786 through 1825, together with the most important New York music publishers from 1836 through 1875**, *see* 62bm[05].

274   RYAN, Thomas. **Recollections of an old musician** (New
bm   York: E.P. Dutton, 1899) 274 p. *Illus., port.*
A personal memoir by the Irish-born musician (1827-1903) and founder in 1849 of the Mendelssohn Quintette Club of Boston, which initially gave local concerts and later toured the United States and Australia between 1859 and the 1880s. Includes 1) anecdotes about early music institutions in Boston, namely, the Boston Academy of Music, Germania Musical Soc., and the Boston Conservatory, 2) reminiscences of performing artists, e.g., Annie Louise Cary, Jenny Lind, Ann Childe Séguin, Cora Miller, Christine Nilsson, and the all-female Viennoise Children's Troupe with 48 members, and 3) a tribute to Margaret Ruthven Lang, with information about her early career and orchestral works. Other women performers known to Ryan through their work in Boston were Camilla Urso and Teresa Carreño.

275   SCANLON, Mary Browning. **Thomas Hastings**, *Musical*
ap   *Quarterly* XXXII/2 (Apr 1946) 265-77. *Illus.*
A biographical study of the prolific hymnist (1784-1872). Hastings's forebears include a namesake (1652-1712), who was the first teacher in Hatfield, Mass. to admit girls in schools, and Margaret Cheney, a musician. Hastings wrote 600 hymn texts and more than 1000 hymn tunes; among his collected works are *The mothers' hymn book* and *Mothers' nursery songs*, both published in 1834. In his preface to the latter, Hastings notes that the child, as imitative pupil of the mother or nurse, must first be instructed by them if he is to "perfect God's praises", and that the 65 nursery songs will "aid mothers in attuning the voices of their infant offspring and inspiring them with the love of vocal music".

276   SCHULTZ, Ferdinand P. **Music in the pioneer days of the**
bm   **Twin Cities area** ([Minneapolis]: [U. of Minnesota], n.d.) 84 p. (typescript, microfilm). *Bibliog.*
Discusses Fort Snelling as the first home for music in the St. Paul-Minneapolis area, where Mrs. Plimpton and Mrs. Taliaferro owned the first pianos in the state ca. 1830. Traces the activity of women as early teachers of music in the 1840s-50s and the growth of female seminaries in the 1850s. Music gained a firm stronghold in the homes of settlers during the 1850s, e.g., the J.W. North home, where Mrs. North--an amateur pianist--held musicales. The acquisition of pianos as an advance over crude frontier conditions is considered.

277   STOUTAMIRE, Albert. **Music of the old South: colony to**
bm   **Confederacy** (Rutherford, N.J.: Fairleigh Dickinson U., 1972) 349 p. *Illus., bibliog., index.*
This history of music in the southern United States from colonial times to 1865 focuses on musical life in Richmond, Va., and discusses concert performances and related activities of the following women singers: Anna Bishop, Mme. Bonavita, Mara De Estvan and her sister L. De Lacy, Rosa Fay, Mme. Feron, Teresa Parodi, Adelina and Amalia Patti, Bertha Ruhl, and Mrs. Sully. Information about numerous less-prominent women musicians is also included.

278   TEAL, Mary Evelyn Durden. **Musical activities in Detroit**
dd   **from 1701 through 1870** (PhD diss., Music: U. of Michigan, 1964) 2v. 445; 611 p. *Bibliog., index.*
Focuses on the years 1850-70, when Detroit's musical consciousness had only just become aroused. 1) Established in 1853, the Detroit Philharmonic Soc. was the subject of heated debate because of the appearance of women chorus members on the concert platform. Defenders of women noted their right to determine their own modesty and demeanor, as well as their right to dress as they pleased. 2) Jenny Centemeri, who arrived in the city in 1854, contributed more than any other person to the development of the public's musical taste in the course of the 19th c. A pianist and singer, Centemeri was the accompanist for the Philharmonic Soc., an organizer of benefit concerts during the Civil War and many other concert events, and a piano teacher for more than 40 years

until her death in 1895. Numerous other women who appeared in Detroit as concert artists between 1850 and 1870 are cited, and educational institutions for women are considered. An index of people active in Detroit's musical life from 1701-1870 is included.

→   WILLARD, Frances. **Woman of the century, A**, *see* 66bm[05].

279   WOODBRIDGE, William C. **Lecture on vocal music as a**
bm   **branch of common education delivered in the Representa-**
tives' Hall, Boston, before the American Institute of In-
struction, 24 August 1830, A (Boston: Hilliard, Gray, Little, &
Watkins, 1831) 25 p. *Music.*
Discusses the general importance of music education for the young, citing Germany as an advanced model for the United States. In Germany, women are educated in music. It is salutary for women to sing: as an accomplishment, as a means of preserving their good health by salubrious exercise to prevent consumption and diseases affecting the "organs of the breast", and finally to "soothe the cares of domestic life and quiet sorrow by the united assistance of the sound and sentiment in a properly chosen song".

280   WOODBRIDGE, William C. **On vocal music as a branch of**
ap   **common education, communicated to the American Lyceum,**
American Annals of Education and Instruction III/5 (May 1833) 193-212. *Music.*
A revised version of the author's first lecture with a similar title (*WIAM* 279) of 1831, which he updates to include discussion of recent events at the Boston Academy of Music and innovations in school music and singing introduced by Elsam Ives, Jr., George Kingsley, and Lowell Mason. Restating his belief that women should be educated in music, Woodbridge nonetheless regrets that conventional attitudes of the day persist in viewing regular musical pursuits as "the mark of a trifling or a feminine mind", suited only to professional musicians and women. Fortunately, Woodbridge notes, this situation is changing.

281   **Young ladies' musical education,** *Musical Reporter* I/1 (Jan
ap   1841) 22-26.
Gives advice on the training and repertory of singers. Those with talent deserve the most thorough training, while those without should not be trained at all. "There can be no severer infliction of penances on the cultivated ear than to be compelled by the conventional rules of society to listen to the jejune and mawkish lullabies that are frequently offered as [drawing room] entertainment". The female singer should sing about friendship, rational love, innocent joys, home, and domestic blessings rather than about "foreign subjects such as the sea, the hunt, war, or chivalry", e.g., *The captive knight* a song by Harriet Browne with words by Felicia Dorothea Heman.

46   Literature about women as composers of art music

282   HODGES, Faustina Hasse. **Edward Hodges** (New York: AMS,
bf   1970) 302 p. *Illus.*
A reprint of the 1896 edition (New York: n.n.). This biography by Faustina Hasse Hodges about her father's work in music includes a portrait of Faustina, a brief biographical sketch of her own career as a composer and performing musician (1822-95), and other biographical information about her formative years as interspersed in the text. Faustina Hasse Hodges "devoted her life to the study and practice of her musical art with unabated vigor and enthusiasm". She was known for her interpretations of Bach fugues, while her songs *Dreams* (*WIAM* 377), *The rose bush* (*WIAM* 384), and *Suffer little children* (*WIAM* 386) were extremely popular. Edward Hodges came to the United States from Bristol, England in 1838. Beginning in 1839 he served as music director of Trinity Parish Church in New York for 35 years.

283   HOOGERWERF, Frank W. **Confederate sheet music at the**
ap   **Robert W. Woodruff Library, Emory University,** *Notes. Music Library Association* XXXIV/1 (Sept 1977) 7-26.
This collection of Confederate sheet music at Emory U. contains music by the following women composers: A lady of Baltimore, A lady of Richmond, Mrs. V.G. Cowdin, Julia Daly, Mrs. Harrill, the Hon. Mrs. Norton, Lizzie C. Orchard, and Ella Wren.

284   LANDAUER, Bella C. **My city 'tis of thee. New York City**
bm   **on sheet music covers** (New York: New York Historical Soc.,
1951) 105 p. *Illus.*
Describes 80 sheet music covers dating from the 1820s-1920s in the music collection of Bella C. Landauer at the New York Historical Soc. The covers illustrate a range of musical and pictorial responses to New York, to both its physical features and events of cultural or historical significance. Two of the

pieces are by women: *Fairest flower so palely drooping* by Augusta Browne (1847), and *Staten Island march* by Maud Mortimore Johnson (1898)..

285   TICK, Judith. **History of American women composers before**
dd   **1870, A** (PhD diss., Musicology: City U. of New York, 1978) 2v.
400 p. (typescript). *Illus., music, bibliog., list of works.*
Surveys the social history of music education for women in private seminaries and academies. Investigates the ideology of music as a feminine accomplishment, as found in etiquette books and educational treatises. Traces the change in status of composition for women as a social skill for the lady amateur in the late 18th c. to a profession for the woman artist at the end of the 19th c.--in the context of changing definitions of women's place in American society. The repertory of music by women composers before 1870 consists of parlor songs and keyboard music. About 50 complete pieces are included together with an appendix listing nearly 200 works that had demonstrable popularity. Biographies of 5 outstanding composers are included, i.e., Augusta Browne, Faustina Hasse Hodges, Susan Parkhurst, Jane Sloman, and Marion Dix Sullivan.
(Author)

286   YERBURY, Grace Helen. **Styles and schools of art song in**
dd   **America 1720-1850** (PhD diss., Music: Indiana U., 1953) 1v. 422
p. (typescript, microfilm). *Music, bibliog.*
This history of art song in United States to 1850 includes brief references to Augusta and Harriet Browne and lists of their works.

47   Literature about women as patrons and educators in art music

→   **America's momentous contribution to public school music,**
see 259ap[44].

→   DEXTER, Elisabeth. **Career women of America 1776-1840,**
see 206bm[38].

→   **Early music teachers,** *see* 766bm[57].

287   GRANT, Francis. **Mary Cushing Webster: pioneer music**
ap   **educator,** *Journal of Research in Music Education* XIV/2 (summer
1966) 99-114.
Discusses Mary Cushing Webster's work in Cleveland between 1837 and 1839, when she established a music school for children and successfully advocated the introduction of music into the public school curriculum in the Cleveland area. At her own school Webster utilized teaching methods based on Pestalozzian principles, which she had brought from Boston. Together with her husband, William C. Webster, she also contributed to the cultural life of the city by giving concerts and through service to the church. Although their efforts were hailed enthusiastically by numerous residents, the Websters were forced to leave Cleveland for financial reasons. Subsequently they worked in Buffalo, Brooklyn, and Rochester, N.Y., and the author recommends that further research should attempt to document their activities in those cities. Mary Cushing Webster died in Canton, Ohio in 1903.

→   HANAFORD, Phebe. **Women of the century,** *see* 53bm[05].

→   MADEIRA, Louis. **Annals of music in Philadelphia and**
history of the Musical Fund Society, *see* 306bf[48].

→   **Mrs. Ann Séguin,** *see* 311an[48].

288   **Music in the public schools of Boston,** *Dwight's Journal of*
ap   *Music* XXIX/1-3 (29 Mar-29 Apr 1869) 4; 12-14; 18-19.
A report by the Committee on Music submitted to the Boston School Committee, which recommends expanded and improved music instruction. In addition to the grammar schools, music is presently taught in only one high school, namely, Girls' High and Normal School, where prospective teachers are trained to "effectively assist the special music teacher in his duties by rehearsing the lesson with the pupils".

→   **Music of the Gold Rush era,** *see* 312bm[48].

289   SMITH, David Stanley. **Gustave J. Stoeckel. Yale pioneer in**
bm   **music** (New Haven: Yale U., 1939) 31 p. *Port., list of works.*
When Gustave J. Stoeckel emigrated from Germany in 1848 and settled in New Haven, Conn. he was befriended by Irene Battell Larned, the wife of a professor of English language and literature at Yale Col. Largely through Larned's help Stoeckel secured pupils in New Haven and subsequently in 1855

was appointed organist and chapelmaster at Yale. Later in his life Stoeckel acknowledged Larned as the "almost solitary friend of music at the college" during the mid-century period. Larned was a prime force behind the establishment of the Battell professorship of music at Yale in 1890; Stoeckel occupied the position until his retirement in 1894. Larned's private music library became the nucleus of the Yale music library. New music in New Haven in the 19th c. and Stoeckel's work in composition are also discussed.

290   **TEMPO Musical correspondence**, *Dwight's Journal of Music*
ap   *XVIII/15 (7 July 1860) 118.*
Reports on the improvements in the music program at Ohio Female Co. in Cincinnati since Fanny Raymond Ritter became an associate in music there. Ritter has upgraded the musical standards by introducing students to fine performances of great music. The school has also profited from her vocal and pianistic skills. The recent commencement exercises featured choruses, songs, and piano compositions by Donizetti, Haydn, and Louis Moreau Gottschalk among others, rather than the usual spectacle, fancy dress, and "wishy-washy music".

48   Literature about women as performers of art music

291   **American prima donna, An**, *Dwight's Journal of Music* IV/22 (4
ap   Mar 1854) 170-71.
Discusses the work of Dolorès Nau, who is appearing at the Paris Opera. The New York-born singer studied voice with Mme. Cinti-Damoureau at the Paris Conservatory, where she soon won first prize for vocalization and singing. She also studied Italian opera with Rossini. Her performance as Urbain in *Les Huguenots* had great success, while her London debut in *Lucia di Lammermoor* was well received. Nau's voice has a "sonorous and silvery sound, and through all its registers is of incomparable purity and sweetness". She plans to return to New York this year.

292   **Career of Mme. Anna Bishop Schulz, The**, *New York Times* 20
an   Mar 1884, 5.
Reports the death of the soprano (1814-84) in New York at the age of 70. Bishop's reputation extended "over the entire civilized, and a great part of the uncivilized world". Her travels were "more extensive than those of any artist of the age". Beginning in 1837, Bishop made concert appearances throughout Europe and the United States, in Mexico, South America, Hawaii, Australia, New Zealand, China, India, and South Africa. Bishop trained initially as a pianist at the Royal Conservatory in London under Moscheles. When she first performed as a singer she sang the music of Händel, Haydn, Mozart, and Beethoven almost exclusively. After 1839 she began to sing Rossini's music and to appear in his operas.

293   **Celebrities in El Dorado 1850-1906**. Ed. by Cornel LENGYEL.
bm   *History of music project* 4 (San Francisco: Works Progress Administration, 1940) 270 p. (typescript). *Bibliog., list of works, index.*
A bibliographical record of 111 prominent musicians who visited San Francisco and performed there between the Gold Rush of 1848 and the Great Fire of 1906, with additional lists of visiting celebrities from 1906-40, chamber music ensembles, bands, orchestras, and other music-making organizations. The careers of the following women active in American music in San Francisco are discussed. Pre-1880: Ruby Hurwitz Jaffa, pianist; Giovanna Bianchi, Eliza Biscaccianti, Mary Goodenow Robb, Josephine d'Ormay, Euphrosyne Parepa-Rosa, and Minnie Walton, singers; Camilla Urso, violinist. Post-1880: Teresa Carreño and Julie Rivé-King, pianists; Annie Louise Cary, Zelie De Lussan, Emma Eames, Olive Fremstad, Johanna Gadski, Louise Homer, Emma Juch, Emma Nevada, Alice Nielsen, Christine Nilsson, Lillian Russell, Ernestine Schumann-Heink, and Marcella Sembrich, singers.

294   **Concerts. Virginia Whiting Lorini**, *Dwight's Journal of Music*
ap   XXV/1 (1 Apr 1865) 8.
An obituary for the operatic soprano (ca. 1840-65). Born in New York, Virginia Whiting Lorini was educated in the Boston public schools. After performing in Castle Garden in New York and elsewhere in the Northeast in 1850, she went to Europe to study. In the summer and fall of 1864 Lorini toured the western United States, after which she went to the West Indies as prima donna with the troupe of S. De Vivo, intending to return to New York in April of 1865. She died of a hemorrhage in February at Santiago de Cuba. Lorini spoke 5 or 6 languages, "knew 40 or 50 operas, was ready at a moment's notice to sing any role a soprano is ever called upon to undertake, and did this with a kindness and good humor rare in any profession".

295   **Death of Parepa-Rosa. A sketch of her life and professional**
ap   **career**, *Dwight's Journal of Music* XXXIII/22 (7 Feb 1874) 170.
An obituary for the Scottish-born soprano (1836 or 1839-74). Euphrosyne Parepa-Rosa first sang in the United States on a concert tour in 1865-66, and the following season she continued to tour, performing in opera as well. Subsequently Parepa-Rosa and her husband, violinist Carl Rosa, formed an

opera troupe to tour America, with Rosa as director and conductor. Besides Parepa-Rosa as the leading soprano, the troupe featured Rose Hersee and Zelda Harrison Séguin in 1869, and Jennie Van Zandt and Clara Doria, stage name of Clara Kathleen Rogers, in 1871. At the National Peace Jubilee held in Boston in 1869 Parepa-Rosa and Adelaide Phillipps were the featured soloists. The Scottish singer last performed in Boston on 27 Jan. 1872. This article originally appeared in the *Boston Daily Advertiser*, 24 Jan. 1874.

→   DEXTER, Elisabeth. **Career women of America 1776-1840**,
see 206bm[38].

296   DOBBIN, Isabel L. **Lanier at the Peabody**, *Peabody Bulletin*
ap   VII/6 (Apr-May 1911) 4, 5.
Discusses Sidney Lanier's music studies in Baltimore and his connections with Asger Hamerik and Nannette Falk Auerbach of the Peabody Conservatory. As first flutist of the Peabody orchestra, Lanier met Auerbach, who often performed piano concertos with the orchestra. The two admired each other and often played together. Lanier also "wrote a sonnet in which he makes Beethoven claim her [Auerbach] as his daughter".

→   GRAU, Robert. **Strange public aversion to contraltos as compared with sopranos of great fame**, *see 1003ap*[58].

297   **Great singer is dead. Sister Agnes Gubert, the famous nun,**
an   **dies in Baltimore**, *New York Times* 9 Aug 1882, 1.
Sister Agnes Gubert was "the most noted teacher of vocal music associated with the Roman Catholic church [in the United States]". Née Louise Gubert, the singer grew up in Philadelphia, where she received excellent instruction in music. Gubert became a nun despite the protestations of her mother and "even some clergy, who appealed to her that by the wonderful powers of her voice she might delight multitudes and thus confer a benefit upon humanity". Euphrosyne Parepa-Rosa and Max Strakosch heard Gubert sing during her years in the convent and attested to her greatness.

298   GREENWOOD, Grace. **Appeal, An**, *Dwight's Journal of Music*
ap   XXXVI/26 (31 Mar 1877) 413.
A letter date-lined Washington, D.C., in which Greenwood appeals for contributions to help support Eliza Biscaccianti. The Boston-born singer is living in Rome to be near her son. As daughter of Luigi Ostinelli and Sophia Hewitt Ostinelli, Biscaccianti was the first native American to sing in Italian opera in the United States. Having lost her voice because of illness, she became a teacher and is now unable to support herself.

299   HALE, Philip. **Dramatic and musical review**, *Boston Sunday*
an   *Herald* 16 Dec 1917, F-6.
Includes discussion of a series of programs given by the Apollo Soc. of Boston in 1824-26. These programs were discovered too late to be included in Oscar Sonneck's *Early concert life in America 1731-1800 (WIAM 219)*. Among the performers listed is Sophia Hewitt Ostinelli, the daughter of James Hewitt, composer and music publisher. Hale describes Ostinelli as the leading professional pianist of her time in Boston. She was also the organist for the Handel and Haydn Soc. Her replacement in the latter position by a German immigrant, Charles Zeuner, caused complaints that a "stranger was replacing a native artist of high merit".

300   HERZ, Henri. **New Orleans**. Trans. by Henry Bertram HILL, *My*
bd   *travels in America* (Madison, Wis.: State Historical Soc. of Wisconsin, 1963) 83-93.
During concert tours in the United States in 1846-51, Henry Herz gave performances in New Orleans and thereby became acquainted with Mrs. Soulé, a fine amateur pianist and patron of music in the city. While in the United States Herz oversaw concerts of "financial music" for 16 women pianists at 8 pianos--so named by his business manager since the phenomenon drew crowds "especially when the concert consisted of national airs". During one concert of financial music in New Orleans, Herz had to substitute a non-pianist for a woman who failed to appear at performance time. The substitute merely pretended to play.

301   **Hint to musical ladies, A**, *Musical Visitor* III/14 (6 Jan 1844)
ap   113.
Advises the " lady who plays well on the pianoforte" to choose her selections for company with care and particularly to look for pieces which "combine brevity with excellence"--so that those who don't care for music will not be wearied, yet those with the most cultivated tastes will enjoy the music.

302   **History of opera in San Francisco I**. Ed. by Lawrence ESTA-
bm   VAN. *San Francisco theater research project* 7 (San Francisco: Works Progress Administration, 1938) 136 p. (typescript). *Illus., facsim., bibliog.*
A general history of opera in San Francisco from the 1840s to 1900. Discusses the heyday of visiting companies in the 1850s-70s, the growth of local theater companies, repertory, and pioneer local musicians. Biographical sketches for

successful American women singers in this history are included as follows: Giovanna Bianchi; Eliza Biscaccianti; Anna Bishop; Maud Fay, who returned to her native San Francisco from Germany in 1916; Emma Nevada; Caro Roma, née Carrie Northey in Oakland; and Sibyl Sanderson, the pupil and protégé of Massenet.

→   HOWARD, John. **Hewitt family in American music, The**, *see* 210ap[38].

303   Jenny Lind's triumph, *New York Times* 3 Nov 1887, 5.
an
Reports the death of Jenny Lind (1820-87). The soprano studied with Henry Berg in her native Stockholm and with Manuel Garcia in Paris. Through the influence of Meyerbeer, Lind studied in Berlin in 1844 and sang the leading role in his *L'étoile du nord*. She made her final operatic appearance in 1849 and thereafter sang only in recitals. On her tour to the United States from 1850-52, Lind sang in the following cities among others: New York, Philadelphia, Boston, Baltimore, Memphis, St. Louis, and Louisville, Ky. The soprano devoted her American earnings to endowing art scholarships and other charities in Sweden. A critique of her voice is included.

→   KLEIN, Herman. **Reign of Patti, The**, *see* 1047bf[58].

304   Late Mme. Christine Dossert, The, *American Art Journal*
ap   XLVII/22 (17 Sept 1887) 341.
An obituary for the concert and oratorio soprano (1855-87). Christine Dossert was born into a family of church singers and organists in Buffalo. After her debut at age 16 she sang with Caroline Richings's concert company, the Brooklyn Philharmonic Orchestra, Theodore Thomas's orchestra, and in 1886 with the American Opera.

305   Letters of Miska Hauser 1853, The. Ed. by Cornel LENGYEL.
bm   *History of music project 3* (San Francisco: Works Progress Administration, 1939) 185 p. (typescript). *Illus., music, bibliog., list of works, index.*
Presents selections in English translation from Miska Hauser's unpublished letters of 1853 and his book entitled *Aus dem Wanderbuche eines Österreichischen Virtuosen* [From the travel book of an Austrian virtuoso] (Leipzig, 1859), regarding the violinist's impressions of music in California during his visits between 1849 and 1855. Hauser toured with singers Anna Bishop and Eliza Biscaccianti, among others. California society, manners, morals, and musical life--including the scandalous alcoholic decline of Biscaccianti--are discussed.

306   MADEIRA, Louis C. **Annals of music in Philadelphia and**
bf   **history of the Musical Fund Society** (New York: Da Capo, 1873) iv, 202 p. $22.50. *Illus., index.*
A reprint of the 1896 edition (Philadelphia: J.B. Lippincott). Although the Musical Fund Soc. of Philadelphia was founded in 1820 exclusively by men, women were soon invited to join. The members of the society--both amateurs and professionals--performed at concerts for which additional professional musicians were hired, and the society also sponsored recitals by visiting artists. A measure of the distrust of musicians at the time is indicated by the 1820 rule that no female professional could perform at a society function without a "written certificate from a lady of established character" in the city. By June 1821 the society had progressed sufficiently to give a performance of Haydn's *Creation*, and in 1824 a hall was built that drew musicians on tour to Philadelphia. In 1847 women in the society held a Ladies' Bazaar to raise money to enlarge the hall. Jenny Lind gave 2 concerts at the hall in 1850, for which first choice of seats sold for $625 a ticket.

→   MARKS, Edward. **They all had glamour from the Swedish Nightingale to the Naked Lady**, *see* 1078bf[58].

307   MAUDE, Jenny Maria Catherine Goldschmidt. **Life of**
bf   **Jenny Lind, The** (New York: Arno, 1977) 222 p. *Illus., index.*
A reprint of the 1926 edition (London: Cassell) by the singer's daughter. Born in Stockholm in 1820, Jenny Lind made her operatic debut as Agathe in *Der Freischutz* in 1838. She sang leading soprano roles in 30 operas from 1838-49, including *I puritani* and *Norma*. The impresario P.T. Barnum organized her American tour of 150 concerts within a period of 18 months in 1850-52. Lind's programs in the United States featured well-known Italian arias and Swedish songs. She performed her final American concert in New York in May 1852. Subsequently Lind was offered a 2nd American contract, which she refused. The soprano retired to her home in Malvern, England, where she died in 1887.

308   Miss Adelaide Phillipps, *Dwight's Journal of Music* VII/24 (15
ap   Sept 1855) 188.
Adelaide Phillipps was born in Bristol, England and came to the United States via Canada at age 7, by which time she had already begun performing as a dancer. At age 15 she discovered her vocal potential, and a year later sang for Jenny Lind, who said that she had a "valuable voice" and donated $1000 for Phillipps's training. Subsequently others added to the fund. Phillipps gave a

series of concerts in various towns before leaving for London to study with Manuel Garcia. Later in Italy she sang Rosina in *Il barbiere di Siviglia* and Arsace in *Semiramide*, all to high praise from demanding audiences. A critic in Milan wrote that Phillipps has "a beautiful voice, incomparable facility, an exquisite feeling which manifests itself in modulations, accents, and gestures nobly expressive". This article is reprinted from the *Boston Daily Advertiser*.

309   Miss Elise Hensler, *Dwight's Journal of Music* III/20 (20 Aug
ap   1853) 159.
Elise Hensler took 2nd prize in a voice contest at the Paris Conservatory, despite the fact that she had been a student there for less than 6 months. Among the judges were Auber, Adolphe Adam, Halévy, and Michele Enrico Carafa de Colobrano.

310   Monster concert by young ladies, A, *Dwight's Journal of Music*
ap   III/18 (6 Aug 1853) 142.
A report of the annual concert by pupils of the Madison Female Col. in Madison, Ga. On the program were 130 performers, including 97 pianists, 11 guitarists, 3 harpists, 13 violinists, 1 violist, 4 cellists, and 1 contrabassist. François Adrien Boieldieu's overture to *The caliph of Bagdad* was played on 1, 3, 7, and 9 pianos, and George C. Taylor's celebration of the Revolutionary War, *Battle*, was performed on 9 pianos by 17 players. Marion Dix Sullivan's *Gypsey* for solo voice and chorus was also performed in a version for several pianos.

311   Mrs. Ann Séguin, *New York Times* 25 Aug 1882, 4.
an
An obituary for Ann Childe Séguin (1808?-82), "who 45 years ago was New York's favorite opera singer". Educated at the Royal Academy, the soprano had already established herself as a performer and teacher in London before emigrating to the United States with her husband, Edward Séguin, who was also a singer. After her husband's death in 1852 Séguin left the stage, continuing to teach in New York.

312   Music of the Gold Rush era. Ed. by Cornel LENGYEL. *History*
bm   *of music project 1* (San Francisco: Works Progress Administration, 1939) 212 p. (typescript). *Illus., music, bibliog., list of works.*
Traces the growth of music in San Francisco from 1849-59, during which time the population increase was largely due to the Gold Rush, and also because the reactionary purge in Germany following political upheavals in 1848 brought many German musicians to the city. Outstanding American women singers included Anna Bishop, Eliza Biscaccianti, Giovanna Bianchi, Anna Griswold, and Marie and Georgina Leach. Women patronized matinee minstrel shows (in which male impersonators took female roles as "wenches"), masked balls, musical soirees, hotel concerts, and the first oratorio concerts in 1852. Women also sang with male *Turnvereins*, the German choral societies, and at May Day festivals. While they were vastly outnumbered, women refined the multi-racial city, although there were always women performers in bars, gambling halls, and makeshift theaters that featured popular dance and folk troupes such as Stephan Leach's Mountaineers in 1854.

313   Musical intelligence, *Dwight's Journal of Music* II/3 (23 Oct
ap   1852) 23.
An announcement of the schedule for Anna Bishop's new opera in English troupe, that will open its New York season with a performance of *Martha*. The company, consisting of soloists, chorus, and orchestra, will travel to Boston, Baltimore, Richmond, Washington, D.C., and Charleston, S.C.

314   Obituary. Caroline Richings Bernard, *New York Times* 15 Jan
an   1882, 5.
Caroline Richings came to the United States with her parents from England. She was adopted by the actor Peter Richings, who directed her education and whose name she assumed. Richings made her professional debut as a pianist in Philadelphia in 1847 at the first concert of the Philharmonic Soc. Later she trained as a singer and appeared with the Richings Opera, which was founded by her adopted father in 1859. In 1867 she succeeded to the management, and under her direction the company toured extensively in the United States and to Australia. This venture ruined her financially, however, and Richings retired from the stage to Richmond, where she headed a music school and became well-known as a teacher.

315   Obituary. Elizabeth Taylor Greenfield, *New York Times* 2 Apr
an   1876, 2.
Reports the death of the singer known as the Black Swan (1809-76). When Elizabeth Taylor Greenfield was still a small child, her mistress moved to Philadelphia, became a Quaker, and later manumitted the few slaves in her household. Although Greenfield was refused as a student by a noted music teacher because of her race, she nonetheless persevered. She made her first public appearance before the Buffalo Music Assoc. Greenfield's successes in Europe eventually paved the way for her acceptance in the United States.

→   SEWALL, Maud. **Washington and its musical history**, *see* 217ac[38].

316 STOWE, Harriet Beecher. **Sunny memories of foreign lands**
bm   (Boston: Phillips, Sampson, 1854) 2v. v, 326; 432 p.
A collection of letters by Harriet Beecher Stowe recounting her travels in 1853 in England and on the Continent. Among the people Stowe met while in England was the singer Elizabeth Taylor Greenfield. Born a slave to a kind mistress who however did not educate her, Greenfield was later freed to pursue her singing. Like others of her race, Greenfield had "a passion for music, and could sing and play by ear". Her singing voice was powerful and beautiful, although unschooled and with "occasional rusticities and artistic defects". She had a range of 3 1/2 octaves and an acute ear for pitch. Aided by Stowe and some members of the British aristocracy, Greenfield was introduced to Sir George Smart, one of the leading figures in London's musical life, who honored her by offering to coach her for any public appearances she might be preparing.

317 SWAYNE, Egbert. **Boston music in 1851 and 1852**, *Music*
ap   [Chicago] VII (Mar 1895) 427-40. *Illus.*
A summary, with programs, of orchestral concerts in Boston, 1851-54. Solo singers with the Boston Musical Fund Soc. included Mlle. Borghese, Emma G. Bostwick, Goria Bothe, Caroline Lehmann, Sophie Anna Thillon, and Mary Isabella Webb--who was the daughter of conductor-composer George James Webb and later the wife of William Mason. Concerts given by the Germania Musical Soc. in 1853 included appearances by Adelina Patti, singer, and young Camilla Urso, violinist, "a sallow, little girl in short gowns, rather sad-looking, the victim of parental driving". The Germania Soc. originated in Baltimore and was reorganized in Boston.

→   UPTON, George. **Musical memories**, *see* 1230bm[58].

318 WATERSTON, Anna Cabot Lowell. **Adelaide Phillipps. A**
bm   **record** (Boston: Cupples, Upham, 1883) 170 p. *Illus.*
Born in England, Adelaide Phillipps (1833-82) began her career as a child singer and dancer in performances at the Boston Museum. In 1851 she traveled with her father to London to study with Manuel Garcia, and she subsequently went on to Italy to gain experience in opera. Phillipps made her American debut in Philadelphia as Arsace in *Semiramide* in 1855. The contralto continued in opera both in the United States and abroad, but her greatest triumphs came in oratorio and concert work with the Handel and Haydn Soc. in the 1860s-70s and at the National Peace Jubilee in Boston in 1869.

319 **Woman and her work**, *Musical World and New York Musical*
ap   *Times* XIX/20 (15 May 1858) 312.
Discusses the necessity of reducing housework for women in light of their expanding rights and opportunities, and views the newly-invented sewing machine as an important agent for change. Concerning music, while most young women receive instruction in music, after marriage music is typically displaced by the demands of housework.

320 **Woman's influence**, *Musical World and New York Musical Times*
ap   XXIV/5 (4 Feb 1860) 2-3.
American women seem to regard music as a "species of fashionable accomplishment"; their entire musical knowledge rests on being able to play a few tunes. Instead young women should study music seriously, so that they can instill an appreciation for music in their children.

321 **Woman's musical influence**, *Message Bird* [New York] XI/25 (1
ap   Aug 1850) 409.
1) "The harp, guitar, or piano are usually permitted after marriage to rust out in silence. Few American homes afford any irresistible attraction in the form of music". 2) "Every young wife, whose musical education has been thorough and comprehensive, can materially aid in expanding in her offspring that love for the divine art which is more or less inherent in every human being".

49   Art music by women (including concert and parlor music)

Choral music

322 BROWNE, Augusta. **Grand vesper chorus** (New York: W.
mm   DuBois, 1842) 4 p.
Sacred chorus. *Dn* 2'. *At* Bishop Heber. *Pf* choral SATB, org or pno. Dedicated to Fanning C. Tucker.   *(Judith Tick)*

323 BROWNE, Augusta. **Hear therefore O Israel** (New York: S.
mm   Ackerman, 1842) 4 p.
Sacred chorus. *Dn* 2'. *Pf* choral SATB, org.   *(Judith Tick)*

324 HODGES, Faustina Hasse. **Blessed are the pure in heart**
md   (1465; New York: G. Schirmer, 1873) 3 p.
Sacred chorus. *Dn* 1'. *Pf* choral SSA, org. *Tm Cloister memories of sacred song.*   *(Judith Tick)*

325 HODGES, Faustina Hasse. **Chant Te Deum** (1122; New York:
md   G. Schirmer, 1870) 3 p. (score).
Choral recitation. *Dn* 3'. *Pf* choral SATB, org. *Tm Cloister memories of sacred song.*   *(Judith Tick)*

326 HODGES, Faustina Hasse. **Holy dead, The** (1612; New York:
mm   Firth, Pond, n.d.) 5 p.
Sacred chorus. *Dn* 2'. *At* Friedrich Gottlieb Klopstock. *Tr* Longfellow. *Pf* solo A, choral SSA, org.   *(Judith Tick)*

327 HODGES, Faustina Hasse. **I heard a voice from Heaven**
md   (634; New York: G. Schirmer, 1867) 3 p.
Sacred chorus. *Dn* 1'. *Pf* solo T or S, choral SATB, org. *Tm Cloister memories of sacred song.*   *(Judith Tick)*

328 SLOMAN, Jane, ed. **Melodist, The. Selected gems and**
ma   **celebrated composers, arranged for the use of female seminaries** (New York: W. Hall, 1850) 112 p.
Sacred and secular songs and hymns. *Pf* solo S, pno; solo or choral SA, SSA, SATB, pno. Presents the following hymns by Sloman: Alise, Cardross, Dismission hymn (*At* Elizabeth Brewer), Holmes, Mutter, Parsons, Prosser, and The academy hymn (*At* Miss Chase). Arrangements of music by Mozart, Rossini, Jenny Lind, and others are also included.

Solo instrumental music

329 BROWNE, Augusta. **American bouquet, The** (Philadelphia:
mm   Osbourn's Music Saloon, 1844) 4 p.
Dn 5'. *Pf* pno.   *(Judith Tick)*

330 BROWNE, Augusta. **Angels whisper. With variations for the**
mm   **pianoforte** (Philadelphia: G.E. Blake, [185-]) 3 p.
Dn 3'.   *(Judith Tick)*

331 BROWNE, Augusta. **Caledonian boquet, The, op. 33** (New
mm   York: C.B. Christian, 1841) 6 p.
Dn 8'. *Pf* pno. *Ct* Scots wha hae, The poor but honest soldier, Burns's farewell, Roslin castle, Braes o' busby.   *(Judith Tick)*

332 BROWNE, Augusta. **De Meyer grand waltz, op. 73** (New
mm   York: Firth & Hall, 1846) 7 p.
Dn 4'. *Pf* pno.   *(Judith Tick)*

333 BROWNE, Augusta. **Ethereal grand waltz** (New York: Firth,
mm   Hall, & Pond, n.d.) 2 p.
Dn 2'. *Pf* pno.   *(Judith Tick)*

334 BROWNE, Augusta. **Merry mountain horn, The. With**
mm   **variations for the pianoforte or harp** (Philadelphia: G.E. Blake, [185-]) 7 p.
Dn 5'. Dedicated to Miss G.W. Crawford of Philadelphia.   *(Judith Tick)*

335 BURTIS, Sarah R. **Lady's book polka, The** (Philadelphia: T.C.
mm   Andrews, 1852) 5 p.
Dn 2'. *Pf* pno.   *(Judith Tick)*

336 BURTIS, Sarah R. **Morning star and Evening star polkas**
mm   (Philadelphia: T.C. Andrews, 1853) 5 p.
Dn 2'. *Pf* pno.   *(Judith Tick)*

337 CLARK, Caroline. **Lafayette's march** (Boston: [author], 1824) 2
mm   p.
Dn 2'. *Pf* pno. "Composed for the Boston Independent Cadets and performed by their band at the review in honor of General LaFayette, 30 Aug. 1824".   *(Judith Tick)*

338 DE LISLE, Estelle. **Cape cottage waltz** (Philadelphia: J.E.
mm   Gould, 1856) 5 p.
Dn 3'. *Pf* pno.   *(Judith Tick)*

339 GARRETT, Mrs. William. **Emily polka** (3110; Boston: Russell
mm   & Richardson, 1857) 5 p.
Dn 2′ . *Pf* pno.   *(Judith Tick)*

340 GERARD, Miss. **Fire polka** (New York: Dressler & Clayton,
mm   1854) 5 p.
Dn 5′ . *Pf* pno.   *(Judith Tick)*

341 HEWITT, Estelle. **Snow-drop, The. A waltz** (1116; Baltimore:
mm   F.D. Benteen, 1847) [2] p.
Dn 2′ . *Pf* pno.   *(Judith Tick)*

342 HODGES, Faustina Hasse. **Marigena. Three reveries by the**
mm   **waterside** (New York: Beer & Schirmer, 1863) 5, 5, 5 p.
Dn 4′ . *Pf* pno. *Ct* Moonlight on the river, Sea shore dream, By the lake shore.
                                                                 (Judith Tick)

343 HODGES, Faustina Hasse. **Pensées du coeur. Nocturne**
mm   (1522; New York: G. Schirmer, 1873) 5 p.
Dn 3′ . *Pf* pno.   *(Judith Tick)*

344 HODGES, Faustina Hasse. **Song of little May. Piano tran-**
mm   **scription** (New York: G. Schirmer, 1862) 5 p.
Dn 2′ . *Pf* pno. Originally for solo voc, pno (earliest copy located: New York,
W.A. Pond, 1873).   *(Judith Tick)*

345 HOHNSTOCK, Adele. **Hohnstock concert polka with varia-**
mm   **tions for the pianoforte** (Philadelphia: A. Fiot, 1849) 5 p.
Dn 2′ .   *(Judith Tick)*

346 HUTET, Josephine. **Sigma waltz, The** (Albany, N.Y.: L.F.
mm   Newland, 1848) 3 p.
Dn 2′ . *Pf* pno.   *(Judith Tick)*

347 LADY, A. **Oft in a stilly night. With variations for the**
mm   **pianoforte** (Philadelphia: G. Willig, 1827) 5 p.
Dn 4′ .   *(Judith Tick)*

348 LADY OF BALTIMORE. **Titus march** (Baltimore: J. Cole,
mm   [1824]) 1 p.
Dn 2′ . *Pf* pno.   *(Judith Tick)*

349 LADY OF CHARLESTON. **United States Marine march**
mm   (108; Philadelphia: G.E. Blake, [1814-15]) 2 p.
Dn 4′ . *Pf* pno.   *(Judith Tick)*

350 LADY OF VIRGINIA, A. **Wild Ashe deer. Brilliant varia-**
mm   **tions for the piano** (2649; Baltimore: Miller & Beacham, 1854) 5
p.
Dn 3′ .   *(Judith Tick)*

351 LOUD, Emily L. **Mountain of light valse, The. Koh I Noor**
mm   (ELL 1; n.p., Penn.: composer, 1851) 2 p.
Dn 2′ . *Pf* pno.   *(Judith Tick)*

352 MARY. **Rosebud quickstep** (5016; New York: Firth, Pond,
mm   1848) 5 p.
Dn 1′ . *Pf* pno. *Rg* Piano music in America I, Vox, SVBX 5302. *(Judith Tick)*

353 MYERS, Emma F. **Capitol march** (842; Philadelphia: Lee &
mm   Walker, 1850) [2] p.
Dn 2′ . *Pf* pno.   *(Judith Tick)*

354 PARKER, Mrs. **Malibran waltz** (Boston: H. Prentiss, 1841) 3 p.
mm
Dn 3′ . *Pf* pno.   *(Judith Tick)*

355 SLOMAN, Jane. **Ericsson schottisch, The** (New York: W. Hall,
mm   1853) 5 p.
Dn 2′ . *Pf* pno.   *(Judith Tick)*

Vocal music

356 ABLAMOWICZ, Anna. **Vale of Avoca, The** (569; Louisville,
mm   Ky.: G.W. Brainard, 1852) 3 p.

Dn 3′ . *Pf* solo voc, pno.

357 BELLCHAMBERS, Julliet. **Spell is broken, The** (New York:
mm   Atwill, 1842) 5 p.
Dn 2′ . *Pf* solo voc, pno.   *(Judith Tick)*

358 BLAKE, Mary. **Beautiful star of the twilight** (Boston: O.
mm   Ditson, 1857) 4 p.
Dn 2′ . *At* composer. *Pf* solo SA, pno.   *(Judith Tick)*

359 BRANDLING, Mary. **I pray for thee or The farewell**
mm   (Philadelphia: G. Hewitt, [1840]) 7 p.
Dn 3′ . *At* composer. *Pf* solo ST, pno.   *(Judith Tick)*

360 BROWNE, Augusta. **Chieftain's halls, The** (Boston: H. Pren-
mm   tiss, 1844) 4 p.
Dn 3′ . *Pf* solo voc, pno.   *(Judith Tick)*

361 BROWNE, Augusta. **Family meeting, The** (376; New York: W.
mm   Hall, 1842) 7 p.
Dn 5′ . *At* Charles Sprague. *Pf* solo voc, pno.   *(Judith Tick)*

362 BROWNE, Augusta. **Reply of the messenger bird, The**
mm   (Philadelphia: A. Fiot, 1848) 5 p.
Dn 4′ . *At* Edward Young. *Pf* solo voc, pno.   *(Judith Tick)*

363 BROWNE, Augusta. **Song of mercy** (New York: Firth, Pond,
mm   1851) 5 p.
Sacred song. *Dn* 3′ . *At* Bunyan. *St* Pilgrim's progress. *Pf* solo voc, pno.
Dedicated to Rev. George B. Cheever.   *(Judith Tick)*

364 BROWNE, Augusta. **Volunteer's war song, The** (New York:
mm   C. Holt, 1847) 5 p.
Dn 3′ . *At* Mrs. Balmanno. *Pf* solo voc, pno. Dedicated to the composer's
brother, Lt. W.H. Browne, who served in the war with Mexico. *(Judith Tick)*

365 BROWNE, Augusta. **Warlike dead in Mexico, The** (New
mm   York: C. Holt, 1848) 8 p.
Dn 5′ . *At* Mrs. Balmanno. *Pf* solo voc, pno. Dedicated to Hon. Henry Clay.
                                                                 (Judith Tick)

366 BURNHAM, Georgiana. **O worship not the beautiful** (18668;
mm   Boston: O. Ditson, [1858]) 5 p.
Dn 3′ . *At* Lucy Linwood. *Pf* solo voc, pno.   *(Judith Tick)*

367 DALY, Julia. **Dying Camille** (Philadelphia: Lee & Walker, 1856)
mm   5 p.
Dn 2′ . *At* W.K. McCurdy. *Pf* solo voc, pno.   *(Judith Tick)*

368 DANA, Mary S.B. **Flee as a bird to your mountain** (8907;
mm   Boston: O. Ditson, 1857) 5 p.
Sacred song. "Words written and adapted to a Spanish melody" by Mary Dana
Shindler. *Dn* 2′ . *Pf* solo voc, pno. Published under the composer's maiden
name, Dana. *Rg* Angels' visits and other vocal gems of Victorian America, New
World, NW 220.   *(Judith Tick)*

369 DEMING, Mrs. L.L. **I cannot sing tonight** (2198; Boston: H.
mm   Tolman, 1854) 5 p.
Dn 3′ . *At* composer. *Pf* solo voc, pno.   *(Judith Tick)*

370 DOLE, Mrs. Caroline. **Answer to the messenger bird** (Boston:
mm   C.H. Keith, 1848) 4 p.
Dn 2′ . *At* American Quaker lady. *Pf* solo SA, pno.   *(Judith Tick)*

371 HABICHT, Mrs. C.E. **Sun is in the west, The** (Boston: G.P.
mm   Reed, 1848) 5 p.
Dn 3′ . *Pf* solo voc, pno.   *(Judith Tick)*

372 HART, Imogine. **Gaily smiles the earth before me** (18786;
mm   Boston: O. Ditson, 1859) 5 p.
Dn 3′ . *Pf* solo voc, pno.   *(Judith Tick)*

373 HODGES, Faustina Hasse. **Alphorn, The** (763; New York:
mm   Firth, Pond, n.d.) [3] p.
Dn 2′ . *At* E. Jennie Warner. *Pf* solo voc, pno.   *(Judith Tick)*

374 HODGES, Faustina Hasse. **Amicizia, L'** (272; New York: G.
mm Schirmer, 1863) 7 p.
Polka duet. *Dn* 3'. *Pf* solo SS, pno.   *(Judith Tick)*

375 HODGES, Faustina Hasse. **As the hours pass on** (New York:
mm Luckhardt & Belder, 1912) 5 p.
Dn 2'. *At* Thomas S. Henry. *Pf* solo voc, pno.   *(Judith Tick)*

376 HODGES, Faustina Hasse. **Blessed are the merciful** (278;
md New York: G. Schirmer, 1863) 3 p.
Sacred song. *Dn* 2'. *Pf* solo voc, pno. *Tm Cloister memories of sacred song.*
                                                          (Judith Tick)

377 HODGES, Faustina Hasse. **Dreams** (633; New York: G.
mm Schirmer, 1869) 11 p.
Dn 5'. *At* H.C.L. *Pf* solo voc, pno.   *(Judith Tick)*

378 HODGES, Faustina Hasse. **Dreary day, The** (New York: Beer
mm & Schirmer, 1860) 5 p.
Dn 2'. *At* Longfellow. *Pf* solo voc, pno.   *(Judith Tick)*

379 HODGES, Faustina Hasse. **In the summer house** (7971;
mm Cincinnati: J. Church, 1892) 5 p.
Dn 2'. *At* Arthur M. Morgan. *Pf* solo voc, pno.   *(Judith Tick)*

380 HODGES, Faustina Hasse. **Indignant spinster, The** (6176;
mm New York: W. Hall, 1867) 11 p.
Dn 5'. *At* composer. *Pf* solo voc, pno.   *(Judith Tick)*

381 HODGES, Faustina Hasse. **Old crow, The** (8312; New York:
mm W.A. Pond, 1872) 5 p.
Dn 1'. *At* H.C.L. *Pf* solo voc, pno.   *(Judith Tick)*

382 HODGES, Faustina Hasse. **Psalm of life, A** (3472; New York:
mm G. Schirmer, 1884) 7 p.
Dn 3'. *At* Longfellow. *Pf* solo voc, pno.   *(Judith Tick)*

383 HODGES, Faustina Hasse. **Remember me** (47-5625; Boston: O.
mm Ditson, 1893) 7 p.
Dn 3'. *At* William Henry Gardner. *Pf* solo voc, pno. *(Judith Tick)*

384 HODGES, Faustina Hasse. **Rose bush, The** (274; New York:
mm G. Schirmer, 1859) 7 p.
Dn 2'. *Tr* W. Caldwell, from German. *Pf* solo AA, pno. Also for solo SA, pno
(273; G. Schirmer, 1881).   *(Judith Tick)*

385 HODGES, Faustina Hasse. **Still o'er the waters** (1899; New
mm York: W. Hall, 1852) 5 p.
Dn 2'. *Pf* solo MBar, pno.   *(Judith Tick)*

386 HODGES, Faustina Hasse. **Suffer little children** (Cincinnati: J.
mm Church, 1860) 5 p.
Dn 2'. *Pf* solo SA, pno.   *(Judith Tick)*

387 HODGES, Faustina Hasse. **Three roses** (8577; New York:
mm W.A. Pond, 1874) 5 p.
Dn 2'. *At* Adelaide A. Proctor. *Pf* solo voc, pno.   *(Judith Tick)*

388 HODGES, Faustina Hasse. **Wishes** (8578; New York: W.A.
mm Pond, 1874) 5 p.
Dn 2'. *Pf* solo voc, pno.   *(Judith Tick)*

389 HODGES, Faustina Hasse. **Yearnings** (47-56250; Boston: O.
mm Ditson, 1893) 7 p.
Dn 3'. *At* William Henry Gardner. *Pf* solo voc, pno. *(Judith Tick)*

390 KERBY, Caroline. **Thornless rose, The** (Philadelphia: R.H.
mm Hobson, 1829) 3 p.
Dn 3'. *At* S. Wild. *Pf* solo voc, pno.   *(Judith Tick)*

391 KING, Frances Isabella. **Fly, fly away or The dream** (New
mm York: H. Waters, 1853) 6 p.
Dn 3'. *At* composer. *Pf* solo voc, pno.   *(Judith Tick)*

392 LADY, A. **Thou hast wounded the spirit that loved thee**
mm (Baltimore: F.D. Benteen, [1846]) 5 p.

Dn 2'. *Pf* solo voc, pno.   *(Judith Tick)*

393 LUYSTER, Mrs. A.R. **Mary, dear Mary** (New York: F. Riley,
mm 1847) 5 p.
Dn 2'. *At* composer. *Pf* solo voc, pno.   *(Judith Tick)*

394 MARY. **Adieu sweet companion** (306; New York: Firth, Pond,
mm 1849) 5 p.
Dn 3'. *At* Eliza C. Hurley. *Pf* solo voc, pno.   *(Judith Tick)*

395 MARY. **Oh! leave me not in sorrow** (182; New York: Firth,
mm Pond, 1848) 4 p.
Dn 2'. *At* Eliza C. Hurley. *Pf* solo voc, pno.   *(Judith Tick)*

396 MARY. **Ring my mother wore** (Cincinnati: J. Church, 1860) [3]
mm p.
Dn 3'. *At* Louis Dela. *Pf* solo voc, pno.   *(Judith Tick)*

397 MOTT, Valentine. **Forget thee, ah never!** (New York: Firth,
mm Hall, Pond, 1846) 3 p.
Dn 1'. *At* V.D.M. *Pf* solo voc, pno.   *(Judith Tick)*

398 PARKHURST, Susan. **Angel Mary** (New York: H. Waters,
mm 1863) 5 p.
Dn 3'. *At* composer. *Pf* solo voc, pno.   *(Judith Tick)*

399 PARKHURST, Susan. **Angels are hovering near** (New
mm York: H. Waters, 1863) 5 p.
Dn 5'. *At* H.W. Adams. *Pf* solo voc, pno.   *(Judith Tick)*

400 PARKHURST, Susan. **Beautiful angel band, The** (New
mm York: H. Waters, 1863) 5 p.
Song with chorus. *Dn* 3'. *At* M.W. *Pf* solo voc, choral SATB, pno. *(Judith Tick)*

401 PARKHURST, Susan. **Give to me those moonlit hours**
mm (6015; New York: W. Hall, 1865) 5 p.
Dn 3'. *At* Francis B. Murtha. *Pf* solo SA, pno.   *(Judith Tick)*

402 PARKHURST, Susan. **Home on the mountain, A** (1081;
mm New York: H. Waters, 1865) 7 p.
Dn 5'. *At* Sidney Dyer. *Pf* solo voc, pno.   *(Judith Tick)*

403 PARKHURST, Susan. **Patter of the rain** (1267; New York:
mm H. Waters, 1866) 5 p.
Song with chorus. *Dn* 3'. *Pf* solo voc, choral SATB, pno.   *(Judith Tick)*

404 PARKHURST, Susan. **There are voices, spirit voices**
mm (1040; New York: H. Waters, 1864) 5 p.
Dn 2'. *At* Fanny Crosby. *Pf* solo voc, pno.   *(Judith Tick)*

405 PARKHURST, Susan. **Weep no more for Lily** (New York:
mm H. Waters, 1864) 5 p.
Song with chorus. *Dn* 2'. *At* Mrs. W.V. Porter. *Pf* solo S, choral SATB, pno.
                                                          (Judith Tick)

406 SANDFORD, Lucy A. **Stars of the summer night** (New York:
mm W. Hall, 1849) 3 p.
Dn 1'. *At* Longfellow. *Pf* solo SA, pno.   *(Judith Tick)*

407 SCOTT, M.B. **Bird of beauty** (6200; Boston: O. Ditson, 1856) 5
mm p.
Dn 2'. *At* Ella of Woodlawn. *Pf* solo voc, pno.   *(Judith Tick)*

408 SLOMAN, Jane. **Forget thee?** (Boston: W.H. Oakes, 1843) 6 p.
mm
Dn 3'. *Pf* solo voc, pno.   *(Judith Tick)*

409 SLOMAN, Jane. **Queen of the night (Del ciel regina)** (1773;
mm Boston: White-Smith, 1873) 9 p.
Dn 4'. *At* Mrs. Brine. *Tr* A.M. *Lt* English, Italian. *Pf* solo voc, pno. *(Judith Tick)*

410 SLOMAN, Jane. **Roll on silver moon.** Arr. by N. BARKER
mm (125; New York: Firth, Pond, 1848) 4 p.
Song with chorus. *Dn* 3'. *Pf* solo S, choral SATB, pno.   *(Judith Tick)*

411 SLOMAN, Jane. **So far away** (6408; New York: W. Hall, 1868)
mm 5 p.

Dn 2′. Pf solo voc, pno.   (Judith Tick)

412 SMITH, Miss. **Place in thy memory, dearest** (New York:
mm   DuBois & Bacon, [183–]) 3 p.
Dn 1′. At composer. Pf solo voc, pno.   (Judith Tick)

413 STITH, Mrs. Townsend. **Our friendship** (Philadelphia: G.
mm   Willig, 1830) 3 p.
Dn 2′. Pf solo voc, pno.   (Judith Tick)

414 SULLIVAN, Marion Dix. **Field of Monterey, The** (Boston: O.
mm   Ditson, 1846) 2 p.
Dn 2′. Pf solo voc, pno.   (Judith Tick)

415 SULLIVAN, Marion Dix. **Jessie Cook** (Boston: Prentiss &
mm   Clark, 1844) 2 p.
Dn 3′. Pf solo voc, pno.   (Judith Tick)

416 SULLIVAN, Marion Dix. **Juniata ballads** (Boston: N. Rich-
ma   ardson, 1855) 64 p.
An album of 48 songs. Dn 60′. At composer. Pf solo voc, pno. (Judith Tick)

417 SULLIVAN, Marion Dix. **Marion Day** (Boston: O. Ditson,
mm   1844) [2] p.
Dn 3′. At composer. Pf solo voc, pno.   (Judith Tick)

418 SULLIVAN, Marion Dix. **Mary Lindsey** (1575; Boston: O.
mm   Ditson, 1848) 2 p.
Dn 3′. Pf solo voc, pno.   (Judith Tick)

419 SULLIVAN, Marion Dix. **O'er our way when first we parted**
mm   (1709; Boston: O. Ditson, [184–]) 2 p.
Dn 3′. Pf solo voc, pno.   (Judith Tick)

420 SULLIVAN, Marion Dix. **Oh! boatman row me o'er the**
mm   **stream** (Boston: O. Ditson, 1844) 3 p.
Dn 3′. At composer. Pf solo SS, pno.   (Judith Tick)

421 SULLIVAN, Marion Dix. **We cross the prairie as of old**
mm   (Boston: E.H. Wade, 1854) 5 p.
Dn 4′. At John Greenleaf Whittier. Pf solo voc, pno.   (Judith Tick)

422 VANE, Florence. **Are we almost there?** (1026; Boston: O.
mm   Ditson, 1845) 5 p.
Dn 5′. Pf solo voc, pno.   (Judith Tick)

1870 TO 1920

50   Literature about women in
vernacular music

423 ALBERTSON, Chris. **Bessie** (New York: Stein & Day, 1974)
bm   253 p. Illus., bibliog., discog.
When Bessie Smith (1894-1937) was born in Chattanooga, Tenn., there were 2
chief areas of employment open to black Americans--manual or domestic labor,
and employment in traveling shows. The latter option increased during the
1890s as white managers realized the great potential in black talent. Smith
entered the entertainment field during the period of transition from Victorian
propriety to the more relaxed age of the 1920s. Beginning in vaudeville, her
fame as a blues singer grew steadily, and after World War I she secured leading
engagements at the Paradise Gardens in Atlantic City. She appeared mainly in
race theaters, though also in some white theaters as well. In 1923 Smith made
her first records for Columbia Phonograph Co., including the sensational hits
Downhearted blues and *Gulf Coast blues*. Her financial success in the 1920s
mirrored the boom in the economy as a whole, and her records drew audiences
to performances of the touring company that she headed and vice versa. In
1925 Smith was billed as the "greatest and highest salaried race star in the
world". She shared her prosperity with her family in the South and also with
those family members who moved north to join her in Philadelphia. With the
rise of the talking motion picture in the late 1920s and the Depression,
vaudeville declined, and the pace of Smith's professional life slackened. For
many years troubled by unrest and heavy drinking, Smith was working for a
comeback when she was fatally injured in a car accident in 1937.

→   ALDRICH, Richard. **Music.** [Natalie Curtis-Burlin], *see*
562an[55].

424 AMES, Morgan. **First lady of the blues**, *High Fidelity/Musical*
rr   *America* XX/10 (Oct 1970) 86-87. *Illus.*
Reviews the initial installment of Columbia Records Division's reissue of the
complete recordings of Bessie Smith entitled *The world's greatest blues singer*,
Columbia, GC 33. 10 albums are projected.

425 BARNETT, Lincoln. **Music used to go roun' and roun' when**
an   **May Irwin sang forty years ago, The**, *New York Herald Tribune*
26 Jan 1936, V-6.
May Irwin recalls her work as a singer and comedienne in the Gay Nineties.
She introduced ragtime in her show *The sweet Miss Fitzwell*, knowing quite well
that ragtime would change the entire character of popular music. In her
retirement Irwin raises race horses.

426 **Born in God's country--California**, *Musical America* XIV/10 (16
ap   Jan 1909) 2.
Caro Roma states in an interview that she was born in California, made her
debut as a singer at age 3, and has "appeared in every city in the United States
and abroad as well as a prima donna". She is proud of her American training,
having graduated from the New England Conservatory with honors. Among
her many operatic roles is Santuzza, which she sang for the composer,
Mascagni. Her songs include *Violets, Resignation, Faded rose* (*WIAM* 542), and
Thinking of thee (*WIAM* 546). At a concert for Queen Victoria that celebrated
the end of the Boer War, Caro Roma sang her *Prayer* and *When I'm big I'll be a
soldier*, moving the queen to tears with her performance.

→   B.R. **Mary Jordan urges artists to champion earlier Ameri-**
can music, *see* 905ap[58].

→   **Caro Roma charms the South**, *see* 916ap[58].

→   **Christian Science hymnal**, *see* 93bc[17].

427 **Classic rags composed by May Aufderheide. Talented**
ap   **Minneapolis girl is achieving enviable reputation**, *American*
Musician and Art Journal XXV/15 (13 Aug 1909) 20.
May Aufderheide, who first became known in her native Indianapolis as a
pianist, lately has been composing "classic rags". Her first, *Dusty* (*WIAM* 468),
was so successful that her father decided to go into the music publishing
business. Other works by Aufderheide include *Richmond rag* (*WIAM* 469),
Buzzer rag (*WIAM* 467), and *Thriller* (*WIAM* 92).

→   DAVENPORT, M. Marguerite. **Azalia. The life of Madame**
E. Azalia Hackley, *see* 575bm[55].

428 **Emily Swan Perkins**, *The Hymn* III/1 (Jan 1952) [2].
ap
Born in 1886, Emily Swan Perkins began her career playing the piano for
Sunday School services in Chicago. In 1900 she started writing hymn tunes, and
she published *Stonehurst hymn tunes* in 1921 and *Riverdale hymn tunes* in 1938.
Perkins was one of the founders of the Hymn Soc. of America in 1922.

→   F.L.C.B. **Show beauty of Negro folk songs in unique concert**
in St. Paul, *see* 776ap[57].

429 FLETCHER, Alice Cunningham. **Study of Omaha Indian**
bf   **music, A.** *Archaeological and ethnological papers of the Peabody*
Museum, Harvard University I/5 (New York: Kraus Reprint, 1967)
152 p. *Music.*
A reprint of the June 1893 issue (Cambridge, Mass.: Peabody Museum of
Archaeology and Ethnology, Harvard U.). Describes types of songs sung by
Omaha Indians, with examples transcribed and harmonized by Fletcher. Only 1
category of songs is associated with women: namely, the Wae-ton wa-an songs,
which are sung by the older women when members of the family are on the
war path. The songs are intended to aid the warrior by sending him power.

430 FULD, James J. **American popular music 1875-1950** (Phila-
bm   delphia: Musical Americana, 1950) 94, 9 p. *Index.*
Lists popular songs still well-known in 1950, together with publication data for
each imprint. The works by women are: Ida Emerson and Joseph E. Howard's
Hello! ma baby (*WIAM* 513); Nora Bayes and Jack Norworth's *Shine on,
harvest moon* (*WIAM* 506); Mildred J. Hill's *Happy birthday to you*; Carrie
Jacobs-Bond's *I love you truly* in her *Seven songs*. *As unpretentious as the wild
rose* (*WIAM* 1741), and in her *Songs everybody sings* (*WIAM* 1743); Jacobs-
Bond's *A perfect day*, also in *Songs everybody sings*; Effie I. Canning's *Rock-
a-bye baby* (*WIAM* 510); and Maude Nugent's *Sweet Rosie O'Grady* (*WIAM*
533).

431 GELLER, James J. **Somebody loves me**, *Famous songs and their*
bd   *stories* (New York: Macauley, 1931) 127-31. *Music.*
Hattie Starr, who wrote both the text and the music for *Somebody loves me*
(*WIAM* 551), was the "first woman to defy convention and enter Tin Pan
Alley". She left the South for New York in 1893, taking along a roll of
manuscripts. After vain attempts to sell her songs to publishers, she approached
the "Queen of song", Josephine Sabel, who agreed to introduce Starr's
Somebody loves me. As a result, Starr's career as a song writer was successfully
launched.

432 **Gifted American woman, A**, *Musical Courier* LII/4 (25 July
ap   1906) 7.
Reports that Clare Kummer is "already a household word" as a composer of
popular music. Her songs *Dearie* (*WIAM* 525), *Egypt* (*WIAM* 526), *Sufficiency*,
June, *My very own*, and *In the wilderness* are well-known in America as well as
abroad. The grandniece of Henry Ward Beecher and Harriet Beecher Stowe,
Kummer has had little formal education in music in the past; currently she is
studying orchestration, composition, and music literature.

433 GILBERT, Douglas. **Maude Nugent launched** *Sweet Rosie*
an   *O'Grady*, [her] **own song, at Tony Pastor's**, *New York World*
      Telegram 17 Apr 1934, 21.
Maude Nugent recalls how her *Sweet Rosie O'Grady* (*WIAM* 533) became a
great hit in 1896. It was only by plugging the song herself in her appearances at
the Madison Square Roof Garden and Tony Pastor's Theater that the song first
became popular, and in turn that the publisher J.W. Stern became interested in
publication. Nugent's MS had been in Stern's office for some time.

→   GILMAN, Charlotte. **Suffrage songs and verses**, *see* 95bc[17].

→   GRANT, Frances. **Recognizing our debt to Negro music**, *see*
      584ap[55].

434 GREENWAY, John. **Aunt Molly Jackson**, *American folksongs*
bd   *of protest* (Philadelphia: U. of Pennsylvania, 1953) 252-75. *Index.*
Born in 1880 as Mary Magdalene Garland in mining country in Kentucky,
Aunt Molly Jackson began writing songs about everyday life and the problems
of poor people at age 4, and from the age of 5 she was involved in union
activities, because her father was an ardent union man. Jackson trained and
worked as a registered nurse and midwife for 47 years, while also being active
as a union organizer. At union rallies and other meetings Jackson typically
performed her own songs—for which she wrote both the text and the music.

→   HALL, J.H. **Biography of gospel song and hymn writers**, *see*
      555bf[54].

→   **Indian music truly American**, *see* 592an[55].

435 JONES, Hettie. **Big star fallin' mama** (New York: Viking, 1974)
bm   150 p. *Illus., discog., index.*
Presents biographies of the blues singers Gertrude ("Ma") Rainey and Bessie
Smith. Gospel singer Mahalia Jackson, jazz singer Billie Holiday, and soul
singer Aretha Franklin are also discussed.

→   **Kate Vannah, American composer**, *see* 693ap[56].

436 K.S.C. **Cherokee singer of Indian melodies pays her first visit**
ap   **to New York**, *Musical America* XXIII/5 (4 Dec 1915) 49. *Illus.*
Reports that Tsianine Redfeather—a Cherokee Indian—is in New York on tour
with Charles Wakefield Cadman in a series of lecture-recitals about American
Indian music. Redfeather grew up on a reservation in Oklahoma, and she
studied voice with John C. Wilcox in Denver. The young mezzo-soprano sings
tribal melodies and idealized Indian songs on her programs with Cadman.
Cadman advocates the use of Indian melodies by contemporary composers in
their compositions.

→   LOVE, William G. **Ma Rainey. Discography**, *see* 21ap[01].

437 MANTLE, Burns. **Passing of May Irwin recalls fruitful life;**
an   **memory of Lederer**, *New York Daily News* 25 Oct 1938, 45.
Reports the death of 2 prominent stage figures: George W. Lederer, theatrical
promoter, and May Irwin, singer and comedienne. Irwin began performing in
the theater at age 9 together with her older sister Flo, who was then 11. She
was one of the first singers to sing ragtime and coon songs, and she introduced
the hit song *After the ball is over*. Irwin was born Georgia Campbell in Whitby,
Ontario, Canada in 1861.

438 MARSH, J.B.T.; LOUDIN, Frederick J. **Story of the Jubilee**
bm   **Singers, The** (Cleveland: Cleveland Printing & Publishing, 1892)
      311 p. *Illus., port., music.*

Considers the origins, concert tours, and personnel of the Jubilee Singers of
Fisk U. in Tennessee. Part I presents an abridged version of earlier accounts of
the group by the first director, Gustavus D. Pike, together with biographies of
the singers—including Georgia Gordon, Mabel Lewis, Patti J. Malone, Ella
Sheppard, and Minnie Tate—and information about the group's fund-raising
activities and early tours in the United States and England. Part II is written by
Loudin, the 2nd director and the 1st black, and describes later tours of the
Jubilee Singers throughout the world. Part III contains transcriptions of
selected songs of the Jubilee Singers.

→   **Mary A. Lathbury**, *see* 558ap[54].

439 MATTFELD, Julius. **Variety music cavalcade 1620-1969**.
bm   With an introduction by Abel GREEN (3rd ed.; Englewood Cliffs:
      Prentice-Hall, 1971) 766 p. *Index.*
A chronologically-ordered book listing the most popular melodies of each year.
Among the songs are over 30 by women to 1920. These include: Effie I.
Canning's *Rock-a-bye baby* (*WIAM* 510); May Irwin's *Mamie! come kiss your
honey* (*WIAM* 518); Anita Owen's *Sweet bunch of daisies* (*WIAM* 537); Maude
Nugent's *Sweet Rosie O'Grady* (*WIAM* 533); Ida Emerson and Joseph E.
Howard's *Hello! ma baby* (*WIAM* 513); Carrie Jacobs-Bond's *I love you truly*
published in her *Seven songs*. As unpretentious as the wild rose (*WIAM* 1741)
and in her *Songs everybody sings* (*WIAM* 1743); Jacobs-Bond's *A perfect day*,
also in *Songs everybody sings*; Nora Bayes and Jack Norworth's *Shine on,
harvest moon* (*WIAM* 506), Caro Roma's *Can't yo' heah me callin', Caroline*
(*WIAM* 541); Lillian Ray's *The sunshine of your smile* (*WIAM* 539); Mana
Zucca's *The big brown bear* (*WIAM* 2586); and Lily Strickland's *Mah Lindy
Lou* (*WIAM* 1946).

440 **Maude Nugent, 85, song writer, dies**, *New York Times* 4 June
an   1958, 31.
Maude Nugent (1873-1958), composer and performer, made her professional
vaudeville debut at age 13 in Brooklyn. She composed her most famous song,
Sweet Rosie O'Grady (*WIAM* 533), at age 19. Nugent retired professionally at
age 28 in order to look after her husband and 3 children, but missing life on the
stage, she returned 7 years later. Her other well-known songs were *Mamie Reilly*
(*WIAM* 530) and *I can't forget you, honey*.

→   MCGILL, Anna. **On the trail of song ballads**, *see* 604ap[55].

441 MCRAE, Barry. **"Ma" Rainey and Bessie Smith accompa-**
ap   **niments, The**, *Jazz Journal* XIV/3 (Mar 1961) 6-8. *Illus.*
Gertrude ("Ma") Rainey's style of blues singing changed little from her first
recording to her last. She seems to have preferred simple accompaniments
because they set off her voice well, and she made little use of progressive
musicians for her ensembles. Bessie Smith began recording with simple piano
backings by ordinary players, but as her musical style developed she turned to
more polished performers, e.g., Fletcher Henderson's Hot Six. Smith had no
interest in the "knockabout" groups with toy instruments that were associated
with Rainey. Numerous individual recordings by the 2 singers are discussed.

→   MCRAE, Lynn T. **Computer catalogue of 19th-century**
      American-imprint sheet music, A, *see* 24bm[01].

→   **Mme. Powell devotes her superb art to aiding music settle-**
      ment, *see* 1108ro[58].

→   MORELL, Parker. **Lillian Russell. The era of plush**, *see*
      1111bm[58].

442 **Mrs. Carlton dies; composed lullaby**, *New York Times* 7 Jan
an   1940, 48.
Effie I. Canning (1872-1940) wrote *Rock-a-bye baby* (*WIAM* 510) in 1886
under a pseudonym because she feared her father's disapproval. Sales from the
song, which was originally published by C.D. Blake of Boston, exceeded
$20,000 within a few months. Canning composed numerous other songs and
acted on the stage for 30 years, retiring in 1922 at the death of her husband,
Harry J. Carlton, who was also an actor.

443 **Mrs. Joseph F. Knapp. The American song and hymn com-**
ap   **poser**, *Musical Courier* XLII/3 (16 Jan 1901) 29.
Phoebe Knapp has written over 500 hymn tunes, the best known being *Blessed
assurance* (*WIAM* 457). She is also highly regarded as a music patron. She
regularly holds musicales at her suite in the Hotel Savoy in New York at which
she features young, aspiring talents. Several years ago Knapp held recitals in
her home in Brooklyn.

→   **New York, New York Public Library, Theater Division. A
      checklist of scrapbooks about women in American music**, *see*
      34bm[01].

444 PEELER, Clare P. **U.S. Army's only woman song-leader tells**
ap   **of her work,** *Musical America* XXVIII/12 (20 July 1918) 9. *Illus.*
Estelle Cushman, who has a bachelor's degree in music from Yale U. and is
supervisor of music in the public schools of Savannah, also directs singing at
Fort Scriven in Tytes, Ga. She finds men in the troops enthusiastic about
"sings", and she estimates that about 40% enjoy light classical music.

445 PIKE, Gustavus D. **Jubilee Singers, and their campaign for**
bm   **twenty thousand dollars, The** (Boston: Lee and Shepard, 1873)
219 p. *Port., music.*
Discusses the activities of the Jubilee Singers during their first year and their
fund-raising activities. This choir of Fisk U. students was formed under George
L. White in Oct. 1871 to raise money for the all-black Tennessee school. Brief
biographies of the singers in their own words and portraits are included. Of the
5 women--Jennie Jackson, Maggie Porter, Ella Sheppard, Minnie Tate, and
Eliza Walker--and 3 men, Sheppard is the most important, being a pianist for
the group as well as a singer. By the 1871-72 season she was also serving on the
faculty of Fisk U.

446 **Popularity of community singing in Brockton due to efforts**
ap   **of Mrs. Nellie Evans Packard,** *Musical America* XXVIII/4 (25
May 1918) 29. *Illus.*
Reports that Nellie Evans Packard--a Boston voice teacher and choral
conductor, who resides in Brockton, Mass.--can claim to be among the first in
New England to introduce community singing. In 2 years Packard has
organized and conducted about 20 public "sings" in Brockton with an average
attendance of over 1000 people.

447 PRIDGETT, Thomas. **Life of Ma Rainey, The,** *Jazz Informa-*
ap   *tion* II/4 (6 Sept 1940) 7-8.
Born in Georgia, Gertrude ("Ma") Rainey first appeared in the Springer Opera
House in Columbus, Ga. with the show Bunch of Blackberries. Together with
her husband, Pa Rainey, she traveled extensively with a road company called
the Rabbit Foot Minstrels, and she headed 2 theaters in Rome, Ga. for 35
years. Rainey recorded nearly 100 blues and related songs for Paramount
Records in Chicago.

→ RAYE-SMITH, Eugénie. **Equal suffrage songsheaf,** *see*
96bc[17].

→ RUFFIN, Bernard. **Fanny Crosby,** *see* 559bm[54].

→ SCHULTZ, Ferdinand. **Andrews family, The,** *see* 1181bm[58].

448 SCHULLER, Gunther. **Bessie Smith,** *Early jazz. Its roots and*
bd   *musical development* (New York: Oxford U., 1968) 226-41. *Music,*
discog., index.
Discusses Bessie Smith's years of apprenticeship with Gertrude ("Ma")
Rainey's Rabbit Foot Minstrels and the development of Smith's style of blues
singing. Considers Smith's performances on recordings and her accompanying
musicians.

449 SILBER, Irwin. **Singing suffragettes sang for women's votes,**
ap   **equal rights,** *Sing-Out!* VI/4 (winter 1957) 4-12. *Music.*
Considers songs generated by the women's suffrage movement in 2 categories:
1) inspirational songs with texts written to a patriotic tune or well-known hymn
that were meant for those already in favor of suffrage and intended primarily
for use at rallies and other suffrage meetings, and 2) "logical argument songs"-
-e.g., *An appeal to American manhood,* and *The taxation tyranny*--which
attempted to convince people that suffrage was not only a right of women, but
also a positive value to the nation and a logical extension of American
democracy. In 1896 the National American Woman Suffrage Assoc. published
a manual for new groups that recommended the singing of a least 2 songs per
meeting. Not all songs dealing with women's suffrage were favorable towards
the cause; rather, many lampooned women. Texts of suffrage songs and 2 songs
with notation are included.

450 SMITH, Charles Edward. **Ma Rainey and the minstrels,**
ap   *Record Changer* XVI/6 (June 1955) 5-6.
Although Gertrude ("Ma") Rainey performed in northern theaters on the
vaudeville circuit and recorded for Paramount Records in Chicago, she was
essentially a singer from the South. Rainey passed the blues repertory on to
Bessie Smith and to jazzmen such as Louis Armstrong, Charles ("Cow Cow")
Davenport, and Johnny Dodds. Rainey's repertory, its origins in Afro-
American music, and the type of life she lived while traveling with tent shows
are discussed.

451 SMITH, Eva Munson. **Woman as composer,** *American Art*
ap   *Journal* LXII/9 (16 Dec 1893) 185-87.
Smith recalls that 30 years previously--at the age of 16--she began to develop
the plan for compiling *Women in sacred song* (*WIAM* 91), in order to honor the

achievements of 19th-c. women as writers of hymn texts and music. The work
of women as composers and performers of art music in the 1890s is also
discussed.

→ SMITH, Eva. **Women in sacred song. A library of hymns,**
religious poems, and sacred music by woman, *see* 91ma[15].

→ **Song festivals among Negroes,** *see* 633ap[55].

452 SPAETH, Sigmund. **Enter the woman in the domain of song-**
ap   **leading,** *Musical America* XXIX/26 (26 Apr 1919) 9. *Illus.*
Robert Lawrence, director of the school for song leaders associated with the
Young Men's Christian Assoc. in New York, has accepted all women
candidates who are sufficiently musical for training as leaders of community
singing. Helen Marie Clarke was the first female graduate of Lawrence's
course, and she has proven extremely valuable in training song leaders for the
United States Army.

453 S.S.B. **Song leader trains college girls in music leading,**
ap   *Musical America* XXX/15 (9 Aug 1919) 13. *Illus.*
Bryn Mawr Col. is the first women's college to support the serious study of
community singing--"a democratic form of music which promises to become a
movement of national significance". Robert Lawrence, director of the school
for song leaders associated with the Young Men's Christian Assoc. in New
York, recently conducted classes in song leading for Bryn Mawr students, with
the result that many young women have enrolled themselves in Lawrence's
complete course in New York.

→ STOLBA, K. Marie. **In memoriam: Fanny Crosby, lyricist,** *see*
561ap[54].

→ STRANG, Lewis. **Prima donnas and soubrettes of light**
opera and musical comedy in America, *see* 1209bm[58].

454 **Successful women song writers,** *Literary Digest* LV/15 (13 Oct
ap   1917) 87-91.
"In song writing as in every other branch or profession women are now pushing
mere man very hard". The work of Anne Caldwell, Clare Kummer, Mana
Zucca, Elsa Maxwell, and Blanche Merrill is discussed.

→ WILLHARTITZ, Adolph. **Some facts about women in**
music, *see* 178bm[25].

→ WILLHARTITZ, Adolph. **Woman in music,** *see* 179ap[25].

455 WITMARK, Isadore; GOLDBERG, Isaac. **House of Wit-**
bf   **mark, The. From ragtime to swingtime** (New York: Da Capo,
1976) 480 p. *Port., music, bibliog., index.*
A reprint of the 1939 edition (New York: L. Furman). Traces the history of the
publishing firm from its establishment ca. 1886 to the death of Julius Witmark
in 1929. The Witmarks published songs by a number of women, including
those whom they called "one-hitters": Lily May Hall, composer of *Pretty pond
lilies;* Hattie Marshall, composer of *Little Willie;* Maude Nugent, *Sweet Rosie
O'Grady (WIAM 533);* Anita Owen, *Just a chain of daisies (WIAM 535);* and
Ella Wheeler Wilcox, who with an L.F. Gottschalk wrote *Laugh and the world
laughs with you.* Among those with more than a single big hit were Hattie Starr
and Caro Roma. Caro Roma had a lifelong professional relationship with the
firm and also was a close friend of the Witmark family. In the estimation of the
authors, Caro Roma was "one of the foremost women composers of the
country". Her many accomplishments included her stage performances from
the age of 3, her career as a prima donna in opera, her direction--while still in
her teens--of an opera company which toured Canada, her work as an
orchestral conductor, and her 2500 poems, many of which she set to music.
Among the most famous of her songs are *Resignation, My Jean (WIAM 544),*
and *Can't yo' heah me callin', Caroline (WIAM 541).* She also wrote sea songs,
sacred songs, and a cycle entitled *The wandering one.* Following Julius
Witmark's death, Caro Roma gave a radio concert in his memory on 6 July
1929, and 3 years later she gave a Golden Jubilee concert of her own,
celebrating her 50th anniversary as a performer.

→ WRIGHT, Josephine. **Sissieretta Jones, 1868-1933,** *see*
1254ap[58].

→ WYNN, Edith. **How the war helped women orchestra and**
hotel musicians, *see* 1257ap[58].

51   Vernacular music by women

Choral music

456   BROWNE, Pauline Russell. **Woman's suffrage songs** (India-
ma   napolis: composer, 1913) 18 p.
A collection of 7 secular choruses. *Dn* 15'. *At* composer. *Pf* choral SATB, pno.
Ct Votes for women, Taxation without representation, Beloved America, We'll
score a victory, Persistence in the cause of right, What some people say, That
suffragette.

457   KNAPP, Phoebe. **Blessed assurance**, *Gospel hymns nos. 1 to 6*
mc   *complete.* Ed. by Ira A. SANKEY, James MCGRANAHAN, and
George C. STEBBINS (Cincinnati: J. Church, 1895) 222.
Hymn. *Dn* 3'. *At* Fanny Crosby. *Pf* choral SATB.   *(Judith Tick)*

458   KNAPP, Phoebe. **Jesus Christ is passing by**, *Gospel hymns nos.*
mc   *1 to 6 complete.* Ed. by Ira A. SANKEY, James MCGRANAHAN,
and George C. STEBBINS (Cincinnati: J. Church, 1895) 443.
Hymn. *Dn* 4'. *At* J. Denham Smith. *Pf* choral SATB.   *(Judith Tick)*

459   KNAPP, Phoebe. **Nearer the cross**, *Gospel hymns nos. 1 to 6*
mc   *complete.* Ed. by Ira A. SANKEY, James MCGRANAHAN, and
George C. STEBBINS (Cincinnati: J. Church, 1895) 288.
Hymn. *Dn* 3'. *At* Fanny Crosby. *Pf* choral SATB.   *(Judith Tick)*

460   KNAPP, Phoebe, ed. **Notes of joy** (New York: W.C. Palmer, Jr.,
ma   1869) 176 p.
Hymn collection. *Pf* choral SATB, org or pno. Knapp was the chief contributor
to this collection of 100 hymns as well as its editor.   *(Judith Tick)*

461   KNAPP, Phoebe. **Nothing but leaves** (6702; New York: W.A.
mm   Pond, 1868) 7 p.
Sacred chorus. *Dn* 2'. *Pf* solo S, choral SATB, pno.   *(Judith Tick)*

462   KNAPP, Phoebe. **Reign of Christ, The** (0931; New York: W.A.
mm   Pond, 1903) 7 p.
Sacred chorus. *Dn* 3'. *At* Elizabeth Cheney. *Pf* solo S or T, choral SATB, org.
    (Judith Tick)

463   KNAPP, Phoebe. **Sabbath closing hymn** (6869; New York:
mm   W.A. Pond, 1868) 5 p.
Dn 2'. *At* Fanny Crosby. *Pf* choral SATB, pno.   *(Judith Tick)*

464   METHVEN, Florence. **When you look in the heart of a rose**
mm   (4076; New York: F. Feist, 1918) 5 p.
Secular chorus. *Dn* 2'. *At* Marian Gillespie. *Pf* choral TTBarB. Arranged by
Stephen O. Jones.

465   WARE, Harriet. **Woman's triumphal march** (New York: H.
mm   Ware, 1927) 6 p.
Secular chorus. *Dn* 3'. *At* Josephine M. Fabricant. *Pf* choral SSA, pno.

Solo instrumental music

466   AUFDERHEIDE, May. **Blue ribbon rag** (Indianapolis: J.H.
mm   Aufderheide, 1910) 5 p.
Dn 4'. *Pf* pno.

467   AUFDERHEIDE, May. **Buzzer rag** (Indianapolis: J.H. Auf-
mm   derheide, 1909) 5 p.
Dn 4'. *Pf* pno.

468   AUFDERHEIDE, May. **Dusty rag** (Indianapolis: D. Crabb,
mm   1908) 5 p.
Dn 4'. *Pf* pno. Reprinted in *Ragtime rarities* (*WIAM* 92).

469   AUFDERHEIDE, May. **Richmond rag, The** (Indianapolis: J.H.
mm   Aufderheide, 1908) 5 p.
Dn 4'. *Pf* pno.

470   BARTLETT, Elinore C.; VANNAH, Kate. **Little corporal,**
mm   **The. Two-step** (12259; Boston: White-Smith, 1916) 7 p.
Dn 5'. *Pf* pno.

471   BLAKE, Charlotte. **Curly. March, Two-step** (EN 548; Detroit:
mm   J.H. Remick, 1907) 7 p.
Dn 5'. *Pf* pno.

472   BLAKE, Charlotte. **Gravel rag, The** (Detroit: J.H. Remick,
mm   1908) 5 p.
Dn 4'. *Pf* pno.

473   BLAKE, Charlotte. **Hip, hip, hoorah! March, Two-step**
mm   (Detroit: J.H. Remick, 1907) 6 p.
Dn 4'. *Pf* pno.

474   BLAKE, Charlotte. **Mascot, The** (Detroit: J.H. Remick, 1905) 5
mm   p.
Dn 2'. *Pf* pno.

475   BLAKE, Charlotte. **Poker rag** (Detroit: J.H. Remick, 1909) 5 p.
mm
Dn 4'. *Pf* pno. *Rg The ragtime women*, Vanguard, VSD 79402.

476   BLAKE, Charlotte. **That tired rag** (New York: J.H. Remick,
mm   1911) 5 p.
Dn 4'. *Pf* pno. Includes quotations from 3 of her songs: *Sweet dreams, Getting
rested*, and *What time is it*.

477   BOYDE, Betty K. **Cotton States' march** (Atlanta: composer,
mm   1895) 5 p.
Dn 4'. *Pf* pno. Dedicated to the Women's Board of the Cotton States'
International Exposition in Atlanta, 1895.

478   BUTLER, Helen May. **Cosmopolitan America. March and**
mm   **Two-step** (Denver: T.B. Ingram, 1904) [6] p.
Dn 4'. *Pf* pno. The composer is identified on the score as the Directress of
Helen May Butler's Ladies' Military Band. The piece was "designated by the
Republican National Committee as the only authentic official campaign march
for the Presidential election of 1904". The trio section of the march includes
unidentified quotations from *O Tannenbaum, Die Wacht am Rhein, Du, du
liegst mir im Herzen*, and the *Star-spangled banner*. Further information on the
score indicates that the piece was "also arranged for orchestra, military band,
mandolins, and guitars".

479   GIBLIN, Irene. **Sleepy Lou. A raggy two-step** (Detroit: J.H.
mm   Remick, 1906) 5 p.
Dn 4'. *Pf* pno.

480   GILES, Imogene. **Red peppers. Two-step** (Quincy, Ill.: Giles,
mm   1907) 5 p.
Dn 4'. *Pf* pno.

481   GILMORE, Maude. **Splinters. Two-step** (Chicago: W. Rossiter,
mm   1909) 5 p.
Dn 4'. *Pf* pno.

482   GOODING, Grace. **Fadette's call, The. Rag one-step trot**
mm   (New York: J.H. Remick, 1914) 5 p.
Dn 4'. *Pf* pno.

483   GUSTIN, Louise V. **Soldiers of fortune. March** (Detroit: W.
mm   Warner, 1901) 5 p.
Dn 4'. *Pf* pno.

484   HAWN, Zena A. **Fall in line. Suffrage march** (New York:
mm   A.W. Tams, 1914) 5 p.
Dn 2'. *Pf* pno. Copyrighted by the New York State's Women's Suffrage Assoc.

485   KONINSKY, Sadie. **Phoebe Thompson's cakewalk** (New
mm   York: S.W. Koninsky, 1899) 5 p.
Dn 4'. *Pf* pno.

486   LE BOY, Grace. **Everybody rag with me. One-step** (New York:
mm   J.H. Remick, 1914) 5 p.
Dn 4'. *Pf* pno.

487   LE BOY, Grace. **Lay down your arms. Grand march** (New
mm   York: J.H. Remick, 1915) 5 p.
Dn 3'. *Pf* pno.

488 LICHTENSTEIN, Bessie Florence. **Triumphal America.**
mm   **March militaire** (57651; Boston: O. Ditson, 1894) 5 p.
Dn 4'. *Pf* pno.

→   MORATH, Max, ed. **One hundred ragtime classics,** *see*
78ma[15].

489 NIEBERGALL, Julia Lee. **Hoosier rag** (New York: J.H.
mm   Remick, 1907) 6 p.
Dn 4'. *Pf* pno. *Rg The ragtime women,* Vanguard, VSD 79402.

490 NIEBERGALL, Julia Lee. **Horseshoe rag** (Indianapolis: J.H.
mm   Aufderheide, 1911) 5 p.
Dn 4'. *Pf* pno.

491 POLLOCK, Muriel. **Rooster rag** (8273; New York: J.W. Stern,
mm   1907) 5 p.
Dn 4'. *Pf* pno. Reprinted in *One hundred ragtime classics* (*WIAM* 78).

492 RICHMOND, Dolly. **Sunflower tickle. A rag** (1193; Chicago:
mm   McCauly Music, 1908) 3 p.
Dn 4'. *Pf* pno.

493 ROMA, Caro. **Black butterflies** (New York: Temple Music,
mm   1906) 4 p.
Dn 2'. *Pf* pno.

494 SANBORN, Carrie Phippen. **Cosmos. March and Two-step**
mm   (EM 360; Boston: Evans Music, 1907) 5 p.
Dn 4'. *Pf* pno.

495 SHEPHERD, Adeline. **Live wires. Rag** (Chicago: H. Rossiter,
mm   1910) 5 p.
Dn 4'. *Pf* pno.

496 SHEPHERD, Adeline. **Pickles and peppers. A rag oddity**
mm   (Milwaukee: J. Flammer, 1906) 7 p.
Dn 5'. *Pf* pno. Reprinted in *One hundred ragtime classics* (*WIAM* 78). *Rg The
ragtime women,* Vanguard, VSD 79402.

497 SHEPHERD, Adeline. **Wireless rag** (Chicago: Standard Music,
mm   1909) 5 p.
Dn 4'. *Pf* pno.

498 SMITH, Ethyl B.; WOOSTER, Frank. **Black cat rag, The.**
mm   **March, Two-step** (New York: J.H. Remick, 1905) 5 p.
Dn 4'. *Pf* pno. Reprinted in *Ragtime rarities* (*WIAM* 92).

499 STARR, Hattie. **Society buds. March, Two-step** (New York:
mm   M. Witmark, 1897) 5 p.
Dn 4'. *Pf* pno.

500 STEINER, Emma Roberto. **Emma R. Steiner's three-step.**
mm   **Mazurka russe** (New York: MacDonald & Steiner, 1914) 3 p.
Dn 2'. *Pf* pno.

501 STOKES, Nellie W. **Snowball rag** (Detroit: J.H. Remick, 1906)
mm   6 p.
Dn 5'. *Pf* pno.

502 TEST, Nellie Donnan. **Panama march and Two-step** (New
mm   York: C. Fischer, 1905) 5 p.
Dn 4'. *Pf* pno.

503 WILLIAMSON, Carlotta. **Fifth Massachusetts. March**
mm   (Boston: Colonial Music, 1909) 5 p.
Dn 4'. *Pf* pno.

504 WILLIAMSON, Carlotta. **Smiling Susan. Characteristic**
mm   **march, Two-step** (Boston: Colonial Music, 1906) 5 p.
Dn 4'. *Pf* pno. A note from the publisher indicates that this piece was also
arranged for 1) piano, 4 hands, 2) small orchestra and piano, 3) full orchestra
and piano, 4) band, 5) mandolin, and 6) guitar or banjo.

Stage work

505 WILSON, Ira B. **Suffragettes, The** (Dayton, Ohio: Lorenz,
mm   1914) 59 p.
Musical comedy in one act. *Dn* 40'. *At* Harriet D. Castle. *Pf* solo S-3A-T-2Bar,
choral duo (boys), choral duo (girls), choral SATB.

Vocal music

506 BAYES, Nora; NORWORTH, Jack. **Shine on, harvest moon**
mm   (New York: J.H. Remick, 1909) 5 p.
Dn 2'. *Pf* solo voc, pno. *Rg Follies, scandals, and other diversions,* New World,
NW 215.

507 BEACH, Amy Cheney. **On a hill. Negro lullaby** (APS 14377;
mm   Boston: A.P. Schmidt, 1929) 7 p.
Folk tune arranged. *Dn* 2'. *Pf* solo voc, pno.

508 BLAKE, Charlotte. **Harbor of love, The** (New York: J.H.
mm   Remick, 1911) 5 p.
Dn 2'. *At* Earle C. Jones. *Pf* solo voc, pno.

509 BLAKE, Charlotte. **Roses remind me of you** (New York: J.H.
mm   Remick, 1910) 5 p.
Dn 2'. *At* Earle C. Jones. *Pf* solo voc, pno.

510 CANNING, Effie I. **Rock-a-bye baby** (144; Boston: C.D. Blake,
mm   1887) 5 p.
Dn 2'. *At* composer. *Pf* solo voc, pno.

511 CANNING, Effie I. **Safely rocked in mother's arms** (157;
mm   Boston: C.D. Blake, 1887) 5 p.
Dn 2'. *At* composer. *Pf* solo voc, pno.

→   CHARTERS, Ann, ed. **Ragtime song book, The,** *see* 82ma[15].

512 DUGGAN, Maggie. **For goodness sake, don't say I told you**
mm   (Boston: G.O. Russell, 1881) 5 p.
Dn 3'. *At* Joe Bradford. *Pf* solo voc, pno.

513 EMERSON, Ida; HOWARD, Joseph E. **Hello! ma baby**
mm   (New York: T.B. Harms, 1899) [6] p.
Dn 2'. *At* composers. *Pf* solo voc, pno. Reprinted in *The ragtime song book*
(*WIAM* 82). *Rg And then we wrote,* New World, NW 272.

514 EMERSON, Ida; HOWARD, Joseph E. **Honey will you miss**
mc   **me?,** *Max Morath's guide to ragtime.* Ed. by Max MORATH (New
York: Hollis Music, 1964) 12-13.
Dn 1'. *At* composers. *Pf* solo voc, pno.

515 EMERSON, Ida; HOWARD, Joseph E. **My Georgia lady**
mm   **love** (New York: T.B. Harms, 1899) 5 p.
Dn 3'. *At* Andrew B. Sterling. *Pf* solo voc, pno.

516 EMERSON, Ida; HOWARD, Joseph E. **Queen of Charcoal**
mm   **Alley, The** (New York: T.B. Harms, 1899) 5 p.
Dn 2'. *At* Andrew B. Sterling. *Pf* solo voc, pno.

517 HOFFMAN, Gertrude. **On San Francisco Bay** (New York: M.
mm   Witmark, 1906) 5 p.
Dn 2'. *At* Vincent Bryan. *Pf* solo voc, pno.

→   HOPEKIRK, Helen, ed. **Seventy Scottish songs,** *see* 86ma[15].

518 IRWIN, May. **Mamie! Come kiss your honey** (9105; Boston:
mm   White-Smith Music, 1893) 5 p.
Dn 3'. *At* composer. *Pf* solo voc, pno.

519 KNAPP, Phoebe. **As thy days thy strength shall be** (13325;
mm   New York: W.A. Pond, 1897) 5 p.
Sacred song. *Dn* 2'. *At* William Fairchild Lloyed. *Pf* solo voc, pno. *(Judith Tick)*

520 KNAPP, Phoebe. **Bird carol, The** (7796; New York: W.A.
mm   Pond, 1898) 7 p.
Dn 4'. *Pf* solo voc, flu, pno. *(Judith Tick)*

521 KNAPP, Phoebe. **Open the gates of the temple** (3668; New
mm   York: Robbins Music, 1951) 7 p.
Sacred song. *Dn* 2′. *At* Fanny Crosby. *Pf* solo S, org or pno. Previously
published in 1892 (New York: W.A. Pond).   *(Judith Tick)*

522 KNAPP, Phoebe. **Watching for Pa** (6558; New York: W.A.
mm   Pond, 1867) 6 p.
Song with chorus. *Dn* 3′. *Pf* solo S, choral SA, pno.   *(Judith Tick)*

523 KONINSKY, Sadie. **Eli Green's cakewalk** (New York: J.W.
mm   Stern, 1896) 5 p.
Dn 2′. *At* Dave Reed Jr. *Pf* solo voc, pno. Reprinted in *Ragtime rarities* (*WIAM*
92), and in *Ragtime song book* (*WIAM* 82).

524 KUMMER, Clare. **Bluebird** (New York: J.H. Remick, 1916) 5 p.
mm
Dn 2′. *At* composer. *Pf* solo voc, pno.

525 KUMMER, Clare. **Dearie** (4352; New York: J.W. Stern, 1905) 5
mm   p.
Dn 2′. *Pf* solo voc, pno.

526 KUMMER, Clare. **Egypt** (3620; New York: J.W. Stern, 1903) [4]
mm   p.
Dn 2′. *At* composer. *Pf* solo voc, pno.

527 LINDSAY, Jennie. **Always take mother's advice**, *Old time hits*
mc   *of the Gay Eighties and Nineties* (New York: E.B. Marks, 1931) 2-4.
Dn 2′. *Pf* solo voc, pno.

528 NEVADA, Hattie. **Letter edged in black, The** (New York:
mm   Mills, 1925) 5 p.
Dn 2′. *At* composer. *Pf* solo voc, pno. According to Sigmund Spaeth, *A history
of popular music in America* (New York: Random House, 1948), this song was
originally published in 1897.

529 NUGENT, Maude. **Down at Rosie Riley's flat** (New York:
mm   Shapiro, Bernstein & Von Tilzer, 1902) 5 p.
Dn 2′. *At* composer. *Pf* solo voc, pno.

530 NUGENT, Maude. **Mamie Reilly** (New York: J.W. Stern, 1897)
mm   5 p.
Dn 2′. *At* composer. *Pf* solo voc, pno.

531 NUGENT, Maude. **My sweet kimona** (New York: Shapiro,
mm   Bernstein & Von Tilzer, 1901) 5 p.
Dn 2′. *At* composer. *Pf* solo voc, pno.

532 NUGENT, Maude. **Somebody wants you** (New York: Shapiro
mm   Music, 1909) 5 p.
Dn 2′. *At* composer. *Pf* solo voc, pno.

533 NUGENT, Maude. **Sweet Rosie O'Grady** (3-644; New York:
mm   J.W. Stern, 1896) 5 p.
Dn 2′. *At* composer. *Pf* solo voc, pno.

534 OWEN, Anita. **Daisies won't tell. Waltz song** (Detroit: J.H.
mm   Remick, 1908) 4 p.
Dn 1′. *At* composer. *Pf* solo voc, pno.

535 OWEN, Anita. **Just a chain of daisies** (New York: J.H. Remick,
mm   1911) 5 p.
Dn 2′. *At* composer. *Pf* solo voc, pno.

536 OWEN, Anita. **Only a rosebud that she wore in her hair**
mm   (Chicago: Wabash Music, 1896) 5 p.
Dn 3′. *At* Arthur J. Lamb. *Pf* solo voc, pno.

537 OWEN, Anita. **Sweet bunch of daisies. Waltz song and**
mm   **refrain** (Chicago: Wabash Music, 1894) 5 p.
Dn 2′. *At* composer. *Pf* solo voc, pno.

538 PHILLEO, Estelle. **Out where the West begins** (Chicago:
mm   Forster Music, 1917) 5 p.
Dn 2′. *At* Arthur Chapman. *Pf* solo voc, pno.

539 RAY, Lillian. **Sunshine of your smile, The** (New York: T.B.
mm   Harms, 1915) 5 p.
Dn 2′. *At* Leonard Cooke. *Pf* solo voc, pno.

540 ROMA, Caro. **Bamboo baby. Listen to dis jungle lullaby**
mm   (MW 16154; New York: M. Witmark, 1920) 4 p.
Dn 2′. *At* William H. Gardner. *Pf* solo voc, pno.

541 ROMA, Caro. **Can't yo' heah me callin', Caroline** (MW
mm   13313; New York: M. Witmark, 1914) 4 p.
Dn 2′. *At* William H. Gardner. *Pf* solo voc, pno.

542 ROMA, Caro. **Faded rose** (New York: M. Witmark, 1908) 5 p.
mm
Dn 2′. *At* composer. *Pf* solo voc, pno.

543 ROMA, Caro. **Liza dear** (MW 16134; New York: M. Witmark,
mm   1920) 4 p.
Dn 1′. *At* William H. Gardner. *Pf* solo voc, pno.

544 ROMA, Caro. **My Jean** (MW 16131; New York: M. Witmark,
mm   1920) 4 p.
Dn 1′. *Pf* solo voc, pno.

545 ROMA, Caro. **Ring out! Sweet bells of peace** (MW 15902;
mm   New York: M. Witmark, 1918) 4 p.
Dn 2′. *At* William H. Gardner. *Pf* solo voc, pno.

546 ROMA, Caro. **Thinking of thee** (New York: Temple Music,
mm   1906) 5 p.
Dn 2′. *La* NN. *At* composer. *Pf* solo voc, pno.

547 SEELEY, Blossom. **My sweet Suzanna** (New York: Shapiro,
mm   1911) 5 p.
Dn 2′. *At* composer. *Pf* solo voc, pno.

→   SMITH, Eva. **Woman in sacred song. A library of hymns,
      religious poems, and sacred music by woman**, *see* 91ma[15].

548 STARR, Hattie. **Grandma's last Amen** (New York: R.A.
mm   Saalfield, 1899) [4] p.
Dn 1′. *At* composer. *Pf* solo voc, pno.

549 STARR, Hattie. **Little Alabama coon** (New York: W. Wood-
mm   ward, 1893) 7 p.
Song with chorus. *Dn* 3′. *At* composer. *Pf* solo S, choral SATB, pno.

550 STARR, Hattie. **My chilly baby** (New York: Feist & Franken-
mm   thaler, 1900) 5 p.
Dn 2′. *Pf* solo voc, pno.

551 STARR, Hattie. **Somebody loves me. Ballad** (1125; New York:
mm   W. Woodward, 1893) 5 p.
Dn 2′. *At* composer. *Pf* solo voc, pno. Also published in James J. Geller's
Famous songs and their stories (*WIAM* 431).

552 TEMPLETON, Fay. **I want yer, ma honey. An Ethiopian**
mm   **oddity** (New York: T.B. Harms, 1895) 6 p.
Dn 2′. *At* composer. *Pf* solo voc, pno.

553 TOMKINS, Celia; ERDMAN, Ernie. **Dreamland brings**
mm   **memories of you** (4341; New York: L. Feist, 1919) 2 p.
Dn 1′. *At* composers. *Pf* solo voc, pno.

54   Literature about women in related
arts and disciplines

554 **Anne Caldwell, 60, librettist, is dead**, *New York Times* 24 Oct
an   1936, 17.
Anne Caldwell (1867-1936) was the librettist of at least 25 successful musical
comedies and the author of lyrics for many more. As a child she wrote plays for
her schoolmates, and she began her professional career as an actress. Her most
successful shows were *Chin-chin* (1914) with music by Ivan Caryll, *Good
morning dearie* (1921), *Stepping stones* (1923) and *Crisscross* (1926) with

Jerome Kern, and *Take the air* (1927) with Dave Stamper. In 1931 Caldwell left New York for Hollywood, Calif., where she worked in the movie industry.

→   **Christian Science hymnal**, *see* 93bc[17].

→   FOOTE, Henry. **Three centuries of American hymnody**, *see* 261bm[44].

→   FREER, Eleanor. **Our poets. Read by Eleanor Everest Freer, before the Chicago Friday Club, November 5, 1915**, *see* 675ap[56].

555   HALL, J.H. **Biography of gospel song and hymn writers** (New
bf   York: AMS, 1971) 419 p. *Illus*.
A reprint of the 1914 edition (New York: F.H. Revell). Presents sketches of leading representatives of gospel song and hymn text writers active in the 19th and early 20th c. The following women writers are included: Carrie B. Adams, Emma Ashford, Flora H. Cassel, Fanny Crosby, Eliza Edmunds Hewitt, Harriet E. Jones, Laura Emeline Newell, Ida L. Reed, and Jennie Wilson.

556   HOLLAND, J.G. **Visit to a boarding school Miss, A**, *Etude*
ap   XI/3 (Mar 1893) 65.
The limited accomplishments of a young woman in French, painting, and music are revealed. The young woman had been a student at a seminary for 3 years.

557   LONG, Edwin M. **Leafy closet of prayer, The**, *Illustrated*
bd   *history of hymns and their authors* (Philadelphia: P.W. Ziegler, 1885) 74-80. *Illus*.
Describes the origins of 19th-c. hymn texts. Considers the work of Phoebe Brown and Phoebe Cary as authors of hymn texts.

558   **Mary A. Lathbury**, *Musical America* XVIII/26 (1 Nov 1913) 35.
ap
Reports the death of Mary A. Lathbury (1841-1913), who was the author of hymns as well as children's stories. Her hymns include *Break thou the bread of life* and *Day is dying in the west*.

→   **Miss Clara Louise Kellogg**, *see* 1099ap[58].

559   RUFFIN, Bernard. **Fanny Crosby** (Philadelphia: United Church,
bm   1976) 257 p.
Fanny Crosby, known as the Queen of the Gospel Hymnwriters, was born Frances Jane Crosby in 1820 in Putnam County, N.Y. She became blind, partly or wholly because of lack of skilled care for an eye infection when she was 6 weeks old. It was apparent from early childhood that Crosby had poetic talent. At 15 she was enrolled in the newly organized New York Inst. for the Education of the Blind in Manhattan. She became a teacher there in 1843, and later the principal. By the mid-1840s she was well-known as the Blind Poetess, and by 1858 she had published 3 volumes of poetry and had appeared in Washington before Congress to recite her poetry as well as to urge legislation to create institutions and libraries for the blind in every state. Leaving the institute in 1858 after her marriage to Alexander Van Alstyne, a blind professor of music, Fanny Crosby devoted most of the rest of her life to work among the unfortunate in the slums of New York and to the writing of hymns. Before her death in 1915, she wrote the lyrics for nearly 9000 hymns, many of which were immensely popular in their day. Crosby's conception of hymnody, her views on life, and the impact of her work are discussed.   *(Author)*

560   SANDERSON, Lydia A. **Contribution of women to the**
ap   **hymnody of this century, The**, *Hartford Seminary Review* VIII/3 (May 1898) 227-34.
"In all the volumes that have been written on hymns and hymn writers, comparatively little has ever been said about the contributions of women writers". The author contends that hymn texts by women usually are subjective and display simplicity in thought and expression, while those by men tend to be objective and expansive. Typical women's themes concern the assurance, joy, and peace achieved through inner communication with Christ, while men stress the idea of God's power and glory. The work of the following American women as hymn writers, among others, is cited: Phoebe Brown, Phoebe Cary, and Harriet Beecher Stowe.

→   SMITH, Eva. **Woman as composer**, *see* 451ap[50].

→   SMITH, Eva. **Woman in sacred song. A library of hymns, religious poems, and sacred music by woman**, *see* 91ma[15].

561   STOLBA, K. Marie. **In memoriam: Fanny Crosby, lyricist**,
ap   *Brethren Herald* XXXVI/4 (16 Feb 1974) 20. *Music*.
A brief biography of Fanny Crosby. Discusses her teaching career in New York

and her work as a writer of hymn texts. Settings of Crosby's lyrics as hymns are still contained in present-day hymnals of major religious denominations and are in use in churches in both the United States and Europe.   *(Author, abridged)*

→   THOMAS, Augustus. **Print of my remembrance, The**, *see* 1222bm[58].

55   General literature about women in art music

562   ALDRICH, Richard. **Music. [Natalie Curtis-Burlin]**, *New*
an   *York Times* 6 Nov 1921, VI-4.
In the final item of his regular column Aldrich discusses the accomplishments of Natalie Curtis-Burlin, following her tragic death on 23 Oct. in Paris after being run down by a taxi cab. A pioneer ethnomusicologist, Curtis-Burlin collected and transcribed 4 published collections of music: 1) *Songs of ancient Americans* (1905), a collection of Pueblo Indian corn-grinding songs, 2) *The Indians' book* (1907), containing 200 songs and chants from 18 different tribes, 3) *Negro folk songs* (1918), and 4) *Songs and tales from the dark continent* (1920), a study of the songs and stories of 2 African-born students at the Hampton Normal and Agricultural Inst. in Hampton, Va.

563   **Anthology of music criticism, An**. Ed. by Cornel LENGYEL.
bm   *History of music project 7* (San Francisco: Works Progress Administration, 1942) 473 p. (typescript). *Bibliog., index*.
Discusses music criticism in California newspapers and journals in 3 time periods as follows: 1850-79, the *belles lettres* of 1876-1906, and 1906-40. Presents a chronology of the major musical events between 1849 and 1940, together with a list of local critics. Leading women critics who began their careers before 1906 are Marie Hicks Davidson, who became editor of the *Tulane Advance* at the age of 21, and Marjory Markres Fisher, who started as a West Coast critic for *Musical America*. After 1906 women music critics include the following: Helen Bonnet, Helen Dare, Ada Hanifin, Grace Rollins Hunt, Frances Joliffe, Mollie Merrick, Blanche Partington, and Anna Cora Winchell.

564   BALTZELL, W. J. **Music in American cities. The three lake**
ap   **cities: Buffalo, Cleveland, and Detroit**, *Musician* XVIII/6 (June 1913) 369-73. *Illus*.
Describes contemporary musical institutions and leading personalities in the 3 cities, stressing that music--a democratic, rather than aristocratic art in the United States--has reached the masses. In Buffalo, important women in music include Amy Graham, music critic and one of the few American exponents of Dalcroze eurhythmics, Flora E. Locke, music educator, and Mai Davis Smith, leading local concert manager. In Cleveland, there are 750 married women enrolled among 1700 music pupils at the Bailey School of Music; its 27 teachers are female. Adella Prentiss Hughes is a concert manager and a supporter of the Cleveland Orchestra. In Detroit, 3 sisters--Kate, pianist, Charlotte, violinist, and Emma McDonald, cellist--established the McDonald School of Music in 1909 with 400 pupils and a faculty of 16. Two other Detroit women are notable in education: Jennie Louise Thomas and Katharine Burrowes.

565   BAUER, Emilie Frances. **Student life in New York**, *Etude* XX/
ap   6 (June 1902) 216.
This item on the *Woman's work in music* page (*WIAM* 645) decries the number of young women who come to New York to further their music studies and the lack of proper living accommodations for them in the city. Parents "should give more care and encouragement to music in their own cities". Also, a healthy household should be provided in New York for those really in earnest about music study.

566   BAUER, Emilie Frances. **Young woman in music, The**,
ap   *Musician* XI/1 (Jan 1906) 42.
1) At the present time so many different employment possibilities are open to women that it is no longer necessary for women without sufficient talent to look to music for an occupation. 2) Significant numbers of women are relocating in New York and other cities in the interests of expanding their opportunities for music study, and accordingly proper, restful housing accommodations for them are needed. Also, women students should not move to major centers without sufficient funds, including monies that will allow them to attend concerts. 3) Qualified women who contemplate careers in music must be prepared to make untold sacrifices.

567   BEDFORD, William C. **Musical apprentice, A: Amy Lowell**
ap   **to Carl Engel**, *Musical Quarterly* LVIII/4 (Oct 1972) 519-42. *Port*.
Discusses the correspondence of the poet Amy Lowell with Carl Engel between 1909 and her death in 1925, at which time Engel was an editor with the Boston Music Co. and, after 1921, chief of the Music Division of the Library of Congress. Lowell's letters show her to have been well acquainted with musical life in Boston, New York, and London. Her description of the first American performance of Schönberg's *Pierrot lunaire* (New York, 4 Feb. 1923) is well

informed and penetrating. Her assessment of *Le sacre du printemps* (London, July 1913) is less kind; she called it "insanity".

568 BLAKE, Dorothy Gaynor. **Genius of Jessie L. Gaynor**, *Etude*
ap   LI/7 (July 1933) 447-48.
Born in St. Louis in 1863, Jessie L. Gaynor attended Pritchett Col. in Glasgow, Mo. After graduation she spent 2 years in St. Louis, where she studied violin and worked as an accompanist for a choral society, in turn learning a great deal of oratorio and lieder repertory. She also spent a year in Boston studying piano with Louis Maas. Subsequently she married and settled in a small town in Kansas that was devoid of musical life. Always resourceful, Gaynor formed a church choir and soon was directing performances of oratorios and operettas. Gaynor taught and composed for 6 years in Chicago before returning to Missouri, where she headed a music school in St. Joseph. She began writing songs for children in the late 1890s because the current literature for young people typically used slang, baby talk, and bad grammar. Gaynor's ideas on teaching children are discussed. Gaynor was a descendant of James Fenimore Cooper.

→   **Boston, New England Conservatory of Music, Spaulding Library. A checklist of source materials by and about women in American music**, *see* 6bm[01].

569 B.R. **Vassar's president champions music as college study**,
ap   *Musical America* XXX/2 (10 May 1919) 1-2. *Illus.*
Noble MacCracken, president of Vassar Col., believes that music deserves a far more honored place than it is now accorded in the average American university or college. This is not the case at Vassar however, where the discipline of music is well-established and students also can receive credit for lessons and practicing. Music appreciation courses are open to the entire student body, as are concerts sponsored by the college. A note from the editors of *Musical America* indicates that this article is the first in a series discussing whether the discipline of music is yet properly recognized by colleges and universities in the United States.

570 **Carolyn Beebe to book own organization**, *Musical Courier*
ap   LXXIII/11 (14 Sept 1916) 18.
Discusses the formation of the New York Chamber Music Soc. under the direction of Gustave Langenus, clarinetist, and Carolyn Beebe, a pianist known for her ensemble playing as well as her ability as a soloist. Beebe will also be business manager for the 1916~17 season. An important asset of the society is Beebe's extensive library of chamber music, which in large part she gathered abroad.

571 CLARK, Kenneth S. **Seek "protection for women" against**
ap   **malignant evils of the musical world**, *Musical America* XXV/22
(31 Mar 1917) 38.
Announces the formation of a Musical Union of Women Artists as an American branch of the Union des Femmes Artistes Musiciennes of France. In France the union has a powerful position due to the support of the government. The American branch has 2 chief aims: 1) to stamp out the practice of imposing on young artists to perform gratis, and 2) to discourage young women who do not have the requisite talent for a career in music. If the union proves successful in its 2nd aim, managers will no longer be able to obtain large sums from mediocre performers to secure bookings. On the other hand--union officials note--the union is willing to put forward funds for a needy artist to obtain a worthy manager. Giulio Gatti-Casazza is honorary president; Frances Alda, Frank Damrosch, Geraldine Farrar, and Ysaÿe are on the advisory committee.

572 **Colonel Fuller's views on the employment of female tuners**,
ap   *American Art Journal* XLV/19 (28 Aug 1886) 311.
In response to a recent article in the journal that included a photograph of women attending piano and organ-tuning classes, Colonel Levi K. Fuller defends the Estey Organ and Piano Co.'s policy of training women. The Estey Co. has employed "more than 30 female organ tuners for upward of 19 years". Fuller asserts that women have the same capacity for the work as men, and that the outcry about flooding the market with tuners should be aimed at second-rate tuners, not women.

573 **Congresses of music, The. The American College of Musi-**
ap   **cians and the Music Teachers National Association**, *Freund's*
Weekly III/2 (19 July 1893) 5.
Presents the official programs for the convention of the Music Teachers National Assoc. and the American Col. of Musicians, which met in Chicago, 4-8 July 1893. The Woman's Musical Congress held 3 sessions, at which women educators and performers read papers, and compositions by women were performed.

574 **C.R. Bostonians honor Helen Hopekirk on eve of departure**,
ap   *Musical America* XXX/13 (26 July 1919) 26. *Illus.*
After 24 years in which she has endeared herself to the public and her fellow musicians, Helen Hopekirk will take final leave of Boston and return to her native Scotland. A group of Hopekirk's colleagues recently presented her with a silver plate bearing an inscription. Some pupils gave her $400 towards the furnishing of her new home in Scotland. Hopekirk decided to devote the monies to a new music room.

575 DAVENPORT, M. Marguerite. **Azalia. The life of Madame**
bm   **E. Azalia Hackley** (Boston: Chapman & Grimes, 1947) 196 p.
Illus., bibliog.
Emma Azalia Hackley (1867-1922) was the first black graduate of the Denver U. School of Music in 1899. Throughout her career in music she worked to preserve traditional spirituals, to encourage black performers to become professional singers of classical music, and to stimulate interest in the music of black composers. While in Denver Hackley organized programs of poetry and songs by blacks for presentation at local churches. In 1901 she settled in Philadelphia, where she founded a chorus of 100 singers. Hackley frequently sang with the chorus as a soloist, and she featured other chorus members as soloists as well--among them Marian Anderson. In 1905 Hackley organized a highly successful concert at the Academy of Music in Philadelphia, in which she appeared with 2 of her students, Charles Marshall and Mary Saunders Peterson. This was a notable event for the black community of the city. In 1910 Hackley embarked on a world-wide tour of lectures about black Americans in music.

→   **Detroit, Michigan, Detroit Public Library, Music and Performing Arts Division. A checklist of source materials by and about women in American music**, *see* 12bm[01].

576 E.C.S. **Woman's business sense a cause of country's musical**
ap   **prosperity**, *Musical America* XX/12 (1 Aug 1914) 13-14.
The foresight and ingenuity of women managers in various cities throughout the country are responsible for the remarkable "enlargement of America's concert map". Only 15 years ago there were fewer than 25 cities that a singer, for instance, could visit on tour. Now there are more than 300. The activities of women managers in the following cities are discussed: Nettie Snyder in St. Paul, Ella May Smith in Columbus, Ohio, Mai Davis Smith in Buffalo, Adella Prentiss Hughes in Cleveland, Mrs. John M. Slaton and Mrs. John L. Meek in Atlanta, Hattie B. Gooding in St. Louis, Mrs. E.B. Douglas in Memphis, Alma Voedish and Gertrude V. O'Hanlon in Chicago, Frances Wright in Des Moines, Myrtle Irene Mitchell in Kansas City, Mo., Mrs. T.H. Wear in Fort Worth, Tex., and Harriet Bacon McDonald in Dallas. Some of these women are affiliated with local women's music clubs.

577 EGGLESTON, George Cary. **Education of women, The**,
ap   *Harpers New Monthly Magazine* LXVII (July 1883) 292-96.
Recommends the study of music for woman as a "resource for her own entertainment, as means of adding to the attractiveness of her home and more than all, as a refining, softening influence on children". Music is as necessary to a girl as arithmetic to a boy. However, the author also believes that each girl should be taught a marketable skill in case she must support herself.

578 **Emilie Frances Bauer dies in New York**, *Musical Digest* IX/22
ap   (16 Mar 1926) 1.
Emilie Frances Bauer (1865-1926) was editor of the *Musical Leader* in Chicago for 26 years. Born in Walla Walla, Wash., Bauer gained her early experience as a writer on the staff of the *Portland Oregonian*. Bauer was also a linguist, pianist, and benefactor to struggling musicians. She composed songs under the pseudonym of Francesco Nogero, and she wrote the texts of many songs composed by her sister, Marion Bauer.

→   FFRENCH, Florence. **Music and musicians in Chicago**, *see* 52bm[05].

579 FINCK, Henry T. **Place of music in American life, The**,
ap   *Etude* XXII/12 (Dec 1904) 490, 511.
Discusses press influence, changing tastes in music, and grand opera, and stresses the importance of music in church, the home, and at all social functions. Praises the work of women's music clubs and notes that women are slowly replacing men in the music profession, except in the highest branches where creative power and sustained effort are necessary. While suffrage for women is not a viable goal, women should "get on" with culture.

580 FINCK, Henry T. **Woman's conquest of music**, *Musician* VII/
ap   5 (May 1902) 186.
As singers and concert-goers women rule the music world. Will they extend their conquest over the entire field? 1) Women excel as solo artists, and in orchestras they might take over the woodwinds and violins, but not other ultra-masculine instruments such as the double bass and drums. 2) Men are still in the lead in music teaching in terms of the best positions, although women are more numerous. 3) Women are composing more than ever before, but quantity is not quality. Music written by men is far better than music by women, and "probably will remain so for centuries to come, if not always".

581
bm
FOSTER, Agnes Greene. **Eleanor Everest Freer--patriot--and her colleagues** (Chicago: Musical Art, 1927) 186 p. *Illus., port., list of works.*
The daughter of a noted Philadelphia musician, Eleanor Everest Freer (1864-1942) grew up hearing performances by singers such as Clara Louise Kellogg, Adelina Patti, and Christine Nilsson in her parents' home. These women in large part inspired Freer to a career as a singer, and while she inwardly rebelled at the prevailing opinion that she should finish her musical education abroad, Freer went to Paris to study with Mathilde Marchesi between 1883 and 1886. When her father died, the possibility of Freer's continuing with Marchesi was thrown into doubt; she managed to complete the degree, however, by becoming Marchesi's accompanist and coaching new students. Freer then returned to Philadelphia and assumed the teaching of her father's pupils, while also commuting twice a week to New York where she taught at the National Conservatory as the sole official representative of the Marchesi Method in the United States. She married Archibald Freer in 1891 and subsequently lived in Leipzig, while he completed his medical studies. In 1899 the Freers settled in Chicago; Eleanor quickly became involved in the musical life of the city, sponsoring musicales in her home. She soon found the need for a greater challenge, and she began studying composition with Bernhard Ziehn. Freer was a founder of the American Opera Soc. of Chicago, and during World War I she was active in raising funds for relief work. Contemporary evaluations of Freer's compositions are included together with lists of the English texts she set and then provided with French and German translations, in accordance with her belief that vocal music should always be sung in the native language of a country.

582
bf
GERSON, Robert A. **Music in Philadelphia** (Westport, Conn.: Greenwood, 1970) 422 p. $19.25.
A reprint of the 1940 edition (Philadelphia: T. Presser). Discusses the activities to 1940 of the following music organizations in Philadelphia run by and for women: the Matinee Musical Club, which was founded in 1894; the Women's Committee of the Philadelphia Orchestra; the Philadelphia Women's Symphony Orchestra; and the Philadelphia Music Club. In addition to performing artists of national prominence who made appearances in the city to 1940, the varied pursuits of the following women who were active locally and/or were native-born are considered: Evelyn Berckman and Eleanor Everest Freer, composers; Mme. Knitel, clarinetist; F. Edna Davis and Margaret Shane, educators; Mary Curtis Bok (Zimbalist), educator and patron; Dorothy Johnstone Baseler, harpist; Emma Feldman, Helen Polaski Innes, and Adele Gilpin Yarnell, managers; Mary Vogt and Alma Wilson, organists; Clara Barnes, Mrs. Alexander Cassatt, and Mary Margaret Zimmerman, patrons; Marian Anderson, Cynthia Bare, and Margaret Cheer, singers; and Helen Ware, violinist.

583
ap
GETHER, Alice E. **Music for the sick**, *Music* [Chicago] VII (Jan 1895) 254-57.
A brief description of the successful use of music for therapy at a Chicago mental health sanitorium, especially among women patients. Some of the women were already musical--including one young pianist "mentally deranged from over-study".

584
ap
GRANT, Frances R. **Recognizing our debt to Negro music**, *Musical America* XXXI/7 (13 Dec 1919) 36. *Illus.*
Discusses the work of Natalie Curtis-Burlin in making recordings of Negro songs and spirituals, and reports that the Musical Art Soc. in New York under the direction of Frank Damrosch will perform 2 Negro songs--transcribed and arranged by Curtis-Burlin--on a forthcoming program. Curtis-Burlin views Damrosch's inclusion of Negro folk music on his first post-war program as prophetic of the true democracy "which should be accorded those black men who fought in Europe for the rights of the oppressed races" and yet "are asked to accept peaceful oppression at home".

585
bm
GRAU, Robert. **Forty years observations of music and the drama** (New York: Broadway, 1909) 370 p. *Illus., port.*
Discusses theater history, leading entrepreneurs and impresarios, and the "star system", chiefly in New York. Includes a chapter about the following women active as theater managers in 1909: Lillian and Minnie Conway, Mrs. John Drew of Philadelphia, Harriet Holman, who also conducted light opera in Toronto, and Fanny Marsh. The following singers, who were active at the turn of the century, are also considered: Mary Anderson, Bessie Abott, Annie Louise Cary, Clara Clemens, Emma Eames, Kate Fisher, Johanna Gadski, Mathilda Heron, Louise Homer, Emma Howson, Sadie Martinot, Lillian Russell, Fritzi Scheff, Ernestine Schumann-Heink, Marcella Sembrich, Emma Cecilia Thursby, and Ellen Beach Yaw.

586
ap
HARRIS, Henry J. **Occupation of musician in the United States, The**, *Musical Quarterly* I/2 (Apr 1915) 299-311.
The occupation returns of the decennial U.S. censuses taken between 1870 and 1910 show that in the 1880 census--the first to categorize male and female separately--men constituted 58% and women 42% of the musicians and teachers of music in 1880, while in 1910 the men represented 39% and the women 61%. The period from 1880 to 1890 showed the greatest increase in the number of women, following a similar trend in many industrial and commercial occupations. The significant majority of women in 1910 reflects their majority as teachers of music. Men, however, still dominated the "musician" category in 1910.

587
bm
HAST, Lisette. **Classical music in early Kentucky, 1850-89** (Louisville, Ky.: author, 1947) 114 p. (typescript). *Illus., port., facsim.*
Presents biographical information for the musician Louis Hast and memorabilia--e.g., photographs, local concert programs, letters, and testimonials--about Hast's work in Louisville. Includes reminiscences of visits of notable performers in the city, for instance, Jenny Lind and Adelina Patti. Contains information about the all-female Beethoven club that was organized in 1869 under Hast's leadership for the purpose of studying and performing the composer's piano music.

588
bm
Helen Hopekirk, 1856-1945. Ed. by Constance Huntington HALL and Helen Ingersoll TETLOW (Cambridge, Mass.: privately printed, 1954) 41 p. *Bibliog., list of works.*
Hopekirk's long career as a concert pianist, composer, and educator is documented by her associates and friends. Constance Huntington Hall wrote the biography, and Helen Ingersoll Tetlow wrote the chapter about Hopekirk's activities as a teacher at the New England Conservatory. George Steward McManus critically reviewed Hopekirk's compositions, and Josephine Allen described Hopekirk as a social being--her appearance and her presence. A catalogue of both published and unpublished works, lists of her concert repertory and performances (chamber as well as with orchestra), and a bibliography of literature are included.

589
an
Helen Hopekirk, pianist, 89, dead, *New York Times* 20 Nov 1945, 21.
Helen Hopekirk (1856-1945) who made her American debut with the Boston Symphony Orchestra in Dec. 1883, made frequent appearances with the orchestra in subsequent years. In 1897 she settled in Boston and began teaching at the New England Conservatory. Hopekirk was an early champion of the music of MacDowell, Debussy, and Ravel. Her own compositions include a piano concerto, a *Konzertstück* for piano and orchestra, 2 violin sonatas, many piano pieces, and more than 100 songs.

590
bm
HOFMANN, Charles. **Frances Densmore and American Indian music** (New York: Museum of the American Indian, Heye Foundation, 1968) 127 p. *Illus., bibliog.*
A memorial volume for Densmore (1867-1957), who did pioneer work among Indian tribes from British Columbia to Florida, transcribing their music. As an undergraduate at Oberlin Col., Densmore studied piano, organ, and harmony, and she continued piano later with John Knowles Paine and Leopold Godowsky. Her first contacts with American Indian music came when she witnessed performances of song and dance at the Columbian Exposition of 1893 in Chicago, and also when she read the writings of Alice Cunningham Fletcher on the music of the Omaha tribes. A chronology of Densmore's life, selected articles by Densmore on Indian texts and music, and excerpts from her reports to the Bureau of American Ethnology at the Smithsonian Inst. in Washington, D.C. between 1907 and 1946 are included.

591
bm
HUGHES, Adella Prentiss. **Music is my life** (Cleveland: World, 1947) 319 p. *Illus., index.*
Adella Prentiss Hughes (1869-1950) was a concert manager and a leading patron of music in Cleveland. Raised in a musical family, Hughes attended Vassar Col. from 1886-90, where she first became committed to encouraging the American musician. Upon graduation Hughes went to Berlin to study piano and theory. She returned to Cleveland in 1891, launched a career as a professional accompanist, and became associated with the Friday Morning Music Club. Her work as an accompanist subsequently led her to become the manager for many of the artists with whom she collaborated in performance, although in time her roster included other musicians as well. Hughes was influential in establishing the Cleveland Orchestra in 1918 and in the building of Severance Hall in 1931, and she also served as the orchestra's manager. Among the highlights of her career are the first American tour of the Diaghilev ballet company in 1916 and the establishment of children's concerts by the Cleveland Orchestra.

592
an
Indian music truly American, *New York Sun* 3 Apr 1920, 18.
Natalie Curtis-Burlin's *The Indians' book* represents the first comprehensive compilation of American Indian songs made by anyone outside of the United States Bureau of Ethnology. During her field work Curtis-Burlin traveled extensively--often on foot and by horseback--and she made many friends among the tribes. Initially she encountered problems in carrying out her research, but after she successfully sought the endorsement of President Theodore Roosevelt all barriers disappeared. Curtis-Burlin believes that the music of the Indians could serve as material for a distinctly American idiom by composers of art music. Frank Damrosch has programmed 3 American Indian songs on a forthcoming program of the Musical Art Soc. in New York.

593   Isabella Beaton, gifted pianist and composer, *Musical Courier*
ap   LXI/1 (5 Jan 1910) 13.
Discusses Beaton's studies in Paris and Berlin, and her versatile work as a singer, composer, pianist, and educator. "Believing that American musicians should stand for the highest type of culture and refinement", Beaton earned 2 advanced degrees at Western Reserve U. upon completion of her studies in Europe. Her first orchestral work, a scherzo, was performed by the New York Philharmonic under the direction of Emil Pauer. She currently heads the department of history at the Cleveland School of Music.

594   J.B. Women who are managing important musical undertak-
ap   **ings,** *Musical America* IX/15 (20 Feb 1909) 6. *Illus.*
Reports on the work of women as managers of the following organizations in New York: A. Lenalie, manager of the People's Symphony Orchestra concerts at Cooper Union and Carnegie Hall; Laura J. Post, manager of the Musical Art Soc.; Mrs. Charles B. Foote, manager of the Russian Symphony Orchestra; Frances Seaver, manager of the Kneisel Quartet and personal representative for David and Clara Damrosch Mannes; Adelaide Lander, manager of her deceased father's orchestra; and Mrs. George R. Sheldon, who is active on behalf of both the New York Philharmonic and the New York Symphony societies. Adelaide Lander is also an assistant to Frida Ashforth, the voice teacher. Mrs. George R. Sheldon has been instrumental in engaging Mahler as conductor of the Philharmonic for the 1909-1910 season.

→   JONES, F.O. **Handbook of American music and musicians,**
    see 57bm[05].

595   KREBS, T.L. Women as musicians, *Sewanee Review* II/1 (Nov
ap   1893) 76-87.
20 years ago a woman carrying a violin case was a strange sight. Now there are significant numbers of good female violinists and cellists; furthermore, all orchestral and band instruments "have been attempted by women, and, in most cases, with marked success". As composers, however, women are pronounced failures. Women can inspire male composers and teach music, with the exception of music theory.

596   LEWANDO, Ralph. Kate DeNormandie Wilson retires,
ap   *Musical Courier* CI/8 (23 Aug 1930) 23.
Reports that Kate DeNormandie Wilson is now retiring after working 35 years to "awaken a music consciousness in Pittsburgh". Born in Brooklyn, Conn. in 1855, at age 22 she married George H. Wilson, then a prominent figure in cultural circles in Boston. In 1895 George H. Wilson assumed management of the Carnegie Music Hall in Pittsburgh and the newly-organized Pittsburgh Symphony Orchestra. After her husband's death, Kate DeNormandie Wilson took over both positions and came to be highly regarded in Pittsburgh for her work. She also served as secretary-treasurer of the Tuesday Musical Club in Pittsburgh for 22 years.

597   Lily Strickland. Maker of music, *Etude* LXI/9 (Sept 1943) 561-
ap   62.
Born in Anderson, S.C., Lily Strickland majored in music at Converse Col. in nearby Spartanburg and subsequently continued her studies at the Inst. of Musical Art and with William H. Humiston in New York. During World War I she worked as an entertainer for military camps. After the war she lived in India and wrote articles for *Etude* about Indian music. Some of her piano works make use of aspects of eastern music. Strickland returned to the United States several years ago.

598   MACDOUGALL, Hamilton C. College girl in music, The,
ap   *Musician* IX/8 (Aug 1904) 301.
At Radcliffe, Smith, Mount Holyoke, Wellesley, Barnard, and Vassar colleges, at the women's college of Brown U. and coeducational institutions as well, courses in music theory and history are now given credit toward the bachelor's degree. However, since the study of voice and instruments is not awarded credit and the typical academic schedule in colleges does not allow much time for practicing, the college girl studying music is often at a disadvantage when compared with her non-college sister. There is a real demand, nonetheless, for the college-trained musician, whose intellectual understanding of music and knowledge of theory and history are typically better than those of a conservatory graduate.

599   MAGUIRE, Helena M. Evening with Mme. Helen Hopekirk,
ap   **An,** *Musician* XVII/6 (June 1912) 369-70.
Helen Hopekirk presently divides her time between teaching piano, performing as a pianist, and composition in Boston as opposed to sojourns in Europe that are devoted to composition exclusively. Following her concert tour in the United States in 1883, she made Vienna her base for 5 years while she studied with Theodor Leschetizky and also developed her own teaching techniques. Hopekirk finds many of her American students clever, but not especially musical. She also believes that the lack of a folk song tradition in the United States is detrimental to the progress of native composers.

600   MARSH, Robert C. Cleveland Orchestra, The (Cleveland:
bm   World, 1967) 205 p. *Illus.*
This history of the Cleveland Orchestra traces the activity of Adella Prentiss Hughes, who in 1903 raised the money to establish the orchestra, and continued to work in the organization's behalf into the 1930s. Personnel rosters indicate that while several women were employed during the orchestra's initial season in 1918-19, no women were included in the ranks 10 years later when the orchestra had become well-established.

601   MARTENS, Frederick Herman. Women's colleges as a
ap   **factor in musical culture,** *Musical America* XXIV/1 (6 May
    1916) 39-40. *Illus.*
While only 20 years ago music was not accepted as an academic subject within institutions of higher education, American colleges and universities are now playing an important role in the development of music in the United States. Women's colleges have been in the forefront in bringing about this change. The music curriculum at Wellesley Col. is discussed, and the question of giving academic credit for the study of instruments and voice is reviewed. Wellesley has a choir of 40 members that was founded in 1900 and an orchestra of 25 players.

602   MATHEWS, William S.B. Hundred years of music in
bf   **America, A** (New York: AMS, 1971) 715 p. $30. *Port.*
A reprint of the 1889 edition (Chicago: G.L. Howe). This history of American music and musical life contains biographies for the following women musicians: composer Constance Faunt Le Roy Runcie; music educators Clara M. Brinkerhoff, Sara Hershey Eddy, F. Jeannette Hall, Clara E. Munger, and Ellen Varesi; performers Emma Abbott, Caroline Richings Bernard, Fannie Bloomfield-Zeisler, Teresa Carreño, Annie Louise Cary, Jessie Bartlett Davis, Zelie De Lussan, Emma Eames, Amy Fay, M. Estelle Ford, Hope Glenn, Helene Hastreiter, Minnie Hauk, Grace Hiltz, Emma Juch, Clara Louise Kellogg, Pauline L'Allemand, Marie Litta (Marie Eugenia Von Elsner), Emma Nevada, Lillian Norton-Gower (Nordica), Adelina Patti, Adelaide Phillipps, Julie Rivé-King, Julie Rosewald, Ella Russell, Lillian Russell, Alice Ryan, Sibyl Sanderson, Antoinette Sterling, Neally Stevens, Emma Cecilia Thursby, and Marie Van Zandt.

603   MATHEWS, William S.B. Musical congresses at Chicago,
ap   **The,** *Freund's Weekly* III/3 (9 Aug 1893) 5.
A brief report on the convention of the Music Teachers National Assoc. and the American Col. of Musicians, which was held in Chicago between July 4 and 8, 1893. The sessions of the Woman's Musical Congress attracted the largest audiences because of 1) the participation of leading women in music, 2) the interesting subject matter of the papers, and 3) the fact that the sessions had a unifying theme, namely, the accomplishments of American women in music.

604   MCGILL, Anna Blanche. On the trail of song ballads,
ap   *Kentucky Folk-lore and Poetry Magazine* I/2-3 (July-Oct 1926) 13-16;
    10-14.
Discusses Josephine McGill's work during the 1910s gathering English folk songs in Kentucky. McGill was asked to undertake the project by Mary Stone, head of the Hindman Settlement School in Knott County, who--"in her zeal in behalf of the mountain people and her appreciation of their goodly heritage"--wanted the ballads recorded before they vanished from the mountaineers' memories. McGill's courtesy and gentleness inspired confidence in the local performers, and she notated over 100 songs--some in several versions. (*Folk songs of the Kentucky mountains, WIAM* 89, is a selection). McGill traveled in Kentucky on horseback.

605   Miss Kellogg and English opera, *New York Times* 20 Feb 1874,
an   2.
A discussion of the influence of Clara Louise Kellogg on the development of opera in English, a cause for which she has provided strong leadership. The soprano lends to the effort musicianship, intelligence, and business ability as head of her troupe. Kellogg's light, flexible voice makes the English language sound more melodious.

606   Miss Selma Borg at Chickering Hall, *New York Times* 11 Dec
an   1878, 5.
Reports on a lecture and concert given by Selma Borg on the subject of Finnish folk music. Borg, a devotee of the music of her homeland, is also the manager of a vocal ensemble, the Swedish Ladies' Quartet. Her success in disseminating Finnish music is indicated by the recent publication of piano arrangements of some Finnish folk songs by a prominent New York publisher, and by the enthusiasm of her audience at this recent concert. After her lecture Borg conducted arrangements of Finnish music, assisted by Lander's orchestra, a group composed of prominent members of Theodore Thomas's former orchestra.

→   MOORE, John. **Appendix to** *Encyclopaedia of music* **contain-**
    ing events and information occurring since the main work
    was issued, *see* 59bm[05].

→   MOORE, John. **Dictionary of musical information 1640-**
1875, A, *see* 60bm[05].

607   Mrs. Babcock, a clever woman manager, *Musical Courier* LXI/
ap   21 (20 May 1908) 12.
Charlotte Babcock runs the International Musical and Educational Exchange
from offices in Carnegie Hall in New York. She places teachers with a wide
variety of specializations and also concert artists for musicales in private homes.
Biographical sketches for a number of Babcock artists are included.

608   Mrs. Emily Tripp, of Louisville, *American Art Journal* XXXIV/
ap   24 (9 Apr 1881) 475.
An account of Emily Tripp's success as a dealer in instruments and sheet music
in Louisville, Ky. Aided by her husband, who entered the music trade in 1856,
she has established a thriving business in pianos and organs.

609   Mrs. Greenwalt, pianist, lecturer, *New York Times* 28 Nov
an   1950, 31.
Reports the death of Mary Elizabeth Hallock Greenwalt (1871-1950), an
internationally-known specialist in the piano works of Chopin and Schumann,
and a pioneer in the use of lighting effects to enhance the emotional and
aesthetic effects of music. Greenwalt first introduced lighting effects in 1915 in
her recitals in Egyptian Hall in New York. Subsequently she invented and
patented light-color players, and she wrote *The fine art of light-color playing,*
which was published privately in 1946. Greenwalt's background and her work
as a lecturer are discussed.

610   Music in Chicago. [Anna Miller], *Musical Courier* XXXII/11 (11
ap   Aug 1896) 28. *Illus.*
The lead article of this column discusses the background and career of Anna
Miller, who in 1894 assumed charge of the Chicago Symphony Orchestra's
ticket sales and increased the receipts over the previous season by $12,000.
Subsequently she was hired as manager.

611   Music in Denver and Colorado. Ed. by Malcolm WYER and
bm   Edwin J. STRINGHAM (Denver: Carson, 1927) 162 p. *Bibliog., list*
of works, index.
A collection of miscellaneous writings on early music in Colorado and the city
of Denver, which was settled in 1858. Discusses activity in the following areas
to 1927: early concert performances, public school music, choral singing, and
orchestral music--i.e., the civic symphony orchestra in Denver. In the 1890s
women founded the first music clubs in the state and the Denver Women's
Press Club. Singers active before 1896 included Bella Cole, Hattie Louise Sims,
and visitor Emma Abbott. Cateau Stegeman Tracy became an influential
pianist and teacher in Denver beginning in 1896. Lists of works by women
composers active in Colorado in 1927 are included.

612   Musical congresses in Chicago, The, *American Art Journal*
ap   LXI/13 (8 July 1893) 292-93.
The opening day of the Musical Congresses--held 4-8 July at the Art Inst.,
Chicago--included a demonstrative examination of a candidate for the
associate degree in the American Col. of Musicians. Among the judges were
Fannie Bloomfield-Zeisler, William H. Sherwood, and Emil Liebling all of
Chicago, Charles H. Jarvis of Philadelphia, and Albert Ross Parsons of New
York. The following papers were read by women during the first 2 general
sessions: "Music as an element in character building" by Alice Putnam, "Use of
music" by Josephine Rand, and "Music as found in certain North American
Indian tribes" by Alice C. Fletcher, Peabody Museum of Archaeology and
Ethnology, Harvard U.

613   Musical congresses in Chicago, The [Women's sessions],
ap   *American Art Journal* LXI/14 (15 July 1893) 317-21.
The Woman's Musical Congress-a participant in the Musical Congresses held at
the Art Inst. in Chicago--convened for 3 sessions on 4-6 July. Mrs. George B.
Carpenter, who chaired the opening session, told an audience of 1500 that
women have made important progress in music and that "the superiority of
men to women in the field has been due to the difference in education". Papers
by Amy Fay, Maud Morgan, Luisa Cappiani, Maud Powell, Charlotte
Mulligan, and Clara E. Munger were read. Performers were Amy Cheney
Beach, Catherine Fisk, Corinne Moore Lawson, and Priscilla White. Outstanding events of the 2nd session were performances by Beach and Maud Powell of
Beach's *Romance, op. 23 (WIAM* 1269), 4 songs by Clara Kathleen Rogers sung
by Caroline Clark, and compositions by Adele Lewing sung by Miss Crum with
the composer at the piano. The papers included Lillian Nordica's "Women of
the lyric stage", in which she recommended that girls who study in Europe take
with them business-minded chaperones of good character. For the 3rd session
Rose Fay Thomas spoke on "The work of women's amateur musical clubs", as
a means of elevating the standards of music in the United States. Camilla
Urso's paper, "Women violinists as performers in the orchestra", praised
women instrumentalists and noted that they often are more diligent and
accomplished than men. Urso expressed her hope that other music organizations would follow the lead of the Music Union in San Francisco--which
invited Urso to join--and open their doors to women.

614   Musical stupefaction, *New York Times* 31 July 1877, 4.
an
An unsigned editorial ridiculing the American fashion of routinely training girls
in music. Because no one finds out first whether girls have talent, the vast
majority are at best able to become decent technicians. Overly ambitious voice
students aspire to stardom, wasting years of their lives and their own as well as
others' money. Young American women are expected to learn to play piano,
however mechanically, even if at the expense of other studies. Their parents
think them prodigies; yet upon marriage of the young women the piano is
immediately abandoned. "Marriage is beneficial sometimes in unexpected
ways".

615   MUSSULMAN, Joseph A. The role of women; the parlor
bd   **piano,** *Music in the cultured generation. A social history of music in*
America, 1870-1900 (Evanston, Ill.: Northwestern U., 1971) 63-66;
171-74.
Discusses the extensive activity of women in American music, 1870-1900, and
notes that there was serious concern among men of the time that music be
reclaimed as a masculine pursuit. "Since so much of America's musical life was
patronized and conducted by women, especially in the parlor where the average
man encountered it, music was popularly regarded as a woman's affair; male
musicians were feminized by implication. Therefore critics were careful to call
attention to notable manifestations of the opposite tendency when they were
present". Hans von Bülow became the hero of music: "Every musician who
values his manhood owes to [Bülow] an opportunity of self-respect heretofore
undreamed of". Manliness in dress, manner, and approach to performance
were consciously cultivated as a way of "clarifying" the roles of the sexes in
music. Mussulman also discusses woman as parlor pianist and her generally low
level of taste and technique. Although playing the piano was not ruled out as a
hobby for men, playing a cabinet organ was considered more manly.

→   **New York, New York Public Library, Theater Division. A**
checklist of scrapbooks about women in American music, *see*
34bm[01].

616   Nuggets from the Chicago musical congresses, *Freund's*
ap   *Weekly* III/3 (26 July 1893) 5.
Presents excerpts from papers delivered at the Woman's Musical Congress in
Chicago, 4-6 July 1893, by the following women: Nellie Strong, "Teaching as
an art"; Lillian Nordica, "Women of the lyric stage"; Camilla Urso, "Women
violinists as performers in the orchestra"; Julia Ettie Crane, "Public school
music"; Josephine Chatterton, "On method, position, and tone reproduction on
the harp as an instrument of musical art"; Octavia Hensel, "The English
language in song"; Maud Powell, "Women and the violin"; and Luisa
Cappiani, "Phonation and guidance of the voice". The Woman's Musical
Congress was held during the convention of the Music Teachers National
Assoc. and the American Col. of Musicians.

617   PEELER, Clare P. Leginska becomes devotee of outdoor
ap   **life,** *Musical America* XXX/9 (28 June 1919) 13.
Ethel Leginska will not appear as pianist during the 1919-20 season in order to
rest herself from the strain of giving concerts regularly over many years.
Instead she will devote herself to teaching piano and to composition. Leginska
discusses her *Gargoyles of Notre Dame,* for piano, and its "modern tendencies".

618   PETRIDES, Frederique Joanne. Some reflections on women
ap   **musicians,** *American Music Lover* I/10 (Feb 1936) 291-94, 314-15.
Traces the following developments that influenced women in American music
after the Civil War: 1) the appearance of a lady's orchestra from Vienna in
New York in Sept. 1871, 2) the rise of opportunities for serious study of the
piano, 3) the publication in 1876 of Fanny Raymond Ritter's *Woman as a*
musician (WIAM 621) and George Upton's *Woman in music (WIAM* 177) in
1880, and 4) the formation in 1888 of the Boston Fadette Lady Orchestra,
which in 1902 succeeded in obtaining a summer engagement that regularly had
been filled by players from the Boston Symphony Orchestra.

619   PRICE, Isabel M. Hunter College gives music study a
ap   **leading place in curriculum,** *Musical America* XXVIII/19 (7 Sept
1918) 4.
In no other institution has there been a greater progress "towards placing music
on a dignified basis" than at Hunter Col. in New York. Music is now a possible
major at the all-female institution. 50 courses in music theory, history,
performance, and education--exclusive of the summer and evening sessions--are
offered as well as concerts and lectures by well-known artists.

620   RAINES, Leonora. "Will American students stay at home
ap   **after the war?" asks Paris,** *Musical America* XXIX/3 (16 Nov
1918) 30.
1) Many music teachers have relocated in the United States during the war, and
it is not reasonable to expect them to return to Europe afterwards. New York
has become the chief music center of the world. Also, American students are
finally realizing that their needs for study can be fully met at home. 2) Because
of their generosity during the war, Americans have more than ever acquired the

reputation of being millionaires, and Americans who go to Europe in the future can expect "to be handled without conscience".

621 RITTER, Fanny Raymond. **Woman as a musician. An art-**
bm **historical study** (New York: E. Schuberth, 1876) 18 p.
An expanded version of the author's address to the meeting of the Assoc. for the Advancement of Women at the Centennial Congress in Philadelphia, 1876. Ritter proposes that 1) composition should become an elective, if not a required, subject at women's colleges, 2) women should pay more attention to the study of instruments other than piano, and 3) since American men are totally occupied with business or politics, American women should assume the role of patron in the formation of music libraries, collections of rare musical instruments, and private societies for music performance. The contributions of women to western music history in general are also discussed.

622 ROGERS, Clara Kathleen. **Memoirs of a musical career**
bm ([Norwood, Mass.]: privately printed, 1932) 503 p. *Illus., index.*
Clara Kathleen Rogers (1844-1931) was the daughter of John Barnett, an English composer, and Eliza Barnett, an amateur singer. Her father intended that Clara and her older sister Rosamund would become singers, but he wanted them to train first as thorough musicians. Accordingly he sent them with their mother and younger brothers to the Leipzig Conservatory for the full 3-year course, while he remained at work in England. Rogers was only 12 years old when she was accepted by the conservatory. She notes that when she began her studies in Leipzig, composition classes were not open to female students, and she feels that the string quartet she composed at age 14 was influential in breaking down the barrier to women in composition--which occurred during her final months at the conservatory. After graduation Rogers and her sister began operatic careers in Italy, changing their last name to Doria. In 1867 they left Italy, however, as their mother wanted to complete the rearing of her youngest children in England. Rogers was not able to break into opera in London, possibly because of her father's disadvantageous position in certain operatic circles, and she therefore decided to travel to the United States in 1871 with the Parepa-Rosa company. At first she made her base in New York, but eventually she found the musical atmosphere of Boston more congenial to her interests. She settled in Boston--singing at Trinity Church and teaching voice--and in 1878 she married Henry Rogers, a prominent Boston lawyer. Rogers wrote about the later phases of her career in *The story of two lives (WIAM* 623).

623 ROGERS, Clara Kathleen. **Story of two lives, The** ([Norwood,
bm Mass.]: privately printed, 1932) 348 p. *Illus., port., index.*
In this sequel to *Memoirs of a musical career (WIAM* 622), Rogers (1844-1931) recalls her career in music in Boston after her marriage to Henry Rogers in 1878. Increasingly she turned away from performance to teaching, composing, and writing books. She composed songs and chamber music--publishing first in 1882--and she reflects that had she been able to study orchestration in her student days at the Leipzig Conservatory, she might have written for orchestra as well. Rogers was active in many aspects of musical life in Boston, e.g., the formation of the Bach Club under Otto Dressel, the Boston Symphony Orchestra, and the Manuscript Club in 1888. She also made friendships with many leading musicians active in Boston at the turn of the century, among them Teresa Carreño, Charles Martin Loeffler, and Benjamin J. Lang. Rogers wrote 3 books about singing technique: 1) *The philosophy of singing*, 1899, 2) *My voice and I*, 1910, and 3) *English diction in song and speech*, 1912. In 1902 Rogers agreed to join the faculty of the New England Conservatory at George W. Chadwick's express urging, although she continued to prefer teaching in her own private studio. An afterword by Henry Rogers comments upon the establishment of the Clara Kathleen Rogers Scholarship at the New England Conservatory.

→ RYAN, Thomas. **Recollections of an old musician,** *see* 274bm[45].

624 S. Antonia Sawyer--pioneer woman musical manager, *Musical*
ap *Courier* LXXXI/22 (25 Nov 1920) 42.
Antonia Sawyer has become one of New York's most successful managers, despite "4 lean years wrought by war in any business concerned with the entertainment of the public". Originally a contralto soloist in New York churches, Sawyer began as a manager by placing local artists from an office in her home. Her business is now incorporated with offices in Aeolian Hall, and Sawyer is managing American tours for major artists--both European and American, e.g.: Katherine Goodson, the English pianist, Kathleen Parlow, the Canadian violinist, and Lillian Nordica. Sawyer's career is illustrative of what a "woman can accomplish in a sphere hitherto considered the legitimate field for men".

625 SAWYER, Antonia. **Songs at twilight** (New York: Devin-Adair,
bm 1939) 204 p. *Illus.*
Born in Maine, Antonia Sawyer (1856-1941) moved to New York in 1888, where she studied lieder with George Henschel and performed in churches and synagogues. After several successful recitals in New York, Sawyer went to France to study voice and diction with Leon Jancey. Upon returning to the United States, the contralto sang in a nationwide concert tour under the direction of Anton Seidl. In 1910 she decided to stop singing professionally and

become a manager instead. Her clients included Kathleen Parlow, Percy Grainger, Albert Spalding, Ferruccio Busoni, and Artur Schnabel. Personal recollections of Annie Louise Cary, Emma Eames, and Lillian Nordica are included.

626 rb —
R. by H., *Musical America* LX/7 (10 Apr 1940) 25.

627 SLONIMSKY, Nicolas. **Plush era in American concert life,**
bd **The**, *One hundred years of music in America.* Ed. by Paul Henry LANG (New York: Grosset & Dunlap, 1961) 109-11.
Discusses opera and concert performances in the 1860s-90s. Considers Jeanette Thurber's American Opera, through which she attempted to champion both opera in English and native American singers, while also abandoning the star system. The first season in 1885-86 was auspicious artistically, but not financially. Renamed the National Opera in 1886-87, the company was returning from a tour on the West Coast when bankruptcy was declared. Lawsuits against Thurber followed. Thurber was more successful with the National Conservatory, which she also founded in 1885 in New York. In 1888 she petitioned Congress for funding to make the conservatory a truly national institution, but her idea was hardly timely.

628 SMITH, Caroline Estes. **Philharmonic Orchestra of Los**
bm **Angeles, The; the first decade 1919-29** (Los Angeles: Putnam, 1930) 283 p. *Illus., port., index.*
While primarily concerned with conductors, artists, and organizers in the early history of the Los Angeles Philharmonic Orchestra, this study also discusses the continual activity of individual women as patrons, lists many leading female singers, and describes the Los Angeles Woman's Symphony Orchestra under the direction of Harley Hamilton. The woman's orchestra features men only as solo vocalists, just as the Los Angeles Philharmonic employs women only as harpists.

629 SMITH, Fanny Morris. **On the housing of self-supporting**
ap **women,** *Etude* XIX/6 (June 1901) 228-29.
Apropos of the numbers of women musicians moving to cities, Smith argues in favor of the hotel with apartments for small groups of women and a family wing, as being the best response to the needs of self-supporting women. The curfew is not necessary for mature women. This article appears on the *Woman's work in music* page (*WIAM* 645).

630 SMITH, Fanny Morris. **Record of woman in music, The,**
ap *Etude (WIAM* 74) 317.
"A woman's number would be incomplete without a review of women's relations to music up to the year 1901". The status of women as professionals in music has been limited for the most part to the last 20 years. Women did not compose a great deal before the late 19th c. because as a class they had no money: they did not support themselves and had no control over the funds necessary for a composer's education or for publication. Therefore women were restricted to music teaching or to performance.

631 SMITH, Fanny Morris. **Women as tuners,** *Etude* XVIII/1 (Jan
ap 1900) 26.
While piano tuning is being advocated as a means of livelihood for women, and women have indeed entered the field, Smith disapproves. The nervous constitution of females is not well-suited to piano tuning. This article appears on the *Woman's work in music* page (*WIAM* 645).

632 SMITH, Fanny Morris. **Women in the practical production**
ap **of music,** *Etude* XVIII/4 (Apr 1900) 146-47.
This article on the *Woman's work in music* page (*WIAM* 645) reports that significant numbers of women are making their livings in music engraving, designing, and publishing. Philadelphia, Boston, and Cincinnati can boast of the largest numbers of women involved in these pursuits.

633 **Song festivals among Negroes,** *Musical America* XXIX/22 (29
ap Mar 1919) 17.
For a number of years Emma Azalia Hackley has been active in black communities in New York and other cities in holding music conventions, organizing choruses, and giving concerts. In these ventures she has had the support of many prominent artists, among them David and Clara Damrosch Mannes. Recently she has been organizing festivals in the South at which Negro songs and spirituals are performed by choruses and soloists. Hackley is successfully arousing interest among both blacks and whites in this music.

634 STANLEY, May. **Girl music students brought face to face**
ap **with New York's serious housing problem,** *Musical America* XXX/18 (30 Aug 1919) 3-4. *Illus.*
During the war New York became the mecca for musicians from abroad and American students of music. All indications point to an even greater influx of students than before during the forthcoming season, as young men and women are discovering they can find gifted teachers of all types in the city. There are

not enough residences for young women students, however, and New York clearly has an obligation to provide adequate housing immediately. On the other hand, it is to be regretted that young people are now adopting the same attitude toward New York that their counterparts held toward Europe years ago. They rush to study in New York, whereas they could complete all basic work in their native cities while living at home.

635 STERNBERG, Constantin. **Are girls taught music to the**
ap **exclusion of boys?**, *Etude* XII/3 (Mar 1894) 66.
While music is not "unsafe in the hands of women", as long as finances and legislation are run by men it is important that more boys study and become interested in music. No longer is interest in the arts considered effeminate.

636 **Successful manager and vocal teacher**, *Musical Courier* XLIX/
ap 26 (28 Dec 1904) 35.
Discusses Kate V. Wilson's work as a concert manager and voice teacher at the Washington Col. of Music in her native Washington, D.C. Wilson recently arranged local appearances of Nellie Melba and Paderewski.

→ TEAL, Mary. **Musical activities in Detroit from 1701**
through 1870, *see* 278dd[45].

637 TICK, Judith. **Women as professional musicians in America,**
ap **1870-1900**, *Yearbook for Inter-American Musical Research* IX
(1973) 95-133.
Discusses the entrance of significant numbers of women into the profession as teachers and performers beginning in the 1870s, and as composers of art music beginning in the 1880s. Considers 1) the changing sexual definition of performance and composition as no longer being exclusively male sex-typed, 2) the taking up of instruments previously considered unfeminine by women--e.g., the violin and the flute, 3) the activity of lady orchestras in New York and Boston in beer gardens and theaters, and the emergence of groups playing classical repertory by 1900, e.g., the Boston Fadette Lady Orchestra, and 4) the establishment of women as composers and the rise of music as a feminist issue in the 1890s. Reviews the development of sexual aesthetics by which both the virtues and the faults of music by women composers were judged as illustrations of the "eternal feminine". Sexual aesthetics functioned so as to assign women composers a peripheral place within composition, chiefly as song composers. Music by the following women is discussed: Amy Cheney Beach, Carrie Jacobs-Bond, Margaret Ruthven Lang, Mary Turner Salter, and Mary Knight-Wood.

638 **Troubles of a feminine impresario**, *Musical America* X/26 (6
ap Nov 1909) 11.
At the urging of Guzman Blanco, her cousin and an official in the Venezuelan government, Teresa Carreño organized an opera company in Europe and brought it to Caracas for a short season in 1886. Carreño recalls how activity by revolutionists disrupted the season and forced her to become the conductor of the company as well as the impresario.

→ TUTHILL, Burnet. **Fifty years of chamber music in the**
United States, *see* 1988ac[65].

639 WARE, Helen. **Motherhood and careers: or, the mother**
ap **artist**, *Musician* XXI/12 (Dec 1916) 728.
The author, a violinist, believes that the truly dedicated woman musician is able to combine matrimony and motherhood with her career. Those women who do not succeed in the combination have been either unfortunate in their choice, or have put their career ahead of their obligations as wife and mother.

640 WATSON, Dorothy DeMuth. **Alice Cunningham Fletcher**,
ap *Musical America* XXXVII/25 (14 Apr 1923) 47.
Reports the death of the anthropologist and authority on American Indian music (1845-1923). Fletcher was one of the first persons to make a systematic study of Indian music, which she notated. She was also active as a lobbyist in Congress in behalf of Indian affairs. In 1882 Fletcher became an assistant in ethnology at the Peabody Museum of Archaeology and Ethnology at Harvard U.

641 **What it means to be the wife of an operatic star**, *Musical*
ap *America* XVII/23 (12 Apr 1913) 5. *Illus.*
An interview with Mrs. Putnam Griswold, wife of the basso at the Metropolitan Opera and a "striking example of the 'power behind the throne' in the career of a successful artist". Mrs. Griswold notes that typically the wife of a performer is his business manager and the organizer of the couple's social life.

→ WILLARD, Frances. **Woman of the century, A**, *see* 66bm[05].

642 WILLETS, Gilson. **Our women musicians and composers: an**
ap **interview with Mrs. Theodore Sutro**, *Midland Monthly* X/5
(Nov 1898) 401-08. *Port.*

Two years ago the Music Teachers National Assoc. asked Florence Edith Sutro to organize the participation of women musicians at its forthcoming convention. The Woman's Department of the association was subsequently founded with Sutro as president, and in turn the National Federation of Music Clubs, which Sutro currently heads. As of 1898 the federation represents 250 clubs, with 25,000 members--including thousands of performers and composers. Sutro, who is a composer herself, has assembled a library of 1400 compositions by women in every genre and 73 books about music by female authors. In compiling the library she met with considerable skepticism from men regarding whether women were indeed active as composers.

→ WILLHARTITZ, Adolph. **Some facts about women in**
music, *see* 178bm[25].

→ WILLHARTITZ, Adolph. **Woman in music**, *see* 179ap[25].

643 **Woman manages an opera company**, *Musical America* V/4 (8
ap Dec 1906) 15. *Illus.*
After working for a number of years as an office manager for an insurance firm and traveling in the South for another commercial enterprise, Margaret H. Brown of Chicago decided she wanted a business of her own, and she founded the Standard Opera, which is currently touring the Northwest with productions of *Martha* and Michael Balfe's *The Bohemian girl*. Brown's company is modeled to a certain extent on the Church Choir Co. of Chicago, but it is presenting operas rather than Gilbert and Sullivan operettas. Although some performances had less than capacity audiences, many were well-attended and thus ensured the survival of the company.

644 **Woman's page**. Ed. by Miss S.C. VERY, *Musician* IV/1 (Jan 1899)
ap 23.
The *Woman's page* is introduced as a new feature of the journal "in view of the increasing activity of women in all phases of music life, her [sic] aggressive and authoritative entrance into spheres heretofore monopolized by men, viz., orchestral and chamber music, and her important labors in the organization and development of music clubs, which are exerting an ever wider influence on music life at large". Brief articles on the Boston Women's Symphony Orchestral Soc., the Women's String Orchestra of New York, and music in the curriculum at Wellesley Col. are included. The *Woman's page* was discontinued after Apr. 1902 (VII/4), when it was replaced by a page devoted to music clubs and fraternities.

645 **Woman's work in music**, *Etude* XV/12 (Dec 1897) 312-13.
ap
The first appearance in *Etude* of a "woman's page", which later became a monthly feature through Feb. 1903 (XXI/2). Considers the newly heightened activity of women in the music clubs and as composers.

→ **Woman's work in music number [I]**, *see* 74bp[10].

→ **Woman's work in music number [II]**, *see* 75bp[10].

→ **Woman's work in music number [III]**, *see* 76bp[10].

646 **Women as piano tuners**, *Etude* XV/10 (Oct 1897) 259.
ap
Piano tuning is a new profession open to women: it is easy to learn, the pay is good, and it does not require a substantial investment in equipment. Any piano maker will gladly explain the intricacies of the piano to a prospective female piano tuner, especially when he thinks she might be able to sell new pianos to some of her customers.

56   Literature about women as composers of art music

647 ADAMS, Juliette A. Graves. **American genius of world**
ap **renown: Mrs. H.H.A. Beach**, *Etude* XLVI/1 (Jan 1928) 34, 61,
69. *Illus.*
The author recalls her first acquaintance with Amy Cheney Beach and Beach's husband at the Columbian Exposition in Chicago in 1893--at which point Beach's music was just becoming known in the Chicago area. Beach's associations with Marcella Craft during Craft's early years in Boston and with Helen Pugh, a young pianist who played Beach's piano concerto in C-sharp minor, op. 45 (*WIAM* 1369) at a convention of the National Federation of Music Clubs in 1923, are discussed as examples of Beach's great kindness toward others. Biographical information about the composer's early years is included.

648 ADAMS, Juliette A. Graves. **Musical creative work among**
ap   **women**, *Music* [Chicago] IX (Jan 1896) 263-72.
The often-posed question "Shall women--can women compose?" is best
answered by the fact that women are active as composers, whether or not they
have composed large-scale works. The work of contemporary women--notable
among them Amy Cheney Beach and Margaret Ruthven Lang--is briefly
considered.

649 A.L.S. **Women and music**, *Musical Courier* XLI/5 (1 Aug 1900)
ap   33.
This article, which is reprinted in *Musical Courier* from the London *Musical
Times*, contends that while women have not been handicapped in music--and in
fact more girls than boys study music (i.e., the piano)--the record of women in
composition is dismal.

650 **American composer still under the rule of Europe, says Mrs.**
ap   **Heckscher**, *Musical America* XXVII/25 (20 Apr 1918) 18. *Illus.*
Celeste D. Heckscher believes that an American school of composition is not yet
in evidence. She is drawn to French models. Her opera, *The rose of destiny*, will
be performed by the Philadelphia Opera Soc. in May. Heckscher began
composing as a child, and despite the protests of her parents, she persisted in
studying composition and piano both in Philadelphia and abroad.

651 APTHORP, William F. **Mrs. H.H.A. Beach; symphony in E**
bd   **minor, "Gallic", op. 32**, *Boston Symphony Orchestra. Programmes
      of the rehearsals and concerts, Music Hall, Boston, 1896-97* (Boston:
      C.A. Ellis, 1896-97) 77-82.
A program for the public rehearsal and concert of the Boston Symphony
Orchestra on 30-31 Oct. 1896, at which Amy Cheney Beach's symphony in E
minor, op. 32 (*WIAM* 1370) was first performed. A biographical sketch of the
composer's career to 1896 and program notes about the symphony are included.

→   BARNES, Edward. **American composers of church and**
     choral music since 1876, *see* 1999ac[66].

→   BEACH, Amy. **Twenty-fifth anniversary of a vision, The**, *see*
     2073ac[67].

652 BLOOMFIELD-ZEISLER, Fannie. **Woman in music**, *Ameri-*
ap   *can Art Journal* LVIII/1 (17 Oct 1891) 1-3.
"There has existed, and exists to this day, the most obstinate prejudice against
female composers. They have, until within a half-century, been excluded from
all higher schools. They have, by social conditions of former times, been
assigned almost exclusively to menial duties. Now that social barriers have been
removed and woman can receive the benefit of a liberal education, she will
develop her creative powers".

653 BROOKS, Benjamin. **"How" of creative composition, The. A**
ap   **conference with Mrs. H.H.A. Beach**, *Etude* LXI/3 (Mar 1943)
      151, 208-09.
Discusses 1) the compositional genesis of the *Canticle of the sun, op. 123*
(*WIAM* 1294) and *The year's at the spring, op. 44, no. 1* (*WIAM* 1623), and 2)
Amy Cheney Beach's self-instruction in music. She copied out the *Well-
tempered clavier*, S.846/93, from memory and then compared her version with
Bach's.

654 BROWER, Edith. **Is the musical idea masculine?**, *Atlantic*
ap   *Monthly* LXXIII (Mar 1894) 332-39.
"Woman has of late fallen into the way of posing as the greater man, and
people are found everywhere who believe her capable of anything she may be
allowed to try her head or hands at". Women have not produced great music-
-or even remarkably good music--because they are deficient in emotional force
and their imaginations cannot handle the abstract. Women deal best with
concrete situations and therefore are good at housekeeping and managing
families.

655 BROWER, Harriette. **Mrs. H.H.A. Beach. How a composer**
bd   **works**, *Piano mastery* (New York: F.A. Stokes, 1917) 179-87.
An interview with Amy Cheney Beach, who--Brower reports--is emerging from
seclusion "after years of quiet study and home life in Boston" and a lengthy
sojourn in Europe. Beach notes that when she is not playing, she is composing.
In order to save her sensitive hearing she practices on a soundless keyboard,
preferably an hour a day for scales and exercises alone. She composes only
when inspired and likes to compose out-of-doors. Her first draft of a
composition is usually fragmentary; the notation resembles shorthand. Often
she lets a musical idea rest quietly in her mind for a long time before putting it
on paper. Beach also discusses her early self-education in music and her
extensive personal library.

656 *Brownings go to Italy, The*, *Musical Leader* LXVIII/21 (19 Dec
ap   1936) 3. *Illus.*
Discusses Eleanor Everest Freer's *The Brownings go to Italy, op. 43* (*WIAM*
1454), a short opera for 4 characters based on the lives of Robert and Elizabeth
Barrett Browning. Freer has included 3 songs from her *Sonnets from the
Portuguese, op. 22* (*WIAM* 1694) in the opera. The composer has also written
11 other operas and numerous orchestral, vocal, and piano works.

657 **California honors Mrs. Beach**, *Musical Courier* LXX/25 (30
ap   June 1915) 15.
Reports that Amy Cheney Beach is presently being given an unprecedented
number of receptions in her honor by music clubs and individuals, such as
Charles Wakefield Cadman, during her visit to California. Despite the frequent
entertainments, Beach still manages to practice the piano every day in the
morning hours.

658 **California's brilliant composer-pianist, Fannie Dillon**, *Musi-*
ap   *cal Courier* LXXIII/20 (16 Nov 1916) 45.
Reports that Fannie Charles Dillon is in demand on the West Coast for piano
recitals and lecture-recitals about various trends in contemporary music.
Includes a chronological list of Dillon's works to op. 39, in which the following
genres are represented: orchestral, choral, chamber, solo vocal, operatic, and
solo instrumental.

→   **Carreño believes in women's rights**, *see* 917ap[58].

→   **Claremont, California, Scripps College Music Library. A**
     checklist of compositions in manuscript by American women
     composers, *see* 9bm[01].

659 CLARKE, Helen A. **Nature of music and its relation to the**
ap   **question of women in music, The**, *Music* [Chicago] VII (Mar
      1895) 453-61.
An answer to Edith Brower's *Is the musical idea masculine?* (*WIAM* 654). Even
in recent years German teachers have refused to teach women the "science of
harmony" on the grounds that women could not understand it. Until women
have had the same training and opportunity to devote themselves to musical
composition as men, it is unfair to declare them incapable of great work.

660 CLIPPINGER, D.A. **Songs of Mary Turner Salter, The**,
ap   *Musical West* VI/4 (Feb 1929) 22.
Discusses how and when Mary Turner Salter composed the following works:
Come to the garden, love (*WIAM* 1898), *The swan* (*WIAM* 1928), *Serenity*
(*WIAM* 1921), *The cry of Rachel* (*WIAM* 1900), *A night in Naishapur* (*WIAM*
1916), *Lyrics from Sappho* (*WIAM* 1912), and *Love's epitome* (*WIAM* 1911).

661 **Columbian Exposition announcement**, *American Art Journal*
ap   LXI/2 (22 Apr 1893) 29.
Announces the musical events planned for the opening day of the Columbian
Exposition in Chicago, 1 May 1893, as well as the program for the dedication
of the Woman's Building. The latter--to be held in the Music Hall of the
Woman's Building--will feature performances of a march for orchestra by
Ingeborg von Bransart of Weimar, an overture for orchestra by Francis Ellicott
of London, and Amy Cheney Beach's *Festival jubilate, op. 17* (*WIAM* 1305),
for which a mixed chorus of 300 singers with orchestra is planned.

662 COWEN, Gertrude. **Mrs. H.H.A. Beach, the celebrated**
ap   **composer**, *Musical Courier* LX/23 (6 June 1910) 14-15.
Numerous honors have been bestowed upon Amy Cheney Beach in recent
years: e.g., an invitation from the French government to enter an autograph
MS in an exhibit at the Paris Opera, the performance of a group of her songs at
the Royal Palace in Sweden, and another invitation to attend the unveiling of a
monument to Wagner in Berlin. Born in Henniker, N.H. in 1867, Beach began
composing short pieces at age 4, and at age 6 she undertook formal study of the
piano with her mother, a gifted singer and pianist. Beach excelled in her school
studies as a youngster, and after some debate her parents decided she should
remain in Boston to complete her general education as well as her musical
training, rather than go abroad. Beach studied music theory and instrumentation on her own. At age 16 she made her debut as a pianist in Boston,
performing Moscheles's concerto in G minor, op. 60. Subsequently she
appeared with the Boston and Chicago symphony orchestras among others,
playing all the major concertos, and she has performed extensively at solo
recitals as well. In 1885 she married Henry Harris Aubrey Beach, a physician in
Boston.

663 CRAIN, Hal Davisson. *Rizzio*, **opera by Mary Carr Moore**,
rm   **is given first hearing in Los Angeles**, *Musical America* LII/11
      (June 1932) 12. *Illus.*
A review of Mary Carr Moore's 2-act opera *David Rizzio, op. 89* (*WIAM* 1456)
performed in the Shrine Auditorium in Los Angeles on 26 May 1932 under the
direction of Alberto Conti.

664   CRAVENS, Kathryn. Carrie Jacobs-Bond, *Christian Science*
an   *Monitor* 26 Mar 1943, 10.
Now 80, Jacobs-Bond is not content to sit around and just be an "old lady". She
has recently written 2 stirring songs for the war effort. Her most famous song, *A
perfect day* (*WIAM* 1743), has been translated into many different languages
and sung around the world. Jacobs-Bond's long and successful career is
reviewed.

665   CROTHERS, Stella Reid. Women composers of America,
ap   **1-45**, *Musical America* X/4-XI/22 (5 June 1909-9 Apr 1910)
pagination noncontinuous. *Illus.*
A series of 45 profiles of the composers listed below, that reports on the
activities of contemporary women in composition rather than reviews their
works. The women are listed in the order of their profiles' publication: Grace
Wassells, Florence Newell Barbour, Margaret Ruthven Lang, Anita Owen,
Clara Anna Korn, Dorothy Temple Brown, Elsie Maxwell, Abbie Gerrish Jones,
Helena Bingham, Lillian Taih Sheldon, Cora S. Briggs, Constance Faunt Le
Roy Runcie, Bertha Remick, Helen Hopekirk, Carrie B. Adams, Katherine
Heyman, Nanka Faucette, Eulalie Andreas, Isidora Martinez, Lily Strickland,
Eleonore MacLean, Anna Connable Meeks, Sarah Ferris Read, Grace Wilbur
Conant, Jessie L. Gaynor, Edythe Pruyn Hall, Etta Larkin, Gena Branscombe,
Fannie Snow Knowlton, Juliette A. Graves Adams, Grace Mayhew Stults,
Edith Dalton, Rose McCoy, Mrs. C.A. Boyle, Minnie E. Gillett, Lelia
Waterhouse-Wilson, Ayers Garnett, Maude E. Batcheller, Emma Ashford,
Mary Turner Salter, Mildred J. Hill, Edith Haines-Kuester, Lucille Mandsley
Sanford, Harriet Ware, and Laura Sedgwick Collins.

→   DAVIS, Mrs. Charles. **Recent performances of American
music [I]**, *see* 2007ap[66].

666   DEN BERG, Henri van. Eleanor Everest Freer. An appreci-
ap   **ation of the work of the talented Chicago composer, with
some consideration of her style and status**, *Musical Leader*
XXVI/9 (28 Aug 1913) 245.
"In the midst of the battle of opinions regarding American music and its future
expression, Mrs. Freer quietly pursues her course". Freer regrets the fact that
"our best musicians too often use foreign languages, whereas our best music
can just as well be set to the best English". The composer's background and
training are also discussed.

→   EBEL, Otto. **Women composers. A biographical handbook of
women's work in music**, *see* 50bm[05].

667   ELDER, Dean. Where was Amy Beach all these years? An
ap   **interview with Mary Louise Boehm**, *Clavier* XV/9 (Dec 1976)
14-17.
A pianist, Boehm has been in the forefront of reviving "next-to-the-greats":
e.g., Arthur Foote, Hummel, Kalkbrenner, Daniel Gregory Mason, and
Moscheles. She first came in contact with Beach's music when she recorded the
piano quintet in F-sharp minor, op. 67 (*WIAM* 1606), a work which she likens
to the Brahms piano quintet in F minor, op. 34, and the Fauré piano quintet in
C minor, op. 115. Boehm thinks that the Beach piano concerto in C-sharp
minor, op. 45 (*WIAM* 1369)--which she finds very challenging to play--could
become a repertory piece along with the Chaikovskii and Rachmaninoff
concertos, at least for a change. The interview also deals with other works in the
piano literature by Beach and Beach's influence on MacDowell.

→   ELSON, Arthur. **Woman's work in music**, *see* 137bf[25].

668   ELSON, Louis Charles. American women in music, *The history*
bd   *of American music* (New York: Macmillan, 1904) 293-310. *Port.*
This landmark history of American music includes a substantial discussion of
Amy Cheney Beach's music and also considers the work of Margaret Ruthven
Lang, Helen Hood, Jessie L. Gaynor, Edith Noyes Porter, Clara Kathleen
Rogers, Helen Hopekirk, and Julie Rivé-King. Elson contends that "insufficient
musical education and male prejudice have prevented female composers [in
Europe] from competing with their male brethren in art. In the United States,
where this prejudice has not existed, the female composer was in the field
contemporaneously with our Chadwicks, Parkers, and MacDowells; and
America can boast at least one female composer [Beach] who can compare
favorably with any woman who has yet entered creative music art".

→   ELSON, Louis. **Woman in music**, *see* 138bf[25].

669   ENDE, Amelia von. Woman as a creative force in music,
ap   *Musical America* XX/11 (18 July 1914) 3-4. *Illus.*
Reviews the history of women as composers and discusses the status of women
in composition as of 1914. 1) Now that educational opportunities are no longer
denied to women, the chief obstacle facing a woman's creative activity in music
seems due to her "lack of perspective about her domestic environment--unless
she chooses chastity". 2) Much of the simple justice in earlier times that
prompted men to encourage women in many pursuits as amateurs, now has

disappeared because women have established themselves as professionals. 3)
Despite the current climate which is hostile to women in composition, it is
hardly likely that they are accomplishing less than their counterparts did in the
past. Rather, men seem to fear competition in a field where previously they
have been supreme.

670   EWEN, David, comp. and ed. Carrie Jacobs-Bond, 1862-
bd   **1946**, *Popular American composers. From revolutionary times to the
present* (New York: H.W. Wilson, 1962) 34-35.
Carrie Jacobs-Bond composed art songs that were so successful that they
became "popular". Born in Janesville, Wis., she was a child prodigy. Later, after
2 marriages and an injury, and after being widowed while still comparatively
young, she began to support herself by publishing her songs and promoting
them at her song recitals. Her first publication, *Seven songs* (*WIAM* 1741),
included *Just a-wearyin' for you*, and *I love you truly*. Later hits included *A
perfect day* of 1909 (*WIAM* 1743), that was promoted by David Bispham and
eventually sold over 5 million copies. Other highly successful songs by Jacobs-
Bond were *God remembers when the world forgets* (*WIAM* 1743), *Life's garden*
(*WIAM* 1743), *A little bit o' honey* (*WIAM* 1743), *I've done my work* (*WIAM*
1743), *His lullaby* (*WIAM* 3088), *Roses are in bloom* (*WIAM* 1740), and *A little
pink rose* (*WIAM* 1743). The composer was honored by the National
Federation of Music Clubs in 1941.

671   Fannie Dillon composes a *Celebration of victory*, *Musical*
ap   *Courier* LXXVII/24 (12 Dec 1918) 9. *Illus.*
Discusses recent works by the Los Angeles composer. Upon receiving news of
the end of the war, Fannie Charles Dillon wrote her *Celebration of victory, 11
November 1918*--a large-scaled, triumphal piece for orchestra. Dillon's piano
compositions, e.g., her *Birds at dawn* and the sonata, op. 27, have delighted
Harold Bauer and Teresa Carreño.

672   Fannie Dillon teaches under the pines, *Musical Courier* LXXV/
ap   3 (19 July 1917) 33. *Illus.*
Discusses Fannie Charles Dillon's courses in piano, ear-training, music history,
and composition, which she teaches in her studio atop Mt. Wilson in California.
These courses have especially attracted the patronage of music teachers. While
Dillon has studied with a number of composers--notably Hugo Kaun and
Rubin Goldmark--her method of teaching composition is not wholly character-
istic of any one of her mentors.

673   FARWELL, Arthur; DARBEY, W. Dermot, eds. Music in
bm   **America**. *The art of music* 4 (New York: National Soc. of Music,
1915) 478 p. *Illus., bibliog., index.*
This history of American music from colonial times to 1915 includes a section
devoted to the following women composers within the chapter "Romanticists
and neo-classicists": Mabel Wheeler Daniels, Fannie Charles Dillon, Eleanor
Everest Freer, Celeste D. Heckscher, Helen Hopekirk, Clara Anna Korn, Mary
Carr Moore, Mary Turner Salter, and Gertrude Norman Smith. The same
chapter also discusses the music of MacDowell, Edgar Stillman Kelley, and
Frederick Converse, etc. Elsewhere in the book the works of Amy Cheney
Beach, Gena Branscombe, and Margaret Ruthven Lang are considered.

674   FAY, Amy. Women and music, *Music* [Chicago] XVIII (Oct
ap   1900) 505-07.
An answer to *Women and music* by A.L.S. (*WIAM* 649). Fay argues that
traditionally women have been preoccupied with encouraging men in composition, rather than developing their own talents. Now that women are realizing
they have brains and are studying composition seriously, the status of women
as composers will improve. Fay also notes that it is wrong to equate the study
of piano at beginning levels with the study of composition.

→   FISHER, Marjory. **Coast WPA men led by Mary Carr
Moore**, *see* 2207ap[68].

→   **Former concert singer a composer**, *see* 982ap[58].

675   FREER, Eleanor Everest. Our poets. Read by Eleanor
ap   **Everest Freer, before the Chicago Friday Club, November 5,
1915**, *Musical Courier* LXXI/20 (18 Nov 1915) 56.
The composer presents her case for vocal music in the English language for
English-speaking countries and discusses the work of contemporary poets in the
Chicago area. Freer delivered this address in connection with a short concert of
her songs.

676   FREER, Eleanor Everest. Recollections and reflections of an
bm   **American composer** (n.p.: author, 1929) 122 p. *Illus.*
A brief autobiography of the composer's professional and personal life. Born
into a musical family, Freer (1864-1942) was still in her teens when she went to
Paris to study voice with Mathilde Marchesi. Three years later she returned to
the United States, married Archibald Freer of Chicago, and subsequently gave
birth to a daughter. She returned to active professional life 10 years later when
she began the study of theory and composition with Bernhard Ziehn. The

composer stresses the importance of native American opera and opera in translation in the United States; she is active herself in both areas.

677 Freer's *Frithiof* [a] vivid Scandinavian opera, *Musical Leader*
ap   LXIX/10 (22 May 1937) 12.
Discusses Eleanor Everest Freer's *Frithiof, op. 40* (*WIAM* 1446) and the composer's long-term association with Scandinavian art and music. The opera is based on a legend that is Scandinavia's equivalent of the *Iliad*. Thus far Freer's work has only been heard in concert form; it would certainly add color and variety to the repertory of American opera companies.

→   FULD, James. **American popular music 1875-1950**, *see*
       430bm[50].

678 GALDBERT, Albert. **American Opera gives native work**,
rm   *Musical America* XLVIII/29 (3 Nov 1928) 27.
A review of Eleanor Everest Freer's one-act opera, *The legend of the piper* (*WIAM* 1449), as performed by the American Opera Soc. of Chicago. The fact that more than 20 characters moved in and out of the 45-minute opera, sometimes "worked havoc for the continuity. Occasional lyric phrases--reminiscent of Puccini--and short motives were woven into the score, which is chiefly distinguished by its economy and taste". A performance of *I pagliacci* followed Freer's opera.

679 GILMAN, Lawrence. **Women in modern music**, *Phases of*
bd   *modern music* (New York: Harper, 1904) 93-101.
Departs from George P. Upton's *Woman in music* (*WIAM* 177) and James Gibbons Huneker's *The eternal feminine* (*WIAM* 1028). Woman's failure to produce music of power and intensity is no doubt partly due to the "lack of urgent inspiration which she herself furnishes to her brother composers".

680 **Gives lecture on women composers**, *Musical America* XI/21 (2
ap   Apr 1910) 15.
Reports that Emma W. Hodkinson gave a lecture-recital on American women composers on 19 Mar., sponsored by the Women's Philharmonic Soc. in New York. The program included songs, piano music, and works for violin and piano by Mary Turner Salter, Clara Anna Korn, Florence Newell Barbour, Dora Becker, Amy Cheney Beach, and Gena Branscombe. Salter, Korn, Barbour, and Becker participated in the performances.

681 GOETSCHIUS, Percy. **Mrs. H.H.A. Beach** (Boston: A.P.
bm   Schmidt, 1906) 134 p. *Illus., music, list of works.*
A tribute to Amy Cheney Beach including 1) an overview of her early career and compositions, 2) extensive quotations from contemporary reviews of her works in all genres, and 3) a list of works by opus number up to 1906. "How completely the sex question (in its popular form) vanishes out of the scrutiny of Mrs. Beach's music might easily be demonstrated by a recital of some of her works before a discriminating audience, under substitution of a fictitious name, without sex clue".

682 HALE, Philip. **With musicians. Women in the list of**
an   **symphony makers**, *Boston Morning Journal* 4 Nov 1896, 9.
Discusses Amy Cheney Beach's symphony in E minor, op. 32 (*WIAM* 1370) given a première performance by the Boston Symphony Orchestra on 30 Oct., and reviews the activity of women as symphonists in Europe. Although Hale thinks the slow movement of the Beach symphony is too long, he finds much to admire in the other movements. "The only trace of woman" in the work is a certain boisterousness, which Hale thinks is the result of the composer's feeling that she must be "virile at any cost".

683 **Handel and Haydn Society gives reception to distinguished**
an   **woman composer of music**, *Boston Globe* 25 Oct 1935, 30.
The Handel and Haydn Soc. gave a reception for Amy Cheney Beach following a retrospective concert of Beach's smaller works by the Manuscript Soc. at the New England Conservatory. The composer reminisced about her long association with Boston musical organizations, which began at the age of 8 when her mother--a singer in the chorus of the Handel and Haydn Soc.--took her to her initial performance sponsored by the society. Subsequently the society gave the première of Beach's Mass in E-flat major, op. 5 (*WIAM* 1316). As another "first", Beach performed as a pianist for the first time with the Boston Symphony Orchestra at age 17.

684 H.A.S. **At 74, Mrs. Beach recalls her first critics**, *Musical*
ap   *Courier* CXXIII/10 (15 May 1941) 7.
An interview with Amy Cheney Beach, who will soon make her annual pilgrimage to the MacDowell Colony in Peterborough, N.H. Since 1921 practically all of her compositions have been inspired by summers spent at the colony. Despite her age--"which she is not ashamed to admit"--Beach is still alert to opportunities for composition. Her first critics were her mother and her husband; both were merciless, but also extremely supportive of her work.

685 HIPSHER, Edward Ellsworth. **American opera and its com-**
bf   **posers**. With a new intro. by H. Earle JOHNSON (New York: Da Capo, 1978) 478 p. $29.50. *Illus., bibliog., index.*
A reprint of the 1934 edition (Philadelphia: T. Presser). This history of opera in the United States aims to bring recognition to Americans as opera composers and includes sections about the following women who were active early in the 20th c.: Adeline Carola Appleton, Eleanor Everest Freer, Shirley Graham, Edith Noyes-Greene, Celeste D. Heckscher, Abbie Gerrish-Jones, Kathleen Lockhart Manning, Lucille Crews Marsh, Mary Carr Moore, Constance Faunt Le Roy Runcie, Jane Van Etten, and Harriet Ware. Biographical information for the composers, synopses of plots, and casts of characters together with the names of the singers who created the roles at first performances are included. Eleanor Everest Freer's advocacy of American opera and her work with the American Opera Soc. are discussed.

686 **How the woman composer is coming to the front**, *New York*
an   *Press* 18 May 1913, IV-8. *Illus.*
Discusses the activities of the following women composers: Marion Bauer, Gena Branscombe, Mabel Wheeler Daniels, Jessie L. Gaynor, Margaret Ruthven Lang, Caro Roma, Emma Roberto Steiner, and Harriet Ware.
                                                    (*Laurine Elkins-Marlow*)

687 HUGHES, Edwin. **Outlook for the young American com-**
ap   **poser, The**, *Etude* XXXIII/1 (Jan 1915) 13-14.
An interview with Amy Cheney Beach upon the composer's return from her European sojourn. 1) The American composer should go abroad to experience European musical life. There is a tremendous respect for music in Europe that is almost impossible to convey to persons who have never been outside the United States. 2) American orchestras and performers don't give the native composer a fair place on their programs, although the women's clubs have accomplished an enormous amount in popularizing American works. 3) It seems unlikely that Indian and Negro melodies will figure importantly in the future development of composition in the United States.

688 HUGHES, Rupert; ELSON, Arthur. **American composers**
bm   (rev. ed.; Boston: Page, 1914) 582 p.
A revised edition of *Contemporary American composers* (*WIAM* 690). Presents 3 supplementary chapters by Arthur Elson that report on the continuing activity of composers included in Hughes's earlier book, as well as on the activity of newly-emerging composers who were considered significant in 1914. The following women, among others, are represented with brief information about their compositions: Amy Cheney Beach, Gena Branscombe, Mabel Wheeler Daniels, Helen Hopekirk, Margaret Ruthven Lang, Grace Marshall, Marguerite Melville, Mary Carr Moore, Edna Rosalind Park, Mary Turner Salter, Harriet Ware, and Lola Carrier Worrell.

689 HUGHES, Rupert. **Women composers**, *Century Magazine* LV/5
ap   (Mar 1898) 768-79.
"It has, then, taken men whole centuries to learn music. They do not yet seem able to write it well in isolated communities without the benefits of association with old and new masters, and the chance for the publishing of ambitious work to a competent audience. America, through pilgrimage to Europe, is only now giving hope of a national school of music. Women have been, as a sex, just such an isolated community". Among Americans, the work of Amy Cheney Beach, Mary Knight-Wood, Margaret Ruthven Lang, Elisa Mazzucato, and Clara Kathleen Rogers is cited.

690 HUGHES, Rupert. **Women composers, The**, *Contemporary*
bd   *American composers* (Boston: L.C. Page, 1900) 423-41. *Port., facsim.,*
      music.
The works of Amy Cheney Beach and Margaret Ruthven Lang--described respectively as "markedly virile" and "supremely womanly"--are discussed in some detail with an emphasis on Beach's *Festival jubilate, op. 17* (*WIAM* 1305), her Mass in E-flat major, op. 5 (*WIAM* 1316), and the songs of both composers. Irene Baumgras and Mary Knight-Wood are also considered. The author of this pioneer work on American music contends that "it is impossible for a rational mind to deny that the best work done in the arts by women is of better quality than the average work done by men".

691 **In memoriam. Mary Turner Salter** (n.p.: S. Salter, 1939) 60 p.
bm   *Port.*
Contains 1) an autobiographical sketch by the song composer, 2) excerpts from reviews and letters about her performances as a singer and her compositions, and 3) poems which she wrote and set herself. Mary Turner Salter (1856-1938) was born in Peoria, Ill. to musical parents who had recently moved from Portland, Me., bringing a piano among their belongings. As a youngster she was far more interested in making up tunes at the piano than in practicing, and she also showed vocal promise at an early age. Her father had ambitions for her in opera, and accordingly she attended the New England Conservatory in her late teens. Salter launched a successful career as a singer in Boston and elsewhere in the eastern United States, but then abandoned it in 1893 because of conflicting domestic and professional interests that had prevailed since her

marriage in 1881. She continued to teach voice however, and she began composing songs. In addition to her work in music, Salter raised 5 children.

692 JACOBS-BOND, Carrie. **Music composition as a field for**
ap   **women,** *Etude* XXXVIII/9 (Sept 1920) 583-84. *Illus.*
Noting that only a few years ago the prevalent opinion was that women should only be homemakers, Carrie Jacobs-Bond discusses her success as a song composer in Chicago. She moved to Chicago from a small town in Michigan and turned to composition when the death of her husband left her practically penniless. She has found women's clubs to be extremely supportive of her work both as a composer and a performer of her own songs. Also the assistance of friends has been invaluable: e.g., David Bispham and Ernestine Schumann-Heink have frequently performed her music, while Jessie Bartlett Davis loaned Jacobs-Bond the $250 that enabled her to publish her first book of songs. The composer recalls that when she began as a song writer she couldn't afford to hire someone to write verses, and therefore she wrote the texts herself. She also designed the cover pages for her publications. Jacobs-Bond and her son started their music publishing business in a spare bedroom of their home; it grew steadily and now is located in the business district on Michigan Avenue. Jacobs-Bond feels strongly about the need for bringing music to the general public, and accordingly she proposes 1) programs by symphony orchestras that will attract the uninitiated, and 2) the availability of seats for concerts and opera performances at nominal prices.

693 **Kate Vannah, American composer,** *Musical Courier* LXIV/12
ap   (20 Mar 1912) 41. *List of works.*
Kate Vannah's songs have world-wide fame both in the home and the concert hall. Her 2 most celebrated songs are *Goodby, sweet day!* (*WIAM* 1951) and the *Cradle song.* The composer graduated from St. Joseph's Col. in Emmittsburg, Md., and she subsequently studied in Boston with Ernst Perabo and George W. Marston. A list of her most successful songs is included.

694 KING, Edith Gertrude. **Mrs. Beach,** *Musician* IV/9 (Sept 1899)
ap   334-35.
This biographical sketch of Amy Cheney Beach's career to 1899 appears together with a similar sketch for Cécile Chaminade and brief stylistic considerations of the music of the 2 composers by Percy Goetschius. Information on Beach's working habits as a composer is included.

695 KING, Mrs. A.T. **Women as composers,** *Musical Courier*
ap   LXXIX/7 (14 Aug 1919) 8-9.
Presents a brief history of women as composers in Europe together with a list of approximately 150 contemporary American women composers. "It is so few years, comparatively speaking, since the work of women composers has been treated seriously, that the progress made, or rather the position of women today in the world of composition is a remarkable one".

696 KINSCELLA, Hazel Gertrude. **How Mary Turner Salter**
ap   **composes her songs,** *Musical America* XXIX/18 (1 Mar 1919) 29.
      Illus.
An interview with Mary Turner Salter and Sumner Salter in their home in Williamstown, Mass., where the couple spends many hours reading piano duets together. Mary Turner Salter discusses the way in which she works and describes the genesis of *The sweet of the year, Pine tree,* and *The swan* (*WIAM* 1928). As organist at Williams Col., Sumner Salter has charge of the chapel choir. When he began in the position he found that there was very little appropriate music for men's voices, and so he "set himself the task of supplying it".

697 KORN, Clara Anna. **Women composers and the federation,**
ap   *Musical Courier* LV/6 (7 Aug 1907) 26.
The author replies to Mrs. John McCarthy's letter to the editor of *Musical Courier* (*WIAM* 708) and notes that it is an error to think that women are not writing for orchestra. Women do write orchestral music, and like men, they need performances. Women face a handicap as orchestral composers in that the practical experience which results from playing in an orchestra is difficult to obtain.

698 KROHN, Ernst C. **Missouri music** (New York: Da Capo, 1971)
bf   380 p. $32.50. *Index.*
A reprint of the 1924 edition *A century of Missouri music* (St. Louis: author) and selected essays by Krohn that appeared individually in different periodicals. *A century of Missouri music* includes information on the work of the following composers, among others: Jessie L. Gaynor, Constance Faunt Le Roy Runcie, and Frances Marion Ralston.

699 K.S.C. **Hearing for women composers of four cities,** *Musical*
ap   *America* XVIII/2 (10 May 1913) 32.
While suffragists were striving for the cause of political equality for women with a pageant at the Metropolitan Opera on 2 May, a concert sponsored by the Manuscript Soc. in New York offered recognition to American women composers. Songs and chamber music by Laura Sedgwick Collins, Susannah

Macaulay, Bertha Remick, Margaret Ruthven Lang, and Eleanor Everest Freer were performed.

700 K.S.C. **Our women composers find recognition in new cam-**
ap   **paign,** *Musical America* XXIV/6 (10 June 1916) 13. *Illus.*
Louise Mertens, contralto, and Lola Carrier Worrell, composer-pianist, will make an extensive tour next season in concerts featuring works by American women composers for women's clubs, women's colleges, and other organizations. Mertens notes that she has planned the venture because she is proud of the accomplishments of American women in composition and also because she feels that women's works are not as well-known as they should be. Songs by the following composers--among others--will be presented on Mertens and Worrell's programs: Amy Cheney Beach, Gena Branscombe, Mabel Wheeler Daniels, Carrie Jacobs-Bond, Margaret Ruthven Lang, Mary Turner Salter, and Kate Vannah.

701 LADD, George Trumbull. **Why women cannot compose**
ap   **music,** *Yale Review* VI/4 (July 1917) 789-806.
Women do not lack incentive or opportunity for composition, rather they lack native ability: women do not possess strength of will. Similarly in architecture, sculpture, and the pictorial arts women are unable to achieve "supremely high creations of the imagination". Singing and playing the piano and violin are viewed as proper spheres of activity for women in music.

→   LANDAUER, Bella. **My city 'tis of thee. New York City on**
      sheet music covers, see 284bm[46].

702 **Letter from Mrs. Beach, A,** *Etude* XVI/5 (Apr 1898) 100.
ap
In response to a request from *Etude* to write a column, Amy Cheney Beach declines, stating that she is too busy composing and practicing for occasional recitals. A brief biographical sketch of Beach is included along with favorable comments about her *Festival jubilate* , *op.* 17 (*WIAM* 1305) and her symphony in E minor, op. 32 (*WIAM* 1370), which was performed to good reviews on 12 Feb. 1898 by the Boston Symphony Orchestra. This article appears on the *Woman's work in music* page (*WIAM* 645).

703 **Lily Strickland,** *Musical Courier* LXIX/17 (28 Oct 1914) 32.
ap
Although she is still relatively young, Lily Strickland has published between 50 and 60 works, and she has 100 more compositions of various types in manuscript, including 3 operas. In the past 4 years since she has settled in New York, Strickland has grown to major status as a composer.

→   **Los Angeles, University of California Music Library. A**
      checklist of materials by and about women in American
      music, see 19bm[01].

→   **Los Angeles, University of Southern California Music**
      Library. A checklist of compositions in manuscript by Mary
      Carr Moore, see 20bm[01].

→   MACDONALD, Margaret I. **Greatest battles ever fought**
      are the silent ones fought by women, The. Some interesting
      facts about Miss Emma R. Steiner, see 1069bm[58].

704 **Margaret R. Lang's music. An afternoon of song and sym-**
ap   **posium,** *Brooklyn Daily Eagle* 20 Apr 1896, 9.
Margaret Ruthven Lang is "considered the foremost woman composer of the younger generation in America". At a private home in Brooklyn, baritone John A. Dempsey gave a brief biographical sketch of the composer's life and performed a number of her songs. Others who have performed Lang's works are Theodore Thomas, Arthur Nikisch, Max Bendix, and the Boston Cecilia Soc. She is the daughter of Benjamin J. Lang of Boston, who taught Arthur Foote, MacDowell, and George W. Chadwick as well as his daughter.

705 MATHEWS, William S.B. **American composer and American**
ap   **concert programs, The. A study,** *Musician* VIII/6 (June 1903)
      204-05.
Discusses the activity of American composers in the areas of popular, salon, and art music, noting that it is most difficult for the native musician to succeed in art music due to the overwhelming German influence. Amy Cheney Beach is listed as a successful art music composer. The author wishes that there was a greater emphasis on "light" orchestral music in the United States. Unfortunately "our excellent women and preachers have done all they could to bar out the lighter orchestras, such as those that give concerts in beer gardens in Germany". This narrow elitism--Mathews argues--has proved detrimental.

706 MATHEWS, William S.B. **Masters and their music, The**
bf   (New York: AMS, 1971) 262 p. *List of works.*
A reprint of the 1898 edition (Philadelphia: T. Presser). Discusses music from

Bach to Liszt in the first section and American and more modern composers in the second. Amy Cheney Beach is the only woman considered, and the only composer for whom a list of major works is not included. Mathews comments about Beach's work: "These are not women's compositions. The musical spirit is unquestionable, the technique of developing ideas is that of a well-trained artist, and the writing for the instrument [the piano] that of an accomplished pianist. At the same time, she makes no effort to be boisterous and to prove that she is a man by the brute force necessary to play her works". Mathews adds that Beach's music deserves a wider audience.

707 MCARTHUR, Alexander. **Women and originality**, *Etude* XX/
ap 2 (Feb 1902) 53.
1) Critics have become so used to berating the efforts of women composers that a hearing, if it is given at all, is biased. 2) While Anton Rubinstein's dictum on women in music is disheartening (*A conversation on music*, *WIAM* 1168), women composers must cultivate effort and confidence. From confidence comes originality.

708 MCCARTHY, Mrs. John. **National Federation of Musical**
ap **Clubs**, *Musical Courier* LV/5 (31 July 1907) 26.
In this letter to the editor, Mrs. John McCarthy argues that it is wrong for the National Federation of Music Clubs to give a $1000 prize for the best orchestral composition by an American since women do not write for orchestra. A better solution would be to award $500 to both the best orchestral piece and the best choral work, thus matching the $500 awards for the best song and the best piano composition. Since the music clubs are chiefly female in membership, they should not reward men at the expense of women.

709 MERRILL, E. Lindsay. **Mrs. H.H.A. Beach. Her life and**
dd **music** (PhD diss., Theory: U. of Rochester, 1963) vii, 303 p. *Music, bibliog., list of works.*
Includes a biography, general information about Amy Cheney Beach's compositions, stylistic analysis of a selected group of her works--with an emphasis on harmonic analysis--and a psychological summary. Beach is viewed as a composer of extraordinary talent, whose *oeuvres* are uneven, and who never developed originality of expression. Her compositions without piano are "less sentimental", more straightforward, and better able to stand the test of time. Merrill suggests that if Beach's life had not been so comfortable financially, and if she had had to struggle, perhaps her music would be bolder. The biographical section makes note of Beach's work for charity and with music clubs, her assistance to young artists, and her work as an educator through her teaching pieces.

→ MERZ, Karl. **Woman in music**, *see* 157ac[25].

710 M.J.C. **American opera in first performance**, *Musical Digest*
rm VIII/23 (22 Sept 1925) 7.
Discusses the first San Francisco performance of Mary Carr Moore's opera *Narcissa* (*WIAM* 1457), with Alice Gentle in the title role. *Narcissa* is the first opera to be written, staged, and directed by an American woman. Excerpts from reviews in San Francisco newspapers are included.

→ MÖLLER, Dr. Heinrich. **Can women compose?**, *see* 158ap[25].

711 **More women composers**, *Musical Courier* LXXIX/13 (25 Sept
ap 1919) 7.
A supplement to Mrs. A.T. King's *Women as composers* (*WIAM* 695). Lists about 80 additional women composers active at the time, chiefly as writers of songs and piano music.

712 **M.R. Lang, composer of *Heavenly noël***, *Boston Globe* 31 May
an 1972, 40.
Reports the death of Margaret Ruthven Lang (1867-1972), who was a life-long resident of Boston. Lang initially studied composition with her father, Benjamin J. Lang, and she published her first work at age 12. She wrote over 200 songs and was best-known for her Christmas cantata, *The heavenly noël*, *op. 57* (*WIAM* 1357), and her *Dramatic overture*, which in 1881 became the first work by a woman to be performed by the Boston Symphony Orchestra. On Lang's 100th birthday the Boston Symphony Orchestra played a special concert of her music.

→ **Mrs. Crosby Adams, teacher of wide reputation, dies**, *see* 811ap[57].

713 **Mrs. General Hancock's *Te Deum laudamus***, *American Art*
ap *Journal* XXXXIII/20 (5 Sept 1885) 309.
A brief description of the *Te Deum laudamus* for male chorus, orchestra, and organ, written by Mrs. General Hancock and performed at Brighton Beach, N.Y. on 27 Aug. 1885. The anthem is Mrs. Hancock's only published work, perhaps her only composition to date. Without apologies and "whatever may exist in the minds of musical thinking people regarding the merits of the musical compositions of women", the work stands on its own. "We hope to see

other ladies emulate Mrs. General Hancock's worthy example, and we may yet boast of brilliant representatives of musical composition among the women of America".

714 **New composer, A**, *New York Times* 22 June 1876, 5.
an
Describes a performance at Chickering Hall in New York of 12 pieces by Corinne Young. The music was written with the intention of adding words and eventually assembling it as an opera. Young's piano score was orchestrated by the conductor and performed competently by the orchestra. The music, entertaining if not especially original, was judged good material for an opéra comique. This article appears as part of a regular column headed *Amusements*.

715 **New composer interests celebrities. Works of Fannie C.**
ap **Dillon, of Los Angeles, to be brought out by leading firm**,
Musical America VIII/14 (15 Aug 1908) 9.
Teresa Carreño considers Fannie Charles Dillon one of the "finds" of her recent American tour, and as a result of Carreño's endorsement together with those of Ignace Jan Paderewski and Harold Bauer, the John C. Church Co. will publish some of Dillon's music. Dillon spent 1901-06 in Berlin, where she studied piano with Leopold Godowsky and composition with Heinrich Urban, Rubin Goldmark, and Hugo Kaun.

716 NILLSON, Victor. **American composer [sic] hold honor**
rm **place. Chadwick and Beach compositions heard at symphony**
orchestra concert, *Minneapolis Journal* 15 Dec 1917, 5.
Reports that at a recent concert by the Minneapolis Symphony Orchestra, 3 works from the "New England Symphonists' School" were performed: George W. Chadwick's *Melpomene overture*, Amy Cheney Beach's symphony in E minor, op. 32 (*WIAM* 1370), and her piano concerto in C-sharp minor, op. 45 (*WIAM* 1369). The New England composers' style--while not American in its cultural roots--produces works which have in common a deep cultural earnestness that is a "mark of character as much as personal distinction". Beach's symphony is full of fire and proves her genuine talent in her ability to strike free and carry out her purpose in the spirit of each movement. The piano concerto is more technically advanced than the symphony; the recurrence of the Largo theme in the final Allegro is supreme among its many points of beauty.

717 **Noteworthy personalities: Mrs. Jessie L. Gaynor**, *Music*
ap [Chicago] XVI (July 1899) 297-98.
The artistic success of Jessie L. Gaynor as a composer and teacher of singing, piano, and harmony has been phenomenal. Nearly 70 of her songs have been published; her children's songs perhaps represent her best work.

718 **Obituaries: Lily Strickland**, *Musical America* LXXVII/9 (Aug
ap 1958) 32.
Lily Strickland died 6 June 1958 at age 71. She held a degree from the Inst. of Musical Art in New York, and she was a member of the American Soc. of Composers, Authors, and Publishers and the National League of American Penwomen. Among her compositions are 3 operas, a symphonic suite on Negro themes, and the *Charleston suite* for piano.

719 PARKER, H.T. **Symphony concert, The. The rich harvest of**
rm **a rare afternoon**, *Boston Evening Transcript* 3 Mar 1917, II-11.
A recent concert by the Boston Symphony Orchestra, Carl Muck conducting, included a performance of Amy Cheney Beach's piano concerto in C-sharp minor, op. 45 (*WIAM* 1369), with the composer as soloist. The Beach work "has withstood 17 years of neglect by almost all pianists but her, yet it holds stoutly beside many a concerto written, applauded, and far more warrantably forgotten within that time". Parker believes that the concerto is Beach's outstanding piece.

720 **Pearl Curran, 65, author, composer**, *New York Times* 17 Apr
an 1941, 23.
An obituary for the composer (1875-1941), who published more than 40 songs and had several recordings to her credit. *Pain*, *Dawn*, and *Life* were among her best known songs and were sung by Caruso, Anna Case, and other noted singers. Curran typically wrote her own texts. In recent years she had her own radio program that was broadcast nationally.

721 PEELER, Clare P. **American woman whose musical message**
ap **thrilled Germany**, *Musical America* XX/24 (17 Oct 1914) 7.
An interview with Amy Cheney Beach on board ship during the composer's return to the United States after a 3-year sojourn in Europe. The outbreak of war precipitated her return. During the first year abroad she could not work; she was recovering from the double loss of her mother and her husband. Then came performances of the violin sonata in A minor, op. 34 (*WIAM* 1270), string quartet, op. 70, symphony in E minor (Gaelic), op. 32 (*WIAM* 1370), and the piano concerto in C-sharp minor, op. 45 (*WIAM* 1369), with the result that Beach began composing again. She is delighted with the enthusiastic critical response that her music received in Germany. For the 1914-15 season Beach is planning a nationwide concert tour of about 30 performances.

722 PEYSER, Herbert F. **Believes women composers will rise to**
ap **greater heights in world democracy**, *Musical America* XXV/25
(21 Apr 1917) 3.
Amy Cheney Beach believes that the continued improvement of the general
status of women will advance women in composition. The composer is also an
enthusiastic pianist on tour, although she may possibly give up traveling in a
few years times to devote herself to a large, sustained effort in composition-
-e.g., an opera, if she can find the right libretto. At the present time she
composes mainly between June and September in New Hampshire, where she
is totally free of distractions. Performances of Beach's works in Germany
during the years she lived abroad prior to the war are discussed.

→ **Philadelphia, Free Library of Philadelphia, Fleisher Collec-**
tion. A checklist of source materials by and about women in
American music, *see* 35bm[01].

723 PRESLEY, Carl. **Historical opera of the Northwest**, *Musical*
rm *America* XVI/1 (11 May 1912) 5. *Illus.*
Reviews the première of Mary Carr Moore's opera *Narcissa* (*WIAM* 1457) in
Seattle, conducted by the composer. A synopsis of the 4-act opera--the libretto
of which is by Sarah Pratt Carr, the composer's mother--is included.

→ RALSTON, Jack. **Treasures from the collection of the**
Institute for Studies in American Music, *see* 39bm[01].

→ REIS, Claire. **Composers in America**, *see* 63bf[05].

724 R.M. **Mme. Carreño will play her compositions**, *Musical*
ap *America* XII/8 (2 July 1910) 7. *Illus.*
The following piano compositions by Fannie Charles Dillon will be featured by
Teresa Carreño in her concert programs during the 1910-11 season: *Eight*
descriptive pieces, op. 20 (*WIAM* 1403), the variations in F-sharp minor, and the
sonata in C minor--which Dillon has dedicated to Carreño. Dillon "bids fair to
become a living refutation of the opinion maintained in some quarters that
women cannot rise to as great heights in creative work as men".

→ RUBINSTEIN, Anton. **Conversation on music, A**, *see*
1168bm[58].

725 SELDEN, Catherine. **Woman before the music tribunal**,
ap *Music* [Chicago] VII (Feb 1895) 322-33.
An answer to *Is the musical idea masculine?* by Edith Brower (*WIAM* 654).
Selden argues that women's failure to develop their creative faculties is due to
lack of encouragement and opportunity. Women have been isolated from the
larger interests of men; their typical work in the home has tended to limit
intellectual development. Selden is optimistic about the future because of the
response by contemporary women to expanding opportunities for their gender.

→ SMITH, Eva. **Woman as composer**, *see* 451ap[50].

→ **Souvenir programme. Emma R. Steiner testimonial comme-**
morating her golden anniversary as American composer and
orchestra director, *see* 1201bm[58].

726 STANLEY, May. **How Fay Foster wrote** *The Americans*
ap *come*, *Musical America* XXIX/7 (14 Dec 1918) 5. *Illus.*
Although Fay Foster didn't want to write a war song because she feels that
many composers are profiteering from the war, Elizabeth A. Wilbur's poem *The*
Americans come gripped her imagination. Fay's song with the same title
(*WIAM* 1627) is one of the most popular of the day; many singers include it on
their programs, choruses of music clubs are singing it, and orchestras and
military bands are playing it in arrangements. The song has also been arranged
as a musical recitation, and translations of the text into French and Italian have
been made. Fay notes that she takes great pleasure in presenting the song in
concerts for soldiers. She performs in military camps 3-4 times a week.

727 STRATTON, Stephen S. **Woman in relation to musical art**,
ap *American Art Journal* XLIV/21-23 (13-27 Mar 1886) 355-56; 373-
74; 391-92.
A feminist discourse disputing the many assertions made about the inferiority
of women in music. Discusses women in musical performance, indicating that
they have always played instruments and scoffing at such prejudices as that
against female violinists. Considers women as composers, admitting that no
woman has achieved the stature of Händel or Beethoven. Stratton credits
society with suppressing the natural abilities of women, particularly through
the institution of matrimony. Having himself compiled a list of hundreds of
women composers from the 12th c. to the present, Stratton deplores the paltry
listings of *Grove's dictionary of music and musicians* and criticizes Fanny
Raymond Ritter for her apologetic tone with regard to women composers.
Ritter has "suggested that woman should be the *genuine* unpretending amateur,

the assistant and befriender of artists". In fact, women have composed in every
genre and will achieve higher stature with increased freedom and education.

→ **Strictly woman's concert**, *see* 1210ro[58].

→ **Successful women song writers**, *see* 454ap[50].

728 SUTRO, Florence Edith. **Woman's work in music**, *Vocalist*
ap VIII/5 (May 1894) 161-65.
An answer to George P. Upton's *Woman in music* (*WIAM* 177). Sutro cites the
names of active women composers and argues that despite the restraints of
social convention, the burdens of housework, and unequal opportunity in
higher education, women have demonstrated themselves capable of original
work as composers. "The dogma that great intellectual effort, strong reasoning,
and original production are exclusively within the capacity and the proprietary
rights of men is a doctrine, which it must be remembered, has been laid down
by men".

729 SUTRO, Florence Edith. **Women in music and law** (New
bc York: Author's Publishing, 1895) 47 p. *Illus.*
A pamphlet containing 3 articles by the author: *Woman composers*, a reprint of
Woman's work in music (*WIAM* 728) by Sutro; *Musical compositions by women*;
and *Women in law*. *Musical compositions by women* is a catalogue of the music
collection that Sutro assembled for an exhibition at the Atlanta Exposition in
Sept.-Dec. 1895. The collection consisted mainly of contemporary songs and
piano music and included works by the following American composers, among
others: Marie Townsend Allen, Amy Cheney Beach, G. Estabrook, Josephine
Gro, Helen Hood, Lydia Kunz-Venth, Adelina Murio-Celli, Anita Owen, Clara
Kathleen Rogers, Hattie P. Sawyer, Fanny M. Spencer, Hattie Starr, Ida
Walker, and Agnes Zimmermann.

730 SUTTONI, Charles. **American Symphony: [Mrs.] H.H.A.**
rm **Beach concerto**, *High Fidelity/Musical America* XXVI/7 (July
1976) MA 29-30. *Illus.*
Reviews Amy Cheney Beach's piano concerto in C-sharp minor, op. 45 (*WIAM*
1369) performed by Mary Louise Boehm with the American Symphony
Orchestra in Hempstead, N.Y.

731 SYFORD, Ethel. **Margaret Ruthven Lang**, *New England Mag-*
ap *azine* XLVI/1 (Mar 1912) 22-23. *Illus.*
A daughter of the musician Benjamin J. Lang, Margaret Ruthven Lang studied
piano, violin, and music theory for 2 years in Munich and also studied
orchestration in the United States with George W. Chadwick and MacDowell.
Several of her large-scale works have been performed by the Boston Symphony
Orchestra under Arthur Nikisch and by the Theodore Thomas Orchestra in
Chicago. The following songs by Lang are discussed: *A song of the lilac, op. 41*
(*WIAM* 1818), *Summer noon, op. 37, no. 4* (*WIAM* 1814), *Somewhere, op. 40,*
no. 1 (*WIAM* 1814), *Tryste noël, op. 37, no. 5* (*WIAM* 1833), *A thought, op. 37,*
no. 1 (*WIAM* 1830), *An Irish love song, op. 22* (*WIAM* 1779), *Song in the*
songless, op. 38, no. 4 (*WIAM* 1816), and *Nonsense rhymes and pictures, op. 42*
(*WIAM* 1799).

→ THOMAS, Jessie. **Women composers hold conference at**
Chautauqua, *see* 2060ap[66].

→ TOWERS, John. **Woman in music**, *see* 65bm[05].

732 TUBBS, Arthur L. **Philadelphia operatic society in Mrs.**
ro **Heckscher's ballet**, *Musical America* XXIII/14 (5 Feb 1916) 52.
Reviews the first performance of Celeste D. Heckscher's "pantomine-ballet",
Dance of the Pyrenees, by the Philadelphia Opera Soc. In its original form the
work was an orchestral suite, which has been played by the Philadelphia and
other leading orchestras. Heckscher is a Philadelphia-based composer.

733 TUTHILL, Burnet Corwin. **Mrs. H.H.A. Beach**, *Musical*
ap *Quarterly* XXVI/3 (July 1940) 297-306. *List of works.*
A review of Amy Cheney Beach's life and works, occasioned by the new
interest in American music as championed by Howard Hanson and others.
Although Tuthill finds an appraisal difficult because Beach's style is passé and
romanticists are generally out of esteem, he concludes her best works are those
composed "when she is away from the hypo-romantic piano". The following
compositions receive individual consideration: *Theme and variations for flute*
and string quartet, op. 80 (*WIAM* 1274), string quartet, op. 70, symphony in E
minor (Gaelic), op. 32 (*WIAM* 1370), and piano concerto in C-sharp minor, op.
45 (*WIAM* 1369).

→ UPTON, George. **Woman in music**, *see* 177bm[25].

734 UPTON, William Treat. **Art song in America** (New York:
bf Johnson Reprint, 1969) 279, 41 p.
A survey of art-song literature and composers in the United States beginning

with the 18th c. to 1930. The songs of Alice Barnett, Amy Cheney Beach, and Clara Kathleen Rogers are discussed with some attention to detail, while the work of numerous other women within the genre is mentioned. This reprint of the 1930 edition (Boston: O. Ditson) includes the author's *A supplement to art-song in America, 1930-38* (also O. Ditson, 1938).

→   V.B.S., **Beloved composer of childhood melodies, A**, *see* 847ap[57].

735   W.H.H. **Noteworthy program of Mrs. Heckscher's composi-**
ap   **tions**, *Musical America* XVIII/19 (22 Mar 1913) 19.
Reports on a concert of works by Celeste D. Heckscher at Aeolian Hall in New York as "the first orchestral concert ever given by an American woman composer". The program included Heckscher's *Dance of the Pyrenees* and the *Asiatic dance* from her opera *The flight of time* as well as songs with orchestra.

736   WIJEYERATNE, James de S. **A perfect day**, *Musical moments*
bd   (London: W. Reeves, [1923]) 110-13.
Although Carrie Jacobs-Bond showed promise early and received a fine education in music, she would not have made music her profession had her husband not died, leaving her and her young son in a precarious financial situation. David Bispham helped Jacobs-Bond to gain recognition by including her songs on his programs, with the composer as accompanist. Jacobs-Bond believes "the multitude needs music--perhaps even more than the cultured few", and she works to supply that need. Her *A perfect day* (*WIAM* 1743) is one of the most successful songs in recent times.

737   **Women as composers**, *Musical Herald* [Boston] IV/1 (Jan 1883)
ap   8.
This editorial argues that since women are now demanding and receiving as thorough a musical education as men, some "thorough women composers" will emerge in the near future.

738   **Women composers honored by Bridgeport musical club**,
ap   *Musical Courier* LXXX/8 (19 Feb 1920) 24.
Describes a program of works by Amy Cheney Beach, Cécile Chaminade, Agatha Backer-Grøndahl, and Augusta Holmes given by the Wednesday Afternoon Musical Club of Bridgeport, Conn.

→   **Worthwhile American composers**, *see* 2067ap[66].

57   Literature about women as educators, patrons, and members of music clubs

739   **Adelina Murio-Celli**, *American Art Journal* XXXIX/25 (13 Oct
ap   1883) 461-62.
Summarizes the career of prima donna Adelina Murio-Celli. Following her studies, which included several years at the Paris Conservatory under Auber, Murio-Celli began a career which took her all over western Europe, to Athens, Constantinople, and finally to Mexico. Since 1867 she has lived in New York, teaching and composing. Emma Juch was one of her pupils.

740   A.F.W. **Choral music to dominate Cleveland season**, *Musical*
ap   *America* X/23 (16 Oct 1909) 28-29.
Four amateur societies, the Mendelssohn Club, the Harmonic Club, the Singers' Club with 110 of the best male voices, and the Rubinstein Club with 95 women directed by Mrs. Seabury Ford, will perform during the 1909-10 season. The Rubinstein Club will give 2 concerts, one featuring the violinist Maud Powell. Among the works this club will perform is *The mermaid* composed by one of its members, Fannie Snow Knowlton.

741   A.I.H. **Musical department at Vassar College, The**, *Dwight's*
ap   *Journal of Music* XXX/9 (16 July 1870) 276.
Describes the courses in music offered at Vassar Col. Although secondary to literary and scientific studies, music is taught well and seriously. Frédéric Louis Ritter, director of the music program, gives free voice lessons to any who are interested. The college library now has the beginnings of a music literature collection. The Cecilia Soc., organized by the students, presents soirées of music by the masters and lectures on music. "Some of the young ladies have attempted to express their thoughts upon various musical subjects in the form of essays, and have received great encouragement from their teachers".

→   ALDA, Frances. **Men, women, and tenors**, *see* 862bm[58].

→   **Alma Clayburgh, soprano, 76, dead**, *see* 871an[58].

742   **Amateur musical club one of Brooklyn's best-trained choral**
ro   **organizations**, *Brooklyn Daily Eagle* 30 Jan 1894, 5.
The Brooklyn Amateur Musical Club, directed by Harry Rowe Shelley, is composed of women with voices of solo calibre. Last night's concert was of uncommon merit and included a lullaby by George W. Chadwick and Cécile Chaminade's *St. John's eve*. "In every instance the club showed promptitude of attack, firmness of tone and harmony, and careful regard for time".

743   BATCHELLOR, Daniel. **Woman's sphere in music teaching**,
ap   *Etude* (*WIAM* 74) 319.
Discusses the teaching of piano to children as woman's proper sphere. Most parents engage a woman teacher in preference to a man not because she is a better teacher but because her fees are lower. While this is not right--and work of equal merit should receive equal remuneration--the fact remains that women are better suited than men to teaching youngsters.

744   BAUER, Emilie Frances. **Among some clubs**, *Etude* XX/6
ap   (June 1902) 216.
Reports on the activities of various women's choral groups, including their participation in performances with men's choral groups. The women's Polyhymnia and the men's Apollo Club, both of Saginaw, Mich., will be part of a "huge presentation" of Mendelssohn's *Elijah, op. 70*. The Musical Club of Peekskill, N.Y. gave a performance of the same composer's *A midsummer night's dream, op. 61*. The Choral Union of Topeka, Kan. has engaged the Chicago Symphony Orchestra for its June festival. This article appears on the *Woman's work in music* page (*WIAM* 645).

745   BAUER, Emilie Frances. **What the club has done for music**
ap   **in America**, *Etude* XX/12 (Dec 1902) 464.
Discusses the wide dissemination of serious music in the United States in recent years, and credits the women's music clubs for much of this progress. The clubs are responsible for the huge growth in music publishing and for the fact that concert-goers have outgrown their interest in bravura pieces only. The clubs benefit music teachers directly by giving them contact with one another, and also indirectly by educating mothers who will, in turn, be more sympathetic to the need for proper musical training for their children. This article appears on the *Woman's work in music* page (*WIAM* 645).

746   BAUER, Emilie Frances. **Women's Philharmonic Society of**
ap   **New York, The**, *Etude* XX/4 (Apr 1902) 148.
One of the largest music clubs in the United States is the Women's Philharmonic Soc. of New York. Recent activities of the society include the sponsoring of concerts at low prices in tenement districts of the city, classes in violin and piano for youngsters, and a children's orchestra. This article appears on the *Woman's work in music* page (*WIAM* 645).

747   **Benefit of individual work**, *Etude* XVII/1 (Jan 1899) 4.
ap
This lead article on the *Woman's work in music* page (*WIAM* 645) reports that it has become fashionable for writers to "sneer, in a mild or covert way", at women in music clubs who have undertaken study programs for which they have no previous training. The editors of *Etude* note that literature for research is just as available to women as to men, and they applaud the activity of women in the clubs.

748   BIRGE, Edward Bailey. **History of public school music in**
bm   **the United States** (Boston: O. Ditson, 1928) 296 p. *Bibliog., index.*
Discusses the contributions of Julia Ettie Crane in Potsdam, N.Y., and Emma A. Thomas in Detroit as music educators beginning ca. 1885. Considers the work of Eleanor Smith as editor of the *Modern music series*, which published song material for elementary school students beginning in 1898, and also the work of Helen Place as editor of *School Music*, a journal founded in 1900 to disseminate new ideas in education within the field of music. In 1900 Frances Elliott Clark and Mary Regal introduced music appreciation courses in high schools in Ottumwa, Iowa and Springfield, Ill., respectively. Later in 1911 Clark joined the educational department of Victor Talking Machine Co. and worked to develop records for classroom use. In 1916 in the schools of Westbury, N.J., Mabel Bray supervised the first "music memory" contest to spur intelligent listening among students. Subsequently the contest became popular and widespread. Numerous women were active as officers and members of national associations of teachers as these began to be organized in the 1890s.

749   BRAINE, Robert. **Keeping up with the times**, *Etude* XV/12
ap   (Dec 1897) 329.
Reports that the standards of piano teaching are rising rapidly in the United States, and urges the large numbers of teachers who are "either standing still in their art or, what is worse, retrograding" to revitalize their work in teaching by giving their own concerts and keeping abreast of the latest compositions and literature on music. Unqualified women who have turned to teaching because of financial necessity are finding it harder every year to make a living in music. These women should not be too proud to resume piano lessons themselves.

750 BROWN, Cora Stanton. **Amateur musical club**, *Etude* XII/11
ap (Nov 1894) 249.
Brown announces a regular *Etude* column to be devoted to the work of women in music clubs throughout the United States and invites clubwomen to report on their successful--as well as their unsuccessful--undertakings. This column continued in *Etude* through May 1895 (XII/5).

751 BROWN, Cora Stanton. **Musical society, The**, *Etude* VIII/10
ap (Oct 1890) 154.
Discusses the formation of the author's club--the Ladies' Musical Soc.--in Schenectady, N.Y. The club aims to advance the members' knowledge about music and musicians and to create more of a general interest in music in the community. Every 8 weeks the club gives a recital for members and their friends, at which members perform pieces they have prepared during earlier meetings.

752 BURGESS, Ruth Payne. **Teresa Carreño as a teacher**, *Etude*
ap XLVIII/11 (Nov 1930) 779-80, 826. *Illus.*
A former pupil of Teresa Carreño's discusses the pianist's technique and methods of teaching. Burgess began work with Carreño in New York in 1888. After Carreño relocated in Berlin in 1889, she sent Burgess "letter lessons".

753 C.A. **Woman--the potent influence in our musical life**, *Musical*
ap *America* XII/22 (8 Oct 1910) 3-4.
"The American woman has decided that musical cultivation contributes to the breadth of view and happiness of the people, and while mere man is indifferent she is working early and late in organizing musical clubs, in getting members for them, in building or leasing club houses or rooms, in completing the arrangements by which famous artists shall appear in communities large and small, [and] in interesting husbands, brothers, and sons in concerts of all kinds. Women are not only active in their own clubs, but exert a colossal influence on the musical life of their communities in the organization of festivals and orchestras, and in the support of other organizations of general musical interest, such as singing societies. The National Federation of Music Clubs is the most potent force in American music".

→ CALDWELL, Belle. **How musical sororities perpetuate**
artistic ties, *see* 2076ap[67].

754 **Cecilia night. The opening concert of the society's season**
ro **successful**, *Brooklyn Daily Eagle* 15 Dec 1892, 5.
The Cecilia Women's Vocal Soc. of Brooklyn, conducted by William Neidlinger, gave its first concert of the season at the Amphion Academy. The musical selections, while not particularly difficult, were well done. Both audience and choir were colorfully dressed.

755 **Cecilia's Vocal Society**, *Brooklyn Daily Eagle* 13 Jan 1894, 7.
ro
The Cecilia Women's Vocal Soc. of Brooklyn under the direction of John Hyatt Brewer sang works by Charles Harford Lloyd, Bertram Luard-Selby, and John Ebenezer West. The program also included solo vocal and instrumental selections. A reception, supper, and dance followed the concert.

756 **Chat with pupils, A. For young ladies**, *Etude* II/5 (May 1884)
ap 74-75.
1) The events of the Civil War era proved that it is clearly wrong to allow young women to reach maturity without a marketable skill. 2) "Not one charm in a woman's character is lessened one degree by a thorough and masterly attainment in music".

757 **Clara Baur, noted educator, is dead**, *Musical America* XVII/7
ap (21 Dec 1912) 1.
Educated at the Stuttgart Conservatory and in Paris, Clara Baur (ca. 1842-1912) emigrated from Germany to the United States, and in 1867 she founded the Cincinnati Conservatory--the first school of its kind in the city. At the conservatory she headed the vocal department, and her students included many who became prominent teachers. Baur was a patron of the Cincinnati Symphony Orchestra.

758 CLARK, Frances Elliott. **Story of American music clubs,**
ap **The**, *Etude* XL/3 (Mar 1922) 161-62. *Illus.*
Traces the background of the music club in the United States as an outgrowth of the singing school and discusses the formation of the National Federation of Music Clubs in 1897. A brief biography of the author as a noted educator and dedicated club woman is included.

759 COLEE, Nema Wethersby. **Mississippi music and musicians**
bm (Magnolia, Miss.: Mississippi Federation of Music Clubs, 1948) 146
p.
Presents a sketch of musical life in Mississippi, and discusses the development

of the Mississippi Federation of Music Clubs. Contains short biographies of numerous women musicians, including the educator Weenonah Poindexter.

760 CORNISH, Nellie C. **Miss Aunt Nellie. The autobiography**
bm **of Nellie C. Cornish**. Ed. by Ellen Van Volkenburg BROWNE
and Edward Nordhoff BECK . With a foreword by Nancy Wilson
ROSS (Seattle: U. of Washington, 1964) 283 p. *Illus., index.*
Born in 1876 in Nebraska, Nellie C. Cornish was educated in convent schools in Portland, Oreg. and Seattle and studied piano with Ebenezer Cook, a pupil of Lowell Mason, and Alfred Venino, a pupil of Theodor Leschetizky. At the age of 14 Cornish began teaching piano for $.50 a lesson. A highpoint of her teens was a concert by Ysäye in Portland. Tired from years of giving lessons in people's parlors, in 1900 Cornish opened a studio in Holyoke Block, a community of artists in Seattle. In 1904 she traveled to Boston to study the Fletcher Music Method with Evelyn Fletcher-Copp, and in 1911 she studied with Calvin Brainerd Cady in Los Angeles. She opened the Cornish School of Music in Seattle in 1914 with her own faculty on a commisssion basis, and at the end of the first season the school already had 85 pupils. After World War I Cornish introduced Dalcroze eurhythmics and folk dancing at the school, and eventually she expanded the curriculum to cover all of the performing and plastic arts. Cornish retired as director in 1939.

761 COURTNEY, Louise George. **Women's Philharmonic Soci-**
ap **ety of New York, The**, *Musical Courier* XXXVIII/17 (26 Apr
1899) 12.
This letter to the editor reports on the recent formation of a musical society for women in New York, with offices at Carnegie Hall. 200 members are already enrolled, and these include established concert artists and teachers, students, and musical amateurs. The society is divided into vocal, piano and organ, string, composition, and music literature departments. General meetings on Saturdays will feature musical programs together with papers on musical subjects. The possibility of developing the following organizations within the Women's Philharmonic Soc. is under consideration: a choral club, string orchestra, and piano-amateur club, a teachers' sodality, students' advisory board, loan fund, and concert bureau.

762 DOUGLASS, Ada B. **Plea for more serious work among the**
ap **so-called music clubs, A**, *Etude* XVI/2 (Feb 1898) 36.
Within the last year the number of music clubs has jumped to 225 partly as a result of the encouragement of Theodore and Rose Fay Thomas. Choral clubs are particularly well represented among the new additions. The author warns, however, against the curse of dilettantism and urges clubs to work with more seriousness of purpose. This article appears on the *Woman's work in music* page (*WIAM* 645).

763 DYKEMA, Peter W. **Musical fraternities and the develop-**
ac **ment of music in America**. *Studies in musical education, history,*
and aesthetics 27 (Oberlin, Ohio: Music Teachers National Assoc.,
1933) 81-93.
Describes early music fraternities, which were organized to raise professional standards and maintain cultural bonding "for the manly musician and the musicianly man". Notes that 2 fraternities--Pi Kappa Lambda and Phi Sigma Nu--admitted women. Discusses 3 all-female organizations: 1) Mu Phi Epsilon, which was founded in 1903, 2) Sigma Alpha Iota, which was also founded in 1903 and became a purely professional organization in 1922, and 3) Delta Omicron International Music Fraternity, which was formed in 1909 for "women of culture and refinement".

764 **E. Fletcher-Copp, a music educator**, *New York Times* 2 Jan
an 1945, 19.
An obituary for Evelyn Fletcher-Copp, who headed the Fletcher Music Method School in Boston between 1893 and 1938. Fletcher-Copp worked to humanize the process of teaching, and children as young as age 7 learned not only to play well, but also to write simple compositions under the Fletcher Method. The educator lectured widely in the United States, Canada, and Europe about her work.

765 **Early music in Minnesota** (Minneapolis: Northwestern National
bm Life Insurance Co., [1949?]) 20 p.
Discusses the singing Andrews family, who owned the first instrument in the state--a reed organ--in 1862, and who later were active as a touring concert and opera company. Considers the work of the following organizations in which women were prominent: 1) the Thursday Musicale of Minneapolis, founded in 1892, 2) the Schubert Club of St. Paul, established in 1882, 3) the Matinee Musicale of Duluth, and 4) the St. Olaf Lutheran Choir, which was organized by F. Melius Christiansen in 1903 at St. Olaf Col.

766 **Early music teachers**. Ed. by Cornel LENGYEL. *History of music*
bm *project* 6 (San Francisco: Works Progress Administration, 1940) 149
p. (typescript). *Port., bibliog., list of works, index.*
Discusses the work of musicians as teachers in San Francisco during the 2nd half of the 19th c., at which time these pioneers had to combat both public

indifference to music and artistic isolation. The following women are considered: 1) Margaret Blake-Alverson, a voice teacher and choral director, who was also known as the "first prima donna of California", 2) Giovanna Bianchi, who traveled to San Francisco from Italy with an opera troupe and stayed to establish a school for vocal studies, 3) Inez Fabbri, née Agnes Schmid, who settled in San Francisco in 1872 and founded a conservatory, and 4) Louisa Marriner-Campbell, a singer from Maine, who came to California in the 1860s and later traveled abroad to study with Mathilde Marchesi and Pauline Viardot-Garcia.

767   Elmira Female College, *Dwight's Journal of Music* XXX/12 (27
ap   Aug 1870) 303-04.
Describes the music department and facilities of Elmira Female Col. in Elmira, N.Y., and praises the directress, Laura A. Wentworth, as an administrator, singer, and teacher. The school has a large new organ, pianos, and "dumb" pianos. Commencement week performances included piano solos, vocal ensembles and choruses, and opera overtures arranged for organ and pianos--16 and 8 hands.

768   Endowed club memberships, *Etude* XXVI/5 (May 1908) 336.
ap
Reports that the initiation fees and dues of many women's music clubs put membership beyond the reach of women with limited means. Endorses the example of the St. Cecilia Club in Grand Rapids, which offers 8 free memberships--typically to young musicians--each year.

769   Erminia Rudersdorff: a great musical personality, *Etude*
ap   XXXIV/5 (May 1916) 373-74.
Erminia Rudersdorff came to the United States at Patrick S. Gilmore's invitation, in order to sing at the World Peace Jubilee of 1872 in Boston. This event was a fitting triumph for the close of her career as a performer. Subsequently she settled in Boston and was a highly regarded teacher of voice. Mary Turner Salter, Emma Cecilia Thursby, Teresa Carreño, and Lillian Bailey were among her most important students. Although she began as an operatic singer in Europe, it was in oratorio and other concert work that Rudersdorff achieved her greatest fame. When Gilmore engaged Rudersdorff in 1872 for the Boston festival, his offer of $3500 a week plus expenses was unprecedented at that time for any comparable engagement in Europe.

770   Evelyn Fletcher-Copp at home, *Musical Courier* LVI/21 (20 May
ap   1908) 27.
An interview with the originator of the Fletcher Music Method for children, which has gained many followers, particularly in the Boston area. In the early 1890s Fletcher-Copp demonstrated her teaching techniques in classes at the New England Conservatory at the express invitation of George W. Chadwick. Since then more than 600 teachers have trained in the Fletcher Method. Fletcher-Copp holds a summer school in Eliot, Me., where new teachers--as well as experienced teachers interested in brushing up--gather to study the method, piano, and voice.

771   Farewell reception and concert for Cappiani, *Musical Courier*
ap   LIV/23 (5 June 1907) 25.
Discusses a reception given by the Women's Philharmonic Soc. of New York for Luisa Cappiani, the vice-president of the society and a distinguished vocal teacher. Amy Fay, president, spoke in behalf of the society in tribute to Cappiani for her valuable service. Cappiani will spend 18 months in Switzerland, resting and also teaching.

772   FAY, Amy. Amateur musical clubs, The, *Etude* V/12 (Dec
ap   1887) 180.
Discusses the evolution of a women's club in Chicago over the preceding 10 years. Originally 4 women met to play orchestral works in arrangements for 2 pianos, 4 hands. Subsequently a larger membership decided to give concerts featuring members with a fee for admission, to rent rooms for the club's quarters, and to hire concert artists on tour to appear at club events. In the early years the club's members were chiefly pupils of 2 leading piano teachers in Chicago--Regina Watson and Emil Liebling--and a great rivalry existed between the 2 groups. As the membership increased, the old rivalry and the old sociability disappeared.

773   FAY, Amy. Woman music-teacher in a large city, The, *Etude*
ap   XX/1 (Jan 1902) 1, 14.
Discusses the principal difficulties a woman music teacher faces in New York at the turn of the 20th c. First, she has difficulty attracting students, because most of the music student population are young girls and girls find it more interesting to study with men teachers. Secondly, the woman teacher who must cope with missed lessons usually ends up not being paid, since parents in general do not pay women teachers in advance as they do men teachers. Should the teacher manage to arrange for make-up lessons, payments are frequently long deferred. A third hardship faces the city teacher as a result of the prevailing tendency of city students to discontinue study during the summer months. Since this period may extend for a time as long as April to late October, by the end of this interval the music teacher suffers from a shortage of funds and cannot afford to advertise for students in the coming year.

(*Sr. Margaret W. McCarthy*)

774   FAY, Amy. Women and the Music Teachers Association,
ap   *Musical Courier* XLVI/24 (17 June 1903) 30.
In this letter to the editor, Amy Fay notes that women are hardly represented on the program for the forthcoming convention of the Music Teachers National Assoc., nor do they figure among the association's officers. Women seem able only to take part in social gatherings and contribute to the expenses of running the association by advertising in its journal. Instead--Fay suggests--women should either give their monies to the National Federation of Music Clubs or establish a Women's Music Teachers National Assoc., inviting men to contribute by advertising.

**775   FINK, Ella Louise. Building teachers who make music live
ap   for the young is steadfast ideal of Julia Crane**, *Musical
America* XXXI/12 (17 Jan 1920) 37. *Illus.*
In 1884 Julia Ettie Crane established a music department within the Normal School of Potsdam in Potsdam, N.Y., with the belief that music was as important as mathematics or any other subject in the elementary school curriculum. Subsequently the demand for trained teachers and supervisors of music became strong, and in response she founded the Crane Normal Inst. of Music. The unique feature of Crane's school is that in training to be teachers the students learn teaching techniques through practical experience at the elementary and high schools in Potsdam. Except for some teaching elsewhere at summer schools, Crane has spent her entire career as an educator furthering her own ideals in her native community. She studied with Luisa Cappiani and Henry Wheeler in the United States and Manuel Garcia in Europe.

**776   F.L.C.B. Show beauty of Negro folk songs in unique concert
ap   in St. Paul**, *Musical America* XXVIII/14 (3 Aug 1918) 10. *Illus.*
Reports on a program of Negro songs and spirituals performed by the Folk Song Coterie in St. Paul. This group of black women banded together to study Negro songs and spirituals as well as art music by contemporary black composers, e.g., Harry T. Burleigh and Robert Nathaniel Dett.

**777   Formation of the National Federation of Women's Musical
ap   Clubs. Mrs. Theodore Sutro's work for this association**,
Musical Age XXI/6 (17 Mar 1898) 6.
Reports that for the June 1897 convention of the Music Teachers National Assoc. Florence Edith Sutro organized a women's department with 14 sub-departments. One of the subdepartments represented music clubs, and during the June convention 52 delegates from the club subdepartment convened, established the National Federation of Music Clubs, and elected Sutro president. Subsequent attempts to broaden the membership of the federation have allegedly been sabotaged by Rose Fay Thomas, who tried to establish a similar federation 4 years ago. Thomas has contended that since Sutro is not president of one of the constituent clubs, she is an outsider. The editors of *Musical Age* endorse Sutro.

778   Frances E. Clark, *Musical America* LXXVII/9 (Aug 1958) 32.
ap
An obituary for Frances Elliott Clark (1860-1958), the noted music educator. She married John Clark at the age of 14, and after his death in 1880 she resumed her education, including college. Between 1888 and 1911 Clark taught in various schools in the Midwest. In 1905 she began to develop educational possibilities for recorded music, and in 1911 the Victor Talking Machine Co. hired her to set up an educational department, which she headed until 1947.

**779   F.W. Psychology and scientific accuracy, key to Dunning
ap   System**, *Musical America* XXXII/24 (9 Oct 1920) 15. *Illus.*
When Carre Louise Dunning presented herself as a piano student to Theodor Leschetizky in Vienna, he told her that she didn't have the temperament of a concert artist, but that she could become a great teacher if she devoted her energies to that end. Dunning returned to Chicago and began to develop the Dunning System, which uses games to help children learn to read and play music.

780   GATES, W. Francis. Woman in the case, The, *Etude* XXIII/10
ap   (Oct 1905) 406.
The female piano teacher of good standing is better paid than the public school teacher of equal position, namely $800 a year versus $550. It is the "underbidding of her own sex, the teaching for $.40 and $.50 a lesson that so many unprepared and prideless young women indulge in, that cheapens the rates of instruction".

781   HALLOCK, Mary. Women's music clubs, *Musician* XVI/9
ap   (Sept 1911) 581, 632.
Discusses the newly revitalized Women's Music Club of Columbus, Ohio under the leadership of Ella May Smith, and commends the National Federation of Music Clubs for providing a uniform study plan available to all constituents--since "it would be quite impossible for individual clubs to do this service for themselves". Urges club leaders to take more risks in engaging relatively unknown artists for concerts at lesser fees, rather than relying upon established performers.

→   HANCHETT, Dr. Henry. **American girls' temperament in relation to music study**, *see* 1008ap[58].

782   HARDING, William G. **Advance of music in Columbus,**
ap   **Ohio,** *Musical Courier* LIV/6 (6 June 1907) 38.
The Women's Music Club has had a renaissance under its new president, Ella May Smith. During Smith's initial year as president, the club grew to include 850 associate members, purchased a Steinway piano, and arranged concerts by Ernestine Schumann-Heink, David Bispham, and Arthur Farwell. The 2nd year under her leadership the club had 1200 and in the 3rd year 2500 associate members. As a result of a fund-raising program, the club has been able to purchase and install an organ in its meeting rooms.

783   HELD, Ernst. **Women's amateur musical clubs,** *Etude* XII/4
ap   (Apr 1894) 80.
During the past 20 years "critical music knowledge has spread in wider and deeper waves through the American people" in large part due to the women's amateur music clubs that have sprung up throughout the country. Various suggestions for running a club are included.

784   HUBERT, Philip G., Jr. **Why not try lecture-recitals?,** *Etude*
ap   XI/12 (Dec 1893) 254.
Lecture-recitals have become a fad in the last 2 years. The idea originated with Jessie Pinney Baldwin, one of the most valued teachers of piano on the faculty of the National Conservatory in New York and formerly a brilliant concert pianist. Partly in self-defense, Baldwin began giving such lectures to her students in 1885. Subsequently she found the lecture-recital to be lucrative, and she addressed a variety of audiences in the metropolitan area.

785   JERVIS, Perlee V. **Practical use of music clubs, The,** *Etude*
ap   XI/12 (Dec 1893) 258.
Most women drop music entirely after marriage because taking care of the home and children absorbs all their attention and leaves them too tired to practice without an additional stimulus. The music club--with its monthly or semi-monthly recital by club members--can provide the additional stimulus.

786   JOHNSON, Frances Hall. **Mrs. Charles Dudley Warner,**
bd   *Musical memories of Hartford* (Hartford: Witkower's, 1931) 239-54.
Illus.
Susan Lee Warner was born in New Haven, Conn., grew up in New York, and married Charles Dudley Warner in 1856. In 1860 the couple settled in Hartford, where Susan Lee Warner became a leader in the musical life of the community for the next 60 years. A pianist, she gave performances of the "finest music" for her friends and family at her "Wednesday evenings". Her "Monday mornings" featured visiting concert artists as well as young pupils. Warner worked with the Memmon Club in Hartford, which sponsored concerts by soloists and chamber groups on tour, and when the club disbanded in 1900 she devoted much energy instead to the Hartford Philharmonic Orchestra, for which she served as vice-president for many years. During World War I Warner gave benefit concerts to aid war relief work. Her friends and associates included Fannie Bloomfield-Zeisler, Helen Hopekirk, Helen Keller, and Harriet Beecher Stowe.

787   **Juliette Crosby Adams: composer, teacher, educator,** *Musi-*
ap   *cian* XXI/4 (Apr 1916) 199-200. *Illus.*
Music education in the United States owes much to the women who have been identified with the pursuit for several generations, especially for their work with children. The career of Juliette A. Graves Adams, wife of Crosby Adams, is discussed.

788   **Kate S. Chittenden honored on eightieth birthday,** *Musical*
ap   *Courier* CXIII/16 (18 Apr 1936) 24.
Together with Albert S. Parson, Kate S. Chittenden developed the Synthetic Method for Piano Playing and founded the Metropolitan Col. of Music in New York. She has a fine record as organist at the Calvary Baptist Church in New York and has taught piano for 62 years.

789   KORN, Clara Anna. **Reply to Amy Fay, A,** *Musical Courier*
ap   XLVI/25 (24 June 1903) 27.
In this reply to Amy Fay's *Women and the Music Teachers Association* (*WIAM* 774), Clara Anna Korn argues that women have very little to gain by isolating themselves from men in music or in club work. Whenever women accomplish anything creditable, men are not backward in displaying their appreciation. For instance, a number of male students study with competent women teachers.

790   KORN, Clara Anna. **Women as teachers,** *Etude* XVII/3 (Mar
ap   1899) 68.
In this lead article on the *Woman's work in music* page (*WIAM* 645), Korn argues that women are more successful pedagogues than men in the training of young people because from their earliest years women are taught to make much of small things and to observe minute details carefully. Also, women are trained early in self-control and do not display their tempers in teaching.

791   KRAMER, A. Walter. **Bertha Feiring Tapper: altruist,**
ap   *Musical America* XXII/21 (25 Sept 1915) 9. *Illus.*
Reports the death of the noted pianist and teacher of pianists. A simple, private funeral was held at Bertha Feiring Tapper's summer home in Blue Hill, Me. and was attended by members of her immediate family and 2 lifelong friends, Franz Kneisel and Horatio Parker. Tapper (1859-1915) was born in Norway and studied piano with Agatha Backer-Grøndahl. Subsequently she studied at the Leipzig Conservatory with Carl Reinecke, Hans Richter, Oscar Paul, and Louis Maas. She married Maas and came to the United States with him in 1880. After Maas's death she joined the faculty of the New England Conservatory, and she also taught at the Inst. of Musical Art in New York. For the past 5 years she had been teaching privately in New York and Boston. Tapper was an indefatigable worker and was known for her devotion to her pupils' futures. She had broad tastes in music and even prepared Leo Ornstein in his own music for recitals he gave during the 1914-15 season. As a pianist she was a distinguished performer, appearing frequently with the Kneisel and Olive Mead quartets. Tapper made many visits to Theodor Leschetizky over the years for study, and she was one of the few people he permitted to observe him giving lessons. Tapper also edited the piano works of Grieg for a recent American publication.

792   KROEGER, Ernest R. **Progress of the Middle West in**
ap   **musical art, The,** *Etude* XVII/5 (May 1899) 145.
In his evaluation of the progress of the Middle West, Kroeger notes the important contribution of the music clubs which have helped to raise musical taste. He also comments that the choral societies are the "nucleus of the musical life of any community".

793   KROEGER, Ernest R. **Changes in piano teaching in fifty**
ac   **years.** *Studies in musical education, history, and aesthetics* 23 (Hartford: Music Teachers National Assoc., 1929) 121-28.
Considers various schools of piano playing that were introduced in the United States between the 1870s and the 1920s by Americans as a result of their studies in Europe with the following masters: Ludwig Deppe, Theodor Leschetizky, Rudolph Breithaupt, Tobias Matthay, and Leopold Godowsky. Amy Fay was a pupil of Ludwig Deppe and Liszt, Julie Rivé-King studied with Liszt, and Fannie Bloomfield-Zeisler finished her training with Theodor Leschetizky. A list of about 80 outstanding and progressive teachers in the United States in the 1870s-90s includes Teresa Carreño, Kate S. Chittenden, and Amy Fay.

794   **Largest women's musical club in world claimed by Colum-**
ap   **bus, O.,** *Musical Courier* LXXII/17 (27 Apr 1916) 45.
Discusses Ella May Smith's multiple activities in music in Columbus, Ohio on the occasion of her retirement from 13 years as president of the Columbus Women's Music Club. Smith was an organist, teacher of singing and piano, composer, writer on music, and one of the organizers of the Edgar Stillman Kelley Publication Soc. for the propagation of orchestral music by American composers. Smith also organized charity concerts and at one time headed an amateur opera troupe.

795   LOCKE, Ralph P. **Charles Martin Loeffler: composer at**
ap   **court,** *Fenway Court* 1974, 30-37. *Illus., port., facsim.*
Isabella Stewart Gardner was not only a leading Boston art collector--her Italianate palazzo known as Fenway Court and its treasures are now a major museum--but she also was an important patron of music. She supported the career of composer Charles Martin Loeffler, organizing and underwriting performances of his music at Fenway Court--notably the first version of *A pagan poem* in 1904. Loeffler, in return, encouraged Gardner's interest in French symbolist poetry and directed her musical taste away from Wagner and toward Bach, Fauré, and d'Indy. In this unusually late case of old-fashioned private patronage, Loeffler often suffered from Gardner's requests for private performances, but in their last years together patron and musician enjoyed a quiet, trusting friendship.   *(Author)*

796   LOCKE, Ralph P. **Letters from Bayreuth,** *Fenway Court* 1975,
ap   19-26. *Illus., facsim.*
Isabella Stewart Gardner, one of Boston's leading art-collectors and patrons of music, was a devoted Wagnerian, remaining so even after her main allegiance shifted to the new French school around 1900. Her papers and travel scrapbook document her interest in the works of Wagner, notably her first trip to Bayreuth in 1889. Among the "leaves" which she brought back from Bayreuth are photos and clippings of the festival and the dying Liszt, a pressed ivy leaf from Wagner's grave, and a letter from the composer to tenor Joseph Tichatscheck (27 Sept. 1858), here reproduced for the first time in its entirety in German and English.   *(Author)*

→   LOMBARD, Louis. **Music as a breadwinner for girls,** *see* 1065ac[58].

797   **Madame Valeri's faith and work,** *Musical Courier* LXV/7 (14
ap   Aug 1912) 19.
Delia M. Valeri is internationally known as a teacher of voice, and she is

regarded as one of the best coaches for Italian opera in the United States. Valeri trained as a pianist and singer in Rome and elsewhere in her native Italy. She regards her teaching as a mission, and during the summer months she continues to work with some students from her New York studio at her cottage on Fire Island, N.Y. Valeri comments that "in America everybody wants to sing, even those without voices; this creates a fertile field for charlatan teachers".

798   MANNES, David. **Music is my faith** (New York: W.W.
bm   Norton, 1938) 270 p. *Illus.*
In this autobiography, David Mannes--violinist and music educator--devotes several chapters to the work of his wife, Clara Damrosch Mannes (1869-1948), the daughter of Leopold Damrosch, who trained as a pianist with Busoni among others. After their marriage in 1898, Clara and David Mannes gave recitals together in the United States and abroad, and Clara taught piano. For 15 years the Mannes were directors of the Music School Settlement in New York on the Lower East Side, and subsequently in 1916 they decided to establish their own school. They intended that the Mannes School of Music should educate the talented amateur as well as the professional.

799   **Mary Wood Chase, pianist and teacher,** *Musical Courier* LVI/
ap   24 (10 June 1908) 29.
Discusses Mary Wood Chase's long association with Chicago musical life as a teacher and a pianist. In 1907 Chase opened studios in the Fine Arts Building, and with a corps of assistant teachers she has enjoyed one of the busiest seasons in her career.

→   MATHEWS, William. **American composer and American concert programs, The. A study,** *see* 705ap[56].

→   MCCARTHY, Mrs. John. **National Federation of Musical Clubs,** *see* 708ap[56].

800   MCCONATHY, Osbourne. **Music in our public schools in**
ac   **1876 and since.** *Studies in musical education, history, and aesthetics* 23 (Hartford: Music Teachers National Assoc., 1929) 186-97.
Discusses developments in pedagogy since Lowell Mason's innovations in Boston in the early 19th c., the growth of summer schools, high school music and school orchestras, community singing, and the first national conference of music supervisors in 1907. Women cited for their significant contributions to music education include: Frances Elliott Clark, director of the Education Department of Victor Talking Machine Co. since 1911, Agnes Moore Fryberger in St. Louis, Mary Regal of New York, Edith Rhetts in Detroit, and Margaret Lowry in Kansas City. Contemporary women composers writing for children include Jessie L. Gaynor and Eleanor Smith.

801   MCELROY, Peter J. **Forty-nine years of making beautiful**
an   **music together,** *New York Post* 15 June 1952, 6.
Henry Holden Huss and Hildegarde Hoffmann Huss have resided at their home on East 150th Street in Bronx, N.Y. since their marriage in 1904, leaving it from time to time for concert tours that have taken them all over the world. On the occasion of his 90th birthday, Henry Holden Huss is being honored with entire programs of his compositions. The pianist-composer still teaches classes of young teachers at Steinway Hall in New York, and his wife--at age 75--still teaches voice. Highlights of their careers are reviewed.

802   MCKNIGHT, Frank T. **National Federation of Musical**
ap   **Clubs,** *Musical Courier* L/25 (21 June 1905) 22-26. *Illus.*
Reports on the 4th annual convention of the National Federation of Music Clubs in Denver, June 1905. The 4-day meeting included concerts that featured the songs of Mary Turner Salter and performances by the Olive Mead Quartet. The federation has not made more rapid progress because many of the larger music clubs have yet to see the virtue of affiliation. One valuable service the clubs provide is sponsoring foreign artists on tour. Otherwise many of these musicians could not afford to come to the United States.

803   **Men versus women teachers,** *Etude* XIII/2 (Feb 1895) 33.
ap
There are many deficient music teachers, and these are by no means all women--as some people charge. However, because women often look upon teaching as temporary work, they do not typically take an interest in the welfare of the profession as men do. Individual teachers should be induced to rise to a higher level of competency, and the general public should be better educated about the qualifications for good teaching.

→   MERZ, Karl. **Woman in music,** *see* 157ac[25].

804   **Mme. Cappiani on singing at the Trade School for Girls,**
ap   *American Art Journal* LXXXIII/7 (21 Nov 1903) 115.
Luisa Cappiani addressed the National Federation of Music Clubs at a meeting in Utica, N.Y. on the desirability of including music in the curriculum of trade schools for girls. Attending the meeting as a delegate from the Women's

Philharmonic Soc. of New York, Cappiani cited her own organization as being successful in disseminating love for music and good fellowship among its members. Choral singing in trade schools for girls could foster the same aims.

805   **Mme. Seiler's School of Vocal Art in Philadelphia,** *Dwight's*
ap   *Journal of Music* XXXVII/10 (18 Aug 1877) 78-79.
An assessment of the educational aims and methods of the School of Vocal Art in Philadelphia, headed by the German-born voice teacher, Emma Seiler. Before opening the school in 1875, Seiler was a successful teacher with 30 pupils. The school, which now has 89 pupils, trains singers as musicians, not just vocalists, and the course of study also includes musical style and acting.

806   MOORE, Aubertine Woodward. **Music and the married**
ap   **mistress of home,** *Etude* XXI/8 (Aug 1903) 308.
"Since so many persons have turned their eyes towards a public career for women, there has come to be an almost total disregard for the mission of music in the home, where it is fully as much needed as in public life". Trained women musicians can find fulfillment in the home in molding the tastes of their children.

807   **Mothers and music,** *Etude* XXVII/4 (Apr 1909) 232.
ap
Advocates the introduction of tuneful nursery rhymes to infants by their mothers, the presence of mothers at their children's piano lessons, and the assistance of mothers to their children during practice sessions.

808   **Mozart Society's brilliant concert,** *Musical Courier* LXIX/25
ap   (23 Dec 1914) 13. *Illus.*
The chorus of the New York Mozart Soc. gave a concert at the Hotel Astor on 16 Dec. 1914. The ladies' chorus of 125 voices was conducted by Walter Henry Hall and sang works by Eduard Lassen, Victor Harris, and Horatio Parker. A special feature of the program was the première of Deems Taylor's cantata *The highwayman*. "The work of the chorus under Mr. Hale is remarkably fine".

809   **Mozart Society's capable president,** *Musical Courier* LXVIII/19
ap   (13 May 1914) 39. *Illus.*
Founded in 1909 with 100 members by Adelaide McConnell, the Mozart Soc. in New York now has 800 members and a choral club of 150 women. McConnell, the society's president, has given freely of her time and financial support--the latter totaling $25,000 over 5 years. McConnell's excellent taste has been exhibited in her choices of artists for concerts sponsored by the society.

810   **Mrs. C. Stoeckel, patron of music,** *New York Times* 6 May
an   1939, 17.
Together with her husband Carl Stoeckel, Ellen Battell Stoeckel (1851-1939) founded the Norfolk Music Festival in Connecticut in 1902. She also founded the Litchfield County U. Club, which awarded scholarships for college education, and she financed private music lessons for promising students as well. In 1906 Mrs. Stoeckel gave Yale U. a valuable library of music, containing autograph MSS by Sibelius and 40 volumes of orchestral scores. She was also active in philanthropies in non-music areas.

811   **Mrs. Crosby Adams, teacher of wide reputation, dies,** *Diapa-*
ap   *son* XLIII/1 (Dec 1951) 20.
An obituary for "the grand old lady of music" (1858-1951), who died in Nashville, S.C. on 9 Nov. Juliette A. Graves Adams studied piano as a young woman, and at age 21 she became a teacher of piano at Ingham Col. in Le Roy, N.Y., where she began work on her teaching pieces. Three months after her marriage, her husband, a steam engineer, suffered severe burns. Adams then resumed her career in music, moved to Chicago, and with her husband established a music school. She also was an organist for a church in Oak Park, Ill. In 1913 the couple relocated in Montreat, N.C. Adams won a wide reputation as a composer of songs, choral works, and piano music. Her teaching materials are well-known.

→   **Mrs. Joseph F. Knapp. The American song and hymn composer,** *see* 443ap[50].

812   **Mrs. Noble McConnell and the Mozart Society,** *Musical*
ap   *Courier* LXVI/4 (22 Jan 1913) 57. *Illus.*
Four years ago Adelaide McConnell withdrew from the Rubinstein Club in New York--of which she had been president for some time--and founded the Mozart Soc. The society's chorus now numbers 135 women. As a girl McConnell was a serious student of piano. In 1905 she graduated from the New York Medical Col. for Women and founded a clinic for women and children in which she is also active. Recent activities of the Mozart Soc. under McConnell's leadership are discussed.

813   **Mrs. Theodore Sutro dead. She was active in musical,**
an   **charitable, and social circles,** *New York Times* 28 Apr 1906, 11.
Née Clinton in England, Florence Edith Sutro (1865-1906) was the first woman

to receive the degree of Doctor of Music from the Grand Conservatory in New York. She graduated in 1891 as class valedictorian. Subsequently Sutro was the founder and the first president of the National Federation of Music Clubs.

814   Musical melting pot in the maze of Greenwich Village,
ap   *Musical America* XXVII/25 (20 Apr 1918) 49-50. *Illus.*
Describes the activities of the Greenwich House Music School, a part of the Greenwich Village Settlement House, in a neighborhood of many recent immigrants in New York. The school was founded and is run by women for the purpose of acclimating neighborhood children and their parents to the United States through the "mutual understanding of music". The teachers are not trying to make musicians of all their students, but rather intelligent concert-goers.

815   Musical women honor Fay, *Musical Courier* LII/11 (14 Mar
ap   1906) 48.
The Women's Philharmonic Soc. of New York gave a musicale and reception in honor of its president, Amy Fay. Luisa Cappiani spoke in tribute to Fay for her work with the society and her help to struggling young artists by offering them scholarships to cover their studies with her. Fay became friendly with d'Indy when they were both studying in Berlin. D'Indy liked her *Music study in Germany* (*WIAM* 970) so much that he helped to bring about the translation of the book into French.

816   National Federation of Musical Clubs, *Musical Courier* L/20
ap   (17 May 1905) 13.
The Music Club of Greenfield, Mass. is embarked on a 7-year course of study divided as follows: 3 years for German music from Bach through Wagner, 1 year for French, Russian, Scandinavian, and Polish music, and 1 year each for Italian and English music. In the future the club plans to study the complete works of selected composers. Three or 4 times per year the club holds musicales and invites the public free of charge.

817   National Federation of Musical Clubs. Board meeting, *Etude*
ap   XVI/11 (Nov 1898) 316-17.
Provides information on activities of the National Federation of Music Clubs, whose current membership is 20,000. Advises constituent clubs to 1) organize circulating libraries of books and music, 2) turn private concerts by well-known artists into public fund-raising events, and 3) avoid the mistake of the Musical Art Club (locale unspecified), which presented on the same program the Kneisel Quartet and its own ladies' choral group. This article appears on the *Woman's work in music* page (*WIAM* 645).

→   **Noteworthy personalities: Mrs. Jessie L. Gaynor,** *see* 717ap[56].

818   Obituary. Jeanette Thurber, *Musical America* LXVI/1 (10 Jan
ap   1946) 24.
Reports the death of the distinguished patron of music at the age of 96. Thurber (1850-1946) first came to prominence when she founded and financed the National Conservatory of New York and the American Opera in 1885. The conservatory was the first music school in the United States to admit highly talented pupils free of charge. Thurber persuaded Dvořák to head the conservatory between 1892 and 1895 during his stay in the United States.

819   PEDERSON, Anne S. Program for the biennial meeting of
ap   **the National Federation of Musical Clubs,** *Etude* XVII/4 (Apr
    1899) 100.
Describes the musical programs planned for the biennial meeting of the National Federation of Music Clubs in St. Louis on 5 May 1899. The Morning Choral Club of St. Louis assisted by the Dominant Ninth, a women's choral group of Alton, Ill., will perform. On May 7 there will be a special program by the combined choirs of St. Louis. This article appears on the *Woman's work in music* page (*WIAM* 645).

820   PERRY, Edward Baxter. Is marriage inimical to music? If
ap   **so, why?,** *Etude* XIV/12 (Dec 1896) 246.
Many women abandon music after marriage because their commitment was not strong initially. Indeed, music has been regarded and even taught as an accomplishment for women. Music clubs, which are being organized throughout the country, augur well as agents for change.

821   Plans and art of Mary Wood Chase, *Musical Courier* LIX/25
ap   (19 June 1907) 17.
Reports that Chase has resigned her position as director of the piano department at the Columbia School of Music in Chicago and has refused offers from other prominent Chicago schools in favor of devoting herself exclusively to independent studio work and her concert engagements. Chase's success as a teacher of teachers is widely acknowledged; her pupils are filling important positions throughout the country.

822   Press women hear music and wit, *Musical Courier* XLIX/22 (30
ap   Nov 1904) 33.

Discusses a recent meeting of the New York Woman's Press Club, which included a concert by the all-female Von Klenner Quartet. Reports that to an outsider the women's club movement is still "as complicated as an Oriental puzzle". While occasional humorists continue to poke fun at the idea of a women's club and old-fashioned husbands protest, the clubs "keep right on in their work of progress".

823   Programs of the National Convention of Women's Amateur
ap   **Musical Clubs held in Recital Hall, Music Hall Building,**
    World's Columbian Exposition, *American Art Journal* LXI/9 (10
    July 1893) 199.
The National Convention of the Women's Amateur Musical Clubs met in Chicago on 21-24 June. Programs for the 4 days included numerous papers on music topics and performances by club members of vocal, choral, and instrumental music. Rose Fay Thomas, who chaired the meeting, stated the aims of the convention: 1) to show the standards of "musical culture among the best class of American women in all parts of the country", 2) to demonstrate the quality of educational work done by women's amateur music clubs, and 3) to encourage the formation of additional clubs.

→   **Pupil of Robert Schumann, A,** *see* 1155ap[58].

824   PUPIN, A. **Ladies' piano club,** *Etude* XI/6 (June 1893) 127.
ap
Advocates the formation of women's music clubs by describing a ladies' piano club in an unspecified location. The club gives its members the opportunities to hear music by great composers, become acquainted with the lives of composers through reports and papers, gain freedom in playing before others, and benefit from each other's encouragement--especially those who are teachers.

825   PUPIN, A. Ladies' piano club and circulating musical
ap   **library,** *Etude* XI/8 (Aug 1893) 172.
Reports on the dedication of the meeting room, circulating library, and reading room of a ladies' piano club in an unspecified locale. Concludes that there is an immense advantage to both teacher and student in having handy access to a good library of music and music literature.

826   PUPIN, A. Timely warning, A, *Etude* XI/12 (Dec 1893) 250.
ap
A fictional account in which the heroine, Ethel Rivers, resolves to equip herself as an able pianist and teacher after she sees a friend forced to take a position as a nursery governess. As a result River's friend "sank out of view beneath the social horizon". Rivers subsequently attends the New England Conservatory and launches a successful teaching career.

827   RITTER, Fanny Raymond. Letters from an island. 1. Vassar
ap   **College,** *Dwight's Journal of Music* XXXIX/995 (7 June 1879) 92-
    93.
A report of music studies at Vassar Col. Students study solo and choral singing, organ, piano, and harmony. The school has a concert series with lectures given by Frédéric Louis Ritter, director of music. In response to the question of whether Vassar has produced famous women, the author points to the recent dearth of famous men from Harvard and Yale universities and continues, "If this be true, why expect so much more from Vassar Col. and the inferior sex"?

→   **Rubinstein Club concert. Harriet Ware's new cantata** *Sir*
    Oluf, *see* 2050ap[66].

828   S. Madame Valeri to teach in Berlin and Vienna, *Musical*
ap   *Courier* LXXX/10 (4 Mar 1920) 7.
During the summer of 1920, Delia M. Valeri will teach in Europe for 8 weeks and also at the Chicago Musical Col. for 5 weeks. Her theories on singing and the teaching of voice are discussed.

829   SESSIONS, Ruth Huntington. Sixty-odd. A personal history
bm   (Brattleboro, Vt.: S. Daye, 1936) 429 p.
Born in 1859, Ruth Huntington Sessions grew up in Boston and Syracuse, N.Y. From 1880-83 she studied piano and voice in Leipzig, and upon her return to the United States she headed the music department of a girls' school in Utica, N.Y. While rearing her children, Sessions was active in a women's music club in Brooklyn, and she also championed the cause of better working conditions for women. One of her children is the composer, Roger Sessions.

830   S.M.C. Music lessons, *Dwight's Journal of Music* XXXI/10 (12
ap   Aug 1871) 79.
An attack against ignorant and incompetent (female) piano teachers and students. Many mothers undergo hardship so that their daughters can become piano teachers, rather than having to work hard for a living. This accounts for the large number of piano teachers, for their poor training, and for the boredom and incompetence of piano students.

831 SMITH, Ella May. **Music life of Columbus**, *Musical Courier*
ap   LIV/6 (6 June 1907) 11-12.
Among the music organizations in Columbus, Ohio are 3 women's choral groups, all conducted by women: the Euterpean Ladies' Chorus of 38 voices, which has competed successfully with several other groups; the Girls' Glee Club of Ohio U., conducted by Ethel Bowman; and the Girls' Music Club, conducted by its president, Emily McCallup.

832 SMITH, Fanny Morris. **Beginning of the club year, The**,
ap   *Etude* XVIII/11 (Nov 1900) 410-11.
As society has grown more complex, the tendency has been to isolate women in the home where they are "obliged to concentrate their thoughts on the administration of a large number of small, vexing, and perplexing details". The music clubs offer women the opportunity for social contacts as well as work that can make them feel useful to their communities. This article appears on the *Woman's work in music* page (*WIAM* 645).

833 SMITH, Fanny Morris. **Belated letter addressed to the**
ap   **convention of the National Federation of Music Clubs, A**,
      Etude XIX/5 (May 1901) 190.
The federation is doing a good job for local talent, but the time has come for it to enlarge its work and undertake the distribution of foreign concert artists as well. Too many leading artists come to the United States and never proceed beyond their landing point of New York. While private management for "grand artists with their railroad cars" will continue to have a place, the town and village circuit would flourish much better if management were handled by the clubs. The federation could provide a central concert bureau and offer a well-planned succession of artists from October to May for a very small outlay by each individual club.

834 SMITH, Fanny Morris. **Have the rich a right to work?**, *Etude*
ap   XVIII/3 (Mar 1900) 106-07.
Discusses the appropriateness of middle-class women becoming piano teachers using as examples fictitious characters and situations. Argues that work is the only way to obtain "life, liberty, and happiness". Concludes that when women with means do not work--or if in working they do not use their talents to the best advantage--"the world is impoverished by the loss of their labor". This article appears on the *Woman's work in music* page (*WIAM* 645).

835 SMITH, Fanny Morris. **On the woman's club as a co-**
ap   **operative business**, *Etude* XIX/11 (Nov 1901) 412-13.
In this item on the *Woman's work in music* page (*WIAM* 645), Smith discusses the excellent training in business that the music clubs offer to women. She advocates turning the well-organized club into a stock company and also recommends that various club activities, e.g., the lending library, lecture series, and recitals, be managed to achieve a slight profit.

836 SMITH, Fanny Morris. **Woman's musical compositions**,
ap   *Etude* XX/1 (Jan 1902) 28.
Florence Edith Sutro's activities on behalf of women in music include the organization of a library of works by women composers for the Atlanta Exposition of 1893, her essays, *Women in music and law* (*WIAM* 729), her organization of the Woman's Department of the Music Teachers National Assoc., her work as first president of the National Federation of Music Clubs, and the impetus she provided for the establishment of the *Woman's work in music* page (*WIAM* 645) in *Etude*, on which this article appears.

837 SMITH, Fanny Morris. **Work of our women's musical clubs,**
ap   **The**, *Etude* (*WIAM* 75) 490-91.
To music clubs that are "struggling against heavy odds in the task of perpetuating a taste for music in their communities", the National Federation of Music Clubs offers several important services: e.g., 1) a Bureau of Reciprocity, which lists all members in the clubs who are willing to give recitals for expenses or a small remuneration, 2) study plans to pursue at club meetings, and 3) a circulating library of music and books. The activities of individual clubs vary from arranging concerts at charitable institutions to encouraging the introduction of music into local schools and publishing lists of music by local composers.

838 SMITH, Margaret A. **Are you a music teacher?**, *New York*
an   *Daily Tribune* 27 Nov 1898, III-2.
Advocates work for women as supervisors of music instruction in the public schools as a better means to a steady income than private teaching. Argues for a strong professional commitment, and suggests that musically-gifted women qualify themselves as supervisors by first assuming positions as general school teachers, and use that income to obtain special training in music education during summer vacations.

839 STANLEY, May. **Singing is chief feature at women worker's**
ap   **league**, *Musical America* XXX/25 (18 Oct 1919) 19. *Illus.*
Discusses the activities of Mrs. Kenneth J. Muir as president of the New York League of Women Workers--an organization of self-supporting women whose members number in the thousands. Muir's chief interest is music, and she has

worked to establish a chorus in every branch of the league. She views choral singing as an excellent way of bringing people of different nationalities together, acclimating immigrants to American traditions, and preserving the ethnic music immigrants bring to the United States. Muir also has been active with the International Music Festival Chorus, which is made up of 36 different ethnic choruses of foreign-born citizens in New York.

840 STODDARD, Eugene M. **Frances Elliott Clark; her life and**
dd   **contributions to music education** (PhD diss., Music: Brigham
      Young U., 1968) 453 p. (typescript, microfilm, xerox).
Investigates the influence and contributions of Frances Elliott Clark in the development of music education from 1885-1958. Born in Indiana, Clark had few educational advantages as a child and learned music at her mother's knee. She began her career as a public school teacher and in 1891 became a supervisor of music in the public school system in Monmouth, Ill. In 1911 she became head of the educational department of the Victor Talking Machine Co. in Camden, N.J. Clark was the founder and a persistent guardian of the Music Educators National Conference.   *(Dissertation Abstracts, abridged)*

841 **Summer takes Huss colony into the Adirondacks**, *Musical*
ap   *America* XLIV/9 (19 June 1926) 28. *Illus.*
Announces the annual summer course to be conducted for teachers and students of piano and voice by Henry Holden Huss and Hildegarde Hoffmann Huss at the Huss Mountainside Studio on Lake George, N.Y. Repertory and teaching methods will be the special features of this year's course, and foreign languages will also be offered.

842 SWAYNE, Egbert. **Musical centers of Chicago VI: the**
ap   **American Conservatory**, *Music* [Chicago] VII (Dec 1894) 170-75.
      Illus.
Discusses the backgrounds of the founding teachers of the American Conservatory, among whom were 2 former piano students of Theodor Leschetizky, Gertrude Hogan-Murdough and Florence Castle, and a pupil of Mathilde Marchesi, Ragna Linne.

→   **Teaching as aid to opera singer**, *see* 1218ap[58].

843 **Thomas Normal Training School**, *Musician* XI/6 (June 1906)
ap   289.
Founded in 1888 by Emma A. Thomas, this Detroit school offers training and placement to music students intent on a career in either private teaching or public school music education. Diplomas are granted after one year of successful training and are accepted by most states in lieu of a teacher's exam. The Thomas Normal Training School is one of the best known institutions of its kind in the Middle West. Living expenses are moderate in Detroit, good accommodations are available near the school, and the city enjoys an active musical life.

844 THOMAS, Rose Fay. **Women's amateur musical clubs**, *Music*
ap   [Chicago] XVI (July 1899) 275-84.
Women's amateur musical clubs aim to develop the talent of their own members and to promote the musical interests of the community and the nation. There are 2 types: in the first the membership participates musically in the meetings, and professional musicians are sometimes hired to broaden the scope of the organization; in the second the members devote themselves to the study of individual works--usually those on the programs of the local symphony orchestra for a given season.

845 TOWNSEND, C.A. **Mother's responsibility**, *Etude* XVII/1
ap   (Jan 1899) 9.
The greatest trials in piano teaching are the indifferent or ignorant mothers of pupils, who studied music as young women all too casually and cannot be depended upon to supervise their children's practice. Therefore the first duty of the piano teacher is to impress pupils with the seriousness of music study, ensuring in turn that there will be a "different set of mothers" for the next generation.

846 **Tribute to the late Carre Louise Dunning, originator of the**
ap   **Dunning System of improved music study for beginners, A**,
      Musical Courier XCIX/12 (21 Sept 1929) 19.
Née Stickle, Carre Louise Dunning (1860-1929) was highly influential in "eliminating the drudgery in the teaching of music to children". 3000 teachers in the United States have been trained in the Dunning method, and looking toward the future, the educator formed an association to perpetuate her goals after her death. Dunning stressed ear-training and notation exercises that interested young people, as opposed to mechanical practicing at the piano as the beginning of a student's work in music.

847 V.B.S. **Beloved composer of childhood melodies, A**, *Musical*
ap   *Observer* XXIII/1 (Jan 1924) 24.
Juliette A. Graves Adams moved with her husband Crosby Adams to the Blue Ridge Mountains in Montreat, N.C. in order to have more time for creative

work, but "her retreat has become a shrine of learning for 21 successive classes of piano teachers". Her course is not about teaching method (indeed, she thinks America is method-ridden), but rather about presenting music as literature. Adams came to specialize in composition for children because she feels that most of the material written for youngsters is uninteresting and trivial.

848 VIRGIL, Mrs. Charles S. **Woman's club as a factor in**
ap   **general musical culture, The**, *Etude* XVI/5 (May 1898) 132.
An assessment of the quality of work in the women's music clubs--a movement of tremendous proportions, part fad and part healthy growth. Even the superficial club program leaves its members somewhat ennobled by the contact with fine music. "Composers are studied, lionized, and even worshipped with an intensity and interest known to no other art". Amy Cheney Beach has commended club members for bringing music into the home, influencing the musical growth of their children, and educating audiences--whose tastes show "a marked advance" over the last 15 years. This article appears on the *Woman's work in music* page (*WIAM* 645).

849 **Wednesday Morning Musicale of Nashville, Tenn.**, *Etude*
ap   XVII/7 (June 1899) 231.
Now in its 9th year, the Wednesday Morning Musicale of Nashville has 25 members, 5 guests, 1 honorary member, and 200 associate members. The last group constitutes the audience, the 3 former the performers. The organization has the only women's club room in Nashville. At a recent concert, Fannie Bloomfield-Zeisler was the guest artist, and other "brilliant soloists and a splendid little chorus of 36" performed Grieg's *Olaf Trygvasson*. The club's president, accompanied by her sister, trained the chorus.

850 W.F.G. **One woman's musical influence. How Weenonah**
ap   **Poindexter developed a musical department at the Missis-**
     sippi State College for Women, *Musical America* XI/17 (5 Mar 1910) 35. *Illus.*
When Weenonah Poindexter became head of the music department at the Mississippi State Col. for Women 15 years ago, only 55 young women in a student body of about 1000 studied music. Now more than 800 students are studying voice, instruments, and teacher-training in music. For a number of years Poindexter lobbied in the state capital to obtain a $40,000 appropriation for a new music building, and ultimately she was successful. She also decided that she needed to bring in fine concert artists in order to make good music students, and for a first concert she engaged Paderewski for a $1000 fee that she herself guaranteed. Now a concert bureau with an annual budget of $4500 arranges concerts at the college by such artists as Harold Bauer, Lillian Nordica, Marcella Sembrich, Johanna Gadski, David Bispham, and Fannie Bloomfield-Zeisler. Poindexter's work has raised music standards throughout the state.

→   W.F.G. **Los Angeles woman sang in** *Stabat Mater* **under Rossini**, *see* 1239ap[58].

→   **What one woman did in Washington. Directing three cho-ruses only a part of Mrs. Blair's many musical activities**, *see* 1241ap[58].

851 WHITCOMB, E.O. **How mother collected her bills**, *Etude*
ap   XLI/5 (May 1923) 296.
Whitcomb relates how his mother, a conservatory graduate, relocated in an unspecified town in the western United States as a piano teacher, and found that she was expected to play the organ and lead the church choir on Sundays as well as to play for funerals--all without remuneration. Also, she frequently was not paid for the lessons she gave. To counter these problems she first established a music club called the Schumann Club for paid-in-full students only. The club was an instant success, and the parents of pupils with arrears settled their accounts shortly. Next she "went to work on other social customs that needed reforming", and 2 years later she was receiving $2 for her Sunday work from the church and $2 for playing at funerals--provided the family could afford to pay. Whitcomb notes that at the present time 4 of his mother's former pupils--all conservatory graduates--carry on his mother's work. The Schumann Club is prominent and has proven highly beneficial to the community.

852 **Who knows?**, *Etude* IX/2 (Feb 1891) 34.
ap
Argues that parents of young women who are studying piano should see that their daughters study seriously, so that if these young women are obliged to support themselves in later life, they are properly prepared. Thousands of women are now teaching piano.

853 **Woman's department of the M.T.N.A.**, *Etude* XV/7 (July 1897)
ap   191.
During a recent convention of the Music Teachers National Assoc., the Woman's Department held sessions at which music by Amy Cheney Beach and Clara Anna Korn was performed, and papers were delivered by Luisa Cappiani, Kate S. Chittenden, Amy Fay, Charlotte W. Hawes, and Mary Gregory Murray. Florence Edith Sutro is highly regarded for her executive ability as president of the department.

854 **Woman's opportunity in music**, *Etude* (*WIAM* 875) 440.
ap
Three-fourths of the music teachers in the United States are women. In no country in the world is woman's position more secure or respected. Nevertheless, there still remains a prejudice in some areas in favor of the man teacher. Equality of opportunity, training for women, and their ability to teach children better than men are considered by noted music teachers. This article is continued in *Etude* XXVII/8 (Aug. 1909, 516).

→   **Women composers honored by Bridgeport musical club**, *see* 738ap[56].

855 **Women in music**, *Etude* XXIII/8 (Aug 1905) 314.
ap
Reports that 9/10ths of the incompetent piano teachers are women, who typically have only 3 terms of lessons of their own to their credit. By way of compensation, the professional musician derives 9/10ths of his income from instructing young women and girls.

856 **Women's musical clubs**, *Musical Courier* XLIX/10 (7 Sept 1904)
ap   6.
Discusses the work of women in the music clubs as amateur managers for concert artists on tour, thereby facilitating performances in small towns. The clubs show how women "can really be useful in advancing the interests of music without endeavoring to compose or to do other creative things of the kind". This article is reprinted in *Musical Courier* from the *New York Sun*.

857 WYNN, Edith Lynwood. **Opposition to the violin for girls**,
ap   *Etude* XVII/3 (Mar 1899) 78.
While some of her pupils' parents are opposed to the idea of young women studying the violin for professional purposes, Wynn argues that giving a daughter the means of a livelihood is of great value. "The time is ripe when everyone should realize that teaching is a noble calling and that the concert performer too is a benefactor, a physician, and a helper of the needy".

58   Literature about women as performers of art music

858 **Adelina Patti souvenir libretto, The. Farewell concerts in the**
ap   **United States and Canada, season 1903-04** (New York: R. Grau, 1903) 53 p. *Illus., music.*
Contains a biographical account of the soprano's career, background information on her farewell tour of 1903-04, and music selections which she performed during the tour. Gounod's *Ave Maria*, Händel's *Angels ever bright and fair* from *Theodora*, and Wagner's *Träume* are included together with popular songs and song texts.

859 **A.H. Bloomfield-Zeisler astounds New York**, *Musical America*
ro   XXXI/17 (21 Feb 1920) 17.
Reviews Fannie Bloomfield-Zeisler's comeback performance at Carnegie Hall after an absence of a number of years from the concert stage due to illness. The pianist gave magnificent performances, with the Victor Herbert Orchestra, of 3 concertos: the Mozart concerto no. 24 in C minor, K.451, the Chopin concerto no. 2 in F minor, op. 21, and Chaikovskii's concerto no. 1 in B-flat minor, op. 23. By the end of the first movement of the rarely heard Mozart concerto "the audience--numbering many pianists--was made to realize that they were assisting at one of the most significant events of the year".

860 AIKEN, Ednah. **Two California songbirds in Europe: Mar-**
ap   **cella Craft**, *Sunset. The Pacific Monthly* XXXIII/3 (Sept 1914) 534-36.
As a young girl in Pasadena, Calif., Marcella Craft borrowed money on her voice, and she subsequently went to Boston where she was successful in concert work. Her dramatic ambitions led her to Italy where she studied with Francesco Mottino and Alessandro Guagni. Later her work in German diction with Eva Wilcke in Berlin helped her gain access to the opera houses of Elberfeld, Keil, and Munich. In Munich especially the soprano achieved great success. Craft believes one reason for her success is her projection of the "ethical purpose" behind an opera. In 1915 Craft plans an American concert tour with composer-pianist Amy Cheney Beach, who regards Craft as her best interpreter. The 2nd California songbird referred to in the title is Maud Fay.

861 AIKEN, Ednah. **Two California songbirds in Europe:**
ap   **Maud Fay--Glückskind**, *Sunset. The Pacific Monthly* XXXIII/3 (Sept 1914) 531-34.
Maud Fay studied in Germany at the recommendation of David Bispham and Walter Damrosch. She made her debut as Marguerite at the Munich Opera, and she also has sung Wagner and Strauss roles with that house. Fay has been

honored with the order of the *Lippische Rose* and the rank of *Kammersängerin*. The 2nd California songbird referred to in the title is Marcella Craft.

862   ALDA, Frances. **Men, women, and tenors** (Boston: Houghton
bm   Mifflin, 1937) 307 p. *Illus*.
Born and raised in New Zealand, Frances Alda (1883-1952) first sang with light opera companies in Australia. At 18 she became a beneficiary of her mother's life insurance, and together with her brother she went on a spending spree through Europe. She remained in Paris to study with Mathilde Marchesi, who assumed direction of all of Alda's activities prior to her debut as Manon at the Opéra-Comique in 1904. Massenet aided her in learning the role. Alda met Gatti-Casazza and Toscanini in 1907 when she was engaged to sing the title role in the first Italian production of *Louise* at La Scala. She followed them to the Metropolitan Opera for the 1908-09 season, and it was around this time that she experienced a new seriousness and deepening commitment within herself as an artist. At the Metropolitan Alda sang 42 roles in 22 years. After her marriage to Gatti-Casazza in 1910 she found herself singing fewer performances at the Metropolitan--presumably because of conflict of interest--and more in concert. Her marriage was chiefly one of convenience and led to divorce in 1921. Among the numerous events Alda recalls are: 1) the first performance of Puccini's *La fanciulla del West*, 2) early recordings she made with Caruso, 3) the final break between Toscanini and Giulio Gatti-Casazza in 1915, and 4) her coaching of Lawrence Tibbett for his great success as Ford in *Falstaff* at the Metropolitan in 1925. After her retirement from public life, Alda taught voice at her estate, Casa mia, in Great Neck, N.Y. She required students to sign contracts as indications of their seriousness, and she secured financial assistance for those students requiring it, allowing them to repay once they were earning their livelihoods as singers.

863   rb --
R. by Olin DOWNES, *New York Times* 26 Dec 1937, VII-6.

864   ALDRICH, Richard. **Adelina Patti in America**, *Musical dis-*
bd   *course from the New York Times* (London: Oxford U., 1928) 242-65.
Discusses Patti's promising career as a young woman in New York and Boston between 1852 and 1860--when she departed to live in England--and considers her return engagements in the United States that began in 1881. The soprano's various farewell tours were ill-advised, since her voice showed wear, and represented an attempt to capitalize on her enormous reputation and "wrest whatever there was left to gain from it". The promoter of the last farewell tour in 1903-04 lost $25,000 "and probably deserved to".

865   ALDRICH, Richard. **Concert life in New York 1902-1923**
ro   (New York: G.P. Putnam's Sons, 1941) 795 p. *Index*.
Aldrich's music reviews for the *New York Times* from 1902-23 include critiques of performances by numerous American women of national and international stature.

866   **Alice Gentle's career one of gradual success**, *Musical Courier*
ap   LXXV/23 (6 Dec 1917) 12. *Illus*.
Born in Seattle, Alice Gentle's career began in 1906 when she joined the chorus of the Manhattan Opera. She is scheduled in the current season to create the leading role in Charles Wakefield Cadman's new opera *Shanewis* at the Metropolitan Opera. In addition to singing leading roles in *Carmen*, *La favorita*, *Il trovatore*, *Aida*, and *La Gioconda*, Gentle has appeared in recitals throughout the United States.

867   **Alice Nielsen dies; operatic star, 66**, *New York Times* 9 Mar
ap   1943, 23.
Nielsen (1877-1943) began her singing career with the Chicago Choir Co., based in Kansas City. Later she studied voice with Ida Valegra in San Francisco and turned to engagements with light opera troupes. Mrs. Victor Herbert heard Nielsen in a New York performance in 1897, and she recommended the soprano to her husband for the leading role in his *The serenade*. Subsequently Herbert wrote the female leads in *The fortune teller* and *The singing girl* for Nielsen. She, however, wished to pursue grand opera, and accordingly she went to Europe, where she made her debut as Violetta in 1903 in Naples. Nielsen sang elsewhere in Europe before returning to the United States on a permanent basis. After her return she appeared with the San Carlo and the Boston Opera companies, as well as at the Metropolitan Opera.

868   A.L.J. **"Changing violin teachers not necessary", says Vera**
ap   **Barstow**, *Musical America* XVI/25 (26 Oct 1912) 11. *Illus*.
Vera Barstow, a young violinist, believes that the best results are gained from studying with one master who helps the pupil to develop individuality. In her case the master is Luigi von Kunits, concertmaster of the Pittsburgh Symphony Orchestra. Barstow's father was a violin maker and repairer; she took her first lessons with a young woman who taught her in lieu of payment for violin repairs.

869   A.L.J. **Mme. Bouton is a champion of women's rights in**
ap   **music**, *Musical America* X/13 (7 Aug 1909) 3. *Illus*.
Isabelle Bouton praises the orchestra's performance at her recent concert

appearance during the Ocean Grove Festival in Ocean Grove, N.J. About 2/3rds of the players were women, and Bouton believes the time is not far off "when her sister artists will be recognized as desirable orchestral and ensemble players". Bouton left opera for concert work because it was not possible to combine regular engagements in opera with her home life.

870   ALLEN, Julia C. **Music in boarding schools**, *Etude* IX/12 (Dec
ap   1891) 229.
1) A first-rate seminary should be able to offer instruction in "harmony, theory, and ensemble playing". 2) Students who might play well the simpler compositions of Haydn and Mozart are often pushed to play more difficult works by Beethoven and Schumann. 3) Teachers should and can find better beginning pieces than the "rubbishy transcriptions and airs with variations which form the repertory of the average school girl".

871   **Alma Clayburgh, soprano, 76, dead**, *New York Times* 6 Aug
an   1958, 25.
Trained by her father as a dramatic soprano with an extensive operatic and concert repertory, Clayburgh sang professionally at churches and charity concerts. She retired from concert life after her marriage in 1908, but maintained her musical interests by giving musical afternoons at her town house. After separating from her husband 8 years later, Clayburgh returned to concert life using her married name--which scandalized her family. Much of Clayburgh's income was used to support the careers of young musicians. She was a patron of the Metropolitan Opera, as well as a sponsor of the Goldman Band, the New York City Symphony Orchestra, and other musical organizations.

872   **Alma Gluck dies; former star of opera, wife of Zimbalist**,
an   *New York Herald Tribune* 28 Oct 1938, 16.
An outstanding singer in opera and on the concert stage, Alma Gluck (1884-1938) rose to fame from obscure beginnings as an immigrant from Bucharest. Upon graduating from Hunter Col. she became a stenographer, and she began to study voice only after her marriage to Bernard Gluck. Her teacher in New York was Arturo Buzzi-Peccia. Gluck made her operatic debut in 1909 as Sophie in *Werther* with a feeder company for the Metropolitan Opera. Between 1914 and 1919 the soprano received $600,000 in royalties from the Victor Talking Machine Co.--her most successful recording being *Carry me back to old Virginny*. After her marriage to the violinist Efrem Zimbalist in 1914, Gluck curtailed her professional engagements, although she gave joint recitals with her husband.

873   **Alma Gluck warns against evils of study-life abroad**, *Musical*
ap   *America* XIX/8 (27 Dec 1913) 1, 3. *Illus*.
The soprano endorses the campaign of John C. Freund--the editor of *Musical America*--to warn American parents about the perils awaiting American students abroad. Many young Americans are living in pensions where the leisure time of students is devoted chiefly to "swapping lies and bedfellows". Gluck is not opposed to the idea of relatively finished singers in their mid-20s going abroad for experience in performance, but she feels strongly that women younger than age 20 should remain in the United States, where there are now many fine teachers. Gluck also discusses her previous summer of study in Europe with Marcella Sembrich.

874   **American art songs for Russia**, *Musical America* XXIII/6 (11
ap   Dec 1915) 25.
Constance Purdy was one of the first singers to introduce Russian art songs in the United States, long before the repertory became so popular that every recitalist now includes at least one Russian song on a program. The soprano is also enthusiastic about songs by contemporary American composers and thinks they should be introduced in Russia. Although her musical training is American, Purdy lived in Russia for 5 years.

875   **American debut of Thelma Given, violinist**, *Musical Courier*
ap   LXXVII/18 (31 Oct 1918) 12. *Illus*.
Born in 1896 in Columbus, Ohio, Thelma Given began violin study with Leopold Auer in St. Petersburg in 1911. She gave her first public concert at the St. Petersburg Conservatory in 1916 and was forced to leave Russia at the outbreak of the Revolution in 1917. Auer's other American pupils include Jascha Heifetz, Max Rosen, and Toscha Seidel.

876   **American girl's success, An**, *Musical Courier* LXVIII/24 (17 June
ap   1914) 12.
Reports that Edyth Walker will return "to her native land after 8 years with a European reputation second to none" and will join the Chicago Opera. Previously she sang at the Metropolitan Opera for 3 seasons, but because German opera is her greatest interest and she didn't find sufficient opportunities to sing German repertory at the Metropolitan, she returned to Germany--where she had originally trained. Walker began as a contralto and became a dramatic soprano; she specializes in Wagnerian roles. Before turning to opera she worked as a grammar school teacher and a teacher of singing in public schools in upstate New York.

877   American musicians in Berlin send greetings to *Musical*
ap   ***America***, *Musical America* XI/3 (27 Nov 1909) 31. *Illus.*
A reproduction of a postcard from musicians in the American colony in Berlin, announcing the great success of the American pianist Wynne Pyle on the occasion of her Berlin debut in Oct. 1909.

878   American Quartet under New York management, *Musical*
ap   *Courier* LXIV/17 (24 Apr 1912) 41.
Organized and sponsored by Charles Martin Loeffler, the American Quartet is now in its 4th season and has the following personnel: Gertrude Marshall, 1st violin, Evelyn Street, 2nd violin, Adeline Packard, viola, and Susan Lord Brandegec, cello.

879   American singers in Europe, *Musical World* II/3 (Apr 1902) 29-
ap   30. *Illus.*
An account of the events leading to Mary Garden's debut at the Opéra-Comique in Paris in 1900. When Martha Rioton could not appear as Louise in Charpentier's opera, Garden substituted for her at the last moment. By the end of Act III, Garden was an established Paris favorite, and she subsequently became one of the few American singers who could be counted upon to draw money at the box office. Her other roles at the Opéra-Comique are listed.

880   American violinist relates trials of study abroad, *Musical*
ap   *Leader* XXVI/10 (4 Sept 1913) 262.
Helen Ware, who is the protégée of several wealthy Philadelphia women, studied abroad with Otakar Sevček in Vienna and Jenő Hubay in Budapest. She cautions that no young musician should be sent abroad without a proper chaperone and adequate finances. Too often young Americans go to Europe only to have their monies run out, and they are forced to teach or to play in smoky cafes, thereby detracting from their own studies.

881   Anna Fitziu, 80, opera soprano early in century, dies on
an   **coast**, *New York Times* 22 Apr 1967, 31.
Born in Huntington, W. Va., Anna Fitziu (1888-1967) came to New York in 1902 and began her career as a chorus girl in musical comedy. She later appeared in comic opera and in concert; she made her operatic debut as Elsa in *Lohengrin* in Milan. Fitziu sang throughout the United States, South America, and Europe until the late 1920s, after which she devoted herself to teaching.

882   ANTRIM, Doron K. American pianists, famous or typical.
ac   *Studies in musical education, history, and aesthetics* 23 (Hartford: Music Teachers National Assoc., 1929) 129-33.
A brief survey of leading men and women pianists from William Mason to George Gershwin, Henry Cowell, and Aaron Copland. Listed "among the ladies" are Dai Buell, Augusta Cottlow, Leonora Cortez, Amy Fay, Julie Glass, Gita Gradova, Georgia Kober, Marian MacDowell, Frances Nash, Julie Rivé-King, Olga Steeb, and Olga Samaroff Stokowski.

883   APOLLO. What is the matter with Clara Louise?, *Dwight's*
ap   *Journal of Music* XXXIV/21 (9 Jan 1875) 368.
A response to Clara Louise Kellogg, who has advised aspiring prima donnas not to have beaux. Ridicules her suggestion, elaborating on the necessity for romantic experience in order for women to give truly dramatic operatic performances. The success of specific singers in operatic roles is attributed to their passions for particular men. This letter to the editor originally appeared in the *Boston Globe*.

884   ARMSTRONG, William. Madame Olive Fremstad and her
ap   **views on the singer's choice of a career**, *Musician* XVI/6 (June 1911) 369-70. *Illus.*
Fremstad has excelled in the 3 areas open to a singer of art music-- church, concert, and opera. A native of Sweden, Fremstad came to New York from Minnesota in 1890 to study voice, and she secured a position as soloist at St. Patrick's Cathedral. In 1895 she made her operatic debut as Azucena at the Cologne Opera. In addition to appearing in opera, Fremstad has sung several lieder recitals each season.

885   ARMSTRONG, William. Romantic world of music, The
bm   (New York: E.P. Dutton, 1922) 239 p. *Illus.*
The author, a friend of many singers, reviews the careers of and his contacts with the following women: Amelita Galli-Curci, Mary Garden, Frieda Hempel, Maria Jeritza, Lillian Nordica, Adelina Patti, and Ernestine Schumann-Heink.

886   ARMSTRONG, William, ed. Teresa Carreño's reminis-
ap   **cences**, *Musical Courier* LXXIV/25-26 (21 June-5 July 1917) 6-7; 6-7.
Near the end of her life, Carreño began work on her memoirs with Armstrong. They progressed only as far as her childhood years in Paris. Carreño recalls her early interest in playing before the public in New York, Boston, and Havana, as well as her youthful encounters with Theodore Thomas and Berlioz. Gounod demonstrated for Carreño how Chopin interpreted his own music.

887   Augusta Cottlow begins her tour, *Musical America* III/18 (17
ap   Mar 1906) 12. *Illus.*
A native of Shelbyville, Ill., Cottlow first studied piano with her mother, a fine amateur musician. When she was 9 years old she began studying with Carl Wolfsohn in Chicago, and in less than a year she was introduced to the Chicago public. Cottlow spent 5 years in Berlin studying piano with Busoni and also composition and theory. She made her mature American debut in 1900 at the Worcester Festival in Massachusetts, appearing with the Boston Symphony Orchestra.

888   Augusta Cottlow to play over WOR, *Musical Courier* CXI/2 (13
ap   July 1935) 17. *Illus.*
Reports that after several years of retirement from the concert stage, Augusta Cottlow will perform as 1 of 12 women pianists in a New York radio series during the summer of 1935. Cottlow is interested in the educational possiblities of radio, and she believes that by playing on the radio, performers of serious music can help to elevate the public's taste.

889   AYRES, E.E. Woman as a musician, *Etude* VI/11 (Nov 1888)
ap   166.
The fact that a large proportion of the graduates from the New England Conservatory and other conservatories are women has been interpreted as unfortunate by *Kunkel's Musical Review*, because this means that music has not yet reached "the position of a serious study worthy of the attention of men". The editors of *Etude* endorse women's achievements--noting that some of the best pianists in America are women--and comment upon the increasing numbers of men studying music as an indication of the advance of serious music in the United States in the previous 25 years.

→   **Baltimore: cradle of municipal music**, *see* 2146bm[68].

890   BARNARD, Charles. Camilla. A tale of a violin (Boston:
bm   Loring, 1874) v, 141 p.
Camilla Urso (1842-1902), who was born in Nantes, France, at age 7, was the first female to be accepted as a violin student at the Paris Conservatory. Three years later upon graduation, she journeyed to the United States with her father and aunt in anticipation of a lucrative concert tour that would ease the financial hardships the family had endured throughout her education. The early years in the United States were similarly difficult however, although Urso found remunerative engagements on tour with the Germania Musical Soc. of Boston and a troupe headed by Henriette Sontag. In 1855 Urso retired to private life in Nashville, and when she resumed her career in 1863 she proved quickly that she had made the transition from child prodigy to mature artist. Especially notable events in this 2nd phase of her career included her trip to California in 1869, where she organized a music festival in San Francisco in 1870 involving choruses, soloists, and an orchestra. Urso participated herself, performing the Beethoven violin concerto in D major, op. 61, at one concert. She also returned to Europe for engagements, spending the 1870-71 season in London working on new music. The author notes that his book stems from conversations he had with the violinist in Boston in Jan.-Feb. 1874, and he credits Urso with bringing about changes in the American public's tastes by playing the Beethoven concerto, the Mendelssohn violin concerto in E minor, op. 64, and other comparable works.

891   BARNES, Harold M., Jr. Mary Garden on records (San
ap   Angelo, Texas: Holcombe-Blanton, 1947) 20 p. *Discog.*
Presents a chronology of Mary Garden's career as a recording artist and a discography. Garden recorded 30 record sides and 3 cylinders between 1902 and 1929. The most significant aspect of the soprano's long career is the large number of operatic roles she helped to create, e.g., Mélisande, Octavian, and Louise.

892   BAUER, Emilie Frances. Geraldine Farrar's early years,
ap   *Musician* XII/2 (Feb 1907) 72-73. *Illus.*
At age 15 Geraldine Farrar was taken to sing for Emma Cecilia Thursby, while the latter was summering in Maine. Subsequently Farrar and her mother lived in New York for more than 2 years, during which time the young woman studied voice with Thursby and also acting, French, and German. It was through Thursby that Farrar met with and sang for Nellie Melba, Lillian Nordica, Marcella Sembrich, and others. Farrar was a born actress, and by age 15 she had developed a distinctive acting style.

893   BAUER, Emilie Frances. Olive Fremstad, *Musician* XII/3 (Mar
ap   1907) 115-16.
Early in her career, Olive Fremstad spent a number of years in Minneapolis, Duluth, Chicago, and New York earning a marginal income by teaching voice and accompanying for other voice teachers. When she finally was able to travel to Berlin in the late 1890s, she studied with Lilli Lehmann and became a great favorite in Berlin musical circles. Fremstad made her European debut in Vienna as Brangäne to Lehmann's Isolde. Prior to her return to the United States, Fremstad studied Wagnerian roles with Cosima Wagner.

894 BELL, Archie. **Voice worth $300,000 a year, A**, *Green Book*
ap *Magazine* X/6 (Dec 1913) 1030-36.
Ernestine Schumann-Heink initially came to the United States because she could not support her family of 10 children on the income she had been earning in Europe. Her earnings in the United States where she is now a citizen have permitted her and her family to live comfortably. Her financial success is somewhat surprising since she is a contralto. Typically she receives $1500 per recital, although she often sings in college towns for half that amount. Schumann-Heink's concert tours bring in higher receipts and higher attendance figures than those of any other artist at the present time. The contralto notes that while many associates thought she was foolish to perform in the operetta *Love's lottery* by Julian Edwards upon leaving the Metropolitan Opera, she did so in order to reach people who were not regular concert-goers, but might become patrons in the future. The major events in Schumann-Heink's career are discussed.

895 **Bifurcated skirt draws. Mrs. Webster-Powell proves to be**
an **magnet at reception**, *New York Tribune* 4 Dec 1910, I-6.
Reports that at a recent reception at City Hall in New York, Alma Webster-Powell sang, talked about dress reform for women, and modeled her outfit consisting of loose trousers, boots, and a long coat--all in black. Webster-Powell is interested primarily in reducing the costs of women's attire.

896 **Birdice Blye, American pianist**, *Musical Courier* LXIII/11 (13
ap Sept 1911) 28.
Reports that Birdice Blye, who is about to begin her 3rd consecutive concert tour in the United States, has become an eminent artist at home and abroad. A pupil of Anton Rubinstein, Blye often performs his music on her programs and also that of MacDowell. In 1911-12 the pianist will play MacDowell's *Keltic sonata, op. 59*, and his *Sonata eroica, op. 50*, which she has already played in more than 70 recitals.

897 **Black Patti, The. Takes high rank in the musical world and**
an **believed to have no superior**, *Brooklyn Daily Eagle* 5 Mar 1893, 9.
Sissieretta Jones, known as the "Black Patti", was born in Portsmouth, Va. on 5 Jan. 1868, but grew up in Providence. Her instrumental studies began at age 15 at Providence's Academy of Music, and her vocal training began at age 18 at the New England Conservatory. In 1887 Jones sang a "grand concert" for the Parnell Defense Fund at the Boston Music Hall, and the following year she was the first black to sing at Wallack's Theater in New York. Her subsequent tour of the West Indies was a phenomenal success. Gifted with a "strong and beautiful voice that sounds with the steadiness of a trumpet", the soprano also has a pleasing appearance.

898 BLAKE-ALVERSON, Margaret. **Sixty years of California**
bm **song** (Oakland, Calif.: author, 1913) 275 p. *Illus., index*.
Margaret Blake-Alverson's father was a minister who left Cincinnati with a grown son in 1849 and mined for gold in California. He was successful and sent monies to his wife and the other 9 children for passage through the Isthmus of Panama. They arrived and settled in Stockton, Calif. in 1851, the children singing in the choir of their father's new church. The family's new piano--which they received for Christmas 1852 from their father--was the first such instrument in Stockton. Margaret Blake-Alverson entered the Young Ladies' Seminary at Benicia as one of 35 pupils during the 2nd term of the school's existence in 1853. After her graduation in 1855, she established a school for children in Stockton. In 1858 Blake-Alverson traveled once again through the Isthmus of Panama with her husband and child of 7 months to Boston, where she spent 4 years studying voice and singing in the chorus of the Handel and Haydn Soc., in a church choir in Needham, Mass., and with other groups. After her return to California, the contralto worked as a church soloist and taught voice in Santa Cruz, San Francisco, and Oakland. In 1876 she traveled and performed with the Vivian Kohler concert troupe in Oregon and Washington. Blake-Alverson discusses the growth of music stores in San Francisco, the 1873 festival in San Francisco headed by Camilla Urso, and the great May Day festival of 1878 in honor of the Mercantile Library in San Francisco. She also includes reminiscences of her pupils and of musicians active in California's early musical life. Blake-Alverson was active in presidential campaigns for Republican candidates from Lincoln through McKinley.

899 BLAUVELT, Lillian. **Reminiscences of a young American**
ap **singer in Europe**, *Metropolitan Magazine* XIII/2 (Feb 1901) 225-31. *Illus*.
The soprano Lillian Blauvelt originally studied violin as well as voice and decided to become a professional violinist, although it was difficult to gain her father's consent. She attended the National Conservatory in New York, then newly founded by Jeanette Thurber, and took advantage of the plan that allowed students to pay back tuition after graduation. While Blauvelt thinks it is unwise for American girls to sacrifice in order to study abroad, she found it necessary to go to Europe to establish her reputation as a singer. In Milan she substituted at the last minute in a performance of the Verdi Requiem Mass, and it was this event that attracted the attention of managers in the United States and in turn led to singing engagements at home.

900 **Blauvelt now a dramatic soprano**, *Musical Courier* LXVII/11 (10
ap Sept 1913) 9.
Reports that Lillian Blauvelt, formerly a coloratura soprano, will be heard in the 1913-14 season as a dramatic soprano. Her teacher, Alex Savine of the Belgrade Opera and the National Opera of Canada, notes that many opera singers become weary of singing the same roles over and over.

901 BLUM, Elsa Proehl. **They pleased world stars. A memoir of**
bm **my parents** (New York: Vantage, 1960) 58 p. *Port*.
A family memoir by the daughter of Paul Proehl, food gourmet and restaurant manager, and Lena Sauter Proehl, a German-born musician whose childhood acquaintances included Wagner's children and Ernestine Schumann-Heink. As a very young woman Lena Sauter Proehl emigrated to the United States and directed an all-women's orchestra in New Orleans. After her marriage to Paul Proehl and their eventual settling in Chicago, Lena Sauter Proehl conducted an orchestra in the Gold Room of the Congress and Auditorium Hotel--the restaurant of which her husband managed. The players in the orchestra were off-duty members of the Chicago Symphony Orchestra, and Lena Sauter Proehl maintained leadership of the group for 17 years. Diners at the Gold Room who became her admirers included Caruso, Johanna Gadski, Carrie Jacobs-Bond, Nellie Melba, Mary Carr Moore, and Lillian Nordica. The composers Charles W. Cadman and Ermanno Wolf-Ferrari were pleased with her appropriate selections from their works for dinner music. Mounting male antagonism in Chicago led to Lena Sauter Proehl's retirement from conducting and orchestral management.

902 BOHM, Jerome D. **Music--a retrospective glance at Olive**
an **Fremstad**, *New York Herald Tribune* 27 May 1951, IV-5.
A tribute to Olive Fremstad discussing her realizations of Wagnerian roles, among which the most memorable are Isolde, Brünnhilde, and Kundry. Her interpretations of Carmen and Tosca are also considered.

→ **Born in God's country--California**, *see* 426ap[50].

903 **Boston women in string trio**, *Musical America* VII/12 (1 Feb
ap 1908) 21. *Illus*.
A. Laura Tolman is one of the few women cellists active at the present time, and she credits much of her success to her first teacher, Erich Loeffler--a cellist with the Boston Symphony Orchestra. After her work with Loeffler, Tolman studied abroad with Julius Klengel, Alwin Schröder, and Leo Schulz, and she has played in more than 800 concerts since her Boston debut in 1890. The cellist presently heads a trio with Gertrude Marshall as violinist and Myra Winslow as pianist.

904 **Boys in camp the audience of the future. So declares Maud**
ap **Powell, who is making a tour of the camps ...**, *Musical Courier* LXXVIII/1 (2 Jan 1919) 12.
Maud Powell has been appearing on tour in Liberty Theater Concerts, under the auspices of the Commission on Training Camp Activities. To the amazement of certain military officials who doubted whether Maud Powell and her violin would be appreciated, the violinist has been drawing large audiences of enthusiastic officers and soldiers. Powell believes that because of the "pleasure they derived through music of a better class during the days of military life", these men will not hesitate to attend concerts in the future.

905 B.R. **Mary Jordan urges artists to champion earlier Ameri-**
ap **can music**, *Musical America* XXX/4 (24 May 1919) 13. *Illus*.
Mary Jordan believes in fostering the songs of John Knowles Paine, George W. Chadwick, and Arthur Foote, as well as composers of a younger generation such as John Alden Carpenter, for whom she has a high regard. The mezzo-soprano has also performed Harry T. Burleigh's arrangements of Negro songs and spirituals on many of her programs, and in presenting them she gives brief talks to the audience explaining that this music is part of the tradition of American folk song. Next season Jordan plans chronologically-arranged recitals of American music.

906 BRAINE, Robert. **Maud Powell's violin**, *Etude* XXXIX/10 (Oct
ap 1921) 686.
On her deathbed Maud Powell requested that her violin--a fine Guadagnini instrument--be used after her death by someone who would appreciate it. Godfrey Turner, Powell's husband, recently loaned the violin to Erica Morini.

907 BROWER, Harriette. **Girl and her music in the small town,**
ap **A**, *Woman's Home Companion* XXXVIII/10 (Oct 1911) 37.
Based on the experiences of her own youth, Brower offers advice to young women who want to pursue their music studies while completing high school. Rising an hour earlier in the morning is suggested as an easy way to increase practice time, while playing Haydn and Mozart symphonies in 4-hand piano versions with a friend is recommended as a means of expanding one's musical horizons. Brower relates how she financed Saturday railroad trips to study piano with a more advanced teacher than her own town offered, and how she organized a music club of fellow high-school students.

908 BROWER, Harriette. **American woman pianists: their views**
ap   **and achievements**, *Musical America* XXVIII/26 (26 Oct 1918) 18-
19.
Discusses the careers of the following women pianists, whose work has helped
to break down the prejudice against native performers in the United States:
Amy Cheney Beach, Carolyn Beebe, Fannie Bloomfield-Zeisler, Ruth Deyo,
Margaret Jamieson, Mana Zucca, Marguerite Melville, Ethel Newcomb,
Wynne Pyle, Eleanor Spencer, and Olga Samaroff Stokowski.

909 BROWER, Harriette. **Are women men's equals as pianists?**
ap   *Musical America* XXV/7 (16 Dec 1916) 19.
An interview with Ethel Leginska, who now stands at the "summit of
achievement" as a pianist. Leginska believes that women are not yet equal to
men as solo artists, chiefly because women lack unity of purpose. She notes that
while it is easy enough for women to achieve a single success or a few of them,
"to hold one's own and go higher all the time--that's the difficult thing". Too
many trivial concerns fill a woman performer's life and take up her thought,
e.g., clothing.

910 BROWER, Harriette. **Augusta Cottlow makes plea for music**
ap   **of the older German masters**, *Musical America* XXVIII/23 (5
Oct 1918) 25-26. *Illus.*
Augusta Cottlow believes it is bigoted of Americans to exclude music by
German composers from concert programs because of the war, although she
notes that she is not performing works by contemporary German composers
because she is not partial to the music. The pianist is, however, enthusiastic
about the music of Busoni, her teacher, and will play several of his works
during the forthcoming season. Cottlow is interested in modern music and has
performed many works by Debussy and MacDowell.

→   BROWER, Harriette. **Mrs. H.H.A. Beach. How a composer**
works, *see* 655bd[56].

911 BULLING, George T. **Household music**, *Dwight's Journal of*
ap   *Music* XL/1027 (28 Aug 1880) 142-43.
A discourse on the benefits of serious music study in the home that includes
several injunctions. 1) In addition to part-singing, household members should
form an orchestra, since "the violin and orchestral instruments generally are
now much studied by ladies". 2) Young amateur female pianists should be
introduced to more and better music. 3) Better care should be taken of pianos;
they are too often allowed "to be exposed to the vagaries of the atmosphere
and of piano-thumping young ladies".

912 BURLEIGH, Cecil. **Pre-eminent American violinists from**
ac   **1876-1926.** *Studies in musical education, history, and aesthetics* 23
(Hartford: Music Teachers National Assoc., 1929) 213-19.
Maud Powell is praised for her musicianship, technical skill, and her devotion-
-like that of Franz Kneisel--to spreading music in the United States through her
extensive concert tours. Amy Neill and Ruth Ray are also considered.

913 BURR, Hobart H. **American women musicians**, *Cosmopolitan*
ap   XXXI/4 (Aug 1901) [357]-64. *Port.*
The United States has cause for pride in its women musicians. However,
whether native-born or immigrants, these women have been instructed by
foreigners and have made their reputations abroad. Adelina Patti is the only
exception; she conquered the "American forum" from the stage of the New
York Academy of Music in 1859 at the age of 16. In addition to Patti's, the
careers of the following performers are considered: Fannie Bloomfield-Zeisler,
Annie Louise Cary, Helene Hastreiter, Clara Louise Kellogg, Maud Powell, and
Sibyl Sanderson.

→   **Cambridge, Massachusetts, Harvard University, Schlesinger**
Library on the History of Women in America. A checklist of
correspondence by Amy Fay, *see* 7bm[01].

914 CAMERON, Allan Gordon. **Helen Hopekirk. A critical and**
bm   **biographical sketch** (n.p.: n.n., [1885]) 16 p.
A pamphlet issued in connection with the pianist's concert tour in the United
States in 1884-85. Born in 1857 near Edinburgh, Helen Hopekirk began to
study piano at age 9, with the support of a father "who spared no pains to
secure the great future foreshadowed by her early promise". In accordance with
her father's wishes, Hopekirk attended the Leipzig Conservatory. She made her
debut at a Gewandhaus concert and subsequently performed for the first time
in London at the Crystal Palace. Anton Rubinstein's playing has influenced
Hopekirk's own. She is married to William A. Wilson, who relinquished his
career in business in order to become the pianist's manager. Press notices from
newspapers in England, Germany, and the United States are included.

915 **Camilla Urso**, *Musical Courier* XLIV/4 (22 Jan 1902) 48.
ap
Reports the death of the violinist in New York on 20 Jan. 1902. Summarizes
her career, and notes that Urso abandoned work as a concert artist from 1853-
63 in part because of her marriage to Frederic Luere. "Necessity, in no doubt,
compelled Urso in recent years to accept engagements from the managers of
high-class vaudeville theaters".

916 **Caro Roma charms the South**, *Musical Courier* LXXIX/10 (11
ap   Dec 1919) 8.
Caro Roma has joined the faculty of the Florida Conservatory of Music and
Art in Miama, Fla., and she is also serving as director of the choir for a large
Presbyterian church in the city. After a lengthy absence from the concert stage,
she is now reappearing as a recitalist, performing her own songs as well as those
of other composers.

917 **Carreño believes in women's rights**, *Musical Courier* LIX/17 (27
ap   Oct 1909) 32.
Reports that Teresa Carreño is not generally considered a woman artist and
that when a German conductor recently said, "But you are not a woman player,
Madame", he was paying the pianist a compliment. Carreño, however, believes
that women can play the piano and compose as well as men.

918 **Caterina Marco, opera star, dead**, *New York Times* 4 Feb 1936,
an   24.
Caterina Marco (ca. 1853-1936) was "the toast of Europe and America" in the
1870s-80s. Née Katherine Smith, the soprano was the 3rd generation of a
theatrical family. Her grandfather was the famous 19th-c. actor Sol Smith.
Marco trained in Milan under Antonio Sangiovanni, and after establishing her
career in Europe she returned to the United States in 1878. Subsequently she
performed in touring opera companies with Clara Louise Kellogg and Annie
Louise Cary. Her declining fortunes occasioned Marco to come out of
retirement for recitals on her 75th and 80th birthdays.

→   **Celebrities in El Dorado 1850-1906**, *see* 293bm[48].

919 **Chat with Bloomfield-Zeisler**, *Musical Courier* LXXV/11 (13
ap   Sept 1917) 40.
Fannie Bloomfield-Zeisler notes that her ancestors on both sides of the family
were intellectuals, many of them active in professional occupations. Her father
was a scholar of Hebrew literature, while her mother was a descendant of a
long line of rabbis. The present relatives of the pianist and her husband
Sigmund Zeisler, a Chicago lawyer, include leading scholars and medical
doctors in the United States and Europe. Bloomfield-Zeisler also discusses the
aptitudes of her children.

920 **Chat with Selma Kronold, A**, *New York Dramatic Mirror* XLII/
ap   1090 (11 Nov 1899) 17.
Originally from Poland, Selma Kronold discusses her European background
and work in the United States. The soprano has created the leading female
roles in the first American performances of *I pagliacci*, *Manon Lescaut*, and
Mascagni's *L'amico Fritz* and *Cavalleria rusticana*.

921 CHRISMAN, Francis Leon. **Afternoon with Mme. Schu-**
ap   **mann-Heink, An**, *Musician* XV/1 (Jan 1910) 9-10, 72.
Ernestine Schumann-Heink reports that her life is simple; she works on concert
programs and then at household chores. She likes to include songs by American
composers for her concerts, and she believes that the work of native Americans
compares favorably with that of song composers from the Old World. Among
her favorite songs by Americans are Ethelbert Nevin's *The rosary*, Margaret
Ruthven Lang's *Irish love song* (*WIAM* 1779), Amy Cheney Beach's song with
the same title, and selected songs by George W. Chadwick. Schumann-Heink
also discusses 1) the qualifications for young women who are thinking in terms
of a stage or concert career, 2) music festivals in the United States, and 3) her
love for home and family.

922 **Church music regulations for the Province of Rome**. Trans.
ap   by Justine Bayard WARD, *Catholic Choirmaster* IV/3-4 (July-Oct
1918) 57-59; 81-82.
The Moto Proprio of His Holiness Pope Pius X concerning sacred music, dated
22 Nov. 1903, contains the following limitations on women as singers in the
Roman Catholic church. 1) Women are forbidden to sing during the liturgical
service except as members of the congregation. 2) Women who are members of
a religious community, however, and their pupils may form choirs to sing in
their own churches and chapels during liturgical services--although solo singing
is forbidden and preference should be given to Gregorian chant rendered by
the entire community both at Mass and Vespers.

923 **Clara Clemens and her cycle. The development of song**,
ap   *Musical Courier* LXXXIX/21 (20 Nov 1924) 54.
Reports that Clara Clemens will give a series of 8 concerts tracing the
development of song from folk song to contemporary art song. While the
Friends of Music Soc., the Beethoven Assoc., and an occasional pianist have
offered concerts with a historical focus in New York in recent years, Clemens is
the first singer to do so.

924 **Clara Clemens at home in every mood**, *Musical Courier* LXXV/
ap   1 (5 July 1917) 15.
The daughter of Mark Twain, Clara Clemens is one of the few instances of a
"distinguished woman making a name for herself irrespective of the reflected
glory of the parent". Clemens notes that she owes a great deal of her
development as a singer to the help of her husband, Ossip Gabrilowitsch.
Clemens's voice, her beauty, and her studies with Delia M. Valeri are briefly
discussed.

925 **Clara Clemens to fill Culp bookings**, *Musical Courier* LXXV/26
ap   (27 Dec 1917) 10. *Illus.*
Clemens found being the daughter of Mark Twain a severe drawback to
establishing herself as a singer because "the public is not prone to accept
offspring of famous people as worthy in their own rights". She notes that she
had been singing professionally for only 6 years when, in 1909, she married
Ossip Gabrilowitsch and made the decision to retire. However, the lure of the
concert stage remained great, and she returned to her profession. In the 1917-
18 season Clemens will fill many of the concert dates planned for Julia Culp,
who is unable to come to the United States.

926 CLEMENS, Clara. **My father Mark Twain** (New York:
bm   Harper, 1931) 292 p. *Illus.*
In this biography of her father, Clara Clemens describes her youth in Hartford,
where the musicales held by Susan Lee Warner did much to further her interest
in music. She also considers her family's extensive sojourn abroad, during
which time the Clemenses lived in Vienna while Clara studied piano with
Theodor Leschetizky in 1898-99.

927 **Clothilde Gobbi, singer, was 104**, *New York Times* 8 Nov 1960,
an   29. *Illus.*
An obituary for Clothilde Operti Gobbi (1856-1960), who was the last
surviving performer of the Metropolitan Opera's opening night production of
Faust in 1883. Born in London of Italian parentage, Gobbi came to the United
States with her father, conductor Alfredo Operti, in 1876. She sang with the
Patti-Nicolini Opera in Philadelphia and with the Metropolitan Opera, before
retiring from professional life in the 1890s.

928 **Concert of the Women's String Orchestra, A**, *Musical Courier*
ro   XXXV/24 (16 Dec 1897) 16.
The Women's String Orchestra of New York has acquired some excellent
masculine qualities in its playing without losing any feminine qualities. Last
year the orchestra's tone was weak. A recent program included a Händel
concerto grosso, Chopin's rondo in E-flat major, op. 16 arranged for piano and
orchestra, and Hans Seeling's *Barcarole*.

929 **Concerts and operas. Close of the Boston Symphony season**
an   **here**, *Brooklyn Daily Eagle* 21 Mar 1897, 4.
Reports that Emma Roberto Steiner will conduct the Brooklyn Philharmonic
Orchestra, an organization of 40 men, in a program of light classics including
her own *Study, The Hungarian*, and *Tecolati* (*WIAM* 1943). Featured
performers are Ida Gray Scott, dramatic soprano, and the entertainer Harriet
Webb. This will be Steiner's 2nd program, the first having been a misfortune
due to the incompetence of the orchestra. In the same column is an
announcement of a performance by the Boston Symphony Orchestra under the
direction of Emil Paur of Amy Cheney Beach's symphony in E minor, op. 32
(*WIAM* 1370). Beach, whose symphony demonstrates "an imagination and
musical power" not shown in earlier works, is the best-known female composer
today of serious music along with Cécile Chaminade and Augusta Holmes.

930 CONE, John Frederick. **Oscar Hammerstein's Manhattan**
bm   **Opera Company** (Norman, Okla.: U. of Oklahoma, 1964) 399 p.
          Illus., bibliog., index.
During the 5 seasons of the Manhattan Opera's existence from 1906-11, Oscar
Hammerstein successfully challenged the dominance of the Metropolitan Opera
in New York. Hammerstein specialized in French opera and gave first-rate
productions of contemporary French works. He was aided by Mary Garden,
who sang the title roles in the first American performances of *Thaïs* in 1907,
Louise in 1908, and *Pelléas et Mélisande* in 1908. Garden also sang Salome with
the company.

931 **Convent music in America, The**, *Etude* III/3 (Mar 1885) 53.
ap
Reports that the study of music in convent schools is not regarded as an
accomplishment, but rather as "something sturdier". Female graduates typically
contribute to the musical life of their home communities.

932 COOK, Ida. **Beloved Butterfly**, *Opera News* XVII/11 (12 Jan
ap   1953) 10-12. *Illus.*
Geraldine Farrar discusses her most popular role. "I just went out on the stage
and was Butterfly. The only real difficulty in the part is to reconcile the
Japanese conception of reserve with the natural outpouring of Puccini melody".
Farrar's meeting with Puccini at the time of the première is described.

933 COOK, John D. **Singer of the golden age of opera, A: Marie**
ap   **Rappold**, *Opera, Concert, and Symphony* XI/10 (Oct 1946) 10-11,
          30-33. *Illus.*
Born in 1880 in Vienna, Rappold came to the United States as a young child
and grew up in Brooklyn. After 7 years of vocal study with Oscar Saenger, she
met Heinrich Conried, who supervised her debut at the Metropolitan Opera as
Sulamith in Rubin Goldmark's *Die Königin von Saba* in 1905. Rappold was
one of the first opera singers to perform on radio.

934 COOKE, James Francis. **Career of the concert singer, The.**
ap   **Opinions and experiences of the noted concert soprano Miss**
          Emma Thursby, *Etude* XXVI/1 (Jan 1908) 14-15.
Emma Cecilia Thursby reflects on the upgraded musical tastes of audiences for
concert programs in recent years as opposed to the standards when she began
singing. Singers are now required to perform in English, French, and German,
and even Slavic is attempted by some. Thursby learned Adelina Patti's practice
techniques from Maurice Strakosch. Information about Thursby's career is
included.

935 **Corinne Rider-Kelsey, prima donna soprano**, *Musical Courier*
ap   LVI/22 (27 May 1908) 12.
Less than 4 years ago Corinne Rider-Kelsey was the soprano soloist with the
First Presbyterian Church in Brooklyn. Since then her rise in the concert field
has been meteoric, and in June 1908 she will make her operatic debut at Covent
Garden. Emma Abbott, Emma Cecilia Thursby, Lillian Blauvelt, and Zelie De
Lussan also began their singing careers in Brooklyn churches. Rider-Kelsey's
appearances in concert in 1907-08 are discussed.

→   COWEN, Gertrude. **Mrs. H.H.A. Beach, the celebrated**
          composer, *see* 662ap[56].

936 **Cremona Ladies' Orchestra leader**, *Musical Courier* LIV/6 (6
ap   Feb 1907) 23.
Jessie Baldwin von Broekhoven is director of and solo violinist with the
Cremona Ladies' Orchestra in New York. The orchestra has just returned from
its 2nd annual tour of 10 weeks, during which 58 concerts were given.

937 **Critical attitude towards women violinists**, *Musical America*
ap   XV/14 (10 Feb 1912) 22.
Maud Powell speaks out against the generally disparaging attitude of music
critics towards women violinists. While she personally believes that women
violinists lack "the tenderness of Ysaÿe and Kreisler", she also feels that female
players are more clearly aware of their shortcomings than men. Critics little
know how much more will power women must exert than men in order to
succeed. Other drawbacks lie in "the discomfort of our clothing, [and] the time
and trouble it takes to keep oneself looking respectable".

938 CUSHING, Mary Watkins. **Rainbow bridge, The** (New York:
bm   G.P. Putnam's Sons, 1954) 318 p. *Illus., index.*
Olive Fremstad's secretary and "buffer" describes her work with the opera star
from 1911-18. Born in Sweden, Fremstad grew up in Minnesota, began her
career as a pianist, and later studied voice with Lilli Lehmann. Best known for
her Wagnerian roles, Fremstad also achieved success in Gluck's *Armide*. Her
last operatic performance was in Minneapolis with the Chicago Opera in 1918.
Fremstad's relationships with Caruso, Geraldine Farrar, Mary Garden, Louise
Homer, and Toscanini are discussed.

939 rb —
R. by Carl VAN VECHTEN, *Saturday Review of Literature* XXXVII/46 (13
Nov 1954) 5.

940 DAUGHTRY, Willia Estelle. **Sissieretta Jones: a study of**
dd   **the Negro's contribution to nineteenth century American**
          concert and theatrical life (PhD diss., Fine Arts: Syracuse U.,
          1968) 257 p. (typescript, microfilm).
Investigates Negro achievement in the fine arts from 1870-1920, while
focussing on the career of Sissieretta Jones. Considers the culture of her day
and its effects on Jones and her fellow performers. As a concert singer, Jones
performed for predominantly white audiences, who greeted her with amazement and reservations. For this reason she was evaluated as the Black Patti--or
a black replica of the white ideal of Adelina Patti. Jones was a pioneer in
establishing blacks' credentials as performers in the art tradition. (*Dissertation
Abstracts, abridged*)

941 DAVENPORT, Marcia. **Too strong for fantasy** (New York: C.
bm   Scribner's Sons, 1967) 483 p. *Illus.*
An autobiography by Marcia Davenport, the daughter of soprano Alma Gluck
and her first husband, Bernard Gluck. Davenport provides considerable
information about her mother's work and personal life. Gluck's gradual loss of
her voice and her dilemma about pursuing her career after her 2nd marriage to
Efrem Zimbalist are discussed.

942 DAVENPORT-ENGBERG, Blanche. **How to start a local**
ap **symphony orchestra**, *Etude* XXXV/5 (May 1917) 309-10.
Blanche Davenport-Engberg notes that when she returned from finishing her
training as a violinist abroad in 1904, not more than 15 people in her native
Bellingham, Wash. played musical instruments. In 1908 she began to organize
a symphony orchestra, and it now numbers 85 members, with every instrument
represented except oboe and bassoon. Substitutes for these instruments are
made during rehearsals; oboe and bassoon players are imported for concerts.
Professional musicians typically hold first-desk positions, while their students
fill out sections. The expenses for the orchestra average $1000 a year and have
been absorbed by a wealthy benefactor. Rehearsals are held at a local Young
Men's Christian Assoc. for a token fee. Davenport-Engberg contributes her
services as conductor, and in the early years of the orchestra's existence she
drilled all the string players individually.

943 **Day of heroic concert stars**, *Musical America* XVIII/4 (31 May
ap 1913) 40. *Illus.*
Marie Rappold's original goal was the concert stage, however she later decided
to pursue opera upon receiving encouragement from Heinrich Conried.
Rappold would like to sing in Europe, but she finds the low salaries abroad a
drawback.

944 DE WEERTH, Ernest. **Why we should listen to Mary**
ap **Garden**, *Opera News* XVIII/22 (5 Apr 1954) 12-14. *Illus.*
Mary Garden's "acting far outshone her voice; her superb diction and
understanding of musical and dramatic phrases were phenomenal". Garden
never attempted to appear with the Metropolitan Opera because she knew that
the details of her extraordinary work would be lost in such a large house.

945 **Death of Bessie Abott**, *New York Times* 10 Feb 1919, 13.
an
Bessie Abott (1878-1919) was a leading American singer when, in 1912, she
retired to marry the sculptor T. Waldo Story. She began her career in
vaudeville, singing with her sister under the management of Edward E. Rice.
After studying with Frida Ashforth in New York and Mathilde Marchesi in
Paris, Abott made her debut in 1901 as Juliette at the Paris Opera. In the
United States she sang at the Metropolitan Opera, with her own company on
tour in *La Bohème*, and as Maid Marion in Reginald De Koven's *Robin Hood*.

946 **Debut of Miss Patti**, *Dwight's Journal of Music* XVI/10 (3 Dec
ro 1859) 283.
Reviews the New York debut of Adelina Patti at the Academy of Music, 24
Nov. 1859. The young soprano is commended on her performance as Lucia, in
which she exhibited a clear voice, excellent enunciation, and "good carriage",
while lacking the passion of an experienced artist.

947 **Della Fox dead here**, *New York Times* 17 June 1913, 11.
an
The daughter of a theatrical photographer, Della Fox (1872-1913) was a
popular comedienne and light opera star in the 1890s. After appearances as a
child actress, Fox performed with the Bennett and Moulton Opera and the
Conried Opera. Highlights of her career were her portrayals as Prince Mataya
in Woolson Morse's *Wang* in 1891 and as Clairette at the Casino in William
Furst and Victor Roger's *The little trooper* in 1894. The soprano retired after a
nervous breakdown in 1900 and subsequently married John D. Levy, a
diamond broker.

948 DENNIS, James. **Olive Fremstad**, *Record Collector* VII/3 (Mar
ap 1952) 53-59. *Illus.*
A biographical summary of the soprano's personal and professional life,
including excerpts from obituaries and a short discography. Fremstad made 15
recordings near the end of her career which are assessed.

949 D.L.L. **Mme. Szumowska to make extended tour of the**
ap **country next season**, *Musical America* VI/1 (18 May 1907) 15.
Reports that the pianist will perform extensively as a soloist and with the
Adamowski Trio in the 1907-08 season. Antoinette Szumowska made her
United States debut in 1895 with the Boston Symphony Orchestra, and she
subsequently appeared in New York and other cities with the Chicago
Symphony Orchestra under Theodore Thomas and the New York Symphony
Orchestra under Walter Damrosch. A native of Poland, Szumowska became a
serious student of piano only upon graduation from college. In Warsaw she
studied with Alexander Michalowski. Later in 1890 she went to Paris, where
she spent 5 years under the tutelage of Paderewski. Szumowska married the
cellist Josef Adamowski in 1896.

950 **Do foreign singers love us?** "Nonsense", says Rita Fornia,
ap *Musical America* XI/15 (19 Feb 1910) 15.
Fornia, a mezzo-soprano with the Metropolitan Opera, contends that European
artists are only interested in the American dollar, and she appeals to the
American public for enthusiastic responses to native performers. Fornia's
training in Berlin and the musical atmosphere in German cities as contrasted
with cities in the United States are also discussed.

951 **Don't give up music at the altar**, *Etude* XXXVII/7 (July 1919)
ap 407-08, 20.
The following women were interviewed by *Etude* and were unanimous about
the value of women's work in perpetuating music in the home: Antoinette
Szumowska, Emma Ashford, Amy Cheney Beach, Mrs. Noah Brandt, Clara
Clemens, Cecile Ayres de Horvath, Hildegarde Hoffmann Huss, Louise Homer,
Gloria Cotton Marshall, and Lily Strickland. Only Horvath makes the
distinction between the amateur and professional musician, noting that it is
wrong to expect the professionally trained woman to abandon her career after
marriage.

952 **Dora Becker, gifted American violinist**, *Musical Courier* LVII/
ap 14 (30 Sept 1908) 6.
A native of Galveston, Tex., Dora Becker first studied with the American
violinist Richard Arnold--who is presently concertmaster of the New York
Philharmonic--who later went to Berlin to work with Joachim and to
concertize. Becker was still in her teens when she returned to the United States
and appeared under the direction of both Anton Seidl and Theodore Thomas.
She has recently made a comeback after several years of retirement because of
nervous exhaustion. As a youthful prodigy, the violinist toured with Olive
Fremstad, Zelie De Lussan, and Emma Cecilia Thursby. Her tours with
Thursby were so successful that Becker was able to buy the Amati violin she
now plays.

953 **Dr. Carl tells of women's success as organists**, *Musical*
ap *America* XXVI/22 (29 Sept 1917) 23. *Illus.*
William Crane Carl, organist of the First Presbyterian Church in New York,
notes that not only are women organists a credit to the profession, they also
hold important positions throughout the country. In New York several
prominent churches have hired women. Perhaps it was the criticism about
women's lack of strength and inability to conduct choirs that made women
organists persevere all the harder and ultimately succeed. "Women understand
organization, patience, and perseverance"--qualities which are essential for the
organist.

954 EAMES, Emma. **Some memories and reflections** (New York:
bf Arno, 1977) 310, [9] p. $24. *Illus., discog.*
A reprint of the 1927 edition (New York: D. Appleton), with a new
discography by W.R. Moran. Emma Eames (1865-1952) was one of the earliest
native-born singers to achieve prominence in opera in the United States. A
soprano, Eames initially had no intention of pursuing opera, because her
teacher and members of her family were of the prevailing opinion that a
woman who went on the stage could not maintain respectability. After
formative years in Bath, Me., she went to Boston to study between 1882 and
1886, accompanied by her mother as chaperone. She recalls the Boston years as
being especially happy and unruffled: she delighted in her first contacts with
concert life, found employment singing in churches, and occasionally performed with the Boston Symphony Orchestra. In 1886 Eames went to Paris to
study with Mathilde Marchesi, and after studying the work with the composer
himself she made her debut at the Opéra in Gounod's *Faust* in 1889. Her
American debut came in 1891 with Maurice Grau's company, and she sang
under Grau's--and later Conried's--management at the Metropolitan Opera and
on tour until her retirement in 1908. Eames was fond of the title roles in *Aida*
and *Tosca*, which she prepared with attention to dramatic details, including
costuming. She chose to retire at the relatively young age of 43 because of
artistic incompatability with the new management at the Metropolitan under
Giulio Gatti-Casazza. For the major share of her professional career, Eames
was plagued with physical and emotional problems.

955 E.H. **Maud Fay's success in Munich**, *Musical America* X/22 (9
ap Oct 1909) 23. *Illus.*
A native of San Francisco, Maud Fay has won distinction at the Munich Opera
for her interpretation of Wagnerian roles and for introducing *Tosca*, despite
German opposition to the performance of Italian opera. Like many American
singers in Germany, the soprano looks forward to being recognized in her own
country.

956 **Eichberg Lady Orchestra, Boston**, *American Art Journal* XLI/20
ap (6 Sept 1884) 308.
In the past it was difficult to organize an all-female orchestra because women
typically played only string instruments. Now young ladies are turning their
attention to other instruments as well. The Eichberg Lady Orchestra, under the
direction of Julius Eichberg, will play overtures and other classical repertory
along with more popular music.

957 E.L. **Chat with Olive Mead, A**, *Musical America* V/25 (4 May
ap 1907) 11. *Illus.*
Violinist Olive Mead was a pupil of Franz Kneisel, and founded the Olive
Mead Quartet in part because of the profound influence the Kneisel Quartet
had upon her. Mead notes that she and Lillian Littlehales, cellist, have no other
commitments except to their solo work, while the other 2 women in the quartet
[Gladys North, 2nd violinist, and Verna Fonaroff, violist] are not dependent
upon the quartet for their livelihoods. Mead has appeared as soloist with the

Boston Symphony Orchestra on 14 occasions, and at the present time she is the conductor of the orchestra of the Women's Philharmonic Soc. of New York.

958 **Emma Abbott**, *Illustrated American* V/49 (24 Jan 1891) 406. *Illus.*
ap
Emma Abbott, the American songstress and prima donna, amassed a fortune through wise investments. Her secret marriage to Eugene Wetherell, a wealthy businessman and investment counselor, created a sensation when it was discovered . She also received publicity for her refusal on moral grounds to sing in *La traviata*. Abbott had the largest repertory of standard operatic roles in English translation of any of her contemporaries.

959 **Emma Nevada, noted American soprano of Mapleson days,**
ap   **dies in London at 78**, *Musical America* LX/12 (July 1940) 28-29.
       Illus.
Born Emma Wixom in Alpha, Calif, Emma Nevada (1859-1940) achieved success in the United States and Europe in the 1880s-90s. During the last years of her retirement, she had grave financial problems until the Bagby Music Lovers' Foundation, which also helped Minnie Hauk near the end of her life, gave Nevada a monthly pension which allowed her to live in relative comfort. During her retirement, Nevada taught voice to her daughter Mignon, who was named after one of Nevada's favorite roles.

→   **Erminia Rudersdorff: a great musical personality**, *see* 769ap[57].

960 **Ethel Leginska plays**, *New York Times* 3 Nov 1916, 11.
ro
Reports that while Leginska offered some splendid playing at a recent concert in Carnegie Hall, the "severely classical program"--which included Bach's *Italian concerto*, S.971, Beethoven's piano sonata no. 8 in C minor, op. 13, and Brahms's waltzes, op. 39 and *Variations on a theme by Paganini, op. 35*--did not show her to her best advantage. Leginska has special gifts as a pianist, and she should continue to display them in lighter repertory, "at the expense of things that might be better left to 6-foot pianists with heavy arms".

961 **Exhibition of violin classes**, *Boston Daily Advertiser* 28 Jan 1882,
an   4.
At a recent recital given by pupils of Julius Eichberg, head of the Boston Conservatory, 2/3rds of the approximately 30 students were young women. There is a growing demand for well-trained violinists "as the public disposition to hear good music increases", and women violinists should find a place in orchestras. Female harpists are currently employed by orchestras in "emergencies".

962 **Fadettes, The--woman's orchestra of Boston**, *Musician* V/8
ap   (Aug 1900) 273.
The Boston Fadette Lady Orchestra was initially organized in 1888 with 6 players. In 1895 the band was reorganized with 20 players and incorporated under the direction of Caroline B. Nichols. At the present time the following instruments are included: flute, piccolo, oboe, bassoon, 2 French horns, 2 cornets, trombone, percussion, and strings.

963 **Fannie Bloomfield-Zeisler, 16 July 1861-20 August 1927**.
ac   *Studies in musical education, history, and aesthetics* 22 (Hartford:
       Music Teachers National Assoc., 1929) 76-83.
Throughout a career of 50 years, Fannie Bloomfield-Zeisler was a leader among native American pianists as well as an equal among the internationally great pianists of her generation. When she gave her first recital in Chicago in 1883 after 5 years of study in Vienna with Theodor Leschetizky, musical life in the United States was just beginning to have an identity of its own. Bloomfield-Zeisler was an important figure in shaping the destiny of the native American artist, both at home and abroad. Prior to her highly successful concert tours in Europe in the 1890s, most Europeans regarded the United States as an artistic wilderness. Her especially noteworthy concert performances in the United States included 1) her appearance with Theodore Thomas's orchestra at the Music Teachers National Convention in Chicago in 1890--which led to numerous subsequent performances under Thomas, 2) a performance after a lengthy illness when, in 1920, she engaged the Chicago Symphony Orchestra and played 3 concertos in succession--including the Chaikovskii concerto no. 1 in B-flat minor, op. 23, and 3) her golden jubilee concert in 1925, at which she played the Schumann concerto in A minor, op. 54, and Chopin's concerto no. 2 in F minor, op. 21. Bloomfield-Zeisler had an extensive repertoire: in 1912 during a concert tour on the West Coast she gave 8 recitals in 18 days with no repetitions in works performed.

964 **Fannie Bloomfield-Zeisler's silver anniversary**, *Musical Courier*
ap   XL/12 (21 Mar 1900) 19-20.
"An entire volume of sermons on woman's sphere is embodied in the home life and public career of Fannie Bloomfield-Zeisler"--concert artist, teacher of piano, wife, and mother. She is about to celebrate the 25th anniversary of her youthful debut in Chicago in a concert of the Beethoven Soc., under the direction of Carl Wolfsohn, her teacher. The pianist is known for an intense, emotional approach in performance, and earlier in time she was criticized for

the rashness of her playing. Bloomfield-Zeisler teaches a select number of students in the congenial atmosphere of her home in Chicago, where she also holds frequent musicales.

965 **Farewell of Miss Anna Mehlig**, *Dwight's Journal of Music*
ro   XXXI/5 (3 June 1871) 36.
Reviews Anna Mehlig's New York recital upon the completion of her American concert tour and assesses her artistic achievements. "It is seldom that a female musician wins so many substantial honors among us as has Miss Mehlig; seldom, indeed, when she is but a pianiste, for it is seldom that all the qualifications of a musician are recognized in the fair claimants. Miss Mehlig proved herself very early in her American tour to be one of the few artists of her sex who depended solely on her art, and not at all on her sex, for public recognition". This article is reprinted from the *New York World*, 20 May 1871.

966 FARRAR, Geraldine. **Story of an American singer, The**
bm   (New York: Houghton-Mifflin, 1916) 116 p. *Illus.*
An autobiography covering the years to 1916. Born in Boston, Geraldine Farrar (1882-1967) was encouraged by her mother to become a singer, and she began performing in her early teens. At 17 she refused a role at the Metropolitan Opera, and instead borrowed money to study in Europe. Lillian Nordica advised Farrar to leave Paris for Berlin, where in 1901 she made her debut in *Faust*. In 1906 she left Berlin and finally made her debut at the Metropolitan under Toscanini's direction. Farrar also describes her early film career.

967 FARRAR, Geraldine. **Such sweet compulsion** (New York: Da
bf   Capo, 1970) 303 p. *Illus., index.*
A reprint of the 1938 edition (New York: Greystone). This 2nd autobiography covers the soprano's life (1882-1967) to 1938. An only child whose musical studies were supervised by her mother, Farrar went to Europe around 1900 and studied with Lilli Lehmann, whom she describes as a great artist and hard taskmaster. While abroad she met Caruso, Isadora Duncan, Massenet, and Nellie Melba. In 1906 Farrar made her debut in *Roméo et Juliette* at the Metropolitan Opera, where she sang 493 performances of 23 roles until her retirement in 1922. The soprano's feelings after her farewell performance, her reasons for retiring from opera at age 40, her film career, and her brief marriage to the actor Lou Tellegen are discussed. An excerpt from a talk given by Farrar in 1937 on the future of opera in the United States and a list of her operatic roles are included.

968 rb —
R. by Francis ROBINSON, *American Music Lover* IV/7 (Nov 1938) 239-42.

969 FASSETT, Stephen. **Emma Eames and her records**, *American*
ap   *Music Lover* IV/11 (Mar 1939) 397-99. *Illus.*
In a radio interview, Eames discusses her career and recordings. She believes her recordings of selections from Gounod's operas are historical documents because she studied the roles with the composer. Among her recordings of lieder, her performance of Schubert's *Gretchen am Spinnrade* has earned especially high praise.

970 FAY, Amy. **Music-study in Germany, from the home corre-**
bf   **spondence of Amy Fay**. With a new introduction by Frances
       DILLON (New York: Dover, 1965) 352 p.
A reprint of the original 1880 edition (Chicago: Jansen, McClurg). The American pianist recounts her life as a student in Germany between 1869 and 1875 when she studied with Carl Tausig, Theodor Kullak, Liszt, and Ludwig Deppe, leading to her successful debut in Berlin in 1875. The book went into 21 printings in the United States in the 19th c., and was also published in London and in French and German translations.

971 F.E.B. **To the** *Woman about town*, *Musical Courier* XXII/2 (8
ap   July 1891) 29-30.
Musical Courier reprints this letter to the editor of a women's column in the *New York Evening Sun*. The author praises the work of Anna M. Winch, harpist, as a pioneer for her gender in the orchestral field. Winch has played in the Metropolitan Opera Orchestra under Anton Seidl and also in Theodore Thomas's orchestra in New York. More women with requisite musical talent and proper training should find a place in the orchestral profession and thereby earn a good living. While increasing numbers of women are taking up the violin, cello, and contrabass, "there is a wide field for them--scarcely touched as yet--in the wind choir".

972 FERRIS, John. **Miss Farrar's 80th birthday recalls "Gerry-**
an   **flapper" days**, *New York World-Telegram* 27 Feb 1962, 23. *Illus.*
When Geraldine Farrar retired from opera in 1922, the "Gerryflappers"--a group of young women who idolized the American soprano--caused the noisiest demonstration at the Metropolitan Opera since Marcella Sembrich retired in 1909. Farrar sang some recitals until 1932, when she officially said farewell to public life and settled in her present home in Connecticut.

973
bm
Fifty local prodigies 1900-1940. Ed. by Cornel LENGYEL.
History of music project 5 (San Francisco: Works Progress Administration, 1940) 203 p. (typescript). *Illus., music, bibliog.*
Discusses 60 (not 50) musical prodigies born and educated in San Francisco between 1900 and 1940. Considers the phenomenon of the prodigy in terms of the subjects' parents, patrons, teachers, and career development. 36 of the 60 prodigies are women. Of the 36, the most extensive studies are presented for the following: Flori Gough, cellist; Patricia Benkman, Violet Blagg, Enid Lillian Brandt, Catherine Carver, Marion Cavenaugh, Cecil Marion Cowles, Laura Dubman, Eula May Howard, Alice Mayer, Reah Sadowski, Ruth Slenczynska, pianists; Lina Pagliughi, singer; and Beverly Blake, Marilyn Doty, Sarah Kriendler, Barbara Lull, and Kayla Mitzel, violinists. Lulu Blumbey and Alice Seckles are noted for their management and promotion of young artists through concerts and competitions.

974
ap
FILLMORE, J.C. **To a strange lady who wrote for information**, *Etude* V/6 (June 1887) 84.
A letter to the editor from a woman conductor has asked whether a woman ought to stand before her chorus of 15-20 women and direct them with a baton at a public concert. Fillmore replies that while rationally he doesn't think it is undignified for a lady to wield a baton, the inquirer would be better off trying to get the results she wants while seated at the piano and thus "avoid shocking the associates who have been opposing her in this move".

975
ap
FINCK, Henry T. **Musical outlook for women, The**, *Etude* XVII/5 (May 1899) 150-51.
Finck comments on the progress of women as pianists (although "the best are still mainly men"), as string players, as orchestral players, and as members of brass bands that play in beer gardens. He cites Sidney Lanier as his authority for the belief that the orchestra of the future will be predominantly female (*The orchestra of today*, WIAM 1053). This item appears on the *Woman's work in music* page (WIAM 645).

976
ap
FISCHER, Mary Chappell. **Women as concert organists**, *Etude* (WIAM 74) 332.
Prejudice against women as church organists is rapidly disappearing as the "new woman" has proven herself to be fully equal to the demands of the organ-loft service. However, for the majority of women organists the church position is a marginal one; they spend their time chiefly in teaching piano and must manage from Sunday to Sunday with the least possible organ preparation. There is no reason why women should not succeed as concert organists provided they have sufficient talent, time, and strength.

977
ap
FLETCHER, Richard D. **Mary Garden of record, The**, *Saturday Review* XXXVI/9 (27 Feb 1954) 47-50, 70. *Illus.*
Evaluates Mary Garden's work as a singer on the occasion of the golden anniversary of her first recording. Maintains that although Garden's dramatic abilities were outstanding, her vocal abilities were just as impressive. Garden was the first soprano to appear in the United States whose training was mainly French. Her first recordings made in Paris with Debussy at the piano, a series of acoustic recordings for the Columbia Gramophone Co. made between 1911 and 1914, and some electrical Victor Talking Machine Co. records issued in the 1920s are discussed.

978
ac
FLINT, Mary H. **Reminiscences of an American artist**, *The music of the modern world*. Ed. by Anton SEIDL (New York: D. Appleton, 1895) I, 133-37.
Since her "Puritan training debarred her from any idea of attempting opera", Annie Louise Cary (1842-1921) began her career as a soloist at conventions of singing societies in New England. While pursuing vocal studies in Boston, Cary sang in the chorus of the Handel and Haydn Soc., and Adelaide Phillipps's appearances with the Soc. inspired her to go abroad for further study. Once in Italy she overcame her reservations about working in opera, and she subsequently made her operatic debut in Copenhagen. Upon her return to the United States, Cary won special acclaim for her performances in 1873 at the Saengerfest in Cincinnati and her creation of Amneris in the first American performance of *Aida* in the same year. She also sang with Clara Louise Kellogg's opera company. Cary divided her work between opera and major festivals until her marriage in 1882 when she ended her career.

979
ap
Florence Austin, a violin virtuosa, *Musical Courier* LXI/18 (2 Nov 1910) 19.
Florence Austin studied in the United States with Henry Schradieck and in Europe with another American living abroad, Camilla Urso. Subsequently Austin entered the Liège Conservatory, where she became the first American to receive highest honors. After extensive concert tours in Belgium and France, she returned to the United States and has quickly taken a place at the head of the younger violinists. Austin possesses "that masculinity of tone which so distinguished Urso's playing".

980
an
Florence Hinkle, singer, dies at 48, *New York Times* 30 Apr 1933, 17.

Florence Hinkle (1885-1933) was known nationally as a concert and oratorio singer. The soprano retired from the concert stage after her marriage in 1917 to Herbert Witherspoon, a leading operatic basso. Hinkle remained active in cultural affairs as a patron in the cities in which she lived, New York, Chicago, and Cincinnati.

981
an
Florence Mulford dies at 86; sang at Met early in century, *New York Times* 10 Sept 1962, 29.
Florence Mulford was active in opera, recital and church work, and as a teacher. While she was a student at the National Conservatory in New York she was encouraged by Dvořák, the conservatory's current director, to continue her studies in Germany and Austria, and upon graduation she followed his advice. The mezzo-soprano sang at the Metropolitan Opera from 1903-06 and again in 1912-17, appearing in the American premières of *Parsifal* in 1903 and *Hänsel und Gretel* in German in 1905. Wagnerian roles were Mulford's specialty.

→   **Florence Wickham, 82, dies**, *see* 2018an[66].

982
ap
Former concert singer a composer, *Musical America* VII/9 (11 Jan 1908) 15. *Illus.*
It is not generally known that before her marriage to Sumner Salter, Mary Turner Salter was a prominent singer in recital, oratorio, and church work. She studied with Max Schilling of Burlington, Iowa, at the New England Conservatory, and also in Boston with Erminia Rudersdorff. Salter had a soprano voice of dramatic quality, which was especially suited to works such as Mendelssohn's *Elijah, op. 70*, and the extended songs of Schubert, Liszt, and Anton Rubinstein. Her fame as a song composer is growing rapidly at the present time. Sumner Salter, an organist and composer, is on the faculty of Williams Col.

983
ap
From coon songs to grand opera. The romantic career of Bessie Abott, who has just signed a contract with Heinrich Conried, *Musical America* III/8 (6 Jan 1906) 5. *Illus.*
On a transatlantic crossing enroute to vaudeville engagements in England, Bessie Abott sang for Jean de Reszke, who encouraged the soprano to train for the opera. Reszke obtained financial assistance from an anonymous patron to enable Abott to study with Frida Ashforth in New York. Ashforth believes that the time has come for the American teacher to receive just recognition.

984
ap
F.W.R. Geraldine Morgan (Mrs. Benjamin F. Roeder), *Musical Courier* LXXVI/22 (30 May 1918) 34. *Illus.*
Reports the death of Geraldine Morgan, the violinist (1867-1918). In the late 1870s Morgan's father, John P. Morgan, was assistant organist at Trinity Church in New York, and she played the violin at services. She also played in a family quartet with her 2 younger sisters and brother. After her father's death in 1881, Morgan went abroad with the rest of her family and studied with Henry Schradieck and Joachim. She also won the Mendelssohn prize. Joachim took a special pride in the young woman's career: he and Morgan played quartets and the Bach concerto for 2 violins in D minor, S.1043, and he introduced her to important people as well. Upon Morgan's return to the United States, she appeared with leading orchestras and played in her own quartet and trio, through which she introduced much new music by Brahms, Grieg, and Debussy. The Joseph Joachim Violin School that she founded in New York was highly successful. After her marriage in 1901 to Benjamin F. Roeder--general manager for David Belasco--Morgan gradually relinquished professional activity and "was delighted with the musical talent and progress of her son".

985
an
Gadski opens suit for $500,000, *New York Times* 7 Feb 1922, 1.
Reports that Johanna Gadski is suing the Chicago Opera for an alleged violation of contract and a statement that the plaintiff would not be welcomed by American audiences because of her German birth and citizenship. Gadski maintains that in Nov. 1921 she was engaged to sing in *Tristan und Isolde* by the Chicago company.

986
bm
GARDEN, Mary; BIANCOLLI, Louis. **Mary Garden's story** (New York: Simon & Schuster, 1951) xii, 302 p. *Illus.*
Born in Aberdeen, Scotland, Mary Garden (1877-1967) came to the United States as a small child and grew up in Chicago. In 1896 she sailed for Europe with her Chicago voice teacher, Mrs. Robinson Duff, intending to study with Mathilde Marchesi. However, because Marchesi wanted to train her as a coloratura soprano, Garden decided instead to study with Lucien Fugère. Discouraged by her lack of progress as a singer in Paris, Garden happened to meet Sibyl Sanderson, who in turn introduced her to Albert Carré, the director of the Opéra-Comique. As a result, Garden made her debut in the title role of *Louise* in 1900. In 1902 she sang Mélisande in the première performance of Debussy's opera, after overcoming Maeterlinck's objections. Garden sang Thaïs at her New York debut in 1907 with Oscar Hammerstein's Manhattan Opera. Strauss wrote the role of Octavian for her; however, World War I intervened, and she never sang it. In her 20-year career with the Chicago Opera beginning in 1910, Garden became both its leading singer and its first

woman director. Her most famous roles--Louise, Mélisande, Salome, and Thaïs--displayed her outstanding talents as both actress and singer. Garden retired to her birthplace in Scotland, but she returned to the United States in 1949 on a lecture tour, the proceeds of which went to benefit American music.

987 rb —
R. by Alfred FRANKENSTEIN, *New York Herald Tribune* 22 Apr 1951, VI-4.

988 rb —
R. by F.T.R., *Record Collector* VII/3 (Mar 1952) 67.

989 rb —
R. by Leo LERMAN, *New York Times* 22 Apr 1951, VII-7.

990   GATES, W. Francis. **Chats with great singers. Emma Eames**, ap   *Musician* XI/4 (Apr 1906) 169.
Asked to comment upon Grover Cleveland's recent statement that a woman's proper place is in the home rather than in public life, Emma Eames notes that a domestic existence is appropriate for perhaps 80% of the women "in the civilized world". It is wrong--she argues--to stifle the individuality of the remaining 20%. Furthermore, women who go before the public as opera singers and concert artists, for instance, feel they have a mission to fulfill besides making a living and gaining applause.

991   **Geraldine Farrar running war relief festival**, *New York Times* an   28 Apr 1918, III-3. *Illus.*
Geraldine Farrar's plans for the forthcoming music festival to benefit the Stage Woman's War Relief have included renting the opera house and countless managerial details. Farrar's administrative ability indicates that "the singer has made just as many strides in her relation to the public world as women have made in general".

992   GIACOMELLI, M. **Camilla Urso**, *Dwight's Journal of Music* II/ ap   15 (15 Jan 1853) 115-16.
Camilla Urso's grandfather and father were both trained musicians. After hearing a violin played at the Church of the Holy Cross in Nantes, France, Urso made an immediate decision to play that instrument. Her first performance at age 7 demonstrated technical command and a pure tone. Urso studied at the Paris Conservatory under Lambert-Joseph Massart, later toured Germany, and then returned to Paris for further studies and to play additional concerts. This article originally appeared in a more lengthy version in *La France musicale*.

993   GILBERT, Morris. **Then and now. Mary Garden is still** ap   **creating operatic personality--by proxy**, *New York Times* 7 Feb
1954, VI-58. *Illus.*
A brief account of Garden's operatic achievements from her debut in Paris in 1900 to her final performance in Chicago in the late 1920s. Garden's current interest is the discovery of new singers. Her views concerning her present life in her native town of Aberdeen, Scotland are discussed.

994   GILL, Lorna. **American woman pianist of today and yester-** ap   **day, The. An entertaining account of the remarkable advance**
in piano playing made by the women of our country during
the last century, *Etude* (*WIAM* 75) 447-48.
In the 1840s, German pianists in the employ of American piano manufacturers traveled throughout the country giving lessons to girls. The ability to play a few, pretty tunes was then considered an accomplishment for young women. With the Civil War, foreign musicians returned to Europe, and the vogue for sentimentality came to an end. After the war, women's education began to be regarded as a more serious matter in all areas, including piano. Conservatories were founded in increasing numbers, and the standards of piano playing in the United States advanced rapidly. Today only the talented girl student pursues piano: "playing at art is out of date".

995   GIPSON, Richard McCandless. **Life of Emma Thursby, The.** bm   **1845-1931** (New York: New York Historical Society, 1940) xxii,
470 p. *Illus., index.*
Emma Cecilia Thursby grew up in Brooklyn and decided to become a singer by the age of 6. Her early progress was slowed, however, by a family financial crisis upon the death of her father, the Civil War, and her choice of the church for musical performance. With income from various church jobs in Brooklyn, she began studying voice with Julius Meyer in New York in 1867, and she also went abroad to study in Italy for 10 months. Thursby's tour of the United States in 1876 as the soprano soloist with Patrick S. Gilmore and his 65-piece band was decisive. Her repertory at this time ranged from the spectacular theme and variations by Heinrich ProSch to selections from Haydn's oratorios. Probably through Gilmore, Thursby came to study with Erminia Rudersdorff, a leading oratorio singer from England whom Gilmore brought to America for his World's Peace Jubilee of 1872. It was Rudersdorff who challenged Thursby to "let the churches go" and establish herself in Europe. Under Maurice Strakosch's management Thursby sang on tour in the United States and Canada in 1877, and in 1878 she turned to Europe where she received instant

and widespread acclaim. For the next 10 years the soprano performed extensively in solo recitals and concert work both at home and abroad. Gipson notes that there was always pressure on Thursby to enter the operatic field, and he speculates that while she may have felt she lacked the temperament for opera, she may also have decided that she would continue to fare better on the concert stage where she did not have significant competition. Thursby's repertory was extensive and mirrored the changes in musical taste in the United States during the 2nd half of the 19th c. Her trademark was Mozart's concert aria *Mia speranza adorato*, K.416. After 1888 she curtailed her touring and established Friday musicales at her home on Gramercy Park in New York. A chronology of Thursby's performances is included.

996 rb —
R. by Ralph THOMPSON, *New York Times* 9 Jan 1941, 19.

997   **Girl violinists: an innovation that has been followed by good** an   **results**, *Boston Herald* 20 Jan 1888, 6.
While 25 years ago young women as violinists were considered oddities, today they are fully accepted, and they excel in the field. This change is due to the influence of Julius Eichberg, head of the Boston Conservatory, who "declares that girls are in every aspect the equal of boys in acquiring proficiency on this instrument".

998   GLACKENS, Ira. **Yankee diva. Lillian Nordica and the** bm   **Golden Days of Opera** (New York: Coleridge, 1963) xiv, 366 p.
Illus., bibliog., discog.
Lillian Nordica's career was built slowly and steadily. Her contemporaries sometimes tired of her references to constant hard work, and yet her career (1857-1914) evidenced it at every turn. Nordica might not have become a singer, had not the death of an older sister with vocal promise allowed for recognition of Nordica's own potential. Her mother and John O'Neill, her teacher at the New England Conservatory, were her first mentors. After further study and performances in Europe between 1878 and 1882, Nordica made her American operatic debut in 1883. In the early years of her career she sang a wide variety of French and Italian roles, but as her voice matured she specialized in Wagner's operas. Nordica was chosen to sing Elsa in the first Bayreuth performance of Lohengrin in 1894--a role which she coached with Cosima Wagner. Subsequently she returned to Bayreuth to prepare the role of Isolde for the American première of *Tristan und Isolde* at the Metropolitan Opera on 27 Nov. 1895. Anton Seidl was the conductor at this memorable performance; Jean de Reszke sang Tristan. Nordica regarded Seidl as one of the most important aides to her artistic growth. She went on to learn the 3 Brünnhilde roles in *Der Ring des Nibelungen* and Kundry, which she performed to great acclaim both at home and abroad. The author notes that Nordica's private life was as unsuccessful as her public life was successful: none of her 3 marriages was happy. Nordica died in Java on a world-wide tour of farewell appearances. Her will was contested by her 3rd husband, and most of the fortune she had earned through her career of 40 years was consumed by legal expenses.

999 rb —
R. by Raymond ERICSON, *New York Times* 3 May 1964, VII-6.

1000   GLUCK, Alma. **Glückliche Reise!** *Opera News* III/2-3 (11 Nov- ap   21 Nov 1938) 1-3; 3-4.
The soprano recalls the poverty of her early years, the unusual way in which she secured a contract at the Metropolitan Opera while still an unknown singer, her debut as Sophie in *Werther* in 1909, and Toscanini's revival of *Orfeo* in 1910--in which Gluck sang the role of the Third Echo. Gluck felt strongly about the necessity for terminating her work at the Metropolitan after 3 seasons in minor roles in order to go to Europe and further her art.

1001   GORDON, Gertrude. **Morning with Gadski, A**, *Green Book* ap   *Album* III/3 (Mar 1910) 632-36.
An interview on tour with Johanna Gadski concerning the management of her career and her private life. The soprano's daughter, Lotta Tauscher, and her husband, Hans Tauscher, take care of all her business and domestic affairs, and while she is grateful she also believes that performers are entitled to this sort of privilege. Gadski married at age 19, and subsequently she left her infant daughter with her husband in Germany in order to come to the United States to further her career. Her family later joined her, and her daughter--now grown--is her constant companion. Gadski sees a great future for music in America and believes that opera houses should be established in small cities throughout the country with the dual purpose of elevating the public's musical tastes and providing ample opportunities for native American singers.

1002   GRAHAM, Katherine. **American girl and her violin, An**, ap   *Metropolitan Magazine* XI/3 (Mar 1900) 281-84.
In only 2 years Leonora Jackson has scored a triumph with leading orchestras in Europe. Her mother, a singer, was her first teacher, and she studied with a number of violinists in Chicago during her formative years. Jackson was in her 2nd year at the Paris Conservatory when she received word of her father's financial failure and accordingly was forced to return to the United States. She raised some monies for a return to Europe by playing concerts at summer

resorts with her brother Ernest--a plan which was devised by their mother. Subsequently 20 women joined to guarantee Jackson 4 years study with Joachim in Berlin, and in 1884 she returned to Europe. Jackson made her debut with the Berlin Philharmonic under the direction of Joachim in the Brahms violin concerto in D major, op. 77. She is a winner of the Mendelssohn prize.

1003 GRAU, Robert. **Strange public aversion to contraltos as**
ap **compared with sopranos of great fame**, *Musician* XXI/11 (Nov 1916) 694-95.
Until the success of Ernestine Schumann-Heink, who has "completely shattered all theories as to the potency of contraltos", no concert manager prospered over the long run by managing a contralto. Schumann-Heink's personality is one reason for her tremendous box-office appeal. Annie Louise Cary was highly successful in appearances with sopranos Clara Louise Kellogg and Christine Nilsson, but in solo performances she did not draw large audiences. Similarly Adelaide Phillipps and Zelda Harrison Séguin lacked box-office appeal as soloists.

1004 GREENWOOD, Grace. **Emma Abbott** (n.p.: author, [1878?])
bm 14 p.
An account of Emma Abbott's personal and professional life prior to her European debut in 1877. Abbott began singing concerts at a young age in the Midwest, and after earning enough money, she moved to New York. There she sang at Dr. Chapin's church, a prestigious establishment whose members Horace Greeley and C.P. Huntington helped send her to Europe in 1872. In Italy she studied with Antonio Sangiovanni, and in Paris with François Wartel and Mathilde Marchesi. Contact with Adelina Patti led to Abbott's Covent Garden debut.

1005 GRIFFITH, M. Dinorben. **Miss Ellen Beach Yaw, "The**
ap **California lark"**, *Strand Magazine* [American ed.] XVII (Dec 1899) 612-17. *Illus.*
A coloratura soprano, Ellen Beach Yaw--sometimes called Lark Ellen--has a vocal compass of 4 octaves; her lower and medium registers possess the rich quality of a contralto. Yaw's mother was her first teacher, and because her father died when she was a child, she could afford professional lessons only intermittently during her formative years as a singer. Typically she would work at a job outside of the music field in order to save money for lessons. Yaw states she owes a great deal to her principal teacher Torpadie Bjorksten in New York, who taught Yaw for 2 years and then financed her way to Paris for further study. The American soprano tours regularly at home and abroad. She is also active for the Lark Ellen Home for New Boys in Los Angeles, singing at benefits and raising monies in related ways as well.

1006 **Growing opportunities for American violinists**, *Etude* XXXIV/
ap 8 (Aug 1916) 602.
Although 25 years ago conductors automatically imported violinists from Europe, in recent years the demand for Americans as both solo and orchestral violinists has increased. The work of the following American concert violinists is cited: Maud Powell, Albert Spalding, Francis Macmillan, and Eddy Brown.

1007 HAENSEL, Fitzhugh W. **Margaret Matzenauer's supremacy**
ap **as an artist**, *Musical Courier* LXIX/11 (16 Sept 1914) 10.
After years of success as a contralto, Margaret Matzenauer has become a dramatic soprano. Intensive training under Felix Mottl in Munich, her strong constitution, and iron nerves enable Matzenauer to sing heavy German roles. For 7 years she was the leading contralto at Wagner festivals in Germany.

→ HANAFORD, Phebe. **Women of the century**, see 53bm[05].

1008 HANCHETT, Dr. Henry G. **American girls' temperament in**
ap **relation to music study**, *Etude* XVII/5 (May 1899) 146.
Now that music is no longer regarded as a mere accomplishment and fewer young women are studying, there is no room on the market for incompetent teachers. Also, music as a study has improved its standing in public opinion. American girls are quick-witted and are learning the value of serious study of music.

→ **Handel and Haydn Society gives reception to distinguished**
woman composer of music, see 683an[56].

1009 HANSLICK, Eduard. **Patti's girlhood**, *Dwight's Journal of*
ap *Music* XXXVII/17 (24 Nov 1877) 136.
An interview with Adelina Patti about her early musical background. Born in Madrid, where her Sicilian father, the tenor Salvatore Patti, and Roman mother, the prima donna Signora Barilla, were singing, she and her family came to New York while she was an infant. As a child the soprano studied voice with her step-brother Ettore Barilli and piano with her sister Carlotta. When the troupe her parents sang in failed, Patti saved her family by performing bravura arias at age 7. She studied the part of Rosina from *Il barbiere di Siviglia* with her brother-in-law, Maurice Strakosch, who later coached her in other roles. Through Strakosch, she was engaged by Bernard

Ullman to sing her debut in 1859 as Lucia with the New York Italian Opera; this was followed by performances as Rosina and Amina in *La sonnambula*. In 1860 she sang in Boston, Philadelphia, and other American cities; her first European appearance was at Covent Garden in London.

1010 **Harp as a profession, The**, *Etude* XVII/8 (Aug 1899) 193.
ap
While at the present time the harp positions in leading orchestras are all filled with foreigners, the fact that the harp is the only instrument which women have been allowed to play in first-class orchestras makes it an appropriate instrument for women to take up. As harpists women can command practically the same fees as men. A letter from Clara Murray is included, in which Murray contends that after 2 years of training a woman harpist can earn her living as an accompanist, particularly with church choirs.

1011 HAUGHTON, John Alan. **Emma Juch, star of the eighties,**
ap **dies in New York**, *Musical America* LIX/5 (10 Mar 1939) 8.
Emma Juch's father was a talented amateur musician who opposed her professional goals until he heard her sing at a student recital. Juch (1863-1939) made debuts in London and New York in 1881 with Colonel Mapleson's company. She was best known in the United States for her association with the American Opera, a company of highly-trained native Americans under the direction of Theodore Thomas. Subsequently she formed the Emma Juch Opera and toured throughout the United States, Canada, and Mexico until 1891. After 1891 the soprano sang chiefly in concerts and at music festivals. When she married Francis L. Wellman she abandoned her career at his insistence, although she later regretted the decision. Juch was a versatile singer, performing roles as different as Aida and Queen of the Night.

1012 HAUK, Minnie. **Memories of a singer** (London: A.M. Philpot,
bm 1925) 295 p. *Illus.*
A child prodigy encouraged by her parents to pursue singing, Minnie Hauk (1851-1929) made her debut in *La sonnambula* at the Academy of Music in Brooklyn when she was 16 years old. Like so many other budding prima donnas of the post-Civil War era, she went to Paris to study while still in her teens, accompanied by her mother as chaperon. Maurice Strakosch assumed the dual role of teacher and manager, and after working with him Hauk began a series of engagements in Europe. She was the first American to appear at leading opera houses in St. Petersburg, Vienna, Budapest, and Berlin. In 1878 she sang the title role in the first performances of *Carmen* in London and New York under Colonel Mapleson's management. This highly successful production--which Hauk was instrumental in creating--was innovative for its realistic acting and scenery. Thereafter Hauk performed in the United States as well as Europe, and among her interests was the popularization of Wagner's operas in America. She notes that when she attended the opening of the Bayreuth Festival in Aug. 1876, she was overwhelmed by the experience and came to appreciate the composer's genius. At the close of her professional career in 1891, Hauk toured the country with her own opera company, finding great success with a new opera she had located a score for in Paris, *Cavalleria rusticana*. Hauk retired with her husband to Wagner's former house in Tribschen, Switzerland, which the couple purchased in 1889.

1013 H.B. **"Give hearing to every new idea", urges Vera Barstow**,
ap *Musical America* XXIII/14 (5 Feb 1916) 47.
"A composition need not necessarily have classical form to possess beauty", argues violinist Vera Barstow in defense of modern music. She believes that new compositions should be heard in the interest of progress. A supporter of suffrage for women, Barstow is also interested in cooking and designing clothes for herself. She asks her critics to make their criticism constructive, i.e., directed toward particular faults.

1014 **Helen Ware will locate in New York**, *Musical Courier* LXIX/12
ap (23 Sept 1914) 13.
The increased demand for Helen Ware's recitals of Hungarian and Slavic music and her joint recitals with Rudoldph Ganz and Harold Bauer have necessitated the removal of her offices from Philadelphia to New York. The violinist plays her own arrangements of Hungarian and Slavic folk tunes, as well as contemporary music by composers such as Jenö Hubay, her teacher.

1015 HEMPEL, Frieda. **Mein Leben dem Gesang [My life in song]**
bm (Berlin: Argon, 1955) 319 p. *Illus., index.* In German.
A pupil of Selma Nicklass-Kempner in Berlin, Frieda Hempel (1885-1955) sang for Hans Conried at a relatively young age and was offered a contract at the Metropolitan Opera; her teacher, however, insisted that Hempel's studies had only begun. Later in 1912 when the coloratura soprano came to the United States, she was a well-established singer with experience at the court opera in Schwerin and the Berlin State Opera. Hempel made her Metropolitan debut in Dec. 1912 as Marguerite de Valois in *Les Huguenots*, appearing with Caruso and Emmy Destinn. In the 1912-13 season she sang the Marschallin--a role she had studied with Strauss--in the American premiére of *Der Rosenkavalier*. Hempel was a tireless traveler on concert tours, and in 1920 she performed in 70 concerts impersonating Jenny Lind for the centenary of the Swedish soprano's birth. She sang the same program Lind sang in 1850 for her first American appearance. Hempel's friendship with Marcella Sembrich, her

making of recordings, and her concerts at the White House for Presidents Hoover and Franklin Roosevelt are considered. This autobiography was published after the soprano's death in Berlin.

1016 HENDERSON, William J. **Why woman loves Chopin**, *Etude*
ap XXVIII/3 (Mar 1910) 160.
"What woman feels in the music of Chopin is the underlying weakness of the personal fiber" of the composer. Woman responds to the elegance and small dimensions of Chopin's shorter works. This article is reprinted by *Etude* from the *New York Sun*.

→ **History of opera in San Francisco I**, *see* 302bm[48].

1017 **History of opera in San Francisco II**. Ed. by Lawrence
bm ESTAVAN. *San Francisco theater research project* 8 (San Francisco: Works Progress Administration, 1938) 165 p. (typescript). *Illus., bibliog., list of works.*
Considers opera in San Francisco from 1900-38. Includes extensive lists of performances, theaters, programs, and singers. Women, naturally, figure importantly in this history. Popular theater and vaudeville stars are also discussed.

1018 **Home for female students of music at Milan**, *Dwight's Journal*
ap *of Music* XXXIV/4 (30 May 1874) 239-40.
Reports of a proposal to found a home for English and American female students of voice in Milan. Students who travel to Milan are often exploited, given false hopes about their careers, and charged high prices for lessons and room and board. They are unprepared for the high expenses and lack the knowledge to choose teachers. The proposed home would protect students by providing residence and instruction in music and language under supervision.

1019 HOMER, Anne. **Louise Homer and the Golden Age of**
bm **Opera** (New York: W. Morrow, 1974) 439 p. *Illus., bibliog., index.*
A biography by the singer's daughter, based on extensive source materials in the possession of the family. Discusses the histories of Louise Homer's parental family--the Beatty's--in Pennsylvania and Sidney Homer's ancestors in Massachusetts. Considers the contralto's formative years in Philadelphia, her studies in Paris and her search for the right teacher, her work at the Metropolitan Opera and on tour in the United States as a recitalist, and the domestic life of the Homer family.

1020 rb —
R. by Louis SNYDER, *Christian Science Monitor* 16 Jan 1974, F-5.

1021 HOMER, Sidney. **My wife and I** (New York: Da Capo, 1977)
bf 269 p. *Illus.*
A reprint of the 1939 edition (New York: Macmillan). Née Beatty, Louise Homer (1871-1947) worked as a stenographer in Philadelphia after her graduation from high school, while also studying voice. In 1893 she made the momentous decision to move to Boston and devote all her energies to music. There she studied harmony with Sidney Homer--who had spent 5 years in Leipzig and Munich under Josef Rheinberger--and in 1895 Louise and Sidney married. At Sidney's urging they borrowed money to go to Paris to further Louise's career as a contralto. Beginning in 1898 she sang with small companies in Vichy and Angers, then in London, and in 1900 she returned to the United States for a 3-year contract at the Metropolitan Opera--with the proviso from Maurice Grau that she could design her own costumes for the "trouser" roles of Siebel in *Faust* and Urbano in *Les Huguenots* in lieu of tights. Homer appeared regularly at the Metropolitan and elsewhere and in concert until her retirement in the 1920s. The revival of Gluck's *Orfeo* in 1909 was perhaps the high point of her career. A firm believer in encouraging native American composers, Homer created the leading female role in Frederick Converse's *The pipe of desire*, and she also collaborated with her husband in performances of his songs. She was the enthusiastic mother of 6 children. After her retirement from public life, Homer became interested in religion and hymn singing.

1022 **Hopekirk recital, The [February 1892]**, *Brooklyn Daily Eagle* 18
ro Feb 1892, 5.
Helen Hopekirk, pianist and composer, played with "unusual power and brilliance in a masculine style". Her performance of Schumann's *Symphonic etudes, op. 13*, was on a par with Paderewski's & better than Pachmann's. Also on the program of her Brooklyn recital were works by Chopin, Arthur Foote, Borodin, Theodor Leschetizky, and 2 Liszt transcriptions of Schubert songs.

1023 **Hopekirk recital, The [May 1892]**, *Brooklyn Daily Eagle* 19 May
ro 1892, 1.
Helen Hopekirk, pianist and composer, gave a recital including works by Rameau, Gluck, Scarlatti, Chopin, Liszt, and her own sonata in F-sharp major. She played Liszt with gravity and force, showing a breadth that men do not often exhibit. She also played Chopin well and without undue sentimentality.

1024 **How one woman carved out a new avenue of bread winning**
an **for her sex**, *Pittsburgh Gazette* 23 Feb 1908, IV-6.
There are 30 women's orchestras in America today, but the Boston Fadette Lady Orchestra is the only one that enjoys a national reputation. This 30-piece orchestra furnishes ample evidence that the "gifts of the fathers" are inherited by their children, even to the 3rd and 4th generation: many players come from musical families. The founder and conductor of the Fadettes, Caroline B. Nichols, believes that young women should be taught a useful vocation, even if they do not need to be self-supporting, and that a career as an orchestral musician offers good pay, respect, and a congenial atmosphere in which to work.

→ HOWARD, John. **Hewitt family in American music, The**, *see* 210ap[38].

1025 HOWARD, Kathleen. **Confessions of an opera singer** (New
bm York: A. Knopf, 1918) 273 p. *Illus.*
Kathleen Howard discusses her 9-year concert and operatic career in Europe as a young artist. Accompanied by her sister Marjorie, the contralto went to Paris to study with Jacques Bouhy, and subsequently she sang at the Metz Opera for 2 years. Howard also studied with Jean de Reszke and sang leading roles for 3 seasons in Darmstadt. Eventually she returned to the United States and sang with the Metropolitan Opera between 1916 and 1927. While Howard speaks favorably of her European experiences, she laments the fact that many American women cannot learn the opera business in their own country. A list of roles in the contralto's repertory is included together with information about her costumer, Marie Muelle, a leading operatic costumer in Paris.

1026 HUME, Paul. **Miss Garden rose to opera's heights from**
an **obscure start**, *Washington Post* 15 Jan 1967, G-2, 7. *Illus.*
A summary of Mary Garden's performances in Chicago, Washington, New York, and Boston, written shortly before her death. Garden spent 20 of the more than 30 years of her active operatic career with the Chicago Opera, singing 24 roles and in 1922 becoming its director for 1 year. The circumstances of her Paris debut in 1900 as well as the making of 2 of her early records are recalled.

1027 HUNEKER, James Gibbons. **Bedouins** (New York: Charles
bm Scribner's Sons, 1920) 271 p. *Illus.*
The first 4 chapters are devoted to the career of Mary Garden and include a critique of the singer-actress in the title roles of *Pelléas et Mélisande*, *Thaïs*, *Carmen*, Massenet's *Cléopâtre*, and Henry Février's *Monna Vanna* and *Gismonda*.

1028 HUNEKER, James Gibbons. **Eternal feminine, The**, *Overtones*
bd (New York: C. Scribner's Sons, 1904) 277-306.
"Piano playing as an accomplishment is passing. The new girl is too busy to play the piano unless she has the gift; then she plays it with consuming earnestness. We listen to her for we know that this is an age of specialization, an age when woman is coming into her own, be it nursing, electoral suffrage, or the writing of plays; men poets no longer make sonnets to our Ladies of Ivories, nor are budding girls chained to the keyboard". The author believes that women pianists should attempt the music of all composers, but he doubts that women are able to interpret some works, e.g., Beethoven's late piano music, and parts of the piano literature by Liszt and Brahms.

1029 HUNEKER, James Gibbons. **Girl who plays Chopin, The**,
ap *Harper's Bazaar* XXXIII/25 (23 June 1900) 466-68.
Chopin is the favorite composer among women and his music is in the repertory of every 18 year-old female pianist. However Huneker believes that young American women are too buoyant, self-reliant, and full of healthy sentiment to confine themselves to Chopin's moody, even morose music.

1030 H.W.L. **"Let stars give their services to help promote**
ap **orchestras"**, Hempel proposes, *Musical Courier* CXXIX/6 (20 Mar 1944) 6.
Frieda Hempel recently appeared with the Peekskill Civic Symphony Orchestra in Peekskill, N.Y. without remuneration, and she found an enthusiastic audience. The soprano suggests that if leading artists would regularly contribute performances in recitals and with orchestra in small communities, the interest of the townspeople would in time permit the charging of entrance fees.

→ **In memoriam. Mary Turner Salter**, *see* 691bm[56].

1031 **Interesting chamber music concerts**, *Musical America* XI/4 (4
ap Dec 1909) 13.
Discusses the backgrounds of Édouard Déthier, violinist, and Carolyn Beebe, pianist, and their sonata recitals for the 1908-09 season in the ballroom of the Hotel Plaza in New York. Their repertory includes Corelli, Bach, Mozart, and Beethoven as well as more "modern music". Beebe studied with Joseph Mosenthal and Paul Tidden in the United States before going to Europe to work further with Moritz Moszkowski and Harold Bauer. Once she returned to

the United States, Beebe became associated with the Inst. of Musical Art in New York and turned her attention to chamber music.

1032 Interview with Augusta Cottlow, An, *Musical Courier* LXXVII/
ap 24 (12 Dec 1918) 14-15. *Illus.*
Cottlow, while primarily a performer, finds teaching piano one day a week fascinating. She espouses her teacher Busoni's ideal of clarity-- of technique, of tone coloring by developing the touch, of rhythm, of form in interpretation, and of spirit or a clearly-defined attitude toward a composer. Known as the leading exponent of MacDowell's piano music, Cottlow believes that Americans have yet to acknowledge MacDowell's importance as the "greatest composer our country has produced". The pianist found her 5 years abroad "broadening and uplifting". However, because of harrowing experiences after the war began, she is grateful to be back in the United States.

1033 Isabella Beaton in New York and Boston, *Musical Courier*
ap LXII/2 (11 Jan 1911) 43.
Isabella Beaton, composer and pianist from Cleveland, gave a concert with soprano Fay Cord in Boston in Jordan Hall. Among the works performed was an excerpt from Beaton's 3-act opera *Anacaona*. A summary of the opera's plot is included.

1034 JACOBS, O.P. Augusta Cottlow's art not forgotten in the
ap **deep joy of her motherhood**, *Musical Courier* XXIII/14 (5 Feb 1916) 29. *Illus.*
In an interview in Berlin, the American pianist discusses her conviction that not only are art and home life compatible, they are mutually helpful. "Hardly anyone would assert that Ernestine Schumann-Heink, Teresa Carreño, or Louise Homer deteriorated with the advent of their children".

1035 J.A.H. Death takes Anne E. Schoen-René, *Musical America*
ap LXII/16 (25 Nov 1942) 15. *Illus.*
Anna Eugénie Schoen-René (1864-1942) studied with Pauline Viardot-Garcia, making her debut as Marcellina in *Fidelio* in Saxe-Altemburg, Germany. In 1906 Schoen-René became an American citizen, but she returned to Paris in 1909 to become an assistant to Viardot-Garcia. In 1925 she joined the faculty at the Juilliard School, where she taught until her death.

1036 Jane Osborn-Hannah, noted Wagnerian soprano, *Musical*
ap *Courier* LXIV/22 (29 May 1912) 38.
After establishing herself as a concert artist in the United States, Jane Osborn-Hannah went to Germany to launch a career in opera in 1903. She prepared a number of Wagnerian roles with Rosa Sucher in Berlin, after which she sang in Leipzig under Arthur Nikisch for 3 years. In Leipzig she performed 20 different operatic roles, and she also won the distinction of singing in 4 Gewandhaus concerts under Nikisch as well as in the first Leipzig performance of Liszt's *Die Legende von der heilige Elisabeth*. Osborn-Hannah returned to the United States in 1909, appearing first with the Metropolitan Opera and subsequently with the Chicago Grand Opera, where she remains the leading Wagnerian soprano. Osborn-Hannah's husband manages all the business aspects of her career.

1037 J.L.H. Maud Powell champions the West's taste for music,
ap *Musical America* VII/5 (14 Dec 1907) 5.
In this interview following upon a concert tour in the western United States, Powell notes that she has inherited her pioneering instincts as a musician from her father, who was a pioneer in education. She delights in the spontaneous enthusiasm of western audiences, which refuse to accept eastern verdicts on certain music and instead decide anew. The violinist also decries the prevalent practice among concert managers of sending 2nd and 3rd rate talents on tour in the West, while advertising them as first rate. Powell plays the same type of program in western locales as in the East, e.g., for the 1907-08 season, Grieg's sonata in G major, op. 14, Vieuxtemps's concerto, op. 31, and only a few popular pieces as encores.

→ JOHNSON, Frances. **Mrs. Charles Dudley Warner**, *see* 786bd[57].

1038 Julia Hostater to return, *Musical Courier* LXXII/23 (8 June
ap 1916) 40.
Announces Julia Hostater's concert tour in the United States for the 1916-17 season. Like so many American singers, the mezzo-soprano is better known abroad than in her own country. Hostater is acknowledged as a supreme interpreter of lieder. Originally she trained as a pianist, which accounts in part for her excellent musicianship.

1039 Julie Rivé-King, *Musical America* LVII/13 (Aug 1937) 36.
ap
An obituary for the pianist (1857-1937). After training in New York and abroad, Rivé-King made the Middle West the principal scene of her activities as a performing artist, and she appeared more than 200 times with orchestra under the direction of Theodore Thomas alone. She married Frank H. King of

Milwaukee in 1876. In 1900 Rivé-King joined the faculty of the Bush Conservatory in Chicago.

1040 J.V. Alice Gentle scores triumph in vaudeville, *Musical Courier*
ap LXXXIX/12 (18 Sept 1924) 22-23.
Reports that Alice Gentle has revealed the American spirit of independence by casting aside a career in opera and concert in favor of an attractive offer in vaudeville. Her success on the West Coast has been impressive, and she may tour the entire vaudeville circuit. Gentle is interested in the money to be made in vaudeville, and notes that the recent influx of foreign artists was limiting her opportunities in opera and concert.

1041 J.V. Johanna Gadski closes third tour with German Grand
ap **Opera**, *Musical Courier* CIII/17 (25 Apr 1931) 6. *Illus.*
An interview with Johanna Gadski at the completion of the 3rd consecutive tour of the German Grand Opera, during which the soprano sang 3 performances a week. Gadski is gratified with the interest of audiences in Wagner's operas during the tour, and she notes that Walter Damrosch's recent radio lectures on Wagner have been instrumental in creating this interest. Gadski wants to impress upon the public that the German Grand Opera is not her company, but rather an American institution organized by Geraldine Hall and J.J. Vincent.

1042 KAGAN, Susan. Camilla Urso: a nineteenth-century violin-
ap **ist's view**, *Signs. Journal of Women in Culture and Society* II/3 (spring 1977) 727-34.
Camilla Urso was a violin virtuoso who began concertizing in the United States at age 10 and pursued a successful career on the concert stage for several decades. Her pioneering efforts on behalf of quality concert music are noteworthy. This article includes a biographical sketch, an assessment of Urso's career, and a reprint of a speech written and delivered by the violinist in 1893 in Chicago at the Woman's Musical Congress. The speech is an argument in favor of economic and professional equality for women as orchestral musicians.
(Author)

→ **Kate S. Chittenden honored on eightieth birthday**, *see* 788ap[57].

→ KEITH, Alice. **Musical Americana**, *see* 2240ap[68].

1043 KELLOGG, Clara Louise. Memoirs of an American prima
bf **donna** (New York: Da Capo, 1978) 382 p. $25. *Illus., port.*
A reprint of the 1913 edition (New York: G.P. Putnam's Sons). One of the first American women to succeed in opera in the United States and abroad, Clara Louise Kellogg (1842-1916) was born into a family of musical amateurs, and she began piano study at age 5 and voice at 15. Initially she did not plan on a career as a singer: her female contemporaries had no professional aspirations, and decent women were assumed not to go on the stage. Nonetheless, Kellogg soon pursued opera, making her debut as Gilda at the Academy of Music in New York in 1861. In 1863 she sang Marguerite in the first American performance of *Faust*--a role, she recalls, she was too naive at the time to understand fully. Kellogg toured extensively in the United States throughout her career, often coping with difficult travel conditions. After the Civil War the soprano made the first of her many trips to Europe, where she performed as far east as St. Petersburg. In 1873 Kellogg organized an opera company which gave performances on tour in English translation; she did the translations herself in addition to singing. Her mother's rigorous chaperonage limited Kellogg's social contacts despite the many interesting people she met as a result of her career. She retired in the late 1880s.

1044 KENDALL, John Smith. Friend of Chopin, and some other
ap **New Orleans musical celebrities**, *Louisiana Historical Quarterly* XXXI/4 (Oct 1948) 856-76.
Considers Minnie Hauk's youth in New Orleans and her voice teacher Gregorio Curo. Discusses the career of singer Caterina Marco, née Catherine Smith in New Orleans. The friend of Chopin referred to in the title is Paul Emile Johns, a New Orleans musician who possibly was influential in dissuading Chopin from settling in the New World in 1832.

1045 KING, Florence M. Women as organists, *Etude* XVII/8 (Aug
ap 1899) 263.
Given dresses of sensible width, a healthy constitution, and determination, there is no reason why women can't succeed as organists. In fact, there are already a few women organists of note.

1046 KINSCELLA, Hazel Gertrude. Half century of piano play-
ap **ing as viewed through Teresa Carreño's eyes**, *Musical America* XXV/9 (30 Dec 1916) 5.
Teresa Carreño scoffs at artists who try to "uplift and educate the public"; instead she plays to please her audiences. She does not like contemporary French music, e.g., the piano works of Ravel. The pianist recalls her associations with Louis Moreau Gottschalk, Anton Rubinstein, Liszt, and

MacDowell and also her composition of a piece that has become one of her most popular encores--namely, *Teresita, kleine Waltzer.*

1047 KLEIN, Herman. **Reign of Patti, The** (New York: Da Capo,
bf   1978) 470 p. $25. *Illus., index.*
A reprint of the 1920 edition (New York: Century). Known as the *prima donna assoluta* of the "Rossini school" of coloratura singing, Adelina Patti (1843-1919) was born in Madrid to Italian parents both of whom were opera singers. The family relocated in New York shortly thereafter, where Patti grew up in a completely musical atmosphere. She studied voice with her half-brother, Ettore Barili, and also Maurice Strakosch, her brother-in-law and later her manager. As a "phenomenal child soprano" Patti toured the United States for 3 years with a company that included Ole Bull, and in 1857 she went on tour with Louis Moreau Gottschalk throughout the southern states and to the West Indies. Realizing full well the enormous potential income Patti's talent represented, her father and Strakosch carefully plotted her career. In 1860 she went to England to gain the necessary foreign reputation, and she remained in Europe for 20 years, during which time she was extremely successful. After 1881 she returned to the United States in a series of tours--some in opera, some in concert with a group of artists. A high point in the American "Patti epidemic" was her appearance in the Mormon Tabernacle in Salt Lake City in 1884. Her American tours included a number of "farewell" concerts. However, by the time she made her final farewell tour in 1903-04, interest in the coloratura repertory had declined. While Marcella Sembrich and Nellie Melba continued as coloratura sopranos after her, Patti represents the last in a line of singers that included Jenny Lind and Giuditta Grisi. Patti was a highly conscientious artist and was always generous with applause for her colleagues.

1048 KRAMER, A. Walter. **Florence Hinkle Witherspoon: a**
ap   **tribute to a great singer,** *Musical America* LIII/7 (25 Apr 1933)
          33. *Illus.*
20 years ago Florence Hinkle was one of America's leading concert sopranos, and there was rarely an important festival for which she was not engaged. Typically she joined a quartet of soloists with a leading symphony orchestra and toured throughout the country, making appearances with local oratorio societies, choruses, etc. Between these engagements she gave solo recitals. A native of Philadelphia, Hinkle relocated in New York early in her career, where she sang at the West End Collegiate Church and studied with Oscar Saenger and Herbert Witherspoon.

→   KRAMER, A. Walter. **Bertha Feiring Tapper: altruist,** *see*
          791ap[57].

→   K.S.C. **Our women composers find recognition in new cam-**
          paign, *see* 700ap[56].

1049 KUTER, Kay Edwin-Emmert. **Carmen incarnate. The story**
ap   **of Marguerite Sylva,** *Opera, Concert, and Symphony* II/7-9 (July-
          Sept 1946) 8, 31-32, 35-36, 42; 9, 32-33, 36-37; 9, 24, 26-27, 38, 42.
          Illus.
Discusses the career of soprano Marquerite Sylva (1875-1957). Born in Brussels, Sylva moved to London, where she made her debut as Carmen at the Drury Lane Theater. She then joined Beerbohm Tree's dramatic company, touring throughout England and the United States. Sylva performed at the Opéra-Comique in Paris, Oscar Hammerstein's Manhattan Opera in 1909, and the Chicago Grand Opera in 1910-11. Her triumphs in Europe included appearances as Salome and Dalila, for which she coached with Strauss and Saint-Saëns respectively. The soprano is best known for her portrayal of Carmen, a role she has sung over 600 times in the United States and abroad. Her work in America in vaudeville, films, Broadway plays, and recordings is also considered.

1050 LAHEE, Henry Charles. **Famous singers of today and yes-**
bm   **terday** (Boston: L.C. Page, 1898) 337 p. *Illus., index.*
Includes biographical information on the following 19th-c. singers active in the United States: Emma Abbott, Annie Louise Cary, Emma Eames, Minnie Hauk, Clara Louise Kellogg, Emma Nevada, Lillian Nordica, Adelina Patti, Sibyl Sanderson, and Marcella Sembrich. A chronological table of birth, debut, retirement, and death dates for singers from 1610-1898 is included.

1051 LAHEE, Henry Charles. **Women as violinists,** *Famous violinists*
bd   *of today and yesterday* (Boston: L.C. Page, 1899) 300-44. *Port.*
"During the past 40 or 50 years the violin has become a fashionable instrument for ladies, and has become correspondingly popular as a profession for those who are obliged to earn a living. Formerly, for many years it seems to have been considered improper, or ungraceful, or unladylike--the reasons are nowhere satisfactorily given, but the fact remains that until recently few women played the violin". Chief among the American women discussed are Maud Powell and Camilla Urso, as well as Leonora Jackson.

1052 LANE, Kenneth. **Memories of Frieda Hempel,** *Opera News*
ap   XX/15 (13 Feb 1956) 10-11, 28. *Illus.*
An appreciation by a devoted voice pupil, who describes Hempel's teaching

abilities and her daily schedule of vocalizing. Hempel, whose repertory included 70 roles, was known for her performances of the same role in 4 languages--namely, Italian, German, French, and English.

1053 LANIER, Sidney. **Orchestra of today, The,** *Music and poetry.*
ac   *Essays upon some aspects and inter-relations of the two arts* (New
          York: Haskell House, 1969) 25-46.
Reviews the individual characteristics of various orchestral instruments, and strongly advocates that women take up the violin, flute, oboe, harp, clarinet, bassoon, and kettledrum. The qualities required to make a perfect orchestral player--patience, fervor, and fidelity--are far more often found in women than in men. This essay originally appeared in *Scribner's Monthly* XIX/4 (Apr. 1880). *Music and poetry* was first published in 1898.

1054 LATHROP, Elsie. **Marcia Van Dresser, American soprano, a**
ap   **"hit" at Covent Garden,** *Musical America* X/4 (5 June 1909) 17.
Although she seemed poised for great success in light opera or on the dramatic stage, Marcia Van Dresser abandoned these prospects to study in Europe for grand opera. Her engagements in Dresden, Dessau, and at Covent Garden as Sieglinde under Hans Richter are discussed. The soprano's interest in American musical affairs remains keen, and she would like to return to the United States now that opportunities for singers are expanding.

1055 LAWTON, Mary. **Schumann-Heink. The last of the titans**
bf   (New York: Arno, 1977) 390, [38] p. $28. *Illus., discog.*
A reprint of the 1928 edition (New York: Macmillan), with a new discography by W.R. Moran. Ernestine Schumann-Heink (1861-1936) made her American debut as Ortrud in *Lohengrin* in Nov. 1898, shortly before the birth of her 7th child, George Washington Schumann. The contralto was born in Prague to parents of limited means, and in her early years as a student and a singer in Dresden, Hamburg, and Berlin she was beset with financial and other problems. Maurice Grau persuaded Schumann-Heink to come to the United States, and she recalls she loved America from the start, mainly for the opportunities she felt it afforded her children. Appearing for the most part in Wagnerian roles, she sang with the Metropolitan Opera until Grau's retirement in 1903. Thereafter she sang in concert, though in Europe she continued in opera. Schumann-Heink became an American citizen in 1905. World War I proved an ordeal for her because she had sons serving in the German and in the United States military forces. She became a great favorite with the American troops as a result of her singing performances.

1056 **Leginska at Carnegie Hall,** *Musical Courier* LXXIII/19 (9 Nov
ro   1916) 38.
While "Bach, Beethoven, and Brahms are names that do not necessarily connote femininity", Ethel Leginska gave admirable performances of works by all 3 composers at a recent Carnegie Hall recital.

1057 LEHMANN, George. **Maud Powell,** *Etude* XXV/1 (Jan 1907)
ap   54.
Of the hundreds, or perhaps thousands, of young American women who have gone to Berlin, Dresden, Leipzig, or Prague to further their violin studies in the past 20 years, Maud Powell is the one artist who has emerged and risen steadily in the esteem of the public. Despite Powell's excellent performance, Sibelius's violin concerto in D minor, op. 47, failed to make a favorable impression at recent hearings. It is hoped that Powell's quest for a new concerto next year will meet with happier results.

1058 LEHMANN, George. **Woman's position in the violin world,**
ap   *Etude* (*WIAM* 74) 334-35.
Society's attitude towards the woman violinist has changed so completely in the past 30 years that "for the young violinist who is possessed of marked artistic ability in conjunction with pleasing personal attributes there are absolutely no limitations to social conquest". However, while the gifted girl player has much more tenacity than the average gifted boy, the limits of her physical endurance will work against the possibility of her achieving greatness as a violinist. Leading women violinists are considered, among them Camilla Urso and Maud Powell.

1059 L.E.M. **Young women as stringed instrumentalists,** *American*
ap   *Art Journal* LI/10 (22 Dec 1888) 146.
Lists some of the activities currently engaged in by female instrumentalists. Besides the growing numbers of female harpists and violinists, there are all-female amateur orchestras. The Marion Osgood Ladies' Orchestra, organized by violinist Marion G. Osgood, includes a wide variety of orchestral instruments and even zithers, while the New York Ladies' Orchestra is composed of violins, violas, guitars, mandolins, harp, kettledrum, banjo, cymbals, piano, and organ.

1060 **Lenten concert by the Women's String Orchestra,** *Musical*
ro   *Courier* XLIV/8 (19 Feb 1902) 189.
Part of the program was offered as a memorial to Camilla Urso, the former honorary president of the orchestra, who died on 20 Jan. 1902. The performers "manifested that seriousness in their playing which has won for them the

support and encouragement of many men and women of wealth and distinction". A roster of the players and lists of the New York orchestra's officers and patrons are included.

1061 LIEBLING, Leonard. **Variations. [Wynne Pyle]**, *Musical*
ap   *Courier* LX/26 (29 June 1910) 21. *Illus.*
In the first item of his regular column, Liebling reports on his recent interview with pianist Wynne Pyle, who was in New York enroute from Europe to her home in Texas for the summer. Pyle was not especially interested in talking about herself; she did note, however, that "if ever equal rights could help, they certainly would be beneficial in music". Because of the numbers of fine pianists, the profession is almost discouragingly difficult for women--even despite the successes of some women, e.g., Fannie Bloomfield-Zeisler, Teresa Carreño, Olga Samaroff Stokowski, and others.

1062 **Lillian Blauvelt to appear in a new comic opera**, *Musical*
ap   *Courier* LIII/10 (5 Sept 1906) 23.
Reports that Blauvelt, who used to earn a few hundred dollars a season singing in a church in Brooklyn, will receive nearly $100,000 for the 1906-07 season in comic opera. The major events in the soprano's career in grand opera and concert up to 1906 are discussed.

1063 **Lillian Nordica, famed American soprano, dies in Batavia,**
ap   **Java**, *Musical America* XX/1 (16 May 1914) 2. *Illus.*
Reports Lillian Nordica's death on 10 May 1914, while the soprano was traveling on a farewell tour around the world, and reviews the major events in her career. "Gifted with personal beauty, dramatic gifts of a very high order, and a voice of rare individuality and beauty, she was likewise extremely versatile and could be convincing in operas of the older order as well as the more dramatic ones of the modern type". Nordica's musicianship, however, was not extraordinary, and studying a new role was often extremely difficult for her.

1064 **Lillian Shattuck**, *Violins and violinists* III/2 (Sept 1940) 72.
ap
An obituary for the violinist (1868-1940), who during the early part of her career was associated with Julius Eichberg at the Boston Conservatory, first as a student and later as a teacher. After a sojourn abroad that included study with Joachim, Shattuck returned to Boston and established the all-female Julius Eichberg Quartet. In her last years she concentrated on teaching in her studio on Copley Square. Her Amati violin has been bequeathed to her life-long friend and associate, Jennie P. Daniel.

1065 LOMBARD, Louis. **Music as a breadwinner for girls**, *Obser-*
ac   *vations of a musician* (Utica, N.Y.: L.C. Childs, 1893) 73-76.
Music study can lead to dependable and lucrative employment for young women in opera and concert work, as organists and singers in churches, and in private teaching. Additional advantages that result from studying music are 1) musically accomplished women are more attractive to suitors, and 2) women can give their children a good start in music. This essay was later reprinted in *Music* [Chicago] IV (Oct. 1893) 650-51.

1066 LOMBARD, Louis. **Why girls should play the violin**, *Observa-*
ac   *tions of a musician* (Utica, N.Y.: L.C. Childs, 1893) 77-79.
Proposes that more young women should study the violin rather than the piano, and discusses the attributes of the violin. This essay was later reprinted in *Music* [Chicago] IV (Oct. 1893) 649.

1067 **Los Angeles boasts of woman's orchestra**, *Musical Courier*
ro   LXVIII/6 (11 Feb 1914) 49.
Reports on the final concert of the Los Angeles Woman's Orchestra in its 1913-14 season. Although many of the orchestra's members are amateurs, the conscientious efforts of the players and conductor Henry Schoenfeld produced a performance that compared favorably with that of any professional organization. The Los Angeles Woman's Orchestra is the oldest women's orchestra in the western United States and the largest women's orchestra active in the country at the present time.

1068 **M. Lady conductors**, *Dwight's Journal of Music* XXXIX/987 (15
ro   Feb 1879) 30.
Reviews Mabel Allen's conducting of Haydn's *Toy symphony* in an amateur performance in Worcester, Mass., and notes that Selma Borg recently conducted Theodore Thomas's orchestra in New York. "The young leader [Allen] is barely out of her teens, and considering the difference of years and experience, it was as great a triumph for Miss Allen to lead these amateurs as for Miss Borg to take the stand before a band of artists. Both are to be congratulated on their successful position. Truly, a woman's sphere widens in this 19th c.".

1069 MACDONALD, Margaret I. **Greatest battles ever fought**
bm   **are the silent ones fought by women, The. Some interesting**
        facts about Miss Emma R. Steiner ([New York?]: [MacDonald
        & Steiner?], [1925]) [8] p.

A composer of 7 light operas, songs, and dance music, Emma Roberto Steiner (1857-1928) was the "first woman to wield a baton in the field of opera" in the United States. For 30 years she conducted over 6000 performances of 50 different operas, while continuing to compose. She conducted over 700 performances of *The mikado* alone. Steiner began her career as assistant musical director with Rice and Collier's Iolanthe Co., and she has worked with a number of other men, including Hans Conried. When Conried became manager of the Metropolitan Opera he admitted he would have engaged Steiner as a conductor--if only he had dared. When Steiner's health began to fail from overwork around 1900 she went to Alaska, where she discovered tin and worked as a prospector for 10 years. This pamphlet was issued in connection with a concert commemorating Steiner's work in music at the Metropolitan Opera on 17 Nov. 1925 (*WIAM* 1201).

1070 MACKAY, Joseph. **Fritzi Scheff reminisces**, *New York Sun* 7
an   Feb 1948, 3. *Illus.*
An account of Fritzi Scheff's professional career and personal life. Born in Vienna in 1879, Scheff made her debut in *Martha* in Nuremberg while still in her teens. She sang at the Metropolitan Opera from 1901-03, after which she abandoned grand opera to appear in Victor Herbert's operetta, *Babette*. Her greatest success was in Herbert's *Mlle. Modiste* in 1905. Scheff performed in vaudeville in the 1920s and sang on radio and in night clubs in the 1930s.

1071 **Madame Bloomfield-Zeisler as a histrione**, *Musical Courier*
ap   LV/13 (25 Sept 1907) 29.
Discusses Fannie Bloomfield-Zeisler's involvement with cultural and civic groups in Chicago: 1) the Little Room Club, an organization of men and women who make their livelihood in the arts in Chicago, and 2) the Book and Play Club, in whose theatrical performances she has participated. For a number of years the pianist has corresponded with George Bernard Shaw; she regrets his turning away from music criticism.

1072 MAGUIRE, Helena M. **Mme. Szumowska's "lesson reci-**
ap   **tals"**, *Musician* XVII/5 (May 1912) 306.
An interview with the pianist in her home in Cambridge, Mass. Antoinette Szumowska describes how she came to develop her "lesson-recitals", in which she discusses the background of the composer of a given piece, the nature and purpose of the music, and some aspects of piano technique that are required. She first used this approach with her students, but now she gives "lesson-recitals" for the public because she feels she has an obligation to make music more meaningful to men who "must attend recitals because their wives will have it so". Szumowska also discusses her studies with Paderewski over a 5-year period.

1073 MAGUIRE, Helena M. **People to whom a girl plays, The**,
ap   *Etude* XVIII/2 (Feb 1900) 94.
Urges young women to continue playing serious music despite the current vogue for ragtime and coon songs. Concludes that young women are really the pioneers of music in the United States, since so many are the first in their families to study music and, in turn, to make serious music a feature of home life.

1074 **Major Pond and the Black Patti**, *Brooklyn Daily Eagle* 18 May
an   1893, 5.
Major Pond, who manages Sissieretta Jones, the "Black Patti", has attempted to prevent the singer from fulfilling engagements he did not secure for her. Jones, however, claims that Pond reneged on his financial obligations: he has taken more than his proper 15% commission and has not paid her salary since Dec. 1892.

1075 MALTBY, Reba Broughton. **How woman organist overcame**
ap   **barriers half a century ago**, *Diapason* XLVI/6 (1 May 1950) 6.
Discusses the prejudice against hiring women organists in New York City in 1900. The author succeeded in counteracting this prejudice by her ability and her courage in standing up to the examining committee members.

→   MANNES, David. **Music is my faith**, *see* 798bm[57].

1076 **Marchesi's opinion of American voices**, *Etude* XV/2 (Feb
ap   1897) 45.
Mathilde Marchesi, the eminent voice teacher in Paris, states that her most promising students now come from the United States. Americans, however, are impatient about their progress, and they lack dramatic temperament. While in the past students typically remained with Marchesi for 3 years, now the average term of study is 2 years or less. Among Marchesi's American pupils are Emma Eames and Sibyl Sanderson. Marchesi's own training and career are discussed.

1077 **Marcia Van Dresser's varied career**, *Musical Courier* LXXV/21
ap   (22 Nov 1917) 42.
Reports that because of the outbreak of war, Marcia Van Dresser has returned to the United States from Frankfurt, where she was the leading lyric soprano for 3 years. Upon her return Van Dresser was engaged by the Chicago Opera, and she has sung with all the leading orchestras. She is now leaving the operatic

stage for the "wider scope" of concert work, which has long been her aim. Van Dresser began her professional career as a young girl with The Bostonians. She was also an actress, appearing with Otis Skinner, Austin Daly, and Viola Allen.

1078 MARKS, Edward B. **They all had glamour from the Swedish**
bf   **Nightingale to the Naked Lady** (Westport, Conn.: Greenwood, 1972) xvii, 448 p. $22.50. *Illus., list of works, index.*
A reprint of the 1944 edition (New York: J. Messner). Discusses the careers of the following singers active in American music in the middle and latter part of the 19th c.: Anna Bishop, Jenny Lind, Euphrosyne Parepa-Rosa, Adelina Patti, Clara Louise Kellogg, and Minnie Hauk. The title refers to Lind as the Swedish Nightingale and Adah Isaacs Menken, the actress. Menken was a sensation when she wore flesh-colored tights for the opening production of George Noel Gordon's *Mazeppa* in 1861.

1079 MARTENS, Frederick Herman. **Maud Powell**, *Violin mastery*
bd   (New York: F.A. Stokes, 1919) 183-97. *Illus.*
Powell is the lone woman and the only American represented in this group of conversations with "master violinists". She discusses certain aspects of technique and speaks eloquently about women as concert violinists, with reference to her own career. "When I began a strong prejudice existed against women fiddlers, which even yet has not altogether been overcome. The fact that I realized my sex was against me in a way led me to be startlingly authoritative and convincing in the masculine manner. When James Gibbons Huneker wrote that I 'was not developing the feminine side of my work', I determined to be just myself and play with no further thought of sex or sex distinctions, which in art, are secondary". Powell also comments upon her commitment to playing works by native American composers.

1080 MARTIN, Sadie E. **Life and professional career of Emma**
bm   **Abbott, The** (Minnneapolis: L. Kimball, 1891) 189 p. *Illus.*
A native of Peoria, Ill., Emma Abbott (1850-91) first studied voice with her father. Clara Louise Kellogg helped raise funds so that Abbott could continue her studies with Mathilde Marchesi in Europe. Her debut as Marie in *La fille du régiment* at Covent Garden in 1877 led to a contract with James Henry ("Colonel") Mapleson, which was later broken because of her refusal to sing in *La traviata*. In 1878 the soprano established the Emma Abbott Opera, which presented operas in English translation on tour throughout the United States. With the financial and managerial help of Abbott's husband, the opera company flourished for 13 years until her death in 1891. Tributes to Abbott's vocal abilities as well as her personal charm and generosity are included.

1081 **Mary Jordan ardent champion of American musical inde-**
ap   **pendence**, *Musical America* XX/12 (25 July 1914) 6. *Illus.*
Trained in the United States, Mary Jordan is committed to including songs by American composers on her recital programs, and she also champions the practice of using English translations for songs and operas written in foreign languages. Jordan discusses the advance in music appreciation among Americans in recent years, noting that the phonograph and the player piano have been chiefly responsible for bringing about the advance. The mezzo-soprano does not believe in "playing down" to audiences in less sophisticated locales.

1082 MATHEWS, William S.B. **Great pianist at home, A**, *Music*
ap   [Chicago] IX (Nov 1895) 1-10.
Although she was born in Bielitz, Austria in 1865, Fannie Bloomfield- Zeisler settled in Chicago with her parents by the age of 2, and Chicago has remained her home. As a youngster she studied with Carl Wolfsohn, the esteemed Chicago musician and pianist, and under Wolfson's direction she made numerous early appearances at concerts of the Beethoven Soc. in Chicago. On the advice of Annette Essipoff--the European pianist and associate of Theodor Leschetizky--Bloomfield-Zeisler went to Vienna to work with Leschetizky between 1878 and 1883, and again in 1888-89. Bloomfield-Zeisler is fortunate to have married a man who is willing to "leave her to her career", while he pursures his own as a lawyer. The pianist's highly successful concert tours in Europe during 1893 and 1894 are discussed.

1083 MATHEWS, William S.B. **New American pianist, Myrtle**
ap   **Elvyn, The.** *Musician* XIII/2 (Feb 1908) 72-73. *Illus.*
Carl Wolfsohn--who earlier had helped to prepare Fannie Bloomfield-Zeisler and Augusta Cottlow for major careers--also taught Myrtle Elvyn for 5 years, then recommended that she continue with Leopold Godowsky. Elvyn spent another another 5 years working with Godowsky in Berlin where she made her debut in 1904, playing the Brahms concerto no. 1 in D minor, op. 15, the Beethoven concerto no. 5 in E-flat major, op. 73, and the Grieg concerto in A minor, op. 16. While in Berlin Elvyn also studied composition with Hugo Kaun, who recommended that she concentrate on composition. However, Elvyn pursued her career as a pianist, and made her American debut in Chicago playing concertos by Beethoven and Chaikovskii,solo works by Chopin, and as an encore, Godowsky's paraphrase of the *Blue Danube* waltz, which Elvyn reconstructed from memory from Godowsky's private performances.

1084 MATHEWS, William S.B. **Young woman pianist and her**
ap   **business prospects, The**, *Etude* XXIV/2 (Feb 1906) 64.

Suggests that the young, would-be concert artist spend 2 years as an assistant teacher in a good seminary, giving a recital every 2 weeks and thereby establishing her reputation. Ideally a woman concert pianist can average between 30 and 50 concerts a year at $40 per engagement, for a total income of $1200-$2000 a year.

1085 **Matzenauer quits the Metropolitan**, *New York Times* 17 Feb
an   1930, 1, 13. *Illus.*
After 19 years at the Metropolitan Opera, Margaret Matzenauer says she is no longer content to sing secondary roles such as Ortrud in *Lohengrin* and Venus in *Tannhäuser*. Her farewell performance was as Amneris, which was also the role of her debut in 1911. Born in Hungary where her father was an opera conductor, Matzenauer made her debut at Strasbourg at age 20, and she sang extensively in Europe before coming to the United States.

1086 **Maud Morgan dies; noted harpist, 81**, *New York Times* 4 Dec
an   1941, 25.
Morgan (1860-1941) was born in New York, the daughter of George Washbourne Morgan, a noted organist. She is believed to have been the first American to appear as a solo harpist on the American concert stage. In 1924 Morgan gave a golden jubilee concert in Carnegie Hall. One of her last public appearances occurred in Nov. 1933, when she played at a concert preceding the unveiling of a memorial in the Brooklyn Museum of Art for Emma Cecilia Thursby.

1087 **Maud Powell**, *Musical Observer* II/2 (Feb 1908) 6.
ap
Born in Peru, Ill. in 1868, Maud Powell notes "it was my mother who first tried music on me to find out if I was musical". Her initial violin lessons at age 8 were with William Lewis of Chicago. Subsequently she went abroad to study with Henry Schradieck in Leipzig, Charles Dancla in Paris, and Joachim in Berlin. Powell made her American debut with the New York Philharmonic in 1884. Her present concert season in widely distant cities is listed.

1088 **Maud Powell a suffragette? "Certainly not", says husband**,
an   *Boston Herald* 8 Mar 1912, 7.
H. Godfrey Turner, the violinist's husband and manager, states that despite Powell's supposed association with the suffrage movement, she has not had the time to become involved. He notes instead her commitment to concertizing in the western United States. The violinist is the founder of the Maud Powell Quartet, and she is known for introducing new works to the American public.

1089 **Maud Powell convinced America is striding ahead in musical**
ap   **appreciation**, *Musical America* XXX/2 (10 May 1919) 13.
Although the influenza epidemic and the "disturbed conditions attending the sudden cessation of the war have made concertizing a hardship", Powell has returned from her western tour in an optimistic state of mind about musical life in the United States. She reports that the number of men attending her concerts in recent years--"without the necessity of accompanying their women folk"--is definitely on the rise.

1090 **Maud Powell, the violinist, is dead**, *New York Times* 9 Jan 1920,
an   17.
Reports the sudden death of the violinist (1868-1920) after a nervous breakdown, and reviews the major events of her career. Concludes that Powell "is entitled to rank as one of the greatest musicians ever produced in the United States. When she first appeared in public in the 1880s she had some of the reputation of a youthful prodigy, but she proved the estimate of the great Joachim by continuous advance to the highest realms of her art".

1091 MAXWELL, Leon R. **Most notable American singers since**
ac   **1876, The**. *Studies in musical education, history, and aesthetics* 23 (Hartford: Music Teachers National Assoc., 1929) 36-46.
Focuses on American-born women (as "few men singers are very good"), and discusses their achievements in opera, oratorio, and recital work. Many women singers have found it helpful to their careers to either Italianize their names, borrow place-names, or use their husbands' names. Most women singers have sought European training and renown, returning to the United States only at the peak of their careers or even afterwards. Antoinette Sterling is a rare example of a brilliant singer who scorned the usual first choice of opera. She did so for moral reasons. The careers of the following singers are considered: Sophie Braslau, Annie Louise Cary, Clara Clemens, Eva Gauthier, and Clara Louise Kellogg. A list of 200 singers active since 1876 is included.

1092 MCCLURE, W. Frank. **Illustrious example of the power of**
ap   **music as a home influence**, *Musical America* XVI/26 (2 Nov 1912) 2. *Illus.*
Discusses the backgrounds and musical interests of Fannie Bloomfield-Zeisler's 3 sons and her husband. "Mrs. Bloomfield-Zeisler's happy domestic life, no less than her talents, has had an ennobling influence on the children". She often plays for and with them, and she gave all 3 children piano lessons before they took up stringed instruments. Occasionally Bloomfield-Zeisler plays ragtime, which she is said to perform excellently.

1093 MCHENRY, Izetta May. **Katherine Heyman**, *Billboard*
ap   XXXIII/14 (2 Apr 1921) 24.
Discusses the pianist's commitment to contemporary music. In 1916 Heyman gave the first American performance of Scriabin's sonata no. 8, op. 66, and since that time it has been chiefly through her efforts that Scriabin's piano works have become known in the United States. The forthcoming publication of Heyman's book, *The relation of ultra modern music to archaic music*, is announced.

1094 **Medal waiting for Marie Rappold**, *Musical America* XIII/16 (25
ap   Feb 1911) 3. *Illus.*
Marie Rappold enjoys the distinction of being one of the first American-trained artists to sing principal roles at the Metropolitan Opera. The soprano, who has achieved success both in the United States and abroad, advocates opera in English translation. Next summer Rappold will receive the Order of Merit from the Rumanian government. A list of her roles in recent seasons is included.

1095 MEPHISTO. **Mephisto's musings. [Julie Rivé-King]**, *Musical*
ap   *America* VIII/5 (13 June 1908) 13.
The first item in this regular column by the editors of *Musical America* recalls the work of Julie Rivé-King, who 25 years previous was regarded as the foremost American pianist. Her husband, Frank King, was associated with the piano manufacturing firm of Decker Brothers and also was totally devoted to Rivé-King's career as a performer. "For many years Mme. Rivé-King's playing together with King's wonderful advertising ability swept everything before them".

1096 MILINOWSKI, Marta. **Teresa Carreño. "By the grace of**
bf   **God"** (New York: Da Capo, 1977) 410 p. $19.50. *Illus., port., bibliog.*
A reprint of the 1940 edition (New Haven, Conn.: Yale U.). Born in Caracas, Teresa Carreño (1853-1917) came with her family to New York in 1862 and made her first public appearances as a pianist soon after with great success. Her father decided to develop the child's genius rather than exploit it, and accordingly he took her to Paris where she played for Rossini, Liszt, and others in select musical circles. She studied with Georges Matthias and Emmanuel Bazin, while also giving concerts in England, France, and Spain to pay for expenses. In 1872 Carreño came to the United States with Maurice Strakosch's company, in which Emile Sauret, a violinist, was also a member. She married Sauret in 1873, but they separated in 1875. Penniless, Carreño launched a new career as a singer in Boston, where she also became associated with the MacDowell family and a mentor of Edward, then in his teens. The opera interlude proved brief; Carreño went back to the piano, touring the country with various companies including her own, the Carreño Concert Co. Artistically this work was hardly rewarding, and thus a season of touring with Leopold Damrosch and the New York Symphony Orchestra in 1882 was an important break, as Carreño had the chance to play Grieg's piano concerto in A minor, op. 16, as well as to refurbish all the other orchestral works in her repertory. In the late 1880s Carreño was able to return to Europe, where she triumphed at her Berlin debut--the "ultimate" test of the time--in 1889. Thereafter she was immensely successful, concertizing for almost 20 years throughout Europe, the United States, Australia, and New Zealand. Carreño did much to popularize the works of MacDowell and Grieg. During the summers she returned to her children and students. Her 2nd and 3rd marriages to Giovanni Tagliapietra, a singer, and Eugen d'Albert, pianist and composer, respectively ended in divorce, while her 4th marriage to Arturo Tagliapietra endured--although the fact that it was a 4th marriage caused a furor even among close friends. The final illness that led to Carreño's death is attributed to overwork throughout the years.

1097 rb —
R. by Carl ENGEL, *Musical Quarterly* XXVI/4 (Oct 1940) 546-49.

1098 rb —
R. by Leslie HODGSON, *Musical America* LX/13 (Sept 1940) 5, 41.

1099 **Miss Clara Louise Kellogg**, *Harper's Bazaar* I/31 (30 May 1868)
ap   481-82.
Numerous American women in literature and the plastic arts have achieved recognition in Europe in the recent past, among them Harriet Beecher Stowe in literature, Charlotte Cushman in drama, and Harriet Hosmer and Emma Stebbins in sculpture. By contrast, American women in music were not similarly distinguished until the 1867 appearances of Clara Louise Kellogg at Her Majesty's Theater in London. With her performances of Marguerite, Violetta, and Gilda, Kellogg has proven that the native American singer can rival the European prima donna.

1100 **Miss Edyth Walker talks very plainly to American girls who**
an   **contemplate studying music abroad and who hope to become**
        prima donnas, *New York Herald* 5 Mar 1905, III-10. *Illus.*
Edyth Walker, who has achieved great success in European opera houses and is currently with the Metropolitan Opera for the 1904-05 season, recalls her decision to leave the United States for study at the Dresden Conservatory. She spent 4 years in Dresden, studying voice with Aglaja Orgeni. Previously she had been a music teacher in the public schools of Rome, N.Y., and she also held a

position as vocalist with a church in Utica. Walker believes that the American girl should go abroad for study if she is earnest about making a public success, but she advises that no one should attempt to do so on as limited a budget as she did. She suggests that $500 a year--including tuition--is sufficient for expenses.

1101 **Miss Emma Thursby**, *New York Daily Graphic* 16 Sept 1882, 537.
an   *Illus.*
Emma Cecilia Thursby, "la belle puritaine", has just returned to New York from a successful concert tour throughout Europe. She won the approval of Parisian concert audiences, and thereafter was a star. Pierre Veron, Jules-Etienne Pasdeloup, and Ambroise Thomas among others heralded her as the heiress of Maria Malibran and Giuditta Pasta, as well as the equal of Adelina Patti.

1102 **Miss Howard, 77, singer, actress**, *New York Times* 17 Aug 1956,
an   19.
Reports the death of Kathleen Howard (1879-1956). In 1916 Howard made her debut at the Metropolitan Opera, where she sang 125 roles in 4 different languages. In 1928 the contralto left the Metropolitan and became the fashion editor of *Harper's Bazaar*. Howard later appeared in Hollywood films in the 1930s-40s.

1103 **Miss Maud Morgan**, *American Art Journal* LVII/8 (6 June 1891)
ap   113-14.
Maud Morgan has reawakened interest in the harp through her concertizing, her lecture-recitals, and her teaching. In recent years the harpist has assisted at various club concerts in New York--e.g., at the Rubinstein, St. Mary's, and the Musurgia clubs--and she plays frequently in churches in New York and Brooklyn. She has also composed and arranged music for harp. Morgan's early appearances with Adelaide Phillipps, Emma Cecilia Thursby, Ole Bull, and her father George Washbourne Morgan are discussed.

1104 **Miss Thursby's new engagement**, *Dwight's Journal of Music*
ap   XXXVI/26 (31 Mar 1877) 416.
Reports that Emma Cecilia Thursby's new contract with Maurice Strakosch is possibly "the most liberal any American singer ever made with a manager". In addition to the fee--more than $100,000 plus expenses for concerts and oratorio work--the contract allows the soprano to fulfill all present engagements and leaves her summers free. Biographical information is also included. This article is reprinted from the *Music Trade Review*.

→   **Mme. Cappiani on singing at the Trade School for Girls**, *see*
        804ap[57].

1105 **Mme. Gadski is dead after motor crash**, *New York Times* 24
an   Feb 1932, 21. *Illus.*
Reports the death of Johanna Gadski (1872-1932) at age 60 in an accident in Berlin. The soprano's career was centered in the United States, and in Berlin she was actually regarded as a German-American. Gadski was 23 years old when Walter Damrosch hired her for his German opera seasons at the Metropolitan Opera, and she only much later told him that she learned all her Wagnerian roles after she came to the United States, for her early repertory in Germany had been mainly light opera and Mozart. Between 1895 and 1917 Gadski was a leading Wagnerian soprano at the Metropolitan, moving from younger parts such as Elsa to Brünnhilde and Isolde. Her outspoken German sentiments during the war aroused protests, and the Metropolitan released her after the 1916-17 season. Gadski's attempts to resume her career immediately after the war were not successful; in recent years, however, she appeared in 3 consecutive seasons with the German Grand Opera, which was founded with the express purpose of bringing Wagner's operas to various small communities throughout the United States.

1106 **Mme. Julie Rivé-King**, *American Art Journal* XLIV/17 (13 Feb
ap   1886) 283.
In the 12 years since her return to the United States from Europe, Rivé-King has performed in 1800 recitals and concerts, appearing with every orchestra in the country. She has presented "to her audiences a repertory greater than that of any artist before the public with the exception of Anton Rubinstein and Hans von Bülow". The American pianist made her European debut in Leipzig at age 16.

1107 **Mme. Nordica gives advice to American girls with voices;**
an   **says they need not go abroad to study**, *New York Herald* 4 Dec
        1904, III-4.
Lillian Nordica relates how she was already a self-supporting singer when she went to Europe in the 1870s to study languages and to gain further professional experience in opera. American girls are too impatient in their vocal studies; hard work is the only answer.

1108 **Mme. Powell devotes her superb art to aiding music settle-**
ro   **ment**, *Musical America* XXX/9 (28 June 1919) 26.

Reviews Maud Powell's benefit concert for the Colored Music School Settlement in New York. The highlight of the evening was the group of Negro songs and spirituals which the violinist played in arrangements. Powell's interest in the settlement school is long-standing.

1109 Mme. Sembrich, 76, dies at home here, *New York Times* 12 Jan
an   1935, 16. *Illus.*
This extensive obituary for the soprano gives a detailed account of her career and attests to her stature as an operatic singer. Sembrich first became famous in the United States with her performances as violinist, pianist, and singer respectively at a benefit concert in Apr. 1884 for the new Metropolitan Opera. The Metropolitan had finished its first season--under the management of Henry E. Abbey--in precarious financial condition.

→   MOORE, Aubertine. **Music and the married mistress of home**, *see* 806ap[57].

1110 MOORE, Edward C. Forty years of opera in Chicago (New
bf   York: Arno, 1977) 430 p.
A reprint of the 1930 edition (New York: H. Liverwright). Discusses the 3 different organizations that constituted Chicago's resident opera company to 1930: the Chicago Grand Opera, 1909-14; the Chicago Opera, 1915-22; and the Chicago Civic Opera, 1922-30. The activities of Johanna Gadski, Mary Garden, and Claudia Muzio among numerous other women are considered. Appendices include lists of operas performed, together with rosters of singers and administrators.

1111 MORELL, Parker. Lillian Russell. The era of plush (New
bm   York: Random House, 1940) 319 p. *Illus., index.*
Considers Lillian Russell's career (1861-1922) with an emphasis on the social history of the period. Born in Clinton, Iowa, the soprano was the daughter of Cynthia Van Names Leonard, a leading feminist, and Charles Leonard, a journalist. Russell made her New York debut in 1880 in vaudeville, but she soon turned to light opera, achieving national acclaim in Gilbert and Sullivan operettas on tour. After a series of triumphs as the Queen of Light Opera--including her appearances in *La grande duchesse de Gérolstein* by Offenbach and *Princess Nicotine* by William Furst, Charles A. Byrne, and Louis Harrison--Russell teamed with Joe Weber and Lew Fields in burlesque beginning in the late 1890s. Part of her success on the stage stemmed from her great beauty. In 1906 she ceased to work as a singer and became a dramatic actress. After retiring from the theater in 1914, Russell became active in politics and worked for women's suffrage.

1112 Mrs. Charles Moulton. A sketch of her musical career (New
bm   York: Baker & Goodwin, 1871) 15 p.
A brief account of the career of Lillie Greenough Moulton. Raised in New England, as a young woman she traveled to Europe for vocal training. Later, as Mrs. Charles Moulton, she sang at soirées in aristocratic circles and was heard by Rossini, who praised her voice. During her travels she met Liszt, Vieux-temps, and other notables. In 1869-70 Moulton came to the United States to sing recitals. This pamphlet announces the mezzo soprano's 2nd series of American concerts, to begin 16 Oct. 1871 at Steinway Hall in New York.

1113 Mrs. Cravath dies; widow of lawyer, *New York Times* 11 Mar
an   1953, 29. *Illus.*
Accompanied by her mother and sister, Agnes Huntington Cravath (1864-1953) went to Dresden in the early 1880s to study voice with Giovanni Battista Lamperti. The mezzo-soprano made her concert debut in Dresden, and later sang with the New York Philharmonic, conducted by Theodore Thomas. After she married Paul D. Cravath in 1892, she retired professionally. Cravath founded the Little Theater Opera in 1930 and was president of the New York Opera Comique.

1114 Music after marriage and motherhood. Opinions of some of
ap   **the most famous living women musicians upon the problem**
          of keeping up musical work without neglecting the home,
          Etude (*WIAM* 75) 443-44.
An appeal to women amateurs to continue their ambitions as singers and players in spite of the domestic duties associated with marriage and mother-hood. Individual assessments of the problem by Amy Cheney Beach, Fannie Bloomfield-Zeisler, Louise Homer, Ernestine Schumann-Heink, and Marcella Sembrich are included. This article is continued in *Etude* XXVII/8 (Aug. 1909, 520).

1115 Musical intelligence. Local, *Dwight's Journal of Music* II/2 (16
ap   Oct 1852) 15.
Reports that Camilla Urso, the young violinist, gave 2 fine concerts in Boston, but could not meet expenses. "Indifference to the flaming advertisement of precocity is well; but it was not well for the taste of Boston to neglect this manifestation of genius".

1116 M.W. Prefers farm to concert honors, *Musical America* XIII/20
ap   (25 Mar 1911) 25. *Illus.*
Reports that Leonora Jackson has temporarily given up public performances in favor of a quiet life on a farm near Albany, N.Y. The violinist comments that she entered public life at a young age, concertized in Europe and in nearly every city in the United States, and now is taking a well-deserved respite. She also is composing. Jackson's family is not pleased with her change of mind.

1117 Myrtle Elvyn, American pianist, *Musical Courier* LVI/22 (27
ap   May 1908) 29.
Elvyn made her American debut with the Theodore Thomas Orchestra in Chicago under the direction of Frederick Stock on 29 Oct. 1907. Elvyn recently returned to the United States after concertizing in Europe. Her European debut was with the Berlin Philharmonic.

1118 Narrow ideas, *Etude* IX/11 (Nov 1891) 210.
ap
Music for women should not be viewed just as a mere accomplishment to entertain company or as a means to livelihood. Rather music enriches the home life, "giving direction to thought and molding taste".

1119 NAYLOR, Blanche. Anthology of the Fadettes, The (Boston:
bm   author, [1941?]) 22 p. *Illus.*
The Boston Fadette Lady Orchestra was founded in 1888 by Caroline B. Nichols, a pupil of Julius Eichberg, Leopold Lichtenberg, and Charles Martin Loeffler. Nichols had the support of her brother-in-law, George H. Chickering. Over the years of the orchestra's existence through 1920, Nichols trained more than 600 young women for self-supporting careers as orchestral players. A "roll of honor" listing these women is included.

1120 Negro singer once had ride in royal coach, A, *New York Herald*
an   *Tribune* 5 Jan 1936, V-5.
Discusses Abbie Mitchell's singing and acting career. Born in New York in 1884, Mitchell went to London at age 15 to perform in the black musical comedy *In Dahomey* with the team of Williams and Walker. She worked with Jean de Reszke in Paris for 2 years and subsequently concertized throughout Europe and the United States. Mitchell is now playing the part of Clara in George Gershwin's *Porgy and Bess*.

1121 Negro talent at the Academy, *Brooklyn Daily Eagle* 19 May 1892,
ro   1.
Sissieretta Jones, Cappa's 7th Regiment Band, the bass C.A. Walker, the raconteur Ernest Jerrold, an unnamed pianist, and a banjo player all performed on the same program. Jones sang an aria from *Robert le diable*, as well as the following songs: *Old-folks at home*, *Maggie, the cows are in the clover*, and *Comin' thro' the rye*. The soprano's voice is "beautiful, well-trained, sweet, clear, steady, and resonant".

1122 New woman in music, The, *Musical America* IX/24 (28 Apr 1906)
ap   8.
This editorial notes that while formerly it was undignified for a woman to play any instrument other than the piano, now women are playing the violin, violoncello, and harp in increasing numbers. Women are advised however not to take up brass instruments, for brass instruments would spoil their appearance.

1123 *New York Herald* on Miss Kellogg, The, *Watson's Art Journal*
ap   XIII/9 (2 July 1870) 88-89.
A recommendation to Clara Louise Kellogg that she use her prestige to influence the development of a national opera in the United States, sung in English. "This young songstress, born in our midst and educated at home with no foreign influence to win her from a loving allegiance to her native country, has steadily worked her way to the highest position of operatic art". She has "but one more duty to pay to the American people--namely, to sing opera in their own language". The quoted passage is reprinted from the *New York Herald*, 1 July 1870.

1124 New York's first *Walkuere*, *New York Sun* 12 July 1908, 4.
an
An interview with Eugenie Pappenheim--the teacher of present-day Brünnhildes--about the first performance of Wagner's opera in New York on 2 Apr. 1877. The soprano recalls that 3 weeks were allowed for rehearsal time, and while the music was quite different from anything the cast had done before, the performance was good and audiences in New York were "prepared to like the advanced Wagner operas". Pappenheim also reflects on changes in operatic life, noting that in the 1870s 1) a few individual artists would typically form their own company, 2) opera companies in Italian, English, and German existed side by side, and 3) repeated performances were as typical of opera as of the dramatic theater.

1125 NIELSEN, Alice. **Born to sing**, *Colliers* LXXXIX/24-26 (11, 18,
ap   25 June)-XC/1-2 (2, 9 July 1932) 9, 44-46; 19, 36, 39; 22, 41-43; 14-
15, 49; 27-29, 37.
As a child Nielsen sang on the streets of Kansas City, and her first professional
engagement was as Nanki Poo during the "*Mikado* epidemic" of 1885. In this
anecdotal autobiography Nielsen also recalls 1) her travels with the Chicago
Choir Co., a small group which she founded in Kansas City and booked
throughout the Midwest, 2) her work with Ida Valegra in light opera in
California, and 3) her association with The Bostonians, a leading operetta
company. Following the success of her appearances in Victor Herbert's *The
serenade* and other Herbert operettas with The Bostonians, Nielsen organized
her own troupe and traveled to England with a production of Herbert's *The
fortune teller*. The venture was not successful, but Nielsen remained abroad,
and with the financial backing of Mrs. Lionel Phillips she prepared for her
debut in grand opera repertory. When she came back to the United States after
singing at numerous opera houses in Europe, Herbert rebuked her for
abandoning light opera at considerable expense to them both.

1126 **Nordica collection**, *New York Times* 22 Mar 1936, XI-5.
an
Organized in 1927, the Nordica Memorial Assoc. of Farmington, Me. has
bought and renovated the family homestead of Lillian Nordica, née Norton, in
Farmington. The soprano's collection of personal effects--including her
costumes and library of music scores--is partially displayed at the homestead,
which was her birthplace. A larger and fireproof building is needed to house the
entire collection.

1127 NORDICA, Lillian. **Lillian Nordica's training for the opera**
bd   **as told in the letters of Amanda Allen Norton and Lillian**
Nordica. Ed. and with an intro. by William ARMSTRONG, *Lillian
Nordica's hints to singers* (New York: E.P. Dutton, [1923]) 3-57.
Lillian Nordica (née Norton) and her mother, Amanda Allen Norton, sailed to
Europe in the spring of 1878. After a series of concerts in England in which the
soprano performed with Patrick S. Gilmore's band, mother and daughter
traveled to Paris, where Nordica studied acting and the French language.
Subsequently they resided in Milan, where Nordica studied with Antonio
Sangiovanni--polishing the roles already in her repertory as well as her
command of Italian. Nordica made a successful Italian debut as Violetta in
Brescia in Apr. 1879, and she appeared in a number of other Italian houses, in
St. Petersburg, and at the Paris Opéra before returning to the United States.
She was aided financially in this European venture by her father, her sister, and
a brother-in-law. Amanda Allen Norton's letters to family members in Boston
display her courage, resourcefulness, and unswerving belief in her daughter's
future greatness. They also give insights into Italian musical life of the period
as well as the final stages in the education of a prima donna in the 1870s.

1128 **Obituary. Madeline Schiller**, *Musical Courier* LXIII/2 (12 July
ap   1911) 42.
Discusses the career of the pianist (185?-1911) in England, on the continent,
and in the United States where she eventually settled. As a Chopin and
Schumann interpreter Schiller had few equals, although she was interested in
more recent music as well. Around the time she settled in New York, Schiller
suffered a nervous collapse, and thereafter she was unwilling to perform
without scores. Because of this circumstance, the pianist was no longer in
demand for concerts, and, in fact, was forced to retire in her prime. Schiller was
"broadly cultured, with a being that was queenly".

1129 O'CONNOR, Eileen. **Girl who would win, The**, *Green Book*
ap   *Magazine* XXIII/4 (Apr 1920) 68.
Born in 1888 the daughter of a blacksmith in New Jersey, Anna Case took her
first voice lessons with money lent to her by neighbors who were interested in
her singing. Case held positions in churches in Plainfield, N.J. and Brooklyn,
and she was appearing in concerts at the Bellevue-Stratford Hotel in
Philadelphia where Andreas Dippel and Geraldine Farrar came to hear her.
Dippel immediately offered Case a contract with the Metropolitan Opera for
the 1909-10 season. Case has been successful financially as well as artistically
in opera, concert, and motion pictures. "For the encouragement of a single
purpose she recommends the single state".

1130 O.D. **Saxophone her medium of musical expression, The.**
ap   **Mrs. R. J. Hall, who appears as soloist with the Boston**
Symphony Orchestra, has developed her art to a high plane
...*, Musical America* XI/16 (26 Feb 1910) 15. *Port.*
The first amateur to perform with the Boston Symphony Orchestra, Elsie Hall is
a "broadly educated musician and saxophonist of uncommon skill". She played
Bizet's *L'Arlesienne suite no. 1* with the orchestra last Dec. Hall trained in Paris,
and she is especially interested in French music. She manages the Orchestral
Club of Boston, conducted by Georges Longy, with whom she studied. This
latter organization has introduced many French "novelties" in America,
including compositions dedicated to Hall that feature the saxophone. Hall is
also concerned with the quality of music education, and she favors a greater
emphasis on solfeggio and class lessons.

1131 OGDEN, Gertrude Paulette. **Growth of violin playing by**
ap   **women**, *Musical Courier* XXXVIII/13 (15 Mar 1899) 17.
Discusses the increasing numbers of female violinists in continental Europe and
England as well as in the United States during the previous 40 years and the
reasons for the change. In the United States Camilla Urso has been the
inspiration for countless young women. The history of women as violinists is
reviewed beginning with Sarah Ottes, who was born in England in 1695.

1132 OGDEN, Gertrude Paulette. **Teresa Liebe**, *Musical Courier*
ap   XL/7 (14 Feb 1900) 20-21.
Together with Camilla Urso, Teresa Liebe inspired many American women to
take up the violin beginning in the 1870s. A native of Strasbourg, Liebe made
her American debut with the orchestra of the Harvard Assoc. in Nov. 1872,
performing the Mendelssohn concerto in E minor, op. 61. She returned to the
United States to concertize in 1874 and again in 1881-83. In 1882 Liebe was
the first woman violinist to appear as soloist with the Boston Symphony
Orchestra. Liebe's teacher and godmother was Teresa Milanollo, one of the first
female violin virtuosi in Europe.

1133 OLD FOGY. **Our girls as piano players**, *Etude* IV/3 (Mar
ap   1886) 79.
1) Women excel at playing Chopin. "His capriciousness, subtlety, and
elusiveness elude masculine minds". 2) While Fannie Bloomfield-Zeisler
recently played Anton Rubinstein's piano concerto no. 4 in D minor, op, 70,
with "nerve of the finest sort", girl players must not attempt to become
"Rubinsteins in petticoats". 3) Young women should be encouraged to continue
studying the piano since they provide income for music teachers and also
support music as concert-goers.

1134 **Olive Mead Quartet opens its season**, *Musical Courier* XIII/4 (3
ro   Dec 1910) 32.
This review of the opening concert by the Olive Mead Quartet in the 1910-11
season notes that the group has "now reached a point of perfection to make
them worthy rivals to the leading chamber music organizations of the day".

1135 **One American singer who has made good**, *Musical Courier*
ap   LXXIV/14 (5 Apr 1917) 10-11. *Illus.*
Anna Fitziu was advised by Ernestine Schumann-Heink and Caruso to go to
Europe to begin an operatic career. After gaining experience in Italy, Fitziu
made her Metropolitan Opera debut as Rosario in the world première of
Granados's *Goyescas* in 1916. The soprano's other roles include Manon, Tosca,
and Thaïs.

1136 ONE OF THE GIRLS. **Sex in piano playing**, *Etude* IV/5 (May
ap   1886) 112.
An answer to Old Fogy's *Our girls as piano players* (*WIAM* 1133). Argues that
brain is not measured by brawn in piano performance, and cites the excellent
work of Fannie Bloomfield-Zeisler, Teresa Carreño, and Sophie Menter.
Denounces Old Fogy's "not so subtle bid" to have women avoid the music of
certain composers and public performance. Our grandmothers might have
subscribed to the "washtub and cradle" theory of women's existence, but "there
seems today a disposition on the part of the world to let the girls have fair
play".

1137 **Open letter and the reply, An**, *Etude* IV/11 (Nov 1886) 259.
ap
A mother queries her daughter's piano teacher, D. de F. Bryant, about the slow
progress of her daughter's studies; the mother wishes to have her daughter
"accomplished for the high society in which it is my desire and intention she
shall move". In his reply Bryant criticizes the concept of accomplishment, and
he affirms both his belief in the real talent of his pupil and his aim to make her
a thorough musician.

1138 **Opinions of some New York leaders on women as orchestral**
ap   **players**, *Musical Standard* [London] XXI (Apr 1904) 217-18.
When the musicians' union became affiliated with the American Federation of
Labor a few months ago, it admitted women musicians for the first time: 4500
members were enrolled in New York, 31 of them women. The reactions of the
men interviewed about the employment of women in orchestras were chiefly
negative: e.g., "It would be like trying to mix oil and water to put men and
women in the same organization".

1139 **Orchestral women**, *Scientific American* LXXIII/21 (23 Nov 1895)
ap   327.
Argues that women lack the stamina for employment as orchestral musicians.
"While as soloist woman can rehearse where and when she pleases, the physical
strain of four-five hours a day rehearsal in orchestral work followed by the
prolonged tax of public performance will bar her against possible competition
with male performers".

1140 OSGOOD, Marion G. **America's first ladies' orchestra**, *Etude*
ap   LVIII/10 (Oct 1940) 713.

A letter to the editor written in response to Frederique Joanne Petrides's *Women in orchestras* (*WIAM* 2327). Osgood points out that the Boston Fadette Lady Orchestra, under the direction of Caroline B. Nichols, was actually predated by her own orchestra--the Marion Osgood Ladies' Orchestra--which Osgood founded in 1884 in Chelsea, Mass. She presided over the orchestra for 10 years, during which time the orchestra played at the finest dances and parties in the Boston area. When Caroline B. Nichols founded her own orchestra in 1888, she used the name as suggested by Osgood's sister.

1141 OWEN, H. Goddard. Recollection of Marcella Sembrich, A
bm   (New York: Marcella Sembrich Memorial Assoc., 1950) 77 p. *Illus.*
Marcella Sembrich (1858-1938) trained as a pianist, a violinist, and a singer at the Lemberg Conservatory in Poland. Later while she was studying piano in Vienna with Julius Epstein, Liszt heard her sing and encouraged her to concentrate on her voice. Accordingly she went to Milan to work with Giovanni Battista Lamperti. After appearing with success at leading opera houses in Europe, Sembrich sang with the Metropolitan Opera in its initial season of 1883-84, when Christine Nilsson had top billing. Sembrich was closely associated with the Metropolitan until her retirement in 1909, and it is a measure of the soprano's distinction that she was chiefly responsible for keeping the Italian repertory alive at the Metropolitan through New York's early and fervid enthusiasm for Wagner's operas. Sembrich was one of the first operatic singers to include lieder on recital programs in the United States. When her husband, Wilhelm Stengel, died in 1917, Sembrich retired from public life and devoted herself to teaching at the Curtis Inst. and the Juilliard School. Stengel was the soprano's first voice teacher in Poland and subsequently her manager.

1142 PATTERSON, Dr. Annie. Woman as organist, The, *Etude*
ap   XXX/11 (Nov 1912) 812.
In the past women were advised not to apply for an organist's job because the organ was considered too difficult an instrument for women and because the duties of the position include directing the choir--which was considered unbecoming to women. With the proper training and a disposition towards developing camaraderie with her choir, the woman organist can certainly succeed. For conducting experience, Patterson recommends drilling school children in hymn singing.

1143 PEELER, Clare P. Mystery of Minnie Hauk, The. Did she
ap   **die eight years ago?**, *Musical America* XXXI/19 (6 Mar 1920) 3.
While newspapers, journals, etc., reported the death of Minnie Hauk in 1912 on the basis of press dispatches from abroad, the former soprano still lives near Lucerne, alone and in poverty. Geraldine Farrar has started a fund to aid Hauk in response to a letter from the retired singer describing her situation.

→   PEELER, Clare. **American woman whose musical message thrilled Germany**, *see* 721ap[56].

→   PEELER, Clare. **U.S. Army's only woman song-leader tells of her work**, *see* 444ap[50].

→   PETRIDES, Frederique. **On women conductors**, *see* 2326ap[68].

1144 PEYSER, Herbert F. Do our singers lack temperament?,
ap   *Musical America* XV/23 (13 Apr 1912) 3.
Sarah Jane Cahier notes that the "Anglo-Saxon habit of self-repression" is a handicap to the American artist that is not easily overcome, and she emphasizes the necessity of a thorough background in the history and theory of music for all singers. She recommends that the young women studying abroad live with a middle-class family and never speak a word of English. A native of Tennessee, Cahier has studied, taught, and performed in Europe; during the present season the contralto is appearing at the Metropolitan Opera. This article is signed H.F.P., and Peyser's name has been supplied.

1145 PEYSER, Herbert F. "Go west, young musician!", Maud
ap   **Powell advises**, *Musical America* XVII/21 (29 Mar 1913) 5. *Illus.*
Maud Powell's popularity in the western half of the United States is enormous. According to 1 manager, only 2 other performers can vie with her success, namely Lillian Russell and David Warfield. Powell believes there is a smugness among easterners that prevents a real understanding of the growth in musical life in the West, and in this connection she points to the organization of a symphony orchestra in Bellingham, Wash., with which she recently appeared. Women's music clubs are viewed as the most active force for the advancement of music in the United States. This article is signed H.F.P., and Peyser's name has been supplied.

1146 PEYSER, Herbert F. Nervousness as aid to singers, *Musical*
ap   *America* XV/2 (18 Nov 1911) 3. *Illus.*
Margaret Matzenauer discusses the circumstances surrounding her debut as Amneris in 1911, her soprano and contralto roles, and American critics. Matzenauer is also an accomplished pianist and likes to accompany herself when practising. This article is signed H.F.P., and Peyser's name has been supplied.

1147 PEYSER, Herbert F. Seeker after novelty in song, A.
ap   **Continually treading the beaten path doesn't appeal to Jane Osborn-Hannah**, *Musical America* XVI/20 (21 Sept 1912) 17.
Although she has devoted herself almost exclusively to opera since her return from Germany in 1909, Osborn-Hannah plans to divide her time more evenly between operatic and recital work in the future. She is always looking for new repertory, and she is interested in music by American composers. The soprano has rejected the theory that there is prestige to be gained by an annual summer trip abroad, and instead she enjoys sports, domestic life with her family, and studying new music at a vacation retreat on the Delaware River. This article is signed H.F.P., and Peyser's name has been supplied.

1148 PEYSER, Herbert F. Using program notes for violin recitals,
ap   *Musical America* XXII/24 (16 Oct 1915) 7.
An interview with Maud Powell at the beginning of her annual coast-to- coast concert tour, which will include performances in Hawaii. Powell notes that audiences in towns where the percentage of knowledgable musicians is small, frequently ask her to talk at the opening of a recital about the works she will perform. Since she dislikes any speaking in connection with a performance, Powell has developed program notes. Typically she writes these during the summer prior to a given season, and she believes that even a brief amount of information about the music to be performed "will improve the attitude of the hearers and gain their sympathy".

1149 PEYSER, Herbert F. Why not viola soloists with our orch-
ap   **estras?**, *Musical America* XVIII/19 (13 Sept 1913) 15.
The violinist Vera Barstow believes that success as a performer is not a sufficient reason to cease study. She has had the same teacher [Luigi von Kunits] throughout her career and considers the continuity gained thereby to be very important. Barstow also plays the viola and regrets its neglect as a solo instrument. This article is signed H.F.P., and Peyser's name has been supplied.

1150 Pianist believes in preparedness, *Musical Courier* LXXII/7 (17
ap   Feb 1916) 31. *Illus.*
Announces the forthcoming American debut of Wynne Pyle in Aeolian Hall in New York, which she will follow with recitals in Boston and Chicago. A native of Texas, Pyle did not decide upon a career as a pianist until she went abroad and had the opportunity to study with both Harold Bauer and Alberto Jonas in Berlin. Jonas was instrumental in arranging Pyle's Berlin debut in 1909, and in the following 5 years Pyle appeared with leading organizations in Europe, including the Berlin Philharmonic. The pianist's chief ambition is to be appreciated by audiences in the United States.

1151 Pioneer work done by the Powell trio, *Musical America* IX/25
ap   (1 May 1909) 21. *Illus.*
The Maud Powell Trio--with Powell as violinist, May Mukle as cellist, and Anne Ford as pianist--has just completed a tour through Iowa, Minnesota, Wisconsin, and Nebraska. The trio played in many small towns "whose audiences were respectful and appreciative to concert programs of strictly high-class chamber music".

→   **Popularity of community singing in Brockton due to efforts of Mrs. Nellie Evans Packard**, *see* 446ap[50].

1152 POWELL, Maud. American girl and her violin, The, *Etude*
ap   (*WIAM* 75) 486-87.
Discusses increasing opportunities for American women violinists in orchestral work. Powell sees "no reason why women should not be regularly employed [as orchestral musicians] if they wish to be. American women, especially, have a good sense of rhythm. They are imitative, adaptable, and conscientious, with endless patience for detail. They are quick to seize the trend of another's thoughts and have marvellous powers of carrying out other people's ideas. If women really want orchestral work, they will get it. Prejudice of the American masculine mind is easily broken down".

1153 POWELL, Maud. Price of fame, The, *New Idea Woman's*
ap   *Magazine* XVIII/6 (Dec 1908) 6. *Illus.*
Maud Powell gives advice to young women intent on becoming professional musicians along with insights into her own career. She recalls that her parents were separated for the better part of 15 years when Powell went to Europe with her mother for study, and then concertized in the eastern United States while her father remained in Illinois. Nonetheless, Powell thinks it is impossible for young American women to study abroad without chaperonage: the independence of American girls, their freedom of speech and manner are misunderstood in Europe. Powell notes that most successful women violinists--e.g., Camilla Urso, Wilma Neruda, Arma Senkrah, and Teresina Tua--have disliked their instrument. She believes she has endured because she is willing to live as quietly as possible in contrast to many men violinists.

1154 Progress of women as Nordica sees it, *Musical America* XVII/
ap   12 (25 Jan 1913) 35.
An ardent advocate of suffrage for women, Lillian Nordica discussed the following points--among others--in her lecture on the progress of women for

the League of Political Action in New York on 14 Jan. 1) In the field of music the only women who escape discriminatory treatment are solo singers. 2) Since the traveling man does not think his necessary absence from the home should disbar him from having a home life, neither should the traveling female performer. 3) A profession makes a woman independent, and independence is far better than indirect influence.

1155 Pupil of Robert Schumann, A. Trans. by Marion Boise ROBIN-
ap   SON, *Peabody Bulletin* XX/1 (fall 1923) 11-12.
Nannette Falk Auerbach, retired from the Peabody Conservatory in Baltimore where she was the chief piano instructor from 1871-83, reminisces about her years with the Schumann family. As Nannette Falk, she studied piano with Robert Schumann, taught piano to his daughters, and substituted for Clara as an accompanist. At age 7 she was introduced on the concert stage by her patroness Jenny Lind. A scrapbook she assembled indicates that she was respected by German and Parisian audiences and was known to Rossini, Liszt, Brahms, Joachim, and many other major musicians. This article originally appeared in the *Danziger Zeitung*, 15 Oct. 1922, when Auerbach was 86.

1156 PUTNAM, Alice. Violin playing as a profession for women,
ap   *Musician* XV/1 (10 Jan 1910) 57.
Reviews the professional opportunities available to women violinists: 1) private teaching of children, 2) teaching positions in secondary boarding schools, but not with state universities as the latter usually hire only men, 3) solo work for the gifted few, 4) playing in chamber groups in hotels, and 5) orchestral work in women's orchestras, which "are as variable and uncertain as the stock market".

1157 REED, Lynnel. Be not afraid. Biography of Madame Rider-
bm   **Kelsey** (New York: Vantage, 1955) 166 p. *Illus.*
While this biography of Corinne Rider-Kelsey (1877-1947) by her 2nd husband focuses mainly on the years of their marriage after 1926--when the soprano taught and was active in musical circles in Cleveland--it also includes information about her earlier career as a highly successful concert artist. A native of Rockville, Ill., Rider-Kelsey came from a modest background, and because of limited family monies she was able to attend the Oberlin Conservatory for only 1 year. Subsequently she studied in New York with Mr. and Mrs. Theodore Toedt, and when she auditioned and was chosen for a church position in Brooklyn, she relocated with her husband in New York. Between 1904 and 1925 the soprano was active in recital and concert work, appearing at the Bach festivals in Bethlehem, Penn. and the Cincinnati festivals. She sang briefly in opera, but did not care for its artificiality. During World War I, Rider-Kelsey found opportunities limited for performers who did not appeal to audiences of servicemen, and she turned increasingly to teaching.

1158 REED, Peter Hugh. Sutro sisters come to town, The, *Musical*
ap   *America* XLVIII/33 (1 Dec 1928) 15.
An interview in New York with Rose and Ottilie Sutro, pioneers in the field of duo-piano playing, who have become widely known in the United States and Europe in the 34 years since their debut in 1894. The Sutro sisters are now planning to settle in Washington, D.C., where they will give "salon recitals", each featuring the works of an American composer. Their first recital will focus on Amy Cheney Beach. In recent years the Sutros have successfully performed Beach's *Suite for two pianos founded upon old Irish melodies, op. 104* (*WIAM* 1272*) which the composer wrote expressly for them.

→   **REED, Peter. Recorded art of Frieda Hempel, The,** *see*
        40ap^01.

1159 REHMANN, J.W. Different courses for different pupils,
ap   *Etude* X/2 (July 1892) 134.
Four-fifths of all piano pupils are young women, and the majority of these are studying music as an enjoyment, rather than with the idea of becoming music teachers. Their interest should be cultivated in learning the works of great composers "that will wear well in later life, rather than in learning pieces of acrobatic skill, which they will soon lose".

1160 RICE, Susan Andrews. Plain talk to girls studying music, A,
ap   *Etude* IX/9 (Sept 1891) 171.
Many young women as conservatory students practice too much and ruin their health. A schedule that calls for time out-of-doors each day as well as a broad range of cultural studies is prescribed.

1161 RIDER-KELSEY, Corinne. Why American girls succeed in
ap   **opera,** *Etude* (*WIAM* 75) 451-52.
American women singers, in general, have remarkable vocal talents, but they lack temperament. The young American woman needs to become established as a singer in Europe prior to securing a position with a company in the United States. While it is difficult to move upwards from the chorus to other roles in America, in Europe the situation is more flexible.

1162 RIDLEY, N.A. Johanna Gadski. With an analysis of the records
ap   by Louis MIGLIORINI, *Record Collector* XI/9-10 (Sept-Oct 1957)
        [197]-231. *Illus., discog.*
Johanna Gadski studied exclusively with Mme. Schröder-Chaloupha in her native Stettin in Poland, and she made her debut at the Krolloper in Berlin at age 16 as Agatha in *Der Freischütz*. Between 1895 and 1917 she was closely bound to the Metropolitan Opera and found it unnecessary to take on any European commitments. During her tenure with the New York house, Gadski was responsible for all the leading soprano roles in the Wagnerian repertory together with Lillian Nordica and later Olive Fremstad. One of Gadski's especially notable performances was in the first *Die Meistersinger* in German at the Metropolitan during the 1900-01 season with Jean and Édouard de Reszke, Ernestine Schumann-Heink, and David Bispham. Anti-German sentiment during World War I led to Gadski's retirement from the Metropolitan at the end of the 1916-17 season and also the termination of all performances of German opera by the company. At the same time the Victor Talking Machine Co. deleted all but one of Gadski's recordings from its catalogue. The soprano's recordings attest to her magnificent instrument and a versatility in opera and art songs that few singers of her day could match.

1163 Rising soprano, A, *American Art Journal* LXXXV/6 (5 Nov 1904)
ap   83.
After attending the Oberlin Conservatory, Corinne Rider-Kelsey spent 3 years in Chicago studying with L.A. Torrens and singing in churches. In 1903 she relocated in New York, where she has been studying with Mrs. Theodore Toedt and launching what promises to be a successful career in concert and oratorio work.

1164 Rita Fornia dies suddenly in Paris, *New York Times* 28 Oct
an   1922, 13.
Rita Fornia, née Newman (1878-1922) decided to pursue a career in singing when as a child she heard Adelina Patti perform in San Francisco. Her father initially would not agree to her goal, but in time he relented and gave her financial assistance to study with Emil Fischer in New York and Selma Nicklass-Kempner in Berlin. With these 2 teachers Fornia worked as a coloratura soprano. Later when studying with Jean de Reszke she became a mezzo-soprano, in which capacity she sang minor roles at the Metropolitan Opera for 14 years.

1165 ROOT, George F. Madame Patti and the old songs, *Music*
ap   [Chicago] I/3 (Mar 1892) 428-31.
A composer's defense of concert audiences and the prevailing public interest in sentimental ballads such as *Home, sweet home*, popularized by Adelina Patti. Hostile music critics have argued for education above entertainment, and for an improvement in public musical taste.

1166 Rosa Olitzka, 76, once with opera, *New York Times* 1 Oct 1949,
an   13.
An obituary for the former leading mezzo-soprano (1873-1949), who special-ized in Wagnerian roles. Born in Berlin, Olitzka came to the United States in 1895 to sing with Walter Damrosch's German opera company. Beginning in 1897 she appeared with the Metropolitan Opera, and later with the Chicago Opera.

1167 ROSENTHAL, Harold, ed. Mapleson memoirs (London:
bm   Putnam, 1966) 346 p. *Illus., index.*
Discusses the careers of Minnie Hauk, Clara Louise Kellogg, Emma Nevada, and Adelina Patti. After 20 years as a manager and director of several opera theaters in England, James Henry ("Colonel") Mapleson launched his first American season at the Academy of Music in New York in 1878. Thereafter until 1886 he presented a regular New York season, introducing many great singers to the American public. The opening of the Metropolitan Opera in 1883 created financial problems for Mapleson and forced him to withdraw.

1168 RUBINSTEIN, Anton. Conversation on music, A. Trans. by
bm   Mrs. John MORGAN (New York: C.F. Tretbar, 1892) 146 p.
In the course of this interview, Anton Rubinstein 1) extols the supremacy of instrumental music over vocal music in general, and 2) surveys the history of music from the Renaissance to his own time, with an emphasis on leading composers. Regarding women in music, Rubinstein views the increasing activity of women as performers and composers in the 2nd half of the 19th c. with alarm. As performers women lack subjectivity, courage, and conviction. As composers women are deficient in concentration, powers of thought and feeling, and freedom of imagination.

1169 Ruth Deyo's achievements, *Musical Courier* LXX/15 (14 Apr
ap   1915) 47. *Illus.*
While Ruth Deyo started to play the piano by ear and to improvise at age 3, her parents carefully guarded her talents, with the result that one of the few appearances she was allowed to make as a child was in a recital of her own works at the Columbian Exposition in Chicago in 1893. Deyo studied with William Mason in New York and also with MacDowell, who advised her to go

abroad. In Europe she studied with and received encouragement from Paderewski, d'Indy, Busoni, Teresa Carreño, Lev Stepanov, and Harold Bauer. Charles Martin Loeffler is Deyo's valued friend. The pianist is now winning acclaim for her performances in the United States, e.g., her recent engagements with the Boston and Cincinnati symphony orhcestras.

1170 SAENGER, Gustav. **Maud Powell. An appreciation**, *Musical*
ap   *Observer* VIII/4 (Aug 1913) 303-05. *Illus.*
"Maud Powell stands at the very top of her profession, worthy to be ranked as the equal of the greatest living violin soloists. She belongs right at the top of the list of masculine players and is equal to many of them in the artistic rendition of every important classic or modern work in the violin literature. She never forgets that it is a violin she is playing, and no matter how delicate, how passionate, or how strong her tone may be, it is always beautiful, sympathetic, and luscious. This is where her femininity stands her in good stead". Saenger also notes that 1) Powell's reputation in Europe is equal to her reputation in the United States, and 2) Powell is interested in playing in small towns across the United States since she feels she has a mission to fulfill.

1171 **Saenger pupils in concert and oratorio**, *Musical Courier* L/20
ap   (17 May 1905) 13.
Hildegarde Hoffmann Huss has won an enviable place among successful concert singers in the United States. She began in a modest way in church work and has now risen to the front ranks of lieder and oratorio singers. She recently married Henry Holden Huss, the pianist-composer, and the 2 musicians plan to concentrate on giving joint recitals. Hildegarde Hoffman Huss studied in New York with Oscar Saenger at a point when he was able to help launch her career. She does not care to work in opera.

1172 **Salzédo delved into antiquity for newest musical ensemble**,
ap   *Musical America* XXX/14 (2 Aug 1919) 1, 6. *Illus.*
Reports the growing popularity of the Salzédo Harp Ensemble, which Carlos Salzédo--the noted harp virtuoso--introduced several seasons ago at Aeolian Hall in New York. In the ensemble Salzédo plays with 6 gifted women. Salzédo has interested a number of contemporary composers in writing for the medium of multiple harps, and the ensemble also plays Baroque music in arrangements.

1173 **Sarah Cahier, 76, diva and teacher**, *New York Times* 16 Apr
an   1951, 25.
An obituary for Sarah Jane Cahier (1870-1951). Cahier studied with Jean de Reszke and Fidèle Koenig in Paris, and with Mahler and Amalie Joachim in Berlin. The contralto made her operatic debut in 1904 in Nice; her Metropolitan Opera debut was in 1912 as Azucena. In the United States Cahier taught at the Curtis Inst. and privately. Among her many pupils were Marian Anderson and Lauritz Melchior.

1174 SAVAGE, Janet L. **Geraldine Farrar finds her Shangri-La**
an   **right at home**, *Boston Herald* 6 Jan 1943, B-1.
Geraldine Farrar lives quietly at her home in Ridgefield, Conn., although she gives much of her time to the war effort. Letter writing is one of her greatest pleasures, and she receives an avalanche of mail daily from former "Gerry-flappers". Unlike most former divas, Farrar has not turned to teaching in her later years.

1175 SAVILLE, Richard L. **Madame Bloomfield-Zeisler**, *Musician*
ap   IX/1 (Jan 1904) 1.
Presents a sketch of Fannie Bloomfield-Zeisler's career to 1904. Her earliest supporters in Chicago included Henry Greenbaum, a patron, and Carl Wolfsohn, her teacher. While still in her teens in the mid-1870s, the pianist gained confidence by appearing regularly in concerts of the Beethoven Soc., which Wolfsohn had just organized. In recent years Anton Rubinstein has said that Bloomfield-Zeisler's performance of his concerto no. 4 in D minor, op. 70, surpasses any other he has heard. An evaluation of Bloomfield-Zeisler's playing in different types of repertory is included.

1176 SAWYER, Frank E. **For musical girls**, *Music* [Chicago] V (Nov
ap   1893) 101-03.
Censors the "piano-playing girl", who typically attempts pieces that are too difficult and tries to impress her friends with technical feats, disregarding expression.

1177 SCHAUENSEE, Max de. **Tribute to Emma Eames, A**, *Opera*
ap   *News* XVII/2 (27 Oct 1952) 15. *Illus.*
Assesses the work of the soprano, whose recent death severed the last link with the legendary Golden Age of Song at the Metropolitan Opera. Eames's recordings offer "precious vocal lessons in placement, classic feeling, and contour".

1178 SCHEFF, Fritzi. **Tales of an *enfant terrible***, *Opera News* VIII/
ap   13 (24 Jan 1944) 8-14. *Illus.*
Presents excerpts from the unpublished memoirs of Fritzi Scheff. Scheff discusses her tour with the Metropolitan Opera during her 2nd season with the

company, her performance in *Die Zauberflöte* with Marcella Sembrich, her decision to leave grand opera in favor of operetta, and her association with Victor Herbert.

1179 SCHOEN-RENÉ, Anna Eugénie. **America's musical inher-**
bm   **itance** (New York: G.P. Putnam's Sons, 1941) 244 p. *Illus., index.*
An autobiography by the German-American singer and voice teacher, Anna Eugénie Schoen-René (1864-1942). Born in Coblenz, Schoen-René studied in Berlin where she met Brahms and Joachim. The soprano came to the United States in 1893 and settled in Minnesota with her sister, a professor at the U. of Minnesota. In 1895 she founded both the music department at the U. of Minnesota and the Northwestern Symphony Orchestra in Minneapolis. A large part of Schoen-René's account is a tribute to her voice teachers, Pauline Viardot-Garcia and Manuel Garcia, with whom she studied for 18 years. Among Schoen-René's best-known pupils were Risë Stevens, Florence Easton, and Karin Branzell.

1180 SCHONBERG, Harold. **Goddess that was Geraldine Farrar,**
an   **The**, *New York Times* 19 Mar 1967, II-21. *Illus.*
A tribute to Geraldine Farrar written shortly after her death at age 85. Discusses her extraordinary appeal, realistic acting, and strong, lyric soprano voice. Farrar was a *prima donna assoluta*. An anecdote about her famous recording with Caruso of the Act I duet from *Madame Butterfly* is included.

1181 SCHULTZ, Ferdinand P. **Andrews family, The. Up from the**
bm   **frontier in music and opera** (Minneapolis: U. of Minnesota,
        1940) 33 p.
A study of the singing Andrews family, based on interviews with a female member of the original generation of the troupe and source materials in the family's possession as well as newspaper reports. Beginning in 1875 the Andrews family toured in Minnesota and throughout the Midwest as a concert and opera company for ca. 30 years, playing in both small communities and major cities. Although the company employed some outside artists, essentially it was family owned and operated. The Andrews were possibly inspired to form a troupe as a result of hearing the Hutchinson family perform in 1874. Also the Leavitt family of Swiss Bell Ringers interested the Andrews in taking up bell playing. A performance of *H.M.S. Pinafore*--which the Andrews attended in Mankato, Minn. in 1883--was influential in their decision to pursue opera. They performed Gilbert and Sullivan repertory, *Carmen, Martha*, and *Cavalleria rusticana*, among other works.

1182 **Schumann-Heink, great singer, dead**, *New York Times* 18 Nov
an   1936, 1, 22. *Illus.*
Reports the death of Ernestine Schumann-Heink in Hollywood, where she was appearing in movies under a 3-year contract with Metro-Goldwyn-Mayer. Once extremely wealthy from her singing, Schumann-Heink's generosity and the Depression made the last years of her life difficult financially. The contralto was affectionately known as "mother" by veterans of World War I, because of her interest in their welfare and her numerous performances at military camps.

1183 **Schumann-Heink's farewell gathers audience of 5000**, *New*
ro   *York Herald Tribune* 11 Dec 1927, 26.
4000 seats in Carnegie Hall were filled for Ernestine Schumann-Heink's farewell performance in New York, while another 1000 people stood. Seldom has a beloved singer received testimonials of such nationwide homage; she was thanked for her lifetime of service and giving joy to others. This was the 25th appearance in a tour of 75 engagements throughout the United States. In the future Schumann-Heink plans to teach and to work for the establishment of opera companies in communities that hitherto have not been able to afford them.

1184 SCHWERKÉ, Irving. **Carmen steps out of the past. A visit**
ap   **to Minnie Hauk in her last days**, *Musical Courier* CVII/14 (30
        Sept 1933) 6.
The earliest and perhaps the most famous of American Carmens, Minnie Hauk influenced operatic acting by the realism of her interpretations. In this interview shortly before her death in 1929, Hauk reminisces about Liszt and Massenet, and about her idols, Jenny Lind and Henriette Sontag.

1185 SCOTT, John M. **Litta, an American singer. A sketch of**
bm   **Marie Eugenia Von Elsner** (Bloomington, Ill.: author, 1897) 160
        p. *Illus.*
A.B. Hough of Cleveland gave Marie Eugenia Von Elsner (1856-83) the funds that enabled her to go to Europe for study in 1874. Her teacher from Cleveland, Dr. Underner, accompanied her abroad. Von Elsner undertook 2 periods of study in Paris with Pauline Viardot-Garcia and Anna-Caroline de La Grange respectively, leading to a debut at the Théâtre-Italien as Lucia under the stage name of Litta. When she returned to the United States in 1878, the soprano joined Max Strakosch's opera company, singing in 2nd position to Clara Louise Kellogg. After 2 seasons she abandoned opera however, with the idea that solo recital work would be more lucrative financially. Traveling on tour injured Von Elsner's health--which had never been robust--and contributed to her death at

an early age. The soprano was known as a convincing actress. Like Jenny Lind, she often sang for the benefit of charities.

1186 SEELEY, Evelyn. **Can you stay _happily_ wed in New York?**
an *New York Telegram* 4 Dec 1930, 17.
An interview with Alma Gluck, the retired singer, and Efrem Zimbalist, violinist, concerning the domestic life of the Zimbalist family. Gluck believes that a woman cannot combine marriage and a career. However, she found it difficult to relinquish hers, and she misses the sense of power the performer feels in making an audience spellbound.

1187 SHAWE-TAYLOR, Desmond. **Gallery of great singers, A.**
ap **8: Emma Eames (1865-1952)**, *Opera* VIII/1 (Jan 1957) 8-13, 64-65. *Illus.*
A critical assessment of the soprano's portrayals of numerous operatic roles, encompassing her work in Paris in the late 1880s and her career at the Metropolitan Opera from 1891-1909. After retiring from the Metropolitan, Eames gave a few recitals, and in 1912 she appeared in several performances as Tosca. Between 1905 and 1911 she made 40 records for the Victor Talking Machine Co. Biographical information about the singer's later years is included.

1188 SHEEAN, Vincent. **Mary Garden. 20 February 1874-3**
ap **January 1967**, *Opera News* XXXI/15 (4 Feb 1967) 6-7.
A personal reminiscence of Mary Garden, whose portrayal of Mélisande impressed the author who heard her in 1927, 25 years after she had appeared in the opera's première in Paris. Garden's flawless diction and mastery of languages as well as an anecdote about her singing Victor Herbert's *Natoma* with John McCormack in 1911 are discussed.

1189 SHIFF, J. Edmund. **Boys and women as choristers in the**
ap **Episcopal church**, *Etude* XXII/2 (Feb 1904) 67.
Reports that the boy chorister is gaining favor over the woman chorister and that the boy choir "is destined to push its way into a large proportion of the Episcopal churches in America".

1190 **Should a woman singer wear a corset? A symposium**, *Musician*
ap XIX/5-6 (May-June 1914) 338-39; 410-11.
A letter to the editor prompted the editors of *Musician* to solicit the views of various singers and voice teachers on the subject of whether a woman singer should wear a corset. The responses were almost unanimously against the wearing of a corset as harmful to the singer in developing adequate breath control and strong muscles.

1191 **Sibyl Sanderson is dead in Paris**, *New York Herald* 17 May
an 1903, I-11. *Illus.*
Reports the death of the American soprano (1865-1903) from pneumonia at the age of 38. A native of Sacramento, Calif., Sanderson studied initially in San Francisco and then at the Paris Conservatory, where Massenet was her mentor. Her Esclarmonde was one of the triumphs of the 1889 Exposition in Paris, and she was the leading exponent at the Opéra of the roles of Manon and Thaïs as well as the title role in Saint-Saëns's *Phryné*.

1192 **Sidelights on the Sutro sisters**, *Musical Courier* LXXIV/16 (19
ap Apr 1917) 10.
Rose and Ottilie Sutro, duo-pianists, are descendents of many generations of native Americans, their male ancestors having been prominent in the military. Both of their parents were musicians: their father founded the Baltimore Oratorio Soc.; their mother was their teacher until they went to Berlin for advanced study. The Sutro sisters began 2-piano playing when youngsters as a pastime, but they were intent on careers as soloists until their teacher in Berlin heard them play together at a social occasion and urged them to take up 2-piano work. During their extensive concertizing abroad as duo-pianists, they formed a friendship with Max Bruch, who wrote his concerto for 2 pianos, op. 88a, for the sisters and gave them exclusive performance rights. The Sutros recently performed the Bruch concerto with the Philadelphia Orchestra under Leopold Stokowski.

1193 SKILTON, Charles S. **Conductors and non-conductors**. *Stud-*
ac *ies in musical education, history, and aesthetics* 6 (Hartford: Music Teachers National Assoc., 1912) 65-78.
Compares training of young musicians in Germany with methods in the United States, where improvements in home, church, and school music are needed. If American boys were encouraged to prefer brass and wind instruments, they might enter the "uniformed masculine ranks", thereby leaving the "irresponsible individualism of the piano" to girls. However, coeducational orchestras have more success that those of single-sex schools, where too few boys play strings and too few girls are accomplished wind players--since these instruments are unsuited to women.

1194 SMITH, A. Philbrook. **Divine endorsement**, *New Jersey Music*
ap II/6 (Feb 1947) 5, 12.
Anna Case began studying voice with a local teacher in New Jersey, who in

turn asked her teacher in New York--Augusta O. Renard--to accept Case as a pupil. Renard was a former student of Mathilde Marchesi and had sung with the Royal Opera in Stockholm prior to settling in the United States. Anna Case already had considerable concert work and a successful Carnegie Hall debut to her credit when Andreas Dippel "discovered" her during an engagement at the Bellevue-Stratford Hotel in Philadelphia in 1909 and offered her a contract with the Metropolitan Opera. The soprano sang at the Metropolitan until 1918, when she decided to devote herself to the concert stage. Case made numerous recordings for Thomas A. Edison, Inc. She retired after her marriage in 1931 to Clarence McKay, the communications magnate.

→ SMITH, Eva. **Woman as composer**, *see* 451ap[50].

1195 SMITH, Fanny Morris. **Amateur versus the professional**
ap **standpoint, The**, *Etude* XIX/4 (Apr 1901) 150-51.
In this lead item on the *Woman's work in music* page (*WIAM* 645), Smith notes that New York and other large cities are filled with "poverty-stricken musicians", who maintain, however, that they cannot exist outside of the musical atmosphere found in major centers. What is needed is a class of trained amateurs that could support a limited class of professional musicians in comfort in all locales. Village orchestras and choruses could promote opportunities for the professional musician.

1196 SMITH, Fanny Morris. **On women in the orchestra**, *Etude*
ap XVIII/5 (May 1900) 186-87.
While women are being told that as violinists their tone is weak or that they should not approach the brass instruments, 2 women's orchestras have, in fact, been successful in New York in the past season, and one of the orchestras intends to add brass in the next season. Another argument being advanced against women as orchestral musicians is that once women are playing in orchestras they will want to become conductors. The general advance of women in all fields of activity is discussed. This article appears on the *Woman's work in music* page (*WIAM* 645).

1197 SMITH, Max. **Mark Twain and music**, *Musical Courier* LX/18
ap (4 May 1910) 17.
Clara and Susan Clemens, daughters of Mark Twain, both began as pianists and later became singers after they went abroad to study. Their taste for good music was formed in the home of Susan Lee Warner, the wife of the Hartford essayist Charles Dudley Warner. In the 1880s concerts in the Hartford area were few, and thus it was at informal weekly musicales organized by Susan Lee Warner that the Clemens sisters read through and learned a large repertory. Although she is now in her 70s, Warner recently gave a piano recital at the Hartford School of Music.

1198 SMITH, May Lyle. **New instrument for women, giving health**
ap **combined with pleasure, The**, *Etude* IX/6 (June 1891) 108.
Reports that increasing numbers of young women are taking up the flute, and recommends the flute as an ideal instrument for women because it requires little exertion, allows the performer a pose of grace and beauty, is easy to carry from place to place, and is beneficial for the lungs. While the violin and piano require much practice, a reasonable amount of skill in flute playing can be acquired more easily.

1199 **Some difficulties confronting American women artists**, *Musi-*
ap *cian* VI/9 (Sept 1901) 275.
Alma Webster-Powell recently resigned from the Berlin State Opera because she was prevented from making appearances by mediocre German artists. Every time Webster-Powell was cast for a performance, these artists planned convenient illnesses, thereby making it necessary for the management to change the bill. If the United States can produce singers like Webster-Powell, who are able to establish themselves abroad as superior to native singers, the time has come for American opera houses to hire such American talent.

1200 **Some tributes to Maud Powell**, *Musical Leader* XII/18 (1 Nov
ap 1906) 9.
Powell made her first appearance in the United States when Theodore Thomas presented her as his "musical grandchild" with the New York Philharmonic. Sibelius has written to thank Powell for planning the performance of his new violin concerto in D minor, op. 47, with the New York Philharmonic this season. Powell's collection of letters and signed photographs also includes tributes from Hans Richter, Saint-Saëns, Henry J. Wood, Anton Seidl, Modest Altschuler, and Vassily Safonoff.

1201 **Souvenir programme. Emma R. Steiner testimonial comme-**
bm **morating her golden anniversary as American composer and**
orchestra director (New York: Metropolitan Opera, 1925) [12] p. *Illus.*
A souvenir program of a concert that featured compositions by Emma Roberto Steiner, conducted by the composer at the Metropolitan Opera on 17 Nov. 1925. Selections from Steiner's comic operas included the overture to *Fleurette* (*WIAM* 1442). Two songs by Irving Berlin were also on the program, together with arias from *Andrea Chenier* and *Il barbieri di Siviglia*. A description of the

Steiner Foundation, which aimed to establish homes for aged and infirm musicians, and a short biography of Steiner are included.

→   SPAETH, Sigmund. **Enter the woman in the domain of song-leading**, *see* 452ap[50].

→   S.S.B. **Song leader trains college girls in music leading**, *see* 453ap[50].

1202   STANLEY, May. **Artist couples uphold feminist belief**,
ap   *Musical America* XXIV/4 (27 May 1916) 3. *Illus.*
While the debate continues as to whether women's proper sphere is in or out of the home, many famous women artists and their husbands have been pursuing careers while raising families. During the 1915-16 season there was a greater number of joint recitals given by married couples than ever before. These included Zabetta Brinska and Paul Althouse, Augusta Cottlow and Edwin Gerst, Alma Gluck and Efrem Zimbalist, Louise and Sidney Homer, Hildegarde Hoffmann Huss and Henry Holden Huss, Margaret Matzenauer and Edouard Ferrari-Fontana, Marguerite Ober and Arthur Arndt, Olga Samaroff Stokowski and Leopold Stokowski, and Rosina Van Dyck and Richard Hageman. In the majority of cases the woman is a singer and her husband, the accompanist.

1203   STANLEY, May. **Believes suffrage will mean more oppor-**
ap   **tunities for young singers**, *Musical America* XXIII/21 (25 Mar 1916) 19. *Illus.*
Minnesota-born Florence Macbeth, who created the leading role in Strauss's *Ariadne auf Naxos* in 1912 in Berlin, sees the feminist movement as an aid to young women performers in obtaining hearings. Macbeth looks forward to the establishment of an indigenous American opera tradition. An account of her European concert and operatic appearances is included.

1204   STANLEY, May. **Here's one American singer who has no**
ap   **operatic yearnings**, *Musical America* XXIV/1 (5 June 1916) 47.
Reports that Florence Hinkle has taken her place in the foremost ranks of concert sopranos. Hinkle recently returned from a tour on the West Coast, where "unheralded, and without the halo that accompanies grand opera stars when they shine upon concert audiences", she was a triumph. The soprano is pleased to note that her training "was American and with an American teacher". Also, she feels that concert work, rather than opera, offers her a wider choice in programs and achievement. Upon her return to the East, Hinkle sang in the first American performance of Mahler's symphony no. 8 in E-flat major with the Philadelphia Orchestra under Leopold Stokowski.

1205   STANTON, H.A. **What is the use of the musical education?**,
ap   *Etude* XIV/5 (May 1896) 104.
While many young women abandon the piano after marriage and children, the time and money spent during their piano studies is not necessarily wasted. Music study teaches discipline, strengthens the memory, develops firm muscles in the arm and hand, and instills a love of music that will be retained in future years when the student becomes an audience member.

1206   STERLING, Elizabeth; NELSON, Cordelia Hulburd. **Queen**
ap   **of American pianists**, *Etude* LVI/8 (Aug 1938) 497-98, 502.
An anecdotal biographical sketch of Teresa Carreño that includes information about her teaching methods. Carreño's physical breakdown and death in 1917 are attributed to anxieties brought about by the war, e.g. financial problems, the difficulties she encountered in returning to the United States from Germany, and the division between her children with German allegiance and those with American allegiance.

1207   STORER, H.J. **Women as orchestral players as illustrated by**
ap   **the Fadettes**, *Musician* XV/8 (Aug 1910) 511.
Considers the marked increase of women studying orchestral instruments as proof of the progress in music education over the past 40 years. Discusses the work of the Boston Fadette Lady Orchestra, under the direction of Caroline B. Nichols. The orchestra has completed 2 transcontinental tours, playing in practically all cities.

1208   STRAKOSCH, Avery. **American singers in opera must**
ap   **become cosmopolites**, *Musical America* XXI/19 (13 Mar 1915) 5. *Illus.*
Vera Curtis believes that American singers should constantly be on the alert to broaden their proficiency in languages, make the most of small roles, and learn new parts. During the 1915-16 season Curtis will sing the role of the Queen in the world première of Giordano's *Madame Sans-Gêne* at the Metropolitan Opera. The soprano's career prior to her joining the Metropolitan in 1912 is discussed.

1209   STRANG, Lewis C. **Prima donnas and soubrettes of light**
bm

opera and musical comedy in America (Boston: L.C. Page, 1900) 270 p. *Illus., index.*
Includes biographical information and appraisals of the work of the following performers active in musical comedy, light opera, and/or vaudeville prior to 1900: Camille d'Arville, Minnie Ashley, Marie Celeste, Hilda Clark, Jessie Bartlett Davis, Marie Dressler, Virginia Earle, Paula Edwards, Della Fox, Mabelle Gilman, Lulu Glaser, Josephine Hall, Pauline Hall, Edna Wallace Hopper, Madge Lessing, Christie MacDonald, Edna May, Alice Nielsen, Maud Raymond, Lillian Russell, Marie Tempest, and Fay Templeton. Most of the women were known primarily as entertainers, rather than as singers or actresses. The coverage is nationwide.

→   STRATTON, Stephen. **Woman in relation to musical art**, *see* 727ap[56].

1210   **Strictly woman's concert**, *Musical America* XV/19 (16 Mar 1912)
ro   29.
Reports on a recent concert of chamber music by Carolyn Beebe, pianist, and the Olive Mead Quartet, composed of Olive Mead, Verna Fonaroff, Gladys North, and Lillian Littlehales. The feature of the program was Amy Cheney Beach's piano quintet in F-sharp minor, op. 67 (*WIAM* 1268).

1211   **String orchestra of women, A**, *Musical Courier* XXXII/10 (4 Mar
ap   1896) 30.
Announces the formation of the Women's String Orchestra of New York under the direction of Carl V. Lachmund, with violinist Camilla Urso as honorary president. Mr. Lachmund, who is aware of the drawing possibilities of an orchestra composed exclusively of women performers, intends to make the orchestra profitable financially as well as artistically. A list of the members is included.

1212   **Study in America. An interview with Schumann-Heink**, *Musi-*
ap   *cal Leader and Concert-goer* XIX/1 (6 Jan 1910) 13.
Ernestine Schumann-Heink notes that on her concert tours throughout the United States she meets young women who think only of further study in New York or Europe. This is wrong because there are fine teachers in every major American city. In many cases, the costly trip abroad--with its inherent danger of homesickness--would better be avoided.

1213   **Success of an American pianist**, *Musical Courier* LVIII/25 (23
ap   June 1909) 34.
Discusses Myrtle Elvyn's 2nd season in the United States on tour to the West Coast with the Chicago Symphony Orchestra, including the hardships she experienced. A pupil of Leopold Godowsky, Elvyn advises young pianists and teachers who have had difficulty in obtaining recognition in the East to travel to the western states, where there is no prejudice in favor of the foreign artist.

1214   **Success of Beebe-Déthier sonata recitals**, *Musical America*
ap   XIII/20 (25 Mar 1911) 35.
Ten years ago the only chamber music organization active in the United States was the Kneisel Quartet. Now the audience for chamber music has grown enough to support as well the Flonzaley Quartet and the Olive Mead Quartet--the latter organization being "composed of 4 young women of decided artistic merit". Even sonata recitals are patronized, chiefly due to the efforts of Carolyn Beebe, pianist, and Édouard Déthier, violinist. Before these artists performed in New York and elsewhere, "the sonata recital did not exist".

1215   **Success of Pittsburgh Ladies' Orchestra**, *Musical Courier*
ap   LXVII/8 (20 Aug 1913) 9.
Albert D. Liefeld organized the Pittsburgh Ladies' Orchestra in 1911. Some of the orchestra's members had previous experience with the Boston Fadette Lady Orchestra and an all-female orchestra in Cleveland. Liefeld is also the director of the Pittsburgh School of Music and head of the Liefeld Orchestra.

1216   **Sweetest singer of ours is back**, *Los Angeles Times* 11 May
an   1906, II-1.
An interview with Ellen Beach Yaw, who has just triumphed in an appearance at the New York Hippodrome upon returning from several years in Europe. When she began singing in the early 1890s, Yaw was regarded as a sensationalist because of her ability to sing unusually high notes "running into dizzy atmospheres far above Patti and her contemporaries". The recognition she has received in recent years in Italy and her work in Paris with Mathilde Marchesi have established her as a true artist. Yaw would like to see an opera season of a few months each year in her native Los Angeles, and she thinks such a venture would be financially viable.

1217   **Talent and dollars**, *Musical Courier* LXXI/4 (28 July 1915) 14-15.
ap
Since she is the daughter of a wealthy industrial magnate in Omaha, Frances Nash's choice of a career as a concert pianist--with its constant effort and self-sacrifice--has amazed many. Nash, however, believes that everyone in life needs a goal. She recently completed 2 years of study in Germany, and she received

considerable recognition for her performances abroad. Upon her return to the United States she appeared with the Minneapolis Symphony Orchestra in her native city. In the 1915-16 season Nash will tour with George Hamlin, tenor. This article is reprinted from the *Omaha Daily News*, 30 May 1915.

1218 **Teaching as aid to opera singer,** *Musical America* XVII/9 (4 Jan
ap   1913) 15. *Illus.*
After appearing at the Metropolitan Opera from 1903-06, Florence Mulford decided to withdraw from the company in order to further her career in Europe. However, her traumatic experiences in San Francisco at the time of the earthquake in Apr. 1906 caused--in part--a nervous breakdown once she reached Berlin, and she returned to the United States to recuperate. In the course of her recovery she turned to teaching as a less arduous profession than performance, and she is emphatic about the benefits she gained as a performer through 7 years of constant teaching. Mulford has returned to the Metropolitan in the current 1912-13 season and is singing 17 roles.

1219 **Teresa Carreño and the Venezuela hymn,** *New York Times* 17
an   June 1917, VIII-7.
A tribute to the "Brünnhilde of the pianoforte", following her death in New York on 12 June 1917. Discusses Carreño's "sturdy Americanism", the long span of her career during which she played at the presidential White House for both Presidents Lincoln and Wilson, and her versatility as a singer, composer, conductor, and pianist. Contrary to the commonly-held assumption, Carreño did not write the Venezuelan national anthem; rather the composer was José Landaeta.

1220 **Theatres and concerts. Boston Symphony Orchestra,** *Boston*
ro   *Evening Transcript* 30 Mar 1885, 1.
Reviews Amy Cheney Beach's performance of the Chopin piano concerto no. 2 in F minor, op. 21, with the Boston Symphony Orchestra on 28 Mar. "Beach played with rare delicacy, warmth, and purity of sentiment, and--as the Germans say--with a totality of conception that one seldom finds in players of her sex".

1221 **THIEDE, Henry A. Scaling opera's ladder,** *Green Book Maga-*
ap   *zine* VII (Nov 1915) 940-44. *Illus.*
The American soprano Marcella Craft relates how she built her career in Europe. After 2 years in Italy she went to Germany, where her interpretation of Salome secured her reputation as a prima donna. Among Craft's future plans is a series of concerts in Germany and the United States devoted to the music of Amy Cheney Beach with Beach as the accompanist.

1222 **THOMAS, Augustus. Print of my remembrance, The** (New
bm   York: C. Scribner's Sons, 1922) 477 p. *Illus., index.*
Contains information about the early career of Della Fox, when as a child actress she appeared in the author's one-act farce *Editha's burglar*, adapted from Frances Hodgson Burnett's story of the same name. Thomas's company toured in the Midwest in 1883-85.

1223 **THOMAS, Fannie Edgar. American girls and musical ca-**
ap   **reers,** *Musical Courier* XXXIII/1 (1 July 1896) 5-6.
Reports that the many young American women who flock to Paris studios to study singing and find engagements are, on the average, not talented enough to succeed professionally. Argues that 1) Americans should exhaust opportunities for training and experience at home before traveling to Europe to finish their studies, and 2) most young American women should "train, entertain, and help art in their own place" as amateurs.

1224 **To play in Saint-Saëns concerto. Katherine Heyman to**
ap   **appear at fair after 10 years abroad,** *Musical America* XXII/8
        (26 June 1915) 23.
Announces that the pianist will play in her native state of California and then tour throughout the United States after 10 years of performing in the major European capitals. Heyman has worked to introduce in Europe the music of American composers--Arthur Farwell, Arthur Foote, MacDowell, and Walter Rummell.

1225 **Too much piano. Outcry of a sufferer,** *Etude* II/3 (Mar 1884)
ap   50.
Proposes a substantial "piano tax" for all purchasers of pianos who, upon examination, do not demonstrate sufficient musical talent. Denounces the social convention that dictates young women should study the piano and be prepared to play at social gatherings, while young men are not expected to do so.

1226 **TRACEY, James M. Some of the world's greatest women**
ap   **pianists,** *Etude* XXV/12 (Dec 1907) 773-74.
While countless numbers of women study the piano, very few emerge as great pianists. The reason for this is that most women lack the necessary physical strength to overcome technical difficulties in playing; those women who do have the strength lack talent. A brief biography is presented for one American pianist, Teresa Carreño, along with similarly brief biographies for the following

European women: Annette Essipoff, Anna Mehlig, Sophie Menter, and Clara Schumann.

1227 **TROTTER, James M. Music and some highly musical people**
bf   (New York: Johnson Reprint, 1968) 152 p. *Illus.*
A reprint of the 1878 edition (Boston: Lee & Shepard). Presents a series of biographical sketches of black musicians in America to 1878, together with an overview of the history of western art music. Includes profiles of Elizabeth Taylor Greenfield and Nellie F. Brown, singers, Anna Madah Hyers and Emma Louise Hyers, singers and pianists, as well as less extensive information about Rachel M. Washington, organist, and Sarah Sedgewick Bowers and Mme. Brown, singers. All of these women were active at the time of the book's publication or slightly earlier.

1228 **TRUETTE, Everett Ellsworth. Women as organists,** *Etude*
ap   (*WIAM* 74) 332.
Until a few years ago the position of organist and choir director in large city churches was closed to women, and women were restricted to smaller city and county churches. Now women hold a number of prominent posts. There are very few organ virtuosi among women players not because women are incapable, but rather because "they generally abandon the chase before the game is won, either from force of circumstances or a sense of self-satisfaction already obtained".

1229 **TUBBS, Arthur L. American teaching behind Florence**
ap   **Macbeth's success,** *Musical America* XIX/17 (28 Feb 1914) 9.
        Illus.
Florence Macbeth, the new coloratura soprano of the Philadelphia-Chicago Opera, has studied voice exclusively in the United States with Yeatman Griffith, although she also has coached and studied diction abroad. She made her operatic debut in Darmstadt in 1912 as Gilda. Her repertory consists of 12 roles at the present time, including Amina in *La sonnambula*, Lucia, and Carmen.

1230 **UPTON, George P. Musical memories** (Chicago: A.C.
bm   McClury, 1908) 345 p. *Illus., index.*
Upton's reminiscences cover the period 1850-1900, when he was active as a music critic in Chicago. The careers of the pianist Teresa Carreño, the violinist Camilla Urso, and the following singers are discussed: Emma Abbott, Anna Bishop, Jessie Bartlett Davis, Minnie Hauk, Euphrosyne Parepa-Rosa, Adelina Patti, Adelaide Phillipps, Caroline Richings, and Erminia Rudersdorff.

1231 **V.E.B. Madame Julie Rivé-King,** *Musician* XV/3 (Mar 1911)
ap   160.
In the 1880s the pianist was the sensation of the American concert world, playing by memory works of European Classic and Romantic composers, as well as compositions by William Mason. Rivé-King's mother was her first teacher, and she also studied with other teachers in her native Cincinnati before going to Weimar to study further with Liszt. Her tour with Theodore Thomas's orchestra in 1882 proved educational for American audiences. Rivé-King's activity as a soloist with orchestras slackened, however, because of a "piano feud". She restricted herself to a piano not esteemed by most conductors, and her appearances with orchestras became infrequent after the 1880s.

1232 **Vera Curtis, soprano, dies at 82; sang at the Met from 1912**
an   **to 1920,** *New York Times* 7 Feb 1962, 37.
Born in Stratford, Conn., Vera Curtis (1880-1962) graduated from the New England Conservatory and the Inst. of Musical Art in New York. The soprano made her Metropolitan Opera debut in 1912 as the First Lady in *Die Zauberflöte*. Among her best-known roles were Marguerite and Desdemona.

1233 **Vienna Lady Orchestra,** *New York Times* 13 Sept 1871, 5.
ro
Reviews the first concert of the women's orchestra from Vienna at Steinway Hall in New York on 11 Sept. 1871. Criticizes the lack of woodwinds other than flutes, of brass and of double bass, and notes its effect on the balance of the ensemble. Praises the "vivacity and unity" of the orchestra's performance. "The sight of an instrumentalist of the gentler sex has little rarity about it, but the view of an organized force of female musicians" has never been offered before in the United States.

1234 **"Violinists shackled", cries Miss Powell,** *New York Times* 4
an   Mar 1912, 11.
The American public is indebted to violinist Maud Powell for her commitment to introducing new compositions. Powell has given the first performances of Sibelius's concerto in D minor, op. 47, and Bruch's violin concerto no. 2 in D minor, op. 44. This summer she will play a new concerto by Samuel Coleridge-Taylor at the Norfolk Music Festival in Connecticut, which has been organized by Carl and Ellen Battell Stoeckel to combat the commercialism they find characteristic of many other festivals in the United States.

1235 WAGENKNECHT, Edward. **Geraldine Farrar. An autho-**
bm   **rized record** (Seattle: U. Book Store, 1929) 91 p. *Illus., bibliog.*
An appreciation of Geraldine Farrar's career. Lists of her operatic roles, motion pictures, and records are included together with 6 typical concert programs from the years 1913-28.

1236 WAGENKNECHT, Edward. **Geraldine the great,** *High Fi-*
ap   *delity* VII/7 (July 1957) 36-38, 89-93. *Illus.*
Discusses Farrar's recordings in light of recent re-releases. With the exception of Alma Gluck, Farrar recorded more works than any other singer of her time. In Germany between 1904 and 1906 she made 18 discs of operatic selections and songs. From 1907 until 1923 she recorded for the Victor Talking Machine Co., which issued 72 recordings of solo songs, 37 of duets, and 64 recordings of operatic selections by Farrar. A personal reminiscence of a Farrar lieder recital is also included.

1237 WAGNALLS, Mabel. **Stars of the opera** (New York: Funk &
bm   Wagnalls, 1907) 402 p. *Illus.*
This series of personal interviews includes the following women in American music: Emma Eames, Geraldine Farrar, Lillian Nordica, and Marcella Sembrich. The interviews, all written in narrative form, discuss the present and early careers of the singers as well as their ideas on the art of singing.

1238 WAGNER, Charles L. **Seeing stars** (New York: G.P. Putnam's
bm   Sons, 1940) 403 p. *Illus., index.*
The author reviews his career as a manager of performing musicians and actors, and discusses his associations with Amelita Galli-Curci, Mary Garden, and Alice Nielsen, among other singers.

1239 W.F.G. **Los Angeles woman sang in** *Stabat Mater* **under**
ap   **Rossini,** *Musical America* XXIV/18 (2 Sept 1916) 17.
The daughter of a New England musician who became a bandmaster during the Civil War, Jennie Twitchell Kempton was a vocal prodigy in her youth, and at age 14 she sang in Mendelssohn's *Elijah, op. 70,* with the Handel and Haydn Soc. While still in her teens she went to Europe for study, and in 1865 she sang in Rossini's *Stabat Mater* in Paris under the direction of the composer. After her return to the United States, Kempton appeared with Theodore Thomas's orchestra, and she took part in the Peace Jubilees organized by Patrick S. Gilmore. During her 15 years in Chicago and 25 years in Los Angeles, Kempton was the teacher and friend of hundreds of aspiring students.

1240 **What one woman did,** *Etude* XXXIV/7 (July 1916) 479.
ap
This editorial discusses the work of Blanche Davenport-Engberg as founder and conductor of an 80-member orchestra in Bellingham, Wash. Davenport-Engberg's success is viewed as an example of what could be accomplished in countless small cities throughout the country. Leading symphony orchestras on tour serve only a small part of the population.

1241 **What one woman did in Washington. Directing three cho-**
ap   **ruses only a part of Mrs. Blair's many musical activities,**
Musical America XV/18 (9 Mar 1912) 25.
Mrs. A.M. Blair is the leader of the Rubinstein Club of Washington, D.C., a women's chorus that is the most active choral organization in the city. She also directs the choruses of the Monday Morning Club and the Young Women's Christian Assoc., and she conducts a women's orchestra, which she organized. Mrs. Blair works without compensation.

→   WHITCOMB, E.O. **How mother collected her bills,** see 851ap[57].

1242 WHITEHEAD, George C. **Being one of the Chautauqua**
ap   **folks. Alice Nielsen of Metropolitan Opera forsakes New**
York ..., *Musical Courier* LXXIII/12 (21 Sept 1916) 27-28. *Illus.*
Discusses Alice Nielsen's 9-week tour to 50 cities in Ohio, West Virginia, and Kentucky on the Redpath Chautauqua circuit. It is estimated that Nielsen sang to 100,000 people, most of whom had never heard an artist of such calibre before. The program included selections by Massenet, Brahms, and Debussy together with popular songs. *Kathleen Mavourneen, Old folks at home,* and *Comin' thro' the rye* were among the encores.

1243 **Who should study music,** *Etude* III/1 (Jan 1885) 6.
ap
Argues that too many young women are being taught to play the piano whether they have "any musical ear or not". There is no reason why unmusical girls should spend an hour or more a day in acquiring the art of playing badly.

1244 WILKINSON, Margaret. **Madame Emma Nevada,** *Metropoli-*
ap   *tan Magazine* XI/1 (Jan 1900) 45-48. *Port.*
Emma Nevada is the only American soprano who has sung in every major

European city. After 3 years of study with Mathilde Marchesi in Paris, Nevada made her operatic debut in 1880 in London as Amina in *La sonnambula.* Five years later she made her American debut with James Henry ("Colonel") Mapleson's opera company in New York.

1245 W.J.Z. **How fashion's dictates handicap woman climbing**
ap   **artistic heights,** *Musical America* XXI/20 (20 Mar 1915) 29.
Discusses the skirt and jacket outfit which Ethel Leginska has designed for her concert appearances: it keeps her warm and at the same time allows for perfect freedom for the arm. The pianist believes women performers have not yet achieved the same overall artistic level that some men have because of the many handicaps that have been put in woman's way, namely, fashions in clothing as well as unequal education and childbearing.

1246 **Woman concertmaster in Des Moines orchestra,** *Musical*
ap   *Courier* LXXI/22 (2 Dec 1915) 12.
Although the choice of Georgine van Aaken as concertmistress of the Des Moines Symphony Orchestra was looked upon with misgivings because of the importance of the post, her performance has dispelled all doubts. Aaken is head of the violin department of the Drake Conservatory in Des Moines.

1247 **Woman's earnings in music,** *Musical Courier* LIII/18 (31 Oct
ap   1906) 24.
1) As singers women are not discriminated against, and many prima donnas have amassed fortunes, e.g., Adelina Patti, Lillian Nordica, Ernestine Schumann-Heink, and Emma Abbott. While successful, Abbott was also grateful; she bequeathed $5000 to the Plymouth Church in Brooklyn where she was employed before she gained renown in opera. 2) The current efforts to replace women with boys in church choirs are meeting with "miserable failure" wherever attempted.

1248 **Woman's orchestra in Los Angeles is an important factor in**
ap   **city's musical life,** *Musical America* V/17 (9 Mar 1907) 15. *Illus.*
Under the direction of Harley Hamilton, the Los Angeles Woman's Orchestra has grown from a handful of players to 50 musicians--both professional and amateur. The young female professional "who may be playing in recitals and cafe orchestras can obtain by membership a learning she could in no other way have. The amateur can get professional training and a familiarity with the best orchestral compositions". A roster of the orchestra's members for the 1906-07 season is included.

1249 **Woman's Orchestral Club concert,** *Musical Courier* LXXII/13
ap   (30 Mar 1916) 58.
Reviews the 2nd concert of the season by the Woman's Orchestral Club at the Young Women's Christian Assoc. on East 15th Street in New York, under the direction of Theodore Spiering. The only all-female orchestra in New York at the present time, the group has graduated from amateur status. The wind parts are played by professional male musicians, but as the membership of the orchestra increases women will assume the wind posts.

1250 **Women composers interpreted,** *Musical Courier* LII/13 (28 Mar
ro   1906) 18.
Reports on a concert given in New York by Mr. and Mrs. A.J. Goodrich, assisted by the violinist Florence Austin. The program included Amy Cheney Beach's *Romance, op. 23 (WIAM* 1269), Margaret Ruthven Lang's *Rhapsody in E minor, op. 21 (WIAM* 1428), and pieces by Clara Schumann and Cécile Chaminade.

1251 **Women in the orchestra,** *American Art Journal* XXXV/5 (28 May
ap   1881) 87.
Urges women to broaden their musical studies and careers to include the playing of string instruments. Despite improvements in their education in recent years, most women still study either piano or voice. There is no reason for women not to study violin--the Bohemian violinist Wilma Neruda demonstrated that women could achieve greatness on that instrument--or indeed the other string instruments. "We shall welcome the day when music's extensive spheres are probed by a keener, if a less stronger [sic], hand".

1252 **Women's String Orchestra,** *Musical Courier* XXXVI/17 (27 Apr
ro   1898) 33.
A recent concert of the 40-piece Women's String Orchestra in New York was distinguished by excellent ensemble playing. Camilla Urso appeared as soloist, performing a caprice by Ernest Guiraud and *The maiden's wish* as an encore.

1253 **Women's String Orchestra gives its second concert,** *Musical*
ap   *America* III/15 (24 Feb 1906) 11.
Now in its 10th anniversary season, the Women's String Orchestra of New York was founded by conductor Carl V. Lachmund to give young women intent on careers as soloists training in ensemble work. Initially Lachmund selected 17 players from 70-80 applicants, and although colleagues told him that he couldn't possibly keep 17 women together in an organization for more than 3 months, the orchestra grew to number 41 players within 4 years. The

orchestra gives 3 concerts a year at Mendelssohn Hall and has also performed in Washington, D.C. at the National Theater. An octet made up of the best players performs on occasion. Dora Becker, a former pupil of Joachim, is concertmistress.

1254 WRIGHT, Josephine; SOUTHERN, Eileen, compilers. **Sis-**
ap   **sieretta Jones, 1868-1933,** *Black Perspective in Music (Bicentennial number)* IV/2 (July 1976) 191-201.
A collection of press items tracing the career of Sissieretta Jones between 1886 and 1899. These source materials document Jones's rise from a lowly, assisting artist as Mrs. M.S. Jones, or Mathilda S. Jones, to the full-fledged prima donna by 1892, known as Mme. Sissieretta Jones, the "Black Patti". In 1896 at the height of her fame, Jones left the concert stage to head her own vaudeville company, Black Patti's Troubadours. Jones studied at the Academy of Music in Providence and the New England Conservatory. Her career was longer than that of most black concert singers, with the exception of Blind Tom. Usually after 2-3 years the novelty of a particular black singer wore off with white audiences.

1255 WYNN, Edith Lynwood. **Cello for women, The,** *Etude* XXVI/
ap   2 (Feb 1908) 129.
Discusses the growing popularity of the cello as a solo instrument and "as a valuable aid in true ensemble work". 30 years ago women as cellists were unknown, even in Europe. The work of Lillian Littlehales, cellist with the Olive Mead Quartet, is cited.

1256 WYNN, Edith Lynwood. **Girl with a bow, The,** *Etude* XXV/9
ap   (Sept 1907) 612-13. *Illus.*
Discusses the increasing activity of women as string players. 1) The first women's string quartet was founded in the 1870s by Julius Eichberg and still exists with the following personnel, all of whom are prominent teachers in Boston: Emma Grebe, Letty Launder, Lillian Shattuck, and Laura Webster. Other women's string quartets currently active include the Olive Mead Quartet, based in New York, and the Carolyn Belcher Quartet, based in Boston. 2) Women who head violin schools in the United States are Geraldine Morgan in New York, Lillian Shattuck in Boston, and Charlotte Demuth Williams in Chicago. 3) There is scarcely a seminary or academy without a violin teacher, and many colleges--particularly in the Midwest--have violin departments within music departments. 4) August Suck, a cellist formerly with the Boston Symphony Orchestra, claims to have been the first male teacher to teach cello to a female student.

1257 WYNN, Edith Lynwood. **How the war helped women**
ap   **orchestra and hotel musicians,** *Musical Observer* XVIII/10 (Oct 1919) 47.
When adequate numbers of male musicians were not available during the war, many hotels hired women, and these women forced hotel managements to pay them wages equal to men's wages since they played just as well as men. Hotel work brings the benefits of a union contract: e.g., a woman cannot be discharged without good reason and a week's notice, and she can furnish a substitute when she wants to fulfill a concert engagement. The atmosphere of hotel work is not one in which the "moral and mental rights" of the female musician might suffer. One obstacle remains: women currently are not allowed to play "late hours" for dancing as hotel managers typically insist that women can't endure 7 hours of playing a day or even 5.

1258 WYNN, Edith Lynwood. **Maud Powell as I knew her--a**
ap   **tribute,** *Musical Observer* XIX/3 (Mar 1920) 58-59.
Maud Powell was the idol of the female violin student. She inspired more young women--including the author--to enter the profession, or at least to study the violin seriously, than any other woman violinist of her time. For Powell it was a sacred trust to play for college audiences, women's clubs, and all other people who ordinarily did not hear artists of her rank. Similarly she felt an obligation to the American composer.

1259 WYNN, Edith Lynwood. **Woman musician, The,** *Etude*
ap   XVIII/9 (Sept 1900) 335.
Describes some of the problems women face as musicians, including less pay than men are given for the same work. Women often are abandoned as teachers when their pupils become advanced, although Wynn thinks it is possible that male teachers make pupils work harder. Wynn believes that the professional woman in music is not less feminine, although she is more independent and business-like, than her sisters. However, no matter what her art or success, home and children must come first. "That is the German idea. I like it. The best type of woman musician is a woman still. Her heart throbs with passion, her soul cries out for sympathy and with sympathy, but she puts her shoulder to the wheel and goes into the profession with all the bravery of a man". This article appears on the *Woman's work in music* page (*WIAM* 645).

→   WYNN, Edith. **Opposition to the violin for girls,** *see* 857ap[57].

1260 **Wynne Pyle to play** *Keltic sonata, Musical Courier* LXXIX/3 (17
ap   July 1919) 27.

Reports that the pianist will make another extensive concert tour in the United States during the 1919-20 season. As part of her program for her first appearance in September at an American music festival in Lockport, N.Y., Pyle will perform MacDowell's *Keltic sonata, op. 59.*

1261 **Youthful martyrs of the keyboard,** *Etude* XVI/12 (Dec 1898)
ap   368.
Parents who look to music and piano playing as a means of upward social mobility for their daughters are misguided. Many young women who are forced to practice will, as a result, hate music.

1262 **Z.A.S. Salt Lake women give worthy orchestral concert,**
ap   *Musical America* XXII/3 (22 May 1915) 27. *Illus.*
Reports on the 2nd annual concert of the Salt Lake Women's Orchestra under the direction of Esther Allen Gaw, and lists the orchestra's players. An organist "interpreted to good advantage the parts usually devoted to brass".

1263 **Zelie De Lussan, noted singer, dies,** *New York Times* 19 Dec
an   1949, 28.
De Lussan (1863-1949) first studied voice with her mother, who had been an operatic singer in France. The mezzo-soprano made her debut at the Academy of Music in New York at age 16, and at age 22 she first sang in opera with the Boston Ideal Opera as Arline in Victor Herbert's *The bohemian girl.* De Lussan's greatest successes came in London at Covent Garden, and she resided in London since 1889. In 1895 she sang in the American première of *Falstaff* at the Metropolitan Opera.

59   Art music by women (including concert and parlor music)

Chamber music

1265 BEACH, Amy Cheney. **Invocation for the violin, op. 55** (APS
mm   6510; Boston: A.P. Schmidt, 1904) 4 p. (score, part).
Dn 2'. *Pf* pno, vln.

1266 BEACH, Amy Cheney. **Mirage, A, op. 100, no. 1** (74674;
md   Boston: O. Ditson, 1924) 5 p. (score, parts).
Dn 2'. *At* Bertha Ochsner. *Pf* solo S, pno, vln, vcl. *Tm Two songs with violin and cello, op. 100* (*WIAM* 1277).

1267 BEACH, Amy Cheney. **Pastorale for woodwind quintet** (CP
mm   125; New York: Composers Press, 1942) 7 p. (score, parts).
Dn 4.' *Rg The flute in American music, Musical Heritage,* MH 3578.

1268 BEACH, Amy Cheney. **Quintet in F-sharp minor, op. 67** (APS
mm   8309; Boston: A.P. Schmidt, 1909) 47 p. (score, parts).
Dn 20'. *Pf* piano quintet. *Rg* Turnabout, TVS 34556.

1269 BEACH, Amy Cheney. **Romance, op. 23** (APS 2368; Boston:
mm   A.P. Schmidt, 1893) 9 p. (score, part).
Dn 4'. *Pf* pno, vln. Dedicated to Maud Powell.

1270 BEACH, Amy Cheney. **Sonate in A moll für Pianoforte und**
mm   **Violine, op. 34** (APS 4756; Boston: A.P. Schmidt, 1899) 35 p. (score, part).
Dn 33'. *Rg* New World, NW 268.

1271 BEACH, Amy Cheney. **Stella viatoris, op. 100, no. 2** (74673;
md   Boston: O. Ditson, 1924) 9 p. (score, parts).
Dn 3'. *At* Jessie Hague Nettleton. *Pf* solo S, pno, vln, vcl. *Tm Two songs with violin and cello, op. 100* (*WIAM* 1277).

1272 BEACH, Amy Cheney. **Suite for two pianos founded upon**
mm   **old Irish melodies, op. 104, nos. 1-4** (18760; Cincinnati: J. Church, 1924) 28, 23, 25, 33 p. (score).
Dn 15'. *Pf* 2 pno, 4 hands. *Ct* Prelude, Old-time peasant dance, The ancient cabin, Finale.

1273 BEACH, Amy Cheney. **Summer dreams, op. 47** (APS 5462;
mm   Boston: A.P. Schmidt, 1901) 31 p. (score).
Dn 12'. *La* DLC, Schmidt Collection. *Pf* pno, 4 hands. *Ct* The brownies, Robin red breast, Twilight, Katydids, Elfin tarantelle, Good night.

1274 BEACH, Amy Cheney. **Theme and variations for flute and**
mm   **string quartet, op. 80** (29793; New York: G. Schirmer, 1920) 37
_Dn_ 19'.   p. (score).

1275 BEACH, Amy Cheney. **Three compositions for violin and**
mm   **piano, op. 40, nos. 1-3** (APS 4550-4552; Boston: A.P. Schmidt,
1898) 3, 5, 7 p. (score).
_Dn_ 9'. _Ct_ La captive, Berceuse, Mazurka.

1276 BEACH, Amy Cheney. **Trio for piano, violin, and violon-**
mm   **cello, op. 150** (CP 145; New York: Composers Press, 1939) 41 p.
(score, parts).
_Dn_ 15'. _Rg_ Dorian, 1007.

1277 BEACH, Amy Cheney. **Two songs for violin and cello, op.**
mm   **100, nos. 1-2** (APS 74673-74674; Boston: A.P. Schmidt, 1924) 5, 9
p. (score, parts).
_Dn_ 5'. _Pf_ solo S, pno, vln, vcl. _Ct_ A mirage (_WIAM_ 1266), Stella viatoris
(_WIAM_ 1271).

1278 BEACH, Amy Cheney. **Variations on Balkan themes, op. 60**
mm   (14907; Boston: A.P. Schmidt, 1942) 23, 19 p. (score).
_Dn_ 23'. _La_ DLC, Schmidt Collection. _Pf_ 2 pno, 4 hands. Also for solo pno
(_WIAM_ 1402).

1279 DILLON, Fannie Charles. **Western concerto, A, op. 117.**
mm   **Descriptive concerto for piano and orchestra** (facsimile of MS
at DLC, 1945) 19, 13, 24 p. (piano reduction).
_Dn_ 26'. _Pf_ orchestration arranged for 2nd pno, solo pno. _Ct_ Mountain wilds,
Desert moonlight, Deerhaven. Also listed as orchestral music (_WIAM_ 1372).

1280 MOORE, Mary Carr. **Chant d'amour, op. 91, no. 3** (facsimile
md   of MS at CLSU, 1942) 4 p. (score, parts).
_Dn_ 3'. _Pf_ flu, pno.

1281 MOORE, Mary Carr. **Four love songs** (San Bruno, Calif.: W.
mm   Webster, 1933) 18 p. (score).
Song cycle. _Dn_ 11'. _Pf_ solo voc, flu, pno, vln, vcl. _Ct_ Renunciation (_At_ Grace E.
Bush), Compensation (_At_ Eleanore Flaig), Consummation (_At_ Whitman),
Desolation (_At_ composer). Also for solo voc, pno (_WIAM_ 1842).

1282 MOORE, Mary Carr. **Message to one absent, op. 87, no. 6**
md   (Lomita Park, Calif.: W. Webster, 1941) 5 p. (score, part).
_Dn_ 2'. _Pf_ pno, vln.

1283 MOORE, Mary Carr. **Nocturne, op. 96, no. 2** (facsimile of MS
md   at CLSU, 1942) 4 p. (score, parts).
_Dn_ 4'. _Pf_ flu, pno.

1284 ROGERS, Clara Kathleen. **Sonata in D minor, op. 25** (APS
mm   2908; Boston: A.P. Schmidt, 1903) 31 p. (score, part).
_Dn_ 18'. _La_ DLC. _Pf_ pno, vln.

Choral music

1285 ASHFORD, Emma. **My task** (Dayton: Lorenz, 1903) 7 p.
mm
Sacred chorus. _Dn_ 2'. _At_ Maude Louise Ray and S.H. Pickup. _Pf_ choral SATB,
org.

1286 BEACH, Amy Cheney. **Ah, love, but a day!, op. 44, no. 2**
md   (APS 13997; Boston: A.P. Schmidt, 1927) 8 p. (choral octavo).
Secular chorus. _Dn_ 2', _At_ Robert Browning. _Pf_ choral SSAA, pno. Also arranged
by Hugo Norden for choral SATB, pno (APS 15433; Schmidt, 1949). Originally
for solo voc, pno (_WIAM_ 1511) in _Three Browning songs, op. 44_.

1287 BEACH, Amy Cheney. **All hail the power of Jesus' name, op.**
mm   **74** (26106; New York: G. Schirmer, 1915) 8 p. (choral octavo).
Sacred chorus. _Dn_ 3'. _At_ Edward Perronet. _Pf_ choral SATB, org. The
composer's _Panama hymn_ (_WIAM_ 1324) is also numbered op. 74.

1288 BEACH, Amy Cheney. **Around the manger, op. 115** (75312;
mm   Boston: O. Ditson, 1925) 7 p. (choral octavo).
Sacred chorus. _Dn_ 1'. _At_ Robert Davis. _Pf_ choral SATB, org or pno. Also for

choral SSAA, org or pno (76514; Ditson, 1929), and for solo voc, org or pno
(_WIAM_ 1516).

1289 BEACH, Amy Cheney. **Benedicite omnia opera Domini, op.**
mm   **121** (APS 14159; Boston: A.P. Schmidt, 1928) 11 p. (choral octavo).
Sacred chorus. _Dn_ 5'. _La_ DLC, Schmidt Collection. _Lt_ English. _Pf_ choral
SATB, org.

1290 BEACH, Amy Cheney. **Benedictus es, Domine, op. 103** (748;
mm   Boston: O. Ditson, 1924) 12 p. (choral octavo).
Sacred chorus. _Dn_ 7'. _Lt_ English. _Pf_ solo B, choral SATB, org.

1291 BEACH, Amy Cheney. **Bethlehem, op. 24** (APS 3246; Boston:
mm   A.P. Schmidt, 1893) 7 p. (choral octavo).
Sacred chorus. _Dn_ 3'. _Pf_ choral SATB, org.

1292 BEACH, Amy Cheney. **Bonum est, confiteri, op. 76, no. 1**
md   (26426; New York: G. Schirmer, 1916) 12 p. (choral octavo).
Sacred chorus. _Dn_ 5'. _Lt_ Latin. _Pf_ solo S, choral SATB, org. The composer's
Separation (_WIAM_ 1592) is also numbered op. 76, no. 1.

1293 BEACH, Amy Cheney. **Candy lion, The, op. 75, no. 1** (26184;
md   New York: G. Schirmer, 1915) 5 p. (choral octavo).
Secular chorus. _Dn_ 2'. _At_ Abbie Farwell Brown. _Pf_ choral SSAA.

1294 BEACH, Amy Cheney. **Canticle of the sun, The, op. 123**
mm   (APS 14158; Boston: A.P. Schmidt, 1928) 35 p. (piano-vocal score).
Sacred chorus. _Dn_ 21'. _At_ St. Francis of Assisi. _Tr_ Matthew Arnold. _Lt_ English.
_Pf_ solo SSTB, choral SATB, org or pno. Originally for voices and orchestra
(autograph at MBNe). Dedicated to the Chautauqua Choir.

1295 BEACH, Amy Cheney. **Chambered nautilus, The, op. 66**
mm   (APS 7699; Boston: A.P. Schmidt, 1907) 51 p. (piano-vocal score).
Secular cantata. _Dn_ 18'. _La_ DLC, Schmidt Collection. _At_ Oliver Wendell
Holmes. _Pf_ solo SA, choral SSAA, org or pno. Originally for voices and
orchestra (MS at MBNe). Dedicated to the St. Cecilia Club, New York.

1296 BEACH, Amy Cheney. **Christ in the universe, op. 132** (New
mm   York: H.W. Gray, 1931) 31 p. (organ-vocal score).
Sacred chorus. _Dn_ 21'. _At_ Alice Meynell. _Pf_ solo AT, choral SATB, org. The
title page indicates that the piece was originally for voices and orchestra.

1297 BEACH, Amy Cheney. **Come unto these yellow sands, op.**
md   **39, no. 2** (APS 4477; Boston: A.P. Schmidt, 1897) 4 p. (choral
octavo).
Secular chorus. _Dn_ 2'. _La_ DLC, Schmidt Collection. _At_ Shakespeare. _St_ The
tempest. _Pf_ choral SSAA, pno for rehearsal only.

1298 BEACH, Amy Cheney. **Constant Christmas, op. 95** (20251;
mm   Philadelphia: T. Presser, 1922) 7 p. (choral octavo).
Sacred chorus. _Dn_ 2'. _Pf_ solo SA, choral SATB, org.

1299 BEACH, Amy Cheney. **Dolladine, op. 75, no. 3** (26186; New
md   York: G. Schirmer, 1915) 7 p. (choral octavo).
Secular chorus. _Dn_ 3'. _At_ William Brightly Rands. _Pf_ choral SSAA.

1300 BEACH, Amy Cheney. **Drowsy dream-town, op. 129** (APS
mm   14566; Boston: A.P. Schmidt, 1932) 7 p. (choral octavo).
Secular chorus. _Dn_ 2'. _At_ Robert Norwood. _St_ Mother and son. _Pf_ solo S, choral
SSA, pno.

1301 BEACH, Amy Cheney. **Dusk in June, op. 82** (27903; New
mm   York: G. Schirmer, 1917) 5 p. (choral octavo).
Secular chorus. _Dn_ 2'. _At_ Sara Teasdale. _Pf_ choral SSAA, pno for rehearsal
only.

1302 BEACH, Amy Cheney. **Evening hymn, op. 125, no. 2. The**
md   **shadows of the evening hours** (APS 14799; Boston: A.P.
Schmidt, 1936) 8 p. (choral octavo).
Sacred chorus. _Dn_ 3'. _At_ Adelaide A. Procter. _Pf_ solo S, choral SATB, pno.
Originally for solo voc, pno (_WIAM_ 1533).

1303 BEACH, Amy Cheney. **Fairy lullaby, op. 37, no. 3** (APS 7617;
md   Boston: A.P. Schmidt, 1907) 5 p. (choral octavo).
Secular chorus. _Dn_ 2'. _At_ Shakespeare. _Pf_ choral SSAA, pno. Originally for solo
voc, pno (_WIAM_ 1535) in _Three Shakespeare songs, op. 37_.

1304 BEACH, Amy Cheney. **Far awa'!, op. 43, no. 4** (APS 11454;
md   Boston: A.P. Schmidt, 1918) 4 p. (choral octavo).
Secular chorus. *Dn* 2'. *At* Robert Burns. *Pf* choral SSA, pno. Also for choral SA,
pno (APS 11455; Schmidt, 1918). Originally for solo voc, pno (*WIAM* 1536) in
Five songs [*to*] *words by Robert Burns, op. 43*

1305 BEACH, Amy Cheney. **Festival jubilate, op. 17** (APS 3040;
mm   Boston: A.P. Schmidt, 1892) 43 p. (piano-vocal score).
Sacred chorus. *Dn* 15'. *Lt* English. *Pf* choral SSAATTB, pno. Originally for
voices and orchestra (autograph at MBNe). Composed for the dedication of the
Women's Building at the Columbian Exposition, Chicago, 1893.

1306 BEACH, Amy Cheney. **Greenwood, The, op. 110** (1095;
mm   Boston: C.C. Birchard, 1925) 8 p. (choral octavo).
Secular chorus. *Dn* 2'. *At* William Lyle Bowles. *Pf* choral SATB.

1307 BEACH, Amy Cheney. **Hearken unto me, op. 139** (APS
mm   14783; Boston: A.P. Schmidt, 1934) 16 p. (choral octavo).
Sacred chorus. *Dn* 14'. *Pf* solo SATB, choral SATB, org. Written for the 100th
anniversary of the founding of St. Bartholomew's Church, New York.

1308 BEACH, Amy Cheney. **Help us, O God, op. 50** (APS 5982;
mm   Boston: A.P. Schmidt, 1903) 23 p. (choral octavo).
Sacred chorus. *Dn* 7'. *La* DLC. *Pf* choral SATB, org for rehearsal only.
Dedicated to Mrs. Louis Agassiz.

1309 BEACH, Amy Cheney. **Hymn of freedom, A, op. 52** (APS
mm   6036; Boston: A.P. Schmidt, 1903) 3 p. (choral octavo).
Secular chorus. *Dn* 1'. *La* DLC, Schmidt Collection. *At* Samuel F. Smith. *Pf*
choral SATB, org or pno. An original setting of the text of *America* ("My
country, tis of thee"). In 1924 the music was published with a new text as *O
Lord our God arise, op. 52* (*WIAM* 1319).

1310 BEACH, Amy Cheney. **Indian lullaby, An**, *The world's best
mc   music.* Ed. by Helen Kendrick JOHNSON and Frederic DEAN (New
York: U. Soc., 1899) I, 169-73. (score).
Secular chorus. *Dn* 2'. *Pf* choral SSAA, pno for rehearsal only. Previously
published in 1895 (n.p.: Bryan & Taylor).

1311 BEACH, Amy Cheney. **June, op. 51, no. 3** (APS 11297; Boston:
md   A.P. Schmidt, 1917) 7 p. (choral octavo).
Secular chorus. *Dn* 1'. *At* Erich Jansen. *Tr* Isadora Martinez from the German.
Pf choral SSAA, pno. Also for choral SATB, pno (APS 14492; Schmidt, 1931).
Originally for solo voc, pno as *Juni (June)* (*WIAM* 1566).

1312 BEACH, Amy Cheney. **Let this mind be in you, op. 105**
mm   (18759; Cincinnati: J. Church, 1924) 9 p. (choral octavo).
Sacred chorus. *Dn* 4'. *Pf* solo SB, choral SATB, org.

1313 BEACH, Amy Cheney. **Little brown bee, The, op. 9** (APS
mm   2213; Boston: A.P. Schmidt, 1891) 4 p. (choral octavo).
Secular chorus. *Dn* 2'. *La* DLC, Schmidt Collection. *Pf* choral SSAA.

1314 BEACH, Amy Cheney. **Lord is my shepherd, The, op. 96**
mm   (20260; Philadelphia: T. Presser, 1923) 15 p. (choral octavo).
Sacred chorus. *Dn* 11'. *Pf* choral SSA, org.

1315 BEACH, Amy Cheney. **Lord of the worlds above, op. 109**
mm   (13892; Boston: O. Ditson, 1925) 11 p. (choral octavo).
Sacred chorus. *Dn* 6'. *At* Isaac Watts. *Pf* solo STB, choral SATB, org.

1316 BEACH, Amy Cheney. **Mass in E-flat [major], op. 5** (APS
mm   2637; Boston: A.P. Schmidt, 1890) 83 p. (organ-vocal score).
Dn 26'. *Lt* Latin. *Pf* solo SATB, choral SATB, org. Originally for voices and
orchestra (MS, parts at MBNe).

1317 BEACH, Amy Cheney. **Minstrel and the king, The (Rudolph
mm   von Habsburg), op. 16** (APS 2963; Boston: A.P. Schmidt, 1894)
43 p. (piano-vocal score).
Ballade. *Dn* 23'. *La* DLC, Schmidt Collection. *At* Schiller. *Lt* German, English.
Pf solo TB, choral TTBB, pno. Dedicated to Theodore Thomas. Originally for
voices and orchestra (MS at MBNe).

1318 BEACH, Amy Cheney. **O Lord God of Israel, op. 141**
mm   (facsimile of MS at DLC, 1941) [14] p. (score).
Sacred chorus. *Dn* 7'. *Pf* solo SAB, choral SATB, org.

1319 BEACH, Amy Cheney. **O Lord our God arise, op. 52** (APS
mm   15204; Boston: A.P. Schmidt, 1924) 3 p. (choral octavo).
Sacred chorus. *Dn* 1'. *Pf* choral SATB, org or pno. Originally published with a
different text as *A hymn of freedom, op. 52* (*WIAM* 1309).

1320 BEACH, Amy Cheney. **O praise the Lord, all ye nations, op.
mm   7** (APS 2309; Boston: A.P. Schmidt, 1891) 7 p. (choral octavo).
Sacred chorus. *Dn* 4'. *Pf* choral SATB, org. Composed for the consecration of
Phillips Brooks, D.D., as Bishop of Massachusetts.

1321 BEACH, Amy Cheney. **One summer day, op. 57, no. 2** (APS
md   6561; Boston: A.P. Schmidt, 1904) 7 p. (choral octavo).
Secular chorus. *Dn* 1'. *La* DLC, Schmidt Collection. *At* Agnes Lockhart
Hughes. *Pf* choral SSAA, pno for rehearsal only.

1322 BEACH, Amy Cheney. **Only a song, op. 57, no. 1** (APS 6560;
md   Boston: A.P. Schmidt, 1904) 7 p. (choral octavo).
Secular chorus. *Dn* 3'. *La* DLC, Schmidt Collection. *At* Agnes Lockhart
Hughes. *Pf* choral SSAA, pno for rehearsal only.

1323 BEACH, Amy Cheney. **Over hill, over dale, op. 39, no. 1**
md   (APS 4476; Boston: A.P. Schmidt, 1897) 4 p. (choral octavo).
Secular chorus. *Dn* 1'. *La* DLC, Schmidt Collection. *At* Shakespeare. *St A
midsummer night's dream. Pf* choral SSAA, pno for rehearsal only.

1324 BEACH, Amy Cheney. **Panama hymn, op. 74** (25474; New
mm   York: G. Schirmer, 1915) 8 p. (choral octavo).
Secular chorus. *Dn* 3'. *At* Wendell Phillips Stafford. *Pf* choral SATB, org or
pno. Written for the Panama Pacific Exposition, 1915. The composer's *All hail
the power of Jesus' name* (*WIAM* 1287) is also numbered op. 74.

1325 BEACH, Amy Cheney. **Pax nobiscum** (1920; New York: H.W.
mm   Gray, 1944) 4 p. (choral octavo).
Sacred chorus. *Dn* 1'. *At* Earl Marlatt. *St The cathedral. Lt* English. *Pf* choral
SSA, org.

1326 BEACH, Amy Cheney. **Peace I leave with you, op. 8, no. 2**
md   (APS 2306; Boston: A.P. Schmidt, 1891) 3 p. (choral octavo).
Sacred chorus. *Dn* 1'. *La* DLC, Schmidt Collection. *Pf* choral SATB, org.

1327 BEACH, Amy Cheney. **Peace on earth, op. 38** (APS 4451;
mm   Boston: A.P. Schmidt, 1897) 11 p. (choral octavo).
Sacred chorus. *Dn* 9'. *La* DLC, Schmidt Collection. *Pf* choral SATB, org.

1328 BEACH, Amy Cheney. **Peter Pan, op. 101** (20298; Philadel-
mm   phia: T. Presser, 1923) 27 p. (choral octavo).
Secular cantata. *Dn* 12'. *At* Jessie Andrews. *Pf* choral SSA, pno.

1329 BEACH, Amy Cheney. **Rose of Avon-town, The, op. 30** (APS
mm   4047; Boston: A.P. Schmidt, 1896) 23 p. (piano-vocal score).
Secular cantata. *Dn* 11'. *At* Caroline Mischka. *Pf* solo SA, choral SSAA, pno.
Originally for voices and orchestra (autograph at MBNe). Dedicated to the
Cecilia Ladies' Vocal Soc., Brooklyn.

1330 BEACH, Amy Cheney. **Sea fever, op. 126** (APS 14506; Boston:
mm   A.P. Schmidt, 1931) 8 p. (choral octavo).
Secular chorus. *Dn* 2'. *At* John Masefield. *Pf* choral TTBB, pno.

1331 BEACH, Amy Cheney. **Sea-fairies, The, op. 59** (APS 6577;
mm   Boston: A.P. Schmidt, 1904) 35 p. (piano-vocal score).
Secular cantata. *Dn* 13'. *La* DLC. *At* Tennyson. *Pf* solo SA, choral SA, pno.
Originally for voices and orchestra (autograph at MBNe, dated 5 Nov. 1904).
Dedicated to the Thursday Morning Musical Club of Boston.

1332 BEACH, Amy Cheney. **Service in A [major], op. 63a-e, op.
mm   121, 122** (APS 7046/14178; Boston: A.P. Schmidt, 1906-28) 19,
12, 15, 15, 7, 11, 12 p. (choral octavo).
Dn 30'. *Da* 1906, op. 63a-e only. *La* DLC, op. 63a-e only. *Pf* solo SATB, choral
SATB, org. *Ct Te Deum, op. 63a* (*WIAM* 1337), Benedictus, op. 63b, Jubilate
Deo, op. 63c, Magnificat, op. 63d, Nunc dimittis, op. 63e, Benedicite, omnia
opera, op. 121, Communion responses, op. 122.

1333 BEACH, Amy Cheney. **Shena Van, op. 56, no. 4** (APS 11329;
md   Boston: A.P. Schmidt, 1919) 7 p. (choral octavo).
Secular chorus. *Dn* 1'. *La* DLC. *At* William Black. *St Yolande. Pf* choral SATB,
pno. Also for choral TTBB, pno (APS 11330; Schmidt, 1917) and choral SSA,
pno (APS 11331; Schmidt, 1917). Originally for solo voc, pno (*WIAM* 1593).

1334 BEACH, Amy Cheney. **Song of welcome, op. 42** (APS 4663;
mm   Boston: A.P. Schmidt, 1898) 8 p. (choral octavo).
Secular chorus. *Dn* 4′. *At* Henry M. Blossom, Jr. *Pf* choral SATB, org.
Composed for the opening ceremonies of the Trans-Mississippi Exposition,
Omaha, 1898.

1335 BEACH, Amy Cheney. **Sylvania, op. 46** (APS 5467; Boston:
mm   A.P. Schmidt, 1901) 67 p. (piano-vocal score).
Secular cantata. *Dn* 32′. *La* DLC. *Tr* Frederick W. Banckroft. *Pf* solo SSATB,
choral SSAATTBB, pno. Originally for voices and orchestra (autograph at
MBNe).

1336 BEACH, Amy Cheney. **Te Deum in F [major], op. 84** (20157;
mm   Philadelphia: T. Presser, 1922) 14 p. (choral octavo).
Sacred chorus. *Dn* 7′. *Pf* solo TTB, org. Also arranged for solo S or T,
choral SATB, org (20158; Presser, 1922). MB has autographs of versions in D
major for solo T, choral TT, org; and in B major for solo T, unison men's voices,
org.

1337 BEACH, Amy Cheney. **Te Deum, op. 63a** (rev. ed.; APS 7046;
md   Boston: A.P. Schmidt, 1905) 16 p. (choral octavo).
Sacred chorus. *Dn* 8′. *Pf* solo SATB, choral SATB, org. *Tm* Service in A [major],
op. 63 (*WIAM* 1332).

1338 BEACH, Amy Cheney. **This morning very early, op. 144** (APS
mm   14864; Boston: A.P. Schmidt, 1937) 7 p. (choral octavo).
Secular chorus. *Dn* 2′. *At* Patricia Louise Hills. *Pf* choral SSA, pno.

1339 BEACH, Amy Cheney. **Thou knowest, Lord, op. 76, no. 2**
md   (25270; New York: G. Schirmer, 1915) 8 p. (choral octavo).
Sacred chorus. *Dn* 9′. *At* Jane Borthwick. *Pf* solo TB, choral SATB, org. The
composer's *Lotos isles* (*WIAM* 1569) is also numbered op. 76, no. 2.

1340 BEACH, Amy Cheney. **Three flower songs, op. 31** (APS 3893;
mm   Boston: A.P. Schmidt, 1896) 11 p. (choral octavo).
Secular choruses. *Dn* 3′. *La* DLC, Schmidt Collection. *At* Margaret Deland. *Pf*
choral SSAA, pno for rehearsal only. *Ct* The clover, The yellow daisy, The
bluebell.

1341 BEACH, Amy Cheney. **Through the house give glimmering
md   light, op. 39, no. 3** (APS 4478; Boston: A.P. Schmidt, 1897) 8 p.
         (choral octavo).
Secular chorus. *Dn* 3′. *La* DLC, Schmidt Collection. *At* Shakespeare. *St* A
midsummer night's dream. *Pf* choral SSAA, pno.

1342 BEACH, Amy Cheney. **We who sing have walked in glory,
mm   op. 140** (14739; Boston: O. Ditson, 1934) 8 p. (choral octavo).
Sacred chorus. *Dn* 3′. *At* Amy Sherman Bridgman. *Pf* choral SATB, pno.

1343 BEACH, Amy Cheney. **When the last sea is sailed, op. 127**
mm   (APS 14536; Boston: A.P. Schmidt, 1931) 8 p. (choral octavo).
Secular chorus. *Dn* 3′. *La* DLC, Schmidt Collection. *At* John Masefield. *Pf*
choral TTBB, pno for rehearsal only.

1344 BEACH, Amy Cheney. **With prayer and supplication, op. 8,
md   no. 3** (APS 2307; Boston: A.P. Schmidt, 1891) 2 p. (choral octavo).
Sacred chorus. *Dn* 1′. *La* DLC, Schmidt Collection. *Pf* choral SATB, org.

1345 BEACH, Amy Cheney. **Wouldn't that be queer, op. 26, no. 4**
md   (APS 11630; Boston: A.P. Schmidt, 1919) 8 p. (choral octavo).
Secular chorus. *Dn* 3′. *La* DLC. *At* Elsie J. Cooley. *Pf* choral SSA, pno.
Originally for solo voc, pno (*WIAM* 1622).

1346 BEACH, Amy Cheney. **Year's at the spring, The, op. 44, no.
md   1** (APS 8450; Boston: A.P. Schmidt, 1909) 5 p. (choral octavo).
Secular chorus. *Dn* 1′. *At* Robert Browning. *St* Pippa passes. *Pf* choral SSAA,
pno. Also for choral SA, pno (APS 11729; Schmidt, 1919); choral SATB, pno
(APS 13792; Schmidt, 1927); and arranged by Frances Moore for choral
TTBB, pno (APS 14659; Schmidt, 1933). Originally for solo voc, pno (*WIAM*
1623) in *Three Browning songs, op. 44*.

1347 FAY, Amy. **Hasten, sinner, to be wise** (New York: New
mm   Singing Soc., 1917) 1 p.
Hymn. *Dn* 1′. *Pf* choral SATB.

1348 FREER, Eleanor Everest. **Part-songs.** *Musical compositions of
ma   Eleanor Everest Freer* 8 (rev. ed.; 34514; Milwaukee: W.A. Kaun
         Music, 1932) 71 p.

Sacred and secular choruses. *Pf* choral SATB, pno. *Ct* For music, op. 8, no. 1 (*At*
Byron); Be true, op. 4, no. 5 (*At* Horatius Bonar); Grace for a child, op. 23, no.
2 (*At* Elia W. Peattie); A Christmas carol, op. 13, no. 4 (*At* Agness Greene
Foster); Unto us a son is born, op. 13, no. 3 (*At* Alice Meynell); Shall I be loved
as I grow old, op. 8, no. 4 (*At* Cornelius Everest); Lord, when the sense of thy
sweet grace, op. 8, no. 3 (*At* Richard Crashaw); When is life's youth?, op. 4, no.
3 (*At* Archibald Freer); An April pastoral, op. 6, no. 3 (*At* William Watson); O
world, be nobler, op. 7, no. 1 (*At* Lawrence Binyon); Children's spring, op. 40,
no. 1 (*At* Barbara Helen Wilson); My garden, op. 10, no. 5 (*At* Thomas Edward
Brown); A carol, op. 21, no. 2 (*At* composer); The wild sea, op. 40, no. 2 (*At* E.
Freer Wilson); Faith, op. 12, no. 1 (*At* Frances Anne Kemble); Old love song,
op. 24, no. 1 (*At* William Gerard Chapman); Étude réaliste, op. 27, no. 8 (*At*
Swinburne). The following are also for solo voc, pno: Be true (*WIAM* 1632),
Grace for a child (*WIAM* 1659), When is life's youth? (*WIAM* 1707), An April
pastoral (*WIAM* 1691), My garden (*WIAM* 1672), A carol (*WIAM* 1635), Faith
(*WIAM* 1650), and Étude réaliste (*WIAM* 1648).

1349 HOPEKIRK, Helen. **Slumber song** (32193; New York: G.
mm   Schirmer, 1925) 7 p. (choral octavo).
Secular chorus. *Dn* 2′. *Pf* choral SSAA, pno for rehearsal only.

1350 HOPEKIRK, Helen. **Song of flowers, A** (APS 993; Boston: A.P.
mm   Schmidt, 1887) 5 p. (choral octavo).
Secular chorus. *Dn* 1′. *At* Mortimer Wheeler. *Pf* choral TTBB, pno.

1351 KNAPP, Phoebe. **Prince of peace** (facsimile of MS at DLC,
mm   1883) 32 p.
Sacred cantata. *Dn* 15′. *Pf* choral SATB, org.   *(Judith Tick)*

1352 LANG, Margaret Ruthven. **Alastair MacAlastair** (APS 5490;
mm   Boston: A.P. Schmidt, 1901) 7 p. (choral octavo).
Secular chorus. *Dn* 3′. *La* DLC, Schmidt Collection. *Pf* choral TTBB, pno.

1353 LANG, Margaret Ruthven. **Boatman's hymn, op. 13** (n.p.:
mm   author, 1892) 26 p. (choral octavo).
Secular chorus. *Dn* 7′. *Tr* Sir Samuel Ferguson. *Pf* choral TTBB, pno. Written
for the Apollo Club.

1354 LANG, Margaret Ruthven. **Bonnie ran the burnie down, op.
mm   25** (APS 4245; Boston: A.P. Schmidt, 1897) 7 p. (choral octavo).
Secular chorus. *Dn* 3′. *La* DLC, Schmidt Collection. *At* Rady Nairne. *Pf* choral
SATB.

1355 LANG, Margaret Ruthven. **Ghosts** (APS 15369; Boston: A.P.
mm   Schmidt, 1889) 4 p.
Secular chorus. *Dn* 1′. *Pf* choral SSA, pno. Originally for solo voc, pno (*WIAM*
1768).

1356 LANG, Margaret Ruthven. **Grant, we beseech thee, merciful
mm   Lord, op. 51** (APS 9802; Boston: A.P. Schmidt, 1912) 7 p. (choral
         octavo).
Sacred chorus. *Dn* 4′. *La* DLC, Schmidt Collection. *Pf* choral SATB, org.

1357 LANG, Margaret Ruthven. **Heavenly noël, The, op. 57** (APS
mm   11040; Boston: A.P. Schmidt, 1916) 19 p. (choral octavo).
Sacred chorus. *Dn* 7′. *La* DLC. *At* Richard Lawson Gales. *St* David in heaven
and other poems. *Pf* solo M, choral SSAA, pno. Originally for voices and
chamber orchestra (autograph at MBNe).

1358 LANG, Margaret Ruthven. **Here's a health to ane I lo'e dear**
mm   (APS 5491; Boston: A.P. Schmidt, 1901) 4 p. (choral octavo).
Secular chorus. *Dn* 3′. *At* Robert Burns. *Pf* choral TTBB, pno.

1359 LANG, Margaret Ruthven. **In praesepio (In the manger), op.
mm   56** (APS 11035; Boston: A.P. Schmidt, 1916) 7 p. (choral octavo).
Sacred chorus. *Dn* 4′. *At* Richard Lawson Gales. *St* David in heaven and other
poems. *Lt* English. *Pf* choral SSAA, org.

1360 LANG, Margaret Ruthven. **Jumblies, The, op. 5** (APS 2198;
mm   Boston: A.P. Schmidt, 1890) 24 p. (choral octavo).
Secular chorus. *Dn* 7′. *La* DLC, Schmidt Collection. *At* Edward Lear. *Pf* choral
TTBB; 2 pno, 4 hands.

1361 LANG, Margaret Ruthven. **Lonely rose, The, op. 43** (APS
mm   7076; Boston: A.P. Schmidt, 1906) 19 p. (choral octavo).
Secular chorus. *Dn* 5′. *La* DLC, Schmidt Collection. *At* Philip Bourke Marston.
Pf choral SSAA, pno.

1362 LANG, Margaret Ruthven. **Song of the three sisters** (APS
mm   8416; Boston: A.P. Schmidt, 1909) 12 p. (choral octavo).
Secular chorus. *Dn* 3′. *At* John Vance Cheney. *St The time of roses. Pf* choral
SSAA, pno.

1363 LANG, Margaret Ruthven. **Te Deum, op. 34** (APS 5126;
mm   Boston: A.P. Schmidt, 1899) 11 p. (choral octavo).
Sacred chorus. *Dn* 5′. *La* DLC, Schmidt Collection. *Pf* choral SATB, pno.

1364 LANG, Margaret Ruthven. **White butterflies** (Boston: C.C.
mm   Birchard, 1904) 3 p. (choral octavo).
Secular chorus. *Dn* 1′. *At* Swinburne. *Pf* choral SSA, pno, choral B optional.

1365 LANG, Margaret Ruthven. **Wild-brier, The** (APS 8417;
mm   Boston: A.P. Schmidt, 1909) 8 p. (choral octavo).
Secular chorus. *Dn* 2′. *La* DLC, Schmidt Collection. *At* John Vance Cheney. *St
The time of roses. Pf* choral SSAA, pno.

1366 SALTER, Mary Turner. **Vision of the shepherds, The.**
mm   **Christmas anthem** (21114; Philadelphia: T. Presser, 1932) 11 p.
Dn 6′. *At* composer. *Pf* solo SAT, choral SATB, pno.

1367 STRICKLAND, Lily Teresa. **St. John, the beloved** (6251;
mm   New York: J. Fischer, 1930) 66 p. (piano-vocal score).
Sacred cantata. *Dn* 30′. *Pf* solo SSAATTBB, choral SATB, pno.

Orchestral and band music

1368 BEACH, Amy Cheney. **Bal masqué, op. 22** (facsimile of
mm   autograph at PPFleisher, n.d.) 28 p. (score, parts).
Dn 4′. *Pf* 2-2-2-2, 4-2-0-0, tim, per including glk, hrp, str. Also for pno (*WIAM*
1373).

1369 BEACH, Amy Cheney. **Concerto for pianoforte and orches-**
mm   **tra, op. 45** (facsimile of autograph at PPFleisher, n.d.) 141 p.
        (score, parts).
Dn 30′. *Pf* 3pic-2-3bcl-2, 4-2-3-1, tim, per, str, solo pno. Dedicated to Teresa
Carreño. Also with the original orchestration arranged for 2nd pno (APS 5119;
Boston: A.P. Schmidt, 1900). *Rg* Vox, QTBS 34665.

1370 BEACH, Amy Cheney. **Symphony in E minor, op. 32. Gaelic**
mm   (APS 436; Boston: A.P. Schmidt, 1897) 220 p. (score).
Dn 35′. *La* DLC, Schmidt Collection. *Pf* 3pic-3enh-3bcl-2, 4-2-3-1, tim, per,
str. Dedicated to Kapellmeister Emil Pane. Facsimile of the published score,
parts at PPFleisher. *Rg* Soc. for the Preservation of American Music, MIA 139
(1968).

1372 DILLON, Fannie Charles. **Western concerto, A, op. 117.**
mm   **Descriptive concerto for piano and orchestra** (facsimile of MS
        at DLC, 1945) 19, 13, 24 p. (piano reduction).
Dn 26′. *Pf* orchestration arranged for 2nd pno, solo pno. *Ct* Mountain wilds,
Desert moonlight, Deerhaven. Also listed as chamber music (*WIAM* 1279).

Solo instrumental music

1373 BEACH, Amy Cheney. **Bal masqué, op. 22** (APS 3259; Boston:
mm   A.P. Schmidt, 1894) 7 p.
Dn 4′. *La* DLC, Schmidt Collection. *Pf* pno. Also for orchestra (*WIAM* 1368).

1374 BEACH, Amy Cheney. **Ballad for the pianoforte, op. 6** (APS
mm   2953; Boston: A.P. Schmidt, 1894) 11 p.
Dn 9′. *La* DLC, Schmidt Collection. Dedicated to Fannie Bloomfield-Zeisler.
Rg Piano music of Mrs. H.H.A. Beach, Genesis, GS 1054.

1375 BEACH, Amy Cheney. **Bit of Cairo, A** (24030; Philadelphia: T.
mm   Presser, 1928) 7 p.
Dn 2′. *Pf* pno.

1376 BEACH, Amy Cheney. **Cadenza, op. 3, to the first movement**
mm   **of the third concerto for the pianoforte (C minor, op. 37) by**
        Ludwig van Beethoven (APS 1639; Boston: A.P. Schmidt, 1888)
        11 p.
Dn 7′.

1377 BEACH, Amy Cheney. **Children's album, op. 36, nos. 1-5**
mm   (APS 4327-4331; Boston: A.P. Schmidt, 1897) 3, 3, 3, 3, 3 p.
Dn 10′. *La* DLC, Schmidt Collection, Waltz only. *Pf* pno. *Ct* Minuet, Gavotte,
Waltz, March, Polka.

1378 BEACH, Amy Cheney. **Cradle song of the lonely mother, A,**
mm   **op. 108** (74803; Boston: O. Ditson, 1924) 7 p.
Dn 6′. *Pf* pno.

1379 BEACH, Amy Cheney. **Eskimos, op. 64, nos. 1-4. Four**
mm   **characteristic pieces for the pianoforte** (APS 7425-7428;
        Boston: A.P. Schmidt, 1907) 11 p.
Dn 6′. *Ct* Arctic night, The returning hunter, Exiles, With dog teams.

1380 BEACH, Amy Cheney. **Fair hills of Eire, O!, The, op. 91**
mm   (APS 12715; Boston: A.P. Schmidt, 1922) 7 p.
Dn 3′. *Pf* pno. *La* DLC as *An old folk song. The fair hills of Eire, O!.* Also for
org (*WIAM* 1395).

1381 BEACH, Amy Cheney. **Fantasia fugata, op. 87** (18654;
mm   Philadelphia: T. Presser, 1923) 10 p.
Dn 5′. *Pf* pno.

1382 BEACH, Amy Cheney. **Five improvisations for piano, op.**
mm   **148, nos. 1-5** (CP 191-195; New York: Composers Press, 1938) 2,
        2, 2, 2, 2 p.
Dn 9′. *Rg Piano music of Mrs. H.H.A. Beach*, Genesis, GS 1054; *Contemporary
American piano classics*, Dorian, 1006.

1383 BEACH, Amy Cheney. **Four sketches, op. 15, nos. 1-4** (APS
mm   2870-2873; Boston: A.P. Schmidt, 1892) 5, 5, 5, 9 p.
Dn 11′. *Pf* pno. *Ct* In autumn, Dreaming, Phantoms, Fireflies. *Rg Piano music
of Mrs. H.H.A. Beach*, Genesis, GS 1054.

1384 BEACH, Amy Cheney. **From blackbird hills, op. 83. An**
mm   **Omaha tribal dance** (APS 12714; Boston: A.P. Schmidt, 1922) 9
        p.
Dn 6′. *Pf* pno.

1385 BEACH, Amy Cheney. **From grandmother's garden, op. 97,**
mm   **nos. 1-5** (APS 18436-18440; Boston: A.P. Schmidt, 1922) 5, 3, 5, 7,
        6 p.
Dn 12′. *Pf* pno. *Ct* Morning glories, Heartsease, Mignonette, Rosemary and
rue, Honeysuckle.

1386 BEACH, Amy Cheney. **From six to twelve** (75929/75934;
mm   Boston: O. Ditson, 1927) 5, 5, 3, 3, 3, 3 p.
Dn 6′. *Pf* pno. *Ct* Sliding on the ice, The first May flowers, Canoeing, Secrets of
the attic, A camp-fire ceremonial, Boy Scouts march.

1387 BEACH, Amy Cheney. **Gavotte fantastique, op. 54, no. 2**
md   (APS 6152; Boston: A.P. Schmidt, 1903) 7 p.
Dn 3′. *Pf* pno.

1388 BEACH, Amy Cheney. **Hermit thrush at eve, A, op. 92, no. 1**
md   (APS 12437; Boston: A.P. Schmidt, 1922) 7 p.
Dn 4′. *Pf* pno. *Rg Piano music of Mrs. H.H.A. Beach*, Genesis, GS 1054.

1389 BEACH, Amy Cheney. **Hermit thrush at morn, A, op. 92, no.**
md   **2** (APS 12438; Boston: A.P. Schmidt, 1922) 9 p.
Dn 6′. *Pf* pno. *Rg Piano music of Mrs. H.H.A. Beach*, Genesis, GS 1054.

1390 BEACH, Amy Cheney. **Nocturne, op. 107** (18758; Cincinnati:
mm   J. Church, 1924) 5 p.
Dn 2′. *Pf* pno. *Rg Piano music of Mrs. H.H.A. Beach*, Genesis, GS 1054.

1391 BEACH, Amy Cheney. **Old chapel by moonlight, op. 106**
mm   (18757; Cincinnati: J. Church, 1924) 5 p.
Dn 2′. *Pf* pno.

1392 BEACH, Amy Cheney. **Out of the depths, op. 130** (APS
mm   14606; Boston: A.P. Schmidt, 1932) 5 p.
Dn 2′. *La* DLC, Schmidt Collection. *Pf* pno.

1393 BEACH, Amy Cheney. **Piano compositions, op. 102, nos. 1-2**
mm   (74761-74762; Boston: O. Ditson, 1924) 5, 5 p.

Dn 4′. *Ct* Farewell summer, Dancing leaves. Dedicated to Olga Samaroff Stokowski.

1394 BEACH, Amy Cheney. **Prelude and fugue for pianoforte, op.**
mm   **81** (28386; New York: G. Schirmer, 1918) 21 p.
Dn 10′. *Rg Piano music of Mrs. H.H.A. Beach*, Genesis, GS 1054.

1395 BEACH, Amy Cheney. **Prelude on an old folk tune.** *The fair*
mm   ***hills of Eire, O*** (New York: H.W. Gray, 1943) 4 p.
Dn 3′. *Pf* org.

1396 BEACH, Amy Cheney. **Rêves de Colombine, Les, op. 65,**
mm   **nos. 1-5. Suite française pour le pianoforte** (APS 7637;
Boston: A.P. Schmidt, 1907) 29 p.
Dn 18′. *La* DLC, Schmidt Collection. *Ct* La fée de la fontaine, Le prince gracieux, Valse amoureuse, Sous les étoiles, Danse d'Arlequin.

1397 BEACH, Amy Cheney. **Scottish legend, op. 54, no. 1** (APS
md   6151; Boston: A.P. Schmidt, 1903) 3 p.
Dn 1′. *La* DLC, Schmidt Collection. *Pf* pno.

1398 BEACH, Amy Cheney. **Three pianoforte pieces, op. 128, nos.**
mm   **1-3** (25530-25532; Philadelphia: T. Presser, 1932) 5, 7, 5 p.
Dn 3′. *Ct* Scherzino. A Peterborough chipmunk; Young birches; A humming bird. Dedicated to Marian MacDowell.

1399 BEACH, Amy Cheney. **Trois morceaux caracteristiques, op.**
mm   **28, nos. 1-3** (APS 3408-3410; Boston: A.P. Schmidt, 1894) 7, 7, 7
p.
Dn 19′. *La* DLC, Schmidt Collection. *Pf* pno. *Ct* Barcarolle, Minuet italien, Dance des fleurs. *Rg Piano music of Mrs. H.H.A. Beach*, Genesis, GS 1054.

1400 BEACH, Amy Cheney. **Tyrolean valse-fantasie, op. 116**
mm   (75318; Boston: O. Ditson, 1926) 16 p.
Dn 10′. *Pf* pno.

1401 BEACH, Amy Cheney. **Valse-caprice for the pianoforte, op.**
mm   **4** (APS 2517; Boston: A.P. Schmidt, 1889) 11 p.
Dn 5′. *Rg Piano music of Mrs. H.H.A. Beach*, Genesis, GS 1054.

1402 BEACH, Amy Cheney. **Variations on Balkan themes, op. 60**
mm   (APS 7196; Boston: A.P. Schmidt, 1906) 27 p.
Dn 23′. *Pf* pno. A note from Schmidt indicates that an orchestral version was available at the time of publication. Beach also arranged the piece for 2 pno, 4 hands (*WIAM* 1278).

1403 DILLON, Fannie Charles. **Eight descriptive compositions,**
mm   **op. 20, nos. 1-8** (17662-17669; Cincinnati: J. Church, 1917) 5, 7,
7, 2, 7, 7, 9, 7 p.
Dn 16′. *Pf* pno. *Ct* April moods, Birds at dawn, The desert, Evening, Forest mourning dove, Ocean depths, A song of the Sierras, Under the pines.

1404 DILLON, Fannie Charles. **From the Chinese, op. 93** (CP 151-
mm   153; New York: Composers Press, 1944) 15 p.
Dn 11′. *Pf* pno. *Ct* Butterfly wings, Winter moonlight, Chinese temple scene. *Rg* Dorian, 1014.

1405 DILLON, Fannie Charles. **Heroic etude, op. 6** (15901; Cin-
mm   cinnati: J. Church, 1917) 15 p.
Dn 4′. *Pf* pno. Dedicated to Teresa Carreño.

1406 DILLON, Fannie Charles. **Six preludes, op. 8, nos. 1-6**
mm   (15902-07; Cincinnati: J. Church, 1908) 3, 5, 5, 5, 3, 7 p.
Dn 15′. *Pf* pno. *Ct* Prelude I (Melody on E-flat and B-flat), Prelude II (In character of a nocturne), Prelude III (In passacaglia style), Prelude IV, Prelude V (Chromatic), Prelude VI.

1407 DILLON, Fannie Charles. **Songs of the seven hills, op. 65,**
mm   **nos. 1-3** (32992-32994; New York: G. Schirmer, 1927) 5, 9, 11 p.
Dn 9′. *Pf* pno. *Ct* Panorama, On the olive hill, Shimmering pool.

1408 DILLON, Fannie Charles. **Woodland flute call** (Glen Rock,
md   N.J.: J. Fischer, 1953) 6 p.
Dn 3′. *Pf* org. *Tm Twenty-five pieces for small organ.* Dedicated to Clement Sampson of Arcadia, Calif.

1409 FREER, Eleanor Everest. **Lyric studies for the pianoforte,**
mm   **op. 3, nos. 1-8** (Milwaukee: W.A. Kaun Music, 1904) 27 p.

Dn 14′.

1410 HOPEKIRK, Helen. **Five Scottish folk songs transcribed for**
mm   **the piano** (5874; Boston: Boston Music, 1919) 17 p.
Dn 8′. *Ct* The lof the Leal; Turn ye to me; Gaelic lullaby and love song; Aye, wakin O!; Eilidh Bhan.

1411 HOPEKIRK, Helen. **Gavotte** (3873; New York: G. Schirmer,
mm   1885) 5 p.
Dn 2′. *Pf* pno.

1412 HOPEKIRK, Helen. **Iona memories** (21277; New York: G.
mm   Schirmer, 1909) 25 p.
Dn 13′. *Pf* pno. *Ct* Wandering, Cronan, In the ruins, A twilight tale.

1413 HOPEKIRK, Helen. **Norland eve, A** (BM 5999; Boston: Boston
mm   Music, 1919) 7 p.
Dn 5′. *Pf* pno. Dedicated to Amy Cheney Beach.

1414 HOPEKIRK, Helen. **Robin good-fellow** (BM 6957; Boston:
mm   Boston Music, 1923) 5 p.
Dn 2′. *Pf* pno.

1415 HOPEKIRK, Helen. **Serenade for piano** (London: Paterson,
mm   1895) 8 p.
Dn 5′.

1416 HOPEKIRK, Helen. **Serenata. Suite for the piano** (BM 6473-
mm   6477; Boston: Boston Music, 1920) 20 p.
Dn 10′. *Ct* Maestoso, Minuet, Sarabande, Arioso, Rigaudon. Dedicated to Arthur Foote.

1417 HOPEKIRK, Helen. **Suite for the pianoforte** (BM 5177-5181;
mm   Boston: Boston Music, 1917) 3, 5, 5, 7, 7 p.
Dn 16′. *Ct* Sarabande, Minuet, Air, Gavotte, Rigaudon. Dedicated to Fannie Bloomfield-Zeisler.

1418 HOPEKIRK, Helen. **Sundown** (21276; New York: G. Schirmer,
mm   1909) 7 p.
Dn 3′. *Pf* pno.

1419 HOPEKIRK, Helen. **Three pieces for the piano** (25329-25331;
mm   New York: G. Schirmer, 1915) 7, 7, 6 p.
Dn 11′. *Ct* Dance (*La* DLC), Prelude, A revery (All soul's day, *La* DLC).

1420 HOPEKIRK, Helen. **Tone pictures** (ECS 508; Boston: E.C.
mm   Schirmer, 1930) 7, 5 p.
Dn 6′. *Pf* pno. *Ct* Dance to your shadow, The seal-woman's sea-joy. Based on melodies from *Songs of the Hebrides*, ed. by Marjory Kennedy-Fraser.

1421 HOPEKIRK, Helen. **Two compositions for the pianoforte**
mm   (BM 7041; Boston: Boston Music, 1924) 7 p.
Dn 5′. *Ct* Shadows, Brocade.

1422 JACOBS-BOND, Carrie. **Betty's music box** (Hollywood, Calif.:
mm   C. Jacobs-Bond & Son, 1917) 5 p.
Dn 4′. *Pf* pno.

1423 JACOBS-BOND, Carrie. **Blue flag, The. Military march for**
mm   **piano** (Chicago: C. Jacobs-Bond & Son, 1907) 6 p.
Dn 4′.

1424 JACOBS-BOND, Carrie. **Reverie pour piano** (ES 3833; New
mm   York: E. Schuberth, 1902) 6 p.
Dn 2′. *Pf* pno. Dedicated " À Amy Fay".

1425 LANG, Margaret Ruthven. **Meditation, op. 26** (APS 4452;
mm   Boston: A.P. Schmidt, 1897) 5 p.
Dn 2′. *La* DLC, Schmidt Collection. *Pf* pno.

1426 LANG, Margaret Ruthven. **Petit roman pour le piano en six**
mm   **chapitres, op. 18** (APS 2984; Boston: A.P. Schmidt, 1894) 31 p.
Dn 16′. *La* DLC, Schmidt Collection. *Ct* Le chevalier, Madame la princesse, Bal chez madame la princesse, Monsieur le prince, L'épée de monsieur le prince, La mort du chevalier.

1427 LANG, Margaret Ruthven. **Revery, op. 31** (13166; Cincinnati:
mm   J. Church, 1899) 7 p.
Dn 2'. *Pf* pno.

1428 LANG, Margaret Ruthven. **Rhapsody in E minor, op. 21**
mm   (APS 3882; Boston: A.P. Schmidt, 1895) 9 p.
Dn 7'. *La* DLC, Schmidt Collection. *Pf* pno.

1429 LANG, Margaret Ruthven. **Spirit of the old house, The, op.**
mm   **58** (APS 11369; Boston: A.P. Schmidt, 1917) 5 p.
Dn 2'. *Pf* pno.

1430 LANG, Margaret Ruthven. **Spring idyl, A, op. 33** (13165;
mm   Cincinnati: J. Church, 1889) 5 p.
Dn 3'. *Pf* pno.

1431 LANG, Margaret Ruthven. **Springtime, op. 30**, *The world's*
mc   *best composers.* Ed. by Victor HERBERT (New York: U. Soc., 1899)
      IV, 967-70.
Dn 4'. *Pf* pno.

1432 LANG, Margaret Ruthven. **Starlight**, *Half hours with the best*
mc   *composers, part 10.* Ed. by Karl KLAUSER (Boston: J.B. Millet,
      1894) 478-82.
Dn 2'. *Pf* pno.

1433 LANG, Margaret Ruthven. **Twilight**, *Half hours with the best*
mc   *composers, part 10.* Ed. by Karl KLAUSER (Boston: J.B. Millet,
      1894) 473-77.
Dn 3'. *Pf* pno.

1434 MOORE, Mary Carr. **Barcarolle for piano, op. 75, no. 8** (San
md   Bruno, Calif.: W. Webster, 1935) 7 p.
Dn 10'.   *(Joan M. Meggett)*

1435 MOORE, Mary Carr. **Before the dawn, op. 100, no. 1** (28710;
md   New York: C. Fischer, 1939) 5 p.
Dn 2'. *Pf* pno. *Tm Forest sketches, op. 100, nos. 1-4.*

1436 MOORE, Mary Carr. **Beyond these hills. Prelude, op. 86, no.**
md   **1** (facsimile of MS at CLSU, n.d.) 2 p.
Dn 4'. *La* CLSU. *Pf* pno.   *(Stephen M. Fry)*

1437 MOORE, Mary Carr. **Murmur of pines, op. 100, no. 4**
md   (28713; New York: C. Fischer, 1939) 9 p.
Dn 2'. *Pf* pno. *Tm Forest sketches, op. 100, nos. 1-4.*

1438 MOORE, Mary Carr. **Song of a faun, op. 81, no. 13** (San
md   Bruno, Calif.: W. Webster, 1922) 1 p.
Dn 8'. *Pf* flu.   *(Joan M. Meggett)*

1439 MOORE, Mary Carr. *Song of the world, The* (facsimile of MS
md   at CLSU, n.d.) 1 p.
Excerpt from an operetta. *Dn* 1'. *At* Laura Sweeney Moore. *Pf* flu. *Tm Flutes of
jade happiness*, operetta in 3 acts.

1440 ROGERS, Clara Kathleen. **Romanza, op. 31**, *Half hours with*
mc   *the best composers, part 24.* Ed. by Karl KLAUSER (Boston: J.B.
      Millet, 1895) 1201-08.
Dn 3'. *Pf* pno.

1441 ROGERS, Clara Kathleen. **Scherzo, op. 32**, *Half hours with the*
mc   *best composers, part 24.* Ed. by Karl KLAUSER (Boston: J.B. Millet,
      1895) 1209-12.
Dn 3'. *Pf* pno.

1442 STEINER, Emma Roberto. **Fleurette. Overture for the**
mm   **pianoforte** (New York: MacDonald & Steiner, n.d.) 8 p.
Dn 3'. *Pf* pno. This overture to Steiner's opera includes the following note on
the score: "Composed in 1877 without any hope of getting a production,
E.R.S.".

1443 STEINER, Emma Roberto. **Gavotte Mengeli. For piano and**
mm   **orchestra, op. 400** (New York: MacDonald & Steiner, 1914) 5 p.
Dn 2'. *Pf* pno. Despite the title, this version is for piano only.

Stage works

1444 FREER, Eleanor Everest. **Chilkoot maiden, The, op. 32**
mm   (Milwaukee: W.A. Kaun Music, 1926) 43 p. (piano-vocal score).
Opera in 1 act. *Dn* 18'. *At* J.J. Underwood. *Li* composer. *St Alaska, an empire
in the making. Pf* solo SMATB, choral SATB, pno.

1445 FREER, Eleanor Everest. **Christmas tale, A, op. 35** (Milwau-
mm   kee: W.A. Kaun Music, 1928) 55 p. (piano-vocal score).
Opera in 1 act. *Dn* 20'. *At* Maurice Boucher. *Li* Barrett H. Clark. *Pf* solo
SMTBar, chorus of men and boys, pno. A facsimile of the autograph at DLC is
numbered op. 33.

1446 FREER, Eleanor Everest. **Frithiof, op. 40** (Milwaukee: W.A.
mm   Kaun Music, 1929) 86 p. (piano-vocal score).
Opera in 2 acts. *Dn* 25'. *At* Esaias Tegner. *Li* Clement B. Shaw. *St Frithiof's
saga. Pf* solo S-5T-2Bar-B, choral SATB, pno.

1447 FREER, Eleanor Everest. **Joan of Arc, op. 38** (Milwaukee:
mm   W.A. Kaun Music, 1929) 86 p. (piano-vocal score).
Opera in 1 act. *Dn* 25'. *La* DLC. *Li* composer. *Pf* solo 2S-A-5T-5B, pno.

1448 FREER, Eleanor Everest. **Legend of Spain, A, op. 35** (29629;
mm   Milwaukee: W.A. Kaun Music, 1931) 42 p. (piano-vocal score).
Opera in 1 act. *Dn* 20'. *La* DLC. *Li* composer. *Pf* solo SSTTBarB, choral SATB,
pno.

1449 FREER, Eleanor Everest. **Legend of the piper, The, op. 28**
mm   (Boston: C.C. Birchard, 1922) 78 p. (piano-vocal score).
Opera in 1 act. *Dn* 35'. *Li* Josephine Preston Peabody. *Pf* solo 2S-2M-7T-6B,
pno.

1450 FREER, Eleanor Everest. **Masque of Pandora, The, op. 36**
mm   (29636; Milwaukee: W.A. Kaun Music, 1930) 88 p. (piano-vocal
      score).
Opera in 1 act. *Dn* 40'. *La* DLC. *At* Longfellow. *St The masque of Pandora. Pf*
solo 5S-2A-2T-3B, choral SATB, pno.

1451 FREER, Eleanor Everest. **Massimilliano, the court jester, or**
mm   **The love of a caliban, op. 30** (23154; Chicago: composer, 1925)
      43 p. (piano-vocal score).
Opera in 1 act. *Dn* 18'. *Li* Elia W. Peattie. *Pf* solo SSTTBB, choral SATB, pno.

1452 FREER, Eleanor Everest. **Preciosa, or The Spanish student,**
mm   **op. 37** (Milwaukee: W.A. Kaun Music, 1928) 64 p. (piano-vocal
      score).
Opera in 1 act. *Dn* 30'. *La* DLC. *At* Longfellow. *St The Spanish student. Pf*
solo 3S-6T-7Bar-2B, choral SATB, pno.

1453 FREER, Eleanor Everest. **Scenes from *Little women*, op. 42**
mm   (36021; Chicago: Music Library, 1934) 72 p. (piano-vocal score).
Opera in 2 acts. *Dn* 20'. *At* Louisa May Alcott. *Li* composer. *Pf* solo 3S-2M-
2A-2T-3Bar, pno.

1454 FREER, Eleanor Everest. **The Brownings go to Italy, op. 43**
mm   (38977; Chicago: Music Library, 1936) 64 p. (piano-vocal score).
Opera in 1 act. *Dn* 20'. *Li* G.A. Hawkins-Ambler. *St* poetry of Robert and
Elizabeth Barrett Browning, freely adapted. *Pf* solo SMTBar, pno.

1455 MOORE, Mary Carr. **Cho Lin's song** (San Bruno, Calif.: W.
md   Webster, 1939) 5 p.
Excerpt from an operetta. *Dn* 5'. *At* Laura Sweeny Moore. *Pf* solo voc, pno. *Tm
Flutes of jade happiness*, operetta in 3 acts.   *(Joan M. Meggett)*

1456 MOORE, Mary Carr. **David Rizzio, op. 89. A grand opera in**
mm   **two acts** (San Bruno, Calif.: W. Webster, 1937) 157 p. (piano-vocal
      score).
Dn 120'. *At* Emmanuel Browne. *Lt* Italian, English. *Pf* solo S-M-3T-2Bar-B,
choral SATB, pno. First performed on 26 May 1932 in Los Angeles at the
Shrine Auditorium, under the direction of Albert Conti.

1457 MOORE, Mary Carr. **Narcissa** (New York: M. Witmark, 1912)
mm   267 p.
Opera in 4 acts. *Dn* 133'. *La* DLC, sketch materials. *At* Sarah Pratt Carr. *Pf*
solo S-M-A-2T-2Bar-B, choral SSAATTBB, pno.

1458 STEINER, Emma Roberto. **Trio from Fleurette. Comic**
mm   **opera in 2 acts** (New York: MacDonald & Steiner, n.d.) 11 p.

Dn 2′ . *Da* 1877. *At* Bessie Ward-Doremus and Edgar Smith. *Pf* solo SAT, pno.

Vocal music

1459 ASHFORD, Emma. **Beware** (Indianapolis: Wulschner Music,
mm   1902) 5 p.
Dn 2′ . *At* Longfellow. *Pf* solo voc, pno.

1460 ASHFORD, Emma. **Blow thou winter wind** (Indianapolis:
mm   Wulschner Music, 1902) 5 p.
Dn 1′ . *Pf* solo voc, pno.

1461 ASHFORD, Emma. **Moods** (New York: Lorenz, 1903) 22 p.
mm
Song cycle. *Dn* 15′ . *Pf* solo voc, pno. *Ct* The search (*At* Ernest Crosby), Night
song (*At* Andrew Hedbrook), My own true love (*At* Arthur Grissom), Sunset
and dawn (*At* Louise Chandler Moulton), Evening (*At* S. Weir Mitchell), Ever a
song somewhere (*At* James Whitcomb Riley), Good night (*At* Arthur S. Hardy).

1462 ASHFORD, Emma. **Rose and love** (Indianapolis: Wulschner
mm   Music, 1902) 7 p.
Dn 2′ . *At* R.A. Halley. *Pf* solo voc, pno.

1463 ASHFORD, Emma. **When love is done** (Indianapolis: Wulsch-
mm   ner Music, 1902) 5 p.
Dn 1′ . *Pf* solo voc, pno.

1464 AYLWARD, Florence. **Beloved, it is morn** (5010; New York:
mm   Chappell, 1895) 7 p.
Dn 2′ . *At* Emily Hickey. *Pf* solo voc, pno.

1465 BARNETT, Alice. **Agamede's song** (31356; New York: G.
md   Schirmer, 1923) 5 p.
Dn 2′ . *At* Arthur Upton. *Pf* solo voc, pno. *Tm Three songs of musing* (*WIAM*
1500).

1466 BARNETT, Alice. **Another hour with thee** (29941; New York:
md   G. Schirmer, 1921) 5 p.
Dn 1′ . *At* Jessie B. Rittenhouse. *Pf* solo voc, pno. *Tm Three love songs* (*WIAM*
1499).

1467 BARNETT, Alice. **As I came down from Lebanon** (32051;
mm   New York: G. Schirmer, 1924) 11 p.
Dn 4′ . *At* Clinton Scollard. *Pf* solo voc, pno.

1468 BARNETT, Alice. **At twilight** (CFS 1039; Chicago: C.F. Summy,
mm   1908) 3 p.
Dn 1′ . *At* William Allingham. *Pf* solo voc, pno.

1469 BARNETT, Alice. **Banjo player, The** (BM 7111; Boston: Boston
mm   Music, 1925) 5 p.
Dn 2′ . *At* F.M. *Pf* solo voc, pno.

1470 BARNETT, Alice. **Beyond** (28553; New York: G. Schirmer,
mm   1918) 3 p.
Dn 1′ . *At* Thomas S. Jones, Jr. *Pf* solo voc, pno.

1471 BARNETT, Alice. **Caravan from China comes, A** (32066;
mm   New York: G. Schirmer, 1924) 7 p.
Dn 1′ . *At* Richard Le Gallienne. *Pf* solo voc, pno.

1472 BARNETT, Alice. **Chanson of the bells of Osenèy** (31892;
mm   New York: G. Schirmer, 1924) 9 p.
Dn 3′ . *At* Cale Young Rice. *Pf* solo voc, pno.

1473 BARNETT, Alice. **Constancy** (31208; New York: G. Schirmer,
mm   1923) 5 p.
Dn 2′ . *At* John Suckling. *Pf* solo voc, pno.

1474 BARNETT, Alice. **Cool of the night, The. A nocturne for
mm   voice and piano** (29130; New York: G. Schirmer, 1919) 5 p.
Dn 2′ . *At* Egmont H. Arens.

1475 BARNETT, Alice. **Days that come and go** (29940; New York:
md   G. Schirmer, 1921) 5 p.

Dn 1′ . *At* John Vance Cheney. *Pf* solo voc, pno. *Tm Three love songs* (*WIAM*
1499).

1476 BARNETT, Alice. **Drums of the sea** (32052; New York: G.
mm   Schirmer, 1925) 5 p.
Dn 1′ . *At* Frederic Mertz. *Pf* solo voc, pno.

1477 BARNETT, Alice. **Ebb tide** (31357; New York: G. Schirmer,
md   1923) 7 p.
Dn 3′ . *At* Ella Higginson. *Pf* solo voc, pno. *Tm Three songs of musing* (*WIAM*
1500).

1478 BARNETT, Alice. **Evening** (CFS 1038; Chicago: C.F. Summy,
mm   1908) 5 p.
Dn 1′ . *At* Goethe. *Pf* solo voc, pno.

1479 BARNETT, Alice. **Harbor lights** (BM 7188; Boston: Boston
mm   Music, 1927) 5 p.
Dn 1′ . *Pf* solo voc, pno.

1480 BARNETT, Alice. **In a gondola** (29146-29153; New York: G.
mm   Schirmer, 1920) 7, 5, 5, 5, 5, 5, 7, 5 p.
Song cycle. *Dn* 30′ . *At* Robert Browning. *Pf* solo voc, pno. *Ct* Serenade; Boat-
song; The moth's kiss, first; What are we two?; He muses--drifting; Dip your
arm o'er the boatside; To-morrow, if a harp string, say; It was ordained to be
so, sweet.

1481 BARNETT, Alice. **In May** (74969; Boston: O. Ditson, 1925) 4 p.
mm
Dn 2′ . *At* Paul Laurence Dunbar. *Pf* solo voc, pno.

1482 BARNETT, Alice. **In the time of saffron moons** (821; New
md   York: Composers' Music, 1924) 5 p.
Dn 2′ . *At* F.M. *Pf* solo voc, pno. *Tm Panels from a Chinese screen* (*WIAM*
1494).

1483 BARNETT, Alice. **Indian serenade, An** (CFS 1040; Chicago:
mm   C.F. Summy, 1908) 7 p.
Dn 2′ . *At* Shelley. *Pf* solo voc, pno.

1484 BARNETT, Alice. **Inspiration** (28671; New York: G. Schirmer,
mm   1919) 5 p.
Dn 1′ . *At* Arthur Stringer. *Pf* solo voc, pno.

1485 BARNETT, Alice. **Lamplit hour, The** (29939; New York: G.
md   Schirmer, 1921) 5 p.
Dn 2′ . *At* Thomas Burke. *Pf* solo voc, pno. *Tm Three love songs* (*WIAM* 1499).

1486 BARNETT, Alice. **Merry, merry lark** (CFS 1094; Chicago: C.F.
mm   Summy, 1909) 6 p.
Dn 1′ . *At* Charles Kingsley. *Pf* solo voc, pno.

1487 BARNETT, Alice. **Mood** (28673; New York: G. Schirmer, 1919)
mm   5 p.
Dn 2′ . *At* A.B. [composer?]. *Pf* solo voc, pno.

1488 BARNETT, Alice. **Mother moon. A lie-awake song** (30141;
md   New York: G. Schirmer, 1921) 5 p.
Dn 2′ . *At* Amelia Josephine Burr. *Pf* solo voc, pno. *Tm Two even-songs* (*WIAM*
1507).

1489 BARNETT, Alice. **Music, when soft voices die** (32743; New
mm   York: G. Schirmer, 1926) 5 p.
Dn 2′ . *At* Shelley. *Pf* solo voc, pno.

1490 BARNETT, Alice. **Night song at Amalfi** (28674; New York: G.
mm   Schirmer, 1919) 5 p.
Dn 1′ . *At* Sara Teasdale. *Pf* solo voc, pno.

1491 BARNETT, Alice. **Nightingale lane** (28552; New York: G.
mm   Schirmer, 1918) 5 p.
Dn 2′ . *At* William Sharp. *Pf* solo voc, pno.

1492 BARNETT, Alice. **Nirvana** (35528; New York: G. Schirmer,
mm   1932) 5 p.
Dn 2′ . *At* John Hall Wheelock. *Pf* solo voc, pno.

1493 BARNETT, Alice. **On a moonlit river** (820; New York: Com-
md   posers' Music, 1924) 5 p.
Dn 2′. *At* F.M. *Pf* solo voc, pno. *Tm Panels from a Chinese screen* (*WIAM*
1494).

1494 BARNETT, Alice. **Panels from a Chinese screen, nos. 1-3**
mm   (819-821; New York: Composers' Music, 1924) 5, 5, 5 p.
Songs. *Dn* 6′. *At* F.M. *Pf* solo voc, pno. *Ct The singing girl of Shan* (*WIAM*
1496), *On a moonlit river* (*WIAM* 1493), *In the time of saffron moons* (*WIAM*
1482).

1495 BARNETT, Alice. **Serenade** (26614; New York: G. Schirmer,
mm   1916) 7 p.
Dn 3′. *At* Clinton Scollard. *Pf* solo voc, pno. Dedicated to Alma Gluck.

1496 BARNETT, Alice. **Singing girl of Shan, The** (819; New York:
md   Composers' Music, 1924) 5 p.
Dn 2′. *At* F.M. *Pf* solo voc, pno. *Tm Panels from a Chinese screen* (*WIAM*
1494).

1497 BARNETT, Alice. **Song at Capri** (31355; New York: G.
md   Schirmer, 1923) 5 p.
Dn 1′. *At* Sara Teasdale. *Pf* solo voc, pno. *Tm Three songs of musing* (*WIAM*
1500).

1498 BARNETT, Alice. **Sonnet** (28551; New York: G. Schirmer,
mm   1918) 5 p.
Dn 2′. *At* Elizabeth Barrett Browning. *Pf* solo voc, pno.

1499 BARNETT, Alice. **Three love songs** (29939-29941; New York:
mm   G. Schirmer, 1921) 5, 5, 5 p.
Dn 4′. *Pf* solo voc, pno. *Ct The lamplit hour* (*WIAM* 1485), *Another hour with
thee* (*WIAM* 1475), *Days that come and go* (*WIAM* 1466).

1500 BARNETT, Alice. **Three songs of musing** (31355-31357; New
mm   York: G. Schirmer, 1923) 5, 5, 7 p.
Dn 6′. *Pf* solo voc, pno. *Ct Song at Capri* (*WIAM* 1497), *Agamede's song*
(*WIAM* 1465), *Ebb tide* (*WIAM* 1477).

1501 BARNETT, Alice. **Thy cheek incline** (CFS 1092; Chicago: C.F.
mm   Summy, 1909) 5 p.
Dn 1′. *At* Heine. *Pf* solo voc, pno.

1502 BARNETT, Alice. **Time of roses, The** (35529; New York: G.
mm   Schirmer, 1932) 5 p.
Dn 2′. *At* Thomas Hood. *Pf* solo voc, pno.

1503 BARNETT, Alice. **To an impromptu of Chopin** (CFS 1093;
mm   Chicago: C.F. Summy, 1909) 5 p.
Dn 2′. *At* Gabriele D'Annunzio. *Pf* solo voc, pno.

1504 BARNETT, Alice. **Tonight** (30140; New York: G. Schirmer,
md   1921) 5 p.
Dn 2′. *At* Sara Teasdale. *Pf* solo voc, pno. *Tm Two even-songs* (*WIAM* 1507).

1505 BARNETT, Alice. **Tryst** (28672; New York: G. Schirmer, 1919)
mm   5 p.
Dn 1′. *At* Clinton Scollard. *Pf* solo voc, pno.

1506 BARNETT, Alice. **'Twas in the glorious month of May** (CFS
mm   1037; Chicago: C.F. Summy, 1908) 6 p.
Dn 1′. *At* Heine. *Pf* solo voc, pno.

1507 BARNETT, Alice. **Two even-songs** (30140-30141; New York:
mm   G. Schirmer, 1921) 5, 5 p.
Dn 4′. *Pf* solo voc, pno. *Ct Mother moon* (*WIAM* 1488), *Tonight* (*WIAM*
1504).

1508 BARTLETT, Elinore C.; VANNAH, Kate. **Love songs** (Bos-
ma   ton: C.W. Thompson, 1899) 24 p.
Dn 10′. *Pf* solo voc, pno. *Ct* by Elinore C. Bartlett: Thinking of you (*At*
composer), Since Mary's gone (*At* George McKenzie), I never forget you, Love
in dreams (*At* Arthur Symons). *Ct* by Kate Vannah: When the clover blooms
again (*At* Charles S.D. Roberts), Daybreak (*At* Victor Hugo), Flower of all the
world (*At* Gilbert Parker), When skies are blue (*At* composer).

1509 BEACH, Amy Cheney. **Across the world, op. 20. Villanelle**
mm   (APS 3493; Boston: A.P. Schmidt, 1894) 9 p.

Dn 3′. *La* DLC, Schmidt Collection. *At* Edith M. Thomas. *Pf* solo voc, pno.

1510 BEACH, Amy Cheney. **After, op. 68** (APS 8311; Boston: A.P.
mm   Schmidt, 1909) 7 p.
Dn 3′. *At* Florence Earle Coates. *Pf* solo voc, pno.

1511 BEACH, Amy Cheney. **Ah, love, but a day!, op. 44, no. 2**
md   (APS 5139; Boston: A.P. Schmidt, 1900) 5 p.
Dn 2′. *At* Robert Browning. *St* James Lee. *Pf* solo voc, pno. *Tm Three
Browning songs, op. 44* (*WIAM* 1607). Also with vln obbligato (APS 12031;
Schmidt, 1900), and in arrangements for solo ST, pno (APS 11295; Schmidt,
1917), solo MBar, pno (APS 11296; Schmidt, 1917), and for choral SSAA, pno,
and choral SATB, pno (*WIAM* 1286).

1512 BEACH, Amy Cheney. **Alone (Allein), op. 35, no. 2** (APS
md   4280; Boston: A.P. Schmidt, 1897) 7 p.
Dn 2′. *La* DLC, Schmidt Collection. *At* Heine. *Lt* German, English. *Pf* solo voc,
pno.

1513 BEACH, Amy Cheney. **Altes Gebet, Ein (An old prayer), op.
md   72, no. 1** (25168; New York: G. Schirmer, 1914) 5 p.
Dn 2′. *Lt* German, English. *Pf* solo voc, pno.

1514 BEACH, Amy Cheney. **Anita, op. 41, no. 1** (APS 4679; Boston:
md   A.P. Schmidt, 1898) 7 p.
Dn 1′. *La* DLC, Schmidt Collection. *At* Cora Fabbri. *Pf* solo voc, pno.

1515 BEACH, Amy Cheney. **Ariette, op. 1, no. 4** (APS 1066; Boston:
md   A.P. Schmidt, 1886) 5 p.
Dn 2′. *At* Shelley. *Pf* solo voc, pno. Also in her *Song album [A]* (*WIAM* 1596)
and *Song album [B]* (*WIAM* 1597).

1516 BEACH, Amy Cheney. **Around the manger, op. 115** (75313;
mm   Bryn Mawr: T. Presser, 1925) 5 p.
Sacred song. *Dn* 1′. *At* Robert Davis. *Pf* solo voc, org or pno. Also for choral
SATB, org or pno, and choral SSAA, org or pno (*WIAM* 1288).

1517 BEACH, Amy Cheney. **Artless maid, The, op. 99, no. 4**
md   (18587; Philadelphia: T. Presser, 1923) 5 p.
Dn 1′. *At* Louise Barili. *Pf* solo voc, pno.

1518 BEACH, Amy Cheney. **Autumn song, op. 56, no. 1** (APS 6438;
md   Boston: A.P. Schmidt, 1904) 5 p.
Dn 1′. *At* Henry Harris Aubrey Beach. *Pf* solo voc, pno.

1519 BEACH, Amy Cheney. **Baby, op. 69, no. 1** (APS 8097; Boston:
md   A.P. Schmidt, 1932) 7 p.
Dn 1′. *At* George MacDonald. *Pf* solo voc, pno.

1520 BEACH, Amy Cheney. **Blackbird, The, op. 11, no. 3** (APS
md   2066; Boston: A.P. Schmidt, 1889) 5 p.
Dn 1′. *La* DLC, Schmidt Collection. *At* William Ernest Henley. *Pf* solo voc,
pno. Also in her *Song album [A]* (*WIAM* 1596) and *Song album [B]* (*WIAM*
1597).

1521 BEACH, Amy Cheney. **Canadian boat song, A, op. 10, no. 1**
md   (APS 2711; Boston: A.P. Schmidt, 1890) 9 p.
Dn 2′. *La* DLC, Schmidt Collection. *At* Thomas Moore. *Pf* solo SBar, pno. *Tm
Songs of the sea, op. 10* (*WIAM* 1599).

1522 BEACH, Amy Cheney. **Canzonetta, op. 48, no. 4** (APS 5753;
md   Boston: A.P. Schmidt, 1902) 5 p.
Dn 1′. *At* Armand Sylvestre. *Pf* solo voc, pno.

1523 BEACH, Amy Cheney. **Chanson d'amour (A song of love),
md   op. 21, no. 1** (APS 2945; Boston: A.P. Schmidt, 1893) 7 p.
Dn 5′. *La* DLC, Schmidt Collection. *At* Victor Hugo. *Lt* French, English. *Pf*
solo voc, pno.

1524 BEACH, Amy Cheney. **Come, ah come, op. 48, no. 1** (APS
md   5750; Boston: A.P. Schmidt, 1902) 5 p.
Dn 1′. *At* Henry Harris Aubrey Beach. *Pf* solo voc, pno.

1525 BEACH, Amy Cheney. **Dark garden, op. 131** (APS 14586;
mm   Boston: A.P. Schmidt, 1932) 6 p.
Dn 1′. *At* Leonora Speyer. *Pf* solo voc, pno.

1526 BEACH, Amy Cheney. **Dark is the night, op. 11, no. 1** (APS
md 2068; Boston: A.P. Schmidt, 1890) 7 p.
Dn 2′. *La* DLC, Schmidt Collection. *At* William Ernest Henley. *Pf* solo voc,
pno. Also in her *Song album* [*A*] (*WIAM* 1596) and *Song album* [*B*] (*WIAM*
1597). *Rg* DLC, Recorded Sound Section.

1527 BEACH, Amy Cheney. **Dearie, op. 43, no. 1** (APS 5040;
md Boston: A.P. Schmidt, 1899) 3 p.
Dn 1′. *At* Robert Burns. *Pf* solo voc, pno. *Tm Five songs [to] words by Robert
Burns, op. 43* (*WIAM* 1538).

1528 BEACH, Amy Cheney. **Deine Blumen (Flowers and fate), op.**
md **72, no. 2** (25167; New York: G. Schirmer, 1914) 5 p.
Dn 2′. *At* Louis Zacharias. *Tr* John Bernhoff. *Lt* German, English. *Pf* solo voc,
pno.

1529 BEACH, Amy Cheney. **Ecstasy, op. 19, no. 2** (APS 3085;
md Boston: A.P. Schmidt, 1892) 5 p.
Dn 2′. *At* composer. *Pf* solo voc, pno. Also in her *Song album* [*A*] (*WIAM*
1596), and with vln obbligato (APS 3559; Schmidt, 1895).

1530 BEACH, Amy Cheney. **Eilende wolken, Segler der Lüfte**
mm **(Wandering clouds, sail through the air), op. 18** (APS 2874;
Boston: A.P. Schmidt, 1892) 15 p. (piano-vocal score).
Opera *scena. Dn* 5′. *At* Schiller. *St Maria Stuart. Lt* German, English. *Pf* solo
A, pno. Originally for voice and orchestra (MS at MBNe). Dedicated to Mrs.
Carl Alves.

1531 BEACH, Amy Cheney. **Elle et moi (My sweetheart and I),**
md **op. 21, no. 3** (APS 2946; Boston: A.P. Schmidt, 1893) 7 p.
Dn 2′. *At* Félix Boret. *Lt* French, English. *Pf* solo voc, pno. Dedicated to
Baroness Hegermann-Lindencrone.

1532 BEACH, Amy Cheney. **Empress of night, op. 2, no. 3** (APS
md 2254; Boston: A.P. Schmidt, 1891) 5 p.
Dn 1′. *At* Henry Harris Aubrey Beach. *Pf* solo voc, pno. Also in her *Song album*
[*A*] (*WIAM* 1596) and *Song album* [*B*] (*WIAM* 1597).

1533 BEACH, Amy Cheney. **Evening hymn, op. 125, no. 2. The**
md **shadows of the evening hours** (APS 14672; Boston: A.P.
Schmidt, 1934) 5 p.
Sacred song. *Dn* 3′. *La* DLC, Schmidt Collection. *At* Adelaide A. Procter. *Pf*
solo voc, pno. Also arranged for solo S, choral SATB, pno (*WIAM* 1302).

1534 BEACH, Amy Cheney. **Extase (Exaltation), op. 21, no. 2**
md (APS 2944; Boston: A.P. Schmidt, 1893) 5 p.
Dn 3′. *At* Victor Hugo. *Lt* French, English. *Pf* solo voc, pno. Also for voice and
orchestra (autograph at MBNe).

1535 BEACH, Amy Cheney. **Fairy lullaby, op. 37, no. 3** (APS 4410;
md Boston: A.P. Schmidt, 1897) 5 p.
Dn 2′. *At* Shakespeare. *Pf* solo voc, pno. *Tm Three Shakespeare songs, op. 37*
(*WIAM* 1608). Also arranged for choral SSAA, pno (*WIAM* 1303).

1536 BEACH, Amy Cheney. **Far awa'!, op. 43, no. 4** (APS 11456;
md Boston: A.P. Schmidt, 1899) 5 p.
Dn 2′. *At* Robert Burns. *Pf* solo voc, pno. *Tm Five songs [to] words by Robert
Burns, op. 43* (*WIAM* 1538). Also arranged for choral SSA, pno, and choral SA,
pno (*WIAM* 1304).

1537 BEACH, Amy Cheney. **Fire and flame, op. 136** (APS 14661;
mm Boston: A.P. Schmidt, 1933) 5 p.
Dn 2′. *At* Anna Addison Moody. *Pf* solo voc, pno.

1538 BEACH, Amy Cheney. **Five songs [to] words by Robert**
mm **Burns, op. 43, nos. 1-5** (APS 5040/11456; Boston: A.P. Schmidt,
1899) 3, 3, 3, 5, 5 p.
Dn 7′. *Pf* solo voc, pno. *Ct Dearie* (*WIAM* 1527), *Scottish cradle song* (*WIAM*
1589), *Oh, were my love yon lilac fair* (*WIAM* 1583), *Far awa'!* (*WIAM* 1536),
My lassie (*WIAM* 1575).

1539 BEACH, Amy Cheney. **For me the jasmine buds unfold, op.**
md **19, no. 1** (APS 3055; Boston: A.P. Schmidt, 1892) 7 p.
Dn 2′. *At* Florence Earle Coates. *Pf* solo voc, pno.

1540 BEACH, Amy Cheney. **Forget me not, op. 35, no. 4** (APS
md 4282; Boston: A.P. Schmidt, 1897) 7 p.
Dn 3′. *At* Henry Harris Aubrey Beach. *Pf* solo voc, pno.

1541 BEACH, Amy Cheney. **Forgotten, op. 41, no. 3** (APS 4681;
md Boston: A.P. Schmidt, 1898) 5 p.
Dn 2′. *La* DLC. *At* Cora Fabbri. *Pf* solo voc, pno.

1543 BEACH, Amy Cheney. **Four brothers, The (Die vier Brüder),**
md **op. 1, no. 2** (APS 1469; Boston: A.P. Schmidt, 1887) 7 p.
Dn 2′. *At* Schiller. *Lt* German, English. *Pf* solo voc, pno.

1544 BEACH, Amy Cheney. **Give me not love, op. 61** (APS 6894;
mm Boston: A.P. Schmidt, 1905) 7 p.
Dn 4′. *At* Florence Earle Coates. *Pf* solo ST, pno.

1545 BEACH, Amy Cheney. **Go not too far, op. 56, no. 2** (APS
md 6439; Boston: A.P. Schmidt, 1904) 5 p.
Dn 1′. *At* Florence Earle Coates. *Pf* solo voc, pno.

1546 BEACH, Amy Cheney. **Golden gates, op. 19, no. 3** (APS 3086;
md Boston: A.P. Schmidt, 1892) 5 p.
Dn 3′. *Pf* solo voc, pno.

1547 BEACH, Amy Cheney. **Good morning, op. 48, no. 2** (APS
md 5751; Boston: A.P. Schmidt, 1902) 5 p.
Dn 1′. *At* Agnes Helen Lockhart. *Pf* solo voc, pno.

1548 BEACH, Amy Cheney. **Good night, op. 48, no. 3** (APS 5752;
md Boston: A.P. Schmidt, 1902) 5 p.
Dn 2′. *At* Agnes Helen Lockhart. *Pf* solo voc, pno.

1549 BEACH, Amy Cheney. **Grossmütterchen (With granny), op.**
md **73, no. 1** (25166; New York: G. Schirmer, 1914) 5 p.
Dn 2′. *At* Louis Zacharias. *Tr* John Bernhoff. *Lt* German, English. *Pf* solo voc,
pno.

1550 BEACH, Amy Cheney. **Haste, O beloved, op. 29, no. 4** (APS
md 3751; Boston: A.P. Schmidt, 1895) 7 p.
Dn 3′. *At* William A. Sparrow. *Pf* solo voc, pno.

1551 BEACH, Amy Cheney. **Host, The, op. 117, no. 2** (18897;
md Cincinnati: J. Church, 1925) 3 p.
Dn 1′. *At* Muna Lee. *St Sea change. Pf* solo voc, pno.

1552 BEACH, Amy Cheney. **Hush baby dear, op. 69, no. 2** (APS
md 8009; Boston: A.P. Schmidt, 1908) 5 p.
Dn 1′. *At* Agnes Lockhart Hughes. *Pf* solo voc, pno. Also arranged by Hugo
Norden for solo SA, pno (APS 15495; Schmidt, 1950).

1553 BEACH, Amy Cheney. **Hymn of trust, op. 13** (APS 5521;
mm Boston: A.P. Schmidt, 1901) 7 p. (score, part).
Dn 4′. *La* DLC, Schmidt Collection. *At* Oliver Wendell Holmes. *Pf* solo voc,
pno, vln obbligato. Also for solo voc, pno in her *Song album* [*A*] (*WIAM* 1596)
and *Song album* [*B*] (*WIAM* 1597).

1554 BEACH, Amy Cheney. **I know not how to find the spring, op.**
md **56, no. 3** (APS 6442; Boston: A.P. Schmidt, 1904) 5 p.
Dn 2′. *At* Florence Earle Coates. *Pf* solo voc, pno.

1555 BEACH, Amy Cheney. **I, op. 77, no. 1** (26960; New York: G.
md Schirmer, 1916) 7 p.
Dn 1′. *At* Cecil Fanning. *Pf* solo voc, pno.

1556 BEACH, Amy Cheney. **I send my heart up to thee, op. 44, no.**
md **3** (APS 5140; Boston: A.P. Schmidt, 1900) 7 p.
Dn 3′. *At* Robert Browning. *St In a gondola. Pf* solo voc, pno. *Tm Three
Browning songs, op. 44* (*WIAM* 1607).

1557 BEACH, Amy Cheney. **I shall be brave, op. 143** (APS 14588;
mm Boston: A.P. Schmidt, 1932) 6 p.
Dn 4′. *At* Katharine Adams. *Pf* solo voc, pno.

1558 BEACH, Amy Cheney. **I sought the Lord, op. 142** (APS
mm 14888; Boston: A.P. Schmidt, 1937) 5 p.
Sacred song. *Dn* 3′. *Pf* solo voc, org.

1559 BEACH, Amy Cheney. **Ich sagete nicht (Silent love), op. 51,**
md **no. 1** (APS 5983; Boston: A.P. Schmidt, 1903) 5 p.
Dn 2′. *At* Eduard Wissmann. *Tr* Isadora Martinez. *Lt* German, English. *Pf* solo
voc, pno.

1560 BEACH, Amy Cheney. **In blossom time, op. 78, no. 3** (27110;
md New York: G. Schirmer, 1917) 6 p.
Dn 1'. *At* Ina Coolbrith. *Pf* solo voc, pno.

1561 BEACH, Amy Cheney. **In the twilight, op. 85** (APS 12713;
mm Boston: A.P. Schmidt, 1922) 10 p.
Dn 3'. *At* Longfellow. *Pf* solo voc, pno.

1562 BEACH, Amy Cheney. **Je demande à l'oiseau (For my love),**
md **op. 51, no. 4** (APS 5986; Boston: A.P. Schmidt, 1903) 5 p.
Dn 1'. *At* Armand Sylvestre. *Tr* Isadora Martinez. *Lt* French, English. *Pf* solo
voc, pno.

1563 BEACH, Amy Cheney. **Jephthah's daughter (La figlia di**
mm **Jephte), op. 53. Aria for soprano** (APS 6218; Boston: A.P.
Schmidt, 1903) 11 p. (piano-vocal score).
Dn 8'. *La* DLC. *Lt* English, Italian. *Tr* Italian version from the original text by
Isadora Martinez; English version based on the Italian by the composer. *Pf* solo
voc, pno. Originally for voice and orchestra (autograph at MBNe).

1564 BEACH, Amy Cheney. **Jesus, my saviour, op. 112** (22514;
mm Philadelphia: T. Presser, 1925) 5 p.
Sacred song. *Dn* 2'. *At* Charlotte Elliott. *Pf* solo voc, org.

1565 BEACH, Amy Cheney. **Jeune fille et jeune fleur, op. 1, no. 3**
md (APS 1406; Boston: A.P. Schmidt, 1887) 7 p.
Dn 3'. *At* Chateaubriand. *Lt* French. *Pf* solo voc, pno.

1566 BEACH, Amy Cheney. **Juni (June), op. 51, no. 3** (APS 5985;
md Boston: A.P. Schmidt, 1903) 5 p.
Dn 1'. *At* Erich Jansen. *Tr* Isadora Martinez. *Lt* German, English. *Pf* solo voc,
pno. Also with vln obbligato (APS 1887; Schmidt, 1903), and for voice and
orchestra (autograph at MBNe). Also arranged for choral SSAA, pno, and
choral SATB, pno (*WIAM* 1311).

1567 BEACH, Amy Cheney. **Just for this, op. 26, no. 2** (APS 3395;
md Boston: A.P. Schmidt, 1894) 5 p.
Dn 1'. *La* DLC. *At* Cora Fabbri. *Pf* solo voc, pno. Also in her *Song album* [A]
(*WIAM* 1596).

1568 BEACH, Amy Cheney. **Little brown-eyed laddie, op. 99, no.**
md **2** (18585; Philadelphia: T. Presser, 1923) 6 p.
Dn 1'. *At* Alice D.O. Greenwood. *Pf* solo voc, pno.

1569 BEACH, Amy Cheney. **Lotos isles, The, op. 76, no. 2** (25276;
md New York: G. Schirmer, 1914) 5 p.
Dn 3'. *At* Tennyson. *Pf* solo voc, pno. The composer's *Thou knowest, Lord*
(*WIAM* 1339) is also numbered op. 76, no. 2.

1570 BEACH, Amy Cheney. **May flowers, op. 137** (APS 14662;
mm Boston: A.P. Schmidt, 1933) 5 p.
Dn 1'. *La* DLC, Schmidt Collection. *At* Anna Addison Moody. *Pf* solo voc,
pno.

1571 BEACH, Amy Cheney. **Meadowlarks, op. 78, no. 1** (27109;
md New York: G. Schirmer, 1917) 7 p.
Dn 2'. *At* Ina Coolbrith. *Pf* solo voc, pno.

1572 BEACH, Amy Cheney. **Message, op. 93** (18102; [Philadelphia]:
mm T. Presser, 1922) 5 p.
Dn 2'. *At* Sara Teasdale. *Pf* solo voc, pno.

1573 BEACH, Amy Cheney. **Mine be the lips, op. 113** (75291;
mm Boston: O. Ditson, 1921) 5 p.
Dn 2'. *At* Leonora Speyer. *St A canopic jar*. *Pf* solo voc, pno.

1574 BEACH, Amy Cheney. **Moon-path, The, op. 99, no. 3** (18586;
md Philadelphia: T. Presser, 1923) 6 p.
Dn 1'. *At* Katharine Adams. *Pf* solo voc, pno.

1575 BEACH, Amy Cheney. **My lassie, op. 43, no. 5** (APS 5045;
md Boston: A.P. Schmidt, 1899) 5 p.
Dn 2'. *At* Robert Burns. *Pf* solo voc, pno. *Tm Five songs [to] words by Robert
Burns, op. 43* (*WIAM* 1538).

1576 BEACH, Amy Cheney. **My luve is like a red, red rose, op. 12,**
md **no. 3** (APS 1954; Boston: A.P. Schmidt, 1889) 7 p.

Dn 3'. *At* Robert Burns. *Pf* solo voc, pno. Also in her *Song album* [B] (*WIAM*
1597).

1577 BEACH, Amy Cheney. **My star, op. 26, no. 1** (APS 3386;
md Boston: A.P. Schmidt, 1894) 7 p.
Dn 3'. *La* DLC, Schmidt Collection. *At* Cora Fabbri. *Pf* solo voc, pno.

1578 BEACH, Amy Cheney. **Night (Nachts), op. 35, no. 1** (APS
md 4279; Boston: A.P. Schmidt, 1897) 5 p.
Dn 2'. *At* Christian Friedrich Scherenberg. *Lt* English, German. *Pf* solo voc,
pno.

1579 BEACH, Amy Cheney. **Night sea, The, op. 10, no. 2** (APS
md 2712; Boston: A.P. Schmidt, 1890) 9 p.
Dn 2'. *At* Harriet Prescott Spofford. *Pf* solo SS, pno. *Tm Songs of the sea, op. 10*
(*WIAM* 1599).

1580 BEACH, Amy Cheney. **Night song at Amalfi, op. 78, no. 2**
md (27111; New York: G. Schirmer, 1917) 5 p.
Dn 2'. *At* Sara Teasdale. *Pf* solo voc, pno.

1581 BEACH, Amy Cheney. **O mistress mine, op. 37, no. 1** (APS
md 4408; Boston: A.P. Schmidt, 1897) 7 p.
Dn 2'. *At* Shakespeare. *Pf* solo voc, pno. *Tm Three Shakespeare songs, op. 37*
(*WIAM* 1608). *Rg* DLC, Recorded Sound Section.

1582 BEACH, Amy Cheney. **O sweet content, op. 71, no. 3** (APS
md 8903; Boston: A.P. Schmidt, 1910) 7 p.
Dn 1'. *At* Thomas Dekker. *Pf* solo voc, pno.

1583 BEACH, Amy Cheney. **Oh, were my love yon lilac fair, op.**
md **43, no. 3** (APS 5042; Boston: A.P. Schmidt, 1899) 3 p.
Dn 1'. *At* Robert Burns. *Pf* solo voc, pno. *Tm Five songs [to] words by Robert
Burns, op. 43* (*WIAM* 1538).

1584 BEACH, Amy Cheney. **Old love-story, An, op. 71, no. 2** (APS
md 8904; Boston: A.P. Schmidt, 1910) 5 p.
Dn 2'. *At* Belle Lowe Stathem. *Pf* solo voc, pno.

1585 BEACH, Amy Cheney. **Prayer of a tired child, op. 75, no. 4**
md (25274; New York: G. Schirmer, 1914) 5 p.
Dn 2'. *At* Abbie Farwell Brown. *Pf* solo voc, pno.

1586 BEACH, Amy Cheney. **Prelude, A, op. 71, no. 1** (APS 8901;
md Boston: A.P. Schmidt, 1910) 5 p.
Dn 1'. *At* composer. *Pf* solo voc, pno.

1587 BEACH, Amy Cheney. **Rainy day, The** (49478; Boston: O.
mm Ditson, 1883) 5 p.
Dn 2'. *Da* Christmas 1880. *La* MBNe. *At* Longfellow. *Pf* solo voc, pno. *Rg*
DLC, Recorded Sound Section.

1588 BEACH, Amy Cheney. **Rendezvous, op. 120** (76314; Boston:
mm O. Ditson, 1928) 13 p. (score, part).
Dn 3'. *At* Leonora Speyer. *Pf* solo voc, pno, vln obbligato.

1589 BEACH, Amy Cheney. **Scottish cradle song, op. 43, no. 2**
md (APS 5041; Boston: A.P. Schmidt, 1899) 3 p.
Dn 1'. *At* Robert Burns. *Pf* solo voc, pno. *Tm Five songs [to] words by Robert
Burns, op. 43* (*WIAM* 1538).

1590 BEACH, Amy Cheney. **Sea song, op. 10, no. 3** (APS 2713;
md Boston: A.P. Schmidt, 1890) 9 p.
Dn 2'. *At* William Ellery Channing. *Pf* solo SS, pno. *Tm Songs of the sea, op. 10*
(*WIAM* 1599).

1591 BEACH, Amy Cheney. **Secret, Le (The secret), op. 14, no. 2**
md (APS 5522; Boston: A.P. Schmidt, 1901) 7 p.
Dn 4'. *La* DLC, Schmidt Collection. *At* Jules de Resseguier. *Lt* French, English.
Pf solo voc, pno. Also in her *Song album* [A] (*WIAM* 1596) and *Song album* [B]
(*WIAM* 1597).

1592 BEACH, Amy Cheney. **Separation, op. 76, no. 1** (25275; New
md York: G. Schirmer, 1914) 6 p.
Dn 1'. *At* John L. Stoddard. *Pf* solo voc, pno. The composer's *Bonum est,
confiteri* (*WIAM* 1292) is also numbered op. 76, no. 1.

1593 BEACH, Amy Cheney. **Shena Van, op. 56, no. 4** (APS 6444;
md   Boston: A.P. Schmidt, 1904) 5 p.
Dn 1′. *La* DLC, Schmidt Collection. *At* William Black. *St Yolande. Pf* solo voc,
pno. Also with vln obbligato (APS 11784; Schmidt, 1919), and arranged for
choral SATB, pno; choral TTBB, pno; and choral SSA, pno (*WIAM* 1333).

1594 BEACH, Amy Cheney. **Singer, The, op. 117, no. 1** (18896;
md   Cincinnati: J. Church, 1925) 5 p.
Dn 1′. *At* Muna Lee. *St Sea change. Pf* solo voc, pno.

1595 BEACH, Amy Cheney. **Sleep, little darling, op. 29, no. 3**
md   (APS 3750; Boston: A.P. Schmidt, 1895) 7 p.
Dn 3′. *At* Harriet Prescott Spofford. *Pf* solo voc, pno.

1596 BEACH, Amy Cheney. **Song album [A]. A cyclus of fourteen
ma   selected songs.** *Edition Schmidt* 23 (APS 1066/3085; Boston: A.P.
Schmidt, 1886) 59 p.
Pf solo voc, pno. *Ct Ariette, op. 1, no. 4* (*WIAM* 1515), *Dark is the night, op. 11,
no. 1* (*WIAM* 1526), *The western wind, op. 11, no. 2* (*WIAM* 1613), *The
blackbird, op. 11, no. 3* (*WIAM* 1520), *Empress of night, op. 2, no. 3* (*WIAM*
1532), *Le secret, op. 14, no. 2* (*WIAM* 1591), *Sweetheart, sigh no more, op. 14,
no. 3* (*WIAM* 1604), *The summerwind, op. 14, no. 1* (*La* DLC, Schmidt
Collection, *At* Walter Learned), *Hymn of trust, op. 13* (*WIAM* 1553), *The
thrush, op. 14, no. 4* (*La* DLC, Schmidt Collection, *At* E.R. Sill), *Wilt thou be
my dearie, op. 12, no. 1* (*La* DLC, Schmidt Collection, *At* Robert Burns), *Ye
banks and braes o' bonnie Doon, op. 12, no. 2* (*La* DLC, Schmidt Collection, *At*
Robert Burns), *Just for this, op. 26, no. 2* (*WIAM* 1567), *Ecstasy, op. 19, no. 2*
(*WIAM* 1529).

1597 BEACH, Amy Cheney. **Song album [B]. A cyclus of thirteen
ma   selected songs** (APS 1066/2809; Boston: A.P. Schmidt, 1891) 57
p.
Pf solo voc, pno. *Ct Ariette, op. 1, no. 4* (*WIAM* 1515), *Dark is the night, op. 11,
no. 1* (*WIAM* 1526), *The western wind, op. 11, no. 2* (*WIAM* 1613), *The
blackbird, op. 11, no. 3* (*WIAM* 1520), *Empress of night, op. 2, no. 3* (*WIAM*
1532), *Le secret, op. 14, no. 2* (*WIAM* 1591), *Sweetheart, sigh no more, op. 14,
no. 3* (*WIAM* 1604), *The summerwind, op. 14, no. 1* (*La* DLC, Schmidt
Collection, *At* Walter Learned), *Hymn of trust, op. 13* (*WIAM* 1553), *The
thrush, op. 14, no. 4* (*La* DLC, Schmidt Collection, *At* E.R. Sill), *Wilt thou be
my dearie, op. 12, no. 1* (*La* DLC, Schmidt Collection, *At* Robert Burns), *Ye
banks and braes o' bonnie Doon, op. 12, no. 2* (*La* DLC, Schmidt Collection, *At*
Robert Burns), *My luve is like a red, red rose, op. 12, no. 3* (*WIAM* 1576).

1598 BEACH, Amy Cheney. **Song in the hills, op. 117, no. 3**
md   (18897; Cincinnati: J. Church, 1925) 2 p.
Dn 1′. *At* Muna Lee. *Pf* solo voc, pno.

1599 BEACH, Amy Cheney. **Songs of the sea, op. 10, nos. 1-3**
mm   (APS 2711-2713; Boston: A.P. Schmidt, 1890) 9, 9, 9 p.
Dn 6′. *Pf* no. 1 for solo SBar, pno; nos. 2-3 for solo SS, pno. *Ct A Canadian
boat song* (*WIAM* 1521), *The night sea* (*WIAM* 1579), *Sea song* (*WIAM* 1590).

1600 BEACH, Amy Cheney. **Spirit divine, op. 88** (18101; Philadel-
mm   phia: T. Presser, 1922) 6 p.
Sacred duet. *Dn* 1′. *At* Andrew Read. *Pf* solo SA, org.

1601 BEACH, Amy Cheney. **Spirit of mercy, op. 125, no. 1** (APS
md   14483; Boston: A.P. Schmidt, 1930) 6 p.
Sacred song. *Dn* 2′. *La* DLC, Schmidt Collection. *Pf* solo voc, org.

1602 BEACH, Amy Cheney. **Spring, op. 26, no. 3** (APS 3388;
md   Boston: A.P. Schmidt, 1894) 5 p.
Dn 2′. *At* Cora Fabbri. *Pf* solo voc, pno.

1603 BEACH, Amy Cheney. **Springtime, op. 124** (34664; New York:
mm   G. Schirmer, 1929) 5 p.
Dn 1′. *At* Susan Merrick Heywood. *Pf* solo voc, pno.

1604 BEACH, Amy Cheney. **Sweetheart, sigh no more, op. 14, no.
md   3** (APS 2803; Boston: A.P. Schmidt, 1891) 3 p.
Dn 2′. *At* Thomas Bailey Aldrich. *La* DLC, Schmidt Collection. *Pf* solo voc,
pno. Also in her *Song album [A]* (*WIAM* 1596), *Song album [B]* (*WIAM* 1597),
and in a revised version (APS 5523; Schmidt, 1901).

1605 BEACH, Amy Cheney. **Take, o take those lips away, op. 37,
md   no. 2** (APS 4409; Boston: A.P. Schmidt, 1897) 5 p.
Dn 1′. *At* Shakespeare. *Pf* solo voc, pno. *Tm Three Shakespeare songs, op. 37*
(*WIAM* 1608).

1606 BEACH, Amy Cheney. **Thanksgiving fable, A, op. 75, no. 2**
md   (25272; New York: G. Schirmer, 1914) 5 p.
Dn 1′. *At* Oliver Herford. *Pf* solo voc, pno.

1607 BEACH, Amy Cheney. **Three Browning songs, op. 44, nos.
mm   1-3** (APS 5137, 5139-5140; Boston: A.P. Schmidt, 1900) 5, 5, 7 p.
Dn 8′. *Pf* solo voc, pno. *Ct The year's at the spring* (*WIAM* 1623), *Ah, love, but
a day!* (*WIAM* 1511), *I send my heart up to thee* (*WIAM* 1556).

1608 BEACH, Amy Cheney. **Three Shakespeare songs, op. 37,
mm   nos. 1-3** (APS 4408-4410; Boston: A.P. Schmidt, 1897) 7, 5, 5 p.
Dn 6′. *Pf* solo voc, pno. *Ct O mistress mine* (*WIAM* 1581), *Take, o take those
lips away* (*WIAM* 1605), *Fairy lullaby* (*WIAM* 1535).

1609 BEACH, Amy Cheney. **Thy beauty, op. 41, no. 2** (APS 4677;
md   Boston: A.P. Schmidt, 1898) 5 p.
Dn 2′. *At* Harriet Prescott Spofford. *Pf* solo voc, pno.

1610 BEACH, Amy Cheney. **Totenkranz, Der (The child's
md   thanks), op. 73, no. 2** (25165; New York: G. Schirmer, 1914) 5 p.
Dn 2′. *At* Louis Zacharias. *Tr* John Bernhoff. *Lt* German, English. *Pf* solo voc,
pno.

1611 BEACH, Amy Cheney. **Twilight, op. 2, no. 1** (APS 1300;
md   Boston: A.P. Schmidt, 1887) 5 p.
Dn 4′. *At* composer. *Pf* solo voc, pno.

1612 BEACH, Amy Cheney. **Wandering knight, The, op. 29, no. 2**
md   (APS 3748; Boston: A.P. Schmidt, 1895) 5 p.
Dn 2′. *Tr* J.G. Lockhart. *Pf* solo voc, pno.

1613 BEACH, Amy Cheney. **Western wind, The, op. 11, no. 2** (APS
md   2067; Boston: A.P. Schmidt, 1889) 4 p.
Dn 2′. *At* William Ernest Henley. *Pf* solo voc, pno. Also in her *Song album [A]*
(*WIAM* 1596) and *Song album [B]* (*WIAM* 1597). *Rg* DLC, Recorded Sound
Section.

1614 BEACH, Amy Cheney. **When far from her, op. 2, no. 2** (APS
md   1931; Boston: A.P. Schmidt, 1889) 5 p.
Dn 1′. *At* Henry Harris Aubrey Beach. *Pf* solo voc, pno.

1615 BEACH, Amy Cheney. **When mama sings, op. 99, no. 1**
md   (18584; Philadelphia: T. Presser, 1923) 5 p.
Dn 1′. *At* composer. *Pf* solo voc, pno.

1616 BEACH, Amy Cheney. **When soul is joined to soul, op. 62**
mm   (APS 6952; Boston: A.P. Schmidt, 1905) 7 p.
Dn 2′. *At* Elizabeth Barrett Browning. *Pf* solo voc, pno. Dedicated to Emma
Eames.

1617 BEACH, Amy Cheney. **Wind o' the westland, op. 77, no. 2**
md   (26965; New York: G. Schirmer, 1916) 6 p.
Dn 2′. *At* Dana Burnett. *Pf* solo voc, pno.

1618 BEACH, Amy Cheney. **Wir drei (We three), op. 51, no. 2**
md   (APS 5984; Boston: A.P. Schmidt, 1903) 7 p.
Dn 3′. *At* Hans Eschelbach. *Tr* Isadora Martinez. *Lt* German, English. *Pf* solo
voc, pno.

1619 BEACH, Amy Cheney. **With thee (Nähe des Geliebten), op.
md   35, no. 3** (APS 4281; Boston: A.P. Schmidt, 1897) 7 p.
Dn 3′. *La* DLC, Schmidt Collection. *At* Goethe. *Lt* German, English. *Pf* solo
voc, pno.

1620 BEACH, Amy Cheney. **With violets, op. 1, no. 1** (APS 300;
md   Boston: A.P. Schmidt, 1885) 5 p.
Dn 1′. *At* Kate Vannah. *Pf* solo voc, pno.

1621 BEACH, Amy Cheney. **Within thy heart, op. 29, no. 1** (APS
md   3746; Boston: A.P. Schmidt, 1885) 5 p.
Dn 2′. *Pf* solo voc, pno.

1622 BEACH, Amy Cheney. **Wouldn't that be queer, op. 26, no. 4**
md   (APS 3389; Boston: A.P. Schmidt, 1894) 7 p.
Dn 3′. *At* Elsie J. Cooley. *Pf* solo voc, pno. Also arranged for choral SSA, pno
(*WIAM* 1345).

1623 BEACH, Amy Cheney. **Year's at the spring, The, op. 44, no.**
md **1** (WM 9271; Cincinnati: Willis Music, n.d.) 4 p.
Dn 1'. *At* Robert Browning. *St Pippa passes. Pf* solo voc, pno. *Tm Three Browning songs, op. 44* (*WIAM* 1607). Previously published in 1928 (APS 14732; Boston: A.P. Schmidt). Also with vln obbligato (APS 11730; Schmidt, 1919), and arranged for choral SSAA, pno; choral SATB, pno; and choral TTBB, pno (*WIAM* 1346). *Rg When I have sung my songs*, New World, NW 247; Victor 87026, 88008.

1624 CURTIS-BURLIN, Natalie. **Songs from** *A child's garden of*
mc *verses, The Wa-Wan Press.* Ed. by Vera Brodsky LAWRENCE (New York: Arno & New York Times, 1970) I, 160-75.
Dn 8'. *At* Robert Louis Stevenson. *St A child's garden of verses. Pf* solo voc, pno. *Ct* Time to rise, Rain, The wind, At the seashore, The swing system, Farewell to the farm. Previously published in 1902 (Newton Center, Mass.: Wa-Wan).

1625 DILLON, Fannie Charles. **April day, An** (New York: Handy
mm Brothers, 1949) 5 p.
Dn 1'. *At* Joseph F. Cotter. *Pf* solo voc, pno.

1626 DILLON, Fannie Charles. **Message of the bells, op. 38** (Los
mm Angeles: C.R. Foster, 1917) 5 p.
Dn 10'. *At* Carlton Russell Foster. *Pf* solo voc, pno.   *(Joan Meggett)*

1627 FOSTER, Fay. **Americans come, The** (JF&B 4527; New York:
mm J. Fischer, 1918) 7 p.
Dn 2'. *At* Elizabeth A. Wilbur. *Pf* solo voc, pno.

1628 FREER, Eleanor Everest. **Advent of spring** (Chicago: National
mm Music, 1941) 2 p.
Dn 1'. *At* Andreas Bard. *Pf* solo voc, pno.

1629 FREER, Eleanor Everest. **Apparitions, op. 9, no. 2** (Milwau-
md kee: W.A. Kaun Music, 1906) 5 p.
Dn 1'. *At* Robert Browning. *Pf* solo voc, pno.

1630 FREER, Eleanor Everest. **Arachne, op. 21, no. 3** (n.p.:
md composer, 1927) 5 p.
Dn 1'. *La* DLC. *At* composer. *Pf* solo voc, pno.

1631 FREER, Eleanor Everest. **August night, op. 12, no. 5** (Mil-
md waukee: W.A. Kaun Music, 1907) 7 p.
Dn 3'. *At* Hester Bancroft. *Pf* solo voc, pno.

1632 FREER, Eleanor Everest. **Be true, op. 4, no. 5** (Milwaukee:
md W.A. Kaun Music, 1905) [3] p.
Dn 1'. *At* Horatius Bonar. *Pf* solo voc, pno. *Tm A book of songs, op. 4* (*WIAM* 1634). Also for choral SATB, pno in her *Part-songs* (*WIAM* 1348).

1633 FREER, Eleanor Everest. **Boat is chafing at our long delay,**
md **The, op. 16, no. 1** (Milwaukee: W.A. Kaun Music, 1909) 3-4.
Dn 1'. *La* DLC. *At* John Davidson. *Pf* solo voc, pno. Bound with *Daughter of Egypt, veil thine eyes!, op. 16, no. 2* (*WIAM* 1642). Also in her *Favorite songs* (*WIAM* 1653).

1634 FREER, Eleanor Everest. **Book of songs, A, op. 4, nos. 1-9**
mm (Milwaukee: W.A. Kaun Music, 1905) 31 p.
Dn 11'. *Pf* solo voc, pno. *Ct* Cradle song (*At* Blake), My star (*At* Robert Browning), When is life's youth (*WIAM* 1707), Like a shooting star (*WIAM* 1705), Be true (*WIAM* 1632), Song (*At* Thomas Hood), Daybreak (*At* Donne), Cherry ripe (*At* Robert Herrick), Time of roses (*At* Thomas Hood).

1635 FREER, Eleanor Everest. **Carol, A, op. 21, no. 2** (Cincinnati:
md Willis Music, 1912) 3 p.
Dn 1'. *La* DLC. *At* composer. *Pf* solo voc, pno. Also in her *Favorite songs* (*WIAM* 1653), and for choral SATB, pno in her *Part-songs* (*WIAM* 1348).

1636 FREER, Eleanor Everest. **Child's quest, The, op. 27, no. 2**
md (1604; Chicago: C.F. Summy, 1915) 6 p.
Dn 1'. *La* DLC. *At* Frances Shaw. *Pf* solo voc, pno. Also in her *Favorite songs* (*WIAM* 1653).

1637 FREER, Eleanor Everest. **Cobra, op. 40, no. 3. The serpent's**
md **story** (Chicago: Music Library, 1935) 7 p.
Dn 3'. *At* Gita Orlova. *Pf* solo voc, pno. Instructions for performance state that should the poem be used for recitation 1) the vocal part can be played by cello, clarinet, or another suitable instrument, or 2) only the piano part need be used.

1638 FREER, Eleanor Everest. **Constant lover, The, op. 9, no. 4**
md (Milwaukee: W.A. Kaun Music, 1906) 5 p.
Dn 1'. *At* John Suckling. *Pf* solo voc, pno.

1639 FREER, Eleanor Everest. **Cup, The, op. 41, no. 10** (Chicago:
md Music Library, 1936) 3 p.
Dn 1'. *At* George Steele Seymour. *Pf* solo voc, pno.

1640 FREER, Eleanor Everest. **Dancers, The, op. 12, no. 2** (Mil-
md waukee: W.A. Kaun Music, 1906) 5 p.
Dn 1'. *At* Michael Field. *Pf* solo voc, pno.

1641 FREER, Eleanor Everest. **Dancing girl, A, op. 40, no. 6**
md (Chicago: Music Library, 1935) 3 p.
Dn 1'. *At* Frances Sargent Locke Osgood. *Pf* solo voc, pno.

1642 FREER, Eleanor Everest. **Daughter of Egypt, veil thine eyes!,**
md **op. 16, no. 2** (Milwaukee: W.A. Kaun Music, 1909) 5-7.
Dn 2'. *La* DLC. *At* Bayard Taylor. *Pf* solo voc, pno. Bound with *The boat is chafing at our long delay, op. 16, no. 1* (*WIAM* 1633). Also in her *Favorite songs* (*WIAM* 1653).

1643 FREER, Eleanor Everest. **Dear, wert thou less than all the**
md **world to me, op. 41, no. 7** (Chicago: Music Library, 1936) 3 p.
Dn 1'. *At* G.A. Hawkins-Ambler. *Pf* solo voc, pno.

1644 FREER, Eleanor Everest. **Devout lover, A, op. 25, no. 3** (New
md York: Church, Paxon, 1912) 5 p.
Dn 1'. *La* DLC. *At* Thomas Randolph. *Pf* solo voc, pno. Also in her *Favorite songs* (*WIAM* 1653).

1645 FREER, Eleanor Everest. **Dream caress, op. 51, no. 1**
md (Chicago: Musical Works, 1942) 2 p.
Dn 1'. *At* George Burt Lake. *Pf* solo voc, pno.

1646 FREER, Eleanor Everest. **Drifting down the river, op. 40, no.**
md **8** (Chicago: Music Library, 1935) 3 p.
Dn 1'. *At* B.H.W. *Pf* solo voc, pno.

1647 FREER, Eleanor Everest. **During music, op. 20, no. 2** (2435;
md Cincinnati: Willis Music, 1913) 5 p.
Dn 1'. *At* Arthur Symons. *Pf* solo voc, pno.

1648 FREER, Eleanor Everest. **Etude réaliste, op. 27, no. 8** (n.p.:
md composer, 1921) 6 p.
Dn 5'. *La* DLC. *At* Swinburne. *Pf* solo voc, pno. Also for choral SATB, pno in her *Part-songs* (*WIAM* 1348).

1649 FREER, Eleanor Everest. **Evening song, op. 20, no. 3** (Mil-
md waukee: W.A. Kaun Music, 1907) 5 p.
Dn 2'. *At* Sidney Lanier. *Pf* solo voc, pno. Dedicated to Ernestine Schumann-Heink.

1650 FREER, Eleanor Everest. **Faith, op. 12, no. 1** (Milwaukee:
md W.A. Kaun Music, 1906) 5 p.
Dn 1'. *At* Frances Anne Kemble. *Pf* solo voc, pno. Also for choral SATB, pno in her *Part-songs* (*WIAM* 1348).

1651 FREER, Eleanor Everest. **Farewell, A, op. 21, no. 5** (Cincin-
md nati: Willis Music, 1912) 3 p.
Dn 1'. *La* DLC. *At* Charles Kingsley. *Pf* solo voc, pno. Also in her *Favorite songs* (*WIAM* 1653).

1652 FREER, Eleanor Everest. **Fate's decree, op. 18, no. 3** (New
md York: Church, Paxon, 1912) 5 p.
Dn 2'. *At* Thomas Moore. *Pf* solo voc, pno.

1653 FREER, Eleanor Everest. **Favorite songs.** *Musical compositions*
ma *of Eleanor Everest Freer* 4 (rev. ed.; Milwaukee: W.A. Kaun Music, 1930) 103 p.
Pf solo voc, pno. *Ct* Sweet and twenty, op. 25, no. 1 (*WIAM* 1697), To a painter, op. 15, no. 6 (*WIAM* 1700), The child's quest, op. 27, no. 2 (*WIAM* 1636), The old boatman, op. 23, no. 1 (*WIAM* 1678), She is not fair to outward view, op. 14, no. 1 (*WIAM* 1686), I have done, put by the lute, op. 14, no. 2 (*WIAM* 1665), A carol, op. 21, no. 2 (*WIAM* 1635), Jenny kiss'd me, op. 25, no. 2 (*At* Leigh Hunt), A farewell, op. 21, no. 5 (*WIAM* 1651), The boat is chafing at our long delay, op. 16, no. 1 (*WIAM* 1633), Daughter of Egypt, veil thine eyes!, op. 16, no. 2 (*WIAM* 1642), The stealer, op. 27, no. 6 (*WIAM* 1695), The flowers of France, op. 27, no. 3 (*WIAM* 1655), Of the need of drinking, op. 15, no. 5 (*WIAM* 1677),

I fear thy kisses, gentle maiden, op. 24, no. 2 (WIAM 1664), Nay, but you who do not love her, op. 18, no. 4 (WIAM 1673), Old love song, op. 24, no. 1 (WIAM 1679), Golden eyes, op. 15, no. 2 (WIAM 1658), She's somewhere in the sunlight strong, op. 17, no. 1 (WIAM 1689), A devout lover, op. 25, no. 3 (WIAM 1644).

1654 FREER, Eleanor Everest. **Five songs to spring, op. 6, nos. 1-5**
mm   (Milwaukee: W.A. Kaun Music, 1905) 22 p.
Dn 7'. *La* DLC. *Pf* solo voc, pno. *Ct* The eternal spring (*At* Milton), Song in March (*At* William Gilmore Simms), *Song* (*WIAM* 1691), Incipit vita nova (*At* William Morton Payne), An April pastoral (*At* Austin Dobson).

1655 FREER, Eleanor Everest. **Flowers of France, The, op. 27,**
md   **no. 3** (Chicago: C.F. Summy, 1916) 5 p.
Dn 1'. *At* Miguel Zamacoïs. *Tr* A.L. *Pf* solo voc, pno. Also in her *Favorite songs* (*WIAM* 1653).

1656 FREER, Eleanor Everest. **For the freedom of all nations, op.**
md   **27, no. 4** (Chicago: W. Rossiter, 1917) 5 p.
Dn 3'. *La* DLC. *At* composer. *Pf* solo voc, pno.

1657 FREER, Eleanor Everest. **Galloping song, op. 12, no. 3**
md   (Milwaukee: W.A. Kaun Music, 1907) 7 p.
Dn 2'. *At* Sara Hamilton Birchall. *Pf* solo voc, pno.

1658 FREER, Eleanor Everest. **Golden eyes, op. 15, no. 2** (New
md   York: Church, Paxon, 1912) 6 p.
Dn 2'. *At* Rufinus. *Tr* Andrew Lang. *Pf* solo voc, pno. Also in her *Favorite songs* (*WIAM* 1653).

1659 FREER, Eleanor Everest. **Grace for a child, op. 23, no. 2**
md   (1229; Cincinnati: W.H. Willis, 1909) 3 p.
Dn 1'. *La* DLC. *At* Elia W. Peattie. *Pf* solo voc, pno. Also for choral SATB, pno in her *Part-songs* (*WIAM* 1348). Dedicated to Donald Peattie.

1660 FREER, Eleanor Everest. **Greater grand Chicago, A, op. 39,**
md   **no. 1** (Chicago: Music Library, 1927) 5 p.
Song with chorus. *Dn* 2'. *La* DLC. *At* Mary L. Peare Taylor. *Pf* solo S, choral SA, pno.

1661 FREER, Eleanor Everest. **Gundi (With raven hair), op. 41,**
md   **no. 3; Kuni-san (Little waif of far Japan), op. 40, no. 4**
(Chicago: Music Library, 1936) 9 p.
Dn 4'. *At* G.A. Hawkins-Ambler. *Lt* English. *Pf* solo voc, pno.

1662 FREER, Eleanor Everest. **How many times do I love thee,**
md   **dear?, op. 19, no. 4** (1435; Cincinnati: Willis Music, 1910) 7 p.
Dn 1'. *La* DLC. *At* Thomas Lovell Beddoes. *Pf* solo voc, pno.

1663 FREER, Eleanor Everest. **Hymn, op. 27, no. 7** (Chicago: C.F.
md   Summy, 1920) 3 p.
Dn 1'. *At* composer. *Pf* solo voc, pno.

1664 FREER, Eleanor Everest. **I fear thy kisses, gentle maiden (Je**
md   **crains tes baisers, douce femme), op. 24, no. 2** (21.386; Paris:
H. Lemoine, 1920) [2] p.
Dn 1'. *La* DLC. *At* Shelley. *Tr* composer, into French. *Lt* English, French. *Pf* solo voc, pno. Also in her *Favorite songs* (*WIAM* 1653).

1665 FREER, Eleanor Everest. **I have done, put by the lute, op. 14,**
md   **no. 2** (Milwaukee: W.A. Kaun Music, 1907) [3] p.
Dn 1'. *La* DLC. *At* Duncan Campbell Scott. *Pf* solo voc, pno. Also in her *Favorite songs* (*WIAM* 1653).

1666 FREER, Eleanor Everest. **Ideal, The, op. 9, no. 3** (Milwaukee:
md   W.A. Kaun Music, 1906) 5 p.
Dn 1'. *At* Duncan Campbell Scott. *Pf* solo voc, pno.

1667 FREER, Eleanor Everest. **Ishtar's song, op. 34** (Milwaukee:
mm   W.A. Kaun Music, 1927) 7 p.
Dn 2'. *La* DLC. *At* composer. *Pf* solo voc, pno.

1668 FREER, Eleanor Everest. **Love and nature, op. 42, no. 2**
md   (Chicago: Music Library, 1936) 5 p.
Dn 1'. *At* G.A. Hawkins-Ambler. *Pf* solo voc, pno.

1669 FREER, Eleanor Everest. **Love call, A, op. 40, no. 9** (Chicago:
md   Music Library, 1935) 3 p.
Dn 1'. *At* B.H.W. *Pf* solo voc, pno.

1670 FREER, Eleanor Everest. **Love in my heart, o heart of me,**
md   **op. 19, no. 2** (1220; Cincinnati: W.H. Willis, 1909) 5 p.
Dn 2'. *La* DLC. *At* William Sharp. *Pf* solo voc, pno.

1671 FREER, Eleanor Everest. **Music of wings, op. 50** (Chicago:
mm   National Music, 1940) 3 p.
Dn 1'. *At* Francesca Falk Miller. *Pf* solo voc, pno.

1672 FREER, Eleanor Everest. **My garden, op. 10, no. 5** (Milwau-
md   kee: W.A. Kaun Music, 1907) 2 p.
Dn 1'. *At* Thomas Edward Brown. *Pf* solo voc, pno. *Tm* Six songs to nature, op. 10 (*WIAM* 1690). Also for choral SATB, pno in her *Part-songs* (*WIAM* 1348).

1673 FREER, Eleanor Everest. **Nay, but you who do not love her,**
md   **op. 18, no. 4** (New York: Church, Paxon, 1912) 3 p.
Dn 1'. *At* Robert Browning. *Pf* solo voc, pno. Also in her *Favorite songs* (*WIAM* 1653).

1674 FREER, Eleanor Everest. **Night of a thousand stars, op. 41,**
md   **no. 8** (Chicago: Music Library, 1936) 5 p.
Dn 1'. *At* G.A. Hawkins-Ambler. *Pf* solo voc, pno.

1675 FREER, Eleanor Everest. **Nights o' spring, The, op. 29, no. 1**
md   (Milwaukee: W.A. Kaun Music, 1923) 7 p.
Dn 3'. *La* DLC. *At* Bertha Ochsner. *Pf* solo voc, pno.

1676 FREER, Eleanor Everest. **O fly not, pleasure, op. 19, no. 3**
md   (1402; Cincinnati: W.H. Willis, 1910) 5 p.
Dn 2'. *At* Wilfrid Scawen Blunt. *Pf* solo voc, pno.

1677 FREER, Eleanor Everest. **Of the need of drinking, op. 15, no.**
md   **5** (New York: Church, Paxon, 1912) 5 p.
Dn 1'. *At* Anacreon Bourne. *St* Ode XIX. *Pf* solo voc, pno. Also in her *Favorite songs* (*WIAM* 1653).

1678 FREER, Eleanor Everest. **Old boat man, The, op. 23, no. 1**
md   (Cincinnati: W.H. Willis, 1909) 5 p.
Dn 1'. *At* Howard Weeden. *Pf* solo voc, pno. Also in her *Favorite songs* (*WIAM* 1653).

1679 FREER, Eleanor Everest. **Old love song, op. 24, no. 1** (New
md   York: Church, Paxon, 1912) 3 p.
Dn 1'. *At* William Gerard Chapman. *Pf* solo voc, pno. Also in her *Favorite songs* (*WIAM* 1653).

1680 FREER, Eleanor Everest. **Our mother tongue, op. 21, no. 3**
md   (2428; Cincinnati: Willis Music, 1913) 5 p.
Dn 1'. *La* DLC. *At* Richard Monckton Milnes. *Pf* solo voc, pno.

1681 FREER, Eleanor Everest. **Outward bound, op. 24, no. 3**
md   (2432; Cincinnati: Willis Music, 1913) 5 p.
Dn 1'. *La* DLC. *At* Harriet Monroe. *Pf* solo voc, pno.

1682 FREER, Eleanor Everest. **Parted, op. 42, no. 1** (Chicago:
md   Music Library, 1936) 6 p.
Dn 2'. *At* G.A. Hawkins-Ambler. *Pf* solo voc, pno.

1683 FREER, Eleanor Everest. **Promise, A, op. 40, no. 4** (Chicago:
md   Music Library, 1935) 3 p.
Dn 2'. *At* Esther Turkington. *Pf* solo voc, pno.

1684 FREER, Eleanor Everest. **Questions, op. 41, no. 6** (Chicago:
md   Music Library, 1936) 6 p.
Dn 2'. *At* G.A. Hawkins-Ambler. *Pf* solo voc, pno.

1685 FREER, Eleanor Everest. **Rondel, op. 41, no. 10** (Chicago:
md   Music Library, 1936) 6 p.
Dn 2'. *At* Max Vivier. *Tr* composer. *Pf* solo voc, pno.

1686 FREER, Eleanor Everest. **She is not fair to outward view, op.**
md   **14, no. 1** (Milwaukee: W.A. Kaun Music, 1907) [2] p.
Dn 1'. *La* DLC. *At* Hartley Coleridge. *Pf* solo voc, pno. Also in her *Favorite songs* (*WIAM* 1653).

1687 FREER, Eleanor Everest. **Shepherd and a shepherdess, A**
mm   (Chicago: Music Library, 1935) 3 p.
Dn 2'. *At* Gita Orlova. *Pf* solo voc, pno.

1688 FREER, Eleanor Everest. **Shepherdess, The, op. 5, no. 1**
md   (Milwaukee: W.A. Kaun Music, 1905) 5 p.
Dn 2′. *La* DLC. *At* Alice Meynell. *Pf* solo voc, pno.

1689 FREER, Eleanor Everest. **She's somewhere in the sunlight**
md   **strong, op. 17, no. 1** (New York: Church, Paxon, 1912) 5 p.
Dn 2′. *At* Richard Le Gallienne. *Pf* solo voc, pno. Also in her *Favorite songs* (*WIAM* 1653).

1690 FREER, Eleanor Everest. **Six songs to nature, op. 10, nos.**
mm   **1-6** (L19; Milwaukee: W.A. Kaun Music, [1913?]) 20 p.
Dn 6′. *La* DLC. *Pf* solo voc, pno. *Ct* The world beautiful (*At* Milton), Before the rain (*At* Thomas Bailey Aldrich), After the rain (*At* Thomas Bailey Aldrich), The harvest moon (*At* Longfellow), My garden (*WIAM* 1672), To the western wind (*At* Robert Herrick).

1691 FREER, Eleanor Everest. **Song (An April pastoral), op. 6, no.**
md   **3** (Milwaukee: W.A. Kaun Music, 1906) 2 p.
Dn 1′. *At* William Watson. *Pf* solo voc, pno. *Tm Five songs to spring* (*WIAM* 1654). Also for choral SATB, pno in her *Part-songs* (*WIAM* 1348) as An April pastoral.

1692 FREER, Eleanor Everest. **Song cycle, op. 29. nos. 4-6**
md   (Milwaukee: W.A. Kaun Music, 1927) 11 p.
Dn 4′. *La* DLC, no. 6 only. *At* Edith Rockefeller McCormick. *Pf* solo voc, pno. *Ct* How can we know; I write not to thee, dearest; Love.

1693 FREER, Eleanor Everest. **Song of the roses, op. 12, no. 4**
md   (Milwaukee: W.A. Kaun Music, 1907) 7 p.
Dn 1′. *At* Elizabeth Barrett Browning. *St Sappho. Pf* solo voc, pno.

1694 FREER, Eleanor Everest. **Sonnets from the Portuguese, op.**
mm   **22** (Chicago: Music Library, 1939) 171 p.
Song cycle of 44 songs. *Dn* 90′. *At* Elizabeth Barrett Browning. *Tr* composer. *Lt* English, French. *Pf* solo voc, pno.

1695 FREER, Eleanor Everest. **Stealer, The, op. 27, no. 6** (Chicago:
md   C.F. Summy, 1918) 5 p.
Dn 3′. *La* DLC. *At* Lee Nichols. *Pf* solo voc, pno. Also in her *Favorite songs* (*WIAM* 1653).

1696 FREER, Eleanor Everest. **Summer night, op. 12, no. 6**
md   (Milwaukee: W.A. Kaun Music, 1907) 5 p.
Dn 2′. *At* Tennyson. *Pf* solo voc, pno.

1697 FREER, Eleanor Everest. **Sweet and twenty, op. 25, no. 1**
md   (Cincinnati: Willis Music, 1912) 3 p.
Dn 1′. *At* Shakespeare. *Pf* solo voc, pno. Also in her *Favorite songs* (*WIAM* 1653).

1698 FREER, Eleanor Everest. **There is a woman like a dew-drop,**
md   **op. 5, no. 2** (Milwaukee: W.A. Kaun Music, 1905) 7 p.
Dn 2′. *At* Robert Browning. *St A blot on the scutcheon. Pf* solo voc, pno.

1699 FREER, Eleanor Everest. **To a dreamer, op. 27, no. 1** (2430;
md   Cincinnati: Willis Music, 1913) 5 p.
Dn 1′. *La* DLC. *At* Agnes Lee. *Pf* solo voc, pno.

1700 FREER, Eleanor Everest. **To a painter, op. 15, no. 6** (Newton
md   Center, Mass.: Wa-Wan, 1907) 5 p.
Dn 1′. *At* Anacreon-Moore. *St Ode LVII. Pf* solo voc, pno. Also in her *Favorite songs* (*WIAM* 1653).

1701 FREER, Eleanor Everest. **Upon Julia's clothes, op. 40, no. 2**
md   (Chicago: Music Library, 1934) 3 p.
Dn 1′. *At* Robert Herrick. *Pf* solo voc, pno.

1702 FREER, Eleanor Everest. **Vagabond song, A, op. 9, no. 1**
md   (Milwaukee: W.A. Kaun Music, 1906) 5 p.
Dn 1′. *At* Bliss Carman. *Pf* solo voc, pno.

1703 FREER, Eleanor Everest. **Valentine, A, op. 21,** *The Wa-Wan*
mc   *Press.* Ed. by Vera Brodsky LAWRENCE (New York: Arno & The New York Times, 1970) V, 138-39.
Dn 1′. *La* DLC. *At* composer. *Pf* solo voc, pno. Previously published in 1907 (Newton Center, Mass.: Wa-Wan). This piece was not assigned a number within the composer's op. 21.

1704 FREER, Eleanor Everest. **Walls of doubt, op. 27, no. 5**
md   (Chicago: C.F. Summy, 1917) 5 p.
Dn 3′. *At* Lee Nichols. *Pf* solo voc, pno.

1705 FREER, Eleanor Everest. **What is life's youth? and Like a**
md   **shooting star, op. 4, nos. 3-4** (n.p.: composer, 1904) 7 p.
Dn 3′. *Pf* solo voc, pno. *Tm A book of songs, op. 4* (*WIAM* 1634). What is life's youth? also published as When is life's youth? (*WIAM* 1707).

1706 FREER, Eleanor Everest. **When I am dead, my dearest, op.**
md   **19, no. 1** (1186; Cincinnati: W.H. Willis, 1909) 5 p.
Dn 2′. *La* DLC. *At* Christina Georgina Rossetti. *Pf* solo voc, pno.

1707 FREER, Eleanor Everest. **When is life's youth?, op. 4, no. 3**
md   (Milwaukee: W.A. Kaun Music, 1905) [3] p.
Dn 1′. *At* Archibald Freer. *Pf* solo voc, pno. *Tm A book of songs, op. 4* (*WIAM* 1634). Also published as *What is life's youth?* (*WIAM* 1705) and for choral SATB, pno in her *Part-songs* (*WIAM* 1348).

1708 FREER, Eleanor Everest. **Whispering winds, op. 41, no. 5**
md   (Chicago: Music Library, 1936) 7 p.
Dn 1′. *At* G.A. Hawkins-Ambler. *Pf* solo voc, pno.

1709 FREER, Eleanor Everest. **Who has robbed the ocean cave,**
md   **op. 19, no. 5** (1483; Cincinnati: Willis Music, 1911) 5 p.
Dn 2′. *La* DLC. *At* John Shaw. *Pf* solo voc, pno.

1710 FREER, Eleanor Everest. **You, op. 23, no. 3** (1335; Cincinnati:
md   W.H. Willis, 1909) 5 p.
Dn 2′. *At* Agness Greene Foster. *Pf* solo voc, pno.

1711 HOPEKIRK, Helen. **Adieu** (APS 995; Boston: A.P. Schmidt,
mm   1887) 2 p.
Dn 1′. *La* DLC, Schmidt Collection. *At* Mortimer Wheeler. *Pf* solo voc, pno.

1712 HOPEKIRK, Helen. **Blows the wind today** (25333; New York:
mm   G. Schirmer, 1915) 6 p.
Dn 3′. *La* DLC. *At* Robert Louis Stevenson. *Pf* solo voc, pno.

1713 HOPEKIRK, Helen. **Bonnie wee thing, cannie wee thing**
mm   (Boston: O. Ditson, 1897) 5 p.
Dn 1′. *Da* 1888, Vienna. *At* Robert Burns. *Lt* English, German. *Pf* solo voc, pno.

1714 HOPEKIRK, Helen. **Eldorado** (APS 992; Boston: A.P. Schmidt,
mm   1887) 7 p.
Dn 2′. *La* DLC, Schmidt Collection. *At* Mortimer Wheeler. *Pf* solo voc, pno.

1715 HOPEKIRK, Helen. **Five songs** (17003; New York: G.
mm   Schirmer, 1904) 16 p.
Dn 6′. *At* Fiona Macleod. *Pf* solo voc, pno. *Ct* Mo-lennav-a-chree; Hushing song; Eilidh, my fawn (*La* DLC); Thy dark eyes to mine; The bandruidh.

1716 HOPEKIRK, Helen. **Good Shepherd, The** (AEE 433; New
mm   York: J.O. von Procházka, 1886) 3 p.
Sacred song. *Dn* 1′. *At* Helen Hunt Jackson. *Pf* solo voc, pno.

1717 HOPEKIRK, Helen. **Highland baloo (Hochlandisches**
mm   **Wiegenlied)** (Boston: O. Ditson, 1897) 5 p.
Dn 2′. *Da* Feb. 1896, London. *La* DLC. *At* Robert Burns. *Lt* English, German. *Pf* solo voc, pno.

1718 HOPEKIRK, Helen. **Hush-a-by** (956; Boston: O. Ditson, 1905)
mm   3 p.
Dn 1′. *St* Songs of the gael. *Pf* solo voc, pno.

1719 HOPEKIRK, Helen. **Jackie's ta'en the parting kiss** (Boston:
mm   O. Ditson, 1897) 5 p.
Dn 2′. *Da* 1896, London. *At* Robert Burns. *Tr* Johanna von Lössl. *Lt* English, German. *Pf* solo voc, pno.

1720 HOPEKIRK, Helen. **Lament, A** (Boston: O. Ditson, 1897) 5 p.
mm
Dn 1′. *Da* Dec. 1893, Paris. *At* Gabriel Seton Craig. *Tr* Johanna von Lössl. *Lt* English, German. *Pf* solo voc, pno.

1721 HOPEKIRK, Helen. **Love me, love** (APS 1013; Boston: A.P.
mm   Schmidt, 1886) 5 p.

Dn 2'. At Mortimer Wilder. Pf solo voc, pno.

1722 HOPEKIRK, Helen. **Minuet, The** (19574; New York: G.
mm   Schirmer, 1907) 7 p.
Dn 2'. At Mary Mapes Dodge. Pf solo voc, pno.

1723 HOPEKIRK, Helen. **My lady of sleep** (AEE 413; New York:
mm   J.O. von Procházka, 1885) 5 p.
Dn 3'. At M.M. Pf solo voc, pno.

1724 HOPEKIRK, Helen. **O can ye sew cushions** (Boston: O. Ditson,
mm   1897) 5 p.
Dn 2'. Da 1893, London. At Robert Burns. Pf solo voc, pno.

1725 HOPEKIRK, Helen. **O, whistle and I'll come to you my lad**
mm   (Boston: O. Ditson, 1897) 5 p.
Dn 2'. Da Nov. 1893, Paris. At Robert Burns. Tr Johanna von Lössl. Lt
English, German. Pf solo voc, pno.

1726 HOPEKIRK, Helen. **Reconciliation** (25644; New York: G.
mm   Schirmer, 1915) 5 p.
Dn 2'. La DLC. At Whitman. St Leaves of grass. Pf solo voc, pno.

1727 HOPEKIRK, Helen. **Requiescat** (AEE 324; New York: J.O. von
mm   Procházka, 1886) 5 p.
Dn 1'. At Matthew Arnold. Pf solo voc, pno.

1728 HOPEKIRK, Helen. **Rosebud** (APS 1011; Boston: A.P. Schmidt,
mm   1886) 5 p.
Dn 2'. At Mortimer Wilder. Pf solo voc, pno.

1729 HOPEKIRK, Helen. **Six poems by Fiona Macleod** (19567;
mm   New York: G. Schirmer, 1907) 23 p.
Dn 10'. Pf solo voc, pno. Ct From the hills of dream, Oh Bonnie Burdeen, The
lonely hunter, When the dew is falling, St. Bride's lullaby, The bird of Christ.

1730 HOPEKIRK, Helen. **Sleep my babe** (Boston: O. Ditson, 1899) 5
mm   p.
Dn 4'. At Evelyn McAdam. Pf solo voc, pno.

1731 HOPEKIRK, Helen. **Song of the glen dun** (25332; New York:
mm   G. Schirmer, 1915) 7 p.
Dn 3'. La DLC. At Moira O'Neill. Pf solo voc, pno.

1732 HOPEKIRK, Helen. **St. Cecilia** (APS 1012; Boston: A.P.
mm   Schmidt, 1886) 7 p.
Dn 4'. At Mortimer Wheeler. Pf solo voc, pno.

1733 HOPEKIRK, Helen. **Under the still, white stars** (61826;
mm   Boston: O. Ditson, 1899) 9 p. (score, part).
Dn 4'. At Mortimer Wheeler. Pf solo voc, pno, vln obligato.

1734 HOPEKIRK, Helen. **Voice in the night, A** (APS 994; Boston:
mm   A.P. Schmidt, 1887) 5 p.
Dn 3'. La DLC, Schmidt Collection. At Mortimer Wheeler. Pf solo voc, pno.

1735 HOPEKIRK, Helen. **Voice of the mountains, The** (25334;
mm   New York: G. Schirmer, 1915) 7 p.
Dn 3'. La DLC. At Barclay Ritchie. Pf solo voc, pno.

1736 JACOBS-BOND, Carrie. **Eleven small songs. As unpreten-
ma   tious as the wild rose** (Chicago: composer, 1901) 21 p.
Pf solo voc, pno. Ct Where youth's eternal, The lily and the rose (At Louise
Chandler Moulton), 'Tis summer in thine eyes (At Heine), A study in symbols
(At Clarence Urmy), When church is out (St Puck), But I have you, Her greatest
charm, When you're so sad, Sunshine; Po li'l lamb (At Paul Laurence Dunbar),
Cupid's home.

1737 JACOBS-BOND, Carrie. **Eleven songs** (New York: S. Brainard,
ma   1911) 39 p.
Pf solo voc, pno. Ct including copyright dates of individual songs: Who is true
(1897), Until death (At Clifford C. Carleton, 1898), If I could hear your voice
again (1897), Write to me often, dear (1896), Someone I love is coming (1898),
Through the mists (1898), Come, Mr. Dream-maker (At Samuel Minturn Peck,
1897), Mother's cradle song (rev., 1895), June and December (1898), Is my
dolly dead? (1895), The pansy and the forget-me-not (1897).

1738 JACOBS-BOND, Carrie. **Half-minute songs** (Chicago: Bond
ma   Shop, 1910-11) 27 p.
Miniature songs. Dn 6'. Pf solo voc, pno. Ct Making the best of it, First ask
yourself, To understand, How to find success, The pleasure of giving, Answer
the first rap, A good exercise, A present from yourself, Now and then, When
they say unkind things, Keep awake, Doan' yo' lis'n.

1739 JACOBS-BOND, Carrie. **Love and sorrow. Song cycle for
mm   barytone** (Chicago: Bond Shop, 1908) 7 p.
Dn 3'. At Paul Laurence Dunbar. Pf solo Bar, pno. Dedicated to David
Bispham.

1740 JACOBS-BOND, Carrie. **Roses are in bloom** (366; Hollywood,
mm   Calif.: composer, 1926) 7 p.
Dn 2'. At Francesca Falk Miller. Pf solo voc, pno.

1741 JACOBS-BOND, Carrie. **Seven songs. As unpretentious as
ma   the wild rose** (Chicago: composer, 1901) 15, [5] p.
Pf solo voc, pno. Ct Shadows (At composer), Parting (At William Ordway
Partridge), Just a-wearyin' for you (At Frank Stanton), De las' long res' (At
Paul Laurence Dunbar), I love you truly (At composer), Still unexprest (At
composer), Des hold my hand tonight (At composer). A quotation by Elbert
Hubbard, a list of Jacobs-Bond's compositions, and 3 poems by the composer-
-Talkin' about little things, Two hard days for mother, and The path o'life--are
included.

1742 JACOBS-BOND, Carrie. **Smile songs, The** (Chicago: P.F.
ma   Volland, 1910) [12] p.
Pf solo voc, pno. At composer. Ct Mother mine, Why, Stop and sing, The good
folk, Please, Almost impossible, Look up, Know and find, A memory, There is a
way, Smile a little, The way of the world. Each song is a few measures long on
a separate page and is hand-decorated with floral designs in color. A final note
reads "The smile songs are published singly so that you can buy one or a dozen
at a time. They are also framed separately in Circassian walnut".

1743 JACOBS-BOND, Carrie. **Songs everybody sings** (B 376;
ma   Boston: C. Jacobs-Bond & Son, 1906) 96 p.
Pf solo voc, pno. Ct I love you truly (At composer), In the meadow (At
composer), Just lonesome (At Harriet Axtell Johnstone), Just a-wearyin' for you
(At Frank Stanton), Shadows (At composer), A song of the hills (At composer),
Through the years (At composer), Until God's day (At Frank Stanton), A
perfect day (At J.P. McEvoy), A study in symbols (At Clarence Urmy), The
golden key (At composer), The hand of you, Good night (At Clarence Ousley),
His lullaby (At Robert Healy), Hush-a-by (At W. Dayton Wegefarth), A little
pink rose (At composer), Birds (At Moira O'Neill), The forget-me-not, God
remembers when the world forgets (At Clifton Bingham), Lazy river (At
composer), Were I (At Nan Terrell Reed), I've done my work (At George W.
Caldwell), When God puts out the light, A little bit o' honey (At W.G. Wilson),
Her greatest charm, Is yo'? Yo' is (At Marjorie Benton Cooke), The sandman
(At Mary White Slater), When church is out (St Puck), Life's garden (At Fred
Jacobs Smith), O time! take me back. An introduction to the collection contains
a short biographical sketch of the composer together with photographs of
Jacobs-Bond and her house and gardens in California.

1744 JACOBS-BOND, Carrie. **Ten songs. As unpretentious as the
ma   wild rose** (Chicago: F.J. Smith, 1905) 27 p.
Pf solo voc, pno. Ct My dearest dear, Good night (At Clarence Ousley), In a
foreign land, The gate of tears (At Mme. Duclaux), Man and woman (At
Wilbur Dick Nesbit), Just by laughing, Just lonesome (At Harriet Axtell
Johnstone), May I print a kiss? When do I want you most? Where to build your
castles.

1745 JACOBS-BOND, Carrie. **Three songs. As unpretentious as
ma   the wild rose** (Chicago: composer, 1904) 11 p.
Dn 4'. Pf solo voc, pno. Ct Nothing but a wild rose, Walking in her garden,
The angelus.

1746 JACOBS-BOND, Carrie. **Twelve songs** (Chicago: composer,
ma   1902) 36 p.
Pf solo voc, pno. Ct When I bid the world goodnight (At Cathcart Bronson, St
Soul immortal), Time makes all but love the past (At composer), Linger not,
Until God's day (At Frank Stanton), Love's sacred trust, Over hills and fields of
daisies (At composer), When I am dead, my dearest (At Christina Georgina
Rossetti), The dear Auf-Wiedersehn (At Grace Duffie Boylan), A bad dream (At
Juliet Wilbur Tomkins), I was dreaming--maybe, The bird song, Mother's three
ages of man (At composer).

1747 LANG, Margaret Ruthven. **April weather, op. 15, no. 3** (APS
md   2925; Boston: A.P. Schmidt, 1893) 5 p.
Dn 2'. La DLC. At Lizette Woodworth Reese. Pf solo voc, pno.

1748 LANG, Margaret Ruthven. **Arcadie, op. 28, no. 2** (APS 4734;
md   Boston: A.P. Schmidt, 1898) 5 p.
Dn 2′. *La* DLC, Schmidt Collection. *At* Arthur Willis Colton. *Pf* solo voc, pno.

1749 LANG, Margaret Ruthven. **Ay de mi** (1078; New York: G.
mm   Schirmer, 1893) 3 p.
Dn 1′. *At* George Eliot. *St* Spanish gypsy. *Pf* solo voc, pno.

1750 LANG, Margaret Ruthven. **Bedtime song, A, op. 6, no. 2**
md   (APS 2797; Boston: A.P. Schmidt, 1891) 5 p.
Dn 3′. *La* DLC, Schmidt Collection. *At* Eugene Field. *Pf* solo voc, pno. Also in
her *Songs* (*WIAM* 1821).

1751 LANG, Margaret Ruthven. **Before my lady's window, op. 19,**
md   **no. 4** (APS 3506; Boston: A.P. Schmidt, 1894) 5 p.
Dn 1′. *At* John Addington Symonds. *Pf* solo voc, pno. *Rg* DLC, Recorded
Sound Section.

1752 LANG, Margaret Ruthven. **Betrayed, op. 9, no. 4** (APS 2867;
md   Boston: A.P. Schmidt, 1892) 5 p.
Dn 2′. *At* Lizette Woodworth Reese. *Pf* solo voc, pno. Also in her *Songs*
(*WIAM* 1821). *Rg* DLC, Recorded Sound Section.

1753 LANG, Margaret Ruthven. **Bird, The, op. 40, no. 3** (APS
md   6334; Boston: A.P. Schmidt, 1904) 7 p.
Dn 2′. *La* DLC, Schmidt Collection. *At* Charles Kingsley. *Pf* solo voc, pno.

1754 LANG, Margaret Ruthven. **Bonnie Bessie Lee, op. 20, no. 1**
md   (APS 3519; Boston: A.P. Schmidt, 1895) 5 p.
Dn 2′. *At* Robert Nicoll. *Pf* solo voc, pno.

1755 LANG, Margaret Ruthven. **Chimes, op. 54, no. 2** (APS 10579;
md   Boston: A.P. Schmidt, 1915) 5 p.
Dn 1′. *La* DLC. *At* Alice Meynell. *St* Collected poems. *Pf* solo voc, pno.

1756 LANG, Margaret Ruthven. **Chinese song, op. 6, no. 1** (APS
md   2796; Boston: A.P. Schmidt, 1891) 5 p.
Dn 1′. *At* Li Tai-pé. *Tr* Stuart Merrill. *Pf* solo voc, pno. *Rg* DLC, Recorded
Sound Section.

1757 LANG, Margaret Ruthven. **Christmas lullaby, op. 8, no. 2**
md   (APS 2862; Boston: A.P. Schmidt, 1892) 5 p.
Dn 2′. *La* DLC, Schmidt Collection. *At* John Addington Symonds. *Pf* solo voc,
pno. *Tm* Three songs of the east, op. 8 (*WIAM* 1831). Also in her *Songs* (*WIAM*
1821).

1758 LANG, Margaret Ruthven. **Cradle song of the war, A, op. 55**
mm   (Boston: O. Ditson, 1916) 5 p.
Dn 2′. *La* DLC. *At* N.S.D. *Pf* solo voc, pno.

1759 LANG, Margaret Ruthven. **Day is gone, op. 40, no. 2** (APS
md   6333; Boston: A.P. Schmidt, 1904) 5 p.
Dn 2′. *At* John Vance Cheney. *St* Evening. *Pf* solo voc, pno.

1760 LANG, Margaret Ruthven. **Dead ship, The, op. 15, no. 3**
md   (APS 2925; Boston: A.P. Schmidt, 1893) 7 p.
Dn 3′. *La* DLC. *At* Lizette Woodworth Reese. *Pf* solo voc, pno.

1761 LANG, Margaret Ruthven. **Dear land of mine (Mein theures**
mm   **Land), op. 16** (APS 2926; Boston: A.P. Schmidt, 1893) 7 p.
Dn 5′. *La* DLC, Schmidt Collection. *At* Rudolf Baumbach. *Lt* German,
English. *Tr* A.M.K. *St* Frau Holde. *Pf* solo voc, pno.

1762 LANG, Margaret Ruthven. **Deserted** (APS 2620; Boston: A.P.
mm   Schmidt, 1890) 5 p.
Dn 2′. *La* DLC, Schmidt Collection. *At* Richard Kendall Munkittrick. *Pf* solo
voc, pno.

1763 LANG, Margaret Ruthven. **Desire, op. 19, no. 5** (APS 3507;
md   Boston: A.P. Schmidt, 1894) 9 p.
Dn 3′. *At* John Addington Symonds. *Pf* solo voc, pno.

1764 LANG, Margaret Ruthven. **Eros** (APS 975; Boston: A.P.
mm   Schmidt, 1889) 2 p.
Dn 1′. *La* DLC, Schmidt Collection. *At* Louise Chandler Moulton. *Pf* solo voc,
pno.

1765 LANG, Margaret Ruthven. **Even psalm, An, op. 46, no. 1**
md   (APS 8365; Boston: A.P. Schmidt, 1909) 5 p.
Dn 4′. *La* DLC, Schmidt Collection. *At* Marguerite Radclyffe-Hall. *St* 'Twixt
earth and stars. *Pf* solo voc, pno.

1766 LANG, Margaret Ruthven. **Garden is a lovesome thing, A,**
md   **op. 50, no. 1** (APS 9864; Boston: A.P. Schmidt, 1912) 5 p.
Dn 1′. *La* DLC, Schmidt Collection. *At* Thomas Edward Brown. *St* Oxford
book of English verse (1908). *Pf* solo voc, pno.

1767 LANG, Margaret Ruthven. **Garden of roses, The, op. 15, no.**
md   **4** (APS 2925; Boston: A.P. Schmidt, 1893) 7 p.
Dn 4′. *La* DLC. *At* F. Marion Crawford. *St* Paul Patoff. *Pf* solo voc, pno.

1768 LANG, Margaret Ruthven. **Ghosts** (APS 1613; Boston: A.P.
mm   Schmidt, 1889) 3 p.
Dn 1′. *At* Richard Kendall Munkittrick. *Pf* solo voc, pno. also in her *Songs*
(*WIAM* 1821) and arranged for choral SSA, pno (*WIAM* 1355). *Rg* DLC,
Recorded Sound Section.

1769 LANG, Margaret Ruthven. **Grandmama's song book for the**
mm   **children, op. 44** (APS 8477; Boston: A.P. Schmidt, 1909) 39 p.
Dn 20′. *St* The daisy and the cowslip (1907). *Pf* solo voc, pno. *Ct* The good girl,
Dancing, The worm, The purloiner, The truant, Come when you are called,
Dressed and undressed, Faithful Pompey, The new book, The beautiful doll,
The greedy boy, The bird-catcher, Look at your copy, Miss Sophia, At church,
Going to school, Dangerous sport, Politeness, Hymn.

1770 LANG, Margaret Ruthven. **Grief of love, The, op. 19, no. 3**
md   (APS 3505; Boston: A.P. Schmidt, 1894) 3 p.
Dn 1′. *At* John Addington Symonds. *Pf* solo voc, pno. *Rg* DLC, Recorded
Sound Section.

1771 LANG, Margaret Ruthven. **Harbor of dreams, The, op. 7,**
md   **no. 3** (APS 2801; Boston: A.P. Schmidt, 1891) 5 p.
Dn 2′. *La* DLC, Schmidt Collection. *At* Frank Dempster Sherman. *Pf* solo voc,
pno. *Tm* Three songs of the night, op. 7 (*WIAM* 1832). Also in her *Songs*
(*WIAM* 1821).

1772 LANG, Margaret Ruthven. **Heliotrope, op. 9, no. 1** (APS
md   2864; Boston: A.P. Schmidt, 1892) 5 p.
Dn 2′. *La* DLC, Schmidt Collection. *At* Frank Dempster Sherman. *Pf* solo voc,
pno.

1773 LANG, Margaret Ruthven. **Hills o' Skye, op. 37, no. 3** (APS
md   5565; Boston: A.P. Schmidt, 1901) 5 p.
Dn 1′. *La* DLC, Schmidt Collection. *At* William McLennan. *Pf* solo voc, pno.

1774 LANG, Margaret Ruthven. **I knew the flowers had dreamed**
mc   **of you,** The world's best music. Ed. by Helen Kendrick JOHNSON
        and Frederic DEAN (New York: U. Soc., 1899) I, 603-05.
Dn 1′. *At* John T. Tabb. *Pf* solo voc, pno. Previously published in 1896 (n.p.:
G.J. Bryan).

1775 LANG, Margaret Ruthven. **In a garden** (APS 2621; Boston:
mm   A.P. Schmidt, 1890) 3 p.
Dn 1′. *La* DLC, Schmidt Collection. *At* Swinburne. *Pf* solo voc, pno. Also in
her *Songs* (*WIAM* 1821).

1776 LANG, Margaret Ruthven. **In the greenwood, op. 19, no. 2**
md   (APS 3504; Boston: A.P. Schmidt, 1894) 5 p.
Dn 2′. *At* John Addington Symonds. *Pf* solo voc, pno. *Rg* DLC, Recorded
Sound Section.

1777 LANG, Margaret Ruthven. **In the twilight** (APS 1614; Boston:
mm   A.P. Schmidt, 1889) 3 p.
Dn 1′. *At* H. Bowman. *Pf* solo voc, pno. Also in her *Songs* (*WIAM* 1821). *Rg*
DLC, Recorded Sound Section.

1778 LANG, Margaret Ruthven. **Into my heart, op. 54, no. 1** (APS
md   10571; Boston: A.P. Schmidt, 1915) 5 p.
Dn 2′. *La* DLC. *At* A.E. Housman. *St* A Shropshire lad. *Pf* solo voc, pno.

1779 LANG, Margaret Ruthven. **Irish love song, op. 22** (APS
mm   10351; Boston: A.P. Schmidt, 1895) 5 p.
Dn 1′. *Pf* solo voc, pno. *Rg* Victor 64195, Brunswick 5129, Victrola 87022;
DLC, Recorded Sound Section.

1780 LANG, Margaret Ruthven. **Irish mother's lullaby, An, op. 34**
mm (APS 5189; Boston: A.P. Schmidt, 1900) 6 p.
Dn 1'. *La* DLC, Schmidt Collection. *At* Mary Elizabeth Blake. *Pf* solo voc, pno.
A note from Schmidt indicates the song was also published with violin obbligato. *Rg* DLC, Recorded Sound Section.

1781 LANG, Margaret Ruthven. **Jock O'Hazeldean, op. 20, no. 6**
md (APS 3524; Boston: A.P. Schmidt, 1895) 3 p.
Dn 2'. *At* Sir Walter Scott. *Pf* solo voc, pno.

1782 LANG, Margaret Ruthven. **King is dead, The, op. 27** (APS
mm 4577; Boston: A.P. Schmidt, 1898) 5 p.
Dn 2'. *At* Mme. Darmesteter. *Pf* solo voc, pno.

1783 LANG, Margaret Ruthven. **King Olaf's lilies, op. 15, no. 1**
md (APS 2925; Boston: A.P. Schmidt, 1893) 6 p.
Dn 3'. *La* DLC. *At* Lizette Woodworth Reese. *Pf* solo voc, pno.

1784 LANG, Margaret Ruthven. **Lament, op. 6, no. 3** (APS 2798;
md Boston: A.P. Schmidt, 1891) 5 p.
Dn 2'. *La* DLC, Schmidt Collection. *At* S. Galler (1525). *Lt* French, English. *Pf* solo voc, pno. Also in her *Songs* (*WIAM* 1821). *Rg* DLC, Recorded Sound Section.

1785 LANG, Margaret Ruthven. **Love is everywhere, op. 40, no. 4**
md (APS 6335; Boston: A.P. Schmidt, 1904) 7 p.
Dn 2'. *La* DLC, Schmidt Collection. *At* John Vance Cheney. *Pf* solo voc, pno.

1786 LANG, Margaret Ruthven. **Love's fear, op. 20, no. 4** (APS
md 3522; Boston: A.P. Schmidt, 1895) 3 p.
Dn 2'. *At* Robert Tannahill. *Pf* solo voc, pno.

1787 LANG, Margaret Ruthven. **Lydia, op. 32, no. 2** (13168;
md Cincinnati: J. Church, 1899) 7 p.
Dn 2'. *At* Lizette Woodworth Reese. *Pf* solo voc, pno.

1788 LANG, Margaret Ruthven. **Maggie away, op. 20, no. 3** (APS
md 3521; Boston: A.P. Schmidt, 1895) 3 p.
Dn 1'. *At* James Hogg. *Pf* solo voc, pno.

1789 LANG, Margaret Ruthven. **Meg Merriles** (APS 2619; Boston:
mm A.P. Schmidt, 1890) 3 p.
Dn 1'. *La* DLC, Schmidt Collection. *At* Keats. *Pf* solo voc, pno.

1790 LANG, Margaret Ruthven. **Menie, op. 20, no. 5** (APS 3523;
md Boston: A.P. Schmidt, 1895) 3 p.
Dn 1'. *At* Robert Nicoll. *Pf* solo voc, pno.

1791 LANG, Margaret Ruthven. **More nonsense rhymes and**
mm **pictures, op. 43, nos. 1-10** (APS 7556; Boston: A.P. Schmidt, 1907) 35 p.
Songs. *Dn* 10'. *At* Edward Lear. *St Nonsense books. Pf* solo voc, pno. *Ct* The old man of Dumbree, The old man with a beard, The young lady in blue, The old person of Ware, The old person of Rimini, The young lady whose eyes ..., The old person of Jodd, The young lady in white, The young lady of Parma, The old person of Ischia.

1792 LANG, Margaret Ruthven. **My ain dear somebody, op. 20,**
md **no. 2** (APS 3520; Boston: A.P. Schmidt, 1895) 3 p.
Dn 1'. *At* Robert Tannahill. *Pf* solo voc, pno.

1793 LANG, Margaret Ruthven. **My garden, op. 28, no. 3** (APS
md 4735; Boston: A.P. Schmidt, 1898) 5 p.
Dn 2'. *At* Philip Bourke Marston. *Pf* solo voc, pno.

1794 LANG, Margaret Ruthven. **My Lady Jacqueminot** (APS
mm 1610; Boston: A.P. Schmidt, 1889) 5 p.
Dn 2'. *At* Julie M. Lippincott. *Pf* solo voc, pno.

1795 LANG, Margaret Ruthven. **My true love** (1079; New York: G.
mm Schirmer, 1893) 5 p.
Dn 2'. *At* Lizette Woodworth Reese. *Pf* solo voc, pno.

1796 LANG, Margaret Ruthven. **My turtle-dove, op. 19, no. 1**
md (APS 3503; Boston: A.P. Schmidt, 1894) 5 p.
Dn 2'. *At* John Addington Symonds. *Pf* solo voc, pno. *Rg* DLC, Recorded Sound Section.

1797 LANG, Margaret Ruthven. **Nameless pain** (APS 1612; Boston:
mm A.P. Schmidt, 1889) 5 p.
Dn 2'. *At* Thomas Bailey Aldrich. *Pf* solo voc, pno.

1798 LANG, Margaret Ruthven. **Night, op. 7, no. 1** (APS 2799;
md Boston: A.P. Schmidt, 1891) 7 p.
Dn 2'. *La* DLC, Schmidt Collection. *At* Louise Chandler Moulton. *Pf* solo voc, pno. *Tm Three songs of the night, op. 7* (*WIAM* 1832). Also in her *Songs* (*WIAM* 1821). *Rg* DLC, Recorded Sound Section.

1799 LANG, Margaret Ruthven. **Nonsense rhymes and pictures,**
mm **op. 42, nos. 1-12** (APS 6826; Boston: A.P. Schmidt, 1905) 35 p.
Songs. *Dn* 12'. *At* Edward Lear. *St Nonsense books. Pf* solo voc, pno. *Ct* The person of Filey, The old man of Cape Horn, The person of Skye, The old man in the kettle, The old man who said "Hush!", The old man who said "Well!", The old lady of France, The young lady of Lucca, The old man with a gong, The old person of Cassel, The old man in a tree, The lady of Riga.

1800 LANG, Margaret Ruthven. **Northward, op. 37, no. 6** (APS
md 5568; Boston: A.P. Schmidt, 1901) 7 p.
Dn 2'. *At* Henry Copley Greene. *Pf* solo voc, pno.

1801 LANG, Margaret Ruthven. **Oh, what comes over the sea?**
mm (APS 976; Boston: A.P. Schmidt, 1889) 2 p.
Dn 1'. *La* DLC, Schmidt Collection. *At* Christina Georgina Rossetti. *Pf* solo voc, pno.

1802 LANG, Margaret Ruthven. **Ojala** (APS 1611; Boston: A.P.
mm Schmidt, 1889) 2 p.
Dn 1'. *At* George Eliot. *St Spanish gypsy. Pf* solo voc, pno.

1803 LANG, Margaret Ruthven. **On an April apple bough,** *The*
mc *world's best music.* Ed. by Helen Kendrick JOHNSON and Frederic DEAN (New York: U. Soc., 1899) I, 128-30.
Dn 1'. *At* Sylvia. *Pf* solo voc, pno. Previously published in 1895 (n.p.: Bryan & Taylor).

1804 LANG, Margaret Ruthven. **Oriental serenade, op. 8, no. 1**
md (APS 2861; Boston: A.P. Schmidt, 1892) 3 p.
Dn 1'. *La* DLC, Schmidt Collection. *Pf* solo voc, pno. *Tm Three songs of the east, op. 8* (*WIAM* 1831). *Rg* DLC, Recorded Sound Section.

1805 LANG, Margaret Ruthven. **Orpheus, op. 38, no. 1** (APS 5899;
md Boston: A.P. Schmidt, 1902) 6 p.
Dn 2'. *La* DLC, Schmidt Collection. *At* Mrs. Fields. *St Orpheus. Pf* solo voc, pno.

1806 LANG, Margaret Ruthven. **Out of the night, op. 46, no. 3**
md (APS 8367; Boston: A.P. Schmidt, 1909) 5 p.
Dn 2'. *La* DLC, Schmidt Collection. *Pf* solo voc, pno.

1807 LANG, Margaret Ruthven. **Out of the past, op. 37, no. 2**
md (APS 5564; Boston: A.P. Schmidt, 1901) 5 p.
Dn 2'. *La* DLC, Schmidt Collection. *Pf* solo voc, pno.

1808 LANG, Margaret Ruthven. **Poet gazes on the moon, A, op.**
md **8, no. 3** (APS 2863; Boston: A.P. Schmidt, 1892) 5 p.
Dn 2'. *La* DLC, Schmidt Collection. *At* Tang, Jo-su. *Tr* Stuart Merrill. *Pf* solo voc, pno. *Tm Three songs of the east, op. 8* (*WIAM* 1831). Also in her *Songs* (*WIAM* 1821).

1809 LANG, Margaret Ruthven. **Sky-ship, The, op. 9, no. 3** (APS
md 2866; Boston: A.P. Schmidt, 1892) 3 p.
Dn 1'. *At* Frank Dempster Sherman. *Pf* solo voc, pno. *Rg* DLC, Recorded Sound Section.

1810 LANG, Margaret Ruthven. **Sleepy-man, op. 38, no. 2** (APS
md 5900; Boston: A.P. Schmidt, 1902) 7 p.
Dn 2'. *At* Charles George Douglas Roberts. *Pf* solo voc, pno.

1811 LANG, Margaret Ruthven. **Slumber song, op. 7, no. 2** (APS
md 2800; Boston: A.P. Schmidt, 1891) 5 p.
Dn 1'. *La* DLC, Schmidt Collection. *Pf* solo voc, pno. *Tm Three songs of the night, op. 7* (*WIAM* 1832).

1812 LANG, Margaret Ruthven. **Snowflakes, op. 50, no. 3** (APS
md 9691; Boston: A.P. Schmidt, 1912) 7 p.
Dn 3'. *At* John Vance Cheney. *St Lyrics. Pf* solo voc, pno. *Rg* DLC, Recorded Sound Section.

1813 LANG, Margaret Ruthven. **Sometimes, op. 46, no. 2** (APS
md   8366; Boston: A.P. Schmidt, 1909) 3 p.
Dn 1'. *At* Thomas S. Jones. *Pf* solo voc, pno.

1814 LANG, Margaret Ruthven. **Somewhere, op. 40, no. 1** (APS
md   6332; Boston: A.P. Schmidt, 1904) 5 p.
Dn 2'. *At* John Vance Cheney. *Pf* solo voc, pno.

1815 LANG, Margaret Ruthven. **Song for Candlemas, A, op. 28,**
md   **no. 1** (APS 4733; Boston: A.P. Schmidt, 1898) 5 p.
Dn 2'. *At* Lizette Woodworth Reese. *Pf* solo voc, pno.

1816 LANG, Margaret Ruthven. **Song in the songless, op. 38, no.**
md   **4** (APS 5902; Boston: A.P. Schmidt, 1902) 6 p.
Dn 2'. *At* George Meredith. *St* A reading of life. *Pf* solo voc, pno. *Rg* DLC,
Recorded Sound Section.

1817 LANG, Margaret Ruthven. **Song of May, A, op. 32, no. 1**
md   (13167; Cincinnati: J. Church, 1899) 5 p.
Dn 2'. *At* Lizette Woodworth Reese. *Pf* solo voc, pno.

1818 LANG, Margaret Ruthven. **Song of the lilac, A, op. 41** (APS
mm   6621; Boston: A.P. Schmidt, 1904) 7 p.
Dn 4'. *At* Louise Imogen Guiney. *Pf* solo voc, pno. *Rg* DLC, Recorded Sound
Section.

1819 LANG, Margaret Ruthven. **Song of the rival maid (Lied der**
mm   **Nebenbuhlerin)** (APS 1615; Boston: A.P. Schmidt, 1889) 5 p.
Dn 2'. *At* Joseph Victor von Scheffel. *Lt* English, German. *Pf* solo voc, pno.

1820 LANG, Margaret Ruthven. **Song of the Spanish gypsies, A**
md   **(Soleà), op. 50, no. 2** (APS 9690; Boston: A.P. Schmidt, 1912) 3
p.
Dn 1'. *Tr* Alma Strettell. *Pf* solo voc, pno. *Rg* DLC, Recorded Sound Section.

1821 LANG, Margaret Ruthven. **Songs.** *Edition Schmidt* 27 (APS
ma   1613/2867; Boston: A.P. Schmidt, 1893) 35 p.
Pf solo voc, pno. *Ct* Ghosts (*WIAM* 1768), In the twilight (*WIAM* 1777), In a
garden (*WIAM* 1775), A bed-time song, op. 6, no. 2 (*WIAM* 1750), Lament, op.
6, no. 3 (*WIAM* 1784), Night, op. 7, no. 1 (*WIAM* 1798), The harbor of dreams,
op. 7, no. 3 (*WIAM* 1771), Christmas lullaby, op. 8, no. 2 (*WIAM* 1757), A poet
gazes on the moon, op. 8, no. 3 (*WIAM* 1808), Betrayed, op. 9, no. 4 (*WIAM*
1752).

1822 LANG, Margaret Ruthven. **Songs for lovers of children, op.**
mm   **39, nos. 1-8** (APS 6084; Boston: A.P. Schmidt, 1903) 31 p.
Dn 13'. *At* Harriet Fairchild Blodgett. *Pf* solo voc, pno. *Ct* Merry Christmas,
Just because, In the night, Morning, Evening, The sandman, To-morrow, Three
ships.

1823 LANG, Margaret Ruthven. **Span-o'-life, The, op. 38, no. 3**
md   (APS 5901; Boston: A.P. Schmidt, 1902) 7 p.
Dn 3'. *At* William McLennan. *St* The span-o'-life. *Pf* solo voc, pno.

1824 LANG, Margaret Ruthven. **Spinning song, op. 15, no. 2** (APS
md   2925; Boston: A.P. Schmidt, 1893) 5 p.
Dn 2'. *La* DLC. *At* H.P. Kimball. *Pf* solo voc, pno.

1825 LANG, Margaret Ruthven. **Spinning song, op. 9, no. 2** (APS
md   2865; Boston: A.P. Schmidt, 1892) 5 p.
Dn 2'. *At* Lizette Woodworth Reese. *Pf* solo voc, pno. *Rg* DLC, Recorded
Sound Section.

1826 LANG, Margaret Ruthven. **Spring, op. 47** (APS 8368; Boston:
mm   A.P. Schmidt, 1909) 7 p.
Dn 3'. *Pf* solo voc, pno.

1827 LANG, Margaret Ruthven. **Spring song, A** (APS 2622; Boston:
mm   A.P. Schmidt, 1890) 3 p.
Dn 1'. *La* DLC, Schmidt Collection. *At* Charlotte Pendleton. *Pf* solo voc, pno.

1828 LANG, Margaret Ruthven. **Summer noon, op. 37, no. 4** (APS
md   5566; Boston: A.P. Schmidt, 1901) 7 p.
Dn 2'. *La* DLC, Schmidt Collection. *At* John Vance Cheney. *Pf* solo voc, pno.

1829 LANG, Margaret Ruthven. **There would I be, op. 50, no. 4**
md   (APS 9692; Boston: A.P. Schmidt, 1912) 5 p.

Dn 2'. *La* DLC, Schmidt Collection. *At* John Vance Cheney. *St* At the silver
gate. *Pf* solo voc, pno. *Rg* DLC, Recorded Sound Section.

1830 LANG, Margaret Ruthven. **Thought, A, op. 37, no. 1** (APS
md   5563; Boston: A.P. Schmidt, 1901) 5 p.
Dn 1'. *La* DLC, Schmidt Collection. *At* John Vance Cheney. *St* Out of the
silence. *Pf* solo voc, pno.

1831 LANG, Margaret Ruthven. **Three songs of the east, op. 8,**
mm   **nos. 1-3** (APS 2861-2863; Boston: A.P. Schmidt, 1892) 3, 5, 5 p.
Dn 5'. *La* DLC, Schmidt Collection. *Pf* solo voc, pno. *Ct* Oriental serenade
(*WIAM* 1804), Christmas lullaby (*WIAM* 1757), A poet gazes on the moon
(*WIAM* 1808).

1832 LANG, Margaret Ruthven. **Three songs of the night, op. 7,**
mm   **nos. 1-3** (APS 2799-2801; Boston: A.P. Schmidt, 1891) 7, 5, 5 p.
Dn 5'. *La* DLC, Schmidt Collection. *Pf* solo voc, pno. *Ct* Night (*WIAM* 1798),
Slumber song (*WIAM* 1811), The harbor of dreams (*WIAM* 1771).

1833 LANG, Margaret Ruthven. **Tryste noël, op. 37, no. 5** (APS
md   5567; Boston: A.P. Schmidt, 1901) 7 p.
Dn 2'. *La* DLC, Schmidt Collection. *At* Louise Imogen Guiney. *Pf* solo voc,
pno.

1834 MCGILL, Josephine. **Duna** (1193; New York: Boosey, 1914) 5 p.
mm
Dn 2'. *At* Marjorie Pickthall. *Pf* solo voc, pno.

1835 MILLER, Anne Stratton. **Boats of mine** (260; New York: H.
mm   Flammer, 1919) 6 p.
Dn 2'. *At* Robert Louis Stevenson. *Pf* solo voc, pno.

1836 MILLER, Anne Stratton. **Parting at morning** (270; New York:
mm   H. Flammer, 1920) 3 p.
Dn 1'. *At* Robert Browning. *Pf* solo voc, pno.

1837 MOORE, Mary Carr. **Blue herons, op. 91, no. 2** (Hollywood,
md   Calif.: R.P. Saunders, 1937) 3 p.
Dn 2'. *At* Eleanor Allen. *Pf* solo voc, pno.

1838 MOORE, Mary Carr. **Brooklet, The** (San Bruno, Calif.: W.
mm   Webster, 1922) 5 p.
Dn 1'. *At* Harriet McEwan Kimball. *Pf* solo voc, pno.

1839 MOORE, Mary Carr. **Call of the open sea** (11214; New York:
mm   M. Witmark, 1910) 5 p.
Dn 2'. *At* Daisy Rineheart. *Pf* solo voc, pno.

1840 MOORE, Mary Carr. **Cicina mia** (San Francisco: Sherman, Clay,
mm   1925) 5 p.
Dn 2'. *At* Fay Jackson van Norden. *Pf* solo voc, pno.

1841 MOORE, Mary Carr. **Dawn, op. 77, no. 1** (San Francisco: J.M.
md   Byron, 1917) 3 p.
Dn 1'. *Pf* solo voc, pno.

1842 MOORE, Mary Carr. **Four love songs. A cycle for medium**
mm   **voice** (San Bruno, Calif.: W. Webster, [1939]) 18 p. (score).
Dn 11'. *Pf* solo M or Bar, pno. *Ct* Renunciation (*At* Grace E. Bush),
Compensation (*At* Eleanore Flaig), Consummation (*At* Whitman), Desolation
(*At* composer). Obbligato parts for flute and violin available at time of
publication. Also for solo M or Bar, flu, vln, vcl, pno (*WIAM* 1281). Originally
for voice and small orchestra. The piece won first prize in the 1932 music
contest of the National League of American Penwomen.

1843 MOORE, Mary Carr. **Homebound, op. 91, no. 14** (San
md   Francisco: W. Webster, 1948) 3 p.
Dn 1'. *At* George E. Curran. *Pf* solo voc, pno.

1844 MOORE, Mary Carr. **I had no songs until today, op. 91, no.**
md   **6** (77914; Boston: O. Ditson, 1936) 4 p.
Dn 2'. *At* Edward Lynn. *Pf* solo voc, pno.

1845 MOORE, Mary Carr. **I love thee, op. 58, no. 2** (11346; New
md   York: M. Witmark, 1910) 5 p.
Dn 2'. *At* Thomas Hood. *Pf* solo SA, pno.

1846 MOORE, Mary Carr. **Japanese night song, op. 87, no. 13**
md   (New York: G. Schirmer, 1930) 5 p.
Dn 2′. *At* Ellen Sanson. *Pf* solo voc, pno.

1847 MOORE, Mary Carr. **May with life and music, op. 28, no. 1**
md   (11215; New York: M. Witmark, 1912) 4 p.
Dn 2′. *At* William Cullen Bryant. *Pf* solo voc, pno.

1848 MOORE, Mary Carr. **Message, op. 98, no. 6** (San Francisco:
md   W. Webster, 1947) 3 p.
Dn 1′. *Pf* solo voc, pno.

1849 MOORE, Mary Carr. **Midsummer, op. 63, no. 3** (Seattle:
md   Sterling Music, 1907) 5 p.
Dn 2′. *At* John Curtis Underwood. *Pf* solo voc, pno.

1850 MOORE, Mary Carr. **My dream, op. 79, no. 3** (San Bruno,
md   Calif.: W. Webster, 1935) 7 p.
Dn 6′. *At* Charles Phillips. *Pf* solo voc, pno.

1851 MOORE, Mary Carr. **Northern love song, A** (Spokane: H.L.
mm   Store, 1906) 7 p. (score, part).
Dn 3′. *At* Sarah Pratt Carr. *Pf* solo voc, pno, vln obbligato.

1852 MOORE, Mary Carr. **Oh sweet, thou little knowest. Sere-**
mm   **nade** (11294; New York: M. Witmark, 1910) 5 p.
Dn 1′. *At* Thomas Hood. *Pf* solo voc, pno.

1853 MOORE, Mary Carr. **Ramoncita mia [My dear Ramona]** (San
md   Bruno, Calif.: W. Webster, 1940) 5 p.
Operatic excerpt. *Dn* 5′. *Lt* English. *Pf* solo Bar, pno. *Tm* Los rubios, a 3 act
opera about early California.   *(Joan M. Meggett)*

1854 MOORE, Mary Carr. **Road song, A, op. 63, no. 1** (11295; New
md   York: M. Witmark, 1910) 5 p.
Dn 2′. *At* Mary Lowell. *Pf* solo voc, pno.

1855 MOORE, Mary Carr. **Shadows, op. 81, no. 12** (San Francisco:
md   W. Webster, 1923) 5 p.
Dn 1′. *At* Fay Jackson van Norden. *Pf* solo voc, pno.

1856 MOORE, Mary Carr. **Song of a faun, op. 81, no. 13** (San
md   Bruno, Calif.: W. Webster, 1922) 7 p. (score, part).
Dn 3′. *At* Fay Jackson van Norden. *Pf* solo voc, pno, flu obbligato.

1857 MOORE, Mary Carr. **Sunset, op. 85, no. 9** (33363; New York:
md   G. Schirmer, 1927) 11 p.
Dn 3′. *At* John Wesley Moore. *Pf* solo voc, pno.

1858 MOORE, Mary Carr. **To mother, op. 79, no. 1** (San Francisco:
md   J.M. Byron, 1917) 3 p.
Dn 1′. *At* Unintah Ruple Boyd. *Pf* solo voc, pno.

1859 MOORE, Mary Carr. **Tryst, The** (11216; New York: M.
mm   Witmark, 1910) 7 p.
Dn 2′. *At* Winston Churchill. *Pf* solo voc, pno.

1860 MOORE, Mary Carr. **Vision, op. 98, no. 11** (San Francisco: W.
md   Webster, 1948) 5 p.
Dn 2′. *At* William Preston Bentley. *Pf* solo voc, pno.

1861 MOORE, Mary Carr. **When thou art near me, op. 35, no. 2**
md   (Seattle: Sterling Music, 1907) 5 p.
Dn 2′. *At* Lady John Scott. *Pf* solo voc, pno.

1862 MOORE, Mary Carr. **Winter** (San Francisco: W. Webster, 1922)
mm   2 p.
Dn 1′. *At* Fay Jackson van Norden. *Pf* solo voc, pno.

1863 MOORE, Mary Carr. **You, op. 77, no. 2** (30225; New York: G.
md   Schirmer, 1921) 3 p.
Dn 1′. *At* George Mellen. *Pf* solo voc, pno.

1864 ROGERS, Clara Kathleen. **Adieu, op. 33, no. 2** (APS 5039;
md   Boston: A.P. Schmidt, 1900) 7 p.

Dn 3′. *La* DLC, Schmidt Collection. *At* Dante Gabriel Rossetti. *Pf* solo voc,
pno. *Rg* DLC, Recorded Sound Section.

1865 ROGERS, Clara Kathleen. **At break of day. Six songs, no. 4**
md   (APS 527; Boston: A.P. Schmidt, 1882) 5 p.
Dn 2′. *La* DLC, Schmidt Collection. *Pf* solo voc, pno. Also in her *Song album*
(*WIAM* 1890).

1866 ROGERS, Clara Kathleen. **Aubade, op. 16** (APS 800; Boston:
mm   A.P. Schmidt, 1924) 5 p.
Dn 2′. *La* DLC, Schmidt Collection. *At* Victor Hugo. *Pf* solo voc, pno, vln
obbligato.

1867 ROGERS, Clara Kathleen. **Browning songs, second series,**
mm   **op. 32, nos. 1-6** (APS 5037; Boston: A.P. Schmidt, 1900) 23 p.
Song cycle. *Dn* 12′. *La* DLC, Schmidt Collection. *At* Robert Browning. *Pf* solo
voc, pno. *Ct* My star, Appearances, A woman's last word, Good to forgive (*St
Pisgah's sights*), One way of love, Love. *Rg* DLC, Recorded Sound Section.

1868 ROGERS, Clara Kathleen. **Clover blossoms, The. Six songs,**
md   **no. 2** (APS 525; Boston: A.P. Schmidt, 1882) 5 p.
Dn 2′. *La* DLC, Schmidt Collection. *At* Oscar Leighton. *Pf* solo voc, pno. Also
in her *Song album* (*WIAM* 1890).

1869 ROGERS, Clara Kathleen. **Come not when I am dead, op.**
md   **24, no. 4** (APS 1505; Boston: A.P. Schmidt, 1887) 5 p.
Dn 2′. *La* DLC, Schmidt Collection. *At* Tennyson. *Pf* solo voc, pno. Also in her
Song album (*WIAM* 1890). *Rg* DLC, Recorded Sound Section.

1870 ROGERS, Clara Kathleen. **Confession, op. 20, no. 2** (APS
md   587; Boston: A.P. Schmidt, 1894) 5 p.
Dn 2′. *La* DLC, Schmidt Collection. *Pf* solo voc, pno. *Rg* DLC, Recorded
Sound Section.

1871 ROGERS, Clara Kathleen. **Heath this night must be my bed,**
md   **The, op. 22, no. 3** (APS 846; Boston: A.P. Schmidt, 1885) 7 p.
Dn 2′. *La* DLC, Schmidt Collection. *At* Sir Walter Scott. *Pf* solo voc, pno. Also
in her *Song album* (*WIAM* 1890).

1872 ROGERS, Clara Kathleen. **I dare not ask, op. 26, no. 3** (APS
md   1633; Boston: A.P. Schmidt, 1888) 3 p.
Dn 2′. *La* DLC, Schmidt Collection. *At* Robert Herrick. *Pf* solo voc, pno. *Rg*
DLC, Recorded Sound Section.

1873 ROGERS, Clara Kathleen. **If we but knew, op. 37** (APS 7301;
mm   Boston: A.P. Schmidt, 1906) 7 p.
Dn 2′. *La* DLC. *At* Clarence Hawkes. *Pf* solo voc, pno.

1874 ROGERS, Clara Kathleen. **Kiss my eyelids, lovely morn** (APS
mm   2221; Boston: A.P. Schmidt, 1890) 7 p. (score, part).
Dn 1′. *La* DLC, Schmidt Collection. *Pf* solo voc, pno, vln obbligato. The
autograph has a variant title: Kiss mine eyelids, lovely maiden.

1875 ROGERS, Clara Kathleen. **Little love song, A** (APS 5367;
mm   Boston: A. P. Schmidt, 1901) 5 p.
Dn 1′. *La* DLC, Schmidt Collection. *At* Clarence Urmy. *Pf* solo voc, pno.

1876 ROGERS, Clara Kathleen. **Look out, o love, op. 22, no. 1**
md   (APS 844; Boston: A.P. Schmidt, 1885) 5 p.
Dn 2′. *La* DLC, Schmidt Collection. *Pf* solo voc, pno. Also in her *Song album*
(*WIAM* 1890).

1877 ROGERS, Clara Kathleen. **Love lies a dying, op. 24, no. 3**
md   (APS 1504; Boston: A.P. Schmidt, 1887) 5 p.
Dn 2′. *La* DLC, Schmidt Collection. *At* Philip Bourke Marston. *Pf* solo voc,
pno. Also in her *Song album* (*WIAM* 1890).

1878 ROGERS, Clara Kathleen. **Mona, op. 20, no. 3** (APS 588;
md   Boston: A.P. Schmidt, 1884) 9 p.
Dn 3′. *La* DLC, Schmidt Collection. *At* Alice Cary. *Pf* solo voc, pno.

1879 ROGERS, Clara Kathleen. **My dark to light** (APS 3966;
mm   Boston: A.P. Schmidt, 1896) 5 p.
Dn 2′. *La* DLC, Schmidt Collection. *At* Newman Hall. *Pf* solo voc, pno.

1880 ROGERS, Clara Kathleen. **Night and sleep, op. 30, no. 1**
md   (APS 2904; Boston: A.P. Schmidt, 1893) 5 p.
Dn 2′. *La* DLC, Schmidt Collection. *Pf* solo voc, pno.

1881 ROGERS, Clara Kathleen. **Oh my garden full of roses, op.**
md   **26, no. 5** (APS 1635; Boston: A.P. Schmidt, 1888) 5 p.
Dn 2′. *La* DLC, Schmidt Collection. *At* Philip Bourke Marston. *Pf* solo voc, pno. *Rg* DLC, Recorded Sound Section.

1882 ROGERS, Clara Kathleen. **Overhead the treetops meet, op.**
mm   **36** (APS 5987; Boston: A.P. Schmidt, 1903) 5 p.
Dn 2′. *La* DLC, Schmidt Collection. *At* Robert Browning. *St Pippa passes. Pf* solo voc, pno. *Rg* DLC, Recorded Sound Section.

1883 ROGERS, Clara Kathleen. **Rhapsody, op. 20, no. 4** (APS 589;
md   Boston: A.P. Schmidt, 1884) 7 p.
Dn 3′. *La* DLC, Schmidt Collection. *At* J. Berry Bensel. *Pf* solo voc, pno. *Rg* DLC, Recorded Sound Section.

1884 ROGERS, Clara Kathleen. **Rose and the lily, The. Six songs,**
md   **no. 5** (APS 528; Boston: A.P. Schmidt, 1882) 3 p.
Dn 2′. *La* DLC, Schmidt Collection. *Pf* solo voc, pno. Also in her *Song album* (*WIAM* 1890). *Rg* DLC, Recorded Sound Section.

1885 ROGERS, Clara Kathleen. **She is not fair, op. 24, no. 5** (APS
md   1506; Boston: A.P. Schmidt, 1887) 3 p.
Dn 1′. *La* DLC, Schmidt Collection. *At* Hartley Coleridge. *Pf* solo voc, pno. Also in her *Song album* (*WIAM* 1890). *Rg* DLC, Recorded Sound Section.

1886 ROGERS, Clara Kathleen. **She never told her love. Six**
md   **songs, no. 1** (APS 524; Boston: A.P. Schmidt, 1882) 5 p.
Dn 2′. *La* DLC, Schmidt Collection. *At* Shakespeare. *Pf* solo voc, pno. Also in her *Song album* (*WIAM* 1890).

1887 ROGERS, Clara Kathleen. **She was more fair than beauty,**
md   **op. 24, no. 1** (APS 1502; Boston: A.P. Schmidt, 1887) 6 p.
Dn 2′. *La* DLC, Schmidt Collection. *At* Julia R. Anagnos. *Pf* solo voc, pno. Also in her *Song album* (*WIAM* 1890).

1888 ROGERS, Clara Kathleen. **Six folk songs, op. 34, nos. 1-6**
mm   (APS 5262; Boston: A.P. Schmidt, 1900) 19 p.
Dn 8′. *Pf* solo voc, pno. *Ct* For love is blind (*At* Helen M. Hutchinson), My heart is sair (*At* Thomas Faed), The stars are with the voyager (*At* Thomas Hood), An Irish love song (*At* Robert Underwood Johnson), Jenny kissed me (*At* Leigh Hunt), When one has a sweetheart (*At* Charles J. Sprague).

1889 ROGERS, Clara Kathleen. **Six love songs, first series, op.**
mm   **27, nos. 1-6** (APS 2910; Boston: A.P. Schmidt, 1893) 23 p.
Song cycle. *Dn* 11′. *La* DLC, Schmidt Collection. *At* Robert and Elizabeth Barrett Browning. *Pf* solo voc, pno. *Ct* Out of my own great woe; Summum bonum; Apparitions; Ah, love, but a day; I have more than a friend; The year's at the spring. No. 6 is also in her *Song album* (*WIAM* 1890). *Rg* for nos. 1-3: DLC, Recorded Sound Section.

1890 ROGERS, Clara Kathleen. **Song album.** *Edition Schmidt* 14
ma   (524/1506; Boston: A.P. Schmidt, 1882-87) 47 p.
Pf solo voc, pno. *Ct* She never told her love (*WIAM* 1886), The clover blossoms, (*WIAM* 1868), At break of day (*WIAM* 1865), The year's at the spring in *Six songs, first series, op. 27, no. 6* (*WIAM* 1889), Nothing (*At* Alice Cary), Look out, o love, op. 22, no. 1 (*WIAM* 1876), Those eyes, op. 22, no. 2 (*WIAM* 1893), The heath this night must be my bed, op. 22, no. 3 (*WIAM* 1871), The sweetest dream, op. 24, no. 2 (*WIAM* 1892), She was more fair than beauty, op. 24, no. 1 (*WIAM* 1887), Love lies a-dying, op. 24, no. 3 (*WIAM* 1877), Come not when I am dead, op. 24, no. 4 (*WIAM* 1869), She is not fair, op. 24, no. 5 (*WIAM* 1885).

1891 ROGERS, Clara Kathleen. **Sudden light, op. 33, no. 1** (APS
md   5038; Boston: A.P. Schmidt, 1900) 5 p.
Dn 2′. *La* DLC, Schmidt Collection. *At* Dante Gabriel Rossetti. *Pf* solo voc, pno. *Rg* DLC, Recorded Sound Section.

1892 ROGERS, Clara Kathleen. **Sweetest dream, The, op. 24, no.**
md   **2** (APS 1503; Boston: A.P. Schmidt, 1887) 5 p.
Dn 2′. *La* DLC, Schmidt Collection. *At* Philip Bourke Marston. *Pf* solo voc, pno. Also in her *Song album* (*WIAM* 1890). *Rg* DLC, Recorded Sound Section.

1893 ROGERS, Clara Kathleen. **Those eyes, op. 22, no. 2** (APS
md   845; Boston: A.P. Schmidt, 1885) 5 p.
Dn 1′. *La* DLC, Schmidt Collection. *At* Ben Jonson. *Pf* solo voc, pno. Also in her *Song album* (*WIAM* 1890). *Rg* DLC, Recorded Sound Section.

1894 ROGERS, Clara Kathleen. **Too young for love, op. 30, no. 2**
md   (APS 2905; Boston: A.P. Schmidt, 1893) 5 p.
Dn 2′. *La* DLC, Schmidt Collection. *Pf* solo voc, pno.

1895 ROGERS, Clara Kathleen. **Under a cherry tree, op. 28, no. 3**
md   (APS 2207; Boston: A.P. Schmidt, 1890) 5 p.
Dn 1′. *La* DLC, Schmidt Collection. *At* William James Linton. *Pf* solo voc, pno.

1896 ROGERS, Clara Kathleen. **Voice that sang alone, The** (APS
mm   4023; Boston: A.P. Schmidt, 1896) 7 p.
Sacred song. *Dn* 3′. *La* DLC, Schmidt Collection. *At* Waldo Clellan Fisher. *Pf* solo voc, pno. Based on a chorale from J.S. Bach's *St. Matthew Passion*, S.244.

1897 RUNCIE, Constance Faunt Le Roy. **My spirit rests** (10500;
mm   New York: W.A. Pond, 1882) 5 p.
Sacred song. *Dn* 1′. *Pf* solo voc, pno. Dedicated to Frank C. Walker. (*Judith Tick*)

1898 SALTER, Mary Turner. **Come to the garden, love** (17464;
mm   New York: G. Schirmer, 1904) 3 p.
Dn 1′. *Pf* solo voc, pno.

1899 SALTER, Mary Turner. **Contentment** (Boston: O. Ditson, 1905)
mm   5 p.
Dn 2′. *At* composer. *Pf* solo voc, pno.

1900 SALTER, Mary Turner. **Cry of Rachel, The** (21324; New
mm   York: G. Schirmer, 1905) 7 p.
Dn 2′. *At* Lizette Woodworth Reese. *Pf* solo voc, pno.

1901 SALTER, Mary Turner. **East wind, The** (19321; New York: G.
md   Schirmer, 1907) 4 p.
Dn 1′. *At* Edwin Warren Guyol. *Pf* solo voc, pno. *Tm Songs of the four winds* (*WIAM* 1924).

1902 SALTER, Mary Turner. **Elves, The** (20484; New York: G.
mm   Schirmer, 1908) 4 p.
Dn 2′. *At* Louise Medbery. *St The Vassar miscellany. Pf* solo voc, pno.

1903 SALTER, Mary Turner. **Fair white flower, A** (14670; Cincin-
mm   nati: J. Church, 1902) 9 p.
Dn 3′. *Pf* solo voc, pno.

1904 SALTER, Mary Turner. **Für Musik (For music)** (19354; New
md   York: G. Schirmer, 1907) 3 p.
Dn 2′. *At* Emmanuel Giebel. *Lt* German, English. *Pf* solo voc, pno. *Tm Three German songs* (*WIAM* 1931).

1905 SALTER, Mary Turner. **Her love-song** (19265; New York: G.
md   Schirmer, 1907) 5 p.
Dn 1′. *At* Frank Dempster Sherman. *Pf* solo voc, pno. *Tm Three love songs* (*WIAM* 1932).

1906 SALTER, Mary Turner. **I breathe thy name** (19266; New
md   York: G. Schirmer, 1907) 4 p.
Dn 1′. *At* composer. *Pf* solo voc, pno. *Tm Three love songs* (*WIAM* 1932).

1907 SALTER, Mary Turner. **In some sad hour** (Boston: O. Ditson,
mm   1904) 5 p.
Dn 1′. *At* Henry Elliot Harman. *Pf* solo voc, pno.

1908 SALTER, Mary Turner. **Lady April, The** (25457; Philadelphia:
mm   T. Presser, 1931) 5 p.
Dn 2′. *At* composer. *Pf* solo voc, pno.

1909 SALTER, Mary Turner. **Lamp of love, The** (19267; New York:
md   G. Schirmer, 1907) 4 p.
Dn 2′. *At* Paracelsus, adapted. *Pf* solo voc, pno. *Tm Three love songs* (*WIAM* 1932).

1910 SALTER, Mary Turner. **Little while, A** (18046; New York: G.
mm   Schirmer, 1905) 3 p.
Dn 1′. *Pf* solo voc, pno.

1911 SALTER, Mary Turner. **Love's epitome** (18008; New York: G.
mm   Schirmer, 1905) 14 p.
Song cycle. *Dn* 8′. *At* composer. *Pf* solo voc, pno. *Ct* Since first I met thee; In the garden; She is mine; Dear hand, close held in mine; Requiem.

1912 SALTER, Mary Turner. **Lyrics from Sappho** (20980; New
mm   York: G. Schirmer, 1909) 19 p.

Song cycle. *Dn* 12′. *Tr* Bliss Carman. *Pf* solo voc, pno. *Ct* Hesperus, bringing together; Well I found you; There is a medlar tree; If death be good; It can never be mine; I grow weary; Over the roofs.

1913 SALTER, Mary Turner. **Maid o' mine** (18643; Philadelphia: T.
mm   Presser, 1923) 3 p.
Dn 1′. *At* Neva McFarland Wadhams. *Pf* solo voc, pno.

1914 SALTER, Mary Turner. **March wind** (114084; New York: G.
md   Schirmer, 1904) 5 p.
Dn 1′. *At* composer. *Pf* solo voc, pno. *Tm* Three spring songs (*WIAM* 1933).

1915 SALTER, Mary Turner. **My lady** (Boston: O. Ditson, 1905) 5 p.
mm
Dn 1′. *At* composer. *Pf* solo voc, pno.

1916 SALTER, Mary Turner. **Night in Naishapûr, A. Six songs**
mm   (18617; New York: G. Schirmer, 1906) 13 p.
Song cycle. *Dn* 7′. *At* Nathan Haskell Dole. *Pf* solo voc, pno. *Ct* Long, long ago; In the city the misgar; The song; The moon has long since wandered; If I could prove my love; The farewell.

1917 SALTER, Mary Turner. **North wind, The** (19324; New York:
md   G. Schirmer, 1907) 4 p.
Dn 1′. *At* Edwin Warren Guyol. *Pf* solo voc, pno. *Tm* Songs of the four winds (*WIAM* 1924).

1918 SALTER, Mary Turner. **Pine tree, The** (17466; New York: G.
mm   Schirmer, 1904) 3 p.
Dn 1′. *At* composer. *Pf* solo voc, pno. Dedicated to Carrie Boeckh White.

1919 SALTER, Mary Turner. **Primavera** (19263; New York: G.
mm   Schirmer, 1907) 3 p.
Dn 2′. *At* Edwin Bjorkman. *Pf* solo voc, pno.

1920 SALTER, Mary Turner. **Schmetterling, Die (The butterfly)**
md   (19356; New York: G. Schirmer, 1907) 4 p.
Dn 1′. *At* Heine. *Lt* German, English. *Pf* solo voc, pno. *Tm* Three German songs (*WIAM* 1931).

1921 SALTER, Mary Turner. **Serenity** (Boston: O. Ditson, 1904) 3 p.
mm
Dn 1′. *At* composer. *Pf* solo voc, pno.

1922 SALTER, Mary Turner. **Slumber sea** (18188; Cincinnati: J.
mm   Church, 1919) 3 p.
Dn 1′. *At* Jean Stansbury Holden. *Pf* solo voc, pno.

1923 SALTER, Mary Turner. **Song of April** (114085; New York: G.
md   Schirmer, 1904) 5 p.
Dn 1′. *At* composer. *Pf* solo voc, pno. *Tm* Three spring songs (*WIAM* 1933).

1924 SALTER, Mary Turner. **Songs of the four winds** (19321-
mm   19324; New York: G. Schirmer, 1907) 4, 4, 4, 4 p.
Dn 6′. *Pf* solo voc, pno. *Ct* The east wind (*WIAM* 1901), The south wind (*WIAM* 1925), The west wind (*WIAM* 1938), The north wind (*WIAM* 1917).

1925 SALTER, Mary Turner. **South wind, The** (19322; New York:
md   G. Schirmer, 1907) 4 p.
Dn 2′. *At* Edwin Warren Guyol. *Pf* solo voc, pno. *Tm* Songs of the four winds (*WIAM* 1924).

1926 SALTER, Mary Turner. **Spring wonder** (New York: G.
mm   Schirmer, 1923) 6 p.
Dn 1′. *At* Cornelia M.J. Howe. *Pf* solo voc, pno.

1927 SALTER, Mary Turner. **Stille Wasserrose, Die (The tranquil**
md   **water lily)** (19355; New York: G. Schirmer, 1907) 4 p.
Dn 3′. *At* Emmanuel Giebel. *Lt* German, English. *Pf* solo voc, pno. *Tm* Three German songs (*WIAM* 1931).

1928 SALTER, Mary Turner. **Swan, The** (18057; New York: G.
mm   Schirmer, 1905) 3 p.
Dn 2′. *At* composer. *Pf* solo voc, pno.

1930 SALTER, Mary Turner. **Sweet o' the year, The** (APS 9388;
mm   Boston: A.P. Schmidt, 1912) 5 p.
Dn 1′. *At* composer. *Pf* solo voc, pno. Dedicated to Clara Tippett.

1931 SALTER, Mary Turner. **Three German songs** (19354-19356;
mm   New York: G. Schirmer, 1907) 3, 4, 4 p.
Dn 6′. *Pf* solo voc, pno. *Ct* Für Musik (*WIAM* 1904), Die stille Wasserrose (*WIAM* 1927), Die Schmetterling (*WIAM* 1920).

1932 SALTER, Mary Turner. **Three love songs** (19265-19267; New
mm   York: G. Schirmer, 1907) 5, 4, 4 p.
Dn 4′. *Pf* solo voc, pno. *Ct* Her love-song (*WIAM* 1905), I breathe thy name (*WIAM* 1906), The lamp of love (*WIAM* 1909).

1933 SALTER, Mary Turner. **Three spring songs** (114084-114086;
mm   New York: G. Schirmer, 1904) 5, 5, 5 p.
Dn 4′. *Pf* solo voc, pno. *Ct* March wind (*WIAM* 1914), Song of April (*WIAM* 1923), The time of May (*WIAM* 1934).

1934 SALTER, Mary Turner. **Time of May, The** (114086; New
md   York: G. Schirmer, 1904) 5 p.
Dn 2′. *At* composer. *Pf* solo voc, pno. *Tm* Three spring songs (*WIAM* 1933).

1935 SALTER, Mary Turner. **Toast, A** (New York: G. Schirmer,
mm   1905) 4 p.
Dn 2′. *At* Ernest Whitney. *Pf* solo voc, pno.

1936 SALTER, Mary Turner. **Ulysses** (18206; Cincinnati: J. Church,
mm   1919) 6 p.
Dn 2′. *At* Burton Braley. *Pf* solo voc, pno.

1937 SALTER, Mary Turner. **Vox invicta** (72831; Boston: O. Ditson,
mm   1919) 7 p.
Dn 3′. *At* Nina Salamon. *Pf* solo voc, pno.

1938 SALTER, Mary Turner. **West wind, The** (19323; New York: G.
md   Schirmer, 1907) 4 p.
Dn 2′. *At* Edwin Warren Guyol. *Pf* solo voc, pno. *Tm* Songs of the four winds (*WIAM* 1924).

1939 SALTER, Mary Turner. **Willow, The** (Boston: O. Ditson, 1905)
mm   5 p.
Dn 2′. *At* composer. *Pf* solo voc, pno.

1940 STEINER, Emma Roberto. **Beautiful eyes** (New York: Mac-
mm   Donald & Steiner, 1921) 7 p.
Dn 2′. *At* Marguerite Linton Glentworth. *Pf* solo voc, pno.

1941 STEINER, Emma Roberto. **Florence Laurence, op. 417** (New
mm   York: MacDonald & Steiner, n.d.) 5 p.
Dn 2′. *At* Margaret M. MacDonald. *Pf* solo voc, pno. Subtitle: "Foxtrot and one-step, two-step or waltz. All in one. Dashing and winsome. For piano and voice, orchestra, and bands. Sung whilst dancing".

1942 STEINER, Emma Roberto. **I envy the rose** (New York:
mm   MacDonald & Steiner, 1921) 5 p.
Dn 2′. *At* M.G. Millais. *Pf* solo voc, pno.

1943 STEINER, Emma Roberto. **Tecolate** (New York: MacDonald
mm   & Steiner, 1921) 5 p.
Dn 2′. *At* Dom St. Henri. *Pf* solo voc, pno. A note from the publisher indicates Steiner also scored the piece for voice and orchestra.

1944 STRICKLAND, Lily Teresa. **At eve I heard a flute** (74323;
mm   Philadelphia: O. Ditson, 1923) 5 p.
Dn 2′. *Pf* solo voc, pno.

1945 STRICKLAND, Lily Teresa. **Ma li'l batteau** (JF&B 4992;
mm   New York: J. Fischer, 1921) 3 p.
Dn 3′. *At* Michael de Longpré. *Pf* solo voc, pno.

1946 STRICKLAND, Lily Teresa. **Mah Lindy Lou. A banjo song**
mm   **with piano accompaniment** (30367; New York: G. Schirmer,
          1948) 5 p.
Dn 2′. *At* composer. *Pf* solo voc, pno. A reprint of the 1920 publication (30367; Schirmer). *Rg* Victor 1544.

1947 STRICKLAND, Lily Teresa. **My Jeanie** (14917; Cincinnati: J.
mm   Church, 1905) 5 p.
Dn 2′. *At* composer. *Pf* solo voc, pno.

1948 STRICKLAND, Lily Teresa. **My lover is a fisherman** (74332;
mm   Philadelphia: O. Ditson, 1922) 5 p.
Dn 3'. *At* composer. *Pf* solo voc, pno.

1949 STRICKLAND, Lily Teresa. **When your ship comes in** (558;
mm   New York: Hinds, Hayden & Eldredge, 1919) 5 p.
Dn 2'. *At* composer. *Pf* solo voc, pno.

1950 VANNAH, Kate. **Come back to me!** (L&B 1793; New York:
mm   Luckhardt & Belder, 1902) 5 p.
Dn 1'. *Pf* solo voc, pno.

1951 VANNAH, Kate. **Good bye, sweet day!** (224; Boston: L.H.
mm   Ross, 1891) 3 p.
Dn 2'. *At* Celia Thaxter. *Pf* solo voc, pno. *Rg* DLC, Recorded Sound Section.

1952 VANNAH, Kate. **'Tis home where the heart is** (LHR 297;
mm   Boston: L.H. Ross, 1894) 5 p.
Dn 3'. *At* George Horton. *Pf* solo voc, pno.

1920 TO 1950

64   Literature about women in related arts and disciplines

1953 ARMSTRONG, Elizabeth. **Taylor opera ready for Metro-**
ap   **politan**, *Musical America* XLIV/23 (25 Sept 1926) 1, 4. *Illus.*
The king's henchman by Deems Taylor on a libretto by Edna St. Vincent Millay
will be Giulio Gatti-Casazza's "especially commissioned American novelty" for
the 1929-30 season at the Metropolitan Opera. The all-American cast will be
headed by Edward Johnson, Florence Easton, and Lawrence Tibbett. Millay
notes that while this is her first libretto, music has always been important in her
life, and that she has been careful to use words which are easy to sing. There
has been some curiosity about the subject of the opera; Millay insists the plot
substantiates the title.

→   BATSON, Charlene. **Naomi Carroll Haimsohn (b. 1894): a**
     history of her contributions to music as an educator,
     composer, and performer; and a study of some social and
     cultural influences on her life as an American woman both in
     music and the arts, *see* 1958dm[65].

1954 **Cadman's gifted collaborator**, *Musical Courier* LXVII/8 (27 Aug
ap   1913) 6.
Charles Wakefield Cadman's first librettist was his talented cousin, Avery
Hassler. Following Hassler's death, Nelle Richmond Eberhart became Cadman's collaborator.

1955 **Nelle Richmond Eberhart, a noted lyricist**, *New York Times* 16
an   Nov 1944, 23.
Reports the death of Nelle Richmond Eberhart in Kansas City, Mo., where she
had settled 2 years previously with her daughter who teaches at a local
conservatory. Eberhart collaborated with Charles Wakefield Cadman for many
years, her best known lyrics being those for Cadman's songs *At dawning* and
From the land of the sky blue water. Their operas included *The robin woman*
(1918), *Garden of mystery* (1925), and the first opera produced on radio, *The
willow tree* (1932).

→   STANLEY, May. **Students may be "farmerettes" under**
     Harriet Ware's plan, *see* 2058ap[66].

65   General literature about women in art music

→   ABDUL, Raoul. **Blacks in classical music. A personal his-**
     tory, *see* 2967bm[75].

→   **Anthology of music criticism, An**, *see* 563bm[55].

1956 ANTRIM, Doron K. **Music therapy**, *Musical Quarterly* XXX/4
ap   (Oct 1944) 409-20.
Discusses the healing powers of music and the use of music as an antidote to
psychic and physical pain. Describes recent pioneer work by the following
women in music therapy: 1) Loretta Bender, a child psychiatrist at Bellevue
Hospital in New York and an advocate of treating hyperkinetic children
through music, 2) Adela Lane, a psychologist and pianist who uses piano
vibrations to help deafened and other patients, 3) Frances Paperte, director of a
clinic for the treatment of the war-wounded at the Inst. of Music Therapy in
New York, and 4) Harriet Seymour, founder of the National Foundation of
Music Therapy, who has treated hysterical blindness with music.

1957 **At the Drinkers**, *Newsweek* XXXI/5 (2 Feb 1948) 69.
ap
For 20 years Henry S. and Sophie Drinker have held choral singing sessions in
their home in Merion, Penn. on the outskirts of Philadelphia. Entitled the
Accademia dei Dilletanti di Musica, the Drinker's chorus is made up of
amateurs, semi-professionals, and professionals who join together regularly for
the pleasure of reading through choral literature.

1958 BATSON, Charlene. **Naomi Carroll Haimsohn (b. 1894): a**
dm   **history of her contributions to music as an educator,**
     composer, and performer; and a study of some social and
     cultural influences on her life as an American woman both in
     music and the arts (MM thesis, Music Education: Roosevelt U.,
     1978) 83 p. *Facsim., music, bibliog., list of works.*
Naomi Carroll Haimsohn was born to Jewish immigrant parents and was raised
on the Lower East Side in New York. She was precocious musically and made
her debut as a pianist in 1902 at the age of 8. She studied chiefly with private
tutors and from the age of 15 on was self-taught. In 1911 the family relocated
in Memphis, and Haimsohn has spent most of her life in that city. From 1921-
48 she was director of the Central Academy of Music, which she located in her
home. Her activities as a music educator included teaching piano, voice, and
music theory as well as developing teaching aids and games for students.
Haimsohn contributed to the musical life of Memphis as a conductor of school
choruses and instrumental groups, and by performing as a pianist and singer.
Her compositions include songs and piano music, and she also published a book
of poetry, *The happy tree and other poems* (1974). This study--which is based on
taped interviews with the educator-composer--also investigates the relationship
between Haimsohn's contributions to music and her childhood socialization,
educational opportunities, and social, domestic, and cultural values.
(Author, abridged)

1959 BAUER, Marion; REIS, Claire. **Twenty-five years with the**
ap   **League of Composers**, *Musical Quarterly* XXXIV/1 (Jan 1948)
     1-14. *Illus.*
A summary of the aims and activities of the League of Composers since its
founding in 1923, written by 2 women who were charter members. Other
women closely associated with the league's early history were Minna Lederman
and Alma Morgenthau Wiener. While the league aims to "unite all musical
creative forces," as of 1948 only 1 of 80 commissioned works by American
composers is by a woman--Marion Bauer. The league frequently has relied on
singers Eva Gauthier and Greta Torpadie for premières in a continuing search
for artists and interested in performing new music. Lists of notable singers
and dancers in stage productions sponsored by the League of Composers and
an evaluation of *Modern Music*--a quarterly edited by Minna Lederman from
1924-46--are included.

1960 **B.F. Cecil Arden talks on women's clubs**, *Musical Courier*
ap   LXXXIV/22 (1 June 1922) 31.
Cecil Arden, the young American mezzo-soprano, praises women in general for
their way of staging and presenting concerts, whether in connection with
particular music clubs or as independent managers. Women are practical about
good lighting and proper footlights, and they often have good taste in the
decoration of a stage.

→   **Boston, New England Conservatory of Music, Spaulding**
     Library. A checklist of source materials by and about women
     in American music, *see* 6bm[01].

1961 BOULTON, Laura. **Music hunter, The** (New York: Doubleday,
bm   1969) 513 p. *Illus., discog., index.*
An autobiography by the ethnomusicologist, who over a period of 35 years
studied ethnic music and customs in Eskimo territories, Sub-Sahara Africa,
Nepal, and Thailand. Religious music was Boulton's major interest, and being
female she was allowed to observe certain female rituals. Initially a singer,
Boulton decided in 1929 to join an African expedition sponsored by the
Museum of Natural History in New York in order to study native music. Now
after 28 subsequent expeditions she has collected over 30,000 recordings and
many musical instruments, which are housed in the Laura Boulton Collection of
World Music and Musical Instruments at Arizona State U. A list of record
albums made from Boulton's field recordings is included.

1962 BRADLEY, Ruth. **Music in hospitals**. *Studies in musical*
ac   *education, history, and aesthetics* 38 (Pittsburgh: Music Teachers
National Assoc., 1944) 453-55.
Reports on a wartime project of the National Federation of Music Clubs that
investigated the use of music therapy among the wounded and disabled.
Suggests that entertainment programs should offer popular music, develop
mobile groups with small pianos and phonographs to reach isolated hospitals,
and enlist teachers as well as performers--especially those prepared to
"abandon platform manners and subordinate the ego" in favor of healing and
educational tasks.

1963 **Claire Raphael Reis dies at 89; leader in New York cultural**
an   **life**, *New York Times* 13 Apr 1978, B-2.
Claire Reis (1888-1978) was active in New York musical circles for over 50
years as a founding member of the League of Composers in 1923 and its
executive chairwoman for 25 years, as the author of books on music, as the
director of the People's Music League in 1912-22, and as the member of
numerous advisory boards. Among other honors, Reis was awarded New York
City's Handel Medallion in 1969.

1964 CRAIG, Mary. **Mary Howe, composer, honored for works**,
ap   *Musical Courier* CXLVII/3 (1 Feb 1953) 22. *Illus.*
1) On 21 Dec. the National Symphony Orchestra under the direction of
Howard Mitchell gave an entire program of Mary Howe's works, and on 24
Feb. Arthur Judson is presenting a Town Hall concert of Howe's choral
compositions and songs. 2) When her daughter and 2 sons reached an
appropriate age for recital work, Howe initiated a series of madrigal concerts in
which they all participated, singing mostly at schools and local festivals. 3)
Despite her prolific output as a composer, Howe finds time and energy to
devote to music organizations, e.g., the National Federation of Music Clubs,
the Music Division of the Library of Congress, and the National Symphony
Orchestra.

→   **Detroit, Michigan, Detroit Public Library, Music and**
Performing Arts Division. A checklist of source materials by
and about women in American music, *see* 12bm[01].

1965 DOWNES, Olin. **Librarian retires. A tribute to Dorothy**
an   **Lawton--her contribution to our musical life**, *New York Times*
8 July 1945, 4.
Lawton was chief music librarian of the circulation department of the New
York Public Library for 25 years. During that time she developed the "most
important circulating library of music in the United States". Trained as a
pianist, Lawton gave up teaching for war work at the outbreak of World War I
before joining the staff of the New York Public Library. She successfully
negotiated donations from the libraries of Henry Edward Krehbiel, James
Gibbons Huneker, and William J. Henderson, and she created special
collections such as the De Coppet collection of chamber music, the Mailamm
collection for Jewish music, and an orchestral collection sponsored by the
Works Progress Administration. In 25 years time the circulating library's
original 1000 items grew to 30,000. Lawton also developed a course in music
librarianship at the New York Col. of Music and a music history course for
librarians.

1966 DOWNES, Olin. **London library. Music institution formed**
an   **along lines of 58th Street branch here**, *New York Times* 10 Aug
1947, II-6.
Dorothy Lawton, head of the music circulating division of the New York
Public Library at the 58th Street branch, returned to her native England upon
retirement. At the suggestion of the English pianist, Winifred Christie, Lawton
helped to found a similar music library in London. Among her innovations at
the New York Public Library were a record library and chamber music
performances on Sunday afternoons for servicemen and the general public.

→   ERICSON, Raymond. **Mezzo becomes an opera manager, A**,
see 2975an[75].

1967 FISHER, William Arms. **Song sharks and their victims**.
ac   *Studies in musical education, history, and aesthetics* 17 (Hartford:
Music Teachers National Assoc., 1923) 110-21.
Deplores publishing swindles of the 1920s, notably songs that attached
plagiarized tunes to newly-solicited texts in evasion of copyright laws. Notes
that women's clubs have been successful in their campaigns against some other
unsavory aspects of popular publishing, e.g., suggestive texts.

→   GERSON, Robert. **Music in Philadelphia**, *see* 582bf[55].

1968 **Graham, Shirley**, *Current biography*. Ed. by Anna ROTHE (New
ac   York: H.W. Wilson, 1946) 221-22. *Illus.*
Shirley Graham's great-grandfather was a freed slave, whose farm in
Evansville, Ind. was used as a station on the underground railway to Canada.
Her father was a minister. Graham graduated from high school in Spokane,

Wash., taught music at Morgan Col. in Baltimore, and then attended the
Oberlin Conservatory--earning a bachelor's degree in 1934 and a master's
degree in 1935. Her *Tom-tom* was originally a musical play, which she made
into an opera at the suggestion of the director of the Cleveland Summer Opera.
The company gave the première performance of the work in 1932. Under the
Works Progress Administration Graham was associated with the Negro unit of
the theater project, and she subsequently attended the Yale School of Drama
and started writing plays. During World War II she directed theatricals for
military entertainments. Graham's writings on notable blacks for young people
include books on George Washington Carver, Paul Robeson, and Frederick
Douglass.

1969 GRANT, Frances R. **Providing young genius with bed and**
ap   **board**, *Musical America* XXXI/17 (21 Feb 1920) 3. *Illus.*
Because of a scarcity of proper housing for women students of music, a
committee headed by Frances McMillan has supervised the renovation of an
apartment building near the Institute of Musical Art, now called the Parnassus
Club.

1970 HILL, Roy. **Fannie Douglass. Reminiscences of yesteryear**,
ap   *Black Perspective in Music* II/1 (spring 1974) 54-62. *Illus.*
An interview with Fannie Douglass, who trained as a pianist at Oberlin
Conservatory and, through much of her career, taught music in junior high
schools in Washington, D.C. Douglass discusses her associations with Hazel
Harrison, pianist, Mary Europe, pianist and music educator, and Marian
Anderson and Lillian Evanti, singers, as well as with noted black male
musicians.

1971 JOHNSON, Harriet. **Olga Samaroff as teacher**, *Musical*
ap   *America* LXVII/11 (Oct 1948) 27, 31, 38.
A tribute to Olga Samaroff Stokowski as pianist, music educator, and critic
upon her death in May 1948. 1) Samaroff Stokowski decried what she called
"teaching-coaching" and instead aimed to make her piano students independent musicians, providing each with the fundamental tools of the craft. 2) For
15 years in her Layman's Music Courses, Samaroff Stokowski sought to bridge
the gap between audience and performer. 3) She firmly believed that a
knowledge of the history of western music was essential for all performers, and
she strove in her teaching to instill this tradition.

1972 KROKOVER, Rosalyn. **Women in music. Who's who among**
ap   **concert executives in the New York offices**, *Musical Courier*
CXXV/3 (5 Feb 1942) 12-14, 116.
"The concert business really came into its own after the end of World War I. It
was about this time that women in large numbers began to enter industry, and
it is more than coincidence that many fresh ideas were adopted in this
particular field. Women have attained positions of paramount importance in
the areas of managing, publicity, and personal representation". The careers of
contemporary women active in the concert business in New York are briefly
considered.

→   MARSH, Robert. **Cleveland Orchestra, The**, *see* 600bm[55].

1973 **Mary C. Dawson dies, founder of Negro opera**, *New York*
an   *Herald Tribune* 21 Mar 1962, 26.
Mary Cardwell Dawson founded the National Negro Opera in 1941 to give
black singers with operatic talent the opportunity to be heard. In 1956 the
company performed Clarence Cameron White's *Ouanga*, an opera with a
Haitian setting, in a semi-concert version at the Metropolitan Opera. Trained at
the New England Conservatory and Chicago Musical Col., Dawson also
founded a music school and the Cardwell Dawson Chorus in her native
Pittsburgh.

1974 MASON, Daniel Gregory. **Tune in, America: a study of our**
bf   **coming musical independence** (New York: AMS, 1976) 205 p.
A reprint of the 1931 edition (New York: A.A. Knopf). 1) Deplores the effects
of radio, pianolas, jazz, and Stravinsky's music on the American public--whose
taste is still generally indifferent to fine music. 2) Observes that while music is
fortunately no longer the preserve of women, the field has become "too Jewish"
and too menaced by facile intellectualism. 3) Advocates singing as an
amusement for women, since men are too busy providing their wives with the
leisure time and monies for music lessons in order to have time for singing
themselves.

1975 MASSMANN, Richard Lee. **Lillian Baldwin and the Cleve-**
dd   **land Plan for educational concerts** (PhD diss., Music: U. of
Michigan, 1972) 236 p. (typescript, microfilm).
Presents a brief history of pioneer efforts in orchestral concerts for school-age
children. Discusses Lillian Baldwin's roles as a musician, teacher, writer, and
administrator. With the collaboration of the Cleveland Board of Education, the
Cleveland Orchestra, and the community, Baldwin developed an internationally
recognized plan for children's concerts known as the Cleveland Plan from
1929-56. Baldwin's ability to write colorful, yet educational, preparatory
material was important in the success of the plan. An appendix containing a list

of concert programs from 1929-72 and examples of the children's materials for the concerts are included. *(Dissertation Abstracts, abridged)*

→ **Memphis, Tennessee, Memphis/Shelby County Library and Information Center. A checklist of works by Naomi Carroll Haimsohn**, *see* 26bm[01].

1976 **Miss Annie Friedberg**, *New York Times* 19 Nov 1952, 26.
an
An obituary for Annie Friedberg (1878-1952), who established her concert management business in New York about 40 years ago. Born in Bingen, Germany, Friedberg studied at the Frankfurt Conservatory and sang in concert and church work before emigrating to the United States. Among the artists and organizations she brought to the United States were Myra Hess, the Budapest String Quartet, Vladimir Horowitz, and Elisabeth Schumann.

1977 **Mrs. Henry Drinker, choral enthusiast**, *New York Times* 10
an   Sept 1967, 82.
Reports the death of Sophie Drinker, who was a promoter of choral singing by women and president of the Montgomery Singers--a women's chorus in suburban Philadelphia. Drinker was the author of several books, among them *Music and women* (*WIAM* 126), *Brahms and his women's choruses* (1952), and *Hannah Penn and the proprietorship of Pennsylvania* (1958).

1978 M.S. **"Public service must be aim of manager", says Mrs.**
ap   **Colbert**, *Musical America* XXXIII/23 (2 Apr 1921) 29. *Illus.*
As director of the Colbert Concert Course in San Francisco, Jessica Colbert is one of the leading managers in the West and the only female impresario in California. Colbert believes that the interest in serious music "throughout the Pacific Coast territory" is considerable indeed; the war turned the thoughts of many Americans towards music. Colbert attributes her success to her tendency to under- rather than overstate the abilities of her artists, and accordingly music clubs and other organizations do not hesitate to accept any musician she endorses.

→ **Music in Denver and Colorado**, *see* 611bm[55].

→ **New York, New York Public Library, Theater Division. A checklist of scrapbooks about women in American music**, *see* 34bm[01].

1979 NICKELL, Marion Fairfield. **Music as a field for women**,
ap   *Musical America* LXVIII/21 (8 Sept 1928) 14.
Grace Spofford, dean of the Curtis Inst., notes that although women have made significant contributions as performers, music educators, patrons, and writers, in composition women "have yet to make their mark". As educators women have held many positions of importance, e.g., Clara Baur, founder of the Cincinnati Conservatory, Mrs. Franklyn Sanders, director of the Cleveland Inst. of Music, Nellie C. Cornish, founder and director of the Cornish School of Music in Seattle, and May Garretson Evans, founder and director of the preparatory department at the Peabody Conservatory. On the faculty of the Curtis Inst. women are well represented at the present time: Marcella Sembrich heads the vocal department, Lea Luboshutz teaches violin, Isabella Vengerova is on the piano faculty, and Renée Longy Miquelle teaches solfège. 45% of the 215 students currently enrolled at Curtis are female, although it is true that women are working almost entirely in the traditional fields of voice, violin, and piano. Spofford stresses that women attending professional schools such as Curtis must have a professional attitude toward their studies.

1980 PARKER, D.C. **Is woman a failure as a musician?**, *Musical*
ap   *America* XXXV/7 (10 Dec 1921) 45.
Discusses J. Swinburne's article in the *Proceedings of the Musical Association* of London for 1919-20, wherein Swinburne argues that women in music have accomplished nothing as creators, interpreters, or critics. After noting the dangers involved in such generalizations, Parker reinforces Swinburne's premise, although he thinks that contemporary woman is "coming into her own" and might make strides in the next decades.

→ PETRIDES, Frederique. **Outline of a prejudice**, *see* 163ap[25].

1981 PORTER, Quincy. **Effects of the national emergency on**
ac   **conservatories and schools of music, The**. *Studies in musical education, history, and aesthetics* 38 (Pittsburgh: Music Teachers National Assoc., 1944) 112-18.
56 respondent schools from 100 surveyed provide data showing that conscription has reduced the number of male students by 19%. A gain of almost 12% in women students was reported, with 27 schools indicating a rise in female enrollment of up to 95%. Despite the emergency, pre-war standards are being maintained.

1982 RANDOLPH, Harold. **Feminization of music, The**. *Studies in*
ac   *musical education, history, and aesthetics* 17 (Hartford: Music Teachers National Assoc., 1923) 194-200.
Notes that 85% of the current music students are female, as are 75% of audience members at concerts. Since Plato, music has been a "man's job", while women have traditionally been wives and mothers. At the present time, however, music in the United States is considered a sissy pursuit; male players outnumber females on "feminine" instruments such as the violin, and Chopin is preferred to the "male" composers, e.g., Bach, Beethoven, and Brahms. While women do have an important role through their emphasis on the more emotional aspects of music, men have a finer sense of rhythm and proportion. To avoid becoming "freaks", schoolboys should be taught only by men and should concentrate on "he-man" bass instruments such as the cello, trombone, or bassoon.

1983 REIS, Claire. **Composers, conductors, and critics** (New York:
bm   Oxford U., 1955) 282 p. *Illus., index.*
The author (1888-1978) reviews her 25 years as executive chairwoman of the League of Composers in New York between 1923--when she worked to found the league--and 1948. During the 1920s-30s the league played a vital role in introducing new music by European composers to American audiences, and also in commissioning and overseeing performances of new works by Americans. Reis felt strongly about the advantages of commissions over competitions, and she was instrumental in establishing a commission fund for the league. She also raised the money that allowed the league to sponsor the first American staged performances of Stravinsky's *Le sacre du printemps* and Schönberg's *Die glückliche Hand, op. 18* in 1930, and Stravinsky's *Oedipus Rex* and Prokofiev's *Pas d'acier, op. 41b* in 1931, as well as other major works. The performances were under the direction of Leopold Stokowski; Reis coordinated the theatrical production. Reis was educated in France, Berlin, and at the Inst. for Musical Art in New York. Under the auspices of the People's Music League, Reis organized free concerts for recent immigrants at Cooper Union in 1912-22. During the last season of the People's Music League she featured works by living composers, and she notes in hindsight that she was already becoming committed to contemporary music.

1984 rb —
R. by Abram CHASINS, *New York Times* 2 Oct 1955, VII-3.

→ SMITH, Caroline. **Philharmonic Orchestra of Los Angeles, The; the first decade 1919-29**, *see* 628bm[55].

1985 SMITH, Cecil Michener. **Worlds of music** (Philadelphia: J.B.
bm   Lippincott, 1952) 328 p. *Index.*
A comprehensive survey of music institutions and the music business at mid-century. 1) Many women have worked independently of major concert management organizations: e.g., Annie Friedberg and Dema Harschbanger, concert managers in New York, and Muriel Francis from New Orleans, who has her own personal-representation office in New York. Emma Feldman presently manages the Philadelphia All-Star Concert Series, and Edna Saunders manages opera and concerts in Houston, Tex. 2) Music clubs and related organizations have a current adult membership of about 300,000, mostly women. Too often the clubs are misdirected towards "pretentious cultural endeavors". 3) In 1931 Anne Evans and Ida Kruse McFarland led a campaign to restore the opera house in Central City, Colo. 4) When the Daughters of the American Revolution snubbed Marian Anderson in 1939, Sol Hurok saw the opportunity to make Anderson a national and international star through a variety of publicity procedures. 5) The present activity of Margaret Webster in stage direction and the past activity of Frances Elliott Clark as a music educator are discussed.

1986 STEVENSON, Robert. **Music in El Paso 1919-39** (El Paso: U.
bm   of Texas, 1970) 40 p. *Illus.*
Presents biographical information for the following women active in music in El Paso between 1919 and 1939: Lillian Hague Corcoran, Elizabeth Garrett, and Helen Roberts, composers; Mrs. William R. Brown, patron; Birdie Alexander, Margaret Vear Conkling, Abbie Marguerite Durkee, Dorothy Learmonth, Virginia Link, and Mary Goodbar Morgan, piano teachers; Edna Andrews, singer; Frances Newman, theory teacher; and Florence Crissey and Virginia Lawrence Bean, violin teachers.

1987 STOKOWSKI, Olga Samaroff. **American musician's story,**
bm   **An** (New York: W.W. Norton, 1939) 326 p. *Illus.*
Olga Samaroff Stokowski (1882-1948) lived a rich and diversified life in music as a concert pianist, the wife of a conductor of a leading orchestra between 1911 and 1923, a teacher at the Juilliard School from the mid-1920s onwards, a music critic for the *New York Evening Sun* beginning in 1925, and the founder of the Layman's Music Courses. Née Hickenlooper in Galveston, Tex., Samaroff Stokowski studied piano initially with her grandmother, who had trained to be a concert pianist in the 1850s. And it was with her grandmother that Samaroff Stokowski subsequently went to Paris to study at the conservatory--where she was the first American girl to win a scholarship in piano--and later to Berlin. Although she assumed the Russian surname Samaroff when she was launching

her career as a pianist in New York in 1905, Samaroff Stokowski was always a staunch advocate of the American musician, and her autobiography focuses upon aspects of musical life in the United States rather than solely upon her personal experiences. She discusses, for instance, 1) the sacrifices made by so many American families to send their musically-gifted children abroad before World War I, as contrasted with the changes in music education in the United States after the war, 2) American symphony orchestras in the early 1900s--their European personnel, their conductors, and the role of the wife of a conductor in the community, 3) her sponsorship of the Schubert Memorial, which offered young American concert artists the opportunity to appear with leading orchestras, and 4) her development of the Layman's Music Courses, which she held at Juilliard and elsewhere in New York and other cities as a pioneer effort in music appreciation.

1988 TUTHILL, Burnet Corwin. **Fifty years of chamber music in**
ac **the United States.** *Studies in musical education, history, and aesthetics* 23 (Hartford: Music Teachers National Assoc., 1929) 163-75.
This survey praises women patrons: e.g., Elizabeth Sprague Coolidge, who established the Berkshire Festival of Chamber Music in 1918; Mrs. Ralph Pulitzer, who sponsored the New York String Quartet; and Carolyn Beebe, the pianist, who was a founder of the New York Chamber Music Soc. All 3 women have commissioned compositions by Americans. The sole female member of the Musical Art Quartet in New York is its female cellist [Marie Roemaet-Rosanoff]. Amy Cheney Beach and Marion Bauer are among the leading American composers of chamber music. The work of the Olive Mead and Marianne Kneisel quartets is noted.

1989 WHITE, William Braid. **Profitable musical calling for**
ap **women, A,** *Etude* LX/9 (Sept 1942) 585-86.
At the convention of the American Soc. of Piano-Tuner Technicians last year, it was reported that there are fewer than 3000 men now working as piano tuners and about 6 million pianos in the United States. Such an imbalance offers employment opportunities to women. The qualifications necessary for tuning pianos--e.g., neatness, patience, attention to detail, and a good sense of pitch-"are as much feminine as masculine traits".

1990 WOLLSTEIN, R.H. **Mrs. Bok. A portrait in action,** *Musical*
ap *America* XLIX/17 (Aug 1929) 7, 32. *Illus.*
Together with Josef Hofmann, Mary Curtis Bok (Zimbalist) presently directs the Curtis Inst., which she founded in 1924 and has sustained by her labors and generous contributions. While she was president of the Philadelphia Settlement Music School Bok developed a "conservatory branch", where advanced instruction was given and more emphasis was placed on music for its own sake, as opposed to the settlement school approach toward music as a means for making better citizens. From this conservatory branch, the beginnings of the Curtis Inst. evolved. Bok represents a 3rd generation in her family with a devotion to music. The philosophy and curriculum of the Curtis Inst. are discussed.

→ **Woman's work in music number [IV],** *see* 77bp[10].

1991 **Women in music,** *New York Times* 6 Feb 1937, 16.
an
This item on the editorial page supports José Iturbi's recent controversial statement that women cannot achieve greatness in music. Iturbi said no more than physicians, anthropologists, and psychologists have been saying for many years: men and women are physically as well as temperamentally different, and these differences account for man's supremacy in art.

1992 WOOLF, S.J. **Music's the thing, The,** *New York Times* 31 Oct
an 1943, VI-14, 37.
The New Friends of Music was founded in 1936 in New York by Hortense Monath, the concert pianist, and her husband Ira Hirschmann, a businessman who also trained as a musician. This organization provides chamber music programs, with an emphasis on the composer rather than the particular performer. Monath decides upon the artistic policies of the New Friends of Music as well as the programs and the performers for concerts.

1994 ZANZIG, Augustus Delafield. **Music in American life,**
bm **present and future** (London: Oxford U., 1932) 560 p. *Illus., bibliog., index.*
Advocates the cultivation of music in all aspects of community life for educational and recreational purposes. Suggests musical activities for women, e.g., choral singing in mothers' clubs, rural festivals of music for families, and radio-listeners' clubs. Through such pursuits a mother can "gain a new kind of distinction in the minds of her children". Music in the home is therapeutic for the diseases of daily life and will nourish future generations of composers and performers. Also, the mother who plays music at home will be more influential than the mother who merely talks about music.

66 **Literature about women as composers of art music**

1995 ADLER, Valerie. **Goossens conducts Cole divertimento,**
ro *Musical America* LIX/7 (10 Apr 1939) 37. *Illus.*
Ulric Cole was the pianist in her *Divertimento for string orchestra and piano* (*WIAM* 2617) at a pair of recent concerts given by the Cincinnati Symphony Orchestra under the direction of Eugene Goossens. Opinions about the merit of Cole's work were divided, perhaps because audiences in Cincinnati are often conservative.

1996 ALDERSON, Margaret. **Opera by young composer features**
ap **Cleveland's season,** *Musical America* LII/13 (Aug 1932) 20. *Illus.*
Discusses Shirley Graham's opera *Tom-tom,* which was first performed by the Cleveland Summer Opera during the summer of 1932. The opera's 3 scenes are placed in Africa before Africans were brought to the United States as slaves, in the ante-bellum South, and in Harlem, N.Y. Graham, who is a student at the Oberlin Conservatory, has done extensive research on African music. Her opera incorporates Negro songs.

1997 **American youth to have its fling in league concert,** *Musical*
ap *America* XLV/17 (12 Feb 1927) 27. *Illus.*
Announces that a forthcoming concert sponsored by the League of Composers will include the works of Randall Thompson, Aaron Copland, Ruth Crawford (Seeger), Evelyn Berckman, Theodore Chanler, and Marc Blitzstein. Crawford, who studied with Adolf Weidig in Chicago, will be represented by her violin sonata. She has also written *Four preludes for piano* (*WIAM* 2725), *Adventures of Tom Thumb* for piano, and 2 pieces for small orchestra. Berckman, a Philadelphia composer who studied with Lazare Saminsky, will be represented by 2 songs--*Limpidité* and *Le baptême de la cloche.*

1998 A.M.P. **Gena Branscombe, a new American composer,** *Musi-*
ap *cal Leader and Concert-goer* XIII/23 (6 June 1907) 13-14. *Illus.*
Discusses Gena Branscombe's works, including the following songs: *Love in a life* (*WIAM* 2806), *In Granada* (*WIAM* 2800), *To Mirza* (*WIAM* 2825), *An epitaph* (*WIAM* 2790), *Deserted gypsy's song* (*WIAM* 2789), and *Starlight* (*WIAM* 2820). G. Schirmer and Wa-Wan Press have recently accepted some of Branscombe's compositions for publication.

1999 BARNES, Edward Shippen. **American composers of church**
ac **and choral music since 1876.** *Studies in musical education, history, and aesthetics* 23 (Hartford: Music Teachers National Assoc., 1929) 101-20.
Discusses the most prolific composers and their works between 1876 and 1928, among whom the only women are Patty Stair of Cleveland and Frances McCollin of Philadelphia, a pupil of H.A. Matthews.

→ BARNES, Edwin. **American women in creative music,** *see* 49bm[05].

2000 **Branscombe conducts own compositions with Chicago wom-**
rm **en's symphony,** *Musical Courier* C/6 (8 Feb 1930) 28.
Reports that on 8 Jan. Gena Branscombe conducted the 2nd half of the program of the Woman's Symphony Orchestra of Chicago, which was devoted entirely to her music. The following works were performed: *The dance of Fjaard* for women's voices and chamber orchestra (*WIAM* 2507), a trio from the choral drama *Pilgrims of destiny* (*WIAM* 2517), and the symphonic suite *Quebec.* Excerpts from reviews by Chicago critics are included.

2001 BRANSCOMBE, Gena. **Sound of trumpets, The,** *Showcase.*
ap *Music Clubs Magazine* XLII/2 (1962) 8-10 *Illus.*
At the age of 81, Gena Branscombe discusses 1) her experiences as a composer and conductor, 2) other women composers she has known, 3) her association with the publishers A.P. Schmidt and G. Schirmer and their support for young composers of her generation, and 4) performances of her works sponsored by the National Federation of Music Clubs and the General Federation of Women's Clubs. A biographical sketch of Branscombe is included.
(Laurine Elkins-Marlow)

2002 **Branscombe's *Pilgrims of destiny* given by New York Matinee**
rm **Musicale,** *Musical Courier* XCV/23 (8 Dec 1927) 24.
Reviews Gena Branscombe's choral drama *Pilgrims of destiny* (*WIAM* 2517) as performed by the Matinee Musicale club of New York at the Hotel Ambassador. The composer conducted. The performance offered "further proof that American music and musicians have made great strides in recent years".

→ BROOKS, Katherine. **Washington interest in music has centered around inspiring leadership of Mary Howe,** *see* 2074an[67].

→   **Claremont, California, Scripps College Music Library. A checklist of compositions in manuscript by American women composers,** *see* 9bm[01].

2003 COOKE, James Francis. **Breaks,** *Etude* LI/11 (Nov 1933) 729.
ap   *Port.*
Describes the recent successes of Evangeline Lehman. After graduating from Oberlin Col. with first prize in singing and piano, Lehman studied in Paris for 5 years. Her first compositions--songs with her own texts and piano pieces dating from 1932--were accepted for publication as a group. She subsequently wrote the oratorio *Ste. Thérèse of the Child Jesus,* which earned her a medal presented to her by the French Ministère des Affaires Étrangères.

2004 C.S. **Mana Zucca. The 'three-in-one artist",** *Prompter* I/3 (Aug
ap   1920) 70.
Mana Zucca studied piano with Alexander Lambert as a young child, and at age 8 she played a Beethoven concerto with the New York Symphony Orchestra under Walter Damrosch. After a concert tour of the United States 3 years later, she went abroad to study piano with Busoni and Leopold Godowsky, and composition with Max Vogrich and Herman Spielter. Mana Zucca concertized extensively in Europe, but upon her return to the United States she concentrated on composition. Her works have been played by the New York Philharmonic, and the Cincinnati, San Francisco, Russian, and Los Angeles symphony orchestras. In 1917 Mana Zucca founded the American Optimist Soc. to promote the interests of American composers and performers.

2005 DANIELS, Mabel Wheeler. **American girl in music, An**
bm   (Boston: Little, Brown, 1905) 286 p.
The composer's letters to a friend in Boston describe her year at the Munich Conservatory in 1902-03. George W. Chadwick, Daniels's composition teacher in Boston, recommended that she study composition with his former Munich classmate, Ludwig Thuile. Daniels also studied voice and devoted considerable time to choral singing. She stresses that only 5 years prior to her coming to Munich, women were not allowed to study composition or even counterpoint, and that when she presented herself as a candidate for the *Partitur-lesen* [score reading] class, she was accepted by the faculty only after deliberation. Fellow male students accepted her once she had proven her sight-reading ability at the keyboard. Performances of Wagner's operas in Munich were Daniels's chief musical enthusiasm during her year abroad. She was accompanied abroad by her mother.

2006 DANIELS, Mabel Wheeler. **Woman composer of yesterday**
ap   **and today, The,** *Music Clubs Magazine* XXXIX/5 (May-June 1960) 12-13. *List of works.*
Includes biographical information about Daniels, a list of her works, and a statement from the composer in which she assesses the improving climate for women as composers in the 20th c.

2007 DAVIS, Mrs. Charles D. **Recent performances of American**
ap   **music [I],** *Music Clubs Magazine* XI/4 (Mar-Apr 1932) 20-21.
A list of some recent performances of American music, including: 1) Amy Cheney Beach's *The chambered nautilus, op. 66* (*WIAM* 1295), 2) works by Beach, Harriet Ware, and Gena Branscombe at the Thursday Musical Club of Minneapolis, 3) an entire program of chamber music in Seattle by women composers, including Beach and Amy Worth, and 4) the Columbia Broadcasting System's "Musical Americana" hours presenting works by Mabel Wheeler Daniels, Ware, Beach, Branscombe, Carrie Jacobs-Bond, Mana Zucca, and Clara Edwards.

2008 DEVRIES, Herman. **Reviews first Tuesday symphony con-**
rm   **cert,** *Chicago American* 26 Oct 1932, 14.
A review of Florence G. Galajikian's *Symphonic intermezzo* (*WIAM* 2622), as performed by the Chicago Symphony Orchestra under the direction of Frederick Stock. Galajikian has written "an interesting and worthwhile score, which we trust will find a regular place in the repertory".

2009 DEYO, Felix. **Women as composers,** *International Lyric Courier*
ap   II/10-11 (Oct-Nov 1947) 5.
Reviews the status of women as composers at mid-century, and concludes that there is no major woman composer. As an explanation Lawrence Gilman's opinion of 1904 (*Women in modern music, WIAM* 679) is recalled: namely, that woman lacks the urgent inspiration she herself furnishes to her brother composer.

2010 D.J.T. **Give program of Branscombe works,** *Musical America*
rm   XXIX/1-2 (2,9 Nov 1918) 48.
Reviews a benefit concert for the Broadway Tabernacle Red Cross in New York on 22 Oct. that featured songs and solo vocal duets by Gena Branscombe, with the composer at the piano.

2011 D.J.T. **Pioneer virtues exalted in Gena Branscombe's Pilgrim**
ap   **opera,** *Musical America* XXXIII/5 (27 Nov 1920) 29, 31. *Illus.*
Discusses Gena Branscombe's *Pilgrims of destiny* (*WIAM* 2517), a choral drama. To date Branscombe has published 80 songs, 5 song cycles, 3 piano suites, 14 choruses for women's voices, and several orchestral works. Aspects of the composer's personal life as the mother of 3 young children and her professional growth are also considered.   (*Laurine Elkins-Marlow*)

2012 DOWNES, Olin. **Miss Bauer's work makes up concert,** *New*
rm   *York Times* 9 May 1951, 41.
Reviews the following works by Marion Bauer, which were performed at an all-Bauer concert at Town Hall in New York sponsored by the Phi Beta National Fraternity of Music and Speech: *Duo for oboe and clarinet, op. 25* (*WIAM* 2405), *Sonata for viola and piano, op. 22* (*WIAM* 2408), *Minstrel of romance* (*WIAM* 2744), the sonata for flute, violoncello, and piano, op. 47, *Moods for dance impressions,* and *Dance sonata.*

→   **Durham, New Hampshire, University of New Hampshire Library, Special Collections. A checklist of correspondence by Amy Cheney Beach,** *see* 13bm[01].

2013 E.A. **Wherein Harriet Ware, composer, announces herself a**
ap   **publisher,** *Musical America* XLV/8 (11 Dec 1926) 27. *Illus.*
Harriet Ware, who recently established a music-publishing business, notes that the only other woman to do so is Carrie Jacobs-Bond. The first publications of H. Ware, Inc. are her own works.

2014 ELKINS-MARLOW, Laurine. **Gena Branscombe, American**
dd   **composer and conductor** (PhD diss., Musicology: U. of Texas at Austin, 1978) 450 p. (typescript). *Bibliog., list of works.*
Gena Branscombe (1881-1977) was born in Canada, received her musical education in Chicago at the turn of the century, and spent her professional life in New York. She first became known as a composer of songs, and later was known for her choral works and arrangements, particularly those for women's voices. In addition to her composing, she conducted women's choruses for 30 years. Branscombe was an advocate of contemporary American music, and through her work with the General Federation of Women's Clubs and the National Federation of Music Clubs, as well as her programming compositions by other Americans along with her own works, she brought this music to the attention of amateur and professional musicians. Analysis of selected songs and choral works together with a catalogue of works are included.   (*Author*)

→   ELSON, Arthur. **Woman's work in music,** *see* 136bm[25].

2015 **Eternal youth effervesces from all compositions of Harriet**
ap   **Ware,** *New Jersey Music* I/1 (Sept 1945) 5-6, 18.
Discusses Ware's early work in music with her mother and her piano studies with William Mason in New York and later Sigismund Stojowski in Paris. Stojowski urged Ware to devote her major efforts to composition. At age 21 she experienced her first success with *The boat song,* which David Bispham helped to popularize. Ware studied composition in Berlin with Hugo Kaun, and during her year there was befriended by Rosalie Spohr, niece of the composer and harpist who toured with Jenny Lind. Ware's *The love wagon,* a light opera, will soon be produced on Broadway. One of her recently composed songs, *This day is mine,* has become a best seller.

2016 **Ethel Leginska directs her opera,** *New York Times* 24 Nov 1935,
an   II-9.
Reports that with the première of her opera *Gale* by the Chicago City Opera, Leginska became "the first woman in history" to write for and conduct in a major opera house. John Charles Thomas created the title role.

→   EWEN, David. **Composers since 1900,** *see* 51bm[05].

→   **Exhibition. Contemporary women composers in the United States,** *see* 3035ap[76].

→   **Fayetteville, Arkansas, University of Arkansas Library, Special Collections Division. A checklist of source materials by and about Florence B. Price,** *see* 16bm[01].

2017 FISHER, Barbara E. Scott. **Woman composer conducts too,**
an   *Christian Science Monitor* 12 June 1956, 10. *Illus.*
An interview with Gena Branscombe, composer and conductor, whom the author found to be a "decisive and independent spirit". Branscombe notes that she felt forced to take up conducting in order to obtain adequate performances of her works. She studied conducting first at New York U. and then worked with Chalmers Clifton and the orchestra of the American Orchestral Soc. in New York. She founded the Branscombe Choral, a women's chorus, in 1934 in New York, and soon after she inaugurated programs of Christmas music by the chorus in railroad stations in the city. In addition to her own compositions, Branscombe has published arrangements of 55 works, chiefly for women's chorus. Information on her training and early career is included.

2018 **Florence Wickham, 82, dies,** *New York Times* 21 Oct 1962, 89.
an
A native of Pennsylvania, Florence Wickham (1880-1962) made her operatic debut in Weisbaden in Meyerbeer's *Le prophète*. The mezzo-soprano also sang in Munich and at Covent Garden before she made her debut at the Metropolitan Opera in 1909 as Emilia in Toscanini's revival of *Otello*. After 3 seasons at the Metropolitan, Wickham retired from the stage in 1912 and began composing songs, ballet scores, and light operas. Among her best-known operettas were *Rosalind* (1938), *Legend of Hex Mountain* (1950), and *Ancestor maker* (1957).

2019 **Frances McCollin wins Federation prize for women's choral**
ap   **setting,** *Musical America* LI/9 (10 May 1931) 22. *Illus.*
Reports that the Philadelphia composer has won the $500 choral prize in the National Federation of Music Clubs' 11th prize competition for American composers with her *Spring in heaven*, on a text by Louise Driscoll. In addition to winning a variety of other prizes, McCollin is well-known for her weekly lectures on the programs of the Philadelphia Orchestra, which she illustrates with examples at the piano.

→   GALT, Martha. **To the ladies,** *see* 17bd[01].

2020 GAUME, Mary Matilda. **Ruth Crawford Seeger: her life and**
dd   **works** (PhD diss., Music: Indiana U., 1973) 331 p. (typescript, microfilm). *Them. cat.*
Presents biographical information for Ruth Crawford Seeger and detailed analyses of her extant art music. Discusses her studies in Chicago and New York, her experience in Europe, and her work with American folk song to determine influences on her style. Considers the evolution of her compositional approach. Also discusses the experimental aspects of Seeger's music and her position as an innovative figure in the first half of the 20th c. Includes a thematic catalogue which lists dates, places of origin, and locations of MSS together with dates of publication and information on first performances.
(Dissertation Abstracts, abridged)

2021 **Gena Branscombe, at 95, composer and conductor,** *New York*
an   *Times* 27 July 1977, B-2.
An obituary for Gena Branscombe (1881-1977), who had been working with a musicologist [Laurine Elkins-Marlow] on her biography until just before her death. Branscombe attended Chicago Musical Col., where she studied composition with Felix Borowski and piano with Arthur Friedheim and Rudolph Ganz. She also studied conducting with Frank Damrosch and Albert Stoessel, and she subsequently founded the Branscombe Choral in 1934, which gave annual concerts in Town Hall through 1954. Branscombe published more than 150 songs. She was especially noted for her choral works, e.g., *Coventry's choir* (*WIAM* 2506), *The phantom caravan* (*WIAM* 2516), *A wind from the sea* (*WIAM* 2522), *Youth of the world* (*WIAM* 2516), and *Pilgrims of destiny* (*WIAM* 2517).

2022 GILBERT, Steven E. **Ultra-modern idiom, The: a survey of**
ap   *New music,* *Perspectives of New Music* XII/1-2 (fall-winter 1973, spring-summer 1974) 282-314. *Music.*
Presents an overview of the music published by Henry Cowell as editor of the *New music edition*, beginning in 1927. Includes analyses of Ruth Crawford Seeger's *Three songs* (*WIAM* 2480) and Vivian Fine's *Four songs* (*WIAM* 3471).

→   G.M.S. **Boston women hold composers contest,** *see* 2088ap[67].

2023 GOSS, Madeline. **Modern music-makers** (New York: Da Capo,
bf   1970) 499 p. $22.50. *Illus.*
A reprint of the 1952 edition (New York: E.P. Dutton). Discusses the careers and works of 36 composers, 6 of whom are women: Marion Bauer, Gena Branscombe, Radie Britain, Mabel Wheeler Daniels, Mary Howe, and Louise Talma. Presents biographical imformation for each composer, a chronology of main events in her life, and a list of works organized by genre with dates and publication information.

2024 HACKETT, Karleton. **Chicago Symphony Orchestra concert**
rm   **at Orchestra Hall,** *Chicago Evening Post* 26 Oct 1932, 8.
Reviews Florence G. Galajikian's *Symphonic intermezzo* (*WIAM* 2622), as performed by the Chicago Symphony Orchestra under the direction of Frederick Stock. Galajikian's work was 1 of 5 prizewinners in the 1932 contest sponsored by the National Broadcasting Co.

2025 H.G.K. **F. Marion Ralston gives program at Peterborough**
ap   **colony,** *Musical America* XXVIII/26 (26 Oct 1918) 19. *Illus.*
Reports that events of the summer at the MacDowell Colony in Peterborough, N.H. included a recital by Frances Marion Ralston of the piano compositions she completed during her residence, e.g., a sonata (*WIAM* 2720) and a theme and variations set (*WIAM* 2722). Ralston is a member of the faculty of Wellesley Col.

→   HILL, Tremont. **Siren serenade,** *see* 143ap[25].

→   HIPSHER, Edward. **American opera and its composers,** *see* 685bf[56].

→   **How the woman composer is coming to the front,** *see* 686an[56].

2026 HOWARD, John Tasker; MENDEL, Arthur. **Our contem-**
bm   **porary composers** (New York: T.Y. Crowell, 1941) 447 p. *Illus., list of works, discog., index.*
A supplementary volume to *Our American music* (*WIAM* 685), covering the decade 1930-40. Prominent composers, new techniques of composition, and performing and other music institutions are discussed. The appendices list recordings, prize-winning compositions, and commissions. Information regarding the following women composers is included: Marion Bauer, Gena Branscombe, Ulric Cole, Mabel Wheeler Daniels, Eleanor Everest Freer, Mary Howe, Frances McCollin, Mary Carr Moore, and Frances Terry.

2027 HOWE, Mary. **Jottings** (Washington, D.C.: author, 1959) 181 p.
bm   *Illus., list of works.*
The composer (1882-1964) discusses her career in music, including 1) her education at the Peabody Conservatory, from which she graduated in 1922, and 2) her association with the MacDowell Colony, the Elizabeth Sprague Coolidge Foundation concerts, and the National Symphony Orchestra, which Howe and her husband were instrumental in founding in 1930. Reviews and lists of performances and publishers are included.

2028 HUDGINS, Mary D. **Chicago school named for state com-**
an   **poser,** *Arkansas Gazette* 30 June 1968, E-5. *Illus.*
Florence B. Price, a native of Little Rock, Ark., was recently honored in Chicago by having a public school dedicated to her memory. She graduated from the New England Conservatory, having studied with George W. Chadwick and Frederick S. Converse. In 1932 she won the Wanamaker Prize for her symphony in E minor, which was subsequently performed by the Chicago Symphony Orchestra. Excerpts from Price's piano concerto and her violin concerto no. 2 were presented at the dedication.

→   HUGHES, Rupert. **American composers,** *see* 688bm[56].

2029 HUME, Paul. **Mary Howe honored on 80th year with concert**
an   **of her own works,** *Washington Post* 5 Apr 1962, C-27.
This concert, which was sponsored by the Elizabeth Sprague Coolidge Foundation at the Library of Congress, is viewed as an appropriate gesture since the foundation became associated with the Library of Congress in large part due to the efforts of Mary Howe. The program included a representative selection of Howe's chamber, choral, and solo vocal works.

2030 **Introducing Ethel Leginska, composer,** *Musical Courier*
ap   LXXVII/13 (26 Sept 1918) 42.
Reports that the pianist has turned to composition and has spent the summer working under the guidance of Ernest Bloch in New York. To date Leginska has completed some songs, a piano composition, and a string quartet.

2031 JACKSON, Barbara Garvey. **Florence Price, composer,** *Black*
ap   *Perspective in Music* V/1 (spring 1977) 30-43. *Port.*
An introduction to the composer's life and works. Née Smith in 1888, Florence Price grew up in Little Rock, Ark. Between 1903 and 1906 she studied at the New England Conservatory, and subsequently she taught in Little Rock and at Clark U. in Atlanta. She married Thomas Price, a lawyer from Little Rock, in 1912. In 1927 the family moved to Chicago, where Price spent the rest of her life as a composer, teacher, pianist, and organist. She was the first black woman to have a symphony performed by a major American orchestra, the Chicago Symphony Orchestra in 1933. *(Author)*

2032 JANSON, Blanche Barney. **Dresden locally premières Flor-**
ap   **ence Wickham's opera,** *Musical Courier* CXIX/4 (15 Feb 1939) 11.
Reports that the European première of Florence Wickham's operetta *Rosalind* took place during the 1938-39 season in Dresden with Kurt Striegler as conductor.

2033 JEPSON, Barbara. **Ruth Crawford Seeger: a study in "mixed**
ap   **accents",** *Feminist Art Journal* VI/1 (spring 1977) 13-16. *Port., bibliog.*
Summarizes the life and works of Ruth Crawford Seeger (1901-53), and attempts to determine why this talented composer stopped writing music after her marriage to Charles Seeger in 1931. Discusses briefly Seeger's activities as a collector and transcriber of folk music. *(Author)*

2034 JOHNSON, Christopher. **Rebecca Clarke. A catalogue of**
bm   **her works** (facsimile of typescript at NNCU-G, 1977) 40 p.
(typescript, xerox). *Bibliog., them. cat., index.*
Rebecca Clarke--an English-American composer of songs and chamber works-
-trained at the Royal Col. of Music, where she was the first woman to study
composition with Sir Charles Stanford. She was well-known as a violist and
chamber musician in England and the United States. Subsequently she settled
in New York, where she married James Friskin, the pianist. This thematic
catalogue includes all her compositions, with data on instrumentation, first
performances, awards, location of MSS, etc. A bibliography of all of Clarke's
published writings, portraits, and all significant writings about the composer
and her works is presented.   *(Author)*

2035 KINSCELLA, Hazel Gertrude. **F. Marion Ralston joins**
ap   **ranks of Pacific Coast notables**, *Musical America* XXXII/21 (25
Sept 1920) 5. *Illus.*
Frances Marion Ralston has recently relocated in Los Angeles, and during the
1920-21 season she will give recitals on the West Coast. The pianist-composer's
first teacher was her mother, who was the leading voice teacher in St. Louis for
30 years. Ralston graduated from the New England Conservatory, and she later
continued her piano studies with Carl Faelten and her work in composition
with Arthur Foote, Ernest R. Kroeger, and Adolph Weidig. For 10 years
Ralston was the director of music at Rockford Col. in Rockford, Ill.
Subsequently she joined the faculty of Wellesley Col., although she resigned
after 1 year in order to relocate in California and devote herself to composition
and performance--with the exception of a few talented piano pupils. Many of
Ralston's piano compositions and songs have been published. Her piano sonata
(*WIAM* 2720) is discussed.

2036 KIRK, Elise Kuhl. **Chamber music of Charles Koechlin, The**
dd   (PhD diss., Musicology: Catholic U. of America, 1977) 390 p.
(typescript, microfilm). *Port., music, bibliog., list of works.*
Considers the chamber music of the French composer Charles Koechlin (1867-
1950), as well as biographical and critical writings about his life and works.
Catherine Murphy Urner began her studies with Koechlin in 1920 and
subsequently became active as a composer, concert singer, and teacher in the
United States, France, and Italy. Urner wrote over 100 songs, 30 choral pieces,
20 piano works, and 14 orchestral transcriptions. Koechlin considered Urner his
favorite pupil and orchestrated several of her works, e.g., *Equisses normandes*
(1929). The major share of Urner's works remains unpublished; her MSS are
deposited at the U. of California at Berkeley and with Charles Shatto in San
Francisco.   *(Author, abridged)*

2037 KIRK, Elise Kuhl. **Parisian in America, A: the lectures and**
ap   **legacies of Charles Koechlin**, *Current Musicology* 25 (1978) 50-
68. *Music.*
Charles Koechlin visited the United States in 1918, 1928-29, and 1937,
lecturing and teaching harmony and counterpoint--mainly in California. These
sojourns are documented through his voluminous notes, diaries, and correspondence. His teachings were transmitted south along the California coast
from Berkeley to San Diego through a small group of devoted American pupils,
one of whom--Catherine Murphy Urner--became Koechlin's life-long friend.
Urner promoted Koechlin's music and also influenced his compositional style.
Catherine Urner's own output as a composer is discussed.   *(Author, abridged)*

2038 KNERR, R.M. **Noted feminist views woman's place in music**,
ap   *Musical America* XXXV/13 (21 Jan 1922) 5.
An interview with W.L. George, a noted English writer and feminist who is
currently on a lecture tour in the United States, regarding women's lack of
stature in composition as contrasted with other areas of creative endeavor.
George suggests that women lack adequate powers of concentration, and that
women's great capacity for "direct emotional expression" is antithetical to the
capacity for creative work. Women do excel as singers, and it is significant that
singing is a personal adornment, or a form of direct emotional expression.

→   KROHN, Ernst. **Missouri music**, *see* 698bf[56].

→   **Los Angeles, University of California Music Library. A**
checklist of materials by and about women in American
music, *see* 19bm[01].

2039 **Mabel Daniels [is] winner of Girl Scouts' song contest**,
ap   *Musical America* XXVIII/21 (21 Sept 1918) 19. *Illus.*
Reports that Mabel Wheeler Daniels's *On the trail* won first place in a contest
for a marching song for the Girl Scouts of the United States of America. The 5
judges were all leading American women composers: Amy Cheney Beach, Gena
Branscombe, Fay Foster, Margaret Ruthven Lang, and Harriet Ware.

2040 **Mana Zucca, humorist**, *Musical Courier* LXXV/3 (19 July 1917)
ap   42.
Mana Zucca discusses incidents in her varied career as singer, pianist,

accompanist, violinist, and composer that have had amusing consequences, e.g.,
her audition for Busoni's master class in piano, a duo-piano recital with Teresa
Carreño, and a private competition for which Mana Zucca and the song
composer Francesco Paolo Tosti set the same texts. Her performances in light
opera and her work as a piano prodigy are also considered.

2041 **Mana Zucca piano concerto, The**, *Musical Courier* LXXXI/19
ap   (4 Nov 1920) 27.
Announces Mana Zucca's forthcoming performance of her piano concerto no. 1
in E-flat major, op. 49 (*WIAM* 2646) with the National Symphony Orchestra,
as one of the rare instances of an American composer being invited to perform
his or her work with a leading orchestra. Mana Zucca played the concerto in
Feb. 1920 in Los Angeles and received excellent critical notices as well as a
good response from the audience.

2042 **Marion Bauer, composer, is dead**, *New York Times* 11 Aug
an   1955, 21.
Marion Bauer was born in Walla Walla, Wash. in 1887, and she studied
composition in Paris with André Gedalge and Nadia Boulanger. A prolific
composer influenced by French impressionism, Bauer wrote for both symphonic
and chamber orchestra, and she published many works for piano, voice, and
chorus. Bauer was a member of the American Composers Alliance, the
American Musicological Soc., and the Soc. for Comparative Musicology.

2043 MARTENS, Frederick Herman. **Champions American poetry**
ap   **as inspiration to composers**, *Musical America* XXI/22 (3 Apr
1915) 27.
Harriet Ware, the composer, is a champion of American poets. Of the 22 songs
and choral works Ware has written to date, the texts of all but 3 are by
Americans. Edwin Markham is Ware's collaborator in her new cantata, *Undine*.

2044 M.B.S. **Rebecca Clarke. Violist and composer**, *Strad* LXXVII
ap   (Dec 1966) 297-99.
Born in Harrow, England in 1886, Rebecca Clarke began her public career as a
violist in the Nora Clench Quartet. She was one of the first 6 women players
chosen by conductor Henry Wood for the Queen's Hall Orchestra in London in
1914. After World War I she performed on tour with a piano quartet in Europe
and the United States. High points in her career have included winning 2nd
prize in the chamber music competition sponsored by Elizabeth Sprague
Coolidge for her viola sonata (*WIAM* 2422) in 1919 and for her piano trio in
1921 (*WIAM* 2425), as well as a 1942 performance of her suite for clarinet and
viola during a festival of the International Soc. for Contemporary Music. In
1944 Clarke married James Friskin, a pianist on the faculty of the Juilliard
School, who had been a fellow student at the Royal Col. of Music in London.

→   MEAD, Janet. **Catalog of Composers Library**, *see* 25bm[01].

2045 **Mrs. M. Wood-Hill, composer, was 83**, *New York Times* 3 Mar
an   1954, 27.
Born in Brooklyn, Mabel Wood-Hill (1870-1954) graduated from Smith Col.
and studied in New York with Walter Henry Rothwell and Cornelius Rybner.
Wood-Hill's compositions include numerous songs and several stage works. She
also orchestrated a number of preludes and fugues by Bach and trio sonatas by
Couperin. Her transcriptions have been performed by the New York Philharmonic among other organizations.

2046 PEYSER, Ethel R. **In memory--Marion Bauer**, *Baton of the Phi*
ap   *Beta Fraternity* XXXV/1 (Nov 1955) 5, 8.
A tribute to Marion Bauer by her friend and co-author of *How music grew*
(1925), *Music through the ages* (1932), and *How opera grew* (1955). Bauer, who
was active in the League of Composers and the International Soc. for
Contemporary Music, taught at New York U. from 1926-51 and received an
honorary doctorate from the New York Col. of Music in 1954.

→   **Philadelphia, Free Library of Philadelphia, Fleisher Collec-**
tion. A checklist of source materials by and about women in
American music, *see* 35bm[01].

→   **Philadelphia, Free Library of Philadelphia, Music Depart-**
ment. A checklist of source materials by and about Frances
McCollin, *see* 36bm[01].

2047 **Proviso's band to play Easter concert today**, *Chicago Tribune*
an   25 Apr 1943, III-4. *Illus.*
Reports that Florence G. Galajikian's *For freedom* will be performed by the
band of Proviso Township High School in Maywood, Ill. Also cites the
composer's *Girl with a Spanish shawl* (*WIAM* 2436) and *Song of joy* (*WIAM*
2559).

2048 **R. Harriet Ware interviewed**, *Musical Courier* XCV/24 (15 Dec
ap   1927) 31.

1) Ware is currently working on a song cycle for children and a suite for piano. The piano suite "is anticipated with interest" because Ware trained as a concert pianist before turning to composition. 2) The composer acknowledges a great debt to the National Federation of Music Clubs for programming her songs at meetings. 3) H. Ware Publishers, Inc. has relocated to a new office on lower Broadway in New York.

→   REIS, Claire. **Composers in America**, *see* 63bf[05].

2049   ROCKWELL, John. **Musical spotlight puts Ruth Seeger in**
rm   **focus sharply**, *New York Times* 21 Feb 1975, 13.
Reviews a retrospective concert of Ruth Crawford Seeger's works given under the auspices of the Performers Committee for 20th-c. Music at Columbia U. The program "ranged from surprisingly mature student works through major masterpieces such as the string quartet (*WIAM* 2477), *Three songs* (*WIAM* 2480) to texts by Carl Sandburg, and the suite for woodwind quintet (*WIAM* 2478).

→   ROSEN, Judith. **Why haven't women become great composers?**, *see* 3130ap[76].

2050   **Rubinstein Club concert. Harriet Ware's new cantata** *Sir*
rm   *Oluf*, *Musical Courier* LXI/25 (21 Dec 1910) 10.
Harriet Ware's cantata *Sir Oluf* is her first large work. The performance at the Rubinstein Club in New York featured Alma Gluck and Cecil Fanning as soloists with a 125-member female chorus. During the intermission a member of the audience was overheard as follows: "What will become of us men, if women can write such good things and have them presented under such glowing circumstances"? While Victor Hugo said the 19th c. was "woman's century", the 20th c. may well "be the period when the woman composer will ultimately rise up and enrich the world".

2051   **Ruth Deyo, author of Egyptian opera**, *New York Times* 20 Jan
an   1930, 16.
Reports that Ruth Deyo--the former American pianist now living in Egypt--recently left Cairo for New York in order to make preliminary arrangements for the production of her music drama, *The diadem of stars*, in which she has attempted a reconstruction of ancient Egyptian music. The supporters of the project include Otto Kahn and Leopold Stokowski. Deyo made her last public performance in New York on 17 Jan. 1925, when she gave a joint recital with George Enesco and Hans Kindler.

2052   SEASHORE, Carl E. **Why no great women composers?**, *In*
bd   *search of beauty in music* (New York: Ronald, 1947) 363-67.
"The absence of women from the higher fields of achievement in creative music does not lie in any form of limitation by heredity, nor does it lie to any great extent in present limitations of opportunity, environment, or woman's particular obligations". Rather, the fundamental cause is her urge to be beautiful and adored as a person. Marriage, as a career in itself, makes music an avocation for women.

2053   SEEGER, Charles. **Ruth Crawford**, *American composers on*
bd   *American music*. Ed. by Henry COWELL (Stanford, Calif.: Stanford U., 1933) 110-18. *Music, index*.
The works of 20 composers are discussed and general trends in composition as of 1933 are considered. Charles Seeger reports on the music of Ruth Crawford (Seeger) and analyzes her *Three songs* (*WIAM* 2480), string quartet (*WIAM* 2477), and her suite for solo flute. A brief biographical sketch of the composer's early career and a list of her principal works written from 1925-32--together with publication information--are included. "One can find only a few men among American composers who are as uncompromisingly and successfully radical" as Ruth Crawford.

2054   SHARPE, Estelle. **Mary Howe, independent composer**,
an   *Washington Post* 26 Dec 1952, 25.
"During 28 years as a composer, Howe has given allegiance to no school of composition--modern or otherwise". While stressing that she is not a feminist, Howe notes that it was considered a handicap to be a woman when she started composing, and she states she would have gotten along faster if she had been a man. Instances of the international recognition that her music has received are discussed.

2055   SHEPLER, David. **More glory than profit in music. But**
an   **Mabel Daniels just can't help turning out her tuneful**
        melodies, *Boston Sunday Herald* 24 May 1934, C-4.
An interview with Mabel Wheeler Daniels, occasioned by the Boston Symphony Orchestra's performance of her *Pirates' island, op. no. 2* (*WIAM* 2621). "Orchestras in many parts of the world and choirs in great cathedral churches sing and play her music continually". At St. Bartholomew's Church in New York includes in its library Daniels's *Exultate Deo* for chorus and orchestra, and her sacred chorus *The Christ child, op. 32, no. 2* (*WIAM*

2529). Daniels mentions several performances of *Deep forest, op. 34, no. 1* (*WIAM* 2619, 2620) and discusses the economic burdens borne by composers.

→   SMITH, Julia. **Directory of American women composers**, *see* 64bm[05].

2056   **Society to publish chamber music works**, *Musical America* LXI/
ap   10 (25 May 1941) 10.
Reports that the Soc. for the Publication of American Music will publish Ulric Cole's piano quintet, dated 1936 (*WIAM* 2429). Several years ago Cole won the publication prize for her violin sonata no. 1 (*WIAM* 2430). Cole studied piano with Josef Lhevinne and composition with Rubin Goldmark at the Juilliard School.

2057   STANLEY, May. **Mana Zucca tells why *Rachem* was writ-**
ap   **ten**, *Musical America* XXXI/4 (22 Nov 1919) 19.
In *Rachem* (*WIAM* 2929)--the Hebrew word for mercy--Mana Zucca has attempted to capture the spiritual yearnings of all races. The song is currently a favorite with recitalists. Mana Zucca's views on song composition are discussed.

2058   STANLEY, May. **Students may be "farmerettes" under**
ap   **Harriet Ware's plan**, *Musical America* XXVII/20 (16 Mar 1918) 13.
Ware plans to hold summer classes in repertory at her newly purchased farm in New Jersey. Numerous musicians--especially singers--have asked to work with her in the past, but the composer has not been able to accommodate them. Ware anticipates holding gatherings at which her students can meet with prominent men and women active in music as well as the plastic arts and literature. Ware also discusses her work habits as a composer, her interest in MacDowell's songs, and her mother's encouragement during her formative years as a musician.

2059   STRONGIN, Theodore. **Study for piano is showcase hit**,
rm   *New York Times* 5 May 1966, 58.
Reviews Ruth Crawford Seeger's *Piano study in mixed accents* (*WIAM* 2726), as performed by Paul Jacobs at the Eisner and Lubin Auditorium of New York U. Other works on the program included Elliott Carter's cello sonata and Charles Schwartz's *Neuma*.

→   **Successful women song writers**, *see* 454ap[50].

2060   THOMAS, Jessie M. **Women composers hold conference at**
ap   **Chautauqua**, *Musical America* LV/13 (Aug 1935) 34. *Illus*.
A conference of American women composers was held at the Chautauqua Summer Festival in Chautauqua, N.Y. on 26-29 July. Albert Stoessel conducted the Chautauqua Symphony Orchestra in performances of Amy Cheney Beach's symphony in E minor, op. 32 (*WIAM* 1370), and Mabel Wheeler Daniels's *Pirates' island, op. 34, no. 2* (*WIAM* 2621). Works by Radie Britain, Mary Howe, and other women were also presented during the conference.

2061   THOMPSON, Oscar. **Former opera singer turns composer**,
ap   *Musical America* LVIII/13 (Aug 1938) 19. *Illus*.
Discusses the première performance of Florence Wickham's operetta *Rosalind* in Carmel, N.Y. at the Rockridge Theater. Wickham's libretto is based on an adaptation of Shakespeare's *As you like it. Rosalind* is reminiscent of Reginald de Koven's *Robin Hood*, in which Wickham appeared after she left the Metropolitan in 1912.

2062   **Two sets of delightful songs by Kathleen Lockhart Manning**,
ap   *Musical America* LI/19 (10 Dec 1931) 28. *Illus*.
Reports that works by women composers are included in G. Schirmer's recent list of song publications. Kathleen Lockhart Manning's *Five fragments* (*WIAM* 2939) and *Chinese impressions* (*WIAM* 2937) are recommended to the concert singer. A photograph of the composer is included.

2063   W. **Convention of American Pen Women hears works by**
ap   **composer-members**, *Musical America* L/10 (25 May 1930) 6.
At a recent convention of the National League of American Pen Women in Washington, D.C., the following compositions, among others, were performed: a string quartet by Mary Howe that won first prize in the Pen Women's music competition, Dorothy Radde Emery's *Flower cycle*, Marianne Genet's *Arabian caravan suite*, and *Day dreams* by Phyllis Fergus. In addition, Gena Branscombe conducted scenes from her choral work *Pilgrims of destiny* (*WIAM* 2517).

2064   **Washington holds a Festival of American Women Compos-**
ap   **ers**, *Musical Courier* XC/21 (28 May 1925) 14.
At the Festival of American Women Composers in Washington, D.C. on 28-30 Apr., works by the following composers were performed at 3 concerts: Karolyn Wells Bassett, Amy Cheney Beach, Gena Branscombe, Ulric Cole, Mabel Wheeler Daniels, Ethel Glenn Hier, Mary Howe, Florence Parr-Gene, Frances

Marion Ralston, Mary Turner Salter, Helen Sears, Harriet Ware, and Mabel Wood-Hill. Many of the composers assisted in the performances. It has been proposed that the festival become an annual event.

2065 WATSON, Dorothy DeMuth. **American women composers**
ap **hold festival in Washington,** *Musical America* LII/9 (10 May 1932) 20, 40.
During the convention of the National League of American Pen Women on April 22-28, an elaborate festival program included 23 recitals and a "national concert" of compositions that were awarded prizes by the league for 1932. Works by the following women, among others, were performed: Mary Carr Moore, Mary Howe, Amy Cheney Beach, Ruth Crawford Seeger, Dorothy Radde Emery, Gena Branscombe, Pearl Adams, and Marjorie Dudley.

2066 **Wins Bearnes Prize,** *Musical America* LVI/8 (25 Apr 1936) 31.
ap *Illus.*
Announces that Jeanne Behrend, pianist-composer, is the winner of the 1936 Bearnes Prize for composition with her songs on texts by Sara Teasdale (*WIAM* 2760). Behrend studied composition with Rosario Scalero and piano with Josef Hofmann.

2067 **Worthwhile American composers,** *Musician* XXVIII/12-XXXII/
ap 3 (Dec 1923-Mar 1927) pagination noncontinuous.
This series of 40 biographical sketches includes articles on 13 women, listed in the order of publication as follows: Florence Newell Barbour, Gena Branscombe, Floy Little Bartlett, Mari Paldi, Amy Cheney Beach, Anna Priscilla Risher, Cora Jenkins, Mabel Madison Watson, Mildred Weston, Edith Hatch, Mabel Lee Hatch, Ida Mae Crombie, and Marion Bauer.

2068 **Wrote second best sonata in the Coolidge contest,** *Musical*
ap *America* XXX/21 (20 Sept 1919) 27. *Illus.*
Reports that Rebecca Clarke won 2nd prize for her viola sonata (*WIAM* 2422) in the chamber music competition sponsored by Elizabeth Sprague Coolidge. Clarke is a violist herself and gives concerts with May Mukle, pianist. She came from England to the United States 3 years ago because of war conditions. Clarke's other compositions to date are briefly discussed.

2069 WURM, Marie. **Women's struggle for recognition in music,**
ap *Etude* LIV/11 (Nov 1936) 687, 746.
Reviews the history of women as composers and discusses the problems traditionally experienced by women in gaining performances of their works. In prefatory remarks the editors of *Etude* note that 1) Wurm speaks for the situation in Europe, whereas in the United States women composers have always received a great deal of attention, and 2) musical clubs in the United States--for which continental European countries have no counterpart--have been especially supportive of the woman composer.

67 Literature about women as educators, patrons, and members of music clubs

2070 A.B. **America's oldest music club celebrates golden jubilee,**
ap *Musical America* XXXIII/15 (5 Feb 1921) 33. *Illus.*
The Rossini Club of Portland, Me., was founded in 1868, when 5 women met to form an association for the advancement of music in their city. By 1871 the club had grown sufficiently to become incorporated. At the Columbian Exposition in Chicago in 1893, Rose Fay Thomas identified the Rossini Club as the oldest music club in the United States.

2071 ANDERTON, Margaret. **What women are doing for music**
ap **in America. The story of Mrs. William Arms Fisher,** *Musician*
XXXIV/1 (Jan 1929) 33.
After graduating from college, Emma Roderick (later Mrs. William Arms Fisher) taught music in the Illinois public school system, and she subsequently was appointed supervisor of music in the schools of Peoria. While in Peoria she became active in the local music club, enlisting the aid of the business and civic communities to secure local performances by internationally known concert artists as well as prominent orchestras such as the Boston Symphony Orchestra. Roderick has held many offices in the National Federation of Music Clubs from state vice-president in the Illinois federation to vice-president of the national federation--a position she currently occupies. At the present time she lives in Boston; she was instrumental in organizing the Boston Music Week that has now evolved into the New England Festival Assoc.

2072 B.E. **Mother Georgia Stevens: R.I.P.,** *Catholic Choirmaster*
ap XXXII/2 (28 June 1946) 60-61, 92.
Mother Georgia Stevens (1870-1946) founded the Pius X School of Liturgical Music at the Manhattanville Col. of the Sacred Heart in New York beginning in 1916. Stevens and her financial backer, Justine Ward, conceived of the

school as a response to Pius X's appeal for the restoration of authentic music within the Roman Catholic church in his *Motu proprio* of 1903. The traditions of the Benedictine monks of Solesmes were followed at the school in teaching Gregorian chant, and choir work and pedagogy were stressed. Mother Stevens developed the Pius X Choir, an all-female ensemble, with the intention of popularizing chant by presenting it with highly-trained voices. Her Tone and Rhythm Series incorporated her ideas on teaching music to children in the elementary grades. Originally Mother Stevens trained as a violinist with Charles Martin Loeffler among others. She made her final profession as a religious in 1914 at Ixelles, Belgium.

2073 BEACH, Amy Cheney. **Twenty-fifth anniversary of a vision,**
ac **The.** *Volume of proceedings of the Music Teachers National Association* 27 (Oberlin, Ohio: Music Teachers National Assoc., 1932) 45-48.
An appeal for financial support for the MacDowell Colony in Peterborough, N.H., which was founded as a memorial to the composer by his wife, Marian MacDowell, in 1907. Beach delivered this paper at the annual meeting of the Music Teachers National Assoc. in 1932, in which she expresses her gratitude for the beauty, solitude, and "inner life" that the colony offers to creative artists.

2074 BROOKS, Katherine. **Washington interest in music has**
an **centered around inspiring leadership of Mary Howe,** *Washington Sunday Star* 2 May 1943, D-6.
Discusses Mary Howe's work as head of the Woman's Committee of the National Symphony Orchestra, which she organized. Howe began piano studies as a girl in Washington and then continued at the Peabody Conservatory, where she was a student of Ernest Hutcheson and Harold Randolph, duopianists. Howe did not pursue composition until her 3 children reached school age, at which point she returned to Peabody for study.

2075 BROWN, Nona. **At 96, a green bough and a singing bird,** *New*
an *York Times* 22 Dec 1963, II-13.
In 1935 Gertrude Clark Whittall presented the Library of Congress with a matched set of Stradivarius instruments and established a foundation to provide free chamber music concerts played on these instruments. The instruments are kept in the Whittall Pavilion, a room donated to the library by Whittall. During World War II she assembled and deposited in the library a collection of autographed MSS by European composers.

2076 CALDWELL, Belle. **How musical sororities perpetuate**
ap **artistic ties,** *Musical America* XLVI/10 (25 June 1927) 3-4. *Illus.*
Five national sororities for music have been established since 1900: Mu Phi Epsilon (founded 1903), Sigma Alpha Iota (1903), Delta Omicron International Music Fraternity (1909), Phi Beta (1912), and Lambda Phi Delta (1917), which includes the fields of dance and speech in addition to music. Each sorority consists of a national society, chapters at conservatories and at colleges, and alumni clubs. Typical interests of the music sororities include the funding of scholarships for worthy students, the encouragement of young composers, and the maintenance of academic standards. Sigma Alpha Iota has endowed a cottage at the MacDowell Colony in Peterborough, N.H.

2077 **Carolina Lazzari, contralto is dead,** *New York Times* 18 Oct
an 1946, 24.
Carolina Lazzari (1891-1946) sang with the Chicago Opera from 1917 to 1920, when she was engaged by the Metropolitan Opera. The contralto taught for many years in a studio at the Metropolitan. Among her pupils were Judy Garland, Doris Duke Cromwell, and Dennis Day.

2078 COOLIDGE, Elizabeth Sprague. **Da capo** (Washington, D.C.:
bm Library of Congress, 1952) 14 p.
Presents the text of a paper Elizabeth Sprague Coolidge delivered to the Mother's Club of Cambridge, Mass. on 13 Mar. 1951. Coolidge relates how in 1916 Hugo Kortschak of the Chicago Symphony Orchestra approached her as a possible sponsor for the string quartet with which he was playing. Subsequently Coolidge signed a 3-year contract with Kortshak's quartet to give performances at her apartment in New York and her summer home in Pittsfield, Mass. In 1917 Frederick Stock took Coolidge to meet Carl and Ellen Battell Stoeckel and visit their music shed in Norfolk, Conn., with the result that Coolidge decided to build a similar establishment in Pittsfield. Coolidge discusses the prize competitions for chamber music she established, the festivals for chamber music she sponsored in Europe, and the beginnings of her association with the Library of Congress. She notes it was at her insistence that major radio networks broadcasted chamber music programs sponsored by the Coolidge Foundation in the 1930s--at a time when radio stations, some of the performers involved, and even Carl Engel were not enthusiastic.

2079 DOWNES, Olin. **Friend of music, A. Mrs. Coolidge, patron**
an **of the art, will be honored at Washington festival,** *New York Times* 22 Oct 1950, II-7.
The 25th anniversary of the Elizabeth Sprague Coolidge Foundation occasioned the honoring of Coolidge, the "patron saint" of chamber music. Before 1918, performance of new chamber works was rare; with the founding, in that

year, of the Berkshire Festival of Chamber Music at South Mountain in the Berkshires, chamber music organizations began to multiply and so did the opportunities for native composers to be heard. The gift of an auditorium to the Library of Congress in 1925 and the establishment of the foundation to insure its use gave the project national scope and significance.

2080 EATON, Frances Q. **Mrs. MacDowell: champion of an**
ap   **ideal**, *Musical America* LX/3 (10 Feb 1940) 106. *Illus.*
Marian MacDowell discusses the damage the 1938 hurricane made at the MacDowell Colony in Peterborough, N.H., and notes that the colony will again be operating during the summer of 1940. The colony's main asset is a $200,000 endowment fund. Colonists pay only a modest fee for board, and the large deficit each year is met by gifts and the receipts from MacDowell's piano recitals.

2081 EATON, Frances Q.; SCHELLSCHMIDT, Pauline. **Music**
ap   **federation looks to youth**, *Musical America* LVII/9 (10 May 1937) 4, 36-38.
A report on the 20th biennial convention of the National Federation of Music Clubs in Apr. 1937 at Indianapolis. Developments of interest included 1) the federation's endorsement for the post of Secretary of Fine Arts in the presidential cabinet, 2) the decision to work for state-wide opera projects, and 3) a challenge by Olga Samaroff Stokowski that the federation give women musicians equal opportunity with men.

2082 EATON, Frances Q. **Symphony women's groups hold fifth**
ap   **biennial in New York**, *Musical America* LXV/6 (25 Apr 1945) 8. *Illus.*
Delegates from the women's committees associated with symphony orchestras in 17 cities convened in New York to share information about their activities. Fund-raising--including the need for government support--union problems, and the importance of concerts for young people were the main themes of the meeting. This article is signed F.Q.E., and Eaton's name has been supplied.

2083 EDWARDS, E. Harlow. **Shall I study with a man or**
ap   **woman?**, *Etude* L/10 (Oct 1932) 756a.
1) In evaluating a teacher, talent for teaching--and not gender--should be the determining factor. 2) While some women singers have trained with men, e.g., Jenny Lind, Lillian Nordica, and Adelina Patti, no woman has yet had outstanding success in training a male voice. However, the promising young singer Nino Martini is studying voice with Maria Gay-Zenatello. Should he become successful, he will be a living refutation of the belief that women cannot teach men.

2084 ENGEL, Carl. **Mrs. Coolidge: sponsor of modern art**, *Singing*
ap   *and Playing* III/5 (June 1928) 20-21, 32.
In 1918 Elizabeth Sprague Coolidge founded the Berkshire Festival of Chamber Music. In 1924 she endowed the Music Division of the Library of Congress, and through the Coolidge Foundation her work begun in Pittsfield, Mass. is now being perpetuated in chamber music concerts in Washington, D.C. and elsewhere. Her aim has been to encourage the composition and performance of music of the highest calibre, which might otherwise have been considered too esoteric or too expensive to perform.

2085 **Estelle Liebling dies here at 90; was a leading operatic**
an   **coach**, *New York Times* 26 Sept 1970, 33. *Illus.*
A graduate of Hunter Col., Estelle Liebling (1884-1970) studied voice in Germany and made her debut at the Metropolitan Opera in 1903--the same year that Caruso made his. She preferred concert work and teaching to opera, however. For over 50 years she coached singers including Amelita Galli-Curci, Frieda Hempel, Miliza Korjus, Max Lorenz, Titta Ruffo, and Beverly Sills. Liebling's family was musical: her father Max studied with Liszt, while her brother Leonard was a critic and for many years the editor of *Musical Courier*.

→   FAIR, Ernest. **Women help Oklahoma symphony**, *see*
      2203ap[68].

2086 FLAGG, Marion. **Music teaching changes its tune**, *Indepen-*
ap   *dent Woman* XX/7 (July 1941) 206-08.
Urges women to enter music teaching and supervision in the public schools, even though men have increasingly come to be preferred as supervisors. This attitude represents a change from the past when women supervisors were in the majority.

→   **Frances E. Clark**, *see* 778ap[57].

2087 **F.W.R. Mozart Society plans for 1922-23**, *Musical Courier*
ap   LXXXV/15 (12 Oct 1922) 41. *Illus.*
An interview with Adelaide McConnell, president of the Mozart Soc. in New York, about her work with the society. Now in its 14th season, the society sponsors monthly Saturday musicales, evening concerts, a women's chorus, and

a variety of social events for charitable purposes. The chorus recently sang at a concert in Washington, D.C. with the United States Marine Corps Band.

2088 G.M.S. **Boston women hold composers contest**, *Musical*
ap   *America* LX/9 (10 May 1940) 15.
Announces that the Boston Women's Symphony Soc. is holding a national prize competition to encourage women to enter the field of orchestral composition. The judges are Walter Piston, Edward Burlingame Hill, Randall Thompson, Frederick S. Converse, Quincy Porter, and Richard Burgin.

2089 **Grace Spofford, 87, was music director**, *New York Times* 7 June
an   1974, 38.
Reports the death of Grace Spofford (1888?-1974), who was head of the Henry Street Settlement Music School in New York from 1935 until her retirement in 1954. Spofford trained at the Peabody Conservatory, and taught piano there prior to becoming a dean. She also served as dean at both the Curtis Inst. from 1924-31 and the New York Col. of Music.

2090 HAGEMAN, Richard. **Shall the young woman choose music**
ap   **as a profession?**, *Musician* XXX/3 (Mar 1925) 9-10.
Discusses music teaching as an excellent vocation for women because of the distinction and respectability it conveys. Also endorses work for women as music supervisors in the public schools and as choir singers and organists.

→   HOWARD, John. **Hewitt family in American music, The**, *see*
      210ap[38].

2091 HOWE, M.A. DeWolfe. **Tale of Tanglewood, The**. With a
bm   foreword by Serge KOUSSEVITZKY (New York: Vanguard, 1946) 101 p. *Illus.*
The initiative and sustained activity of several women played an important part in the early years of the Berkshire Music Festival in western Massachusetts. Gertrude Robinson Smith and Mrs. Owen Johnson of Stockbridge were key figures in the festival's organization, together with Mrs. William Fulton Barrett of Great Barrington. Elizabeth Sprague Coolidge served as honorary president when the festival was incorporated in 1934. In the summer of 1936 Mary Aspinwall Tappan and her niece Mrs. Andrew H. Hepburn gave their Stockbridge estate, Tanglewood, to the Boston Symphony Orchestra as a permanent home for the festival.

→   HUME, Paul. **Mary Howe honored on 80th year with concert**
      of her own works, *see* 2029an[66].

→   **Josephine Antoine**, *see* 2235ap[68].

2092 J.V. **Heeding musical "handwriting on the wall"**, *Musical*
ap   *Courier* CXVI/8 (1 Oct 1937) 19. *Illus.*
Estelle Liebling has been teaching in her private studio in New York for 15 years, and she is also currently on the faculty of the Curtis Inst. She notes that she began her work as a teacher when she herself was a student of Selma Nicklass-Kempner in Berlin and of Mathilde Marchesi in Paris. Liebling is enthusiastic about increasing job opportunities for musicians in the movie, radio, and television industries, and she prepares her students for work in these areas.

2093 KELLEY, Jessie. **Nation's federated music clubs drive for-**
ap   **ward**, *Musical America* XLII/27 (24 Oct 1925) 7.
Kelley, president of the National Federation of Music Clubs, outlines the federation's chief areas of sponsorship for the 1925-26 season as follows: 1) American opera, 2) performance contests for young American artists, 3) competitions for American composers, and 4) music education in the public schools. The federation has 1900 constituent organizations.

2094 KLEINST, M.; RITTENHOUSE, C.H.; FARNSWORTH,
ac   Paul R. **Two new Strong vocational interest scales for musicians**. *Studies in musical education, history, and aesthetics* 43 (Pittsburgh: Music Teachers National Assoc., 1951) 131-33.
Discusses the Strong Vocational Interest Blank, developed by E.K. Strong, Jr., for the purpose of forecasting relative success in occupations. Considers the application of the test on sex-differentiated groups of music teachers and supervisors in California in 1948. The men had an average age of 38.8 years, 12 years of schooling, and 17 years of teaching experience. The comparable women's scale resulted in a mean age of 48.2 years, 13.9 years of completed schooling, and teaching experience ranging from 3-50 years.

2095 KRAMER, A. Walter. **Annual festival draws pilgrims to**
ro   **Pittsfield's shrine of music**, *Musical America* XXXIV/24 (8 Oct 1921) 1, 2, 4. *Illus.*
Reviews the 4th annual Berkshire Festival of Chamber Music in Pittsfield, Mass., to which 400 musicians and music lovers were invited by Elizabeth Sprague Coolidge. Coolidge was presented with a bronze tablet in tribute to her

work as a music patron. The program included performances of Schubert's piano quintet in A major, D.667 (the "Trout"), Beethoven's string quartet no. 13 in B-flat major, op. 130, and Brahms's string quintet no. 2 in G major, op. 111, as well as performances of Leo Sowerby's woodwind quintet and Harry Waldo Warner's prize-winning piano trio.

→   **Lea Luboshutz, artist, teacher**, see 2250an[68].

2097   **Lorraine Foster gives a résumé of the founding of the**
ap   **Stephen Foster Society in New York**, Musical Courier CI/26 (27 Dec 1930) 12, 33.
Together with Alfred Hunan, Lorraine Foster has founded a society to promote the works of Stephen Foster and also American folk song. The soprano grew up in Kentucky, and she regularly includes Kentucky mountain songs on her programs. Lorraine Foster is distantly related to the composer.

→   **LOVINGGOOD, Penman. Famous modern Negro musicians**, see 2264bf[68].

→   **Lucile Lawrence an ardent exponent of contemporary harpism**, see 2266ap[68].

→   **M. Lea Luboshutz, first woman violinist to become member of faculty at Curtis Institute of Music**, see 2269ap[68].

→   **Mabel Garrison, opera singer, 77**, see 2270an[68].

2098   MAIER, Guy. **Shall I major in music?**, Etude LXXII/8 (Aug 1948) 468.
ap
The author notes that as a consultant in music for Stephens Col., he is often asked by young women whether they should major in music. Given an individual student's real talent and interest in music, Maier recommends the music major, because after years of raising children it is relatively easy to refurbish one's piano technique and become a piano teacher for beginning students. By contrast the student who majors in English literature or mathematics will have little opportunity for earning income or regaining purposeful activity after years in the home.

→   **Marianne Kneisel, violinist, 75, dead**, see 2275an[68].

→   **Marie Sundelius, ex-opera singer**, see 2277ap[68].

→   **Mary Flagler Cary Music Collection, The**, see 23bm[01].

2099   MCKEE, Nancy. **Valiant woman** (San Antonio: Naylor, 1962)
bm   79 p. Illus.
Née Nevins, Marian MacDowell (1857-1956) first studied piano with her aunt, a gifted musician. Later she went abroad and became the pupil of Edward MacDowell, while he was on the faculty of Darmstadt U. They married in 1884 on the condition that Edward would give up teaching and devote 5 years to composition while living on Marian's legacy. Marian MacDowell also relinquished all plans for a concert career, believing that her husband's creative talents were more important than her interpretive talents. After the couple returned to the United States they lived in New York, while Edward taught at Columbia U., and in Peterborough, N.H. during the summers. Some of Edward's students from Columbia often joined him in Peterborough, paying weekly board and thereby becoming the first colonists. In 1907 the MacDowell Assoc. was formed to develop the colony, and after the composer's death in 1908 Marian MacDowell devoted her energies to the expansion of the colony's facilities. She planned and supervised the construction of 25 new buildings, retrained as a pianist and concertized nationwide to raise monies for the colony, and personally directed the colony until she was 91 years of age. Throughout much of her lifetime Marian MacDowell suffered from paralysis that affected her ability to walk.

→   **Merle Alcock, a contralto at Met in 1920s, is dead**, see 2286an[68].

2100   **Miss Elsie Sweeney, music patron, dead**, New York Times 3
an   May 1972, 50.
The influence of Elsie Irwin Sweeney, a student of Josef Lhevinne, was felt in the musical world through her membership on the boards of the Friends of Music at Indiana U. and the National Federation of Music Clubs, as well as her work on the executive committee of the National Council of the Metropolitan Opera.

2101   MITCHELL, Elizabeth. **Music with a feather duster** (Boston:
bm   Little, Brown, 1941) 280 p. Illus., index.
An autobiography by a socialite, who has used her considerable musical talents as a hobby. Born in 1881, Elizabeth Mitchell studied piano with Rudolph Ganz

at the Chicago Musical Col., and after she married and relocated in New York, she continued with Yolande Méró. She also studied harmony with Rubin Goldmark in New York. During the 1910s-20s private musicales were a popular form of entertainment, and Mitchell became active in this area featuring the Flonzaley Quartet, George Gershwin, Fritz Kreisler, and Andres Segovia among others. She also has been a supporter of the New York Philharmonic. Although Mitchell has had some of her songs published and her Chopin and Bach orchestrations have been performed, she feels women face restrictions. "There are certain things a lady doesn't do: she doesn't smoke cigars in public or put her feet up in barrooms; nor does she write great symphonies".

2102   **Mme. Van der Veer, singer, teacher, 74**, New York Times 27
an   Sept 1958, 21.
An obituary for Nevada Van der Veer, who was well known as a recitalist in the 1920s throughout the United States and Europe. With her husband, tenor Reed Miller, she founded the Van der Veer-Miller summer school in Lake George, N.Y. From 1934-50 Van der Veer was head of the voice department at the Cleveland Inst. of Music, and she taught privately in New York until a year before her death.

2103   **Mme. Vengerova**, New York Times 8 Feb 1956, 33.
an
Reports the death of Isabella Vengerova (1877-1956), a pianist and teacher, who studied in Vienna with Theodor Leschetizky and Annette Essipoff. She taught at the Imperial Conservatory in St. Petersburg from 1906-20--when she decided to leave her native country--and after 1924 she was on the faculties of the Curtis Inst. and the Mannes School of Music. Her American pupils include Leonard Pennario, Jacob Lateiner, Gary Graffman, Lillian Kallir, and Abby Simon.

2104   **Mrs. Dickinson dies; sacred music expert**, New York Herald
an   Tribune 27 Aug 1957, II-8.
Helen Adell Dickinson (1875-1957) was a founder of the School of Sacred Music at Union Theological Seminary with her husband Clarence Dickinson in 1928. A graduate of Queen's U. in Kingston, Ontario in Canada, she subsequently became the first woman to receive a doctoral degree from the U. of Heidelberg. Dickinson was a lecturer on sacred music, art, architecture, and liturgy at the School of Sacred Music, and she also collaborated with her husband on many of his 500 sacred compositions.

2105   **Mrs. Efrem Zimbalist, Sr., Curtis heiress, is dead**, New York
an   Times 6 Jan 1970, 41.
Mary Curtis Bok Zimbalist (1876-1970) founded the Curtis Inst. in 1924 and effected an affiliation between the institute and the Philadelphia Grand Opera in 1929. Among her other philanthropic activities were the founding of the Philadelphia Settlement Music School in 1917, the donation of the Annie Russell Theater at Rollins Col., and the gift of an organ to the Philadelphia Academy of Music in 1960.

2106   **Mrs. E.S. Coolidge, music patron, dies**, New York Times 5 Nov
an   1953, 31.
Elizabeth Sprague Coolidge (1864-1953) was an outstanding patron of music in the United States and one of the nation's wealthiest women. While the music festivals she sponsored in Pittsfield, Mass. attracted wide attention, Coolidge shunned personal publicity, with the result that the extent of her philanthropies was not generally known. These included the establishment of numerous scholarships for students and a pension fund for the Chicago Symphony Orchestra, the construction of Sprague Hall at Yale U., and the endowment of the Library of Congress for activities in chamber music and a chair for the head of the Music Division.

2107   **Mrs. Julia Cassebeer Steinway, 86**, Musical Courier CLVII/4
ap   (Mar 1958) 6.
An obituary for Julia Cassebeer Steinway (1872-1958), who served as a member of the board of the New York Philharmonic since 1934, vice-president of the Musicians' Emergency Fund in the 1930s, and vice-president of the National Orchestral Assoc. She was the widow of Frederick T. Steinway.

2108   **Mrs. Randall-MacIver, 87, dies; music patron cited by**
an   **France**, New York Times 17 May 1961, 37.
Mabel Holden Randall-MacIver received the Legion of Honor in 1923 for her part in developing understanding between American and French musicians. Her interest in French music and musicians dated from just after World War I, when she was instrumental in helping restore the war-torn Rheims Conservatory and in founding a summer school at Fontainebleau for American music students. During World War II Randall-MacIver was chairwoman of the board of directors of the American Assoc. for Assistance to French Artists.

2109   **Mrs. Sokoloff, 69, a patron of music**, New York Times 21 July
an   1955, 23.
An obituary for Ruth Haller Ottaway Sokoloff (1886-1955), who was president of the National Federation of Music Clubs in 1929-33 and a delegate to the

Anglo-American Music Conference in Lucerne in 1929. Sokoloff was also chairwoman of the music committee within the National Council of Women.

2110 Music takes its true place in this working girls' club, *Musical*
ap *America* XXXI/16 (14 Feb 1920) 19. *Illus.*
The Kittredge Club was founded in New York in 1887 by Abbott E. Kittredge under the name of the Manhattan Working Girls' Soc. Kittredge's aim was to provide young women "who had been forced or had otherwise gone into the business and industrial world" with opportunities to socialize with one another and to engage in meaningful leisure pursuits. The Kittridge Glee Club, under the direction of Ida Seymour Hutcheson, leads the "sings" that are open to all members of the club and gives an annual concert as well as programs for Christmas and Easter.

2111 National Music Week May 1-7 offers opportunity for many
ap **and varied activities,** *General Federation News* VII/7 (Apr 1927) 1.
Discusses National Music Week as an opportunity for a community to take stock of its musical assets and upgrade them. Urges women's clubs in communities presently not involved to support the week and to investigate the status of music in Sunday schools of churches and the public schools, as well as the availability of music books in public libraries and good concerts for young people.

2112 NEWTON, Ivor. Accompanying Lotte Lehmann's classes,
ap *Opera* VIII/12 (Deç 1957) 742-49. *Illus.*
Lotte Lehmann's accompanist describes the master classes Lehmann has given in London and Santa Barbara, Calif. since her retirement from the stage in 1947. The soprano's associations with Puccini, Strauss, Toscanini, and Otto Klemperer are also discussed.

→ **Obituary. Dorothee Manski,** *see* 2310ap[68].

→ PELTZ, Mary. **Obituaries. Karin Branzell,** *see* 2322ap[68].

→ PEYSER, Ethel. **In memory--Marion Bauer,** *see* 2046ap[66].

2113 Place aux jeunes! is slogan of Leginska's coast studio,
ap *Musical Courier* CXXXVI/5 (15 Oct 1942) 19.
Several years ago "this first-rate pianist and the first woman to successfully conduct symphony orchestras" opened a studio for pianists in Hollywood, Calif. Part of the work that pupils receive with Leginska is the opportunity to play concertos with the Leginska Little Symphony Orchestra under Leginska's direction. The high points in Ethel Leginska's career are reviewed.

→ **Queena Mario resigns from the Metropolitan,** *see* 2336an[68].

2114 REVELLI, William D. Women can teach instrumental
ap **music,** *Etude* LXI/5 (May 1943) 311.
Because of the current shortage of men as music educators, women are needed--especially as teachers at the elementary and junior high levels.

2115 ROGERS, Delmer. Memorial tribute to Lota May Spell
ap **(1885-1972), A,** *Yearbook for Inter-American Musical Research* X (1974) 194-98. *Bibliog.*
As a first-year graduate student in 1918 at the U. of Texas in Austin, Spell began her association with the people and data that were to shape her future. She subsequently became a librarian in the Latin American section of the university library, where one of the prime collections of Latin Americana was gradually collected. Spell wrote on a wide range of topics including education, music, printing, and theater in the southwestern United States. Both her master's thesis and doctoral dissertation dealt with early music education in North America. *Pioneer printer: Samuel Bangs in Mexico and Texas* (Austin: U. of Texas, 1963) is Spell's most important work. *(Author, abridged)*

2116 ROSENFELD, Jay C. Elizabeth Sprague Coolidge: a tribute
bm **on the one-hundredth anniversary of her birth** (n.p.: privately printed, 1964) 8 p.
Coolidge's early training as a pianist and composer allowed her to manage her musical philanthropies both wisely and sympathetically, because she was able to associate with her beneficiaries as an equal. Highpoints of her philanthropies are described, including the founding of the Berkshire Festival of Chamber Music in Pittsfield, Mass. in 1918 and the construction of the Coolidge Auditorium at the Library of Congress in the 1920s.

2117 SCHONBERG, Harold C. Rosina Lhevinne--the total piano
an **teacher,** *New York Times* 21 Nov 1976, D-17. *Illus.*
A tribute to Rosina Lhevinne (1880-1976) following her death in California at the age of 96. 1) The pianist might well have abandoned her career as a solo artist following her marriage to Josef Lhevinne because of the frustration she envisioned in competing with her husband's flawless technique. On the other hand, Josef tended to be unambitious and was in need of Rosina's energy and

drive. 2) In the 1950s Rosina Lhevinne's pupils began putting their mark on international pianism, e.g., Van Cliburn, John Browning, Daniel Pollack, Mischa Dichter, Olegna Fuschi, David Bar-Ilan, and Garrick Ohlsson. 3) After World War II, Rosina Lhevinne was one of the last pianists who represented the traditions of late 19th-c. piano playing as opposed to modern attempts towards literalism.

2118 SCOFIELD, Ronald D. Some wonderful things go on here,
an *Santa Barbara (Calif.) News-Press* 23 July 1961, C-12.
Discusses Lotte Lehmann's master classes in song interpretation and operatic roles held for the previous 16 years in Santa Barbara, Calif. at the Music Academy of the West. Future plans include the staging of *Fidelio* and the American première of Eugen d'Albert's *Die toten Augen*, in which Lehmann created the leading role at its Viennese première in 1919.

2119 Short sketch of the Mana Zucca Music Club, *Musical Courier*
ap XCVIII/25 (22 June 1929) 12.
In May 1928 Mana Zucca enlisted 15 members as a nucleus for the Mana Zucca Music Club in Miama, Fla. When the club formally commenced in October, it had more than 100 members, and at the present time it numbers approximately 260. The Mana Zucca Music Club provides performance opportunities for local musicians, sponsors appearances by artists of national stature, and offers lectures on music and composers. Given the enthusiasm of the club's members, Miami should become a music center in the South.

2120 STEFAN, Paul. Mrs. E.S. Coolidge carries premières to
ro **Vienna,** *Musical America* XLVI/25 (8 Oct 1927) 8. *Illus.*
Reviews 2 concerts of chamber music in Vienna sponsored by Elizabeth Sprague Coolidge for invited audiences; the programs included premières of Frank Bridge's string quartet no. 3, Respighi's *Trittico botticelliano*, and Schönberg's string quartet no. 3, op. 30. Stefan comments upon the importance of this opportunity to hear works of significance in excellent performances and also notes that the American works on the programs--by Charles Martin Loeffler and Frederick Jacobi--were of special interest to the audiences. "It is difficult to express the joy and satisfaction with which Elizabeth Sprague Coolidge's undertaking was greeted here".

2121 Talented federation chairman, *New Jersey Music* I/5 (20 Jan
ap 1946) 14. *Illus.*
Ethel Glenn Hier--chairwoman of the Young Composers Contest of the New Jersey Federation of Music Clubs--has studios in New York City, New Jersey, and Connecticut, where she teaches private pupils and classes in duo-piano playing. A native of Cincinnati, Hier studied at the conservatory there and subsequently at the Juilliard School. Her theory and composition teachers included Percy Goetschius, Hugo Kaun, Ernest Bloch, Egon Wellesz, Berg, and Malipiero. Hier's *Asolo bells* (*WIAM* 2626) was recently performed by the Cincinnati Symphony Orchestra under the direction of Eugene Goossens.

2122 Teacher's teacher, *New Yorker* XXXIV/31 (20 Sept 1958) 33-34.
ap
An interview with Angela Diller at age 80, who notes that above all she likes to teach teachers. Born in Brooklyn as a daughter of a clergyman, Diller learned to read music at age 3, and at age 8 she played the piano in school for choral singing in exchange for German lessons. Subsequently for 7 years she studied music at Columbia Col., including composition with MacDowell. Diller taught at the Music School Settlement in New York and the Mannes School of Music, and then in 1921 she founded the Diller-Quaile School of Music with Elizabeth Quaile. To date the Diller-Quaile instruction books have sold approximately 2 million copies.

2123 TURNER, Chittenden. Music and the women's crusade, *Arts*
ap *and Decoration* XIX/5 (Sept 1923) 29, 70-71, 73. *Illus.*
The National Federation of Music Clubs presently enrolls 1800 musical organizations with more than 100,000 individual members. 400 clubs joined in 1922. While the federation believes firmly in the international character of music, it also has a special commitment to ensuring that American composers and performers receive a fair hearing. The activities of numerous clubwomen and women composers and performers in the clubs are discussed.

2124 UNTERMEYER, Sophie Guggenheimer; WILLIAMSON,
bm **Alix. Mother is Minnie** (New York: Doubleday, 1960) 213 p. *Illus.*
An anecdotal biography by Minnie Guggenheimer's daughter, which traces the development of the Lewissohn Stadium concerts in New York. Musicians and patrons who came into Guggenheimer's orbit are discussed. Guggenheimer (1882-1966) herself is portrayed as an eccentric, whose only goal in life was to promote the stadium concerts.

2125 WALLACE, Robert Kimball. Century of music making, A:
bm **the lives of Josef and Rosina Lhevinne** (Bloomington, Ind.: Indiana U., 1976) xi, 350 p. $17.50. *Illus., bibliog., discog.*
Rosina Bessie (1880-1976) and Josef Lhevinne (1875-1944) trained at the Moscow Conservatory and married at the ages of 18 and 23 respectively.

Following Josef's early triumphs in Europe and the United States, they worked as duo-pianists and teachers in Berlin until World War I, when they were interned as enemy aliens. In 1919 they emigrated to the United States. The account of their American years traces Josef's evolution as a pianist, his and Rosina's achievements as a duo-piano team, their involvement with the Juilliard School from its inception, and the many adjustments necessary to preserve the vitality of a marriage of 2 disparate personalities. After Josef's death, Rosina Lhevinne emerged as a soloist and teacher in her own right. Highlights of this later phase in her career include her resumption of work as a soloist at the age of 76, her performances with Leonard Bernstein and the New York Philharmonic at age 82, and the success of her students, e.g., Van Cliburn, John Browning, Mischa Dichter, and Garrick Ohlsson.   *(Author, abridged)*

→   WATSON, Dorothy. **Washington hears Mrs. E.S. Coolidge as pianist**, *see* 2386ro[68].

2126   Women in musical service, *Musical Courier* CXXVIII/7 (20 Nov
ap   1943) 30.
This editorial commends the work of the War Service Committee of the National Federation of Music Clubs in collecting 40,000 musical instruments and 50,000 recordings during the past 2 years for use by American armed forces abroad.

68   Literature about women as performers of art music

2127   About Mildred Dilling's summer class, *Musical Courier*
ap   LXXVI/24 (13 June 1918) 40.
Mildred Dilling is a young concert harpist who is giving solo recitals at private musicales, as well as performing as assisting artist with singers Alma Gluck, Claudia Muzio, Anna Case, and Frances Alda. Dilling teaches at her studio on West 85th Street in New York, and this summer she will hold classes at a girls' summer camp in upstate New York.

**2128   AHLERS, Margaret Ann. Value of music study to a business
ap   woman, The**, *Etude* LII/1 (Jan 1934) 56.
Advocates the study of a musical instrument for the mature student as a broadening experience, a form of relaxation, and a means of enriching the spirit.

2129   Aida without make-up, *Time* XXII/5 (31 July 1933) 28. *Illus.*
ap
Born in Wilmington, N.C., Caterina Jarboro made her operatic debut in Milan in 1930. She then performed regularly in leading opera houses in France, Italy, and Switzerland. The first Negro soprano to appear with an American opera group, Jarboro sang Aida with Alfredo Salmaggi's Chicago Opera Co. in 1933 at the New York Hippodrome.

**2130   A.K.C. Chicago women musicians win success with own
ap   orchestra**, *Musical Courier* XCII/23 (2 Dec 1926) 27.
An interview with Lillian Poenisch, a clarinetist with and one of the founders of the Woman's Symphony Orchestra of Chicago in 1924. Poenisch is optimistic about both the orchestra's growth and women's eventual success in gaining employment in all-male orchestras.

**2131   A.K.C. Woman's Symphony Orchestra of Chicago com-
ap   pletes successful season**, *Musical Courier* C/21 (24 May 1930)
    16.
During the 1929-30 season concert attendance increased, and the orchestra's financial status improved. Another problem near solution is securing competent women players for instruments not typically played by women, e.g., oboe, bassoon, French horn, and double bass. The orchestra's conductor, Ebba Sundstrom, proposes a scholarship fund to encourage more women to take up these instruments and thereby increase the pool of qualified female players from which the orchestra can select in the future.

2132   Aline Van Bärentzen a brilliant concert pianist, *Musical
ap   Courier* LXX/16 (21 Apr 1915) 8. *Illus.*
Born in Boston, Aline Van Bärentzen studied piano with E.M. Delaborde at the Paris Conservatory and with Ernst von Dohnanyi in Berlin. In 1905 she made her European debut at age 8 and subsequently performed throughout the continent. During the 1914-15 season, the pianist gave 2 solo recitals in Aeolian Hall in New York and was a soloist with the Boston Symphony Orchestra.

**2133   ALLEN, Montagu. From fourteen to sixty. Martha Lipton
ap   discusses her roles**, *Opera News* XI/16 (3 Feb 1947) 26-29. *Illus.*
During Martha Lipton's 3 seasons with the Metropolitan Opera she has sung roles ranging from 14-year old Hänsel to 60-year old Cieca in *La Gioconda*. The mezzo-soprano is appearing as Amneris for the first time this season. Among

Lipton's other roles are Emilia in *Otello*, Annina in *Der Rosenkavalier*, Maddalena in *Rigoletto*, and her favorite, the Nurse in *Boris Godunov*.

2134   ALTMAN, Thelma. Neglected contralto, The, *Music Journal*
ap   [New York] VII/6 (Nov 1950) 15, 50.
Deplores the replacement of the contralto--with a typical 3 octave range--by the mezzo-soprano in opera after 1920 and the disappearance of operas with leading contralto parts from the repertory, e.g., *Le prophète*, *Lucrezia Borgia*, *La Cenerentola*, and *L'Italiana in Algeri*. Most of the mezzo-sopranos singing Carmen, Mignon, and Dalila--the 3 starring roles left for contraltos--do not have the requisite range.

2135   Amy Ellerman, singer, teacher, *New York Times* 6 June 1960, 29.
an
Reports the death of the mezzo-soprano, who had been a soloist at the First Presbyterian Church in New York for 26 years. A native of South Dakota and a graduate of the American Conservatory, Ellerman made extensive appearances on tour during the 1920s to demonstrate the fidelity of the records she made for Thomas A. Edison, Inc.

2136   ANDERSON, Marian. My Lord, what a morning (New York:
bm   Viking, 1956) 312 p. *Illus.*
An autobiography by the American contralto. Born in Philadelphia in 1902, Marian Anderson began her singing career in local churches, using that income to pay for vocal lessons with Giuseppe Boghetti. She sang at Negro colleges in the South for several years before winning a Lewisohn Stadium concert in 1925 and making her debut with the New York Philharmonic. Even though Anderson received favorable reviews, it was not until she returned from a successful European concert tour in 1935 that she was given proper recognition in the United States. In 1939 the Daughters of the American Revolution refused to let Anderson sing in Washington's Constitution Hall; with the aid of Eleanor Roosevelt, an outdoor concert was held instead at the Lincoln Memorial with 75,000 people in attendance. Anderson's operatic debut took place in 1955 when she became the first Negro singer to appear at the Metropolitan Opera. Her concert repertory includes lieder as well as spirituals. The contralto's accompanists, audiences, recordings, and future plans are discussed.

2137   rb —
R. by Rex STOUT, *New York Herald Tribune* 28 Oct 1956, VI-1.

**2138   ANDERTON, Margaret. It is woman who keeps our music
ap   a-going**, *Musician* XXXIII/8 (Aug 1928) 11-12. *Illus.*
The origins of the Chicago Woman's Symphony Orchestra, which was founded by Elena Moneak in 1924, and its offspring--the Woman's Symphony Orchestra of Chicago--are discussed.

2139   Annie Louise David, *Musical America* LXXX/7 (June 1960) 44.
ap
An obituary for the harpist, who also performed as a concert pianist. Annie Louise David studied harp with Heinrich Schücker, Van Veachen Rogers, and Ada Sassoli and piano with Arthur Foote, MacDowell, and Heinrich Gebhardt. Settling in San Francisco, David became active in the city's artistic life and taught at several conservatories.

2140   Antoine, Josephine, *Current biography*. Ed. by Anna ROTHE
ac   (New York: H.W. Wilson, 1944) 13-15.
In 1936 Josephine Antoine moved from operatic productions at the Juilliard School directly to the Metropolitan Opera, where she has sung only leading roles. A coloratura soprano, Antoine majored in English at the U. of Colorado, and she used income from teaching English to further her preparation as a singer. After winning a fellowship through a competition, she went to the Curtis Inst. to study with Marcella Sembrich, and she continued with Sembrich at Juilliard. Antoine has done considerable work on radio, e.g., the Chase and Sanborn opera in English hours and the Sunday symphonic hours sponsored by the Ford and Packard motor companies.

**2141   Antonia Brico's triumph: first of sex to wield baton over the
ap   New York Philharmonic**, *Newsweek* XII/5 (1 Aug 1938) 21.
Discusses Brico's training, previous background, and her appearance with the New York Philharmonic at Lewisohn Stadium.

→   ANTRIM, Doron. **American pianists, famous or typical**, *see* 882ac[58].

2142   Are women musicians people?, *Musical Courier* CXV/8 (20 Feb
ap   1937) 18.
An editorial discussing the recent statement by José Iturbi, who in an interview in Toronto, Canada noted that women cannot achieve greatness in music because of physical and temperamental limitations. Includes a letter from Suzanne D'Olivera Jackowska of the Soc. of Authors and Composers in defense of women musicians.

2143 ARNDT, Jessie Ash. **Concert singer just grew up with music,**
an   **but earnest work counted too,** *Christian Science Monitor* 2 June
         1948, 10. *Illus.*
Carol Brice was born in Indianapolis to a musical family, and from kindergarten onwards she attended the Palmer Inst. in Sedalia, N.C., which was founded by Charlotte Hawkins Brown--Brice's aunt and a noted Negro educator. With the financial help of Mrs. Galen Stone of Boston, Brice subsequently attended Talladega Col., majoring in music education. She then won a fellowship in voice to the Juilliard School where she studied for 5 years with Francis Rogers. During the 1946-47 season Brice sang Brahms's *Alto rhapsody, op. 53,* with the Boston Symphony Orchestra. She recently completed 63 concerts on tour with the San Francisco Symphony Orchestra under the direction of Pierre Monteux.

2144 **Artist chooses artist's hands as subject for exhibition por-**
ap   **trait,** *Musical America* L/6 (25 Mar 1930) 33. *Illus.*
Reports that J. Blair-Leighton has recently painted a study of the hands of Martha Baird (Rockefeller). A native of California, Baird studied and won prizes under George Proctor--a pupil of Theodor Leschetizky--and Artur Schnabel. She made her debut with the Boston Symphony Orchestra at a relatively young age. During 1929 the pianist performed 11 concerts for the British Broadcasting Co., 7 of which were all-Schubert programs.

2145 **Aux armes, citoyennes,** *Musical Courier* CXVIII/9 (1 Nov 1938)
ap   18.
This editorial generally endorses the campaign of the Committee for the Recognition of Women in the Musical Profession in New York to secure employment for women instrumentalists in symphony orchestras and other performing organizations. The women have proposed "an heroic ordeal--nothing less than a sort of blindfold test in which they would hide their charms behind screens at auditions".

2146 **Baltimore: cradle of municipal music** (Baltimore: City of
bm   Baltimore, 1934) 15 p. *Illus.*
This tribute to the Baltimore Symphony Orchestra on the 18th anniversary of its founding lists outstanding occasions in the orchestra's history to date. Notable performances by the following women are cited: Mary Howe and Anne Hull, duo-pianists; and Elsa Alsen, Sophie Braslau, Johanna Gadski, Margaret Matzenauer, and Gladys Swarthout, singers.

2147 BARNES, Harold M., Jr. **Claudia Muzio. A biographical**
bm   **sketch and discography** (Princeton, N.J.: author, 1941) 18 p.
         Illus., discog.
Born in Pavia, Italy, Claudia Muzio (1889-1938) was a singer of international acclaim. Between 1916 and 1922 the soprano appeared at the Metropolitan Opera, where she sang in the world première of *Il trittico* in 1918, the first American performance of *Eugen Onegin* in 1920, and the first Metropolitan performance of *Andrea Chenier* in 1921. From 1922-32 Muzio was responsible for all the leading soprano roles in the Italian repertory of the Chicago Opera. Her career in Europe and elsewhere is also considered. The discography gives information on 108 recordings--including a wide range of operatic excerpts and songs--that Muzio made over a period of 24 years.

2148 BEESON, Edith. **Styling gowns to fit the artist. Wrong ones**
ap   **may handicap the woman recitalist,** *Musical Courier* CXXXI/1
         (15 June 1945) 8.
Offers suggestions for dress for women performers. Pianists should wear full skirts and sleeves long enough to camouflage unladylike muscles, yet short enough to allow freedom while playing. In small towns the artist is typically met at the train station by a committee from the local women's music club, and therefore care should be taken to make a good impression in dress.

2149 BERGER, Meyer. **Other instruments may come and go, but**
an   **this musician strings along with harps,** *New York Times* 4 Jan
         1957, 17.
In small cities Mildred Dilling usually includes brief lectures about the history of the harp and its repertoire on her recital programs. Dilling's collection of harps now numbers 60 instruments--both ancient and modern. At age 17 Dilling came to New York from Indiana to study with Carlos Salzedo. Subsequently she studied in Paris with Henriette Renié, "whom she still worships". This article appeared in connection with Dilling's forthcoming recital in Town Hall.

2150 BIDDLE, Mark. **All-girl band of Winthrop College, The,**
ap   *Etude* LIX/6 (June 1941) 385-86, 417-18. *Illus.*
When in 1938 the author joined the music faculty of Winthrop Col., a women's college in Rock Hill, S.C., he distributed a questionnaire among the students regarding the feasibility of a band at the college. The results indicated that while very few students played band instruments--because high school bands were not encouraging women as players--260 women in a student body of 1600 were interested in playing in a band. Biddle subsequently formed a band at Winthrop Col. that has become an important feature of student life. He notes that young women obviously like to play wind instruments and that the band

has given the music program "a scope that previously was impossible". The growth and activities of the Winthrop band are discussed.

2151 B.L.H. **Los Angeles, California [Los Angeles Woman's**
ap   **Symphony Orchestra],** *Musical Courier* XCVIII/11 (14 Mar 1929)
         49.
The first item of the column reports on a recent concert by the Los Angeles Woman's Symphony Orchestra, under the direction of Henry Schoenefeld. Founded in 1893, the orchestra was organized to give women the opportunity to play large-scale orchestral works.

2152 BOJANOWSKY, Jerzy. **Championing the woman orchestral**
ap   **player,** *Musical Courier* CXXXI/2 (15 Jan 1945) 42.
Speculates that prejudices against women as orchestral players might return given peace-time conditions. Argues that each woman player must be judged individually for her merits and that if a woman can meet the obligation of continuous service, her gender should not stand in her way. Similarly, some women have the strength to play large instruments and should not be prejudged. While a sizeable number of players from the ranks of the Woman's Symphony Orchestra of Chicago have been engaged by other orchestras because of the military draft, the membership currently totals 92 players, and applications are being received daily.

2153 BORROFF, Edith. **Fairbank Collection, The,** *College Music*
ap   *Symposium* XVI (spring 1976) 105-22. *List of works.*
The Newberry Library in Chicago houses a distinguished collection of songs that comprised the working library of Janet Fairbank, soprano. A member of a wealthy and prominent Chicago family, Fairbank pursued her career in the face of the traditional prejudice against women of means who have sought a place on the stage. Given her vocal limitations and the impossibility of achieving critical success in operatic and standard concert repertory, Fairbank came to specialize in contemporary music. The collection of songs she gathered as possible repertory for her recitals in the 1930s-40s--both published and in MS--represents a remarkable achievement for one individual and indicates a keen judgment of musical value. American composers are predominant, a significant proportion being women, i.e., Marion Bauer, Amy Cheney Beach, Jeanne Behrend, Helen Louise Birch, Radie Britain, Alice de Cevee, Vera Eakin, Beatrice Fenner, Vivian Fine, Florence G. Galajikian, Peggy Glanville-Hicks, Betty S. Hall, Mary Howe, Kathleen Lockhart Manning, Elizabeth C. Marshall, Ruth Wright Vanderlip, and Helen Searles Westbrook.

2154 BRAGGIOTTI, Mary. **Brünnhilde at the ball game--an**
an   **American story,** *New York Post* 2 June 1946, 43. *Illus.*
Helen Traubel was criticized for returning to St. Louis instead of accepting a contract with the Metropolitan Opera in 1926, and her career suffered some setbacks before the Metropolitan Opera offered her another contract in the late 1930s. Traubel considers her mother and Lulu Vetta-Karst, her voice teacher of 17 years, to be the greatest influences on her work. The soprano is an avid baseball fan.

2155 BRAINE, Robert. **Women symphony players,** *Etude* XLII/8
ap   (Aug 1925) 591.
Reviews the progress of women as orchestral players, and announces the formation of the American Women's Symphony Orchestra in New York under the direction of Elizabeth Kuyper.

→   BRAINE, Robert. **Maud Powell's violin,** *see* 906ap[58].

→   **Branscombe conducts own compositions with Chicago wom-**
      en's symphony, *see* 2000rm[66].

2156 **Branzell, Karin,** *Current biography.* Ed. by Anna ROTHE (New
ac   York: H.W. Wilson, 1946) 70-73. *Illus., bibliog.*
Karin Branzell, whose first patron was the late Crown Princess Margaret of Sweden, made her operatic debut at the Stockholm Opera in 1912. 12 years later she made her American debut at the Metropolitan Opera as Fricka in *Die Walküre.* Although best known for her Wagnerian roles, the contralto also sang French and Italian repertory in opera and recital. In 1944 she retired from the Metropolitan Opera, and in 1946 she joined the faculty at the Juilliard School.

2157 **Braslau song MSS bought by library,** *New York Times* 29 Apr
an   1936, 19.
The entire music collection of Sophie Braslau, contralto at the Metropolitan Opera and a concert artist, has been acquired by the Brooklyn Public Library. Autograph MSS of songs by Chaikovskii, Charles Griffes, MacDowell, Rachmaninoff, and Sibelius are included. Braslau, who died in 1935, introduced many of the songs to the American public in her recitals.

2158 BUGBEE, Emma. **Hortense Monath says music is essential**
an   **even during war,** *New York Herald Tribune* 28 Sept 1942, 11. *Illus.*
Discusses the career of Hortense Monath as a concert pianist and head of the New Friends of Music. A native of New York, Monath's first teacher was her

mother. She made her debut in Hamburg at age 19, after 4 years of study with Artur Schnabel. Monath thinks that given wartime conditions, women musicians should find their rightful place in orchestras.

2159 C. **Benefit concert for Finland, A**, *Musical America* LXI/10 (25
ap   May 1941) 23.
Reports on a benefit concert in Town Hall featuring three choruses regularly conducted by Antonia Brico and brought together for the first performance of Joyce Barthelson's *In the beginning*, with text by Nancy Byrd Turner adapted from the Book of Genesis. Brico conducted the work with the composer at the piano.

2160 CARACAPPA, Michael. **Mother Hilger: the cellist who**
ap   **conquered**, *Music Journal* [New York] XXVII/1 (Jan 1969) 34-35,
75, 86. *Illus.*
When she was hired by the Philadelphia Orchestra in 1935, Elsa Hilger became the first woman instrumentalist--other than harpists--to join a leading symphony orchestra. Her career and philosophy of teaching the cello are discussed.

→   **Carolina Lazzari, contralto, is dead**, *see* 2077an[67].

2161 CARROLL, Amy Keith. **Is conductor's vocabulary bar to**
ap   **women players?**, *Musical Opinion* XXII/4 (Apr 1923) 31.
An interview with Richard Czerwonky, conductor of the Bush Conservatory Orchestra in Chicago. Czerwonky believes that women can perform in orchestras just as well as men, provided that they assume equality with male players and submit to the discipline and freedom of rehearsals. His aim at Bush is to prepare students to enter major American orchestras, so that conductors do not automatically look to Europe for new personnel, and he welcomes women players. At present women in the Bush Orchestra hold positions as concertmistress, first chair in all the other string sections, and clarinetist.

2162 **Cellist Elsa Hilger retires**, *Pan Pipes of Sigma Alpha Iota* LXI/4
ap   (May 1969) 26.
Elsa Hilger has been a member of the Philadelphia Orchestra for 34 years. A native of Vienna, Hilger came to the United States in 1920 on tour with her sisters in a piano trio. A recommendation from Pablo Casals helped Hilger to obtain an audition with Leopold Stokowski, who hired her for the Philadelphia Orchestra. Around the same time the cellist also became head of the cello department at the Philadelphia Conservatory. Hilger's husband and son are amateur cellists. She expects to perform as a guest artist with orchestras in the future.

2163 **Chat with a great artist of yesteryear, A**, *Opera and Concert* XI/
ap   5 (May 1946) 22-23, 25. *Illus.*
An interview with Rosa Ponselle, who retired from the Metropolitan Opera in 1937, although she continues to sing at home and for friends. Ponselle made her Metropolitan debut in 1918 as Leonora in *La forza del destino* with Caruso. The soprano studied with Romano Romani and sang leading roles in Spontini's *La vestale* and Halévy's *La juive* at the Metropolitan in the 1920s. Her favorite roles were Norma, Violetta, and Gioconda.

2164 **Chicago women who triumph in orchestral field**, *Musical*
ap   *America* XLIV/5 (22 May 1926) 11.
Discusses the newly formed Woman's Symphony Orchestra of Chicago, conducted by Richard Czerwonky. The founders of the orchestra--Lillian Poenisch (clarinetist), Lois Colburn Bichl (cellist), Adeline Schmidt (flutist), and Gertrude Early (violinist)--accomplished its organization despite the widespread assumption that women cannot accept the discipline involved in orchestral work. Among the possible successors to Czerwonky are Amy Neill, Theodora Sturkow-Ryder, and Ebba Sundstrom.

2165 CLARK, Kenneth S. **Carrying music to many lands privilege**
ap   **of reproductive artist**, *Musical America* XXI/12 (23 Jan 1915) 2.
Illus.
A native of Sweden, Julia Claussen came to the United States for artistic and financial reasons at the invitation of Andreas Dippel, director of the Chicago Opera. She now resides in Chicago and intends to become a citizen. The mezzo-soprano has had to relearn 10 operas in German, Italian, and French, but she notes that Scandinavians are good linguists. She specializes in Wagnerian roles. Ortrud and Amneris are her favorite parts.

→   CONTOS, Catherine. **Brava, maestra!**, *see* 3209ap[78].

2166 COST, Herbert W. **St. Louis welcomes women's symphony**,
ap   *Musical America* LIX/6 (25 Mar 1939) 11.
The St. Louis Women's Symphony Orchestra--which has been organized by conductor Edith Gordon--made its first appearance on 27 Feb. in a local high-school auditorium. The standard of performance was admirable considering that the orchestra has only a few hours of rehearsal each week. Schubert's symphony no. 8 in B minor, D.759, and Liszt's *Les preludes* were on the program.

2167 COX, Jeanette. **Bush Conservatory Orchestra receives warm**
ap   **reception at first concert of the season**, *Musical Courier*
LXXXVII/24 (13 Dec 1923) 29, 48-49.
The Bush Conservatory Orchestra offers students experience in orchestral routine and repertory so that upon graduation some members are able to find positions with leading symphony orchestras. The women players for 1923-24 are singled out as follows: Adeline Schmidt, flute, Lillian Poenisch, clarinet, Olga Eitner, principal violin, Marion Levin, violin, Ethel Murray, principal cello, and Anne Slack and Miriam Little, cello.

2168 COX, Jeanette. **Woman's Symphony of Chicago prospering**
ap   **under Leginska**, *Musical Courier* XCIV/3 (19 Jan 1928) 48.
Under the guidance of Ethel Leginska as conductor, the orchestra is "forging its way to the foremost rank of symphonic ensembles".

2169 CRAIG, Mary. **Ellabelle Davis reports on "a short tour" of**
ap   **Europe**, *Musical Courier* CXLI/1 (June 1950) 24. *Illus.*
During recent seasons, American-born and trained singers have established attendance records in European concert halls where audiences now hold American artists in higher regard. Ellabelle Davis is one of these singers, and she has just completed her 3rd European concert tour. The soprano comments that she would like to spend an entire season in her own country.

2170 CRAIG, Mary. **Success saga**, *Musical Courier* CXXXIII/3 (1
ap   Feb 1946) 12.
While she is proud to continue the tradition of artistic achievement that has been established by black musicians in the United States, Ellabelle Davis feels that a performer should be judged on merit alone, without discrimination or favors because of race, color, or creed. She is also in disagreement with those people who think she should sing spirituals because she is black. Davis notes that she grew up in New Rochelle, N.Y. and has never attended a revival meeting. The major events in the singer's career are discussed.

→   CRAIG, Mary. **Women at work**, *see* 2972ap[75].

2171 **Dame Myra Hess is dead at 75; one of world's leading**
an   **pianists**, *New York Times* 27 Nov 1965, 1, 28.
Myra Hess (1890-1965) first studied piano with Julian Pascal and Robert O. Morgan in her native London. She continued her studies with Tobias Matthay at the Royal Academy of Music beginning in 1902. In 1908 Hess made both her solo recital debut at Aeolian Hall in London and her orchestral debut with the London Philharmonic, conducted by Thomas Beecham. The pianist made her American debut in 1922 and concertized throughout the United States annually except for the years during World War II. From 1939-46 Hess organized and performed in lunchtime concerts at the National Gallery in London, which were attended by more than 700,000 people. Her repertory included Mozart, Beethoven, Schubert, and Brahms; unlike most pianists of her generation she rarely performed Chopin or Liszt. Hess retired from public life in 1961 and had been teaching in London until shortly before her death.

2172 DE CISNEROS, Eleanora. **Are American artists being denied**
ap   **a square deal in their own country?**, *Etude* XL/10 (Oct 1922)
665-66.
An appeal to the National Federation of Music Clubs for a policy of employing native-born and trained musicians at club concerts. The author notes that the post-war years have brought about an influx of foreign artists to the United States, and she argues that the directors of leading orchestras and opera companies--all Europeans--are not committed to musical life in America other than as a means for revenue.

→   DENNIS, Charles. **California Parent-Teacher Association**
Mothersingers, *see* 3219ap[78].

2173 DEVRIES, Renee. **Chicago. Woman's Symphony Orchestra**
ro   **of Chicago**, *Musical Courier* XCIV/17 (28 Apr 1927) 32.
Ethel Leginska's debut with the Woman's Symphony Orchestra of Chicago on 19 Apr. was a much heralded event and a great success. Devries comments that the orchestra has a special place in Chicago's musical life because its members are women and suggests that an emphasis on the performance of works by American composers would give the orchestra still another special role.

2174 **Distinguished career, A**, *Musical Leader* LX/24 (11 June 1931)
ap   26. *Illus.*
Discusses Elisabeth Rethberg's career in the United States and Europe. For the past 7 years Rethberg has been singing at the Metropolitan Opera and at the Ravinia Opera in Chicago. In 1927 the soprano performed with opera companies in Los Angeles and San Francisco. In 1928 she created the leading soprano roles in the world premières of Respighi's *La campana sommersa* at the Metropolitan and Richard Strauss's *Die Ägyptische Helena* in Dresden.

2175   D.L.L. **Finds lieder singing more fatiguing than opera roles,**
ap   *Musical America* XXII/5 (5 June 1915) 9. *Illus.*
Reports that Povla Frijsh is returning to Europe after her first season in the United States as a recitalist with the impression that good performance conditions and discriminating audiences prevail in America. Frijsh studied voice with Sarah De Lande in Paris, and she subsequently made concert tours in Europe with Raoul Pugno, the pianist, and Pablo Casals. Notable events in the soprano's career to date include her performances in Paris in Mahler's symphony no. 4 in G major, with the Cologne Orchestra under the composer's direction, and in Monteverdi's *L'incoronazione di Poppea*.

2176   D.L.L. **Sophie Braslau began career as Metropolitan's**
ap   **youngest singer,** *Musical America* XXXIV/4 (21 May 1921) 1, 8.
Illus.
Reports that Sophie Braslau gave 70 concerts during her recently-completed second annual tour. The contralto, whose Russian repertory includes songs by Rachmaninoff, Musorgski, and Aleksandr Grechaninov, plans to add to her next-year's programs lesser-known works by American composers. When Braslau, who sang at the Metropolitan Opera for 5 seasons, joined the company in 1914, she was its youngest singer.

2177   **Dorothy Speare, novelist, is dead,** *New York Times* 5 Feb 1951,
an   23. *Illus.*
Born in Newton Center, Mass., Dorothy Speare graduated from Smith Col. in 1919. After her instant success as a novelist, Speare studied voice with Jean de Reszke in France, and in 1927 she made her American operatic debut in Washington, D.C. in Thomas's *Mignon*. In 1931 the soprano was forced to retire from singing for health reasons. Speare wrote the play *Prima donna*, which was later adapted for film as *One night of love* with Grace Moore.

2178   DOWNES, Olin. **250 in chorus sing *Hora novissima*,** *New York*
ro   *Times* 31 Mar 1937, 28.
A review of the 30 Mar. concert of the New York Women's Symphony Orchestra, which featured a performance of Horatio Parker's *Hora novissima*. Soloists and a chorus made up of various choral groups in the metropolitan area joined the orchestra for the Parker work. As conductor, Antonia Brico "again gave convincing proof of a great talent and of her sincere desire to be of musical service to her community".

2179   DOWNES, Olin. **Brico Orchestra at Carnegie Hall,** *New York*
ro   *Times* 26 Jan 1939, 16.
Reviews the first concert of the newly organized Brico Symphony Orchestra--which includes both male and female players--and notes the careful selection of the membership from numerous applicants. The best players from the New York Women's Symphony Orchestra have been retained.

2180   DOWNES, Olin. **New chamber orchestra, A,** *New York Times*
an   23 Oct 1938, IX-7.
Announces the forthcoming debut of the orchestra of the New Friends of Music in New York. The orchestra's 40 players are young Americans averaging 25 years of age, and include the following women: Frances Blaisdell, 1st flute; Lois Wann, 1st oboe; and Ellen Stone, 1st horn. The New Friends of Music has 2 goals in organizing an orchestra: 1) to add to the repertory of the New Friends, and 2) to give competent American players orchestral experience.

2181   DOWNES, Olin. **Successful debut by Antonia Brico,** *New*
ro   *York Times* 11 Jan 1933, 23.
Reviews Brico's New York debut with the Musicians' Symphony Orchestra at the Metropolitan Opera on 10 Jan., and describes her as a conductor of "real acquirements and conspicuous talent. Miss Brico knew what she was doing a good deal better than many a young man who has been touted and feted and given golden opportunities in this city".

2182   DOWNES, Olin. **Two anniversaries,** *New York Times* 6 Dec
an   1936, XIII-11. *Illus.*
Reports that Eva Gauthier will give 3 retrospective recitals of songs she has introduced in the United States over a period of 22 years. These songs are chiefly by living composers. Gauthier's associations with George Gershwin (her accompanist at one time), Ravel, John Singer Sargent, and *Les Six* are discussed. A reproduction of one of Sargent's portraits of the mezzo-soprano is included. A 2nd anniversary is being celebrated by Efrem Zimbalist, who will play a concert in honor of the 25th anniversary of his American debut.

2183   DOWNES, Olin. **Verdi's Requiem heard in concert,** *New York*
ro   *Times* 27 Apr 1938, 19.
An enthusiastic review of the final concert by the New York Women's Symphony Orchestra in its 4th season, under the direction of Antonia Brico. "The uncommon unity and contagious feeling of the performance emanated as a central force from the conductor".

2184   DRAGONETTE, Jessica. **Faith is a song. The odyssey of an**
bm   **American artist** (New York: D. McKay, 1951) 322 p. *Illus.*
An autobiography by the radio star. Born in Calcutta, Dragonette came to the United States at age 6, and she grew up in a conventual orphanage in New Jersey after the death of her mother. In the early 1920s she studied in New York with Estelle Liebling, her first voice teacher. Dragonette's 10-year radio career began in 1925 with her performance in the first singing-acting serial written for radio. In 1935 she appeared on the first experimental television broadcast. Dragonette's repertory for both broadcasts and concerts included selections from operettas and operas as well as popular songs.

2185   DREYFUS, Sylvia G. **American songbird,** *Liberty* XVII/48 (30
ap   Nov 1940) 55-57. *Illus.*
Born in Norfolk, Va., Dorothy Maynor studied for 11 years at Hampton Inst., where she sang in the Hampton Choir under Nathaniel Dett. With the financial help of Harriet Curtis, dean of women at Hampton, Maynor studied voice with Wilfried Klamroth for 2 years and then with John Alan Haughton. In the summer of 1939, the singer auditioned for Serge Koussevitsky, whose endorsement helped secure several offers of contracts for Maynor, who went on to give a successful Town Hall debut in the fall of that year.

→   DRINKER, Sophie. **What price women's chorus?,** *see*
    3224ap[78].

2186   **Duplicates foreign success here,** *Musical America* IX/21 (3 Apr
ap   1909) 13. *Illus.*
Born in New York, Nevada Van der Veer studied voice with Victor Beigel in New York and London and was coached by Marie Roze in Paris. Her American concert debut was in Debussy's *La damoiselle elue* in 1908 with the New York Oratorio Soc., conducted by Frank Damrosch at Carnegie Hall. Van der Veer will sing with the New York Symphony Orchestra under Walter Damrosch on the orchestra's spring tour.

2187   E.A. **Wherein Frances Nash refuses to talk about novelties,**
ap   **jazz, and drudgery,** *Musical America* XLV/12 (8 Jan 1927) 36.
Illus.
Reports that the pianist has been busy studying contemporary music and her audiences on a series of coast-to-coast tours. She believes that performers have an obligation to play contemporary works, but she finds she cannot play more than a short piece on a program and sustain her audiences' interest. Nash wishes that more American artists had the now-listen-to-me-and-you'll-hear-something-really-wonderful demeanor typical of European performers.

2188   EASTON, Florence. **Open door to opera, The,** *Etude* XXXVI/4
ap   (Apr 1918) 229-30.
Florence Easton advocates the establishment of small opera houses in the United States, which would give native singers the opportunity to mature and gain experience as they do in Europe. Her own career--the soprano notes--is a good example of how thorough preparation led to success. Biographical information about Easton is included.

2189   EASTON, Florence. **Winning success without "pull",** *Musi-*
ap   *cian* XXVII/10 (Oct 1922) 7, 24.
Florence Easton discusses the 18 years of hard work that led to her engagement by the Metropolitan Opera. Initially Easton studied at the London Academy of Music, and at age 14 she went to Paris to further her vocal studies. When her father died she no longer had the financial resources to continue in Paris, and she began singing with opera companies touring the provinces in England. Shortly after her marriage to Francis Maclennan in 1904, Easton came to the United States because of her husband's contract with Henry W. Savage's opera company. In time Easton was also engaged by Savage. Easton and Maclennan have plotted their careers around their marriage and have sung together at the Berlin Opera, at Covent Garden, and in 1915 with the Chicago Opera.

2190   EATON, Quaintance. **How eighty-eight roles are sung,**
ap   *Musical America* XLVIII/1 (21 Apr 1928) 19.
Florence Easton's gift for learning roles quickly and her extensive repertory have brought her into great demand among managers. The soprano particularly enjoys singing Isolde, Tosca, and the Marschallin, and she has performed Butterfly over 300 times--perhaps the world's record. Her 88 roles are listed.

2191   EATON, Frances Quaintance. **Marjorie Lawrence sings from**
ap   **a wheelchair,** *Musical America* LXII/13 (Sept 1942) 15. *Illus.*
Discusses the soprano's professional comeback after being stricken with polio in Mexico in June 1941. Lawrence recently appeared as a soloist with Andre Kostelanetz on a radio broadcast and has sung several concert benefits. This article is signed F.Q.E., and Eaton's name has been supplied.

→   EATON, Frances. **Music federation looks to youth,** *see*
    2081ap[67].

→   EATON, Frances. **Women come into their own in our orchestras**, *see* 3229ap[78].

2192   Ebba Sundstrom new conductor of Woman's Symphony of
ap   **Chicago**, *Musical Courier* XCIX/14 (5 Oct 1929) 23.
Reports that Ebba Sundstrom was chosen to replace Ethel Leginska as conductor of the Woman's Symphony Orchestra of Chicago when Leginska's absences for other engagements made it impossible for her to continue. Sundstrom formerly was concertmistress with the orchestra and also with other orchestras in the Chicago area. The current subscription campaign for the women's orchestra is proving successful.

2193   Edith Mason dies, leading soprano, *New York Times* 27 Nov
an   1973, 47.
Edith Barnes Mason (1893-1973) sang at the Metropolitan Opera from 1915-17 and again in 1935-36. She appeared with the Chicago Opera from 1921-23 and again from 1934-42. Among her best-known roles were Micaela, Madame Butterfly, Violetta, and Marguerite.

2194   Eleanor Spencer, the American pianist, *Musical Courier* LXVI/
ap   23 (4 June 1913) 7.
Born in 1890 in Chicago, Eleanor Spencer began studying the piano seriously at age 6, and when she was 10 years old appeared in Chicago and New York as a child prodigy. Her mother, a former singer, took charge of Spencer's career and carefully avoided exploiting her talent. Spencer studied for 2 years in New York with William Mason, and subsequently she worked with Harold Bauer in Paris and Theodor Leschetizky in Vienna. Although her mother died when Spencer was only 18, she went on to make a successful debut in London in 1910. Her first American concert tour for 1913-14 is announced.

2195   Elfrieda B. Mestechkin dies; concert violinist and teacher,
an   *New York Times* 31 July 1963, 29.
Elfrieda Boss Mestechkin was a contemporary of Efrem Zimbalist and Mischa Elman. Her husband, the violinist Jacob Mestechkin, had been a classmate in St. Petersburg. After the couple emigrated from Russia to the United States in 1919, Mestechkin concentrated on appearances with chamber music ensembles as well as radio engagements. She was the concertmistress of both the New York Women's Symphony Orchestra under Antonia Brico and the New York City Symphony Orchestra.

2196   Elisabeth Schumann dies at 63; operatic soprano, lieder
an   **singer**, *New York Herald Tribune* 24 Apr 1952, 26.
Born in Germany, Elisabeth Schumann (1888-1952) made her debut at age 18 at the Hamburg Opera. She came to the United States in 1921 to perform in concerts under the direction of Richard Strauss. In 1938 Schumann assumed direction of the vocal department at the Curtis Inst., and she became a United States citizen in 1944.

→   ELKINS-MARLOW, Laurine. **Gena Branscombe, American composer and conductor**, *see* 2014dd[66].

2197   Ellabelle Davis dies at 53. Negro singer a Cinderella, *New*
an   *York Herald Tribune* 16 Nov 1960, 25.
Ellabelle Davis was working as a seamstress for Josephine Crane--the noted patron--when Crane overheard her singing and offered to support her vocal studies. Crane also backed Davis's debut recital in Town Hall in 1942. In 1945 Davis sang Aida, her first operatic role, at the National Opera in Mexico City. Lukas Foss wrote his cantata *Song of songs* for Davis in 1947 with a commission from the League of Composers.

2198   Elsa Alsen dead; opera singer, 94, *New York Times* 2 Feb 1975,
an   I-49.
Elsa Alsen (1880-1975) appeared in 200 roles from 1900-35, first as a mezzo-soprano and later as a dramatic soprano. She came to the United States in 1924 and sang with the Chicago Civic Opera as well as companies in San Francisco and Los Angeles. She also sang widely in concert. Alsen was a voice teacher in New York until her retirement in 1970.

→   **Ethel Leginska directs her opera**, *see* 2016an[66].

2199   Ethel Leginska's activities, *Musical Courier* XCVIII/11 (14 Mar
ap   1929) 14.
Leginska now seems to be coming into her own as a conductor. Undaunted by lack of encouragement after her debut in New York, she went on to conduct the People's Symphony Orchestra in Boston, the Boston Woman's Symphony Orchestra, and the Woman's Symphony Orchestra of Chicago. Currently she is making plans for an opera company in Boston, which will give performances in English; the Boston Woman's Symphony Orchestra will participate.

2200   "Europeans should come to U.S. to learn to sing", says

ap   **Marie Sundelius**, *Musical America* XXIII/15 (12 Feb 1916) 34.
Illus.
The Swedish-American soprano notes that she received all her fundamental voice training in the United States. She began singing as a church soloist and in recitals when she was age 19, but she did not think of becoming a professional until her husband--a physician and accomplished amateur musician--challenged her to do so. Sundelius observes that husbands and wives who have their own individual work are inevitably happier in their marriages.

2201   Eva Gauthier, 73, a singer, is dead, *New York Times* 27 Dec
an   1958, 2.
The Canadian-American singer (1885-1958) was known for her programs of contemporary music, her first performances of many American works, and her inclusion of jazz and show tunes in recitals. She also sang Oriental music as well as less well-known European music of the 17th and 18th c. Since World War II Gauthier had devoted most of her time to teaching and coaching young singers.

2202   F. Eleanor Spencer returns to America, *Musical Courier* C/6 (8
ap   Feb 1930) 8, 39. *Illus.*
The American pianist has been living abroad and concertizing in central Europe for several years. Her recent Carnegie Hall recital received reviews commending her taste and solid musicianship. Spencer's views on contemporary piano music and the vogue for music by Spanish composers are discussed.

2203   FAIR, Ernest W. Women help Oklahoma symphony, *Musical*
ap   *America* XLVII/11 (31 Dec 1927) 6. *Illus.*
The Oklahoma City Symphony Orchestra had its beginnings within the Women's Music Club of the city when, in 1922, Mrs. George Forsythe organized a string orchestra and engaged Frederick Holmberg of Oklahoma City U. as conductor. Gradually men joined the orchestra which expanded to include all the choirs, and public concerts became a regular feature. The women of the orchestra raised funds within the business community of the city in order to establish the orchestra financially. At the present time the orchestra numbers 68 players; the majority are teachers and students of music, although a few firemen, clerks, and other business men are also members.

→   **Fifty local prodigies 1900-1940**, *see* 973bm[58].

2204   Final concert of Sinfonetta set Sunday, *Stockton [Calif.] Record*
an   4 Nov 1938, 19.
As a result of a controversy with the local musicians' union, 4 key players in the orchestra--who are union members, but who have played with the group since its inception 2 seasons ago--are now forced to retire. Since there are no other comparable women players in the community, La Sinfonetta is expected to disband.

2205   First Metropolitan debutante of the season, The: Martha
ap   **Lipton**, *Opera News* IX/3 (20 Nov 1944) 24-26. *Illus.*
A native of New York, Martha Lipton studied voice with Paul Reimers at the Juilliard School between 1937 and 1940. Also in 1940 she won first prize in a contest sponsored by the National Federation of Music Clubs, and in 1941 she gave a debut recital in Town Hall in New York. The mezzo-soprano has studied operatic roles with Ettore Verna and Kurt Adler, and during the 1944-45 season she will make her debut at the Metropolitan Opera as Siebel in *Faust*.

2206   First women's band of the Marines, *Musician* L/2 (Feb 1945)
ap   56-57. *Illus.*
Discusses the women's band of the United States Marine Corps, which has been in existence for a year at Camp Lejeune, N.C. The band plays for military reviews, marches, etc., for women's units of the Marines, and it also breaks into smaller groups to supply music for dancing and other recreational activities.

2207   FISHER, Marjory Markres. Coast WPA men led by Mary
ap   **Carr Moore**, *Musical America* LVIII/10 (25 May 1938) 29. *Illus.*
At the invitation of Alfred Hertz, Mary Carr Moore recently conducted the Federal Symphony Orchestra in San Francisco in performances of 2 of her works: the intermezzo from *David Rizzio, op. 89* (*WIAM* 1456) and *Kamiakin*, a tone poem. The Federal Symphony Orchestra operates under the auspices of the Works Progress Administration (WPA).

2208   Florence Lennon, *New York Times* 11 Nov 1972, 36.
an
An obituary for Florence Lennon, who--as "Roxanne"--led a 26-man orchestra in the 1930s on New York's radio station WOR. After an early and brief career in vaudeville, Lennon played organ for silent films in various movie theaters in New York.

2209   F.R.G. Making choristers of New York's business women,
ap   *Musical America* XXXIII/26 (23 Apr 1921) 9.
While much attention is paid to the tired business man in the United States, comparatively little is paid to the business woman, who is now taking a definite part in social life. The New York Woman's Choir, organized and conducted by

Jean Whitcomb Fenn, aims to give young women between the ages of 17 and 26 a "medium for self-expression". After 1 year, its membership numbers 75, with branches of the chorus in Manhattan, Brooklyn, and Newark, N.J. Fenn's husband has provided practically all of the financial support for the choir.

2210 GAUTHIER, Eva. **On the edge of opera**, *Opera News* XIX/13
ap (31 Jan 1955) 10-11. *Illus.*
Eva Gauthier studied voice with Jacques Bouhy at the Paris Conservatory and was coached by Rina Giachetti in Italy. The soprano began her career singing opera, but later devoted herself to solo recitals. In her New York appearances she introduced arias from Rimski-Korsakov's *Le coq d'or* and Erich Wolfgang Korngold's *Die tote Stadt*.

2211 GELATT, Roland. **Music makers** (New York: A.A. Knopf,
bm 1953) 286 p. *Illus., index.*
This collection of biographical sketches includes essays about Myra Hess and Wanda Landowska, keyboard players, and Lotte Lehmann, singer.

2212 G.F. **Chapmans of Florence, The**, *Opera News* XXV/3 (19 Nov
ap 1960) 16, 31. *Illus.*
Gladys Swarthout recalls her singing career with pride and regret. After vocal study at the Bush Conservatory in Chicago, Swarthout sang with the Chicago Opera and later with the Metropolitan Opera. She considers the conductor Tullio Serafin to have been the greatest influence on her career. Swarthout left opera to appear in films and on radio, and in hindsight she notes that she lost sight of her original artistic goals. She now lives in retirement in Italy with her husband, Frank Chapman.

2213 **Giannini engaged by Metropolitan**, *New York Times* 24 Oct
an 1935, 18. *Illus.*
Reports that Dusolina Giannini will make her debut at the Metropolitan Opera in 1936. Born in Philadelphia of Italian parentage, Giannini studied voice with her father, tenor Feruccio Giannini, and with Marcella Sembrich. Her repertory includes the roles of Carmen, Donna Anna, Aida, and Santuzza. Edward Johnson, general manager of the Metropolitan, notes that Giannini should have been singing at the Metropolitan 10 years ago. To date she has sung only in recitals and with orchestras in the United States.

2214 GILBERT, Douglas. **Dorothée Manski; one-woman Wagner,**
ap **knows every note of all his operas**, *New York World-Telegram* 9
Jan 1935, 4. *Illus.*
Dorothée Manski began her work in opera at the Berlin Opera in 1911. She has specialized in Wagnerian roles at the Metropolitan Opera since 1927. The highlight of her career to date has been a performance as Isolde at the Salzburg festival in 1933, conducted by Bruno Walter.

2215 GILBERT, Gama. **Katherine Bacon in sonata recital**, *New*
ro *York Times* 17 Oct 1939, 31.
Reviews the opening concert of a series in which the pianist will perform 16 of the Beethoven sonatas. Bacon presented a Beethoven cycle earlier in 1927 and a Schubert cycle in 1928. Her readings were "reverent, devoted, and poetic", but she did not convey "Beethoven's physical energy in the fullest measure. Many passages of these sonatas seem never to have been intended for feminine hands".

2216 **Grace Moore fooled critics**, *New York Sun* 27 Jan 1947, 3.
an
After Grace Moore's success as a musical comedy star, she was told by critics and voice teachers that she would never reach the Metropolitan Opera. Although she failed several auditions, the soprano finally made her debut as Mimi in 1928, and she continued at the Metropolitan for 3 seasons.

2217 G.V. **Persecution in Russia drove Rosa Raisa to vocal**
ap **career**, *Musical America* XXV/5 (2 Dec 1916) 19. *Illus.*
An account of Rosa Raisa's early career. Born in Russian-occupied Poland in 1893, Raisa fled from a pogrom to Naples, where she studied voice with Barbara Marchisio, her only teacher. The soprano made her operatic debut at the Verdi centenary in Parma in 1913. The same year she also made her American debut in *Aida* with the Chicago Grand Opera. A list of the roles in Raisa's repertory is included.

→ HAGEMAN, Richard. **Shall the young woman choose music**
as a profession?, *see* 2090ap[67].

2218 HANSEN, Ruth. **These Portlanders cooked and sewed their**
an **way to concerts**, *Portland Sunday Oregonian* 19 May 1935, 8.
The Portland Women's Symphony Orchestra has given 60 concerts since its organization in Mar. 1934 under the direction of D'Zama Murielle. The players prepared food to serve at the luncheons associated with their earliest concerts, which were popular in nature, and they have made their own dresses to wear for performances. D'Zama Murielle's background as a conductor in the Boston area is discussed.

2219 **Happy heroine**, *Time* 11 Nov 1946, 61-62, 64, 67. *Illus.*
ap
Helen Traubel is the first American-born and trained soprano to sing Wagnerian roles exclusively at the Metropolitan Opera. Her background and her relationships with Kirsten Flagstad and Lauritz Melchior are discussed.

2220 **Harmati seeks native works for women's string orchestra**,
ap *Musical America* XXXI/26 (24 Apr 1920) 33. *Illus.*
Sandor Harmati, conductor of the Women's Orchestral Club in New York, announces his interest in receiving scores for string orchestra for performance by his women's orchestra during the 1920-21 season. Harmati would like to increase the number of string players in the orchestra and to add winds and brass. The 6-year history of the Women's Orchestral Club is reviewed.

2221 HARRISON, Jay S. **Tippy tells all (almost) about her life at**
an **the Met**, *New York Herald Tribune* 6 Dec 1959, IV-6.
Thelma Votipka, known as "Tippy" to her friends, specialized in small roles at the Metropolitan Opera for 26 years. She believes that singing with the famous singers of the time, from Mary Garden to Maria Callas and Renata Tebaldi, was her principal reward. As a teacher, she has trained a number of prize-winning students.

2222 H.A.S. **Newspaper prize launched diva's career**, *Musical*
ap *Courier* CXX/12 (15 Dec 1939) 9. *Illus.*
Marjorie Lawrence discusses her experiences in the United States, where she was the first Brünnhilde at the Metropolitan Opera to ride her horse directly into Siegfried's pyre in *Götterdämmerung*. The soprano believes that American women are doing wonderful work in organizing concerts and sponsoring performances. The inspiration of winning a newspaper prize in her native Australia sent Lawrence to Paris for further vocal study at the beginning of her career.

2223 HAUGHTON, John Alan. **"Make every thought and experi-**
ap **ence count for your art", is Mabel Garrison's motto**, *Musical*
America XXXII/9 (26 June 1920) 9. *Illus.*
Mabel Garrison discusses her forthcoming European trip--her first--to sing and to absorb the culture. The soprano also reminisces about the risks she and her husband/accompanist George Siemonn took when they left Baltimore for New York, where she eventually achieved success at the Metropolitan Opera.

2224 HAVENER, Helen. **Girl with a baton**, *Independent Woman*
ap XXVII/11 (Nov 1948) 328-30. *Illus.*
A protégé of Ferdinand Schaefer in Indianapolis, Ann Kullmer attended the Leipzig Conservatory, where after some initial resistance from the faculty she was accepted as a student in conducting. She made her debut as a conductor in Berlin at the age of 21. Like many young American women, Kullmer had intended to launch her career abroad and then return to the United States, but she found an abundance of engagements in Germany, primarily as a violinist, but also in conducting. During World War II her fluency in German led her to intelligence work, and she developed a radio program tailored to expressing American ideals to German women. Recently she has begun to re-establish herself as a conductor at guest appearances with leading European orchestras. She would prefer the directorship of an orchestra of her own in the United States.

2225 H.B. **"Back to nature" [is] Frances Nash's slogan**, *Musical*
ap *America* XXIV/8 (24 June 1916) 47. *Illus.*
An interview with Frances Nash at her summer home in Heath, Mass., prior to the pianist's New York debut in the fall of 1916. While Nash was studying in Berlin, twice a week an orchestra of students and members of the State Opera Orchestra played at her home, thereby giving her the opportunity to rehearse many difficult works. When the war broke out Nash and her associates gave up practicing to assist in preparing provisions for the German army. Although she is shy about the fact, Nash is a wealthy woman who has helped many struggling artists.

2226 HENDERSON, William J. **Music and musicians. [Lucrezia**
an **Bori]**, *New York Sun* 28 Mar 1936, 11.
Written shortly after Lucrezia Bori's farewell performance at the Metropolitan Opera, this tribute in Henderson's regular column presents a summary of Bori's career. Her portrayal of Fiora in Montemezzi's *L'amore dei tre re* established Bori in 1914 as a first-rank dramatic soprano. Among her many popular roles were Manon, Mélisande, Mimi, and Violetta.

2227 HENDERSON, William J. **Music and musicians [Women as**
an **orchestral musicians]**, *New York Sun* 16 Nov 1935, 8.
Henderson argues, in his regular column, that there is no reason why qualified women shouldn't be hired for orchestral work. The questions of rehearsal fatigue and discipline depend on the individual woman. This article was occasioned by the recent appearance of a female player [Elsa Hilger] in the cello section of the Philadelphia Orchestra.

2228 HENSCHEL, Horst; EHRHARD, Friedrich. **Elisabeth**
bf   **Rethberg. Ihr leben und Künstlertum** [Elisabeth Rethberg. Her
      life and genius] (New York: Arno, 1977) 115 p. $11. In German.
A reprint of the 1928 edition (Schwarzenberg: Städtischer Geschichtsverein).
Traces the soprano's career in Europe and the United States to 1928. Includes
excerpts from numerous reviews of her performances.

→   HILL, Tremont. **Siren serenade**, *see* 143ap[25].

→   **History of opera in San Francisco II**, *see* 1017bm[58].

2229 HORSLEY, Carter B. **Gladys Swarthout dies at 64; popular**
an   **mezzo-soprano at Met**, *New York Times* 9 July 1969, 34. *Illus.*
Born in Missouri, Gladys Swarthout (1904-69) sang boy soprano parts with the
Chicago Opera in her early years. She made her Metropolitan Opera debut in
1929 in *La Gioconda* and retired in 1945. Swarthout was best known for her
interpretation of Carmen, a role she sang for the first operatic production
staged exclusively for television in 1950.

2230 H.S. **Brodsky and Triggs champion the cause of American**
ap   **music**, *Musical Courier* CVII/8 (19 Aug 1933) 8. *Illus.*
Vera Brodsky (Lawrence) and Harold Triggs are both pupils of Josef Lhevinne,
and a year ago they decided to join their talents and perform works for 2
pianos on radio stations in New York. They are interested in American music,
and they believe they have a commitment as young musicians to play the works
of young American composers. To date 15 compositions have been written
expressly for Brodsky and Triggs by George Newell, Henry Brant, Dana Suesse,
Charles Haubiel, and Evelyn Berckman. The Berckman piece--*Hateful city*--is
for 2 pianos and orchestra.

2231 **Italian aspect of the art of pianoforte playing, An**, *Etude*
ap   XLIII/11 (Nov 1925) 763. *Illus.*
Reports that Maria Carreras has been touring the United States since her New
     debut in Jan. 1923. At age 6, Carreras won a scholarship to the Academy
of St. Cecilia in Rome. Later she finished her piano studies with Giovanni
Sgambati, who also conducted for Carreras's debut with orchestra in Rome
when she was 21 years old. The pianist discusses the piano playing of Liszt,
Busoni, Sgambati, and Beniamo Cesi.

2232 J.A.H. **Role of impressario as Lucy Gates interprets it**,
ap   *Musical America* XXXIII/26 (23 Apr 1921) 15. *Illus.*
Lucy Gates discusses her production of Pergolesi's *La serva padrona*, which she
will include as part of a concert program on tour. The soprano has studied the
score and early 18th-c. paintings in detail in order to make the production as
authentic as possible. She is enjoying the executive aspects of the production.

2233 J.E. **Young American woman conductor trained abroad**
ap   **begins home career**, *Musical America* LXV/11 (Aug 1945) 28.
      Illus.
Ann Kullmer won a scholarship in 1936 to study at the Leipzig Conservatory,
and it was only after 6 months of persistence on her part that she was accepted
as a student in conducting as well as violin. Subsequently, performances
Kullmer conducted in Berlin occasioned Wilhelm Fürtwangler's interest in her
talent, and he offered to work on scores with her. This was a rare honor since
Fürtwangler had never previously accepted a pupil. With the outbreak of the
war Kullmer was interned in Frankfurt, and when she returned to New York
the only employment she was able to secure was playing in nightclubs.
Presently Kullmer is the conductor of a women's orchestra that has been
featured in concerts on radio and at military camps.

2234 JERITZA, Maria. **Sunlight and song**. Trans. from German by
bf   Frederick Herman MARTENS (New York: Arno, 1977) 262 p. $21.
      Illus.
A reprint of the 1928 edition (New York: Appleton), tracing the soprano's
career to that year. Born in Brünn, Austria, Jeritza made her operatic debut as
Elsa in *Lohengrin* in 1910 in Olmütz. Two years later she made her Viennese
debut as Elisabeth in *Tannhäuser* and sang the title role in the world première
of Strauss's *Ariadne auf Naxos* in Stuttgart. Beginning in 1922 the soprano
appeared in leading roles at the Metropolitan Opera; among her best known
were Tosca and Turandot, which she studied with Puccini. Although she had
not sung in concert in Europe, once she was in the United States Jeritza
followed the example of other operatic stars who went on concert tours after
the termination of the opera season, and she worked hard to perfect her English
so as to include songs by American composers on her programs. While in New
York Jeritza studied with Marcella Sembrich.

2235 **Josephine Antoine**, *Opera News* XXXVI/10 (29 Jan 1972) 36.
ap
An obituary for Josephine Antoine (1908-71), who made her Metropolitan
Opera debut as Philine in Thomas's *Mignon*. The soprano's most popular roles
included Lucia, Gilda, and Rosina. After her retirement in the late 1940s,
Antoine taught voice at the Eastman School until her death in Nov. 1971.

2236 J.V. **"An artist is no different from anyone else", says Povla**
ap   **Frijsh, the distinguished soprano**, *Musical Courier* LXXIX/2 (10
      July 1919) 18. *Illus.*
An interview with Povla Frijsh, who thinks it is wrong to put artists on
pedestals. Besides giving recitals throughout the United States during the 1918-
19 season, the soprano toured as a soloist with the Minneapolis Symphony
Orchestra under the direction of Artur Bodanzky and made appearances as
soloist with the Philadelphia Orchestra in Washington, D.C., Baltimore, and
Philadelphia. In the future she plans to include more modern French songs on
her programs and songs by contemporary Americans, e.g., John Alden
Carpenter, Charles Martin Loeffler, and Charles Griffes.

2237 KAHN, Dorothea. **Women build a symphony**, *Christian Sci-*
an   *ence Monitor* 4 Jan 1941, weekly magazine-5, 13.
A brief history of the Woman's Symphony Orchestra of Chicago on the
occasion of the orchestra's debut season in radio broadcasting under the
direction of Izler Solomon. Lillian Poenisch--a founder and charter member-
-notes that the most important goal before the orchestra at the present time is
the guarantee of a season of 10-15 weeks, which would mean more regular
work for the members than they have had in the past. Information about
Poenisch's orchestral career is included.

2238 KAHN, E.J., Jr. **Profiles. The harp lady**, *New Yorker* 3 Feb
ap   1940, 25-29.
A native of Indiana, Mildred Dilling took up the harp at age 12, and after
graduating from high school she came to New York where she continued her
studies and secured her first professional engagements at the Central Presbyterian Church. Her most important period of study was with Henriette Renié in
Paris. Dilling made her first cross-country tour in 1924 with 4 male singers who
called themselves the Reszke Quartet after their teacher Jean de Reszke.
Typically the harpist spends 6 months of the year on tour, and now that the
war prevents her from concertizing in Europe, she is considering traveling to
Australia. Harpo Marx became Dilling's pupil in 1928. After losing considerable money in the stock market crash in 1929, Dilling decided that harps would
be a better investment, and she currently owns a collection of 32 instruments,
almost all of which she keeps in her living room. Her favorite is a French 18th-
c. instrument made by Jacques-Georges Cousineau. The most expensive
instruments in the collection are the American-made Lyon & Healy harps that
Dilling plays in concerts. Dilling would like to see the harp replace the piano as
the favorite instrument for amateurs.

2239 **Kathryn Meisle, 75, sang with the Met**, *New York Times* 19 Jan
an   1970, 47.
An obituary for the contralto (1894-1970), who sang at the Metropolitan Opera
from 1935-38. Azucena was her most popular role. Meisle made her debut as a
soloist with the Minneapolis Symphony Orchestra in 1921. In 1923 she made
her operatic debut as Erda in *Siegfried* with the Chicago Civic Opera.

2240 KEITH, Alice. **"Musical Americana"**, *Music Clubs Magazine*
ap   XI/4 (Mar-Apr 1932) 15.
A description of the current radio series, "Musical Americana", produced by the
Columbia Broadcasting System in cooperation with the National Federation of
Music Clubs. Marion Bauer and Amy Cheney Beach are featured playing their
own compositions, together with performances of works by Rosalie Housman
and Annabel Buchanan.

2241 KINDLER, Hans. **Support for women players**, *New York*
an   *Times* 20 Oct 1946, II-7.
A letter to the editor in response to the recent statement by Thomas Beecham
that "women in symphony orchestras constitute a disturbing element". Kindler
argues that the women players in orchestras he has conducted were not only
fully equal to the men, but sometimes more imaginative, and always especially
cooperative. Since women players served so well during World War II, it would
be wrong to dismiss them now.

2242 KLEIN, Howard. **Marian Anderson will return in 1965 after**
an   **tour of world**, *New York Times* 12 Dec 1963, 40. *Illus.*
On the occasion of President Johnson's presentation of the Freedom Medal to
her, Marian Anderson recalls her White House performances for Presidents
Roosevelt and Truman, and her singing at the inaugurations of Presidents
Eisenhower and Kennedy. After her farewell American appearance in 1965,
Anderson plans to become more active in the civil rights movement.

2243 LA HINES, Elizabeth. **Orchestral field opening to women**,
an   *New York Times* 11 Apr 1937, VI-6.
Reports on Frederique Joanne Petrides's research and articles about women as
orchestral musicians, and discusses the work of women's orchestras active both
in the past and at the present time in Los Angeles, Philadelphia, Long Beach,
Calif., Chicago, and New York. Petrides contends that women's orchestras have
traditionally faced a handicap because the public views them as novelty items
rather than ensembles of artists.

2244 LA HINES, Elizabeth. **Orchestral posts urged for women**,
an   *New York Times* 2 Oct 1938, II-5.
The Committee for the Recognition of Women in the Musical Profession in
New York--which now numbers approximately 800 members--has formulated
plans for breaking down resistance to the "mixed" orchestra made up of both
male and female players. 1) The committee proposes that auditions for
employment should be held behind screens. 2) The committee is appealing to
women's and other appropriate organizations for support, e.g., the New York
League of Business and Professional Women. 3) The committee is offering
recent female graduates of the Juilliard School and Curtis Inst. the opportunity
to play orchestral repertory in informal groups, so that these women do not lose
the orchestral routine acquired during schooling. The officers of the committee
include Joyce Barthelson, Mildred Hunt, Catherine Newton, Jean Schneider,
and Ruth Wilson.

2245 LASSIMONNE, Denise. **Myra Hess by her friends** (London:
bm   Hamish, Hamilton, 1966) 119 p. *Illus., discog.*
A collection of informal sketches by Myra Hess's friends, written shortly after
her death. Contains 2 essays about her work in the United States from 1922-61
by Bruce Simonds and by Anita Gunn, Hess's secretary, who traveled with the
pianist on her American tours.

2246 LAWRENCE, Marjorie. **Interrupted melody** (Sydney, Aus-
bm   tralia: Invincible, 1949) 261 p. *Illus.*
An autobiography by the soprano Marjorie Lawrence. Born in Australia in
1908, Lawrence won a singing contest which enabled her to study in Paris with
Cécile Gilly in 1928. She sang in Monte Carlo and Lille before making her
Paris debut in 1933 as Ortrud. Her American debut as Brünnhilde took place in
1935 at the Metropolitan Opera, where she sang for 6 seasons. In 1941
Lawrence was stricken with polio, but she managed to appear on radio
broadcasts only a year later. The soprano gave a Town Hall recital in 1942 and
sang Isolde from a wheelchair in 1944. Best known for her Wagnerian roles,
Lawrence also achieved success as Elektra, Salome, Tosca, Carmen, and Thaïs.

2247 **Lawrence of Australia**, *Opera News* II/12 (31 Jan 1938) 1-3. *Illus.*
ap
Discusses Marjorie Lawrence's repertory, which includes the roles of Elisabeth,
Brünnhilde, Ortrud, Aida, Donna Anna, and Salome. In 1934 she sang her first
Salome in Paris in French, and she is now learning the role in German for the
current Metropolitan Opera production.

2248 L.B. **Kathryn Meisle spells health with a capital "H"**, *New*
an   *York World-Telegram* 25 Jan 1936, 23. *Illus.*
Kathryn Meisle is "purely an American product", having been educated
exclusively in the United States. The mezzo-soprano--whose most famous roles
include Fricka, Waltraute, Amneris, Azucena, and Erda--appears regularly with
the San Francisco Opera.

2249 LE MASSENA, C.E. **Galli-Curci's life of song** (New York:
bm   Paebar, 1945) 336 p. *Illus., discog.*
A biography describing the Italian-born soprano's professional career and
personal life. Prior to coming to the United States, Amelita Galli-Curci (1889-
1963) sang throughout Europe, Central America, and in South America, where
she appeared with Caruso in 1915. She made her American debut in Chicago in
1916, but it was not until 1921 that she sang at the Metropolitan Opera,
appearing in *La traviata*. In 1918 the soprano became an American citizen and
married her accompanist, Homer Samuels. Galli-Curci settled in Los Angeles in
1938. Lists of her roles and recordings are included.

2250 **Lea Luboshutz, artist, teacher**, *New York Times* 19 Mar 1965,
an   35.
Reports the death of the former concert violinist in Philadelphia at age 80.
Born in Odessa, Russia, Lea Luboshutz studied with her father before
attending the Moscow Conservatory. Later she completed her training with
Ysaÿe in Belgium. She appeared as soloist with many of the world's great
orchestras and conductors, and she was also well-known for her joint recitals
with Josef Hofmann. Luboshutz settled in the United States in 1927 and
taught many leading violinists at the Curtis Inst. until her retirement in 1945.
The violinist created a fund to assist young musicians.

2251 LEGGE, Walter. **Rosa**, *Opera News* XLI/18 (12 Mar 1977) 10-
ap   15. *Illus.*
Reviews Rosa Ponselle's career on the occasion of her 80th birthday. Almost 60
years after her Metropolitan Opera debut in 1918 and nearly 40 years after her
retirement, Ponselle remains active as a consultant to the Baltimore Opera. The
soprano's voice, recordings, and her decision to retire at the height of her career
in 1937 are discussed.

2252 **Leginska enlivens** *Boccaccio*, *Musical Courier* CIII/22 (28 Nov
ro   1931) 5, 51.
Reviews the revival of Franz von Suppe's *Boccaccio* in an English version, and

describes Ethel Leginska as an able conductor. Leginska achieved a far more
successful ensemble of soloists and chorus than is usual in light opera.

2253 **Leginska, guest conductor of Chicago Woman's Symphony,**
ap   **to play solo**, *Musical Courier* XCIV/15 (14 Apr 1927) 33.
Reports that Ethel Leginska--the dynamic conductor of the Boston Philharmonic Orchestra and the only woman director to command international
attention--will be guest conductor of the Woman's Symphony Orchestra of
Chicago at its last concert of the 1926-27 season and will play Mozart's piano
concerto no. 23 in A major, K.488.

2254 **Leginska is found, her mind a blank; reported in Boston**, *New*
an   *York Times* 2 Feb 1925, 1, 15.
Reports that Ethel Leginska--who disappeared just before she was scheduled to
give a recital in Carnegie Hall on 26 Jan.--has been found. The pianist and her
friends are keeping all details secret. A statement from the Bureau of Missing
Persons attributes Leginska's disappearance to a "nervous breakdown caused
by overwork".

2255 **Leginska not found; nerves are blamed**, *New York Times* 28 Jan
an   1925, 1.
Reports that Ethel Leginska is still missing after she disappeared on her way to
give a concert at Carnegie Hall 2 days earlier, and speculates that she fled
because her hands were not in good shape. Various friends of the pianist insist
that she did not disappear for the sake of publicity.

2256 **Leginska's orchestra in concert**, *Boston Post* 14 Oct 1929, 11.
ro
Announces a 10-week tour in the United States by the Boston Woman's
Symphony Orchestra under the direction of Ethel Leginska, and reviews the
orchestra's farewell concert. Reports that when the orchestra was first
organized it was treated with polite condescension, but that this situation has
since changed. "Granted that women performers are not likely to attain
masculine proficiencies with such unfeminine instruments as the double bass,
French horns, trombones, and tuba, the players of these instruments in Miss
Leginska's present orchestra are at least adequate to any ordinary demands that
may be placed upon them. The band as a whole plays with a gratifying, even a
surprising effectiveness".

2257 LEHMANN, Lotte. **Midway in my song**. Trans. from German
bm   by Margaret LUDWIG (New York: Bobbs-Merrill, 1938) 250 p.
      Illus., index.
A translation of the soprano's autobiography, *Anfang und Aufstieg. Lebenser-
innerungen* (Wien: H. Reichner, 1937), tracing her career through 1936. Born in
Perleberg, Germany, Lotte Lehmann (1888-1976) studied with Mathilde
Mallinger and made her operatic debut in Hamburg as Freia in *Das Rheingold*
in 1910. In 1914 she sang Sophie in *Der Rosenkavalier*, which marked the
beginning of her long personal and professional association with Strauss. In
1916 the soprano sang the title role in *Ariadne auf Naxos*, and in 1919 she
appeared as the Dyer's wife in the première of *Die Frau ohne Schatten*.
Lehmann's most popular role is the Marschallin, which she has performed over
300 times; her other roles include Tosca, Desdemona, Mimi, and Manon.
Lehmann made her American debut with the Chicago Civic Opera in 1930 and
her Metropolitan Opera debut 4 years later as Sieglinde.

2258 LEHMANN, Lotte. **My many lives**. Trans. by Frances HOL-
bm   DEN (New York: Boosey & Hawkes, 1948) 262 p. *Illus.*
Lotte Lehmann discusses her experiences with and ideas about the opera roles
she has sung. Wagnerian roles for which she is famous are Elsa, Elisabeth, Eva,
and Sieglinde. Lehmann is probably best-known for her interpretations of
Strauss roles, including the Marschallin, Sophie, Octavian, Arabella, and
Ariadne.

2259 **Lev, Ray**, *Current biography*. Ed. by Anna ROTHE (New York:
ap   H.W. Wilson, 1949) 353-55. *Illus.*
Born in Russia, Ray Lev (1912-68) came to the United States as a child with
her parents, who were both singers. Inspired by a Paderewski recital at age 13,
she began to study piano with Gaston-Marie Déthier. Later she won the
American Matthay Prize, which enabled her to study with Tobias Matthay in
London. In 1931 Lev made her London debut, in 1933 her American debut,
and she has appeared regularly in solo recitals and concerts in both Europe and
the United States. The pianist is known especially for her performance of
contemporary works.

2260 LIEBLING, Leonard. **Ethel Leginska, pianist, leads orches-
ro   tra**, *New York American* 10 Jan 1925, 14.
Leginska's debut as a conductor with the New York Symphony Orchestra
"occasioned curiosity, skepticism, and even some hardly suppressed merri-
ment". She displayed a thorough knowledge of the scores and got the effects
she wanted from the orchestra. Following the performance of Beethoven's
symphony no. 7 in A minor, op. 92, Leginska played the Bach concerto in F
minor, S.1056, conducting from the piano.

2261 Long Beach woman's unit has civic backing, *Musical Courier*
ap   CXX/11 (1 Dec 1939) 70-71. *Illus.*
The only municipally sponsored women's orchestra of its kind, the Long Beach Women's Symphony Orchestra in California has provided experience for more than 600 young women during its 14 year history. The orchestra has never had to hire male players to complete the personnel. With Eva Anderson as conductor, the membership at present numbers 120.

→   **Lorraine Foster gives a résumé of the founding of the Stephen Foster Society in New York**, *see* 2097ap[67].

2262 Lotte Lehmann, U.S. citizen aids in war benefit concerts,
ap   *Musical Courier* CXXV/6 (5 Apr 1942) 37.
Lotte Lehmann--who will receive her final United States citizenship papers in 1943--states she is merely doing her duty for her adopted country. Lehmann's recitals with Bruno Walter accompanying her at the piano were notable events of the past 2 seasons. One of these concerts alone raised more than $12,000 for the American Red Cross. When Lehmann renounced her Austrian citizenship in 1938, a group of 1000 leading Americans in literature, music, and art gave the soprano a testimonial dinner in tribute to her work.

2263 Lotte Lenya, *Current biography.* Ed. by Charles MORITZ (New
ac   York: H.W. Wilson, 1959) 254-56. *Illus.*
Born in Vienna, Lotte Lenya began her career as a dancer. In 1926 she married Kurt Weill, and in 1928 she sang the role of Jenny in the première of Weill and Bertold Brecht's *Die Dreigroschenoper* in Berlin. In 1935 Lenya and Weill fled from Germany to New York, where she appeared in dramatic plays before retiring in 1945. Following Weill's death in 1950, the soprano performed in a revival of the Weill-Brecht operetta and made several recordings of her husband's music.

2264 LOVINGGOOD, Penman. Famous modern Negro musi-
bf   **cians.** With a new intro. by Eileen SOUTHERN (New York: Da Capo, 1979) 69 p. 010,60; *Illus. index.*
A reprint of the 1921 edition (Brooklyn: Press Forum). Considers the work of the following women active in 1921: patron and educator Emma Azalia Hackley, pianist Helen E. Hagen, and singers Marian Anderson, Florence Cole-Ralbot, and Cleota J. Collins.

2265 LOW, Beth. People versus Ruth Breton, The, *Musical Digest*
ap   XIII/1 (Jan 1928) 25, 63.
Born in Kentucky into a musical family, Ruth Breton was inspired to become a professional violinist by Mischa Elman, Franz Kneisel, and Leopold Auer. A turning point in her career came in 1926, when she was chosen by the American Academy of Arts and Letters to perform at the opening concert of a series designed to promote American music and native performers at Carnegie Hall. Breton is interested in playing new or virtually unheard works.

2266 Lucile Lawrence an ardent exponent of contemporary harp-
ap   **ism**, *Musical Courier* CIV/18 (30 Apr 1932) 27. *Illus.*
Lucile Lawrence is a 4th-generation harpist whose great-grandmother, Sallie Ward Davis Smith, performed for President Polk in the 1840s but was subsequently denied a professional career by her mother. Lawrence is well-known as a teacher and performer. Her pupils include Edna Phillips, Flora Greenwood, and Alice Chalifoux, who are harpists with the Philadelphia and Cleveland orchestras.

2267 Lucy Gates, *Musical America* LXXI/7 (May 1951) 24.
ap
An obituary for the American soprano Lucy Gates (1880-1951). Gates initially studied violin and piano in her native Salt Lake City. In 1897 she went abroad to study voice with Blanche Corelli in Berlin, and she remained abroad pursuing her career until the outbreak of World War I. Gates made her American debut in 1916 in Mozart's *Der Schauspieldirektor* at the Empire Theater in New York. Subsequently the soprano and her brother B. Cecil Gates, a conductor and composer, organized the Lucy Gates Opera, which performed in the Salt Lake City area.

2268 LYON, Jean. Antonia Brico, first woman to conduct in
an   **Metropolitan, pleases her orchestra. Tonight she meets her audience**, *New York Sun* 10 Jan 1933, 28.
Discusses Brico's New York debut at a forthcoming concert of the Musicians' Symphony Orchestra, and notes that the male musicians are somewhat resentful about having a woman conductor--an attitude Brico is used to dispelling from her appearances as a conductor in Europe. The orchestra has 3 women players: Frances Blaisdell, flute, Jeanette Scheerer, clarinet, and Olga Attl, harp.

2269 M. Lea Luboshutz, first woman violinist to become member
ap   **of faculty at Curtis Institute of Music**, *Musical Courier* XCIV/11 (17 Mar 1927) 14.
A pupil of Ysaÿe, Lea Luboshutz has concertized extensively in Europe and

during the last 3 seasons in the United States as well. She is considered "one of the great women geniuses of the violin". Luboshutz left Soviet Russia after World War I and the Revolution, and she has been intent on settling in the United States for some time.

2270 Mabel Garrison, opera singer, 77, *New York Times* 22 Aug
an   1963, 27.
An obituary for Mabel Garrison (1886-1963), who was a native of Baltimore. Garrison made her operatic debut as Philine in Thomas's *Mignon* in 1912 with the Aborn Opera in Boston. From 1914-22 she sang at the Metropolitan Opera, where her best-known roles were the Queen of the Night, Lucia, and Gilda. In 1927 the soprano toured China and Japan as a recitalist and oratorio singer. Garrison was appointed professor of music at Smith Col. in 1933.

2271 Mabel Swint Ewer, organizer of orchestra, *Musical Courier*
ap   LXXXVI/19 (17 May 1923) 12.
Discusses the career of Mabel Swint Ewer, a trumpet player and graduate of the New England Conservatory, who founded the Philadelphia Women's Symphony Orchestra in 1921.

2272 Make way for the ladies, *Musical America* LV/19 (10 Dec 1935)
ap   16.
An editorial arguing in favor of the "mixed" orchestra. The accomplishments of contemporary women conductors are also noted.

2273 MARCUS, J. Anthony. Recognition for woman, *New York*
an   *Times* 12 Feb 1939, IX-6.
Departing from findings of the National Women's Inst. that American women as concert artists are not receiving recognition, the author of this letter to the editor argues that women in the audiences are to blame. They will accept any musician in trousers--above all a foreigner--before a woman. Also, women in the music clubs are intimidated by the woman musician because of her superior intellect and culture, and therefore will not encourage her.

2274 Margarete Dessoff to retire, *New York Times* 8 Mar 1936, IX-7.
an
Reports that for reasons of health the choral conductor is retiring from her musical activities; in the future she will spend most of her time abroad. Since her arrival from Germany in 1923, Dessoff's fine work has influenced the standards of choral concerts and particularly of *a cappella* singing throughout the United States. She is known for her encouragement of contemporary composers and has presented many important premières of works by both Europeans and Americans.

2275 Marianne Kneisel, violinist, 75, dead, *New York Times* 4 Mar
an   1972, 30.
Marianne Kneisel was the daughter of Franz Kneisel, the founder and first violinist of the Kneisel Quartet. She studied violin at the Inst. of Musical Art in New York, and at age 25 she joined the faculty of the school. Shortly thereafter she founded her own all-female string quartet, which toured throughout the United States for more than 25 years as the Marianne Kneisel Quartet. In the 1950s Kneisel turned the Kneisel family residence in Blue Hill, Me. into a summer music school for the teaching and performance of chamber music.

2276 Marie Morraisey voted the first honorary member of Organ-
ap   **ized Women Musicians**, *Musical Leader* LXX/6 (26 Mar 1938) 16.
The Organized Women Musicians of Chicago represent 200 professional players for the purpose of securing employment. Many of the women play with the Woman's Symphony Orchestra of Chicago.

2277 Marie Sundelius, ex-opera singer, *New York Times* 4 July 1958,
ap   19.
Reports the death in Boston of the Swedish-American soprano (1884-1958). Sundelius, who came to the United States as a child, received all her vocal training in America, and sang with the Metropolitan Opera between 1916 and 1924. She was active in Swedish-American musical circles, and in 1923 she received a medal from Gustav V of Sweden for her work in advancing the music of Swedish composers in the United States. After retiring from the operatic and concert stage, Sundelius taught for many years on the faculty of the New England Conservatory, where a scholarship was established in her honor in 1957.

2278 MARION, John Francis. Lucrezia Bori of the Metropolitan
bm   **Opera** (New York: P.J. Kennedy, 1962) 189 p. *Illus., index.*
A biography of the Spanish-American soprano (1887-1960). Born in Valencia, Spain, Bori trained in Milan, appeared at La Scala and in Paris, and subsequently made her debut at the Metropolitan Opera in 1912 as Manon Lescaut. She continued at the Metropolitan until her retirement in 1936, although she was forced to abandon the stage for several years beginning in 1915, when she lost her voice and had to undergo operations on her vocal cords. Bori, who raised funds for the Metropolitan, headed the Save the Metropolitan

Committee during the Depression. She continued to be active in opera production after her retirement as a singer.

2279 Martha Attwood, retired soprano, *New York Times* 8 Apr 1950,
an   I-78. *Illus.*
An obituary for Martha Attwood (1887-1950), who studied abroad and made her operatic debut in Siena. Subsequently she made her American debut in 1926 as Liu in the first performance of *Turandot* at the Metropolitan Opera. Attwood continued at the Metropolitan through the 1929-30 season, and she was also active in recital work. In 1938 the soprano founded the Cape Cod Inst. of Music in Brewster, Mass., which she directed until 1943. During World War II Attwood was instrumental in organizing musical entertainments at Camp Edwards on Cape Cod and in bringing music and music lessons to servicemen in hospitals.

2280 Martha Baird, now playing Chopin series, to write book on
ap   **composer**, *Musical America* L/1 (10 Jan 1931) 25. *Illus.*
Martha Baird's series of 4 Chopin recitals that began this month is the result of a 10-year study of the complete works of and the literature about the composer. Although Baird (Rockefeller) has played all-Chopin programs in the past, she waited to do a series until her interpretations had adequate time to develop and mature. She used the same approach to her work on Schubert in previous years. The pianist's program notes for the Chopin series give a hint about the nature of her proposed book. Baird's other recent activities in performance are discussed.

2281 MARTIN, Mylas. Mme. Carreras, piano great, *New York*
an   *Herald Tribune* 18 Apr 1966, 16.
Reports the death in New York of Maria Carreras (1877-1966), the pianist who was especially known for her interpretations of the works of Beethoven, Liszt, and Chopin during an international career that lasted for more than 20 years. Although Carreras was a tiny woman, "her power at the keyboard forced comparisons with the foremost of male pianists". She was a close friend of Busoni, whose work she esteemed.

2282 Mary Lewis dies after career as opera singer, *New York Herald*
an   *Tribune* 1 Jan 1942, 26.
The soprano from Little Rock, Ark. (1900-42) ran away from home at the age of 14 to join a vaudeville troupe. Later she worked in New York in night clubs in Greenwich Village and with the Ziegfield Follies. Lewis went abroad in the 1920s to study opera, and after appearances in major European opera houses she made her debut at the Metropolitan Opera as Mimi in 1926. With her 3rd marriage in 1931, Lewis retired from the stage. The soprano was acclaimed for her beauty as well as her voice.

→   MAXWELL, Leon. **Most notable American singers since 1876, The**, *see* 1091ac[58].

2283 MCCARRELL, Lamark. Impact of World War II on the
ap   **college band, The**, *Journal of Band Research* X/1 (fall 1973) 3-8.
Prior to World War II, women played only in bands at small colleges and in all-female bands at 2 women's colleges, Winthrop Col. in South Carolina and Florida State Col. for Women. When the war effort depleted the numbers of available men, band directors at larger colleges and universities included women players for the first time in order to fill their ranks. Some institutions were willing to utilize women in concert bands, but not in marching bands. After the war, returning veterans did not generally displace women players. Instead women remained, and college band enrollments reached unprecedented highs.

2284 MCKENNA, Marian C. Myra Hess. A portrait (London: H.
bm   Hamilton, 1976) 319 p. *Illus., facsim., music, discog., index.*
Myra Hess (1890-1965) successfully launched an international career with a recital in New York in 1922. She came to the United States from England under the management of Annie Friedberg. Hess belonged to the modern school of piano playing that emphasized clarity, textual accuracy, and delicate color in contrast to the older school of romantic pianists.

2285 MELLISH, Mary. Sometimes I reminisce. An autobiography
bm   (New York: G.P. Putnam's Sons, 1941) 336 p. *Illus.*
Mary Mellish was a member of the Metropolitan Opera for 7 years during the 1920s, singing small parts. She often sang in operas in which Geraldine Farrar starred, and her autobiography is a source of information about the work of Farrar and other leading artists as well as new productions during the 1920s at the Metropolitan. Mellish also appeared in concert, light opera, and in Broadway shows. Her reminiscences of her early days in New York include her search for a voice teacher, attending performances at the Metropolitan, and her work as assistant to conductor Clara Novello-Davies of the Woman's Choral Soc. during World War I. The chorus sang in connection with the Liberty Loan Drive.

2286 Merle Alcock, a contralto at Met in 1920s, is dead, *New York*
an   *Times* 4 Mar 1975, 36.
From 1923-29 Merle Alcock (1890-1975) sang at the Metropolitan Opera, where she was best known for her portrayal of the role of Beppe in Mascagni's *L'amico Fritz*. The contralto also made numerous appearances as soloist with the New York Philharmonic and the Boston Symphony Orchestra. Alcock taught voice for many years in New York; her most famous pupil is Eileen Farrell.

2287 MÉRÖ, Yolande. Hungarian rhapsody, *Musical Digest* XIII/3
ap   (Mar 1928) 32.
Mérö asserts that a woman can combine home and career. The Hungarian pianist married soon after coming to the United States. She is able to devote substantial time to music, both as composer and performer, because her households are run by well-trained servants and her child is supervised by a governess.

2288 Mestechkin studio faculty, The, *Musical Courier* LXXXIX/15 (9
ap   Oct 1924) 19.
Jacob Mestechkin and his wife Elfrieda Boss Mestechkin, violinists, left Russia at the time of the Revolution and came to the United States with the Zimbro Ensemble. They are now located in New York at a studio with Leonid Mestechkin, pianist. Elfrieda Boss Mestechkin was a student of Leopold Auer in St. Petersburg, where she was a solo violinist and assistant concertmistress with a summer series of popular orchestral concerts.

2289 METZ, Mary Jane. All pepper, *Opera News* XXXI/21 (18 Mar
ap   1967) 26-27. *Illus.*
A biographical sketch of Edith Barnes Mason. Born in St. Louis, the lyric soprano studied with Enrico Bertrand and Edmond Clément in Paris. In 1912 she made her American debut as Nedda in *I pagliacci* with the Boston Opera. Mason subsequently went to Europe for further training, but the outbreak of World War I forced her return. In 1915 she made her Metropolitan Opera debut as Sophie in *Der Rosenkavalier*, and she went on to sing 26 other roles at the Metropolitan. Puccini coached her in the role of Madame Butterfly, which she sang in 1921 as her debut with the Chicago Opera. Since her retirement in 1942, Mason has divided her time between Chicago and Italy.

2290 Miss Brico forms mixed orchestra, *New York Times* 4 Jan 1939,
an   24.
Antonia Brico has decided to disband the New York Women's Symphony Orchestra in favor of the formation of a new, mixed ensemble, to be known as the Brico Symphony Orchestra. The conductor's experience with orchestras sponsored by the Works Progress Administration has convinced her that men and women can work together effectively in a symphony orchestra.

2291 Miss Hilda Ohlin, 45, operatic soprano, *New York Times* 13
an   Feb 1954, 13. *Illus.*
An obituary for the soprano, who was a native of Denver. Hilda Ohlin studied at the Chicago Musical Col. and with Paul Althouse and Povla Frijsh. While she was a member of the Chicago City Opera, the soprano sang in the American première of Respighi's *La fiamma* in 1935. Ohlin was also active in recital and concert work.

2292 Miss Lazzari on the study of opera, *Christian Science Monitor*
an   13 July 1918, 20.
Carolina Lazzari describes her regimen of study during 3 years in New York that led to her successful debut in Nov. 1917 with the Chicago Opera as Giglietta in Mascagni's *Isabeau*. The contralto hopes that her example will prove to American women that they can study and succeed as native artists without going abroad.

2293 M.L.S. American singer finds new opportunities in musical
ap   **productions of this country**, *Musical Courier* CXII/9 (29 Feb
1936) 27. *Illus.*
Helen Jepson discusses her career in opera and concert, as well as her future plans for work in the motion picture field. Born to a musical family, the soprano attended the Curtis Inst., where she studied voice with Horatio Connell and operatic roles with Richard Hageman. She has sung with the Philadelphia Orchestra, the New York Philharmonic, and the Baltimore Symphony Orchestra. Jepson notes that radio and movies increased public interest in opera, and that because the movies present actors in close-up, the public expects opera singers to act convincingly and look attractive.

2294 M.L.S. Chance to sing Wagnerian role arrived unexpectedly,
ap   **says Margaret Halstead**, *Musical Courier* CXIII/18 (2 May 1936)
12. *Illus.*
Born in Pittsfield, Mass., Margaret Halstead spent much of her childhood abroad because her father was a foreign diplomat, but studied voice in the United States. The soprano unexpectedly made her operatic debut in Cologne in 1931 as Venus in *Tannhaüser* and subsequently made her debut at the

Metropolitan Opera in the same role in 1932. Halstead has specialized in German dramatic soprano repertory, with the exception of Lady Marigold in Howard Hanson's *Merry mount* in 1934.

2295 M.L.S. **Radio loses lyric favorite as Jessica Dragonette says**
ap   **"Au revoir",** *Musical Courier* CXVI/11 (15 Nov 1937) 11. *Illus.*
Jessica Dragonette looks forward to singing for live audiences in her forthcoming cross-country concert tour. For the last decade she has been a featured performer on major radio broadcasts.

2296 M.L.S. **Versatile harpsichord can play both old and modern**
ap   **scores,** *Musical Courier* CXXXIV/1 (July 1946) 15.
Yella Pessl has helped to give the harpsichord a place in contemporary musical life through her solo, chamber, and orchestral performances. She is interested in contemporary as well as Baroque music for her instrument, and she recently played the American première of Poulenc's *Concert champêtre* for harpsichord and orchestra. Pessl often includes pieces by early American composers on her programs.

2297 **Mme. De Cisneros, opera singer dies,** *New York Times* 4 Feb
an   1934, 31.
Eleanora De Cisneros (1878-1934) was, in 1919, one of the first native Americans to make a debut at the Metropolitan Opera without foreign experience. Subsequently the mezzo-soprano went abroad, singing in virtually every major opera house. Her specialities included Strauss and Verdi roles. De Cisneros was fluent in several languages and also was widely read.

2298 **Mme. Leginska leads New York Symphony, plays Bach**
ro   **concerto,** *New York Herald Tribune* 10 Jan 1925, 10.
A review of Ethel Leginska's New York debut as a conductor. Considers Leginska no more than an earnest student of conducting, but notes it is to her credit that nothing serious occurred to mar the performance.

2299 **Mme. Peralta, retired soprano, dies,** *New York Herald Tribune*
an   23 Dec 1933, 17.
Frances Peralta had sung leading roles at the Metropolitan Opera for more than 10 years when illness forced her to retire in 1930. The dramatic soprano also made several operatic tours throughout the United States, singing the role of Aida more than any other part. Peralta was a linguist and a versatile artist; reportedly she could fill any role within her voice range at a moment's notice. She made her New York stage debut to instant acclaim in Lehár's *Zigeunerliebe*, under her real name, Phyllis Partington.

→   **Mme. Vengerova,** *see* 2103an[67].

2300 MOLLESON, John. **Helen Traubel defies Met's night club**
an   **ban,** *New York Herald Tribune* 28 Sept 1953, 1, 25. *Illus.*
Discusses the circumstances surrounding Helen Traubel's resignation from the Metropolitan Opera. Traubel has accused Rudolph Bing of "rank snobbery" for asking her to refrain from appearing in night clubs while singing in opera. The soprano states she is proud to perform songs by George Gershwin, Jerome Kern, Irving Berlin, and Richard Rodgers in night clubs, since, after all, she can't sing them at the Metropolitan.

2301 **Monroe, Lucy,** *Current biography.* Ed. by Maxine BLOCK (New
ac   York: H.W. Wilson, 1942) 603-04. *Illus.*
The daughter of actress Anna Laughlin, Lucy Monroe studied voice with Estelle Liebling and Queena Mario in New York. She began her career in musical comedy in 1925 and made her Metropolitan Opera debut as Musetta in *La bohème* in 1937. Dubbed the "star-spangled soprano", Monroe has sung the national anthem over 1800 times in the past 2 years at appearances promoting the sale of defense bonds and stamps. Monroe is currently director of patriotic music for RCA Victor Co.

2302 MOORE, Earl V. **Men, music, and morale. The case for the**
ap   **federal project,** *Musical America* LXIII/8 (25 Apr 1942) 5, 41.
Discusses the proliferation of music performance groups under the Works Progress Administration (WPA) and the importance of music as a morale builder in wartime. Focuses on the activity of WPA orchestras in major cities throughout the United States, and notes that experience with WPA orchestras has given many musicians the opportunity to secure positions with leading symphony orchestras, as well as with orchestras for opera and ballet companies, and radio stations.

→   MOORE, Edward. **Forty years of opera in Chicago,** *see*
1110bf[58].

2303 MOORE, Grace. **You're only human once** (New York: Arno,
bf   1977) 275 p. $17.
A reprint of the 1944 edition (Garden City, N.Y.: Doubleday, Doran). Born in Jellicoe, Tenn., Grace Moore (1901-47) studied voice at the Wilson-Green

School of Music in Washington, D.C. She went to Paris in 1921 to study with Roger Thiral, but she was unsuccessful in her attempts to become a member of an opera company. Moore subsequently moved to New York where she appeared on Broadway for 3 years in Irving Berlin's *Music box revue.* After several unsuccessful auditions, the soprano finally made her debut at the Metropolitan Opera as Mimi in 1928. In 1930 she began making films in Hollywood, including *One night of love* and *Louise,* based on the opera by Charpentier (who collaborated on the screen play). The challenge of her 3 careers in musical comedy, film, and opera is discussed.

2304 rb —
R. by Jack GOULD, *New York Times* 19 Mar 1944, VII-7.

→   MORINI, Erica. **Women as musicians,** *see* 159ac[25].

2305 **Mrs. Mabel Swint Ewer,** *New York Times* 1 July 1974, 32.
an
Reports the death of Mabel Swint Ewer, who founded the Philadelphia Women's Symphony Orchestra in 1921. The orchestra remained in existence for over 30 years. In 1923 Ewer joined a Philadelphia radio station as program director and subsequently became the first female radio announcer in Pennsylvania.

2306 **"Much money spent on European study is wasted", says**
ap   **Mme. Mérö,** *Musical America* XIX/17 (28 Feb 1914) 11.
Virtuosi do not take the same interest in their pupils as a regular teacher does, Yolande Mérö believes. Students may, however, want to go to Europe for the benefits of travel and the more intense musical atmosphere. Mérö suggests that artists make their debuts in cities other than New York, so that if the concert is not successful, no great harm has been done. A performer who is not well received by New York critics at a debut recital has no future in the United States whatsoever.

2307 **Negro singer seeks opportunities for youth of her race,** *New*
an   *York Herald Tribune* 26 Oct 1947, X-5. *Illus.*
Reports that Dorothy Maynor spends much of her time doing research on Negro songs and spirituals, which she promotes through her recitals. The soprano supports groups throughout the United States that are devoted to increasing opportunities for young blacks. She also champions the arts and believes that government support for the arts is both necessary and justifiable.

2308 **New concert star an all-American product,** *Musical America*
ap   XXIII/3 (20 Nov 1915) 19.
Merle Alcock graduated from the Drake Conservatory in Des Moines and subsequently studied with William Wade Hinshaw and Paul Savage. The contralto has appeared in private musicales and has been a soloist with the New York Symphony Orchestra, conducted by Walter Damrosch.

→   **New Haven, Connecticut, New Haven Historical Society. A**
checklist of source materials by and about women in
American music, *see* 29bm[01].

2309 **N.S. Women's orchestra to include 10 men,** *New York Times* 29
an   Nov 1936, II-1.
A small number of positions in the New York Women's Symphony Orchestra that have been vacated by women players moving on to other employment, are now being filled by men. Antonia Brico, the orchestra's conductor, states that since she has proven the competence of women as orchestral musicians, it is no longer necessary to limit the membership of the orchestra to women.

2310 **Obituary. Dorothée Manski,** *Opera* XVIII/7 (July 1967) 587.
ap
Born in New York, Dorothée Manski (1891-1967) made her Metropolitan Opera debut as the Witch in *Hänsel und Gretel* in 1927. After her retirement from the Metropolitan in 1941, Manski joined the faculty of Indiana U. at Bloomington. Her famous roles included Venus, Gutrune, Sieglinde, and Herodias.

2311 **Obituary. Julia Claussen,** *Musical America* LXI/9 (10 May 1941)
ap   28.
After 9 years at the Royal Opera in Stockholm, Clausson (1879-1941) came to the United States in 1913 and joined the Chicago Opera. She made her debut at the Metropolitan Opera as Dalila to Caruso's Samson in Nov. 1917, and she continued to sing at the Metropolitan until 1932. Subsequently she returned to Sweden and taught voice.

2312 O'CONNELL, Charles. **Other side of the record, The** (New
bm   York: A. Knopf, 1947) 332 p. *Index.*
Personal reminiscences by the former musical director of RCA Victor Co. Includes chapters written in anecdotal style on Grace Moore, Lily Pons, and Helen Traubel.

2313 Old-timers greet the new Kneisels, *New York Times* 2 Feb 1927,
ro 23.
Reports the successful debut of the Marianne Kneisel Quartet in New York at
Aeolian Hall with Marianne Kneisel--the daughter of Franz Kneisel--as 1st
violinist, Elizabeth Worth as 2nd violinist, Lillian Fuchs as violist, and Phyllis
Kraeuter as cellist. "From the first authoritative note of leadership the young
Miss Kneisel proved herself the rightful heir of a musical tradition". Among the
audience were colleagues of the performers from the New York Inst. of
Musical Art, former subscribers to concerts of the Kneisel Quartet under Franz
Kneisel, and members of the Olive Mead Quartet.

2314 Olga Samaroff finds a real message in Beethoven's thirty-two
ap **sonatas**, *Musical Courier* LXXXI/25 (16 Dec 1920) 39.
Discusses Olga Samaroff Stokowski's artistic development in anticipation of her
forthcoming performances of the complete Beethoven piano sonatas. Early in
her career, the pianist had her chief successes in the Chaikovskii concerto no. 1
in B-flat major, op. 23. Ossip Gabrilowitsch interested Samaroff Stokowski in
many of the lesser-known Beethoven sonatas, and her Beethoven programs to
date and her lecture-recitals on Beethoven with Leopold Stokowski have been
highly regarded by the public.

2315 Opera has lost Grace Moore, *Opera News* XI/17 (10 Feb 1947)
ap 4-7. *Illus.*
A tribute to the soprano Grace Moore, who died in an airplane crash en route
to Stockholm on 26 Jan. 1947. Highlights of her operatic career are recalled;
among her best-known roles were Mimi, Manon, Louise, Juliette, and Tosca.
Excerpts from reviews of performances and films are included.

2316 Orchestra posts open to women, *New York Times* 24 Aug 1929,
an 11.
Michel Bernstein, chairman of the executive committee of the 2-year old
Conductorless Symphony Orchestra in New York, recently announced a new
policy: women players will be admitted on the basis of ability to fill openings in
the string sections. Bernstein noted that the committee wants to make the
orchestra democratic in fact as well as in name. Ten women have already
applied.

2317 O.T. Woman conductor leads Schola Cantorum, *Musical*
ro *America* XLV/12 (8 Jan 1927) 7. *Illus.*
For the first concert of its 18th season in New York the Schola Cantorum
"offered the novelty of a woman guest conductor, Margarete Dessoff"--who
conducted with dignity and intelligence. "If it sometimes seemed that more
exertion was necessary on her part than would have been required of one of the
better-known conductors of the opposite sex in achieving the same effects, this
may have been because the same exertion appeared more strenuous in a
woman". For the Schola Cantorum the program was an orthodox one; works
by Bach, Gibbons, Sweelinck, Brahms, and Schubert were included. Dessoff
came to the United States in 1923 to assume the position of director of choral
music at the Inst. of Musical Art in New York.

2318 OWEN, H. Goddard. Elisabeth Schumann, *Record Collector*
ap VII/10 (Oct 1952) 217-40. *Illus.*
Discusses recordings made by Elisabeth Schumann from 1914 through the
1930s. Includes biographical information, a list of operas in which Schumann
sang, and anecdotes about her association with Richard Strauss.

2319 PANZER, Raymond M. Stepdaughters of Orpheus, *Inde-*
ap *pendent Woman* XV/2 (Feb 1936) 39, 40, 58.
1) Music is not attractive financially as a profession: radio, the talkies, and the
Depression have put thousands of musicians out of work. Therefore, fewer men
in the future will look to music as a career, and women can step in. Once they
are entrenched in the interpretive field, women will naturally branch out into
the creative sphere. 2) One fallacy about women in music has been completely
demolished by the women's orchestras: that women lack the necessary physical
stamina to play mouth-cup instruments such as the trumpet and trombone.

2320 PASATIERI, Thomas. From the Villa pace, *Opera News* XLI/
ap 18 (12 Mar 1977) 16-18. *Illus.*
Born in Meriden, Conn., Rosa Ponselle was, in 1918, the first American artist to
make a Metropolitan Opera debut without prior European experience. The
soprano sang art songs at a supper club in New Haven in an early professional
engagement and subsequently joined her sister Carmela in a vaudeville show in
New York. Caruso heard Ponselle sing and obtained an audition for her with
Giulio Gatti-Casazza. The soprano sang in only 2 opera houses abroad, Covent
Garden from 1929-31, and the Teatro Communale in Florence in 1933. A
victim of constant stage fright, Ponselle decided to retire in 1937 when the
Metropolitan refused to stage a new production of Cilea's *Adriana Lecouvreur*
for her. The Villa pace is Ponsell's home in Baltimore.

2321 PEAKE, Harvey. Julia Claussen likes Chautauqua audi-
ap **ences**, *Musical America* XXIV/13 (29 July 1916) 11.
Discusses the mezzo-soprano's Chautauqua tour of 70 concerts throughout the
South and Midwest under the management of the Redpath Concert Bureau of
Chicago. Claussen finds her audiences like art songs--especially those by
Schubert and Schumann--better than lighter numbers.

2322 PELTZ, Mary Ellis. Obituaries. Karin Branzell, *Opera News*
ap XXXIX/12 (25 Jan 1975) 30. *Illus.*
Karin Branzell (1891-1974) came to the United States from Germany, and
between 1924 and 1944 she sang 19 roles in over 300 performances at the
Metropolitan Opera. Branzell retired from the Metropolitan in 1944 in protest
over a major cut in a role she was to sing; later, however, Rudolph Bing
persuaded her to return to sing Erda in several performances in 1951. Best
known for her performances as Brangäne and Waltraute, the contralto also
sang Klytämnestra at the Metropolitan première of Strauss's *Elektra* in
German. Among Branzell's pupils were Jean Madeira, Nell Rankin, and
Mignon Dunn.

2323 PERKINS, Francis D. Play recorder, harpsichord, and early
ro **lute. Yella Pessl, Suzanne Bloch, and Carl Dolmetsch give**
program at Town Hall, *New York Herald Tribune* 18 Mar 1936,
17.
A concert of "marked musical appeal as well as musicological interest" was
presented by Yella Pessl, harpsichordist, Suzanne Bloch, lutenist and recorder
player, and Carl Dolmetsch, recorder player. The program included harpsichord
pieces by John Bull, Bach's *Italian concerto* in F major for harpsichord, S.971,
lute pieces by Pierre Attaingnant and John Dowland, a Händel sonata for
recorder and harpsichord, and Bach's *Brandenburg concerto no. 4 in G major*,
S.1049, for 2 recorders and a string ensemble.

2324 PERKINS, Francis D. Youth Orchestra, *New York Herald*
an *Tribune* 21 July 1940, VI-6.
Discusses the organization of the All-American Youth Orchestra during the
winter months of 1939-40, under the direction of Leopold Stokowski.
Stokowski decided to form the orchestra, which has no restrictions on "race,
color, or sex", because of the rapidly increasing numbers of young and talented
musicians in the orchestral field. The author thinks the Youth Orchestra will
provide a pool of qualified players for the major orchestras.

2325 Personality. Wanda Landowska, *Time* LX/22 (1 Dec 1952) 31.
ap
Around 1900, Wanda Landowska began collecting MSS of Baroque music and
examining harpsichords in European museums. Based on her research, she
commissioned a harpsichord from the Pleyel firm in Paris. In 1940 Landowska
settled in the United States, and she has since performed as many as 150
concerts per season throughout the country. Now age 73, she is completing her
recording of Bach's *Well-tempered clavier*, S.846/93.

2326 PETRIDES, Frederique Joanne. On women conductors,
ap *American Music Lover* II/3 (July 1936) 75-77.
Discusses the work of Emma Roberto Steiner, Caroline B. Nichols, and Ethel
Leginska as conductors. Petrides concludes: "When one expects to consider the
increasing numbers of young American women who are now studying, or who
aspire to study in the near future, the art of directing an orchestra, one's
conviction grows stronger and stronger that the day is not far distant when the
sight of women conductors will no longer evoke feelings of curiosity and
surprise".

2327 PETRIDES, Frederique Joanne. Women in orchestras, *Etude*
ap LVI/7 (July 1938) 429-30, 474.
In 1916 Leopold Stokowski spoke out regarding the exclusion of women from
symphony orchestras as being a waste of fine talent. Since then there has been
some improvement in orchestral opportunities for women, and it seems
probable that more and more women will find their way into standard
symphony orchestras in the future. Women's symphonies still continue to fill a
need. All-female orchestras active in 1938 are listed and discussed, and the
early history of women as orchestral players and conductors in both Europe and
the United States is surveyed.

→ PETRIDES, Frederique. **Women in music I-VI**, *see* 70bp[10].

2328 PEYSER, Ethel R. Some prima donnas I have known, *Musi-*
ap *cian* XXXIV/5 (May 1929) 11-12. *Illus.*
The author reminisces about the following singers active in American music:
Elsa Alsen, Martha Attwood, Lucrezia Bori, Florence Easton, Mary Garden,
Rosa Ponselle, and Elisabeth Rethberg.

2329 PEYSER, Herbert F. American soprano refuses to sing for
ap **Kaiser**, *Musical America* XXI/1 (7 Nov 1914) 3. *Illus.*
Lucy Gates has ignored a royal order to return to her position at the Kassel
Opera and will instead pursue an American concert tour. Gates went to
Germany to acquire operatic experience at the urging of Marcella Sembrich-
-even though her family opposed the idea of a stage career. Gates's operatic
roles and work in Germany are discussed. This article is signed H.F.P., and
Peyser's name has been supplied.

2330 Philharmonic women both wed and modern, *New York World* 1
an Apr 1928, M-8.
An interview with Bertha Vandenburg, pianist and celesta player, and Steffy Goldner, harpist, about their backgrounds in music and their present work with the New York Philharmonic. Both women feel that they have been accepted by their male colleagues.

2331 Phyllis Kraeuter, American cellist, *Musical Courier* XCVII/19
ap (8 Nov 1928) 49. *Illus.*
In 1926 Phyllis Kraeuter graduated from the Inst. of Musical Art in New York with highest honors and a cash prize of $1000. In 1927 Kraeuter won a Naumburg prize, which entitled her to a solo recital in New York. While she is in demand as a soloist, Kraeuter also plays a great deal of chamber music with the Marianne Kneisel Quartet and the Helen Teschner Tas Quartet. Last summer Kraeuter performed with the South Mountain Quartet in a series of 10 concerts sponsored by Elizabeth Sprague Coolidge at the Temple of Music in Pittsburgh.

2332 Phyllis Kraeuter receives ovation in native city, *Musical*
ap *Courier* C/15 (12 Apr 1939) 20.
Reports on Phyllis Kraeuter's triumphant return to her native Columbus, Ohio as cello soloist with the Minneapolis Symphony Orchestra. During the 1929-30 season Kraeuter has also played with the New York Philharmonic under Arthur Bodanzky and the St. Louis Symphony Orchestra under Enrique Arbos. While it is rare that cellists are able to interest American audiences in solo recitals, Kraeuter has been successful due to her wide repertory and choice of programs.

→ **Place aux jeunes! is slogan of Leginska's coast studio**, *see* 2113ap[67].

2333 PREDMORE, George V. Different kinds of choirs. The,
bd *Sacred music and the Catholic church* (Boston: McLaughlin & Reilly, [1936]) 115-20.
Defines the liturgical choir as one composed only of male singers, in accordance with rules found in the *Motu proprio* of 1903. Choirs of mixed voices are forbidden; women may sing only as part of the congregation. Nuns may sing in their own churches and chapels during liturgical services, but in a place where they cannot be seen by the people. Popular opinion which suggests that women may sing in choirs if they are separated from the men is wrong.

2334 P.S. Concert by harp ensemble delights Indianapolis, *Musical*
ro *America* XXX/1 (3 May 1919) 13. *Illus.*
Reviews a concert by the Louise Schellschmidt-Koehne Harp Ensemble Class with Mildred Dilling as soloist. Schellschmidt-Koehne was Dilling's first teacher. 10 harpists--all women--performed in the ensemble.

2335 Queena Mario, Metropolitan soprano, to give summer opera
an **on Connecticut farm**, *New York Sun* 26 July 1938, 14.
Queena Mario plans to produce acts of operas in a theater made out of a rebuilt barn at her residence in Connecticut. Her intention is to give young women singers the opportunity to perform with established artists in opera and radio. 12 young women are currently in residence with Mario, and they manage the theater as well as rehearse for performances. Mario notes the lack of opportunities for young singers in the United States to make their debuts.

2336 Queena Mario resigns from the Metropolitan, *New York*
an *Herald Tribune* 16 Nov 1938, 19.
The lyric soprano has submitted her resignation to the Metropolitan Opera in order to gain more time for teaching, which has become her major interest. Queena Mario first studied with Oscar Saenger and Marcella Sembrich, paying for her lessons by writing syndicated columns in newspapers. She made her debut with the San Carlo Opera in 1918 and first sang with the Metropolitan Opera in 1922. The role she has most closely been identified with is Gretel in Humperdinck's *Hänsel und Gretel*. Mario's teaching career began when she took over Marcella Sembrich's duties at the Curtis Inst. after Sembrich fell ill in 1933.

2337 RASPONI, LanFranco. Women and music, *New York Times* 29
an Sept 1940, IV-10.
Izler Solomon, conductor of the Woman's Symphony Orchestra of Chicago, discusses the question of women as orchestral musicians on the occasion of the orchestra's debut in a nationwide radio series.

2338 Ray Lev is dead; concert pianist, *New York Times* 21 May 1968,
an 47.
Ray Lev (1912-68) made her New York debut as a soloist with the National Orchestral Assoc., performing Chaikovskii's piano concerto no. 1 in B-flat minor, op. 23, in Carnegie Hall in 1933. Later an international artist, Lev was the first American to serve on the faculty of the Tokyo U. of the Arts. In addition to her recital work, the pianist also performed with the Budapest and Gordon quartets. Lev made many recordings for the Concert Hall Soc.

2339 REAMER, Lawrence. Girl singer's dream of fame nets
an **$50,000**, *New York Herald* 14 Oct 1923, 4. *Illus.*
Dusolina Giannini made her New York debut in 1923, singing Italian folk songs with the Schola Cantorum under the direction of Kurt Schindler. She substituted for an indisposed singer [Anna Case]; otherwise she would have probably been compelled--as so many singers are--to pay the expenses of about $1500 for a debut recital. During the 1923-24 season the soprano will earn not less than $50,000, which is unprecedented for a beginner. Her appearances will include engagements with the Philadelphia Orchestra under Willem Mengelberg and the New York Symphony Orchestra under Walter Damrosch. Giannini is a pupil of Marcella Sembrich.

2340 RICH, Alan. Lotte Lehmann co-directs *Rosenkavalier* at
an **Met**, *New York Times* 10 Nov 1962, 15. *Illus.*
Discusses Lotte Lehmann's return to the Metropolitan Opera as director, following her retirement from the company in 1946. Well-known for her interpretation of the Marschallin, the soprano is working on "intimate aspects of the singers' performance". Lehmann has been a teacher and a coach in the United States and England for the past 15 years.

2341 RICH, Alan. Marian Anderson: she opened the door, *New*
an *York Herald Tribune* 24 Jan 1965, 29. *Illus.*
In anticipation of Marian Anderson's farewell concert, the author discusses the contralto's career in relation to the progress of the American Negro singer in the 20th c. Roland Hayes's work in the 1920s helped to pave the way for Anderson. Although her belated debut at the Metropolitan Opera in 1955 was "little more than a gesture", it provided the opportunity for other singers to follow in Anderson's footsteps.

→ **RICHARDS, J.B. Recordings of Lucrezia Bori, The**, *see* 41ap[01].

2342 ROCKWELL, John. Lily Pons, star coloratura of the Met,
an **dead**, *New York Times* 14 Feb 1976, 1, 32. *Illus.*
Born near Cannes, Lily Pons (1904-76) made her operatic debut in Mulhouse, Alsace in 1928 and performed intermittently in the French provinces for the next 2 years. She was still unknown when the tenor Giovanni Zenatello heard her and persuaded Pons to audition for Giulio Gatti-Casazza, who offered her a Metropolitan Opera contract on the spot in 1931. The soprano sang 10 roles in more than 200 performances at the Metropolitan. In the 1930s and 1940s Pons was internationally known for her interpretation of coloratura roles such as Lucia di Lammermoor, Gilda, and Lakmé. She also sang with major orchestras throughout the United States and appeared in 3 Hollywood films. In 1972 the soprano sang her last public performance with the New York Philharmonic, conducted by Andre Kostelanetz.

→ **ROESCH, Clara. Plight of the woman symphony player, The**, *see* 3315ap[78].

2343 Rose Bampton [I], *Current biography*. Ed. by Maxine BLOCK
ac (New York: H.W. Wilson, 1940) 44-46. *Illus.*
Rose Bampton studied voice with Horatio Connell and Queena Mario at the Curtis Inst. for 5 years. In 1928 she began her operatic career as a contralto with the Chautauqua Opera Assoc., and she subsequently sang leading roles with the Philadelphia Grand Opera until 1932, when she joined the Metropolitan Opera. Tired of playing secondary roles and wanting instead to be the heroine, Bampton developed the top of her voice and in 1936 began appearing as a soprano.

2344 Rose Bampton [II], *Opera News* VI/23 (30 Mar 1942) 5. *Illus.*
ap
Rose Bampton grew up in Buffalo and later studied voice at the Curtis Inst. In 1932 she sang in the American première of Schönberg's *Gurrelieder* with the Philadelphia Orchestra. Also in the same year, Bampton made her Metropolitan Opera debut as Laura in *La Gioconda*.

2345 ROSS, Betsy. American Women's Symphony Orchestra, The,
ap *Musical Courier* LXXXIX/14 (2 Oct 1924) 17, 52. *Illus.*
Discusses the activity of Elizabeth Kuyper--a European composer and conductor--as director of women's orchestras in Berlin in 1910, The Hague in 1922, and London in 1922-23. All 3 orchestras disbanded because of inadequate finances. Kuyper is presently in New York organizing the American Women's Symphony Orchestra. "It is now up to the women of America whether their women musicians shall remain in the movies, the restaurants, and hotels, or enter the concert hall".

2346 R.P. Orchestrette plays to large audience, *New York Times* 3
ro Feb 1942, 22.
Reviews the 2nd concert in the 9th season of the Orchestrette Classique, an all-female chamber orchestra in New York under the direction of Frederique Joanne Petrides. While the orchestra may not have the finesse of a first-rank organization, it provided a highly interesting evening of music including

performances of Ralph Vaughan Williams's *Flos campi*, Mozart's piano concerto no. 21 in D minor, K. 466, with Lonny Epstein as soloist, and Paul Creston's *Prelude and dance, op. 25.*

2347 SABIN, Robert. **Povla Frijsh**, *Musical America* LXXX/9 (Aug
ap   1960) 40. *Illus.*
Reports the death of the song interpreter (1881-1960) in Blue Hill, Me. Born in Denmark and trained in Paris, Frijsh was active as a song recitalist in the United States from 1915-47. Her extensive repertory included songs by such diverse composers as Gluck and Randall Thompson. Songs by Poulenc and Milhaud were among her specialties. Frijsh was "a woman of high culture", and a typical concert program of hers included songs in 4 or 5 languages. After her retirement from the concert stage, Frijsh worked as a teacher and coach.

→   **Santa Barbara, California, University of California Library, Lotte Lehmann Archive. A checklist of source materials by and about Lotte Lehmann,** *see* 43bm[01].

2348 SAXON, Wolfgang. **Elisabeth Rethberg, star of the Met, is**
an   **dead at 81**, *New York Times* 7 June 1976, 32. *Illus.*
Born in Germany, Elisabeth Rethberg (1894-1976) was a graduate of the Dresden Conservatory. With the help of Fritz Reiner the soprano made her operatic debut in Dresden in Johann Strauss's *Der Zigeunerbaron* in 1915. She made her Metropolitan Opera debut in 1922 as Aida--the role which she also sang for her farewell performance at the Metropolitan in 1942. Her best-known roles included Desdemona, Sieglinde, Elsa, Elisabeth, and especially Aida, and she also was a distinguished recitalist. Rethberg made few public appearances after her retirement.

2349 SCHAUENSEE, Max de. **Lucrezia Bori**, *Musical America*
ap   LXXX/7 (June 1960) 24, 30. *Illus.*
A critical assessment of the soprano's career (1887-1960), following her death in New York. Despite Bori's conservative and religious background, she was able to persevere in her goal of becoming a singer, and she enjoyed a brilliant career at the Metropolitan Opera. A fine actress, Bori sang 29 roles; Mimi, Violetta, Manon, Juliette, and Mélisande were her most popular portrayals. Bori was the first singer elected to the board of directors of the Metropolitan, and in 1942 she became the chairwoman of the Metropolitan Opera Guild.

2350 SCHONBERG, Harold C. **Traubel, great soprano**, *New York*
an   *Times* 31 July 1972, 23.
A tribute to Helen Traubel, who "loved baseball, worked with Groucho Marx and Jimmy Durante, and was also a great singer". Discusses her voice and her operatic repertory, which was limited chiefly to Wagnerian roles. Traubel considered herself an entertainer, and she made no distinction between Wagner's *Liebestod* and a song by Cole Porter.

2351 SEDGWICK, Ruth Woodbury. **Darned stocking, A**, *New York*
an   *Herald Tribune* 2 June 1935, VII-6, 15. *Illus.*
Discusses Helen Jepson's career from 1925-35. Born in Titusville, Penn., Jepson saved enough money by working in a music store to attend the Chautauqua Festival one summer. There she met Horatio Connell, who advised her to study with him at the Curtis Inst. The soprano made her operatic debut in 1930 as Nedda in *I pagliacci* with the Philadelphia Grand Opera, and she remained with the company for 2 years. Jepson then studied in New York with Queena Mario and began singing on nationwide radio programs. In 1935 she made her Metropolitan Opera debut as Helene in John Lawrence Seymour's *In the pasha's garden*. The title of this article refers to an early audition that Jepson allegedly won because her darned stocking aroused sympathy among the judges.

2352 SEWARD, William. **Conversation with Amelita Galli-Curci,**
ap   **A**, *Hi-Fi/Stereo Review* XIII/1 (July 1964) 50-55. *Illus.*
Galli-Curci discusses how Mascagni discovered her voice, how piano study helped to develop her musicality, and how she reacted to her first operatic performance in *Rigoletto* in Trani, Italy. Advice on voice development and dramatic interpretation is included. The best advice for the young girl who leaves home to establish an operatic career is: take your mother along.

2353 SHEEAN, Vincent. **Jeritza**, *Show. The magazine of the arts* III/2
ap   (Feb 1963) 68-71, 114. *Illus.*
A reminiscence of Maria Jeritza's early career at the Metropolitan Opera. Her portrayals in 1921 of Marietta in Erich Wolfgang Korngold's *Die tote Stadt* and of Tosca may have influenced Geraldine Farrar's decision to retire at age 40. Of Jeritza's many roles--over 50--her greatest was Turandot, which she first sang in 1925.

→   SHERMAN, Rose. **Cleveland Women's Symphony Orches-**
       tra, *see* 3333ap[78].

2354 **Sigrid Onégin dies; once opera star**, *New York Times* 19 June
an   1943, 13. *Illus.*

Sigrid Onégin (1889-1943) was equally successful in opera and on the concert stage. A native of Stockholm, the contralto grew up in Paris and studied voice in Germany and Milan. In 1912 she made her operatic debut in Stuttgart as Carmen with Caruso as her Don José. Subsequently in 1922 Onégin made an American debut as soloist with the Philadelphia Orchestra, under the direction of Leopold Stokowski. Later in the same year she gave her debut performance at the Metropolitan Opera as Amneris. Onégin appeared regularly in recitals in New York and elsewhere through 1938. In the early years of her performing career, she continued her vocal studies with her first husband, Baron Lvoff Onégin, a Russian composer who was killed during the Revolution.

2355 SLENCZYNSKA, Ruth; BIANCOLLI, Louis. **Forbidden**
bm   **childhood** (Garden City, N.Y.: Doubleday, 1957) 263 p.
An autobiography by the pianist Ruth Slenczynska. Born in Sacramento, Calif. in 1925, Slenczynska was forced to practice 9 hours a day by her tyrannical father, Josef Slenczynsky. After beginning study with her father, Slenczynska became a student of Isabella Vengerova at the Curtis Inst., and she also worked in Europe with Egon Petri, Artur Schnabel, Alfred Cortot, and Rachmaninoff. She made her debut in 1933 at the age of 8 and subsequently performed in a series of tours both abroad and in the United States, attracting interest as a child prodigy. Despite her father's opposition, Slenczynska ceased to perform publicly after receiving several poor reviews during her teens. In 1944 the pianist married George Born, who managed to overcome her reservations about resuming a concert career. Slenczynska began a comeback in 1951.

2356 SMITH, Leona May. **Is there a career for women musicians?**
ap   *Metronome* LIV/1 (Jan 1938) 48, 50.
In recent years there has been a growth in the numbers of women's dance orchestras and symphonic ensembles, although the work they provide is not as financially remunerative as that of men's orchestras. This situation will change once women's performances are judged on a par with men's. Teaching offers the steadiest income for women musicians.

2357 **So practical a contribution, 1930-40** (New York: National
bm   Orchestral Assoc., 1940) 86 p. *Illus.*
Founded in 1930, the National Orchestral Assoc. in New York offers advanced training to young American players and conductors and also aids young American composers by reading through their orchestral works. The orchestra consists of 130 students, whose average age is 23 years. Between 14 and 22 women play with the orchestra each year. 137 former students are now playing in 29 major organizations throughout the United States. A list of the 137 graduates and their affiliations is included.

2358 **Sophie Braslau is dead; noted concert singer**, *New York Herald*
an   *Tribune* 23 Dec 1935, 12. *Illus.*
Born in 1892, the contralto was 21 when she auditioned for Giulio Gatti-Casazza and subsequently was engaged by the Metropolitan Opera. Braslau sang with the Metropolitan for 5 seasons, and then devoted herself to recitals and to concert work with leading symphony orchestras throughout the United States.

2359 SPEARE, Dorothy. **Prelude**, *Pictorial Review* XXVIII/11 (Aug
ap   1927) 12-13, 59-60, 62. *Illus.*
An account of the author's operatic debut. In 1922 following the publication of her first novel, *Dancers in the dark*, Speare went to France and Italy to study voice. After several setbacks and last-minute cancellations, the soprano finally made her debut in Asti, Italy in 1927 as Lucia.

2360 STANLEY, May. **When Sophie Braslau was a standee at the**
ap   **Metropolitan**, *Musical America* XXVII/11 (12 Jan 1918) 11.
The contralto recalls standing for performances at the Metropolitan Opera with her parents, who were recent immigrants from Russia, and she notes that her parental background has been the determining factor in her thirst for education and knowledge. Braslau was trained as an accompanist as well as a singer. Arturo Buzzi-Peccia and Gabrielle Sibella were her only voice teachers.

2361 STODDARD, Hope. **Fine musicianship knows no sex**, *Inde-*
ap   *pendent Woman* XXVI/11 (Nov 1947) 316-18, 331.
While considerable attention is being paid to the recent comments by Thomas Beecham and Hans Kindler (*Support for women players, WIAM* 2241) about the work of women as orchestral musicians, the fact remains that at the present time the 18 major symphony orchestras all employ 1 or more female players for a total of 155 women. The majority are quite expectedly violinists and harpists, although other instruments are represented, indicating that the choice of instrument by women is widening. These qualified women players should be retained even though the wartime shortage of men is no longer in effect.

2362 STODDARD, Hope. **Women's activities in the field of**
ap   **music**, *International Musician* XLVI/12 (June 1948) 24-25. *Illus.*
Reports on a recent survey about the activity of women as orchestral musicians: small numbers of women now hold positions with major orchestras in the United States, although many women play with 200 secondary orchestras. In

general, the women queried felt that female players must be better qualified than their male competitors in order to secure orchestral work.

2363 STOKOWSKI, Olga Samaroff. **Women in music**, *Music Clubs*
ap   *Magazine* XVII/1 (Sept-Oct 1937) 7-9, 12.
An appeal to build conditions in the United States that eliminate prejudice and baseless discrimination against women in music. There are no physical, mental, or temperamental reasons why women cannot play musical instruments and conduct orchestras as well as men. Women musicians should be hired and paid fees according to their merit.

2364 STOLFUS, Mary L. **Eve in the ensemble**, *Musical Courier*
ap   CXXXVI/8 (1 Dec 1947) 9, 17.
Evaluates the progress of women as orchestral players immediately after World War II. While veterans are displacing some women players, the situation for women in orchestras is still more promising than it was before the war. The reasons for prejudice against women players are discussed.

2365 STRAKOSCH, Avery. **Lived in sultan's harem to glean Java**
ap   **folk songs**, *Musical America* XXI/16 (20 Feb 1915) 15. *Illus.*
Reports that with the outbreak of war in Europe, Eva Gauthier has returned from the Orient and settled in New York. The mezzo-soprano spent 4 years in Malay and Java giving concerts and studying native music. In Java she accepted an invitation to live amongst the sultan's 400 wives in order to attend performances of music in the palace.

2366 STUTSMAN, Grace May. **Women's symphony formed in**
ro   **Boston**, *Musical America* LX/3 (10 Feb 1940) 306. *Illus.*
Announces the recent formation of the Boston Women's Symphony Orchestra under the direction of Alexander Thiede. The orchestra's opening program included a performance of Mabel Wheeler Daniels's *Deep forest for symphony orchestra, op. 34, no. 1* (*WIAM* 2619, 2620). On the orchestra's board of directors are Mrs. Frederick S. Converse, Mrs. Archibald T. Davison, Mrs. Henry Hadley, and Mrs. Philip Hale.

2367 SUNDSTROM, Ebba. **Women as conductors**, *Who is who in*
ac   *music* (Chicago: L. Stern, 1940-41) 756-57.
Argues that there are large numbers of women musicians who deserve livelihoods in reward for the effort and monies that went into their training. Considers the upsurge in activity by women in women's orchestras since 1930, the continuing need for the women's orchestra, and reasons for the relatively small number of women orchestral conductors.

2368 **Survey of musicians at work**, *New York Times* 13 Oct 1946, II-7.
an
Based on a report of the American Federation of Musicians, numbers of musicians employed and minimum salaries in 1944-45 are presented for 5 areas of employment as follows: motion picture studios, symphony orchestras, radio stations, theatrical employment, and the recording industry.

2369 **Symphony goes co-ed, The**, *Newsweek* XXII/23 (6 Dec 1943) 86,
ap   88.
The draft, jobs in defense industries, and the lure of about $90 a week minimum on Broadway as contrasted with $45-$55 per week paid by many symphony orchestras have reduced the numbers of men available for orchestral work and thereby opened the ranks of symphonies to women. Figures indicate that women are now employed in all but 3 of the nation's 19 leading orchestras.

2370 TAUBMAN, Howard. **Building a career**, *Music as a profession*
bd   (New York: C. Scribner's Sons, 1939) 88-146.
Women, like Negroes, have the accident of birth to contend with in addition to all the other problems faced by musicians in finding employment. Only as singers do women enjoy equality of opportunity, and even then women recitalists receive lower fees than men. The Committee for the Recognition of Women in the Musical Profession in New York recently presented its grievances to Local 802. Prejudice is not the fault of the union, however; rather prejudice lies with the public and employers. As a solution to the problem, Taubman suggests the founding of a national bureau of fine arts to develop more professional opportunities in music.

2371 TAUBMAN, Howard. **Marian Anderson wins ovation in first**
an   **opera role at the Met**, *New York Times* 7 Jan 1955, 1, 11. *Illus.*
Marian Anderson is the first Negro singer to perform at the 71-year old Metropolitan Opera. The contralto's long-awaited debut as Ulrica in *Un ballo in maschera* represents the culmination of a brilliant international career. Perhaps the Metropolitan will now consider other Negro singers, particularly Mattiwilda Dobbs and Leontyne Price.

2372 TAUBMAN, Howard. **Miss Brico leads women musicians**,
ro   *New York Times* 19 Feb 1935, 27.
Reviews the debut of the New York Women's Symphony Orchestra at Town Hall on 18 Feb., and commends the good start the orchestra has made.

"Considering the difficulties encountered in rehearsal period--many of the players have other jobs and some live out of town, making full attendance a trying problem--Miss Brico obtained remarkably unified performances". The program included a concerto grosso by Händel, Schumann's symphony no. 1 in B-flat major, op. 38, and Chaikovskii's *Romeo and Juliet*. This article is signed H.T., and Taubman's name has been supplied.

2373 TAUBMAN, Howard. **Powell is soloist in own rhapsody.**
ro   **Pianist also plays Mozart with Women's Orchestra under**
        Antonia Brico, *New York Times* 18 Dec 1935, 33.
Reviews the 2nd concert of the season by the New York Women's Symphony Orchestra at Carnegie Hall, and notes the orchestra's steady development. While not yet a major orchestra, the Women's Symphony "is progressing toward balance of its choirs and is beginning to gain a distinctive individuality under Brico's vigorous guidance". The performance of John Powell's well-known *Negro rhapsody* was impressive. This article is signed H.T., and Taubman's name has been supplied.

2374 TAUBMAN, Howard. **Voice of a race**, *New York Times* 6 Apr
an   1941, VII-9.
Reports that Marian Anderson has been honored with the $10,000 Bok award, which is given annually to the citizen who has done the most to advance the interests of Philadelphia. The contralto is using her prize money to establish the Marian Anderson Award for young artists. Anderson's early struggles as a concert artist are discussed.

2375 TAYLOR, Deems. **Woman's place**, *Well-tempered listener* (New
bd   York: Simon & Schuster, 1940) 199-202.
1) Even though American women are accepted in most professions, in the orchestral field the outlook has remained a European one: "woman's place is not in the trombones". 2) In the past music students have tended to think only in terms of careers as solo artists. 3) Prejudice against women as orchestral musicians is rapidly declining, chiefly because of the activity of young women in high school orchestras and bands as players of many different instruments.

2376 **Ten years of activity by Dessoff Choirs marked by many**
ap   **pioneering achievements**, *Musical Courier* CX/1 (5 Jan 1935) 13.
In Oct. 1924 Margarete Dessoff founded the Adesdi Chorus in New York with 35 women's voices, and while the women had little previous experience, given Dessoff's training and her unusual programs, the chorus soon attracted interest. In 1927 a group of professional singers appealed to Dessoff to establish a mixed chorus, which she did as the A Cappella Singers. Subsequently the 2 choruses combined as the Dessoff Choirs with about 130 voices--both amateur and professional. Dessoff's primary aim in all her work has been to present unknown music, whether by 16th-17th c. composers or contemporary composers. She has been responsible for many first performances of older European works in the United States, e.g., Orazio Vecchi's *L'Amfiparnasso*, which she introduced in New York and then conducted in repeated performances at Harvard U., Vassar and other colleges, and at the Library of Congress. Dessoff's father, Otto Felix Dessoff, was a conductor in Vienna and Frankfurt. She trained at the Frankfurt Conservatory, and later formed the Dessoff Frauenchor, which rose to prominence in Germany in 1912.

2377 **Thirty-one women play in major orchestras**, *New York Herald*
an   *Tribune* 23 Aug 1942, VI-6.
A survey conducted by the National Music Council indicates that during the 1941-42 season there was no great necessity for symphony orchestras to replace drafted men with women players. This trend may change dramatically, however, with the 1942-43 season. Among the 31 women employed by the 16 major orchestras, most are harpists and violinists.

2378 **This golden voice is Chicago's own**, *Opera Topics* VIII/2 (May
ap   1931) 1. *Illus.*
Discusses Rosa Raisa's activity in Chicago. A native of Poland, Raisa was trained in Italy, where she created the title role of *Turandot*. Since 1916 the soprano's career has been closely identified with the Chicago Opera. Raisa was a protégée of Eva Tetrazzini and her husband Cleofonte Campanini.

2379 THOMSON, Virgil. **Musical scene, The** (New York: A.A.
ap   Knopf, 1945) xiv, 301, xv p. *Index.*
This collection of the author's music reviews for the *New York Herald Tribune* from 1940-44 contains considerable information about the activity of women as performers.

2380 TOLL, Katherine. **Seventy-five girls and one man. Our**
an   **women's symphony orchestra**, *Boston Post* 13 July 1941, A-1.
Discusses the Boston Women's Symphony Orchestra at the onset of its 3rd season under the direction of Alexander Thiede, and considers the backgrounds of a number of the players.

2381 TRAUBEL, Helen; HUBER, Richard G. **St. Louis woman.**

bf   With an intro. by Vincent SHEEAN (New York: Arno, 1977) 296 p.
      $19. *Illus.*
A reprint of the 1959 edition (New York: Duell, Sloan, & Pierce). Born in St.
Louis, Helen Traubel (1903-72) left high school at age 13 to study voice with
Lulu Vetta-Karst, her only teacher. In 1924 the soprano made her debut with
the St. Louis Symphony Orchestra; in 1926 she sang in Lewisohn Stadium
under Rudolph Ganz. Also in 1926, she was offered a Metropolitan Opera
contract which she refused, and she returned to St. Louis to continue her vocal
studies. Walter Damrosch persuaded Traubel to sing the leading role in his
opera *Man without a country* at the Metropolitan Opera in 1937. Her first Town
Hall recital in 1939 was followed shortly thereafter by her official Metropolitan
Opera debut as Sieglinde. Traubel discusses the myth of her feud with Kirsten
Flagstad, her tumultuous relationship with Rudolph Bing which led to her
resignation from the Metropolitan in 1953, and her association with Margaret
Truman. Excerpts from critical reviews and a list of her performances at the
Metropolitan Opera are included.

2382   Unique organization, A. Nuns band at De Paul University
ap   **probably the first of its kind,** *Etude* LXIII/4 (Apr 1945) 196.
         Illus.
Presents a group of annotated illustrations about a band whose members are
Roman Catholic nuns, who attended a summer session at De Paul U. The
women are music teachers in parochial schools.

2383   VEHANEN, Kosti. Marian Anderson. A portrait (Westport,
bf   Conn.: Greenwood, 1970) 270 p. $13.50. *Illus.*
A reprint of the 1941 edition (New York: Whittlesey House). Marian
Anderson's accompanist discusses the contralto's concert tours in Europe and
the United States from 1931-41. In 1930 Anderson received an award from the
Julius Rosenwald Fund to study in Berlin, and she worked there with Sarah
Jane Cahier, the American-born singer. Subsequently the contralto performed
in concerts in Scandinavia for 3 seasons and then made concert debuts in Paris,
London, and other major cities. In 1935 Anderson returned to the United States
to give recitals in Town Hall in Dec. and Carnegie Hall in Mar. 1936, and in
choosing Vehanen as her accompanist for these performances she went against
the wishes of her manager, who felt that it was inappropriate for a black singer
to have a white accompanist in the United States. On a tour in the Soviet Union
in 1936 Anderson met Konstantin Stanislavski, who offered to coach her in the
role of Carmen--an offer which she did not accept and later regretted. An
appendix contains a list of the important dates in Anderson's career to 1941,
excerpts from reviews, and a few typical concert programs.

2384   Voice like a cello, *Time* XLVII/10 (11 Mar 1946) 74. *Illus.*
ap
While she was a student at the Juilliard School, Carol Brice won a Naumburg
award in 1944 that entitled her to a Town Hall debut. In 1945 Serge
Koussevitzky became interested in Brice, and he has indicated he would like to
commission a symphony with a contralto part for her. Brice has recorded de
Falla's *El amor brujo* with the orchestra of the Columbia Broadcasting System,
under the direction of Fritz Reiner.

→   WAGNER, Charles. **Seeing stars,** *see* 851bm[58].

→   WALLACE, Robert. **Century of music making, A: the lives**
     of Josef and Rosina Lhevinne, *see* 2125bm[67].

2385   Wanda Landowska dies at 80; won fame as harpsichordist,
an   *New York Times* 17 Aug 1959, 23. *Illus.*
Wanda Landowska (1879-1959) graduated from the Warsaw Conservatory at
age 14 and settled in Paris in 1900 to teach at the Schola Cantorum. In 1919
the harpsichordist established her École de Musique Ancienne in St.-Leu-la-
Forêt, a suburb of Paris. Landowska made her American debut in 1923 with
the Philadelphia Orchestra conducted by Leopold Stokowski, and from 1924-
32 she performed solo recitals frequently in New York. Landowska stimulated
interest in Baroque music for the harpsichord and also performed contemporary
works--e.g., de Falla's concerto and Poulenc's *Concert champêtre*, which were
composed specifically for her. Landowska gave her last public performance at
the Frick Museum in New York in 1954 and afterwards devoted her time to
making recordings.

2386   WATSON, Dorothy DeMuth. Washington hears Mrs. E.S.
ro   **Coolidge as pianist,** *Musical America* XLV/5 (20 Nov 1926) 2.
Reviews Elizabeth Sprague Coolidge's performance as pianist in the Brahms
piano quartet no. 2 in A major, op. 26, with 3 members of the Lenox String
Quartet. This was the first time Coolidge performed in Washington; previously
she has been known only as a benefactor of music.

2387   W.B.M. Philadelphia women form new orchestra, *Musical*
ap   *America* XXXV/6 (3 Dec 1921) 43.
Reports the formation of the Philadelphia Women's Symphony Orchestra with
Mabel Swint Ewer as chairwoman of the executive committee. Thaddeus Rich,
dean of music at Temple U., is chairman of the screening committee. Two flute
players and a clarinetist have already been recruited, and efforts are being made

to complete the wind and brass sections. Several of the new orchestra's
members played with the Boston Fadette Lady Orchestra. The Philadelphia
Women's Symphony Orchestra has progressed so far as to rent club rooms, and
Ewer has plans for 6 concerts a season.

2388   When women blow horns, *Literary Digest* CXIII/1 (2 Apr 1932)
ap   19-20.
Discusses the newly formed National Women's Symphony Orchestra in New
York under the direction of Ethel Leginska, and quotes from W.J. Henderson's
review of the orchestra's recent debut in Carnegie Hall in the *New York Sun* (3
Mar. 1932, 15). Henderson is amazed that Leginska could muster a symphonic
force of 100 women players of all instruments, but he endorses the concept of
women's orchestras and women as conductors.

2389   W.J.Z. New exemplar of American training, *Musical America*
ap   XIX/15 (14 Feb 1914) 13. *Illus.*
Reports that Mabel Garrison is the first American-trained coloratura soprano to
sing leading roles at the Metropolitan Opera. She studied with Lucien
O'dendthal at the Peabody Conservatory in Baltimore and with Oscar Saenger
in New York. Through Saenger's efforts, Garrison was heard by Giulio Gatti-
Casazza, who subsequently offered her a 3-year contract for 24 roles.

2390   WOLLSTEIN, R.H. Fame overnight. An interview with the
ap   **operatic sensation of the year, Lily Pons,** *Etude* XLIX/6 (June
         1931) 393-94. *Illus.*
Lily Pons discusses her career up to her Metropolitan Opera debut in 1931 as
Lucia di Lammermoor. She began piano studies at age 14, but was forced to
discontinue them due to illness. With financial help from her husband, Pons
began voice lessons at age 21 and made her operatic debut 3 years later. The
soprano describes the practice methods she used to develop the upper range of
her voice.

2391   Women as musicians, *New Republic* LXXXXV (13 July 1938)
ap   263.
Reports on the newly-founded Committee for the Recognition of Women in
the Musical Profession in New York. Notes that while the city's 17,000 male
musicians average $90 a week minimum under union conditions, female
musicians earn only $30 to $35 a week, and fewer than 100 women have
steady positions.

2392   Women in orchestras, *Musical Courier* XCI/10 (3 Sept 1925) 20.
ap
An editorial arguing that women are not excluded from orchestras for lack of
ability, but rather for lack of strength. Concludes that the recently announced
plan for organizing a full symphony orchestra of women in New York has
merit and seems more feasible than opening standard organizations to women.

2393   Women indignant at jibe by Iturbi, *New York Times* 5 Feb 1937,
an   23.
Presents the reactions of various individuals gathered at a fund-raising event
for the New York Women's Symphony Orchestra, regarding José Iturbi's
recent statement that women are incapable of achieving greatness in music.
Antonia Brico, the orchestra's conductor, proposes a contest in which her
players would compete with male players, unseen by the judges.

2394   Women musicians urge equal rights, *New York Times* 19 May
an   1938, 24.
Reports on a rally held in New York by the Committee for the Recognition of
Women in the Musical Profession, which was founded 6 weeks previously.
Speakers at the rally included Antonia Brico, who noted that while educational
opportunities in music are generally available to women, employment as
orchestral musicians--or even auditions for such employment--is, not. Jean
Schneider, the director of the committee, stressed that the group has 2 chief
purposes: 1) to press for the recognition of women's rights within the American
Federation of Musicians, and 2) to focus attention on the problems faced by
women in gaining employment in orchestras.

2395   Women on their own, *Time* XXVI/25 (16 Dec 1935) 52-53.
ap
Discusses the Woman's Symphony Orchestra of Chicago, under the direction of
Ebba Sundstrom, on the occasion of its 10th anniversary season.

2396   Women's group in recital, *New York Times* 5 Nov 1935, 33.
ro
The opening concert in the 3rd season of the Orchestrette Classique, a chamber
orchestra of 24 players under the direction of Frederique Joanne Petrides in
New York, is reviewed favorably. The group has worked hard to develop a
repertory and find an audience.

2397   Women's symphony orchestra of eighty will make its debut
an   **here Monday,** *New York Times* 24 Jan 1935, 21.
The New York Women's Symphony Orchestra, under the direction of Antonia

Brico, has been founded to provide "a medium for serious women musicians to practice their art and perhaps make a living at it". Four concerts are planned for the first season. All of the players have had professional experience, and practically all are local residents--although Brico had to look elsewhere for several important players, including a tympanist from Boston. The orchestra's sponsors include Harold Bauer, Ossip Gabrilowitsch, Eleanor Roosevelt, and Bruno Walter.

2398 Women's symphony under Brico in debut before invited
ap   **audience,** *Musical America* LV/4 (25 Feb 1935) 11. *Illus.*
Discusses the recent preview concert given by the New York Women's Symphony Orchestra in Town Hall before an invited audience, which was "one of the most brilliant--socially and musically--audiences of the season". The executive board of the orchestra consists of Mrs. James H. Perkins, chairwoman, Olga Samaroff Stokowski, Sigismund Stojowski, and Alma Clayburgh as chairwoman of the junior committee. Antonia Brico's progress as a conductor will be interesting to watch.

2399 WOOLF, S.J. **Lily Pons in a new role,** *New York Times* 5 Jan
an   1941, VII-9. *Illus.*
Reports that during the current 1940-41 season Lily Pons's new role is Marie in Donizetti's *La fille du régiment* at the Metropolitan Opera. Pons studied coloratura repertory with Alberti di Gorostigia for 3 years and then sang throughout Europe in the late 1920s. Since her Metropolitan Opera debut in 1931 as Lucia di Lammermoor, the soprano has sung the title roles in Donizetti's *Linda di Chamounix* and Delibe's *Lakmé.* A native of France, Pons recently became an American citizen.

2400 Y.M.C.A. **problem bigger than ever,** *Musical Courier* LXXVIII/
ap   18 (1 May 1919) 12.
Martha Baird (Rockefeller) will perform for armed forces in France for 6 months under the auspices of the Young Men's Christian Assoc. The pianist has been learning ragtime pieces so that if she is called upon to play popular music she will not disappoint her audiences. Now that the war is over, there is an even greater need for providing entertainment for troops than before. Baird graduated from the New England Conservatory in 1917, and she first gained recognition as an assisting artist with Nellie Melba on tour in New England.

2401 YOST, Dr. Gaylord. **En passant,** *Musical Forecast* XXXV/6
ap   (Aug 1938) 11.
In his monthly column Yost argues that women have no place in orchestras, except women's orchestras. Women are physically inferior and mentally immature.

69   Art music by women

Chamber music

2402 BAUER, Marion. **American youth concerto for piano and**
mm   **orchestra, op. 36** (41276; New York: G. Schirmer, 1946) 32 p.
(piano reduction).
Dn 13'. *Pf* orchestration arranged for 2nd pno, solo pno.

2403 BAUER, Marion. **Aquarelle [II], op. 39, no. 2** (facsimile of
md   autograph at PPFleisher, n.d.) 7 p. (score, parts).
Dn 4'. *Pf* flu, pic, 2 obo, 2 cla, 2 hrn, 2 cbs. Originally for pno (*WIAM* 2655).

2404 BAUER, Marion. **Concertino for oboe, clarinet, and string**
mm   **quartet, op. 32b** (New York: Arrow Music, 1944) 32 p. (miniature
score).
Dn 9'. *Pf* string orchestra may be used instead of string quartet.

2405 BAUER, Marion. **Duo for oboe and clarinet, op. 25** (6014;
mm   New York: C.F. Peters, 1953) 10 p. (score).
Dn 7'. *La* DLC. *Ct* Prelude, Improvisation, Pastoral, Dance.

2406 BAUER, Marion. **Fantasia quasi una sonata, op. 18** (34056;
mm   New York: G. Schirmer, 1928) 35 p. (score, part).
Dn 23'. *Pf* pno, vln.

2407 BAUER, Marion. **Five pieces for string quartet, op. 41, nos.**
mm   **1-5** (facsimile of autograph at DLC, NN, n.d.) [5], [4], 7, 5, 10 p.
(score).
Dn 8'. *La* DLC.

2408 BAUER, Marion. **Sonata for viola (or clarinet) and piano,**
mm   **op. 22** (New York: G. Schirmer, 1951) 32 p. (score, parts).
Dn 14'.

2409 BAUER, Marion. **Up the Ocklawaha, op. 6** (APS 9818; Boston:
mm   A.P. Schmidt, 1913) 7 p. (score).
Dn 4'. *La* DLC, Schmidt Collection. *Pf* pno, vln.

2410 BEHREND, Jeanne. **Lamentation** (Philadelphia: composer,
mm   1944) 6 p. (score, part).
Dn 8'. *Pf* pno, vla.   *(Composer)*

2411 BEHREND, Jeanne. **String quartet** (Philadelphia: composer,
mm   1940) 20 p. (score, parts).
Dn 10'.   *(Composer)*

2412 BRANSCOMBE, Gena. **At the fair, op. 21, no. 2** (APS 9061;
md   Boston: A.P. Schmidt, 1911) 6 p. (score).
Dn 4'. *Pf* pno, vln. *Tm* Three compositions for violin and pianoforte, op. 21
(*WIAM* 2416).   *(Laurine Elkins-Marlow)*

2413 BRANSCOMBE, Gena. **Carnival fantasy, A** (APS 11905;
mm   Boston: A.P. Schmidt, 1920) 10 p. (score, part).
Dn 5'. *Pf* pno, vln. Also for hrp, vln, vla, vcl, cbs (autograph score at NN).
Dedicated to Samuel Gardner.   *(Laurine Elkins-Marlow)*

2414 BRANSCOMBE, Gena. **Memory, A, op. 21, no. 3** (APS 9062;
md   Boston: A.P. Schmidt, 1911) 3 p. (score).
Dn 2'. *La* NN. *Pf* pno, vln. *Tm* Three compositions for violin and pianoforte, op.
21 (*WIAM* 2416).   *(Laurine Elkins-Marlow)*

2415 BRANSCOMBE, Gena. **Old love tale, An, op. 21, no. 1** (APS
md   9060; Boston: A.P. Schmidt, 1911) 3 p. (score, part).
Dn 2'. *Pf* pno, vln. *Tm* Three compositions for violin and pianoforte, op. 21
(*WIAM* 2416). Also for pno, vcl (APS 13936; Schmidt, 1927). These are
instrumental versions of the song, *Autumn wind so wistful* (*WIAM* 2779).
                                                   (Laurine Elkins-Marlow)

2416 BRANSCOMBE, Gena. **Three compositions for violin and**
mm   **pianoforte, op. 21, nos. 1-3** (APS 9060-9062; Boston: A.P.
Schmidt, 1911) 3, 6, 3 p. (score).
Dn 8'. *Ct* An old love tale (*WIAM* 2415), At the fair (*WIAM* 2412), A memory
(*WIAM* 2414).   *(Laurine Elkins-Marlow)*

2417 CLARKE, Rebecca. **Chinese puzzle** (London: Oxford U., 1925)
mm   3 p. (score, part).
Dn 3'. *Da* 1921. *La* publisher. *Pf* pno, vln.   *(Christopher Johnson)*

2418 CLARKE, Rebecca. **Combined carols (get 'em all over at**
mm   **once)** (facsimile of MS at NN, n.d.) 7 p. (score, parts).
Dn 6'. *Da* 1941. *La* composer. *Pf* string quartet, optional cbs
                                                     (Christopher Johnson)

2419 CLARKE, Rebecca. **Midsummer moon** (London: Oxford U.,
mm   1926) 8 p. (score, part).
Dn 5'. *Da* 1924. *La* publisher. *Pf* pno, vln.   *(Christopher Johnson)*

2420 CLARKE, Rebecca. **Passacaglia on an old English tune**
mm   (40192; New York: G. Schirmer, 1943) 7 p. (score, part).
Dn 8'. *Da* 1941. *La* publisher. *Pf* pno, vla.   *(Christopher Johnson)*

2421 CLARKE, Rebecca. **Prelude, allegro, and pastorale** (facsimile
mm   of MS at NN, n.d.) 12 p. (score).
Dn 15'. *Da* 1941. *La* DLC. *Pf* cla, vla.   *(Christopher Johnson)*

2422 CLARKE, Rebecca. **Sonata for viola (or violoncello) and**
mm   **piano** (805; London: J. & W. Chester, 1921) 41 p. (score, part).
Dn 25'. *Da* 1919. *La* DLC. This composition won 2nd prize in the 1919
Elizabeth Sprague Coolidge chamber music competition. *(Christopher Johnson)*

2423 CLARKE, Rebecca. **Three Irish country songs** (London:
mm   Oxford U., 1928) 8 p. (score).
Song cycle. *Dn* 10'. *Da* 1926. *La* publisher. At Herbert Hughes, ed. *St Irish
country songs. Pf* solo voc, vln. *Ct* I know my love, I know where I'm goin', As I
was goin' to Ballynure.   *(Christopher Johnson)*

2424 CLARKE, Rebecca. **Three old English songs** (4175; London:
mm Winthrop Rogers, 1925) 7 p. (score).
Song cycle. *Dn* 12′. *Da* 1924. *La* publisher. *Pf* solo voc, vln. *Ct* It was a lover
and his lass (*At* Shakespeare, *St As you like it*), Phillis on the new mown hay,
The tailor and his mouse. *(Christopher Johnson)*

2425 CLARKE, Rebecca. **Trio for violin, violoncello, and piano**
mm (4333; London: Winthrop Rogers, 1928) 41 p. (score, parts).
Dn 15′. *Da* 1921. *La* DLC. *(Christopher Johnson)*

2426 CLARKE, Rebecca. **Two pieces for viola (or violin) and cello**
mm (London: Oxford U., 1930) 3, 5 p. (score).
Dn 8′. *Da* 1918. *La* publisher. *Ct* Lullaby, Grotesque. *(Christopher Johnson)*

2427 COLE, Ulric. **Divertimento for two pianos** (facsimile of MS at
mm NN, 1971) 37 p. (score).
Dn 16′. Originally for string orchestra and piano (*WIAM* 2617).

2428 COLE, Ulric. **Man-about-town** (41631; New York: G. Schirmer,
md 1947) 11 p. (score, parts).
Dn 5′. *Pf* 2 pno, 4 hands. Also for solo pno in *Metropolitones* (*WIAM* 2678).

2429 COLE, Ulric. **Quintet for piano and strings** (New York: G.
mm Schirmer, 1941) 49 p. (score, parts).
Dn 20′. This composition won the 1941 publication prize from the Soc. for the
Publication of American Music.

2430 COLE, Ulric. **Sonata for violin and piano** (New York: G.
mm Schirmer, 1930) 42 p. (score, part).
Dn 12′. This sonata won a publication prize from the Soc. for the Publication
of American Music.

2431 COLE, Ulric. **String quartet no. 1** (facsimile of MS at NNAMC,
mm 1932) 29 p. (score).
Dn 15′.

2432 COLE, Ulric. **Suite for piano, violin, and cello** (facsimile of
mm MS at NNAMC, 1931) 39 p.
Dn 16′.

2433 DANIELS, Mabel Wheeler. **In a manger lowly. Christmas**
mm **song** (26227; New York: G. Schirmer, 1915) 13 p.
Dn 5′. *Pf* pno, vln.

2434 DANIELS, Mabel Wheeler. **Pastoral ode, op. 40 for flute**
mm **and strings** (JF&B 0407; New York: J. Fischer, 1940) 27 p. (score).
Dn 9′. *Pf* flu, string quartet. *Rg* NN, Rogers and Hammerstein Archives of
Recorded Sound.

2435 DANIELS, Mabel Wheeler. **Three observations for three**
mm **woodwinds, op. 41** (1850; New York: C. Fischer, 1953) 15 p.
(score, parts).
Dn 7′. *Pf* flu or obo, cla, bsn. *Ct* Ironic, Canonic, Tangonic. *Rg* Four American
composers, Desto 7117.

2436 GALAJIKIAN, Florence G. **Girl with a Spanish shawl**
mm (27735; New York: C. Fischer, 1937) 7 p. (score, part).
Dn 2′. *Pf* pno, vln.

2437 GALAJIKIAN, Florence G. **Hillbilly's dance** (28878; New
mm York: C. Fischer, 1940) 5 p. (score, part).
Dn 2′. *Pf* pno, vcl.

2438 HIER, Ethel Glenn. **Asolo bells** (CP 140; New York: Composers
mm Press, 1946) 11 p. (score).
Dn 6′. *Pf* 2 pno, 4 hands. Originally for solo pno as *Campane d'Asolo* (*WIAM*
2685); also arranged for orchestra (*WIAM* 2626).

2439 HIER, Ethel Glenn. **Down in the glen** (New York: Composers
mm Press, 1958) 3 p. (score, parts).
Dn 2′. *At* Katharine Adams. *Pf* solo voc, pno, vln, vcl.

2440 HIER, Ethel Glenn. **If you must go, go quickly** (New York:
mm composer, 1925) 7 p. (score, parts).
Dn 3′. *At* Eloise Robinson. *Pf* solo voc, pno, vln, vcl.

2441 HIER, Ethel Glenn. **Joy of spring** (CFS 2385; Chicago: C.F.
mm Summy, 1926) 5 p. (score).
Dn 3′. *Pf* pno, vln.

2442 HIER, Ethel Glenn. **Poem** (facsimile of MS at NNAMC, n.d.) 9
mm p. (score, part).
Dn 8′. *Pf* pno, vln.

2443 HIER, Ethel Glenn. **Poems for remembrance. Suite for**
mm **violin, viola, cello, and piano** (New York: Composers Facsimile
Ed., 1957) 22 p. (score, parts).
Dn 8′. *Ct* This twilight, Junes they have loved, It should be always winter.

2444 HIER, Ethel Glenn. **Quintet for voice, flute, viola, cello, and**
mm **harp** (New York: Composers Facsimile Ed., 1965) 17 p. (score,
parts).
Dn 11′. *Pf* vln may be substituted for flu, pno for hrp. *Ct* Approach (*At*
Frances Frost), Swans (*At* Leonora Speyer), Gulls (*At* Leonora Speyer). *Gulls*
also for solo voc, pno (*WIAM* 2891).

2445 HIER, Ethel Glenn. **Rhapsody for violin and piano** (New
mm York: Composers Facsimile Ed., 1955) 9 p. (score, part).
Dn 6′.

2446 HIER, Ethel Glenn. **Scherzo for trio** (New York: Composers
mm Facsimile Ed., 1952) 11 p. (score, parts).
Dn 5′. *Pf* flu, pno, vcl.

2447 HIER, Ethel Glenn. **Study in blue** (New York: Composers
mm Facsimile Ed., 1953) 8 p. (score, parts).
Dn 5′. *Pf* 2 pno, 4 hands.

2448 HIER, Ethel Glenn. **Suite for chamber ensemble** (facsimile of
mm MS at NNAMC, n.d.) 27 p. (score, parts).
Dn 15′. *Pf* flu, obo, pno, vln, vla, vcl. *Ct* Night wind sings, Foreboding,
Caprice, Intermezzo, Dance.

2449 HIER, Ethel Glenn. **Theme and variations for two pianos**
mm (facsimile of MS at NNAMC, n.d.) 23 p. (score).
Dn 8′. *Pf* 2 pno, 4 hands.

2450 HOWE, Mary. **Ballade fantasque for cello and piano** (facsimm mile of MS at NN, n.d.) 10 p. (score).
Dn 6′. *La* DLC.

2451 HOWE, Mary. **For four woodwinds and French horn** (facsimm mile of MS at NN, [1958?]) 30 p. (score).
Dn 15′. *La* DLC. *Pf* woodwind quintet.

2452 HOWE, Mary. **Fugue in A minor for string quartet** (facsimile
mm of MS at NN, n.d.) 6 p. (score, parts).
Dn 6′.

2453 HOWE, Mary. **Grave piece for strings. From a devotion by**
mm **John Donne** (facsimile of autograph at NN, [1951?]) 5 p. (score,
parts).
Dn 6′. *La* DLC. *Pf* string quartet.

2454 HOWE, Mary. **Interlude between two pieces for alto re-**
mm **corder and harpsichord** (facsimile of autograph at NN, n.d.) 6, 3,
5 p. (score).
Dn 10′. *La* DLC. *Ct* Traits, Interlude, Tactics. *Rg* NN, Rogers and Hammerstein Archives of Recorded Sound.

2455 HOWE, Mary. **Patria** (facsimile of autograph at NN, [194-]) 3 p.
mm (score, part).
Dn 2′. *Pf* pno, vcl (or vla).

2456 HOWE, Mary. **Quatuor I** (facsimile of autograph at NN, n.d.) 12
mm p. (score, parts).
Dn 8′. *Pf* string quartet.

2457 HOWE, Mary. **Quatuor II** (facsimile of autograph at NN, n.d.) 7
mm p. (score, parts).
Dn 5′. *Pf* string quartet.

2458 HOWE, Mary. **Quatuor III** (facsimile of MS at NN, n.d.) 8 p.
mm   (score, parts).
Dn 6′. *Pf* string quartet.

2459 HOWE, Mary. **Sonata for violin and piano** (New York: C.F.
mm   Peters, 1962) 28 p. (score, part).
Dn 15′.

2460 HOWE, Mary. **Song for cello. Über allen Gipfeln** (facsimile
mm   of autograph at NN, [194-]) 3 p. (score, part).
Dn 2′. *Pf* pno, vcl. Originally for solo voc, pno in her *German songs* (*WIAM*
2906).

2461 HOWE, Mary. **Spring pastoral** (facsimile of MS at NN, n.d.) 7
mm   p. (score).
Dn 7′. *Pf* flu, obo, bsn, hrn, str. Also for choral SSA, pno (*WIAM* 2572).

2462 HOWE, Mary. **Stars for two pianos, four hands** (facsimile of
mm   autograph at NN, [194-]) 7 p.
Dn 5′. Originally for chamber orchestra (*WIAM* 2641, 2642).

2463 HOWE, Mary. **Suite for string quartet and piano, nos. 1-3**
mm   (facsimiles of MSS at NN, n.d.) 12, 10, 11 p. (score, parts).
Dn 15′. *Ct* Romanza, Scherzo, Finale. *Rg* NN, Rogers and Hammerstein
Archives of Recorded Sound.

2464 HOWE, Mary. **Suite mélancolique for piano, violin, and**
mm   **cello** (facsimile of MS at NN, n.d.) 10 p. (score, parts).
Dn 5′. *La* DLC. *Ct* Prelude, Chanson grave, Air gai, Elégiaque.

2465 HOWE, Mary. **Three Emily Dickinson pieces for string**
mm   **quartet** (facsimile of MS at NN, [1941?]) 17 p. (score, parts).
Dn 10′. *La* DLC. *Ct* The summers of Hesperides, Birds by the snow, God for a
frontier. *Rg* NN, Rogers and Hammerstein Archives of Recorded Sound.

2466 HOWE, Mary. **Three restaurant pieces** (facsimiles of MSS at
mm   NN, [194-]) 6, 5, 9 p. (score).
Dn 12′. *Pf* pno, vln. *Ct* Melody at dusk, Valse, Fiddler's reel.

2467 HOWE, Mary. **Three Spanish folk tunes transcribed for two**
mm   **pianos** (BM 7559-7561; Boston: Boston Music, 1926) 7, 7, 7 p.
      (score).
Dn 9′. *Pf* 2 pno, 4 hands. *Ct* Peteñera, Spanish folk dance, Habañera de Cinna.

2468 HOWE, Mary. **Trifle for piano duo** (facsimile of MS at NN,
mm   n.d.) 18 p. (score).
Dn 5′. *Pf* 2 pno, 4 hands.

2469 MANA ZUCCA. **Ballade and caprice, op. 28** (6120; Boston:
mm   Boston Music, 1923) 13 p. (score, part).
Dn 3′. *Pf* pno, vln. Also for pno, vcl (6679; Boston Music, 1923).

2470 MANA ZUCCA. **Concerto no. 1 for piano and orchestra, op.**
mm   **49** (Miami, Fla.: Congress Music, 1948) 53 p. (piano reduction).
Dn 30′. *Pf* orchestration arranged for 2nd pno, solo pno.

2471 MANA ZUCCA. **Sonata for violin and piano, op. 132**
mm   (27759; New York: C. Fischer, 1937) 41 p. (score, part).
Dn 12′.

2472 MANA ZUCCA. **Trio for violin, cello, and piano, op. 40**
mm   (18418; Cincinnati: J. Church, 1921) 48 p. (score, parts).
Dn 14′.

2473 RALSTON, Frances Marion. **Sonate spirituel** (New York:
mm   Breitkopf, 1927) 32 p. (score, part).
Dn 15′. *Pf* vln, pno.

2474 SEEGER, Ruth Crawford. **Diaphonic suite no. 2 (1930)**
mm   (New York: Continuo Music, 1972) 8 p. (score, parts).
Dn 3′. *La* DLC. *Pf* bsn, vcl; 2nd vcl can replace bsn.

2475 SEEGER, Ruth Crawford. **Diaphonic suite no. 3 (1930)**
mm   (New York: Continuo Music, 1972) 8 p. (score, parts).
Dn 3′. *La* DLC. *Pf* 2 cla.

2476 SEEGER, Ruth Crawford. **Diaphonic suite no. 4 (1930)**
mm   (New York: Continuo Music, 1972) 12 p. (score, parts).
Dn 5′. *La* DLC. *Pf* obo, vcl.

2477 SEEGER, Ruth Crawford. **String quartet, 1931**, *New Music*
mp   XIV/2 (Jan 1941) 2-22. (score).
Dn 11′. *La* DLC. *Rg* Nonesuch, H 71280.

2478 SEEGER, Ruth Crawford. **Suite for wind quintet.** Ed. by Kurt
mm   STONE (AB 172; New York: A. Broude, 1969) 26 p. (score, parts).
Dn 10′. *La* DLC. *Rg* Composers Recordings, CRI SD 249.

2479 SEEGER, Ruth Crawford. **Suite no. 2 for strings and piano**
mm   (facsimile of autograph at DLC, 1929) 30 p. (score, parts).
Dn 6′. *Pf* piano quintet.

2480 SEEGER, Ruth Crawford. **Three songs.** *New music orchestra*
mm   *series* 5 (San Francisco: New Music Ed., 1933) 58 p. (score).
Dn 7′. *La* DLC. *At* Sandburg. *St* Good morning America, Cornhuskers. *Pf* solo
contralto, obo, per, pno; optional cla, bcl, bsn, cbn, hrn, tpt, str. *Ct* Rat riddles,
Prayers of steel, In tall grass. *Rg* Cowell, Riegger, Becker, and Seeger, New
World, NW 285.

2481 URNER, Catherine Murphy. **Jubilee suite for flute and**
mm   **piano** (facsimile of MS at CU, 1978) 17 p. (score, part).
Dn 10′. *Da* 1931.   (*Elise Kuhl Kirk*)

2482 URNER, Catherine Murphy. **Petite suite for flute, violin,**
mm   **viola, and cello** (facsimile of MS at CU, 1978) 37 p. (score, parts).
Dn 18′. *Da* 1930. *La* CU.   (*Elise Kuhl Kirk*)

2483 URNER, Catherine Murphy. **Quartet in C-sharp minor**
mm   (facsimile of MS at CU, 1978) 44 p. (score, parts).
Dn 12′. *Pf* string quartet.   (*Elise Kuhl Kirk*)

2484 URNER, Catherine Murphy. **Sonata in C [major] for violin**
mm   **and piano** (facsimile of MS at CU, 1978) 51 p. (score, part).
Dn 20′. *Da* 1942.   (*Elise Kuhl Kirk*)

2485 URNER, Catherine Murphy. **Sonata in C-sharp minor for**
mm   **violin and piano** (facsimile of MS at CU, 1978) 47 p. (score, part).
Dn 18′. *Da* 1939. *La* CU.   (*Elise Kuhl Kirk*)

Choral music

2486 BAUER, Marion. **At the new year, op. 42** (New York: Associ-
mm   ated Music, 1950) 13 p. (choral octavo).
Secular chorus. *Dn* 3′. *Da* 1947. *At* Kenneth Patchen. *St* First will and testament.
Pf choral SATB, pno.

2487 BAUER, Marion. **China, op. 38** (JF&B 8021; New York: J.
mm   Fischer, 1944) 17 p. (choral octavo).
Secular chorus. *Dn* 6′. *La* DLC. *At* Boris Todrin. *Pf* choral SATB, pno.

2488 BAUER, Marion. **Death spreads his gentle wings** (New York:
mm   Associated Music, 1952) 5 p. (choral octavo).
Secular chorus. *Dn* 2′. *At* Eunice Prosser Crain. *Pf* choral SATB, pno for
rehearsal only.

2489 BAUER, Marion. **Fair daffodils** (APS 10298; Boston: A.P.
mm   Schmidt, 1914) 8 p. (choral octavo).
Secular chorus. *Dn* 3′. *La* DLC, Schmidt Collection. *At* Robert Herrick. *Pf*
choral SSA, pno.

2490 BAUER, Marion. **Foreigner comes to earth on Boston**
mm   **Common, A** (New York: Composers Facsimile Ed., 1953) 19 p.
      (choral octavo).
Secular cantata. *Dn* 6′. *La* DLC. *At* Horace Gregory. *Pf* solo ST, choral SATB,
pno for rehearsal only.

2491 BAUER, Marion. **Garden is a lovesome thing, A, op. 28**
mm   (36767; New York: G. Schirmer, 1938) 7 p. (choral octavo).
Secular chorus. *Dn* 4′. *At* Thomas Edward Brown. *Pf* choral SSATBB, pno for
rehearsal only.

2492 BAUER, Marion. **Here at high morning, op. 27** (New York:
mm   H.W. Gray, 1931) 10 p. (choral octavo).
Secular chorus. *Dn* 2′. *Da* 23 July 1931, Peterborough, N.H. *At* May Lewis. *Pf*
choral TTBB, pno for rehearsal only.

2493 BAUER, Marion. **Lay of the four winds, The, op. 8** (APS
mm   10472; Boston: A.P. Schmidt, 1915) 15 p. (choral octavo).
Secular chorus. *Dn* 6′. *La* DLC. *At* Cale Young Rice. *Pf* choral TTBB, pno.

2494 BAUER, Marion. **Lobster quadrille** (facsimile of MS at NN,
mm   1953) 2 p. (parts).
Secular chorus. *Dn* 2′. *At* Lewis Carroll. *St Alice in wonderland. Pf* choral
SSAA.   *(Laurine Elkins-Marlow)*

2495 BAUER, Marion. **Three noëls, op. 22, nos. 1-3** (APS 14467;
mm   Boston: A.P. Schmidt, 1930) 16 p. (choral octavo).
Sacred choruses. *Dn* 10′. *La* DLC, Schmidt Collection. *Pf* choral SSA, pno. *Ct*
Tryste noël (*At* Louise Imogen Guiney), I sing of a maiden, Lullaby.

2496 BAUER, Marion. **Wenn ich rufe zu dir, Herr, mein Gott, op.
mm   3 [When I call to thee, Lord, my God]. Der 28 Psalm** (GH
3542; Leipzig: Gebrüder Hug, 1903) 17 p. (choral octavo).
Sacred chorus. *Dn* 4′. *Pf* solo S, choral SSA, org or pno.

2497 BEHREND, Jeanne. **Easter hymn** (rev. ed.; Philadelphia: com-
mm   poser, 1941) 11 p. (score, parts).
Sacred cantata. *Dn* 10′. *At* A.E. Housman. *Pf* solo S, choral SS, per, hrp, org. A
revision of the original version for small orchestra, 1940.   *(Composer)*

2498 BEHREND, Jeanne. **Fantasy on Shostakovitch's** *Song of the
mm   United Nations* (facsimile of MS at NNAMC, 1942) 15 p.
Secular chorus. *Dn* 6′. *Pf* solo S, choral SA, 2 pno.   *(Composer)*

2499 BOYD, Jeanne M. **Have you seen but a whyte lillie grow**
mm   (41255; New York: G. Schirmer, 1946) 7 p. (choral octavo).
Folk tune arranged. *Dn* 1′. *At* Ben Jonson. *Pf* choral SSA, pno.

2500 BOYD, Jeanne M. **Hunting of the snark, The** (Chicago: H.T.
mm   FitzSimons, 1929) 40 p.
Secular chorus. *Dn* 12′. *At* Lewis Carroll. *St The hunting of the snark. Pf* solo
Bar, choral duo (children), pno.

2501 BOYD, Jeanne M. **Mr. Frog** (3074; Chicago: H.T. FitzSimons,
mm   1948) 8 p. (choral octavo).
Secular chorus. *Dn* 2′. *At* Elvera Spivey. *Pf* choral SSA, pno.

2502 BOYD, Jeanne M. **On a winding way** (3069; Chicago: H.T.
mm   FitzSimons, 1948) 8 p.
Secular chorus. *Dn* 2′. *Pf* choral SSA, pno.

2503 BOYD, Jeanne M. **Three sea chanties** (New York: H.W. Gray,
mm   1950) 8, 8, 6 p. (choral octavo).
Secular choruses. *Dn* 5′. *At* Stanton H. King. *Pf* choral TTBB, pno rehearsal
only. *Ct* A-roving; Farewell and adieu; Blow, boys, blow.

2504 BRANSCOMBE, Gena. **All a-maying go! From** *Pilgrims of
md   destiny* (78208; Boston: O. Ditson, 1929) 7 p. (choral octavo).
Secular chorus. *Dn* 3′. *La* DLC, NN. *At* composer. *Pf* choral SA (children),
pno. *Tm Pilgrims of destiny* (*WIAM* 2517).   *(Laurine Elkins-Marlow)*

2505 BRANSCOMBE, Gena. **Arms that have sheltered us** (To-
mm   ronto: G.V. Thompson, 1958) 5 p. (choral octavo).
Secular chorus. *Dn* 4′. *La* NN. *At* composer. *Pf* choral TTBB, pno. Dedicated to
the Royal Canadian Navy on its 50th anniversary.   *(Laurine Elkins-Marlow)*

2506 BRANSCOMBE, Gena. **Coventry's choir** (40941; New York:
mm   G. Schirmer, 1944) 15 p. (choral octavo).
Sacred chorus. *Dn* 8′. *La* NN. *At* Violet B. Alvarez. *Pf* solo S, choral SSAA,
pno. Also for solo voc, pno (autograph at NN) and for choral SSAA, string
orchestra (autograph score and parts at NN).   *(Laurine Elkins-Marlow)*

2507 BRANSCOMBE, Gena. **Dancer of Fjaard, The** (APS 13659;
mm   Boston: A.P. Schmidt, 1926) 24 p. (choral octavo).
Secular chorus. *Dn* 10′. *La* NN. *At* composer. *Pf* solo SA, choral SSAA, pno.
Also for solo SA, choral SSA, 1-1-1-1, 1-0-0-0, tim, hrp, str (autograph score at
NN). Accompaniment also arranged for chamber orchestra: 1-0-0-0, 0-0-0-0,
per, hrp, str (autograph score at NN, voice parts lacking). *(Laurine Elkins-Marlow)*

2508 BRANSCOMBE, Gena. **Dear lad o' mine** (APS 10761; Boston:
mm   A.P. Schmidt, 1915) 8 p. (choral octavo).
Secular chorus. *Dn* 2′. *At* Katherine Hale. *Pf* choral SSAA, pno. Also for solo S
or T, pno (*WIAM* 2787).   *(Laurine Elkins-Marlow)*

2509 BRANSCOMBE, Gena. **God of the nations** (APS 11365;
mm   Boston: A.P. Schmidt, 1917) 7 p.
Sacred chorus. *Dn* 3′. *At* Sara E. Branscombe. *Pf* solo SB, choral SATB, pno.
Also for choral SATB (APS 11364; Schmidt, 1917) and for solo SB, pno
(*WIAM* 2793).   *(Laurine Elkins-Marlow)*

2510 BRANSCOMBE, Gena. **I bring you heartsease** (APS 10819;
mm   Boston: A.P. Schmidt, 1916) 7 p. (choral octavo).
Dn 2′. *At* composer. *Pf* choral SSA, pno. Also for choral SSA, chamber
orchestra: 1-0-1-1, 1-0-0-0, per, hrp, str (autograph score and parts at NN); and
for solo voc, pno (*WIAM* 2796).   *(Laurine Elkins-Marlow)*

2511 BRANSCOMBE, Gena. **Mary at Bethlehem** (NY 964; New
mm   York: G. Ricordi, 1934) 9 p. (choral octavo).
Sacred chorus. *Dn* 5′. *Tr* composer. *St* France, 15th c. *Pf* solo SA, choral SSA,
pno.   *(Laurine Elkins-Marlow)*

2512 BRANSCOMBE, Gena. **May Day dancing** (New York: G.
mm   Ricordi, 1931) 11 p. (choral octavo).
Secular chorus. *Dn* 5′. *At* composer. *Pf* choral SSA, pno. Also for choral SSA,
chamber orchestra: 1-1-0-0, 0-0-0-0, per, str (autograph score and parts at NN).
Dedicated to the Clifton Music Club, Cincinnati, Ohio.   *(Laurine Elkins-Marlow)*

2513 BRANSCOMBE, Gena. **O love that guides our way** (CMR
mm   2416; New York: H.W. Gray, 1956) 6 p. (choral octavo).
Sacred chorus. *Dn* 3′. *At* composer. *Pf* choral SATB, pno. Also for solo voc, pno
(*WIAM* 2810).   *(Laurine Elkins-Marlow)*

2514 BRANSCOMBE, Gena. **Ol' Marse Winter** (APS 10453; Bos-
mm   ton: A.P. Schmidt, 1914) 7 p. (choral octavo).
Secular chorus. *Dn* 3′. *At* Mary Alice Ogden. *Pf* choral SSA, pno. Also for solo
voc, pno (autograph score at NN). Dedicated to the Lyric Club of Newark,
N.J., Arthur P. Woodruff, director.   *(Laurine Elkins-Marlow)*

2515 BRANSCOMBE, Gena. **Our Canada, from sea to sea** (To-
mm   ronto: G.V. Thompson, 1939) 1 p. (choral octavo).
Secular chorus. *Dn* 2′. *Pf* choral SATB.   *(Laurine Elkins-Marlow)*

2516 BRANSCOMBE, Gena. **Phantom caravan, The** (18994; Cin-
mm   cinnati: J. Church, 1926) 25 p. (choral octavo).
Secular chorus. *Dn* 10′. *La* NN. *At* Kendall Banning. *Pf* choral TTBB, pno.
Also for choral TTBB, chamber orchestra: 1-1-1-0, 1-0-0-0, tim, str (autograph
score at NN).   *(Laurine Elkins-Marlow)*

2517 BRANSCOMBE, Gena. **Pilgrims of destiny** (76444; Boston: O.
mm   Ditson, 1929) 133 p. (piano-vocal score).
Secular choral drama. *Dn* 30′. *Da* 1919. *La* NN, DLC. *At* composer. *Pf* solo 4S-
2A-3T-2Bar-B, choral SATB, SA (children), pno. Originally for solo 4S-2A-3T-
2Bar-B, choral SATB, SA (children), 1pic-1-1-1, 1-1-1-1, tim, per, hrp, str
(autograph score at DLC).   *(Laurine Elkins-Marlow)*

2518 BRANSCOMBE, Gena. **Prayer for song** (NY 1268; New York:
mm   G. Ricordi, 1942) 11 p. (choral octavo).
Sacred chorus. *Dn* 5′. *At* Ruth MacDonald. *Pf* choral SSAA, pno. Also for
choral SATB, pno (NY 2318; New York: F. Colombo, 1964). Written for and
dedicated to the Branscombe Choral.   *(Laurine Elkins-Marlow)*

2519 BRANSCOMBE, Gena. **Roses in Madrid** (APS 10542; Boston:
mm   A.P. Schmidt, 1915) 15 p. (choral octavo).
Secular chorus. *Dn* 8′. *At* Isabella Valency Crawford. *Pf* choral SSA, pno.
    (Laurine Elkins-Marlow)

2520 BRANSCOMBE, Gena. **Spirit of motherhood** (APS 13320;
mm   Boston: A.P. Schmidt, 1924) 8 p. (choral octavo).
Secular chorus. *Dn* 4′. *La* NN. *At* Louise Driscoll. *Pf* choral SSA, pno. Also for
solo voc, pno (*WIAM* 2818).   *(Laurine Elkins-Marlow)*

2521 BRANSCOMBE, Gena. **Sun and the warm brown earth**
mm   (1675; Boston: C.C. Birchard, 1935) 5 p. (choral octavo).
Secular chorus. *Dn* 2′. *At* Mary Henderson. *Pf* choral SSA, pno. Also for choral
SSA, 1-1-2-1, 2-1-1-0, tim, per including cel, str (autograph score at NN).
    (Laurine Elkins-Marlow)

2522 BRANSCOMBE, Gena. **Wind from the sea, A** (13077; Boston:
mm   A.P. Schmidt, 1924) 8 p. (choral octavo).
Secular chorus. *Dn* 3'. *Pf* choral SSA, pno. Also for choral SSA, flu, obo, and
string quartet (autograph score at NN).   *(Laurine Elkins-Marlow)*

2523 BRANSCOMBE, Gena. **Wind is blowing soft today, The.**
md   **From** *Pilgrims of destiny* (78194; Boston: O. Ditson, 1929) 3 p.
(choral octavo).
Secular chorus. *Dn* 1'. *La* DLC, NN. *At* composer. *Pf* choral unison (children),
pno. *Tm Pilgrims of destiny* (*WIAM* 2517).   *(Laurine Elkins-Marlow)*

2524 BRANSCOMBE, Gena. **Woodwinds** (3076; Chicago: H.T.
mm   FitzSimons, 1949) 7 p. (choral octavo).
Secular chorus. *Dn* 3'. *At* composer. *Pf* choral SSA, pno. *(Laurine Elkins-Marlow)*

2525 BRANSCOMBE, Gena. **Wreathe the holly, twine the bay**
mm   (7463; New York: J. Fischer, 1938) 8 p. (choral octavo).
Secular chorus. *Dn* 4'. *At* composer. *Pf* choral SSA, pno, optional 2nd alto. Also
for choral SATB, pno (JF&B 7464; Fischer, 1938), and for choral SATB, 2 flu,
cla, bsn, tim, per including chimes (autograph at NN).   *(Laurine Elkins-Marlow)*

2526 BRANSCOMBE, Gena. **Youth of the world** (MW 19282; New
mm   York: M. Witmark, 1932) 32 p. (choral octavo).
Secular choral cycle. *Dn* 10'. *At* composer. *Pf* choral SSA, pno. *Ct* Airmen,
Maples, Youth of the world.
                                                 (Laurine Elkins-Marlow)

2527 DANIELS, Mabel Wheeler. **Canticle of wisdom** (676; New
mm   York: H.W. Gray, 1958) 11 p. (choral octavo).
Sacred chorus. *Dn* 2'. *Pf* choral SSA, pno.

2528 DANIELS, Mabel Wheeler. **Carol of a rose** (44398; New
mm   York: G. Schirmer, 1958) 7 p. (choral octavo).
Secular chorus. *Dn* 5'. *Pf* choral SSA, pno for rehearsal only.

2529 DANIELS, Mabel Wheeler. **Christ child, The, op. 32, no. 2**
md   (APS 14553; Boston: A.P. Schmidt, 1931) 4 p. (choral octavo).
Sacred chorus. *Dn* 2'. *La* DLC, Schmidt Collection. *At* Gilbert Keith
Chesterton. *Pf* choral SATB, pno for rehearsal only.

2530 DANIELS, Mabel Wheeler. **Christmas in the manger, op. 35,**
md   **no. 2** (JF&B 6841; New York: J. Fischer, 1934) 4 p. (choral octavo).
Sacred chorus. *Dn* 2'. *At* Katharine Shepard Hayden. *Pf* choral SATB, pno for
rehearsal only.

2531 DANIELS, Mabel Wheeler. **Christmas in the wood, op. 35,**
md   **no. 1** (JF&B 6840; New York: J. Fischer, 1934) 5 p. (choral octavo).
Secular chorus. *Dn* 3'. *At* Frances Frost. *Pf* choral SATB, pno for rehearsal
only.

2532 DANIELS, Mabel Wheeler. **Collinette, op. 4** (APS 6813;
mm   Boston: A.P. Schmidt, 1905) 11 p. (choral octavo).
Secular chorus. *Dn* 4'. *At* John Winwood. *Pf* choral SSAA, pno.

2533 DANIELS, Mabel Wheeler. **Dream song, op. 6, no. 2** (1056;
md   New York: G. Schirmer, 1905) 5 p. (choral octavo).
Secular chorus. *Dn* 1'. *At* Gertrude Craven. *Pf* choral SSAA, pno for rehearsal
only.

2534 DANIELS, Mabel Wheeler. **Dum Dianae vitrea (When**
md   **Diana's silver light), op. 38, no. 2** (JF&B 7876; New York: J.
Fischer, 1942) 11 p. (choral octavo).
Secular chorus. *Dn* 4'. *St* Benedictbeurn MS, 1100-1200. *Lt* Latin, English. *Pf*
choral SSA, pno for rehearsal only.

2535 DANIELS, Mabel Wheeler. **Eastern song, op. 16, no. 1** (APS
md   9265; Boston: A.P. Schmidt, 1911) 15 p. (piano-vocal score).
Secular chorus. *Dn* 5'. *Pf* choral SSA, pno, 2 vln. A note from Schmidt
indicates Daniels also scored the piece for voices and orchestra and that parts
were available at the time of publication.

2536 DANIELS, Mabel Wheeler. **Exultate Deo, op. 33** (APS
mm   14331; Boston: A.P. Schmidt, 1929) 19 p. (piano-vocal score).
Sacred chorus. *Dn* 5'. *Pf* choral SATB, pno. Originally for voices and orchestra
(autograph at MBNe [1929?]). Composed for the 50th anniversary of Radcliffe
Col.

2537 DANIELS, Mabel Wheeler. **Festival hymn, op. 38, no. 1.**
md   **Salve, festa dies** (JF&B 7474; New York: J. Fischer, 1939) 11 p.
(choral octavo).
Sacred chorus. *Dn* 3'. *At* Fortunatus. *Pf* choral SATB, pno for rehearsal only.

2538 DANIELS, Mabel Wheeler. **Flower-wagon, op. 42, no. 1**
md   (JF&B 8137; New York: J. Fischer, 1945) 16 p. (choral octavo).
Secular chorus. *Dn* 4'. *At* Frances Taylor Patterson. *Pf* choral SSA, pno.

2539 DANIELS, Mabel Wheeler. **Holiday fantasy, A, op. 31, no. 2**
md   (APS 14143; Boston: A.P. Schmidt, 1928) 19 p. (choral octavo).
Secular chorus. *Dn* 5'. *At* composer. *Pf* choral SATB, pno. The title page
indicates that the piece was originally for voices and orchestra. *Tm Two
choruses for mixed voices, op. 31* (*WIAM* 2555).

2540 DANIELS, Mabel Wheeler. **Holy star, The, op. 31, no. 1**
md   (APS 14142; Boston: A.P. Schmidt, 1928) 11 p. (choral octavo).
Sacred chorus. *Dn* 5'. *At* Nancy Byrd Turner. *Pf* choral SATB, pno. *Tm Two
choruses for mixed voices, op. 31* (*WIAM* 2555).

2541 DANIELS, Mabel Wheeler. **June rhapsody, op. 20, no. 1**
md   (APS 10215; Boston: A.P. Schmidt, 1914) 8 p. (choral octavo).
Secular chorus. *Dn* 2'. *La* DLC, Schmidt Collection. *At* Minnie L. Upton. *Pf*
choral SSA, pno.

2542 DANIELS, Mabel Wheeler. **Mavourneen, op. 12, no. 1** (APS
md   7150; Boston: A.P. Schmidt, 1906) 4 p. (choral octavo).
Secular chorus. *Dn* 2'. *At* composer. *Pf* choral SATB, pno.

2543 DANIELS, Mabel Wheeler. **Midsummer, op. 10** (APS 7066;
mm   Boston: A.P. Schmidt, 1906) 11 p. (choral octavo).
Secular chorus. *Dn* 4'. *Pf* choral SATB, pno.

2544 DANIELS, Mabel Wheeler. **Night in Bethlehem, A** (CMR
mm   2316; New York: H.W. Gray, 1953) 8 p. (choral octavo).
Sacred chorus. *Dn* 3'. *At* composer. *Pf* choral SATB, org.

2545 DANIELS, Mabel Wheeler. **O'er brake and heather, op. 18,**
md   **no. 1** (APS 8403; Boston: A.P. Schmidt, 1909) 5 p. (choral octavo).
Secular chorus. *Dn* 1'. *At* Abbie Farwell Brown. *Pf* choral SATB, pno. A note
from Schmidt indicates Daniels also scored the piece for voices and orchestra
and that parts were available at the time of publication.

2546 DANIELS, Mabel Wheeler. **Oh God of all our glorious past**
mm   (1459; Boston: C.C. Birchard, 1930) 3 p. (choral octavo).
Sacred chorus. *Dn* 2'. *At* Amelia Ely Howe. *Pf* choral SATB, pno.

2547 DANIELS, Mabel Wheeler. **Peace in liberty, op. 25** (APS
mm   11356; Boston: A.P. Schmidt, 1929) 12 p. (piano-vocal score).
Secular chorus. *Dn* 6'. *At* Abbie Farwell Brown. *Pf* choral SATB, pno.
Originally for voices and orchestra (autograph at MBNe). *Peace in liberty* was
published initially as *Peace with a sword* (APS 11356; Schmidt, 1917).

2548 DANIELS, Mabel Wheeler. **Piper, play on!** (ECS 1842;
mm   Boston: E.C. Schirmer, 1961) 20 p. (choral octavo).
Secular chorus. *Dn* 6'. *Pf* choral SATB, pno for rehearsal only.

2549 DANIELS, Mabel Wheeler. **Psalm of praise, A** (CCS 19; New
mm   York: H.W. Gray, 1955) 24 p. (score).
Sacred chorus. *Dn* 5'. *Pf* choral SATB, 3 tpt, tim, per. Published score, parts,
and organ reduction on rental at Belwin-Mills, Melville, N.Y. Daniels wrote this
piece for the 75th anniversary of the founding of Radcliffe Col.

2550 DANIELS, Mabel Wheeler. **Secrets, op. 22, no. 1** (APS 9819;
md   Boston: A.P. Schmidt, 1913) 4 p. (choral octavo).
Secular chorus. *Dn* 4'. *La* DLC, Schmidt Collection. *At* Frederic Lawrence
Knowles. *St On life's stairway. Pf* choral TTBB, pno.

2551 DANIELS, Mabel Wheeler. **Song of Jael, The, op. 37** (JF&B
mm   7330; New York: J. Fischer, 1937) 59 p. (piano-vocal score).
Sacred cantata. *Dn* 20'. *La* MB. *At* Edward Arlington Robinson. *St Sisera. Pf*
solo S, choral SATB, pno. Originally for voices and orchestra (autograph, parts
at MB).

2552 DANIELS, Mabel Wheeler. **Song of the Persian captive, op.**
md   **24, no. 2** (APS 10750; Boston: A.P. Schmidt, 1915) 8 p. (choral
octavo).

Secular chorus. *Dn* 3'. *La* DLC, Schmidt Collection. *Pf* choral SSA, pno.

2553 DANIELS, Mabel Wheeler. **Songs of elfland, op. 28** (APS
mm 13124-13125; Boston: A.P. Schmidt, 1924) 19, 24 p. (choral octavo).
Secular choruses. *Dn* 7'. *At* composer. *Pf* choral SSA, flu, hrp, pno. *Ct* Fairy
road, Fairy ring. A note from Schmidt indicates Daniels scored the piano part
for strings and that string parts were available at the time of publication.

2554 DANIELS, Mabel Wheeler. **Through the dark the dreamers**
md **came, op. 32, no. 1** (rev. ed.; ECS 1843; Boston: E.C. Schirmer,
1961) 7 p. (choral octavo).
Sacred chorus. *Dn* 4'. *La* DLC, Schmidt Collection. *At* Earl Marlatt. *Pf* choral
SSATB, pno. Previously published in 1929 (ECS 1843; Schirmer). Also for
choral SSA, pno (rev. ed.; ECS 1844; Schirmer, 1961).

2555 DANIELS, Mabel Wheeler. **Two choruses for mixed voices,**
mm **op. 31, nos. 1-2** (APS 14142-14143; Boston: A.P. Schmidt, 1928)
11, 19 p. (choral octavo).
Sacred chorus, secular chorus. *Dn* 10'. *Pf* choral SATB, pno. *Ct* The holy star
(*WIAM* 2540), A holiday fantasy (*WIAM* 2539).

2556 DANIELS, Mabel Wheeler. **Veni creator spiritus** (APS 9800;
mm Boston: A.P. Schmidt, 1912) 7 p. (choral octavo).
Sacred chorus. *Dn* 4'. *Pf* solo S, choral SSA, pno.

2557 DANIELS, Mabel Wheeler. **Voice of my beloved, The, op.**
md **16, no. 2** (APS 9266; Boston: A.P. Schmidt, 1911) 12 p. (choral
octavo).
Sacred chorus. *Dn* 5'. *Pf* choral SSA, pno, 2 vln.

2558 DANIELS, Mabel Wheeler. **Wild ride, The** (APS 13683;
mm Boston: A.P. Schmidt, 1926) 16 p. (choral octavo).
Secular chorus. *Dn* 5'. *La* DLC, Schmidt Collection. *At* Louise Imogen Guiney.
Pf choral TTBB, pno.

2559 GALAJIKIAN, Florence G. **Song of joy** (29031; New York: C.
mm Fischer, 1941) 9 p.
Dn 3'. *At* Ina Coolbrith. *Pf* choral SSA, pno.

2560 HIER, Ethel Glenn. **America the beautiful** (facsimile of MS at
mm NNAMC, n.d.) 5 p. (score).
Secular chorus. *Dn* 2'. *At* Katherine Lee Bates. *Pf* choral SATB, 2-2-2-2, 4-3-
3-1, tim, per.

2561 HIER, Ethel Glenn. **Mountain preacher** (New York: Composers
mm Facsimile Ed., 1966) 18 p. (score, parts).
Secular cantata. *Dn* 10'. *At* James Still. *Pf* choral SATB, 2-2-2-2, 2-2-2-0, per,
hrp, pno, str, narrator. *Ct* Death on the mountain, When the dulcimers are
gone, Journey beyond the hills, A cappella, Epitaph for Uncle Ira Combs.

2562 HIER, Ethel Glenn. **Then shall I know** (facsimile of MS at
mm NNAMC, n.d.) 14 p. (score).
Sacred chorus. *Dn* 9'. *Pf* choral SATB.

2563 HOWE, Mary. **Catalina** (30249; New York: C. Fischer, 1948) 7
mm p. (choral octavo).
Secular chorus. *Dn* 3'. *La* DLC. *Pf* choral SATB, pno.

2564 HOWE, Mary. **Chain-gang song** (32287; New York: G.
mm Schirmer, 1925) 16 p. (choral octavo).
Secular chorus. *Dn* 9'. *Pf* choral TTBB, pno. *Rg* NN, Rogers and Hammerstein
Archives of Recorded Sound.

2565 HOWE, Mary. **Christmas song** (40084; New York: G. Schirmer,
mm 1942) 12 p. (choral octavo).
Sacred chorus. *Dn* 5'. *La* DLC. *Pf* choral SSTB, org.

2566 HOWE, Mary. **Devotion, A** (CCS 18; New York: H.W. Gray,
mm 1955) 16 p. (choral octavo).
Secular chorus. *Dn* 8'. *La* DLC. *At* Donne. *Pf* choral TTBB, pno for rehearsal
only.

2567 HOWE, Mary. **Laud for Christmas** (37410; New York: G.
mm Schirmer, 1936) 7 p. (choral octavo).
Sacred chorus. *Dn* 4'. *La* DLC. *At* Nancy Byrd Turner. *Pf* choral SATB, pno
for rehearsal only.

2568 HOWE, Mary. **Pavilion of the Lord, The. Domine illumina-**
mm **tio** (facsimile of autograph at NN, n.d.) 13 p. (choral octavo).
Sacred chorus. *Dn* 4'. *La* DLC. *Pf* choral SATB, org.

2569 HOWE, Mary. **Prophecy (1792)** (New York: H.W. Gray, 1955)
mm 38 p. (choral octavo).
Secular chorus. *Dn* 11'. *La* DLC. *At* Blake. *St* A song of liberty. *Pf* choral TTBB,
pno.

2570 HOWE, Mary. **Song of palms** (30287; New York: C. Fischer,
mm 1947) 27 p. (choral octavo).
Secular chorus. *Dn* 14'. *La* DLC. *At* A. O'Shaugnessy. *Pf* choral SSAA, pno.

2571 HOWE, Mary. **Song of Ruth** (38879; New York: G. Schirmer,
mm 1940) 11 p. (choral octavo).
Sacred chorus. *Dn* 7'. *La* DLC. *Pf* choral SATB, org. *Rg* NN, Rogers and
Hammerstein Archives of Recorded Sound.

2572 HOWE, Mary. **Spring pastoral** (38152; New York: G. Schirmer,
mm 1938) 11 p. (choral octavo).
Secular chorus. *Dn* 7'. *La* DLC. *At* Elinor Wylie. *Pf* choral SSA, pno. Also for
chamber ensemble (*WIAM* 2461). *Rg* Composers Recordings, CRI SRD 145.

2573 HOWE, Mary. **Williamsburg Sunday** (2172; New York: C.
mm Fischer, 1955) 9 p. (choral octavo).
Secular chorus. *Dn* 3'. *La* DLC. *At* Katherine Garrison Chapman. *Pf* choral
SATB, pno for rehearsal only. *Rg* NN, Rogers and Hammerstein Archives of
Recorded Sound.

2574 HOWE, Mary. **Yule catch** (facsimile of autograph at NN, 1940)
mm 3 p. (score).
Secular chorus. *Dn* 1'. *Da* Christmas 1940. *Pf* choral SSA.

2575 JACKSON, Elizabeth B. **Beauty of God's world, The,**
mp *Younger Choir* VIII/3 (Mar 1965) 6-7. (choral octavo).
Secular chorus. *Dn* 3'. *Da* 1962. *La* publisher. *At* composer. *Pf* choral SA.
(Composer)

2576 JACKSON, Elizabeth B. **Boy Jesus, The,** *Younger Choir* VIII/4
mp (Apr 1965) 10-11.
Sacred chorus. *Dn* 3'. *Da* 1960. *La* publisher. *At* Bible, composer. *Pf* choral SA.
(Composer)

2577 JACKSON, Elizabeth B. **Christmas prayer for peace** (975;
mm New York: Belwin-Mills, 1949) 8 p. (choral octavo).
Sacred chorus. *Dn* 4'. *Da* 1949. *La* publisher. *At* composer. *Pf* choral SATB,
pno. *(Composer)*

2578 JACKSON, Elizabeth B. **O God thou art my God** (956; New
mm York: Belwin-Mills, 1949) 8 p. (choral octavo).
Sacred chorus. *Dn* 4'. *Da* 1949. *La* publisher. *Pf* choral SATB, pno. *(Composer)*

2579 JAMES, Dorothy. **Christmas night** (2046; Chicago: H.T. Fitz-
mm Simons, 1934) 4 p. (choral octavo).
Sacred chorus. *Dn* 2'. *Da* 1934. *La* publisher. *At* Edith Tatum. *Pf* choral
SSAATB, pno for rehearsal only. *(Composer)*

2580 JAMES, Dorothy. **Envoy** (JF&B 9254; Glen Rock, N.J.: J.
mm Fischer, 1955) 4 p. (choral octavo).
Secular chorus. *Dn* 3'. *Da* 1955. *La* publisher. *At* Francis Thompson. *Pf* choral
SSA. *(Composer)*

2581 JAMES, Dorothy. **Jumblies, The** (facsimile of MS on rental;
mm Chicago: H.T. FitzSimons, 1935) 63 p. (score, parts).
Secular cantata. *Dn* 15'. *Da* 1935. *La* composer. *At* Edward Lear. *Pf* choral
SSAA, 2pic-2-2-2, 2-2-2-0, tim, hrp, str, optional cel. Also published in a piano-
vocal score (FitzSimons, 1935) *(Composer)*

2582 JAMES, Dorothy. **Little Jesus came to town, The. A legend**
mm (2053; Chicago: H.T. FitzSimons, 1935) 6 p. (choral octavo).
Sacred chorus. *Dn* 2'. *At* Lizette Woodworth Reese. *Pf* choral SATB, pno for
rehearsal only. *(Composer)*

2583 JAMES, Dorothy. **Mary's lullaby** (3066; Chicago: H.T. FitzSi-
mm mons, 1946) 4 p. (choral octavo).
Sacred chorus. *Dn* 3'. *Da* 1942. *La* composer. *At* Elizabeth Coatsworth. *Pf*
choral SSAA. *(Composer)*

2584 JAMES, Dorothy. **Nativity hymn** (9179; Glen Rock, N.J.: J.
mm   Fischer, 1957) 10 p. (choral octavo, parts).
Sacred chorus. *Dn* 5'. *Da* 1957. *At* Milton. *Pf* choral SATB, 2 hrn, 2 tbn. Also
published in *The son of man*, Howard D. McKinney, ed. (Fischer, 1964).
(Composer)

2586 MANA ZUCCA. **Big brown bear, The, op. 52, no. 1** (29530;
md   New York: G. Schirmer, 1919) 4 p.
Secular chorus. *Dn* 2'. *At* H.A. Heydt. *Pf* choral SSA, pno. Originally for solo
voc, pno (*WIAM* 2922).

2587 PRICE, Florence B. **Heav'n bound soldier** (New York: Handy
mm   Brothers Music, 1959) 3 p. (choral octavo).
Spiritual arranged. *Dn* 1'. *Pf* choral SSA, pno.

2588 PRICE, Florence B. **Nature's magic** (4501; Chicago: C.F.
mm   Summy, 1953) 7 p. (choral octavo).
Secular chorus. *Dn* 2'. *Pf* choral SSA, pno.

2589 PRICE, Florence B. **New moon, The** (964; Chicago: Gamble
mm   Hinged Music, 1930) 12 p.
Secular chorus. *Dn* 3'. *Pf* choral SSAA, pno, optional solo S.

2590 PRICE, Florence B. **Nod** (facsimile of autograph at ArU, n.d.) 5
mm   p.
Secular chorus. *Dn* 2'. *At* Walter de la Mare. *Pf* choral TTBB. *(Barbara Garvey Jackson)*

2591 PRICE, Florence B. **Song for snow** (2640; New York: C.
mm   Fischer, 1957) 5 p.
Secular chorus. *Dn* 2'. *At* Elizabeth Coatsworth. *Pf* choral SATB, pno. *(Barbara Garvey Jackson)*

2592 PRICE, Florence B. **Witch of the meadow** (1785; Chicago:
mm   Gamble Hinged Music, 1937) 7 p. (choral octavo).
Secular chorus. *Dn* 2'. *At* Mary Rolofson Gamble. *Pf* choral SSA, pno.

2593 SEEGER, Ruth Crawford. **Chant, 1930** (AB 701; New York:
mm   A. Broude, 1971) 7 p. (choral octavo).
Secular chorus. *Dn* 5'. *La* DLC. *Pf* solo S, choral SATB, pno for rehearsal only.

2594 TYSON, Mildred Lund. **Lilacs are in bloom, The** (36279;
mm   New York: G. Schirmer, 1934) 4 p. (choral octavo).
Secular chorus. *Dn* 3'. *At* George Moore. *Pf* choral SSA, pno.   *(Composer)*

2595 TYSON, Mildred Lund. **May in Japan** (6793; New York: J.
mm   Fischer, 1934) 5 p. (choral octavo).
Secular chorus. *Dn* 4'. *La* NN. *Pf* choral SSA, pno.   *(Composer)*

2596 TYSON, Mildred Lund. **One little cloud** (37065; New York:
mm   G. Schirmer, 1936) 2 p. (choral octavo).
Secular chorus. *Dn* 2'. *Pf* choral SSA, pno.   *(Composer)*

2597 TYSON, Mildred Lund. **Sea moods** (39189; New York: G.
mm   Schirmer, 1941) 6 p. (choral octavo).
Secular chorus. *Dn* 4'. *At* Kenneth Benham. *Pf* choral SATB, pno. Also for
choral SSA, pno (39188; Schirmer, 1941). *Rg* RCA Victor, LM 1870. *(Composer)*

2598 URNER, Catherine Murphy. **Mystic trumpeter, The** (facsimm   mile of MS at CU, 1978) 61 p. (score, parts).
Secular cantata. *Dn* 11'. *At* Whitman. *St* Leaves of grass. *Pf* choral SATB,
2-2enh-2-2, 2-0-1-0, tim, per, str, solo tpt.   *(Elise Kuhl Kirk)*

2599 URNER, Catherine Murphy. **Rhapsody of Aimairgin of the
mm   Golden Knee** (facsimile of MS at CU, 1978) 42 p. (score, parts).
Secular chorus. *Dn* 9'. *Da* 1936. *St* 11th-c. Celtic poem. *Pf* solo B, choral SATB,
2pic-2enh-2bcl-2, 3-2-2-1, tim, per, pno, str.
(Elise Kuhl Kirk)

Orchestral and band music

2600 BAUER, Marion. **American youth concerto for piano and
mm   orchestra, op. 36** (41276; New York: G. Schirmer, 1946) 32 p.
        (score).
Dn 13'. *Pf* orchestration arranged for 2nd pno, solo pno.

2601 BAUER, Marion. **Indian pipes, op. 12, no. 2a**. Arr. by Martin
md   BERNSTEIN (facsimile of autograph at PPFleisher, 1927-28) 25 p.
        (score, parts).
Dn 3'. *Pf* 2-2enh-2-2, 4-2-3-0, hrp, str. First performed in 1928 by the
Chautauqua Symphony Orchestra under the direction of Albert Stoessel.
Originally for pno (*WIAM* 2661). *Tm From the New Hampshire woods, op. 12*
(*WIAM* 2659).

2602 BAUER, Marion. **Lament on an African theme, A, op. 20a**
mm   (facsimile of autograph at PPFleisher, 1927) 10 p. (score, parts).
Dn 6'. An arrangement for string orchestra of the composer's string quartet, op.
20, first performed by the Washington Square String Orchestra at New York
U., Apr. 1935, under the direction of Martin Bernstein.

2603 BAUER, Marion. **Patterns, op. 41, no. 2** (facsimile of MS at
md   PPFleisher, n.d.) 7 p. (score, parts).
Dn 1'. *La* DLC. *Pf* for chamber orchestra: 2pic-2-2-2, 2-0-0-0, str.

2604 BAUER, Marion. **Prelude and fugue for flute and string
mm   orchestra, op. 43** (facsimile of autograph at DLC, n.d.) [8] p.
        (score).
Dn 4'. *La* DLC. *Rg* Composers Recordings, CRI SRD 101.

2605 BAUER, Marion. **Symphonic suite for string orchestra, op.
mm   33** (facsimile of MS at DLC, n.d.) 14 p. (score).
Dn 15'. *La* PPFleisher. *Rg* Composers Recordings, CRI SRD 101.

2606 BAUER, Marion. **Symphony no. 1, op. 45** (facsimile of MS at
mm   NN, n.d.) 70 p. (score).
Dn 16'. *Pf* 3pic-3enh-4bcl-2, 4-3-3-1, tim, 2 hrp, str.

2607 BEHREND, Jeanne. **Festival fanfare** (facsimile of autograph at
mm   PPFleisher, 1959) 7 p. (score, parts).
Dn 2'. *Pf* 2-2-2-2, 4-3-3-1, tim, per, str.   *(Composer)*

2608 BERCKMAN, Evelyn. **County fair** (facsimile of MS at PPFle-
mm   isher, n.d.) 146 p. (score, parts).
Ballet. *Dn* 25'. *Li* May Borland. *Pf* 3pic-3-3-2; 2-2-1-0; tim; per including glk,
vib, mba; hrp; str. Cornets may be substituted for trumpets.

2609 BERCKMAN, Evelyn. **Orage, L' (Sturm)** (EMS 6890; Paris:
mm   Editions M. Senart, 1926) 9 p. (score).
Dn 2'. *At* Heine. *Lt* French, German. *Pf* solo S, 2-1-2-2, 2-3-0-0, hrp, str. Also
for solo S, pno (*WIAM* 2763).

2610 BERCKMAN, Evelyn. **Return of song, The** (facsimile of MS
mm   at PPFleisher, n.d.) 42 p. (score, parts).
Dn 12'. *Pf* 3-3enh-3bcl-2, 4-3-0-0, tim, hrp, pno, str.

2611 BERCKMAN, Evelyn. **Sorbonne** (facsimile of autograph at
mm   NNAMC, n.d.) 34 p.
Dn 20'. *Pf* 3pic-2-3-2, 4-2-2-0, tim, per, 2 hrp, str.

2612 BERCKMAN, Evelyn. **Tours. Fifteenth century** (facsimile of
mm   MS at PPFleisher, n.d.) 25 p. (score, parts).
Dn 5'. *Pf* 2-2-2-2; 4-4-3-0; tim; per including cel, vib; 2 hrp; str.

2613 BERCKMAN, Evelyn. **Ville des nuages, La (Die Nebelstadt)**
mm   (EMS 6892; Paris: Editions M. Senart, 1926) 13 p. (score).
Dn 3'. *At* Heine. *Lt* French, German. *Pf* solo S, 2-2-2-2, 2-2-0-0, cel, hrp, str.
Also for solo S, pno (*WIAM* 2764).

2614 BOYD, Jeanne M. **Eleventurous dances** (facsimile of autograph
mm   at PPFleisher, 1951) 82 p. (score, parts).
Dn 21'. *Pf* 3pic-2-3bcl-3cbn, tim, per, pno, str. *Ct* Preludicrous, Allemandarin,
Courantics, Sarabandon, Habanearly, Minuetiquette, Polkaleidoscope, Pavan-
illa, Valsetting, Marchness, Giguerilla. Originally for 2 flu, cla, pno, string
quartet (1943) and first performed at the Festival of Women Composers in
Basel, 1950. Boyd arranged the piece for full orchestra in 1951. *Eleventurous
dances* was commissioned by the Sigma Alpha Iota music fraternity and is
dedicated to the memory of Lewis Carroll.

2615 BOYD, Jeanne M. **Introduction and fugue** (facsimile of MS at
mm   PPFleisher, 1949) 34 p. (score, parts).
Dn 7'. *Pf* 2-2-2-2, 4-2-3-1, tim, per, str. First performed in 1960 by the
Rochester Symphony Orchestra under the direction of Howard Hanson.

2616 BOYD, Jeanne M. **Symphonic poem. Song against ease**
mm   (facsimile of MS at PPFleisher, 1940) 66 p. (score).
Dn 17′. *Pf* 3pic-3enh-3bcl-2, 4-2-3-1, tim, per, hrp, str. First performed in 1946 by the Rochester Symphony Orchestra under the direction of Howard Hanson. Boyd based the piece on Scharmel Iris's poem *Song against ease* from the author's *Bread out of stone*.

2617 COLE, Ulric. **Divertimento for string orchestra and piano**
mm   (JF&B 0368; New York: J. Fischer, 1939) 48 p. (score).
Dn 16′. Also arranged for 2 pno (*WIAM* 2427).

2618 COLE, Ulric. **Sunlight channel** (facsimile of MS at NN, [194-])
mm   28 p.
Dn 10′. *Pf* 3pic-2-2-2, 4-3-3-0, tim, per including cel, hrp, str.

2619 DANIELS, Mabel Wheeler. **Deep forest for symphony**
md   **orchestra, op. 34, no. 1** (facsimile of autograph at PPFleisher, n.d.) 31 p. (score, parts).
Prelude. *Dn* 6′. *Da* Aug. 1933. *Pf* 2-2-2-2, 4-2-3-1, tim, per, hrp, str. Facsimile of MS, parts on rental at C. Fischer, New York. Originally for chamber orchestra (*WIAM* 2620).

2620 DANIELS, Mabel Wheeler. **Deep forest, op. 34, no. 1** (JF&B
md   0296; New York: J. Fischer, 1932) 26 p. (score, parts).
Prelude. *Dn* 6′. *Pf* 1-1-1-1, 1-1-0-0, tim, per. Score, parts on rental at C. Fischer, New York. Dedicated to the Barrère Little Symphony. Also for full orchestra (*WIAM* 2619). *Rg Survey of American women composers*, Composers Recordings, CRI SRD 145.

2621 DANIELS, Mabel Wheeler. **Pirates' island, op. 34, no. 2**
md   (facsimile of autograph at PPFleisher, n.d.) 66 p. (score, parts).
Dn 9′. *La* MB, score and string parts only. *Pf* 3pic-2-2-2, 4-2-3-1, tim, per including xyl, str.

2622 GALAJIKIAN, Florence G. **Symphonic intermezzo** (facsimile
mm   of MS at PPFleisher, 1931) 40 p. (score, parts).
Dn 12′. *Pf* 3-3enh-3bcl-2cbn, 4-3-3-1, tim, per, hrp, str.

2623 GALAJIKIAN, Florence G. **Tragic overture for full orches-**
mm   **tra** (facsimile of MS at PPFleisher, 1934) 53 p. (score, parts).
Dn 12′. *Pf* 3-3enh-3bcl-2cbn, 4-3-3-1, tim, per, hrp, str.

2624 HIER, Ethel Glenn. **Carolina Christmas** (New York: Compos-
mm   ers Facsimile Ed., 1952) 25 p. (score).
Suite. *Dn* 10′. *Pf* 2-2-2-2, 4-0-0-0, str. *Ct* Cousin Callie's garden, A tramp to holly hedge, Mocking birds at Johnson's pond, Twilight on the plantation. Also for 2 pno, 4 hands (facsimile of MS at NNAMC, 1927); for pno, 4 hands (facsimile of MS at NNAMC, 1927); and for string quartet (facsimile of MS at NNAMC, n.d.).

2625 HIER, Ethel Glenn. **Choreographe. Ballet suite for orchestra**
mm   (New York: Composers Facsimile Ed., 1952) 31 p. (score).
Dn 10′. *Pf* 2-2-2-2, 4-2-3-1, str.

2626 HIER, Ethel Glenn. **Three pieces for orchestra** (CP 353; New
mm   York: Composers Press, 1954) 63 p. (score).
Dn 12′. *Pf* 3pic-2-3bcl-2; 4-3-3-1; tim; per including cel, glk; hrp; pno; str. *Ct* Foreboding, *Asolo bells*, *Badinage*. Given the 1953 Symphonic Award sponsored by Composers Press. *Asolo bells* originally for pno as *Campane d'Asolo* (*WIAM* 2685), and also arranged for 2 pno, 4 hands (*WIAM* 2438). *Badinage* also for pno (*WIAM* 2683). Hier transcribed *Asolo bells* for orchestra in 1938, and the orchestral version was first performed in Rochester, N.Y. under the direction of Howard Hanson. Score and parts are at PPFleisher.

2627 HOWE, Mary. **Agreeable overture for chamber orchestra**
mm   (facsimile of autograph at NN, n.d.) 32 p. (score).
Dn 8′. *La* DLC. *Pf* 2pic-2enh-2-1, 2-2-1-0, tim, per including xyl, str. The composer's name is inked out, and "by Oriana" inserted.

2628 HOWE, Mary. **Ambience** (facsimile of MS at NN, n.d.) 16 p.
md   (score).
Dn 6′. *Pf* 2-1-1-1, 2-2-1-1, tim, str. *Tm Three scores for orchestra* (*WIAM* 2643).

2629 HOWE, Mary. **American piece** (facsimile of autograph at NN,
mm   n.d.) 55 p. (score).
Dn 20′. *La* DLC. *Pf* 3pic-2-2-2, 4-3-3-1, tim, per, hrp, str.

2630 HOWE, Mary. **Attente** (facsimile of MS at NN, n.d.) 15 p.
md   (score).
Dn 6′. *Pf* 3pic-1-1-1, 3-2-3-1, tim, str. *Tm Three scores for orchestra* (*WIAM* 2643).

2631 HOWE, Mary. **Axiom. Free passacaglia with fugue for**
mm   **chamber orchestra** (facsimile of autograph at NN, [1932?]) 45 p. (score).
Dn 19′. *Pf* 1-2enh-2-1, 2-2-1-0, tim, per including cel, hrp, str.

2632 HOWE, Mary. **Castellana. Romanesca on Spanish themes**
mm   (facsimile of MS at NN, [1935?]) 63 p. (score).
Dn 30′. *La* DLC. *Pf* 3pic-2-2-2; 4-3-3-1; tim; per; str; solo 2 pno, 4 hands. *Rg* Composers Recordings, CRI 124.

2633 HOWE, Mary. **Coulennes. Tableau de genre** (facsimile of
mm   autograph at NN, [1936]) 14 p. (score).
Dn 10′. *La* DLC. *Pf* 1-0-0-0, 1-0-0-0, tim, per, str. Facsimile of MS, parts on rental at C. Fischer, New York.

2634 HOWE, Mary. **Dirge** (facsimile of autograph at NN, 1931) 18 p.
mm   (score).
Dn 11′. *Pf* 2-2-2-2, 4-3-3-1, tim, per, str.

2635 HOWE, Mary. **Irish lullaby** (facsimile of MS on rental; New
mm   York: C. Fischer, n.d.) 6 p. (score, parts).
Dn 2′. *At* Helen Coale Crew. *Pf* solo voc, flu or cla, 4 hrn, str. Also for solo voc, pno (*WIAM* 2910).

2636 HOWE, Mary. **Ombrine** (facsimile of MS at NN, n.d.) 26 p.
md   (score).
Dn 8′. *Pf* 2-2-1-1, 2-0-0-0, tim, str. *Tm Three scores for orchestra* (*WIAM* 2643).

2637 HOWE, Mary. **Paean for orchestra** (facsimile of autograph at
mm   NN, [194-]) 38 p. (score).
Dn 15′. *Pf* 3pic-2-2-2, 4-3-3-1-sax, tim, per including xyl, hrp, str. Facsimile of MS, parts on rental at C. Fischer, New York.

2638 HOWE, Mary. **Poema for orchestra** (facsimile of autograph at
mm   NN, [194-]) 38 p. (score).
Dn 15′. *Pf* 3pic-2-2-2, 4-2-2-1, tim, hrp, str.

2639 HOWE, Mary. **Potomac. Suite for orchestra** (facsimile of MS
mm   at NN, [1940]) 64 p. (score).
Dn 25′. *La* DLC. *Pf* 3pic-2-2-1, 2-2-2-1, tim, per, str. *Ct* Prelude, Mt. Vernon, Arlington, Watergate. Facsimile of MS, parts on rental at C. Fischer, New York.

2640 HOWE, Mary. **Rock** (2295; New York: Galaxy Music, 1963) 38
mm   p. (score).
Dn 9′. *La* DLC. *Pf* 3pic-3enh-2-1, 3-3-3-1, tim, per, hrp, str.

2641 HOWE, Mary. **Stars and Sand** (2299; New York: Galaxy Music,
mm   1963) 16 p. (score).
Dn 3′. *La* DLC, *Stars* only. *Pf* 2pic-1-1-1, 1-0-0-0, per, str. *Stars* also with *Whimsy* (*WIAM* 2642), and arranged for pno (*WIAM* 2701) and 2 pno (*WIAM* 2462). *Rg* Composers Recordings, CRI SRD 103 and CRI 124.

2642 HOWE, Mary. **Stars, Whimsy for small orchestra** (New York:
mm   Composers Press, 1939) 13 p. (score).
Dn 5′. *La* DLC. *Pf* 2pic-1-1-1, 2-1-0-0, tim, per, hrp, str. *Stars* also with *Sand* (*WIAM* 2641), arranged for pno (*WIAM* 2701) and 2 pno (*WIAM* 2462). *Whimsy* also arranged for pno (*WIAM* 2703).

2643 HOWE, Mary. **Three scores for orchestra** (facsimiles of MSS
mm   at NN, n.d.) 26, 15, 16 p. (score).
Dn 20′. *Ct Ombrine* (*WIAM* 2636), *Attente* (*WIAM* 2630), *Ambience* (*WIAM* 2628).

2644 JAMES, Dorothy. **Pastorales** (facsimile of MS at PPFleisher,
mm   1934) 16 p. (score).
Dn 8′. *Da* 1933. *La* composer. *Pf* hrp, str, solo cla.   *(Composer)*

2645 JAMES, Dorothy. **Symphonic fragments** (facsimile of MS at
mm   PPFleisher, 1932) 36 p. (score, parts).
Dn 8′. *La* composer. *Pf* 3-3-3-3, 4-2-3-1, tim, per, str.   *(Composer)*

2646 MANA ZUCCA. **Concerto no. 1 for piano and orchestra, op.**
mm **49** (Miami, Fla.: Congress Music, 1948) 53 p. (piano reduction).
Dn 30'. *Pf* original orchestration arranged for 2nd pno, solo pno. First
published by Boston Music, 1920.

2647 MANA ZUCCA. **Violin concerto, op. 224** (Miami, Fla.:
mm Congress Music, 1955) 47 p. (piano reduction).
Dn 30'. *Pf* original orchestration arranged for pno, solo vln.

2648 RALSTON, Frances Marion. **Rhapsodie for piano and**
md **orchestra, op. 50, no. 1** (Los Angeles: composer, 1938) 40 p.
(piano reduction).
Dn 11'. *Pf* original orchestration arranged for 2nd pno, solo pno.

2649 URNER, Catherine Murphy. **Concerto for flute and orches-**
mm **tra** (facsimile of MS at CU, 1978) 85 p. (score, parts).
Dn 17'. *Da* 1940. *Pf* 2-2-2bcl-2, 2-2-2-1, tim, per, str, solo flu.   *(Elise Kuhl Kirk)*

2650 URNER, Catherine Murphy. **Esquisses normandes** (facsimile
mm of MS at CU, 1978) 71 p. (score, parts).
Dn 17'. *Da* 1929. *Pf* 1-1-1-1, 1-1-0-0, tim, per, str. Orchestrated by Charles
Koechlin in 1945.   *(Elise Kuhl Kirk)*

2651 URNER, Catherine Murphy. **Three movements for chamber**
mm **orchestra** (facsimile of MS at CU, 1978) 59 p. (score).
Dn 12'. *Da* 1940. *Pf* 2-2enh-2-2, 2-0-0-0, str.   *(Elise Kuhl Kirk)*

Solo instrumental music

2653 BAUER, Marion. **Anagrams, op. 38** (New York: Composers
mm Facsimile Ed., 1959) 5 p.
Dn 1'. *Da* 19 June 1950. *Pf* pno.

2654 BAUER, Marion. **Aquarelle [I], op. 39, no. 1** (Providence:
md Axelrod, 1944) 4 p.
Dn 1'. *Pf* pno.

2655 BAUER, Marion. **Aquarelle II, op. 39, no. 2** (facsimile of
md autograph at DLC, [1950?]) 3 p.
Dn 2'. *Pf* pno. Also arranged for chamber ensemble (*WIAM* 2403).

2656 BAUER, Marion. **Eight diversions from a composer's note-**
mm **book** (9118; New York: Chappell, 1953) 16 p.
Dn 10'. *Pf* pno.

2657 BAUER, Marion. **Fancy, A, op. 21, no. 1** (Providence: Axelrod,
md 1939) 3 p.
Dn 2'. *Pf* pno.

2658 BAUER, Marion. **Four piano pieces, op. 21, nos. 1-4** (CC 2;
mm New York: Cos-Cob, 1930) 12 p.
Dn 6'. *Ct* Chromaticon, Ostinato, Toccata, Syncope.

2659 BAUER, Marion. **From the New Hampshire woods, op. 12,**
mm **nos. 1-3** (30797, 31199-31200; New York: G. Schirmer, 1923) 7, 5,
7 p.
Suite. *Dn* 11'. *Da* 1921. *Pf* pno. *Ct* White birches (*WIAM* 2672), Indian pipes
(*WIAM* 2661), Pine trees (*WIAM* 2664). *Indian pipes* arranged for orchestra by
Martin BERNSTEIN (*WIAM* 2601).

2660 BAUER, Marion. **In the country, op. 5, nos. 1-4. Four little**
mm **piano pieces** (APS 9847-9850; Boston: A.P. Schmidt, 1913) 3, 5, 3,
5 p.
Dn 5'. *La* DLC, Schmidt Collection. *Pf* pno. *Ct* At the cross roads, In the
market place, The village gossips, The trysting hour.

2661 BAUER, Marion. **Indian pipes, op. 12, no. 2** (31199; New
md York: G. Schirmer, 1923) 5 p.
Dn 3'. *Da* 1921. *Pf* pno. *Tm From the New Hampshire woods, op. 12.* Also
arranged for orchestra by Martin Bernstein (*WIAM* 2601).

2662 BAUER, Marion. **New solfeggietto after C.P.E. Bach, A**
mm (168; New York: Mercury Music, 1948) 3 p.
Dn 1'. *Pf* pno.

2663 BAUER, Marion. **Parade** (169; New York: Mercury Music, 1948)
mm 3 p.
Dn 1'. *Pf* pno.

2664 BAUER, Marion. **Pine trees, op. 12, no. 3** (31200; New York:
md G. Schirmer, 1923) 7 p.
Dn 3'. *Pf* pno. *Tm From the New Hampshire woods, op. 12* (*WIAM* 2659).

2665 BAUER, Marion. **Six preludes for the pianoforte, op. 15**
mm (APS 12716; Boston: A.P. Schmidt, 1922) 23 p.
Dn 13'. Dedicated to Amy Cheney Beach.

2666 BAUER, Marion. **Spring day** (170; New York: Mercury Music,
mm 1948) 5 p.
Dn 2'. *Pf* pno. *Ct* In a swing, Cherry blossoms, Drifting down a stream.

2667 BAUER, Marion. **Summertime suite. Eight pieces for stu-**
mm **dents** (New York: Leeds Music, 1953) 20 p.
Dn 9'. *Pf* pno. *Ct* A rainy day, A gallop in the park, Pond lilies, Whippet race,
Nodding mandarins, The waterwheel, Fireflies, Mermaids.

2668 BAUER, Marion. **Three preludettes. Melodic studies for**
mm **pianoforte** (31421; New York: G. Schirmer, 1923) 7 p.
Dn 5'.

2669 BAUER, Marion. **Tumbling Tommy** (171; New York: Mercury
mm Music, 1948) 3 p.
Dn 1'. *Pf* pno.

2670 BAUER, Marion. **Turbulence, op. 17, no. 2** (11805; New York:
md E.B. Marks, 1942) 6 p.
Dn 1'. *Pf* pno.

2671 BAUER, Marion. **Water wheel, The** (New York: MCA Music,
mm 1953) 5 p.
Dn 1'. *Pf* pno.

2672 BAUER, Marion. **White birches, op. 12, no. 1** (30797; New
md York: G. Schirmer, 1923) 7 p.
Dn 5'. *Pf* pno. *Tm From the New Hampshire woods, op. 12* (*WIAM* 2659).

2673 BEHREND, Jeanne. **Dance into space** (Delaware Water Gap,
mm Penn.: Shawnee, 1942) 5 p.
Dn 3'. *Da* Jan. 1933. *La* composer. *Pf* pno.   *(Composer)*

2674 BEHREND, Jeanne. **From dawn until dusk. A child's day**
mm (Bryn Mawr, Penn.: Elkan-Vogel, 1936) 21 p.
Dn 15'. *Da* Aug. 1934. *La* composer. *Pf* pno.   *(Composer)*

2675 BEHREND, Jeanne. **Quiet piece** (Delaware Water Gap, Penn.:
mm Shawnee, 1941) 3 p.
Dn 4'. *Da* Jan. 1932. *La* composer. *Pf* pno.   *(Composer)*

2676 CLARKE, Rebecca. **Cortege** (facsimile of MS at NN, n.d.) 4 p.
mm
Dn 4'. *Da* 1930. *La* composer. *Pf* pno.   *(Christopher Johnson)*

2677 COLE, Ulric. **Above the clouds** (18777; Cincinnati: J. Church,
mm 1924) 7 p.
Dn 4'. *Pf* pno.

2678 COLE, Ulric. **Metropolitones** (40143/45; New York: G.
mm Schirmer, 1943) 6, 5, 6 p.
Dn 5'. *Pf* pno. *Ct* Harlem meander, Lullaby in the park, Man-about-town. Man-
about-town also for 2 pno, 4 hands (*WIAM* 2428)

2679 COLE, Ulric. **Vignette I** (JF&B 7191; New York: J. Fischer,
mm 1936) 7 p.
Dn 5'. *Pf* pno.

2680 COLE, Ulric. **Vignette II** (JF&B 7192; New York: J. Fischer,
mm 1936) 5 p.
Dn 3'. *Pf* pno.

2681 COLE, Ulric. **Vignette III** (JF&B 7193; New York: J. Fischer,
mm 1936) 7 p.

Dn 5'. Pf pno.

2682 GALAJIKIAN, Florence G. **Piece for organ** (facsimile of MS
mm   at NN, n.d.) 4 p.
Dn 3'.

2683 HIER, Ethel Glenn. **Badinage** (CP 304; New York: Composers
mm   Press, 1949) 5 p.
Dn 2'. Pf pno. Also for orchestra (WIAM 2626).

2684 HIER, Ethel Glenn. **Ballade** (New York: Composers Facsimile
mm   Ed., 1952) 6 p.
Dn 8'. Pf pno.

2685 HIER, Ethel Glenn. **Campane d'Asolo** (CP 47; New York:
mm   Composers Press, 1938) 7 p.
Dn 4'. Pf pno. Also arranged for 2 pno, 4 hands (WIAM 2438) and for
orchestra (WIAM 2626) as Asolo Bells.

2686 HIER, Ethel Glenn. **Day in the Peterborough woods, A, op.
mm   19, nos. 1-5. Suite for piano** (GM 104-108; Chicago: Gilbert
        Music, 1924) 5, 5, 5, 5, 5 p.
Dn 10'. Ct The robin, Bobolink, The wood-thrush, Sunset at Hillcrest, The
whippoorwill.

2687 HIER, Ethel Glenn. **Dragon-flies, op. 16. Barcarole** (2443;
mm   Cincinnati: Willis Music, 1913) 7 p.
Dn 2'. Pf pno.

2688 HIER, Ethel Glenn. **Prelude** (CP 46; New York: Composers
mm   Press, 1938) 5 p.
Dn 2'. Pf pno.

2689 HIER, Ethel Glenn. **Study in fourths and fifths** (New York:
mm   Composers Facsimile Ed., 1953) 4 p.
Dn 3'. Pf pno.

2690 HIER, Ethel Glenn. **Study in thirds** (New York: Composers
mm   Facsimile Ed., 1953) 4 p.
Dn 3'. Pf pno.

2691 HOWE, Mary. **Berceuse** (32297; New York: G. Schirmer, 1925)
mm   5 p.
Dn 2'. La DLC. Pf pno. Also for solo voc, pno (WIAM 2899).

2692 HOWE, Mary. **Blue hills. Sketch for piano** (facsimile of
mm   autograph at NN, [1941?]) 3 p.
Dn 1'.

2693 HOWE, Mary. **Clog-dance (Possum-a-lah). Sketch for piano**
mm   (facsimile of autograph at NN, [194-]) 6 p.
Dn 3'.

2694 HOWE, Mary. **Elegy** (COS 21; New York: H.W. Gray, 1948) 7 p.
mm
Dn 3'. La DLC. Pf org.

2695 HOWE, Mary. **Estudio brillante for piano** (facsimile of auto-
mm   graph at NN, [194-]) 6 p.
Dn 3'.

2696 HOWE, Mary. **For a wedding** (facsimile of autograph at NN,
mm   n.d.) 4 p.
Dn 5'. La DLC. Pf org.

2697 HOWE, Mary. **Intermezzo in B-flat major for piano** (facsimile
mm   of autograph at NN, [194-]) [2] p.
Dn 2'.

2698 HOWE, Mary. **Intermezzo [in E-flat major for piano]** (facsimm   mile of autograph at NN, [194-]) [3] p.
Dn 2'.

2699 HOWE, Mary. **Nocturne** (32441; New York: G. Schirmer, 1925)
mm   5 p.
Dn 2'. Pf pno.

2700 HOWE, Mary. **Prelude** (32173; New York: G. Schirmer, 1925) 5
mm   p.
Dn 2'. Pf pno.

2701 HOWE, Mary. **Stars** (CP 49; New York: Composers Press, 1938)
mm   5 p. (piano reduction).
Dn 3'. La DLC. Pf pno. Originally for chamber orchestra (WIAM 2641, 2642).

2702 HOWE, Mary. **Trifle for piano** (facsimile of autograph at NN,
mm   n.d.) [6] p.
Dn 5'.

2703 HOWE, Mary. **Whimsy** (CP 48; New York: Composers Press,
mm   1938) 3 p. (piano reduction).
Dn 2'. La DLC. Pf pno. Originally for chamber orchestra (WIAM 2642).

2704 JACKSON, Elizabeth B. **Berceuse**, Organ Portfolio III/17 (June
mp   1940) 59-60.
Dn 4'. Da 1940. La publisher. Pf org.   (Composer)

2705 JACKSON, Elizabeth B. **Tranquillity**, Organ Portfolio II/12
mp   (Aug 1939) 66-67.
Dn 2'. Da 1939. La publisher. Pf org.   (Composer)

2706 JACKSON, Elizabeth B. **Worship**, Organ Portfolio I/4 (Apr
mp   1938) 6-7.
Dn 3'. Da 1938. La publisher. Pf org.   (Composer)

2707 JAMES, Dorothy. **Autumnal** (632; New York: H.W. Gray, 1937)
mm   3 p.
Dn 2'. Da 1937. La publisher. Pf org.   (Composer)

2708 MANA ZUCCA. **Jocosity, op. 283** (Miami, Fla.: Congress
mm   Music, 1972) 5 p.
Dn 4'. Pf pno.

2709 MANA ZUCCA. **Moment espagnol for pianoforte, op. 293**
mm   (Miami, Fla.: Congress Music, 1977) 5 p. $1.
Dn 4'.

2710 MANA ZUCCA. **My musical calendar, book no. 3, op. 183,
mm   nos. 1-31. Southern California impressions** (Miami, Fla.:
        Congress Music, 1940) 42 p.
Dn 29'. Pf pno. Ct Southern Californians, Blue Pacific, Los Angeles, Overland
trail, Catalina Island, Glass bottom boats, Dancing spray, A memoir, Resignation, Poppy fields, The Mission play, Santa Ana, Agua Caliente, Sombrero
dance, Tia Juana, A thought, Another thought, No use thinking, A Pasadena
garden, Grimaces, A preview, Hollywood studios, Dusk, Mid-night, Starlit
nights, A picnic lunch, A whiff, Santa Monica, Nature's grandeur, Lovely
Coronado, Lazy Beach.

2711 MANA ZUCCA. **My musical calendar, book no. 5, op. 185,
mm   nos. 1-30. Yosemite Valley impressions** (Miami, Fla.: Congress
        Music, 1942) 38 p.
Dn 31'. Pf pno. Ct Yosemite valley; Valley sunset; Redwood trees; Sequoia
grove; Tenaya Lake; The donkey ride up the trail; The trail; A pleasant
memory; Mirror Lake; Towers; The gazelle; Camp fires; Expectancy; Glacier
Point; Angry streams; Emerald Isle; Boundless canyon; Bridalveil Fall; Deep
grassy valley; A cliff; Hiking; Hitchhiking; A sigh; Zephyr Cove, Shimmering
skies; Tioga Pass; Green, green meadows; Tiny falls; O lovely night; Wawona.

2712 MANA ZUCCA. **My musical calendar, book no. 6, op. 186,
mm   nos. 1-30. New York impressions** (Miami, Fla.: Congress Music,
        1940) 39 p.
Dn 22'. Pf pno. Ct New York harbor--fog-bound, Terrific traffic, Wall Street,
Fifth Avenue cathedral, Side streets, A tranquil night, Greenwich Village,
Rockefeller Center, Bell boys, Sky scrapers, Chic women, At St. Bartholomew's,
The mall, Skyline, Grant's Tomb, Harlemites, Columbus Circle orators, Drizzle,
The sophisticates, Park Avenue, Hustle-bustle, Washington Bridge, A bleak
day, The ghetto, Torn-up streets, More torn-up streets, And more torn-up
streets, Memories, The Bronx Zoo, New York fugue (free style).

2713 MANA ZUCCA. **Piano sonata no. 3, op. 281** (Miami, Fla.:
mm   Congress Music, 1973) 34 p. $5.
Dn 20'.

2714 PRICE, Florence B. **Adoration**, Organ Portfolio XV/86 (Dec
mp   1951) 34-35.
Dn 4'. Pf org.
                                              (Barbara Garvey Jackson)

2715 PRICE, Florence B. **At the cotton gin. A southern sketch**
mm   (33200; New York: G. Schirmer, 1927) 5 p.
Dn 3′. *Pf* pno.

2716 PRICE, Florence B. **Dances in the canebrakes** (AMI 3201; Los
mm   Angeles: Affiliated Musicians, 1953) 13 p.
Dn 7′. *Pf* pno. *Ct* Nimble feet, Tropical noon, Silk hat and walking cane.

2717 PRICE, Florence B. **In quiet mood** (1822; New York: Galaxy,
mm   1951) 5 p.
Dn 3′. *Pf* org.

2718 PRICE, Florence B. **Levee dance** (26545; Philadelphia: T.
mm   Presser, 1937) 7 p.
Dn 3′. *Pf* pno.

2719 RALSTON, Frances Marion. **Scotch idyll** (1666; Chicago: C.F.
mm   Summy, 1916) 5 p.
Dn 10′. *Pf* org.   *(Joan M. Meggett)*

2720 RALSTON, Frances Marion. **Sonata for piano** (Chicago: C.F.
mm   Summy, 1921) 28 p.
Dn 15′.

2721 RALSTON, Frances Marion. **Song without words, op. 10,**
md   **no. 1** (5426; St. Louis: Balmer & Weber, 1905) 6 p.
Dn 2′. *Pf* pno.

2722 RALSTON, Frances Marion. **Theme and variations** (Chicago:
mm   C.F. Summy, 1919) 17 p.
Dn 20′. *Pf* pno.   *(Joan M. Meggett)*

2723 RALSTON, Frances Marion. **Three little waltzes** (CP 214-
mm   216; New York: Composers Press, 1946) 5, [2], 5 p.
Dn 6′. *Pf* pno.

2724 SEEGER, Ruth Crawford. **Diaphonic suite no. 1** (1930)
mm   (New York: Continuo Music, 1972) 6 p.
Dn 3′. *La* DLC. *Pf* flu or obo.

2725 SEEGER, Ruth Crawford. **Four preludes for piano [nos.**
mp   **6-9],** *New Music* II/1 (Oct 1928) 1-15.
Dn 5′. *Rg* Composers Recordings, CRI SD 247.

2726 SEEGER, Ruth Crawford. **Piano study in mixed accents,** *New*
mp   *Music* VI/1 (Oct 1932) 2-5.
Dn 1′. *Rg* Composers Recordings, CRI SD 247.

2727 URNER, Catherine Murphy. **Barcarolle** (facsimile of MS at
mm   CU, 1978) 3 p.
Dn 3′. *Da* 1932. *Pf* org.   *(Elise Kuhl Kirk)*

2728 URNER, Catherine Murphy. **Piano suite for children** (facsimm   mile of MS at CU, 1978) 5 p.
Dn 3′.   *(Elise Kuhl Kirk)*

2729 URNER, Catherine Murphy. **Two traditional American**
mm   **Indian songs for organ** (facsimile of MS at CU, 1978) 5 p.
Dn 4′.   *(Elise Kuhl Kirk)*

Stage works

2730 BOYD, Jeanne M. **My divinity. A musical comedy in three**
mm   **acts** ([Chicago]: composer, 1911) 50 p.
Dn 30′. *Li* composer, Winifred Seeger. *Pf* solo 7 girls, 4 boys, choral unison or
duo (children). Written for and presented by the Frances Shimer School, U. of
Chicago, Mt. Carroll, Ill.

2731 DANIELS, Mabel Wheeler. **Copper complication, A** (Boston:
mc   White-Smith, 1900) 48 p. (piano reduction).
Selections from the musical comedy. *Dn* 33′. *At* composer. *Li* Rebecca L.
Hooper. *Pf* 3S-3A, choral SSA, pno. *Ct* Click-clack, Gay Nannette, Love's a
dream, From over the sea, Winter man, Boating song, For the king, Entrance of
robber band, Nightingale's song, Love steals softly, Finale. Written for
Radcliffe Col. for a 60-member women's chorus and orchestra. Daniels and
Hooper were members of the class of 1900.

2732 DANIELS, Mabel Wheeler. **Court of hearts, The. Selections**
mm   (Boston: White-Smith, 1901) 32 p. (piano-vocal score).
Comic opera. *Dn* 13′. *At* Rebecca L. Hooper. *Pf* solo SSAA, choral SSAA, pno.
Ct The hunting fete, Song of the Jacks, Cupid is roving, Song of the jolly joker,
Dear one I love thee, Ching-a-ling, The fountains of Ambrosia, Serenade. First
performed under the auspices of the composer's class of 1900, Radcliffe Col.

2733 HOWE, Mary. **Cards. A game in one trick** (facsimile of
mm   autograph at NN, n.d.) 32 p. (piano reduction).
Ballet. *Dn* 15′. *La* DLC. *Pf* per, 2 pno. Originally with chamber orchestra. *Ct*
March dance of the King of Spades, Rolic of the Ace of Clubs, Intermezzo,
Polka of the Knave of Diamonds, Entrance and waltz of the Queen of Hearts,
Finale.

2734 HOWE, Mary. **Jongleur de Notre Dame, Le** (facsimile of MS
mm   at NN, [1959?]) 51 p. (score).
Ballet. *Dn* 15′. *Pf* 1-1-1-1, 2-2-2-1, tim, str.

Vocal music

2735 BAUER, Marion. **By the Indus** (APS 11046; Boston: A.P.
mm   Schmidt, 1917) 7 p.
Dn 3′. *La* DLC. *At* Cale Young Rice. *St* Song surf. *Pf* solo voc, pno.

2736 BAUER, Marion. **Coyote song** (APS 9651; Boston: A.P.
mm   Schmidt, 1912) 7 p.
Dn 2′. *La* DLC, Schmidt Collection. *At* John S. Reed. *Pf* solo voc, pno.

2737 BAUER, Marion. **Epitaph of a butterfly, The** (73759; Boston:
mm   O. Ditson, 1921) 5 p.
Dn 1′. *At* Thomas Walsh. *Pf* solo voc, pno.

2738 BAUER, Marion. **Four poems, op. 16, nos. 1-4** (31827; New
mm   York: G. Schirmer, 1924) 40 p.
Dn 15′. *At* John Gould Fletcher. *Pf* solo voc, pno. *Ct* Through the upland
meadows, I love the night, Midsummer dreams, In the bosom of the desert.

2739 BAUER, Marion. **Gold of the day** (APS 12251; Boston: A.P.
mm   Schmidt, 1921) 7 p.
Dn 1′. *La* DLC, Schmidt Collection. *At* Katharine Adams. *Pf* solo voc, pno.

2740 BAUER, Marion. **Harp, The** (New York: Broadcast Music, 1947)
mm   5 p.
Dn 1′. *At* Edna Castleman Bailey. *Pf* solo voc, pno.

2741 BAUER, Marion. **Linnet is tuning her flute, The** (APS 10653;
mm   Boston: A.P. Schmidt, 1915) 6 p.
Dn 1′. *La* DLC, Schmidt Collection. *At* Louis Untermeyer. *St* First love. *Pf* solo
voc, pno.

2742 BAUER, Marion. **Little lane, A** (APS 10374; Boston: A.P.
mm   Schmidt, 1914) 5 p.
Dn 2′. *At* Ellen Glasgow. *Pf* solo voc, pno.

2743 BAUER, Marion. **Malay to his master, The** (New York:
mm   Composers Facsimile Ed., 1959) 8 p.
Dn 5′. *At* Cale Young Rice. *Pf* solo voc, pno.   *(Rosalie Calabrese)*

2744 BAUER, Marion. **Minstrel of romance, The** (APS 11045;
mm   Boston: A.P. Schmidt, 1917) 5 p.
Dn 2′. *La* DLC, Schmidt Collection. *At* John S. Reed. *Pf* solo voc, pno.

2745 BAUER, Marion. **Night in the woods** (29985; New York: G.
mm   Schirmer, 1921) 5 p.
Dn 3′. *At* Edward Rowland Sill. *Pf* solo voc, pno.

2747 BAUER, Marion. **Nocturne** (facsimile of MS at NN, n.d.) 3 p.
mm
Dn 1′. *At* Herbert French. *Pf* solo voc, pno.

2749 BAUER, Marion. **Only of thee and me** (APS 10372; Boston:
mm   A.P. Schmidt, 1914) 5 p.
Dn 2′. *La* DLC, Schmidt Collection. *At* Louis Untermeyer. *St* First love. *Pf* solo
voc, pno.

2750 BAUER, Marion. **Parable, A. The blade of grass** (30961; New
mm   York: G. Schirmer, 1922) 5 p.

Dn 2′ . At Stephen Crane. St Dark riders. Pf solo voc, pno.

2751 BAUER, Marion. **Phillis** (APS 10377; Boston: A.P. Schmidt,
mm   1914) 5 p.
Dn 2′ . La DLC, Schmidt Collection. At Charles Riviere Defresny. Pf solo voc,
pno.

2752 BAUER, Marion. **Red man's Requiem** (APS 9653; Boston: A.P.
mm   Schmidt, 1912) 7 p.
Dn 2′ . La DLC, Schmidt Collection. At Emilie Frances Bauer. Pf solo voc, pno.

2753 BAUER, Marion. **Roses breathe in the night** (29986; New
mm   York: G. Schirmer, 1921) 7 p.
Dn 2′ . At Margaret Widdemer. Pf solo voc, pno.

2754 BAUER, Marion. **Send me a dream (Intuition)** (APS 9648;
mm   Boston: A.P. Schmidt, 1912) 7 p.
Dn 2′ . La DLC, Schmidt Collection. At Emilie Frances Bauer. Pf solo voc, pno.

2755 BAUER, Marion. **Star trysts** (APS 9654; Boston: A.P. Schmidt,
mm   1912) 7 p.
Dn 2′ . At Thomas Walsh. Pf solo voc, pno.

2756 BAUER, Marion. **Swan** (New York: Broadcast Music, 1947) 5 p.
mm
Dn 1′ . At Edna Castleman Bailey. Pf solo voc, pno.

2757 BAUER, Marion. **Thoughts** (APS 12253; Boston: A.P. Schmidt,
mm   1921) 5 p.
Dn 1′ . La DLC, Schmidt Collection. At Katharine Adams. Pf solo voc, pno.

2758 BAUER, Marion. **To losers** (facsimile of MS at NN, 1932) 3 p.
mm
Dn 1′ . At Frances Frost. Pf solo voc, pno.

2759 BAUER, Marion. **Wood song of Triboulet, op. 33, no. 1**
md   (facsimile of autograph at DLC, n.d.) [4] p.
Dn 2′ . La DLC. At William Rose Benét. Pf solo voc, pno.

2760 BEHREND, Jeanne. **Six Teasdale songs** (Philadelphia: com-
mm   poser, 1943) 10 p.
Dn 12′ . At Sara Teasdale. Pf solo voc, pno. Ct Faults, The look, Late October, I
shall not care, Advice to a girl, Debt. Awarded the Bearnes Prize for
composition in 1936.   (Composer)

2761 BEHREND, Jeanne. **Songs** (Philadelphia: composer, 1943) 8 p.
mm
Dn 7′ . La composer. Pf solo voc, pno. Ct Righteous indignation (At James
Stephens), Procne (At Peter Quennell), A minor bird (At Robert Frost).
                                             (Composer)

2762 BEHREND, Jeanne. **Songs of a soldier** (Philadelphia: com-
mm   poser, 1944) 8 p.
Dn 8′ . Pf solo voc, pno. Ct Together (At Nathan Cohen), Plea for grace (At
Katherine J. Krause), Coming home.   (Composer)

2763 BERCKMAN, Evelyn. **Orage, L' (Sturm)** (6889; Paris: Edi-
mm   tions M. Senart, 1926) 9 p.
Dn 2′ . At Heine. Lt French, German. Pf solo S, pno. Also for voice and
orchestra (WIAM 2609).

2764 BERCKMAN, Evelyn. **Ville des nuages, La (Die Nebelstadt)**
mm   (6891; Paris: Editions M. Senart, 1926) 5 p.
Dn 3′ . Lt French, German. Pf solo S, pno. Also for voice and orchestra (WIAM
2613).

2765 BOYD, Jeanne M. **Adoration** (GM 1374; New York: Galaxy
mm   Music, 1943) 5 p.
Dn 3′ . At Scharmel Iris. Pf solo voc, pno.

2766 BOYD, Jeanne M. **At morning** (26742; New York: G. Schirmer,
mm   1916) 7 p.
Dn 2′ . At Scharmel Iris. St Lyrics of a lad. Pf solo voc, pno.

2767 BOYD, Jeanne M. **Canzonetta. A little song** (26741; New
mm   York: G. Schirmer, 1914) 5 p.
Dn 1′ . At Scharmel Iris. St Lyrics of a lad. Pf solo voc, pno.

2768 BOYD, Jeanne M. **Cape Horn gospel I** (1488; New York:
mm   Galaxy Music, 1945) 9 p.
Dn 3′ . At John Masefield. Pf solo voc, pno.

2769 BOYD, Jeanne M. **I have a rendezvous with death** (27990;
mm   New York: G. Schirmer, 1918) 7 p.
Dn 2′ . At Alan Seeger. St Poems by Alan Seeger (1916). Pf solo voc, pno.

2770 BOYD, Jeanne M. **In Italy** (416; Chicago: Gamble Hinged
mm   Music, 1915) 6 p.
Dn 1′ . At Scharmel Iris. St Lyrics of a lad. Pf solo voc, pno.

2771 BOYD, Jeanne M. **In the cool of the evening** (Fremont, Nebr.:
mm   composer, 1914) 5 p.
Dn 4′ . At composer. Pf solo voc, pno.

2772 BOYD, Jeanne M. **Invitation** (28077; New York: G. Schirmer,
mm   1918) 7 p.
Dn 2′ . At Scharmel Iris. St Lyrics of a lad. Pf solo voc, pno.

2773 BOYD, Jeanne M. **Invocation** (28079; New York: G. Schirmer,
mm   1918) 6 p.
Dn 2′ . At Scharmel Iris. St Lyrics of a lad. Pf solo voc, pno.

2774 BOYD, Jeanne M. **Tarantella, La (Italian folk dance)** (417;
mm   Chicago: Gamble Hinged Music, 1914) 9 p.
Dn 2′ . At Scharmel Iris. St Lyrics of a lad. Pf solo voc, pno.

2775 BOYD, Jeanne M. **When the bobolink sings high** (468;
mm   Chicago: Gamble Hinged Music, 1916) 7 p.
Dn 2′ . At Fanny Sage Stone. Pf solo voc, pno.

2776 BOYD, Jeanne M. **Wind from the south** (469; Chicago: Gamble
mm   Hinged Music, 1916) 9 p.
Dn 1′ . At composer. Pf solo voc, pno.

2777 BRANSCOMBE, Gena. **Across the blue Aegean Sea** (GM
mm   540; New York: Galaxy Music, 1935) 5 p.
Dn 3′ . La NN. At Anna Moody. Pf solo voc, pno.   (Laurine Elkins-Marlow)

2778 BRANSCOMBE, Gena. **Ah, love, I shall find thee** (2860; New
md   York: Boosey, 1927) 6 p.
Operatic excerpt. Dn 3′ . La NN. At composer. Pf solo voc, pno. Tm The bells of
circumstance (unfinished).   (Laurine Elkins-Marlow)

2779 BRANSCOMBE, Gena. **Autumn wind so wistful** (APS 10459;
mm   Boston: A.P. Schmidt, 1911) 5 p.
Dn 2′ . At composer. Pf solo voc, pno. Also for pno, vln with the title An old love
tale, op. 21, no. 1 (WIAM 2415).   (Laurine Elkins-Marlow)

2780 BRANSCOMBE, Gena. **Best is yet to be, The** (APS 12140;
mm   Boston: A.P. Schmidt, 1921) 7 p.
Dn 3′ . At Robert Browning. Pf solo voc, pno. (Laurine Elkins-Marlow)

2781 BRANSCOMBE, Gena. **Blow softly, maple leaves** (New
mm   York: H.W. Gray, 1945) 5 p.
Dn 2′ . At Arthur Stringer. Pf solo voc, pno. Also published with a sacred text, O
love that guides our way (WIAM 2810).   (Laurine Elkins-Marlow)

2782 BRANSCOMBE, Gena. **Bluebells drowsily ringing** (APS
mm   10751; Boston: A.P. Schmidt, 1916) 6 p.
Dn 3′ . At composer. Pf solo voc, pno.   (Laurine Elkins-Marlow)

2783 BRANSCOMBE, Gena. **Boot and saddle** (Boston: O. Ditson,
mm   1907) 5 p.
Dn 3′ . At Robert Browning. St Cavalier tunes. Pf solo voc, pno. (Laurine Elkins-
Marlow)

2784 BRANSCOMBE, Gena. **By St. Lawrence water** (APS 12144;
mm   Boston: A.P. Schmidt, 1921) 5 p.
Dn 1′ . La NN. At composer. Pf solo voc, pno. (Laurine Elkins-Marlow)

2785 BRANSCOMBE, Gena. **Changes** (APS 10684; Boston: A.P.
mm   Schmidt, 1915) 5 p.
Dn 1′ . At Paris Nesbit. Pf solo voc, pno.   (Laurine Elkins-Marlow)

2786 BRANSCOMBE, Gena. **Dear is my inlaid sword** (Boston: O.
mm   Ditson, 1911) 5 p.
Dn 2′. *At* Laurence Hope. *St* India's love lyrics. *Pf* solo voc, pno. *(Laurine Elkins-Marlow)*

2787 BRANSCOMBE, Gena. **Dear lad o' mine** (APS 10721; Boston:
mm   A.P. Schmidt, 1915) 5 p.
Dn 2′. *At* Katherine Hale. *Pf* solo voc, pno. Also for choral SSAA, pno (*WIAM* 2508). *(Laurine Elkins-Marlow)*

2788 BRANSCOMBE, Gena. **Dear little hut by the rice fields** (APS
mm   9191; Boston: A.P. Schmidt, 1911) 5 p.
Dn 1′. *At* Laurence Hope. *St* India's love lyrics. *Pf* solo voc, pno. *(Laurine Elkins-Marlow)*

2789 BRANSCOMBE, Gena. **Deserted gipsy's song** (19793; New
mm   York: G. Schirmer, 1907) 7 p.
Dn 2′. *La* NN. *At* Laurence Hope. *St* India's love lyrics. *Pf* solo voc, pno. *(Laurine Elkins-Marlow)*

2790 BRANSCOMBE, Gena. **Epitaph, An** (19989; New York: G.
mm   Schirmer, 1908) 3 p.
Dn 1′. *At* Arthur Stringer. *Pf* solo voc, pno. *(Laurine Elkins-Marlow)*

2791 BRANSCOMBE, Gena. **Eskimo cradle song,** *Canadian Music*
mp   *and Trade Journal* (1901) 13-16.
Dn 2′. *At* Sara E. Branscombe. *Pf* solo voc, pno. *(Laurine Elkins-Marlow)*

2792 BRANSCOMBE, Gena. **Every town's your home town** (New
mm   York: War Camp Community Service, 1918) 3 p.
Dn 3′. *At* Margaret Widdemer. *Pf* solo voc, pno. *(Laurine Elkins-Marlow)*

2793 BRANSCOMBE, Gena. **God of the nations** (APS 11582;
mm   Boston: A.P. Schmidt, 1917) 7 p.
Dn 3′. *At* Sara E. Branscombe. *Pf* solo SB, pno. Also for solo SB, choral SATB, pno (*WIAM* 2509). *(Laurine Elkins-Marlow)*

2794 BRANSCOMBE, Gena. **Hail ye tyme of holiedayes. A song**
mm   **of Chrystmasse** (APS 9721; Boston: A.P. Schmidt, 1912) 5 p.
Dn 2′. *At* Kendall Banning. *Pf* solo voc, pno. *(Laurine Elkins-Marlow)*

2795 BRANSCOMBE, Gena. **Happiness (Glück)** (APS 9252; Bos-
mm   ton: A.P. Schmidt, 1911) 7 p.
Dn 1′. *La* NN. *At* Joseph Freiherr von Eichendorff. *Tr* composer. *Pf* solo voc, pno.
(Laurine Elkins-Marlow)

2796 BRANSCOMBE, Gena. **I bring you heartsease** (APS 10657;
mm   Boston: A.P. Schmidt, 1915) 5 p.
Dn 2′. *At* composer. *Pf* solo voc, pno. Piano accompaniment arranged for 1-1-0-0, 2-0-1-0, str in *Orchestral accompaniments to favorite songs* (APS 11210; Schmidt, 1915) parts only; and for choral SSA, pno (*WIAM* 2510). *(Laurine Elkins-Marlow)*

2797 BRANSCOMBE, Gena. **I love you** (WR 950; Toronto: Whaley,
mm   Royce, 1903) 5 p.
Dn 1′. *At* Sara E. Branscombe. *Pf* solo voc, pno. *(Laurine Elkins-Marlow)*

2798 BRANSCOMBE, Gena. **I send my heart up to thee. Serenade**
mm   (APS 9363; Boston: A.P. Schmidt, 1905) 3 p.
Dn 2′. *La* NN. *At* Robert Browning. *St* In a gondola. *Pf* solo voc, pno. Originally published as *Serenade (Song)* (Newton Center, Mass.: Wa-Wan, 1905) and reprinted in *The Wa-Wan Press* (Ed. by Vera Brodsky Lawrence; New York: Arno & the New York Times, 1970) III, 81-82. *(Laurine Elkins-Marlow)*

2799 BRANSCOMBE, Gena. **I shall hold to life** (New York: E.F.
mm   Kalmus, 1934) 7 p.
Dn 3′. *La* NN. *At* Josephine Hancock Logan. *St* Light and darkness. *Pf* solo voc, pno. *(Laurine Elkins-Marlow)*

2800 BRANSCOMBE, Gena. **In Granada** (19794; New York: G.
mm   Schirmer, 1907) 5 p.
Dn 3′. *At* Sara E. Branscombe. *Pf* solo voc, pno. *(Laurine Elkins-Marlow)*

2801 BRANSCOMBE, Gena. **In my heart there lives a song** (5039;
mm   New York: J. Fischer, 1922) 4 p.
Dn 3′. *At* composer. *Pf* solo voc, pno. *(Laurine Elkins-Marlow)*

2802 BRANSCOMBE, Gena. **Into the light** (25831; New York: C.
mm   Fischer, 1929) 5 p.
Dn 3′. *At* composer. *Pf* solo SA, pno. Also for solo SA, 1-1-2-1, 2-2-0-0, tim, hrp, str (autograph score and parts at NN). Dedicated to the National Assoc. of Altrusa Clubs. *(Laurine Elkins-Marlow)*

2803 BRANSCOMBE, Gena. **Just before the lights are lit** (APS
mm   11305; Boston: A.P. Schmidt, 1917) 5 p.
Dn 2′. *At* composer. *Pf* solo voc, pno. *(Laurine Elkins-Marlow)*

2804 BRANSCOMBE, Gena. **Just in the hush before the dawn**
mm   (19791; New York: G. Schirmer, 1907) 4 p.
Dn 1′. *At* Laurence Hope. *St* Indian love lyrics. *Pf* solo voc, pno. Also arranged for solo voc, 1-1-2-2, 2-0-2-0, str (autograph score at NN). *(Laurine Elkins-Marlow)*

2805 BRANSCOMBE, Gena. **Krishna** (APS 9189; Boston: A.P.
mm   Schmidt, 1911) 5 p.
Dn 2′. *At* Laurence Hope. *St* India's love lyrics. *Pf* solo voc, pno. *(Laurine Elkins-Marlow)*

2806 BRANSCOMBE, Gena. **Love in a life** (19523; New York: G.
mm   Schirmer, 1907) 19 p.
Song cycle. *Dn* 15′. *At* Elizabeth Barrett Browning. *St Sonnets from the Portuguese. Pf* solo voc, pno. *Ct* I thought once how Theocritus had sung, But only three in all God's universe, How do I love thee?, The widest land, The face of all the world is changed, My own beloved. *(Laurine Elkins-Marlow)*

2807 BRANSCOMBE, Gena. **Lute of jade, A** (APS 10023/10030;
mm   Boston: A.P. Schmidt, 1913) 5, 5, 4, 6 p.
Song cycle. *Dn* 9′. *Pf* solo voc, pno. *Ct* A lovely maiden roaming, My fatherland, There was a king of Liang, Fair is the pine grove. *(Laurine Elkins-Marlow)*

2808 BRANSCOMBE, Gena. **Marching along!** (19593; New York:
mm   G. Schirmer, 1907) 4 p.
Dn 2′. *At* Robert Browning. *Pf* solo voc, pno. *(Laurine Elkins-Marlow)*

2809 BRANSCOMBE, Gena. **My love is like a tempting peach**
mm   (APS 9262; Boston: A.P. Schmidt, 1911) 5 p.
Dn 1′. *Pf* solo voc, pno. Dedicated to David Bispham. *(Laurine Elkins-Marlow)*

2810 BRANSCOMBE, Gena. **O love that guides our way** (New
mm   York: H.W. Gray, 1959) 4 p.
Sacred song. *Dn* 3′. *At* composer. *Pf* solo voc, pno. Also for choral SATB, pno (*WIAM* 2513). First published with a secular text, *Blow softly, maple leaves* (*WIAM* 2781). *(Laurine Elkins-Marlow)*

2811 BRANSCOMBE, Gena. **Of my ould loves** (APS 9250; Boston:
mm   A.P. Schmidt, 1911) 5 p.
Dn 2′. *La* NN. *At* Arthur Stringer. *Pf* solo voc, pno. Also for choral TTBB, flu, vln (autograph at NN). *(Laurine Elkins-Marlow)*

2812 BRANSCOMBE, Gena. **Old woman rain,** *Contemporary Amer-*
mc   *ican songs.* Ed. by Bernard TAYLOR (5371; Evanston, Ill.: Summy-Birchard, 1960) 32-35.
Dn 3′. *At* Louise Driscoll. *Pf* solo voc, pno. *(Laurine Elkins-Marlow)*

2813 BRANSCOMBE, Gena. **Ould Doctor Ma'Ginn** (APS 9341;
mm   Boston: A.P. Schmidt, 1911) 5 p.
Dn 3′. *At* Arthur Stringer. *Pf* solo voc, pno. *(Laurine Elkins-Marlow)*

2814 BRANSCOMBE, Gena. **Radiant as the morning** (APS 11457;
mm   Boston: A.P. Schmidt, 1918) 7 p.
Dn 3′. *At* Kendall Banning. *Pf* solo voc, pno. *(Laurine Elkins-Marlow)*

2815 BRANSCOMBE, Gena. **Resentful lover, The** (APS 10685;
mm   Boston: A.P. Schmidt, 1915) 5 p.
Dn 2′. *At* Paris Nesbit. *Pf* solo voc, pno. Dedicated to Paul Dufault. *(Laurine Elkins-Marlow)*

2816 BRANSCOMBE, Gena. **Song of a wanderer** (19760; New
mm   York: G. Schirmer, 1907) 7 p.
Dn 3′. *At* Ruth Davenport Holmes. *Pf* solo voc, pno. Dedicated to Herbert Witherspoon. *(Laurine Elkins-Marlow)*

2817 BRANSCOMBE, Gena. **Songs of the unafraid, nos. 1-6** (APS
mm   11552/11561; Boston: A.P. Schmidt, 1919) 7, 5, 5, 7, 5, 9 p.
Song cycle. *At* Kendall Banning. *Pf* solo voc, pno. *Ct* At the postern gate, The

lass of the glad gray eyes, The great adventure, An' if I had a true love, Within the walls of London, The call of the seven seas. *(Laurine Elkins-Marlow)*

2818 BRANSCOMBE, Gena. **Spirit of motherhood** (APS 13519; mm Boston: A.P. Schmidt, 1924) 7 p. (score, part).
Dn 4′. *La* NN. *At* Louise Driscoll. *Pf* solo voc, pno, optional vln. Piano part arranged for flu, obo, 2 vln, vla, vcl without vocal part (autograph score at NN). Also for choral SSA, pno (*WIAM* 2520). *(Laurine Elkins-Marlow)*

2819 BRANSCOMBE, Gena. **Sprightly Mrs. Grasshopper** (APS mm 12556; Boston: A.P. Schmidt, 1922) 5 p.
Dn 2′. *At* composer. *Pf* solo voc, pno. *(Laurine Elkins-Marlow)*

2820 BRANSCOMBE, Gena. **Starlight** (19796; New York: G. mm Schirmer, 1907) 5 p.
Dn 3′. *At* Laurence Hope. *St* Indian love lyrics. *Pf* solo voc, pno. *(Laurine Elkins-Marlow)*

2821 BRANSCOMBE, Gena. **Tender sweetness, The** (19524; New mm York: G. Schirmer, 1907) 4 p.
Dn 2′. *La* NN. *At* composer. *Pf* solo voc, pno. *(Laurine Elkins-Marlow)*

2822 BRANSCOMBE, Gena. **Then tell me how to woo thee, love** mm (19988; New York: G. Schirmer, 1908) 5 p.
Dn 2′. *At* Graham of Gartmore. *Pf* solo voc, pno. Dedicated to Herbert Witherspoon. *(Laurine Elkins-Marlow)*

2823 BRANSCOMBE, Gena. **There's a woman like a dewdrop** mm (APS 9138; Boston: A.P. Schmidt, 1911) 7 p.
Dn 3′. *La* NN. *At* Robert Browning. *St* A blot on the 'scutcheon. *Pf* solo voc, pno. *(Laurine Elkins-Marlow)*

2824 BRANSCOMBE, Gena. **Three mystic ships** (APS 11250; mm Boston: A.P. Schmidt, 1917) 5 p.
Dn 2′. *At* Katherine Tynan. *Pf* solo voc, pno. *(Laurine Elkins-Marlow)*

2825 BRANSCOMBE, Gena. **To Mirza. Persian serenade** (19594; mm New York: G. Schirmer, 1907) 7 p.
Dn 3′. *At* Sara E. Branscombe. *Pf* solo voc, pno. *(Laurine Elkins-Marlow)*

2826 BRANSCOMBE, Gena. **What are we two?**, *The Wa-Wan* mc *Press*. Ed. by Vera Brodsky LAWRENCE (New York: Arno & New York Times, 1970) III, 83-85.
Dn 2′. *At* Robert Browning. *St* In a gondola. *Pf* solo voc, pno. Previously published in 1905 (Newton Center, Mass.: Wa-Wan).

2827 BRANSCOMBE, Gena. **With rue my heart is laden** (19748; mm New York: G. Schirmer, 1907) 2 p.
Dn 1′. *At* A.E. Housman. *St* A Shropshire lad. *Pf* solo voc, pno. Dedicated to Herbert Witherspoon. *(Laurine Elkins-Marlow)*

2829 CLARKE, Rebecca. **Donkey, The** (facsimile of MS at NN, n.d.) mm 4 p.
Dn 3′. *Da* 1942. *La* composer. *At* G.K. Chesterton. *St* The donkey. *Pf* solo voc, pno. *(Christopher Johnson)*

2830 CLARKE, Rebecca. **Lethe** (facsimile of MS at NN, n.d.) 4 p. mm
Dn 5′. *Da* 1941. *La* composer. *At* Edna St. Vincent Millay. *St* Lethe. *Pf* solo voc, pno. *(Christopher Johnson)*

2831 CLARKE, Rebecca. **Shy one** (2847; London: Winthrop Rogers, mm 1920) 5 p.
Dn 2′. *Da* 1912. *La* publisher. *At* Yeats. *Pf* solo voc, pno. *(Christopher Johnson)*

2832 CLARKE, Rebecca. **Tiger, tiger** (facsimile of MS at NN, n.d.) 7 mm p.
Dn 5′. *Da* 1933. *La* composer. *At* Blake. *St* The tyger. *Pf* solo voc, pno. *(Christopher Johnson)*

2833 DANIELS, Mabel Wheeler. **At evening, op. 13, no. 2** (APS md 7394; Boston: A.P. Schmidt, 1907) 5 p.
Dn 2′. *At* composer. *Pf* solo voc, pno.

2834 DANIELS, Mabel Wheeler. **Awake my heart** (36; Boston: mm C.W. Thompson, 1901) 7 p.
Dn 3′. *Pf* solo voc, pno.

2835 DANIELS, Mabel Wheeler. **Before the king, op. 7, no. 1** md (APS 6973; Boston: A.P. Schmidt, 1905) 7 p.
Dn 3′. *La* DLC, Schmidt Collection. *At* composer. *Pf* solo voc, pno. *Tm Songs of Damascus, op. 7 (WIAM 2860).*

2836 DANIELS, Mabel Wheeler. **Beyond, op. 24, no. 1** (APS md 10655; Boston: A.P. Schmidt, 1915) 5 p.
Dn 2′. *La* DLC, Schmidt Collection. *At* Kendall Banning. *Pf* solo voc, pno.

2837 DANIELS, Mabel Wheeler. **Blue bonnet, The** (11814; Boston: mm White-Smith Music, 1902) 5 p.
Dn 1′. *At* composer. *Pf* solo voc, pno.

2838 DANIELS, Mabel Wheeler. **Call of spring, The, op. 13, no. 1** md (APS 7392; Boston: A.P. Schmidt, 1907) 5 p.
Dn 1′. *At* composer. *Pf* solo voc, pno.

2839 DANIELS, Mabel Wheeler. **Cherry flowers, op. 29, no. 1** md (APS 13615; Boston: A.P. Schmidt, 1925) 7 p.
Dn 2′. *La* DLC, Schmidt Collection; MB. *At* Agnes Campbell. *Pf* solo voc, pno.

2840 DANIELS, Mabel Wheeler. **Could I catch the wayward** md **breeze, op. 7, no. 2** (APS 6974; Boston: A.P. Schmidt, 1905) 5 p.
Dn 1′. *La* DLC, Schmidt Collection. *At* composer. *Pf* solo voc, pno. *Tm Songs of Damascus, op. 7 (WIAM 2860).*

2841 DANIELS, Mabel Wheeler. **Daybreak, op. 18, no. 2** (APS md 8576; Boston: A.P. Schmidt, 1909) 5 p.
Dn 2′. *La* DLC, Schmidt Collection. *Pf* solo voc, pno.

2842 DANIELS, Mabel Wheeler. **Desolate city, The, op. 21** (APS mm 10167; Boston: A.P. Schmidt, 1914) 15 p.
Dn 8′. *Da* 1913. *La* DLC, Schmidt Collection. *At* Wilfrid Scawen Blunt. *Pf* solo Bar, pno. Originally for voice and orchestra (autograph at MB): 1-1-2-2, 4-2-3-1, tim, hrp, str, solo Bar.

2843 DANIELS, Mabel Wheeler. **Einst (Then and now), op. 15,** md **no. 1** (APS 8203; Boston: A.P. Schmidt, 1909) [2] p.
Dn 1′. *La* DLC. *At* J. Bodenstedl. *Tr* composer. *Lt* German, English. *Pf* solo voc, pno.

2844 DANIELS, Mabel Wheeler. **Fields o' Bally close, The** (APS mm 9027; Boston: A.P. Schmidt, 1911) 5 p.
Dn 2′. *La* DLC, Schmidt Collection. *At* Denis A. McCarthy. *St* Voices from Erin. *Pf* solo voc, pno.

2845 DANIELS, Mabel Wheeler. **Glory and endless years, op. 27,** md **no. 1** (APS 12395; Boston: A.P. Schmidt, 1921) 5 p.
Dn 2′. *At* William Dean Howells. *Pf* solo voc, pno.

2846 DANIELS, Mabel Wheeler. **Highland love song, op. 9, no. 1** md (APS 7068; Boston: A.P. Schmidt, 1906) 5 p.
Dn 1′. *La* DLC, Schmidt Collection. *At* composer. *Pf* solo voc, pno. *Tm Three love songs, op. 9 (WIAM 2861).*

2847 DANIELS, Mabel Wheeler. **I cannot bide, op. 29, no. 2** (APS md 13616; Boston: A.P. Schmidt, 1925) 7 p.
Dn 3′. *La* DLC, Schmidt Collection; MB. *At* Ellen Janson. *Pf* solo voc, pno.

2848 DANIELS, Mabel Wheeler. **If love should fly away, op. 13,** md **no. 3** (APS 7396; Boston: A.P. Schmidt, 1907) 5 p.
Dn 3′. *At* composer. *Pf* solo voc, pno.

2849 DANIELS, Mabel Wheeler. **In the dark, op. 8, no. 2** (APS md 6977; Boston: A.P. Schmidt, 1905) 5 p.
Dn 2′. *La* DLC, Schmidt Collection. *At* James B. Pratt. *Pf* solo voc, pno. *Tm Two Irish songs, op. 8 (WIAM 2864).*

2850 DANIELS, Mabel Wheeler. **Irish coquette, An, op. 8, no. 1** md (APS 6976; Boston: A.P. Schmidt, 1905) 7 p.
Dn 2′. *La* DLC, Schmidt Collection. *At* Henry Morgan Stone. *Pf* solo voc, pno. *Tm Two Irish songs, op. 8 (WIAM 2864).*

2851 DANIELS, Mabel Wheeler. **Kilties pass, The** (JF&B 7937; mm New York: J. Fischer, 1943) 5 p.
Dn 2′. *At* A.H. Spicer. *Pf* solo voc, pno.

2852 DANIELS, Mabel Wheeler. **Lady of dreams, The** (APS 8300;
mm   Boston: A.P. Schmidt, 1909) 5 p.
Dn 2′. *La* DLC, Schmidt Collection. *At* Richard Lincoln. *Pf* solo voc, pno.

2853 DANIELS, Mabel Wheeler. **Lied des Einsamen (Lonely lies**
md   **my way), op. 15, no. 3** (APS 8204; Boston: A.P. Schmidt, 1909)
[3] p.
Dn 1′. *La* DLC. *Tr* composer. *Lt* German, English. *Pf* solo voc, pno.

2854 DANIELS, Mabel Wheeler. **Love, how green the world, op.**
md   **5, no. 2** (BM 1058; Boston: Boston Music, 1905) 6 p.
Dn 1′. *At* Omar Khayyám. *St* Rubáiyát. *Tr* Richard Le Gallienne. *Pf* solo SA,
pno. *Tm Two duets for soprano and alto, op. 5* (*WIAM* 2863).

2855 DANIELS, Mabel Wheeler. **Love, the fair day, op. 5, no. 1**
md   (BM 1057; Boston: Boston Music, 1905) 7 p.
Dn 3′. *At* Omar Khayyám. *St* Rubáiyát. *Tr* Richard Le Gallienne. *Pf* solo SA,
pno. *Tm Two duets for soprano and alto, op. 5* (*WIAM* 2863).

2856 DANIELS, Mabel Wheeler. **Love, when I sleep, op. 7, no. 3**
md   (APS 6975; Boston: A.P. Schmidt, 1905) 5 p.
Dn 2′. *La* DLC, Schmidt Collection. *At* composer. *Pf* solo voc, pno. *Tm Songs
of Damascus, op. 7* (*WIAM* 2860).

2857 DANIELS, Mabel Wheeler. **Love's gift, op. 9, no. 2** (APS
md   7070; Boston: A.P. Schmidt, 1906) 3 p.
Dn 2′. *La* DLC, Schmidt Collection. *At* composer. *Pf* solo voc, pno. *Tm Three
love songs, op. 9* (*WIAM* 2861).

2858 DANIELS, Mabel Wheeler. **My soul doth call, op. 9, no. 3**
md   (APS 7071; Boston: A.P. Schmidt, 1906) 5 p.
Dn 3′. *La* DLC, Schmidt Collection. *At* composer. *Pf* solo voc, pno. *Tm Three
love songs, op. 9* (*WIAM* 2861).

2859 DANIELS, Mabel Wheeler. **Soldier cap (The scarlet cap)**
mm   (11480; Boston: White-Smith, 1902) 5 p.
Dn 1′. *At* composer. *Pf* solo voc, pno.

2860 DANIELS, Mabel Wheeler. **Songs of Damascus, op. 7, nos.**
mm   **1-3** (APS 6973-6975; Boston: A.P. Schmidt, 1905) 7, 5, 5 p.
Dn 6′. *At* composer. *Pf* solo voc, pno. *Ct Before the king* (*WIAM* 2835), *Could I
catch the wayward breeze* (*WIAM* 2840), *Love, when I sleep* (*WIAM* 2856).

2861 DANIELS, Mabel Wheeler. **Three love songs, op. 9, nos. 1-3**
mm   (APS 7068, 7070-7071; Boston: A.P. Schmidt, 1906) 5, 3, 5 p.
Dn 6′. *Pf* solo voc, pno. *Ct Highland love song* (*WIAM* 2846), *Love's gift*
(*WIAM* 2857), *My soul doth call* (*WIAM* 2858).

2862 DANIELS, Mabel Wheeler. **Tree and the image, The** (JF&B
mm   7194; New York: J. Fischer, 1936) 5 p.
Dn 3′. *At* Alice Brown. *Pf* solo voc, pno.

2863 DANIELS, Mabel Wheeler. **Two duets for soprano and alto,**
mm   **op. 5, nos. 1-2** (BM 1057-1058; Boston: Boston Music, 1905) 7, 6
p.
Dn 4′. *Pf* solo SA, pno. *Ct Love, the fair day* (*WIAM* 2855), *Love, how green the
world* (*WIAM* 2854).

2864 DANIELS, Mabel Wheeler. **Two Irish songs, op. 8, nos. 1-2**
mm   (APS 6976-6977; Boston: A.P. Schmidt, 1905) 7, 5 p.
Dn 4′. *Pf* solo voc, pno. *Ct An Irish coquette* (*WIAM* 2850), *In the dark* (*WIAM*
2849).

2865 DANIELS, Mabel Wheeler. **Two triolets** (APS 11452; Boston:
mm   A.P. Schmidt, 1918) 5 p.
Dn 3′. *At* William Lindsey. *Pf* solo voc, pno. *Ct Solitaire, The mistletoe.*

2866 DANIELS, Mabel Wheeler. **Undaunted, op. 26, no. 1** (APS
md   11358; Boston: A.P. Schmidt, 1917) 5 p.
Dn 2′. *La* DLC, Schmidt Collection. *At* Blanche M. Kelly. *Pf* solo voc, pno.

2867 DANIELS, Mabel Wheeler. **Verborgener Schimmer (Star-**
md   **light), op. 15, no. 2** (APS 8205; Boston: A.P. Schmidt, 1909) [2] p.
Dn 1′. *La* DLC. *At* Hans Gabriel. *Tr* composer. *Lt* German, English. *Pf* solo
voc, pno.

2868 DANIELS, Mabel Wheeler. **Villa of dreams** (APS 9263;
mm   Boston: A.P. Schmidt, 1911) 7 p.
Dn 3′. *La* DLC, Schmidt Collection. *At* Arthur Symons. *Pf* solo voc, pno.

2869 DANIELS, Mabel Wheeler. **Waterfall, The, op. 27, no. 2**
md   (APS 12494; Boston: A.P. Schmidt, 1922) 7 p.
Dn 2′. *La* DLC, Schmidt Collection. *At* Eleanor Hammond. *Pf* solo voc, pno.

2870 DANIELS, Mabel Wheeler. **When shepherds come wooing,**
md   **op. 13, no. 4** (APS 7398; Boston: A.P. Schmidt, 1907) 7 p.
Dn 3′. *At* composer. *Pf* solo voc, pno.

2871 EDWARDS, Clara Gerlich. **All thine own** (27185; New York:
mm   C. Fischer, 1935) 5 p.
Dn 2′. *At* composer. *Pf* solo voc, pno.

2872 EDWARDS, Clara Gerlich. **At twilight** (40625; New York: G.
mm   Schirmer, 1944) 6 p.
Dn 2′. *At* composer. *Pf* solo voc, pno.

2873 EDWARDS, Clara Gerlich. **Awake, beloved** (32330; New
mm   York: G. Schirmer, 1925) 5 p.
Dn 1′. *At* Thekla Hollingsworth. *Pf* solo voc, pno.

2874 EDWARDS, Clara Gerlich. **Benediction, A** (35061; New York:
mm   G. Schirmer, 1930) 5 p.
Dn 2′. *At* composer. *Pf* solo voc, pno.

2875 EDWARDS, Clara Gerlich. **By the bend of the river** (33189;
mm   New York: G. Schirmer, 1927) 5 p.
Dn 4′. *At* Bernhard Haig. *Pf* solo voc, pno. A note from the publisher indicates
Edwards also arranged the song for a variety of solo vocal, choral, and
instrumental combinations.

2876 EDWARDS, Clara Gerlich. **Day's begun, The** (35099; New
mm   York: G. Schirmer, 1930) 5 p.
Dn 2′. *At* composer. *Pf* solo voc, pno.

2877 EDWARDS, Clara Gerlich. **Fisher's widow, The** (34237; New
mm   York: G. Schirmer, 1929) 5 p.
Dn 1′. *At* Arthur Symons. *Pf* solo voc, pno.

2878 EDWARDS, Clara Gerlich. **Into the night** (37357; New York:
mm   G. Schirmer, 1939) 6 p.
Dn 2′. *At* composer. *Pf* solo voc, pno.

2879 EDWARDS, Clara Gerlich. **Lady moon** (75962; Boston: O.
mm   Ditson, 1927) 5 p.
Dn 1′. *At* Thekla Hollingsworth. *Pf* solo voc, pno.

2880 EDWARDS, Clara Gerlich. **Little shepherd's song, The** (New
mm   York: Mills Music, 1922) 6 p.
Dn 2′. *At* William Alexander Percy. *Pf* solo voc, pno.

2881 EDWARDS, Clara Gerlich. **Sometimes at close of day**
mm   (32494; New York: G. Schirmer, 1925) 5 p.
Dn 2′. *At* Bernhard Haig. *Pf* solo voc, pno.

2882 EDWARDS, Clara Gerlich. **With the wind and the rain in**
mm   **your hair** (34829; New York: G. Schirmer, 1930) 5 p.
Dn 2′. *At* composer. *Pf* solo voc, pno.

2883 GALAJIKIAN, Florence G. **Lilt of spring, A** (Chicago: G.
mm   Galajikian, 1924) 5 p.
Dn 2′. *At* Lillian Gard. *Pf* solo voc, pno.

2884 HIER, Ethel Glenn. **Avalon** (CP 39; New York: Composers Press,
mm   1938) 5 p.
Dn 2′. *At* Nancy Byrd Turner. *Pf* solo voc, pno.

2885 HIER, Ethel Glenn. **Bird in the rain, The** (New York: Compos-
mm   ers Facsimile Ed., 1955) 4 p.
Dn 1′. *At* Elinor Wylie. *Pf* solo voc, pno.

2886 HIER, Ethel Glenn. **Chanson du cordonnier, La [The song of**
mm   **the shoemaker]** (New York: Composers Facsimile Ed., 1953) 3 p.

2887 HIER, Ethel Glenn. **Click o' the latch** (CP 38; New York:
mm   Composers Press, 1938) 7 p.
Dn 2'. *At* Nancy Byrd Turner. *Pf* solo voc, pno.

2888 HIER, Ethel Glenn. **Dreamin' town** (3738; Cincinnati: Willis
mm   Music, 1919) 7 p.
Dn 3'. *At* Paul Laurence Dunbar. *Pf* solo voc, pno.

2889 HIER, Ethel Glenn. **Dusk in the hill country** (New York:
mm   Composers Facsimile Ed., 1953) 3 p.
Dn 2'. *At* Julia Collins Ardayne. *Pf* solo voc, pno.

2890 HIER, Ethel Glenn. **Fairy ring, The** (New York: Composers
mm   Press, 1938) [4] p.
Dn 2'. *At* Abbie Farwell Brown. *Pf* solo voc, pno.

2891 HIER, Ethel Glenn. **Gulls** (CP 92; New York: Composers Press,
mm   1940) 7 p.
Dn 1'. *At* Leonora Speyer. *Pf* solo voc, pno. Also for chamber ensemble
(*WIAM* 2444).

2892 HIER, Ethel Glenn. **Hour, The and The return** (CP 308-309;
mm   New York: Composers Press, 1949) 7 p.
Dn 4'. *Pf* solo voc, pno. *Ct* The hour (*At* Jessie B. Rittenhouse), The return (*At*
Sara Teasdale).

2893 HIER, Ethel Glenn. **Japanese lullaby** (New York: composer,
mm   1925) 5 p.
Dn 2'. *At* Eugene Field. *Pf* solo voc, pno.

2894 HIER, Ethel Glenn. **Lonely cabin, The** (CP 93; New York:
mm   Composers Press, 1940) 5 p.
Dn 3'. *At* Herbert Gorman. *Pf* solo voc, pno.

2895 HIER, Ethel Glenn. **My kite** (2687; Cincinnati: Willis Music,
mm   1914) 5 p.
Dn 1'. *At* Mabel Hubbard Birch. *Pf* solo voc, pno.

2896 HIER, Ethel Glenn. **Song sparrow, The** (New York: Composers
mm   Facsimile Ed., 1955) 4 p.
Dn 2'. *At* Alfred Kreymborg. *Pf* solo voc, pno.

2897 HIER, Ethel Glenn. **Time to woo, The** (2760; Cincinnati: Willis
mm   Music, 1914) 5 p.
Dn 1'. *At* Samuel Minturn Peck. *Pf* solo voc, pno.

2898 HOWE, Mary. **Baritone songs**. *Songs by Mary Howe* 3 (2149;
ma   New York: Galaxy Music, 1959) 23 p.
Dn 13'. *Pf* solo voc, pno. *Ct* The lake isle of Innisfree (*At* Yeats); The rag
picker (*La* DLC, *At* Frances Shaw); Now goes the light (*La* DLC, *At* Cecilia
Lee); Lullaby for a forester's child (*At* Frances Frost); Spring, come not too
soon (*At* Charles Norman); Reach (*At* Cecilia Lynch); Little fiddler's green (*La*
DLC). *Rg* The ragpicker and Lullaby for a forester's child: NN, Rogers and
Hammerstein Archives of Recorded Sound.

2899 HOWE, Mary. **Berceuse** (40704; New York: G. Schirmer, 1925)
mm   5 p.
Dn 2'. *Pf* solo voc, pno. Also for pno (*WIAM* 2691).

2900 HOWE, Mary. **Christmas story, The** (30566; New York: C.
mm   Fischer, 1949) 5 p.
Sacred song. *Dn* 3'. *La* DLC. *At* Lisenka Ourusoff. *Pf* solo voc, org or pno.

2901 HOWE, Mary. **Cossack cradle song** (74253; Boston: O. Ditson,
mm   1922) 5 p.
Dn 2'. *At* composer. *Tr* Constance Purdy, from French to English. *Lt* French,
English. *Pf* solo voc, pno. Also in her *French songs* (*WIAM* 2905) as Berceuse
cossaque.

2902 HOWE, Mary. **English songs, part I**. *Songs by Mary Howe* 2
ma   (2148; New York: Galaxy Music, 1959) 31 p.
Dn 17'. *Pf* solo voc, pno. *Ct* Fragment (*At* Cecilia Lee); O Proserpina (*At*
Shakespeare, *St* A winter's tale); The bailey and the bell (*At* anon., 15th c.);
Horses (*La* DLC, *At* Rose Fyleman); Fair Annet's song (*La* DLC, *At* Elinor
Wylie); The birds (*La* DLC, *At* D.C.); There has fallen a splendid tear (*La*

DLC, *At* Tennyson). *Rg* O Proserpina: NN, Rogers and Hammerstein Archives
of Recorded Sound.

2903 HOWE, Mary. **English songs, part II**. *Songs by Mary Howe* 6
ma   (2152; New York: Galaxy Music, 1959) 34 p.
Dn 28'. *Pf* solo voc, pno. *Ct* You (*La* DLC, *At* Alice Dows); Viennese waltz
(*La* DLC, *At* Elinor Wylie); My lady comes (*La* DLC, *At* Chard Powers Smith);
Hymne (*At* Donne); Three hokku (*WIAM* 2918); Men (*At* Dorothy E. Reid); In
Tauris (*At* Euripides, *Tr* Gilbert Murray).

2904 HOWE, Mary. **English songs, part III**. *Songs by Mary Howe* 7
ma   (2172; New York: Galaxy Music, 1959) 27 p.
Dn 12'. *Pf* solo voc, pno; *The horseman* is scored for SS or TT, pno (*WIAM*
2909). *Ct* Avalon (*At* Nancy Byrd Turner), O mistress mine (*WIAM* 2915),
Where I die tonight (*At* Marie Valeur), Old English lullaby (*At* anon., 15th c.),
The prinkin' leddie (*At* Elinor Wylie), The horseman (*WIAM* 2909), Red fields
of France (*At* Charles Going).

2905 HOWE, Mary. **French songs**. *Songs by Mary Howe* 4 (2150; New
ma   York: Galaxy Music, 1959) 32 p.
Dn 18'. *Lt* French, English. *Pf* solo voc, pno. *Ct* Chanson souvenir (*At* Viele
Griffin); L'amant des roses (Lover of roses, *At* Jules Ruelle); Poème de Thalia
(Thalia's poem, *At* Thalia Gage); Berceuse cossaque (Cossack lullaby, *At*
composer); Rêve (The dream, *At* Victor Hugo); Soit (So be it, *At* M. Mahtrow);
Ma douleur (Torment of mine, *At* Baudelaire). Berceuse cossaque also
published as *Cossack cradle song* (*WIAM* 2901). *Rg* Ma douleur: NN, Rogers
and Hammerstein Archive of Recorded Sound.

2906 HOWE, Mary. **German songs**. *Songs by Mary Howe* 5 (2151;
ma   New York: Galaxy Music, 1959) 28 p.
Dn 18'. *Lt* German, English. *Pf* solo voc, pno. *Ct* Mein Herz (My heart, *At*
Mirza Schaffy, *Tr* F. Bodenstaedt into German); Über allen Gipfeln (Over
every summit, *La* DLC, *At* Goethe); Nicht mit Engeln (Not with angels, *La*
DLC, *At* Mirza Schaffy); Der Einsame (The lonely one, *La* DLC, *At* Rilke);
Liebeslied (Love song, *La* DLC, *At* Rilke); Schaflied (Slumber song, *La* DLC,
At Rilke); Herbsttag (Autumn day, *La* DLC, *At* Rilke). Howe also arranged
Über allen Gipfeln for pno, vcl (*WIAM* 2460).

2907 HOWE, Mary. **Go down, death** (facsimile of autograph at NN,
mm   [194-]) 14 p.
Dn 3'. *At* James Weldon Johnson. *Pf* solo voc, pno.

2908 HOWE, Mary. **Great land of mine** (311; New York: Mercury
mm   Music, 1955) 5 p.
Dn 2'. *La* DLC. *Pf* solo voc, org or pno.

2909 HOWE, Mary. **Horseman, The** (facsimile of autograph at NN,
mm   n.d.) 1 p. (score).
Dn 1'. *At* Walter de la Mare. *Pf* SS or TT, pno. Also in her *English songs, part
III* (*WIAM* 2904).

2910 HOWE, Mary. **Irish lullaby** (30248; New York: C. Fischer,
mm   1948) 7 p.
Dn 2'. *La* DLC. *At* Helen Coale Crew. *Pf* solo voc, pno. Also for voice and
orchestra (*WIAM* 2635).

2911 HOWE, Mary. **Let us walk in the white snow. Velvet shoes**
mm   (30247; New York: C. Fischer, 1948) 7 p.
Dn 4'. *La* DLC. *At* Elinor Wylie. *Pf* solo voc, pno.

2912 HOWE, Mary. **Little elegy** (38298; New York: G. Schirmer,
mm   1939) 5 p.
Dn 1'. *La* DLC. *At* Elinor Wylie. *Pf* solo voc, pno.

2913 HOWE, Mary. **Little rose, The** (38299; New York: G. Schirmer,
mm   1939) 3 p.
Dn 1'. *At* Grace Hazard Conkling. *St* Wilderness songs. *Pf* solo voc, pno.

2914 HOWE, Mary. **Needle in the knee: A travesty** (facsimile of
mm   autograph at NN, [194-]) 6 p.
Dn 3'. *Pf* solo voc, pno.

2915 HOWE, Mary. **O mistress mine** (33472; New York: G. Schirmer,
mm   1927) 5 p.
Dn 2'. *La* DLC. *At* Shakespeare. *St* Twelfth night. *Pf* solo voc, pno. Also in her
English songs, part III (*WIAM* 2904).

2916 HOWE, Mary. **Ripe apples** (38297; New York: G. Schirmer,
mm   1939) 5 p.
Dn 2' *At* Leonora Speyer. *St* The naked heel. *Pf* solo voc, pno.

146

2917 HOWE, Mary. **Seven Goethe songs.** *Songs by Mary Howe* 1
ma   (2147; New York: Galaxy Music, 1959) 24 p.
Dn 18′. *At* Goethe. *Lt* German, English. *Pf* solo voc, pno. *Ct* Zweifel
(Hesitation), Die Götter (The gods), Heute geh' ich (Now I leave you), Mailied
(May song), Ich denke dein (I think of thee), Die Jahre (The years), Am Flusse
(By the river).

2918 HOWE, Mary. **Three hokku. From the Japanese** (GM 2157;
mm   New York: Galaxy Music, 1959) 5 p.
Dn 3′. *At* Amy Lowell. *Pf* solo voc, pno. Dedicated to Adele Addison. Also in
her *English songs, part II* (*WIAM* 2903).

2919 HOWE, Mary. **To the unknown soldier** (41066; New York: G.
mm   Schirmer, 1945) 5 p.
Dn 3′. *La* DLC. *At* Nicholas G. Lely. *Tr* Joseph Auslander. *Pf* solo voc, pno.

2920 HOWE, Mary. **When I died in Berners Street** (41475; New
mm   York: G. Schirmer, 1947) 10 p.
Dn 3′. *La* DLC. *At* Elinor Wylie. *St* Collected poems. *Pf* solo voc, pno. *Rg* NN,
Rogers and Hammerstein Archives of Recorded Sound.

2921 MANA ZUCCA. **A-whispering, op. 24** (27930; New York: G.
mm   Schirmer, 1917) 5 p.
Dn 1′. *At* Carter S. Cole. *Pf* solo voc, pno.

2922 MANA ZUCCA. **Big brown bear, The, op. 52, no. 1** (28839;
md   New York: G. Schirmer, 1948) 4 p.
Dn 1′. *At* Herman August Heydt. *Pf* solo voc, pno. A reprint of the 1919
publication (28839; Schirmer). Also arranged for choral SSA, pno (*WIAM*
2586).

2923 MANA ZUCCA. **Eve, and a glowing west, op. 33** (5826;
mm   Boston: Boston Music, 1918) 6 p.
Dn 2′. *At* G. Hubi Newcombe. *Pf* solo voc, pno.

2924 MANA ZUCCA. **Fairest of all, op. 35** (5843; Boston: Boston
mm   Music, 1918) 5 p.
Dn 2′. *At* E. Casalino. *Pf* solo voc, pno.

2925 MANA ZUCCA. **First love, op. 31** (5758; Boston: Boston
mm   Music, 1918) 6 p.
Dn 2′. *At* Etienne. *Pf* solo voc, pno.

2926 MANA ZUCCA. **I love life, op. 83** (30012; Philadelphia: T.
mm   Presser, 1923) 7 p.
Dn 2′. *At* Irwin M. Cassel. *Pf* solo voc, pno. *Rg* Victor 1986.

2927 MANA ZUCCA. **Nichavo!** (18462; Cincinnati: J. Church, 1921)
mm   7 p.
Dn 2′. *At* Helen Jerome. *Pf* solo voc, pno.

2928 MANA ZUCCA. **Query, A, op. 47, no. 2** (30211; New York:
md   G. Schirmer, 1921) 5 p.
Dn 1′. *At* Robert Browning. *Pf* solo voc, pno.

2929 MANA ZUCCA. **Rachem, op. 60, no. 1** (30021; Miami, Fla.:
md   Congress Music, 1957) 7 p.
Sacred song. *Dn* 3′. *At* Max S. Brown. *Tr* Elsie Jean, into English; Arturo
Papolardo, into Italian. *Lt* Hebrew, English, Italian. *Pf* solo voc, pno.
Previously published in 1919 (18289; Cincinnati: J. Church). *Rg* Victor 1986.

2930 MANA ZUCCA. **Rose-Marie, op. 36, no. 1** (5780; Boston:
md   Boston Music, 1918) 7 p.
Dn 2′. *At* A.H. Clements. *Pf* solo voc, pno.

2931 MANA ZUCCA. **Sleep, my darling, op. 39, no. 12** (5942;
md   Boston: Boston Music, 1918) 6 p.
Dn 2′. *At* Elsie Jean Stearn. *Pf* solo voc, pno.

2932 MANA ZUCCA. **Speak to me!, op. 18, no. 1** (27328; New
md   York: G. Schirmer, 1917) 4 p.
Dn 1′. *At* Ben Altheimer. *Pf* solo voc, pno.

2933 MANA ZUCCA. **Tear drops, op. 32** (5757; Boston: Boston
mm   Music, 1918) 7 p.
Dn 2′. *At* Carter S. Cole. *Pf* solo voc, pno.

2934 MANA ZUCCA. **Tell me if this be true, op. 34** (5781; Boston:
mm   Boston Music, 1918) 7 p.
Dn 2′. *At* Rabindranath Tagore. *Pf* solo voc, pno.

2935 MANA ZUCCA. **Top o' the morning, The, op. 67, no. 1**
md   (18376; Cincinnati: J. Church, 1920) 5 p.
Dn 1′. *At* Benjamin Mark Kaye. *Pf* solo voc, pno.

2936 MANA ZUCCA. **When the day has flown, op. 36, no. 2**
md   (5844; Boston: Boston Music, 1918) 7 p.
Dn 2′. *At* John H. Bacon. *Pf* solo voc, pno.

2937 MANNING, Kathleen Lockhart. **Chinese impressions**
mm   (35421/35454; New York: G. Schirmer, 1931) 5, 5, 5, 5, 5 p.
Song cycle. *Dn* 9′. *At* composer. *Pf* solo voc, pno. *Ct* Pagoda bells; Incense;
Chinoise; Nang-ping; Hop-li, the rickshaw man.

2938 MANNING, Kathleen Lockhart. **Cocktails** (Hollywood,
mm   Calif.: composer, 1929) 7 p.
Song cycle. *Dn* 5′. *At* composer. *Pf* solo voc, pno. *Ct* Temptation, Attraction,
Dregs, Reflection, Infidelity.

2939 MANNING, Kathleen Lockhart. **Five fragments** (35236;
mm   New York: G. Schirmer, 1931) 13 p.
Songs. *Dn* 3′. *At* composer. *Pf* solo voc, pno. *Ct* Streets, Image, Silhouette, Miss
Wing-fu, Voyage.

2940 MANNING, Kathleen Lockhart. **Japanese ghost songs** (839;
mm   New York: Composers' Music, 1924) 14 p.
Dn 2′. *At* composer. *Pf* solo voc, pno. *Ct* In the bamboo, The maid of mystery.

2941 MANNING, Kathleen Lockhart. **Nostalgia** (35238; New
mm   York: G. Schirmer, 1931) 5 p.
Dn 3′. *At* composer. *Pf* solo voc, pno.

2942 MANNING, Kathleen Lockhart. **Sketches of London**
mm   (25084; New York: C. Fischer, 1929) 19 p.
Songs. *Dn* 10′. *At* composer. *Pf* solo voc, pno. *Ct* The Thames, Fog, Windsor
Castle, Toys, June in London.

2943 MANNING, Kathleen Lockhart. **Sketches of New York**
mm   (36596; New York: G. Schirmer, 1936) 12 p.
Songs. *Dn* 6′. *At* composer. *Pf* solo voc, pno. *Ct* Along the East River, Street
scene, Tenement windows, Greenwich Village nights, Fifth Avenue, The St.
Regis roof.

2944 MANNING, Kathleen Lockhart. **Sketches of Paris** (35042;
mm   New York: G. Schirmer, 1925) 23 p.
Songs. *Dn* 12′. *At* composer. *Pf* solo voc, pno. *Ct* Riverboats, Lamplighter, The
street fair, In the Luxembourg Gardens, Absinthe, Paris: an ode.

2945 MANNING, Kathleen Lockhart. **Songs of Egypt. Five song**
mm   **impressions** (28910; New York: C. Fischer, 1934) 22 p.
Dn 25′. *At* composer. *Pf* solo voc, pno. *Ct* Sphinx, Moonrise, Love song, Camel
rider, Dusk on desert.
(Joan M. Meggett)

2946 MANNING, Kathleen Lockhart. **Tale a garden told, The.**
mm   **Burlesque en miniature** (25085; New York: C. Fischer, 1929) 18
p.
Song cycle. *Dn* 20′. *At* composer. *Pf* solo voc, pno. *Ct* The big potato, Carrots,
Cabbages, Lettuce patch, Strawberry bed, What the parsley said.
(Joan M. Meggett)

2947 MANNING, Kathleen Lockhart. **Vignettes** (35853; New
mm   York: G. Schirmer, 1933) 49 p.
Songs. *Dn* 25′. *At* composer. *Pf* solo voc, pno. *Ct* Offering, Illusion, By a lonely
river, Siren, Frost, House-guest, Departed, L'Amour, Barren, Promenade,
Beloved, Throb, In retrospect, Along the shore, Funeral, Maiden, Footfall,
Transition, A winter afternoon, Treasure, Brooding, Monotone, Destiny,
Harbinger, Finis.

2948 MANNING, Kathleen Lockhart. **Water lily, The** (2570;
mm   London: Boosey, 1923) 4 p.
Dn 1′. *At* composer. *Pf* solo voc, pno.

2949 PRICE, Florence B. **Dreamin' town** (facsimile of autograph at
mm   ArU, 1934) 4 p.

Dn 2'. Da 5 Jan. 1934. At Paul Laurence Dunbar. *Pf* solo voc, pno. *(Barbara Garvey Jackson)*

2950 PRICE, Florence B. **Envious wren, The** (facsimile of autograph
mm   at ArU, n.d.) 6 p.
Dn 3'. At Alice and Phoebe Carey. *Pf* solo voc, pno.   *(Barbara Garvey Jackson)*

2951 PRICE, Florence B. **Fantasy in purple** (facsimile of autograph
mm   at ArU, n.d.) 3 p.
Dn 2'. At Langston Hughes. *Pf* solo voc, pno.   *(Barbara Garvey Jackson)*

2952 PRICE, Florence B. **Forever** (facsimile of autograph at ArU,
mm   n.d.) 3 p.
Dn 2'. At Paul Laurence Dunbar. *Pf* solo voc, pno.   *(Barbara Garvey Jackson)*

2953 PRICE, Florence B. **I am bound for the kingdom, and I'm**
mm   **workin' on my buildin'** (New York: Handy Brothers Music, 1949)
     5 p.
Spirituals arranged. *Dn 2'. Pf* solo voc, pno.

2954 PRICE, Florence B. **Love-in-a-mist** (facsimile of autograph at
mm   ArU, n.d.) 4 p.
Dn 2'. At Mary Rolofson Gamble. *Pf* solo voc, pno.   *(Barbara Garvey Jackson)*

2955 PRICE, Florence B. **Moonbridge** (937; Chicago: Gamble Hinged
mm   Music, 1930) 6 p.
Dn 2'. At Mary Rolofson Gamble. *Pf* solo voc, pno.

2956 PRICE, Florence B. **My soul's been anchored in the Lord**
mm   (1292; Chicago: Gamble Hinged Music, 1937) 5 p.
Spiritual arranged. *Dn 2'. Pf* solo voc, pno. *Rg* Victor 1799.

2957 PRICE, Florence B. **Night**, *Negro art songs.* Ed. by Willis C.
mc   PATTERSON (New York: E.B. Marks, 1977) 82-83.
Dn 1'. At Louise B. Wallace. *Pf* solo voc, pno.

2958 PRICE, Florence B. **Nightfall** (facsimile of autograph at ArU,
mm   n.d.) 3 p.
Dn 2'. At Paul Laurence Dunbar. *Pf* solo voc, pno.   *(Barbara Garvey Jackson)*

2959 PRICE, Florence B. **Out of the South blew a wind**, *Negro art*
mc   *songs.* Ed. by Edgar Rogie CLARK (1220; New York: E.B. Marks,
     1936) 33-35.
Dn 1'. At Fannie Carter Woods. *Pf* solo voc, pno.

2960 PRICE, Florence B. **Song to the dark virgin**, *Negro art songs.*
mc   Ed. by Willis C. PATTERSON (New York: E.B. Marks, 1977) 98-
     101.
Dn 1'. At Langston Hughes. *Pf* solo voc, pno.

2961 PRICE, Florence B. **To my little son** (facsimile of MS at DLC,
mm   n.d.) 2 p.
Dn 1'. At Julia Johnson Davis. *Pf* solo voc, pno.

2963 TYSON, Mildred Lund. **Great divide, The** (38451; New York:
mm   G. Schirmer, 1938) 3 p.
Dn 2'. At Lew Sarett. *Pf* solo voc, pno.   *(Composer)*

2964 TYSON, Mildred Lund. **Noon and night** (38183; New York: G.
mm   Schirmer, 1939) 3 p.
Dn 3'. At Herbert French. *Pf* solo voc, pno.   *(Composer)*

2965 URNER, Catherine Murphy. **Quatre mélodies** (Paris: Edition
mm   M. Senart, 1928) 15 p.
Dn 8'. Lt French. *Pf* solo S, pno. *Ct* La lune se lève (*At* Madeleine Jacques), Ici-
bas (*At* Sully Prudhomme), Le papillon (*At* Alphonse de Lamartine), Colloque
sentimental (*At* Verlaine).

2966 URNER, Catherine Murphy. **Six songs** (Paris: Editions M.
mm   Senart, 1928) 22 p.
Dn 11'. Pf solo S, pno. *Ct* Sonnet (*At* Maude Meagher), Song (*At* Irene
Rutherford McLeod), Come away, death (*At* Shakespeare, *St* Twelfth night),
Music I heard with you (*At* Conrad Aiken), Dusk at sea (*At* Thomas Jones, Jr.),
The lake isle of Innisfree (*At* Yeats).

1950 TO 1978

75   General literature about women in art music

2967 ABDUL, Raoul. **Blacks in classical music. A personal his-**
bm   **tory** (New York: Dodd, Mead, 1977) 253 p. *Illus., index.*
Considers the careers of the following women: composers Margaret Bonds,
Dorothy Rudd Moore, Florence B. Price, and Julia Perry; conductor Eva Jessye;
harpsichordist Frances Cole; pianists Hazel Harrison, Natalie Hinderas, and
Philippa Duke Schuyler; and singers Marian Anderson, Martina Arroyo, Joyce
Britton, Grace Bumbry, Clamma Dale, Jessye Norman, and Shirley Verrett,
among others.

2968 **Another distaff victory**, *Diapason* LX/7 (June 1969) 14.
ap
1) Barbara Kolb is the first woman composer to win the Rome Prize
Fellowship. 2) As organists, American women have received more recognition
than women in other areas of music. 3) In the 41 years since its founding, the
Chicago Club of Women Organists has sponsored recitals by women organists,
an annual playing contest for women, and a variety of other professional
activities.

2969 BARZUN, Jacques. **Music in American life** (Gloucester, Mass.:
bm   P. Smith, 1958) 126 p. *Bibliog.*
Appraises the cultural revolution that since the 1920s has changed popular
attitudes regarding music as the province of only "wretched professionals and
scheming young ladies", sissy schoolboys, and male pianists considered to be
"long-haired animals of dubious habits". Barzun attributes the welcome change
to the permeation of music throughout society due to technology in radio, film,
and the record industries.

2970 CARACAPPA, Michael. **Wonder woman of 42nd street**,
ap   *Music Journal* [New York] XXIV/5 (May 1966) 18-20, 60, 71. *Illus.*
Relates how Lee Wurlitzer, widow of Rembert Wurlitzer and president of
Rembert Wurlitzer, Inc., recently competed in a profession heretofore dominated by men by successfully negotiating the purchase of 38 rare violins from
the collection of Henry Hottinger. The collection included instruments made by
Stradivarius, Guarneri, Amati, and other masters.

2971 **Career alternatives in music: some advice from outstanding**
ap   **women musicians**, *Instrumentalist* XXXI/5 (Dec 1976) 34-39.
     Illus.
The following women discuss their careers in music and the necessary
qualifications for pursuing employment in their particular areas: Victoria Bond,
orchestral conductor; Wanda Lathom, music therapist; Jennifer A. Becker,
violin maker and repairer; Eve Queler, opera conductor; Carole Dawn
Reinhart, trumpet soloist; Karen Monson, music critic; Clara Steuermann,
music librarian; and Diane Thome, Nancy Van de Vate, and Shulamit Ran,
composers. An introduction to the 10 profiles indicates that the article was
planned in part with the idea of providing role models for young female
students.   *(Nancy Van de Vate)*

2972 CRAIG, Mary. **Women at work**, *Musical Courier* CLIII/2 (15
ap   Jan 1956) 7, 14. *Illus.*
Discusses the careers of Mildred Dilling, harpist, Nina Gordani, singer, and
Janet Schenck, director of the Manhattan School of Music in 1956.

2973 **Defining their role**, *Opera News* XL/14 (14 Feb 1976) 18-19. *Illus.*
ap
The following women discuss briefly the ramifications of the women's
movement in their particular areas of work, as well as how being female has
affected their careers to date: Anne Howard Bailey, librettist; Charlotte Curtis,
journalist; Doriot Anthony Dwyer, flutist; Martha Graham, choreographer;
Nancy Hanks, arts administrator; Adela Holzer, Broadway producer; Thea
Musgrave, composer; Beverly Sills, singer; Risë Stevens, music administrator
and former singer; and Violette Verdy, dancer.

2974 **Dr. Montgomery honored in Oklahoma**, *Music Clubs Magazine*
ap   LVI/3 (1977) 21.
At Merle Montgomery's induction into the Oklahoma Hall of Fame by the
Oklahoma Heritage Assoc., Van Cliburn described Montgomery's background
and contributions to the music world. A native of Oklahoma and a graduate of
the U. of Oklahoma, Montgomery studied in Paris with Nadia Boulanger and
Isidore Philipp and earned her master's degree and Ph.D. from the Eastman
School. She has taught piano and theory, worked for Carl Fischer, Inc. and
Oxford U. Press, and published a number of books and articles. Currently she
serves as vice-president of the New York City Opera Guild and as president of
the National Music Council.   *(Julia Smith, abridged)*

→   EATON, Frances. **Renaissance woman**, *see* 3228ap[78].

2975 ERICSON, Raymond. **Mezzo becomes an opera manager, A,**
an   *New York Times* 25 June 1967, II-13.
A mezzo-soprano at the Metropolitan Opera since 1944, Blanche Thebom is now artistic director for the opera division of Atlanta's Municipal Theater. Other women opera directors in the 20th c. include Mary Garden of the Chicago Opera, Carol Fox of the Chicago Lyric Opera, Sarah Caldwell of the Boston Opera, and Risë Stevens, co-director of the Metropolitan Opera National Co.

→   **Evanston, Illinois, Northwestern University Library, The Women's Collection. A checklist of source materials by and about women in American music,** *see* 15bm[01].

→   **Focus on women: composers, musicians--a not so silent minority,** *see* 67bp[10].

2976 **Gateway to honor, The. Helen Hewitt,** *Notes. Music Library*
ap   *Association* IV/4 (Sept 1947) 436-37.
A biographical sketch of the musicologist Helen Hewitt, who is currently an associate professor at North Texas State Col. in Denton. Born in Granville, N.Y. in 1900, Hewitt majored in music and mathematics at Vassar Col. In 1933 she received her master's degree from Columbia U. and in 1938 her doctoral degree from Radcliffe Col., where she worked with Hugo Leichentritt and Edward Burlingame Hill of Harvard U. Hewitt's major work to date is her edition of Petrucci's *Harmonices musices odhecaton A* (Cambridge, Mass.: Medieval Academy of America, 1942). Her work on *Canti B, numero cinquanta* is substantially completed, and during 1947-48 she has a Guggenheim fellowship to prepare an edition of Petrucci's 3rd collection, *Canti C, numero cento cinquanta.*

2977 HANDY, D. Antoinette. **Conversation with Lucille Dixon.**
ap   **Manager of a symphony orchestra,** *Black Perspective in Music* III/3 (fall 1975) 299-311.
A bass player, since Apr. 1972 Lucille Dixon has been the manager as well as a member of the Symphony of the New World--a professional orchestra that was founded in New York in 1964 to give minorities the opportunity for orchestral work. Dixon was born in 1923, and she notes that while she studied classical music, she was unable to pursue it because of discrimination against blacks in the classical field. Due to this experience she is committed to the Symphony of the New World. Between 1946 and 1960 Dixon ran her own jazz band, and she has continued to perform both jazz and classical music.

2978 **Helen M. Thompson, 66, dead; ex-head of orchestra league,**
an   *New York Times* 26 June 1974, 46. *Illus.*
Born in Greenville, Ill., Helen M. Thompson (1908-74) received a bachelor's degree from the U. of Illinois and did graduate work in psychology and sociology. An amateur musician, in 1940 she became manager of the Charleston Symphony Orchestra in Charleston, W. Va., and in 1950 she assumed the post of executive secretary of the American Symphony Orchestra League. Thompson worked for the league until 1970, when she was appointed manager of the New York Philharmonic. Since her mandatory retirement in 1973 she had been a private arts consultant in California. As a lobbyist for the performing arts in the United States, Thompson furthered the growth of American orchestras through her travels, workshops, speeches, and publications.

→   **I am woman. A tribute to women in music,** *see* 55bp[05].

2979 **Introducing Radie Britain,** *Musical Courier* XCIII/25 (16 Dec
ap   1926) 10.
Radie Britain trained as a pianist and organist at Clarendon Col. in her native Amarillo, Tex., and later graduated from the American Conservatory. She spent 2 lengthy sojourns abroad, returning after the first to teach in Amarillo and thereby earn sufficient monies to finance the second. During the first stay Britain studied organ in Paris with Marcel Dupré and Isidore Philipp. During the second she studied piano in Munich with Joseph Pembaur, who also encouraged her in composition. Recently Britain made her Chicago debut, playing her *Western suite* and her prelude in G-flat major for piano.

2980 **JONES, Robert. Ragtime's reluctant queen,** *New York Sunday*
an   *News* 8 June 1975, L-6. *Illus.*
Although 24 publishers rejected Vera Brodsky Lawrence's edition of Scott Joplin's collected works before the New York Times and Arno Press accepted it, Joplin's music has since become popular as a result of her pioneer work. Brodsky Lawrence's earlier career as a pianist is briefly discussed, including her world première of Shostakovich's piano sonata no. 2, op. 64, and her work as staff pianist for the Columbia Broadcasting System at a time when the position was an important one.

2981 KEPPLER, Philip. **Sylvia Kenney,** *Journal of the American*
ap   *Musicological Society* XXII/3 (fall 1969) 528.
An obituary for the musicologist (1923-68) who studied at Wellesley Col., Yale U., and in Brussels. Kenney's doctoral dissertation was published under the title *Walter Frye and the contenance angloise,* and she edited the complete edition of Frye's works. Kenney held positions at Wells and Bryn Mawr colleges, Yale U., the U. of California, and finally Smith Col.

2982 MELONE, Halsey. **People love music out of our past,**
an   *Washington Post* 6 Aug 1972, F-1, 5. *Illus.*
In less than 8 years of her career as a music historian, Vera Brodsky Lawrence has published a 5 vol. edition of the complete piano works of Louis Moreau Gottschalk (1969), a 5 vol. edition of the publications of the Wa-Wan Press from 1901-11 (1970), and a 2 vol. edition of the collected works of Scott Joplin (1971). Her book *Music for patriots, politicians, and presidents* is currently in preparation. Brodsky Lawrence's first career in music was as a pianist in the 1930s-40s, when she played both as a soloist and in duo-piano recitals with Harold Triggs. In 1944 she married Theodore Lawrence, a noted sound and lighting engineer, and gradually she gave up playing. After her husband's death in 1964, Brodsky Lawrence took a position with a music publisher.

2983 NEULS-BATES, Carol. **Foundation support for women.** *The*
as   *status of women in college music: preliminary studies.* Ed. by Carol NEULS-BATES (*WIAM* 73) 10-15. *College Music Society report no. 1*
In her *Women in fellowship and training programs* (Washington, D.C.: Assoc. of American Colleges, 1972), Cynthia Attwood concludes that qualified women have been less likely to apply for foundation support in the recent past than qualified men. The participation of women in music in the programs of the John Simon Guggenheim Memorial Foundation, the National Endowment for the Humanities, the American Council of Learned Societies, and the Martha Baird Rockefeller Fund for Music, Inc. is reviewed together with statistics for earned degrees conferred to women in music. Since fellowships have traditionally molded and advanced the careers of leaders, society will benefit if more women achieve recognition as recipients of foundation support. Also, women's taxes--as well as men's--subsidize tax-exempt foundations.

2984 ROBBINS, Jack. **Daily closeup. Black music,** *New York Post* 22
an   July 1971, 31.
With her book *The music of black Americans: a history* (*WIAM* 170), Eileen Southern feels that she has made a contribution to her people. A musicologist on the faculty of York Col. of the City U. of New York, Southern grew up in the Midwest and was trained as a pianist. Her mother insisted that she stay with classical music rather than take up jazz. Southern earned a master's degree at Prairie View Col. in Texas when she was 21, and she taught 8-9 years in schools in the South before working for her Ph.D. at New York U.

→   SMITH, Cecil. **Worlds of music,** *see* 1985bm[65].

2985 **Society elects Knapp and Benton,** *Newsletter. American Musico-*
ap   *logical Society* IV/1 (15 Jan 1974) 1.
Reports that for 1974-76 the American Musicological Soc. has elected Janet Knapp president and re-elected Rita Benton as secretary. The backgrounds of both women are briefly reviewed.

2986 **This month we salute Mrs. Helen M. Thompson,** *Music Clubs*
ap   *Magazine* XXXII/1 (Sept 1952) 7. *Illus.*
Helen M. Thompson, a trained psychologist and social worker, played 2nd violin and managed the Charleston Symphony Orchestra in Charleston, W. Va. for 10 years. In 1946 she began volunteer work with the American Symphony Orchestra League, which serves as a clearing house for the problems of 700 symphony orchestras, and in 1950 she became its executive secretary. This summer she will teach a course in community symphony management in Brevard, N.C. As a spokeswoman for American orchestras, Thompson was responsible for the repeal of the 20% federal excise tax on concert admissions in 1951.

2987 **Women in music,** *Pan Pipes of Sigma Alpha Iota* LXVII/2 (Jan
ap   1975) 2-7. *Illus.*
Reports on the lecture and recital series entitled "Encounters with Women in Music", which was held during the summer of 1974 at California State U. at Los Angeles. The series included a concert by pianist Nancy Fierro, and panel discussions about women as music educators, women in musicology, and women poets and composers. Biographical sketches for the following women composers are included: Esther Williamson Ballou, Radie Britain, Ruth Brush, Jean Eichelberger Ivey, Ethel Harnden, Barbara Kolb, Shirley Mackie, Ursula Mamlok, Joyce Mekeel, Dika Newlin, Gertrud Roberts, and Nancy Van de Vate.

2988 **You won't have "lady musicians" to kick around much**
ap   **longer,** *Music Educators Journal* LIX/1 (Sept 1972) [i].
Challenges women in music to break away from elementary school teaching and enter the field in greater numbers in other areas. A recent sample of

members of the Music Educators National Conference indicates that 80% of the music teachers in elementary schools are women, while in high schools and colleges 75% of the teachers are men. A recent survey conducted by the *Music Journal* found that of the 1427 musicians under concert management only 31% are women, and of these 74% are singers. The 5 leading symphony orchestras in the United States--i.e., the Boston, Chicago, Cleveland, New York, and Philadelphia orchestras--include only 38 women in their ranks within a total of 527 musicians.

76   Literature about women as composers of art music

2989 **A.H. Several works given Town Hall premières**, *New York*
rm *Times* 2 Feb 1970, 28.
Reviews Vally Weigl's *Songs from Do not awake me* (*WIAM* 3794) and Alida Vazquez's *Watercolors of Mexico* (*WIAM* 4995). Other composers whose works were performed included Paul Reif, Eugene Seaman, Harold Branch, and Charles Haubiel.

→ **Albuquerque, New Mexico, University of New Mexico, Fine Arts Library. A checklist of music in manuscript by Eunice Lea Kettering**, *see* 1bm[01].

2990 ALSTON, Vernon. **Festival of Contemporary Music's fourth**
rm **program is presented here**, *Baton Rouge (La.) State-Times* 23 Feb 1976, B-6.
Reviews Gloria Coates's *Voices of women in wartime* (*WIAM* 3425).

→ ANDERSON, E. **Contemporary American composers: a biographical dictionary**, *see* 48bm[05].

2991 ANTHEIL, George. **Peggy Glanville-Hicks**, *Bulletin. American*
ap *Composers Alliance* IV/1 (1954) 2-9. *Illus., list of works.*
Discusses Peggy Glanville-Hicks's *Letters from Morocco* (*WIAM* 4423), *Sinfonia da pacifica* (*WIAM* 4424), sonata for piano and percussion (*WIAM* 3501), harp sonata (*WIAM* 4639), and *The transposed heads* (*WIAM* 4804). Includes a biographical sketch, a list of works arranged by genre with complete publication information, and excerpts from reviews.

2992 **Anthem notes [I]**, *Journal of Church Music* XVI/10 (Nov 1974)
rm 18.
Reviews Natalie Sleeth's *We had a share* (*WIAM* 4194).

2993 **Anthem notes [II]**, *Journal of Church Music* XVI/8 (Sept 1974) 31.
rm
Reviews Natalie Sleeth's *Noël, noël, a boy is born* (*WIAM* 4182).

2994 ANTHONY, Michael. **Orchestra plays composer's *Lament***,
rm *Minneapolis Tribune* 22 Oct 1956, B-5.
Reviews Marga Richter's *Lament for string orchestra* (*WIAM* 4504).

2995 ARCHIBALD, Bruce. **Reviews of records**, *Musical Quarterly*
rr LXI/4 (Oct 1975) 638-41.
Reviews Jean Eichelberger Ivey's *Aldebaran* (*WIAM* 4332), *Hera, hung from the sky* (*WIAM* 4333), *Terminus* (*WIAM* 4336), and *Three songs of night* (*WIAM* 4337) as recorded on Folkways, FTS 33439.

2996 ASHLEY, Patricia. **Here they are--one plastic platter**, *Ms.* III/
rr 5 (Nov 1975) 111-14.
Reviews recordings of the following works: selected piano music by Amy Cheney Beach on Genesis 1054, entitled *Piano music of Mrs. H.H.A. Beach*; Netty Simons's *Music for young listeners* on Composers Recordings, CRI 309; and Ruth Crawford Seeger's *Two movements for chamber orchestra*, Thea Musgrave's *Chamber concerto no. 2* (*WIAM* 3616), and Joyce Mekeel's *Planh* on Delos 25405. A discography of currently available recordings by 46 women composers--chiefly contemporary and American--is included.

→ **Available recordings of works by women composers**, *see* 2ap[01].

2997 BAKER, David N.; BELT, Lida M.; HUDSON, Herman,
bd eds. **Undine Smith Moore**, *The black composer speaks* (Metuchen, N.J.: Scarecrow, 1978) 172-202. *Port., bibliog., list of works, discog., index.*
As one of 15 black composers interviewed, Undine Smith Moore discusses the following topics: 1) defining black music, 2) black music and the educational system, 3) advice for the aspiring young black composer, 4) compositional

techniques and style, and 5) her personal philosophy as reflected in her music. A biographical sketch is included.

2998 BARKIN, Elaine. **Louise Talma: *The tolling bell***, *Perspectives*
ap *of New Music* X/2 (spring-summer 1972) 142-52. *Facsim., music.*
Discusses Louise Talma's triptych *The tolling bell* (*WIAM* 4537), set to texts by Shakespeare, Marlowe, and Donne. Talma's orchestration, text-setting, and pitch-organizing procedures are considered.

2999 ***Beguine* to bow at youth concert**, *Washington Post* 8 Oct 1962,
an B-4.
Esther Williamson Ballou wrote *Beguine* (*WIAM* 3359) for 2 pianos, 4 hands, to be performed at a recital by 2 of her students. Subsequently she orchestrated the work, and it is the orchestral version that will be performed at a forthcoming youth concert by the National Symphony Orchestra. Ballou seemed destined for a brilliant career when she was crippled by arthritis in 1943. Although the disease consumed 10 years of her life, she has recovered and now teaches on the faculty of the American U.

3000 BELT, Byron. **Oratorio's bicentennial salute witty and noble**,
rm *Long Island (N.Y.) Press* 21 May 1976, 12.
Reviews Vivian Fine's *Meeting for equal rights 1866* (*WIAM* 3930).

3001 B.J. **Buebendorf work has première here**, *New York Times* 25
rm Feb 1955, 16.
Reviews Julia Smith's *Two pieces for viola and piano* (*WIAM* 3738), performed by violist Eugenie Dengel and the composer. Other composers represented on the program included Francis Buebendorf, Darius Milhaud, Aaron Copland, and Paul Hindemith.

3002 BLECHNER, Mark. **Van de Vate, Tucker**, *High Fidelity/*
rm *Musical America* XXVII/3 (Mar 1977) MA 26-27.
Reviews Nancy Van de Vate's *Trio for strings* (*WIAM* 3780). Works by Tui St. George Tucker were also on the program.

→ BLOCK, Adrienne. **Women in composition**, *see* 99as[20].

3003 BOAL, Sara. *Cycle of love, A. Four art songs*, *Composers and*
rm *Authors Association of America Magazine* XXXII/1-2 (Nov 1976) 12.
Reviews Jeanne Singer's song cycle (*WIAM* 4962).

3004 BRODER, Nathan. **Columbia's modern American music**
rm **series**, *Musical Quarterly* XLI/4 (Oct 1955) 551-55.
Reviews 24 recorded works by 15 composers, including Peggy Glanville-Hicks's sonata for piano and percussion (*WIAM* 3501) and *Concertino da camera* (*WIAM* 3500). This article is signed N.B., and Broder's name has been supplied.

3005 **Broude Brothers Limited**, *Choral Journal* XVII/5 (Jan 1977) 35.
rm
Reviews Judith Lang Zaimont's *O mistress mine* (*WIAM* 2663).

3006 BURFORD, Exie. **Salute to American composers: Julia**
ap **Smith, woman of talents**, *Music Clubs Magazine* XLVII/3 (Feb 1968) 20. *Port., list of works.*
At the meeting of the National Federation of Music Clubs held in St. Louis in the fall of 1967, Julia Smith's *Invocation* (*WIAM* 4199) was chosen as the federation's official invocation song. A brief résumé of the composer's background and lists of her principal compositions and première performances are included.
(Julia Smith, abridged)

→ **Catalogue of contemporary American women composers. Harold Branch Publishing, Inc.; Jelsor Music Co.**, *see* 8bm[01].

3007 CHERRY, Robert L. **Tucson Symphony: Richter première**,
rm *High Fidelity/Musical America* XXVI/7 (July 1976) MA 34.
Reviews Marga Richter's piano concerto entitled *Landscapes of the mind I* (*WIAM* 4505).

3008 **Choral music reviews**, *Choral Journal* X/7 (Apr 1970) 23.
rm
Reviews Emma Lou Diemer's *For ye shall go out with joy* (*WIAM* 3917).

3009 ***Cockcrow* is smashing hit. Audience captivated by composer,**
rm **colorful music, and costuming**, *Marshall (Tex.) News Messenger* 7 Feb 1964, A-2.
Reviews Julia Smith's opera *Cockcrow* (*WIAM* 4837).

3010 COMMANDAY, Robert. **Women composers: a place to**
rm   **stand**, *High Fidelity/Musical America* XXV/1 (Jan 1975) MA 23, 39.
Reviews the following works as performed at the Cabrillo Music Festival in
Aptos, Calif., under the direction of Dennis Russell Davies: Beth Anderson's
She wrote (*WIAM* 3358), *Joan* (*WIAM* 4787), and *Tulip clause*; Victoria
Bond's *Suite aux troubadors* (*WIAM* 3399) and *C-A-G-E-D* (*WIAM* 4372); and
Netty Simons's *Pied Piper of Hamlin*. Women composers from the past who
were represented at the festival by performances of their works included Clara
Schumann, Ruth Crawford Seeger, and Barbara Strozzi.

3011 CORY, Eleanor. **Review of records. Martin Boykan: string**
rr   **quartet no. 1 (1967); Elaine Barkin: string quartet (1969)**,
Musical Quarterly LXII/4 (Oct 1976) 616-20. *Music.*
Reviews Elaine Barkin's string quartet (*WIAM* 3383) and Martin Boykan's
string quartet no. 1, as performed by the American Quartet on Composers
Recordings, CRI SD 338.

3012 CROWDER, Charles. **Gallery concert**, *Washington Post* 18 Oct
rm   1971, B-6.
Reviews Margaret Garwood's *The cliff's edge* (*WIAM* 4914), performed at the
National Gallery, Washington, D.C.

3013 DALLMAN, Paul. **Chinese songs engaging**, *Washington Eve-*
rm   *ning Star* 29 Feb 1972, A-11.
Reviews Emma Lou Diemer's *Four Chinese love-poems for soprano and harp or
piano* (*WIAM* 4905), performed by Phyllis Bryn-Julson, soprano, and Sylvia
Meyer, harpist.

→   DANIEL, Oliver. **New festival, The**, *see* 10ap[01].

3015 DAVIS, Peter G. **Concert is salute to Dorothy Moore**, *New*
rm   *York Times* 25 Feb 1975, 28.
Reviews Dorothy Rudd Moore's *Dream variations* (*WIAM* 4680).

3016 DAVIS, Peter G. **Moore shows flair and polish on cello**, *New*
rm   *York Times* 15 May 1972, 44.
Reviews Dorothy Rudd Moore's *Dirge and deliverance* (*WIAM* 3607),
performed by Kermit Moore.

3017 DAVIS, Peter G. **Moore song cycle heard in première**, *New*
rm   *York Times* 30 Oct 1972, 39.
Reviews Dorothy Rudd Moore's song cycle *From the dark tower* (*WIAM* 4466),
sung by Hilda Harris with the Symphony of the New World under the direction
of George Byrd.

3018 DAVIS, Peter G. **Music: chamber society**, *New York Times* 19
rm   Oct 1975, I-53.
Reviews the American première of Thea Musgrave's *Space play. A concerto for
9 instruments* (*WIAM* 3626), as performed by the Chamber Music Soc. of
Lincoln Center.

3019 DAVIS, Peter G. **Music: tribute. Howard Swanson is**
rm   **honored by Triad Chorale**, *New York Times* 13 June 1977, 35.
Reviews Dorothy Rudd Moore's *In celebration* (*WIAM* 4066). Other composers
represented on the program honoring black composer Howard Swanson were
Irwin Bazelon, Arthur Cunningham, John Childs, and Hale Smith.

3020 DAVIS, Peter G. **Recital: Miller at piano**, *New York Times* 17
rm   Nov 1976, C-24.
Reviews Joan Tower's *Black topaz* (*WIAM* 3763). Other composers whose
works were performed by the Group for Contemporary Music and pianist
Robert Miller at the Manhattan School of Music included John Cage, Milton
Babbitt, David Del Tredici, and Gregory Ballard.

3021 DAVIS, Peter G. **Violinist and soprano offer Dorothy**
rm   **Moore's** *Sonnets*, *New York Times* 24 May 1976, 36.
Reviews the composer's song cycle *Sonnets on love, rosebuds, and death* (*WIAM*
3610), performed by violinist Sanford Allen and soprano Miriam Barton.

3022 DOWNES, Edward O.D. **Notes on the program. Julia**
ap   **Perry's** *Study for orchestra*, *Programmes. Philharmonic Symphony
Soc. of New York* 9 May 1965, B.
Julia Perry's *Study for orchestra* was composed in Florence in 1952 and was
first performed by the Turin Symphony Orchestra under the direction of Dean
Dixon. Born in Lexington, Ky., Perry was trained at Westminster Choir Col. in
Princeton, N.J. and at the Juilliard School. She also studied abroad with Luigi
Dallapiccola and Nadia Boulanger.

3023 DOWNES, Edward O.D. **Clio Concert Trio presents pro-**
rm   **gram**, *New York Times* 30 Oct 1956, 43.
Reviews the première performance of Julia Smith's *Trio--Cornwall for violin,
cello, and piano* (*WIAM* 3737) by the Clio Concert Trio in New York.

3024 D.R.H. **Owen, Blythe.** *Sarabande and gigue*, *Instrumentalist*
rm   XXIX/8 (Apr 1975) 80.
Reviews Blythe Owen's *Sarabande and gigue* (*WIAM* 3651).

3025 DYER, Richard. **Muddled finale to Music Days, A**, *Boston*
rm   *Evening Globe* 1 Nov 1976, 39.
Reviews Ellen Taaffe Zwilich's string quartet (*WIAM* 3819), performed by the
New York String Quartet at a concert sponsored by the International Soc. for
Contemporary Music/World Music Days. Other composers whose works were
on the program included Donald Sur, Jacques-Louis Monod, Jacob Druckman,
and Ezra Laderman.

3026 DYER, Richard. **New work proves effective**, *Boston Evening*
rm   *Globe* 14 Aug 1975, 26.
Reviews Shulamit Ran's *Ensembles for 17* (*WIAM* 3687).

3027 EATON, Quaintance. **Women composers honored**, *Music*
ap   *Clubs Magazine* XLVIII/4 (Apr 1969) 42.
Works by American women were performed to a capacity audience of 250 at
the Donnell Library Center at a concert sponsored by the Musicians Club of
New York. The 5 composers represented were Mabel Wheeler Daniels,
Elizabeth Gould, Julia Smith, Louise Talma, and Elinor Remick Warren. All
were present, except Daniels, and stated that they had not felt the effects of sex
discrimination. However, Warren noted her displeasure with press comments
that her works sounded as if composed by a man, and Julia Smith remarked
that opera houses frequently take risks in producing new works by men, but are
not willing to take similar risks for works by women.   *(Julia Smith, abridged)*

3028 **Elinor Remick Warren honored in Israel**, *Music Clubs Magazine*
ro   LVI/2 (winter 1976-77) 13.
Elinor Remick Warren's *Abram in Egypt* (*WIAM* 4242) was the featured work
in 2 concerts honoring the United States at the Israel Festival in 1976.
Commissioned by musicologist Louis Sudler and based on the text of one of the
Dead Sea Scrolls, Warren's composition was first performed in Los Angeles in
1961.   *(Julia Smith, abridged)*

→   ELKINS-MARLOW, Laurine. **Have women in this country**
written for full orchestra?, *see* 14ap[01].

3029 ERICSON, Raymond. **Celebrating Louise Talma**, *New York*
an   *Times* 4 Feb 1977, 7. *Illus.*
On the occasion of her 50th year of teaching at Hunter Col., Louise Talma was
honored by a program of her compositions that included *Terre de France*
(*WIAM* 4987), *Voices of peace* (*WIAM* 4236), *All the days of my life: cantata
for tenor, clarinet, violoncello, percussion, piano, and celesta* (*WIAM* 3751),
Summer sounds (*WIAM* 3757), and her piano sonata no. 2 (*WIAM* 4756). The
composer grew up in New York and studied with Nadia Boulanger and Isidore
Philipp in France. Talma is the only composer who has collaborated with
Thornton Wilder on an opera, *The Alcestiad* (*WIAM* 4846), which was
performed in Frankfurt in 1962.

3030 ERICSON, Raymond. **Clamma Dale at best in Falla**, *New*
rm   *York Times* 7 May 1977, 36.
Reviews Ellen Taaffe Zwilich's *Trompeten* (*WIAM* 5024), performed by
soprano Clamma Dale. Manuel de Falla's *Seguidilla* was also on the program.

3031 ERICSON, Raymond. **Concert offers young composers**, *New*
rm   *York Times* 22 May 1963, 37.
Reviews Ursula Mamlok's *Variations for solo flute* (*WIAM* 4673), performed at
Carnegie Recital Hall. The program also included works by Howard Rovics,
Harvey Sollberger, Charles Wuorinen, Charles Whittenberg, and M. William
Kerlins.

3032 ERICSON, Raymond. **First for sonata by Luening, A**, *New*
rm   *York Times* 20 Nov 1975, 50.
Reviews Judith Lang Zaimont's *Greyed sonnets* (*WIAM* 5021). A 3rd composer
represented on the program was Eric Salzman.

3033 ERICSON, Raymond. **Ingenious** *Solitaire* **stands out in an**
rm   **evening for new music**, *New York Times* 17 Feb 1972, 32.
Reviews Barbara Kolb's *Solitaire* (*WIAM* 4339), performed by Richard
Trythall at Carnegie Recital Hall. The program also included works by Lukas
Foss, Leo Smit, Makoto Shinohara, and Julius Eastman.

3034 ERICSON, Raymond. **Patricia Morehead plays courageous**
rm   **oboe program**, *New York Times* 12 June 1977, 59.
Reviews Eleanor Cory's *Trio for flute, oboe, and piano* (*WIAM* 3431).

→   EWEN, David. **Composers since 1900**, *see* 51bm[05].

3035 **Exhibition. Contemporary women composers in the United**
ap   **States**, *Musical America* LXXXIII/8 (Aug 1963) 12.
Reports that scores for a wide range of vocal and instrumental compositions by
the following composers are on exhibit in the Music Division of the New York
Public Library: Gena Branscombe, Mabel Wheeler Daniels, Vivian Fine,
Miriam Gideon, Elizabeth Gould, Mary Howe, Netty Simons, Julia Smith,
Louise Talma, and Elinor Remick Warren.

3036 FARNSWORTH, Paul R. **Effects of role-taking on artistic**
ap   **achievement, The**, *Journal of Aesthetics and Art Criticism* XVIII/3
(Mar 1960) 345-49.
"In this sample of the American population, men believe creativity in the arts
has a much closer linkage to their own interest patterns than those of women.
The more passive artistic activities and those that deal with performance are
deemed to be more in the feminine role. Women appear to be so impressed by
the dismal picture history has so far given of their contributions to the arts that
they picture creativity as an enduring characteristic of the masculine role. So
long as they retain this image, it is likely that relatively few will be willing to
put forth the effort essential to sustained creativity".

3037 FINE, Vivian; DLUGOSZEWSKI, Lucia. **Composer/cho-**
ap   **reographer. Choreographer/composer**, *Dance Perspectives* 16
(1963) 8-11, 21-25. *Illus.*
Vivian Fine and Lucia Dlugoszewski discuss the relationship of their music to
dance in this symposium of composers and choreographers. The following
works by Fine are considered: *The race of life* (*WIAM* 4412), which was
written for Doris Humphrey; *Opus 51*, written for Charles Weidman; and
Alcestis, written for Martha Graham. Biographical sketches of the 2 composers
and chronological lists of their dance scores are included.

3038 FISHER, Barbara E. Scott. **Women today: piano keys career**,
an   *Christian Science Monitor* 21 Feb 1956, 12. *Illus., port.*
Summarizes the career of Julia Smith, who grew up in a musical household and
attended North Texas State Col. When she began at the Juilliard School in
1930, her piano teacher, Carl Friedberg, persuaded her to focus on composition.
Subsequently she received a composition fellowship and studied with Rubin
Goldmark. Smith's interest in Aaron Copland was inspired by *Billy the kid*, an
interest she ascribes in part to her Texas origins; her doctoral dissertation on
Copland resulted. A composer of large scale works including a chamber
symphony (*WIAM* 4519) and a piano concerto (*WIAM* 4516) that have been
played by leading orchestras, Smith performs as a pianist and has taught theory
at Juilliard.   *(Julia Smith, abridged)*

3039 FLANNAGAN, William. **Miss Renzi sings, four composers**
rm   **accompany her**, *New York Herald Tribune* 19 May 1959, 19.
Reviews Marga Richter's *Transmutation. Eight songs to Chinese poems* (*WIAM*
4952), performed by Dorothy Renzi. Other composers represented on the
program were John Edmunds, John La Montaine, and Lee Hoiby.

3040 FLEMING, Shirley. **Thea Musgrave's elusive** *Ariadne*, *New*
an   *York Times* 25 Sept 1977, II-19, 22. *Illus.*
Discusses Thea Musgrave's *The voice of Ariadne* (*WIAM* 4824) and *Mary,
Queen of Scots*. Conducted by the composer, the 2 operas will receive their
American premières during the 1977-78 season in New York and Norfolk, Va.,
respectively. Musgrave studied composition at Edinburgh U. and then
continued with Nadia Boulanger in Paris. Last year she conducted her *Concerto
for orchestra* (*WIAM* 4470) in her American debut as a conductor with the
Philadelphia Orchestra. Musgrave's works to date include 4 operas, and choral,
solo vocal, chamber, and orchestral works.

3041 GALKIN, Elliott. **Baltimore Symphony; Jean Eichelberger**
rm   **Ivey première**, *High Fidelity/Musical America* XXVI/8 (Aug 1976)
MA 22.
Reviews the première of Jean Eichelberger Ivey's *Testament of Eve* (*WIAM*
4443), sung by Elaine Bonazzi with the Baltimore Symphony Orchestra under
the direction of Leon Fleisher.

3042 GETLEIN, Frank. **Two blows for women's liberation**, *Wash-*
an   *ington Star-News* 22 Dec 1973, B-7.
Discusses the film *A woman is ...* about composer-teacher Jean Eichelberger
Ivey. During the film Ivey is interviewed regarding the problems of musicians-
-especially women composers--and is seen at work as a teacher and a composer
instructing a woodwind ensemble in the performance of one of her compositions. The other "blow" in the title refers to the film of Ibsen's play, *A doll's
house*, starring Jane Fonda.

→   GILBERT, Steven. **Ultra-modern idiom, The: a survey of**
New music, *see* 2022ap[66].

3043 *Glittering gate, Rapunzel* **in first performances**, *Musical Amer-*
rm   *ica* LXXIX/7 (June 1959) 20.
Reviews the premières of Peggy Glanville-Hicks's *The glittering gate* (*WIAM*
4799) and of Lou Harrison's *Rapunzel*.

3044 GOLDSMITH, Harris. **Daniel Heifetz, violin**, *High Fidelity/*
rm   *Musical America* XXVII/9 (Sept 1977) MA 24.
Reviews Marga Richter's *Landscapes of the mind II* (*WIAM* 3691), performed
by violinist Daniel Heifetz.

3045 GRUEN, John. **Miriam Gideon's music heard at recital hall**,
rm   *New York Herald Tribune* 15 Apr 1961, 6.
Reviews Miriam Gideon's cello sonata (*WIAM* 3494), string quartet (*WIAM*
3490), and 2 groups of songs--*The hound of heaven* (*WIAM* 3487) and *Sonnets
from Shakespeare* (*WIAM* 3496). The performance took place at Carnegie
Recital Hall.

3046 GUSSOW, Mel. **Elizabeth Swados--a runaway talent**, *New*
an   *York Times* 5 Mar 1978, VI-18, 19-22, 52-59. *Illus.*
Discusses *Runaways*, a musical theater piece by Elizabeth Swados. The
composer describes her method of choosing a company of actors and her
conception of music and theater. She has collaborated with Andrei Serban on
Euripides's *Medea* and *The Trojan women*--which have toured throughout
Europe and the Middle East. Her most recent musical creation is *Nightclub
cantata*, composed in 1977.

3047 GUSSOW, Mel. **Elizabeth Swados writes cantata for ca-**
an   **baret**, *New York Times* 7 Jan 1977, C-3.
Discusses Elizabeth Swados's *Nightclub cantata*, a musical revue. Born in
Buffalo, Swados studied composition with Henry Brant at Bennington Col. She
has written the music for Joseph Papp's productions of Chekhov's *The cherry
orchard* and Aeschylus's *Agamemnon* in New York.

3048 GUZZO, R. Louis. **Memorial work crowns program of new**
rm   **music**, *Seattle Times* 8 Dec 1964, 24.
Reviews Ursula Mamlok's *Stray birds. Five aphorisms for soprano, flute, and
violoncello* (*WIAM* 3589), dedicated to the memory of John F. Kennedy.

3049 HARMAN, Carter. **Forum hears music by Richter, Sokoloff**,
rm   *New York Times* 5 Feb 1951, 18.
Reviews Marga Richter's clarinet sonata (*WIAM* 3695), performed by Herbert
Tichman and the composer. Works by Noel Sokoloff were also heard.

3050 HARRIS, Carl G., Jr. **Unique world of Undine Smith Moore,**
ap   **The**, *Choral Journal* XVI/5 (Jan 1976) 2, 6-7. *List of works.*
Presents a biographical sketch of the composer, who was born in 1905, and a
selected list of her published choral compositions. Discusses the influences
found in Moore's choral writing, which include the heritage of her devoutly
religious parents, her association with Dr. John Work as a student at Fisk U.,
her contacts with the Harlem Renaissance as a graduate student in New York,
and other influences including Negro spirituals, ragtime, blues, jazz, and gospel
music. Special mention is made of her choral works on the texts of famous
poets, and those settings written in a black idiom based on the composer's
personal collection of Negro folk songs and spirituals as recorded in "south-
side" Virginia. The influence of Undine Smith Moore on the careers of many of
her students who have become professional musicians in the United States and
abroad is considered.   *(Author)*

3051 HASKINS, John. **Anniversary concert honors Kindler**, *Wash-*
rm   *ington Evening Star* 8 Jan 1963, B-11.
Reviews Emma Lou Diemer's *Sextet for winds and piano* (*WIAM* 3452),
performed at the 11th anniversary concert of the Hans Kindler Foundation.

3052 HENAHAN, Donal. **Concert honors black composers**, *New*
rm   *York Times* 29 May 1968, 20.
Reviews Dorothy Rudd Moore's *Modes for string quartet* (*WIAM* 3609). Other
composers represented on the program were Ulysses Kay, Carman Moore, Noel
da Costa, Hale Smith, William Fischer, and Stephen Chambers.

3053 HENAHAN, Donal. **Music: American range**, *New York Times*
rm   18 Mar 1976, 51.
Reviews the New York première of Louise Talma's *Summer sounds* (*WIAM*
3757), as performed in the Bicentennial Chamber Music Series at Carnegie
Hall. Other composers represented on the program included Charles Ives,
George Rochberg, and George Gershwin.

3054 HENAHAN, Donal. **Music by Vivian Fine**, *New York Times* 17
rm   Apr 1973, 35.
Reviews Vivian Fine's *Concerto for piano strings and percussion for one player*
(*WIAM* 4625).

3055 HENAHAN, Donal. **Music: moderns' hearing**, *New York*
rm   *Times* 19 Aug 1970, 34.
Reviews Barbara Kolb's *Trobar clus* (*WIAM* 3563), commissioned by the
Berkshire Music Center and the Fromm Music Foundation. The concert--which
also included performances of works by Mario Davidowsky, John Heiss,
Donald Lybbert, and George Wilson--was the 2nd in the Festival of Contemporary Music at the Berkshire Music Center.

3056 HENAHAN, Donal. **Music: two "firsts" for Sarah Caldwell**,
ro   *New York Times* 12 Nov 1975, 48.
Reviews the first concert by the New York Philharmonic exclusively devoted to
works by women composers. Conducted by Sarah Caldwell, the program
included an overture by Grazyna Bacewicz, the Andante from Ruth Crawford
Seeger's string quartet (*WIAM* 2477) played by string orchestra, Lili Boulanger's tone poem *Faust et Hélène*, Pozzi Escot's *Sands* (*WIAM* 4409), and Thea
Musgrave's clarinet concerto (*WIAM* 3622). The other "first" in the article's
title refers to the fact that Caldwell became the first woman to conduct a New
York Philharmonic Pension Fund concert.

3057 HENAHAN, Donal. **Rebel who found a cause**, *New York*
an   *Times* 17 Nov 1976, C-21. *Illus.*
A native of Hartford, Barbara Kolb majored in clarinet as an undergraduate at
Hartt Col. of Music. Despite parental opposition and the opinion of her first
composition teacher--Arnold Franchetti--that "there never has been a good
woman composer", Kolb persevered and earned a master's degree in composition from Hartt. Of her subsequent teachers, Gunther Schuller and Lukas Foss
have been major influences. She achieved her first success with *Trobar clus*
(*WIAM* 3563) at the Festival of Contemporary Music in 1970. Since 1970 Kolb
has won the Rome Prize Fellowship and prestigious commissions.

3058 HENAHAN, Donal. **Singer with flair**, *New York Times* 26 Sept
rm   1972, 40.
Reviews Ursula Mamlok's *Haiku settings* (*WIAM* 3587), performed by Lee
Dougherty at Alice Tully Hall in New York.

3059 HIGGINS, Ardis O. **Brilliant program of organ music**, *Santa*
rm   *Barbara (Calif.) News Press* 13 May 1973, D-11.
Reviews the following organ works composed and performed by Emma Lou
Diemer: *Fantasy on O sacred head* (*WIAM* 4609), *Declarations for organ*
(*WIAM* 4607), and *Toccata and fugue for organ* (*WIAM* 4616).

3060 HIGGINS, Ardis O. **Rare musical offering, A**, *Santa Barbara*
rm   *(Calif.) News Press* 30 Apr 1976, C-10.
Reviews Emma Lou Diemer's *Pianoharpsichordorgan* (*WIAM* 3450) and
Declarations for organ (*WIAM* 4607).

3061 HOROWITZ, Joseph. **Music: Xenakis, Wuorinen et al.**, *New*
rm   *York Times* 4 Feb 1977, C-18.
Reviews Joan La Barbara's *Vocal extensions* (*WIAM* 4345). Other composers
represented on the program were Iannis Xenakis, Charles Wuorinen, and
Milton Babbitt.

3062 HRUBY, Frank. **Toledo teacher is winner in Shepherd**
rm   **contest**, *Cleveland Press* 5 May 1969, C-8.
Reviews Elizabeth Gould's *Personal and private* (*WIAM* 3505).

3063 HUGHES, Allen. **Choral work built on Kennedy words**, *New*
rm   *York Times* 13 May 1968, 52.
Reviews Louise Talma's *A time to remember* (*WIAM* 4235), performed by the
Hunter Col. Choir, conducted by Ralph Hunter. The choral work is based on
speeches and favorite quotations of John F. Kennedy.

3064 HUGHES, Allen. **Composers' group plays seven pieces in**
rm   **Carnegie debut**, *New York Times* 19 Apr 1975, 26.
Reviews Alison Nowak's *Musica composita I for piano and chamber players*
(*WIAM* 3638).

3065 HUGHES, Allen. **Concert centers on Miriam Gideon**, *New*
rm   *York Times* 15 Apr 1961, 14.
Reviews a concert in Carnegie Recital Hall devoted to music by Miriam
Gideon. Her string quartet (*WIAM* 3490), sonata for cello and piano (*WIAM*
3494), *The hound of heaven* (*WIAM* 3487), and *Sonnets from Shakespeare*
(*WIAM* 3496) were included on the program.

3066 HUGHES, Allen. **Music: a Boulez evening**, *New York Times* 2
rm   Feb 1975, 47.
Reviews Ellen Taaffe Zwilich's *Symposium for orchestra* (*WIAM* 4564),
performed by the Juilliard Orchestra under the direction of Pierre Boulez. Other
composers represented on the program were Paul Alan Levi and Ira Taxin.

3067 HUGHES, Allen. **Reston Trio offers first of two concerts**,
rm   *New York Times* 27 Mar 1970, 24.
A review of Dorothy Rudd Moore's piano trio no. 1 (*WIAM* 3612).

3068 HUMPHREY, Doris. **Music for an American dance**, *Bulletin*.
ap   *American Composers Alliance* VIII/1 (1958) 4.
Discusses Vivian Fine's *The race of life* (*WIAM* 4412), written expressly for the
author in 1937, and *Opus 51*, composed in 1938 for Charles Weidman.

3069 HUNSBERGER, Donald R. **New music reviews. Wind and**
rm   **percussion ensemble grade V**, *Instrumentalist* XXXI/11 (June
      1977) 86.
Reviews Emma Lou Diemer's *Music for woodwind quartet* (*WIAM* 3449).

3070 ISAAC, Merle. **New music reviews. Orchestra grade IV**,
rm   *Instrumentalist* XXVI/1 (Aug 1971) 62.
Reviews Emma Lou Diemer's *Rondo concertante* (*WIAM* 4401).

3071 IVEY, Jean Eichelberger; OLIVEROS, Pauline. **Observations**
bd   **by composers**, *Electronic music: a listener's guide*. Ed. by Elliott
      SCHWARTZ (New York: Praeger, 1973) 230-34, 246-49.
Jean Eichelberger Ivey and Pauline Oliveros are among the composers who
contributed untitled essays to Part IV of this book. Ivey discusses works which
combine live performers and tape, the aesthetics of tape music, her *Terminus*
(*WIAM* 4336) and *Three songs of night* (*WIAM* 4337). Oliveros considers her
Valentine, a mixed-media work.   *(Jean Eichelberger Ivey)*

→   IVEY, Jean. **Composer as teacher, The**, *see* 3179ap[77].

3072 JEPSON, Barbara. **Music review: music by women--a fall**
rm   **1976 roundup**, *Feminist Art Journal* V/4 (winter 1976-77) 40-41.
Reviews Ellen Taaffe Zwilich's string quartet (*WIAM* 3819) and Jean
Eichelberger Ivey's *Testament of Eve* (*WIAM* 4443).

3073 JOHNSON, Lawrence B. **Milwaukee Symphony: Richter**
rm   **première**, *High Fidelity/Musical America* XXVII/7 (July 1977) MA
      34-35.
Reviews Marga Richter's *Blackberry vines and winter fruit* (*WIAM* 4500).

3074 JOHNSON, Tom. **Lucia Dlugoszewski**, *High Fidelity/Musical*
ap   *America* (*WIAM* 67) MA 4-5.
Discusses Dlugoszewski's evolution as a composer and her present concerns.
Dlugoszewski, who uses both traditional and non-traditional sound sources,
avoids rigid compositional procedures. Although Dlugoszewski is known and
admired among musicians, her music has received relatively little attention
from conductors, recording companies, or the media. The composer studied
with Varèse.

3075 JOHNSON, Tom. **Research and development**, *Village Voice* 27
rm   Jan 1975, 106.
Reviews Joan La Barbara's *Voice piece. One-note internal resonance investigation* (*WIAM* 4935) and *Hear what I feel. A vocal experiment* (*WIAM* 4934). La
Barbara is experimenting with the use of vocal sounds.

3076 JULIUS, Ruth. **Showcasing woman composers**, *Feminist Art*
ap   *Journal* VI/2 (summer 1977) 39-40. *Illus.*
Evaluates a series of 11 concerts at the New School for Social Research during
the fall of 1976 that were devoted to works by women. Entitled "Meet the
woman composer", the series was planned and moderated by Beth Anderson
and Doris Hays. Each concert was followed by an informal discussion with the
composer. The 18 composers who were featured represented a wide variety of
musical styles, ranging from improvisatory, mixed-media pieces to neo-
romantic string quartets.   *(Author)*

3077 KEFALAS, Elinor. **Pauline Oliveros: an interview**, *High*
ap   *Fidelity/Musical America* (*WIAM* 67) MA 24-25.
Oliveros expresses reservations about the new wave of the women's movement
and its importance for women in composition, arguing that the development of
an individual's strength comes through a balance of resistance and support.
However, she feels it is important for women who want to compose to find a
sympathetic environment, and in this respect women's groups of various kinds
can be helpful. Women have been excluded from composition in the past
because composing is telling others what to do. Oliveros prefers to write with a
specific performance in mind.

3078 KLEIN, Howard. **Weekend's other music events. Julia**
rm **Smith plays own works,** *New York Times* 29 Mar 1965, 44.
A review of the composer's string quartet (*WIAM* 3736) and *Three love songs*
(*WIAM* 4973).

3079 LANG, Janice Miller. *Journeys: pilgrims and strangers.* **Alice**
rm **Parker conducts a première,** *Choral Journal* XVI/9 (May 1976)
10-11. *Illus.*
Reviews Alice Parker's *Journeys: pilgrims and strangers* (*WIAM* 4101), as
performed at a convention of the North Central American Choral Director's
Assoc. in Columbus, Ohio. Includes a synopsis of the text of each movement
together with comments by the composer about her aesthetics and philosophy.
(Author, abridged)

3080 LARSEN, Arved M. **Contemporary woman composer, The,**
ap *Pan Pipes of Sigma Iota* LXVIII/1 (Nov 1975) 2.
Discusses a conference held at Southern Connecticut State Col. on 30 Apr. 1975
that brought together 4 leading composers for a panel discussion and included
a concert of their works. The composers were Vivian Fine, Jean Eichelberger
Ivey, Joyce Mekeel, and Joan Panetti. The panel discussed the handicaps faced
by women composers amd possibilities for improvement.

3081 LAUFER, Beatrice. **Woman composer speaks out, A,** *ASCAP*
ap *Today* I/2 (June 1967) 9. *Illus.*
Advocates that other organizations in music follow the example of the
American Soc. for Composers, Authors, and Publishers (ASCAP) in accepting
the woman composer as an integral part of the field of composition. ASCAP
includes women among the recipients for awards in creative achievement.

3082 LAWSHE, Mark. **Cabrillo Festival off to startling, puzzling**
rm **start,** *Santa Cruz (Calif.) Sentinel* 16 Aug 1974, 4.
Reviews the performance of Beth Anderson's *She wrote* (*WIAM* 3358) at
Cabrillo Col., Aptos, Calif.

3083 LERNER, Ellen. **Music of selected contemporary American**
dm **women composers, The: a stylistic anaylsis** (MM thesis,
Musicology: U. of Massachusetts at Amherst, 1976) 124 p. (typescript, xerox). *Music, bibliog., list of works, discog.*
Part I presents biographical information for 22 composers of contemporary art
music and discusses the general stylistic characteristics of their music. Elinor
Remick Warren, Vivian Fine, Joan Tower, and Lucia Dlugoszewski are
included among others. Part II examines in detail Miriam Gideon's *The seasons
of time* (*WIAM* 3493, 4920), Jean Eichelberger Ivey's *Terminus* (*WIAM* 4336),
and Daria Semegen's *Jeux des quatres* (*WIAM* 3707). An extensive list of
contemporary American women composers--with information regarding date
of birth and works published--is included together with a discography of
recordings available through June 1976. *(Author)*

3084 LEVIN, Gregory. **Current chronicle. American Society of**
rm **University Composers,** *Musical Quarterly* LX/4 (Oct 1974) 625-
32.
Reviews Jean Eichelberger Ivey's *Hera, hung from the sky* (*WIAM* 4333) and
Joan Tower's *Breakfast rhythms I and II for clarinet and five instruments*
(*WIAM* 3764).

3085 LIMMERT, Erich. **Hannover Nostalgie Welle in der**
rm **jüngsten Tonkunst Tage Neuer Musik** [Hannover: wave of
nostalgia in the latest music at the Conference of New Music], *Melos*
I/2 (Feb 1975) 117-18. In German.
Reviews Gloria Coates's *Planets* (*WIAM* 4393).

3086 LIMMERT, Erich. **Vier Tage-Festival in Hannover: so**
rm **spassig war neue Music noch nie** [Four-day festival in Hannover: new music was never so amusing], *Hamburger Abendblatt* 5 Feb
1975, 9.
Reviews Gloria Coates's *Planets* (*WIAM* 4393).

3087 L.T. **Composers Forum held at Columbia,** *New York Herald*
rm *Tribune* 16 Jan 1956, 8.
Reviews a Composers Forum concert at Columbia U. that featured the works
of Miriam Gideon and Avery Claflin. Gideon's *The hound of heaven* (*WIAM*
3487), *Three sonnets from Fatal interview* (*WIAM* 3499), and her *Air for violin
and piano* (*WIAM* 3482) were included on the program.

3088 MAIER, Guy. **Great woman composer? When?,** *Etude* LXXII/
ap 5 (May 1954) 21, 59.
"The day of the eminent woman composer is not distant. Today women are
writing better early-grade educational music than most men, and women are
just as good students as men. As theory and piano teachers they excel".

3089 MAMLOK, Ursula. *Polyphony for solo clarinet,* *Contemporary*
rm *Music Newsletter* III/1-2 (Jan 1969) 2.
Mamlok analyzes her *Polyphony I for solo clarinet* (*WIAM* 4672).

3090 MARGRAVE, Wendell. **Diemer piano etudes acclaimed at**
rm **première,** *Washington Evening Star* 21 Apr 1966, D-[22].
Reviews the world première of Emma Lou Diemer's *Seven etudes for piano*
(*WIAM* 4613), performed by Stewart Gordon.

3091 MCCANN, Anabel Parker. **Texas girls to give own opera--on**
rm **a Texas heroine. Composer, librettist, and prima donna all**
from the Lone Star state, *New York Sun* 2 Feb 1939, 12.
Reviews the première of Julia Smith's opera, *Cynthia Parker*, produced at
North Texas State U. Discusses the background of Leonora Corona, who sang
the title role, and circumstances surrounding composition of the opera. A brief
summary of the plot is included. *(Julia Smith)*

3092 MCGRAW, Cameron. **Piano music for children,** *Notes* XXIX/
rm 2 (Dec 1972) 336-41.
Includes a review of Emma Lou Diemer's *Sound pictures for piano* (*WIAM*
4614).

→ MEAD, Janet. **Catalog of Composers Library,** *see* 25bm[01].

3093 MOMA: women composers, *High Fidelity/Musical America*
rm XXV/12 (Dec 1975) MA 27-28.
Reviews the following works by women, which were performed in the
Summergarden of the Museum of Modern Art (MOMA) on 15 Aug. 1975:
Victoria Bond's *Conversation piece* (*WIAM* 3396); Nancy Chance's *Daysongs*
(*WIAM* 3413) and *Three Rilke songs* (*WIAM* 3418); Claire Polin's *O, aderyn
pur* (*WIAM* 4354); Daria Semegen's *Quattro for flute and piano* (*WIAM* 3709);
and Ruth Shaw Wylie's *Psychogram for piano* and *Three pieces for clarinet and
piano* (*WIAM* 3710).

3094 MONSON, Karen. **Contemporary chamber players: Ran**
rm **première,** *High Fidelity/Musical America* XXVII/5 (May 1977) MA
20.
Reviews Shulamit Ran's *Double vision for two quintets and piano* (*WIAM*
3686).

3095 MONTGOMERY, Merle. **We're on the air! It's time to tune**
ap **in!,** *Music Clubs Magazine* LI/5 (summer 1972) 5, 12-14.
72 radio stations in 34 states as well as the District of Columbia and Okinawa
have agreed to broadcast one or both of 2 thirteen-week radio programs
prepared by Julia Smith, National Chairwoman of American Women Composers, which is a division of the National Federation of Music Clubs. Series I
is devoted to works by the following women: Esther Williamson Ballou,
Marion Bauer, Mabel Wheeler Daniels, Emma Lou Diemer, Judith Dvorkin,
Vivian Fine, Miriam Gideon, Peggy Glanville-Hicks, Elizabeth Gyring, Mary
Howe, Jean Eichelberger Ivey, Ursula Mamlok, Dika Newlin, Pauline Oliveros,
Julia Perry, Claire Polin, Ruth Crawford Seeger, Julia Smith, Louise Talma,
and Elinor Remick Warren. *(Julia Smith, abridged)*

3096 MOOR, Paul. **Louise Talma's** *The Alcestiad* **in première at**
rm **Frankfurt Opera,** *New York Times* 2 Mar 1962, 25.
A review of Louise Talma's *The Alcestiad* (*WIAM* 4846), the first work by an
American woman composer to be produced by a major European opera house.
Talma did not set Thornton Wilder's original play, but rather a new libretto in
free verse that Wilder prepared from his play with a musical setting in mind.
Biographical information on Talma is included.

3097 MORIN, Raymond. *Millenium* **offered at Atlantic Union,**
rm *Worcester (Mass.) Telegram* 22 Apr 1974, 9.
Reviews Margarita Merriman's *The millenium* (*WIAM* 4065), performed at
Atlantic Union Col., South Lancaster, Mass.

3098 MORROW, Grace. **Many women composers hold academic**
an **posts,** *Abilene (Tex.) Reporter-News* 25 Mar 1976, B-1, 2.
Considers briefly the work of the following composers, the majority of whom
are (or were) on music faculties at American colleges and universities: Esther
Williamson Ballou, Margaret Bonds, Vivian Fine, Miriam Gideon, Jean
Eichelberger Ivey, Mana Zucca, Elinor Remick Warren, and Marilyn Ziffrin.
(Author)

3099 MORROW, Grace. **Texas can brag about its women com-**
an **posers,** *Abilene (Tex.) Reporter-News* 23 Mar 1976, B-3. *Illus.*
Discusses briefly the work of the following women, who are either native-born
Texans or are presently active in the state: Radie Britain, Dawn C. Crawford,
Sr. Elaine Gentemann, Shirley Mackie, Julia Morrison, Pauline Oliveros,
Annette Myers Planick, Julia Smith, and Mary Jeanne Van Appledorn. *(Author)*

3100 NAIRN, Norman. *Alice in wonderland*, Rochester (N.Y.) Demo-
rm   crat and Chronicle 7 Nov 1951, 11, 13.
Reviews Florence DuPage's *Alice in wonderland* (*WIAM* 4792), conducted by
Howard Hanson.

3101 **National Federation of Music Clubs' official benediction. A**
ap   **salute to its composer**, *Music Clubs Magazine* XLIX/1 (fall 1969)
        6.
Reports that *Bless us O God* by Glad Robinson Youse was voted the official
benediction song by the National Federation of Music Clubs at its fall meeting
in Charlotte, N.C. Proceeds from the sale of the song will be donated to the
federation's building fund. Youse's career and works are discussed.
(Julia Smith, abridged)

3102 **National Federation of Music Clubs salutes the Decade of**
ap   **Women in a concert of international women composers**,
        Music Clubs Magazine LVI/1 (autumn 1976) 17-21. *Port.*
Reports that a concert at Columbia U. on 7 Nov. 1976 sponsored by the
National Federation of Music Clubs in celebration of the Decade of Women
(1975-85) will consist of works by 5 women composers, including Americans
Jean Eichelberger Ivey and Julia Smith. The Columbia U. Orchestra will be
conducted by Victoria Bond and Joyce Keshner, with mezzo-soprano Elaine
Bonazzi, violist Karen Phillips, and pianist Tana Bowden as soloists. Ivey,
whose work *Testament of Eve* (*WIAM* 3546) uses a text by the composer, is on
the faculty of the Peabody Conservatory. Smith, the composer of the piano
concerto (*WIAM* 4516) to be featured on the concert program, is also known as
an author and an advocate for women composers. Brief biographies of the
conductors and soloists are included.   (Julia Smith, abridged)

3104 NELSON, Boris. **Local composer's music played**, *Toledo*
rm   *Blade* 8 Nov 1976, 6.
Reviews Elizabeth Gould's piano sonata no. 2 (*WIAM* 4641).

3105 NELSON, Boris. **Seventy five hundred attend young people's**
rm   **concerts opened by Toledo Symphony**, *Toledo Blade* 14 Nov
        1973, 26.
Reviews Elizabeth Gould's *Mini-symphony with an introduction to the instruments* (*WIAM* 4427) for young people, performed by the Toledo Symphony
Orchestra.

3106 NELSON, Boris. **Toledo composer wins Delta Omicron**
rm   **contest**, *Toledo Blade* 8 Sept 1971, 18.
Reviews Elizabeth Gould's *(F)Raileries* (*WIAM* 4927).

3107 NELSON, Boris. **Toledo orchestra tries new peristyle enclo-**
rm   **sure**, *Toledo Blade* 16 Oct 1965, 4.
Reviews Elizabeth Gould's *Suite for woodwinds, brass, and percussion* (*WIAM*
4328), performed by the Toledo Symphony Orchestra.

3108 **Netty Simons**, *Composers of the Americas* XVIII (1972) 94-101.
ap   *Illus., music, list of works.*
Presents a biographical sketch of the composer and a classified, chronological
catalogue of her works to 1972.

3109 **New organ music [I]**, *Musical Opinion* XCV/1134 (Mar 1972) 323.
rm
Reviews Emma Lou Diemer's *Fantasy on O sacred head* (*WIAM* 4609).

3110 **New organ music [II]**, *Music. The American Guild of Organists and*
rm   *Royal Canadian College of Organists Magazine* IV/5 (May 1970) 27.
Reviews Emma Lou Diemer's *He leadeth me. Hymn setting for organ* (*WIAM*
4611).

→   **New York, Graduate Center of the City University of New**
        York, Project for the Oral History of Music in America. A
        checklist of oral history materials about women in American
        music, *see* 31bm[01].

3111 OLIVEROS, Pauline. **And don't call them lady composers**,
an   *New York Times* 13 Sept 1970, II-23, 30. *Illus., discog.*
Discusses the question of why there have been no great women composers in
the past and how roles for women are slowly changing at the present time.
Reports that of 1000 composers listed in a current Schwann record catalogue,
75% are contemporary. Of the 75%, only 24 composers are women. A
discography of works by women is included.

3112 OVERTON, Hall. **Classics, The**, *Metronome* LXXII/12 (Dec
rr   1956) 42.
Reviews Marga Richter's piano sonata (*WIAM* 4715), recorded by Menahem
Pressler on MGM E-3244.

3113 PAIGE, Paul. **New choral music**, *Choral Journal* XI/6 (Feb
rm   1971) 24.
Reviews Emma Lou Diemer's *Verses from the Rubáiyát* (*WIAM* 3928).

3114 PANEKY, Claire. **American composer in Germany, An**, *Music*
ap   *Clubs Magazine* LVI/3 (1977) 10-11, 30. *Illus.*
Presents biographical information about and a list of works by Gloria Coates,
who is a European representative of the League of Women Composers. Coates
currently resides in Munich.

3115 PARMENTER, Ross. **Orchestrette is heard**, *New York Times* 4
rm   Mar 1941, 21.
Reviews Julia Smith's *Hellenic suite* (*WIAM* 4520), performed by the
Orchestrette Classique under the direction of Frederique Joanne Petrides.

3116 PARMENTER, Ross. **Recital by Miss Michna**, *New York*
rm   *Times* 31 Oct 1949, 21.
Reviews Julia Smith's *Characteristic suite* (*WIAM* 4737), performed by the
pianist Marienka Michna.

3117 **Peggy Glanville-Hicks**, *Composers of the Americas* XIII (1967)
ap   53-59. *Illus., music, list of works.*
Presents a biographical sketch of the composer and a classified, chronological
catalogue of her works to 1967.

3118 PERKINS, Francis D. **Two orchestras give concerts in**
rm   **Carnegie Hall**, *New York Herald Tribune* 22 Apr 1941, 18.
Reviews Julia Smith's *Liza Jane* (*WIAM* 4521), performed by the Orchestrette
Classique under the direction of Frederique Joanne Petrides. A 2nd orchestral
performance conducted by Otto Klemperer is also reviewed.

3119 PERLE, George. **Music of Miriam Gideon, The**, *Bulletin.*
ap   *American Composers Alliance* VII/4 (1958) 2-9. *Illus., music, list of*
        works.
Analyzes Miriam Gideon's *The hound of heaven* (*WIAM* 3487), string quartet
(*WIAM* 3490), and *Three sonnets from Fatal interview* (*WIAM* 3499). Includes
a brief biographical sketch, a list of works arranged by genre with publication
information, and excerpts from reviews.

→   **Philadelphia, Free Library of Philadelphia, Fleisher Collec-**
        tion. A checklist of source materials by and about women in
        American music, *see* 35bm[01].

3120 PORTER, Andrew. **Musical events: getting to know you**, *New*
rm   *Yorker* 10 Feb 1975, 113-14.
Reviews Ellen Taaffe Zwilich's *Symposium for orchestra* (*WIAM* 4564),
performed by Pierre Boulez with the New York Philharmonic.

3121 **Pozzi Escot**, *Composers of the Americas* XVII (1971) 63-69. *Illus.,*
ap   *music, list of works.*
Presents a biographical sketch of the composer and a classified, chronological
catalogue of her works to 1971.

3122 **Radie Britain wins composers prize**, *New York Times* 28 Mar
an   1941, 27. *Illus.*
Reports that Radie Britain's *Light* (*WIAM* 4383) is the winner of the national
prize competition sponsored by the Boston Women's Symphony Soc. The work
will be performed by the Boston Women's Symphony Orchestra in May.
Honorable mention went to Florence DuPage for *The pond* (*WIAM* 4407) and
to Estelle Cover for *The Mississippi River*.

3123 RICE, Curtis E. *Transposed heads*, *Musical Courier* CLVII/5
rm   (Apr 1958) 31.
Reviews Peggy Glanville-Hicks's *The transposed heads* (*WIAM* 4804). The
article is signed C.E.R., and Rice's name has been supplied.

3124 RICHTER, Marion Morrey. **National Federation of Music**
ap   **Clubs salute to the United Nations features music of Israel**,
        Music Clubs Magazine LIV/3 (1975) 16. *Port.*
A concert featuring the music of Israeli-born Shulamit Ran was broadcast over
the New York radio station WNYC as part of the 1974 "Hands across the sea"
concert, given as the National Federation of Music Clubs's annual salute to the
United Nations. Works performed were Ran's *Structures* composed in 1968,
Toccata for piano composed in 1965, and *O the chimneys* (*WIAM* 4356), all
with the composer at the piano. Speakers included Merle Montgomery,
president of the federation, Marion Morrey Richter, federation chairwoman
for the broadcasts, and Herman Neuman, music director emeritus of WNYC
and originator of the program.   (Julia Smith, abridged)

→   RICHTER, Marion. **Fanfare for the 1969 Parade**, *see* 3183ap[77].

3125   RIEGGER, Wallingford. **Music of Vivian Fine, The**, *Bulletin.*
ap   *American Composers Alliance* VIII/1 (1958) 2-6. *Illus., music, list of works.*
Analyzes Vivian Fine's *A guide to the life expectancy of a rose* (*WIAM* 3473) and *Four pieces for two flutes* (*WIAM* 3470). Includes a biographical sketch and a list of works arranged by genre together with publication information.

3126   RINGENWALD, Richard D. **Music of Esther Williamson**
dm   **Ballou, The: an analytical study** (M.A. diss.: American U., 1960) 20 p. (typescript). *Port., music, list of works, index.*
Summarizes Esther Williamson Ballou's musical training and her work as a composer and teacher. Discusses selected representative compositions, e.g., her sonata for 2 pianos (*WIAM* 3372), *Prelude and allegro for string orchestra and piano* (*WIAM* 4370), piano sonata (*WIAM* 4572), and piano sonatina (*WIAM* 4573).   *(James R. Heintze)*

3127   ROCKWELL, John. **Concert: afternoon premières**, *New York*
rm   *Times* 8 Nov 1976, 45.
Reviews a concert devoted to women composers at Columbia U. in McMillin Theater. Conducted by Victoria Bond, the Columbia U. Orchestra gave the first New York performances of Jean Eichelberger Ivey's *Testament of Eve* (*WIAM* 4443) and Julia Smith's piano concerto (*WIAM* 4516). Other composers represented on the program included Elizabeth Lutyens, Germaine Tailleferre, and Grete von Zieritz.

3128   ROCKWELL, John. **New music: Pauline Oliveros**, *New York*
an   *Times* 23 Sept 1977, C-26.
A native of Houston, Tex., Pauline Oliveros has lived in California since 1952. She began her work in composition with group improvisation, moving on to electronic experimentation and music that includes elements of theater and ritual. In recent years she has devoted herself increasingly to Tibetan Buddhism. Oliveros is director of the Center for Music Experiment at the U. of California at San Diego. A review of her *Horse sings from a cloud*--performed by the composer at the Samaya Foundation--is included.

3129   ROCKWELL, John. **Opera: "Passion of Shaw"**, *New York*
rm   *Times* 3 Apr 1976, 20.
Reviews Alison Nowak's *Musica composita II for solo percussion* (*WIAM* 4687). The program also featured the first performance of Bruce J. Taub's one-act opera *Passion, poison, and petrification or the fatal gozogene*, based on the play by George Bernard Shaw.

→   ROREM, Ned. **Ladies' music**, *see* 166bd[25].

3130   ROSEN, Judith. **Why haven't women become great compos-**
ap   **ers?**, *High Fidelity/Musical America* XXIII/2 (Feb 1973) MA 46, 51-52.
"The woman composer, the patron, and music itself are all victims of traditionally imposed sex roles". The male patron-employer has limited the opportunities available to women composers. Ruth Crawford Seeger and Pauline Oliveros are cited as successful women composers.

3131   R.S. **New music reviews**, *Musical America* LXII/16 (15 Dec 1952)
rm   26.
Reviews Peggy Glanville-Hicks's *Five songs* (*WIAM* 4924), together with other new songs and song cycles by American composers.

3132   RUBIN-RABSON, Grace. **Why haven't women become great**
ap   **composers?**, *High Fidelity/Musical America* XXIII/2 (Feb 1973) MA 47-50.
In Paul Farnsworth's *The effects of role taking on artistic achievement* (*WIAM* 3036), those artistic activities rated most masculine were found to be predominantly of the creative type. The author believes that male-female differences in creative areas have a deep-lying cause: men are active, messianic; women are not, except as regarding their children. Women, who show early verbal competence, usually lack interest in abstract or quantitative thinking, both of which are requisites for serious musical composition.

3133   SAMINSKY, Lazare. **New faces among our composers**,
ap   *Musical Courier* CXXVII/3 (1 Feb 1943) 13, 34. *Illus.*
The early works of Miriam Gideon and Vivian Fine are briefly discussed in this survey of young composers. Other featured composers are Elliott Carter, Normand Lockwood, Edward Cone, and Alvin Etler.

3134   SAMINSKY, Lazare. **Today in the United States**, *Living*
bd   *music of the Americas* (New York: Howell, Soskin, and Gown, 1949) 40-116. *Music, index.*
In this chapter devoted to contemporary American composers, Saminsky

discusses the following works by Vivian Fine: *Allegro concertante*, the oboe sonata, and the songs *Epigram, Bloom*, and *Dirge* (*WIAM* 4908). The following works by Miriam Gideon are also considered: *Dances for two pianos, Slow, slow, fresh fount* (*WIAM* 3949), *Three motets, Lyric piece for string orchestra* (*WIAM* 4416), string quartet (*WIAM* 3490), *The hound of heaven* (*WIAM* 3487), and *Incantation on a Chippewa chant*.

3135   SAMSON, Blake A. **Lovely one-act opera**, *San Mateo (Calif.)*
rm   *Times* 19 Aug 1976, 15.
Reviews Margaret Garwood's *The nightingale and the rose* (*WIAM* 4797), performed in the California Music Center program at the Col. of Notre Dame, Belmont, Calif.

3136   SAMSON, Valerie Brooks. **Valerie Samson: Betty Wong**,
ap   *EAR Magazine* [San Francisco] IV/2 (Feb 1976) 5, 6.
Valerie Samson interviews composer Betty Wong about her background, the responsibilities she feels to audiences, Eastern concepts of music and her current work with the Flowing Stream Ensemble, and her experiences in the San Francisco area.   *(Author)*

3137   SAMSON, Valerie Brooks. **Valerie Samson: Elinor Armer**,
ap   *EAR Magazine* [San Francisco] V/1 (Feb 1977) 3, 6, 7.
Armer talks about her work as a composer, and also about *Music-west*, the inner versus the outer landscape, problems of teaching in the university, and the hazards of role-playing.   *(Author)*

3138   SAMSON, Valerie Brooks. **Valerie Samson interviews Janice**
ap   **Giteck**, *EAR Magazine* [San Francisco] IV/1 (Jan 1976) 3, 6, 7. *Music.*
Composer Janice Giteck talks about her work to Valerie Samson. They discuss the value of studying music theory, methods of education, a method of using chance in composition, reaching an audience, being a woman composer, and the advantages of being a parent at the same time.   *(Author)*

3139   SAMSON, Valerie Brooks. **Valerie Samson interviews Marta**
ap   **Ptaszynska**, *EAR Magazine* [San Francisco] IV/3 (Mar 1976) 2, 3, 7. *Music.*
Ptaszynska, a composer, discusses the difference between experimentation and composition, methods of developing skills in composition, contemporary music in Poland, her impressions of the United States, achieving performances of her works, and her forthcoming book on percussion.   *(Author)*

3140   SCANLAN, Roger. **Spotlight on contemporary American**
rm   **composers**, *Bulletin. National Association of Teachers of Singing* XXXII/4 (May 1976) 36-37, 42.
Reviews the following works by Jan Pfischner McNeil: *Prayers from the ark, In soundless grasses, Aureate earth* (*WIAM* 3597), *Songs of commitment* (*WIAM* 4938), *Three preludes to the aureate earth* (*WIAM* 3598), and *And when the soul*.

3141   SCHAEFER, Theodore. **Music reviews. Solo songs**, *Notes.*
rm   *Music Library Association* VIII/4 (Sept 1951) 751-52.
Reviews Peggy Glanville-Hicks's *Thirteen ways of looking at a blackbird* (*WIAM* 4926) and *Profiles from China* (*WIAM* 4925), together with songs by 7 other composers.

3142   SCHONBERG, Harold C. **Music: a chamber society pro-**
rm   **gram**, *New York Times* 31 Oct 1972, 50.
Reviews the première of Barbara Kolb's *Soundings,* performed by the Chamber Music Soc. of Lincoln Center.

3143   SCHONBERG, Harold C. **Thea Musgrave, at City Opera,**
rm   **introduces** *Voice of Ariadne, New York Times* 2 Oct 1977, I-67.
Reviews the American première of Thea Musgrave's *The voice of Ariadne* (*WIAM* 4824), produced by the New York City Opera and conducted by the composer.

3144   SCHREIBER, Wolfgang. **Aus der Alten Welt** [From the Old
rm   World], *Munich Süddeutsche Zeitung* 14 July 1976, 30. In German.
Reviews Gloria Coates's string quartet no. 3 (*WIAM* 3423).

→   **Scores and parts presented to the Music Library by the Center of the Creative and Performing Arts, State University of New York, Buffalo**, *see* 44bm[01].

3145   SEARS, Lawrence. **Maryland University has fine symphony**,
rm   *Washington Evening Star* 17 Nov 1965, C-27.
Reviews Emma Lou Diemer's *Festival overture* (*WIAM* 4400), performed at the U. of Maryland.

3146 SEGAL, Lewis. **Delcina Stevenson in Westwood**, *Los Angeles*
rm   *Times* 16 June 1976, 12.
Reviews Sharon Davis's *Though men call us free* (*WIAM* 3441), performed by soprano Delcina Stevenson, clarinetist David Atkins, and the composer.

3147 SHERMAN, Robert. **Perlman is soloist with Philharmonic**,
rm   *New York Times* 10 May 1965, 39.
Reviews Julia Perry's *Study for orchestra*, performed by the New York Philharmonic. Also included on the program was Bruch's violin concerto no. 1 in G minor, op. 26, with Itzhak Perlman as soloist.

3148 SHERMAN, Robert. **Precision shown by young mezzo**, *New*
rm   *York Times* 24 Jan 1972, 21.
Reviews Shulamit Ran's *Hatzvi Israel eulogy* (*WIAM* 3688), sung by Susan Reid-Parsons. Other composers represented on the program were Mitya Stillman and Alberto Ginastera.

3149 SINGER, Samuel. **Philadelphia Orchestra**, *Philadelphia In-*
rm   *quirer* 31 Mar 1976, E-2.
Reviews Nancy Chance's *Ritual sounds* (*WIAM* 3417), performed by the Philadelphia Orchestra.

3150 SMITH, Julia. **Report of International Women's Year**
ap   **Committee**, *Music Clubs Magazine* LIV/5 (summer 1975) 29, 41.
A report on music activities connected with International Women's Year, sponsored by the National Federation of Music Clubs. 1) Among the events planned are concerts featuring women performers and works by women to be given at the United Nations and the New York Public Library in a "Hands across the sea" program and broadcast over radio station WNYC. 2) An exhibit prepared by Jean Bowen of the Music Division of the New York Public Library is on display, entitled "The silent battle: women in American music". 3) A 13-week television series over station WNET in New York will feature women composers in a program conducted by women and chaired by pianist Claudette Sorel.   *(Author, abridged)*

→   SMITH, Julia. **Directory of American women composers**, *see* 64bm[05].

3151 SNOW, Harlan. **Symphony, Price unite for interesting con-**
rm   **cert**, *Shreveport (La.) Times* 20 Feb 1977, B-7.
Reviews Beatrice Laufer's *Cry* (*WIAM* 4446), performed by the Shreveport Symphony Orchestra. The actor Vincent Price was featured in another work.

3152 STILMAN, Julia. *Barcarola* (DMA diss., Composition: U. of
dd   Maryland, 1973) 22 p.
Discusses the poetical and theoretical background of Stilman's *Barcarola. Cantata no. 3* (*WIAM* 4224) and includes a score of the work.

3153 STRONGIN, Theodore. **Avant-garde unit plays new works**,
rm   *New York Times* 9 Feb 1970, 47.
Reviews Thea Musgrave's *Music for horn and piano* (*WIAM* 3623), performed by Ralph Froelich, horn, and Gilbert Kalish, piano. Other composers represented on this program sponsored by the League of Composers-International Soc. for Contemporary Music at Carnegie Recital Hall were Erich-Itor Kahn, Richard Ronsheim, Edward Steuermann, and Chinary Ung.

3154 STRONGIN, Theodore. **Concert is given for the fun of it**,
rm   *New York Times* 27 Mar 1968, 40.
Reviews Pauline Oliveros's *Theatre piece*, presented at the Evenings for New Music series at Carnegie Recital Hall.

3155 STRONGIN, Theodore. **New works heard in concert here**,
rm   *New York Times* 23 May 1968, 52.
Reviews Miriam Gideon's *Spiritual madrigals* (*WIAM* 3950) and *Rhymes from the hill* (*WIAM* 3492). Mark Brunswick's *Four madrigals and a motet* were also on the program at Carnegie Hall.

3156 STRONGIN, Theodore. **Richard Elias gives bold violin**
rm   **recital**, *New York Times* 3 Mar 1967, 25.
Reviews the first performance of Dorothy Rudd Moore's *Three pieces for violin and piano* (*WIAM* 3611) by the violinist Richard Elias.

3157 SYKES, Martha M. **Joyce Barthelson**, *Music Clubs Magazine*
ap   XLVII/3 (Feb 1968) 18.
Reports that Joyce Barthelson received first prize for her one-act opera *Chanticleer* in the 1967 contest sponsored by the National Federation of Music Clubs and the American Soc. of Authors, Composers, and Publishers. The award involves cash and a reading by the Metropolitan Opera Studio.

Barthelson is a choral director and both co-founder and co-director of the Hoff-Barthelson Music School in White Plains, N.Y.

3158 **Talma première, opening event, A. Milwaukee Center for**
ap   **Performing Arts**, *Pan Pipes of Sigma Alpha Iota* LXII/2 (Jan 1970) 36, 42. *Illus.*
Discusses Louise Talma's *The tolling bell. Triptych for baritone and orchestra* (*WIAM* 4537), as performed by the Milwaukee Symphony Orchestra under the direction of Kenneth Schermerhorn. The work was commissioned by the MacDowell Club of Milwaukee, and its première was planned to highlight the opening of the city's new Center for the Performing Arts. Talma's *The Alcestiad* (*WIAM* 4846) is also discussed.

3159 TAUBER, Violetta. **Elizabeth Gyring: profile in music**, *Amer-*
ap   *ican-German Review* XXVIII/6 (Aug-Sept 1962) 30-32. *Illus., music.*
Elizabeth Gyring was born and spent the early years of her career in Vienna. Since relocating in New York in 1939, she has doubled her output in composition for a total of more than 100 pieces in practically all genres. Recent performances of Gyring's works include that of her Fantasy for organ at Longwood Gardens in Pennsylvania in 1960, her Adagio for clarinet at a festival in New York also in 1960, and her woodwind quintet at Carnegie Recital Hall in New York in 1961. Most of her music has been published in the American Composers Ed. series (New York).

3160 THOMSON, Virgil. **American music since 1900** (London:
bm   Weidenfeld & Nicolson, 1970) 204 p. *Illus., bibliog., index.*
Among the biographical sketches of more than 100 composers, the following women are represented: Lucia Dlugoszewski, Vivian Fine, Ruth Crawford Seeger, and Louise Talma.

3161 THOMSON, Virgil. **Music: Composers' Forum. For teaching**
rm   **and for the mind**, *New York Herald Tribune* 17 Apr 1950, 10. *Illus.*
Reviews Julia Smith's *Characteristic suite* (*WIAM* 4737) and excerpts from her one-act opera *The gooseherd and the goblin* (*WIAM* 4840), performed by the Teachers Col. Little Symphony Orchestra under the direction of the composer at Columbia U.

3162 TIPTON, Albert. **Flute music review**, *School Musician* XLV/5
rm   (Jan 1974) 60.
Reviews Emma Lou Diemer's *Sonata for flute and piano or harpsichord* (*WIAM* 3453).

3163 VAN CAMP, Martha F. **Opera's good deed**, *Christian Science*
an   *Monitor* 7 Nov 1973, B-10. *Illus.*
A description of Julia Smith's opera *Daisy* (*WIAM* 4838) on the occasion of its recent première at the Dade County Auditorium in Miami, Fla. The work, a setting of a libretto by Bertita Harding, is based on the life of Juliette Low, founder of the Girl Scouts of the United States of America. Commissioned by Arthuro di Filippi of the Opera Guild of greater Miami, the opera was sponsored by the Girl Scouts, the National Endowment for the Arts, and the Fine Arts Council of Florida. Elizabeth Volkman sang the lead; other performances are scheduled in Fort Meyers, Va. and Fort Lauderdale, Fla.
                                   (Julia Smith, abridged)

3164 VAN DE VATE, Nancy. **American woman composer, The:**
ap   **some sour notes**, *High Fidelity/Musical America* (*WIAM* 67) MA 18-20. *Discog.*
Considers the question of why women have made little apparent contribution to the history of composition in the United States. The numerous articles devoted to women as composers that have appeared in 1975 as a result of International Women's Year may represent only a brief fad. A complete discography of works listed in the *Schwann-1 Record and Tape Guide* XXVII/3 (Mar. 1975) points up the paucity of their recorded works. Ways in which the temporary interest in women composers can be sustained, and the relationship between originality and professional opportunity for composers are discussed.
                                   (Author)

3165 VAN DE VATE, Nancy. **Every good boy (composer) does**
ap   **fine**, *Symphony News* XXIV/6 (Dec 1973-Jan 1974) 11-13. *Discog.*
Discusses the dearth of recordings of serious music by women composers, explanations for this situation, and possible remedies. Presents lists of recorded works by women for 8 half-hour radio programs, which were prepared by the National Federation of Music Clubs with the cooperation of record companies and a grant from the American Soc. of Composers, Authors, and Publishers. The 8 programs were chosen by the author from a total of 13 programs because each included orchestral works.   *(Author)*

3166 VAN DE VATE, Nancy. **Notes from a bearded lady: the**
ap   **American woman composer**, *International Musician* LXXIV/1 (July 1975) 9, 22. *Port.*
Discusses circumstances that limit the development of women as composers. Many of the standard avenues of professional activity have not been, and are

still not generally open to women, e.g., recordings, commissions, orchestral performances, academic positions, and grants. Opportunities for women composers can be increased by 1) the anonymous submission of scores to all competitions and grant-awarding bodies, and 2) organized action on the part of women composers themselves to make the profession more aware of their music. To implement this 2nd goal, the author suggests membership in the League of Women Composers, an action group of established professionals which she founded in 1975. *(Author)*

3167 VOUGHT, Ruby S. **Winner of National Federation of**
ap **Music Clubs' Distinguished Women Composers Award has commissioned work,** *Music Clubs Magazine* L/3 (1971) 10.
Reports that Emma Lou Diemer, who in 1969 was one of the winners of the $1000 Award for Distinguished Composers, was commissioned to write a work for the tricentennial anniversary of the founding of South Carolina. She composed 3 *Anniversary choruses* (*WIAM* 3916), which were given their first performance at a meeting of the South Carolina Music Teachers Assoc., 25 Apr. 1970. *(Julia Smith, abridged)*

3168 WASSON, D. DeWitt. **New organ music,** *Music. The American*
rm *Guild of Organists and Royal Canadian College of Organists Magazine* X/10 (Oct 1976) 20.
Reviews Emma Lou Diemer's *Jubilate and Contrasts* (*WIAM* 4612).

3169 WASSON, D. DeWitt. **Reviews: hymn materials,** *Music. The*
rm *American Guild of Organists and Royal Canadian College of Organists Magazine* XI/1 (Jan 1977) 8.
Reviews Emma Lou Diemer's *Celebration. Seven hymn settings for organ* (*WIAM* 4606).

3170 WEST, Richard. **Lost valley,** *Chautauquan (N.Y.) Daily* 18 July
rm 1946, 4.
Reviews Florence DuPage's *Lost valley* (*WIAM* 4406).

3171 Women composers: en route, *High Fidelity/Musical America*
ap (*WIAM* 67) MA 21.
Reports on a survey conducted by *Musical America* regarding the status of women as faculty and students in composition at major univerities, colleges, and conservatories in the United States. A total of 23 institutions --or 66% of those queried--responded. The results indicate that while in 1975, 13% of the undergraduates in composition at the 23 schools were women, 14% on the graduate level were women, and 16% of the doctoral candidates were women, only 4% of the faculties in composition were women. Information about performances by 5 major orchestras of works by women composers is included.

3172 Women honored for composition, *Albuquerque (N.M.) Journal*
ap 21 Apr 1969, A-12.
Three outstanding American women composers were honored recently by the National Federation of Music Clubs and the American Soc. of Composers, Authors, and Publishers (ASCAP) at the federation's national convention in Albuquerque, N.M. The winners were Hansi Alt, Washington, D.C., for piano teaching material; Emma Lou Diemer, Falls Church, Va., for choral and instrumental music for high school and college; and Miriam Gideon, New York, for symphonic and concert music. Marion Morrey Richter, national chairwoman of the federation's American Music Department, presented each composer with a $1000 award. *(Julia Smith)*

3173 ZUMMO, Peter. **Bas-relief in time,** *Soho (New York) Weekly*
rm *News* 16 Dec 1976, 17.
Reviews Beth Anderson's *Good-bye Bridget Bardot or Hello Charlotte Moorman* (*WIAM* 4317). The title refers to the critic's description of the piece as a "bas-relief".

77   Literature about women as educators, patrons, and members of music clubs

3174 American Symphony Orchestra League Women's Council.
bm **Women's Association reports 1975-76 season** (Vienna, Va.:
American Symphony Orchestra League, 1976) 186 p.
Presents fact sheets describing the 1975-76 activities of 76 women's symphony orchestra associations in the United States in the areas of fund raising, ticket sales, and educational projects, in order to share new ideas and methods and to pay tribute to the work of these women. Includes background information about the American Symphony Orchestra League, founded lin 1942, and the Women's Council of the League, established in 1964.

→ BARNES, Nancy. **Women in music: a preliminary report,** *see* 97ap[20].

→ BLOCK, Adrienne. **Introduction. The woman musician on campus: hiring and promotion patterns,** *see* 98as[20].

→ BLOCK, Adrienne. **Women in composition,** *see* 99as[20].

→ ELROD, Elizabeth. **Women in music: result of the CMS questionnaire,** *see* 104as[20].

→ ERICSON, Raymond. **Eleanor Steber concert may be a family affair,** *see* 3233an[78].

→ ERICSON, Raymond. **Teacher takes time out to play, A,** *see* 3241an[78].

3175 FLEMING, Shirley. **Jennie Tourel,** *High Fidelity/Musical*
ap *America* XVII/12 (Dec 1967) MA 19. *Illus.*
Considers Jennie Tourel's 10-year teaching career at the Juilliard School, Hartt Col. of Music, Aspen in Colorado, and U. of North Carolina and her current master classes at Carnegie Recital Hall. The singer's New York recital debut in 1943 and her performance in Hebrew on a recent recording of Mahler's symphony no. 2 in C minor are also discussed.

→ GETLEIN, Frank. **Two blows for women's liberation,** *see* 3042an[76].

→ GRUEN, John. **I am a very normal human being,** *see* 3257an[78].

3176 HEBSON, Ann. **Women can become successful university**
ap **music professors,** *School Musician* XL/5 (Jan 1969) 52-53. *Illus.*
Discusses the careers of Dorothy Ziegler and Constance Weldon as professors at the U. of Miami in Coral Gables, Fla. Ziegler teaches trombone and is director of the opera theater. She studied trombone and piano at the Eastman School in the 1940s and in 1961 studied conducting with Max Rudolph. A principal trombonist with the St. Louis Symphony Orchestra for 14 years, Ziegler has also been music director of the St. Louis Opera Guild and opera director at Washington U. Weldon teaches tuba and is associate director of the preparatory division of the U. of Miami, of which she is herself a graduate. Formerly, Weldon taught at the U. of Kansas, and she has performed with the Boston Pops Orchestra. Both Ziegler and Weldon now play with the Fort Lauderdale Symphony Orchestra and are members of the U. of Miami Faculty Brass Quintet.

3177 HENAHAN, Donal. **Training grant for conductors,** *New York*
an *Times* 17 May 1978, C-17.
Reports that Lila Acheson Wallace, a member of the board of trustees of the Juilliard School and co-director of the Reader's Digest Assoc., has made a $3 million grant to the Juilliard School to establish a long-range program for the development of young American conductors. In announcing Wallace's grant, Peter Mennin, president of Juilliard, said he expected female candidates to audition and that they were welcome. The unique aspect of the proposed program is that the selected conductors will have the opportunity of working twice a week under the guidance of senior conductors--not only with symphony orchestras, but also in opera.

3178 HENAHAN, Donal. **Vocal virtuosos teach stars of the**
an **future,** *New York Times* 2 Dec 1976, 45, 56. *Illus.*
Reports that Elisabeth Schwarzkopf and her husband Walter Legge are teaching their first master classes at the Juilliard School during 1976-77. The soprano gave her New York farewell recital at Carnegie Hall in 1975 after 40 years of singing lieder and opera. Schwarzkopf's concentration on details and technique in teaching is contrasted with Lotte Lehmann's approach, which was more intuitive and worked on students' imaginations.

3179 IVEY, Jean Eichelberger. **Composer as teacher, The,** *Peabody*
ap *Conservatory Alumni Bulletin* XIV/1 (1974) 4-6.
Ivey discusses her experiences in teaching composition at the Peabody Conservatory, stressing that the composer-teacher must not impose his or her own personal style, but rather must help students to find their own. Methods of identifying a student's problems, helping the student over unproductive periods, and the ways in which the mature composer-teacher can serve as a role model are considered. The problems of earning a living in composition are investigated briefly. Ivey believes that given the changing climate, women composers will be in the field in equal numbers to men in 100 years. *(Author, abridged)*

→ MAYER, Anne. **Women in applied music teaching,** *see* 106as[20].

3180 Mrs. John D. Rockefeller, Jr., dies at 75, *New York Times* 25
an   Jan 1971, 39.
A native of Madiera, Calif., Martha Baird Rockefeller (1895-1971) graduated
from Occidental Col. in Los Angeles and the New England Conservatory,
where she was trained as a pianist. She later studied with Artur Schnabel in
Berlin, and during the 1920s she toured in the United States and Europe, giving
solo recitals and appearing with orchestras. She retired from the concert stage
in 1931 at the time of her 2nd marriage, although she maintained an active
interest in music. Her 3rd marriage to John D. Rockefeller occurred in 1951,
and upon his death in 1960 the former pianist inherited approximately half of
Rockefeller's estate. In 1961 she established the Martha Baird Rockefeller
Fund for Music, Inc., with the chief aim of aiding young musicians of unusual
promise. For a number of years Martha Baird Rockefeller was a major patron
of the Boston Symphony Orchestra, City Center of Music and Drama in New
York, Lincoln Center for the Performing Arts, Manhattan School of Music, and
the New England Conservatory.

3181 New chamber music society founded, *Music of the West* XVI/1
ap   (Sept 1960) 14.
Announces the formation of the Women's Chamber Music Soc. in Los Angeles
by Vahdah Olcott Bickford, a classical guitar player. The society aims to foster
chamber music in concerts and workshops, build a library for its members,
sponsor young artists in performance, and encourage composers with good
performances of their works.

3182 PERLIS, Vivian. Boulanger--20th century music was born in
an   **her classroom**, *New York Times* 11 Sept 1977, II-25, 26. *Illus.*
Several months before her 90th birthday, Nadia Boulanger was interviewed by
Perlis in her Paris apartment, where she has lived and taught since 1900.
Noting that she was interested only in the student and had nothing to say
about herself, Boulanger proceeded to discuss Aaron Copland, her sister Lili
Boulanger, who encouraged Nadia to teach, and her current students.
Boulanger presented concerts of American music in Paris in 1926 and 1929. In
1937-38 she came to Boston to teach at the Longy School of Music and to
conduct major American orchestras. Boulanger has always been interested in
new music, and she introduced Serge Koussevitzky to many 20th-c. American
works.

3183 RICHTER, Marion Morrey. Fanfare for the 1969 Parade,
ap   *Music Clubs Magazine* XLVIII/5 (summer 1969) 53.
This year's Parade of American Music sponsored by the National Federation of
Music Clubs was the largest to date and gave 1082 Awards of Merit. Among
the awards were those to women who participated in a new competition, the
American Women Composers Award Program, which was designed to promote
the performance of works by women.   *(Julia Smith, abridged)*

3184 RICHTER, Marion Morrey. National Federation of Music
ap   **Clubs salute to the United Nations on WNYC October 21,**
      1967, *Music Clubs Magazine* XLVII/2 (Dec 1967) 14-15.
A report by the chairwoman of the American music department of the
National Federation of Music Clubs (NFMC) about the federation's 22nd
annual broadcast salute to the United Nations, "Hands across the sea", on New
York radio station WNYC. Among the participants were Mrs. Maurice
Honigman, president of the federation, Mrs. Warren Knox, the federation's
representative to the United Nations, and Benno and Sylvia Rabinof, violin
and piano duo. Mrs. Honigman noted that "the 600,000 members of the
NFMC, the world's largest philanthropic organization, have taken pride in
using music to strengthen and promote friendships, understanding, and good
will among the nations and peoples". The NFMC is the only organization in
the United States that has a representative at the United Nations, and as a
result has made major contributions to world music and musicians.
                                                        (Julia Smith, abridged)

→   RICHTER, Marion. **National Federation of Music Clubs**
     salute to the United Nations features music of Israel, *see*
     3124ap[76].

→   SABIN, Robert. **Povla Frijsh**, *see* 2347ap[68].

3185 SHEPARD, Richard F. Dorothy Maynor helps bring har-
an   **mony to Harlem**, *New York Times* 5 Apr 1966, 43.
In 1963 Dorothy Maynor founded the Harlem School of the Arts in New York
in order to make music training available within the black community to gifted
children. As of 1966 the school has 23 part-time teachers, 13 pianos, and many
clarinets and string instruments that are available on loan to individual
students. The following women were among the first benefactors of the school:
Mrs. Samuel Dushkin, Wanda Horowitz, Olga Naoumoff Koussevitzky, and
Mrs. Arthur Rodzinski.

→   SMITH, Barbara. **Women in ethnomusicology**, *see* 107as[20].

→   SOUTHERN, Eileen. **Partial report on black women in**
     college music teaching, A, *see* 108as[20].

→   **Statistics in music**, *see* 109ap[20].

→   **Status of women in college music, The: preliminary studies**,
     see 73bs[10].

→   **Thelma Votipka, soprano, dies; with the Met for 28 years**,
     see 3345an[78].

3186 THOMPSON, Helen M. Handbook for symphony orchestra
bm   **women's associations** (Vienna, Va.: American Symphony Orches-
      tra League, 1963) 56 p.
A corps of women workers is vital to a symphony orchestra, and women's
associations have existed since 1898 when women in New York founded a
committee in support of the New York Symphony Orchestra. The legal
structure of the women's association and its relationship to the total orchestral
association are discussed. Initial steps in forming a women's association,
suggestions for building and maintaining the membership, and the activities of
the women's association are also considered.

3187 THOMSON, Virgil. Greatest music teacher--at 75, *New York*
an   *Times* 4 Feb 1962, VI-24, 33, 35. *Illus.*
Reports that Nadia Boulanger will conduct 4 concerts with the New York
Philharmonic during her forthcoming visit to the United States. For more than
40 years Boulanger has taught composition to Americans, among them Elliott
Carter, Aaron Copland, Peggy Glanville-Hicks, Roy Harris, Douglas Moore,
Roger Sessions, Louise Talma, and the author--Virgil Thomson. In addition to
teaching privately in her Paris apartment, Boulanger has also been affiliated
with the Paris Conservatory, the École Normale de Musique de Paris, and the
American Conservatory at Fontainebleau. She understands "at sight any piece
of music--its meaning, its nature, its unique existence--and can reflect this back
to a student like a mirror".

→   TICK, Judith. **Women in musicology**, *see* 110as[20].

→   WRIGHT, Gladys. **Career opportunities for the young**
     woman graduate, *see* 111ap[20].

78   Literature about women as
           performers of art music

3188 "All South American girls play the piano", says Guiomar
ap   **Novaes**, *Musical Courier* LXXVI/26 (27 June 1918) 7. *Illus.*
Guiomar Novaes studied piano with Isidore Philipp at the Paris Conservatory,
and after 2 years on tour in Europe she made her New York recital debut in
1915. The pianist recently returned from a nationwide tour of 51 concerts, and
she notes that young women in the United States all seem to pursue singing,
whereas young women in South America typically study the piano.

3189 Angeles, Victoria de los, *Current biography*. Ed. by Margaret
ac   Dent CANDEE (New York: H.W. Wilson, 1955) 18-20. *Illus.*
Born in Barcelona, Victoria de los Angeles won first prize in an international
singing contest in Geneva in 1947. Many concert engagements in Europe,
Africa, and South America followed. The soprano made her Carnegie Hall
debut in 1950 and her Metropolitan Opera debut in 1951 as Marguerite in
Faust. She has also appeared as orchestral soloist with the Pittsburgh, Chicago,
and Detroit symphony orchestras.

3190 Anne Bollinger, *Opera News* XIII/10 (3 Jan 1949) 11-12, 31. *Illus.*
ap
Born in Lewiston, Idaho, Anne Bollinger graduated in 1943 from the U. of
Southern California, where she studied voice with Lotte Lehmann for 2 years.
The soprano sang with major orchestras conducted by William Steinberg and
Robert Shaw, and subsequently made her Metropolitan Opera debut during the
1948-49 season.

3191 Anne Bollinger, soprano, was 39, *New York Times* 17 July 1962,
ap   25. *Illus.*
An obituary for Anne Bollinger (1923-62), who made her debut as Frasquita in
Carmen at the Metropolitan Opera in 1949. Her roles at the Metropolitan also
included Mimi, Micaela, Cherubino, and Siebel. In 1953 the soprano made her
Hamburg debut as Zdenka in Richard Strauss's *Arabella*, and in 1957 she sang
Pamina for the opening of the new Hamburg opera house.

3192 ARDOIN, John. **Irene Dalis: villainess with charm**, *Musical*
ap   *America* LXXXIII/3 (Mar 1963) 44. *Illus.*
Born in San José, Calif. in 1925, Irene Dalis studied voice with Edyth Walker
and Paul Althouse in New York and with Otto Mueller in Milan. In 1953 the
mezzo-soprano made her operatic debut in Berlin as Princess Eboli in *Don
Carlo*, the role she also sang for her Metropolitan Opera debut in 1957. Her
repertory of over 40 roles includes Amneris, Azucena, Venus, Ortrud, and
Brangäne.

3193 ARELL, Ruth. **Muscle men and maids of music**, *Music Journal*
ap   [New York] VII/6 (Nov 1950) 22-23, 54.
While years ago music was regarded as a "sissy occupation", and many boys
had to be forced to practice the violin or piano, today music is a big business.
Performers have to be in top shape to meet the exhausting demands of the
profession, and because of their sports activities, many performing musicians in
turn are making converts for music. The favorite sports of numerous singers-
-both male and female--are discussed.

3194 ASKLUND, Gunnar. **Hints for the young violinist**, *Etude*
ap   LXI/12 (Dec 1943) 773, 824. *Illus.*
While "there used to be a feeling that a woman violinist was a commercial
question mark", Carroll Glenn has thoroughly dispelled it with a schedule of
more than 60 concerts a year. Born in South Carolina, Glenn received her first
lessons from her mother, and she later studied with Édouard Déthier at the
Juilliard School. She has won 4 major awards, which led to appearances with
the New York Philharmonic and the Philadelphia Orchestra. Glenn believes
that the fact of being female poses no obstacles to the serious student.

3195 BARTHEL, Ivan. **"Gee, what would happen if I were just
an   me"?**, *New York Times* 8 May 1966, II-13. *Illus.*
Judith Raskin discusses her roles as professional singer, wife, and mother. After
graduation from Smith Col., Raskin raised 2 children and continued studying
voice with Anna Hamlin and acting with Ludwig Donath. In 1957 she began
singing with the National Broadcasting Co. Opera in television productions and
on tour, directed by George Schick. Raskin made her Metropolitan Opera debut
as Susanna in *Le nozze di Figaro* in 1962. In 1964 the soprano sang 52
performances, including her first lieder recital. She would now like to learn
more Spanish, French, and English songs and also to teach voice.

3196 BERNHEIMER, Martin. **Schwarze Venus, Die [The black
ap   Venus]**, *Opera News* XXVI/2 (28 Oct 1961) 21.
Reports that Grace Bumbry is the first black to have sung at Bayreuth. In
defense of Bumbry, Wieland Wagner noted, "My grandfather wrote for vocal
colors, not skin colors". After early periods of study in St. Louis, Boston, and
Chicago, the mezzo-soprano was invited by Lotte Lehmann to attend her
master classes in Santa Barbara, Calif. In 1960 Bumbry gained operatic
experience in Basel, which led in turn to her engagement at Bayreuth.

3197 **Blegen, Judith**, *Current biography*. Ed. by Charles MORITZ (New
ac   York: H.W. Wilson, 1977) 69-72. *Illus.*
Judith Blegen grew up in Missoula, Mont., where she studied the violin first
with her mother. At age 14 she began taking voice lessons and applied her
violin technique to vocal practice. From 1959-64 Blegen pursued vocal study at
the Curtis Inst. with Euphemia Gregory and Martial Singher. After 6 years of
operatic experience in Europe, the soprano made her Metropolitan Opera debut
in 1970 as Marcellina in *Fidelio*. Blegen has appeared as a soloist with
orchestras and in solo recitals throughout the United States and Europe.

3198 BLYTH, Alan. **Accent on drama**, *Music and Musicians* XVII/2
ap   (Oct 1968) 33. *Illus.*
Montserrat Caballé studied with Eugenia Kemeny for 6 years at the conservatory in her native Barcelona. The soprano sang in Basel for 4 years and in
Bremen for 2 years, and then made her debut in Vienna in 1958. In 1965 she
made her New York debut with the American Opera Soc. in Donizetti's *Roberto
Devereux*.

3199 BRAGGIOTTI, Mary. **She gives the same way for everybody**,
an   *New York Post* 10 May 1946, 43. *Illus.*
Jennie Tourel discusses American audiences upon the completion of her first
cross-country tour. One of her first performances in the United States was in
1942 in Berlioz's *Roméo et Juliette*, under the direction of Toscanini.

3200 BREUER, Gustl. **Every thing in its time**, *Opera News* XXIX/6
ap   (19 Dec 1964) 26-28. *Illus.*
Elisabeth Schwarzkopf discusses the Marschallin, the role of her Metropolitan
Opera debut during the 1964-65 season. The soprano made her operatic debut
in Berlin in the 1930s singing light roles such as Violetta and Sophie in *Der
Rosenkavalier*. Subsequently her husband, Walter Legge, advised her to sing
Eva, Donna Elvira, and the Countess in *Le nozze di Figaro*, so as to provide
herself with new artistic challenges and a longer operatic career. Although
Schwarzkopf's debut at the Metropolitan is belated, the soprano believes,
"Jedes Ding hat seine Zeit" (*Der Rosenkavalier*, Act I).

3201 BRIGGS, Marion L. **Breaking a Boston Symphony tradition**,
ap   *Etude* LXXII/9 (Sept 1954) 13, 63. *Illus.*
A biographical sketch of the flutist Doriot Anthony Dwyer, who, when hired by
the Boston Symphony Orchestra in 1952, became the first woman in the United
States to hold a first chair position with a leading orchestra. Dwyer's attitudes
about teaching the flute are briefly discussed.

3202 BROZEN, Michael. **Reri Grist**, *Musical America* LXXXIII/10
ap   (Oct 1963) 24. *Illus.*
An interview with Reri Grist, who discusses her operatic experiences in New
York, Santa Fe, and Washington, D.C. Based on his knowledge of Grist's work
as a member of the cast of *West Side story*, Leonard Bernstein asked the
soprano to sing in a performance of Mahler's symphony no. 4 in G major with
the New York Philharmonic. Stravinsky chose Grist to sing the title role in *Le
rossignol* for a performance in Washington, D.C. This article is signed M.B.,
and Brozen's name has been supplied.

3203 BUEHLMAN, Barbara. **Should a woman be a band direc-
ap   tor?**, *Instrumentalist* XXI/2 (Sept 1966) 56. *Illus.*
Contends that a woman with musical talent, administrative ability, personality,
and intelligence will be an excellent band director. A national association of
women band directors is proposed.

3204 CHAMBERS, Marcia. **Shirley Verrett takes up the challenge**,
an   *New York Times* 22 Oct 1973, 44.
Reports that Shirley Verrett will sing the roles of both Dido and Cassandra in
Berlioz's *Les Troyens* at the Metropolitan Opera this season. She made her
Metropolitan debut in 1968 as Carmen, but she was not pleased with the roles
Rudolf Bing offered her in subsequent years. The mezzo-soprano notes, "Had I
not been black, I would have long ago gotten the kind of opportunities that I'm
getting now", and she also discusses Marian Anderson and Leontyne Price who
paved the way for her and other black artists.

3205 **Claramae Turner**, *Opera News* XI/11 (30 Dec 1946) 10-11. *Illus.*
ap
Born in Dinuba, Calif., Claramae Turner began her career singing Gilbert and
Sullivan repertory with the Savoy Opera in San Francisco. She married at age
19 and subsequently gave up the music profession. However, during World
War II when her husband was in the armed forces, Turner decided to resume
her career, studying in New York with Alberto Sciarretti and Ernesto Barbini.
In 1946 Turner sang the title role in Gian-Carlo Menotti's *The medium*. The
contralto will make her Metropolitan Opera debut during the present season as
Martha in *Faust*.

3206 COLEMAN, Emily. **Leontyne makes a date with history**, *New*
an   *York Times* 11 Sept 1966, II-21. *Illus.*
Reports that Leontyne Price will sing the role of Cleopatra in the première of
Samuel Barber's *Anthony and Cleopatra* for the opening performance at the
new Metropolitan Opera house in Lincoln Center. The role was written for
Price, and in preparation the soprano has worked for a year with her voice
teacher, Florence Page Mitchell, and also with the British actress Irene Worth in
studying Shakespearean English. Price sang Barber's *Hermit songs* at her Town
Hall recital debut in 1954, accompanied by the composer. In 1955 she was the
first black to appear in opera on television, and in 1961 she became the first
black to sing in an opening performance for the season at the Metropolitan.

3207 COLEMAN, Emily. **Non-prima-donnaish prima donna**, *New*
an   *York Times* 22 Feb 1959, VI-23, 34-38. *Illus.*
Eleanor Steber will create the role of Marie in the Metropolitan Opera's first
production of *Wozzeck* in March. Born in Wheeling, W. Va., Steber studied
with William L. Whitney at the New England Conservatory and made her
Metropolitan debut as Sophie in *Der Rosenkavalier* in 1940. In 1953 Steber and
Astrid Varnay were the first Americans to open a Bayreuth festival since Lillian
Nordica did so in 1894. Steber has also traveled to the Far East as part of an
international cultural exchange program. The soprano has sung 40 roles at the
Metropolitan, including the title role in the 1958 world première of Samuel
Barber's *Vanessa*, which she performed on short notice when Sena Jurinac-
-who was scheduled to sing--became ill.

3208 COMMANDAY, Robert. **Symphony scandal, The**, *High*
ap   *Fidelity/Musical America* XXIV/9 (Sept 1974) MA 28-29. *Illus.*
Reports that the 7-man Players Committee of the San Francisco Symphony
Orchestra overrode the wishes of director Seiji Ozawa and denied contract
renewal to Elayne Jones, a black timpanist, and Ryohei Nakagawa, a Japanese-
born bassoonist. Jones plans to take the Symphonic Assoc. and the union to
court, to fight for her job, her integrity, and the principles involved. Before
joining the San Francisco Symphony, Jones was timpanist for 10 years with the
American Symphony Orchestra under the direction of Leopold Stokowski, and
she also played with the orchestra of the New York City Opera, among others.

3209 CONTOS, Catherine. **Brava, maestra!**, *High Fidelity/Musical*
ap   *America* XXI/5 (May 1971) MA 7-10. *Illus.*
Discusses American women who are presently active as conductors, e.g.,

Antonia Brico and Eve Queler, and traces the history of women as conductors through anecdotes about Ethel Leginska and Ann Kullmer among others. Suggests that the small number of women active as conductors is due to discouragement at all levels of music education.

3210 COOK, Joan. **Piano prodigy at 3, now the conductor of** *Hair*,
an   A, *New York Times* 5 Nov 1970, 62.
Born in Chicago in 1943, Margaret Harris is the first black and the first woman to conduct the hit Broadway musical. She was trained at the Curtis Inst. and the Juilliard School, and she has toured Europe as musical director, conductor, and pianist in the Black New World production. Later this year Harris will make her piano debut in New York and London.

3211 COOKE, Charles. **Ann Schein's career is now an interna-**
an   **tional one,** *Washington Evening Star* 30 Jan 1966, D-1, 4. *Illus.*
Ann Schein studied piano with Mieczyslaw Munz at the Peabody Conservatory and made her recital debut at age 17 in Washington, D.C. In 1957 she performed Rachmaninoff's piano concerto no. 3 in D minor, op. 30, with the National U. Symphony Orchestra in Mexico City, and she performed the same work for her New York Philharmonic debut in 1960. Schein made her debut as a recitalist in Carnegie Hall in 1962 and since then has divided her time between recitals and orchestral appearances in many countries.

3212 CORRY, John. **Conductor hums, cues, sings, and says that**
an   **security is involvement in music,** *New York Times* 22 Mar 1973,
45. *Illus.*
Reports that Eve Queler will conduct the Opera Orchestra of New York in a concert version of Riccardo Zandonai's *Francesca da Rimini* at Carnegie Hall. Queler was an assistant conductor to Julius Rudel for 5 years at the New York City Opera, resigning because she was not allowed to conduct a performance. Queler then formed the Opera Orchestra to present concert versions of little-known operas. Other women conductors mentioned include Sarah Caldwell in Boston, Margaret Harris on Broadway, and Beatrice Brown in Scranton.

3213 CRICHTON, Kyle Samuel. **Subway to the Met: Risë Stev-**
bm   **ens's story** (Garden City, N.Y.: Doubleday, 1959) 240 p. *Illus.*
Born in the Bronx, N.Y., Risë Stevens sang on radio broadcasts as a child and subsequently studied voice with Anna Eugénie Schoen-René at the Juilliard School. The mezzo-soprano next performed with the New York Opera Comique and studied further with Marie Gutheil-Schoeder in Salzburg. Stevens sang in Prague for several seasons before making her Metropolitan Opera debut as Octavian in 1938. She has also appeared in the Hollywood film *Going my way* with Bing Crosby, as well as on radio and television. Among her other roles are Carmen and Orfeo in Gluck's *Orfeo ed Euridice*.

3214 DANIELS, Robert D. **Eye on tomorrow,** *Opera News* XXXI/21
ap   (18 Mar 1967) 16. *Illus.*
An interview with Brooklyn-born Evelyn Lear, who is making her Metropolitan Opera debut as Lavinia in the world première of Marvin David Levy's *Mourning becomes Elektra*. In 1957 Lear and her husband Thomas Stewart received Fulbright grants to study voice in Berlin, and within 2 years they both were singing leading roles with the German Opera. The soprano is known for her interpretation of 20th-c. operatic roles and also sings in recitals and concerts. This article is signed R.D.D., and Daniels's name has been supplied.

3215 DANIELS, Robert D. **Only way, The,** *Opera News* XXXIV/24
ap   (11 Apr 1970) 13. *Illus.*
Born in San Pedro, Calif., Maralin Niska taught elementary school for several years before pursuing a vocal career. From 1965-67 the soprano sang throughout the United States with the Metropolitan Opera National Co. In 1967 she joined the New York City Opera, where her roles have included Mimi, Madame Butterfly, and the governess in Benjamin Britten's *Turn of the screw*. In performance Niska is an intense actress--"the only way she knows". This article is signed R.D.D., and Daniels's name has been supplied.

3216 DANIELS, Robert D. **Triple threat,** *Opera News* XXVII/22 (6
ap   Apr 1963) 14. *Illus.*
Mignon Dunn discusses the roles of the Nurse, the Innkeeper, and Marina in *Boris Godunov*, which she is singing during the 1962-63 season. A native of Memphis, the mezzo-soprano has performed at the Metropolitan Opera since 1958; her repertory includes Carmen, Azucena, Amneris, and Dalila. This article is signed R.D.D., and Daniels's name has been supplied.

3217 DAVIS, Peter G. **Ample recordings allow posterity to judge**
an   **Callas,** *New York Times* 4 Oct 1977, 48. *Illus.*
Written shortly after Maria Callas's death, this article discusses a representative selection of her numerous recordings made from 1949-74. The soprano recorded 26 complete operas; among the best are *Lucia di Lammermoor* on Seraphim, and *Tosca* and *Norma* on Angel.

3218 **Debut in opera was gamble to Regina Resnik,** *New York Herald*
an   *Tribune* 8 Dec 1944, 20. *Illus.*

Reports that Regina Resnik made her Metropolitan Opera debut as Leonora in *Il trovatore* with much critical and popular acclaim, replacing Zinka Milanov on 24 hours notice. The soprano had been scheduled to make her debut as Santuzza in *Cavalleria rusticana* later in the season. Born and raised in New York, Resnik graduated from Hunter Col. in 1942. She has sung with the New York City Opera and with the National Opera in Mexico City.

3219 DENNIS, Charles M. **California Parent-Teacher Associa-**
ap   **tion Mothersingers,** *Music Educators Journal* XLI/2 (Nov-Dec
1954) 45.
Reports that the highlight of the congress of Parent-Teacher Associations (PTA) in California was the performance by a 700-member women's chorus, which combined various groups of Mothersingers affiliated with local PTA groups throughout the state. Some groups of Fathersingers are active, but they "have failed so far to attain the prestige of the female contingent". The Mothersingers project originated in 1930, and 3500 groups were active by 1935.

3220 DIDIER, Curt. **Ida Krehm rehearses with foreign ensembles.**
ap   **National Federation of Music Clubs artist winner distin-**
guished as international pianist-composer, *Music Clubs Maga-*
zine XLIX/3 (1970) 8-9.
Pianist-conductor Ida Krehm rehearses orchestras around the world. The Canadian-born musician has recently worked with the Prague Chamber Orchestra and the Melos Ensemble of London, as well as with ensembles in Norway, India, Bulgaria, and the Philippines. Formerly a student of Rudolph Ganz in Chicago, Krehm is respected by orchestral players and has been praised by such musicians as Otto Klemperer and Leopold Stokowski.
(Julia Smith, abridged)

3221 **Distaff side, The,** *New York Times* 25 Mar 1962, II-15.
an
In trying to gain acceptance as soloists, women instrumentalists face 2 basic problems: 1) women concert-goers prefer male performers, and 2) virtuosos are popular in direct proportion to the strength they employ, while women lack the strength of men. Women may play beautifully, but men provide more excitement with their playing.

3222 **Dobbs, Mattiwilda,** *Current biography.* Ed. by Marjorie Dent
ac   CANDEE (New York: H.W. Wilson, 1955) 172-73. *Illus.*
Born in Atlanta in 1925, Mattiwilda Dobbs studied voice with Lotte Leonard in New York and Pierre Bernac in Paris. After winning an international music competition in Geneva in 1950, Dobbs became the first black to sing at La Scala. The soprano made her New York debut in 1954 with Thomas Scherman's Little Orchestra Soc.

3223 **Dorothy Kirsten,** *Opera and Concert* XII/10 (Oct 1947) 14-15.
ap   *Illus.*
Born in Brooklyn to a musical family, Dorothy Kirsten began her singing career in radio. Encouraged by Grace Moore to pursue opera, Kirsten followed in Moore's footsteps by studying the role of Louise with the composer, Charpentier. The soprano will sing Louise and Fiora in Montemezzi's *L'amore dei tre re* with the San Francisco Opera this season.

3224 DRINKER, Sophie. **What price women's chorus?,** *Music*
ap   *Journal* [New York] XII/1 (Jan 1954) 19, 42.
Women's choruses have experienced a tremendous boom since World War I, due to the increased attendance of young women in high schools as well as of women in clubs. The literature for women's choruses is inadequate however: voice treatment and the selection of texts deserve fresh approaches. Possible departures from the stereotyped SSAA and SSA settings are suggested, and the need for texts that do not emphasize "activities which are supposed to be characteristically feminine"--e.g., spinning and singing children to sleep--is discussed.

3225 DYER, Richard. **Sarah Caldwell--her genius is her gimmick,**
an   *New York Times* 11 Jan 1976, II-1, 17. *Illus.*
The author maintains that the implication of Sarah Caldwell's total devotion to musical and dramatic art as being eccentric is ill-founded and obscures her accomplishments as a conductor, stage director, and impresario. A critique of her skills in each of these areas is presented.

3226 DYER, Richard. **Spell of Jennie Tourel, The,** *New York Times*
an   22 Sept 1974, 32, 33. *Illus.*
Discusses recordings Tourel made in 1944-52, which have been reissued, as well as 2 live recordings of concerts with Leonard Bernstein in 1969 and James Levine in 1970. Tourel helped rekindle interest in the works Berlioz and Mahler.

3227 DYER, Richard. **Sutherland, Bonynge, and "The voice",** *New*
an   *York Times* 22 Feb 1976, II-1, 17. *Illus.*
Reports that Joan Sutherland will sing Elvira in *I puritani*, conducted by Richard Bonynge during the current season at the Metropolitan Opera.

Sutherland and Bonynge will also join forces in Massenet's *Esclarmonde* and *Le roi de Lahore* with the Vancouver Opera. Sutherland's voice--which has a solid, yet flexible, middle and low range as well as the necessary coloratura top range for bel canto repertory--is also discussed.

3228 EATON, Frances Q. **Renaissance woman**, *Opera News* XXVIII/
ap   23 (18 Apr 1964) 26. *Illus.*
An interview with the conductor Sarah Caldwell, who has established a new resident opera company in Boston. In 1943 Caldwell entered the New England Conservatory intending to become a violinist, but she quickly switched to the opera department, where she studied under Boris Goldovsky. She became fascinated with the prospect of an opera company in Boston, and to date she has developed a local audience, enlisted the support of 3 industrial sponsors, and assembled a board of directors that represents a wide range of community interests. Recent productions that have attracted national interest include the East Coast première of *Lulu* and *I puritani* with Joan Sutherland. Caldwell directs all of the company's productions and serves as conductor for many.

3229 EATON, Frances Q. **Women come into their own in our**
ap   **orchestras**, *Musical America* LXXV/4 (15 Feb 1955) 30, 179, 183.
Reports that women constitute 18.4% of the personnel in 31 major symphony orchestras in the United States. Even when male players returned to orchestras after World War II, many women remained, and their numbers have grown since. Older orchestras are still conservative about hiring women, particularly in the eastern part of the country. The previous history of women as instrumentalists is reviewed, and the domestic arrangements of husbands and wives who are employed by the same orchestra are considered.

3230 **Elias, Rosalind**, *Current biography*. Ed. by Charles MORITZ (New
ac   York: H.W. Wilson, 1967) 105-07. *Illus.*
Born in Lowell, Mass., Rosalind Elias studied voice with Gladys Miller at the New England Conservatory. In 1948 the mezzo-soprano made her debut as Maddalena in *Rigoletto* with the New England Opera. During her first season at the Metropolitan Opera in 1954-55, Elias sang 55 performances of 7 minor roles. Samuel Barber chose Elias to create the role of Erika in the world première of his opera *Vanessa* in 1958.

3231 ELSON, James. **Practical aspects of our art. Music selection**
ap   **and program building for the women's chorus**, *Choral Journal* XIII/2 (Oct 1972) 18-19.
Offers suggestions for variety in programming and discusses the following bibliographic guides: 1) Arthur Ware Locke and Charles K. Fassett, *Selected list of choruses for women's voices* (3rd ed.; Northampton, Mass.: Smith Col., 1964), 2) Charles C. Burnsworth, *Choral music for women's voices. An annotated bibliography of recommended works* (Metuchen, N.J.: Scarecrow, 1968), and 3) Richard Cox's list of larger choral works in *Choral Journal* XII/9 (May 1972).

3232 ERICSON, Raymond. **Colored girl like you can't play in**
an   **Hollywood Bowl, A**, *New York Times* 19 Nov 1972, II-15, 26.
      Illus.
Born in Oberlin, Ohio, to a musical family, Natalie Hinderas was the youngest graduate in the history of Oberlin Conservatory up to that time. Subsequently the pianist studied with Olga Samaroff Stokowski at the Juilliard School and for 5 additional years with Edward Steuermann. She made her New York recital debut in 1954. Hinderas reports being told by Columbia Artists Management that the firm found it difficult to obtain engagements for women pianists, and she also notes the double handicap for black women--although she feels resistance began to lessen in the late 1960s. Hinderas played as a soloist with the Los Angeles Philharmonic during the summer of 1972, and in the course of the 1972-73 season she will appear with the New York Philharmonic, Atlanta Symphony Orchestra, and Cleveland Orchestra.

3233 ERICSON, Raymond. **Eleanor Steber concert may be a**
an   **family affair**, *New York Times* 17 Dec 1976, C-8. *Illus.*
Reports that Eleanor Steber will sing 3 recitals for the benefit of the music foundation she has established to aid young singers. A number of her friends will participate as instrumentalists, and she may also include on the program her brother, an amateur tenor, and her mother, who was once the leading soprano of Wheeling, Va. From 1963-72 Steber was head of the voice department at the Cleveland Inst. of Music, and she now teaches at the Juilliard School as well as privately. The soprano is currently preparing materials for an autobiography and for a book on the vocal method taught to her by William L. Whitney in Boston.

3234 ERICSON, Raymond. **Eve Queler of the dauntless baton**, *an*
an   *New York Times* 7 Jan 1977, C-22. *Illus.*
Eve Queler studied conducting with Carl Bamberger and was a rehearsal accompanist, coach, and conductor with the New York City Opera and the Metropolitan Opera National Co. In 1967 she founded the Opera Orchestra of New York with the idea of giving young singers and orchestral players experience in standard repertory. Later she branched out to more exotic repertory, such as Smetana's *Dalibor*. Queler has been a guest conductor for the

San Antonio Symphony Orchestra and the Philadelphia Orchestra. Her goal is to secure a full-time conductorship with a major orchestra.

3235 ERICSON, Raymond. **In the Granados tradition**, *New York*
an   *Times* 2 Jan 1966, II-11. *Illus.*
Alicia de Larrocha inherited the Granados "tradition" from her mother, her aunt, and her piano teacher Frank Marshall--all of whom studied with Granados. A specialist in the works of Albéniz, de Falla, and Granados, de Larrocha was not allowed to study this music until she was 15 and had acquired the necessary base in Bach and Mozart. Prior to her present group of appearances, the pianist has appeared in the United States only in 1954-55.

3236 ERICSON, Raymond. **Maria Callas, 53, is dead of heart**
an   **attack in Paris**, *New York Times* 17 Sept 1977, 1, 26.
Born in New York to Greek parents, Maria Callas (1923-77) moved to Athens with her family at age 13 and studied voice there with Elvira de Hidalgo. The soprano made her operatic debut in Athens at age 15, and in 1947 she won international recognition for her appearances in Venice as Brünnhilde and Elvira in *I puritani*. Callas made her American debut in 1954 with the Chicago Lyric Opera and her Metropolitan Opera debut in 1956. After an absence of 7 seasons, Callas returned to the Metropolitan in 1965 as Tosca. In 1974 she sang her last public performance in Carnegie Hall with Giuseppe di Stefano. By appearing in the roles of Norma, Lucia, and Medea, the soprano revived interest in the bel canto repertory and paved the way for such singers as Beverly Sills and Joan Sutherland.

3237 ERICSON, Raymond. **Met engages first woman conductor**,
an   *New York Times* 3 Apr 1975, 44. *Illus.*
Reports that Sarah Caldwell will lead 11 performances of *La traviata* at the Metropolitan Opera with Beverly Sills as Violetta. The founder of the Boston Opera in 1957, Caldwell has presented the American premières of Prokofiev's *War and peace*, op. 91, and Rameau's *Hippolyte et Aricie*. The conductor has also staged *Ariadne auf Naxos* and Hans Werner Henze's *Der junge Lord* at the New York City Opera. In 1967 she conducted the American National Opera in 3 productions.

3238 ERICSON, Raymond. **Miss Hillis carries her baton lightly**,
an   *New York Times* 2 Nov 1977, C-17. *Illus.*
Born in Kokomo, Ind., Margaret Hillis studied piano, several wind instruments, and contrabass at Indiana U. and subsequently studied conducting at the Juilliard School. In the early 1950s she formed the American Concert Choir and Orchestra in New York, which presented concert versions of Rameau's *Hippolyte et Aricie* and Gluck's *Paride ed Elena*. At the request of Fritz Reiner, Hillis founded the Chicago Symphony Orchestra Chorus in 1957, and she has been active as its conductor for 20 years.

3239 ERICSON, Raymond. **Some sopranos just love those lurid**
an   **roles**, *New York Times* 25 July 1971, II-15, 18.
Discusses the careers of Arlene Saunders and Carole Farley. Arlene Saunders will sing the title role in the forthcoming world première of Alberto Ginastera's *Beatrix Cenci* in the Opera Soc. of Washington (D.C.) production at the new John F. Kennedy Center for the Performing Arts. In the early 1960s the soprano sang with the New York City Opera, and for the past 7 years she has appeared in leading roles at the Hamburg State Opera. Carole Farley has sung the title role in *Lulu* in Cologne and in an English translation in Wales. Born in Moscow, Idaho, the soprano studied piano and voice at Indiana U. and in Austria.

3240 ERICSON, Raymond. **Step forward for a woman conductor**,
an   **A**, *New York Times* 8 May 1977, II-17.
Judith Somogi will shortly become the 3rd woman to conduct the New York Philharmonic, following in the footsteps of Nadia Boulanger and Sarah Caldwell. Since 1974 Somogi has conducted 5 operas with the New York City Opera, including a live television performance of Douglas Moore's *The ballad of Baby Doe*. She has also conducted the Oklahoma Symphony Orchestra, the Tulsa Philharmonic Orchestra, and at the Hollywood Bowl.

3241 ERICSON, Raymond. **Teacher takes time out to play, A**, *New*
an   *York Times* 5 Jan 1975, II-17.
A native of Kansas City, Adele Marcus studied piano with Josef Lhevinne in Chicago and with Artur Schnabel in Berlin. The pianist now has 22 pupils at the Juilliard School and in addition teaches at Temple U. and privately. Among her best known students are Byron Janis and Agustin Anievas. Marcus's forthcoming recital is her first in New York since 1963.

3242 EYER, Ronald. **Man and wife**, *Opera News* XXXI/8 (17 Dec
ap   1966) 15. *Illus.*
Discusses the careers of mezzo-soprano Christa Ludwig and baritone Walter Berry. For the past 8 years Ludwig has been singing such trouser roles as Cherubino, Octavian, and Prince Orlofsky. In 1959 Ludwig made her Metropolitan Opera debut as Cherubino. This season she will be singing the Dyer's wife in Richard Strauss's *Die Frau ohne Schatten* and Elsa in *Lohengrin*

at the Metropolitan. Ludwig has also sung with the American Opera Soc. and in Chicago and Dallas.

3243 **Farrell, Eileen**, *Current biography*. Ed. by Charles MORITZ (New
ac   York: H.W. Wilson, 1961) 153-54. *Illus.*
Eileen Farrell was born in Willimantic, Conn. to parents who had worked in vaudeville, and she came to New York after graduating from high school in 1939 for 5 years of intensive vocal study with Merle Alcock. Farrell began her performing career as a singer on radio programs, and then in 1947 she turned to concert work--both as a recitalist and a soloist with orchestras. On the occasion of her Oct. 1950 recital in Carnegie Hall Farrell was hailed as one of the most important concert stars to have emerged since the end of World War II. Before turning to opera in the mid-1950s, the soprano was a member of the Bach Aria Group and was active as a church and oratorio singer. Her tastes in music include "everything from Bach to the blues".

3244 FERGUSON, Charles W. **Americans not everyone knows:**
ap   **Philippa Duke Schuyler**, *PTA Magazine* LXII/4 (Dec 1967) 12-
        14.
The black pianist's career (1933-67) was cut short by her death in a helicopter crash in Vietnam, where she had just completed her 2nd concert tour. The daughter of 2 writers, Schuyler began to play in public at age 4 with the encouragement of her parents. She performed in 80 countries and appeared with such artists as Marian Anderson and Artur Rubinstein. As an author and composer, Schuyler wrote 6 books and a number of compositions, including *The cockroach ballet, Manhattan nocturne*, and *The Nile fantasy*.

3245 FITZGERALD, Gerald. **Heroine at home**, *Opera News* XXV/
ap   13 (4 Feb 1961) 14-15. *Illus.*
Born in Laurel, Miss., Leontyne Price attended Central State Col. in Wilberforce, Ohio and then studied voice at the Juilliard School. Her student performance in *Falstaff* at Juilliard led to an engagement for Virgil Thomson's *Four saints in three acts* in New York and Paris, and the role of Bess in *Porgy and Bess* on Broadway in 1952. In 1957 Price made her American operatic debut as Madame Lidoine in Poulenc's *Les dialogues des Carmélites* in San Francisco. She then sang at the Vienna State Opera for several years before making her Metropolitan Opera debut as Leonora in *Il trovatore* in 1961. This article is signed G.F., and Fitzgerald's name has been supplied.

3246 FITZGERALD, Gerald. **Kammersängerin**, *Opera News* XXVI/
ap   22 (14 Apr 1962) 14. *Illus.*
A native of West Hartford, Conn., Teresa Stich-Randall studied voice at the Hartford School of Music and at Columbia U. Virgil Thomson chose her for the role of Susan B. Anthony in the première of *The mother of us all*, and she also sang the title role in Otto Luening's *Evangeline*. Since 1951 the soprano has been a soloist with the Vienna State Opera, and in 1956 she appeared with the Chicago Lyric Opera. This article is signed G.F., and Fitzgerald's name has been supplied.

→   FLEMING, Shirley. **Jennie Tourel**, see 3175ap[77].

3247 FRAME, Florence K. **Women also conduct orchestras**, *Music
ap   Journal* [New York] XV/2 (Feb 1957) 25, 31. *Illus.*
Surveys the history of women as orchestral conductors, and discusses the work of the following 3 conductors: Antonia Brico, Denver Businessmen's Orchestra; Ruth Haroldson, California Women's Symphony Orchestra, and Margaret Hillis, New York Concert Choir.

3248 FREEMAN, John W. **Quiet type, The**, *Opera News* XXVIII/16
ap   (29 Feb 1964) 33. *Illus.*
Rosalind Elias briefly discusses her Lebanese heritage and the role of Olga in *Eugen Onegin*, which she is singing in the current Metropolitan Opera production of Chaikovskii's opera. Elias's model during the early years of her career was Risë Stevens. This article is signed J.W.F., and Freeman's name has been supplied.

3249 GALATOPOULOS, Stelios. **Callas: La divina** (London: J.M.
bm   Dent, 1966) 218 p. *Illus., discog., index.*
A biography of Maria Callas in 3 chronological sections: 1) early life in New York and operatic experience in Greece, 2) Italian appearances in 1947 and Callas's subsequent meeting with Tullio Serafin, who helped launch her international career, and 3) operatic performances at La Scala, Covent Garden, the Chicago Lyric Opera, and the Metropolitan Opera. An analysis of Callas's most famous roles, a complete list of her public performances in opera and concert, and a list of recordings are included.

3250 **Girl from Radnor High, The**, *Time* LXXIV/21 (23 Nov 1959)
ap   70. *Illus.*
Born in Wayne, Penn., Anna Moffo studied voice at the Curtis Inst. and then won a Fulbright scholarship to study in Italy. The soprano made her American debut in 1957 with the Chicago Lyric Opera and her Metropolitan Opera debut in 1959 as Violetta in *La traviata*.

3251 GLEASON, Gene. **Bronx girl makes debut at Met when**
an   **Nadine Conner becomes ill**, *New York Herald Tribune* 18 Nov
        1950, 1, 6. *Illus.*
Reports Roberta Peters's successful Metropolitan Opera debut as Zerlina in *Don Giovanni*. The 20-year old soprano, who had had no previous stage experience, was given only 5 hours notice to prepare for the performance. Peters began intensive vocal and linguistic study with William Herman at age 13. She was originally scheduled to make her Metropolitan debut in 1951.

3252 GLENN, Clark. **In quest of answers. Women conductors**,
ap   *Choral Journal* XVI/4 (Dec 1975) 24-25.
The following women discuss their experiences in both choral and orchestral conducting: Elaine Browne, Jane Skinner Hardester, Iva Dee Hiatt, Margaret Hillis, and Lois Wells.

3253 GRAHAM, Desmond. **Very private person, A**, *Opera News*
ap   XXXIV/8 (20 Dec 1969) 26.
A native of New York, Claire Watson studied voice with Elisabeth Schumann and made her operatic debut as Desdemona in *Otello* in Graz, Austria. She made her American debut as soloist with the Boston Symphony Orchestra in 1969 and will sing the roles of Donna Anna and Arabella this season in Chicago and New Orleans, respectively. The soprano has just made her first recording of Schubert and Wolf lieder.

3254 GREENFIELD, Edward. **Joan Sutherland** (New York: Drake,
bm   1973) 64 p. *Illus., discog.*
Born in 1926, Joan Sutherland won several singing contests in her native Sydney, Australia, which enabled her to study in London with Clive Carey. In the 1950s the soprano initially sang as a dramatic soprano, although as early as 1951 Richard Bonynge, a vocal coach and later Sutherland's husband, encouraged her to develop her voice for coloratura repertory. She launched her international career in 1959 with a Covent Garden performance of *Lucia di Lammermoor*. In 1961 Sutherland made her Metropolitan Opera debut as Lucia, and she also has sung Norma and Donna Anna at the Metropolitan. A list of the soprano's operatic debuts is included.

3255 GRUEN, John. **Betty is busy figuring out Betty**, *New York*
an   *Times* 19 Aug 1973, II-13, 24. *Illus.*
Born in Campbell, Ohio in 1930, Betty Allen studied voice with Theodor Heimann and Sarah Peck Moore, the latter a pupil of Lilli Lehmann. In 1952 Allen won a scholarship to study at Tanglewood, and in 1953 she sang in Virgil Thomson's *Four saints in three acts* in New York and Paris. Best known as an orchestral soloist and lieder interpreter, the mezzo-soprano has also appeared with the New York City Opera in the roles of Azucena, Dame Quickly, and Jocasta in Stravinsky's *Oedipus Rex*.

3256 GRUEN, John. **Delicate lass with the sensuous flute, The**,
an   *New York Times* 9 Jan 1977, II-13, 20. *Illus.*
Born in Nashville, Tenn., Paula Robison grew up in Los Angeles and studied flute with Julius Baker at the Juilliard School. After graduation in 1963, she studied with Marcel Moyse in Paris and played at the Marlboro Festival in Vermont, where she worked with Rudolf Serkin. Since 1970 Robison has been a member of the Chamber Music Soc. of Lincoln Center, and she is also a member of the Orpheus Trio. The flutist is artist-in-residence at the New England Conservatory and performs 100 solo recitals each year. Robison states that she has found support in the women's movement for her aspirations as a soloist.

3257 GRUEN, John. **I am a very normal human being**, *New York*
an   *Times* 31 Oct 1971, II-15, 28. *Illus.*
Reports that Maria Callas is teaching 12 master classes at the Juilliard School and is making her screen debut in a film about the Medea legend, directed by Pier Paolo Pasolini. The soprano, who has not sung publicly since her appearance as Tosca at the Metropolitan Opera in 1965, plans to perform again when ready. Callas refuses to comment on her personal life, stating, "I am a very normal human being".

3258 GRUEN, John. **Lady tiger at the keyboard, A**, *New York Times*
an   15 Dec 1974, II-21, 22. *Illus.*
Born in Detroit, Ruth Laredo studied piano initially with her mother and then became the pupil of Rudolf Serkin for 6 years. She began her performing career as an accompanist to violinist Jaime Laredo; by 1969 they were known as the Jaime and Ruth Laredo Duo. In 1973 the pianist gave a solo recital in Tully Hall in New York, and in 1974 she made her debut with the New York Philharmonic in Ravel's concerto in G major. Laredo's most recent accomplishment has been recording all the solo piano works of Rachmaninoff.

3259 GRUEN, John. **Love story plays the Met**, *New York Times* 20
an   Feb 1972, II-13, 32. *Illus.*
Evelyn Lear first achieved success abroad in 1962 by singing the title role in *Lulu*, Marie in *Wozzeck*, and the woman in Schönberg's monodrama, *Erwartung*. In 1968 the soprano stopped singing 20th-c. repertory because she felt it was hurting her voice, and she began study with Daniel Ferro, head of

the voice department at the Manhattan School of Music. In the last few years she has sung Octavian and Cherubino at the Metropolitan Opera, and she would like to sing Tosca and the Marschallin. Lear discusses her early life and subsequent marriage to Thomas Stewart, a baritone at the Metropolitan.

3260 GUSSOW, Mel. **Clamma Dale sings way to top and seeks**
an **out new challenges**, *New York Times* 29 Sept 1976, 28. *Illus.*
Born in Chester, Penn., Clamma Dale studied voice at the Settlement Music School in Philadelphia and at the Juilliard School. After graduation Dale taught music, painting, and poetry to prisoners on Riker's Island in New York. In 1975 the soprano won a Naumburg Foundation award and made her New York City Opera debut as Antonia in *Les contes d'Hoffmann*. She discusses her current role of Bess in *Porgy and Bess* on Broadway.

3261 HAYBURN, Robert F. **Law of the church, The**, *Digest of*
bd *regulations and rubrics of Catholic church music* (Boston: McLaughlin & Reilly, 1961) 1-15. *Index.*
Reports that the 25 Dec. 1955 encyclical letter of Pope Pius XII, *Musica sacrae disciplina*, permits mixed choirs of men and women or girls--located outside of the sanctuary--to sing liturgical texts "as long as the men are completely separated from the women, and everything unbecoming is avoided".

→   HEBSON, Ann. **Women can become successful university music professors**, *see* 3176ap[77].

3262 HENAHAN, Donal. **Antonia Brico, at 72, finds her baton in**
an **high demand**, *New York Times* 19 May 1975, 22. *Illus.*
Since the release of the film *Antonia: a portrait of the woman* in 1974, Antonia Brico has begun once again to receive national recognition. She will conduct in forthcoming months at the Hollywood Bowl and in New York, Washington, D.C., and Seattle. Born in Holland in 1902, Brico was raised in the United States and subsequently went abroad to study in Germany. She made her conducting debut with the Berlin Philharmonic at the age of 28. Despite the support of Sibelius, Albert Schweitzer, and Bruno Walter in the 1930s, Brico was unable to secure a permanent position in New York or elsewhere in the eastern United States, and she therefore relocated in Denver where, for 27 years, she has conducted the Denver Businessmen's Orchestra. Recently the Denver orchestra was renamed the Brico Symphony Orchestra.

3263 HENAHAN, Donal. **Primavera String Quartet performs at**
ro **Tully Hall**, *New York Times* 18 Apr 1978, 44.
Reviews the New York debut of the all-female Primavera String Quartet, winner of the 1977 Naumburg Chamber Music Award. The program included works by Haydn, Shostakovitch, Schubert, and Paul Chihara.

3264 HENAHAN, Donal. **Prodigious Sarah**, *New York Times* 5 Oct
an 1975, VI-21, 93-98. *Illus.*
Raised in Fayetteville, Ark., Sarah Caldwell attended the New England Conservatory and subsequently became a faculty member in the opera departments of the Berkshire Music Center and Boston U. Currently she is active as the conductor and director of the Boston Opera, which she founded in 1957. The company has given the American premières of Schönberg's *Moses und Aron*, the original Musorgskii version of *Boris Godunov*, and Berlioz's *Les Troyens* in its entirety. Caldwell will conduct the New York Philharmonic in a forthcoming program devoted to works by the women composers, Grazyna Bacewicz, Ruth Crawford Seeger, Pozzi Escot, Thea Musgrave, and Lili Boulanger. Other women who have led the Philharmonic are Nadia Boulanger, who conducted in 1939 and 1962, and Rosalyn Tureck, who led a program in 1958 from the keyboard.

3265 HENAHAN, Donal. **Queen of Wagnerians. Birgit Nilsson**,
an *New York Times* 20 Nov 1971, 23. *Illus.*
Since her debut in Stockholm almost 25 years ago, Birgit Nilsson has developed a monopoly on the major Wagnerian soprano roles. Her international career dates from 1955 with performances of Brünnhilde and Salome in Munich. Since 1959 the soprano has appeared regularly at the Metropolitan Opera. Nilsson has established her position as one of the of leading female Wagnerian singers along with Kirsten Flagstad, Olive Fremstad, Johanna Gadski, Lilli Lehmann, Lillian Nordica, and Helen Traubel.

3266 HENAHAN, Donal. **They're mad about Alicia**, *New York*
an *Times* 18 July 1976, VI-12, 13-16. *Illus.*
Alicia de Larrocha's steep rise to fame began in 1965 when Herbert Breslin, a public-relations director in New York, heard one of her recordings and offered to represent the pianist in the United States. She now plays about 50 concerts and recitals in the United States a year, her repertory ranging from Bach and Couperin to Rachmaninoff and Granados. De Larrocha has appeared regularly at the Mostly Mozart Festival in New York during its 10-year history. Other women pianists including Gina Bachauer, Fannie Bloomfield-Zeisler, Teresa Carreño, Myra Hess, Sophie Menter, and Clara Schumann are discussed. The changing climate for women as pianists is also considered.

3267 HENAHAN, Donal. **Victoria de los Angeles states Carmen**
an **[is] being misinterpreted**, *New York Times* 26 Nov 1977, 12. *Illus.*
Victoria de los Angeles discusses her career in the United States. She sang at the Metropolitan Opera from 1951-63, and although she now prefers recitals to opera, she would like to sing Carmen to "redress the wrongs done to her by current interpreters" who don't understand Spanish women. Family obligations and tax laws have kept de los Angeles away from the United States for the past 5 years, but she is presently on a 2-month recital tour throughout the country.

3268 HENAHAN, Donal. **Woman steps in for Solti, wins Carne-**
ro **gie Hall ovation**, *New York Times* 1 Nov 1977, 1, 46. *Illus.*
Reviews the New York performance of Mahler's symphony no. 8 in E-flat major by the Chicago Symphony Orchestra under the direction of Margaret Hillis. A last-minute replacement for Georg Solti, who had suffered an accident, Hillis as assistant conductor had prepared the 2 adult choirs and the children's choir for the Mahler work. In the 1950s Hillis conducted performances of the Robert Shaw Chorale and the American Opera Soc., and she has frequently conducted the Chicago Symphony in works for chorus and orchestra.

→   HENAHAN, Donal. **Music: two "firsts" for Sarah Caldwell**, *see* 3056ro[76].

→   HENAHAN, Donal. **Training grant for conductors**, *see* 3177an[77].

→   HENAHAN, Donal. **Vocal virtuosos teach stars of the future**, *see* 3178an[77].

3269 HIEMENZ, Jack. **Tale of the impatient diva, The**, *New York*
an *Times* 7 Mar 1976, II-17. *Illus.*
A native of New York, Tatiana Troyanos studied voice with Hans Heinz and began her career singing in musical comedy on Broadway. After appearing in several small roles at the New York City Opera, the mezzo-soprano joined the Hamburg State Opera in 1966, and she has sung throughout Europe for the last 10 years. Troyanos has appeared with opera companies in Boston and San Francisco and is making her Metropolitan Opera debut during the 1975-76 season as Octavian in *Der Rosenkavalier*.

3270 HUGHES, Allen. **Jennie Tourel, mezzo-soprano in opera, is**
an **dead**, *New York Times* 25 Nov 1973, 84. *Illus.*
Born in Montreal of Russian parents, Jennie Tourel (1910-73) grew up in Paris. She began to study voice at age 16 with Anna El-Tour. In 1933 Tourel made her debut at the Opéra-Comique in *Carmen*, and she made her Metropolitan Opera debut in 1943. She was noted for performing Rosina in *Il barbiere di Siviglia* in the original mezzo-soprano version. Tourel was best known as an orchestral soloist and as an interpreter of art songs.

3271 HUGHES, Allen. **Maureen Forrester turns clock back 20**
an **years**, *New York Times* 12 Nov 1976, C-23.
Reports that Maureen Forrester will return to Town Hall on 12 Nov. 1976 to repeat the program of her American debut of 12 Nov. 1956 with the same accompanist, John Newmark. At the present time Forrester sings about 120 performances a year in opera, solo recitals, and guest appearances with orchestras and chamber groups. Her 5 children live in Ottawa.

3272 HUGHES, Allen. **Woman conductor warms up baton**, *New*
an *York Times* 15 Mar 1974, 18. *Illus.*
Reports that Judith Somogi will become the first woman to conduct the New York City Opera in a forthcoming performance of *The mikado*. Born in Brooklyn, the conductor studied at the Juilliard School, at the Berkshire Music Center and in Spoleto, Italy. Somogi was assistant conductor to Leopold Stokowski with the American Symphony Orchestra and has conducted Menotti's *Amahl and the night visitors* and *Help, help the globolinks* on Broadway. She joined the New York City Opera in 1966 as a vocal coach and rehearsal pianist.

3273 JACOBSON, Robert. **Joanna Simon sings "pieces I love to**
ap **sing ..."**, *Cue* XLIV/15 (21 Apr 1975) 72.
Discusses the forthcoming New York debut recital by Joanna Simon at Hunter Col. The mezzo-soprano studied voice with Beverly Johnson and Daniel Ferro, and Risë Stevens coached her in the role of Carmen. Simon made her New York City opera debut as Cherubino in 1962 and sang in the world premières of Alberto Ginastera's *Bomarzo* in Washington, D.C., and Thomas Pasatieri's *Black widow* in Seattle.

3274 JEPSON, Barbara. **American women in conducting**, *Feminist*
ap *Art Journal* IV/4 (winter 1976) 13-18. *Port., bibliog.*
Discusses the problems and progress of the following women conductors, who as of Nov. 1975 either held positions as music directors of professional orchestras or had appeared as guest conductors: Victoria Bond, Antonia Brico, Beatrice Brown, Sarah Caldwell, Margaret Harris, Margaret Hillis, Carolyn Hills, Joyce Johnson, Eve Queler, Judith Somogi, and Frances Steiner. All of

these women were personally interviewed by the author except Sarah Caldwell and Antonia Brico, for whom published information was utilized. This article is written from a feminist perspective, although not all of the women interviewed consider themselves feminists. Frequent obstacles encountered by women conductors, stereotyped notions about what women can and cannot conduct, problems of tokenism, advantages of being female, and resistance from women's symphony guilds are considered. Short personal profiles for each conductor, a historical overview of women conductors from the 17th to the early 20th c., and a letter from Columbia Artists Management to Beatrice Brown--giving reasons why the firm could not manage a woman conductor--are included.   *(Author)*

3275 JEPSON, Barbara. **Looking back: an interview with Doriot**
ap   **Anthony Dwyer**, *Feminist Art Journal* V/3 (fall 1976) 21-24.
Doriot Anthony Dwyer, 1st flutist with the Boston Symphony Orchestra since 1952, was the first woman to be appointed to a principal position with a major orchestra in the United States. The interview focuses on Dwyer's experiences as a 2nd flutist with the Los Angeles Philharmonic under Alfred Wallenstein and her attempts to become a 1st flutist with a leading orchestra, which culminated in her appointment to the Boston Symphony under Charles Munch. Dwyer's mother was a professional flutist who played in Chautauquas and traveling outdoor entertainments; her great-grandaunt was suffragist Susan B. Anthony. This article is written by a feminist and is presented as one woman's struggle and triumph over discrimination. Statistics from the American Symphony Orchestra League regarding the numbers of women presently in major orchestras, the number of women holding principal positions, and the number of major orchestras allowing preliminary auditions behind screens are included.
(Author)

3276 JOHNSON, Helen. **California Women's Symphony Orches-**
ap   **tra, The**, *Etude* LXXIII/8 (Aug 1955) 11, 48.
Formerly called the Los Angeles Women's Symphony Orchestra, this semi-professional orchestra of about 50 players has been in continual existence for 61 years. Ruth Haroldson, who has been its conductor since 1935 and a long-time advocate of women as instrumentalists and conductors, believes "it is immaterial whether a man or a woman is the physical medium through which the finest symphonic literature is presented".

3277 KETTRING, Donald D. **Mr. and Mrs. ministries in church**
ap   **music**, *Journal of Church Music* XV/6 (June 1973) 2-6. *Illus.*
Considers the work of 3 husband and wife teams in dividing the traditional choir director-organist position in church work. In 2 of the 3 situations the women do the major share of the conducting.

3278 KLEIN, Howard. **She's come a long way from St. Louis**, *New*
an   *York Times* 10 Dec 1967, II-21, 36. *Illus.*
Born in St. Louis in 1937, Grace Bumbry studied voice with Lotte Lehmann and Armand Tokatyan. After several years of singing at Bayreuth, La Scala, and Covent Garden, the mezzo-soprano made her Metropolitan Opera debut in 1965 as Princess Eboli in *Don Carlo*. She is best known for her portrayal of Carmen, a role she has sung over 95 times.

3279 KLEIN, Howard. **Woman conductor, a rara avis, finds a rest**
an   **in Scranton, Penn.**, *New York Times* 20 Feb 1964, 25.
Beatrice Brown, the only woman under contract as a regular conductor in the eastern United States, is director of the Scranton Philharmonic Orchestra. Born in England, Brown graduated from Hunter Col. and subsequently became the only woman awarded Fulbright and Rockefeller grants in conducting prior to 1964. Brown studied with Serge Koussevitzky at the Berkshire Music Center in 1949 and with Hermann Scherchen in Europe. The work of other conductors including Margaret Hillis in Chicago, Antonia Brico in Denver, and Dorothy Ziegler in St. Louis is also noted.

3280 KLEMSRUD, Judy. **Is women's lib coming to the Philhar-**
an   **monic?**, *New York Times* 11 Apr 1971, 19, 29.
A discussion with 4 women who joined the New York Philharmonic in recent years about their acceptance by the previously all-male orchestra. The women are: Michele Saxon and Orin O'Brien, bassists, and Evangeline Benedetti and Toby Saks, cellists. O'Brien was the first woman hired as a regular member of the Philharmonic in 1966.

3281 KOZINN, Allan. **Rosalyn Tureck's 40-year search for Bach**,
an   *New York Times* 9 Oct 1977, II-19, 38. *Illus.*
Reports that Rosalyn Tureck will perform Bach's *Goldberg variations*, S.988, on both the piano and harpsichord to commemorate her 40th anniversary of Bach recitals. Since 1937 Tureck has been active in researching, performing, recording, and lecturing on Bach's music. In 1969 she formed the Tureck Bach Players, a chamber ensemble, and in 1966 she organized the International Bach Soc. to promote a closer association between performers and musicologists. Tureck has long been interested in the performance of contemporary music, and accordingly she founded the Composers of Today concert series in the early 1950s. She has also introduced piano works by David Diamond, William Schuman, and Aaron Copland. In 1958 Tureck conducted the New York Philharmonic from the keyboard.

3282 LEVY, Alan. **Life at the opera with "Madame Butterball"**,
an   *New York Times* 14 May 1972, VII-20, 26-38. *Illus.*
Born and raised in Harlem, New York, Martina Arroyo graduated from Hunter Col. in 1956. In 1958 she won the Metropolitan Opera auditions and within a year sang the offstage celestial voice in *Don Carlo*. The soprano appeared in concerts in the United States and Europe before her success as Aida at the Metropolitan in 1965, when she replaced Birgit Nilsson. Arroyo has sung in performances opening 2 recent seasons at the Metropolitan, i.e., as Elvira in *Ernani* in 1970 and Elisabetta in *Don Carlo* in 1971. "Madame Butterball" refers to the opera *Madama Butterfly*.

3283 LINGG, Ann M. **Girl with everything, The**, *Opera News* XXVI/
ap   3 (18 Nov 1961) 16. *Illus.*
Discusses Mary Costa's early professional life. Born in Knoxville, Tenn. in 1934, Costa began her career singing in Walt Disney films. On Jack Benny's advice, the soprano studied voice with Mario Chamlee, and subsequently she appeared at the Hollywood Bowl and at the Glyndebourne Festival in Cimarosa's *Il segreto di Susanna*. This article is signed A.M.L., and Lingg's name has been supplied.

3284 LINGG, Ann M. **Melody recaptured**, *Reader's Digest* LVI/334
ap   (Feb 1950) 113-15. *Illus.*
Discusses the life and career of Maryla Jonas, a pupil of Paderewski. During the German invasion of Poland in 1939, Jonas fled her native country and escaped ultimately to Rio de Janeiro. Artur Rubinstein persuaded the pianist to come to New York to pursue her concert career. Using earnings from her South American recitals, Jonas made her New York debut in 1946.

3285 LYON, Hugh Lee. **Leontyne Price: highlights of a prima**
bm   **donna** (New York: Vantage, 1973) 218 p. *Illus.*
This biography of Leontyne Price includes a list of principal events and honors, operatic debuts, and a discography. The following black singers are also discussed: Marian Anderson, Martina Arroyo, Grace Bumbry, Gloria Davy, Mattiwilda Dobbs, Reri Grist, and Shirley Verrett.

3286 **Madeira, Jean (Browning)**, *Current biography*. Ed. by Anna
ac   ROTHE (New York: H.W. Wilson, 1963) 258-60. *Illus.*
Née Browning in Illinois, Jean Madeira auditioned for the Juilliard School as a pianist before Olga Samaroff Stokowski and was accepted. When Madeira mentioned that she had also studied voice, Samaroff Stokowski asked her to sing and promptly recommended Madeira to the voice department. Madeira presently divides her time between the Metropolitan and Vienna State operas, her successes in Vienna having increased her stature at the Metropolitan. She is best known for her interpretation of Carmen and also has sung Amneris, Azucena, Dalila, and Klytämnestra.

3287 **Martina Arroyo**, *Current biography*. Ed. by Charles MORITZ
ac   (New York: H.W. Wilson, 1971) 11-14. *Illus.*
Martina Arroyo studied music at Hunter Col., participating in the opera workshop, and subsequently she became a voice pupil of Marinka Gurewich. An international star, Arroyo is best known for her interpretations of the roles of Madame Butterfly, Leonora in *Il trovatore*, and Amelia in *Un ballo in maschera*. In 1968 the soprano became the first black to sing Elsa at the Metropolitan Opera.

→   MAYER, Anne. **Women in applied music teaching**, *see*
106as[20].

3288 MAYER, Martin. **Marilyn Horne becomes a prima donna**,
an   *New York Times* 17 Jan 1971, VI-14, 15, 42-47. *Illus.*
Discusses Marilyn Horne's wide vocal range and variety of operatic roles. In 1970 Horne made her debut at the Metropolitan Opera as Adalgisa, or *secunda donna*, to Joan Sutherland's Norma. Now in the 1971-72 season the Metropolitan has added *Il barbiere di Siviglia* to the schedule to allow Horne to become a *prima donna assoluta*. In addition to singing such diverse roles as Fidès in Meyerbeer's *Le prophète* and Zerlina, the mezzo-soprano has recorded Mahler's *Kindertotenlieder*. She would like to venture into Wagnerian repertory.

3289 MEISLIN, Richard J. **Gina Bachauer, 63, piano virtuoso,**
an   **dies before concert appearance in Athens**, *New York Times* 23
Aug 1976, 26.
Gina Bachauer (1913-76) studied with Waldemar Freeman in her native Athens and with Alfred Cortot in Paris. The pianist made her debut in 1935 as orchestral soloist with the Athens National Symphony. Subsequently the events of World War II thwarted her career. During the war, however, Bachauer played more than 600 concerts for soldiers in the Near East, and she later credited that experience with developing her musical maturity. In 1950 the pianist made her American debut, and for the past 26 years she made annual tours throughout the United States.

3290 MERKER, Ethel. **Case for women in brass, The**, *Musart*
ap   XXVIII/2 (winter 1975) 30-32.

Women can, and many women already have, become first-rate French horn players. Girl students tend to have smaller lung capacities than boys and therefore must work harder for copious amounts of air. For performance attire, women should by all means wear a loose-fitting garment that allows ease in breath management. Women as players of other brass instruments are not considered.

3291 MERKLING, Frank. **Lyric graduate**, *Opera News* XXVII/12
ap   (26 Jan 1963) 15. *Illus.*
A graduate of Smith Col. where she studied with Anna Hamlin, Judith Raskin began her professional career specializing in Baroque music, e.g., Monteverdi's *Orfeo*, *L'incoronazione di Poppea*, and Purcell's *The fairy queen*. In 1959 she made her New York City Opera debut as Despina in *Cosi fan tutti* and in 1961 sang Sophie in *Der Rosenkavalier*. Mozart and Strauss roles are now her favorites. Raskin has been a soloist with the Philadelphia, Cincinnati, Minneapolis, and Cleveland orchestras. This article is signed F.M., and Merkling's name has been supplied.

3292 MERKLING, Frank. **Regina Resnik**, *Musical America*
ap   LXXVIII/6 (May 1958) 9, 39. *Illus.*
After more than a decade of singing soprano roles in the United States and Europe, Regina Resnik made her mezzo-soprano debut as Marina in *Boris Godunov* in 1956 at the Metropolitan Opera. Resnik says she prefers mezzo-soprano roles because the mezzo usually has to act, while the "sweet heroines in opera [the soprano roles] are frequently symbols or types rather than women". She discusses her interpretation of Carmen, which she has sung 80 times, and the role of Klytämnestra in *Elektra*.

3293 **Milanov from Ternina to Toscanini**, *Opera News* IV/11 (25 Dec
ap   1939) 12-14. *Illus.*
A native of Zagreb, Yugoslavia, Zinka Milanov studied for 3 years with Milka Ternina, who sang Kundry in the first Metropolitan Opera production of *Parsifal* in 1903. Toscanini chose Milanov as his soprano soloist for recent performances of Verdi's *Requiem Mass* in London, Salzburg, and Lucerne.

3294 M.L.S. **Irra Petina, born in Russia, found opera career after**
ap   **American training**, *Musical Courier* CXI/4 (14 Sept 1935) 18.
        Illus.
Irra Petina studied voice with Harriet van Emden at the Curtis Inst. The mezzo-soprano sang with the Philadelphia Grand Opera for 2 years and also was a soloist with the Philadelphia Orchestra. In 1934 Petina made her Metropolitan Opera debut as Fyodor in *Boris Godunov*.

3295 MOVSHON, George. **Grace Melzia Bumbry--from playgirl**
an   **to soprano**, *New York Times* 2 Jan 1977, II-13, 16. *Illus.*
Discusses Grace Bumbry's 2 careers as a mezzo-soprano and as a dramatic soprano. In 1960 Bumbry began her operatic career in Basel as the leading mezzo-soprano in the roles of Amneris and Carmen. Now an international star, Bumbry has recently expanded her repertory to include the roles of Tosca and Salome, and she would like to add the leading roles in *Ernani* and *Nabucco*.

3296 MOVSHON, George. **What next for this charming Cheru-**
an   **bino?**, *New York Times* 29 Feb 1976, II-17, 19. *Illus.*
Born in Somerville, N.J., Frederica Von Stade studied voice with Sebastian Engelberg at the Mannes School of Music. In 1969 she began singing trouser roles such as Siebel in *Faust* and Nicklausse in Offenbach's *Les contes d'Hoffmann* at the Metropolitan Opera. The mezzo-soprano has also sung Penelope in Monteverdi's *Il ritorno d'Ulisse* at the New York City Opera. Her portrayal of Cherubino at the Metropolitan and throughout Europe has been widely acclaimed.

3297 **Nan Merriman, mezzo-soprano, retires after Amsterdam**
an   **recital**, *New York Times* 1 May 1965, 18.
A native of Pittsburgh, Nan Merriman won a $1000 award from the National Federation of Music Clubs in 1943. In 1946 she made her debut with the New York Philharmonic and subsequently appeared in concert versions of operas conducted by Toscanini. Known for her numerous recordings and radio broadcasts, Merriman was soloist for the première recording of Leonard Bernstein's *Jeremiah symphony*, conducted by the composer. She has always intended to retire while at the height of her abilities, and it was her express wish to finish her career in Amsterdam with the Concertgebouw Orchestra.

3298 **Negro soprano sings** *Butterfly* **role tonight**, *New York Herald*
an   *Tribune* 15 May 1946, 19. *Illus.*
Reports that Camilla Williams, the first Negro to sing Madame Butterfly, will make her debut in that role with the New York City Opera. Born in Danville, Va., Williams graduated from Virginia State Col. in 1941. The following year an alumni group awarded her a scholarship to study voice with Marian Szekely-Freschl in Philadelphia. In 1943 the soprano won the Marian Anderson Award, which led to a series of concerts in New Jersey.

3299 **New Fricka, A**, *Opera News* IX/6 (11 Dec 1944) 5-6. *Illus.*
ap
Reports that Blanche Thebom will sing Fricka in *Die Walküre* at the Metropolitan Opera during the 1944-45 season. Initially Thebom worked as a secretary in Canton, Ohio for 7 years. While traveling with her parents on an ocean voyage to their native Sweden in 1938, Thebom met and sang for Kosti Vehanen, Marian Anderson's accompanist. Vehanen in turn encouraged Thebom to pursue a vocal career. With financial help from her Ohio employer's parents, Thebom studied voice with Edyth Walker in New York. In 1941 the mezzo-soprano made her debut with the Philadelphia Orchestra, conducted by Eugene Ormandy, and in 1944 she made her Town Hall debut.

3300 **Norman, Jessye**, *Current biography*. Ed. by Charles MORITZ
ac   (New York: H.W. Wilson, 1976) 292-95. *Illus.*
Born in Augusta, Ga., Jessye Norman studied voice at Howard U. and continued her work with Pierre Bernac at the U. of Michigan. From 1969-72 the soprano sang leading roles with the German Opera in Berlin, and in 1973 she made her New York recital debut. Highlights of Norman's career from 1974-76 are reviewed.

3301 ONE OF YOUR FANS. **Ladies, bless 'em, The**, *Musical*
ap   *America* LXXIII/4 (Mar 1953) 21.
This letter to the editor states that the Portland Symphony Orchestra and the Portland Junior Symphony Orchestra include numerous women within their ranks. "Out here in the West only the percussion and brass sections are still a man's world".

3302 **Operatic volcano, An**, *New York Times* 30 Oct 1956, 43. *Illus.*
an
Reports that Maria Callas finally made her debut at the Metropolitan Opera in the title role of *Norma*. The soprano was offered the roles of Leonora in *Fidelio* and Madame Butterfly at the Metropolitan earlier in 1947, but she refused to sing *Fidelio* in English as requested and felt she was too heavy for Butterfly. In 1952 Rudolph Bing again invited Callas to the Metropolitan, but at that time her Italian husband was unable to obtain a visa. Callas maintains she enters opera houses only on her own terms.

3303 PAIGE, Raymond. **Why not women in our orchestras?**, *Etude*
ap   LXX/1 (Jan 1952) 14-15. *Illus.*
The taboo against women in orchestras is dying out in keeping with women's general advance in the professions and also because the military situation makes it hazardous for an orchestra manager to hire men. Women who want orchestral work should avoid instruments heavier than the cello, clarinet, and French horn.

3304 PARMENTER, Ross. **Callas is dropped by Metropolitan**,
an   *New York Times* 7 Nov 1958, 1, 20. *Illus.*
Rudolph Bing announces that Maria Callas has failed to fulfill the terms of her contract with the Metropolitan Opera and will therefore be dropped from its roster. Callas's departure from the Metropolitan is the latest in a series of similar departures from opera houses in Chicago, San Francisco, and Milan. Earlier this year the soprano nearly caused a riot in Rome by refusing to finish a performance of *Norma*.

3305 PAUL, Doris A. **This I believe**, *Music Journal* [New York] XII/3
ap   (Mar 1954) 83, 92, 94, 96.
Paul challenges conductors of women's choruses to consider the singers they are directing as serious musicians, rather than housewives who merely seek a release from domestic work. Suggestions for repertory are included.

3306 PHILLIPS, Harvey E. **Introspective prima donna**, *New York*
an   *Times* 17 Aug 1975, II-13. *Illus.*
Benita Valente studied voice with Martial Singher at the Curtis Inst. and with Margaret Harshaw. She was a soloist with the Robert Shaw Chorale for many years and made her Metropolitan Opera debut as Pamina in *Die Zauberflöte* in 1973. The soprano has enjoyed the demanding standards of performance at the Marlboro Music Festival and her collaboration with Rudolf Serkin.

3307 PHILLIPS, Harvey E. **Irra**, *Opera News* XXXIV/1 (6 Sept 1969)
ap   17. *Illus.*
A native of Russia, Irra Petina came to the United States in the wake of the Revolution. In 1934 she began singing minor roles at the Metropolitan Opera, and in the 1940s she advanced to leading parts, including Octavian in *Der Rosenkavalier* and Carmen. Petina subsequently became active in operetta and musical comedy performances, e.g., Robert Wright and George Forrest's *The song of Norway* (based on Grieg's music), Sigmund Romberg's *The student prince*, and Leonard Bernstein's *Candide*. Petina's next operatic engagement is in Seattle as Prince Orlofsky in *Die Fledermaus*.

3308 PHILLIPS, Harvey E. **Reri**, *Opera News* XXX/20 (19 Mar 1966)
ap   16. *Illus.*
Reri Grist, a native of New York, studied voice with Claire Gelda. The soprano

began her operatic career with the Santa Fe Opera in 1959, and in the early 1960s she made appearances in Europe. Grist's favorite roles are Rosina in *Il barbieri di Siviglia*, Sophie in *Der Rosenkavalier*, and Zerbinetta in *Ariadne auf Naxos*.

3309 Polyna Stoska to make Guild debut, *Opera News* XII/3 (3 Nov
ap   1947) 6-8. *Illus.*
Reports that Polyna Stoska will sing Donna Elvira in a benefit performance for the Metropolitan Opera Guild. Born in Worcester, Mass., Stoska studied voice with Frank E. Doyle and drama with Charlotte Gadski-Busch--the daughter of Johanna Gadski--in Berlin in 1938. The soprano returned to the United States in 1941 and made her New York City Opera debut in 1944. Stoska subsequently sang the role of Mrs. Maurrant in Kurt Weill's *Street scene* on Broadway.

3311 RIZZO, Eugene R. Adventuress, *Opera News* XXXI/12 (14 Jan
ap   1967) 13. *Illus.*
Born in Clarksburg, W. Va. in 1922, Phyllis Curtin attended Wellesley Col. and the New England Conservatory, where she studied operatic staging with Boris Goldovsky. Since her debut at the New York City Opera as Salome in 1954, the soprano has sung over 50 roles at the Vienna State Opera, La Scala, and the Metropolitan Opera. The title refers to Curtin's adventurous repertory. This article is signed E.R.R., and Rizzo's name has been supplied.

3312 RIZZO, Eugene R. Costa diva, *Opera News* XXIX/21 (3 Apr
ap   1965) 30. *Illus.*
Mary Costa discusses the title role in Samuel Barber's *Vanessa*--a role with which she has been closely identified. The soprano sang in musical comedy and television commercials before changing to an operatic career. Costa made her Metropolitan Opera debut as Violetta in 1964; her other roles include Alice Ford in *Falstaff* and Marguerite. This article is signed E.R.R., and Rizzo's name has been supplied.

3313 RIZZO, Eugene R. Singing for the sky, *Opera News* XXXI/3
ap   (15 Oct 1966) 19. *Illus.*
A native of Toronto, Maureen Forrester studied with Bernard Diamant, who encouraged her to concentrate on classical repertory. In 1956 the contralto made her New York recital debut and also sang in Bruno Walter's farewell concert with the New York Philharmonic. During the 1966-67 season she is making her stage debut with the New York City Opera in Händel's *Giulio Cesare*. This article is signed E.R.R., and Rizzo's name has been supplied.

3314 ROCKWELL, John. Guiomar Novaes declines to call it a
an   **piano finale**, *New York Times* 2 Dec 1972, 42.
While announcements of Guiomar Novaes's forthcoming recital at Hunter Col. indicate that it will be a farewell performance, the pianist disagrees. She maintains that she will continue touring throughout the United States and South America, and she also plans to make more recordings. Novaes's early career in the United States and how her appearances in New York "opened the doors of the country for her" are discussed.

3315 ROESCH, Clara Burling. Plight of the woman symphony
ap   **player, The**, *Music Clubs Magazine* XXXI/4 (Mar 1952) 5, 36-37.
Discusses the formation of the National Women's Symphony Orchestra under the direction of the author, who studied conducting with Dmitri Mitropoulos. This orchestra, which will tour nationally, aims to provide employment and an artistic outlet for women instrumentalists at a time when the number of women employed by major symphony orchestras and radio orchestras has been cut back to accommodate returning veterans. The National Women's Symphony will also offer women composers the opportunity of hearing their works played in rehearsal sessions. During the war Roesch toured military camps with the Roesch Little Symphony Orchestra, a group of 13 female string players who were students at the Juilliard School. The work of women as orchestral musicians in the 1920s and 30s, together with changing employment patterns in the music field are considered.

3316 RUBIN, Stephen E. Better hurry. Caballé is retiring in three
an   **years**, *New York Times* 4 Mar 1973, II-17, 35. *Illus.*
Montserrat Caballé studied piano, theory, harmony, composition, and voice at the Barcelona Conservatory with the financial help of Bertrand Mata. Since her American debut in 1965, Caballé has sung a wide range of roles at the Metropolitan Opera including Norma, Salome, and Donna Elvira. The soprano's trademark is her pianissimo sound. She plans to retire in 3 years to devote more time to her family.

3317 RUBIN, Stephen E. But she's not Italian, *New York Times* 14
an   May 1972, II-15, 24. *Illus.*
Phyllis Curtin discusses her career as an operatic singer, orchestral soloist, and recitalist. In 1956 the soprano sang in the première of Carlisle Floyd's *Susannah* at the New York City Opera. Curtin has introduced more than 100 contemporary works in a variety of genres.

3318 RUBIN, Stephen E. "I'm not scared any more", *New York
an   Times* 16 Sept 1973, II-1, 28. *Illus.*
Leontyne Price discusses her career as the first black international star in opera. She notes that being a token black in the past involved pressure not to make a mistake. The climate has improved in the past 10 years however, and now she is not afraid to fail on occasion. Price sang 118 performances at the Metropolitan Opera and is now returning to sing Madame Butterfly, a role she has not sung anywhere since 1961. The soprano wants to correct the myth about the Chisholm family in her native Laurel, Miss. Although the Chisholms contributed financially to Price's studies, her parents gave her the greatest moral and financial support.

3319 RUBIN, Stephen E. She plays her vocal cords like violin
an   **strings**, *New York Times* 9 June 1974, II-13, 16. *Illus.*
Judith Blegen was a student of both violin and voice at the Curtis Inst. before she decided to concentrate on a career in singing. Her favorite roles are Sophie in *Der Rosenkavalier*, Marcellina in *Fidelio*, Susanna in *Le nozze di Figaro*, and Adina in *L'elisir d'amore*. Blegen discusses how she approaches a role vocally and dramatically, and how she studies notes separately from the text.

3320 RUBIN, Stephen E. Troubled prima donna tries for a
an   **comeback**, *New York Times* 15 May 1977, II-17, 24. *Illus.*
Anna Moffo discusses her early career in the 1960s. The coloratura soprano was pressured into singing new roles at the rate of 12 a year, and she also appeared on television and in films. Now after an absence of several years from public life, Moffo is beginning to perform again in recitals and orchestral concerts.

3321 Ruth Bradley opens New York studio, *Musical America* LVI/17
ap   (10 Nov 1936) 33.
Reports that Ruth Bradley is working as a pianist, accompanist, piano teacher, and coach in New York. Formerly Bradley was on the faculty of the Bush Conservatory in Chicago. She is a pupil of Fannie Bloomfield-Zeisler.

3322 SARGEANT, Winthrop. Divas (New York: Coward, McCann,
bm   and Geoghegan, 1973) 192 p. *Illus.*
Discusses the professional and personal lives, and the voices and roles of the following international singers: Eileen Farrell, Marilyn Horne, Birgit Nilsson, Leontyne Price, Beverly Sills, and Joan Sutherland.

3323 rb —
R. by Donal HENAHAN, *New York Times* 18 Mar 1973, 6.

3324 SARGEANT, Winthrop. Doing what comes naturally, *Opera
ap   News* XXXII/6 (9 Dec 1967) 28-29. *Illus.*
Eileen Farrell discusses her vocal range and technique, which enable her to sing Wagner as well as Bellini. In 1955 the soprano made her operatic debut in Cherubini's *Medea* with the American Opera Soc. Among the roles Farrell has sung at the Metropolitan Opera since her debut in 1960 are Santuzza, Gioconda, Leonora in *La forza del destino*, and Alcestis in *Alceste*.

3325 SATZ, Arthur. Musician of the month: Carole Farley, *High
ap   Fidelity/Musical America* XXVII/1 (Jan 1977) MA 4-5.
Reports that Carole Farley will make her Metropolitan Opera debut in March in the title role of *Lulu*, a role for which she is well-known in Europe. In 1968 the soprano won a Fulbright scholarship to study in Munich and subsequently was engaged by the Cologne Opera. Farley has sung Rosalinda in *Die Fledermaus* and Hélène in Offenbach's *La belle Hélène* with the New York City Opera.

3326 SAYRE, Nora. Antonia. Film portrait of a conductor, *New
an   York Times* 19 Sept 1974, 50. *Illus.*
Reviews the documentary film produced by Judy Collins and Jill Godmilow about the career of Antonia Brico. After making her debut as a conductor with the Berlin Philharmonic in 1930, Brico appeared twice in concerts at the Metropolitan Opera, but she was denied a 3rd performance because of baritone John Charles Thomas's refusal to work with a woman conductor. In 1934 Brico founded the New York Women's Symphony Orchestra, which performed regularly for several seasons. Since the 1940s she has been teaching and conducting in Denver. The film alternates Brico's narration of events in her career with glimpses of her at work in rehearsing and teaching. Brico notes that not being able to conduct more than 4 or 5 times a year from the 1940s onwards has been a source of perpetual heartbreak.

3327 SCHONBERG, Harold C. Ho-yo-to-ho! A new Brünnhilde,
an   *New York Times* 10 Jan 1960, VI-17, 92-95. *Illus.*
Discusses Birgit Nilsson's career in light of those of other Wagnerian sopranos, e.g., Olive Fremstad, Lilli Lehmann, and Lillian Nordica. In addition to singing Wagnerian roles at the Metropolitan Opera, Nilsson will also appear as Aida, Turandot, and Salome in the future. A critique of Nilsson's voice and acting abilities is included, together with a discussion of the physical requirements necessary to sing her roles.

3328 SCHUYLER, Philippa Duke. **Adventures in black and white.**
bm   With a foreword by Deems TAYLOR (New York: R. Speller, 1960)
302 p. *Illus., index.*
A chronicle by the pianist of her travels on concert tours around the world
during the 1950s. Beginning as a child prodigy, Schuyler (1933-67) accomplished a series of breakthroughs for the black musician in the classical field.

3329 SEROFF, Victor. **Renata Tebaldi. The woman and the diva**
bm   (New York: Appleton-Century-Crofts, 1961) 213 p. *Illus., discog.,
index.*
Born in Pesaro, Italy in 1922, Renata Tebaldi studied voice with Carmen Melis.
In 1944 the soprano made her operatic debut in Parma as Mimi in *La bohème.*
In 1946 she sang at the inaugural concert of the reconstructed opera house at
La Scala under the direction of Toscanini. Her first American appearance was
in San Francisco as Desdemona in 1950, and she made her Metropolitan Opera
debut in the same role 5 years later. In 1958 Tebaldi sang Madame Butterfly at
the Metropolitan, coached by the Japanese stage director, Yoshio Aoyama. A
list of the soprano's performances and a discography of her recordings issued in
the United States are included. R. by Eric SALZMAN, *New York Times*, 19 Feb
1961, VII-14.

3330 SHANNON, Anthony. **Gypsy whose dream came true,** *New*
an   *York World Telegram and Sun* 2 Feb 1957, 5. *Illus.*
Discusses Jean Madeira's association with the role of Carmen, the part in which
she made her debut at the Vienna State Opera in 1955. Madeira had been
singing minor roles at the Metropolitan Opera for 7 years when, in 1955, she
decided to pursue a European career. She is scheduled to sing Carmen as well as
several other major roles at the Metropolitan this season.

3331 SHEPARD, Richard F. **About New York; plaudits for a**
an   **silver anniversary,** *New York Times* 17 Nov 1975, 35. *Illus.*
Reports that the Metropolitan Opera has honored Roberta Peters--the youngest
singer to date to celebrate a 25th anniversary with the opera house. With the
help of Jan Peerce, a family friend, Peters auditioned for Sol Hurok while still
in her teens. Through Hurok and after 6 years of further study, the soprano
joined the Metropolitan in an apprentice capacity. Peters discusses the details
of her debut in 1950 as a last-minute replacement and her subsequent successes
in opera and concert as well as her recent debut as an actress on television.

3332 SHERMAN, John K. **Woman harpist or cellist is top sight at**
ap   **concerts,** *American String Teacher* XII (Mar-Apr 1962) 1-2.
Discusses the appropriateness of different instruments for women on the basis
of how graceful women look when playing. Women as players of winds--other
than flute--brass, and percussion are not "top sights" at concerts.

3333 SHERMAN, Rose. **Cleveland Women's Symphony Orches-**
ap   **tra,** *International Musician* LXVII/6 (Dec 1968) 5, 20-21.
Founded in 1935, this amateur orchestra of 70-90 players has always had a
nucleus of professional musicians and music teachers. Many members have
gone on to play in professional orchestras.

3334 SILLS, Beverly. **Bubbles** (New York: Bobbs Merrill, 1976) 240 p.
bm   *Illus., index.*
An autobiography by Beverly Sills, who has been known as "Bubbles" since
childhood. Born in Brooklyn in 1929, Sills began vocal study with Estelle
Liebling at age 7. She sang commercials on radio broadcasts and learned 20
operas by age 15. The soprano gained operatic experience in Philadelphia,
Baltimore, and San Francisco before making her New York City Opera debut
as Rosalinda in *Die Fledermaus* in 1955. In 1958 Sills sang the title role in
Douglas Moore's *The ballad of Baby Doe* and later appeared with the Boston
Opera, directed by Sarah Caldwell. Her performances as Cleopatra in Händel's
Giulio Cesare at the New York City Opera in 1966 launched her international
career. In 1968 Sills made her debut at La Scala as Pamira in Rossini's *La siège
de Corinthe,* the role she also sang for her Metropolitan Opera debut in 1975.
She has furthered the revival of bel canto repertory by appearing in Donizetti's
Maria Stuarda, Anna Bolena, and *Roberto Devereux.*

3335 S.J. **Blonde with brains,** *Opera News* XXXII/5 (25 Nov 1967) 18.
ap   *Illus.*
Arlene Saunders discusses the role of Freia, which she is singing in the new San
Francisco production of *Das Rheingold.* A native of Cleveland, the soprano first
appeared with the Grass Roots Opera in Raleigh, N.C. and then made her New
York City Opera debut as Giorgetta in Puccini's *Il tabarro* in 1961. Saunders
made her European debut in Hamburg as Agathe in *Der Freischutz* in 1963.
The same year she also sang German repertory with the Metropolitan Opera on
tour.

3336 SMITH, Patrick J. **Spanish treasure: Montserrat Caballé,**
ap   *Opera News* XXX/1 (25 Sept 1965) 13. *Illus.*
Discusses Montserrat Caballé's recent international success. In 1960 she sang in
the world première of de Falla's *Atlantida,* and in 1964 she made her Mexico
City debut as Manon. This year she will sing in Dallas and make her debut at
the Metropolitan Opera in *Faust.*

3337 **Soprano from Spokane,** *Time* LVIII/23 (3 Dec 1951) 50-56. *Illus.*
ap
Originally from Spokane, Patrice Munsel relocated in New York to study with
William Herman. In 1943 at the age of 18, she made her debut at the
Metropolitan Opera somewhat prematurely and received mixed reviews.
Subsequently her career suffered further reverses. She had the continuing
support, however, of Edward Johnson as general manager of the Metropolitan,
and in 1949 she achieved acclaim for her performance of Zerlina in *Don
Giovanni.* Munsel is now the leading soubrette at the Metropolitan. During the
current season she is singing Musetta in *La bohème,* Adele in *Die Fledermaus,*
and Despina in *Così fan tutti.*

3338 STARR, Susan. **Prejudice against women, The,** *Music Journal*
ap   [New York] XXXII/3 (Mar 1974) 14-15, 28. *Illus.*
The author discusses her experiences as a pianist. Starr studied with Eleanor
Sokoloff and later with Rudolf Serkin at the Curtis Inst. After graduating from
Curtis in 1961, she sought a manager and was told: "If only you were a man,
I'd sign you up in a minute". The pianist won a 2nd prize at the Chaikovskii
Competition in 1962 and subsequently began concertizing in Europe. It is
Starr's opinion that women are encouraged to specialize or to play unknown
repertory as a means of establishing themselves and that prejudice extends to
all women instrumentalists--both solo performers and orchestral musicians. She
notes further that women earn less than men as teachers in colleges and
conservatories.

→   **Statistics in music,** *see* 109ap[20].

3339 STEINBERG, Michael. **Women's symphony orchestra plays.**
ro   **R. Gregorian conducts,** *Boston Globe* 12 July 1965, 24.
Reviews an outdoor concert by the 70-member women's "pops" orchestra.
Marion Sutcliffe organized the orchestra in 1963 to provide much-needed
employment for women and to fill the hiatus between the end of the Boston
Symphony Orchestra's season and the beginning of the Boston Pops Orchestra
concerts. The financial difficulties of the women's orchestra and its disagreements with the musicians' union over wages are discussed.

3340 STODDARD, Hope. **Ladies of the symphony,** *International*
ap   *Musician* LI/11 (May 1953) 24-25.
Discusses sexual stereotyping regarding instruments and the employment of
women players by major and secondary orchestras.

3341 STRONGIN, Theodore. **Jane Marsh tells of tough Russian**
an   **competition,** *New York Times* 12 July 1966, 35.
Reports that Jane Marsh is the first American to win a first prize in the
Chaikovskii Competition since Van Cliburn won in 1958. Marsh graduated
from Oberlin Col. and then studied voice in New York with Otto Guth and Lili
Wexberg. The soprano made her operatic debut in 1965 at the Spoleto Festival
as Desdemona. She has been offered a Metropolitan Opera contract, which she
does not feel ready to accept.

3342 STRONGIN, Theodore. **Milanov, at the Met since 1937,**
an   **will retire next Wednesday,** *New York Times* 8 Apr 1966, 26.
Illus.
Zinka Milanov made both her initial operatic debut in Ljubljana, Yugoslavia in
1927 and her Metropolitan Opera debut in 1937 as Leonora in *Il trovatore.* The
soprano was offered a contract at the Metropolitan provided she agreed to learn
Italian and lose 25 lbs. Milanov has appeared 453 times with the Metropolitan
and will sing her farewell performance as Madeleine in *Andrea Chénier.*

3343 TAUBMAN, Howard. **Birgit Nilsson as Isolde flashes like**
ro   **new star in "Met" heaven,** *New York Times* 19 Dec 1959, 1, 31.
Illus.
Reviews Birgit Nilsson's debut at the Metropolitan Opera as Isolde, and reports
that the soprano is the finest Isolde to appear at the Metropolitan since Kirsten
Flagstad sang the role in the 1930s. Born in Karup, Sweden, Nilsson began her
operatic career in Stockholm in 1947 as Lady Macbeth in Verdi's opera. Her
previous American operatic appearances have been in Chicago and San
Francisco.

3344 TAUBMAN, Howard. **Pianist's story,** *New York Times* 10 Mar
an   1946, II-5.
Born in Warsaw in 1911, Maryla Jonas began piano study at age 7 and made
her debut with the Warsaw Philharmonic at age 9. She studied with Emil Saur
for 3 years and subsequently won several international prize competitions in
the early 1930s. Her career was interrupted in 1939 when she chose to leave
Poland and take refuge in South America. Finally in 1946 she launched her
career in the United States with a successful Carnegie Hall debut.

3345 **Thelma Votipka, soprano, dies; with the Met for 28 years,**
an   *New York Times* 27 Oct 1972, 44. *Illus.*
Born in Cleveland, Thelma Votipka (1898-1972) studied voice at Oberlin Col.
She sang 70 small roles with the Metropolitan Opera from 1935-63. Among her

favorite roles were Martha in *Faust* and the Witch in Humperdinck's *Hänsel und Gretel*. Votipka had been a voice teacher for many years.

3346 Thirty years at the Met: three stars reminisce, *New York Times*
an   30 Dec 1975, 27, 45. *Illus.*
Dorothy Kirsten, Robert Merrill, and Jerome Hines--each American-born and trained--discuss their careers on the occasion of their 30th anniversary with the Metropolitan Opera. Kirsten, who is retiring at the close of the current season, made her debut in 1945 as Mimi in *La bohème*. She will sing Tosca for her farewell performance. Kirsten has sung 12 roles in 169 performances and has had the longest career of any leading soprano at the Metropolitan. The soprano's association with Grace Moore and her early years in Chicago and San Francisco are considered.

3347 Town Hall prize to Miss Tureck, *New York Times* 22 May 1938,
an   XI-5.
Reports that Rosalyn Tureck is the first winner of the newly created Town Hall Young Artist Award for her performances of Bach's *Well-tempered clavier*, S.846/93, and other works by the composer in 6 recitals. Born in Chicago, Tureck first studied with Sophia Brilliant-Liven and Jan Chiapusso, and subsequently at the Juilliard School with Olga Samaroff Stokowski. In 1935 the pianist won a $1000 prize from the National Federation of Music Clubs and the Schubert Memorial award, which entitled her to an appearance with the Philadelphia Orchestra.

3348 Two to perform in recital at H-SU, *Abilene (Tex.) Reporter-*
an   *News* 15 Feb 1976, A-21.
Announces the 2nd concert in a 2-part series entitled "Women in American song", to be given in Feb. 1976 by Grace Morrow, soprano and associate professor of voice and music education at Hardin-Simmons U. Works by the following composers will be included, among others: Amy Cheney Beach, Natalie Curtis-Burlin, Eleanor Everest Freer, Nancy Van de Vate, Elinor Remick Warren, and Marilyn Ziffrin. Grace Morrow and her accompanist, Thurman Morrison, undertook considerable research in compiling the programs. *(Grace Morrow)*

3349 Vignettes [I], *Music Clubs Magazine* LIII/2 (winter 1973-74) 29-30.
ap   *Port.*
Presents short summaries of the careers of some past winners of the National Federation of Music Clubs' Young Artist Award, including pianists Eunis Podis and Claudette Sorel, singer Shirley Verrett, and violinist Sylvia Rosenberg. *(Julia Smith, abridged)*

3350 Vignettes [II], *Music Clubs Magazine* LIII/3 (1974) 23-24.
ap
A summary of the professional activities of some past winners of the National Federation of Music Clubs' Young Artist Award, including keyboard player Rosalyn Tureck, pianist Tana Bowden, singer Lee Dougherty, and violinist Eudice Shapiro.

3351 WARNKE, Frank J. New faces: Marilyn Horne, *Opera News*
ap   XXV/8 (31 Dec 1960) 14, 32. *Illus.*
Discusses Marilyn Horne's early career leading to her San Francisco debut as Marie in *Wozzeck* in 1960. Born in Branford, Penn., Horne studied voice with William Venard at the U. of Southern California. She sang with the Roger Wagner Chorale and in the Monday Evening Concerts in Los Angeles, and then in 1954 she made her operatic debut in Smetana's *The bartered bride* with the Los Angeles Guild Opera. Subsequently the mezzo-soprano appeared at the Venice Biennale and became a regular member of the opera house in Gelsenkirchen, West Germany.

3352 WARREN, Dale. Disappearing contralto, The, *American*
ap   *Record Guide* XXVII/4 (Dec 1960) 276-79.
Reviews the work of contraltos in opera early in the 20th c. in the United States, and discusses the current preference for the mezzo-soprano voice. The chief virtue of the contralto voice lies in its contrast with dramatic soprano parts, as for instance when Amneris is sung by a contralto in contrast to the dramatic soprano heroine, Aida.

3353 WILLS, Garry. Shirley Verrett gambles on superstardom,
an   *New York Times* 30 Jan 1977, VI-15, 16, 20, 56-58. *Illus.*
Born in New Orleans, Shirley Verrett grew up in Los Angeles and studied voice with Anna Fitziu. After receiving a degree in business and selling real estate for several years, Verrett won the Arthur Godfrey Talent Show in 1955, which enabled her to pursue vocal study at the Juilliard School with Marian Szekely-Freschl. Leopold Stokowski chose her for an orchestral performance in Houston in the late 1950s, but blacks were excluded at that time. Verrett has recently won acclaim for her dramatic interpretation of the roles of Azucena and the Second Prioress in Poulenc's *Les dialogues des Carmélites*. Now in her mid-40s, Verrett is changing from mezzo-soprano to soprano roles.

3354 Women band directors national association holds first
ap   **official meeting in Chicago**, *School Musician* XLI/8 (Apr 1970)
70. *Illus.*
Reports that the first meeting of the Women Band Directors National Assoc. was held in Dec. 1969 in Chicago. Consisting of 40 charter members, the organization plans to publish 3 issues of a newsletter annually and *Ladies of the Podium*, a publication featuring articles about women band directors. The organization aims to provide a forum on problems unique to women in the profession.

3355 Women in American symphony orchestras, *Symphony News*
ap   XXVII/2 (Apr 1976) 13, 14.
Between 1964 and 1974, the percentage of women players in the major orchestras grew from 18.3% to 21.8%, in the metropolitan orchestras from 36.5% to 39.7%. In community orchestras in 1973-75, 47.4% of the players were women. One-third of all the major orchestras currently hold preliminary auditions behind a screen, and 3 orchestras--each with a high percentage of female players--use a screen in the final audition. Contemporary women conductors and women active in the American Symphony Orchestra League are noted.

→   **Women of music, The**, *see* 181ap[25].

→   WRIGHT, Gladys. **Career opportunities for the young woman graduate**, *see* 111ap[20].

79   Art music by women

Chamber music

3356 ANDERSON, Beth. Argument, An (facsimile of MS at
mm   NNACA, 1977) 1 p. (score, parts).
Dn 4'. *Da* 1970. *La* composer. *Pf* solo AB, tba. *(Composer)*

3357 ANDERSON, Beth. Paranoia (facsimile of MS at NNACA,
mm   1977) 1 p. (score, parts).
Dn 1'. *Da* 1967. *La* composer. *At* composer. *Pf* solo M, pno. 2 flu can replace pno. *(Composer)*

3358 ANDERSON, Beth. She wrote (facsimile of MS at NNACA,
mm   1977) 11 p. (score, parts).
Dn 7' (expandable). *Da* Jan. 1974. *La* composer. *At* Gertrude Stein, composer. *St* Q.E.D. *Pf* solo S, 2 vln amplified. *(Composer)*

3359 BALLOU, Esther Williamson. Beguine for two pianos (New
mm   York: Composers Facsimile Ed., 1958) 10 p. (score, parts).
Dn 4'. *Da* 1957. *Pf* 2 pno, 4 hands. Also for orchestra (*WIAM* 4362) and for 4 pno, 8 hands (*WIAM* 3368). *(James R. Heintze)*

3360 BALLOU, Esther Williamson. Brass sextette with pianoforte
mm   (New York: Composers Facsimile Ed., 1962) 21 p. (score, parts).
Dn 10'. *Pf* 2 tpt, 2 hrn, 2 tbn, pno. *(James R. Heintze)*

3361 BALLOU, Esther Williamson. Capriccio for violin and piano
mm   (New York: Composers Facsimile Ed., 1963) 13 p. (score).
Dn 10'. *Da* 1963.

3362 BALLOU, Esther Williamson. Christmas variations (facsimile
mm   of autograph at NNACA, 1954) 6 p. (score).
Dn 4'. *Da* 1954. *Pf* obo, rec, hps.

3363 BALLOU, Esther Williamson. Dialogues (facsimile of auto-
mm   graph at NNACA, 1966) 8 p. (score).
Dn 6'. *Da* 29 Nov. 1966, revised 1969. *Pf* obo, gtr. *(James R. Heintze)*

**3364 BALLOU, Esther Williamson. Divertimento for string quar-
mm   tet** (New York: Composers Facsimile Ed., 1958) 17 p. (score).
Dn 10'. *Da* Jan. 1958. *(James R. Heintze)*

**3365 BALLOU, Esther Williamson. Fantasia brevis for oboe and
mm   strings** (New York: Composers Facsimile Ed., 1952) 5 p. (score, parts).
Dn 2'. *Da* 1950. *Pf* obo, string trio.

3366 BALLOU, Esther Williamson. **Fantasia brevis II** (New York:
mm   Composers Facsimile Ed., 1952) 13 p. (score, parts).
Dn 3' . *Pf* obo, string quartet.

3367 BALLOU, Esther Williamson. **Five-Four-Three** (New York:
mm   Composers Facsimile Ed., 1936) 21 p. (score).
Dn 11' . *At* E.E. Cummings. *St* 73 poems (1963). *Pf* solo voc, hrp, vla. *Ct* All
which isn't singing is mere talking; Who is this; May I be gay; A great; ! Hope.
Commissioned by the Hans Kindler Foundation and first performed 12 June
1966 in Washington, D.C.

3368 BALLOU, Esther Williamson. **Forty-finger beguine** (New
mm   York: Composers Facsimile Ed., 1952) 4 p. (score, parts).
Dn 3' . *Da* 1950. *Pf* 4 pno, 8 hands. Also for orchestra (*WIAM* 4362) and for 2
pno, 4 hands (*WIAM* 3359).   *(James R. Heintze)*

3369 BALLOU, Esther Williamson. **Plaintive note, A, [and] A**
mm   **cheerful note** (New York: Composers Facsimile Ed., 1952) 3 p.
       (score, part).
Dn 3' . *Da* 29 Aug. 1951. *Pf* pno, vcl.   *(James R. Heintze)*

3370 BALLOU, Esther Williamson. **Prism for string trio** (facsimile
mm   of autograph at NNACA, 1969) 17 p. (score).
Dn 14' . *Da* 1969.

3371 BALLOU, Esther Williamson. **Romanza** (facsimile of auto-
mm   graph at NNACA, 1969) 3 p. (score, part).
Dn 3' . *Da* June 1969. *Pf* pno, vln.   *(James R. Heintze)*

3372 BALLOU, Esther Williamson. **Sonata for two pianos** (New
mm   York: Merrymount Music, 1949) 28 p. (score).
Dn 10' . *Pf* 2 pno, 4 hands. The 1969 revision is in MS at DAU.
                                                              (James R. Heintze)

3373 BALLOU, Esther Williamson. **Sonata no. 2 for two pianos**
mm   (New York: Composers Facsimile Ed., 1959) 29 p. (score, parts).
Dn 14' . *Da* 1958. *Pf* 2 pno, 4 hands.

3374 BALLOU, Esther Williamson. **Suite for violoncello and**
mm   **piano** (New York: Composers Facsimile Ed., 1952) 6, 6, 1 p. (score).
Dn 7' . *Da* 1945-51.   *(James R. Heintze)*

3375 BALLOU, Esther Williamson. **Suite for winds** (New York:
mm   Composers Facsimile Ed., 1957) 23 p. (score, parts).
Dn 9' . *Da* Mar. 1957. *Pf* 2 flu, 2 obo, 2 cla, 2 bsn, 2 hrn. *(James R. Heintze)*

3376 BALLOU, Esther Williamson. **Trio for violin, 'cello, and**
mm   **pianoforte** (New York: Composers Facsimile Ed., 1956) 40 p.
       (score).
Dn 18' . *Da* 1955, Peterborough, N.H.

3377 BALLOU, Esther Williamson. **What if a much of a which of**
mm   **a wind** (New York: Composers Facsimile Ed., 1959) 27 p. (score,
       parts).
Dn 4' . *At* E.E. Cummings. *Pf* solo SBarB, woodwind quintet. *(James R. Heintze)*

3378 BARKIN, Elaine. **Inward and outward bound** (New York:
mm   Composers Facsimile Ed., 1975) 40 p. (score, parts).
Dn 13' . *Da* 1975. *La* composer. *Pf* flu alternating with pic, obo, cla alternating
with bcl, bsn, hrn, tpt, tbn, tba, tim, per for 2 players including vib and mba,
vln, vla, vcl, cbs.   *(Composer)*

3379 BARKIN, Elaine. **Mixed modes** (Hillsdale, N.Y.: Mobart, 1976)
mm   28 p. $12. (score, parts).
Dn 13' . *Da* 1975. *La* composer. *Pf* obo, pno, vln, vla, vcl. *(Composer)*

3380 BARKIN, Elaine. **Plus ça change [The more things change]**
mm   (New York: Composers Facsimile Ed., 1973) 50 p. (score, parts).
Dn 10' . *Da* 1972. *La* composer. *Pf* per for 3 players including mba, vib, and
xyl; 4 vln; 2 vla; 2 vcl; 2 cbs.   *(Composer)*

3381 BARKIN, Elaine. **Prim cycles** (Hillsdale, N.Y.: Mobart, 1976) 13
mm   p. (score).
Dn 9' . *Da* 1972. *La* composer. *Pf* flu, obo, vln, vcl.   *(Composer)*

3382 BARKIN, Elaine. **Refrains** (New York: Composers Facsimile
mm   Ed., 1967) 19 p. (score, parts).
Dn 8' . *Da* 1967. *La* composer. *Pf* flu, obo, cel, vln, vla, vcl. *(Composer)*

3383 BARKIN, Elaine. **String quartet** (New York: Composers Fac-
mm   simile Ed., 1969) 33 p. (score, parts).
Dn 17' . *Da* 1969. *La* composer. First movement also published in *American
Society of University Composers Journal of Music Scores* II (1974), 5-22. *Rg*
Composers Recordings, CRI SD 338.   *(Composer)*

3384 BARKIN, Elaine. **Triode** (Hillsdale, N.Y.: Mobart, 1977) 22 p.
mm   (score).
Dn 14' . *Da* Oct. 1976. *La* composer. *Pf* vln, vla, vcl.   *(Composer)*

3385 BARRETT-THOMAS, N. **Gregarious chants II for viola and**
mm   **clarinet** (Boston: Artists' Forum, 1974) 8 p. (score).
Dn 5' . *Da* May 1974. *La* composer.   *(Paula Ann Ross)*

3386 BARRETT-THOMAS, N. **Gregarious chants III for percus-**
mm   **sion and flute** (Boston: Artists' Forum, 1975) 8 p. (score).
Dn 5' . *Da* May 1974. *La* composer. *Pf* flu, per including mba. *(Paula Ann Ross)*

3387 BARRETT-THOMAS, N. **Perpetuum mobile, 1969** (Boston:
mm   Artists' Forum, 1969) 18 p. (score, parts).
Dn 10' . *Da* Apr. 1969. *La* composer. *Pf* flu, bsn, vln, vla. *(Paula Ann Ross)*

3388 BARRETT-THOMAS, N. **Posauna in the highest** (Boston:
mm   Artists' Forum, 1970) 27 p. (score, parts).
Dn 10' . *La* composer. *Pf* 18 tbn, tim, per including xyl. *(Paula Ann Ross)*

3389 BARRETT-THOMAS, N. **Refractions** (Boston: Artists' Forum,
mm   1969) 13 p. (score, parts).
Dn 10' . *Da* Sept. 1969. *La* composer. *Pf* flu, obo, cla, bsn, pno. *(Paula Ann Ross)*

3390 BARRETT-THOMAS, N. **Sonata for viola and piano** (Bo-
mm   ston: Artists' Forum, 1976) 34 p. (score, part).
Dn 20' . *Da* Mar. 1976.   *(Paula Ann Ross)*

3391 BARRETT-THOMAS, N. **Songs of singing** (Boston: Artists'
mm   Forum, 1970) 21 p. (score, parts).
Song cycle. *Dn* 15' . *Da* Apr. 1970. *At* Stephen Crane. *Pf* solo A, pno, vcl. *Ct*
Once I knew a fine song, Each small gleam, The livid lightnings flashed, Tongue
of wood, I have heard the sunset song.   *(Paula Ann Ross)*

3392 BARRETT-THOMAS, N. **Three psalms for tenor voice,**
mm   **viola, and piano** (Boston: Artists' Forum, 1977) 15 p. (score, parts).
Dn 10' . *Da* Aug. 1977. *La* composer. *Ct* Ps 23, 40, and 98. *(Paula Ann Ross)*

3393 BELL, Carla Huston. **Ode to Martin Luther King** (New York:
mm   Caaron Music, 1977) 9 p.
Dn 5' . *Da* 1977. *La* composer. *At* composer. *Pf* solo S, vcl, cbs. Also for choral
S, vcl, cbs (*WIAM* 3830).   *(Composer)*

3394 BOLZ, Harriett. **Pageant for woodwind quintet** (West Babylon,
mm   N.Y.: H. Branch, 1976) 36 p. (score).
Dn 10' . *Da* 1973. *La* publisher.   *(Composer)*

3395 BOND, Victoria. **Can(n)ons for clarinet and violin** (New
mm   York: Seesaw Music, 1974) 11 p. (score, parts).
Dn 5' . *Da* 1970. *La* publisher.   *(Composer)*

3396 BOND, Victoria. **Conversation piece** (New York: Seesaw Music,
mm   1975) 13 p. (score, parts).
Dn 10' . *Da* 1975. *La* publisher. *Pf* vib, vla.   *(Composer)*

3397 BOND, Victoria. **Cornography** (New York: Seesaw Music, 1974)
mm   9 p. (score, parts).
Dn 5' . *Da* 1970. *La* publisher. *Pf* bsn, hrn.   *(Composer)*

3398 BOND, Victoria. **Sonata for cello and piano** (New York:
mm   Seesaw Music, 1974) 26 p. (score, part).
Dn 10' . *Da* 1971. *La* publisher. *Rg* Twentieth century cello, Laurel-Protone, LP
13.   *(Composer)*

3399 BOND, Victoria. **Suite aux troubadours** (New York: Seesaw
mm   Music, 1974) 30 p. (score, parts).
Dn 15' . *Da* 1970. *La* publisher. *Pf* solo S, flu, obo, enh, lute or hrp, vla, vcl.
                                                              (Composer)

3400 BOND, Victoria. **Trio for brass** (New York: Seesaw Music,
mm   1974) 17 p. (score, parts).
Dn 8' . *Da* 1969. *La* publisher. *Pf* hrn, tpt, tbn.   *(Composer)*

3401 BOONE, Clara Lyle. **Americas trio for flute, clarinet, and
mm   bassoon, The** (62; Washington, D.C.: Arsis, 1976) 10 p. $2.50.
(score, parts).
Dn 5'. *Da* 1960. Published under the pseudonym of Lyle de Bohun.   *(Composer)*

3402 BOONE, Clara Lyle. **Slumber song** (Washington, D.C.: Arsis,
mm   1975) 3 p. $1.50. (score).
Dn 3'. *Da* 1957. *At* composer. *Pf* solo A, flu or vln or rec. Published under the
pseudonym of Lyle de Bohun.   *(Composer)*

3403 BOONE, Clara Lyle. **Songs of estrangement** (58; Washington,
mm   D.C.: Arsis, 1975) 16 p. $3.50. (score, parts).
Dn 7'. *Da* 1958. *At* composer. *Pf* solo S, string quartet. Published under the
pseudonym of Lyle de Bohun.   *(Composer)*

3404 BRITAIN, Radie. **Dance grotesque** (New York: Seesaw Music,
mm   1976) 5 p. (score).
Dn 3'. *Pf* 2 flu.

3405 BRITAIN, Radie. **Four sarabandes for woodwind quintet**
mm   (New York: Seesaw Music, 1974) 15 p. (score, parts).
Dn 7'.

3406 BRITAIN, Radie. **In the beginning** (New York: Seesaw Music,
mm   1976) 6 p. (score).
Dn 4'. *Pf* 4 hrn.

3407 BRITAIN, Radie. **Recessional** (West Babylon, N.Y.: H. Branch,
mm   1977) 5 p. $3. (score, parts).
Dn 2'. *Pf* 4 tbn.

3408 BRUSH, Ruth. **Duets for flute and bassoon** (facsimile of MS at
mm   NNAMC, 1970) 4 p. (score, parts).
Dn 4'.   *(Composer)*

3409 BRUSH, Ruth. **Sarabande from** *Suite for string sextette or
md   orchestra* (facsimile of MS at NNAMC, 1952) 7 p. (score, parts).
Dn 5'. *Pf* 3 vln, vla, vcl, cbs. Also for string orchestra (*WIAM* 4389). *(Composer)*

3410 BRUSH, Ruth. **Valse joyeuse** (CP 408; New York: Composers
mm   Press, 1960) 5 p. (score).
Dn 5'. *Pf* pno, vln.   *(Composer)*

3411 CHANCE, Nancy Laird. **Ceremonial for percussion quartet**
mm   (New York: Seesaw Music, 1976) 24 p. $7. (score).
Dn 14'. *Da* 1 June 1976. *La* publisher.

3412 CHANCE, Nancy Laird. **Darksong** (New York: Seesaw Music,
mm   1972) 41 p. $16. (score, parts).
Dn 8'. *Da* 10 Nov. 1970. *La* publisher. *At* composer. *Pf* solo S, 2 flu, 2 cla, 2
hrn, per for 5 players, hrp, pno, gtr.   *(Composer)*

3413 CHANCE, Nancy Laird. **Daysongs for alto flute and per-
mm   cussion** (New York: Seesaw Music, 1974) 20 p. $6. (score, parts).
Dn 10'. *Da* 15 May 1974. *La* publisher. *Pf* alto flu, per for 2 players. *(Composer)*

3414 CHANCE, Nancy Laird. **Declamation and song** (New York:
mm   Seesaw Music, 1977) 38 p. (score, parts).
Dn 13'. *Da* 1 June 1977. *La* publisher. *Pf* vib, pno, vln, vcl.   *(Composer)*

3415 CHANCE, Nancy Laird. **Duos I for soprano voice and flute**
mm   (New York: Seesaw Music, 1966) 9 p. (score).
Dn 7'. *Da* 15 Dec. 1975. *La* publisher.   *(Composer)*

3416 CHANCE, Nancy Laird. **Edensong** (New York: Seesaw Music,
mm   1974) 21 p. $6. (score, parts).
Dn 9'. *Da* 8 Mar. 1973. *La* publisher. *At* Elizabeth Barrett Browning. *Pf* solo S,
flu, cla, vcl, per for 3 players, hrp.   *(Composer)*

3417 CHANCE, Nancy Laird. **Ritual sounds for brass and per-
mm   cussion** (New York: Seesaw Music, 1975) 11 p. $4. (score, parts).
Dn 7'. *Da* 10 Jan. 1975. *La* publisher. *Pf* hrn, 2 tpt, 2 tbn, per for 3 players.
(Composer)

3418 CHANCE, Nancy Laird. **Three Rilke songs** (New York:
mm   Seesaw Music, 1973) 16 p. $4. (score).

Dn 14'. *Da* 28 Sept. 1966. *La* publisher. *St* Sonnets to Orpheus. *Pf* solo S, flu,
enh, vcl.   *(Composer)*

3419 COATES, Gloria. **Fantasy on** *How lovely shines the morning
mm   star* **for viola and organ** (facsimile of MS at NNAMC, 1973) 12
p. (score).
Dn 13'. *Da* 1973. *La* composer. *Pf* org, vla with contact microphone. *Rg* tape at
Bayerischer Rundfunk, Munich; available through the Assoc. of German
Broadcasters, New York.   *(Composer)*

3420 COATES, Gloria. **Five abstractions from poems of Emily
mm   Dickinson for woodwind quartet** (facsimile of MS at NNAMC,
1975) 17 p. (score).
Dn 13'. *Da* 1975. *La* composer. *Pf* flu, obo, cla, bsn. *Ct* I shall keep singing,
Had I known that the first was the last, He fumbles at your soul, Under the
light, I felt a cleavage in my mind. *Rg* tape at Südwestfunk, Baden-Baden,
West Germany; available through the Assoc. of German Broadcasters, New
York.   *(Composer)*

3421 COATES, Gloria. **My country 'tis of thee** (facsimile of MS at
mm   NNAMC, 1976) 12 p. (score).
Dn 12'. *Da* 1976. *La* composer. *Pf* pno 4 hands, vla alternating with vln. *Rg*
tape at Bayerischer Rundfunk, Munich; available through the Assoc. of
German Broadcasters, New York.   *(Composer)*

3422 COATES, Gloria. **String quartet no. 2** (Munich, West Germany:
mm   composer, 1972) 12 p. (score).
Dn 11'. *Da* 1972. *La* composer. *Rg* tape at Radio Bremen, West Germany;
available through the Assoc. of German Broadcasters, New York.   *(Composer)*

3423 COATES, Gloria. **String quartet no. 3** (facsimile of MS at
mm   NNAMC, 1976) 16 p. (score).
Dn 13'. *Da* 1976. *La* Moldenhauer Archives, Spokane, Wash. *Rg* tape at Radio
Bremen, West Germany; available through the Assoc. of German Broadcasters,
New York.   *(Composer)*

3424 COATES, Gloria. **Trio for three flutes** (facsimile of MS at
mm   NNAMC, 1967) 12 p. (score).
Dn 8'. *Da* 1967. *La* composer. *Rg* tape at Westdeutscher Rundfunk, Cologne;
available through the Assoc. of German Broadcasters, New York.   *(Composer)*

3425 COATES, Gloria. **Voices of women in wartime** (facsimile of
mm   MS at NNAMC, 1973) 18 p. (score, parts).
Song cycle. *Dn* 16'. *Da* 1973. *La* composer. *Pf* solo S, tim, pno, 3 vcl. *Ct* Junge
Witwe (*At* Charlotte Hagedorn, *Lt* German); The flying bombers (*At* Angela
Paris, *Lt* English); Rinne, Regen, Rinne (*At* Elfriede Brindorfer, *Lt* German);
All the world is an orphan's home (*At* Lillian Tysdal, *Lt* German). *Rg* tape at
Bayerischer Rundfunk, Munich; available through the Assoc. of German
Broadcasters, New York.   *(Composer)*

3426 CODY, Judith. **Dances for guitar and flute, op. 8, nos. 1-2**
mm   (Los Altos, Calif.: Kikimora, 1977) 2 p. $4. (score).
Dn 2'. *Da* 1977. *La* composer.   *(Composer)*

3427 CODY, Judith. **Trio for poem, classical guitar, and flute** (Los
mm   Altos, Calif.: Kikimora, 1977) 16 p. $15. (score).
Dn 10'. *Da* Aug 1974. *La* composer. *At* composer. *Pf* flu, gtr, narrator.
(Composer)

3428 COOPER, Rose Marie. **Chamber suite** (Greensboro, N.C.:
mm   composer, 1959) 7 p. (score, parts).
Dn 7'. *Pf* flu, oboe d'amore, hrp.   *(Composer)*

3429 CORY, Eleanor. **Octagons** (facsimile of MS at NNACA, 1976)
mm   23 p. (score, parts).
Dn 9'. *La* NNACA. *Pf* 3 flu, vib, gtr, pno, 2 vla.   *(Composer)*

3430 CORY, Eleanor. **Trio for clarinet (bass clarinet), cello, and
mm   piano** (facsimile of MS at NNACA, 1973) 33 p. (score, parts).
Dn 10'. *La* NNACA.   *(Composer)*

3431 CORY, Eleanor. **Trio for flute (piccolo), oboe (English
mm   horn), and piano** (facsimile of MS at NNACA, 1977) 27 p. (score,
parts).
Dn 8'. *La* NNACA.   *(Composer)*

3432 CORY, Eleanor. **Waking for soprano and ten instruments**
mm   (facsimile of MS at NNACA, 1974) 93 p. (score, parts).

171

Dn 22′. *La* composer. *At* Muriel Rukeyser. *Pf* solo S, flu, hrn, tim, per including mba, pno, vln, vla, vcl, cbs.   *(Composer)*

3433 CRANE, Joelle Wallach. **Amen for solo instrument and solo**
mm   **voice** (New York: Composers Facsimile Ed., 1976) 1 p. (score).
Dn 1′. *Da* 1976. *La* NNACA. *Pf* solo S, oboe or flu or vln.   *(Composer)*

3434 CRANE, Joelle Wallach. **Cords** (New York: Composers Facsimm   mile Ed., 1973) 7 p. (score).
Dn 10′. *Da* 1973. *La* NNACA. *At* composer. *Pf* solo S, 2 cbs.   *(Composer)*

3435 CRANE, Joelle Wallach. **Movement for string quartet** (New
mm   York: Composers Facsimile Ed., 1968) 7 p. (score, parts).
Dn 8′. *Da* 1968. *La* NNACA.   *(Composer)*

3436 DAIGLE, Sr. Anne Cecile. **American folk tune suite** (Maryl-
mm   hurst, Oreg.: Marylhurst, 1976) 20 p. $3.50. (score, part).
Dn 11′. *Da* 1970. *La* publisher. *Pf* pno, vln. *Ct* Skip to my Lou; Black is the color; The lone, wild bird; Country reel.   *(Composer)*

3437 DAVIS, Sharon. **Fantasy for B-flat, alto, and bass clarinets,**
mm   **and piano** (AV 215; Los Angeles: Avant Music, 1977) 20 p. $10. (score, parts).
Dn 8′. *Da* 1976. *La* composer.   *(Composer)*

3438 DAVIS, Sharon. **Old King Cole variations** (AV 210; Los
mm   Angeles: Avant Music, 1977) 14 p. $8. (score, parts).
Dn 5′. *Da* 1974. *La* composer. *Pf* oboe, pno, vla.   *(Composer)*

3439 DAVIS, Sharon. **Prelude and dance** (AV 216; Los Angeles:
mm   Avant Music, 1977) 20 p. $6. (score, part).
Dn 10′. *Da* 1977. *La* composer. *Pf* hrn, pno.   *(Composer)*

3440 DAVIS, Sharon. **Suite of wildflowers** (AV 208; Los Angeles:
mm   Avant Music, 1977) 12 p. $15. (score, parts).
Dn 12′. *Da* 1973. *La* composer. *At* composer. *Pf* solo S, flu, oboe, pno, vln, vcl.   *(Composer)*

3441 DAVIS, Sharon. **Though men call us free** (AV 207; Los
mm   Angeles: Avant Music, 1976) 19 p. $10. (score, parts).
Dn 10′. *Da* 1975. *La* composer. *At* Oscar Wilde. *St* The young king. *Pf* solo S, cla, pno. *Rg Sharon Davis: pianist/composer*, WIM Records, WIMR 13.   *(Composer)*

3442 DAVIS, Sharon. **Three moods of Emily Dickinson** (AV 209;
mm   Los Angeles: Avant Music, 1977) 24 p. $13. (score, parts).
Dn 8′. *Da* 1976. *La* composer. *Pf* solo S, pno, vln, vcl.   *(Composer)*

3443 DAVIS, Sharon. **Three poems of William Blake for soprano**
mm   **and one clarinetist** (AV 217; Los Angeles: Avant Music, 1977) 17 p. $10. (score, parts).
Dn 9′. *Da* 1977. *La* composer. *Pf* solo S, cla or bcl or cbc.   *(Composer)*

3444 DENBOW, Stefania Björnson. **Surtsey string quintet** (New
mm   York: Seesaw Music, 1974) 38 p. $15. (score, parts).
Dn 11′. *Da* 1974. *La* composer.   *(Composer)*

3445 DENBOW, Stefania Björnson. **Trio Íslandia** (New York:
mm   Seesaw Music, 1976) 25 p. $16. (score, parts).
Dn 12′. *Da* 1975. *La* composer. *Pf* pno, vln, vcl.   *(Composer)*

3446 DIEMER, Emma Lou. **Four poems by Alice Meynell for**
mm   **soprano and chamber ensemble** (facsimile of MS on rental; New York: C. Fischer, 1976) 82 p. (score, parts).
Dn 13′. *Da* 1976. *La* publisher. *Pf* solo S, 2 flu, hrp, hps, pno, per, str. A piano-vocal score is available from the publisher.   *(Composer)*

3447 DIEMER, Emma Lou. **Movement for flute, oboe, and organ.**
mm   **September 8, 1974** (New York: C. Fischer, 1976) 18 p. (score, parts).
Dn 10′. *Da* 1974. *La* composer.   *(Composer)*

3448 DIEMER, Emma Lou. **Movement for flute, oboe, clarinet,**
mm   **and piano** (New York: Seesaw Music, 1976) 26 p. (score, parts).
Dn 10′. *Da* 1976. *La* publisher.   *(Composer)*

3449
mm   DIEMER, Emma Lou. **Music for woodwind quartet** (New York: Oxford U., 1976) 14 p. (score, parts).
Dn 10′. *Da* 1972. *La* composer.   *(Composer)*

3450 DIEMER, Emma Lou. **Pianoharpsichordorgan** (New York:
mm   Seesaw Music, 1976) 23 p. (score).
Dn 7′. *Da* 1974. *La* publisher. *Pf* pno, hps, org live or taped.   *(Composer)*

3451 DIEMER, Emma Lou. **Quartet for piano, violin, viola, and**
mm   **cello** (New York: Seesaw Music, 1976) 23 p. (score, parts).
Dn 12′. *Da* 1954. *La* publisher.   *(Composer)*

3452 DIEMER, Emma Lou. **Sextet for winds and piano** (New York:
mm   Seesaw Music, 1976) 73 p. (score, parts).
Dn 18′. *Da* 1963. *La* composer. *Pf* woodwind quintet, pno.   *(Composer)*

3453 DIEMER, Emma Lou. **Sonata for flute and piano or harp-**
mm   **sichord** (ST-43; San Antonio, Tex.: Southern Music, 1973) 24 p. $4. (score, part).
Dn 10′. *Da* 1958. *La* composer.   *(Composer)*

3454 DIEMER, Emma Lou. **Sonata for violin and piano** (New
mm   York: Seesaw Music, 1976) 20 p. (score, part).
Dn 12′. *Da* 1949. *La* composer.   *(Composer)*

3455 DIEMER, Emma Lou. **Toccata for flute chorus** (New York:
mm   C. Fischer, 1972) 20 p. $5. (score, parts).
Dn 8′. *Da* 1968. *La* composer. *Pf* pic, E-flat flu, C flu, alto flu, bass flu. *Rg Quartet music for flute with the Armstrong flute ensemble*, Golden Crest, CR 4088.   *(Composer)*

3456 DIEMER, Emma Lou. **Woodwind quintet no. 1** (New York:
mm   Boosey & Hawkes, 1962) 18 p. (score, parts).
Dn 9′. *Da* 1960. *La* composer.   *(Composer)*

3457 DRAKE, Elizabeth Bell. **Fantasy-sonata** (facsimile of MS at
mm   NNAMC, 1971) 15 p. (score, part).
Dn 11′. *Da* 1971. *La* composer. *Pf* pno, vcl.   *(Composer)*

3458 DRAKE, Elizabeth Bell. **First string quartet** (facsimile of MS
mm   at NNAMC, 1958) 41 p. (score, parts).
Dn 21′. *Da* 1958. *La* composer.   *(Composer)*

3459 DU PAGE, Florence. **Fantasy for violin and piano** (Atlanta:
mm   Porter, 1977) 8 p. (score, part).
Dn 7′.

3460 ESCOT, Pozzi. **Cristos** (facsimile of MS at PPFleisher, 1963) 15
mm   p. (score, parts).
Dn 15′. *Pf* alto flu, cbn, per, 3 vln.   *(Composer)*

3461 ESCOT, Pozzi. **Lamentus** (facsimile of MS at PPFleisher, 1962)
mm   28 p. (score, parts).
Dn 15′. *At* James Joyce. *St* Finnegan's wake, adapted. *Pf* per for 3 players, pno, 2 vln, 2 vcl.   *(Composer)*

3462 ESCOT, Pozzi. **Three movements for violin and piano** (Cam-
mm   bridge, Mass.: Publications Contact International, 1975) 9 p. $3. (score).
Dn 5′. *Da* 1960.   *(Composer)*

3463 ESCOT, Pozzi. **Three poems of Rilke** (Cambridge, Mass.:
mm   Publications Contact International, 1975) 15 p. $10. (score).
Dn 9′. *Da* 1959. *Lt* German. *Pf* string quartet, speaking part. *Ct* Du entfernst dich von mir, du Stunde; Welt war in dem Antlitz der Geliebten; Der Tod ist gross.   *(Composer)*

3464 ESCOT, Pozzi. **Visione** (facsimile of MS at PPFleisher, 1964) 22
mm   p. (score, parts).
Dn 10′. *At* Jean Arthur Rimbaud, Wassily Kandinsky, Gertrude Stein, and Günther Grass, adapted by composer. *Pf* solo S, pic, flu, alto flu, sax, per including vib, ghost speaker amplified.   *(Composer)*

3465 FINE, Vivian. **Concertino for piano and percussion** (Shafts-
mm   bury, Vt.: Catamount Facsimile Ed., 1972) 24 p. $6. (score, parts).
Dn 11′. *Da* 1965. *La* composer. *Pf* tim; per for 4 players including xyl, vib, mba; solo pno.   *(Composer)*

3466 FINE, Vivian. **Confession, The** (Shaftsbury, Vt.: Catamount
mm   Facsimile Ed., 1972) 25 p. $6. (score, parts).
Dn 11'. *Da* 1963. *La* composer. *At* Racine. *Pf* solo M, flu, pno, vln, vla, vcl.
(Composer)

3467 FINE, Vivian. **Divertimento for cello and percussion**
mm   (Shaftsbury, Vt.: Catamount Facsimile Ed., 1972) 11 p. $4. (score).
Dn 5'. *Da* 1951. *La* composer. *Pf* per for 1 player, vcl.   *(Composer)*

3468 FINE, Vivian. **Duo for flute and viola** (New York: C. Fischer,
mm   1976) 6 p. (score).
Dn 6'. *Da* 1961. *La* publisher.   *(Composer)*

3469 FINE, Vivian. **Fantasy for cello and piano** (Shaftsbury, Vt.:
mm   Catamount Facsimile Ed., 1972) 13 p. $4. (score, part).
Dn 7'. *Da* 1962. *La* composer.   *(Composer)*

3470 FINE, Vivian. **Four pieces for two flutes** (Shaftsbury, Vt.:
mm   Catamount Facsimile Ed., 1974) 12 p. $3.50. (score).
Dn 5'. *Da* 1930. *La* composer.   *(Composer)*

3471 FINE, Vivian. **Four songs,** *New Music* VI/4 (July 1933) 16-23.
mp   (score).
Dn 6'. *Da* 1933. *Pf* solo A, 2 vln, vla, vcl. *Ct* The lover in winter plaineth for
the spring, Comfort to a youth that had lost his love (*At* Robert Herrick), She
weeps over Rahoon (*At* James Joyce), Tilly (*At* James Joyce).   *(Composer)*

3472 FINE, Vivian. **Great Wall of China, The,** *New Music* XXI/3
mp   (Apr 1948) 3-26. (score).
Dn 14'. *Da* 1947. *At* Kafka. *Pf* solo A, flu, pno, vcl.   *(Composer)*

3473 FINE, Vivian. **Guide to the life expectancy of a rose, A**
mm   (Shaftsbury, Vt.: Catamount Facsimile Ed., 1972) 47 p. $8. (score,
        parts).
Dn 16'. *At* S.R. Tilley. *Pf* solo ST, flu, cla, pno, vln, vcl.   *(Composer)*

3474 FINE, Vivian. **Quintet for string trio, trumpet, and harp**
mm   (Shaftsbury, Vt.: Catamount Facsimile Ed., 1972) 32 p. $7. (score,
        parts).
Dn 15'. *Da* 1967. *La* composer.   *(Composer)*

3475 FINE, Vivian. **Sonata for violin and piano** (Shaftsbury, Vt.:
mm   Catamount Facsimile Ed., 1972) 30 p. $7. (score, part).
Dn 16'. *Da* 1952. *La* composer.   *(Composer)*

3476 FINE, Vivian. **String quartet** (Shaftsbury, Vt.: Catamount
mm   Facsimile Ed., 1972) 38 p. $8. (score, parts).
Dn 19'. *Da* 1957. *La* composer.   *(Composer)*

3477 FINE, Vivian. **Teisho for eight solo singers or small chorus
mm   and string quartet** (Shaftsbury, Vt.: Catamount Facsimile Ed.,
        1976) 124 p. $15. (score, parts).
Dn 30'. *Da* 1975. *La* composer. *Pf* solo SSAATTBB, string quartet. Also for
choral SATB, string quartet (*WIAM* 3933).   *(Composer)*

3478 FINE, Vivian. **Three Buddhist evocations for violin and
mm   piano** (Shaftsbury, Vt.: Catamount Facsimile Ed., 1977) 15 p. $4.
        (score).
Dn 11'. *Da* 1977. *La* composer.   *(Composer)*

3479 FINE, Vivian. **Trio for strings** (Shaftsbury, Vt.: Catamount
mm   Facsimile Ed., 1974) 18 p. $4.50. (score, parts).
Dn 10'. *Da* 1930. *La* composer.   *(Composer)*

3480 GARWOOD, Margaret. **Six Japanese songs for voice,
mm   clarinet, and piano** (E. Greenville, Penn.: composer, 1966) 12 p.
        (score, parts).
Song cycle. *Dn* 6'. *Ct* Loneliness, From "essences", Iris, Death song, Two white
butterflies, Snow.   *(Composer)*

3481 GIDEON, Miriam. **Adorable mouse, The** (Hastings-on-Hud-
mm   son, N.Y.: General Music, 1973) 15 p. (score).
Dn 12'. *At* La Fontaine, adapted. *Pf* solo M, flu, cla, bsn, hrn, tim, hps. Also for
narrator and chamber orchestra (*WIAM* 4415). *Rg* Serenus, SRS 12050.

3482 GIDEON, Miriam. **Air for violin and piano** (New York:
mm   American Composers Ed., 1957) 6 p. (score, part).

Dn 5'.

3483 GIDEON, Miriam. **Condemned playground, The** (Hillsdale,
mm   N.Y.: Mobart, 1976) 30 p. (score, parts).
Song cycle. *Dn* 14'. *La* DLC. *Pf* solo ST, flu, bsn, string quartet. *Ct* Pyrrha (*At*
Horace, *Tr* Milton, *Lt* English), Hiroshima (*At* Gary Spokes, *Tr* Satoka Akiya,
Lt Japanese), The litanies of Satan (*At* Baudelaire, *Tr* Edna St. Vincent Millay,
Lt English). *Rg* Composers Recordings, CRI SD 343.

3484 GIDEON, Miriam. **Divertimento for woodwind quartet** (New
mm   York: American Composers Ed., 1948) 14 p. (score, parts).
Dn 10'.

3485 GIDEON, Miriam. **Fantasy on a Javanese motive** (New York:
mm   American Composers Ed., 1948) 4 p. (score).
Dn 3'. *Pf* pno, vcl.

3486 GIDEON, Miriam. **Fantasy on Irish folk motives** (New York:
mm   American Composers Ed., 1975) 28 p. (score, parts).
Dn 13'. *Pf* oboe, vla, bsn or vcl, per including vib, glk.

3487 GIDEON, Miriam. **Hound of Heaven, The** (New York:
mm   Columbia U. Music, 1975) 9 p. (score, parts).
Dn 8'. *At* Francis Thompson. *Pf* solo M, oboe, vln, vla, vcl. *Rg* Composers
Recordings, CRI SD 286.

3488 GIDEON, Miriam. **Lyric piece for string quartet** (New York:
mm   American Composers Ed., 1955) 22 p. (score, parts).
Dn 9'.

3489 GIDEON, Miriam. **Nocturnes** (New York: American Composers
mm   Ed., 1976) 11 p. (score, parts).
Dn 8'. *Pf* solo S, flu, oboe, vib, vln, vcl. *Ct* Prelude, To the moon (*At* Shelley),
Hayride (*At* Jean Starr Untermeyer), Interlude, Witchery (*At* Frank Dempster
Sherman).

3490 GIDEON, Miriam. **Quartet for strings** (New York: American
mm   Composers Ed., 1946) 29 p. (score, parts).
Dn 12'.

3491 GIDEON, Miriam. **Questions on nature** (Hillsdale, N.Y.:
mm   Mobart, 1976) 32 p. (score, parts).
Dn 10'. *La* DLC. *At* Adelard of Bath (12th c.), adapted. *Pf* solo M, oboe, per
including glk, pno. *Rg* Composers Recordings, CRI SD 343.

3492 GIDEON, Miriam. **Rhymes from the hill** (Hillsdale, N.Y.:
mm   Mobart, 1976) 13 p. (score, parts).
Song cycle. *Dn* 8'. *At* Christian Morgenstern. *Tr* Max Knight. *St* Galgenlieder.
Lt German, English. *Pf* solo M, cla, mba, vcl. *Ct* Bundeslied der Galgenlieder
(Chorus of the gallows gang), Galgenkindes Wiegenlied (Gallows child's
lullaby), Die korfsche Uhr (Korf's clock), Palmström's Uhr (Palmstroem's
clock), Der Seufzer (The sigh). Also for solo M, pno (*WIAM* 4919). *Rg*
Composers Recordings, CRI SD 286.

3493 GIDEON, Miriam. **Seasons of time, The** (Hastings-on-Hudson,
mm   N.Y.: General Music, 1971) 22 p. (score).
Song cycle. *Dn* 10'. *St* Tanka poetry of ancient Japan, adapted. *Pf* solo M, flu,
pno alternating with cel, vcl. *Ct* Now it is spring (*At* Yakamochi, *Tr* Robert H.
Brower and Earl Miner), The wild geese returning (*At* Kunimoto, *Tr* Arthur
Waley), Can it be that there is no moon? (*At* Narihira, *Tr* Arthur Waley),
Gossip grows like weeds (*At* Hitomaro, *Tr* Kenneth Rexroth), Each season
more lovely (*At* Yakamochi, *Tr* J.L. Pierson), In the leafy tree-tops (*At*
Yakamochi, *Tr* Nippon Shinkokai), A passing show'r (*Tr* Nippon Shinkokai), I
have always known (*At* Narihira, *Tr* Kenneth Rexroth), To what shall I
compare this world? (*At* Mansei, *Tr* Arthur Waley), Yonder in the plum tree
(*Tr* Nippon Shinkokai). *Rg* Desto, 7117. Also for solo M, pno (*WIAM* 4920).

3494 GIDEON, Miriam. **Sonata for cello and piano** (New York:
mm   American Composers Ed., 1961) 26 p. (score, part).
Dn 13'.

3495 GIDEON, Miriam. **Sonata for viola and piano** (New York:
mm   American Composers Ed., 1948) 23 p. (score, part).
Dn 17'.

3496 GIDEON, Miriam. **Sonnets from Shakespeare** (New York:
mm   American Composers Ed., 1959) 20 p. (score, parts).
Dn 18'. *Pf* solo S or A, tpt, string quartet. String orchestra may be used instead
of string quartet. *Ct* Music to hear (VIII), Devouring time (XIX), Full many a

173

glorious morning (XXXIII), No longer mourn for me (LXXI), No, time, thou shall not boast (CXXIII).

3497 GIDEON, Miriam. **Suite for clarinet and piano** (New York:
mm   American Composers Ed., 1972) 16 p. (score, part).
Dn 7′.

3498 GIDEON, Miriam. **Three biblical masks for violin and piano**
mm   (New York: American Composers Ed., 1960) 14 p. (score, part).
Dn 10′. La DLC. Ct Haman, Esther, Mordecai. Also for org (WIAM 4638).

3499 GIDEON, Miriam. **Three sonnets from Fatal interview** (New
mm   York: American Composers Ed., 1952) 13 p. (score, parts).
Dn 10′. At Edna St. Vincent Millay. Pf solo M, vln, vla, vcl.

3500 GLANVILLE-HICKS, Peggy. **Concertino da camera** (OL
mm   170; Monaco: Editions de l'Oiseau-Lyre, 1950) 24 p. (score).
Dn 10′. Pf flu, cla, bsn, pno. Rg Columbia ML 4990.

3501 GLANVILLE-HICKS, Peggy. **Sonata for piano and percus-**
mm   **sion** (AMP 96033; New York: Associated Music, 1954) 24 p. (score,
      parts).
Dn 10′. Pf per including xyl, pno. Rg Columbia ML 4990.

3502 GLANVILLE-HICKS, Peggy. **Sonatina for treble recorder**
mm   **or flute and piano** (S 5112; London: B. Schott, 1941) 12 p. (score,
      part).
Dn 10′.

3503 GLANVILLE-HICKS, Peggy. **Three gymnopédies** (facsimile
mm   of MS at DLC, 1953) 6, 5, 6 p. (score).
Dn 15′. Pf obo, hrp, cel, str. No. 3 is published separately, but as no. 1 (WIAM
4422).

3504 GOULD, Elizabeth. **Music for trio** (facsimile of MS at
mm   NNAMC, 1977) 31 p. (score, parts).
Dn 14′. Da 1964. La composer. Pf pno, vln, vcl.   (Composer)

3505 GOULD, Elizabeth. **Personal and private** (facsimile of MS at
mm   NNAMC, 1977) 15 p. (score, parts).
Song cycle. Dn 13′. Da 1969. At Phyllis McGinley. St Times three. Pf solo S, 2
flu. Ct Apology for husbands, One crowded hour of glorious strife, Report on a
situation, Notes for a southern roadmap.   (Composer)

3506 GOULD, Elizabeth. **Sonata for cello and piano** (facsimile of
mm   MS at NNAMC, 1977) 35 p. (score, part).
Dn 18′. Da 1959. La composer. Awarded 1st prize in the Mu Phi Epsilon
composition competition, 1961.   (Composer)

3507 GOULD, Elizabeth. **Sonata for viola and piano** (facsimile of
mm   MS at NNAMC, 1977) 36 p. (score, part).
Dn 17′. Da 1963. La composer.   (Composer)

3508 GOULD, Elizabeth. **String quartet** (facsimile of MS at
mm   NNAMC, 1977) 53 p. (score, parts).
Dn 19′. Da 1960. La composer. Awarded 2nd prize in the 3rd international
competition for women composers (GEDOK), Mannheim, Germany, 1961.
        (Composer)

3509 GOULD, Elizabeth. **Triadic suite for flute and piano** (facsimm   mile of MS at NNAMC, 1977) 15 p. (score).
Dn 8′. Da 1974. La composer.   (Composer)

3510 GREENE, Margo. **Movement for string quartet** (facsimile of
mm   MS at NNAMC, 1969) 8 p. (score, parts).
Dn 5′. Da 1969. La composer.   (Composer)

3511 GREENE, Margo. **Quintet** (facsimile of MS at NNACA and
mm   NNAMC, 1977) 10 p. (score, parts).
Dn 8′. Da 4 Sept. 1977. La composer. Pf flu, obo, cla, vln, vcl.   (Composer)

3512 GREENE, Margo. **Suite from Coo-me-doo. They're only**
mm   **made of clay** (New York: Associated Music, 1977) 7 p. (score,
      parts).
Dn 10′. Da May 1977. La composer. Pf whistles, 3 rec, per, hps and/or pno,
gtr.   (Composer)

3513 HAYS, Doris. **Pieces from last year** (New York: Quinska
mm   Music, 1976) 10 p. $10. (score, parts).
Dn 8′. Da 1975. La composer. Pf alto flu, 3 alto rec, 2 ocarina, pno, 3 vln, 3 vla,
3 vcl.   (Composer)

3514 HAYS, Doris. **Scheveningen Beach** (New York: Seesaw Music,
mm   1973) 5 p. $3. (score).
Dn 5′. Da 1973. La publisher. Pf 5 flu.   (Composer)

3515 HOOVER, Katherine. **Divertimento** (facsimile of MS at
mm   NNAMC, 1976) 16 p. (score, parts).
Dn 13′. Da Dec. 1975. La composer. Pf flu, vln, vla, vcl.   (Composer)

3516 HOOVER, Katherine. **Homage to Bartók** (facsimile of MS at
mm   NNAMC, 1976) 20 p. (score, parts).
Dn 14′. Da 1974. La composer. Pf flu, obo, cla, bsn, hrn.   (Composer)

3517 HOOVER, Katherine. **Seven haiku** (facsimile of MS at
mm   NNAMC, 1976) 6 p. (score).
Dn 8′. Da 1973. La composer. At Gyodai, Basho, Shiki, Kyoshi. Pf solo S, flu.
        (Composer)

3518 HOOVER, Katherine. **Trio for flutes** (facsimile of MS at
mm   NNAMC, 1976) 12 p. (score, parts).
Dn 8′. Da 1974. La composer.   (Composer)

3519 HOOVER, Katherine. **Two dances for flute, oboe, and guitar**
mm   (facsimile of MS at NNAMC, 1977) 12 p. (score, parts).
Dn 7′. Da 1976. La composer.   (Composer)

3520 HSU, Wen-ying. **Capriccio** (West Babylon, N.Y.: H. Branch,
mm   1977) 6 p. (score).
Dn 3′. Da 1976. La composer. Pf flu, pno.   (Composer)

3521 HSU, Wen-ying. **Fantasia for two pianos** (Los Angeles: com-
mm   poser, 1955) 29 p. (score).
Dn 12′. Da 1955. La composer.   (Composer)

3522 HSU, Wen-ying. **Percussions East and West** (Los Angeles:
mm   composer, 1966) 9 p. (score, parts).
Dn 12′. Pf for 8 players: tim; per including glk, xyl, chimes, Chinese drums,
and gongs. Chinese instruments can be rented from the composer.   (Composer)

3523 HSU, Wen-ying. **Songs of nature** (Los Angeles: composer, 1974)
mm   18 p. (score, parts).
Song cycle. Dn 10′. At composer. Pf solo S; tim; per including glk, xyl; pno. Ct
Rain, Moon, Storm.   (Composer)

3524 HSU, Wen-ying. **Sonorities of Chinese percussions with tune**
mm   **of three variations of Plum blossoms** (Los Angeles: composer,
      1973) 4 p. (score, parts).
Dn 10′. Da 1973. La composer. Pf per for 8 players including xyl, glk, Chinese
drum. This piece was awarded first prize by the Manuscript Club of Los
Angeles in 1973.   (Composer)

3525 HSU, Wen-ying. **String quartet no. 2** (Los Angeles: composer,
mm   1968) 37 p. (score, parts).
Dn 15′.   (Composer)

3526 HSU, Wen-ying. **Theme and variations for woodwind trio**
mm   (Los Angeles: composer, 1964) 12 p. (score, parts).
Dn 15′. Pf flu, cla, bsn.   (Composer)

3527 HSU, Wen-ying. **Traveler's suite** (Los Angeles: composer, 1960)
mm   70 p. (score, parts).
Dn 24′. Pf piano quintet. Ct Morning in an inn, Rugged way, Under the
moonlight, Falling petals on a running stream.   (Composer)

3528 HSU, Wen-ying. **Trio for violin, cello, and piano** (Los Angeles:
mm   composer, 1955) 31 p. (score).
Dn 20′. Da 1955. La composer. This piece won first prize from the Manuscript
Club in 1969 and an award from the MacDowell Club, both of Los Angeles.
        (Composer)

3529 HSU, Wen-ying. **Violin pieces** (Los Angeles: composer, 1977) 28
mm   p. (score, parts).
Dn 20′. Da 1977. La composer. Pf vln, pno, optional flu.   (Composer)

3530 HSU, Wen-ying. **Violin suite** (Los Angeles: composer, 1966) 18
mm p. (score).
Dn 8′ . *Pf* pno, vln. (Composer)

3531 HSU, Wen-ying. **Vocal series no. II. Songs of Sung cycle**
mm (Los Angeles: composer, 1972) 42 p.
Song cycle. *Dn* 20′ . *Da* 1972. *La* composer. *Tr* composer. *St* Chinese poems,
10th-13th c. *Pf* solo S, flu, obo, cla, vcl, pno. *Ct* Waves on sand (*At* Li Yu),
Prelude to the water tune (*At* Su Shih), Ugly six (*At* Chou Pang-yen), Slow
sound (*At* Li Ching-chao), River of red (*At* Yo Fe). (Composer)

3532 HUGHES, Sr. Martina. **Jolie** (Duluth, Minn.: composer, 1945)
mm 14 p. (score, parts).
Dn 2′ . *Da* 1945. *La* composer. *Pf* flu, cla, pno. (Composer)

3533 HUGHES, Sr. Martina. **Occasional music** (Duluth, Minn.:
mm composer, 1947) 25 p. (score, parts).
Dn 7′ . *Da* 1947. *La* composer. *Pf* pno, vln, vla, vcl. (Composer)

3534 HYSON, Winifred. **Memories of New England** (facsimile of
mm MS at NN, 1975) 63 p. (score).
Dn 18′ . *La* composer. *At* Maxine Kumin. *St* Up country. *Pf* solo S, per, pno, vln.
(Composer)

3535 HYSON, Winifred. **Three love songs from the Bengali**
mm (facsimile of MS at NN, 1975) 22 p. (score).
Dn 9′ . *Da* 1975. *La* composer. *At* Rabindranath Tagore. *St* The gardener. *Pf*
solo A, flu, vcl. (Composer)

3536 HYSON, Winifred. **Three night pieces** (facsimile of MS at NN,
mm 1976) 22 p. (score).
Dn 9′ . *Da* 1976. *La* composer. *Pf* flu, cla, vcl. *Ct* When I go at night to my love-
tryst; I run as the musk-deer runs; Speak to me, my love. (Composer)

3537 HYSON, Winifred. **Winter triptych. A fantasy for soprano,
mm flute, violin, and piano** (facsimile of MS at NN, 1972) 44 p.
(score).
Dn 14′ . *Da* 1972. *La* composer. *At* Maxine Kumin, *St* Nightmare factory; *At*
Ruth Stone, *St* Typography and other poems; and *At* Jean Starr Untermeyer, *St*
Job's daughter. (Composer)

3538 IVEY, Jean Eichelberger. **Absent in the spring** (New York:
mm composer, 1977) 6 p. (score, parts).
Dn 5′ . *Da* 1977. *La* composer. *At* Shakespeare. *St* Sonnet XCVIII. *Pf* solo M,
vln, vla, vcl. (Composer)

3539 IVEY, Jean Eichelberger. **Androcles and the lion. A suite for
mm woodwind quintet** (facsimile of MS at NNAMC, 1963) 23 p.
(score).
Dn 10′ . *Ct* Overture, Waltz, March, Hymn, Trio, Caper.

3540 IVEY, Jean Eichelberger. **Carol of animals, A** (New York:
mm composer, 1976) 7 p. (score, parts).
Dn 5′ . *Da* 1976. *La* composer. *St* O magnum mysterium, A Christmas carol (*At*
Christina Georgina Rossetti). *Lt* Latin, English. *Pf* solo M, obo, pno.
(Composer)

3541 IVEY, Jean Eichelberger. **Dinsmoor suite** (facsimile of MS at
mm NNAMC, 1963) 24 p. (score).
Dn 10′ . *Pf* 2 cla, tbn, per including xyl. *Ct* Prairie artist, The garden of Eden,
Cain and Abel, Labor crucified, Modern civilization, Tomb with angel, Codetta.

3542 IVEY, Jean Eichelberger. **Music for viola and piano** (FE 87;
mm New York: C. Fischer, 1975) 12 p. (score).
Dn 10′ . *Da* 1974. *La* publisher. (Composer)

3543 IVEY, Jean Eichelberger. **Ode for violin and piano** (facsimile
mm of MS at NNAMC, 1965) 8 p. (score, parts).
Dn 5′ .

3544 IVEY, Jean Eichelberger. **Scherzo for wind septet** (facsimile of
mm MS at NNAMC, 1953) 7 p. (score).
Dn 3′ . *Pf* flu, obo, cla, bsn, hrn, tpt, tbn.

3545 IVEY, Jean Eichelberger. **Six inventions for two violins**
mm (facsimile of MS at NNAMC, 1959) 14 p. (score, parts).
Dn 10′ .

3546 IVEY, Jean Eichelberger. **Song of Pan for alto recorder or
mm flute and piano** (facsimile of MS at NNAMC, 1954) 6 p. (score,
parts).
Dn 5′ .

3547 IVEY, Jean Eichelberger. **String quartet** (facsimile of MS at
mm NNAMC, 1960) 53 p. (score).
Dn 20′ .

3548 IVEY, Jean Eichelberger. **Suite for cello and piano** (facsimile
mm of MS at NNAMC, 1960) 36 p. (score, part).
Dn 25′ . *Ct* Aria, Divisions on a ground, Bourreé, Barcarolle, Finale.

3549 IVEY, Jean Eichelberger. **Tonada. Duo for violin and cello**
mm (facsimile of MS at NNAMC, 1966) 5 p. (score, parts).
Dn 5′ .

3550 IVEY, Jean Eichelberger. **Two songs for high voice, flute, and
mm piano** (New York: composer, 1975) 9, 9 p. (score).
Dn 10′ . *Ct* Night voyage (*At* Matthew Arnold), Iliad (*At* Humbert Wolfe).
(Composer)

3551 KETTERING, Eunice Lea. **Fifteen carols arranged for two
mm instruments** (97-4898; St. Louis: Concordia, 1969) 13 p. (score).
Dn 10′ . *Da* 1967. *La* NmU. *Pf* any 2 treble instruments. (Composer)

3552 KETTERING, Eunice Lea. **Paddy O'Hara** (46729; New York:
mm G. Schirmer, 1970) 10 p. $1.50. (score).
Dn 2′ . *Da* 1960. *La* NmU. *Pf* 2 pno, 4 hands. (Composer)

3553 KETTERING, Eunice Lea. **Rigadoon** (46730; New York: G.
mm Schirmer, 1970) 10 p. $1.50. (score).
Dn 2′ . *Da* 1934. *La* NmU. *Pf* 2 pno, 4 hands. (Composer)

3554 KETTERING, Eunice Lea. **Three Spanish folk dances**
mm (47149; New York: G. Schirmer, 1972) 14 p. $1.25. (score).
Dn 5′ . *Da* 1971. *La* NmU. *Pf* pno, 4 hands. (Composer)

3555 KOLB, Barbara. **Chansons bas** (New York: C. Fischer, 1972) 22
mm p. $5. (score, parts).
Dn 15′ . *Da* 1966. *At* Mallarmé. *Pf* solo S; hrp; per for one player including glk,
vib, xyl. *Ct* Le cantonnier, Le marchand d'ail et
d'oignons, Le vitrier, Le crieur d'imprimés, La marchande d'habits. *Rg* Desto,
7143.

3556 KOLB, Barbara. **Figments for flute and piano** (New York: C.
mm Fischer, 1972) 14 p. $5. (score).
Dn 10′ . *Da* Nov. 1969. *Rg* Desto, 7143.

3557 KOLB, Barbara. **Homage to Keith and Gary** (New York:
mm Boosey & Hawkes, 1976) 10 p. (score).
Dn 7′ . *Da* 1976. *Pf* flu, vib.

3558 KOLB, Barbara. **Musique pour un vernissage** (New York:
mm Boosey & Hawkes, 1977) 18 p. (score).
Dn 10′ . *Pf* flu, vln, vla, gtr.

3559 KOLB, Barbara. **Percussion quartet. New York, Le Havre**
mm (facsimile of MS at NNAMC, 1968) 13 p.
Dn 10′ . *Pf* per including vib, xyl.

3560 KOLB, Barbara. **Rebuttal** (facsimile of MS at DLC, 1965) 7 p.
mm (score).
Dn 6′ . *Pf* 2 cla. *Rg* Opus One, 14.

3561 KOLB, Barbara. **Sentences, The** (New York: Boosey & Hawkes,
mm 1976) 6 p.
Dn 5′ . *At* Robert Pinsky. *Pf* solo S, gtr.

3562 KOLB, Barbara. **Three place settings for violin, clarinet,
mm double bass, percussion, and narrator** (04906; New York: C.
Fischer, 1972) 16 p. (score).
Dn 8′ . *Pf* cla; per including vib, xyl; vln; cbs; narrator. *Ct* I think I'll have (*At*
Irving Diamond), Roast peacock (*At* Cora, Rose, and Bob Brown), Automart
(*At* Ronald F. Costa). *Rg* Desto, 7143.

3563 KOLB, Barbara. **Trobar clus** (New York: Boosey & Hawkes,
mm   1973) 24 p. $4.
Dn 9′. *Pf* flu; alto flu; 2 tpt; 2 tbn; per including vib, mba; hps; gtr; vln; 2 vla;
vcl; cbs. *Rg* Turnabout, TV 34487. Commissioned by the Fromm Foundation
in cooperation with the Berkshire Music Center.

3564 LA BARBARA, Joan. **Chords and gongs** (facsimile of MS at
mm   NN, 1976) 1 p. $.30. (score, parts).
Dn 3′. *Pf* any voice type, per.   *(Composer)*

3565 LA BARBARA, Joan. **Ides of March no. 1** (facsimile of MS at
mm   NN, 1975) 3 p. (score, parts).
Dn 20′. *Pf* any 3 voice types, per, 2 vln, vla, vcl, cbs.   *(Composer)*

3566 LA BARBARA, Joan. **Ides of March no. 2** (facsimile of MS at
mm   NN, 1975) 3 p. (score, parts).
Dn 20′. *Pf* any voice type, soprano sax, per.   *(Composer)*

3567 LA BARBARA, Joan. **Ides of March no. 4** (facsimile of MS at
mm   NN, 1975) 3 p. (score, parts).
Dn 20′. *Pf* any voice type, tbn, tenor sax, per.   *(Composer)*

3568 LA BARBARA, Joan. **Ides of March no. 5** (facsimile of MS at
mm   NN, 1975) 3 p. (score, parts).
Dn 20′. *Pf* any voice type, enh, per.   *(Composer)*

3569 LA BARBARA, Joan. **Ides of March no. 5a** (facsimile of MS
mm   at NN, 1975) 3 p. (score, parts).
Dn 20′. *Pf* any voice type, enh, per including bowed vib.   *(Composer)*

3570 LOMON, Ruth. **Dialogue for harpsichord and vibraphone**
mm   (facsimile of MS at NNAMC, 1964) 12 p. (score).
Dn 8′. *Da* 1964. *La* composer.   *(Composer)*

3571 LOMON, Ruth. **Five songs after poems by William Blake**
mm   (facsimile of MS at NNAMC, 1962) 12 p. (score).
Dn 8′. *Da* 1962. *La* composer. *Pf* solo A, vla. *Ct* The sunflower, Little fly, The
sick rose, The clod and the pebble, Injunction.   *(Composer)*

3572 LOMON, Ruth. **Phase I for cello and piano** (facsimile of MS
mm   at NNAMC, 1969) 8 p. (score).
Dn 7′. *Da* 1969. *La* composer.   *(Composer)*

3573 LOMON, Ruth. **Phase II for soprano, cello, and piano**
mm   (facsimile of MS at NNAMC, 1975) 10 p. (score).
Dn 8′. *Da* 1975. *La* composer. *At* Whitman. *St* Leaves of grass.   *(Composer)*

3574 LOMON, Ruth. **Songs for a Requiem** (facsimile of MS at
mm   NNAMC, 1977) 28 p. (score, parts).
Sacred songs. *Dn* 15′. *Da* 1977. *La* composer. *At* composer. *Pf* solo S, flu, 2 cla,
bcl, bsn. Excerpts from the composer's *Requiem* (*WIAM* 4045).   *(Composer)*

3575 LOMON, Ruth. **Soundings** (Washington, D.C.: Arsis, 1977) 8 p.
mm
Dn 7′. *Da* 1975. *La* composer. *Pf* pno, 4 hands.   *(Composer)*

3576 LORENZ, Ellen Jane. **Bell jubilee** (Dallas: Choristers Guild,
mm   1969) 2 p. (score).
Dn 2′. *Pf* handbells (3 octaves).   *(Composer)*

3577 LORENZ, Ellen Jane. **Cathedral, The** (89; Dallas: Choristers
mm   Guild, 1970) 4 p. (score).
Dn 4′. *Pf* handbells (3 octaves).   *(Composer)*

3578 LORENZ, Ellen Jane. **Fanfare for nine** (Dallas: American
mm   Guild of English Handbell Ringers, 1977) 7 p. $.65. (score).
Dn 3′. *Pf* hrn, 3 tpt, 2 tbn, tba, per.   *(Composer)*

3579 LORENZ, Ellen Jane. **Nocturne** (AGEHR 4002; Dallas: Ameri-
mm   can Guild of English Handbell Ringers, 1970) 4 p. (score).
Dn 4′. *Pf* flu, handbells (4 octaves).   *(Composer)*

3580 LORENZ, Ellen Jane. **Phrygian suite** (AGEHR 3015; Dallas:
mm   American Guild of English Handbell Ringers, 1972) 8 p. $.40.
(score).
Dn 7′. *Da* 1971. *Pf* handbells (3 octaves).   *(Composer)*

3581 LORENZ, Ellen Jane. **String quartet** (facsimile of MS at Mu
mm   Phi Epsilon, Los Angeles, 1972) 35 p. (score, parts).
Dn 11′. *Da* 1972. *La* composer. Published under the composer's married name,
Porter.   *(Composer)*

3582 LORENZ, Ellen Jane. **Variations on a Welsh tune** (Dallas:
mm   Psaltery Music, 1977) 3 p. $.50. (score).
Dn 5′. *Pf* handbells (3 octaves).   *(Composer)*

3583 MAMLOK, Ursula. **Concert piece for four for flute, oboe,
mm   viola, percussion** (facsimile of MS at NNACA, 1964) 32 p. (score,
parts).
Dn 11′. *Rg* tape at NNACA.   *(Composer)*

3584 MAMLOK, Ursula. **Designs for violin and piano** (facsimile of
mm   MS at NNACA, 1962) 24 p. (score, part).
Dn 9′. *Rg* tape at NNACA.   *(Composer)*

3585 MAMLOK, Ursula. **Divertimento for flute, violoncello, and
mm   two percussionists** (facsimile of MS at NNACA, 1976) 22 p.
$7.70. (score, parts).
Dn 11′. *Pf* flu, vcl, per including glk, xyl.   *(Composer)*

3586 MAMLOK, Ursula. **Five capriccios for oboe and piano** (P
mm   66497; New York: C.F. Peters, 1975) 7 p. $8. (score, parts).
Dn 7′. *La* publisher. *Rg* tape at NNACA.   *(Composer)*

3587 MAMLOK, Ursula. **Haiku settings** (facsimile of MS at
mm   NNACA, 1967) 8 p. (score, parts).
Dn 7′. *At* Peter Beilenson and Harry Behn. *Pf* solo S, flu. *Rg* Grenadilla, GS
1015.   *(Composer)*

3588 MAMLOK, Ursula. **Sextet for flute, clarinet, bass clarinet,
mm   violin, double bass, piano** (facsimile of MS at NNACA, 1977) 43
p. (score, parts).
Dn 13′.   *(Composer)*

3589 MAMLOK, Ursula. **Stray birds. Five aphorisms for soprano,
mm   flute, and violoncello** (facsimile of MS at NNACA, 1963) 21 p.
(score, parts).
Dn 14′. *At* Rabindranath Tagore. Dedicated to the memory of John F.
Kennedy. *Rg* Composers Recordings, CRI 301.   *(Composer)*

3590 MAMLOK, Ursula. **String quartet** (facsimile of MS at NNACA,
mm   1962) 34 p. (score, parts).
Dn 9′. *Rg* tape at NNACA.   *(Composer)*

3591 MAMLOK, Ursula. **Variations and interludes for four per-
mm   cussionists** (P 66498; New York: C.F. Peters, 1977) 12 p. (score,
parts).
Dn 6′. *La* publisher. *Pf* per including glk, mba, vib, xyl. *Rg* tape at NNACA.
                                                        (Composer)

3592 MARCUS, Adabelle Gross. **Blue flute** (West Babylon, N.Y.: H.
mm   Branch, 1977) 5 p. $3. (score, part).
Dn 5′. *Pf* flu, pno.   *(Composer)*

3593 MARCUS, Adabelle Gross. **Sonata** (facsimile of MS at
mm   NNAMC, 1974) 36 p. (score, part).
Dn 20′. *Pf* pno, vln.   *(Composer)*

3594 MARCUS, Adabelle Gross. **Song for flute** (Chicago: Tempo
mm   Music, 1970) 8 p. (score, part).
Dn 12′. *Pf* flu, pno.   *(Composer)*

3595 MCLEAN, Priscilla. **Fire and ice** (Austin, Tex.: composer, 1978)
mm   33 p. (score).
Dn 17′. *Da* 1977. *La* composer. *Pf* tbn, pno duo.   *(Composer)*

3596 MCLEAN, Priscilla. **Interplanes for two pianos** (New York: A.
mm   Broude, 1978) 32 p. (score).
Dn 13′. *Da* 1970. *La* publisher. Also published in *American Society of
University Composers Journal of Music Scores* V (New York: J. Boonin, 1978).
Rg American Society of University Composers, Advance, FGR-195.   *(Composer)*

3597 MCNEIL, Jan Pfischner. **Aureate earth**, *American Society of*

mp   *University Composers Journal of Music Scores* I (1973) 31-38, $8. (score).
Dn 12′. *Da* 1972. *At* Omar Khayyám. *Tr* Edward Fitzgerald. *St Rubáiyát. Pf* solo T, tim, per including marimbaphone, pno, prepared pno.   *(Composer)*

3598   MCNEIL, Jan Pfischner. **Three preludes to the *Aureate earth***
mm   (New York: C. Fischer, 1975) 6 p. $3. (score, parts).
Dn 15′. *Da* 1974. *At* Omar Khayyám. *Tr* Edward Fitzgerald. *St Rubáiyát. Pf* solo S, any 6 instruments.   *(Composer)*

3599   MEACHEM, Margaret M. **Dragon fly** (facsimile of MS at
md   NNAMC, 1976) 2 p. (score).
Dn 3′. *Da* 1976. *La* composer. *At* Chisaku. *Pf* solo S, tpt, vln, *Tm Haiku kaleidoscope* (*WIAM* 3600).   *(Composer)*

3600   MEACHEM, Margaret M. **Haiku kaleidoscope** (facsimile of
mm   MS at NNAMC, 1977) 12, 7, 17 p. (score).
Dn 21′. *Da* 1977. *La* composer. *Ct Six gaping beaks* (*WIAM* 3602), *Dragon fly* (*WIAM* 3599), *In icy moonlight* (*WIAM* 3601).   *(Composer)*

3601   MEACHEM, Margaret M. **In icy moonlight** (facsimile of MS at
md   NNAMC, 1977) 17 p. $10. (score, parts).
Dn 20′. *Da* 1977. *La* composer. *At* Buson. *Pf* solo S; flu; per including vib, glk; pno. *Tm Haiku kaleidoscope* (*WIAM* 3600).   *(Composer)*

3602   MEACHEM, Margaret M. **Six gaping beaks** (facsimile of MS
md   at NNAMC, 1976) 12 p. (score).
Dn 3′. *Da* 1976. *La* composer. *At* Issa. *Pf* solo S, flu, cla, bsn, tpt, hrn, per. *Tm Haiku kaleidoscope* (*WIAM* 3600).

3603   MEACHEM, Margaret M. **Three French songs** (facsimile of
mm   MS at NNAMC, 1974) 13 p. $5. (score, parts).
Dn 15′. *Da* 1974. *La* composer. *Pf* solo S, pic, flu, pno. *Ct* Le papillon (*At* Alphonse de Lamartine), Le cigale et la formi (*At* La Fontaine), L'hippopotame (*At* Théophile Gautier).   *(Composer)*

3604   MEACHEM, Margaret M. **Trio for winds** (facsimile of MS at
mm   NNAMC, 1972) 15 p. $5. (score, parts).
Dn 15′. *Da* 1972. *Pf* flu, cla, bsn.   *(Composer)*

3605   MEACHEM, Margaret M. **Variations for two flutes** (facsimile
mm   of MS at NNAMC, 1972) 4 p. $2.50. (score, parts).
Dn 3′. *Da* 1972. *La* composer.   *(Composer)*

3606   MERRIMAN, Margarita L. **Sonata for cello and piano**
mm   (facsimile of MS at Atlantic Union Col., South Lancaster, Mass., 1977) 27 p. $7. (score, part).
Dn 15′. *Da* 1973. *La* composer.

3607   MOORE, Dorothy Rudd. **Dirge and deliverance** (New York:
mm   Composers Facsimile Ed., 1971) 23 p. $7.70. (score, part).
Dn 16′. *Da* 1971. *La* composer. *Pf* pno, vcl.   *(Composer)*

3608   MOORE, Dorothy Rudd. **From the dark tower** (New York:
mm   Composers Facsimile Ed., 1970) 44 p. $12.10. (score, parts).
Song cycle. *Dn* 34′. *Da* 1970. *La* composer. *Pf* solo M, pno, vcl. Arranged for solo M, orchestra (*WIAM* 4466). *Ct* O black and unknown bards (*At* James Weldon Johnson), Southern mansion (*At* Arna Bontemps), Willow bend and weep (*At* Herbert Clark Johnson), Old black men (*At* Georgia Douglass Johnson), No images (*At* Waring Cuney), Dream variation (*At* Langston Hughes), For a poet (*At* Countee Cullen), From the dark tower (*At* Countee Cullen).   *(Composer)*

3609   MOORE, Dorothy Rudd. **Modes for string quartet** (New
mm   York: Composers Facsimile Ed., 1968) 15 p. (score, parts).
Dn 12′. *Da* 1968. *La* composer.   *(Composer)*

3610   MOORE, Dorothy Rudd. **Sonnets on love, rosebuds, and**
mm   **death** (New York: Composers Facsimile Ed., 1976) 34 p. $9.90.
Song cycle. *Dn* 25′. *Da* 1976. *La* composer. *Pf* solo S, pno, vln. *Ct* I had no thought of violets of late (*At* Alice Dunbar Nelson), Joy (*At* Clarissa Scott Delaney), Some things are very dear to me (*At* Gwendolyn B. Bennett), He came in silver armour (*At* Gwendolyn B. Bennett), Song for a dark girl (*At* Langston Hughes), Idolatry (*At* Arna Bontemps), Youth sings a song of rosebuds (*At* Countee Cullen), Invocation (*At* Helene Johnson).   *(Composer)*

3611   MOORE, Dorothy Rudd. **Three pieces for violin and piano**
mm   (New York: Composers Facsimile Ed., 1967) 10 p. (score, part).
Dn 10′. *Da* 1967. *La* composer.

3612   MOORE, Dorothy Rudd. **Trio no. 1 for violin, cello, and**
mm   **piano** (New York: Composers Facsimile Ed., 1970) 36 p. $8.80. (score, parts).
Dn 15′. *Da* 1970. *La* composer.   *(Composer)*

3613   MOORE, Dorothy Rudd. **Weary blues** (New York: Composers
mm   Facsimile Ed., 1972) 9 p. $3.30.
Dn 5′. *Da* 1972. *La* composer. *Pf* solo B, pno, vcl.   *(Composer)*

3614   MUSGRAVE, Thea. **Cantata for a summer's day** (facsimile of
mm   MS on rental; New York: Belwin-Mills, 1954) 56 p. (score, parts).
Secular vocal chamber music. *Dn* 33′. *At* Alexander Hume and Maurice Lindsay. *Pf* solo SATB, flu, cla, string quartet, speaking part. Also for solo SATB, 1-0-1-0, 0-0-0-0, str, speaking part (*WIAM* 4467); for choral SATB, flu, cla, string quartet, speaking part (*WIAM* 4067), and for choral SATB, 1-0-1-0, 0-0-0-0, str, speaking part (*WIAM* 4067).

3615   MUSGRAVE, Thea. **Chamber concerto no. 1** (London: J. &
mm   W. Chester, 1977) 22 p. (score, parts).
Dn 11′. *Da* 1962. *Pf* oboe, cla, bsn, hrn, tpt, tbn, vln, vla, vcl.

3616   MUSGRAVE, Thea. **Chamber concerto no. 2** (JWC 438;
mm   London: J. & W. Chester, 1967) 59 p. (score).
Dn 15′. *Pf* pic, flu, cla, bcl, pno, vln, vla, vcl. *Rg* Delos, 25405.

3617   MUSGRAVE, Thea. **Chamber concerto no. 3** (JWC 444;
mm   London: J. & W. Chester, 1968) 82 p. (score).
Dn 25′. *Pf* cla, bsn, hrn, 2 vln, vla, vcl, cbs.

3618   MUSGRAVE, Thea. **Colloquy for violin and piano** (JWC 428;
mm   London: J. & W. Chester, 1961) 16 p. (score).
Dn 11′. *Rg* Argo, ZRG 5328.

3619   MUSGRAVE, Thea. **Elegy for viola and cello** (London: J. &
mm   W. Chester, 1971) 19 p. (score).
Dn 8′. *Da* 1970.

3620   MUSGRAVE, Thea. **Excursions** (JWC 2647; London: J. & W.
mm   Chester, 1966) 19 p. (score).
Dn 8′. *Pf* pno 4 hands. *Rg* Argo, ZRG 704.

3621   MUSGRAVE, Thea. **Impromptu for flute and oboe** (JWC
mm   442; London: J. & W. Chester, 1968) 7 p. (score).
Dn 4′.

3622   MUSGRAVE, Thea. **Impromptu no. 2** (JWC 8902; London: J.
mm   & W. Chester, 1974) 14 p. (score).
Dn 9′. *Pf* flu, oboe, cla.

3623   MUSGRAVE, Thea. **Music for horn and piano** (JWC 448;
mm   London: J. & W. Chester, 1967) 27 p. (score, part).
Dn 10′.

3624   MUSGRAVE, Thea. **Primavera** (London: J. & W. Chester,
mm   1976) 8 p. (score, parts).
Dn 4′. *Da* 1971. *Pf* solo S, flu. *Rg* Caprice, RIKS LP 59.

3625   MUSGRAVE, Thea. **Serenade for flute, clarinet, harp, viola,**
mm   **and cello** (JWC 283; London: J. & W. Chester, 1962) 40 p. (score).
Dn 13′.

3626   MUSGRAVE, Thea. **Space play. A concerto for nine in-**
mm   **struments** (New York: Novello, 1975) 58 p.
Dn 20′. *Pf* flu, oboe, cla, bsn, hrn, vln, vla, vcl, cbs.

3627   MUSGRAVE, Thea. **String quartet** (JWC 277; London: J. &
mm   W. Chester, 1959) 26 p. (score).
Dn 16′.

3628   MUSGRAVE, Thea. **Trio for flute, oboe, and piano** (JWC
mm   287; London: J. & W. Chester, 1964) 19 p. (score, parts).
Dn 10′. *Rg* Delta, SDel 18005

3629   NOBLE, Ann. **And I saw her standing in the water, with**
mm   **shining ...** (facsimile of MS at Mills Col., Oakland, Calif., 1977) 6 p. (score).
Dn 12′. *La* composer. *Pf* flügelhorn, cbs, pno.   *(Composer)*

3630 NOBLE, Ann. **Dreaming of being taken out and allowed to**
mm   **shine** (facsimile of MS at NNAMC, 1977) 6 p. (score).
Dn 45'. *La* composer. *Pf* flu, obo, cla, bsn, hrn, sax.   *(Composer)*

3631 NOBLE, Ann. **Paler shade of soft, A** (facsimile of MS at
mm   NNAMC, 1976) 5 p. $3.50. (score, parts).
Dn 10'. *La* composer. *Pf* flu; cla; sax; per including vib, cel.   *(Composer)*

3632 NOBLE, Ann. **Percussion trio no. 1** (facsimile of MS at Mills
mm   Col., Oakland, Calif., 1975) 10 p. $5. (score, parts).
Dn 7'. *La* composer. *Pf* tim, per.   *(Composer)*

3633 NOBLE, Ann. **Percussion trio no. 2** (facsimile of MS at
mm   NNAMC, 1975) 21 p. $5.50. (score, parts).
Dn 10'. *La* composer. *Pf* tim, per including mba.   *(Composer)*

3634 NOBLE, Ann. **Piano tinkled like someone breaking glass in a**
mm   **tin box** (facsimile of MS at NNAMC, 1977) 4 p. (score).
Dn 3'. *La* composer. *Pf* cla, hps.

3635 NOBLE, Ann. **Saved in prisms of honey ...**, *Soundings*. Ed. by
mc   Peter GARLAND (Washington, D.C.: P. Garland, 1976) X, 64-73,
$5. (score, parts).
Dn 10'. *Da* June 1976. *At* John Woods. *Pf* solo S, cla, pno.   *(Composer)*

3636 NOWAK, Alison. **Equinox** (facsimile of MS at NNACA, 1977)
mm   23 p. $4. (score, parts).
Dn 10'. *Da* 1977. *Pf* cla, bsn, hrn, vln, vla, cbs.   *(Composer)*

3637 NOWAK, Alison. **Four pieces for three clarinets** (facsimile of
mm   MS at NNACA, 1970) 9 p. $1.75. (score, parts).
Dn 7'. *Da* 1970. *Pf* cla, bcl, cbc.   *(Composer)*

3638 NOWAK, Alison. **Musica composita I for piano and cham-**
mm   **ber players** (facsimile of MS at NNACA, 1974) 21 p. $4. (score,
parts).
Dn 10'. *Pf* flu, cla, bsn, tpt, per, pno, vln, vcl.   *(Composer)*

3639 NOWAK, Alison. **Quartet for flute, violin, clarinet, cello**
mm   (facsimile of MS at NNACA, 1974) 14 p. $3. (score, parts).
Dn 8'. *Da* 1974.   *(Composer)*

3640 NOWAK, Alison. **Quintet for flute, violin, bassoon, guitar,**
mm   **piano** (facsimile of MS at NNACA, 1973) 12 p. $2.50. (score).
Dn 7'. *Da* 1973.   *(Composer)*

3641 NOWAK, Alison. **String trio** (facsimile of MS at NNACA,
mm   1970) 14 p. $2.50. (score, parts).
Dn 10'. *Da* 1970.   *(Composer)*

3642 NOWAK, Alison. **Trio for woodwinds** (facsimile of MS at
mm   NNACA, 1973) 7 p. $1.50. (score, parts).
Dn 7'. *Da* 1973. *Pf* flu, cla, bsn.   *(Composer)*

3643 NOWAK, Alison. **Variations for violin and piano** (facsimile of
mm   MS at NNACA, 1975) 12 p. $2.50. (score).
Dn 9'. *Da* 1975.   *(Composer)*

3644 OLIVEROS, Pauline. **Sonic meditations I-XXV** (Baltimore:
mm   Smith, 1974) 8 p. $7. (score, parts).
Dn variable. *Pf* number and choice of instruments optional. Also listed as
WIAM 4483, 4693.   *(Publisher)*

3645 OLIVEROS, Pauline. **To Valerie Solanas and Marilyn**
mm   **Monroe in recognition of their desperation** (Baltimore: Smith,
1977) 4 p. $4. (score, parts).
Dn 30'. *Pf* may be performed by chamber group, orchestra, or chorus.
Instrumentation not specified. Also listed as *WIAM* 4077, 4484.   *(Publisher)*

3646 OLIVEROS, Pauline. **Trio for accordion, trumpet, and string**
mm   **bass** (Baltimore: Smith, 1977) 12 p. (score, parts).
Dn 10'. *Da* 1961. *La* publisher.   *(Publisher)*

3647 OLIVEROS, Pauline. **Trio for flute, piano, and page turner**
mm   (Baltimore: Smith, 1977) 16 p. $12. (score, parts).
Dn 10'. *Rg* New music for woodwinds, Advance Recordings, FGR-95. *(Publisher)*

3648 OLIVEROS, Pauline. **Variations for sextet** (Baltimore: Smith,
mm   1977) 30 p. (score, parts).
Dn 13'. *Da* 1965. *La* publisher. *Pf* flu (pic), cla, hrn, tpt, pno, vcl.   *(Publisher)*

3649 OLIVEROS, Pauline. **Willowbrook generations and reflec-**
mm   **tions** (Baltimore: Smith, 1977) 4 p. $5.50. (score, parts).
Dn 15-60'. *Pf* any group or groups of 15 or more; audience participation. Also
listed as *WIAM* 4078, 4485.   *(Publisher)*

3650 OWEN, Blythe. **Fanfare and processional, op. 44, no. 1**
md   (Berrien Springs, Mich.: Hall-Orion Music, 1974) 11 p. $7. (score,
parts).
Dn 6'. *Da* 1969. *La* publisher. *Pf* brass quartet, org.   *(Composer)*

3651 OWEN, Blythe. **Sarabande and gigue for tuba quartet, op.**
md   **43, no. 1** (Berrien Springs, Mich.: Hall-Orion Music, 1973) 4 p. $6.
(score, parts).
Dn 4'. *Da* 1969. *La* publisher.   *(Composer)*

3652 OWEN, Blythe. **Trio for oboe, clarinet, and bassoon, op. 18,**
md   **no. 1** (Berrien Springs, Mich.: Hall-Orion Music, 1972) 19 p. $6.75.
(score, parts).
Dn 15'. *Da* 1959. *La* publisher.   *(Composer)*

3653 OWEN, Blythe. **Two-part inventions for woodwinds, op. 35,**
md   **no. 1** (Berrien Springs, Mich.: Hall-Orion Music, 1972) 4 p. $4.
(score, parts).
Dn 3'. *Da* 1964. *La* publisher. *Pf* any two high woodwinds.   *(Composer)*

3654 PARKER, Alice. **Songs for Eve** (facsimile of MS on rental;
mm   Chapel Hill, N.C.: Hinshaw Music, 1976) 138 p. (score, parts).
Dn 70'. *Da* 1976. *La* composer. *At* Archibald MacLeish. *Pf* solo SATB, string
quartet. *Ct* 28 songs. A piano-vocal score is available on rental from the
publisher.   *(Composer)*

3655 PAULL, Barberi. **O wind** (facsimile of MS on rental; New York:
mm   A. Broude, 1975) 36 p. $15.
Dn 12'. *Da* 1975. *La* composer. *At* composer. *Pf* solo M or Bar, string quartet.
(Composer)

3656 PAULL, Barberi. **Two songs for trumpet with piano and**
mm   **electric piano** (facsimile of MS on rental; New York: A. Broude,
1972) 12 p. (score, parts).
Dn 6'. *La* composer.   *(Composer)*

3657 PERRY, Julia Amanda. **Beacon, The** (facsimile of MS at
mm   NNAMC, 1963) 14 p.
Dn 6'. *Pf* 2 enh, 2 sax, 2 bsn, 2 tpt.

3658 PERRY, Julia Amanda. **Homunculus C.F.** (1002; New York:
mm   Southern Music, 1966) 20 p. (score, parts).
Dn 5'. *Pf* tim; per including cel, vib, xyl; hrp. *Rg* Composers Recordings, CRI
SD 252.

3659 PERRY, Julia Amanda. **Pastoral for flute septet** (591; New
mm   York: Southern Music, 1962) 9 p. (score, parts).
Dn 3'. *Da* 1959. *Pf* flu, 2 vln, 2 vla, 2 vcl.

3660 PERRY, Julia Amanda. **Stabat Mater** (213; New York: South-
mm   ern Music, 1954) 32 p. (score, parts).
Dn 20'. *Da* 1951. *At* Jacopone da Todi. *Tr* composer. *Pf* solo A, string quartet.
Also for solo A, string orchestra (*WIAM* 4486). *Rg* Composers Recordings, CRI
SD 133.

3661 PIERCE, Alexandra. **Arabesque** (New York: Seesaw Music,
mm   1977) 10 p. (score, parts).
Dn 7'. *Da* Feb. 1977. *La* composer. *Pf* cla, pno.   *(Composer)*

3662 PIERCE, Alexandra. **Danse Micawber** (New York: Seesaw
mm   Music, 1976) 7 p. $4. (score).
Dn 4'. *Da* fall 1974. *La* composer. *Pf* pno, 4 hands.   *(Composer)*

3663 PIERCE, Alexandra. **My Lady Hunsdon's pavane** (New York:
mm   Seesaw Music, 1976) 3 p. $2. (score).
Dn 5'. *Da* Apr. 1975. *La* composer. *Pf* 2 cla.   *(Composer)*

3664 PIERCE, Alexandra. **Norwich chorale** (New York: Seesaw
mm   Music, 1976) 5 p. (score).
Dn 8′. *Da* Jan. 1976. *La* composer. *Pf* cla, pno.   *(Composer)*

3665 PIERCE, Alexandra. **Sargasso** (New York: Seesaw Music, 1977)
mm   10 p. (score).
Dn 8′. *Da* Mar. 1977. *La* composer. *Pf* cla, pno.   *(Composer)*

3666 PIERCE, Alexandra. **Sweeney among the nightingales** (New
mm   York: Seesaw Music, 1976) 10 p. $5. (score).
Dn 5′. *Da* fall 1974. *La* composer. *Pf* pno, 4 hands.   *(Composer)*

3667 POLIN, Claire. **Cader Idris for brass quintet** (New York: G.
mm   Schirmer, 1971) 10 p. (score, parts).
Dn 12′.

3668 POLIN, Claire. **Consecutivo** (facsimile of MS at NN, 1966) 14
mm   p. (score).
Dn 7′. *Pf* flu, alto flu, cla, bcl, pno, vln, vcl.

3669 POLIN, Claire. **Death of Procris, The. For flute and tuba**
mm   (New York: Seesaw Music, 1973) 10 p. (score, parts).
Dn 8′.

3670 POLIN, Claire. **First flute sonata** (San Antonio: Southern
mm   Music, 1954) 20 p.
Dn 4′. *Pf* flu, pno.

3671 POLIN, Claire. **Journey of Owain Madoc, The** (New York:
mm   Seesaw Music, 1974) 33 p. (score, parts).
Dn 15′. *Pf* hrn, 2 tpt, tbn, tba, per including mba, pno.

3672 POLIN, Claire. **Klockwrk** (Islington, Mass.: Dorn, 1977) 14 p.
mm   (score).
Dn 10′. *Pf* bsn, sax, hrn.

3673 POLIN, Claire. **Makimono I** (New York: Seesaw Music, 1972)
mm   16 p. (score, parts).
Dn 8′. *Pf* flu, cla, pno, vln, vcl. Also published under the title Makimono II, for
hrn, 2 tpt, tbn, tba (Seesaw, 1972).

3674 POLIN, Claire. **No-rai. Songs from the Korean** (facsimile of
mm   MS at NNAMC, 1963) 14 p. (score).
Song cycle. *Dn* 15′. *At* Kim So-wol. *Pf* solo S, flu, cbs. *Ct* Azaleas, Setting sun,
Swallow, Cricket, Untitled.

3675 POLIN, Claire. **Sonata for flute and harp** (New York: Seesaw
mm   Music, 1975) 13 p. (score, parts).
Dn 10′.

3676 POLIN, Claire. **Third string quartet** (facsimile of MS at
mm   NNAMC, 1960) 18 p. (score).
Dn 20′.

3677 POLIN, Claire. **Tower sonata for three winds** (New York:
mm   Seesaw Music, 1975) 14 p. (score, parts).
Dn 15′. *Pf* flu, cla, bsn.

3678 PREOBRAJENSKA, Vera N. **Chamber trio for flute, violin,
mm   and cello** (facsimile of autograph at NNAMC, 1976) 9 p. (score,
        parts).
Dn 3′. *Da* 1976. *La* composer.   *(Composer)*

3679 PREOBRAJENSKA, Vera N. **Classical menuetto for string
mm   quartet** (facsimile of autograph at NNAMC, 1946) 7 p. (score).
Dn 3′. *Da* 1946.   *(Composer)*

3680 PREOBRAJENSKA, Vera N. **Fingerflow. Javanese dance**
mm   (facsimile of autograph at NNAMC, 1960) 19 p. (score).
Dn 10′. *Da* 1960. *At* Lillian V. Inke. *Pf* solo S, flu, tim, per,
mandolin.   *(Composer)*

3681 PREOBRAJENSKA, Vera N. **Mazurka, op. 2, no. 1 for
md   string octet** (facsimile of autograph at NNAMC, 1947) 21 p.
        (score).
Dn 3′. *Da* 1947. *La* composer. *Pf* flu, 2 cla, hrn, string quartet.   *(Composer)*

3682 PREOBRAJENSKA, Vera N. **Petit sonatine for string
mm   quartet, Le** (facsimile of autograph at NNAMC, 1962) 13 p.
        (score).
Dn 5′. *Da* 1972. *La* composer.   *(Composer)*

3683 PREOBRAJENSKA, Vera N. **Preludium for string quintet**
mm   (facsimile of autograph at NNAMC, 1972) 10 p. (score).
Dn 8′. *La* composer. *Pf* flu, cla, pno, vln, vcl.   *(Composer)*

3684 PREOBRAJENSKA, Vera N. **Quintet for solo clarinet with
mm   chamber accompaniment** (facsimile of autograph at NNAMC,
        1976) 20 p. (score, parts).
Dn 4′. *Da* 1976. *La* composer. *Pf* cla, string quartet.   *(Composer)*

3685 PREOBRAJENSKA, Vera N. **Undertones of frost** (facsimile
mm   of autograph at NNAMC, 1960) 49 p. (score).
Dn 20′. *Da* 1960. *La* composer. *At* Lillian V. Inke. *St* Time is a dream. *Pf* solo
S, flu, obo, bsn, tba, vln, vcl, cbs. Originally for solo S, pno (*WIAM* 4950).
                                                               (Composer)

3686 RAN, Shulamit. **Double vision for two quintets and piano**
mm   (facsimile of MS on rental; New York: T. Presser, 1977) 44 p. (score,
        parts).
Dn 22′. *Da* 1976. *La* composer. *Pf* flu (pic), obo, 2 cla (E-flat cla and bcl), bsn,
hrn, 2 tpt, tbn, btn, pno.   *(Composer)*

3687 RAN, Shulamit. **Ensembles for seventeen** (facsimile of MS on
mm   rental; New York: T. Presser, 1975) 49 p. (score, parts).
Dn 18′. *Da* 1975. *La* composer. *At* Shakespeare. *St* Othello. *Pf* solo S amplified,
pic, 2 flu, alto flu, 2 cla (E-flat cla), bcl and sarrousaphone, bsn, hrn, tpt, tbn,
btn, per for 2 players, pno, string quartet.   *(Composer)*

3688 RAN, Shulamit. **Hatzvi Israel eulogy** (facsimile of MS on
mm   rental; New York: C. Fischer, 1972) 17 p. (score, parts).
Dn 7′. *Da* 1969. *La* composer. *Pf* solo S, flu, hrp, string quartet. *Rg* Vocal
chamber music ... Dal Segno ensemble, Critics Choice, CC 1703.   *(Composer)*

3689 RAN, Shulamit. **Ten children's scenes for piano, four hands**
mm   (04807; New York: C. Fischer, 1970) 24 p. $3. (score).
Dn 8′. *Da* 1966. *La* composer. Also for orchestra as Ten children's scenes, 2-2-
2-2, 2-2-1-0, tim, per including cel, str (facsimile of MS on rental; Fischer, n.d.).
                                                               (Composer)

3690 RICHTER, Marga. **Aria and toccata for viola and piano**
mm   (New York: Belwin-Mills, 1958) 19 p. (score).
Dn 9′. *Da* Feb. 1957. *La* composer. Also for string orchestra, solo vla (*WIAM*
4498).   *(Composer)*

3691 RICHTER, Marga. **Landscapes of the mind II** (facsimile of
mm   MS on rental; New York: C. Fischer, 1975) 18 p. (score, part).
Dn 13′. *Da* 1971. *La* composer. *Pf* pno, vln.   *(Composer)*

3692 RICHTER, Marga. **Melodrama** (facsimile of MS on rental; New
mm   York: C. Fischer, 1975) 49 p. (score).
Dn 16′. *Da* 1956. *La* composer. *Pf* 2 pno, 4 hands.   *(Composer)*

3693 RICHTER, Marga. **One for two and two for three** (facsimile
mm   of MS on rental; New York: C. Fischer, 1975) 6 p. (score).
Dn 5′. *Da* 1947, rev. 1974. *La* composer. *Pf* 3 tbn.   *(Composer)*

3694 RICHTER, Marga. **Pastorale for oboe duet** (facsimile of MS
mm   on rental; New York: C. Fischer, 1975) 2 p. (score).
Dn 2′. *Da* 1975. *La* composer.   *(Composer)*

3695 RICHTER, Marga. **Sonata for clarinet and piano** (facsimile of
mm   MS on rental; New York: C. Fischer, 1975) 30 p. (score, part).
Dn 11′. *Da* 1948. *La* composer.   *(Composer)*

3696 RICHTER, Marga. **String quartet no. 2** (facsimile of MS on
mm   rental; New York: C. Fischer, 1975) 20 p. (score, parts).
Dn 16′. *Da* 1958. *La* composer.   *(Composer)*

3697 RICHTER, Marga. **Suite for violin and piano** (facsimile of MS
mm   on rental; New York: C. Fischer, 1975) 9 p. (score, part).
Dn 6′. *Da* 1963. *La* composer.   *(Composer)*

3698 RICHTER, Marga. **Variations on a theme by Latimer** (fac-
mm   simile of MS on rental; New York: C. Fischer, 1975) 16 p. (score).

Dn 9′ . *Da* 1964. *La* composer. *Pf* pno, 4 hands.   *(Composer)*

3699 RICHTER, Marion Morrey. **Sonata for trio** (facsimile of MS
mm   at NN, 1960) 56 p. (score, parts).
Dn 19′ . *Da* 1960. *La* composer. *Pf* pno, vln, vcl.   *(Composer)*

3700 ROSSER, Annetta Hamilton. **Bagatelle** (Madison, Wis.: Gil-
mm   bert, 1977) 5 p. (score, part).
Dn 2′ . *Da* 1976. *Pf* flu, pno.   *(Composer)*

3701 ROSSER, Annetta Hamilton. **Bird song** (Madison, Wis.: Gil-
mm   bert, 1977) 3 p. (score, part).
Dn 2′ . *Da* 1968. *Pf* flu, pno.   *(Composer)*

3702 ROSSER, Annetta Hamilton. **Dialogue for flute and violin**
mm   (Madison, Wis.: Gilbert, 1977) 3 p. (score).
Dn 2′ . *Da* 1976.   *(Composer)*

3703 ROSSER, Annetta Hamilton. **Flute in the night** (Madison,
mm   Wis.: Gilbert, 1977) 5 p. (score, part).
Dn 5′ . *Da* 1976. *Pf* flu, pno.   *(Composer)*

3704 ROSSER, Annetta Hamilton. **Lullaby for an April baby**
mm   (Madison, Wis.: Gilbert, 1977) 4 p. (score, part).
Dn 4′ . *Da* 1948. *Pf* pno, vln.   *(Composer)*

3705 ROSSER, Annetta Hamilton. **Meditation** (Madison, Wis.:
mm   Gilbert, 1977) 7 p. (score, part).
Dn 5′ . *Da* 1970. *Pf* pno, vln.   *(Composer)*

3706 SANDIFUR, Ann. **Shared improvisations** (Berkeley, Calif.:
mm   Arsciene, 1977) 23 p. (score).
Dn 40′ . *Da* 1976. *La* publisher. *Pf* 2 pno, 4 hands.   *(Composer)*

3707 SEMEGEN, Daria. **Jeux des quatres** (New York: Composers
mm   Facsimile Ed., 1971) 16 p. $6. (score, parts).
Dn 12′ . *Da* 1970. *La* composer. *Pf* cla, tbn, pno, vcl.   *(Composer)*

3708 SEMEGEN, Daria. **Lieder auf der Flucht** (New York: Com-
mm   posers Facsimile Ed., 1969) 28 p. $8.50. (score, parts).
Dn 12′ . *Da* 1967. *La* composer. *At* Ingeborg Bachmann. *Pf* solo S, flu, cla, hrn,
per, pno, vln, vcl.   *(Composer)*

3709 SEMEGEN, Daria. **Quattro** (New York: Composers Facsimile
mm   Ed., 1969) 5 p. $3. (score).
Dn 5′ . *Da* 1967. *La* composer. *Pf* flu, pno.   *(Composer)*

3710 SEMEGEN, Daria. **Three pieces** (New York: Composers Fac-
mm   simile Ed., 1971) 7 p. $3. (score).
Dn 5′ . *Da* 1968. *La* composer. *Pf* cla, pno.   *(Composer)*

3711 SILSBEE, Ann. **Bourn** (facsimile of MS at NNAMC, 1974) 20 p.
mm $5.50. (score).
Dn 10′ . *Da* Apr. 1974. *Pf* solo A or Ct, hps, vcl.   *(Composer)*

3712 SILSBEE, Ann. **Canticle, A** (facsimile of MS at NNAMC, 1974)
mm   15 p. $5. (score).
Dn 9′ . *Da* Dec. 1974. *La* composer. *Pf* solo S, obo, hps.   *(Composer)*

3713 SILSBEE, Ann. **Huit chants en brun** (facsimile of MS at
mm   NNAMC, 1975) 28 p. $7.50. (score, parts).
Dn 22′ . *Da* Apr. 1975. *La* composer. *At* Federico Garcia Lorca. *Tr* André
Belamich. *Pf* solo S or A or Ct, obo, vla.   *(Composer)*

3714 SILSBEE, Ann. **Icarus** (facsimile of MS at NNAMC, 1977) 15 p.
mm $4. (score).
Dn 6′ . *Da* Mar. 1977. *La* composer. *At* William Carlos Williams. *St* Landscape
with the fall of Icarus. Pf solo SSAATTBB, 3 rec, bongo drums.   *(Composer)*

3715 SILSBEE, Ann. **Only the cold bare moon** (facsimile of MS at
mm   NNAMC, 1970) 51 p. $6.50. (score).
Dn 22′ . *Da* June 1970. *La* composer. *At* Li Po, Li Yung, Tu Fu, Meng Lai, Jan,
Su Tong Po, Wang Wei, Li Po, Tu Fu. *St Jade flute. Lt* English. *Pf* solo S, flu,
pno.   *(Composer)*

3716 SILSBEE, Ann. **Phantasy** (facsimile of MS at NNAMC, 1973) 16
mm   p. $5. (score).

Dn 9′ . *Da* Dec. 1973. *La* composer. *Pf* obo, hps.   *(Composer)*

3717 SILSBEE, Ann. **Quest** (facsimile of MS at NNAMC, 1977) 16 p.
mm $6. (score, parts).
Dn 15′ . *Da* Jan. 1977. *La* composer. *Pf* string quartet.   *(Composer)*

3718 SILSBEE, Ann. **Raft** (facsimile of MS at NNAMC, 1976) 14 p.
mm $5. (score, parts).
Dn 8′ . *Da* 31 Dec. 1976. *La* composer. *At* A.R. Ammons. *Pf* per for 5 players,
narrator amplified.   *(Composer)*

3719 SILSBEE, Ann. **Scroll** (facsimile of MS at NNAMC, 1977) 16 p.
mm $6. (score, parts).
Songs. *Dn* 11′ . *Da* 1977. *La* composer. *Lt* English. *Pf* solo S, flu, tpt, tim, per,
pno, vln, cbs. *Ct* This road (*At* Basho, *Tr* Harold Henderson), The sea
darkening (*At* Basho, *Tr* Peter Beilenson), Lightning (*At* Basho, *Tr* Harold
Henderson), A storm wind moans (*At* Chora, *Tr* Harold Henderson), In these
dark waters (*At* Ringai, *Tr* Peter Beilenson).   *(Composer)*

3720 SILSBEE, Ann. **Spirals** (facsimile of MS at NNAMC, 1975) 27 p.
mm $6.50. (score, parts).
Dn 19′ . *Da* Oct. 1975. *La* composer. *Pf* pno, string quartet.   *(Composer)*

3721 SILSBEE, Ann. **Trialogue** (facsimile of MS at NNAMC, 1976)
mm   13 p. $5. (score).
Dn 9′ . *Da* Feb. 1976. *La* composer. *Pf* cla, pno, vln.   *(Composer)*

3722 SILVERMAN, Faye-Ellen. **Conversations** (New York: Seesaw
mm   Music, 1975) 6 p. (score).
Dn 6′ . *Da* 1975. *La* publisher. *Pf* alto flu, cla.   *(Composer)*

3723 SILVERMAN, Faye-Ellen. **Dialogue** (New York: Seesaw
mm   Music, 1976) 6 p. (score).
Dn 5′ . *Da* 1976. *La* publisher. *Pf* hrn, tba.   *(Composer)*

3724 SILVERMAN, Faye-Ellen. **For him** (New York: Seesaw Music,
mm   1975) 17 p. (score, parts).
Dn 10′ . *Da* 1975. *La* publisher. *Pf* flu, vib, vcl.   *(Composer)*

3725 SILVERMAN, Faye-Ellen. **In shadow. Three songs and two**
mm   **interludes** (New York: Seesaw Music, 1973) 9 p. (score).
Dn 7′ . *Da* 1972. *La* publisher. *At* Emily Dickinson. *Pf* solo S, cla, gtr. *(Composer)*

3726 SILVERMAN, Faye-Ellen. **String quartet** (New York: Seesaw
mm   Music, 1976) 13 p. (score, parts).
Dn 9′ . *Da* 1976. *La* publisher.   *(Composer)*

3727 SILVERMAN, Faye-Ellen. **Windscape** (New York: Seesaw
mm   Music, 1977) 8 p. (score, parts).
Dn 6′ . *Pf* woodwind quintet.   *(Composer)*

3728 SINGER, Jeanne. **American short subjects for two pianos**
mm   (facsimile of autograph at NNAMC, 1964) 6 p. (score).
Dn 4′ . *La* composer. *Pf* 2 pno.   *(Composer)*

3729 SINGER, Jeanne. **From the Green Mountains** (West Babylon,
mm   N.Y.: H. Branch, 1977) 13 p. $6. (score, parts).
Dn 8′ . *Da* 1974. *La* composer. *Pf* cla, pno, vln. *Ct* Winter identity, Yankee
springtime.   *(Composer)*

3730 SINGER, Jeanne. **Nocturne for clarinet and piano** (facsimile
mm   of autograph at NNAMC, 1972) 8 p. (score, part).
Dn 6′ . *La* composer.   *(Composer)*

3731 SINGER, Jeanne. **Sonnet** (facsimile of autograph at NNAMC,
mm   1972) 5 p. (score, parts).
Dn 4′ . *La* composer. *At* Patricia Benton. *St* Of the heart's own telling. *Pf* solo S
or M, cla, vln.   *(Composer)*

3732 SINGER, Jeanne. **Sweet Stacy suite** (West Babylon, N.Y.: H.
mm   Branch, 1977) 7 p. $5. (score, parts).
Dn 6′ . *Da* 1969. *La* composer. *Pf* cla, pno, vln. *Ct* Sephardic dance, Echoes
from Spain, American tune.   *(Composer)*

3733 SINGER, Jeanne. **To stir a dream** (facsimile of autograph at
mm   NNAMC, 1971) 8 p. (score, parts).
Dn 4′ . *La* composer. *At* Patricia Benton. *Pf* solo S, cla, pno.   *(Composer)*

3734 SINGER, Jeanne. **Trio rhapsody** (facsimile of MS at NNAMC,
mm   n.d.) 6 p. (score, parts).
Dn 4′ . *Da* 1969. *La* composer. *Pf* cla, pno, vln.   *(Composer)*

3735 SMITH, Julia. **American dance suite for two pianos, four
hands** (MM 109; New York: Mowbray Music, 1968) 21 p. (score).
Dn 10′ . *Da* fall 1966. *Ct* One morning in May, Lost my partner, Negro lullaby,
Chicken reel. Originally for small orchestra (*WIAM* 4515).   *(Composer)*

3736 SMITH, Julia. **Quartet for strings** (MM 110; New York:
mm   Mowbray Music, 1968) 27 p. (score, parts).
Dn 15′ . *Da* 1964. *La* composer. *Rg* Four American composers, Desto, D 7117.

3737 SMITH, Julia. **Trio--Cornwall for violin, cello, and piano**
mm   (MM 103; New York: Mowbray Music, 1966) 39 p. (score, parts).
Dn 15′ . *Da* 28 Oct. 1955.

3738 SMITH, Julia. **Two pieces for viola and piano** (MM 102; New
mm   York: Mowbray Music, 1966) 15 p. (score, part).
Dn 8′ . *Da* 1944. *Ct* Nocturne, Festival piece.   *(Composer)*

3739 SPENCER, Williametta. **Adagio and rondo for oboe and
piano** (AV 145; Los Angeles: Western International Music, 1968) 15
p. (score, part).
Dn 10′ . *Da* 1960. *La* composer.   *(Composer)*

3740 STILMAN, Julia. **Cello quartet** (New York: Composers Facsimm   mile Ed., 1977) 17 p. (score, parts).
Dn 6′ . *Da* 1959. *La* composer. *Pf* cla, tpt, xyl, vcl.   *(Composer)*

3741 STILMAN, Julia. **Cuadrados y angulos [Squares and angles]**
mm   (New York: Composers Facsimile Ed., 1977) 15 p. $4.27. (score,
parts).
Dn 4′ . *Da* 1960. *La* composer. *At* Alfonsina Storni. *Lt* Spanish. *Pf* solo A, sax,
tpt, tim, pno. *Rg* Composers of Argentina III, International Recording Club.
                                        (Composer)

3742 STILMAN, Julia. **Etudes for woodwind quintet** (New York:
mm   Composers Facsimile Ed., 1977) 35 p. $6.47. (score, parts).
Dn 10′ . *Da* 1968, rev. 1977. *La* composer.   *(Composer)*

3743 SUCHY, Gregoria Karides. **Argument** (facsimile of MS at
mm   NNAMC, 1960) 5 p. (score, parts).
Dn 4′ . *La* composer. *Pf* 2 pno, 4 hands. Also for orchestra (*WIAM* 4527).
                                        (Composer)

3744 SUCHY, Gregoria Karides. **Ass in the lion's skin, The**
mm   (facsimile of MS at NNAMC, 1974) 49 p. (score, parts).
Dn 5′ . *La* composer. *St* Aesop's fable, adapted. *Pf* solo S; cla; bcl; hrn; tbn; per
including mba, xyl; pno; vln.   *(Composer)*

3745 SUCHY, Gregoria Karides. **Entries** (facsimile of MS at
mm   NNAMC, 1970) 16 p. (score, parts).
Dn 5′ . *La* composer. *At* Charles Wright. *Pf* solo B, tim, per, pno, narrator.
                                        (Composer)

3746 SUCHY, Gregoria Karides. **String quartet no. 1** (facsimile of
mm   MS at NNAMC, 1963) 42 p. (score, parts).
Dn 14′ . *La* composer. Awarded first prize for chamber music in the composers
contest sponsored by the Wisconsin Federation of Music Clubs, 1966. *(Composer)*

3747 SUCHY, Gregoria Karides. **Three lovers** (facsimile of MS at
mm   NNAMC, 1960) 14 p. (score, parts).
Dn 12′ . *La* composer. *Pf* 2 pno, 4 hands. *Ct* Mountain rascal, Wretched loser,
Happy suitor. Also for orchestra (*WIAM* 4530). Awarded first prize in the
composition contest sponsored by the Musicians Club of Women, Chicago,
1960.   *(Composer)*

3748 SUCHY, Gregoria Karides. **Triophony** (facsimile of MS at
mm   NNAMC, 1964) 16 p. (score, parts).
Dn 5′ . *La* composer. *Pf* flu, cla or vla, vcl or bsn.   *(Composer)*

3749 SWISHER, Gloria Wilson. **Sonata for clarinet and piano**
mm   (facsimile of MS at NNAMC, 1977) 18 p. (score, part).
Dn 9′ . *Da* 1959. *La* composer.   *(Composer)*

3750 SWISHER, Gloria Wilson. **Theater trio** (facsimile of MS at
mm   NNAMC, 1977) 13 p. (score, parts).
Dn 9′ . *Da* 1960. *La* composer. *Pf* tpt, sax, pno. *Ct* Fanfare, Thornton Wilder,
Eugene O'Neill, William Saroyan. Published under the composer's maiden
name, Gloria Wilson.   *(Composer)*

3751 TALMA, Louise. **All the days of my life. Cantata for tenor,
clarinet, violoncello, percussion, piano, and celesta** (facsimile
of MS at NN, 1965) 45 p. (score).
Sacred cantata. *Dn* 21′ .

3752 TALMA, Louise. **Birthday song** (New York: composer, 1960) 4
mm   p. (score).
Dn 2′ . *At* Edmund Spenser. *St* Amoretti IV. *Pf* solo T, flu, vla. *(Composer)*

3753 TALMA, Louise. **Four-handed fun** (30162; New York: C.
mm   Fischer, 1949) 15 p. (score, parts).
Dn 4′ . *Pf* 2 pno, 4 hands.

3754 TALMA, Louise. **Sonata for violin and piano** (New York:
mm   composer, 1962) 17 p. (score, part).
Dn 16′ .   *(Composer)*

3755 TALMA, Louise. **Song and dance** (New York: composer, 1951)
mm   5 p. (score, part).
Dn 4′ . *Pf* pno, vln.   *(Composer)*

3756 TALMA, Louise. **String quartet** (facsimile of MS at NN, 1954)
mm   33 p. (score).
Dn 16′ .

3757 TALMA, Louise. **Summer sounds** (FE 88; New York: C.
mm   Fischer, 1976) 17 p. $4.50. (score, parts).
Dn 12′ . *Pf* cla, string quartet.

3758 TALMA, Louise. **Three duologues** (38441; New York: Edition
mm   Musicus, 1969) 16 p. (score, part).
Dn 11′ . *Pf* cla, pno. *Rg* Composers Recordings, CRI SD 374.

3759 TANNER, Hilda. **Modal suite for two flutes** (facsimile of MS
mm   at NIC, 1977) 8 p. $1.50. (score).
Dn 5′ . *Da* Aug. 1977. *La* composer. *Ct* Mimicking modals, Lydian lilt, Flowing
Phrygians.   *(Composer)*

3760 TANNER, Hilda. **Singing bird, The** (facsimile of MS at NIC,
mm   1977) 6 p. $3.75. (score, parts).
Dn 4′ . *Da* 1969. *La* composer. *At* composer. *Pf* solo SM, flu, cla. *(Composer)*

3761 THEMMEN, Ivana Marburger. **Mystic trumpeter, The** (fac-
mm   simile of MS at NNAMC, 1975) 101 p. (score, parts).
Dn 22′ . *At* Whitman. *St* Leaves of grass. *Pf* solo S or M, 2 tpt, pno, string
quintet. Also for solo S or M and orchestra (*WIAM* 4539). A piano-vocal score
is available (facsimile of MS at NNAMC).   *(Composer)*

3762 THEMMEN, Ivana Marburger. **Ten cantos for two horns**
mm   (Massapequa, N.Y.: Cor, 1972) 11 p. (score).
Dn 10′ . *Da* 1972.   *(Composer)*

3763 TOWER, Joan. **Black topaz for piano and six instruments**
mm   (facsimile of MS at NNACA, 1976) 60 p. (score, parts).
Dn 13′ . *Da* 1976. *At* composer. *Pf* flu; pic; cla; tpt; tbn; per including mba,
vib; pno.   *(Composer)*

3764 TOWER, Joan. **Breakfast rhythms I & II for clarinet and
five instruments** (New York: Composers Facsimile Ed., 1974) 47 p.
$34. (score, parts).
Dn 15′ . *Da* 1974-75. *Pf* flu; cla; per including mba, vib; vcl; pno. *Rg*
Composers Recordings, CRI 354.   *(Composer)*

3765 TOWER, Joan. **Brimset** (facsimile of MS at NNACA, 1965) 23 p.
mm   (score).
Dn 10′ . *Pf* 2 flu; per including mba, vib.

3766 TOWER, Joan. **Movements for flute and piano**, *American
mp   Society of University Composers Journal of Music Scores* I (1973)
5-30. (score).
Dn 10′ . *Da* 1970. *La* NNACA.

3767 TOWER, Joan. **Opa eboni** (facsimile of MS at NNACA, 1967)
mm   27 p. (score).
Dn 8′ . *Pf* obo, pno.

3768 TOWER, Joan. **Prelude for five players** (facsimile of MS at
mm   NNACA, 1970) 19 p. (score).
Dn 6′ . *Pf* flu, obo or vln, cla, bsn or vcl, pno. *Rg* Composers Recordings, CRI
302.

3769 VAN DE VATE, Nancy. **Diversion for brass** (Wrightsville,
mm   Penn.: Manuscript, 1973) 6 p. $1.90. (score, parts).
Dn 4′ . *Da* 1964. *La* composer. *Pf* hrn, 2 tpt, tbn.   *(Composer)*

3770 VAN DE VATE, Nancy. **Incidental piece for three saxes**
mm   (facsimile of MS at NNAMC, 1976) 7 p. (score, parts).
Dn 5′ . *Da* 1976. *La* composer. *Pf* 3 alto sax.   *(Composer)*

3771 VAN DE VATE, Nancy. **Letter to a friend's loneliness**
mm   (facsimile of MS at NNAMC, 1977) 24 p. (score, parts).
Dn 11′ . *Da* June 1976. *La* composer. *At* John Unterecker. *Pf* solo S, string
quartet.   *(Composer)*

3772 VAN DE VATE, Nancy. **Music for student string quartet**
mm   (facsimile of MS at NNAMC, 1977) 13 p. (score, parts).
Dn 6′ . *Da* 1977. *La* composer.   *(Composer)*

3773 VAN DE VATE, Nancy. **Music for viola, percussion, and
mm   piano** (facsimile of MS at NNAMC, 1977) 28 p. (score, parts).
Dn 18′ . *Da* Oct. 1976. *La* composer.   *(Composer)*

3774 VAN DE VATE, Nancy. **Quintet (1975)** (facsimile of MS at
mm   NNAMC, 1977) 31 p. (score, parts).
Dn 11′ . *Da* 1975. *La* composer. *Pf* flu, cla, pno, vln, vcl.   *(Composer)*

3775 VAN DE VATE, Nancy. **Quintet for brass** (Wrightsville,
mm   Penn.: Manuscript, 1976) 26 p. $4. (score, parts).
Dn 10′ . *Da* 1974. *La* composer. *Pf* hrn, 2 tpt, tbn, tba.   *(Composer)*

3776 VAN DE VATE, Nancy. **Short suite for brass quartet** (T
mm   117; Bryn Mawr, Penn.: Tenuto, 1972) 12 p. $4. (score, parts).
Dn 6′ . *Da* 1963. *La* composer. *Pf* 2 tpt, 2 tbn.   *(Composer)*

3777 VAN DE VATE, Nancy. **Sonata for viola and piano** (Bryn
mm   Mawr, Penn.: Tenuto, 1966) 19 p. (score, part).
Dn 13′ . *Da* 1964. *La* composer.   *(Composer)*

3778 VAN DE VATE, Nancy. **String quartet no. 1** (facsimile of MS
mm   at NNAMC, 1977) 20 p. (score, parts).
Dn 13′ . *Da* 1964, 1969. *La* composer.   *(Composer)*

3779 VAN DE VATE, Nancy. **Three sound pieces for brass and
mm   percussion** (Wrightsville, Penn.: Manuscript, 1976) 54 p. $6. (score,
parts).
Dn 10′ . *Da* 1973. *La* composer. *Pf* 2 hrn, 2 tpt, 2 tbn, tba, per for 6 players.
    (Composer)

3780 VAN DE VATE, Nancy. **Trio for strings (1974)** (facsimile of
mm   MS at NNAMC, 1977) 29 p. (score, parts).
Dn 15′ . *Da* 1974. *La* composer. *Pf* string trio.   *(Composer)*

3781 VAN DE VATE, Nancy. **Woodwind quartet** (SS 694; San
mm   Antonio: Southern Music, 1966) 10 p. (score, parts).
Dn 8′ . *Da* 1964. *La* composer.   *(Composer)*

3782 VAZQUEZ, Alida. **Music for seven instruments** (New York:
mm   Seesaw Music, 1974) 12 p. $4. (score, parts).
Dn 4′ . *Da* 1974. *La* composer. *Pf* flu, obo, cla, bsn, hrn, tpt, vla.   *(Composer)*

3783 VAZQUEZ, Alida. **Piece for clarinet and piano** (New York:
mm   Seesaw Music, 1974) 5 p. $6. (score, part).
Dn 6′ . *Da* 1971. *La* composer.   *(Composer)*

3784 VAZQUEZ, Alida. **String quartet no. 2** (facsimile of MS at
mm   NNAMC, 1975) 21 p. (score, parts).
Dn 11′ . *Da* 1975. *La* composer.   *(Composer)*

3785 WALDO, Elisabeth. **Gran quivira, El** (Northridge, Calif.:
mm   Mundoamericas Music, 1977) 37 p. $6. (score, parts).
Dn 12′ . *Da* 1977. *La* composer. *Pf* gtr, 2 vln, vla, vcl, cbs.   *(Composer)*

3786 WALKER, Gwyneth. **Rhapsody for clarinet and piano** (New
mm   Canaan, Conn.: Walker, 1976) 23 p. $5. (score, part).
Dn 14′ . *Da* 1974. *La* composer.   *(Composer)*

3787 WARREN, Elinor Remick. **Sonnets for soprano and string
mm   quartet** (New York: C. Fischer, 1965) 17 p. (score, parts).
Dn 12′ . *Da* rev. 1970. *La* composer. *At* Edna St. Vincent Millay. *St Fatal
interview.* Also for solo S and string orchestra (*WIAM* 4556) and published in a
piano-vocal score (Fischer, 1965).   *(Composer)*

3788 WEIGL, Vally. **Dear earth** (New York: Composers Facsimile Ed.,
mm   1956) 24 p. (score, parts).
Dn 14′ . *At* Frederika Blankner. *Pf* solo M, hrn, pno, vln, vcl. *Ct* Evolution,
Redemption, Post factum, Dear earth. *Rg* NNAMC.   *(Composer)*

3789 WEIGL, Vally. **Five songs from** *Take my hand* (New York:
mm   Composers Facsimile Ed., 1975) 10 p. $4.40. (score).
Song cycle. *Dn* 12′ . *At* Edith Segal. *Pf* solo M, flu, cla, pno, bcl or vcl. *Ct* Other
summer, Challenge, I saw two birds, Soon, Other hearts. *Rg* NNAMC.
    (Composer)

3790 WEIGL, Vally. **Lyrical suite from** *All my youth* (New York:
mm   Composers Facsimile Ed., 1956) 23 p. (score, parts).
Song cycle. *Dn* 14′ . *At* Frederika Blankner. *Pf* solo M, flu or cla, pno, vcl. *Ct*
Tide foam, Tryst, Open book, Winter, O love this tree, April woods, Query.
    (Composer)

3791 WEIGL, Vally. **Mood sketches for woodwind quintet** (New
mm   York: Composers Facsimile Ed., 1954) 23 p. (score, parts).
Dn 15′ .   *(Composer)*

3792 WEIGL, Vally. **Nature moods** (New York: Composers Facsimile
mm   Ed., 1956) 13 p. (score, parts).
Dn 12′ . *La* NNACA. *At* Harry Woodbourne. *St The green kingdom.* *Pf* solo S
or T, flu or cla, vln. *Ct* Whippoorwill, Winter reverie, Afterthoughts, Insect
orchestra, Gardener's prayer. *Rg Music of nature and the gods,* Composers
Recordings, CRI SD 326.   *(Composer)*

3793 WEIGL, Vally. **New England suite** (West Babylon, N.Y.: H.
mm   Branch, 1977) 30 p. (score, parts).
Dn 17′ . *Pf* flu or cla, pno, vln, vcl. *Ct* Vermont nocturne, Maine interlude,
Berkshire pastorale, Connecticut country fair. *Rg Music of nature and the gods,*
Composers Recordings, CRI SD 326.   *(Composer)*

3794 WEIGL, Vally. **Songs from** *Do not awake me* (New York:
mm   Composers Facsimile Ed., 1957) 21 p. (score, parts).
Dn 17′ . *At* Marion Edey. *Pf* solo A, pno, vln or hrn. *Ct* Evening out on the rim,
When we wake again, On the top of the hill, Ah angel!, The quiet house, I feel
the autumn grieve me, The wings of the morning.   *(Composer)*

3795 WEIGL, Vally. **Songs of remembrance** (New York: Composers
mm   Facsimile Ed., 1952) 17 p. (score, parts).
Dn 11′ . *At* Emily Dickinson. *Pf* solo M, flu, pno, optional cla or vln. Also for
solo M, string quartet (Composers Facsimile Ed., 1953).   *(Composer)*

3796 WYLIE, Ruth Shaw. **Five occurrences for woodwind quintet,
mm   op. 27** (West Babylon, N.Y.: H. Branch, 1977) 34 p. $3.50. (score).
Dn 8′ . *Da* 1971. *La* composer.   *(Composer)*

3797 WYLIE, Ruth Shaw. **Imagi** (West Babylon, N.Y.: H. Branch,
mm   1977) 6 p. (parts).
Dn variable. *Da* 1974. *La* composer. *Pf* flu, obo, cla, pno, vln, vcl or any
combination of 3 to 6 of these instruments.   *(Composer)*

3798 WYLIE, Ruth Shaw. **Incubus** (West Babylon, N.Y.: H. Branch,
mm   1977) 21 p. (score).
Dn 6′ . *Da* 1973. *La* composer. *Pf* flu, obo, per, 16 vcl. Also published in
American Society of University Composers Journal of Music Scores IV (1976),
73-96   *(Composer)*

3799 WYLIE, Ruth Shaw. **Nova, op. 30, no. 1** (West Babylon, N.Y.:
md   H. Branch, 1977) 26 p. $7.50. (score, parts).
Dn 10′ . *Da* 1975. *La* composer. *Pf* flu, cla, per, vln, vcl, solo mba and vib.
    (Composer)

3800 WYLIE, Ruth Shaw. **Sonata for flute and piano, op. 20** (West
mm Babylon, N.Y.: H. Branch, 1977) 35 p. (score, part).
Dn 15′. *Da* 1960. *La* composer.   *(Composer)*

3801 WYLIE, Ruth Shaw. **Sonata for viola and piano, op. 16, no.**
md **3** (West Babylon, N.Y.: H. Branch, 1977) 35 p. $20.
Dn 15′. *Da* 1954. *La* composer.   *(Composer)*

3802 WYLIE, Ruth Shaw. **String quartet no. 3, op. 17** (New York:
mm Camara, 1962) 51 p. (score, parts).
Dn 20′. *Da* 1956. *La* composer.   *(Composer)*

3803 WYLIE, Ruth Shaw. **Three inscapes** (West Babylon, N.Y.: H.
mm Branch, 1977) 51 p. $5. (score, parts).
Dn 13′. *Pf* flu, per, gtr, pno, vla.   *(Composer)*

3804 WYLIE, Ruth Shaw. **Toward Sirius, op. 31, no. 1** (West
md Babylon, N.Y.: H. Branch, 1977) 28 p. $5. (score, parts).
Dn 12′. *Da* 1976. *La* composer. *Pf* flu, obo, hps, pno, vln, vcl. *(Composer)*

3805 WYLIE, Ruth Shaw. **Wistful piece for flute or oboe or violin**
md **and piano, op. 16, no. 2** (West Babylon, N.Y.: H. Branch, 1977) 5
   p. $5. (score, parts).
Dn 5′. *Da* 1953. *La* composer.   *(Composer)*

3806 ZAIMONT, Judith Lang. **Grand tarantella for violin and**
mm **piano** (facsimile of autograph at NNAMC, 1970) 21 p. (score, part).
Dn 5′. *La* composer.   *(Composer)*

3807 ZAIMONT, Judith Lang. **Music for two** (facsimile of auto-
mm graph at NNAMC, 1971) 14 p. (score, parts).
Dn 7′. *La* composer. *Pf* any 2 equal treble instruments, particularly descant
recorders, flutes, or clarinets.   *(Composer)*

3808 ZAIMONT, Judith Lang. **Snazzy sonata. An entertainment**
mm **for two** (facsimile of autograph at NNAMC, 1972) 59 p. (score,
   parts).
Dn 18′. *La* composer. *Pf* pno, 4 hands or 2 pno, 4 hands. *Ct* Moderate two-
step, Lazy bequine, Be-bop scherzo, Grand valse brilliante.   *(Composer)*

3809 ZAIMONT, Judith Lang. **Songs of innocence for soprano,**
mm **tenor, flute, cello, and harp** (facsimile of autograph at NNAMC,
   1974) 24 p. (score, parts).
Dn 9′. *La* composer. *At* Blake. *Rg* Sunny airs and sober. *Music for voice by
Judith Lang Zaimont*, Golden Crest, ATH 5051.   *(Composer)*

3810 ZAIMONT, Judith Lang. **Woman of valor, A. Tone poem**
mm **for mezzo soprano and string quartet** (facsimile of MS at
   NNACA, 1977) 18 p. (score, parts).
Dn 7′. *Da* Feb. 1977. *La* composer.   *(Composer)*

3811 ZIFFRIN, Marilyn J. **Haiku. Song cycle for soprano, viola,**
mm **and harpsichord** (facsimile of MS at NNAMC, 1971) 24 p. (score,
   parts).
Dn 16′. *Da* 1971. *La* composer. *At* Kathryn Martin.   *(Composer)*

3812 ZIFFRIN, Marilyn J. **In the beginning .... For percussion**
mm **ensemble** (facsimile of MS at NNAMC, 1968) 17 p. (score, parts).
Dn 4′. *Da* 1968. *Pf* per, pno.   *(Composer)*

3813 ZIFFRIN, Marilyn J. **Little prince, The. Suite for B-flat**
mm **clarinet and bassoon** (facsimile of MS at NNAMC, 1953) 6 p.
   (score, parts).
Dn 7′. *Da* 1953. *La* composer.   *(Composer)*

3814 ZIFFRIN, Marilyn J. **Movements for B-flat clarinet and**
mm **percussion** (facsimile of MS at NNAMC, 1972) 17 p. (score, parts).
Dn 12′. *Da* 1972. *La* composer. *Pf* cla, tim, per including mba. *(Composer)*

3815 ZIFFRIN, Marilyn J. **String quartet** (facsimile of MS at
mm NNAMC, 1970) 21 p. (score, parts).
Dn 13′. *Da* 1970. *La* composer.   *(Composer)*

3816 ZIFFRIN, Marilyn J. **Thirteen for chamber ensemble** (facsimm mile of MS at NNAMC, 1969) 18 p. (score, parts).
Dn 12′. *Da* 1969. *La* composer. *Pf* 2 flu, cla, 2 bsn, 2 hrn, tbn, tim, per, 2 vln,
vla, vcl.   *(Composer)*

3817 ZIFFRIN, Marilyn J. **Trio for violin, cello, and piano**
mm (facsimile of MS at NNAMC, 1975) 36 p. (score, parts).
Dn 18′. *Da* 1975. *La* composer.   *(Composer)*

3818 ZWILICH, Ellen Taaffe. **Sonata in three movements for**
mm **violin and piano** (facsimile of MS at NNAMC, 1974) 18 p. (score,
   part).
Dn 12′. *Da* 1973. *La* composer.   *(Composer)*

3819 ZWILICH, Ellen Taaffe. **String quartet** (facsimile of MS at
mm NNAMC, 1974) 31 p. (score, parts).
Dn 17′. *La* composer.   *(Composer)*

Choral music

3820 BALLOU, Esther Williamson. **Babe is born, A** (New York:
mm Composers Facsimile Ed., 1959) 5 p. (choral octavo).
Sacred chorus. *Dn* 3′. *Da* Nov. 1959. *Pf* choral SATB.   *(James R. Heintze)*

3821 BALLOU, Esther Williamson. **Bag of tricks** (facsimile of
mm autograph at NNACA, 1956) 11 p. (choral octavo).
Secular chorus. *Dn* 2′. *Da* 1956. *At* Irene Orgel. *Pf* choral SSAA, pno.

3822 BALLOU, Esther Williamson. **Beatitudes, The** (New York:
mm Composers Facsimile Ed., 1963) 21 p. (choral octavo).
Sacred chorus. *Dn* 10′. *Da* 1957. *Pf* solo SATB, choral SATB, org.

3823 BALLOU, Esther Williamson. **Hear us!** (Waco, Tex.: Word,
mm 1969) 20 p. (choral octavo).
Sacred chorus. *Dn* 7′. *La* DAU. *Pf* choral SATB, org.   *(James R. Heintze)*

3824 BALLOU, Esther Williamson. **May the words for S.A.T.B.**
mm **(a cappella)** (New York: Composers Facsimile Ed., 1967) 10 p.
   (choral octavo).
Sacred chorus. *Dn* 1′. *Da* Oct. 1965. *Pf* choral SATB, org or pno for rehearsal
only.   *(James R. Heintze)*

3825 BALLOU, Esther Williamson. **O the sun comes up-up-up in**
mm **the opening** (New York: Composers Facsimile Ed., 1966) 7 p.
   (choral octavo).
Secular chorus. *Dn* 2′. *Da* 1966. *At* E.E. Cummings. *St* 73 poems. *Pf* choral
SSA.

3826 BARRETT-THOMAS, N. **Boston: alone** (Boston: Artists'
mm Forum, 1977) 18 p. (choral octavo).
Secular chorus. *Dn* 10′. *Da* Feb. 1977. *La* composer. *At* Nikki Flionis. *Pf* choral
SSAA.   *(Paula Ann Ross)*

3827 BARRETT-THOMAS, N. **From the land of the caribou**
mm (Boston: Artists' Forum, 1975) 85 p. (score, parts).
Secular choral cycle. *Dn* 30′. *Da* Aug. 1975. *La* composer. *St* Eskimo folk
songs. *Pf* solo S, choral SSAA, pic, 2 flu, 2 obo, enh, cla, bsn, tim, per including
mba.   *(Paula Ann Ross)*

3828 BARRETT-THOMAS, N. **Songs to a handsome woman**
mm (Boston: Artists' Forum, 1977) 25 p. (choral octavo).
Secular choruses. *Dn* 20′. *Da* May 1977. *La* composer. *At* Rita Mae Brown. *St*
Songs for a handsome woman. *Pf* solo S, choral SSAA, pno. *Ct* Follies, A woman
wronged, I looked for sisters, Spontaneous combustion, Beyond vocabulary.
                                                                (Paula Ann Ross)

3829 BELL, Carla Huston. **Love is the color** (Detroit: Stein & Van
mm Stock, 1965) 5 p.
Dn 5′. *Da* 1963. *La* composer. *At* composer. *Pf* choral SATB. *(Composer)*

3830 BELL, Carla Huston. **Ode to Martin Luther King** (New York:
mm Caaron Music, 1977) 9 p.
Dn 5′. *Da* 1977. *La* composer. *At* composer. *Pf* choral S, vcl, cbs. Also for solo
S, vcl, cbs (*WIAM* 3393).

3831 BELL, Carla Huston. **Suite for a Greek festival** (facsimile of
mm MS at NNAMC, 1976) 12 p. (score, parts).
Dn 15′. *Da* 1976. *La* composer. *At* composer. *Pf* choral 4S, soprano rec, alto
rec, per, pno, 2 vln, 2 vla, 2 vcl.   *(Composer)*

3832 BITGOOD, Roberta. **Alleluia! Christ is risen** (451-590; Nash-
mm ville: Broadman, 1964) 2 p. (choral octavo).

Sacred chorus. *Dn* 2′. *Da* 1963. *La* composer. *Pf* choral unison (children), org or pno. *(Composer)*

3833 BITGOOD, Roberta. **Altogether joyfully sing. Worship**
mm **responses for junior choristers and others** (Dallas: Choristers Guild, 1971) 40 p. $2. (choral octavo).
Sacred choruses. *Dn* 50′. *Da* 1971. *La* composer. *Pf* choral unison and/or SATB. *(Composer)*

3834 BITGOOD, Roberta. **Be still, and know that I am God** (CMR
mm 2230; New York: H.W. Gray, 1952) 8 p. (choral octavo).
Sacred chorus. *Dn* 4′. *Da* 1939. *La* composer. *Pf* solo B, choral SATB. Originally for solo M or Bar, org (*WIAM* 4861). *(Composer)*

3835 BITGOOD, Roberta. **Choral benedictions** (APM 470; Nash-
mm ville: Abingdon, 1965) 5 p. (choral octavo).
Sacred choruses. *Dn* 6′. *Da* 1962. *La* composer. *Pf* choral SSATTBB. *(Composer)*

3836 BITGOOD, Roberta. **Christ the Lord is born** (1886; New
mm York: Galaxy Music, 1952) 5 p. (choral octavo).
Sacred chorus. *Dn* 2′. *Da* 1945. *La* composer. *At* composer. *Pf* choral SSA, org or pno. Also for choral SATB (1943; Galaxy, 1953). *(Composer)*

3837 BITGOOD, Roberta. **Christ went up into the hills alone** (A
mm 152; Dallas: Choristers Guild, 1974) 5 p. $.40. (choral octavo).
Sacred chorus. *Dn* 4′. *Da* 1942. *La* composer. *At* Katherine Adams. *Pf* choral SAB, org or pno. *(Composer)*

3838 BITGOOD, Roberta. **Christmas candle, The** (CMR 1348; New
mm York: H.W. Gray, 1935) 2 p. (choral octavo).
Sacred chorus. *Dn* 2′. *Da* 1935. *La* composer. *At* Anna Hempstead Branch. *Pf* choral unison (children), org. Also for choral SATB, org (CMR 1445; Gray, 1937). *(Composer)*

3839 BITGOOD, Roberta. **Closing responses and amens** (Glen
mm Rock, N.J.: J. Fischer, 1964) 3 p. (choral octavo).
Sacred choruses. *Dn* 16′. *Da* 1960. *La* composer. *Pf* choral SATB. *(Composer)*

3840 BITGOOD, Roberta. **Except the Lord build the house** (3405;
mm New York: H. Flammer, 1956) 9 p. (choral octavo).
Sacred chorus. *Dn* 5′. *Da* 1956. *La* composer. *Pf* choral SATB. *(Composer)*

3841 BITGOOD, Roberta. **Give me a faith** (CMR 2017; New York:
mm H.W. Gray, 1947) 8 p. (choral octavo).
Sacred chorus. *Dn* 4′. *Da* 1945. *La* composer. *At* Charles Lee Reynolds. *Pf* solo SB, choral SATB. *(Composer)*

3842 BITGOOD, Roberta. **Glory to God** (CMR 1872; New York:
mm H.W. Gray, 1943) 8 p. (choral octavo).
Sacred chorus. *Dn* 5′. *Da* 1941. *La* composer. *Pf* choral SA (children), SATB, org. *(Composer)*

3843 BITGOOD, Roberta. **Good thing it is to give thanks, A** (GMC
mm 1515; New York: Galaxy Music, 1945) 9 p. (choral octavo).
Sacred chorus. *Dn* 5′. *Da* 1942. *La* composer. *Pf* solo A or B, choral SATB. *(Composer)*

3844 BITGOOD, Roberta. **Grant us thy peace (Dona nobis pacem)**
mm (CMR 1697; New York: H.W. Gray, 1940) 4 p. (choral octavo).
Sacred chorus. *Dn* 2′. *Da* 1939. *La* composer. *Pf* choral SAB. *(Composer)*

3845 BITGOOD, Roberta. **Greatest of these is love, The** (New
mm York: H.W. Gray, 1936) 8 p. (choral octavo).
Sacred chorus. *Dn* 4′. *Da* 1936. *La* composer. *Pf* choral SATB, org or pno. Originally for solo SB, org, pno (*WIAM* 4862). *(Composer)*

3846 BITGOOD, Roberta. **Holy Spirit, hear us** (S 8633; Dayton:
mm Lorenz, 1976) 3 p. $.35. (choral octavo).
Sacred chorus. *Dn* 2′. *Da* 1959. *La* composer. *At* William Henry Parker. *Pf* choral unison (children), descant. *(Composer)*

3847 BITGOOD, Roberta. **How excellent thy name** (4352; New
mm York: H. Flammer, 1965) 3 p. (choral octavo).
Sacred chorus. *Dn* 3′. *Da* 1964. *La* composer. *Pf* choral SA (children). *(Composer)*

3848 BITGOOD, Roberta. **Job. Cantata for mixed voices** (New
mm York: H.W. Gray, 1948) 34 p. (choral octavo).

Dn 28′. *Da* 1945. *La* composer. *Tr* Newton Mann. *Pf* solo STTB, choral SSATBB, org or pno. *(Composer)*

3849 BITGOOD, Roberta. **Joseph. Cantata for mixed voices** (New
mm York: H.W. Gray, 1966) 48 p. (choral octavo).
Dn 28′. *Da* 1960. *La* composer. *At* Nicolaus Selnecker. *Pf* solo SATB, choral SSAATTBB, org or pno. *(Composer)*

3850 BITGOOD, Roberta. **Joy dawned again on Easter Day** (1416;
mm New York: H.W. Gray, 1965) 6 p. (choral octavo).
Sacred chorus. *Dn* 4′. *Da* 1936. *La* composer. *Tr* J.M. Neale. *Pf* choral SA, choral SATB, org or pno. *(Composer)*

3851 BITGOOD, Roberta. **Let there be light. Christmas cantata**
mm **for children's voices** (Dayton: Lorenz, 1965) 34 p. (choral octavo).
Dn 20′. *Da* 1964. *La* composer. *At* Mildred Kerr. *Pf* choral SA, org or pno. *(Composer)*

3852 BITGOOD, Roberta. **Let us now praise famous ones** (145;
mm Hanover, Penn.: Stone Chapel, 1970) 7 p. $.25. (choral octavo).
Sacred chorus. *Dn* 4′. *Da* 1962. *La* composer. *Pf* choral SSATBB. *(Composer)*

3853 BITGOOD, Roberta. **Lord, guard and guide the men who fly**
mm (9435; Glen Rock, N.J.: J. Fischer, 1963) 6 p. (choral octavo).
Sacred chorus. *Dn* 4′. *Da* 1960. *La* composer. *At* Mary C.D. Hamilton. *Pf* choral SSAATTBB. *(Composer)*

3854 BITGOOD, Roberta. **Lord, guide our thoughts** (A 25; Dallas:
mm Choristers Guild, 1963) 4 p. (choral octavo).
Sacred chorus. *Dn* 3′. *Da* 1962. *La* composer. *At* Louise Whitman. *Pf* choral SA (children). *(Composer)*

3855 BITGOOD, Roberta. **Lord, may we follow** (M 1047; New
mm York: McAfee Music, 1974) 10 p. $.40. (choral octavo).
Sacred chorus. *Dn* 5′. *Da* 1972. *La* composer. *At* Edward Osler. *Pf* solo S, choral SSATBB, org. *(Composer)*

3856 BITGOOD, Roberta. **New meanings for our age** (4431; New
mm York: H. Flammer, 1967) 24 p. (choral octavo).
Sacred chorus. *Dn* 8′. *Da* 1965. *La* composer. *At* Harold Confer. *Pf* choral unison (children), SSATTB, handbells, org. *(Composer)*

3857 BITGOOD, Roberta. **Now a new day opens, now a new year**
mm **opens** (9739; Glen Rock, N.J.: J. Fischer, 1967) 4 p. (choral octavo).
Sacred chorus. *Dn* 2′. *Da* 1962. *La* composer. *Pf* choral SAB. *(Composer)*

3858 BITGOOD, Roberta. **Power of music, The** (M 152; New York:
mm McAfee Music, 1972) 8 p. $.40. (choral octavo).
Sacred chorus. *Dn* 5′. *Da* 1967. *La* composer. *At* composer. *Pf* choral SSATBB, org. *(Composer)*

3859 BITGOOD, Roberta. **Prayer is the soul's sincere desire** (CMR
mm 1611; New York: H.W. Gray, 1967) 6 p. (choral octavo).
Sacred chorus. *Dn* 5′. *Da* 1939. *La* composer. *At* James Montgomery. *Pf* choral SSATBB. *(Composer)*

3860 BITGOOD, Roberta. **Rejoice, give thanks** (333; Carol Stream,
mm Ill.: Hope, 1971) 11 p. $1.95. (score, parts).
Dn 5′. *Da* 1969. *La* composer. *Pf* choral unison, congregation, 2 tpt, 2 tbn, solo org. *(Composer)*

3861 BITGOOD, Roberta. **Rosa mystica** (CMR 1346; New York:
mm H.W. Gray, 1963) 3 p. (choral octavo).
Sacred chorus. *Dn* 2′. *Da* 1932. *La* composer. *At* Mary G. Segar. *Pf* choral SATB. *(Composer)*

3862 BITGOOD, Roberta. **Sixteen amens from the oratorios**
mm (3451; New York: H. Flammer, 1957) 3 p. (choral octavo).
Sacred choruses. *Dn* 8′. *Da* 1954. *La* composer. *Pf* choral SATB. *(Composer)*

3863 BITGOOD, Roberta. **Sons of God, The** (S 2858; Dayton:
mm Lorenz, 1973) 3 p. $.25. (choral octavo).
Sacred chorus. *Dn* 4′. *Da* 1942. *La* composer. *Pf* choral TTBB. *(Composer)*

3864 BITGOOD, Roberta. **That we might find Him still** (A 59;
mm Dallas: Choristers Guild, 1968) 5 p. (choral octavo).
Sacred chorus. *Dn* 3′. *Da* 1966. *La* composer. *At* composer, John Erskine. *Pf* choral unison (children), flu, org. *(Composer)*

3865 BITGOOD, Roberta. **They shall walk** (E 63; Dayton: Lorenz,
mm   1966) 7 p. (choral octavo).
Sacred chorus. *Dn* 4′. *Da* 1965. *La* composer. *At* William Cowper. *Pf* choral
SSATBB.   *(Composer)*

3866 BITGOOD, Roberta. **We come with songs of gladness** (453-
mm   921; Nashville: Broadman, 1968) 4 p. (choral octavo).
Sacred chorus. *Dn* 3′. *Da* 1968. *La* composer. *Pf* choral unison (children).
                                                          (Composer)

3867 BOLZ, Harriett. **Carol of the flowers** (S 165; New York: Choral
mm   Art, 1967) 6 p. (choral octavo).
Sacred chorus. *Dn* 3′. *Da* 1966. *La* publisher. *St* French carol. *Pf* choral SSA,
org or pno.   *(Composer)*

3868 BOLZ, Harriett. **Day and dark. A cantata for chorus and
mm   orchestra with baritone solo** (facsimile of MS at NNAMC, 1958)
      54 p. (score, parts).
Secular cantata. *Dn* 15′. *La* composer. *At* George Cabot Lodge. *Pf* solo Bar,
choral SATB, 2-2-2-2, 2-2-1-0, tim, per, str.   *(Composer)*

3869 BOLZ, Harriett. **Four Christmas songs** (R 198; New York:
mm   Choral Art, 1967) 10 p. (choral octavo).
Sacred choruses. *Dn* 10′. *Da* 1966. *La* publisher. *Pf* choral SATB, org or pno.
Ct Tidings of the bells (*At* composer), Star lullaby (*At* composer), Winter's
night carol (*Tr* F.R. Marvin), May joy come your way (*At* composer). *(Composer)*

3870 BOLZ, Harriett. **Sweet Jesus** (BP 1006; Columbus, Ohio:
mm   Beckenhorst, 1974) 7 p. $.40. (choral octavo).
Sacred chorus. *Dn* 3′. *Da* 1974. *La* publisher. *Pf* choral SAB, org or pno.
                                                          (Composer)

3871 BOLZ, Harriett. **That I may sing!** (PS 168; New York: S. Fox,
mm   1970) 6 p. (choral octavo).
Sacred chorus. *Dn* 3′. *Da* 1969. *La* publisher. *Pf* choral SSA, org or pno.
                                                          (Composer)

3872 BOLZ, Harriett. **Two madrigals for Christmas** (PS 142; New
mm   York: S. Fox, 1968) 5 p. (choral octavo).
Sacred choruses. *Dn* 3′. *Da* 1967. *La* publisher. *Pf* choral SA. *Ct* Child of God,
Lo! a brighter star.   *(Composer)*

3873 BONDS, Margaret. **Ballad of the brown king, The. A
mm   Christmas cantata** (New York: S. Fox, 1961) 56 p. (score).
Dn 22′. *At* Langston Hughes. *Pf* solo SATBar, choral SATB, choral SST, pno.

3874 BONDS, Margaret. **Go tell it on the mountain** (MC 431; New
mm   York: Beekman Music, 1962) 6 p.
Spiritual arranged. *Dn* 3′. *Pf* choral SATB, pno for rehearsal only. Also for solo
S, pno (*WIAM* 4867).

3875 BOONE, Clara Lyle. **Alleluia** (99; Washington, D.C.: Arsis,
mm   1974) 7 p. $.35. (choral octavo).
Sacred chorus. *Dn* 2′. *Da* 1957. *Pf* choral SATB. Published under the
pseudonym of Lyle de Bohun.   *(Composer)*

3876 BOONE, Clara Lyle. **Meditation** (39; Washington, D.C.: Arsis,
mm   1974) 4 p. $.35. (choral octavo).
Sacred chorus. *Dn* 2′. *Da* 1956. *At* composer. *Pf* choral SATB. Published under
the pseudonym of Lyle de Bohun.   *(Composer)*

3877 BOONE, Clara Lyle. **Thou shalt light my lamp** (56; Washing-
mm   ton, D.C.: Arsis, 1976) 6 p. $.35. (choral octavo).
Sacred chorus. *Dn* 4′. *Da* 1955. *Pf* choral SSATB. Published under the
pseudonym of Lyle de Bohun.   *(Composer)*

3878 BRADLEY, Ruth. **Abraham Lincoln walks at midnight** (CPO
mm   65; New York: Composers Press, 1959) 27 p. (choral octavo).
Secular chorus. *Dn* 9′. *At* Vachel Lindsay. *Pf* choral SATB, pno.

3879 BRADLEY, Ruth. **Ballad of Mark Twain** (CPO 73; New York:
mm   Composers Press, 1962) 18 p. (choral octavo).
Secular chorus. *Dn* 6′. *At* Burton Frye. *Pf* choral SATB, pno.

3880 BRADLEY, Ruth. **Ice cream** (3281; [New York]: H. Flammer,
mm   1956) 8 p. (choral octavo).
Secular chorus. *Dn* 2′. *At* Anthony Euwer. *Pf* choral SATB, pno.

3881 BRADLEY, Ruth. **Patchwork quilts** (3155; [New York]: H.
mm   Flammer, 1955) 4 p. (choral octavo).
Secular chorus. *Dn* 1′. *At* Genevieve Lawless. *Pf* choral SSA, org or pno.

3882 BRITAIN, Radie. **Drums of Africa** (19706; New York: M.
mm   Witmark, 1936) 12 p. (choral octavo).
Secular chorus. *Dn* 5′. *At* R.L. Jenkins. *Pf* choral SATB, per, pno for rehearsal
only.

3883 BRITAIN, Radie. **Prayer** (1024; New York: G. Ricordi, 1936) 6
mm   p. (choral octavo).
Secular chorus. *Dn* 3′. *At* Lucille Quarry. *Pf* choral SATB, org or pno.

3884 BRITAIN, Radie. **Star and the child, The** (APS 15725; Boston:
mm   A.P. Schmidt, 1956) 4 p. (choral octavo).
Sacred chorus. *Dn* 3′. *At* John Lancaster. *Pf* choral SSA, pno.

3885 BRUSH, Ruth. **Lord is my shepherd, The** (Cincinnati: Bartles-
mm   ville, 1972) 14 p. (choral octavo).
Sacred chorus. *Dn* 5′. *Pf* choral SATB, org or pno.   *(Composer)*

3886 BRUSH, Ruth. **This same Jesus** (Cincinnati: Bartlesville, 1973)
mm   12 p. (choral octavo).
Sacred chorus. *Dn* 4′. *At* Grace Noll Crowell. *Pf* choral SATB, org or pno.
                                                          (Composer)

3887 CHANCE, Nancy Laird. **Motet for double chorus divided**
mm   (New York: Seesaw Music, 1972) 19 p. $7. (score).
Sacred chorus. *Dn* 11′. *Da* 1965. *La* publisher. *Lt* Latin. *Pf* choral SSAATTBB.

3888 COOPER, Rose Marie. **Christ child come below** (Chapel Hill,
mm   N.C.: Hinshaw Music, 1975) 5 p. $.50. (choral octavo).
Sacred chorus. *Dn* 4′. *At* composer. *Pf* choral SSATB, pno.   *(Composer)*

3889 COOPER, Rose Marie. **Crown of thorns** (New York: C. Fischer,
mm   1961) 5 p. (choral octavo).
Sacred chorus. *Dn* 4′. *At* Jennie Frye. *Pf* choral SSATB, pno.   *(Composer)*

3890 COOPER, Rose Marie. **Hymn of truth** (Cape Girardeau, Mo.:
mm   Julian, 1970) 4 p. $.50. (choral octavo).
Sacred chorus. *Dn* 3′. *At* Thomas Hughes. *Pf* choral SATB.   *(Composer)*

3891 COOPER, Rose Marie. **Hymns to the Trinity** (New York: C.
mm   Fischer, 1964) 4 p.
Sacred chorus. *Dn* 4′. *Pf* choral unison (children), org or pno. *Ct* Lamb of God
(*At* W.W. How), Behold a little child (*At* C.F. Alexander), Father of mercy (*At*
F.G. Moore).   *(Composer)*

3892 COOPER, Rose Marie. **Lord most holy** (Nashville: Broadman,
mm   1963) 28 p. (choral octavo).
Sacred cantata. *Dn* 20′. *Pf* choral SA, org or pno. *Rg* Broadman 452-062.
                                                          (composer)

3893 COOPER, Rose Marie. **Morning star** (New York: C. Fischer,
mm   1970) 32 p. $1.50. (choral octavo).
Sacred cantata. *Dn* 20′. *Pf* solo T, choral SA, org or pno.   *(Composer)*

3894 COOPER, Rose Marie. **Once in royal David's city** (New York:
mm   C. Fischer, 1962) 2 p. (choral octavo).
Sacred chorus. *Dn* 2′. *At* C.F. Alexander. *Pf* choral unison (children), pno.
                                                          (Composer)

3895 COOPER, Rose Marie. **Plainsongs and carols** (New York: H.
mm   Flammer, 1965) 28 p. (choral octavo).
Sacred choruses. *Dn* 20′. *Lt* English. *Pf* choral SSA, org or pno. *Ct* Dies est
laetitiae, Quem pastores, Avison, Chartres, Resonet in laudibus, Frankfort.
                                                          (Composer)

3896 COOPER, Rose Marie. **Psalm 150** (Nashville: Broadman, 1962)
mm   4 p. (choral octavo).
Sacred chorus. *Dn* 3′. *Pf* choral SA, 2 tpt, pno.   *(Composer)*

3897 COOPER, Rose Marie. **Settings of five haiku** (Phoenix: Byron-
mm   Douglas, 1972) 5 p. $.50. (choral octavo).
Secular choruses. *Dn* 5′. *At* Shiki, Buson. *Pf* choral SATB or SSA, pno.
                                                          (Composer)

3898 COOPER, Rose Marie. **Tell the blessed tidings** (Nashville:
mm   Broadman, 1970) 3 p. $.50. (choral octavo).
Sacred chorus. *Dn* 2′. *Pf* choral unison, org or pno. *Rg Lord most holy*,
Broadman, 452-062.
(*Composer*)

3899 COOPER, Rose Marie. **This is the land that I love** (Chapel
mm   Hill, N.C.: Hinshaw Music, 1976) 5 p. $.50. (choral octavo).
Secular chorus. *Dn* 4′. *At* Susan Graham Erwin. *Pf* choral SATB, pno.
(*Composer*)

3900 COOPER, Rose Marie. **Three anthems for junior choir** (St.
mm   Louis: Concordia, 1967) 8 p. (choral octavo).
Sacred choruses. *Dn* 9′. *Pf* choral unison (children), org or pno. *Ct* Come, Holy
Spirit, heavenly dove; For you a child is born; O word of God incarnate.
(*Composer*)

3901 COOPER, Rose Marie; ANGELL, Warren. **Psalm 145.**
mm   **Great is the Lord** (Delaware Water Gap, Penn.: Shawnee, 1960) 6
p. (choral octavo).
Sacred chorus. *Dn* 4′. *Pf* choral SATB, 2 tpt, 2 tbn, org or pno.   (*Composer*)

3902 COOPER, Rose Marie ; ANGELL, Warren. **This is the day**
mm   (New York: C. Fischer, 1959) 5 p. (choral octavo).
Sacred chorus. *Dn* 4′. *Pf* choral SATB, org or pno.   (*Composer*)

3903 CRANE, Joelle Wallach. **Introit I** (New York: Composers
mm   Facsimile Ed., 1974) 1 p. (choral octavo).
Sacred chorus. *Dn* 1′. *Da* 1974. *La* NNACA. *Pf* solo ST, choral SATB, pno for
rehearsal only.
(*Composer*)

3904 CRANE, Joelle Wallach. **Introit II** (New York: Composers
mm   Facsimile Ed., 1976) 1 p. (choral octavo).
Sacred chorus. *Dn* 1′. *Da* 1976. *La* NNACA. *Pf* solo ST, choral SATB, pno for
rehearsal only.
(*Composer*)

3905 CRANE, Joelle Wallach. **Look down fair moon** (New York:
mm   Composers Facsimile Ed., 1976) 5 p. (choral octavo).
Secular chorus. *Dn* 4′. *Da* 1976. *La* NNACA. *At* Whitman. *Pf* choral 4S-4A-
2T-3B, pno for rehearsal only.
(*Composer*)

3906 CRANE, Joelle Wallach. **On the beach at night alone** (New
mm   York: Composers Facsimile Ed., 1977) 27 p. (choral octavo).
Secular chorus. *Dn* 8′. *Da* 1977. *La* NNACA. *At* Whitman. *Pf* solo A, choral
SSAATTBB, pno for rehearsal only.
(*Composer*)

3907 CRANE, Joelle Wallach. **Tears** (New York: Composers Facsi-
mm   mile Ed., 1976) 19 p. (choral octavo).
Secular chorus. *Dn* 8′. *Da* 1976. *La* NNACA. *At* Whitman. *Pf* choral
SSAATTBB, pno for rehearsal only.
(*Composer*)

3908 CRANE, Joelle Wallach. **Three Whitman visions** (New York:
mm   Composers Facsimile Ed., 1977) 51 p. (choral octavo).
Secular chorus. *Dn* 20′. *Da* 1977. *La* NNACA. *At* Whitman. *Pf* solo A, choral
4S-4A-2T-2B, pno for rehearsal only.
(*Composer*)

3909 DAVIS, Katherine K. **Carol of the drum** (7498; Boston: B.F.
mm   Wood Music, 1941) 12 p. (choral octavo).
Sacred chorus. *Dn* 3′. *At* C.R.W. Robertson (pseudonym for the composer). *Pf*
choral SATB. This piece was pirated in 1958 and published under the title *Little
drummer boy*. It subsequently appeared in various choral versions and for large
band, small band, and for solo instruments.
(*Composer*)

3910 DAVIS, Katherine K. **Let all things now living** (1108; Boston:
mm   E.C. Schirmer, 1938) 4 p. (choral octavo).
Sacred chorus. *Dn* 3′. *At* John Cowley (pseudonym for the composer). *Pf*
choral SA, org or pno.
(*Composer*)

3911 DAVIS, Katherine K. **Nancy Hanks** (1529; New York: Galaxy
mm   Music, 1945) 8 p. (choral octavo).
Secular chorus. *Dn* 4′. *At* Rosemary Benet. *Pf* choral SSA, pno. Also for choral
SATB, pno (1569; Galaxy, 1946) and for solo S, pno (*WIAM* 4904). (*Composer*)

3912 DAVIS, Katherine K. **This is Noel** (3737; New York: Remick,
mm   1953) 36 p. (score).
Sacred cantata. *Dn* 25′. *At* John Cowley (pseudonym for the composer). *Pf* solo
SB, choral SATB, oboe, org.
(*Composer*)

3913 DENBOW, Stefania Björnson. **All glory for this blessed**
mm   **morn** (New York: Seesaw Music, 1975) 13 p. $3. (score).

Sacred cantata. *Dn* 6′. *Da* 1974. *La* composer. *At* Coelius Sedulius. *Tr* John
Ellerton. *Pf* solo ST, choral SATB, org. Based on the plainsong *A solis ortus
cardine*.
(*Composer*)

3914 DENBOW, Stefania Björnson. **Christ is risen, alleluia** (New
mm   York: Seesaw Music, 1975) 34 p. $20. (score, parts).
Sacred cantata. *Dn* 20′. *La* composer. *St* 12th-c. German carol. *Pf* solo ST,
choral SATB, flu, str.
(*Composer*)

3915 DENBOW, Stefania Björnson. **Magnificat** (New York: Seesaw
mm   Music, 1976) 30 p. $15. (score, parts).
Sacred chorus. *Dn* 10′. *Da* 1972. *La* composer. *Pf* solo S, choral SATB, flu, obo,
hrp, str.
(*Composer*)

3916 DIEMER, Emma Lou. **Anniversary choruses** (N 5419; New
mm   York: C. Fischer, 1970) 50 p. (score, parts).
Sacred choruses. *Dn* 15′. *Da* 1970. *La* composer. *Pf* choral SATB, 2-2-2-2, 4-3-
3-1, tim, per, str. *Ct* I will sing of mercy and judgment, Sleep sweetly sleep: ode
(*At* Henry Timrod and Archibald Rutledge), Sing aloud unto God.   (*Composer*)

3917 DIEMER, Emma Lou. **For ye shall go out with joy** (New
mm   York: C. Fischer, 1968) 14 p. (choral octavo).
Sacred chorus. *Dn* 5′. *Da* 1967. *La* composer. *Pf* choral SATB, pno. (*Composer*)

3918 DIEMER, Emma Lou. **Four carols** (18; Philadelphia: Elkan-
mm   Vogel, 1962) 19 p. (choral octavo).
Sacred choruses. *Dn* 8′. *Da* 1961. *La* composer. *St* Christmas carols from
different countries. *Pf* choral SSA.
(*Composer*)

3919 DIEMER, Emma Lou. **Madrigals three** (N 5597; New York: C.
mm   Fischer, 1972) 21 p. (choral octavo).
Secular choruses. *Dn* 9′. *Da* 1971. *La* composer. *Pf* choral SATB, pno. *Ct*
Come, O come, my life's delight (*At* Thomas Campion); Daybreak (*At* Donne);
It was a lover and his lass (*At* Shakespeare).
(*Composer*)

3920 DIEMER, Emma Lou. **Now the spring has come again** (5743;
mm   New York: Boosey & Hawkes, 1970) 20 p. (choral octavo).
Sacred chorus. *Dn* 7′. *Da* 1961. *La* composer. *St* Piae cantiones. *Pf* choral
SATB, pno.
(*Composer*)

3921 DIEMER, Emma Lou. **O come, let us sing unto the Lord** (N
mm   3663; New York: C. Fischer, 1961) 15 p. (choral octavo).
Sacred chorus. *Dn* 6′. *Da* 1960. *La* composer. *Pf* choral SATB, pno. (*Composer*)

3922 DIEMER, Emma Lou. **O to make the most jubilant song** (N
mm   5547; New York: C. Fischer, 1972) 32 p. (choral octavo).
Secular chorus. *Dn* 8′. *Da* 1971. *La* composer. *At* Whitman, *St* Leaves of grass;
At Tennyson, *St* In memoriam. *Pf* choral SATB, pno.   (*Composer*)

3923 DIEMER, Emma Lou. **Praise the Lord** (N 5919; New York: C.
mm   Fischer, 1975) 16 p. (score, parts).
Sacred chorus. *Dn* 7′. *Da* 1974. *La* composer. *Pf* choral SATB, brass quintet,
org.
(*Composer*)

3924 DIEMER, Emma Lou. **Prophecy, The** (N 5882; New York:
mm   Boosey & Hawkes, 1974) 19 p. (choral octavo).
Sacred chorus. *Dn* 8′. *Da* 1968. *La* composer. *Pf* choral SSAA.   (*Composer*)

3925 DIEMER, Emma Lou. **Psalm 134** (New York: Seesaw Music,
mm   1976) 8 p. (choral octavo).
Sacred chorus. *Dn* 7′. *Da* 1974. *La* composer. *Pf* choral SATB.   (*Composer*)

3926 DIEMER, Emma Lou. **Sing, O heavens** (N 5888; New York: C.
mm   Fischer, 1975) 10 p. (choral octavo).
Sacred chorus. *Dn* 5′. *Da* 1974. *La* composer. *Pf* choral SATB.   (*Composer*)

3927 DIEMER, Emma Lou. **Three madrigals** (5417; New York:
mm   Boosey & Hawkes, 1962) 12 p. (choral octavo).
Secular choruses. *Dn* 7′. *Da* 1960. *La* composer. *At* Shakespeare. *Pf* choral
SATB, pno. *Ct* O mistress mine, where are you roaming?; Take, O take those
lips away; Sigh no more, ladies.
(*Composer*)

3928 DIEMER, Emma Lou. **Verses from the** *Rubáiyát* (5782; New
mm   York: Boosey & Hawkes, 1970) 24 p. (choral octavo).
Secular chorus. *Dn* 12′. *Da* 1967. *La* composer. *At* Omar Khayyám. *Pf* choral
SATB.
(*Composer*)

3929 ESCOT, Pozzi. **Ainu** (Cambridge, Mass.: Publications Contact
mm International, 1975) 10 p.
Secular chorus. *Dn* 11′. *Da* 1970. *Pf* choral SATB. *(Composer)*

3930 FINE, Vivian. **Meeting for equal rights 1866** (Shaftsbury, Vt.:
mm Catamount Facsimile Ed., 1976) 91 p. $15. (score, parts).
Secular cantata. *Dn* 30′. *Da* 1975. *La* composer. *Pf* solo SB; choral SATB; 2-2-
2-2; 2-2-2-0; tim; per including glk, xyl; str. *(Composer)*

3931 FINE, Vivian. **Morning** (Shaftsbury, Vt.: Catamount Facsimile
mm Ed., 1972) 15 p. $4. (score, parts).
Secular chorus. *Dn* 7′. *Da* 1962. *La* composer. *At* Thoreau. *St* Walden. *Pf*
choral SATB, org or pno, narrator. *(Composer)*

3932 FINE, Vivian. **Paean** (Shaftsbury, Vt.: Catamount Facsimile Ed.,
mm 1972) 26 p. $7.50. (score, parts).
Secular cantata. *Dn* 12′. *Da* 1969. *La* composer. *Pf* solo T, choral SA, 6 tpt, 6
tbn. *Rg Bennington composers*, Composers Recordings, CRI SD 260. *(Composer)*

3933 FINE, Vivian. **Teisho for eight solo singers or small chorus**
mm **and string quartet** (Shaftsbury, Vt.: Catamount Facsimile Ed.,
1976) 124 p. $15. (score, parts).
Dn 30′. *Da* 1975. *La* composer. *Pf* choral SATB, string quartet. Also for solo
SSAATTBB, string quartet (*WIAM* 3477). *(Composer)*

3934 FINE, Vivian. **Valedictions** (Shaftsbury, Vt.: Catamount Facsi-
mm mile Ed., 1972) 72 p. $10. (score, parts).
Secular chorus. *Dn* 18′. *Da* 1959. *La* composer. *At* Donne. *Pf* solo ST, choral
SATB, flu, obo, cla, bsn, hrn, tpt, 2 vln, vla, vcl. *(Composer)*

3935 FRYXELL, Regina Holmen. **Christmas wish** (New York: H.W.
mm Gray, 1957) 7 p. (choral octavo).
Carol. *Dn* 2′. *At* Jean Kenyon Mackenzie. *Pf* choral SATB, org or pno for
rehearsal only. *(Composer)*

3936 FRYXELL, Regina Holmen. **Heaven, peace, and joy!** (New
mm York: H.W. Gray, 1957) 7 p. (choral octavo).
Sacred chorus. *Dn* 3′. *At* Ernest Hargrove. *Pf* choral SATB, org or pno for
rehearsal only. *(Composer)*

3937 FRYXELL, Regina Holmen. **O come, Creator Spirit, come**
mm (New York: H.W. Gray, 1959) 8 p. (choral octavo).
Sacred chorus. *Dn* 4′. *Pf* choral SATB, org or pno. *(Composer)*

3938 FRYXELL, Regina Holmen. **Praise, my soul, the King of**
mm **Heaven. On a melody by J.S. Bach** (New York: C. Fischer,
1963) 6 p. (choral octavo).
Hymn. *Dn* 5′. *Pf* choral SA or TB in unison, org or pno. Also for solo S or T,
org or pno (*WIAM* 4910). *(Composer)*

3939 FRYXELL, Regina Holmen. **Praise to the Lord** (New York:
mm H.W. Gray, 1953) 8 p. (choral octavo).
Sacred chorus. *Dn* 3′. *At* Joachim Neander. *Tr* Catherine Winkworth. *Pf* choral
SSATB, org or pno. *(Composer)*

3940 FRYXELL, Regina Holmen. **To the Christ Child** (New York:
mm H.W. Gray, 1954) 4 p. (choral octavo).
Sacred chorus. *Dn* 2′. *At* Frank Mason North. *Pf* choral unison, org or pno.
Also for solo S or T, org or pno (*WIAM* 4912). *(Composer)*

3941 FRYXELL, Regina Holmen. **To the hills I lift mine eyes**
mm (APM 475; Nashville: Abingdon, 1966) 8 p. (choral octavo).
Sacred chorus. *Dn* 4′. *Pf* choral SATB, org or pno. *(Composer)*

3942 FRYXELL, Regina Holmen. **Unseen presence, The** (APM
mm 474; Nashville: Abingdon, 1965) 6 p. $.25. (choral octavo).
Sacred chorus. *Dn* 3′. *At* Frederick Lucian Hasmer. *Pf* choral SATB, org or
pno; also can be sung by choral unison, org or pno, and by solo S, org or pno.
(Composer)

3943 GARWOOD, Margaret. **Haiku. Six songs for small chorus**
mm (E. Greenville, Penn.: composer, 1974) 18 p. (choral octavo).
Secular choruses. *Dn* 6′. *Pf* choral 4S-4A-4T-4B. *Ct* Arise, old cat; Twilight
whippoorwill; I heard a hushed sound; Where does he wander; Old dark sleepy
pool; Dim the grey cow. *(Composer)*

3944 GIDEON, Miriam. **Adon olom** (New York: American Compos-
mm ers Ed., 1954) 16 p. (score).
Sacred chorus. *Dn* 6′. *Lt* Hebrew. *Pf* choral SATB, cla, tpt, str.

3945 GIDEON, Miriam. **Habitable earth, The** (New York: Ameri-
mm can Composers Ed., 1966) 49 p. (choral octavo).
Sacred cantata. *Dn* 12′. *La* DLC. *Pf* solo SATB, choral SATB, obo, org or pno.

3946 GIDEON, Miriam. **How goodly are thy tents. Psalm 84** (MC
mm 162; New York: Merrymount Music, 1951) 9 p. (choral octavo).
Sacred chorus. *Dn* 2′. *Pf* choral SSA, org or pno. *Rg* Westminster, 9634.

3947 GIDEON, Miriam. **Sacred service (Saturday morning)** (New
mm York: American Composers Ed., 1971) 38 p. (score, parts).
Dn 30′. *Lt* Hebrew. *Pf* solo SATBar, choral SATB, flu, obo, bsn, tpt, org, vla,
vcl.

3948 GIDEON, Miriam. **Sacred service. Shirat Miriam L'Shabbat**
mm **(Friday evening)** (New York: C.F. Peters, 1978) 64 p.
Dn 30′. *Lt* Hebrew, English. *Pf* cantor, choral SATB, org.

3949 GIDEON, Miriam. **Slow, slow fresh fount** (MC 11; New York:
mm Merrymount Music, 1949) 7 p. (choral octavo).
Secular chorus. *Dn* 5′. *At* Ben Jonson. *Pf* choral SATB, pno for rehearsal only.
Also for choral TTBB, pno (facsimile of MS at NNACA, 1968).

3950 GIDEON, Miriam. **Spiritual madrigals for male voices with**
mm **viola, cello, bassoon** (Hillsdale, N.Y.: Mobart, 1976) 23 p. (score,
parts).
Secular choruses. *Dn* 9′. *La* DLC. *Lt* German, English. *Pf* choral TTB, bsn, vla,
vcl. *Ct* Die Engel (*At* Rilke), Wähebûf und Nichtenvint (*At* Süez Kint von
Trimperg), Hallelujah (*At* Heine).

3951 GLANVILLE-HICKS, Peggy. **Choral suite for female cho-**
mm **rus, oboe, and string orchestra** (Paris: Editions de l'Oiseau-Lyre,
1938) 48 p. (score).
Secular chorus. *Dn* 20′. *At* John Fletcher. *Pf* choral SAA, obo, 2 vln, vla, vcl,
cbs. *Ct* Great god Pan, Aspatia's song, Fair cupid!, Weep no more, Song in the
wood. *Rg* Oiseau-Lyre 100.

3952 GLANVILLE-HICKS, Peggy. **Pastoral** (New York: Weintraub
mm Music, 1951) 14 p. (choral octavo).
Secular chorus. *Dn* 5′. *At* Rabindranath Tagore. *St* Fruit-gathering. *Pf* choral
SSAA, cla.

3953 GOULD, Elizabeth. **Drum of morning and the flute of night,**
mm **The. A madrigal cycle** (facsimile of MS at NNAMC, 1977) 155 p.
(score, parts).
Dn 50′. *Da* 1964. *La* composer. *At* Eugene Hochman. *Pf* choral SSATTB, flu,
obo, cla, 2 bsn, cbn, tpt, sax, tim, per including xyl, pno, vcl, cbs. *Ct*
Introduction, Anthem to the sun, The boy and his reflection, Confrontation in
the morning, Chant to the moon, The girl and her reflection, Confrontation in
the evening, The gift of recognition, Resolution. *(Composer)*

3954 HOOVER, Katherine. **Come ye shepherds** (CM 7944; New
md York: C. Fischer, 1975) 8 p. $.45. (score, parts).
Sacred chorus. *Dn* 4′. *Da* 1973. *La* publisher. *St* German carol. *Tr* composer.
Pf choral SSATBB, 2 tpt, 2 tbn. *Tm* Songs of joy (*WIAM* 3964). *(Composer)*

3955 HOOVER, Katherine. **Do you hear?** (CM 7943; New York: C.
md Fischer, 1975) 3 p. $.35. (score, parts).
Sacred chorus. *Dn* 2′. *Da* 1973. *La* publisher. *St* German carol. *Tr* composer.
Pf choral SATB, 2 tpt, 2 tbn. *Tm* Songs of joy (*WIAM* 3964). *(Composer)*

3956 HOOVER, Katherine. **Four English songs** (facsimile of MS at
mm NNAMC, 1976) 6, 4, 3, 4 p. (score, parts).
Secular choruses. *Dn* 11′. *Da* 1976. *La* composer. *Pf* choral SATB, obo, enh,
pno. *Ct* Sabrina fair (*WIAM* 3962), Prayer of Mary, Queen of Scots (*WIAM*
3959), Some have too much (*WIAM* 3963), Heart's music (*WIAM* 3957).
(Composer)

3957 HOOVER, Katherine. **Heart's music** (facsimile of MS at
md NNAMC, 1976) 4 p. (score, parts).
Secular chorus. *Dn* 3′. *Da* 1976. *La* composer. *St* Thomas Campion's *A book of
ayres*, 1601. *Pf* choral SATB, obo, enh, pno. *Tm* Four English songs (*WIAM*
3956). *(Composer)*

3958 HOOVER, Katherine. **Of a young maid** (CM 7941; New York:
md C. Fischer, 1975) 5 p. $.40. (score, parts).

Sacred chorus. *Dn* 3′. *Da* 1973. *La* publisher. *St* German carol. *Tr* composer. *Pf* choral SATB, 2 tpt, 2 tbn. *Tm Songs of joy* (*WIAM* 3964).   *(Composer)*

3959 HOOVER, Katherine. **Prayer of Mary, Queen of Scots**
md   (facsimile of MS at NNAMC, 1976) 4 p. (score, parts).
Secular chorus. *Dn* 4′. *Da* 1976. *La* composer. *At* Mary, Queen of Scots. *Pf* choral SA, enh, pno. *Tm Four English songs* (*WIAM* 3956).   *(Composer)*

3960 HOOVER, Katherine. **Rejoice** (CM 7940; New York: C. Fischer,
md   1975) 4 p. $.40. (score, parts).
Sacred chorus. *Dn* 2′. *Da* 1973. *La* publisher. *St* German carol. *Tr* composer. *Pf* choral SATB, 2 tpt, 2 tbn. *Tm Songs of joy* (*WIAM* 3964).   *(Composer)*

3961 HOOVER, Katherine. **Run, run all ye shepherds** (CM 7942;
md   New York: C. Fischer, 1975) 3 p. $.35. (score, parts).
Sacred chorus. *Dn* 1′. *Da* 1973. *La* publisher. *St* German carol. *Tr* composer. *Pf* choral SATB, 2 tpt, 2 tbn. *Tm Songs of joy* (*WIAM* 3964).   *(Composer)*

3962 HOOVER, Katherine. **Sabrina fair** (facsimile of MS at
md   NNAMC, 1976) 6 p. (score, parts).
Secular chorus. *Dn* 4′. *Da* 1976. *La* composer. *At* Milton. *Pf* choral TB, obo, pno. *Tm Four English songs* (*WIAM* 3956).   *(Composer)*

3963 HOOVER, Katherine. **Some have too much** (facsimile of MS at
md   NNAMC, 1976) 3 p. (score, parts).
Secular chorus. *Dn* 1′. *Da* 1976. *La* composer. *At* Edward Dyer. *Pf* choral SATB, obo, enh. *Tm Four English songs* (*WIAM* 3956).   *(Composer)*

3964 HOOVER, Katherine. **Songs of joy** (CM 7940-7944; New York:
mm   C. Fischer, 1975) 4, 5, 3, 3, 8 p. (score, parts).
Sacred choruses. *Dn* 12′. *Da* 1973. *La* publisher. *St* German carols. *Tr* composer. *Pf* choral SATB, 2 tpt, 2 tbn. *Ct Rejoice* (*WIAM* 3960), *Of a young maid* (*WIAM* 3958), *Run, run all ye shepherds* (*WIAM* 3961), *Do you hear?* (*WIAM* 3955), *Come ye shepherds* (*WIAM* 3954).   *(Composer)*

3965 HOOVER, Katherine. **Three carols** (CM 7787; New York: C.
mm   Fischer, 1972) 9 p. $.40. (score, parts).
Sacred choruses. *Dn* 9′. *Da* 1971. *La* publisher. *St* Stevens, John, ed. *Medieval carols,* Vol. IV of *Musica britannica* (1952). *Pf* solo S, choral SSA, flu. *Ct* Now make we mirthe, Have mercy of me, There is no rose.   *(Composer)*

3966 HRUBY, Dolores. **And let us all be merry** (New York:
mm   Plymouth, 1970) 8 p. $.30. (choral octavo).
Christmas carol arranged. *Dn* 3′. *At* George Wither. *Pf* choral SATB, per.   *(Composer)*

3967 HRUBY, Dolores. **Black is the color of my true love's hair**
mm   (Cincinnati: Westwood, 1969) 7 p. (choral octavo).
Folk song arranged. *Dn* 3′. *Pf* choral SSA, pno.   *(Composer)*

3968 HRUBY, Dolores. **Christ the Lord is risen** (Minneapolis:
mm   Augsburg, 1976) 7 p. $.45. (choral octavo).
Sacred chorus. *Dn* 3′. *At* composer. *Pf* choral unison, org or pno.   *(Composer)*

3969 HRUBY, Dolores. **Come and praise the Lord with joy** (St.
mm   Louis: Concordia, 1974) 7 p. $.35. (choral octavo).
Sacred chorus. *Dn* 3′. *At* composer. *Pf* choral SATB, per.   *(Composer)*

3970 HRUBY, Dolores. **For the least of my brothers** (St. Louis:
mm   Concordia, 1976) 4 p. $.35. (choral octavo).
Sacred chorus. *Dn* 2′. *At* composer. *Pf* choral AB, org or pno.   *(Composer)*

3971 HRUBY, Dolores. **Gather around the Christmas tree** (St.
mm   Louis: Concordia, 1977) 16 p. $1.50. (choral octavo).
Sacred cantata. *Dn* 20′. *At* composer (narration only). *Pf* choral SA, org or pno.   *(Composer)*

3972 HRUBY, Dolores. **He whom joyous shepherds praised** (St.
mm   Louis: Concordia, 1969) 7 p. $.25. (choral octavo).
Christmas carol arranged. *Dn* 3′. *Pf* choral SA, per including xyl.   *(Composer)*

3973 HRUBY, Dolores. **Holy Child, The** (Westbury, N.Y.: Pro Art,
mm   1972) 7 p. $.30. (choral octavo).
Sacred chorus. *Dn* 3′. *St* traditional Puerto Rican carol. *Pf* choral SATB, org or pno. Also for choral SSA, org or pno and choral SAB, org or pno (Pro Art, 1975).   *(Composer)*

3974 HRUBY, Dolores. **I lift my hands to the Lord most high. For**
mm   **voice and sacred dance** (Dallas: Choristers Guild, 1975) 11 p. $.45. (choral octavo).
Sacred chorus. *Dn* 4′. *At* composer. *Pf* choral unison, per, flu, org or pno, dancer(s).   *(Composer)*

3975 HRUBY, Dolores. **Mass. Love thy neighbor** (Boston:
mm   McLaughlin & Reilly, 1967) 11 p. (choral octavo).
Dn 15′. *Lt* English. *Pf* choral SATB, congregation, org.   *(Composer)*

3976 HRUBY, Dolores. **Mass to honor St. Elizabeth** (Boston:
mm   McLaughlin & Reilly, 1967) 12 p. (choral octavo).
Dn 15′. *Lt* English. *Pf* choral SA or TB, org.   *(Composer)*

3977 HRUBY, Dolores. **Peter Piper** (Westbury, N.Y.: Pro Art, 1969)
mm   11 p. (choral octavo).
Secular chorus. *Dn* 3′. *At* composer. *Pf* choral SSA, pno. Also for choral SATB, pno (Pro Art, 1973).   *(Composer)*

3978 HRUBY, Dolores. **Set down servant** (Cincinnati: World Library,
mm   1966) 6 p. (choral octavo).
Folk tune arranged. *Dn* 3′. *Pf* choral SA, pno.   *(Composer)*

3979 HRUBY, Dolores. **Sweet it is to praise the Lord** (Chicago:
mm   Hope, 1969) 4 p. (choral octavo).
Sacred chorus. *Dn* 2′. *At* composer. *Pf* choral SA, handbells.   *(Composer)*

3980 HRUBY, Dolores. **Three sacred songs** (St. Louis: Concordia,
mm   1973) 7 p. $.35. (choral octavo).
Sacred chorus. *Dn* 4′. *Pf* choral SA, org or pno.   *(Composer)*

3981 HRUBY, Dolores. **Your holy cross** (Chicago: G.I.A., 1974) 7 p.
mm $.40. (choral octavo).
Sacred chorus. *Dn* 3′. *At* composer. *Pf* choral SSA or TTB, org.   *(Composer)*

3982 HSU, Wen-ying. **Merciful father** (Los Angeles: composer, 1974)
mm   7 p. (choral octavo).
Sacred chorus. *Dn* 3′. *Pf* choral SSA, pno.   *(Composer)*

3983 HSU, Wen-ying. **Sound and sound** (Los Angeles: composer,
mm   1966) 27 p.
Dn 7′. *Pf* solo S, choral TTBB.   *(Composer)*

3984 HSU, Wen-ying. **Vocal series no. III** (Los Angeles: composer,
mm   1974) 24 p.
Sacred choruses. *Dn* 10′. *Da* 1974. *La* composer. *At* composer. *Pf* solo ST, choral SATB, pno. *Ct* Pray our Lord, Jesus our Saviour, Good news for Christmas.   *(Composer)*

3985 HUGHES, Sr. Martina. **Highwayman, The** (Duluth, Minn.:
mm   composer, 1941) 87 p. (score, parts).
Secular cantata. *Dn* 20′. *Da* 1940. *La* composer. *At* Alfred Noyes. *Pf* choral SATB, 3pic-3enh-3bcl-2, 4-2-3-1, tim, per, str. Also for choral SATB, tpt, tim, per including mba, electronic pno, str (Duluth, Minn.: composer, 1974).   *(Composer)*

3986 HUGHES, Sr. Martina. **Mass in honor of Christ the King**
mm   (Duluth, Minn.: composer, 1964) 15 p. (score, parts).
Dn 5′. *Da* 1964. *La* composer. *Pf* choral SSA, unison (congregation or male voices), org.   *(Composer)*

3987 HUGHES, Sr. Martina. **Psalm 26** (Duluth, Minn.: composer,
mm   1977) 14 p. $1.50. (score, parts).
Sacred chorus. *Dn* 3′. *Da* 1977. *La* composer. *Pf* choral SA or choral SATB, org.   *(Composer)*

3988 HUGHES, Sr. Martina. **Rejoice unto God** (Cincinnati: Willis
mm   Music, 1965) 8 p. (choral octavo).
Sacred chorus. *Dn* 2′. *Da* 1963. *La* composer. *Pf* choral SSA, pno.   *(Composer)*

3989 HUGHES, Sr. Martina. **Stars** (Duluth, Minn.: composer, 1972) 9
mm   p. $1. (choral octavo).
Secular chorus. *Dn* 3′. *Da* 1972. *La* composer. *At* Joyce Kilmer. *Pf* choral SAB.   *(Composer)*

3990 HUNKINS, Eusebia. **Americana. A festive chorus** (04629;
mm   New York: C. Fischer, 1962) 32 p. (choral octavo).

Secular chorus. *Dn* 9'. *Da* 1962. *La* composer. *Pf* solo ABB, choral SSATB, pno. Orchestral or band parts are available on rental from the publisher.   *(Composer)*

3991 HUNKINS, Eusebia. **Appalachian Mass** (04769; New York: C.
mm   Fischer, 1968) 14 p. (score, parts).
Sacred chorus. *Dn* 10'. *Da* 1957. *La* composer. *Pf* solo S, choral unison, hps or org, gtr or lute. Also published in a piano-vocal score (04769A; Fischer, 1968).
(Composer)

3992 HUNKINS, Eusebia. **Forest voices** (CM 7169; New York: C.
md   Fischer, 1960) 4 p. (choral octavo).
Operatic excerpt. *Dn* 2'. *Da* 1958. *La* composer. *At* composer. *St* Ojibwe songs. *Pf* choral SSA, pno for rehearsal only. *Tm Spirit owl* (*WIAM* 4810).   *(Composer)*

3993 HUNKINS, Eusebia. **What wondrous love** (CM 7112; New
md   York: C. Fischer, 1959) 5 p. (choral octavo).
Sacred chorus. *Dn* 2'. *Da* 1958. *La* composer. *At* composer. *St* Appalachian hymn. *Pf* choral SSATBB, org or pno, narrator. *Tm Wondrous love* (*WIAM* 4812).   *(Composer)*

3994 HUNKINS, Eusebia. **Why** (CM 6950; New York: C. Fischer,
md   1957) 3 p. (choral octavo).
Sacred chorus. *Dn* 2'. *Da* 1958. *La* composer. *At* composer. *Pf* choral SSA, pno. *Tm Wondrous love* (*WIAM* 4812).   *(Composer)*

3995 HYSON, Winifred. **Becoming** (facsimile of MS at NN, 1968) 26
mm   p. (score).
Secular chorus. *Dn* 8'. *La* composer. *At* Millicent Spaulding Eifler. *Pf* solo SS, choral SSAA, rec.   *(Composer)*

3996 HYSON, Winifred. **Island of content, An** (facsimile of MS at
mm   NN, 1973) 46 p. (score).
Sacred cantata. *Dn* 15'. *La* composer. *At* Robert Louis Stevenson. *St Prayers from Vailima. Pf* solo S, choral SSAATB, flu, per, org.   *(Composer)*

3997 IVEY, Jean Eichelberger. **Lord, hear my prayer** (Boston:
mm   McLaughlin & Reilly, 1966) 7 p. (choral octavo).
Sacred chorus. *Dn* 5'. *Da* 1960, rev. 1965. *La* composer. *At* composer. *Pf* choral SATB.   *(Composer)*

3998 IVEY, Jean Eichelberger. **O come bless the Lord** (Boston:
mm   McLaughlin & Reilly, 1966) 4 p. (choral octavo).
Sacred chorus. *Dn* 5'. *Da* 1960, rev. 1965. *La* composer. *Pf* choral SATB.
(Composer)

3999 JORDAN, Alice. **All things are thine** (CPO 70; New York:
mm   Composers Press, 1960) 10 p. (choral octavo).
Sacred chorus. *Dn* 4'. *Pf* choral SATB, pno for rehearsal only.   *(Composer)*

4000 JORDAN, Alice. **As Joseph was a-walking** (2766; New York:
mm   H.W. Gray, 1962) 4 p. (choral octavo).
Sacred chorus. *Dn* 2'. *Pf* choral unison, org or pno.   *(Composer)*

4001 JORDAN, Alice. **Beatitudes, The** (APM 464; Nashville:
mm   Abingdon, 1965) 6 p. (choral octavo).
Sacred chorus. *Dn* 3'. *Pf* choral SATB, org.   *(Composer)*

4002 JORDAN, Alice. **Beloved night** (9248; New York: J. Fischer,
mm   1960) 8 p. (choral octavo).
Secular chorus. *Dn* 4'. *At* Longfellow. *Pf* choral SSA, pno.   *(Composer)*

4003 JORDAN, Alice. **Choral service sentences** (S 204; Dayton:
mm   Sacred Music, 1977) 11 p. (choral octavo).
Sacred choruses. *Dn* 5'. *Pf* choral SATB, org.   *(Composer)*

4004 JORDAN, Alice. **Come and dwell with me** (4558; Nashville:
mm   Broadman, 1977) 3 p. (choral octavo).
Dn 3'. *St St. Patrick's breastplate*, adapted. *Pf* choral unison, pno.   *(Composer)*

4005 JORDAN, Alice. **God is here on every hand** (64385; New
mm   York: Belwin-Mills, 1966) 2 p. (choral octavo).
Sacred chorus. *Dn* 1'. *At* Tashunka Withaka. *St* Sioux prayer. *Pf* choral unison, org or pno.   *(Composer)*

4006 JORDAN, Alice. **God who touchest earth with beauty**
mm   (64258; New York: Belwin-Mills, 1960) 6 p. (choral octavo).
Sacred chorus. *Dn* 3'. *At* Mary S. Edgar. *Pf* choral SATB, org.   *(Composer)*

4007 JORDAN, Alice. **God's lark at morning** (3082; Chicago: H.T.
mm   FitzSimons, 1960) 4 p. (choral octavo).
Secular chorus. *Dn* 2'. *St* 13th-c. poem. *Tr* William A. Percy. *Pf* choral SSA, pno for rehearsal only.   *(Composer)*

4008 JORDAN, Alice. **In the calm night** (4546; Nashville: Broadman,
mm   1976) 5 p. (choral octavo).
Sacred chorus. *Dn* 2'. *At* Alfred Dornett. *Pf* choral SATB, org.   *(Composer)*

4009 JORDAN, Alice. **Only a manger** (44-825; New York: Belwin-
mm   Mills, 1963) 5 p. (choral octavo).
Sacred chorus. *Dn* 2'. *Pf* choral SATB, pno for rehearsal only.   *(Composer)*

4010 JORDAN, Alice. **Prayer in winter** (64231; New York: Belwin-
mm   Mills, 1958) 2 p. (choral octavo).
Sacred chorus. *Dn* 1'. *At* Anna H. Yost. *Pf* choral unison, org or pno. *(Composer)*

4011 JORDAN, Alice. **Ring, Christmas bells** (S 8872; Dayton:
mm   Sacred Music, 1973) 3 p. (choral octavo).
Sacred chorus. *Dn* 2'. *St* old German carol, adapted. *Pf* choral unison, handbells, org or pno.   *(Composer)*

4012 JORDAN, Alice. **See the land** (ADM 912; Nashville: Abingdon,
mm   1974) 6 p. $.45. (choral octavo).
Sacred chorus. *Dn* 3'. *Pf* choral SATB, org.   *(Composer)*

4013 JORDAN, Alice. **Suffer the little children** (A 459; Carol
mm   Stream, Ill.: Hope, 1973) 3 p. (choral octavo).
Sacred chorus. *Dn* 2'. *Pf* choral unison, org.   *(Composer)*

4014 KETTERING, Eunice Lea. **And above, singing angels** (60842;
mm   New York: Mills Music, 1969) 7 p. (choral octavo).
Sacred chorus. *Dn* 3'. *Da* 1966. *La* NmU. *At* Melrose Pitman. *Pf* choral SSA, org.   *(Composer)*

4015 KETTERING, Eunice Lea. **A-shining far in the East** (1347;
mm   New York: H.W. Gray, 1935) 7 p. (choral octavo).
Sacred chorus. *Dn* 3'. *Da* 1933. *La* NmU. *At* Garnet Hamrick. *Pf* choral SSAATTBB, org or pno.   *(Composer)*

4016 KETTERING, Eunice Lea. **Bells of Sunday morning [and]**
mm   **Sunday evening, The** (3531; New York: H. Flammer, 1959) 4 p. (choral octavo).
Sacred chorus. *Dn* 2'. *Da* 1954. *La* NmU. *At* Frederick Saur. *Pf* choral SSAATTBB, chimes.   *(Composer)*

4017 KETTERING, Eunice Lea. **Christ, the Christ is risen** (FEC
mm   10091; New York: Belwin-Mills, 1973) 10 p. $.35. (choral octavo).
Sacred chorus. *Dn* 3'. *Da* 1968. *La* NmU. *At* Melrose Pitman. *Pf* choral SATB, org or pno, optional 3 tpt.   *(Composer)*

4018 KETTERING, Eunice Lea. **Christmas sermon, A** (4017; New
mm   York: Chappell Music, 1955) 26 p. (choral octavo).
Sacred chorus. *Dn* 13'. *Da* 1952. *La* NmU. *At* Roark Bradford. *Pf* choral SATB, narrator.   *(Composer)*

4019 KETTERING, Eunice Lea. **Factory windows are always**
mm   **broken** (6811; Cincinnati: Willis Music, 1950) 6 p. (choral octavo).
Secular chorus. *Dn* 2'. *Da* 1942. *La* NmU. *At* Vachel Lindsay. *Pf* choral SATB.   *(Composer)*

4020 KETTERING, Eunice Lea. **Five songs to the texts of Vachel**
mm   **Lindsay** (4049/4172; Chicago: C.F. Summy, 1949) 3, 3, 2, 2, 4 p. (choral octavo).
Secular choral cycle. *Dn* 6'. *Da* 1941-42. *La* NmU. *Pf* choral SSA. *Ct* A dirge for a righteous kitten, Drying their wings, The moon's the north wind's cooky, The sun says his prayers, The old crows.   *(Composer)*

4021 KETTERING, Eunice Lea. **God of the dew** (2434; New York:
mm   H.W. Gray, 1956) 7 p. (choral octavo).
Sacred chorus. *Dn* 3'. *Da* 1951. *La* NmU. *At* Maltbie D. Babcock. *Pf* choral SATB.   *(Composer)*

4022 KETTERING, Eunice Lea. **I hear America singing** (SP 694;
mm   Chicago: Somerset, 1970) 21 p. $.60. (choral octavo).
Secular chorus. *Dn* 5'. *Da* 1968. *La* NmU. *At* Whitman. *Pf* choral SATB, pno.   *(Composer)*

4023 KETTERING, Eunice Lea. **Lamb, The** (6741; Cincinnati:
mm   Willis Music, 1950) 8 p. (choral octavo).
Secular chorus. *Dn* 3'. *Da* 1945. *La* NmU. *At* Blake. *Pf* choral SATB. *(Composer)*

4024 KETTERING, Eunice Lea. **Last song, The** (7064; Cincinnati:
mm   Willis Music, 1954) 4 p. (choral octavo).
Secular chorus. *Dn* 1'. *Da* 1951. *La* NmU. *At* Hartley Alexander. *St Manito masks. Pf* choral TTBB. *(Composer)*

4025 KETTERING, Eunice Lea. **Mysterious cat, The** (6812;
mm   Cincinnati: Willis Music, 1950) 6 p. (choral octavo).
Secular chorus. *Dn* 1'. *Da* 1942. *La* NmU. *At* Vachel Lindsay. *Pf* choral SATB. *(Composer)*

4026 KETTERING, Eunice Lea. **Psalm 86** (289; Melville, N.Y.: Mills
mm   Music, 1955) 10 p. (choral octavo).
Sacred chorus. *Dn* 2'. *Da* 1950. *La* NmU. *Pf* choral SATB. *(Composer)*

4027 KETTERING, Eunice Lea. **Silence** (A 297; New York: Associ-
mm   ated Music, 1958) 8 p. (choral octavo).
Secular chorus. *Dn* 3'. *Da* 1945. *La* NmU. *At* Laurence Henry Blackburn. *Pf* choral SATB. *(Composer)*

4028 KETTERING, Eunice Lea. **Sing unto the Lord** (ESA 1649;
mm   Cincinnati: World Library of Sacred Music, 1969) 9 p. (choral octavo).
Sacred chorus. *Dn* 3'. *Da* 1967. *La* NmU. *Pf* choral SSA, hrp or org or pno. *(Composer)*

4029 KETTERING, Eunice Lea. **Song from St. Matthew** (11534;
mm   New York: G. Schirmer, 1968) 5 p. (choral octavo).
Sacred chorus. *Dn* 3'. *Da* 1966. *La* NmU. *At* Melrose Pitman. *Pf* choral SA, org or pno. *(Composer)*

4030 KETTERING, Eunice Lea. **Spring journey** (6755; Cincinnati:
mm   Willis Music, 1950) 14 p. (choral octavo).
Secular chorus. *Dn* 3'. *Da* 1935. *La* NmU. *At* Eloir Winter Gilmore. *Pf* choral SSA, pno. *(Composer)*

4031 KETTERING, Eunice Lea. **Sun, The. I'll tell you how the
mm   sun rose** (N 2170; New York: C. Fischer, 1955) 5 p. (choral octavo).
Secular chorus. *Dn* 3'. *Da* 1951. *La* NmU. *At* Emily Dickinson. *Pf* choral SSA. *(Composer)*

4032 KETTERING, Eunice Lea. **Tennessee mountain** (3129; Chi-
mm   cago: C.F. Summy, 1950) 10 p. (choral octavo).
Secular chorus. *Dn* 2'. *Da* 1940. *La* NmU. *At* Claudia Lewis. *Pf* choral TTBB. *(Composer)*

4033 KETTERING, Eunice Lea. **Valley Forge** (621; New York:
mm   H.W. Gray, 1942) 6 p. (choral octavo).
Secular chorus. *Dn* 2'. *Da* 1941. *La* NmU. *At* Evelyn Norcross Sherrill. *Pf* choral SSAATTBB. *(Composer)*

4034 LAUFER, Beatrice. **And Thomas Jefferson said ...** (facsimile
mm   of MS at NNAMC, 1975) [100] p. (score).
Secular chorus. *Dn* 50'. *At* Jefferson. *St* Declaration of Independence. *Pf* solo Bar, choral SATB, 3pic-1-2-2, 4-3-3-1, tim, per, str. A piano-vocal score is available (facsimile of MS at NNAMC, 1975). *(Composer)*

4035 LAUFER, Beatrice. **Do you fear the wind?** (New York:
mm   Associated Music, 1948) 5 p. (choral octavo).
Secular chorus. *Dn* 4'. *Da* 1948. *At* Hamlin Garland. *Pf* choral SATB, pno. *(Composer)*

4036 LAUFER, Beatrice. **Everyone sang** (MC 212; New York:
mm   Mercury Music, 1955) 9 p. (choral octavo).
Secular chorus. *Dn* 5'. *At* Philip Sassoon. *Pf* solo S, choral SATB. *(Composer)*

4037 LAUFER, Beatrice. **He who knows not** (MC 213; New York:
mm   Mercury Music, 1955) 6 p. (choral octavo).
Secular chorus. *Dn* 3'. *Pf* choral SATB. *(Composer)*

4038 LAUFER, Beatrice. **Percussion** (Delaware Water Gap, Penn.:
mm   Shawnee, 1950) 10 p. (score, parts).
Secular chorus. *Dn* 5'. *Pf* choral SATB; per including glk, xyl; optional tim. *(Composer)*

4039 LAUFER, Beatrice. **Song of the fountain** (L 278; New York:
mm   Leeds Music, 1952) 10 p. (choral octavo).
Secular chorus. *Dn* 6'. *At* Delphine Krielsheimer. *Pf* choral SATB, pno. Commissioned by the American Assoc. for the United Nations to celebrate the Freedom Fountain. *(Composer)*

4040 LAUFER, Beatrice. **Spring thunder** (New York: Associated
mm   Music, 1948) 5 p. (choral octavo).
Secular chorus. *Dn* 3'. *At* Mark Van Doren. *Pf* choral SATB, pno. *(Composer)*

4041 LAUFER, Beatrice. **Under the pines** (New York: Associated
mm   Music, 1948) 5 p. (choral octavo).
Secular chorus. *Dn* 4'. *Da* 1948. *At* Arthur Burdinot. *Pf* choral SATB, pno. *(Composer)*

4042 LIBBEY, Dee. **Tolling bells** (51721; New York: Lawson-Gould,
mm   1973) 9 p. $.40. (choral octavo).
Sacred chorus. *Dn* 4'. *At* Q'Adrianne Rohde. *Pf* solo AB, choral SSAATTBB. *(Composer)*

4043 LIBBEY, Dee. **Wee little boy** (51686; New York: Lawson-
mm   Gould, 1973) 8 p. $.30. (choral octavo).
Secular chorus. *Dn* 4'. *At* Q'Adrianne Rohde. *Pf* solo S, choral SSA, pno for rehearsal only. *(Composer)*

4044 LOCKSHIN, Florence Levin. **Do not go gentle into that
mm   good night** (New York: Independent Music, 1959) 15 p. (score, parts).
Secular chorus. *Dn* 8'. *Da* 1959. *La* composer. *At* Dylan Thomas. *Pf* choral TTBB, flu, obo, hrn, 2 tpt, tbn, tim, per, cbs. *(Composer)*

4045 LOMON, Ruth. **Requiem** (facsimile of MS at NNAMC, 1977)
mm   72 p. (score, parts).
Dn 40'. *Da* 1977. *La* composer. *At* composer. *Lt* Latin. *Pf* solo S, choral SSAATTB, 1-0-3bcl-1, 0-2-2-1. *(Composer)*

4046 LORENZ, Ellen Jane. **America singing** (Franklin, Ohio: El-
mm   dridge, 1975) 36 p. $.75. (choral octavo).
Secular cantata. *Dn* 50'. *Da* 1970. *Pf* choral unison, or SA, or SATB, speaking choir, narrator, pno. *(Composer)*

4047 LORENZ, Ellen Jane. **Carols of Christmas** (Dayton: Lorenz,
mm   1942) 64 p. (choral octavo).
Sacred cantata. *Dn* 60'. *Da* 1941. *At* composer. *Pf* choral SATB, org or pno. *(Composer)*

4048 LORENZ, Ellen Jane. **Christmas/folk style** (Dayton: Lorenz,
mm   1968) 48 p. (choral octavo).
Sacred cantata. *Dn* 50'. *Da* 1967. *Pf* choral unison, SATB, org or pno; optional gtr, per, cbs. Published under the pseudonym, Rosemary Hadler. *(Composer)*

4049 LORENZ, Ellen Jane. **Easter/folk style** (Dayton: Lorenz,
mm   1969) 48 p. (choral octavo).
Sacred cantata. *Dn* 50'. *Da* 1968. *Pf* choral unison, SATB, org or pno; optional gtr, per, cbs. Published under the pseudonym, Rosemary Hadler. *(Composer)*

4050 LORENZ, Ellen Jane. **Echoing alleluia** (APM 773; Nashville:
mm   Abingdon, 1969) 5 p. (choral octavo).
Sacred chorus. *Dn* 3'. *Pf* choral SATB. Published under the pseudonym, Allen James. *(Composer)*

4051 LORENZ, Ellen Jane. **Festal alleluia, A** (E 21-215; Dayton:
mm   Lorenz, 1962) 14 p. (choral octavo).
Sacred chorus. *Dn* 4'. *At* John M. Neale and Isaac Watts. *Pf* choral 4S-3A-T-2B, handbells (2 octaves), org. *(Composer)*

4052 LORENZ, Ellen Jane. **Gate of Heaven, The** (APS 774;
mm   Nashville: Abingdon, 1976) 6 p. (choral octavo).
Sacred chorus. *Dn* 3'. *At* G. Tersteegen. *Pf* solo S, choral SATB, handbells (2 octaves), org. *(Composer)*

4053 LORENZ, Ellen Jane. **Look to Him and be radiant** (CMR
mm   3221; New York: Belwin-Mills, 1971) 6 p. $.30. (choral octavo).
Sacred chorus. *Dn* 3'. *Pf* choral SATB. Published under the pseudonym, Allen James. *(Composer)*

4054 LORENZ, Ellen Jane. **Love of God, The** (31014; New York: C.
mm   Fischer, 1958) 6 p. (choral octavo).

Sacred chorus. *Dn* 3'. *Pf* choral SATB, org or pno. Published under the pseudonym, Allen James. *(Composer)*

4055 LORENZ, Ellen Jane. **O thou eternal Christ** (A 386; Chicago:
mm   Hope, 1967) 5 p. (choral octavo).
Sacred chorus. *Dn* 3'. *At* Calvin Laufer. *Pf* choral unison, org or pno. Published under the pseudonym, Allen James. *(Composer)*

4056 LORENZ, Ellen Jane. **Psalms for singing. Seven tunes for**
mm   **twelve psalms** (A 115; Dallas: Choristers Guild, 1972) 14 p. $3.50.
      (choral octavo).
Sacred chorus. *Dn* 7'. *Da* 1971. *At* composer. *Pf* choral S (children), handbells, per, pno. Published under the pseudonym, Peter Jerome. *(Composer)*

4057 LORENZ, Ellen Jane. **Ring a bell of joy for the Lord**
mm   (Nashville: Broadman, 1974) 7 p. (choral octavo).
Sacred chorus. *Dn* 4'. *At* composer. *Pf* choral SATB, handbells (3 octaves). *(Composer)*

4058 LORENZ, Ellen Jane. **Sing Jehovah's praise** (Chicago: Hope,
mm   1969) 7 p. (choral octavo).
Sacred chorus. *Dn* 2'. *At* Isaac Watts. *Pf* choral SATB, org or pno; optional tpt or tbn. Published under the pseudonym, Allen James. *(Composer)*

4059 LORENZ, Ellen Jane. **Stand in awe** (L65-36; Dayton: Lorenz,
mm   1958) 4 p. (choral octavo).
Sacred chorus. *Dn* 2'. *Pf* choral SATB. *(Composer)*

4060 LORENZ, Ellen Jane. **Twelve days of Christmas, The** (APM
mm   445; Nashville: Abingdon, 1965) 9 p. (choral octavo).
Christmas carol arranged. *Dn* 4'. *Pf* choral SATB. Published under the pseudonym, Allen James. *(Composer)*

4061 MCLEAN, Priscilla. **Messages** (Austin, Tex.: composer, 1973)
mm   57 p. (score, parts).
Secular cantata. *Dn* 15'. *La* composer. *At* Whitman. *St* Leaves of grass. *Pf* solo SATB, choral SATB, 6 rec amplified, pno, per, autoharp processed through synthesizer. *(Composer)*

4062 MCNEIL, Jan Pfischner. **Sermon in stone** (New York: C.
mm   Fischer, 1975) 3 p. $5. (score, parts).
Secular chorus. *Dn* 10'. *Da* 1974. *At* composer. *Pf* choral SATB, per for 4 players, prepared pno. *(Composer)*

4063 MEACHEM, Margaret M. **Chanson d'automne** (facsimile of
mm   MS at NNAMC, 1975) 10 p. $3. (choral octavo).
Secular chorus. *Dn* 5'. *Da* 1975. *La* composer. *Pf* choral SATB, obo, per including xyl, 3 freakas. *(Composer)*

4064 MEACHEM, Margaret M. **In the beginning** (facsimile of MS at
mm   NNAMC, 1973) 48 p. (score, parts).
Sacred cantata. *Dn* 30'. *Da* 1973. *La* composer. *Pf* solo ST, choral SATB, 2-2-2-2, 2-2-2-1, tim, per, str. *(Composer)*

4065 MERRIMAN, Margarita L. **Millennium, The** (facsimile of MS
mm   at Atlantic Union Col., South Lancaster, Mass., 1977) 208 p. $60.
      (score, parts).
Oratorio. *Dn* 35'. *Da* July 1973. *La* composer. *Pf* solo STB, choral SATB, 2-2-2-2, 4-3-3-1, tim, per, hrp, str. A piano reduction is available at Atlantic Union Col. *(Composer)*

4066 MOORE, Dorothy Rudd. **In celebration** (New York: Compos-
mm   ers Facsimile Ed., 1977) 14 p. $4.95. (score, parts).
Secular chorus. *Dn* 7'. *Da* 1977. *La* composer. *Pf* solo SB, choral SATB, pno. *(Composer)*

4067 MUSGRAVE, Thea. **Cantata for a summer's day** (facsimile of
mm   MS on rental; New York: Belwin-Mills, 1954) 56 p. (score, parts).
Secular chorus. *Dn* 33'. *At* Alexander Hume and Maurice Lindsay. *Pf* choral SATB, flu, cla, string quartet, speaking part. A string orchestra may replace the string quartet. Also for solo SATB, flu, cla, string quartet, speaking part (*WIAM* 3614) and solo SATB, 1-0-1-0, 0-0-0-0, str, speaking part (*WIAM* 4467).

4068 MUSGRAVE, Thea. **Five ages of man, The** (JWC 8846;
mm   London: J. & W. Chester, 1965) 102 p.
Secular chorus. *Dn* 27'. *At* Hesiod. *Tr* Richmond Lattimore. *St* Works and days. *Pf* choral SATB, pno.

4069 MUSGRAVE, Thea. **Four madrigals** (JWC 7742; London: J. &
mm   W. Chester, 1958) 3, 3, 4, 7 p. (choral octavo).
Secular choruses. *Dn* 8'. *At* Thomas Wyatt. *Pf* choral SATB. *Ct* With serving still, Tanglid I was in love's snare, At most mischief, Hate whom ye list.

4070 MUSGRAVE, Thea. **John Cook** (19268; New York: Novello,
mm   1963) 4 p. (choral octavo).
Secular chorus. *Dn* 1'. *Pf* choral SATB.

4071 MUSGRAVE, Thea. **Make ye merry for him that is to come**
mm   (JWC 8834; London: J. & W. Chester, 1963) 8 p.
Sacred chorus. *Dn* 4'. *Pf* choral SA, unison (children), optional org.

4072 MUSGRAVE, Thea. **Memento creatoris** (JWC 8861; London:
mm   J. & W. Chester, 1967) 12 p. (choral octavo).
Secular chorus. *Dn* 4'. *Pf* choral SATB, optional org.

4073 MUSGRAVE, Thea. **Phoenix and the turtle, The** (London: J.
mm   & W. Chester, 1962) 89 p. (score, parts).
Secular chorus. *Dn* 18'. *At* Shakespeare. *Pf* choral SATB, 2pic-2enh-2bcl-2, 4-3-3-1, tim, per, hrp, str.

4074 MUSGRAVE, Thea. **Rorate coeli** (20200; New York: Novello,
mm   1973) 41 p. (choral octavo).
Sacred chorus. *Dn* 11'. *At* William Dunbar. *Pf* solo SSATB, choral SSAATTBB.

4075 MUSGRAVE, Thea. **Two Christmas carols in traditional**
mm   **style** (JWC 8865; London: J. & W. Chester, 1968) 13 p. (choral
      octavo).
Sacred choruses. *Dn* 5'. *At* Norman Nicholson. *Pf* solo S, choral SA or choral SATB, pno for rehearsal only. Also for solo S, choral SA or choral SATB, obo or cla or vln, str without cbs (facsimile of MS, parts on rental; Chester, 1968).

4076 OLIVEROS, Pauline. **Sound patterns** (Hackensack, N.J.: J.
mm   Boonin, 1964) 8 p. (choral octavo).
Secular chorus. *Dn* 5'. *Pf* choral SATB. *Rg* Extended voices, Odyssey 32160156; *20th century choral music*, Ars nova, AN 1005. *(Publisher)*

4077 OLIVEROS, Pauline. **To Valerie Solanas and Marilyn**
mm   **Monroe in recognition of their desperation** (Baltimore: Smith,
      1977) 4 p. $4. (score, parts).
Dn 30'. *Pf* may be performed by chamber group, orchestra, or chorus. Instrumentation not specified. Also listed as *WIAM* 3645, 4484. *(Publisher)*

4078 OLIVEROS, Pauline. **Willowbrook generations and reflec-**
mm   **tions** (Baltimore: Smith, 1977) 4 p. $5.50. (score, parts).
Dn 15-60'. *Pf* any group or groups of 15 or more; audience participation. Also listed as *WIAM* 3649, 4485. *(Publisher)*

4079 OWEN, Blythe. **Easter song, op. 5, no. 1** (UM 107; Miami,
md   Fla.: U. of Miami Music, 1970) 8 p. $.30. (choral octavo).
Sacred chorus. *Dn* 6'. *Da* 1942. *La* publisher. *At* George Herbert. *Pf* choral SATB, optional pno. *(Composer)*

4080 OWEN, Blythe. **Eleven choral responses, op. 33** (3202; Berrien
mm   Springs, Mich.: Hall-Orion Music, 1974) 8 p. $.30. (choral octavo).
Sacred choruses. *Dn* 22'. *Da* 1963-69. *La* publisher. *Pf* choral SATB, org. *(Composer)*

4081 OWEN, Blythe. **Go lovely rose, op. 9, no. 1** (UM 106; Miami,
md   Fla.: U. of Miami Music, 1970) 10 p. $.35. (choral octavo).
Secular chorus. *Dn* 6'. *Da* 1944. *La* publisher. *At* Edmund Waller. *Pf* choral SATB. *(Composer)*

4082 OWEN, Blythe. **Hearken unto me, op. 17, no. 4** (Northfield,
md   Ill.: Composers Press, 1959) 11 p. (choral octavo).
Sacred chorus. *Dn* 6'. *Da* 1957. *La* publisher. *Pf* choral SATB, org. *(Composer)*

4083 OWEN, Blythe. **Little Jesus came to town, The, op. 23, no. 3**
md   (MF 574; Nashville: Broadman, 1960) 6 p. (choral octavo).
Sacred chorus. *Dn* 3'. *At* Lizette W. Reese. *Pf* choral SATB, pno. *(Composer)*

4084 PARKER, Alice. **Angels, supposedly** (108; Chapel Hill, N.C.:
mm   Hinshaw Music, 1975) 7 p. $.40. (choral octavo).
Sacred chorus. *Dn* 3'. *Da* Jan. 1975. *La* composer. *At* Molly Pyle. *Pf* choral SS, pno, optional per. *(Composer)*

4085 PARKER, Alice. **Away, melancholy** (2816; Boston: E.C.
mm   Schirmer, 1973) 15 p. (choral octavo).
Secular chorus. *Dn* 8′. *Da* 1973. *La* publisher. *At* Stevie Smith. *Pf* choral SSAA
and SSA, per.   *(Composer)*

4086 PARKER, Alice. **Blessings** (51592; New York: Lawson-Gould,
mm   1971) 8 p. $.40. (choral octavo).
Sacred chorus. *Dn* 3′. *Da* 1965. *La* publisher. *Pf* choral SATB.   *(Composer)*

4087 PARKER, Alice. **Brotherly love** (2818; Boston: E.C. Schirmer,
mm   1972) 2 p. $.25. (choral octavo).
Secular chorus. *Dn* 1′. *Da* 1972. *La* publisher. *Pf* choral 5A, optional per and
gtr.   *(Composer)*

4088 PARKER, Alice. **Earth now is green** (2965; Boston: E.C.
md   Schirmer, 1972) 10 p. (choral octavo).
Sacred chorus. *Dn* 3′. *Da* 1969. *La* publisher. *Pf* choral SATB. *Tm An Easter
rejoicing* (*WIAM* 4089).   *(Composer)*

4089 PARKER, Alice. **Easter rejoicing, An** (2798; Boston: E.C.
mm   Schirmer, 1972) 76 p. (score, parts).
Sacred cantata. *Dn* 30′. *Da* 1969. *La* composer. *Pf* solo SATB, choral SATB,
per, hrp, org. *Ct* 13 sacred and secular solos and choruses. Two selections, *Earth
now is green* (*WIAM* 4088) and *Gabriel's message* (*WIAM* 4092), are published
separately.   *(Composer)*

4090 PARKER, Alice. **English Mass, An** (107; Chapel Hill, N.C.:
mm   Hinshaw Music, 1975) 4 p. (choral octavo).
Dn 5′. *Da* 1968. *La* composer. *Pf* choral SATB.   *(Composer)*

4091 PARKER, Alice. **Feast of ingathering, The** (New York: C.
mm   Fischer, 1971) 38 p. (piano-vocal score).
Sacred cantata. *Dn* 20′. *Da* 1971. *La* composer. *Pf* solo A, choral SATB, org,
optional per.   *(Composer)*

4092 PARKER, Alice. **Gabriel's message** (2832; Boston: E.C.
md   Schirmer, 1972) 10 p. (choral octavo, parts).
Sacred chorus. *Dn* 4′. *Da* 1969. *La* publisher. *Tr* J.M. Neale. *St Piae cantiones,
1582*. *Pf* solo S, choral SSA, per, pno or hrp. *Tm An Easter rejoicing* (*WIAM*
4089).   *(Composer)*

4093 PARKER, Alice. **Games** (CM 7992; New York: C. Fischer, 1975)
mm   11 p. $.45. (choral octavo).
Secular chorus. *Dn* 3′. *Da* 1975. *La* publisher. *At* composer. *Pf* choral SSA,
pno.   *(Composer)*

4094 PARKER, Alice. **Gaudete. Six Latin Christmas hymns** (fac-
mm   simile of MS on rental; Boston: E.C. Schirmer, 1973) 102 p. (score,
parts).
Sacred cantata. *Dn* 24′. *Da* 1973. *La* composer. *Pf* choral SSAATTBB, 2-2-2-2,
4-2-3-1, tim, hrp, str. Also published in a piano-vocal score (Schirmer, 1973). *Lt*
Latin, English. *Ct* Corde natus (Of the Father's love begotten); Puer nobis
(Unto us a boy is born); Dormi, Jesu (Sleep now, Jesus); Personet hodie (On
this day earth shall ring); Resonet in laudibus (Let our voices sound with joy);
Adeste, fideles (O come, all ye faithful). *Rg Nativity*, Turnabout, QTV 34647/
48.   *(Composer)*

4095 PARKER, Alice. **Grace to you and peace**, *Mennonite hymnal*
mc   (Scottdale, Penn.: Mennonite Publishing, 1969) 646. (choral octavo).
Sacred chorus. *Dn* 1′. *Da* 1969. *La* publisher. *Pf* choral 3A.   *(Composer)*

4096 PARKER, Alice. **Hellos and goodbyes** (CM 7990; New York:
mm   C. Fischer, 1976) 7 p. $.40. (choral octavo).
Secular chorus. *Dn* 2' or more. *Da* 1975. *La* publisher. *At* composer. *Pf* choral
SSAATTBB, pno. Includes 4 rounds.   *(Composer)*

4097 PARKER, Alice. **Holy Spirit, truth divine**, *Mennonite hymnal*
mc   (Scottdale, Penn.: Mennonite Publishing, 1969) 307. (choral octavo).
Sacred chorus. *Dn* 1′. *Da* 1969. *La* publisher. *Pf* choral SATB.   *(Composer)*

4098 PARKER, Alice. **I saw a stable** (2780; Boston: E.C. Schirmer,
mm   1969) 7 p. (choral octavo).
Sacred chorus. *Dn* 3′. *Da* 1969. *La* publisher. *Pf* choral SATB, per, org.
                                                             (Composer)

4099 PARKER, Alice. **In Bethlehem** (2779; Boston: E.C. Schirmer,
mm   1969) 16 p. (choral octavo).
Sacred chorus. *Dn* 3′. *Da* 1969. *La* publisher. *Pf* choral SATB, per, org.
                                                             (Composer)

4100 PARKER, Alice. **Jesus, whom every saint adores** (2970;
md   Boston: E.C. Schirmer, 1972) 3 p. (choral octavo).
Sacred chorus. *Dn* 1′. *Da* 1969. *La* publisher. *At* Isaac Watts. *Pf* choral SATB,
per. *Tm An Easter rejoicing* (*WIAM* 4089).   *(Composer)*

4101 PARKER, Alice. **Journeys: pilgrims and strangers** (facsimile
mm   of MS on rental; Chapel Hill, N.C.: Hinshaw Music, 1976) 133 p.
(score, parts).
Oratorio. *Dn* 50′. *Da* 1975. *La* composer. *St* American hymnals, 1790-1850. *Pf*
solo SB, choral SSATTBB, 3pic-3enh-3bcl-3cbn, 4-2-3-1, tim, per for 4 players,
str, optional improvising jazz band. Also published in a piano-vocal score
(Hinshaw Music, 1977).   *(Composer)*

4102 PARKER, Alice. **Melodious accord. A concert of praise**
mm   (3010; Boston: E.C. Schirmer, 1977) 83 p. (score, parts).
Sacred cantata. *Dn* 30′. *Da* 1974. *La* composer. *Pf* solo SATB, choral
SSAATTBB, brass quartet, hrp.   *(Composer)*

4103 PARKER, Alice. **Most glorious Lord of life** (2968; Boston:
md   E.C. Schirmer, 1972) 5 p. (choral octavo).
Sacred chorus. *Dn* 3′. *Da* 1969. *La* publisher. *At* Edmund Spenser. *Pf* choral
SATB. *Tm An Easter rejoicing* (*WIAM* 4089).   *(Composer)*

4104 PARKER, Alice. **Now glad of heart** (885; New York: Lawson-
mm   Gould, 1960) 12 p. (choral octavo).
Sacred chorus. *Dn* 4′. *Da* 1959. *La* publisher. *Pf* choral SATB, org.   *(Composer)*

4105 PARKER, Alice. **Of a virtuous woman**, *Songs for Sunday*
mc   (51157; New York: Lawson-Gould, 1964) I, 26-30. (choral octavo).
Sacred chorus. *Dn* 3′. *Da* 1964. *La* publisher. *Pf* choral SA, org or pno.
                                                             (Composer)

4106 PARKER, Alice. **Phonophobia** (Chapel Hill, N.C.: Hinshaw
mm   Music, 1977) 19 p. $1. (choral octavo).
Secular chorus. *Dn* 11′. *Da* Apr. 1977. *La* publisher. *Pf* choral SATB, pno or
gtr, optional per.   *(Composer)*

4107 PARKER, Alice. **Play on numbers, A** (2817; Boston: E.C.
mm   Schirmer, 1973) 20 p. $.65. (choral octavo).
Secular chorus. *Dn* 7′. *Da* 1973. *La* publisher. *Pf* choral SA, pno.   *(Composer)*

4108 PARKER, Alice. **Prayer** (51737; New York: Lawson-Gould,
mm   1973) 6 p. (choral octavo).
Secular chorus. *Dn* 4′. *Da* 1971. *La* composer. *At* Isaac Watts. *Pf* choral SATB,
SATB. 4 woodwinds or brass quartet or org may replace 2nd chorus. *(Composer)*

4109 PARKER, Alice. **Psalm 136** (51250; New York: Lawson-Gould,
mm   1966) 11 p. (choral octavo).
Sacred chorus. *Dn* 8′. *Da* 1963. *La* publisher. *Pf* solo B, choral SATB.
                                                             (Composer)

4110 PARKER, Alice. **Psalms of praise** (51385; New York: Lawson-
mm   Gould, 1966) 12 p. (choral octavo).
Sacred chorus. *Dn* 6′. *Da* 1966. *La* composer. *Pf* choral TB, per.   *(Composer)*

4111 PARKER, Alice. **Search me, O God**, *Songs for Sunday* (51157;
mc   New York: Lawson-Gould, 1964) I, 17-19. (choral octavo).
Sacred chorus. *Dn* 2′. *Da* 1964. *La* publisher. *Pf* choral SA, org or pno.
                                                             (Composer)

4112 PARKER, Alice. **Seasons and times** (2967; Boston: E.C.
md   Schirmer, 1972) 6 p. (choral octavo).
Sacred chorus. *Dn* 4′. *Da* 1969. *La* publisher. *At* Isaac Watts. *Pf* choral STB,
per, pno or hrp. *Tm An Easter rejoicing* (*WIAM* 4089).   *(Composer)*

4113 PARKER, Alice. **Sermon from the mountain, A: Martin
mm   Luther King** (facsimile of MS on rental; Boston: E.C. Schirmer,
1971) 131 p. (score, parts).
Sacred cantata. *Dn* 40′. *Da* 1969. *La* composer. *Pf* solo SATB, choral SATB,
per, gtr, str, optional org. Also published in a piano-vocal score (Schirmer,
1971).   *(Composer)*

4114 PARKER, Alice. **Seven carols** (CM 7838-7844; New York: C.
mm   Fischer, 1972) 66 p. (choral octavo).
Sacred choruses. *Dn* 18′. *Da* 1972. *La* composer. *Pf* choral SSAATTBB, org or
pno. Facsimile of MS, parts on rental from the publisher. *Ct* Good Christian
men, rejoice; God rest ye merry, gentlemen; So blest a sight; Masters in this
hall; O come, O come Emmanuel; Away in a manger; Fum, fum, fum.
                                                             (Composer)

4115 PARKER, Alice. **Shrill chanticleer** (2781; Boston: E.C.
mm Schirmer, 1969) 15 p. (choral octavo).
Sacred chorus. *Dn* 2'. *Da* 1969. *La* publisher. *Pf* choral SATB, per, org.
(Composer)

4116 PARKER, Alice. **Six hymns to Dr. Watts** (2940; Boston: E.C.
mm Schirmer, 1977) 11 p. (choral octavo).
Sacred chorus. *Dn* 6'. *Da* 1968. *La* composer. *At* Isaac Watts. *Pf* choral SATB.
(Composer)

4117 PARKER, Alice. **Small rain**, *Songs for Sunday* (51157; New
mc York: Lawson-Gould, 1964) I, 20-22. (choral octavo).
Sacred chorus. *Dn* 3'. *Da* 1964. *La* publisher. *Pf* choral SA, org or pno.
(Composer)

4118 PARKER, Alice. **Street corner spirituals** (51594; New York:
mm Lawson-Gould, 1971) 19 p. $.45. (choral octavo).
Sacred chorus. *Dn* 10'. *Da* 1966. *La* publisher. *Pf* solo B, choral SATB, tpt, per, gtr.
(Composer)

4119 PARKER, Alice. **Sunday rounds** (106; Chapel Hill, N.C.:
mm Hinshaw Music, 1975) 6 p. $.35. (choral octavo).
Sacred chorus. *Dn* 2' or more. *Da* 1975. *La* publisher. *Pf* choral SSAATBB, optional per and gtr.
(Composer)

4120 PARKER, Alice. **There and back again** (facsimile of MS on
mm rental; Chapel Hill, N.C.: Hinshaw Music, 1977) 34 p. (score, parts).
Secular chorus. *Dn* 14'. *Da* 1977. *La* publisher. *At* Katharine Pyle. *Pf* choral SATB, flu, obo, cla, bsn. Also published in a piano-vocal score (Hinshaw Music, 1977).
(Composer)

4121 PARKER, Alice. **Three circles** (CM 7805; New York: C.
mm Fischer, 1972) 16 p. $.40. (choral octavo).
Secular choruses. *Dn* 5'. *Da* 1972. *La* publisher. *Pf* choral SATB, per. *Ct* The moon always follows the sun (*Tr* C. and W. Leslaw), Sleep (*Tr* A.P.), As the world turns (*At* Jonathan Swift).
(Composer)

4122 PARKER, Alice. **True use of music, The** (Chapel Hill, N.C.:
mm Hinshaw Music, 1977) 35 p. $.75. (choral octavo).
Sacred chorus. *Dn* 5'. *Da* Jan. 1977. *La* publisher. *At* Charles Wesley. *Pf* choral SATB, pno. Facsimile of MS, parts on rental from the publisher.
(Composer)

4123 PARKER, Alice. **Wings of the morning, The**, *Songs for Sunday*
mc (51157; New York: Lawson-Gould, 1964) I, 3-6. (choral octavo).
Sacred chorus. *Dn* 2'. *Da* 1964. *La* publisher. *Pf* choral SA, org or pno.
(Composer)

4124 PAULL, Barberi. **Christmas carol, A** (New York: A. Broude,
mm 1978) 50 p. (choral octavo).
Sacred chorus. *Dn* 60'. *La* composer. *At* composer. *Pf* choral SATB, pno, narrator, optional gtr.
(Composer)

4125 PAULL, Barberi. **Ev'ry merry Christmas** (New York: A.
mm Broude, 1977) 8 p. $.75. (choral octavo).
Secular chorus. *Dn* 9'. *La* publisher. *Pf* choral SAB, pno.
(Composer)

4126 PAULL, Barberi. **Peace and joy and love** (New York: A.
mm Broude, 1977) 7 p. $.60. (choral octavo).
Secular chorus. *Dn* 9'. *La* publisher. *Pf* choral SAB, pno.
(Composer)

4127 PAULL, Barberi. **Snowmoth, The** (facsimile of MS at NNAMC,
mm 1974) 56 p. $12. (score).
Secular chorus. *Dn* 17'. *La* composer. *Pf* choral SATB; per including glk, mba, vib.
(Composer)

4128 PERRY, Julia Amanda. **Be merciful unto me, O God** (GMC
mm 1947; New York: Galaxy Music, 1953) 8 p.
Sacred chorus. *Dn* 2'. *Pf* solo SB, choral SATB, org.

4129 PERRY, Julia Amanda. **Carillon heigh-ho** (30357; New York:
mm C. Fischer, 1947) 8 p.
Secular chorus. *Dn* 2'. *Pf* choral SATB.

4130 PERRY, Julia Amanda. **Our thanks to Thee** (GMC 1860; New
mm York: Galaxy Music, 1951) 8 p.
Sacred chorus. *Dn* 2'. *Pf* solo A, choral SATB, org.

4131 PERRY, Julia Amanda. **Song of our Saviour** (GMC 1946;
mm New York: Galaxy Music, 1953) 8 p.
Sacred chorus. *Dn* 3'. *Pf* choral SATB, pno for rehearsal only.

4132 PERRY, Julia Amanda. **Ye who seek the truth** (GMC 1901;
mm New York: Galaxy Music, 1952) 7 p.
Sacred chorus. *Dn* 3'. *Pf* solo T, choral SATB, org.

4133 PREOBRAJENSKA, Vera N. **Christmas prayer** (57; Berkeley,
mm Calif.: Orthodox, 1962) 1 p. (choral octavo).
Sacred chorus. *Dn* 2'. *Pf* choral SATB.
(Composer)

4134 PREOBRAJENSKA, Vera N. **Creation, The** (161; Berkeley,
mm Calif.: Orthodox, 1970) 9 p. (choral octavo).
Sacred cantata. *Dn* 10'. *At* V.O. Smirnoff and M.I. Uspensky. *Pf* solo AAT, choral SATB.
(Composer)

4135 PREOBRAJENSKA, Vera N. **Creed, The** (131; Berkeley,
mm Calif.: Orthodox, 1969) 3 p. (choral octavo).
Sacred chorus. *Dn* 4'. *Pf* choral SATB.
(Composer)

4136 PREOBRAJENSKA, Vera N. **Easter prayer** (48; Berkeley,
mm Calif.: Orthodox, 1960) 2 p. (choral octavo).
Sacred chorus. *Dn* 3'. *Pf* choral SATB.
(Composer)

4137 PREOBRAJENSKA, Vera N. **Lord's prayer** (111; Berkeley,
mm Calif.: Orthodox, 1967) 2 p. (choral octavo).
Sacred chorus. *Dn* 2'. *Pf* choral SATB.
(Composer)

4138 PREOBRAJENSKA, Vera N. **Prayer to Mary** (91; Berkeley,
mm Calif.: Orthodox, 1965) 4 p. (choral octavo).
Sacred chorus. *Dn* 4'. *Pf* choral SATB.
(Composer)

4139 PREOBRAJENSKA, Vera N. **Prayer to the guardian angel**
mm (96; Berkeley, Calif.: Orthodox, 1966) 2 p. (choral octavo).
Sacred chorus. *Dn* 2'. *Pf* choral SATB.
(Composer)

4140 RICHTER, Marga. **Psalm 91** (Bryn Mawr, Penn.: Elkan-Vogel,
mm 1963) 7 p. (choral octavo).
Sacred chorus. *Dn* 4'. *Da* 1962. *La* composer. *Pf* choral SATB.
(Composer)

4141 RICHTER, Marga. **Seek him** (facsimile of MS on rental; New
mm York: C. Fischer, 1975) 8 p.
Sacred chorus. *Dn* 5'. *Da* 1963. *La* composer. *Pf* choral SATB.
(Composer)

4142 RICHTER, Marga. **Three songs of madness and death**
mm (facsimile of MS on rental; New York: C. Fischer, 1975) 18 p.
Secular chorus. *Dn* 6'. *Da* 1956. *La* composer. *At* John Webster. *Pf* choral SATB. *Ct* The white devil, The Devil's law-case, The Duchess of Malfi.
(Composer)

4143 RICHTER, Marion Morrey. **Sea chant for women's voices**
mm (83218; New York: H. Flammer, 1951) 7 p. (choral octavo).
Secular chorus. *Dn* 4'. *Da* 1950. *La* composer. *At* Margaret Raymond. *Pf* choral SSA, pno. Also arranged for choral SATB, pno (Scarsdale, N.Y.: composer, 1976).
(Composer)

4144 RICHTER, Marion Morrey. **Tale of a timberjack** (Scarsdale,
mm N.Y.: composer, 1959) 18 p. (score).
Dn 8'. *Da* 1959. *La* composer. *Pf* choral TTBB, pno. Also for concert band as *Timberjack overture* (*WIAM* 4507).
(Composer)

4145 SANDIFUR, Ann. **Still still** (Berkeley, Calif.: Arsciene, 1977) 18
mm p. (score, parts).
Dn 20'. *Da* 1971. *La* publisher. *At* composer. *Pf* choral SATB, flu, obo, per, electric pno, cbs.
(Composer)

4146 SILSBEE, Ann. **Diffraction** (facsimile of MS at NNAMC, 1974)
mm 25 p. $5.50. (score).
Dn 16'. *Da* June 1974. *La* composer. *At* E.E. Cummings. *St* Stinging gold. *Pf* solo S, choral SATB, flu, per for 2 players, pno.
(Composer)

4147 SILVERMAN, Faye-Ellen. **For showing truth** (New York:
mm Seesaw Music, 1972) 13 p. (score, parts).
Secular chorus. *Dn* 5'. *Da* 1972. *La* publisher. *At* Keats. *Pf* choral SSA.
(Composer)

4148 SINGER, Jeanne. **Carol of the bells** (facsimile of autograph at
mm   NNAMC, 1974) 4 p. (choral octavo).
Sacred chorus. *Dn* 3′. *La* composer. *At* composer. *Pf* choral SSA, pno.
(Composer)

4149 SINGER, Jeanne. **Composers' prayer** (facsimile of autograph at
mm   NNAMC, 1977) 11 p. (choral octavo).
Secular chorus. *Dn* 5′. *La* composer. *At* Ora Pate Stewart. *Pf* choral SSA, pno.
(Composer)

4150 SINGER, Jeanne. **For the night of Christmas** (facsimile of
mm   autograph at NNAMC, 1972) 4 p. (choral octavo).
Sacred chorus. *Dn* 4′. *La* composer. *At* Bernard Grebanier. *St The angel in the
rock. Pf* choral SSA, optional pno. *(Composer)*

4151 SINGER, Jeanne. **Madrigal** (facsimile of autograph at NNAMC,
mm   1976) 5 p. (choral octavo).
Secular chorus. *Dn* 4′. *At* anonymous, 16th c. *Pf* choral SATB. *(Composer)*

4152 SLEETH, Natalie. **Amen, so be it** (New York: C. Fischer, 1973)
mm   11 p. $.35. (choral octavo).
Sacred chorus. *Dn* 2′. *At* composer. *Pf* choral duo, org or pno, optional cbs.
(Composer)

4153 SLEETH, Natalie. **Baby, what you goin' to be?** (New York: C.
mm   Fischer, 1972) 6 p. $.30. (choral octavo).
Sacred chorus. *Dn* 3′. *At* composer. *Pf* solo or choral unison or duo, hps or org
or pno. Also for choral SATB (Fischer, 1972). *(Composer)*

4154 SLEETH, Natalie. **Blessing** (Dallas: Choristers Guild, 1974) 8 p.
mm $.45. (choral octavo).
Sacred chorus. *Dn* 3′. *At* composer. *Pf* choral unison, hps or org or pno,
optional flu. *(Composer)*

4155 SLEETH, Natalie. **Canon of praise, A** (Dallas: Choristers Guild,
mm   1969) 11 p. (choral octavo).
Sacred chorus. *Dn* 3′. *At* composer. *Pf* choral trio, org or pno, optional
handbells. *(Composer)*

4156 SLEETH, Natalie. **Carol of the fishermen** (Minneapolis: Art
mm   Masters Studio, 1971) 7 p. $.40. (choral octavo).
Sacred chorus. *Dn* 2′. *At* composer. *Pf* choral unison or duo, hps or org or pno.
Originally called *A fisherman's carol*. Also published in *I sing to rejoice God II*
(Art Masters Studio, 1971). *(Composer)*

4157 SLEETH, Natalie. **Christmas is a feeling** (Chapel Hill, N.C.:
mm   Hinshaw Music, 1975) 7 p. $.40. (choral octavo).
Secular chorus. *Dn* 2′. *At* composer. *Pf* choral unison or duo, pno, optional flu.
Also for solo S, pno, optional flu (*WIAM* 4972). *(Composer)*

4158 SLEETH, Natalie. **Down the road** (Chapel Hill, N.C.: Hinshaw
mm   Music, 1975) 10 p. $.50. (choral octavo).
Secular chorus. *Dn* 2′. *At* composer. *Pf* choral duo, pno. Also for choral SATB,
pno (Hinshaw, 1975). *(Composer)*

4159 SLEETH, Natalie. **Everywhere I go** (Dallas: Choristers Guild,
mm   1975) 9 p. $.50. (choral octavo).
Sacred chorus. *Dn* 3′. *At* composer. *Pf* choral unison or duo, hps or org or pno,
optional flu. *(Composer)*

4160 SLEETH, Natalie. **Fa la la fantasie** (New York: C. Fischer,
mm   1972) 10 p. $.35. (choral octavo).
Secular chorus. *Dn* 2′. *At* composer. *Pf* choral SATB, optional pno and cbs.
Also published in *Choral sounds*, ed. by Buryl A. Red (New York: Holt,
Rinehart & Winston, 1973). *(Composer)*

4161 SLEETH, Natalie. **Feed my lambs** (New York: C. Fischer, 1972)
mm   6 p. $.35. (choral octavo).
Sacred chorus. *Dn* 2′. *At* composer. *Pf* choral unison, 2 flu, hps or org or pno.
(Composer)

4162 SLEETH, Natalie. **For this was I born** (Nashville: Broadman,
mm   1971) 7 p. $.35. (choral octavo).
Sacred chorus. *Dn* 3′. *At* composer. *Pf* choral SA or SAB, hps or org or pno.
(Composer)

4163 SLEETH, Natalie. **Gaudeamus hodie (Let us rejoice today)**
mm   (New York: C. Fischer, 1972) 12 p. $.40. (choral octavo).

Sacred chorus. *Dn* 2′. *At* composer. *Lt* Latin, English. *Pf* choral trio with
descant, pno 4 hands, calypso instruments. *(Composer)*

4164 SLEETH, Natalie. **God of great and God of small** (New York:
mm   C. Fischer, 1973) 5 p. $.35. (choral octavo).
Sacred chorus. *Dn* 2′. *At* composer. *Pf* choral unison, hps or org or pno.
(Composer)

4165 SLEETH, Natalie. **Hallelujah day** (New York: C. Fischer, 1971)
mm   12 p. $.35. (choral octavo).
Secular chorus. *Dn* 3′. *At* composer. *Pf* choral SATB, pno. *(Composer)*

4166 SLEETH, Natalie. **Hallelujah, glory hallelujah** (Dayton:
mm   Sacred Music, 1976) 8 p. $.40. (choral octavo).
Sacred chorus. *Dn* 3′. *At* composer. *Pf* choral SA, org or pno. *(Composer)*

4167 SLEETH, Natalie. **Have a good day** (New York: C. Fischer,
mm   1974) 8 p. $.40. (choral octavo).
Secular chorus. *Dn* 2′. *At* composer. *Pf* solo S or choral unison, pno, optional
flu. *(Composer)*

4168 SLEETH, Natalie. **Isn't it reassuring?** (New York: C. Fischer,
mm   1973) 11 p. $.35. (choral octavo).
Secular chorus. *Dn* 2′. *At* composer. *Pf* choral duo, pno. *(Composer)*

4169 SLEETH, Natalie. **Jazz Gloria** (New York: C. Fischer, 1970) 12
mm   p. $.40. (choral octavo, parts).
Sacred chorus. *Dn* 3′. *At* composer. *Pf* choral SATB, 3 tpt, cbs, bongo drums,
pno, optional gtr. Also arranged for symphonic band by Eric Osterling (*WIAM*
4514). *(Composer)*

4170 SLEETH, Natalie. **Joy in the morning** (Carol Stream, Ill.: Hope,
mm   1976) 15 p. $.60. (choral octavo).
Secular chorus. *Dn* 4′. *At* composer. *Pf* choral SATB, brass quartet, optional org
or pno. *(Composer)*

4171 SLEETH, Natalie. **Jubilate Deo** (Nashville: Abingdon, 1972) 10
mm   p. $.55. (choral octavo, parts).
Sacred chorus. *Dn* 3′. *At* composer. *Pf* choral SATB (arranged in multiple
mixed choirs) brass quartet, org or pno. *(Composer)*

4172 SLEETH, Natalie. **Just another baby** (Nashville: Broadman,
mm   1972) 5 p. $.35. (choral octavo).
Sacred chorus. *Dn* 3′. *At* composer. *Pf* choral unison, hps or org or pno.
(Composer)

4173 SLEETH, Natalie. **Kingdom of the Lord, The** (Minneapolis:
mm   Art Masters Studio, 1976) 12 p. $.55. (choral octavo).
Sacred chorus. *Dn* 3′. *At* composer. *Pf* choral SA, hps or org or pno, optional
flu. *(Composer)*

4174 SLEETH, Natalie. **Little by little** (Chapel Hill, N.C.: Hinshaw
mm   Music, 1975) 11 p. $.50. (choral octavo).
Secular chorus. *Dn* 4′. *At* composer. *Pf* choral SA or TB, pno. *(Composer)*

4175 SLEETH, Natalie. **Little grey donkey** (Dallas: Choristers Guild,
mm   1970) 6 p. $.35. (choral octavo).
Sacred chorus. *Dn* 2′. *At* composer. *Pf* choral unison, hps or org or pno,
optional obo. *(Composer)*

4176 SLEETH, Natalie. **Long time ago** (Dayton: Sacred Music, 1973)
mm   8 p. $.35. (choral octavo).
Sacred chorus. *Dn* 2′. *At* composer. *Pf* choral SA, hps or org or pno. Also
published in *O come, let us sing* (Nashville: Broadman, 1974). *(Composer)*

4177 SLEETH, Natalie. **Lord, He made the earth and sky, The**
mm   (Minneapolis: Art Masters Studio, 1971) 5 p. $.35. (choral octavo).
Sacred chorus. *Dn* 2′. *At* composer. *Pf* choral unison or duo, hps or org or pno.
Also published in *I sing to rejoice God II* (Art Masters Studio, 1971). *(Composer)*

4178 SLEETH, Natalie. **Lord Jesus, be near me** (New York: C.
mm   Fischer, 1975) 7 p. $.40. (choral octavo).
Sacred chorus. *Dn* 2′. *At* composer. *Pf* solo S or choral unison, hps or org or
pno, optional cla or vcl. *(Composer)*

4179 SLEETH, Natalie. **Lord, make us worthy** (Minneapolis: Art
mm   Masters Studio, 1975) 8 p. $.40. (choral octavo).
Sacred chorus. *Dn* 3′. *At* composer. *Pf* choral SA, hps or org or pno. *(Composer)*

4180 SLEETH, Natalie. **Love is a song** (Chapel Hill, N.C.: Hinshaw
mm   Music, 1976) 19 p. $.60. (choral octavo).
Secular chorus. *Dn* 3′. *At* composer. *Pf* choral trio, per, pno 4 hands, cbs,
optional tpt.   *(Composer)*

4181 SLEETH, Natalie. **Love one another** (Carol Stream, Ill.: Hope,
mm   1975) 6 p. $.35. (choral octavo).
Sacred chorus. *Dn* 2′. *At* composer. *Pf* choral duo, pno. Also published in
Exodus song book (Hope, 1976).   *(Composer)*

4182 SLEETH, Natalie. **Noël, noël, a boy is born** (Minneapolis: Art
mm   Masters Studio, 1973) 9 p. $.45. (choral octavo).
Sacred chorus. *Dn* 2′. *At* composer. *Pf* choral unison or duo, hps or org or pno,
optional handbells.   *(Composer)*

4183 SLEETH, Natalie. **On this day is born a savior**, *Christmas. An*
mc   *American annual of Christmas literature and art* (Minneapolis:
Augsburg, 1976) unpaged. (score).
Sacred chorus. *Dn* 2′. *At* composer. *Lt* Latin, English. *Pf* solo S or duet, or
choral unison or duo.   *(Composer)*

4184 SLEETH, Natalie. **Praise the Lord** (Chapel Hill, N.C.: Hinshaw
mc   Music, 1976) 4 p. $.40. (choral octavo).
Sacred chorus. *Dn* 2′. *At* composer. *Pf* choral unison or duo, hps or org or pno.
Ta Sunday songbook (WIAM 4187).   *(Composer)*

4185 SLEETH, Natalie. **Some day soon** (New York: C. Fischer, 1974)
mm   14 p. $.40. (choral octavo).
Secular chorus. *Dn* 3′. *At* composer. *Pf* choral SATB, pno.   *(Composer)*

4186 SLEETH, Natalie. **Spread joy** (New York: C. Fischer, 1972) 9 p.
mm $.40. (choral octavo).
Secular chorus. *Dn* 2′. *At* composer. *Pf* choral trio, pno, optional tpt.   *(Composer)*

4187 SLEETH, Natalie. **Sunday songbook** (Chapel Hill, N.C.: Hin-
ma   shaw Music, 1976) 32 p. $2.50. (choral octavo).
Sacred chorus. *Dn* 24′. *At* composer. *Pf* choral unison and duo, org or pno. *Ct*
Praise the Lord (WIAM 4184), That's good, For these blessings, Light one
candle, Sing nöel, Lullaby, Part of the plan, *This is the day* (WIAM 4189), You
and I, Children of the Lord, The Holy Book, Go now in peace.   *(Composer)*

4188 SLEETH, Natalie. **They all lived long ago** (Nashville: Broad-
mm   man, 1971) 5 p. $.35. (choral octavo).
Sacred chorus. *Dn* 2′. *At* composer. *Pf* choral unison, hps or org or pno. Flu and
gtr may be used in place of a keyboard instrument.   *(Composer)*

4189 SLEETH, Natalie. **This is the day** (Chapel Hill, N.C.: Hinshaw
mc   Music, 1977) 3 p. $.40. (choral octavo).
Sacred chorus. *Dn* 1′. *At* composer. *Pf* choral unison or duo, hps or org or pno.
Ta Sunday songbook (WIAM 4187).   *(Composer)*

4190 SLEETH, Natalie. **This land of ours**. Arr. by John CACAVAS
mm   (New York: C. Fischer, 1975) 21 p. $3. (score, parts).
Dn 4′. *At* composer. *Pf* choral SATB, 2pic-2-6-2-4sax, 4-2-3-1-3crn-bar, tim,
per, cbs. Originally for choral duo or SATB, per, pno 4 hands, optional 2 tpt
(WIAM 4191).   *(Composer)*

4191 SLEETH, Natalie. **This land of ours** (New York: C. Fischer,
mm   1975) 16 p. $.50. (choral octavo).
Secular chorus. *Dn* 3′. *At* composer. *Pf* choral duo or SATB, per, pno 4 hands,
optional 2 tpt. Also arranged for choral SATB, symphonic band (WIAM 4190).
    (Composer)

4192 SLEETH, Natalie. **Thy church, O God** (Nashville: Broadman,
mm   1970) 6 p. $.35. (choral octavo).
Sacred chorus. *Dn* 3′. *At* composer. *Pf* choral unison with descant, hps or org or
pno.   *(Composer)*

4193 SLEETH, Natalie. **Unto every nation tell**, *Altogether joyfully*
mc   *sing*. Ed by Roberta BITGOOD (Dallas: Choristers Guild, 1971) 37-
38. (choral octavo).
Sacred chorus. *Dn* 1′. *Pf* choral duo.   *(Composer)*

4194 SLEETH, Natalie. **We had a share** (Minneapolis: Art Masters
mm   Studio, 1973) 8 p. $.40. (choral octavo).
Sacred chorus. *Dn* 3′. *At* composer. *Pf* choral SA, hps or org or pno. *(Composer)*

4195 SLEETH, Natalie. **Weekday songbook** (Chapel Hill, N.C.:
ma   Hinshaw Music, 1977) 58 p. $2.95. (choral octavo).
Secular choruses. *Dn* 33′. *At* composer. *Pf* choral unison and duo, pno. *Ct* A
round of greeting, Sharing it with me, Here's to America, Try again, You never
stop learning, Keeping Xmas, The "Winter's a drag" rag, A Valentine wish,
One day at a time, Let's make music, Two roads, We're on our way.   *(Composer)*

4196 SLEETH, Natalie. **Were you there on that Christmas night?**
mm   (Carol Stream, Ill.: Hope, 1976) 6 p. $.35. (choral octavo).
Sacred chorus. *Dn* 3′. *At* composer. *Pf* choral duo, org or pno.   *(Composer)*

4197 SLEETH, Natalie. **What would we do without music?** (New
mm   York: C. Fischer, 1974) 10 p. $.35. (choral octavo).
Secular chorus. *Dn* 3′. *At* composer. *Pf* choral duo, pno. Also for choral SATB,
pno (Fischer, 1974).   *(Composer)*

4198 SMITH, Julia. **Enrich your life with music** (MM 112; New
mm   York: Mowbray Music, 1969) 11 p. (choral octavo).
Secular chorus. *Dn* 3′. *Da* Mar. 1969. *At* Kathleen Lemmon. *Pf* choral SSAA,
pno.   *(Composer)*

4199 SMITH, Julia. **Invocation** (MM 107; New York: Mowbray
mm   Music, 1968) 7 p. (choral octavo).
Sacred chorus. *Dn* 2′. *Da* 28 Feb. 1967. *At* composer. *Pf* choral SSA, pno.
Adopted by the board of directors of the National Federation of Music Clubs
as that organization's official invocation, fall 1967 session in St. Louis.
    (Composer)

4200 SMITH, Julia. **Our heritage. For festival occasions** (MM 125;
mm   New York: Mowbray Music, 1969) 23 p. (choral octavo).
Secular chorus. *Dn* 10′. *Da* fall 1956. *At* Arthur M. Sampley. *St Of the fleet and*
strong. *Pf* solo S, choral SSAATB, pno. Also arranged for solo S, choral
SSAATB, symphonic band; solo S, choral SSAATB, small orchestra; and solo S,
choral SSAATB, large orchestra (facsimiles of MSS, parts on rental; New York:
T. Presser, 1969).   *(Composer)*

4201 SMITH, La Donna. **Amerigreen** (12; Tuscaloosa, Ala.: Trans-
mm   museq, 1976) 12 p. $10. (score, parts).
Secular chorus. *Dn* 9′. *Da* 1976. *La* composer. *Pf* choral 3S-3A-3T-3B, 3-3-
3bcl-0, 3-3-3-3, per, str, 4 lawn mowers amplified. *Rg* Transmuseq, 2002.
    (Composer)

4202 SMITH, La Donna. **Amplified Jude** (28; Tuscaloosa, Ala.:
mm   Transmuseq, 1976) 28 p. $20. (score).
Sacred chorus. *Dn* 20′. *Da* 1976. *Pf* choral SATB, flu, obo, cla, tbn, per, pno.
    (Composer)

4203 SPENCER, Williametta. **At the round earth's imagined**
mm   **corners** (6; Delaware Water Gap, Penn.: Shawnee, 1968) 8 p.
(choral octavo).
Secular chorus. *Dn* 3′. *Da* 1968. *La* composer. *At* Donne. *Pf* choral SATB.
    (Composer)

4204 SPENCER, Williametta. **Death be not proud** (Delaware Water
mm   Gap, Penn.: Shawnee, 1971) 8 p. $.30. (choral octavo).
Secular chorus. *Dn* 3′. *Da* 1970. *La* composer. *Pf* choral SATB. *Rg Spectrum*.
The great American choral sound, Omnisound, N 1009.   *(Composer)*

4205 SPENCER, Williametta. **Four madrigals to poems of James**
mm   **Joyce** (MF 315; Marquette, Mich.: M. Foster Music, 1970) 16 p.
$.55. (choral octavo).
Secular chorus. *Dn* 10′. *Da* 1959. *La* composer. *Pf* choral SATB. *Ct* O cool is
the valley; Lean out of the window, golden hair; Rain has fallen; Who goes
amid the greenwood.   *(Composer)*

4206 SPENCER, Williametta. **Give me the splendid silent sun** (MF
mm   337; Champaign, Ill.: M. Foster Music, 1976) 8 p. $.45. (choral
octavo).
Secular chorus. *Dn* 2′. *Da* 1970. *La* composer. *Pf* choral SATB.   *(Composer)*

4207 SPENCER, Williametta. **Missa brevis** (MF 140; Champaign,
mm   Ill.: M. Foster Music, 1974) 34 p. $2.50. (choral octavo).
Sacred chorus. *Dn* 12′. *Da* 1972. *La* composer. *Pf* choral SATB.   *(Composer)*

4208 SPENCER, Williametta. **Mystic trumpeter, The** (10; Ana-
mm   heim, Calif.: National Music, 1969) 10 p. (choral octavo).
Secular chorus. *Dn* 3′. *Da* 1969. *La* composer. *At* Whitman. *Pf* choral SATB.
    (Composer)

4209 SPENCER, Williametta. **Nova, nova, Ave fit ex Eva** (9;
mm   Anaheim, Calif.: National Music, 1969) 9 p. (choral octavo).
Sacred chorus. *Dn* 3'. *Da* 1968. *La* composer. *Lt* English with Latin refrain. *Pf*
choral SATB.   *(Composer)*

4210 SPENCER, Williametta. **There is no rose of such virtue** (A
mm   601; New York: Associated Music, 1968) 6 p. (choral octavo).
Sacred chorus. *Dn* 2'. *Da* 1968. *La* composer. *Pf* choral SATB. Also published
in *Te Deum laudamus* (A 665; Associated Music, 1971).   *(Composer)*

4211 STEWART, Ora Pate. **Battle line of home, The** (Provo, Utah:
mm   Fernwood, 1966) 7 p. (choral octavo).
Secular chorus. *Dn* 3'. *At* Bertha A. Kleinman. *Pf* choral SSA, pno.   *(Composer)*

4212 STEWART, Ora Pate. **Claim thou my heart** (Provo, Utah:
mm   Fernwood, 1965) 6 p. (choral octavo).
Secular chorus. *Dn* 3'. *At* composer. *Pf* choral SSA, pno.   *(Composer)*

4213 STEWART, Ora Pate. **Crossing the bar** (Provo, Utah: Fern-
mm   wood, 1964) 11 p. (choral octavo).
Secular chorus. *Dn* 2'. *At* Tennyson. *Pf* choral SSA, pno, optional org. *Rg*
Crossing the bar, Pre-View Records, 1.   *(Composer)*

4214 STEWART, Ora Pate. **Golden promise** (Provo, Utah: Fern-
mm   wood, 1968) 8 p. (choral octavo).
Secular chorus. *Dn* 3'. *At* composer. *Pf* choral SSA, pno. *Rg To a child/Golden*
promise, Pre-View Records, 2.   *(Composer)*

4215 STEWART, Ora Pate. **I cried when I sang of the babes in the**
mm   **woods** (Provo, Utah: Fernwood, 1967) 5 p. (choral octavo).
Secular chorus. *Dn* 3'. *At* composer. *Pf* choral SSA, pno.   *(Composer)*

4216 STEWART, Ora Pate. **Jamie's Christmas** (Provo, Utah: Fern-
mm   wood, 1977) 11 p. $1. (choral octavo).
Secular chorus. *Dn* 3'. *At* composer. *Pf* choral SSA, pno. *Rg* Medallion Records,
KM-1421.   *(Composer)*

4217 STEWART, Ora Pate. **Likewise** (Provo, Utah: Fernwood, 1974)
mm   16 p. $1. (choral octavo).
Secular chorus. *Dn* 4'. *At* composer. *Pf* choral SSA, pno. *Rg Country time-*
U.S.A., Pre-View Records, 17.   *(Composer)*

4218 STEWART, Ora Pate. **Mother-song** (Provo, Utah: Fernwood,
mm   1973) 13 p. $.75. (choral octavo).
Secular chorus. *Dn* 4'. *At* composer. *Pf* choral SSA, pno. *Rg Country time-*
U.S.A., Pre-View Records, 3.   *(Composer)*

4219 STEWART, Ora Pate. **Pebble Beach** (Provo, Utah: Fernwood,
mm   1973) 12 p. $.75. (choral octavo).
Secular chorus. *Dn* 4'. *At* composer. *Pf* choral SSA, pno. *Rg Country time-*
U.S.A., Pre-View Records, 6.   *(Composer)*

4220 STEWART, Ora Pate. **This is the land** (Provo, Utah: Fernwood,
mm   1974) 24 p. $1. (score, parts).
Secular chorus. *Dn* 8'. *At* composer. *Pf* choral SATB, pno, optional brass and
str.   *(Composer)*

4221 STEWART, Ora Pate. **To a child** (Provo, Utah: Fernwood,
mm   1964) 1 p. (choral octavo).
Secular chorus. *Dn* 3'. *At* composer. *Pf* choral SSA, pno, optional vln and vla.
Also for solo A, pno (*WIAM* 4976). *Rg To a child*, Kennard, 23041.
    (Composer)

4222 STEWART, Ora Pate. **Tree stood tall, A** (Provo, Utah:
mm   Fernwood, 1967) 6 p. (choral octavo).
Secular chorus. *Dn* 2'. *At* composer. *Pf* choral SSA, pno. *Rg A tree stood tall/*
Crossing the bar, Pre-View Records, 2.   *(Composer)*

4223 STEWART, Ora Pate. **What was that song?** (Provo, Utah:
mm   Fernwood, 1969) 3 p. (choral octavo).
Secular chorus. *Dn* 2'. *At* composer. *Pf* choral SATB, pno.   *(Composer)*

4224 STILMAN, Julia. **Barcarola. Cantata no. 3** (New York:
mm   Composers Facsimile Ed., 1977) 57 p. $21.35. (score, parts).
Secular cantata. *Dn* 14'. *Da* 1973. *La* composer. *At* Pablo Neruda. *Lt* Spanish.
St Residence on the earth. Pf solo SSA, choral 3S-3A-3T-3B, 3 flu, cla, tim, per
for 3 players including cel, 3 vla, 3 vcl, 3 cbs.   *(Composer)*

4225 STILMAN, Julia. **Cantares. Cantata no. 2: Cantares de al**
mm   **madre joven [Songs of the young mother]** (New York: Com-
    posers Facsimile Ed., 1977) 35 p. $12.15. (score, parts).
Secular cantata. *Dn* 12'. *Da* 1963. *La* composer. *At* Rabindranath Tagore. *St*
Gitanjali. Lt Spanish. *Pf* solo S, choral 3S-3A, flu, tim, per for 2 players, gtr, vln,
vla, vcl.   *(Composer)*

4226 STILMAN, Julia. **Magic rituals of the golden dawn. Cantata**
mm   **no. 4** (New York: Composers Facsimile Ed., 1977) 31 p. $13. (score,
    parts).
Secular cantata. *Dn* 11'. *Da* 1975. *La* composer. *At* Yeats. *Pf* choral 4S-4A-4T-
4B, 4pic-0-4bcl-0, 2-0-0-0, tim, per for 3 players including cel, pno, harmonium,
hrp, str.   *(Composer)*

4227 SWISHER, Gloria Wilson. **God be merciful unto us** (facsimile
mm   of MS at NNAMC, 1977) 4 p. (choral octavo).
Sacred chorus. *Dn* 3'. *Da* 1963. *La* composer. *Pf* choral SAATB.   *(Composer)*

4228 SWISHER, Gloria Wilson. **God is gone up with a merry**
mm   **noise** (N 3590; New York: C. Fischer, 1961) 9 p. (choral octavo).
Sacred chorus. *Dn* 3'. *Da* 1961. *Pf* choral SAATB, org or pno.   *(Composer)*

4229 SWISHER, Gloria Wilson. **Two faces of love** (facsimile of MS
mm   at NNAMC, 1977) 17 p. (choral octavo).
Secular choruses. *Dn* 6'. *Da* 1972. *La* composer. *At* Shakespeare. *Pf* choral
SSAATB, pno. *Ct* Shall I compare thee?, O mistress mine.   *(Composer)*

4230 TALMA, Louise. **Carmina Mariana** (New York: composer,
mm   1963) 9 p. (score).
Sacred choruses. *Dn* 6'. *Da* 1963. *La* composer. *Lt* Latin. *Pf* choral SS, org. *Ct*
Ave Maria, Regina caeli, Salve Regina. Also for choral SS, 0-0-0-0, 0-2-2-0, org,
str (composer, 1966); and for solo SS, pno (*WIAM* 4981).   *(Composer)*

4231 TALMA, Louise. **Celebration** (66749; New York: C.F. Peters,
mm   1978) 61 p. (score, parts).
Sacred chorus. *Dn* 12'. *Pf* choral SSA, 2pic-1-1-1, 2-1-0-0, per, pno, str. Also
published in a piano-vocal score (Peters, 1978).   *(Composer)*

4232 TALMA, Louise. **Divine flame, The** (New York: composer,
mm   1948) 275 p. (score).
Oratorio. *Dn* 70'. *Pf* solo M, Bar, choral SATB, 3pic-2-2-2cbn, 4-3-3-1, tim, per,
pno, str. A piano-vocal score is available from the composer.   *(Composer)*

4233 TALMA, Louise. **Holy sonnets** (facsimile of MS at DLC, NN,
mm   1954) 24 p. (choral octavo).
Secular chorus. *Dn* 20'. *At* Donne. *Pf* choral SATB. *Ct* La corona, Annunciation, Nativitie, Temple, Crucifying, Resurrection, Ascension. *Rg* Composers
Recordings, CRI SD 187.   *(Composer)*

4234 TALMA, Louise. **Leaden echo and the golden echo, The**
mm   (New York: composer, 1951) 21 p.
Secular chorus. *Dn* 14'. *At* Gerard Manley Hopkins. *Pf* solo S, choral
SSAATTBB, pno.   *(Composer)*

4235 TALMA, Louise. **Time to remember, A** (facsimile of MS at NN,
mm   1968) 79 p. (score).
Dn 21'. *Pf* choral SSAATTBB, speaking chorus, 1-1-2-2, 0-2-2-1, tim, per, pno,
org, str.

4236 TALMA, Louise. **Voices of peace** (New York: composer, 1973)
mm   44 p. (choral octavo).
Sacred chorus. *Dn* 21'. *At* St. Francis of Assisi, Gerard Manley Hopkins. *Pf*
choral SATB, str.   *(Composer)*

4237 THEMMEN, Ivana Marburger. **Requiem for four solo**
mm   **voices, chorus, and orchestra** (facsimile of MS at NNAMC,
    1973) 247 p. (score, parts).
Dn 60'. *Da* 1973. *Pf* solo SATB, choral SSATTB, 3pic-3enh-4bcl-3cbn, 4-3-3-1,
tim, per, hrp, pno, str. Also for solo SATB, choral SSATTB, 2pic-2enh-2bcl-2,
1-2-1-1, tim, per, hps, pno (facsimile of MS at NNAMC). A piano-vocal score is
available (facsimile of MS at NNAMC).   *(Composer)*

4238 VAN DE VATE, Nancy. **American essay, An** (facsimile of MS
mm   at NNAMC, 1977) 119 p. (score, parts).
Secular choral cycle. *Dn* 30'. *Da* 1972. *La* composer. *Pf* solo S, choral SATB,
tim, per, pno. *Ct* City of ships; Long, too long, O land; Patroling Barnegat; To
the East and to the West; The sobbing of the bells.   *(Composer)*

4239 VAN DE VATE, Nancy. **How fares the night?** (Buffalo:
mm   Montgomery Music, 1977) 7 p. $.50. (choral octavo).
Secular chorus. *Dn* 4'. *Da* 1959. *La* composer. *Tr* Mimi Tsoi from Chinese,
adapted by composer. *Pf* choral SSA, pno.   *(Composer)*

4240 VAN DE VATE, Nancy. **Pond, The** (facsimile of MS at
mm   NNAMC, 1977) 11 p. (choral octavo).
Secular chorus. *Dn* 4'. *Da* 1970. *La* composer. *At* Annette von Droste-Hulshoff.
Tr Herman Salinger. *Pf* choral SATB.   *(Composer)*

4241 WALDO, Elisabeth. **Misa de la raza [Mass of the New
mm   World]** (Northridge, Calif.: Mundoamericas Music, 1976) 67 p. $6.
(score, parts).
Dn 24'. *Da* 1976. *La* composer. *Lt* Spanish. *Pf* solo SSAATTBB, choral
SSAATTBB, flu, per including mba, pno, hps, gtr, str.   *(Composer)*

4242 WARREN, Elinor Remick. **Abram in Egypt** (facsimile of MS
mm   on rental; New York: Belwin-Mills, 1961) 94 p. (score, parts).
Sacred chorus. *Dn* 23'. *Da* 1960. *La* publisher. *St* The dead sea scrolls. *Pf* solo
Bar; choral SATB; 3pic-3enh-2-2; 4-2-3-1; tim; per including cel, xyl; hrp; str.
Also published in a piano-vocal score (Belwin-Mills, 1961). *Rg* Composers
Recordings, CRI 172.   *(Composer)*

4243 WARREN, Elinor Remick. **From this summer garden** (N
mm   5247; New York: C. Fischer, 1970) 6 p. $.25. (choral octavo).
Secular chorus. *Dn* 3'. *Da* 1969. *La* composer. *At* Paula Romay. *Pf* choral SSA,
pno.   *(Composer)*

4244 WARREN, Elinor Remick. **Good morning, America!** (facsimm   mile of MS on rental; New York: C. Fischer, 1976) 53 p. (score,
parts).
Secular chorus. *Dn* 16'. *Da* 1976. *La* composer. *At* Carl Sandburg. *Pf* choral
SATB; 3pic-3enh-2-2; 4-2-3-1; tim; per including cel, glk, xyl; pno; str;
narrator. Also published for reduced orchestra (2-2-2-2, 2-2-2-2) and in a
piano-vocal score (Fischer, 1976). *Rg* publisher.   *(Composer)*

4245 WARREN, Elinor Remick. **Harp weaver, The** (facsimile of
mm   MS on rental; New York: Belwin-Mills, 1933) 79 p. (score, parts).
Secular cantata. *Dn* 10'. *Da* 1933. *La* publisher. *At* Edna St. Vincent Millay. *Pf*
solo Bar, choral SSA, 3pic-3enh-2-2, 4-2-3-1, tim, per, hrp, str. Also published in
a piano-vocal score (Belwin-Mills, 1933).   *(Composer)*

4246 WARREN, Elinor Remick. **Hymn of the city** (facsimile of MS
mm   on rental; New York: C. Fischer, 1970) 19 p. (score, parts).
Secular chorus. *Dn* 5'. *Da* 1969. *La* composer. *At* William Cullen Bryant. *Pf*
choral SATB, 1-1-2-1, 2-1-1-0, tim, str. Also published in a piano-vocal score (N
5248; Fischer, 1970).   *(Composer)*

4247 WARREN, Elinor Remick. **Legend of King Arthur, The**
mm   (facsimile of MS on rental; New York: Belwin-Mills, 1974) 245 p.
(score, parts).
Secular cantata. *Dn* 60'. *Da* 1974. *La* publisher. *At* Tennyson. *St* "Morte
d'Arthur" from *Idylls of the king*. *Pf* solo TBar, choral SATB, 3pic-3enh-3bcl-2,
4-3-3-1, tim, per including cel, hrp, str, optional org. Also published in a piano-
vocal score (Belwin-Mills, 1974).   *(Composer)*

4248 WARREN, Elinor Remick. **Little choral suite** (N 5619; New
mm   York: C. Fischer, 1973) 14 p. $.35. (choral octavo).
Secular choruses. *Dn* 10'. *Da* 1972. *La* composer. *Pf* choral SSA, pno. *Ct* Rain
slippers, Sleep walks over the hill (*At* Rowena Bastin Bennet), Little song of life
(*At* Lizette Woodworth Reese).   *(Composer)*

4249 WARREN, Elinor Remick. **More things are wrought by
md   prayer** (New York: H.W. Gray, 1939) 5 p. (choral octavo).
Sacred chorus. *Dn* 3'. *At* Tennyson. *St* "Morte d'Arthur" from *Idylls of the
king*. *Pf* choral SATB. *Tm* The legend of King Arthur (*WIAM* 4247). Also for
solo S or M, org or pno (*WIAM* 4999).   *(Composer)*

4250 WARREN, Elinor Remick. **Night rider** (51878; New York:
mm   Lawson-Gould, 1975) 9 p. $.45. (choral octavo).
Secular chorus. *Dn* 3'. *Da* 1974. *La* composer. *At* Robert Louis Stevenson. *Pf*
choral SATB, pno.   *(Composer)*

4251 WARREN, Elinor Remick. **Requiem** (facsimile of MS on
mm   rental; New York: Lawson-Gould, 1966) 136 p. (score, parts).
Dn 53'. *Da* 1966. *La* composer. *Tr* composer. *Lt* Latin, English. *Pf* solo SBar;
choral SATB; 3pic-3enh-2-2; 4-2-3-1; tim; per including cel, glk, xyl; hrp; str.
Also published in a piano-vocal score (Lawson-Gould, 1966). *(Composer)*

4252 WARREN, Elinor Remick. **Sanctus** (facsimile of MS on rental;
md   New York: Lawson-Gould, 1967) 13 p. (score, parts).
Sacred chorus. *Dn* 9'. *La* composer. *Pf* solo SBar, choral SATB, tim, org or pno,
str. *Tm* Requiem (*WIAM* 4251). Also published in a piano-vocal score (Lawson-
Gould, 1965).   *(Composer)*

4253 WARREN, Elinor Remick. **To my native land** (facsimile of MS
mm   on rental; Boston: E.C. Schirmer, 1942) 15 p. (score, parts).
Secular chorus. *Dn* 4'. *Da* 1942. *La* composer. *At* Longfellow. *Pf* choral SATB,
2-2-2-2, 3-2-3-0, tim, per, hrp, str. Also published in a piano-vocal score
(Schirmer, 1942).   *(Composer)*

4254 WARREN, Elinor Remick. **Transcontinental** (facsimile of MS
mm   on rental; New York: T. Presser, 1958) 64 p. (score, parts).
Secular chorus. *Dn* 12'. *Da* 1958. *La* publisher. *At* Aloysius Michael Sullivan.
Pf solo Bar, choral SATB, 3pic-1-2-1, 2-2-2-0, tim, per, pno, str. Also published
in a piano-vocal score (Presser, 1958).   *(Composer)*

4255 WARREN, Elinor Remick. **Windy weather** (1315; Boston: E.C.
mm   Schirmer, 1942) 11 p. (choral octavo).
Secular chorus. *Dn* 2'. *Da* 1942. *La* publisher. *At* James Stephens. *Pf* choral
SSA, pno.   *(Composer)*

4256 WEAVER, Mary. **All weary men** (New York: Galaxy Music,
mm   1949) 6 p. (choral octavo).
Sacred chorus. *Dn* 5'. *Da* 1948. *La* MoKU. *At* composer. *Pf* choral SATB, org.
                                                            (Composer)

4257 WEAVER, Mary. **Confess Jehovah** (New York: Galaxy Music,
mm   1951) 5 p. (choral octavo).
Sacred chorus. *Dn* 5'. *Da* 1950. *La* MoKU. *At* composer. *Pf* choral SATB, org.
                                                            (Composer)

4258 WEAVER, Mary. **Enchanted islands** (St. Louis: G. Scholin,
mm   1952) 6 p. (choral octavo).
Secular chorus. *Dn* 5'. *Da* 1951. *La* MoKU. *At* composer. *Pf* choral SSA, org or
pno.   *(Composer)*

4259 WEAVER, Mary. **God's love enfolds** (New York: Belwin, 1952)
mm   5 p. (choral octavo).
Sacred chorus. *Dn* 5'. *Da* 1952. *La* MoKU. *At* composer. *Pf* choral SATB, org.
                                                            (Composer)

4260 WEAVER, Mary. **Hail, Jesu bambino** (Delaware Water Gap,
mm   Penn.: Shawnee, 1967) 6 p. (choral octavo).
Sacred chorus. *Dn* 5'. *Da* 1964. *La* MoKU. *At* composer. *Pf* choral SATB, org.
                                                            (Composer)

4261 WEAVER, Mary. **Like doves descending** (New York: Galaxy
mm   Music, 1952) 8 p. (choral octavo).
Sacred chorus. *Dn* 5'. *Da* 1950. *La* MoKU. *At* composer. *Pf* choral SATB, org.
                                                            (Composer)

4262 WEAVER, Mary. **Like the young sheep** (New York: Galaxy
mm   Music, 1950) 7 p. (choral octavo).
Sacred chorus. *Dn* 5'. *Da* 1949. *La* MoKU. *At* composer. *Pf* choral SATB, org.
                                                            (Composer)

4263 WEAVER, Mary. **New Mexican lullaby** (New York: Belwin,
mm   1953) 6 p. (choral octavo).
Sacred chorus. *Dn* 5'. *Da* 1952. *La* MoKU. *At* composer. *Pf* choral SSA, org or
pno.   *(Composer)*

4264 WEAVER, Mary. **O Holy Child** (St. Louis: G.A. Scholin, 1952)
mm   5 p. (choral octavo).
Sacred chorus. *Dn* 4'. *Da* 1950. *La* MoKU. *At* composer. *Pf* choral SSA, org or
pno.   *(Composer)*

4265 WEAVER, Mary. **On the eve of the first Christmas** (New
mm   York: Galaxy Music, 1948) 5 p. (choral octavo).
Sacred chorus. *Dn* 4'. *Da* 1947. *La* MoKU. *At* composer. *Pf* choral SATB, org.
                                                            (Composer)

4266 WEAVER, Mary. **Rise up all men** (New York: Galaxy Music,
mm   1953) 8 p. (choral octavo).
Sacred chorus. *Dn* 6'. *Da* 1952. *La* MoKU. *At* composer. *Pf* choral SATB, org.
                                                            (Composer)

4267 WEAVER, Mary. **When Jesus lay by Mary's side** (New York:
mm   G. Schirmer, 1951) 8 p. (choral octavo).
Sacred chorus. *Dn* 5′. *Da* 1948. *La* MoKU. *At* composer. *Pf* choral SATB, org.
(Composer)

4268 WEIGL, Vally. **Fear no more** (Bryn Mawr, Penn.: T. Presser,
mm   1958) 9 p. (choral octavo).
Secular chorus. *Dn* 5′. *At* Shakespeare. *Pf* choral SATB.   *(Composer)*

4269 WEIGL, Vally. **Let my country awake** (New York: Composers
mm   Facsimile Ed., 1967) 9 p. (score, parts).
Secular chorus. *Dn* 10′. *At* Richard Davidson. *Pf* solo SATB, choral SATB, pno,
speaking parts.   *(Composer)*

4270 WEIGL, Vally. **People, yes!, The** (New York: Composers
mm   Facsimile Ed., 1977) 93 p. $25. (score, parts).
Secular cantata. *Dn* 75′. *Da* 2 Nov. 1976. *La* Moldenhauer Archives, Spokane,
Wash. *At* Sandburg. *Pf* solo SATB, choral SATB, tpt, tbn, tim, pno, string
quartet.   *(Composer)*

4271 WEIGL, Vally. **Shelter for all** (West Babylon, N.Y.: H. Branch,
mm   1971) 19 p. $.75. (choral octavo).
Dn 9′. *Da* 1963. *La* publisher. *At* Kenneth Boulding. *Pf* solo SATB, choral
SATB, pno, speaking parts.   *(Composer)*

4272 WEIGL, Vally. **Three choral songs of the Southwest** (Bryn
mm   Mawr, Penn.: T. Presser, 1967) 12 p. (choral octavo).
Secular chorus. *Dn* 6′. *At* Patricia Benton. *Pf* choral SATB. *Ct* Life chant,
Desert lullaby, Lantern in the snow.   *(Composer)*

4273 WINTER, Sr. Miriam Therese. **Gold, incense, and myrrh**
mm   (New York: Vanguard Music, 1972) 31 p. (choral octavo).
Sacred choruses. *Dn* 35′. *At* composer. *Pf* solo SA, choral SATB, gtr. *Ct* Song of
glory, Wonderful, Child of morning, Christmas ballad, Sing of birth, In the
beginning, Silent the night, Take courage, No longer alone, Peace upon earth, O
what a happening, He comes. *Rg* Avant Garde, AVS-136.
(Sr. Mary Elizabeth Johnson)

4274 WINTER, Sr. Miriam Therese. **I know the secret** (New York:
mm   Vanguard Music, 1966) 31 p. (choral octavo).
Sacred choruses. *Dn* 32′. *At* composer. *Pf* solo SA, choral SSA, gtr. *Ct* He
bought the whole field, I know the secret, Yet I believe, Don't worry, Ballad of
the prodigal son, God loves a cheerful giver, Come Lord Jesus, Peter, Easter
song, A virgin, Christ is my rock, Come to the springs of living water. *Rg* Avant
Garde, AVS-105.   *(Sr. Mary Elizabeth Johnson)*

4275 WINTER, Sr. Miriam Therese. **Joy is like the rain** (New York:
mm   Vanguard Music, 1966) 24 p. $2.75. (choral octavo).
Sacred choruses. *Dn* 30′. *At* composer. *Pf* solo SA, choral SSA, gtr. *Ct* Joy is like
the rain; Zaccheus; Come down Lord; Spirit of God; It's a long road to
freedom; Howl, my soul; Pilgrim song; How I have longed; Ten lepers; God
gives the people strength; The wedding banquet; Speak to the wind. *Rg* Avant
Garde, AVS-101.   *(Sr. Mary Elizabeth Johnson)*

4276 WINTER, Sr. Miriam Therese. **Knock, knock** (New York:
mm   Vanguard Music, 1968) 32 p. (choral octavo).
Sacred choruses. *Dn* 31′. *At* composer. *Pf* solo SA, choral SSA, gtr, per, cbs. *Ct*
Knock, knock; Song for the sun; Three tents; Christ is King; Father, thy will be
done; Changin'; Song of loveliness; The sower; The visit; John; Night; I built a
garden; Seek first the kingdom. *Rg* Avant Garde, AVS-109
(Sr. Mary Elizabeth Johnson)

4277 WINTER, Sr. Miriam Therese. **Seasons** (New York: Vanguard
mm   Music, 1970) 32 p. $2.50. (choral octavo).
Sacred choruses. *Dn* 30′. *At* composer. *Pf* solo SA, choral SSA, gtr, per, cbs. *Ct*
Lift up your hearts, Let there be peace, Help my unbelief, Ballad of the seasons,
Who is my neighbor?, A long night, Praise God, If you look, Runnin', How
high the sky, Spirit of the Lord, Shout the good news. *Rg* Avant Garde, AVS-
126.   *(Sr. Mary Elizabeth Johnson)*

4278 WYLIE, Ruth Shaw. **Echo for women's chorus and string
mm   orchestra, op. 22** (West Babylon, N.Y.: H. Branch, 1977) 12 p.
$10. (score, parts).
Secular chorus. *Dn* 5′. *Da* 1965. *La* composer. *At* Christina Georgina Rossetti.
Pf choral SSAA, str.   *(Composer)*

4279 WYLIE, Ruth Shaw. **Five madrigals, op. 13, no. 1** (facsimile
mm   of MS on rental; West Babylon, N.Y.: H. Branch, 1977) 24 p. $20.
(score, parts).

Secular chorus. *Dn* 10′. *Da* 1950. *La* composer. *At* Blake. *St Songs of innocence
and experience. Pf* choral SATB.   *(Composer)*

4280 YOUSE, Glad Robinson. **April is forever** (2420; New York:
mm   Bourne, 1952) 4 p. (choral octavo).
Secular chorus. *Dn* 3′. *At* Edythe Hope Genee. *Pf* choral SSA, pno. Also for
solo S, pno (*WIAM* 5006).   *(Composer)*

4281 YOUSE, Glad Robinson. **As long as children pray** (2150; New
mm   York: Bourne, 1941) 5 p.
Sacred chorus. *Dn* 3′. *At* Iris Jean Crawford. *Pf* choral SSA, pno. Also for solo
S, pno (*WIAM* 5007).   *(Composer)*

4282 YOUSE, Glad Robinson. **Behold, God is my salvation** (N
mm   3024; New York: C. Fischer, 1958) 7 p. (choral octavo).
Sacred chorus. *Dn* 3′. *Pf* choral SATB, pno.   *(Composer)*

4283 YOUSE, Glad Robinson. **Glorious Easter morning** (1321; St.
mm   Louis: C.A. Scholin, 1954) 10 p. (choral octavo).
Sacred chorus. *Dn* 5′. *At* composer. *Pf* choral SATB, pno.   *(Composer)*

4284 YOUSE, Glad Robinson. **Great is thy mercy** (N 2278; New
mm   York: C. Fischer, 1955) 6 p. (choral octavo).
Sacred chorus. *Dn* 3′. *At* composer. *Pf* choral SATB, pno.   *(Composer)*

4285 YOUSE, Glad Robinson. **He who believes in me** (4190; New
mm   York: Remick Music, 1960) 7 p. (choral octavo).
Sacred chorus. *Dn* 5′. *Pf* choral SATB.   *(Composer)*

4286 YOUSE, Glad Robinson. **Hear me Lord** (2185; New York:
mm   Bourne, 1942) 6 p. (choral octavo).
Sacred chorus. *Dn* 4′. *At* composer. *Pf* choral SATB, pno. Also for solo S, pno
(*WIAM* 5009).   *(Composer)*

4287 YOUSE, Glad Robinson. **High upon a hilltop** (3618; New
mm   York: Remick Music, 1961) 3 p. (choral octavo).
Secular chorus. *Dn* 2′. *At* composer. *Pf* choral SSA, pno.   *(Composer)*

4288 YOUSE, Glad Robinson. **Hungry pagan** (N 4816; New York:
mm   C. Fischer, 1966) 11 p. (choral octavo).
Sacred chorus. *Dn* 4′. *At* Ralph Spaulding Cushman. *Pf* choral SATB, pno.
(Composer)

4289 YOUSE, Glad Robinson. **I would remember** (3686; New York:
mm   Remick Music, 1962) 5 p. (choral octavo).
Secular chorus. *Dn* 3′. *At* composer. *Pf* choral SSA, pno.   *(Composer)*

4290 YOUSE, Glad Robinson. **If you stand very still** (4174; New
mm   York: Remick Music, 1960) 6 p. (choral octavo).
Secular chorus. *Dn* 3′. *Pf* choral SSA, pno.   *(Composer)*

4291 YOUSE, Glad Robinson. **Man must have a song, A** (020;
mm   Cleveland: Ludwig Music, 1956) 6 p. (choral octavo).
Secular chorus. *Dn* 3′. *Pf* choral TTBB, pno.   *(Composer)*

4292 YOUSE, Glad Robinson. **O, it is lovely, Lord** (N 3592; New
mm   York: C. Fischer, 1961) 5 p. (choral octavo).
Sacred chorus. *Dn* 3′. *At* Ralph Spaulding Cushman. *St More hilltop verses and
prayers. Pf* choral SSA, pno.   *(Composer)*

4293 YOUSE, Glad Robinson. **Ring out ye bells! Sing out ye
mm   voices!** (3904; New York: Remick Music, 1956) 9 p. (choral octavo).
Sacred chorus. *Dn* 4′. *At* composer. *Pf* choral SATB, pno.   *(Composer)*

4294 YOUSE, Glad Robinson. **Salute to America, A** (3776; New
mm   York: Remick Music, 1954) 11 p. (choral octavo).
Secular chorus. *Dn* 6′. *At* composer. *Pf* choral SATB, pno. *Rg* DD Records,
1075.   *(Composer)*

4295 YOUSE, Glad Robinson. **This nation under God** (New York:
mm   Bourne, 1958) 5 p. (choral octavo).
Secular chorus. *Dn* 5′. *At* composer. *Pf* choral SATB, pno. *Rg* DD Records,
1075.   *(Composer)*

4296 YOUSE, Glad Robinson. **Winds of the prairie** (2534; New
mm   York: Bourne, 1954) 8 p. (choral octavo).
Secular chorus. *Dn* 4′. *At* composer. *Pf* choral SSA, pno.   *(Composer)*

4297 ZAIMONT, Judith Lang. **Chase, The** (facsimile of autograph at
mm   NNAMC, 1972) 35 p. (choral octavo).
Secular cantata. *Dn* 6′. *La* composer. *At* composer. *Pf* choral SSAATTBB, pno.
(Composer)

4298 ZAIMONT, Judith Lang. **Man's image and his cry** (facsimile
mm   of MS at NNAMC, 1968) 65 p. (score, parts).
Sacred cantata. *Dn* 17′. *Da* 1968. *La* composer. *St* Jewish high holiday prayer
book. *Pf* solo AB, choral SATB, 1-1-1-1, 2-2-2-0, tim, per including xyl, str.
(Composer)

4299 ZAIMONT, Judith Lang. **Moses supposes. 3-part canon for
mm   treble voices and percussion** (New York: Tetra Music, 1977) 4 p.
(choral octavo).
Secular chorus. *Dn* 4′. *Da* 1975. *La* composer. *St* a nursery rhyme. *Pf* choral 3S,
optional per.
(Composer)

4300 ZAIMONT, Judith Lang. **Sacred service for the Sabbath
mm   evening** (facsimile of MS on rental; New York: Galaxy Music, 1976)
258 p. $9.50. (score).
Dn 68′. *Da* 1976. *La* composer. *St The union prayerbook for Jewish worship. Pf*
solo A or B, choral SSAATTBB, pno. Full score and parts available from
composer. Orchestration: 2-2-2-2; 2-2-2-0; tim; per including glk, chimes; str. A
piano-vocal score is available on rental from the publisher.   *(Composer)*

4301 ZAIMONT, Judith Lang. **Sunny airs and sober. A book of
mm   madrigals** (M 144; New York: Walton Music, 1977) 44 p. $3.
(choral octavo).
Secular choruses. *Dn* 14′. *Da* 1974. *La* composer. *Pf* solo SAT, choral SSATB.
Ct A question answered (*At* Shakespeare), Winter mourning (*At* Shelley), Sigh
no more, ladies (*At* Shakespeare), Come away, death (*At* Shakespeare), Life is a
jest (*At* John Gay). *Rg Sunny airs and sober. Music for voice by Judith Lang
Zaimont*, Golden Crest, ATH 5051.   *(Composer)*

4302 ZAIMONT, Judith Lang. **Three ayres** (BB 5026-5028; New
mm   York: Broude Bros., 1976) 8, 5, 5 p. (choral octavo).
Secular choruses. *Dn* 6′. *Pf* for nos. 1 and 2: choral SSATB; for no. 3: choral
SATB. *Ct* O mistress mine (*At* Shakespeare, *St Twelfth night*); Slow, slow, fresh
fount (*At* Ben Jonson, *St Cynthia's revels*); How sweet I roam'd (*At* Blake, *St
Poetical sketches*). *Rg Sunny airs and sober. Music for voice by Judith Lang
Zaimont*, Golden Crest, ATH 5051.

Electronic music

4303 GREENE, Margo. **Targets for electronic tape** (New York:
mm   composer, 1973). (tape).
Dn 6′. *Da* 1973. *La* composer.   *(Composer)*

4304 IVEY, Jean Eichelberger. **Cortege--for Charles Kent** (New
mm   York: composer, 1973). (tape).
Dn 6′. *La* composer. *Pf* tape. *Rg Music by Jean Eichelberger Ivey for voices,
instruments, and tape*, Folkways, FTS 33439.   *(Composer)*

4305 IVEY, Jean Eichelberger. **Pinball** (New York: composer, 1967).
mm   (tape).
Film score. *Dn* 6′. *Da* 1967. *La* composer. *Pf* tape. *Rg Music by Jean
Eichelberger Ivey for voices, instruments, and tape*, Folkways, FTS 33439.
(Composer)

4306 MCLEAN, Priscilla. **Dance of dawn** (Austin, Tex.: composer,
mm   1974). (tape).
Dn 21′. *La* composer. *Pf* tape. *Rg* Composers Recordings, CRI SD 335.
(Composer)

4307 MCLEAN, Priscilla. **Invisible chariots** (Austin, Tex.: composer,
mm   1978). (tape).
Dn 22′. *Da* 1978. *La* composer. *Pf* tape.   *(Composer)*

4308 MEACHEM, Margaret M. **Kilogram meters/second². An
mm   electronic study in velocity** (tape at NNAMC, 1977) $10. (tape).
Dn 10′. *Da* July 1977. *La* NNAMC. *Pf* tape.   *(Composer)*

4309 SANDIFUR, Ann. **In celebration of movement** (Berkeley,
mm   Calif.: Arsciene, 1977). (tape).
Dn 90′. *Da* 1974. *La* publisher. *Pf* tape.   *(Composer)*

4310 SEMEGEN, Daria. **Electronic composition no. 1** (tape on
mm   rental; New York: American Composers Alliance, 1972) $10. (tape).

Dn 6′. *Da* 1972. *La* Electronic Music Studio, State U. of New York, Stony
Brook. *Pf* tape. *Rg Electronic music winners*, Odyssey, Y 34139.   *(Composer)*

4311 SMITH, La Donna. **Electronic lullaby** (Tuscaloosa, Ala.:
mm   composer, 1976). (tape).
Dn 4′. *Pf* tape.   *(Composer)*

4312 SMITH, La Donna. **Prelude, day music** (Tuscaloosa, Ala.:
mm   composer, 1976). (tape).
Dn 8′. *Pf* tape. *Rg* Transmuseq, 2005.   *(Composer)*

4314 WHITE, Ruth. **Flowers of evil** (Los Angeles: composer, 1968).
mm   (tape).
Dn 33′. *La* composer. *At* Baudelaire. *Tr* composer. *Pf* tape. *Rg* Limelight, LS
86058.   *(Composer)*

4315 WHITE, Ruth. **Seven trumps from the tarot cards** (Los
mm   Angeles: composer, 1967). (tape).
Dn 21′. *La* composer. *Pf* tape. *Rg* Limelight, LS 86058.   *(Composer)*

4316 WHITE, Ruth. **Short circuits** (Los Angeles: composer, 1970).
mm   (tape).
Dn 30′. *La* composer. *Pf* tape. *Rg* Angel, S-36042.   *(Composer)*

Mixed media

4317 ANDERSON, Beth. **Good-bye Bridget Bardot or Hello
mm   Charlotte Moorman** (facsimile of MS at NNACA, 1977) 1 p.
(score, part, tape).
Dn 10-45′. *Da* 1974. *La* composer. *Pf* vcl, tape.   *(Composer)*

4318 ANDERSON, Beth. **They did it** (facsimile of MS at NNACA,
mm   1977) 3 p. (score, part, tape).
Dn 12′. *Da* 1975. *La* composer. *At* W.H. Auden. *St* Vespers. *Pf* pno, tape.
(Composer)

4319 ANDERSON, Beth. **Torero piece** (facsimile of MS at NNACA,
mm   1977) 9 p. (score, parts).
Text-sound. *Dn* 7-90′. *Da* July 1973. *La* composer. *At* composer. *Pf* solo SS or
AA with amplification, red spotlight. *Rg 10 + 2 = 12 American text-sound pieces*,
1750 Arch, no. 1752.   *(Composer)*

4320 CHANCE, Nancy Laird. **Bathsabe's song** (New York: Seesaw
mm   Music, 1972) 37 p. $12. (score, tape).
Dn 7′. *Da* 1971. *La* publisher. *At* George Peele. *Pf* alto sax live, alto sax
recorded, speaker.   *(Composer)*

4321 COATES, Gloria. **Spring morning at Grobholz** (Munich:
mm   composer, 1975) 12 p. (score, parts, tape).
Dn 8′. *La* composer. *Pf* 3 flu, tape. *Rg* tape at Westdeutschen Rundfunk,
Cologne; available through the Assoc. of German Broadcasters, New York.
(Composer)

4322 CORY, Eleanor. **Tempi for clarinet and tape** (facsimile of MS
mm   at NNACA, 1972) 10 p. (score, part, tape).
Dn 9′. *La* NNACA.   *(Composer)*

4323 DAIGLE, Sr. Anne Cecile. **Four temperaments** (Marylhurst,
mm   Oreg.: Marylhurst, 1973) 29 p. $10. (score, parts, tape).
Dn 12′. *Da* 1973. *La* publisher. *Pf* 2 hrp, tape. *Ct* Preludium, Scherzo, Arioso,
Hoe down.   *(Composer)*

4324 DIEMER, Emma Lou. **Quintet for flute, viola, cello, harp-
mm   sichord, and tape** (New York: Seesaw Music, 1976) 46 p. (score,
parts, tape).
Dn 13′. *Da* 1974. *La* composer.   *(Composer)*

4325 DIEMER, Emma Lou. **Trio for flute, oboe, harpsichord, and
mm   tape** (New York: Seesaw Music, 1976) 30 p. (score, parts, tape).
Dn 10′. *Da* 1973. *La* composer.   *(Composer)*

4326 ESCOT, Pozzi. **Interra** (Cambridge, Mass.: Publications Contact
mm   International, 1975) 25 p. $25. (score, tape).
Dn 13′. *Da* 1968. *Pf* pno, tape, spotlights, film slides.   *(Composer)*

4327 FINE, Vivian. **Missa brevis for four cellos and taped voice**

mm (Shaftsbury, Vt.: Catamount Facsimile Ed., 1972) 14 p. $4. (score, tape).
Dn 21'. *Da* 1972. *La* composer.   *(Composer)*

4328 GOULD, Elizabeth. **Suite for woodwinds, brass, and per-**
mm **cussion** (facsimile of MS at PPFleisher, 1977) 88 p. (score, parts, tape).
Dn 17'. *Da* 1965. *La* composer. *Pf* 3pic-3enh-3bcl-3cbn, 4-4-3-1, tim, per
including xyl, tape.   *(Composer)*

4329 HAYS, Doris. **Hands full** (New York: Tetra Music, 1977) 3 p.
mm $8.60. (choral octavo, tape).
Dn 3'. *Da* 1976. *La* composer. *St* African bushman's chant. *Pf* choral SA, tape,
3 tom-toms.   *(Composer)*

4330 HAYS, Doris. **Pamp** (New York: Quinska Music, 1976) 8 p. $4.
mm (score, tape).
Dn 7'. *Da* 1973. *La* composer. *Pf* pno, tape.   *(Composer)*

4331 HAYS, Doris. **Sensevents concert** (New York: Quinska Music,
mm 1975) 4 p. $12. (score, parts, tape).
Dn 60-120'. *Da* 1975. *La* composer. *Pf* flu, obo, bsn, hrn, tbn, pno, vln, vla, vcl,
tape.   *(Composer)*

4332 IVEY, Jean Eichelberger. **Aldebaran** (FE 56; New York: C.
mm Fischer, 1973) 9 p. (score, tape).
Dn 10'. *Da* 1972. *La* publisher. *Pf* vla, tape. *Rg Music by Jean Eichelberger Ivey
for voices, instruments, and tape*, Folkways, FTS 33439.   *(Composer)*

4333 IVEY, Jean Eichelberger. **Hera, hung from the sky** (facsimile
mm of MS on rental; New York: C. Fischer, 1974) 38 p. (score, parts, tape).
Dn 13'. *Da* 1973. *La* publisher. *At* Carolyn Kizer. *Pf* solo M; flu; obo; cla; bsn;
hrn; tpt; tbn; per including vib, xyl; pno or cel, tape. *Rg New vocal music*,
Composers Recordings, CRI SD 325.   *(Composer)*

4334 IVEY, Jean Eichelberger. **Prospero** (facsimile of MS on rental;
mm New York: C. Fischer, 1978) 14 p. (score, parts, tape).
Dn 9'. *La* publisher. *At* Shakespeare. *St The tempest. Pf* solo B, hrn, per, tape.
                                    (Composer)

4335 IVEY, Jean Eichelberger. **Skaniadaryo** (FE 102; New York: C.
mm Fischer, 1975) 14 p. (score, tape).
Dn 11'. *Da* 1973. *La* publisher. *Pf* pno, tape.   *(Composer)*

4336 IVEY, Jean Eichelberger. **Terminus** (FE 22; New York: C.
mm Fischer, 1972) 7 p. (score, tape).
Dn 10'. *Da* 1970. *La* publisher. *At* Ralph Waldo Emerson. *Pf* solo M, tape. *Rg
Music by Jean Eichelberger Ivey for voices, instruments, and tape*, Folkways, FTS
33439.   *(Composer)*

4337 IVEY, Jean Eichelberger. **Three songs of night** (FE 57; New
mm York: C. Fischer, 1973) 29 p. (score, parts, tape).
Song cycle. *Dn* 14'. *Da* 1971. *La* publisher. *Pf* solo S, flu, cla, pno, vla, vcl, tape.
Ct The astronomer (*At* Whitman), I dreamed of Sappho (*At* Richard Hovey),
Heraclitus (*At* Callimachus, *Tr* William Cory). *Rg Music by Jean Eichelberger
Ivey for voices, instruments, and tape*, Folkways, FTS 33439.   *(Composer)*

4338 KOLB, Barbara. **Looking for Claudio** (New York: Boosey &
mm Hawkes, 1975) 19 p. (score, tape).
Dn 15'. *Pf* choral (unspecified voice types), mandolin, per including vib, tape,
solo gtr. *Rg Composers Recordings, CRI SD 361.

4339 KOLB, Barbara. **Solitaire** (66508; New York: C.F. Peters, 1972)
mm 12 p. (score, tape).
Dn 14'. *Pf* pno, tape. *Rg Turnabout, TV 34487.

4340 KOLB, Barbara. **Soundings** (66587; New York: C.F. Peters,
mm 1977) 38 p. (score, parts, tape).
Dn 14'. *Pf* 3-3-3-3, 3-0-0-0, per including vib, hrp, str, tape.

4341 KOLB, Barbara. **Spring river flowers moon night** (New York:
mm Boosey & Hawkes, 1975) 31 p. (score, tape).
Dn 20'. *At* Chang Jo-hsu. *Pf* mandolin; gtr; per including mba, vib; 2 pno;
tape. *Rg Composers Recordings, CRI SD 361.

4342 KOLB, Barbara. **Toccata** (66567; New York: C.F. Peters, 1976)
mm 10 p. (score, part, tape).

Dn 4'. *Pf* hps, tape.

4343 LA BARBARA, Joan. **Cyclone. A sound sculpture** (New York:
mm composer, 1977). (tape).
Dn 30'. *Pf* any voice type, Arp and Moog synthesizers, panning device, tape.
                                    (Composer)

4344 LA BARBARA, Joan. **Thunder** (facsimile of MS at NN, 1976) 4
mm p. (score).
Dn 20'. *Pf* any voice type, tim, phase shifter, frequency analyzer, echo
reverberation unit. *Rg Tapesongs*, Chiaroscuro, CR 196.   *(Composer)*

4345 LA BARBARA, Joan. **Vocal extensions** (New York: composer,
mm 1975) 5 p. (score).
Dn 20'. *Pf* any voice type, phase shifter, frequency analyzer, echo reverberation unit. *Rg Voice is the original instrument*, Wizard, RVW 2266.   *(Composer)*

4346 MUSGRAVE, Thea. **Orfeo I. An improvisation on a theme**
mm **for solo flute and pre-recorded tape** (facsimile of MS on rental;
    New York: Belwin-Mills, 1975) 19 p. (score, tape).
Dn 13'.

4347 MUSGRAVE, Thea. **Soliloquy I** (London: J. & W. Chester,
mm 1969) 17 p. (score, tape).
Dn 9'. *Pf* gtr, tape.

4348 NOWAK, Alison. **Piece for violin and computer** (facsimile of
mm MS at NNACA, 1973) 4 p. $1. (score, part, tape).
Dn 5'. *Da* 1973. *Pf* vln, tape.   *(Composer)*

4349 OLIVEROS, Pauline. **Double basses at twenty paces** (Balti-
mm more: Smith, 1977) 8 p. $6.50. (score, parts, tape).
Dn 12'. *Pf* 2 cbs, tape.   *(Publisher)*

4350 PAULL, Barberi. **Antifon for piano and tape** (facsimile of MS
mm on rental; New York: A. Broude, 1974) 22 p. (score, tape).
Dn 10'. *La* composer.   *(Composer)*

4351 PAULL, Barberi. **In the vast space of world** (facsimile of MS
mm on rental; New York: A. Broude, 1975) 42 p. $15. (score, parts).
Dn 15'. *La* composer. *At* composer. *Pf* solo M, per, pno, electric pno, film slides,
narrator.   *(Composer)*

4352 PAULL, Barberi. **Land, The** (facsimile of MS at NNAMC, 1976)
mm 70 p. $7.50. (score).
Dn 15'. *La* composer. *At* composer. *Pf* solo Bar; per including glk and xyl; org;
pno; film slides.   *(Composer)*

4353 PAULL, Barberi. **Mass, The** (facsimile of MS at NNAMC,
mm 1975) 31 p. (score, parts, tape).
Dn 12'. *La* composer. *Pf* per including glk, mba, vib, xyl; tape; film slides.

4354 POLIN, Claire. **O, aderyn pur** (New York: Seesaw Music, 1973)
mm 8 p. (score, parts, tape).
Dn 10'. *Pf* flu, sax, tape.

4355 POLIN, Claire. **Telemannicon** (New York: Seesaw Music, 1975)
mm 5 p.
Dn 10'. *Pf* solo flu or obo, played canonically with taped or live flu or obo.

4356 RAN, Shulamit. **O the chimneys** (New York: C. Fischer, 1973)
mm 33 p. $9.50. (score, parts, tape).
Dn 19'. *Da* 1969. *La* composer. *At* Nelly Sachs. *Pf* solo S, flu, cla (bcl), tim, per
including vib, pno, vcl, tape. *Rg The contemporary composer in the USA*,
Turnabout, TV 34492.   *(Composer)*

4357 SANDIFUR, Ann. **Double chamber music** (Berkeley, Calif.:
mm Arsciene, 1977) 25 p. (score, parts).
Dn 45'. *Da* 1976. *La* publisher. *Pf* flu, obo, hrp, pno, vln, vla, vcl, all amplified;
electro-acoustically amplified found objects.   *(Composer)*

4358 SILVERMAN, Faye-Ellen. **K. 1971** (New York: Seesaw Music,
mm 1976) 52 p. (score, parts, tape).
Dn 20'. *Da* 1972. *La* publisher. *At* Franz Kafka. *St The trial. Pf* solo TB, choral
SA, flu, obo, str, 2 narrators, tape.   *(Composer)*

4359 VAZQUEZ, Alida. **Electronic moods and piano sounds**
mm (facsimile of MS at NNAMC, 1977) 10 p. (score, tape).

Dn 5′. Da 1977. La composer. Pf pno, tape. *(Composer)*

4360 WYLIE, Ruth Shaw. **Long look home, The, op. 30, no. 2**
md (facsimile of MS on rental; West Babylon, N.Y.: H. Branch, 1977) 76
p. $15. (score, parts, tape).
Dn 30′. Da 1975. La composer. At Jeanne Wylie Torosian. Pf 2pic, alto
flu-2enh-2-2, 4-2-1-1, tim, per, str. Includes tape of spoken poetry and slides of
watercolor paintings. Ct Moon, Clouds, Snow, Desert, Nuclear energy. *(Composer)*

Orchestral and band music

4361 BALLOU, Esther Williamson. **Adagio for bassoon and string**
mm **orchestra** (New York: Composers Facsimile Ed., 1962) 4 p. (score,
parts).
Dn 5′. Da 20 Mar. 1960. La DAU. *(James R. Heintze)*

4362 BALLOU, Esther Williamson. **Beguine** (New York: Composers
mm Facsimile Ed., 1960) 19 p. (score).
Dn 3′. Da 1960. Pf 2-2-2-3cbn, 4-3-3-1, tim, per, str. Also for 2 pno, 4 hands
(*WIAM* 3359) and for 4 pno, 8 hands (*WIAM* 3368).

4363 BALLOU, Esther Williamson. **Concerto for piano and or-**
mm **chestra** (New York: Composers Facsimile Ed., 1965) 94 p. (score).
Dn 32′. Da 10 Aug. 1964. Pf 2pic-2-1-2, 4-2-2-1, tim, per, str, solo pno.

4364 BALLOU, Esther Williamson. **Concerto for solo guitar and**
mm **chamber orchestra** (New York: Composers Facsimile Ed., 1966)
28 p. (score).
Dn 8′. Pf 1-1-1-1, 1-1-1-0, str, solo gtr.

4365 BALLOU, Esther Williamson. **Early American portrait** (New
mm York: Composers Facsimile Ed., 1962) 65 p. (score).
Dn 20′. At Elizabeth Peck. St American frontier. Pf solo S, 2pic-1-1-1, 2-1-1-0,
tim, per including cel, hrp, str. Ct Wild geese, The loiterer, Buffaloes, The
christening, Democracy. Also for solo S, pno as *Five songs for soprano and piano*
(*WIAM* 4854).

4366 BALLOU, Esther Williamson. **In memoriam** (New York:
mm Composers Facsimile Ed., 1952) 6 p. (score).
Dn 4′. Pf for chamber orchestra: obo, str. In memory of Walter Penland.

4367 BALLOU, Esther Williamson. **Intermezzo for orchestra** (New
mm York: Composers Facsimile Ed., n.d.) 18 p. (score).
Dn 10′. Da 1943. Pf 2-2-2-2, 4-3-0-0, str. *(James R. Heintze)*

4368 BALLOU, Esther Williamson. **Konzertstück** (facsimile of MS
mm at NNACA, 1970) 43 p. (score, parts).
Dn 10′. Da Aug. 1969. Pf 2-2-2-2, 4-3-3btb-0, tim, per, str, solo vla.
(James R. Heintze)

4369 BALLOU, Esther Williamson. **Oboe concertino** (New York:
mm Composers Facsimile Ed., 1953) 35 p. (score, parts).
Dn 12′. Da 22 Aug. 1953, Bennington, Vt. Pf for chamber orchestra: str, solo
obo. *(James R. Heintze)*

4370 BALLOU, Esther Williamson. **Prelude and allegro for string**
mm **orchestra and piano** (New York: Composers Facsimile Ed., 1952)
18 p. (score, parts).
Dn 7′. Da 1957. Also entitled *Music for string orchestra and piano*. Rg
Composers Recordings, CRI SD 115.

4371 BARRETT-THOMAS, N. **Chikona** (Boston: Artists' Forum,
mm 1973) 48 p. (score, parts).
Dn 40′. La composer. Pf 3pic-3enh-4bcl-2, 4-3-3-1, tim, per including xyl, str.
(Paula Ann Ross)

4372 BOND, Victoria. **C-A-G-E-D** (New York: Seesaw Music, 1974)
mm 17 p. (score, parts).
Dn 10′. Da 1974. La publisher. Pf str orchestra. *(Composer)*

4373 BOND, Victoria. **Sonata for orchestra** (New York: Seesaw
mm Music, 1974) 33 p. (score, parts).
Dn 6′. Da 1972. La publisher. Pf 2-2-2-2, 2-2-2-1, tim, per including vib, hrp,
str. *(Composer)*

4374 BOONE, Clara Lyle. **Annunciation of spring** (facsimile of MS
mm on rental; Washington, D.C.: Arsis, 1974) 24 p. (score, parts).
Dn 11′. Da 1955. Pf 3-3-3-2, 4-2-2-0, str. Also for pno (*WIAM 4586*).
Published under the pseudonym of Lyle de Bohun. *(Composer)*

4375 BOONE, Clara Lyle. **Motive and chorale** (facsimile of MS on
mm rental; Washington, D.C.: Arsis, 1974) 16 p. (score, parts).
Dn 4′. Da 1962. Pf 2pic-2-2-2, 2-2-2-0, str. *(Composer)*

4377 BRITAIN, Radie. **Cactus rhapsody** (facsimile of MS at PPFlei-
mm sher, 1953) 83 p. (score, parts).
Dn 8′. Pf 3-3-2-2, 4-3-3-1, tim, per, hrp, str. Also for pno (*WIAM 4589*).

4378 BRITAIN, Radie. **Cosmic mist symphony** (facsimile of MS at
mm PPFleisher, 1962) 45 p. (score, parts).
Dn 24′. Pf 3-2-2-2, 4-3-3-1, tim, per, str.

4379 BRITAIN, Radie. **Cowboy rhapsody** (facsimile of MS at
mm PPFleisher, 1962) 63 p. (score, parts).
Dn 13′. Pf 3-2-2-2, 4-3-3-1, tim, per, hrp, str.

4380 BRITAIN, Radie. **Franciscan sketches** (facsimile of MSS at
mm PPFleisher, 1941) 26 p. (score, parts).
Dn 11′. Pf 3-2-2-3cbn, 4-3-3-1, tim, per, hrp, org, pno, str. Ct San Luis Rey, St.
Francis of Assisi.

4381 BRITAIN, Radie. **Heroic poem** (facsimile of MS at NNAMC,
mm 1929) 55 p. (score).
Dn 13′. Pf 3pic-3enh-3bcl-3cbn, 4-3-3-1, tim, per including cel, hrp, str.

4382 BRITAIN, Radie. **Infant suite. Three movements for small**
mm **orchestra** (facsimile of MS at PPFleisher, 1935) 36 p. (score, parts).
Dn 5′. Pf 1-1-1-1, 1-1-0-0, per including cel, hrp or pno, str. Ct The infant,
Berceuse, Toy parade.

4383 BRITAIN, Radie. **Light** (facsimile of MS at PPFleisher, 1935) 57
mm p. (score, parts).
Dn 8′. Pf 3-3-3-3, 4-3-3-1, tim, per, hrp, str.

4384 BRITAIN, Radie. **Ontonagon sketches** (New York: Seesaw
mm Music, 1974) 46 p. (score, parts).
Dn 20′. Da 1929. Pf 3-3-3-3, 4-3-3-1, tim, per, hrp, str. Ct Sunset on Lake
Superior, Woods at dusk, Victoria Falls.

4385 BRITAIN, Radie. **Prelude to a drama** (New York: Seesaw
mm Music, 1974) 36 p. (score, parts).
Dn 6′. Da 1928. Pf 3-2-2-2, 4-3-3-1, tim, per, hrp, str.

4386 BRITAIN, Radie. **Saturnale** (facsimile of MS at PPFleisher,
mm 1939) 105 p. (score, parts).
Dn 9′. Pf 3-3-3-3, 4-3-3-1, tim, per, str.

4387 BRITAIN, Radie. **Southern symphony** (facsimile of MS at
mm PPFleisher, 1935) 190 p. (score, parts).
Dn 23′. Pf 3-3-3-3, 4-3-3-1, tim, per including cel, hrp, str.

4388 BRITAIN, Radie. **This is the place** (facsimile of MS at
mm PPFleisher, 1958) 107 p. (score, parts).
Dn 5′. Pf 2-2-2-2, 4-3-3-1, tim, per, hrp, pno, str.

4389 BRUSH, Ruth. **Sarabande from** *Suite for string sextette or*
md *orchestra* (facsimile of MS at NNAMC, 1952) 7 p. (score, parts).
Dn 5′. Pf str. Also for 3 vln, vla, vcl, cbs (*WIAM* 3409). *(Composer)*

4390 CHANCE, Nancy Laird. **Lyric essays for orchestra** (New
mm York: Seesaw Music, 1972) 64 p. (score, parts).
Dn 15′. La publisher. Pf 3-3-3-3, 4-3-3-1, per including cel for 3 players, hrp,
pno, str. *(Composer)*

4391 COATES, Gloria. **Implorare for string orchestra** (Munich:
mm composer, 1977) 11 p. (score, parts).
Dn 15′. La composer. *(Composer)*

4392 COATES, Gloria. **Music on open strings** (facsimile of MS at
mm NNAMC, 1974) 24 p. (score, parts).
Dn 15′. Da 1974. La composer. Pf chamber or full string orchestra. *(Composer)*

4393 COATES, Gloria. **Planets. Three movements for orchestra**
mm   (facsimile of MS at NNAMC, 1974) 15 p. (score, parts).
Dn 14′. *Da* 1974. *La* composer. *Pf* 3pic-3enh-2bcl-3, 4-0-0-0, str. *Rg* tape at
Radio Bremen, West Germany; available through the Assoc. of German
Broadcasters, New York.   *(Composer)*

4394 DAIGLE, Sr. Anne Cecile. **Chronicle of creation** (Marylhurst,
mm   Oreg.: Marylhurst, 1959) 118 p. (score, parts).
Dn 14′. *Da* 1955. *La* publisher. *Pf* 2-2-2-2, 4-2-3-1, tim, per, hrp, str. *(Composer)*

4395 DAIGLE, Sr. Anne Cecile. **Concerto for trumpet and or-**
mm   **chestra** (Marylhurst, Oreg.: Marylhurst, 1975) 75 p. $25. (score,
parts).
Dn 13′. *Da* 1975. *La* publisher. *Pf* 2-2-2-2, 2-1-1-0, tim, per including glk, hrp,
str, solo tpt.   *(Composer)*

4396 DAIGLE, Sr. Anne Cecile. **Concerto for violin and orchestra**
mm   (Marylhurst, Oreg.: Marylhurst, 1963) 123 p. (score, parts).
Dn 23′. *Da* 1962. *La* publisher. *Pf* 3-3-3-2, 4-3-2-2, tim, per including cel, hrp,
str, solo vln.   *(Composer)*

4397 DIEMER, Emma Lou. **Brass menagerie, The. A suite for**
mm   **band** (85215; New York: Belwin-Mills, 1967) 35 p. (score, parts).
Dn 12′. *Da* 1960. *La* composer. *Pf* 2pic-2-6-2-4sax, 0-4alto hrn-3-3-1, tim, per
including xyl.   *(Composer)*

4398 DIEMER, Emma Lou. **Concert piece for organ and orches-**
mm   **tra** (New York: Seesaw Music, 1977) 70 p. (score, parts).
Dn 9′. *Da* Jan. 1977. *La* composer. *Pf* 2-2-2-2, 4-3-3-1, tim, per, str, solo org. A
piano reduction is available from the publisher.   *(Composer)*

4399 DIEMER, Emma Lou. **Concerto for harpsichord and cham-**
mm   **ber orchestra** (New York: Seesaw Music, 1977) 60 p. (score, parts).
Dn 12′. *Da* 1958. *Pf* 1-1-1-1, 2-2-2-1, tim, str, solo hps.   *(Composer)*

4400 DIEMER, Emma Lou. **Festival overture** (Philadelphia: Elkan-
mm   Vogel, 1968) 36 p. (score, parts).
Dn 7′. *Da* 1961. *La* composer. *Pf* 2-2-2-2, 4-3-3-1, tim, per, str.   *(Composer)*

4401 DIEMER, Emma Lou. **Rondo concertante** (DE 137; New
mm   York: Boosey & Hawkes, 1971) 24 p. (score, parts).
Dn 5′. *Da* 1960. *La* composer. *Pf* 3pic-2-2-2, 4-3-3-1, tim, per, pno, str.
                                                                     (Composer)

4402 DIEMER, Emma Lou. **Symphonie antique** (85075; New York:
mm   Belwin-Mills, 1966) 53 p. (score, parts).
Dn 10′. *Da* 1961. *La* composer. *Pf* 3pic-2-2-2, 4-3-3-1, tim, per, str. *(Composer)*

4403 DIEMER, Emma Lou. **Youth overture for young people's**
mm   **orchestra** (New York: Belwin-Mills, 1961) 12 p. (score, parts).
Dn 6′. *Da* 1960. *La* composer. *Pf* 2-2-2-2, 4-3-3-1, tim, per, str.   *(Composer)*

4404 DRAKE, Elizabeth Bell. **Concerto for orchestra** (Ithaca, N.Y.:
mm   composer, 1976) 58 p. $12. (score, parts).
Dn 9′. *Da* 1976. *La* composer. *Pf* 2pic-2enh-2bcl-2, 4-2-3-1, tim, per, str.
                                                                     (Composer)

4405 DRAKE, Elizabeth Bell. **Symphony no. 1** (Ithaca, N.Y.: com-
mm   poser, 1971) 124 p. $25. (score, parts).
Dn 20′. *Da* 1971. *La* composer. *Pf* 3pic-3enh-3bcl-3cbn, 4-3-3-1, tim, per, str.
                                                                     (Composer)

4406 DU PAGE, Florence. **Lost valley** (facsimile of MS on rental;
mm   Atlanta: Porter, 1976) 11 p. (score, parts).
Dn 5′. *Da* 1946. *La* composer. *Pf* 3pic-2enh-2-2, 2-2-3-1, tim, per, hrp, str.
                                                                     (Composer)

4407 DU PAGE, Florence. **Pond, The** (facsimile of MS on rental;
mm   Atlanta: Porter, 1941) 19 p. (score, parts).
Dn 7′. *Da* 1941. *La* composer. *Pf* 3-3-4-3, 3-3-4-3, cel, hrp. *Rg* NRU, Eastman
School of Music.   *(Composer)*

4408 DU PAGE, Florence. **Two sketches for string orchestra**
mm   (Bryn Mawr, Penn.: Elkan-Vogel, 1946) 9 p. (score, parts).
Dn 4′. *La* composer. *Ct* Prelude to a quiet evening, Jumping jack.   *(Composer)*

4409 ESCOT, Pozzi. **Sands** (facsimile of MS at PPFleisher, 1965) 30 p.
mm   (score, parts).

Dn 12′. *Pf* 5 sax, egr, per, 17 vln, 9 cbs.   *(Composer)*

4410 FINE, Vivian. **Alcestis** (Shaftsbury, Vt.: Catamount Facsimile
mm   Ed., 1972) 55 p. $10. (score, parts).
Dn 11′. *Da* 1960. *La* composer. *Pf* 2-2-2-2; 2-2-2-0; tim; per including vib, xyl;
hrp; str. *Rg* Composers Recordings, CRI SRD 145.   *(Composer)*

4411 FINE, Vivian. **Concertante for piano and orchestra** (Shafts-
mm   bury, Vt.: Catamount Facsimile Ed., 1972) 83 p. $13. (score, parts).
Dn 15′. *Da* 1944. *La* composer. *Pf* 2-2-2-2, 2-2-2-0, tim, str, solo pno. *Rg*
Composers Recordings, CRI SD 135.   *(Composer)*

4412 FINE, Vivian. **Race of life, The** (Shaftsbury, Vt.: Catamount
mm   Facsimile Ed., 1972) 108 p. $15. (score, parts).
Dn 20′. *Da* 1956. *La* composer. *Pf* 2pic-0-2-1, 2-2-2-1, tim, per for 2 players
including xyl.   *(Composer)*

4413 FINE, Vivian. **Romantic ode for string orchestra with solo**
mm   **violin, viola, and cello** (Shaftsbury, Vt.: Catamount Facsimile Ed.,
1976) 42 p. $8. (score, parts).
Dn 12′. *Da* 1976. *La* composer.   *(Composer)*

4414 FINE, Vivian. **Sonnets for baritone and orchestra** (Shafts-
mm   bury, Vt.: Catamount Facsimile Ed., 1976) 31 p. $7. (score, parts).
Dn 10′. *Da* 1976. *La* composer. *At* Keats. *Pf* solo Bar, 2-2-2-2; 4-2-2-0; tim;
per including glk, mba, vib; str.   *(Composer)*

4415 GIDEON, Miriam. **Adorable mouse, The** (Hastings-on-Hud-
mm   son, N.Y.: General Music, 1960) 37 p. (score).
Dn 12′. *At* La Fontaine, adapted. *Pf* 1-0-1-0, 2-0-0-0, tim, pno, str, narrator.
Also for solo M, flu, cla, bsn, hrn, tim, hps (*WIAM* 3481). *Rg* Serenus, SPN
12650.

4416 GIDEON, Miriam. **Lyric piece for string orchestra** (New
mm   York: American Composers Ed., 1961) 22 p. (score).
Dn 9′. *La* DLC. *Rg* Composers Recordings, CRI 170.

4417 GIDEON, Miriam. **Songs of youth and madness** (New York:
mm   American Composers Ed., 1977) 50 p. (score, parts).
Dn 12′. *Da* July 1977. *La* composer. *At* Friedrich Hölderlin. *Pf* solo M; 1-1-
1-1; 1-1-0-0; tim; per including vib, glk; str.   *(Composer)*

4418 GIDEON, Miriam. **Symphonia brevis** (New York: American
mm   Composers Ed., 1953) 34 p. (score, parts).
Dn 8′. *Pf* 2-2-2-2, 4-2-2-0, tim, str. *Rg* Composers Recordings, CRI 128.

4419 GLANVILLE-HICKS, Peggy. **Concerto romantico** (facsimile
mm   of MS on rental; New York: C.F. Peters, 1957) 106 p. (score, parts).
Dn 21′. *Pf* 1-1enh-3bcl-1, 4-0-1-0, hrp, str, solo vla. *Rg* MGM 3559.

4420 GLANVILLE-HICKS, Peggy. **Drama for orchestra** (facsimile
mm   of MS on rental; New York: C.F. Peters, 1961) 85 p. (score, parts).
Dn 17′. *Pf* 0-0-1-0, 0-1-0-0, tim, per including xyl, pno, str.

4421 GLANVILLE-HICKS, Peggy. **Etruscan concerto** (facsimile of
mm   MS on rental; New York: C.F. Peters, 1954) 82 p. (score, parts).
Dn 16′. *Pf* 1-1-1-1, 1-1-0-0, tim, per including xyl, pno, str. *Rg* MGM 3557.

4422 GLANVILLE-HICKS, Peggy. **Gymnopédie no. 1 for oboe,**
md   **harp, and strings** (AMP 95559; New York: Associated Music,
1957) 8 p. (score, parts).
Dn 6′. *Tm* Three gymnopédies (*WIAM* 3503).

4423 GLANVILLE-HICKS, Peggy. **Letters from Morocco** (fac-
mm   simile of MS on rental; New York: C.F. Peters, 1953) 63 p. (score,
parts).
Dn 16′. *At* Paul Bowles. *Pf* solo T, 1-1-0-1, 0-1-0-0, tim, per including xyl, hrp,
str. *Rg* MGM E3549.

4424 GLANVILLE-HICKS, Peggy. **Sinfonia da pacifica** (facsimile
mm   of MS at DLC, 1953) 50 p. (score).
Dn 16′. *Pf* 1-1-1-1, 1-1-1-0, tim, per including mba, str. *Rg* MGM E3336.

4425 GLANVILLE-HICKS, Peggy. **Tapestry for orchestra** (fac-
mm   simile of MS on rental; New York: C.F. Peters, 1958) 75 p. (score,
parts).
Dn 18′. *Pf* 2pic-2-2-2, 2-2-2-0, tim, per including cel, hrp, pno, str.

4426 GOULD, Elizabeth. **Concerto for trumpet and strings** (fac-
mm simile of MS on rental; New York: T. Presser, 1977) 29 p. (score,
parts).
Dn 14′. *Da* 1959. *La* composer. Awarded first prize for orchestral music in the
Mu Phi Epsilon composition competition, 1961.   *(Composer)*

4427 GOULD, Elizabeth. **Mini-symphony with an introduction to
mm the instruments** (facsimile of MS at PPFleisher, 1977) 52 p. (score,
parts).
Dn 16′. *Da* 1973. *La* composer. *At* composer. *Pf* 2-2-2-2, 0-0-0-0, tim, str,
narrator.   *(Composer)*

4428 GREENE, Margo. **Five songs for mezzo-soprano and or-
mm chestra** (facsimile of MS at NNACA, 1972) 42 p. (score, parts).
Dn 15′. *At* Blake. *Pf* solo M, 2-2enh-2bcl-2, 2-1-2-1, per, hrp, str. *Ct* Ah! sunflower, London, A cradle song, I fear'd the fury of my wind, A divine image.
(Composer)

4429 HSU, Wen-ying. **Cello concerto** (facsimile of MS on rental;
mm West Babylon, N.Y.: H. Branch, 1977) 81 p. (score, parts).
Dn 18′. *Da* 1963. *La* composer. *Pf* 2-2-2-2, 2-2-2-1, tim, Chinese per, hrp, str,
solo vcl. Chinese instruments can be rented from the publisher.   *(Composer)*

4430 HSU, Wen-ying. **Concerto for orchestra** (facsimile of MS on
mm rental; West Babylon, N.Y.: H. Branch, 1977) 61 p. (score, parts).
Dn 12′. *Da* 1962. *La* composer. *Pf* 2-2-2-2, 2-2-2-1, tim, Chinese per, str.
Chinese instruments can be rented from the publisher.   *(Composer)*

4431 HSU, Wen-ying. **March of Chinese cadets** (Los Angeles:
mm composer, 1967) 29 p. (score, parts).
Piece for marching band. *Dn* 15′. *Pf* 3pic-2-3bcl-2-3sax; 4-2-2-1; per including
Chinese bells, drum. Chinese instruments can be rented from the composer.
(Composer)

4432 HSU, Wen-ying. **Prelude and Song of old fisherman** (Los
mm Angeles: composer, 1961) 17 p. (score, parts).
Dn 9′. *Da* 1961. *Tr* composer. *St* Chinese folk song. *Lt* Chinese, English. *Pf*
solo Bar, 1-1-1-1, 0-0-0-0, hrp, str.   *(Composer)*

4433 HSU, Wen-ying. **Sky maidens' dance suite** (facsimile of MS on
mm rental; West Babylon, N.Y.: H. Branch, 1977) 47 p. (score, parts).
Dn 15′. *Da* 1966. *La* composer. *Pf* 2-2-2-2; 0-0-0-0; per including Chinese per,
cel, glk; hrp; str. Chinese instruments can be rented from the composer. The
suite is an excerpt from an incomplete opera, *Cowherd and weaving maiden.*
(Composer)

4434 HUGHES, Sr. Martina. **April 1943** (Duluth, Minn.: composer,
mm 1944) 60 p. (score, parts).
Dn 8′. *Da* 1943. *La* composer. *Pf* 3pic-3enh-3bcl-2, 4-2-3-1, tim, per, str.
(Composer)

4435 HUGHES, Sr. Martina. **Invocation** (Duluth, Minn.: composer,
mm 1947) 57 p. (score, parts).
Dn 15′. *La* composer. *Pf* 3pic-3enh-3bcl-2, 4-3-3-1, tim, per, hrp, str. *(Composer)*

4436 HUGHES, Sr. Martina. **Revelation** (Duluth, Minn.: composer,
mm 1963) 40 p. (score, parts).
Dn 12′. *La* composer. *Pf* 3pic-3enh-3bcl-3cbn, 4-3-3-1, tim, per, hrp, str.
(Composer)

4437 HUGHES, Sr. Martina. **Sounds heard from the shore of
mm Lake Superior** (Duluth, Minn.: composer, 1976) 91 p. $25. (score,
parts).
Dn 11′. *Da* 1976. *La* composer. *Pf* 3pic-3enh-2-2; 4-2-3-1; tim; per including
cel, glk, vib; hrp; pno; str.   *(Composer)*

4438 HYSON, Winifred. **Partita for string orchestra** (facsimile of
mm MS at NN, 1970) 31 p. (score).
Dn 13′. *La* composer.   *(Composer)*

4439 HYSON, Winifred. **Suite for young orchestra. Variations on
mm an original theme** (Philadelphia: Elkan-Vogel, 1969) 24 p. (score,
parts).
Dn 11′. *Da* 1964. *La* composer. *Pf* 1-0-1-0, 0-0-0-0, str.   *(Composer)*

4440 IVEY, Jean Eichelberger. **Forms in motion** (facsimile of MS on
mm rental; New York: C. Fischer, 1973) 107 p. (score).
Dn 25′. *Da* 1972. *La* publisher. *Pf* 3-3-3-3, 4-3-3-1, tim, per including cel
alternating with pno, hrp, str.   *(Composer)*

4441 IVEY, Jean Eichelberger. **Ode for orchestra** (facsimile of MS
mm on rental; New York: C. Fischer, 1968) 26 p. (score, parts).
Dn 7′. *Da* 1965. *La* publisher. *Pf* 2-2-2-2, 4-3-3-1, tim, per, str.   *(Composer)*

4442 IVEY, Jean Eichelberger. **Passacaglia for chamber orchestra**
mm (facsimile of MS on rental; New York: C. Fischer, 1968) 19 p. (score,
parts).
Dn 5′. *Da* 1954. *La* publisher. *Pf* 1-1-1-1, 1-1-1-0, per, str.   *(Composer)*

4443 IVEY, Jean Eichelberger. **Testament of Eve** (facsimile of MS
mm on rental; New York: C. Fischer, 1976) 71 p. (score, parts).
Monodrama. *Dn* 20′. *Da* 1976. *La* publisher. *At* composer. *Pf* solo M, 2-2-2-2,
4-2-3-1, tim, per, str, tape.   *(Composer)*

4444 IVEY, Jean Eichelberger. **Tribute: Martin Luther King**
mm (facsimile of MS on rental; New York: C. Fischer, 1969) 81 p. (score,
parts).
Dn 30′. *Da* 1969. *La* publisher. *Pf* solo B, 3-3-3-3, 4-3-3-1, tim, per, str. *Ct* I
never felt such love in my soul before; I made my vow to the Lord; Go down,
Moses; There is a balm in Gilead.

4445 KOLB, Barbara. **Crosswinds for wind ensemble and percus-
mm sion** (New York: Boosey & Hawkes, 1974) 30 p. (score, parts).
Dn 13′. *Pf* 2-2enh-2bcl-2-sax, 2-2-2-0, per including mba.

4446 LAUFER, Beatrice. **Cry!** (facsimile of MS on rental: New York:
mm Belwin-Mills, 1965) 18 p. (score, parts).
Dn 6′. *Pf* 2-1-2-2, 4-3-2-1, per including vib, str. May be performed with *In the
throes* (*WIAM* 4447) and *Resolution* (*WIAM* 4448).   *(Composer)*

4447 LAUFER, Beatrice. **In the throes** (facsimile of MS on rental;
mm New York: Belwin-Mills, 1976) 26 p. (score, parts).
Dn 12′. *Pf* 2-1-2-2, 4-3-2-1, tim, per including vib, str. May be performed with
Cry (*WIAM* 4446) and *Resolution* (*WIAM* 4448).   *(Composer)*

4448 LAUFER, Beatrice. **Resolution** (New York: Belwin-Mills, 1976)
mm 17 p. (score, parts).
Dn 6′. *Pf* 2-1-2-2, 4-3-2-1, tim, per, str. May be performed with *Cry* (*WIAM*
4446) and *In the throes* (*WIAM* 4447).   *(Composer)*

4449 LIBBEY, Dee. **Essence and distractions** (facsimile of MS on
mm rental; New York: Bourne Music, 1963) 38 p. (score, parts).
Dn 8′. *La* composer. *Pf* 3pic-2-3bcl-2, 4-3-3-1, tim, per including xyl, hrp, pno,
str.   *(Composer)*

4450 LIBBEY, Dee. **Impressions of a leaking faucet** (Goodwell,
mm Okla.: composer, 1963) 28 p. (score, parts).
Dn 7′. *La* composer. *Pf* 3pic-2enh-2bcl-1;|4-3-2-0; tim; per including mba, xyl;
hrp; str.   *(Composer)*

4451 LIBBEY, Dee. **Lost forest, The** (Goodwell, Okla.: composer,
mm 1960) 39 p. (score, parts).
Dn 10′. *La* composer. *Pf* 3pic-2enh-2bcl-2, 4-2-3-1, tim, per, str. *(Composer)*

4452 LOCKSHIN, Florence Levin. **Annie Bradley's tune. Fantasy
mm on a Negro folk-song** (New York: Independent Music, 1959) 66 p.
(score, parts).
Dn 15′. *Da* 1959. *La* composer. *Pf* 3pic-3enh-3bcl-3cbn, 2-2-2-0, tim, per, str.
(Composer)

4453 LOCKSHIN, Florence Levin. **Aural. Verse for orchestra**
mm (New York: Independent Music, 1964) 24 p. (score, parts).
Dn 10′. *Da* 1964. *La* composer. *Pf* 3pic-2-3bcl-2, 4-3-3-0, tim, per, str.
(Composer)

4454 LOCKSHIN, Florence Levin. **Cumbia. Fantasy on a Colom-
mm bian folk dance** (New York: Independent Music, 1977) 25 p. $10.
(score, parts).
Dn 7′. *Da* 1977. *La* composer. *Pf* 3pic-2-2-3cbn, 2-2-2-0, tim, per including xyl,
str.   *(Composer)*

4455 LOCKSHIN, Florence Levin. **Cycle, The. Suite from the
mm ballet** (New York: Independent Music, 1956) 128 p. (score, parts).
Dn 25′. *Da* 1956. *La* composer. *Pf* 3pic-3enh-3bcl-3cbn, 2-2-2-1, tim, per, str.
(Composer)

4456 LOCKSHIN, Florence Levin. **Introduction, lament, and**

mm protest. **Memorial to F.A.B.** (New York: Independent Music, 1967) 48 p. $15. (score, parts).
Dn 12′. *Da* 1967. *La* composer. *Pf* 3pic-2-3enh-3bcl, 4-3-3-1, tim, per, str.
(Composer)

4457 LOCKSHIN, Florence Levin. **Paean--Santa Maria de Gua-**
mm **dalupe** (New York: Independent Music, 1962) 47 p. (score, parts).
Dn 10′. *Da* 1962. *La* composer. *Pf* 3pic-2-2-3cbn, 4-3-3-1, tim, per including xyl, str.
(Composer)

4458 LOCKSHIN, Florence Levin. **Scavarr. Songs of the Yuma**
mm **and Mojave Indians** (New York: Independent Music, 1969) 49 p. (score, parts).
Dn 10′. *Da* 1969. *La* composer. *Pf* 3pic-2-3enh-3bcl, 2-2-3-0, tim, per, str.
(Composer)

4459 LOCKSHIN, Florence Levin. **Song form for orchestra** (New
mm York: Independent Music, 1961) 37 p. (score, parts).
Dn 9′. *Da* 1961. *La* composer. *Pf* 3pic-3enh-0-3cbn-sax, 4-3-3-0, tim, per, str.
(Composer)

4460 MAMLOK, Ursula. **Concerto for oboe and orchestra** (facsi-
mm mile of MS at NNACA, 1976) 51 p. $17.60. (score, parts).
Dn 12′. *Pf* 3-3-3-0; 4-3-3-1; per including cel, glk, xyl; hrp; str; solo oboe.
(Composer)

4461 MARCUS, Adabelle Gross. **Symphony of the spheres** (facsi-
mm mile of MS at NNAMC, 1974) 36 p. (score, parts).
Dn 30′. *Pf* 3pic-3enh-3-2, 4-3-3-1, tim, per including cel, hrp, pno, str. *Ct* Depicting: the sounds in the universe; Depicting: the search for life; Depicting: the vastness of the universe.
(Composer)

4462 MCLEAN, Priscilla. **Variations and mozaics on a theme of**
mm **Stravinsky** (facsimile of MS on rental; Austin, Tex.: composer, 1977) 106 p. (score, parts).
Dn 20′. *La* composer. *Pf* 3-2-2-2, 4-2-2-0, tim, per including cel, hrp, str.
(Composer)

4463 MERRIMAN, Margarita L. **Concertante for horn and**
mm **chamber orchestra** (facsimile of MS at Atlantic Union Col., South Lancaster, Mass., 1977) 59 p. $20. (score, parts).
Dn 10′. *Da* Dec. 1976. *La* composer. *Pf* 2-2-2-2, 0-1-1-0, tim, str, solo hrn.
(Composer)

4464 MERRIMAN, Margarita L. **Seventeen-seventy-six** (facsimile
mm of MS at Atlantic Union Col., South Lancaster, Mass., 1977) 84 p. $25. (score, parts).
Dn 9′. *Da* Sept. 1975. *La* composer. *Pf* 1-1-1-1, 1-1-1-0, tim, str. *(Composer)*

4465 MERRIMAN, Margarita L. **Symphony no. 1** (facsimile of MS
mm at NRU, 1959) 127 p. (score, parts).
Dn 20′. *La* composer. *Pf* 3pic-2-2-2, 4-2-3-1, tim, per including xyl, hrp, pno, str. Parts available from the composer. *(Composer)*

4466 MOORE, Dorothy Rudd. **From the dark tower** (New York:
mm Composers Facsimile Ed., 1972) 42 p. $13.75. (score, parts).
Song cycle. *Dn* 22′. *Pf* solo M, 2-3enh-3bcl-2, 4-3-3-0, tim, per including cel, str. Originally for solo M, pno, vcl (*WIAM* 3608). *Ct* O black and unknown bards (*At* James Weldon Johnson), Willow bend and weep (*At* Herbert Clark Johnson), Dream variation (*At* Langston Hughes), From the dark tower (*At* Countee Cullen).
(Composer)

4467 MUSGRAVE, Thea. **Cantata for a summer's day** (facsimile of
mm MS on rental; New York: Belwin-Mills, 1954) 56 p. (score, parts).
Dn 33′. *At* Alexander Hume and Maurice Lindsay. *Pf* solo SATB, 1-0-1-0, 0-0-0-0, str, speaking part. Also for solo SATB, flu, cla, string quartet, speaking part (*WIAM* 3614); for choral SATB, flu, cla, string quartet, speaking part (*WIAM* 4067); and for choral SATB, 1-0-1-0, 0-0-0-0, str, speaking part (*WIAM* 4067).

4468 MUSGRAVE, Thea. **Clarinet concerto** (JWC 452; London: J.
mm & W. Chester, 1969) 136 p. (score).
Dn 22′. *Pf* 3-3enh-bcl-3cbn; 4-3-3-1; tim; per including glk, vib; hrp; accordion; str; solo cla. *Rg* Argo, ZRG 726.

4469 MUSGRAVE, Thea. **Concerto for horn and orchestra** (JWC
mm 483; London: J. & W. Chester, 1974) 88 p. (score).
Dn 21′. *Pf* 2pic-2enh-2bcl-2cbn, 4-3-1-0, per including vib, hrp, prepared pno, str, solo hrn. *Rg* London, Lon. Head-8.

4470 MUSGRAVE, Thea. **Concerto for orchestra** (JWC 445;
mm London: J. & W. Chester, 1968) 114 p. (score).
Dn 20′. *Pf* 3pic-3enh-3bcl-3cbn, 4-3-3-1, tim, per including vib, hrp, str. *Rg* London, Lon. Head-8.

4471 MUSGRAVE, Thea. **Festival overture** (facsimile of MS on
mm rental; New York: G. Schirmer, 1965) 77 p. (score, parts).
Dn 10′. *Pf* 2pic-2-2-2, 4-2-3-0, tim, per including vib, str.

4472 MUSGRAVE, Thea. **Memento vitae** (London: J. & W. Chester,
mm 1975) 105 p. (score, parts).
Dn 18′. *Da* 1970. *Pf* 2-2-2-2, 4-3-3-1, tim, str.

4473 MUSGRAVE, Thea. **Night music for chamber orchestra**
mm (JWC 475; London: J. & W. Chester, 1972) 74 p. (score).
Dn 18′. *Pf* 1-2-0-1, 2-0-0-0, str. *Rg* Argo, ZRG 702.

4474 MUSGRAVE, Thea. **Nocturnes and arias for orchestra**
mm (facsimile of MS on rental; New York: G. Schirmer, 1966) 100 p. (score, parts).
Dn 21′. *Pf* 2pic-2-2bcl-2cbn, 4-3-3-1, tim, per including vib, hrp, str.

4475 MUSGRAVE, Thea. **Obliques for orchestra** (JWC 126; Lon-
mm don: J. & W. Chester, 1961) 62 p. (score).
Dn 12′. *Pf* 3pic-1-3bcl-2; 4-3-3-1; tim; per including cel, glk, xyl; hrp; str.

4476 MUSGRAVE, Thea. **Orfeo II** (New York: Novello, 1976) 35 p.
mm (score, parts).
Dn 14′. *Pf* flu, str.

4477 MUSGRAVE, Thea. **Theme and interludes.** *Music for today* 3
md (London: Novello, 1962) 50 p. (score).
Dn 11′. *Pf* 2-1-3-1, 2-2-1-0, tim, per, str, pno for rehearsal only.

4478 MUSGRAVE, Thea. **Triptych for tenor and orchestra** (JWC
mm 123; London: J. & W. Chester, 1960) 68 p. (score).
Dn 11′. *At* Chaucer. *Pf* solo T; 2pic-2enh-1-1; 3-2-0-0; per including cel, vib; hrp; pno; str. *Rg* HMV, ALP 2279/ASD 2279.

4479 MUSGRAVE, Thea. **Viola concerto** (New York: Novello, 1973)
mm 105 p. (score).
Dn 23′. *Pf* 1-2enh-2bcl-1, 3-2-1-0, per, hrp, str, solo vla.

4480 NOBLE, Ann. **It's nicer down here; or Call on God, but row**
mm **away from the rocks** (facsimile of MS at Mills Col., Oakland, Calif., 1976) 50 p. $12. (score, parts).
Dn 15′. *La* composer. *Pf* 2pic-2enh-6(bcl-cbc)-2cbn, 4-8-2btn-bar-1, tim, per.
(Composer)

4481 NOWAK, Alison. **Piece for strings** (facsimile of MS at
mm NNACA, 1970) 7 p. $1.25. (score, parts).
Dn 6′. *Da* 1970. *(Composer)*

4482 NOWAK, Alison. **Quid pro quo** (facsimile of MS at NNACA,
mm 1972) 80 p. $15. (score, parts).
Dn 15′. *Da* 1972. *Pf* 3-3-3-3, 4-3-3-1, tim, str. *(Composer)*

4483 OLIVEROS, Pauline. **Sonic meditations I-XXV** (Baltimore:
mm Smith, 1974) 8 p. $7. (score, parts).
Dn variable. *Pf* number and choice of instruments optional. Also listed as *WIAM* 4693, 3644. *(Publisher)*

4484 OLIVEROS, Pauline. **To Valerie Solanas and Marilyn**
mm **Monroe in recognition of their desperation** (Baltimore: Smith, 1977) 4 p. $4. (score, parts).
Dn 30′. *Pf* may be performed by chamber group, orchestra, or chorus. Instrumentation not specified. Also listed as *WIAM* 3645, 4077. *(Publisher)*

4485 OLIVEROS, Pauline. **Willowbrook generations and reflec-**
mm **tions** (Baltimore: Smith, 1977) 4 p. $5.50. (score, parts).
Dn 15-60′. *Pf* any group or groups of 15 or more; audience participation. Also listed as *WIAM* 3649, 4078. *(Publisher)*

4486 PERRY, Julia Amanda. **Homage to Vivaldi** (facsimile of MS
mm on rental; New York: Southern Music, 1964) 33 p. (score, parts).
Dn 8′. *Pf* 3pic-2-2-2, 4-2-2-0, tim, per including xyl, str.

4487 PERRY, Julia Amanda. **Short piece for orchestra, A** (facsimm mile of MS on rental; New York: Southern Music, 1962) 35 p. (score, parts).
Dn 10′. *La* DLC. *Pf* 3pic-3enh-3bcl-3cbn; 4-3-2-1; tim; per including xyl, cel; hrp; pno; str. *Rg* Composers Recordings, CRI SD 145.

4488 PERRY, Julia Amanda. **Stabat Mater** (213; New York: Southmm ern Music, 1954) 32 p. (score, parts).
Dn 20′. *Da* 1951. *At* Jacopone de Todi. *Tr* composer. *Pf* solo A, str. Also for solo A, string quartet (*WIAM* 3660).

4489 PIERCE, Alexandra. **Behemoth** (New York: Seesaw Music, mm 1976) 58 p. (score, parts).
Dn 15′. *Da* fall 1976. *La* composer. *Pf* 2-1-1-2, 2-1-1-0, tim, per, str. *(Composer)*

4490 POLIN, Claire. **Scenes from Gilgamesh** (New York: Seesaw mm Music, 1972) 22 p. (score, parts).
Dn 12′. *Pf* str, solo flu.

4491 POLIN, Claire. **Second symphony. Korean** (New York: Seesaw mm Music, 1975) 63 p. (score, parts).
Dn 26′. *Pf* 2pic-2enh-2bcl-2; 4-3-3-1; tim; per including vib, xyl; pno; str.

4492 POLIN, Claire. **Symphony in two movements** (facsimile of MS mm on rental; New York: Seesaw Music, 1961) 59 p. (score, parts).
Dn 22′. *Pf* 1-2-4bcl-2, 4-3-3-1, tim, per, str.

4493 PREOBRAJENSKA, Vera N. **Hebraic suite for string or-**mm **chestra** (facsimile of autograph at NNAMC, 1968) 11 p. (score).
Dn 12′. *Da* 1968. *La* composer. *(Composer)*

4494 PREOBRAJENSKA, Vera N. **Promenade from *Suite for***md ***string orchestra*** (facsimile of autograph at NNAMC, 1946) 5 p. (score).
Dn 3′. *Da* 1946. *La* composer. *Tm Suite for string orchestra* (*WIAM* 4495). *(Composer)*

4495 PREOBRAJENSKA, Vera N. **Suite for string orchestra** mm (facsimile of autograph at NNAMC, 1947) 12 p. (score).
Dn 4′. *La* composer. *(Composer)*

4496 RAN, Shulamit. **Concert piece for piano and orchestra** mm (fascimile of MS on rental; New York: T. Presser, 1970) 36 p. (score, parts).
Dn 14′. *Da* 1970. *La* composer. *Pf* 4pic(pic-alto flu)-2-4bcl-3cbn, 5-4-3-1, tim, per for 4 players, str, solo pno. Also for 2pic-2-2bcl-2, 4-2-2btn-1, tim, per for 3 players, str, solo pno alternating with cel (Presser, 1973). *(Composer)*

4497 RICHTER, Marga. **Abyss** (facsimile of MS on rental; New York: mm Belwin-Mills, 1965) 57 p. (score, parts).
Dn 20′. *Da* 1965. *La* composer. *Pf* 2pic-1-2bcl-1, 2-1-1-0, tim, per, pno, str. *(Composer)*

4498 RICHTER, Marga. **Aria and toccata for viola and strings** mm (facsimile of MS on rental; New York: Belwin-Mills, 1957) 14 p. (score, parts).
Dn 10′. *Da* Feb. 1957. *La* composer. *Pf* string orchestra, solo vla. Also for pno, vla (*WIAM* 3690). *(Composer)*

4499 RICHTER, Marga. **Bird of yearning** (facsimile of MS on rental; mm New York: C. Fischer, 1976) 107 p. (score, parts).
Dn 25′. *Da* 1968. *La* composer. *Pf* 2pic-2-2bcl-2, 4-2-2-0, tim, per including cel, hrp, pno, str. Also can be performed by small orchestra (C. Fischer, 1976): 2pic-1-2bcl-1, 2-1-1-0, tim, per including cel, hrp, pno, str. *(Composer)*

4500 RICHTER, Marga. **Blackberry vines and winter fruit** (facsimm mile of MS on rental; New York: C. Fischer, 1976) 43 p. (score, parts).
Dn 13′. *Da* 1976. *La* composer. *Pf* 3pic-2-2-2; 4-3-2-1; tim; per including cel, mba, vib; hrp; str.

4501 RICHTER, Marga. **Concerto for piano and violas, cellos,** mm **and basses** (facsimile of MS on rental; New York: C. Fischer, 1977) 58 p. (score, parts).
Dn 21′. *Da* 1955. *La* composer. *Rg* MGM, E3547. *(Composer)*

4502 RICHTER, Marga. **Eight pieces for orchestra** (facsimile of MS mm on rental; New York: C. Fischer, 1975) 20 p. (score, parts).

Dn 7′. *Da* 1961. *La* composer. *Pf* 3pic-3enh-3bcl-3cbn, 4-3-3-1, tim, per including cel, hrp, str. *(Composer)*

4503 RICHTER, Marga. **Fragments** (facsimile of MS on rental; New mm York: C. Fischer, 1976) 9 p. (score, parts).
Dn 6′. *Da* Feb. 1976. *La* composer. *Pf* 2pic-2-2-2, 2-1-1-1, tim, per including cel, hrp, str. Also for solo pno (*WIAM* 4713). *(Composer)*

4504 RICHTER, Marga. **Lament for string orchestra** (New York: mm Broude Brothers, 1958) 16 p. (score, parts).
Dn 11′. *Da* 1956. *La* composer. *Rg* MGM, E3422. *(Composer)*

4505 RICHTER, Marga. **Landscapes of the mind I. Concerto for** mm **piano with orchestra** (facsimile of MS on rental; New York: C. Fischer, 1975) 91 p. (score, parts).
Dn 28′. *Da* 1974. *La* composer. *Pf* 3pic-3enh-3bcl-3cbn, 4-4-0-0, tim, per for 3 players, ebs, egr, electric tamboura, str, solo pno. Also with orchestration arranged for 2nd pno (New York: C. Fischer, 1977). *(Composer)*

4506 RICHTER, Marga. **Variations on a sarabande** (facsimile of mm MS on rental; New York: C. Fischer, 1975) 25 p. (score, parts).
Dn 8′. *Da* 1959. *La* composer. *Pf* 2pic-2-2-2, 4-2-2-1, tim, per, hrp, pno, str. *(Composer)*

4507 RICHTER, Marion Morrey. **Timberjack overture for concert** mm **band** (facsimile of autograph at NN, 1961) 32 p. (score, parts).
Dn 8′. *Da* 1961. *La* composer. *Pf* 2pic-1-6bcl-1-3sax, 0-0-0-0, tim, per. Also arranged for choral TTBB, pno (*WIAM* 4144). *(Composer)*

4508 ROBERTS, Gertrud. **Double concerto** (Honolulu, Haw.: com-mm poser, 1976) 139 p. (score, parts).
Dn 25′. *Da* 1976. *La* composer. *Pf* 2-2-2bcl-2, 4-2-3-0, tim, per, hrp, str, solo 2 hps or hps and pno. *(Composer)*

4509 ROBERTS, Gertrud. **Elegy** (facsimile of MS at Kennedy Library, mm Waltham, Mass., 1965) 22 p. (score, parts).
Dn 8′. *Da* 1965. *La* composer. *Pf* 2-2enh-2bcl-2cbn, 4-4-2-1, tim, per, hrp, str. A piano reduction is also available (facsimile of MS at Kennedy Library). *(Composer)*

4510 SEMEGEN, Daria. **Poème premier: dans la nuit [First poem:** mm **At night]** (New York: Composers Facsimile Ed., 1971) 16 p. $8. (score, parts).
Dn 8′. *Da* 1969. *La* composer. *At* Henri Michaux. *Pf* solo Bar, 2pic-1-0-1cbn, 0-1-0-0, per including cel, pno, str. *(Composer)*

4511 SEMEGEN, Daria. **Triptych for orchestra** (New York: Com-mm posers Facsimile Ed., 1975) 30 p. $15. (score, parts).
Dn 18′. *Da* 1965. *La* composer. *Pf* 3pic-2-2-3cbn, 4-3-3-1, tim, per, str. *(Composer)*

4512 SILVERMAN, Faye-Ellen. **Madness. Three bagatelles for** mm **small orchestra and narrator** (New York: Seesaw Music, 1972) 31 p. (score, parts).
Dn 6′. *Da* 1972. *La* publisher. *At* composer. *Pf* 2-2-2-2, 4-2-2-0, tim, per, str, narrator. *(Composer)*

4513 SILVERMAN, Faye-Ellen. **Shadings** (New York: Seesaw mm Music, 1977) 28 p. (score, parts).
Dn 10′. *Da* 1977. *La* publisher. *Pf* 1-1-0-1-sax, 1-1-0-0, per, str. *(Composer)*

4514 SLEETH, Natalie. **Jazz Gloria**. Arr. by Eric OSTERLING (New mm York: C. Fischer, 1973) 10 p. $18.75. (score, parts).
Dn 5′. *Pf* 2pic-2-8-2-4sax, 4-0-3-1-3crn-bar, per for 2 players, ebs. Originally for choral SATB, 3 tpt, cbs, bongo drums, pno, optional gtr (*WIAM* 4169). *(Composer)*

4515 SMITH, Julia. **American dance suite for small orchestra** (rev. mm ed.; facsimile of MS on rental; New York: T. Presser, 1963) 60 p. (score, parts).
Dn 10′. *Da* 3 Apr. 1963. *La* composer. *Pf* 1-1-2-1, 2-2-1-0, per, pno or hrp, str, optional tim. *Ct* Chicken reel, Negro lullaby, Lost my partner, One morning in May. Also arranged for 2 pno, 4 hands (*WIAM* 3735). The original version of 1936 was entitled *Little American suite*. *(Composer)*

4516 SMITH, Julia. **Concerto for piano and orchestra** (facsimile of mm MS on rental; New York: T. Presser, n.d.) 127 p. (score, parts).
Dn 22′. *La* composer. *Pf* 2-2-3-2, 4-3-3-1, tim, per, str, solo pno. Also with the original orchestration arranged for 2nd pno (MM 130; New York: Mowbray Music, 1971). *(Composer)*

4517 SMITH, Julia. **Episodic suite for large orchestra** (facsimile of
mm   MS on rental; New York: T. Presser, 1936) 30 p. (score, parts).
Dn 8'. *Da* 30 Oct. 1936. *La* composer. *Pf* 3-2-2-2, 4-2-3-1, tim, per including
xyl, hrp, str. *Ct* Yellow and blue, Nocturne, Waltz, March, Toccata. First
performed by Frederique Joanne Petrides and the Orchestrette Classique,
Carnegie Recital Hall, New York, 26 Apr. 1937. Originally for pno (*WIAM*
4738). Also arranged for 10 instruments (*WIAM* 4839).   *(Composer)*

4518 SMITH, Julia. **Fanfare for alma mater for full band** (New
mm   York: Mowbray Music, 1971) 7 p. $12. (score, parts).
Dn 4'. *Da* 1970. *Pf* 3-2-5-2-4sax, 4-2-3-epm-3-3crn, tim, per including vib. A
condensed score is also available from the publisher.   *(Composer)*

4519 SMITH, Julia. **Folkways symphony in four movements.**
mm   **Based on western cowboy and fiddle tunes** (facsimile of MS on
rental; New York: T. Presser, 1948) 93 p. (score, parts).
Dn 14'. *Da* 23 Dec. 1948. *La* composer. *Pf* for chamber orchestra: 2-2-2-2;
2-2-1-0; tim; per; hrp; pno, 4 hands; str. *Ct* Day's a-breakin', Night herding
song, Cowboy's waltz, Stomping leather.   *(Composer)*

4520 SMITH, Julia. **Hellenic suite based on Greek folk-melodies**
mm   (facsimile of MS on rental; New York: T. Presser, 1950) 54 p. (score,
parts).
Dn 15'. *Da* 1940-41. *La* composer. *Pf* 2-2-2-2, 4-2-3-1, tim, per, hrp, str. *Ct*
Sirtos (dance), Berceuse, Saga.   *(Composer)*

4521 SMITH, Julia. **Liza Jane** (facsimile of MS on rental; New York:
mm   T. Presser, 1940) 26 p. (score, parts).
Dn 4'. *Da* 1940. *La* composer. *Pf* 1-1-2-1, 2-2-1-0, tim, per, str. Commissioned
by the Columbia Broadcasting System, 1939-40.   *(Composer)*

4522 SMITH, Julia; VASHAW, Cecile. **Remember the Alamo for**
mm   **symphonic band with optional narrator and mixed chorus**
(115-40073; Bryn Mawr, Penn.: T. Presser, 1965) 52 p. (score, parts).
Dn 12'. *Da* 10 Dec. 1964. *At* William J. Marsh and Gladys Yoakum Wright. *St*
Official Texas state song. *Pf* choral SATB, 3-2-7-3-5sax, 4-2-3-3-3crn, tim, per,
cbs, optional male narrator. Also arranged for choral SATB, large orchestra
(facsimile of MS, parts on rental; New York: T. Presser, 1966).   *(Composer)*

4523 SMITH, Julia; VASHAW, Cecile. **Sails aloft. Overture for**
mm   **symphonic band** (New York: Mowbray Music, 1966) 34 p. (score,
parts).
Dn 7'. *Da* June 1966. *Pf* 3-2-7-3-5sax; 4-2-3-2-3crn; tim; per including vib,
xyl; cbs; hrp or pno. A condensed score is also available from the publisher.
          (Composer)

4524 SMITH, La Donna. **Orchestrophes** (49; Tuscaloosa, Ala.:
mm   Transmuseq, 1975) 46 p. $25. (score, parts).
Dn 35'. *Da* 1975. *La* composer. *Pf* 3-2-3-2; 4-4-4-1; per including glk, mba,
xyl; egr; pno; hrp; str.   *(Composer)*

4525 SMITH, La Donna. **Solo for amateur orchestra** (21; Tusca-
mm   loosa, Ala.: Transmuseq, 1976) 21 p. $6. (score, parts).
Dn 20'. *Da* 1976. *La* composer. *Pf* 1-1-1-1, 1-1-1-1, tim, per, egr, org, pno, str,
optional additional instruments and doublings. *Rg* Transmuseq, 2001.
          (Composer)

4526 STILMAN, Julia. **Oro intimo, El. Cantata no. 1 [The**
mm   **intimate gold]** (New York: Composers Facsimile Ed., 1977) 51 p.
$17.20. (score, parts).
Dn 17'. *Da* 1961. *La* composer. *At* Amado Nervo. *St* Elevación. *Lt* Spanish. *Pf*
solo B, 2-enh-3bcl-3cbn-4sax, 2-0-0-1, tim, per for 3 players, 4 vln and 4 vla or
8 vla.   *(Composer)*

4527 SUCHY, Gregoria Karides. **Argument** (facsimile of MS at
mm   NNAMC, 1960) 15 p. (score, parts).
Dn 4'. *Pf* 3pic-2-2-2, 4-3-3-1, per including xyl, str. Also for 2 pno, 4 hands
(*WIAM* 3743).   *(Composer)*

4528 SUCHY, Gregoria Karides. **Greek rhapsody (Ellinike' rap-**
mm   **sodia)** (facsimile of MS at NNAMC, 1951) 90 p. (score, parts).
Dn 10'. *La* composer. *Pf* 3pic-3enh-3bcl-2, 4-3-3-1, per, hrp, str. *(Composer)*

4529 SUCHY, Gregoria Karides. **Symphonic piece with trumpet**
mm   **and piano obbligato** (facsimile of MS at NNAMC, 1962) 109 p.
(score, parts).
Dn 13'. *Pf* 1-1-1-1, 1-1-0-0, tim, per, pno, str.   *(Composer)*

4530 SUCHY, Gregoria Karides. **Three lovers** (facsimile of MS at
mm   NNAMC, 1960) 33 p. (score, parts).
Dn 12'. *La* composer. *Pf* 3pic-2-2-2, 4-3-3-1, tim, per including xyl, hrp, pno,
str. *Ct* Mountain rascal, Wretched loser, Happy suitor. Also for 2 pno, 4 hands
(*WIAM* 3747).   *(Composer)*

4531 SWISHER, Gloria Wilson. **Canción** (facsimile of MS at
mm   NNAMC, 1977) 13 p. (score, parts).
Dn 5'. *Da* 1964. *La* composer. *Pf* 2-2-2-2, 2-2-2-1, str, solo flu. *(Composer)*

4532 SWISHER, Gloria Wilson. **Concerto for clarinet and or-**
mm   **chestra** (facsimile of MS at NNAMC, 1977) 97 p. (score, parts).
Dn 19'. *Da* 1960. *La* composer. *Pf* 3pic-2-0-3cbn, 4-3-3-1, tim, per, str, solo cla.
Published under the composer's maiden name, Gloria Wilson.   *(Composer)*

4533 SWISHER, Gloria Wilson. **Mountain and the island, The**
mm   (facsimile of MS at NNAMC, 1977) 24 p. (score, parts).
Dn 10'. *Da* 1970. *La* composer. *Pf* 3pic-2-5bcl-2-4sax, 4-4alto hrn-3crn-2-3-
bar-1, tim, per.   *(Composer)*

4534 SWISHER, Gloria Wilson. **Processions** (facsimile of MS at
mm   NNAMC, 1977) 33 p. (score, parts).
Dn 8'. *Da* 1973. *La* composer. *Pf* 3pic-2-5bcl-2-4sax, 4-4alto hrn-3crn-2-3-bar-
1, tim, per.   *(Composer)*

4535 TALMA, Louise. **Dialogues for piano and orchestra** (facsimile
mm   of MS on rental; New York: C. Fischer, 1965) 93 p. (score, parts).
Dn 23'. *La* DLC. *Pf* 3pic-2-2-2, 4-3-3-1, tim, per including cel, str, solo pno. *Ct*
Challenge, Struggle, Respite, Pursuit. Also with original orchestration arranged
for 2nd pno (facsimile of autograph at DLC, 1964).

4536 TALMA, Louise. **Toccata** (4008; New York: C. Fischer, 1947)
mm   98 p. (score, parts).
Dn 12'. *Pf* 3pic-3enh-3bcl-3cbn, 4-3-3-1, tim, per, pno, str. *Rg* Composers
Recordings, CRI SD 145.

4537 TALMA, Louise. **Tolling bell, The. Triptych for baritone and**
mm   **orchestra** (facsimile of MS on rental; New York: C. Fischer, 1969)
100 p. (score, parts).
Dn 27'. *Pf* solo Bar, 3pic-3enh-3bcl-3cbn, 4-3-3-1, tim, per including cel, hrp,
pno, str. *Ct* To be or not to be (*At* Shakespeare), Ah, Faustus (*At* Christopher
Marlowe), This is my plates last scene (*At* Donne). A piano-vocal score is
available (facsimile of MS at NN, 1967).

4538 THEMMEN, Ivana Marburger. **Fasching** (facsimile of MS at
mm   NNAMC, 1965) 66 p. (score).
Dn 9'. *Da* 1965. *Pf* 4pic-3enh-4bcl-4cbn, 4-3-3-1, tim, per including cel, hrp,
pno, str.   *(Composer)*

4539 THEMMEN, Ivana Marburger. **Mystic trumpeter, The** (fac-
mm   simile of MS at NNAMC, 1975) 87 p. (score, parts).
Dn 22'. *Da* Sept. 1975. *At* Whitman. *St* Leaves of grass. *Pf* solo S or M, 3pic-
3enh-3bcl-3cbn, 4-3-3-1, tim, per including cel, 2 hrp, pno, str. Also for solo S or
M, 2 tpt, pno, string quintet (*WIAM* 3761).   *(Composer)*

4540 THEMMEN, Ivana Marburger. **Ode to Akhmatova** (facsimile
mm   of MS at NNAMC, 1977) 76 p. (score, parts).
Dn 16'. *At* Anna Akhmatova. *St* Requiem 1935-40. *Pf* solo S, 3pic-2enh-3bcl-
3cbn, 4-3-3-1, tim, per, hrp, pno, str. Also for solo S, pno (*WIAM* 4990).
          (Composer)

4541 THEMMEN, Ivana Marburger. **Shelter this candle from the**
mm   **wind** (New York: composer, 1978) 86 p. (score, parts).
Dn 20'. *Da* 1978. *La* composer. *At* Edna St. Vincent Millay. *Pf* solo S; 3pic-
3enh-3bcl-3cbs; 4-3-3-1; tim; per including glk, xyl; hrp; pnc (cel); str.
          (Composer)

4542 VAN DE VATE, Nancy. **Adagio for orchestra** (facsimile of
mm   MS at NNAMC, 1977) 18 p. (score, parts).
Dn 6'. *Da* 1957. *La* composer. *Pf* 2-2-2-2, 4-2-2-1, tim, per, str.   *(Composer)*

4543 VAN DE VATE, Nancy. **Concerto for piano and orchestra**
mm   (facsimile of MS at NNAMC, 1977) 115 p. (score, parts).
Dn 21'. *Da* 1968. *La* composer. *Pf* 3pic-2-2-2, 4-2-3-1, tim, per, str, solo pno.
          (Composer)

4544 VAZQUEZ, Alida. **Incidental music for strings** (facsimile of
mm   MS at NNAMC, 1970) 19 p. (score).
Dn 6'. *Da* 1970. *La* composer.   *(Composer)*

4545 WALDO, Elisabeth. **Concierto Indo-Americano** (Northridge,
mm   Calif.: Mundoamericas Music, 1977) 25 p. $10. (score, parts).
Dn 13'. *Da* 1976. *La* composer. *Pf* 2-2-2-2, 4-2-3-1, per, pno, str, solo vln. Also
for chamber orchestra: 1-1-1-1, 1-1-1-1, per, pno, str, solo vln (Mundoamericas
Music, 1977).   *(Composer)*

4546 WALDO, Elisabeth. **De Anza march, The** (Northridge, Calif.:
mm   Mundoamericas Music, 1969) 20 p. (score, parts).
Dn 4'. *Da* 1969. *La* composer. *Pf* 2-2-2-2, 4-2-3-1, tim, per, str. Also for
chamber orchestra: 1-1-1-1, 1-1-1-1, str (Mundoamericas Music, 1969). *Rg Viva
California*, Southern Music, PSO 002   *(Composer)*

4547 WALDO, Elisabeth. **Entrance of the conquistadores** (Nor-
mm   thridge, Calif.: Mundoamericas Music, 1975) 19 p. $8.50. (score,
parts).
Dn 4', rev. 1975. *La* composer. *Pf* 2-2-2-2, 4-2-3-1, tim, per, str. *Rg
Realm of the Incas*, GNP Crescendo, 603.

4548 WALDO, Elisabeth. **Incan festival dance** (Northridge, Calif.:
mm   Mundoamericas Music, 1977) 16 p. $8.50. (score, parts).
Dn 3'. *Da* 1960, rev. 1977. *La* composer. *Pf* 2-2-2-2, 4-2-3-1, tim, per, str.

4549 WALDO, Elisabeth. **Jarabes mestizos. Mexican dances**
mm   (Northridge, Calif.: Mundoamericas, 1974) 18 p. $7.50. (score, parts).
Dn 10'. *Da* 1974. *La* composer. *Pf* 2-2-2-2, 4-2-3-1, tim, per, str. Also for
chamber orchestra: 1-1-1-1, 1-1-1-1, tim, per, str (Mundoamericas Music,
1974).   *(Composer)*

4550 WALDO, Elisabeth. **Serpent and the eagle, The** (Northridge,
mm   Calif.: Mundoamericas Music, 1959) 18 p. $8.50. (score, parts).
Dn 4'. *Da* 1959. *La* composer. *Pf* 2-2-2-2, 4-2-3-1, tim, per, str. Also for
chamber orchestra: 1-1-1-1, 1-1-1-1, tim, per, str (Mundoamericas Music,
1959). *Rg Rites of the pagan*, GNP Crescendo, 601.   *(Composer)*

4551 WALKER, Gwyneth. **Upon her leaving. For baritone and
mm   chamber orchestra** (New Canaan, Conn.: Walker, 1977) 80 p. $8.
(score, parts).
Dn 15'. *Da* 1977. *La* composer. *At* Carll Tucker. *Pf* solo Bar, 2-1-2-1, 1-1-1-0,
tim, per including vib, str.   *(Composer)*

4552 WARREN, Elinor Remick. **Along the western shore** (facsimile
mm   of MS on rental; New York: C. Fischer, 1963) 55 p. (score, parts).
Dn 12'. *Da* 1963. *La* publisher. *Pf* 3pic-3enh-3bcl-3cbn, 4-2-3-1, tim, per
including cel, hrp, str. *Ct* Dark hills, Nocturne, Sea rhapsody. *Rg* publisher.
                                                                (Composer)

4553 WARREN, Elinor Remick. **Crystal lake, The** (facsimile of MS
mm   on rental; New York: C. Fischer, 1962) 42 p. (score, parts).
Tone poem. *Dn* 9'. *Da* 1958. *La* publisher. *Pf* 3pic-3enh-2-2; 4-2-3-0; tim; per
including xyl, cel; hrp; str. Facsimile of MS also at PPFleisher. *Rg* publisher.
                                                                (Composer)

4554 WARREN, Elinor Remick. **Fountain, The** (facsimile of MS at
mm   PPFleisher, 1942) 19 p. (score, parts).
Tone poem. *Dn* 5'. *Da* 1942. *La* composer. *Pf* 2-2-2-2, 3-2-3-0, tim, per
including cel, hrp, str.   *(Composer)*

4555 WARREN, Elinor Remick. **Intermezzo** (facsimile of MS on
md   rental; New York: Belwin-Mills, 1974) 21 p. (score, parts).
Dn 6'. *Da* 1970. *La* publisher. *Pf* 2-2-3bcl-2, 4-3-3-1, tim, per, hrp, str. *Tm The
legend of King Arthur* (*WIAM* 4247).   *(Composer)*

4556 WARREN, Elinor Remick. **Sonnets for soprano and string
mm   orchestra** (facsimile of MS on rental; New York: C. Fischer, 1965)
34 p. (score, parts).
Dn 12'. *Da* rev. 1970. *La* composer. *At* Edna St. Vincent Millay. *St Fatal
interview*. Also for solo S and string quartet (*WIAM* 3787).   *(Composer)*

4557 WARREN, Elinor Remick. **Suite for orchestra** (facsimile of
mm   MS on rental; New York: C. Fischer, 1959) 121 p. (score, parts).
Dn 17'. *Da* 1958. *La* publisher. *Pf* 3pic-3enh-2-2; 4-2-3-1; tim; per including
cel, glk, xyl; hrp; str. *Rg* Composers Recordings, CRI 172.   *(Composer)*

4558 WARREN, Elinor Remick. **Symphony in one movement**
mm   (facsimile of MS on rental; New York: C. Fischer, 1972) 79 p. (score,
parts).
Dn 17'. *Da* 1971. *La* composer. *Pf* 3pic-3enh-2-2; 4-2-3-1; tim; per including
cel, glk, xyl; str.   *(Composer)*

4559 WYLIE, Ruth Shaw. **Concerto grosso for solo woodwinds
mm   and string orchestra, op. 15** (West Babylon, N.Y.: H. Branch,
1977) 55 p. (score, parts).
Dn 12'. *Da* 1952. *La* composer. *Pf* 2-1-2-2, 0-0-0-0, str.

4560 WYLIE, Ruth Shaw. **Involution, op. 24, no. 2** (facsimile of MS
mm   on rental; West Babylon, N.Y.: H. Branch, 1977) 31 p. $10. (score,
parts).
Dn 12'. *Da* 1967. *La* composer. *Pf* 2-1-2-2, 0-2-2-0, per, str.   *(Composer)*

4561 WYLIE, Ruth Shaw. **Memories of birds for orchestra, op.
md   31, no. 2** (facsimile of MS on rental: West Babylon, N.Y.: H.
Branch, 1977) 33 p. $10. (score, parts).
Dn 12'. *Da* 1976. *La* composer. *Pf* 3-2-2-3, 4-3-3-1, tim, per for 3 players, str.
                                                                (Composer)

4562 ZAIMONT, Judith Lang. **Concerto for piano and orchestra**
mm   (New York: composer, 1972) 141 p. (score).
Dn 33'. *Da* 1972. *La* composer. *Pf* 3-3-3-2, 4-2-3-1, tim, per, str, solo pno.
                                                                (Composer)

4563 ZIFFRIN, Marilyn J. **Orchestra piece no. 1** (facsimile of MS at
mm   NNAMC, 1977) 39 p. (score, parts).
Dn 9'. *Da* 1977. *La* composer. *Pf* 2-2-2-2, 2-2-2-0, tim, per, str.   *(Composer)*

4564 ZWILICH, Ellen Taaffe. **Symposium for orchestra** (New
mm   York: Elkan-Vogel, 1975) 57 p. (score, parts).
Dn 12'. *Da* 1973. *La* publisher. *Pf* 3-3enh-4bcl-3, 4-3-3-1; tim; per including
cel, xyl; str.   *(Composer)*

Solo instrumental music

4565 BALLOU, Esther Williamson. **Dance suite** (facsimile of auto-
mm   graph at NNACA, 1937) [7] p.
Dn 3'. *Pf* pno.

4566 BALLOU, Esther Williamson. **Elegy** (facsimile of autograph at
mm   NNACA, 1968) 2 p.
Dn 7'. *Da* Aug. 1968. *Pf* vcl.

4567 BALLOU, Esther Williamson. **Eleven piano teaching pieces**
mm   (New York: Composers Facsimile Ed., 1962) [2] p.
Dn 5'. *Pf* pno.   *(James R. Heintze)*

4568 BALLOU, Esther Williamson. **Galliard** (New York: Composers
mm   Facsimile Ed., 1956) 1 p.
Dn 1'. *Pf* pno.

4569 BALLOU, Esther Williamson. **Gigue** (New York: Composers
mm   Facsimile Ed., 1956) 3 p.
Dn 1'. *Pf* pno.

4570 BALLOU, Esther Williamson. **Impromptu** (facsimile of auto-
mm   graph at NNACA, 1968) 2 p.
Dn 2'. *Da* 18 May 1968. *Pf* org.   *(James R. Heintze)*

4571 BALLOU, Esther Williamson. **Passacaglia and toccata** (New
mm   York: Composers Facsimile Ed., 1962) 8 p.
Dn 8'. *Pf* org.   *(James R. Heintze)*

4572 BALLOU, Esther Williamson. **Sonata for piano** (New York:
mm   Composers Facsimile Ed., 1959) 15 p.
Dn 11'. *Da* 1955.

4573 BALLOU, Esther Williamson. **Sonatina for piano** (facsimile
mm   of autograph at NNACA, 1941) 9 p.
Dn 8'. *Da* 1941. Published under the composer's maiden name, Williamson.

4574 BALLOU, Esther Williamson. **Variations, scherzo, and
mm   fugue on a theme by Lou Harrison** (New York: Composers
Facsimile Ed., 1959) 19 p.
Dn 12'. *Da* 15 July 1959. *Pf* pno. *Rg* NNACA.

4575 BARKIN, Elaine. **For suite's sake** (New York: Composers
mm   Facsimile Ed., 1975) 10 p.
Dn 8'. *Da* 1975. *La* composer. *Pf* hps.   *(Composer)*

4576 BARKIN, Elaine. **Six compositions for piano** (New York:
mm   Composers Facsimile Ed., 1969) 10 p.
Dn 7′. *Da* 1969. *La* composer.   *(Composer)*

4577 BITGOOD, Roberta. **Choral prelude on** *Covenanters tune*
mm   (3604; New York: H. Flammer, 1958) 3 p.
Dn 3′. *Da* 1956. *La* composer. *Pf* org.   *(Composer)*

4578 BITGOOD, Roberta. **Choral prelude on** *God himself is with*
mm   *us* (793; New York: H.W. Gray, 1952) 8 p.
Dn 3′. *Da* 1942. *La* composer. *Pf* org. Based on Neander's tune.   *(Composer)*

4579 BITGOOD, Roberta. **Choral prelude on** *Jewels* (746; New
mm   York: H.W. Gray, 1949) 4 p.
Dn 3′. *Da* 1942. *La* composer. *Pf* org.   *(Composer)*

4580 BITGOOD, Roberta. **Choral prelude on** *Siloam* (778; New
mm   York: H.W. Gray, 1952) 3 p.
Dn 2′. *Da* 1936. *La* composer. *Pf* org.   *(Composer)*

4581 BITGOOD, Roberta. **Meditation on** *Kingsfold* (101; Chapel
mm   Hill, N.C.: Hinshaw Music, 1976) 5 p. $1.50.
Dn 4′. *Da* 1975. *La* composer. *Pf* org.   *(Composer)*

4582 BITGOOD, Roberta. **O Master, let me walk with thee.**
mp   **Choral prelude,** *Organ Album* XXXIII (Aug 1961) 68-71.
Dn 3′. *Da* 1956. *La* composer. *Pf* org.   *(Composer)*

4583 BITGOOD, Roberta. **Offertories from afar. Seven pieces for**
mm   **organ based on folk tunes** (4175; New York: H. Flammer, 1964)
   24 p.
Dn 18′. *Da* 1963. *La* composer.   *(Composer)*

4584 BITGOOD, Roberta. **On an ancient Alleluia** (894; New York:
mm   H.W. Gray, 1962) 8 p.
Dn 5′. *Da* 1958. *La* composer. *Pf* org.   *(Composer)*

4585 BITGOOD, Roberta. **Postlude on an old Spanish hymn,**
mp   *Organ Portfolio* XXIX/3 (Feb 1966) 76-77.
Dn 2′. *Da* 1966. *La* composer. *Pf* org.   *(Composer)*

4586 BOONE, Clara Lyle. **Annunciation of spring** (Detroit: Shelby
mm   Music, 1953) 11 p.
Dn 9′. *Da* 1952. *Pf* pno. Also for orchestra (*WIAM* 4374).   *(Composer)*

4587 BRITAIN, Radie. **Adoration** (Hollywood, Calif.: Calvi Music,
mm   1956) [2] p.
Dn 3′. *Pf* pno.

4588 BRITAIN, Radie. **Anima divina for harp** (New York: Seesaw
mm   Music, 1973) 12 p.
Dn 8′.

4589 BRITAIN, Radie. **Cactus rhapsody** (facsimile of MS at NN,
mm   n.d.) 15 p.
Dn 12′. *Pf* pno. Also for orchestra (*WIAM* 4377).

4590 BRITAIN, Radie. **Dance of the clown** (15404; Boston: A.P.
mm   Schmidt, 1948) 3 p.
Dn 2′. *Pf* pno.

4591 BRITAIN, Radie. **Little Spaniard** (APS 15405; Boston: A.P.
mm   Schmidt, 1948) 3 p.
Dn 2′. *Pf* pno.

4592 BRITAIN, Radie. **Reflection for harp** (1091; Hollywood, Calif.:
mm   R.B. Brown, 1966) 4 p.
Dn 4′.

4593 BRITAIN, Radie. **Wings of silver** (WM 7012; Cincinnati: Willis
mm   Music, 1953) 3 p.
Dn 2′. *Pf* pno.

4594 BRUSH, Ruth. **Pastorale,** *Lorenz's organ album* (OP 168-70;
mc   Dayton, Ohio: Lorenz, 1953) 84-86.
Dn 4′. *Pf* org.   *(Composer)*

4595 BRUSH, Ruth. **Two expressive pieces for organ** (8927; New
mm   York: J. Fischer, 1956) 8 p.
Dn 9′. *Ct* Canzona, Canticle.   *(Composer)*

4596 COATES, Gloria. **Structure for piano. Three pieces about C**
mm   (facsimile of MS at NNAMC, 1973) 12 p.
Dn 13′. *Da* 1973. *La* composer.   *(Composer)*

4597 CODY, Judith. **City and country themes in G [major]** (Los
mm   Altos, Calif.: Kikimora, 1977) 2 p. $4.50.
Dn 3′. *Da* Apr. 1976. *La* composer. *Pf* gtr.   *(Composer)*

4598 CODY, Judith. **Etude no. 1** (Los Altos, Calif.: Kikimora, 1977) 2
mm   p. $4.
Dn 1′. *Da* May 1976. *La* composer. *Pf* gtr.   *(Composer)*

4599 CODY, Judith. **Firelights in C [major]** (Los Altos, Calif.:
mm   Kikimora, 1977) 2 p. $5.
Dn 2′. *Da* 1976. *La* composer. *Pf* gtr.   *(Composer)*

4600 CODY, Judith. **Firelights in G major: prelude and theme** (Los
mm   Altos, Calif.: Kikimora, 1977) 4 p. $8.50.
Dn 4′. *Da* July 1977. *La* composer. *Pf* gtr.   *(Composer)*

4601 CODY, Judith. **Nocturne, op. 9, no. 1** (Los Altos, Calif.:
mm   Kikimora, 1977) 8 p. $12.
Dn 10′. *Da* Aug. 1977. *La* composer. *Pf* gtr.   *(Composer)*

4602 CORY, Eleanor. **Combinations** (facsimile of MS at NNACA,
mm   1970) 12 p.
Dn 5′. *La* NNACA. *Pf* pno.   *(Composer)*

4603 CORY, Eleanor. **Epithalamium** (facsimile of MS at NNACA,
mm   1973) 4 p.
Dn 7′. *La* NNACA. *Pf* flu.   *(Composer)*

4604 CRANE, Joelle Wallach. **Moment for solo oboe** (New York:
mm   Composers Facsimile Ed., 1967) 2 p.
Dn 7′. *Da* 1967. *La* NNACA.   *(Composer)*

4605 DENBOW, Stefania Björnson. **Exaltation. Twenty-one vari-**
mm   **ations on tonus peregrinus** (New York: Seesaw Music, 1975) 17
   p. $8.
Dn 11′. *Da* 1972. *La* composer. *Pf* org.   *(Composer)*

4606 DIEMER, Emma Lou. **Celebration. Seven hymn settings for**
mm   **organ** (Minneapolis: Augsburg, 1976) 26 p. $3.50.
Dn 18′. *Da* 1970. *La* composer. *Ct* Wareham, Ancient of days, Hankey,
Wesley, Innsbruck, Gounod, Were you there?   *(Composer)*

4607 DIEMER, Emma Lou. **Declarations for organ** (New York:
mm   Seesaw Music, 1976) 10 p.
Dn 8′. *Da* 1973. *La* publisher.   *(Composer)*

4608 DIEMER, Emma Lou. **Fantasie for organ** (New York: Oxford
mm   U., 1967) 12 p.
Dn 7′. *Da* 1958. *La* composer.   *(Composer)*

4609 DIEMER, Emma Lou. **Fantasy on** *O sacred head* (New York:
mm   Boosey & Hawkes, 1972) 12 p. $3.
Dn 8′. *Da* 1967. *La* composer. *Pf* org.   *(Composer)*

4610 DIEMER, Emma Lou. **Four on a row for piano,** *New Scribner*
mc   *music library.* Ed. by Merle MONTGOMERY (SML 4; New York:
   Scribner's Sons, 1972) IV, 253-56.
Dn 4′. *Da* 1972. *La* composer.   *(Composer)*

4611 DIEMER, Emma Lou. **He leadeth me. Hymn setting for**
mm   **organ** (New York: Oxford U., 1970) 12 p. $3.
Dn 6′. *Da* 1969. *La* composer.   *(Composer)*

4612 DIEMER, Emma Lou. **Jubilate and Contrasts,** *Preludes and*
mc   *postludes* (Minneapolis: Augsburg, 1976) IV, 8-12.
Dn 6′. *Da* 1975. *La* composer. *Pf* org.   *(Composer)*

4613 DIEMER, Emma Lou. **Seven etudes for piano** (New York: C.
mm   Fischer, 1972) 28 p. $5.

Dn 18′ . *Da* 1965. *La* publisher. *(Composer)*

4614 DIEMER, Emma Lou. **Sound pictures for piano** (New York:
mm   Boosey & Hawkes, 1971) 11 p. $3.
Dn 8′ . *Da* 1971. *La* composer. *(Composer)*

4615 DIEMER, Emma Lou. **Three pieces for carillon** (10-C2;
mm   Bloomfield Hills, Mich.: Guild of Carilloneurs in North America,
1976) 8 p.
Dn 8′ . *Da* 1972. *La* composer. *(Composer)*

4616 DIEMER, Emma Lou. **Toccata and fugue for organ** (New
mm   York: Seesaw Music, 1976) 12 p.
Dn 8′ . *Da* 1969. *La* publisher. *(Composer)*

4617 DIEMER, Emma Lou. **Toccata for marimba** (M 1; New York:
mm   Music for Percussion, 1957) 4 p.
Dn 6′ . *Da* 1955. *La* composer. *(Composer)*

4618 DIEMER, Emma Lou. **Toccata for organ** (New York: Oxford
mm   U., 1967) 19 p.
Dn 8′ . *Da* 1964. *La* composer. *(Composer)*

4619 DRAKE, Elizabeth Bell. **Arecibo sonata** (Ithaca, N.Y.: com-
mm   poser, 1968) 14 p. $2.50.
Dn 11′ . *Da* 1968. *La* composer. *Pf* pno. *(Composer)*

4620 DRAKE, Elizabeth Bell. **Second sonata** (facsimile of MS at
mm   NNAMC, 1972) 19 p.
Dn 10′ . *Da* 1972. *La* composer. *Pf* pno. *(Composer)*

4621 DRAKE, Elizabeth Bell. **Variations and interludes** (Ithaca,
mm   N.Y.: composer, 1952) 8 p. $1.50.
Dn 7′ . *Da* 1952. *La* composer. *Pf* pno. *(Composer)*

4622 ESCOT, Pozzi. **Differences group I** (Cambridge, Mass.: Publica-
mm   tions Contact International, 1975) 4 p. $3.
Dn 5′ . *Da* 1961. *Pf* pno. *(Composer)*

4623 ESCOT, Pozzi. **Differences group II** (Cambridge, Mass.: Publi-
mm   cations Contact International, 1975) 6 p. $3.
Dn 6′ . *Da* 1963. *Pf* pno. *(Composer)*

4624 ESCOT, Pozzi. **Fergus are** (Cambridge, Mass.: Publications
mm   Contact International, 1975) 13 p. $25.
Dn 8′ . *Pf* org. *(Composer)*

4625 FINE, Vivian. **Concerto for piano strings and percussion for
mm   one performer** (Shaftsbury, Vt.: Catamount Facsimile Ed., 1973)
23 p. $7.50.
Dn 10′ . *Da* 1972. *La* composer. *(Composer)*

4626 FINE, Vivian. **Four polyphonic piano pieces** (Shaftsbury, Vt.:
mm   Catamount Facsimile Ed., 1974) 11 p. $3.50.
Dn 7′ . *Da* 1932. *La* composer. *(Composer)*

4627 FINE, Vivian. **Second prophet-bird, The** (Shaftsbury, Vt.:
mm   Catamount Facsimile Ed., 1972) 6 p. $3.
Dn 6′ . *Da* 1973. *La* composer. *Pf* flu. *(Composer)*

4628 FINE, Vivian. **Second solo for oboe** (Shaftsbury, Vt.: Cata-
mm   mount Facsimile Ed., 1972) 4 p. $2.50.
Dn 5′ . *Da* 1947. *La* composer. *(Composer)*

4629 FINE, Vivian. **Sinfonia and fugato**, *New music for the piano*. Ed.
mc   by Joseph PROSTAKOFF (New York: Lawson-Gould, 1963) 57-63.
Dn 7′ . *Da* 1952. *La* composer. *Pf* pno. *Rg* Composers Recordings, CRI SD 288.
(Composer)

4630 FINE, Vivian. **Solo for oboe** (Shaftsbury, Vt.: Catamount
mm   Facsimile Ed., 1974) 2 p. $2.
Dn 5′ . *Da* 1929. *La* composer. *(Composer)*

4631 FINE, Vivian. **Song of Persephone, The** (Shaftsbury, Vt.:
mm   Catamount Facsimile Ed., 1972) 6 p. $3.
Dn 8′ . *Da* 1964. *La* composer. *Pf* vla. *(Composer)*

4632 FINE, Vivian. **Suite in E-flat [major]** (Shaftsbury, Vt.: Cata-
mm   mount Facsimile Ed., 1972) 8 p. $3.50.
Dn 7′ . *Da* 1940. *La* composer. *Pf* pno. *(Composer)*

4633 FINE, Vivian. **Variations for harp** (New York: Lyra Music,
mm   1965) 7 p.
Dn 6′ . *Da* 1953. *La* composer. *(Composer)*

4634 GIDEON, Miriam. **Canzona for piano solo**, *New Music XX/2*
mp   (Jan 1947) 3-7.
Dn 4′ .

4635 GIDEON, Miriam. **Of shadows numberless. Suite for piano**
mm   (New York: American Composers Ed., 1966) 21 p.
Dn 9′ . *La* DLC. *At* Keats. *St Ode to a nightingale*, adapted.

4636 GIDEON, Miriam. **Six cuckoos in quest of a composer.
mm   Suite for keyboard** (New York: American Composers Ed., 1953)
26 p.
Dn 15′ . *Pf* pno. *Ct* Il cucolo nel Rinascimento. Ricercar in tre voci, Kleines
Praeludium im Barockstil auf den Namen "Kuku", Klassische Sonatine auf ein
berühmtes Motiv, Le coucou au dix-neuvième siècle. Prelude sentimental,
Impression d'un coucou, The bird.

4637 GIDEON, Miriam. **Sonata for piano** (New York: American
mm   Composers Ed., 1977) 13 p.
Dn 10′ . *Da* 1977. *La* composer. *(Composer)*

4638 GIDEON, Miriam. **Three biblical masks for organ** (New
mm   York: American Composers Ed., 1958) 16 p.
Dn 10′ . *Ct* Haman, Esther, Mordecai. Also for pno, vln (*WIAM* 3498).

4639 GLANVILLE-HICKS, Peggy. **Sonata for harp** (New York:
mm   Weintraub Music, 1953) 14 p.
Dn 10′ . *Rg* Esoteric E5523.

4640 GOULD, Elizabeth. **Sonata for piano no. 1** (facsimile of MS at
mm   NNAMC, 1977) 21 p.
Dn 12′ . *Da* 1958. *La* composer. Awarded first prize for chamber music in the
Mu Phi Epsilon composition contest, 1959. *(Composer)*

4641 GOULD, Elizabeth. **Sonata for piano no. 2** (facsimile of MS at
mm   NNAMC, 1977) 26 p.
Dn 14′ . *Da* 1961. *La* composer. *(Composer)*

4642 GREENE, Margo. **Study for solo clarinet** (facsimile of MS at
mm   NNAMC, 1971) 3 p.
Dn 3′ . *Da* 1971. *La* composer. *(Composer)*

4643 GREENE, Margo. **Variations for clarinet solo** (New York:
mm   Associated Music, 1972) 5 p.
Dn 6′ . *Da* 1972. *La* composer. *(Composer)*

4644 HAYS, Doris. **Breathless for bass flute** (New York: Quinska
mm   Music, 1976) 2 p. $2.
Dn 4′ . *Da* 1976. *La* composer. *(Composer)*

4645 HAYS, Doris. **Sunday nights** (New York: Quinska Music, 1977)
mm   5 p. $3.
Dn 6′ . *Da* 1977. *La* composer. *Pf* pno. *(Composer)*

4646 HSU, Wen-ying. **Perpetual momentum** (West Babylon, N.Y.: H.
mm   Branch, 1977) 6 p.
Dn 4′ . *Da* 1974. *La* composer. *Pf* pno. *(Composer)*

4647 HSU, Wen-ying. **Piano sonata no. 1** (West Babylon, N.Y.: H.
mm   Branch, 1977) 17 p.
Dn 10′ . *Da* 1958. *La* composer. *(Composer)*

4648 HSU, Wen-ying. **Piano suite** (Los Angeles: composer, 1967) 14
mm   p.
Dn 8′ . *Da* 1967. *La* composer. *(Composer)*

4649 HSU, Wen-ying. **Sound of autumn. Piano suite** (West Baby-
mm   lon, N.Y.: H. Branch, 1977) 4 p.
Dn 6′ . *Da* 1975. *La* composer. *Ct* Love song in the moonlight, Autumn breeze,
Grief in autumn. *(Composer)*

4650 HUGHES, Sr. Martina. **Dĭko** (Duluth, Minn.: composer, 1973) 5
mm   p. $1.25.
Dn 4′. *Da* 1973. *La* composer. *Pf* pno.   *(Composer)*

4651 IVEY, Jean Eichelberger. **Prelude and passacaglia** (facsimile
mm   of MS at NNAMC, 1955) 10 p.
Dn 6′. *La* composer. *Pf* pno.   *(Composer)*

4652 IVEY, Jean Eichelberger. **Sonata for piano** (facsimile of MS at
mm   NNAMC, 1958) 26 p.
Dn 20′. *La* composer.   *(Composer)*

4653 IVEY, Jean Eichelberger. **Sonatina for unaccompanied clar-
mm   inet** (New York: C. Fischer, 1972) 6 p.
Dn 10′. *Da* 1963. *La* publisher.   *(Composer)*

4654 IVEY, Jean Eichelberger. **Theme and variations** (facsimile of
mm   MS at NNAMC, 1952) 10 p.
Dn 10′. *Da* 1952. *La* composer. *Pf* pno.   *(Composer)*

4655 JORDAN, Alice. **Elegy on a Norwegian folk melody**, *All hail
mc   the power of Jesus' name.* Ed. by Sharron LYON (4570; Nashville:
Broadman, 1956) 36-38, $3.25.
Dn 4′. *Pf* org.   *(Composer)*

4656 JORDAN, Alice. **Fantasy on** *Foundation*, *All hail the power of
mc   Jesus' name.* Ed. by Sharron LYON (4570; Nashville: Broadman,
1976) 24-27, $3.25.
Dn 4′. *Pf* org.   *(Composer)*

4657 JORDAN, Alice. **Prelude on** *Mercy*, *All hail the power of Jesus'
mc   name.* Ed. by Sharron LYON (4570; Nashville: Broadman, 1976) 46-
48, $3.25.
Dn 4′. *Pf* org.   *(Composer)*

4658 JORDAN, Alice. **Salutation. All hail the power of Jesus'
mc   name**, *All hail the power of Jesus' name.* Ed. by Sharron LYON
(4570; Nashville: Broadman, 1976) 3-6, $3.25.
Dn 4′. *Pf* org.   *(Composer)*

4659 JORDAN, Alice. **Season and a time, A** (4575; Nashville:
mm   Broadman, 1977) 48 p.
Dn 40′. *Pf* org. *Ct* Jubilate, Communion on 2 American folk hymns, Canonic
voluntary on *Dix*, Triumphant gladness, Pastorale on an Austrian carol, Prayer,
Processional on an old English melody, Arioso on a German carol, Fanfare and
trumpet tune, Four familiar Nativity melodies, Adoration on a traditional
English melody, The Lord is my shepherd.   *(Composer)*

4660 JORDAN, Alice. **Worship service music for the organist.** Ed.
mm   by Sharron LYON (4570; Nashville: Broadman, 1975) 47 p. $3.25.
Dn 44′. *Pf* org. *Ct* Adagio on a traditional Swedish hymn tune, Amabile on a
Swedish folk tune, Canticle of praise on *Azmon*, Cantilena on a traditional
Welsh melody, Chorale on *Canonbury*, Entreaty on *Thou didst leave thy throne*
(*Margaret*), Improvisation on *Old hundredth*, Intrada on 2 hymn tunes,
Introduction and chorale on *St. Margaret*, Meditation on *Maryton*, Voluntary
on *Germany*.   *(Composer)*

4661 KETTERING, Eunice Lea. **Clouds, rain, wind suite** (46736;
mm   New York: G. Schirmer, 1970) 8 p. $1.
Dn 5′. *Da* 1947. *La* NmU. *Pf* pno.   *(Composer)*

4662 KETTERING, Eunice Lea. **House of the Lord, The**, *American
mc   organ music.* Ed. by Leslie P. SPELMAN (5062; Chicago: Summy-
Birchard, 1957) I, 24-32.
Dn 5′. *Da* 1945. *La* NmU.   *(Composer)*

4663 KETTERING, Eunice Lea. **Lord into his garden comes, The**
mm   (3473; New York: H. Flammer, 1958) 4 p.
Dn 2′. *Da* 1940. *La* NmU. *Pf* org.   *(Composer)*

4664 KETTERING, Eunice Lea. **Paraphrase on an American folk
mm   hymn** *Kemath* (765; New York: H.W. Gray, 1951) 5 p.
Dn 4′. *Da* 1944. *La* NmU. *Pf* org.   *(Composer)*

4665 KETTERING, Eunice Lea. **Passacaglia in G minor** (Phila-
mm   delphia: Elkan-Vogel, 1953) 6 p.
Dn 4′. *Da* 1929. *La* NmU. *Pf* org.   *(Composer)*

4666 KOLB, Barbara. **Appello** (New York: Boosey & Hawkes, 1976)
mm   15 p.
Dn 10′. *Pf* pno.   *(Composer)*

4667 LOMON, Ruth. **Dust devils** (Washington, D.C.: Arsis, 1977) 8 p.
mm
Dn 7′. *Da* 1976. *La* composer. *Pf* hrp.   *(Composer)*

4668 LOMON, Ruth. **Rondo** (facsimile of MS at NNAMC, 1959) 6 p.
mm
Dn 5′. *Da* 1959. *La* composer. *Pf* pno.   *(Composer)*

4669 LOMON, Ruth. **Toccata and fugue** (facsimile of MS at
mm   NNAMC, 1961) 8 p.
Dn 6′. *Da* 1961. *La* composer. *Pf* pno.   *(Composer)*

4670 LORENZ, Ellen Jane. **Communion hymn sequence** (Dayton:
mm   Lorenz, 1961) 16 p.
Free-style organ accompaniments to Communion hymns. *Dn* 65′. *Pf* org,
optional choral SATB. Published under the pseudonym of Allen James.
                     (Composer)

4671 LORENZ, Ellen Jane. **From an old tune book** (Dayton: Lorenz,
mm   1971) 16 p. $2.50.
Dn 20′. *Da* 1971. *Pf* org.   *(Composer)*

4672 MAMLOK, Ursula. **Polyphony I for solo clarinet** (facsimile of
mm   MS at NNACA, 1969) 7 p.
Dn 7′. *Rg* tape at NNACA.   *(Composer)*

4673 MAMLOK, Ursula. **Variations for solo flute** (facsimile of MS
mm   at NNACA, 1963) 9 p.
Dn 6′. *Da* 1962. *Rg* Samuel Baron plays 20th century American music for solo
flute, Composers Recordings, CRI 212.   *(Composer)*

4674 MARCUS, Adabelle Gross. **Child's day, A** (West Babylon,
mm   N.Y.: H. Branch, 1977) 12 p.
Dn 20′. *Pf* pno.   *(Composer)*

4675 MARCUS, Adabelle Gross. **Etude érotique** (facsimile of MS on
mm   rental; West Babylon, N.Y.: H. Branch, 1977) 9 p.
Dn 6′. *Pf* pno.   *(Composer)*

4676 MARCUS, Adabelle Gross. **Theme and variations** (facsimile
mm   of MS on rental; West Babylon, N.Y.: H. Branch, 1977) 13 p.
Dn 10′. *Pf* pno.   *(Composer)*

4677 MCNEIL, Jan Pfischner. **Antiphons II** (New York: C. Fischer,
mm   1975) 5 p. $2.50.
Dn 7′. *Da* 1973. *Pf* pno.   *(Composer)*

4678 MERRIMAN, Margarita L. **Currents** (facsimile of MS at
mm   Atlantic Union Col., South Lancaster, Mass., 1977) 14 p. $3.
Dn 10′. *Da* 1969. *La* composer. *Pf* pno. *Ct* Grim, Skeptical, Sentimental, Tense.
                     (Composer)

4679 MERRIMAN, Margarita L. **Piano sonata** (facsimile of MS at
mm   Atlantic Union Col., South Lancaster, Mass., 1977) 20 p. $5.
Dn 12′. *Da* 1974. *La* composer. *Pf* pno.   *(Composer)*

4680 MOORE, Dorothy Rudd. **Dream and variations for piano**
mm   (New York: Composers Facsimile Ed., 1974) 21 p. $6.60.
Dn 20′. *Da* 1974. *La* composer.   *(Composer)*

4681 MUSGRAVE, Thea. **Monologue for piano** (2351; London: J.
mm   & W. Chester, 1960) 16 p.
Dn 15′. *Rg* Argo, ZRG 704.   *(Composer)*

4682 NOBLE, Ann. **Breaking of your soul upon my lips, The**
mm   (facsimile of MS at Mills Col., Oakland, Calif., 1977) 5 p.
Dn 10′. *La* composer. *Pf* vln.   *(Composer)*

4683 NOBLE, Ann. **In a harsh, light, gasping whisper** (facsimile of
mm   MS at NNAMC, 1977) 3 p.
Dn 7′. *La* composer. *Pf* pno.   *(Composer)*

4684 NOWAK, Alison. **Cyclorama for solo cello** (facsimile of MS
mm   at NNACA, 1977) 6 p. $1.50.
Dn 9′. *Da* 1977.   *(Composer)*

4685 NOWAK, Alison. **Five bagatelles** (facsimile of MS at NNACA,
mm   1973) 5 p. $1.
Dn 4′. *Da* 1973. *Pf* pno.   *(Composer)*

4686 NOWAK, Alison. **Klavierstück** (facsimile of MS at NNACA,
mm   1973) 6 p. $1.25.
Dn 4′. *Da* 1973. *Pf* pno.   *(Composer)*

4687 NOWAK, Alison. **Musica composita II for solo percussion**
mm   (facsimile of MS at NNACA, 1974) 10 p. $2.25. (score, parts).
Dn 10′. *Da* 1974. *Pf* per including vib, mba.   *(Composer)*

4688 NOWAK, Alison. **Piano piece in three movements** (facsimile
mm   of MS at NNACA, 1970) 9 p. $2.
Dn 6′. *Da* 1970.   *(Composer)*

4689 NOWAK, Alison. **Shifting sands** (facsimile of MS at NNACA,
mm   1977) 5 p. $1.25.
Dn 5′. *Da* 1977. *Pf* flu.   *(Composer)*

4690 NOWAK, Alison. **Three short movements for piano** (facsimile
mm   of MS at NNACA, 1971) 4 p. $.85.
Dn 4′. *Da* 1971.   *(Composer)*

4691 NOWAK, Alison. **Toccata** (facsimile of MS at NNACA, 1974) 5
mm   p. $1.
Dn 3′. *Da* 1974. *Pf* pno.   *(Composer)*

4692 NOWAK, Alison. **Wedding** (facsimile of MS at NNACA, 1975)
mm   6 p. $1.25.
Dn 3′. *Da* 1975. *Pf* org.   *(Composer)*

4693 OLIVEROS, Pauline. **Sonic meditations I-XXV** (Baltimore:
mm   Smith, 1974) 8 p. $7. (score, parts).
Dn variable. *Pf* number and choice of instruments optional. Also listed as
WIAM 3644, 4483.   *(Publisher)*

4694 OWEN, Blythe. **Chorale prelude on** *Rothwell*, op. 51, no.1,
mp   *Sacred Organ Journal* XI/3 (1 Jan 1977) 62-64.
Dn 5′. *Da* 1975. *La* publisher. *Pf* org.   *(Composer)*

4695 OWEN, Blythe. **Game and Swinging, op. 36, nos. 2-3,**
md   *Contemporary collection.* Ed. by Frances GOLDSTEIN, Alice KERN,
Frances LARIMER, Jeanette ROSS, and Harold WEISS (6004;
Evanston, Ill.: Summy-Birchard, 1974) 25-26.
Dn 3′. *Da* 1964. *La* publisher. *Pf* pno.   *(Composer)*

4696 OWEN, Blythe. **Serially serious, op. 46, nos. 1-3** (Berrien
mm   Springs, Mich.: Hall-Orion Music, 1973) 8 p. $2.
Dn 7′. *Da* 1971. *La* publisher. *Pf* pno.   *(Composer)*

4697 PIERCE, Alexandra. **Blending stumps for prepared piano**
mm   (New York: Seesaw Music, 1976) 13 p.
Dn 11′. *Da* Sept. 1976. *La* composer.   *(Composer)*

4698 PIERCE, Alexandra. **Coming to standing for piano** (New
mm   York: Seesaw Music, 1976) 11 p.
Dn 8′. *Da* Dec. 1975. *La* composer.   *(Composer)*

4699 PIERCE, Alexandra. **Greycastle** (New York: Seesaw Music,
mm   1976) 17 p. $5.
Dn 9′. *Da* July 1974. *La* composer. *Pf* prepared pno.   *(Composer)*

4700 PIERCE, Alexandra. **Maola** (New York: Seesaw Music, 1977)
mm   11 p.
Dn 12′. *Da* Jan. 1977. *La* composer. *Pf* hrp.   *(Composer)*

4701 PIERCE, Alexandra. **Orb for prepared piano** (New York:
mm   Seesaw Music, 1976) 16 p. $4.
Dn 9′. *Da* July 1976. *La* composer.   *(Composer)*

4702 PIERCE, Alexandra. **Prelude and fugue for solo flute** (New
mm   York: Seesaw Music, 1976) 7 p. $3.
Dn 6′. *Da* Apr. 1974. *La* composer.   *(Composer)*

4703 PIERCE, Alexandra. **Spectres for piano with five easy eraser
mm   preparations** (New York: Seesaw Music, 1976) 13 p. $6.
Dn 8′. *Da* Jan. 1975. *La* composer. *Pf* prepared pno.   *(Composer)*

4704 POLIN, Claire. **Eligmos archaios for solo harp** (New York:
mm   Seesaw Music, 1973) 11 p.
Dn 10′.

4705 POLIN, Claire. **Laissez sonner!** (New York: Seesaw Music,
mm   1976) 12 p.
Dn 8′. *Pf* pno.

4706 POLIN, Claire. **Margoä for solo flute** (New York: Seesaw
mm   Music, 1972) 4 p.
Dn 5′.

4707 POLIN, Claire. **Out of childhood** (New York: Seesaw Music,
mm   1973) 8 p.
Dn 6′. *Pf* pno.

4708 POLIN, Claire. **Pièce d'encore for solo viola (or violin)** (New
mm   York: Seesaw Music, 1976) 5 p.
Dn 5′.

4709 POLIN, Claire. **Serpentine for solo viola** (New York: Seesaw
mm   Music, 1974) 11 p.
Dn 15′.

4710 POLIN, Claire. **Structures for solo flute** (Bryn Mawr, Penn.:
mm   Elkan-Vogel, 1964) 6 p.
Dn 15′.

4711 POLIN, Claire. **Summer settings for solo harp** (New York:
mm   Lyra Music, 1967) 5 p.
Dn 7′. *Rg Contemporary music for flute and harp*, Ars Nova 1004.

4712 RAN, Shulamit. **Hyperbolae for piano** (6070; Tel Aviv: Israel
mm   Music Inst., 1977) 12 p.
Dn 7′. *Da* 1976. *La* composer. *Pf* pno. Boosey & Hawkes is the U.S. agent for
Israel Music Inst.   *(Composer)*

4713 RICHTER, Marga. **Fragments** (facsimile of MS on rental; New
mm   York: C. Fischer, 1975) 7 p.
Dn 5′. *Da* 1963. *La* composer. *Pf* pno. Also for orchestra (*WIAM* 4503).
                                                                       (Composer)

4714 RICHTER, Marga. **Remembrances** (facsimile of MS on rental;
mm   New York: C. Fischer, 1977) 3 p.
Dn 4′. *Da* 1977. *La* composer. *Pf* pno.   *(Composer)*

4715 RICHTER, Marga. **Sonata for piano** (facsimile of MS on
mm   rental; New York: C. Fischer, 1975) 37 p.
Dn 21′. *Da* 1954. *La* composer. *Rg* MGM, E3244.   *(Composer)*

4716 RICHTER, Marga. **Soundings** (FE 83; New York: C. Fischer,
mm   1976) 9 p. $4.
Dn 9′. *Da* 1965. *La* composer. *Pf* hps.   *(Composer)*

4717 RICHTER, Marga. **Variations on a theme by Neithart von
mm   Reuenthal** (FE 84; New York: C. Fischer, 1976) 22 p. $6.50.
Dn 13′. *Da* 1974. *La* composer. *Pf* org.   *(Composer)*

4718 RICHTER, Marion Morrey. **Capriccio for piano** (facsimile of
mm   autograph at NN, 1955) 7 p.
Dn 4′. *Da* 1955. *La* composer.   *(Composer)*

4719 RICHTER, Marion Morrey. **Prelude on a twelve-tone row
mm   for piano** (facsimile of autograph at NN, 1969) 7 p.
Dn 4′. *Da* 1969. *La* composer.   *(Composer)*

4720 ROBERTS, Gertrud. **Charlot suite** (Honolulu, Haw.: composer,
mm   1965) 15 p.

Dn 20′ . *Da* 1965. *La* composer. *Pf* hps. *(Composer)*

4721 ROBERTS, Gertrud. **Christmas chaconne** (Honolulu, Haw.:
mm   Island Heritage, 1972) 10 p. $3.50.
Dn 9′ . *Da* 1951. *Pf* hps or pno. *(Composer)*

4722 ROBERTS, Gertrud. **Rondo. Homage to Couperin** (Honolulu,
mm   Haw.: Island Heritage, 1972) 8 p. $3.
Dn 4′ . *Da* 1955. *Pf* hps. *(Composer)*

4723 ROBERTS, Gertrud. **Twelve time gardens** (Honolulu, Haw.:
mm   Island Heritage, 1976) 31 p. $4.
Dn 22′ . *Pf* pno. *(Composer)*

4724 ROSSER, Annetta Hamilton. **Alleluia, sing and rejoice**
mm   (Madison, Wis.: Gilbert, 1977) 5 p.
Dn 5′ . *Da* 1977. *Pf* org. *(Composer)*

4725 ROSSER, Annetta Hamilton. **Holy innocents** (Madison, Wis.:
mm   Gilbert, 1977) 2 p.
Dn 2′ . *Da* 1958. *Pf* org. *(Composer)*

4726 SANDIFUR, Ann. **Scored improvisations** (Berkeley, Calif.:
mm   Arsciene, 1977) 8 p. $4.
Dn 15′ . *Da* 1977. *La* publisher. *Pf* acoustic or electric keyboard. *(Composer)*

4727 SEMEGEN, Daria. **Music for violin solo** (New York: Com-
mm   posers Facsimile Ed., 1973) 6 p. $3.
Dn 8′ . *Da* 1973. *La* composer. *(Composer)*

4728 SILSBEE, Ann. **Doors** (facsimile of MS at NNAMC, 1976) 11 p.
mm $5.
Dn 11′ . *Da* Oct. 1976. *La* composer. *Pf* pno. *(Composer)*

4729 SILSBEE, Ann. **Three chants** (facsimile of MS at NNAMC,
mm   1975) 9 p. $4. (score).
Dn 11′ . *Da* 1975. *La* composer. *Pf* flu (alto flu, bass flu). *(Composer)*

4730 SILVERMAN, Faye-Ellen. **Memories** (New York: Seesaw
mm   Music, 1974) 6 p.
Dn 9′ . *Da* 1974. *La* publisher. *Pf* vla. *(Composer)*

4731 SILVERMAN, Faye-Ellen. **Speaking alone** (New York: Seesaw
mm   Music, 1976) 2 p.
Dn 5′ . *Da* 1976. *La* publisher. *Pf* flu. *(Composer)*

4732 SILVERMAN, Faye-Ellen. **Three movements for saxophone
mm   alone** (New York: Seesaw Music, 1972) 7 p.
Dn 7′ . *Da* 1971. *La* publisher. *Pf* soprano sax. *(Composer)*

4733 SINGER, Jeanne. **Four pieces for piano** (facsimile of auto-
mm   graph at NNAMC, 1975) 14 p.
Dn 16′ . *La* composer. *Ct* Etude, Remembrance, Baroque frolic, Toccatina.
(Composer)

4734 SINGER, Jeanne. **Introduction and caprice** (facsimile of
mm   autograph at NNAMC, 1973) 5 p.
Dn 5′ . *La* composer. *Pf* pno. *(Composer)*

4735 SINGER, Jeanne. **Ricky's rondo** (facsimile of autograph at
mm   NNAMC, 1972) 4 p.
Dn 4′ . *La* composer. *Pf* pno. *(Composer)*

4736 SINGER, Jeanne. **Suite in harpsichord style for piano or
mm   harpsichord** (West Babylon, N.Y.: H. Branch, 1976) 9 p. $3.
Dn 6′ . *Da* 1975. *La* composer. *(Composer)*

4737 SMITH, Julia. **Characteristic suite for piano solo** (MM 105;
mm   New York: Mowbray Music, 1967) 16 p.
Dn 10′ . *Da* 30 May 1949. *Ct* Canon, Waltz, Passacaglia, March, Toccata.
(Composer)

4738 SMITH, Julia. **Episodic suite for piano solo** (MM 111; New
mm   York: Mowbray Music, 1966) 12 p.
Dn 8′ . *Da* 1935. *Ct* Yellow and blue, Nocturne, Waltz, March, Toccata. First
published in 1938 (New York: H. Flammer). Also arranged for orchestra
(*WIAM* 4517) and for 10 instruments (*WIAM* 4839). *(Composer)*

4739 SMITH, Julia. **Sonatine in C** (MM 101; New York: Mowbray
mm   Music, 1966) 16 p.
Dn 10′ . *Da* 1943-44. *Pf* pno. *(Composer)*

4740 STEWART, Ora Pate. **March of the Gadiantons** (Provo,
mm   Utah: Fernwood, 1975) 2 p. $1.
Dn 2′ . *Pf* pno. *(Composer)*

4741 STILMAN, Julia. **Visiones. Primera sonata for piano** (New
mm   York: Composers Facsimile Ed., 1977) 18 p. $5.15.
Dn 13′ . *(Composer)*

4742 SUCHY, Gregoria Karides. **Circle dance in seven-eight**
mm   (facsimile of MS at NNAMC, 1963) 4 p.
Dn 4′ . *La* composer. *Pf* pno. Awarded first prize in the composers contest
sponsored by the Wisconsin Federation of Music Clubs, 1964. *(Composer)*

4743 SUCHY, Gregoria Karides. **Fantasy for piano, A** (facsimile of
mm   MS at NNAMC, 1960) 13 p.
Dn 15′ . *La* composer. Awarded first prize in the composers contest sponsored
by the Wisconsin Federation of Music Clubs, 1962. *(Composer)*

4744 SUCHY, Gregoria Karides. **Mother Goose rhymes in twelve
mm   tone** (facsimile of MS at NNAMC, 1964) 39 p.
Dn 13′ . *La* composer. *Pf* pno, optional recitation. *(Composer)*

4745 SUCHY, Gregoria Karides. **Saturn's rings** (facsimile of MS at
mm   NNAMC, 1964) 2 p.
Dn 3′ . *La* composer. *Pf* pno. *(Composer)*

4746 SUCHY, Gregoria Karides. **Soliloquy sans C for unaccom-
mm   panied solo violin** (facsimile of MS at NNAMC, 1974) 5 p.
Dn 9′ . *La* composer. *(Composer)*

4747 SUCHY, Gregoria Karides. **Sousta** (facsimile of MS at
mm   NNAMC, 1960) 2 p.
Dn 1′ . *La* composer. *Pf* pno. Award winner in the composers contest sponsored
by the Wisconsin Federation of Music Clubs, 1962. *(Composer)*

4748 SUCHY, Gregoria Karides. **Suite on Greek themes** (facsimile
mm   of MS at NNAMC, 1959) 9 p.
Dn 8′ . *La* composer. *Pf* pno. Special award winner in the composers contest
sponsored by the Wisconsin Federation of Music Clubs, 1961. *(Composer)*

4749 SUCHY, Gregoria Karides. **Two sketches for piano** (facsimile
mm   of MS at NNAMC, 1969) 4 p.
Dn 4′ . *La* composer. *(Composer)*

4750 SWISHER, Gloria Wilson. **Theme and variations for solo
mm   flute** (facsimile of MS at NNAMC, 1977) 2 p.
Dn 2′ . *Da* 1963. *La* composer. *(Composer)*

4751 SWISHER, Gloria Wilson. **Variations on an original theme**
mm   (facsimile of MS at NNAMC, 1977) 6 p.
Dn 5′ . *Da* 1962. *La* composer. *Pf* pno. *(Composer)*

4752 TALMA, Louise. **Alleluia in form of toccata** (N 1062; New
mm   York: C. Fischer, 1947) 13 p.
Dn 10′ . *Pf* pno. *Rg* Première. Recorded performances of keyboard works by
women, Avant, AV 1012.

4753 TALMA, Louise. **Passacaglia and fugue for piano** (New
mm   York: composer, 1962) 12 p.
Dn 11′ . *(Composer)*

4754 TALMA, Louise. **Pastoral prelude** (30880; New York: C.
mm   Fischer, 1952) 5 p.
Dn 4′ . *Pf* pno.

4755 TALMA, Louise. **Piano sonata no. 1** (30393; New York: C.
mm   Fischer, 1948) 29 p.
Dn 16′ .

4756 TALMA, Louise. **Piano sonata no. 2** (CP 8; New York: C.
mm   Fischer, 1977) 17 p.
Dn 16′ . *Da* Aug. 1955. *Rg* Composers Recordings, CRI SD 281.

4757 TALMA, Louise. **Six etudes for piano** (45014; New York: G.
mm   Schirmer, 1962) 27 p.
Dn 5′. *Rg* Desto, DC 7117.

4758 TALMA, Louise. **Sound shots** (New York: composer, 1974) 23
mm   p.
Dn 24′. *Pf* pno.   *(Composer)*

4759 TALMA, Louise. **Textures** (New York: composer, 1977) 16 p.
mm
Dn 8′. *Pf* pno.   *(Composer)*

4760 TALMA, Louise. **Three bagatelles for piano** (New York:
mm   composer, 1955) 5 p.
Dn 5′.   *(Composer)*

4761 TALMA, Louise. **Venetian folly: overture and barcarolle**
mm   (New York: composer, 1947) 5 p.
Dn 5′. *Pf* pno.   *(Composer)*

4762 TALMA, Louise. **Wedding piece. Where thou goest I go**
mm   (New York: composer, 1946) 3 p.
Dn 5′. *Pf* org.   *(Composer)*

4763 TANNER, Hilda. **Suite for piano** (facsimile of MS at NIC,
mm   1977) 6 p. $1.
Dn 5′. *Da* 1975. *La* composer. *Ct* Waltz, Chorale, Lullaby, Scherzo.   *(Composer)*

4764 TANNER, Hilda. **Three plus three plus two** (facsimile of MS
mm   at NIC, 1977) 3 p. $.50.
Dn 3′. *Da* 1973. *La* composer. *Pf* pno. Also for pno duet (facsimile of MS at
NIC, 1977).   *(Composer)*

4765 TOWER, Joan. **Fantasia for piano** (facsimile of MS at NNACA,
mm   1966) 14 p.
Dn 9′.

4766 TOWER, Joan. **Hexachords for flute** (New York: American
mm   Composers Ed., 1972) 4 p.
Dn 7′. *Rg* Composers Recordings, CRI 354.

4767 TOWER, Joan. **Platinum spirals for violin** (facsimile of MS at
mm   NNAMC, 1977) 3 p.
Dn 7′. *Da* 1977.

4768 VAN DE VATE, Nancy. **Six etudes for solo viola** (facsimile
mm   of MS at NNAMC, 1977) 6 p.
Dn 8′. *Da* 1969. *La* composer.   *(Composer)*

4769 VAN DE VATE, Nancy. **Suite for solo violin** (facsimile of MS
mm   at NNAMC, 1977) 10 p.
Dn 9′. *Da* 1975. *La* composer.   *(Composer)*

4770 WALKER, Gwyneth. **April, Rag, Fantasy** (New Canaan,
mm   Conn.: Walker, 1977) 7 p. $3.
Dn 9′. *Da* 1977. *La* composer. *Pf* pno. *Fantasy* also in her *Complete piano works*
(*WIAM* 4772).   *(Composer)*

4771 WALKER, Gwyneth. **Ayre and variations on a country**
mm   **dance** (New Canaan, Conn.: Walker, 1973) 15 p. $3.
Dn 10′. *Da* 1973. *La* composer. *Pf* org.   *(Composer)*

4772 WALKER, Gwyneth. **Complete piano works** (New Canaan,
ma   Conn.: Walker, 1976) 34 p. $7.
Dn 30′. *Da* 1976. *La* composer. *Ct* Suite for piano: A child's day; Five pieces
for piano; Preludes; Fantasy. *Fantasy* also in *April, Rag, Fantasy* (*WIAM*
4770).   *(Composer)*

4773 WALKER, Gwyneth. **Four pieces for contemporary lute**
mm   (New Canaan, Conn.: Walker, 1977) 11 p. $2.50.
Dn 10′. *Da* 1977. *La* composer.   *(Composer)*

4774 WALKER, Gwyneth. **Passacaglia and fugue for organ** (New
mm   Canaan, Conn.: Walker, 1976) 20 p. $3.50.
Dn 11′. *Da* 6 Dec. 1976. *La* composer.   *(Composer)*

4775
mm   WALKER, Gwyneth. **Sonatina, Rondo, Variations for solo**
   guitar (New Canaan, Conn.: Walker, 1976) 18 p. $2.50.
Dn 16′. *Da* 1976. *La* composer.   *(Composer)*

4776 WARREN, Elinor Remick. **Processional march** (46504; New
mm   York: G. Schirmer, 1969) 5 p.
Dn 3′. *Da* 1969. *La* composer. *Pf* org or pno.   *(Composer)*

4777 WYLIE, Ruth Shaw. **Five piano preludes** (New York: Camara,
mm   1962) 12 p.
Dn 15′. *Da* 1949. *La* composer.   *(Composer)*

4778 WYLIE, Ruth Shaw. **Soliloquy, op. 23, for piano left hand**
mm   (West Babylon, N.Y.: H. Branch, 1976) 5 p. $2.
Dn 5′. *Da* 1966. *La* composer.   *(Composer)*

4779 ZAIMONT, Judith Lang. **Calendar set, A. Twelve preludes**
mm   **for piano** (facsimiles of autographs at NNAMC, 1975) 3, 5, 4, 4, 2,
   5, 3, 5 p.
Dn 17′. *La* composer. *Ct* February. Palace of ice; April. "You know how it is
with an April day"; June. "Then, if ever, come perfect days"; July. The glorious
Fourth!; August. "Dry August and warm"; October. "The wind is rising, and
the air is wild with leaves"; November. "November's sky is chill and drear";
December. The carols. Four pieces were not available when this bibliography
went to press. *Rg* Leonarda Productions, LPI 101.   *(Composer)*

4780 ZAIMONT, Judith Lang. **Capriccio** (facsimile of autograph at
mm   NNAMC, 1971) 4 p.
Dn 3′. *La* composer. *Pf* flu.   *(Composer)*

4781 ZAIMONT, Judith Lang. **Judy's rag for piano solo** (facsimile
mm   of autograph at NNAMC, 1974) 7 p.
Dn 7′. *La* composer.   *(Composer)*

4782 ZAIMONT, Judith Lang. **Reflective rag for piano solo**
mm   (facsimile of autograph at NNAMC, 1974) 5 p.
Dn 5′. *La* composer.   *(Composer)*

4783 ZAIMONT, Judith Lang. **Toccata** (facsimile of autograph at
mm   NNAMC, 1968) 6 p.
Dn 3′. *La* composer. *Pf* pno.   *(Composer)*

4784 ZAIMONT, Judith Lang. **Valse romantique** (facsimile of
mm   autograph at NNAMC, 1972) 4 p.
Dn 4′. *La* composer. *Pf* flu.   *(Composer)*

4785 ZIFFRIN, Marilyn J. **Toccata and fugue for organ** (facsimile
mm   of MS at NNAMC, 1956) 7 p.
Dn 6′. *Da* 1956. *La* composer.   *(Composer)*

Stage works

4787 ANDERSON, Beth. **Joan** (facsimile of MS at NNACA, 1977) 25
mm   p. (score, parts, tape).
Oratorio. *Dn* 18′ (expandable). *Da* July 1974. *La* composer. *At* composer. *St*
Joan of Arc's trial in various translations. *Pf* with amplification: solo SSTB, 3-3-
4-3, 4-2-3-1, tim, per, hrp, str, ring modulator and tape, dancer. The
orchestration is flexible, and substitutions can be made.   *(Composer)*

4788 BRITAIN, Radie. **Ubiquity** (facsimile of MS at DLC, 1937) 103
mm   p. (score).
Opera in 1 act. *Dn* 40′. *At* Lester Luther. *Pf* solo S-A-3T-6Bar-B, choral SATB,
3 speaking parts, tim, per, pno.

4789 COOPER, Rose Marie. **Oh, Penelope** (Greensboro, N.C.:
mm   composer, 1975) 68 p. (score, parts).
Musical. *Dn* 45′. *At* Susan Graham Erwin. *Pf* solo ST, choral SATB, 2-3enh-
2bcl-1, 1-1-2-1, tim, per, pno, str.   *(Composer)*

4790 DAVIS, Katherine K. **Road to Galilee, The** (2305; New York:
mm   Galaxy Music, 1964) 64 p. (piano-vocal score).
Sacred musical drama. *Dn* 37′. *At* composer. *Pf* solo 3S-2A-T-2B; choral unison
(children), SATB; org.   *(Composer)*

4791 DAVIS, Katherine K. **Unmusical impresario, The** (4400; New
mm   York: G. Schirmer, 1956) 82 p. (score, parts).

Musical comedy. *Dn* 55′. *At* composer and Heddie Root Kent. *Pf* solo SSATB, choral SATB, pno. *(Composer)*

4792 DU PAGE, Florence. **Alice in Wonderland** (facsimile of MS on
mm   rental; New York: C. Fischer, 1951) 46 p. (score, parts).
Ballet suite. *Dn* 17′. *Da* Nov. 1947. *La* composer. *Pf* 3-3-3-2, 4-3-3-1, cel, hrp, str. *Ct* Down the rabbit hole, The pool of tears, A caucus race, The queen's croquet ground. *Rg* NRU, Eastman School of Music. *(Composer)*

4793 DU PAGE, Florence. **New world for Nellie** (facsimile of MS on
mm   rental; Atlanta: Porter, 1965) 117 p. (score).
Ballad chamber opera. *Dn* 60′. *Da* 1960. *La* composer. *At* Rowland Emett. *Li* composer. *Pf* solo TB; choral SATB; 1-1-2-1; 2-1-1-0; tim; per including vib, xyl. *(Composer)*

4794 DU PAGE, Florence. **Trial universelle** (Westbury, N.Y.:
mm   Church of the Advent, 1963) 73 p. (score, parts).
Chamber opera. *Dn* 60′. *Da* Jan. 1963. *La* composer. *At* Jean Thompson. *Li* composer. *Pf* solo TB; choral SA; flu; hrn; tpt; tim; per including cel, xyl; org or pno. *(Composer)*

4795 DU PAGE, Florence. **Whither** (facsimile of MS on rental;
mm   Atlanta: Porter, 1964) 38 p. (score, parts).
Music drama in 3 acts. *Dn* 35′. *Da* Feb. 1964. *La* composer. *At* Jean Thompson. *Pf* solo B, choral SA, 2 cla, hrp, org or pno, vcl. *(Composer)*

4796 FINE, Vivian. **Women in the garden, The** (Shaftsbury, Vt.:
mm   Catamount Facsimile Ed., 1977) 136 p. $15. (score, parts).
Chamber opera. *Dn* 60′. *Da* 1977. *La* composer. *At* Virginia Woolf, Gertrude Stein, Isadora Duncan, Emily Dickinson. *Pf* solo SSMAT, flu, cla, bsn, tim, per including vib, pno, vla, vcl, cbs. *(Composer)*

4797 GARWOOD, Margaret. **Nightingale and the rose, The** (East
mm   Greenville, Penn.: composer, 1977) 269 p. (score, parts).
Opera in one act. *Dn* 50′. *Pf* solo SSATB, 2-2-2-2, 2-2-2-2, tim, per including xyl, hrp, str. A piano-vocal score is available (facsimile of MS at NNAMC). *Rg* NNAMC. *(Composer)*

4798 GIDEON, Miriam. **Fortunato** (New York: American Composers
mm   Ed., 1958) 93 p. (piano-vocal score).
Chamber opera in 3 scenes. *Dn* 60′. *La* DLC. *At* Serafin and Joaquin Alvarez Quintero. *Pf* solo 4S-M-T-4Bar, pno. The title page indicates that this piece was originally for voices and orchestra.

4799 GLANVILLE-HICKS, Peggy. **Glittering gate, The** (facsimile
mm   of MS on rental; New York: Belwin-Mills, 1957) 108 p. (score, parts).
Opera in 1 act. *Dn* 30′. *Da* 1956. *At* Lord Dunsany. *Pf* solo TB, 1-1-1-1, 1-1-1-0, tim, per including glk, str, tape.

4800 GLANVILLE-HICKS, Peggy. **Masque of the wild man, The**
mm   (New York: Composers Facsimile Ed., 1958) 78 p. (score).
Ballet. *Dn* 18′. *Pf* flu, cel, hrp, per, str.

4801 GLANVILLE-HICKS, Peggy. **Nausicaa** (facsimile of MS at
mm   DLC, 1960) 153 p. (score).
Opera in 3 acts. *Dn* 120′. *At* Robert Graves. *St* Homer's daughter. *Pf* solo S-A-3T-Bar-2B, choral SATB, pno. Original orchestration: 2pic-1-3bcl-2cbn, 2-2-1-0, per, hrp, pno, str. *Rg* Scenes from the opera, Composers Recordings, CRI 175.

4802 GLANVILLE-HICKS, Peggy. **Saul and the witch of Endor**
mm   (facsimile of MS on rental; New York: C.F. Peters, 1959) 85 p. (score, parts).
Ballet. *Dn* 20′. *Pf* tpt, tim, per including xyl.

4803 GLANVILLE-HICKS, Peggy. **Tragic celebration. Jeptha's**
mm   **daughter** (facsimile of MS on rental; New York: C.F. Peters, 1964) 77 p. (score, parts).
Ballet. *Dn* 19′. *Pf* 1-1-1-1, 0-1-0-1, tim, per, hrp, str.

4804 GLANVILLE-HICKS, Peggy. **Transposed heads, The** (fac-
mm   simile of MS at DLC, 1953) 112 p. (score).
Opera in 6 scenes. *Dn* 90′. *At* Thomas Mann. *Pf* solo STBar, 2 speaking parts, pno. Original orchestration: 1-1-1-1, 1-1-1-0, per for 4 players, hrp, str. *Rg* London, 545-6.

4805 HUNKINS, Eusebia. **Child of promise. Choral dance drama**
mm   (facsimile of MS on rental; New York: C. Fischer, 1962) 28 p. (score, parts).

Dn 15′. *Da* 1962. *La* composer. *At* composer. *Pf* solo SSA, choral SSA, 3 cla, per, hrp, pno, cbs, narrator. Also published in a piano-vocal score (4451; Fischer, 1962). *(Composer)*

4806 HUNKINS, Eusebia. **Happy land. Our American heritage in**
mm   **story and song** (facsimile of MS on rental; New York: C. Fischer, 1975) 48 p. (score, parts).
Opera in 1 act. *Dn* 55′. *La* composer. *At* Emily Hammond. *Pf* choral SATB, flu, pno or reed org, gtr or dulcimer, 5 narrators. Also for choral SSA, flu, pno or reed org, gtr or dulcimer, 5 narrators (facsimile of MS on rental; Fischer, 1975). *(Composer)*

4807 HUNKINS, Eusebia. **Magic laurel trees, The. An opera for**
mm   **children** (facsimile of MS on rental; New York: C. Fischer, 1975) 73 p. (score, parts).
Opera in 2 acts. *Dn* 75′. *Da* 1974. *La* composer. *At* Emily Hammond. *St Les douze princesses dansantes. Pf* solo 3S-3A, choral SA, 2 flu, per including cel, pno. A piano-vocal score is available on rental from the publisher. *(Composer)*

4808 HUNKINS, Eusebia. **Mice in council** (facsimile of MS on
mm   rental; New York: C. Fischer, 1952) 70 p. (score, parts).
Opera in 1 act. *Dn* 40′. *Pf* solo STTBar, choral SATB, 1-1-2-1, 1-2-0-0, tim, per including glk, hrp, str. *(Composer)*

4809 HUNKINS, Eusebia. **Smoky Mountain. American folk opera**
mm   (facsimile of MS on rental; New York: C. Fischer, 1950) 83 p. (score, parts).
Folk opera in 1 act. *Dn* 90′. *La* composer. *At* composer. *Pf* solo SSATTBB, choral SSATTBB, 2-0-2-1, 1-0-0-0, gtr, str. Also published in a piano-vocal score (3830; Fischer, 1950). *(Composer)*

4810 HUNKINS, Eusebia. **Spirit owl** (facsimile of MS on rental; New
mm   York: C. Fischer, 1976) 83 p. (score, parts).
Opera in 2 acts. *Dn* 90′. *Da* 1959. *La* composer. *At* composer. *Pf* solo SSATTBB, choral SATB, 2-2-2-2, 2-4-2-2, tim, per, cbs. A piano-vocal score is available on rental from the publisher. *(Composer)*

4811 HUNKINS, Eusebia. **What have you done to my mountain?**
mm   (facsimile of MS on rental; New York: C. Fischer, 1975) 131 p. (score, parts).
Folk opera in 2 acts. *Dn* 120′. *Da* 1970. *La* composer. *At* composer. *Pf* solo SSATTBB, pno, 2 gtr, autoharp, banjo, cbs. A piano-vocal score is available on rental from the publisher. *(Composer)*

4812 HUNKINS, Eusebia. **Wondrous love** (3948; New York: C.
mm   Fischer, 1951) 47 p. (score, parts).
Sacred choral drama. *Dn* 30′. *Da* 1951. *La* composer. *At* composer. *Pf* solo SSATB, choral SATB, org, pno, narrator. Also for solo SSATB, choral SSA, org, pno, narrator (4108; Fischer, 1951). *Why* and *What wondrous love* are also published separately (*WIAM* 3994, 3993). *(Composer)*

4813 HUNKINS, Eusebia. **Young Lincoln** (facsimile of MS on
mm   rental; New York: C. Fischer, 1958) 42 p. (score, parts).
Folk opera. *Dn* 45′. *Da* 1958. *La* composer. *At* composer. *Pf* solo 3S-2A-T-B, choral SSATB, 2-2-2-2, 1-1-1-1, pno, str. *(Composer)*

4814 HUNKINS, Eusebia. **Young Lincoln II** (facsimile of MS on
mm   rental; New York: C. Fischer, 1958) 50 p. (piano-vocal score).
Folk opera in 1 act. *Dn* 55′. *La* composer. *At* composer. *Pf* solo 3S-2A-T-B, choral SSATB, pno. *(Composer)*

4815 LAUFER, Beatrice. **Great God Brown, The** (facsimile of MS
mm   on rental; New York: Belwin-Mills, 1966) 125 p. (score).
Ballet. *Dn* 30′. *At* Eugene O'Neill. *Pf* 2-1-2-2, 4-3-2-1, tim, per including vib, str. *(Composer)*

4816 LAUFER, Beatrice. **Ile** (facsimile of MS on rental; New York:
mm   Belwin-Mills, 1958) 100 p. (score, parts).
Opera in 1 act. *Dn* 55′. *At* Eugene O'Neill. *St* Long voyage home. *Pf* solo S-3T-4Bar, 2-1-2-1, 2-2-1-0, tim, per, str. *(Composer)*

4817 LORENZ, Ellen Jane. **Johnny Appleseed** (Dayton: Lorenz,
mm   1947) 32 p. (piano-vocal score).
Operetta. *Dn* 60′. *Da* 1947. *At* Mildred Kerr. *Pf* choral S (children), pno. *(Composer)*

4818 MUSGRAVE, Thea. **Abbot of Drimock, The** (facsimile of MS
mm   on rental; New York: G. Schirmer, 1955) 43 p. (score, parts).
Chamber opera in 3 scenes. *Dn* 60′. *At* John Mackay Wilson. *Li* Maurice Lindsay. *St* Tales of the border. *Pf* solo S-M-A-T-2Bar-B, obo, cla, bsn, hrn,

pno, cel, per including xyl, vln, vcl. Also published by J. & W. Chester (London, 1955).

4819 MUSGRAVE, Thea. **Beauty and the beast** (facsimile of MS on
mm rental; New York: G. Schirmer, 1969) 531 p. (score, parts).
Ballet in 2 acts. *Dn* 120'. *Pf* 1-1-2-1, 1-2-1-0, per, str, tape.

4820 MUSGRAVE, Thea. **Decision, The** (facsimile of MS on rental;
mm New York: G. Schirmer, 1965) 334 p. (score, parts).
Opera in 3 acts. *Dn* 120'. *At* Ken Taylor. *Li* Maurice Lindsay. *Pf* solo 2S-M-3A-4T-4Bar-3B, choral SATB, 2-2-3-3, 4-3-3-1, tim, per, hrp, str. Also published in a piano-vocal score (London: J. & W. Chester, 1965).

4821 MUSGRAVE, Thea. **Marko the miser** (London: J. & W.
mm Chester, 1962) 83 p. (score).
Dn 13'. *At* composer, Frederic Samson. *Pf* solo SSAA (children), choral SA (children), 2 rec, cla or vln, gtr, per including glk, pno, narrator.

4822 MUSGRAVE, Thea. **Mary, Queen of Scots** (facsimile of MS
mm on rental; New York: Belwin-Mills, 1978) 621 p. (score, parts).
Opera in 3 acts. *Dn* 129'. *Da* 1977. *Pf* solo 3S-2A-3T-2Bar-2B; choral SATB; 4pic-5enh-3bcl-3cbn; 3-2-1-0, tim; hrp; str; stage band: flu(pic), obo, enh, bsn, tpt, per.

4823 MUSGRAVE, Thea. **Tale for thieves, A** (London: J. & W.
mm Chester, 1954) 66 p. (piano reduction).
Ballet in 2 acts. *Dn* 35'. *Pf* 2 pno. Based on Chaucer's *The pardoner's tale*.

4824 MUSGRAVE, Thea. **Voice of Ariadne, The** (facsimile of MS
mm on rental; New York: Belwin-Mills, 1977) 405 p. (piano-vocal score).
Opera in 3 acts. *Dn* 132'. *Pf* solo S-M-A-2T-2Bar-B, 3pic-3enh-3bcl-3cbn, 1-0-0-0, tim, per, hrp, pno (chamber org), solo string quartet, cbs, taped voices.

4825 NOBLE, Ann. **Juniper tree** (facsimile of MS at Mills Col.,
mm Oakland, Calif., 1977) 50 p. (score, parts).
Chamber opera. *Dn* 70'. *La* composer. *Pf* solo SATBarB, flu or vln, cla, bcl, bsn, egr, 2 pno or vib and cel, cbs. *(Composer)*

4826 NOWAK, Alison. **Diversion and division** (facsimile of MS at
mm NNACA, 1973) 44 p. $6.50. (score, parts).
Opera in one act. *Dn* 30'. *Da* 1973. *Li* composer. *Pf* solo ST, male speaking voice; 1-1-1-1, 0-1-1-0, pno, str. *(Composer)*

4827 OLIVEROS, Pauline. **Bonn Feier** (Baltimore: Smith, 1977) 8 p.
mm $5. (score).
Environmental theater work. *Dn* 15 hrs-1 year. *Pf* specialized and non-specialized performers; intended for a city, or college or university campus. *(Publisher)*

4828 OLIVEROS, Pauline. **Pieces of eight** (Baltimore: Smith, 1977)
mm 15 p. (score, parts, tape).
Theater piece. *Dn* 16'. *Da* 1964. *La* publisher. *Pf* flu, obo, cla, bcl, cbn, hrn, tpt, tbn, film, tape. *(Publisher)*

4829 PARKER, Alice. **Family reunion, The** (facsimile of MS on
mm rental; New York: C. Fischer, 1975) 166 p. (score, parts).
Opera in 1 act. *Dn* 60'. *Da* 1975. *La* composer. *Li* composer. *Pf* solo 4S-4A-2T-2B, choral SSAATTBB, children's chorus, flu, bsn, hrn, tpt, tbn, tba, per, gtr, banjo, vln. *(Composer)*

4830 PARKER, Alice. **Martyrs' mirror, The** (Boston: E.C. Schirmer,
mm 1971) 179 p. (score, parts).
Sacred opera. *Dn* 120'. *Da* 1971. *La* composer. *At* John Ruth. *Pf* solo SATB, choral SSAATTBB, unison (children), obo, bsn, tpt, 3 tbn, 2 rec, per, pump organ. *(Composer)*

4831 PAULL, Barberi. **Time** (tape at NNAMC, 1971). (tape).
mm
Ballet with slide projections. *Dn* 16'. *La* composer. *At* composer. *Pf* tape, film slides, dancers. *(Composer)*

4832 PERRY, Julia Amanda. **Bottle, The** (facsimile of MS on rental;
mm New York: Southern Music, 1953) 85 p. (score, parts).
Opera in 1 act. *Dn* 40'. *At* Poe. *St The cask of Amontillado*. *Li* composer. *Pf* solo MTBar, choral SA, 3pic-2enh-3bcl-1, 2-1-1-1, tim, per including xyl, hrp, pno, str.

4833 POLIN, Claire. **Infinito. A requiem** (New York: Seesaw Music,
mm 1973) 43 p. (score, parts).

Dn 20'. *At* Thomas Wolfe, T.S. Eliot, Rilke, Henry Vaughan, Heledd. *Pf* solo S, choral SATB, sax, narrator, dancer.

4834 RICHTER, Marion Morrey. **This is our camp. Music play
mm for young people** (2167; Boston: C.C. Birchard, 1955) 43 p. (piano-vocal score).
Dn 50'. *Da* 1950. *La* composer. *At* Margaret Raymond. *Pf* choral SS (children), tpt or crn, pno. *(Composer)*

4835 SEMEGEN, Daria. **Arc: music for dancers** (tape on rental;
mm New York: American Composers Alliance, 1977) $15. (tape, graph dance score).
Dn 14'. *Da* May 1977. *La* Electronic Music Studio, State U. of New York, Stony Brook. *Pf* tape. *(Composer)*

4836 SILVERMAN, Faye-Ellen. **Miracle of Nemirov, The** (New
mm York: Seesaw Music, 1975) 150 p. (score, parts).
Opera in 1 act. *Dn* 30'. *Da* 1974. *La* publisher. *At* composer. *Pf* solo 2S-A-4T-2B, 1-1-1-1, 3-0-0-0, per, str, tape. *(Composer)*

4837 SMITH, Julia. **Cockcrow. A fairy-tale opera in one act**
mm (facsimile of MS on rental; New York: T. Presser, 1953) 106 p. (score, parts).
Dn 25'. *Da* 1953. *La* composer. *At* Constance D'Arcy Mackay. *Pf* solo SSAATTBB; 1-1-1-1; 1-1-0-0; tim; per; pno; str. *(Composer)*

4838 SMITH, Julia. **Daisy. An opera in two acts** (facsimile of MS on
mm rental; New York: T. Presser, 1973) 564 p. (score, parts).
Dn 90'. *Da* 1973. *La* publisher. *At* Bertita Harding. *St* Based on the life of Juliette Gordon Low, founder of the Girl Scouts of the United States of America. *Pf* solo 4S-4A-T-Bar-B; choral SSAATB; 1-1-2-1; 2-2-1-0; tim; per including xyl, cel; hrp; str. Also published in a piano-vocal score (MM 140; New York: Mobray Music, 1977). *Rg* Highlights from the opera, Orion 76248.

4839 SMITH, Julia. **Episodic suite. Ballet version for ten instru-
mm ments** (facsimile of MS on rental; New York: T. Presser, 1967) 36 p. (score, parts).
Dn 8'. *Da* 12 Jan. 1967. *La* composer. *Pf* 1-1-1-1, 1-1-1-0, per, pno, cbs. *Ct* Yellow and blue, Nocturne, Waltz, March, Toccata. Originally for pno (*WIAM* 4738). Also arranged for orchestra (*WIAM* 4517). *(Composer)*

4840 SMITH, Julia. **Gooseherd and the goblin, The. Opera in one
mm act with prologue** (facsimile of MS on rental; New York: T. Presser, 1946) 125 p. (score, parts).
Dn 45'. *Da* 1946. *La* composer. *At* Josephine Fetter Royle. *St* Play of the same name by Constance D'Arcy Mackay. *Pf* solo SSAT; choral SSA; 1-1-1-1; 1-1-0-0; per; pno; str. *(Composer)*

4841 SMITH, Julia. **Indian dances. From *Cynthia Parker*, an
mm American opera in three acts** (rev. ed.; facsimile of MS at PPFleisher: 1977) 36 p. (score, parts).
Ballet. *Dn* 15'. *Da* 1943, rev. 1977. *La* composer. *Pf* 3-2-3-2, 4-2-3-1, tim, per including cel, hrp. *Ct* Puwuck tawi (lullaby), Braves' dance, Corn song, Medicine man's dance, Mescal rite. *(Composer)*

4842 SMITH, Julia. **Shepherdess and the chimney sweep, The. A
mm Christmas opera in one act** (facsimile of MS on rental; New York: T. Presser, 1963) 88 p. (score, parts).
Dn 30'. *Da* 1963. *La* Dallas Public Library. *At* Constance D'Arcy Mackay. *Pf* solo STB; choral SSAA; 2-2-2-2; 2-2-2-0; tim; per including xyl, vib, cel; hrp; str. *(Composer)*

4843 SMITH, Julia. **Stranger of Manzano, The. Opera in one act
mm with prologue and ballet** (facsimile of MS on rental; New York: T. Presser, 1943) 382 p. (score, parts).
Dn 45'. *Da* 1943. *La* composer. *At* John William Rogers. *Pf* solo S-A-T-5B, choral SSAATB; 1-1-2-1; 2-2-1-0; tim; per including cel; hrp; str. *(Composer)*

4844 SUCHY, Gregoria Karides. **Skins and exposures** (tape at
mm NNAMC, 1966). (tape).
Ballet. *Dn* 17'. *La* composer. *(Composer)*

4845 SWISHER, Gloria Wilson. **Happy hypocrite, The** (facsimile of
mm MS at NNAMC, 1977) 272 p. (score, parts).
Chamber opera in 3 acts. *Dn* 60'. *Da* 1963. *La* composer. *At* Hugh Funk. *Pf* solo 4S-A-3T-6B; choral SATB; 2pic-1-1-2cbn; 1-1-0-0; tim; per including glk, cel; hrp; str. *(Composer)*

4846   TALMA, Louise. **Alcestiad, The** (facsimile of MS on rental;
mm   New York: C. Fischer, 1960) 561 p. (score, parts).
Opera in 3 acts. *Dn* 148'. *Da* 1958. *La* DLC. *At* Thornton Wilder. *Pf* solo M-A-
Ct-4T-3Bar-B; choral SATB; 3pic-3enh-4-3; 4-2-3-1; tim; per including cel, glk,
vib, xyl; pno; hrp; str.

4847   WALDO, Elisabeth. **Popol vuh, El. Mayan creation myth**
mm   (Northridge, Calif.: Mundoamericas Music, 1972) 26 p. $10. (score,
parts).
Ballet. *Dn* 30'. *Da* 1972. *La* composer. *Pf* 2-2-2-2, 4-2-3-1, tim, per, str,
optional pre-Columbian instruments including multiple and triple flutes,
soprano and alto ocarinas, conch shell trumpets. Also for chamber orchestra:
1-1-1-1, 1-1-1-1, tim, per, str (Mundoamericas Music, 1972).   *(Composer)*

4848   WHITE, Ruth. **Pinions** (Los Angeles: composer, 1966). (tape).
mm
Ballet. *Dn* 24'. *La* composer. *Pf* tape. *Rg* Limelight, LS 86058.   *(Composer)*

4849   ZIFFRIN, Marilyn J. **Drinking song and dance from** *Captain*
mm   ***Kidd*** (facsimile of MS at NNAMC, 1971) 31 p. (score, parts).
Opera excerpt. *Dn* 10'. *Da* 1971. *La* composer. *Pf* solo B, choral TB, rec, per, 2
gtr.   *(Composer)*

Vocal music

4850   ANDERSON, Beth. **Day, A** (facsimile of MS at NNACA, 1977)
mm   1 p.
Dn 1'. *Da* 1967. *La* composer. *At* composer. *Pf* solo M, pno.   *(Composer)*

4851   ANDERSON, Beth. **Postcard, A** (facsimile of MS at NNACA,
mm   1977) 1 p.
Dn 1'. *Da* 1967. *La* composer. *At* composer. *Pf* solo M, pno.   *(Composer)*

4852   ANDERSON, Beth. **Y's swatches?** (facsimile of MS at
mm   NNACA, 1977) 8 p.
Song cycle. *Dn* 8'. *Da* 1966. *La* composer. *At* composer. *Pf* solo M.   *(Composer)*

4853   BALLOU, Esther Williamson. **Bride** (New York: Composers
mm   Facsimile Ed., 1963) 4 p.
Sacred song. *Dn* 4'. *Da* 1962. *At* Virginia Sorenson. *Pf* solo S, org.

4854   BALLOU, Esther Williamson. **Five songs for soprano and**
mm   **piano** (facsimile of autograph at NNACA, 1962) 27 p.
Dn 20'. *Da* 1962. *At* Elizabeth Peck. *St American frontier. Ct* Wild geese, The
loiterer, Buffaloes, The christening, Democracy. Also for solo S and orchestra as
Early American portrait (*WIAM* 4365).

4855   BALLOU, Esther Williamson. **Song, A** (New York: Composers
mm   Facsimile Ed., 1967) 3 p.
Dn 2'. *Da* Feb. 1967. *At* John Ciardi. *Pf* solo M, pno.   *(James R. Heintze)*

4856   BALLOU, Esther Williamson. **Street scenes** (New York:
mm   Composers Facsimile Ed., 1960) 8 p.
Dn 5'. *At* Henri Champers. *Pf* solo S, pno.

4857   BARRETT-THOMAS, N. **Boston: reflected** (Boston: Artists'
mm   Forum, 1976) 23 p.
Song cycle. *Dn* 12'. *Da* Dec. 1975. *La* composer. *At* Nikki Flionis. *St Boston:
reflected. Pf* solo S, pno. *Ct* Necessity, Tremont Street at noon, Commonwealth
Avenue, Waiting for a cab, Sentence.   *(Paula Ann Ross)*

4858   BELL, Carla Huston. **In anticipation** (096; New York: Caaron
mm   Music, 1968) 4 p.
Dn 4'. *Da* Aug. 1968. *La* composer. *At* composer. *Pf* solo A, pno.   *(Composer)*

4859   BELL, Carla Huston. **Let the rain fall on me** (030; New York:
mm   Caaron Music, 1964) 4 p.
Dn 4'. *Da* 1964. *La* composer. *At* composer. *Pf* solo B, pno.   *(Composer)*

4860   BELL, Carla Huston. **Reflection** (063; New York: Caaron Music,
mm   1968) 3 p.
Dn 5'. *Da* 1965. *La* composer. *At* composer. *Pf* solo S or T, pno.   *(Composer)*

4861   BITGOOD, Roberta. **Be still and know that I am God** (GV
mm   55; New York: H.W. Gray, 1951) 6 p.
Sacred song. *Dn* 4'. *Pf* solo M or B, org. Also for solo S or T, org (GV 55; Gray,

1947), solo A or B, org (GV 55; Gray, 1949), and solo B, choral SATB (*WIAM*
3834).

4862   BITGOOD, Roberta. **Greatest of these is love, The** (GV 61;
mm   New York: H.W. Gray, 1964) 6 p.
Sacred song. *Dn* 5'. *Da* 1933. *La* composer. *Pf* solo SB, org or pno. Also for
solo AB, org or pno (Gray, 1961), for solo SA, org or pno(Gray, 1962), and for
choral SATB, org or pno (*WIAM* 3845).   *(Composer)*

4863   BOND, Victoria. **From an antique land** (New York: Seesaw
mm   Music, 1976) 35 p.
Song cycle. *Dn* 12'. *Da* 1976. *La* publisher. *Pf* solo S, pno. *Ct* Recuerdo (*At*
Edna St. Vincent Millay), Ozymandias (*At* Shelley), Spring and fall to a young
child (*At* Gerard Manley Hopkins), In the spring and the fall (*At* Edna St.
Vincent Millay).   *(Composer)*

4864   BONDS, Margaret. **Didn't it rain** (New York: Beekman Music,
mm   1967) 5 p.
Spiritual arranged. *Dn* 5'. *Pf* solo S, pno.

4865   BONDS, Margaret. **Ezek'el saw the wheel** (New York: Beek-
mm   man Music, 1959) 5 p.
Spiritual arranged. *Dn* 3'. *Pf* solo S, pno. Dedicated to Betty Allen.

4866   BONDS, Margaret. **Five spirituals** (M 272; New York: Mutual
mm   Music Soc., 1946) 12 p.
Spirituals arranged. *Dn* 10'. *Pf* solo S, pno. *Ct* Dry bones; Sit down servant;
Lord, I just can't keep from cryin'; You can tell the world; I'll reach to heaven.

4867   BONDS, Margaret. **Go tell it on the mountain** (A 345; New
mm   York: Beekman Music, 1952) 4 p.
Spiritual arranged. *Dn* 2'. *Pf* solo voc, pno. Also for choral SATB, pno for
rehearsal only (*WIAM* 3874).

4868   BONDS, Margaret. **He's got the whole world in his hands** (A
mm   360; New York: Beekman Music, 1963) 5 p.
Spiritual arranged. *Dn* 2'. *Pf* solo S, pno.

4869   BONDS, Margaret. **Hold on** (New York: Mercury Music, 1962)
mm   5 p.
Spiritual arranged. *Dn* 3'. *Pf* solo S, pno.

4870   BONDS, Margaret. **I got a home in that rock** (New York:
mm   Mercury Music, 1968) 6 p.
Spiritual arranged. *Dn* 2'. *Pf* solo M, pno.

4871   BONDS, Margaret. **Joshua fit da battle of Jericho** (New
mm   York: Beekman Music, 1967) 5 p.
Spiritual arranged. *Dn* 2'. *Pf* solo S, pno.

4872   BONDS, Margaret. **Negro speaks of rivers, The** (New York:
mm   Handy Brothers Music, 1935) 7 p.
Dn 2'. *At* Langston Hughes. *Pf* solo M, pno.

4873   BONDS, Margaret. **Rainbow gold** (9274; New York: Chappell,
mm   1956) 7 p.
Dn 2'. *Pf* solo M, pno.

4874   BONDS, Margaret. **Sing aho** (5351; New York: Chappell, 1960)
mm   6 p.
Spiritual arranged. *Dn* 3'. *Pf* solo S, pno.

4875   BONDS, Margaret. **Three dream portraits**, *Anthology of art*
mc   *songs by black American composers*. Ed. by Willis C. PATTERSON
        (New York: E.B. Marks, 1977) 111-25.
Dn 6'. *At* Langston Hughes. *Pf* solo S, pno. *Ct* Minstrel man; Dream variation;
I, too.

4876   BOONE, Clara Lyle. **Beyond the stars** (50; Washington, D.C.:
mm   Arsis, 1975) 3 p. $1.50.
Dn 2'. *Da* 1970. *Pf* solo S or T, pno. Published under the pseudonym of Lyle
de Bohun.   *(Composer)*

4877   BOONE, Clara Lyle. **Celestia** (2; Washington, D.C.: Arsis, 1974)
mm   2 p. $1.50.
Dn 2'. *Da* 1954. *At* composer. *Pf* solo S or T, pno. Published under the
pseudonym of Lyle de Bohun.   *(Composer)*

4878   BOONE, Clara Lyle. **Fantasia** (51; Washington, D.C.: Arsis,
mm   1976) 5 p. $1.50.
Dn 3′. *Da* 1954. *At* composer. *Pf* solo S or T, pno. Published under the
pseudonym of Lyle de Bohun.   *(Composer)*

4879   BOONE, Clara Lyle. **Goodnight kiss** (48; Washington, D.C.:
mm   Arsis, 1975) 3 p. $1.50.
Dn 2′. *Da* 1955. *At* Betty Banister. *Pf* solo S or T, pno. Published under the
pseudonym of Lyle de Bohun.   *(Composer)*

4880   BOONE, Clara Lyle. **Lovely heart** (61; Washington, D.C.: Arsis,
mm   1976) 4 p. $1.50.
Dn 3′. *Da* 1956. *At* Loren Kenneth Davidson. *Pf* solo S, pno. Published under
the pseudonym of Lyle de Bohun.   *(Composer)*

4881   BOONE, Clara Lyle. **Mirrored love** (Washington, D.C.: Arsis,
mm   1975) 2 p. $1.50.
Dn 3′. *Da* 1961. *At* composer. *Pf* solo S or T, pno. Published under the
pseudonym of Lyle de Bohun.   *(Composer)*

4882   BOONE, Clara Lyle. **Sea thoughts** (53; Washington, D.C.:
mm   Arsis, 1976) 2 p. $1.50.
Dn 2′. *Da* 1954. *At* composer. *Pf* solo S or T, pno. Published under the
pseudonym of Lyle de Bohun.   *(Composer)*

4883   BOONE, Clara Lyle. **Sonnet** (7; Washington, D.C.: 1974) 3 p.
mm $1.50.
Dn 3′. *Da* 1957. *At* Shakespeare. *Pf* solo S or T, pno. Published under the
pseudonym of Lyle de Bohun.   *(Composer)*

4884   BOONE, Clara Lyle. **Time cannot claim this hour** (4; Wash-
mm   ington, D.C.: Arsis, 1975) 3 p. $1.50.
Dn 3′. *Da* 1955. *Pf* solo S or T, pno. Published under the pseudonym of Lyle
de Bohun.   *(Composer)*

4885   BOONE, Clara Lyle. **When songs have all been sung** (56;
mm   Washington, D.C.: Arsis, 1976) 2 p. $1.50.
Dn 2′. *Da* 1956. *At* Loren Kenneth Davidson. *Pf* solo A, pno. Published under
the pseudonym of Lyle de Bohun.   *(Composer)*

4886   BOONE, Clara Lyle. **Winter song** (49; Washington, D.C.: Arsis,
mm   1976) 2 p. $1.50.
Dn 2′. *Da* 1968. *At* composer. *Pf* solo S, pno. Published under the pseudonym
of Lyle de Bohun.   *(Composer)*

4887   BRADLEY, Ruth. **Budget** (New York: American Composers Ed.,
mm   1958) 3 p.
Dn 1′. *At* Harry S. Grannatt. *Pf* solo voc, pno.

4888   BRADLEY, Ruth. **Eight abstractions. Series no. 2 for voice**
mm   **and piano** (New York: American Composers Ed., 1960) 20 p.
Dn 8′. *At* Camille Anderson. *St* Abstractions 101. *Pf* solo S, pno.

4889   BRADLEY, Ruth. **Five abstractions. Series no. 5 for voice**
mm   **and piano** (New York: American Composers Ed., 1961) 13 p.
Dn 6′. *At* Camille Anderson. *St* Abstractions 101. *Pf* solo S, pno.

4890   BRADLEY, Ruth. **Four abstractions. Series no. 6 for voice**
mm   **and piano** (New York: American Composers Ed., 1961) 12 p.
Dn 5′. *At* Camille Anderson. *St* Abstractions 101. *Pf* solo S, pno.

4891   BRADLEY, Ruth. **Nine abstractions. Series no. 1 for voice**
mm   **and piano** (New York: American Composers Ed., 1960) 18 p.
Dn 10′. *At* Camille Anderson. *St* Abstractions 101. *Pf* solo S, pno.

4892   BRADLEY, Ruth. **Procrastination** (New York: American
mm   Composers Ed., 1958) 3 p.
Dn 1′. *At* Edith Pinchard. *Pf* solo S, pno.

4893   BRADLEY, Ruth. **Release** (New York: American Composers
mm   Ed., 1958) 3 p.
Dn 1′. *At* Edith Pinchard. *Pf* solo S, pno.

4894   BRADLEY, Ruth. **Seven abstractions. Series no. 3 for voice**
mm   **and piano** (New York: American Composers Ed., 1961) 14 p.
Dn 7′. *At* Camille Anderson. *St* Abstractions 101. *Pf* solo S, pno.

4895   BRADLEY, Ruth. **Six abstractions. Series no. 4 for voice**
mm   **and piano** (New York: American Composers Ed., 1961) 14 p.
Dn 6′. *At* Camille Anderson. *St* Abstractions 101. *Pf* solo S, pno.

4896   BRADLEY, Ruth. **Three abstractions. Series no. 7 for voice**
mm   **and piano** (New York: American Composers Ed., 1961) 8 p.
Dn 3′. *At* Camille Anderson. *St* Abstractions 101. *Pf* solo S, pno.

4897   BRADLEY, Ruth. **Two abstractions. Series no. 8 for voice**
mm   **and piano** (New York: American Composers Ed., 1961) 6 p.
Dn 6′. *At* Camille Anderson. *St* Abstractions 101. *Pf* solo S, pno.

4898   BRITAIN, Radie. **Lasso of time, The** (facsimile of MS at NN,
mm   n.d.) 3 p.
Dn 2′. *At* Alice McKenzie. *Pf* solo A, pno.

4899   BRITAIN, Radie. **Stillness** (Hollywood, Calif.: Stockton Studios,
mm   1943) 3 p.
Dn 1′. *At* Lester Luther. *Pf* solo M, pno.

4900   BRITAIN, Radie. **Withered flowers (Welke Blumen)** (CP
mm   387; New York: Composers Press, 1957) 5 p.
Dn 2′. *Lt* English, German. *At* Friedl Schreyvogl. *Pf* solo S, pno.

4901   COATES, Gloria. **Five poems of Emily Dickinson for voice**
mm   **and piano** (facsimile of MS at NNAMC, 1973) 15 p.
Song cycle. *Dn* 10′. *Da* 1972. *La* composer. *Pf* solo S or M, pno. *Ct* I'm nobody;
I've seen a dying eye; I held a jewel in my fingers and went to sleep; Wild
nights, wild nights; They dropped like flakes, they dropped like stars. *(Composer)*

4902   COOPER, Rose Marie. **Trilogy** (Greensboro, N.C.: composer,
mm   1959) 7 p.
Songs. *Dn* 5′. *At* Jennie Frye. *Pf* solo S, pno. *Ct* Silence; O, Kitty; Absent.
                                                                (Composer)

4903   CRANE, Joelle Wallach. **Five-fold amen** (New York: Compos-
mm   ers Facsimile Ed., 1974) 1 p.
Dn 1′. *Da* 1974. *La* NNACA. *Pf* solo SA.   *(Composer)*

4904   DAVIS, Katherine K. **Nancy Hanks** (1158; New York: Galaxy
mm   Music, 1941) 3 p.
Dn 4′. *At* Rosemary Benet. *Pf* solo S, pno. Also for choral SSA and choral
SATB (*WIAM* 3911).   *(Composer)*

4905   DIEMER, Emma Lou. **Four Chinese love-poems for soprano**
mm   **and harp or piano** (New York: Seesaw Music, 1976) 16 p.
Dn 10′. *Da* 1965. *La* publisher. *St* ancient Chinese poetry. *Ct* People hide their
love (*At* Wu-ti), Wind and rain, By the willows, The mulberry on the lowland.
                                                                (Composer)

4906   DIEMER, Emma Lou. **Three mystic songs for soprano and**
mm   **baritone** (New York: Seesaw Music, 1976) 20 p.
Dn 12′. *Da* 1963. *La* publisher. *St* Hindu poetry. *Pf* solo SBar, pno. *Ct* He is
the sun (*St* Upanishads), To the great self (*St* Upanishads), God: there is no god
but He (*St* Koran).   *(Composer)*

4907   DRAKE, Elizabeth Bell. **Songs of here and forever** (facsimile
mm   of MS at NNAMC, 1970) 34 p.
Song cycle. *Dn* 20′. *Da* 1970. *La* composer. *At* composer. *Pf* solo S, pno. *Ct*
Cache Lake, Communication, Harlem Bridge, Light, Song of worship, Storm.
                                                                (Composer)

4908   FINE, Vivian. **Four Elizabethan songs** (Shaftsbury, Vt.: Cata-
mm   mount Facsimile Ed., 1972) 10 p. $4.
Dn 6′. *Da* 1941. *La* composer. *Pf* solo M, pno. *Ct* Daybreak (*At* Donne),
Spring's welcome (*At* John Lyly), Dirge (*At* Shakespeare), The bargain (*At*
Philip Sidney).   *(Composer)*

4909   FINE, Vivian. **Two Neruda poems** (Shaftsbury, Vt.: Catamount
mm   Facsimile Ed., 1972) 12 p. $4.
Songs. *Dn* 14′. *Da* 1971. *La* composer. *At* Pablo Neruda. *Pf* solo M, pno. *Lt*
Spanish. *Ct* La tortuga, Oda al piano.   *(Composer)*

4910   FRYXELL, Regina Holmen. **Praise, my soul, the King of**
mm   **Heaven. On a melody by J.S. Bach** (New York: C. Fischer,
       1963) 6 p.

Dn 5′. *Pf* solo S or T, org or pno. Also for choral SA or TB in unison, org or pno (*WIAM* 3938).

4911 FRYXELL, Regina Holmen. **Psalm 67** (New York: H.W. Gray,
mm   1954) 4 p.
Sacred song. *Dn* 2′. *Pf* solo S or T, org or pno; also can be sung by choral unison, org or pno with optional 2nd voice.   *(Composer)*

4912 FRYXELL, Regina Holmen. **To the Christ Child** (New York:
mm   H.W. Gray, 1954) 4 p.
Sacred song. *Dn* 2′. *At* Frank Mason North. *Pf* solo S or T, org or pno. Also for choral unison, org or pno (*WIAM* 3940).   *(Composer)*

4913 FRYXELL, Regina Holmen. **Vision, A** (New York: H.W. Gray,
mm   1956) 4 p.
Sacred song. *Dn* 2′. *St* 15th-c. English carol. *Pf* solo S, org or pno. *(Composer)*

4914 GARWOOD, Margaret. **Cliff's edge, The. Songs of a psy-
mm   chotic** (facsimile of MS at NNAMC, 1969) 18 p.
Song cycle. *Dn* 9′. *At* Eithne Tabor. *St* The cliff's edge. *Pf* solo S, pno. *Ct* O thou twin-blossoming rose (schizophrenia), The child in the sunlight dancing (hebephrenia), And is there anyone at all (panic), This is how it starts (breakdown), And with what silence (asylum).   *(Composer)*

4915 GARWOOD, Margaret. **Lovesongs. 6 songs to poems of
mm   E.E. Cummings** (E. Greenville, Penn.: composer, 1963) 30 p.
Dn 15′. *Pf* solo S, pno. *Ct* Who knows if the moon's a balloon; Now all the fingers of this tree; It may not always be so; A wind has blown the rain away; Cruelly, love; What a proud dreamhouse.   *(Composer)*

4916 GARWOOD, Margaret. **Springsongs. 5 songs to poems of
mm   E.E. Cummings** (facsimile of MS at NNAMC, 1970) 25 p.
Song cycle. *Dn* 10′. *Pf* solo S, pno. *Ct* O sweet spontaneous earth, Trees were in (give give), Until and I heard, Thy fingers make early flowers of all things, Before the fragile gradual throne of night.   *(Composer)*

4917 GIDEON, Miriam. **Epitaphs from Robert Burns** (New York:
mm   American Composers Ed., 1957) 4 p.
Dn 4′. *Pf* solo S or A, pno.

4918 GIDEON, Miriam. **Mixco** (New York: American Composers Ed.,
mm   1959) 10 p.
Dn 5′. *At* Miguel Angel Asturias. *Pf* solo S, pno.

4919 GIDEON, Miriam. **Rhymes from the hill** (facsimile of MS at
mm   NN, 1968) 11 p.
Song cycle. *Dn* 8′. *At* Christian Morgenstern. *Tr* Max Knight. *St* Galgenlieder. *Lt* German, English. *Pf* solo M, pno. *Ct* Bundeslied der Galgenlieder (Chorus of the gallows gang), Galgenkindes Wiegenlied (Gallows child's lullaby), Die korfsche Uhr (Korf's clock), Palmströms Uhr (Palmstroem's clock), Der Seufzer (The sigh). Also for solo M, chamber ensemble (*WIAM* 3492). *Rg* Composers Recordings, CRI SD 286.

4920 GIDEON, Miriam. **Seasons of time, The** (Hastings-on-Hudson,
mm   N.Y.: General Music, 1971) 15 p.
Song cycle. *Dn* 10′. *St* Tanka poetry of ancient Japan, adapted. *Pf* solo M, pno. *Ct* Now it is spring (*At* Yakamochi, *Tr* Robert H. Brower and Earl Miner), The wild geese returning (*At* Kunimoto, *Tr* Arthur Waley), Can it be that there is no moon? (*At* Narihira, *Tr* Arthur Waley), Gossip grows like weeds (*At* Hitomaro, *Tr* Kenneth Rexroth), Each season more lovely (*At* Yakamochi, *Tr* J.L. Pierson), In the leafy tree-tops (*At* Yakamochi, *Tr* Nippon Shinkokai), A passing show'r (*Tr* Nippon Shinkokai), I have always known (*At* Narihira, *Tr* Kenneth Rexroth), To what shall I compare this world? (*At* Mansei, *Tr* Arthur Waley), Yonder in the plum tree (*Tr* Nippon Shinkokai). Also for solo M, flu, vcl, pno (cel) (*WIAM* 3493).

4921 GIDEON, Miriam. **Songs of voyage** (New York: American
mm   Composers Ed., 1964) 5, 9 p.
Dn 8′. *Pf* solo S, pno. *Ct* Farewell tablet to Agathocles (*At* Florence Wilkinson), The nightingale unheard (*At* Josephine Preston Peabody).

4922 GIDEON, Miriam. **To music** (New York: American Composers
mm   Ed., 1964) 7 p.
Dn 5′. *At* Robert Herrick. *Pf* solo S, pno.

4923 GLANVILLE-HICKS, Peggy. **Ballade** (New York: Hargail
mm   Music, 1949) 8 p.
Songs. *Dn* 5′. *At* Paul Bowles. *Pf* solo M, pno. *Ct* Yet in no sleep, How in this garden, But no!.   *(Publisher)*

4924 GLANVILLE-HICKS, Peggy. **Five songs** (New York: Wein-
mm   traub Music, 1952) 12 p.
Dn 10′. *At* A.E. Housman. *Pf* solo M, pno. *Ct* Mimic heaven, He would not stay, Stars, Unlucky love, Homespun collars.

4925 GLANVILLE-HICKS, Peggy. **Profiles from China** (New
mm   York: Weintraub Music, 1951) 8 p.
Songs. *Dn* 6′. *At* Eunice Tietjens. *Pf* solo M, pno. *Ct* Poetics, A lament of scarlet cloud, The dream, Crepuscle, The son of heaven.

4926 GLANVILLE-HICKS, Peggy. **Thirteen ways of looking at a
mm   blackbird** (New York: Weintraub Music, 1951) 19 p.
Dn 10′. *At* Wallace Stevens. *Pf* solo M, pno.

4927 GOULD, Elizabeth. **(F)Raileries** (facsimile of MS at NNAMC,
mm   1977) 22 p.
Song cycle. *Dn* 14′. *Da* 1970. *La* composer. *At* Irja Friend. *Pf* solo S, pno. *Ct* Item: time + item: mite = emit, The strange house, Crazy quilt lilting song, Charm for dea(th) fear, So-long song, Breakawa(y)ken(n)ed. Awarded 1st prize in the Delta Omicron music composition contest, 1971.   *(Composer)*

4928 HSU, Wen-ying. **Vocal series no. I** (Los Angeles: composer,
mm   1972) 32 p.
Dn 18′. *Dn* 1972. *La* composer. *Pf* solo S, pno, optional flu. *Ct* Evening prayer, Alleluja, Light of God (*At* composer, *Lt* English, Chinese), Regret (*At* Hsu Yu), Song of Ching Hai (*At* Lo Chai-lun), Parting song, At a glance (*At* Sun Ju-lin).   *(Composer)*

4929 HYSON, Winifred. **Songs of Job's daughter** (facsimile of MS
mm   at NN, 1970) 18 p.
Song cycle. *Dn* 12′. *La* composer. *At* Jean Starr Untermeyer. *St* Job's daughter. *Pf* solo S, pno. *Ct* Injunction, High tide, Lullaby for a man-child, Two and a child, Birthday, My phoenix.   *(Composer)*

4930 JORDAN, Alice. **Bless the Lord O my soul** (APM 800;
mm   Nashville: Abingdon, 1970) 4 p. $1.
Sacred song. *Dn* 2′. *Pf* solo M or Bar, org or pno.   *(Composer)*

4931 KETTERING, Eunice Lea. **Compensation,** *Contemporary*
mc   *American songs.* Ed. by Bernard TAYLOR (5371B; Evanston, Ill.:
        Summy-Birchard, 1960) I, 40-42.
Dn 2′. *Da* 1955. *La* NmU. *At* Sara Teasdale. *Pf* solo A or B, pno.   *(Composer)*

4932 KETTERING, Eunice Lea. **Gifts** (2081; New York: Galaxy
mm   Music, 1955) 4 p.
Dn 3′. *Da* 1954. *La* NmU. *At* Martha E. Holmes. *Pf* solo A or B, pno.
          (Composer)

4933 LA BARBARA, Joan. **Circular song** (New York: composer,
mm   1976) 4 p. $25.
Dn 8′. *Da* Aug. 1976. *La* composer. *At* composer. *Pf* any voice type. *Rg* Voice is the original instrument, Wizard, RVW 2266.

4934 LA BARBARA, Joan. **Hear what I feel: a vocal experiment,**
mc   *Soundings 10.* Ed. by Peter GARLAND (Berkeley, Calif.: P. Garland,
        1976) 82-93.
Dn 10′. *La* composer. *At* composer. *Pf* any voice type.   *(Composer)*

4935 LA BARBARA, Joan. **Voice piece. One-note internal reso-
mm   nance investigation** (New York: composer, 1976) 9 p. $25.
Dn 35′. *Da* 23 Aug. 1976. *At* composer. *Pf* any voice type. *Rg* Voice is the original instrument, Wizard, RVW 2266.   *(Composer)*

4936 LAUFER, Beatrice. **Soldier's prayer** (AMP 9546; New York:
mm   Associated Music, 1955) 6 p.
Dn 5′. *Da* 1943. *At* Hugh Rowell Brodie. *Pf* solo B, pno.   *(Composer)*

4937 LORENZ, Ellen Jane. **Three songs for sacred occasions**
mm   (APM 348; Nashville: Abingdon, 1966) 8 p.
Dn 6′. *Da* 1965. *Pf* solo A or B, pno. *Ct* Here in our upper room (*At* Paul Robinson); Little ones we bring to thee (*At* Philip Gregory); Bless us, God of loving (*At* Jan Struther).   *(Composer)*

4938 MCNEIL, Jan Pfischner. **Opus 10: songs of commitment**
mm   (New York: C. Fischer, 1975) 29 p. $7.50. (score, parts).
Dn 18′. *Da* 1974. *At* composer. *Pf* solo ST, pno.   *(Composer)*

4939 MERRIMAN, Margarita L. **Tunnels and sidewalks** (facsimile
mm of MS at Atlantic Union Col., South Lancaster, Mass., 1977) 12 p. $5.
Song cycle. *Dn* 10'. *Da* 1974. *La* composer. *At* R. Lynn Sauls. *Pf* solo S, pno. *Ct*
The mole's prayer, Reflections on seeing a raccoon skull, Rawback and
bloodybones, Enlightenment, Love song, Pragmatism.

4940 MUSGRAVE, Thea. **Five love songs** (London: J. & W. Chester,
mm 1970) 15 p.
Dn 10'. *Da* 1955. *Pf* solo S, gtr. *Ct* Except I love, I cannot have delight (*At*
Robert Parry); O love, how strangely sweet are thy weak passions (*At* John
Marston); Poor is the life that misses the lover's greatest treasure; Weep eyes,
break heart, my love and I must part (*At* Thomas Middleton); The spring of joy
is dry, that ran into my heart.

4941 MUSGRAVE, Thea. **Sir Patrick Spens** (London: J. & W.
mm Chester, 1976) 10 p.
Dn 7'. *Da* 1961. *Pf* solo T, gtr.

4942 MUSGRAVE, Thea. **Song for Christmas, A** (London: J. & W.
mm Chester, 1963) 8 p.
Dn 5'. *Pf* solo S, pno.

4943 MUSGRAVE, Thea. **Suite o' bairnsangs, A** (JWC 4063;
mm London: J. & W. Chester, 1962) 15 p.
Dn 5'. *At* Maurice Lindsay. *Pf* solo M, pno. *Ct* The man-in-the-mune, Daffins,
Willie Wabster, A bairn's prayer at night, The green.

4944 NOBLE, Ann. **Child saint, A** (facsimile of MS at Mills Col.,
mm Oakland, Calif., 1976) 8 p. $2.50.
Dn 7'. *La* composer. *At* Alva Svoboda. *Pf* solo Bar, pno. *(Composer)*

4945 PERRY, Julia Amanda. **Free at last** (GM 1826; New York:
mm Galaxy Music, 1951) 5 p.
Spiritual arranged. *Dn* 2'. *Pf* solo S or T, pno.

4946 PERRY, Julia Amanda. **How beautiful are the feet** (GMC
mm 1978; New York: Galaxy Music, 1954) 5 p.
Sacred song. *Dn* 4'. *Pf* solo M or Bar, org.

4947 PERRY, Julia Amanda. **I'm a poor li'l orphan in this world**
mm (GMC 1874; New York: Galaxy Music, 1952) 3 p.
Spiritual arranged. *Dn* 2'. *Pf* solo M or Bar, pno.

4948 PERRY, Julia Amanda. **Lord! what shall I do?** (Boston:
mm McLaughlin & Reilly, 1949) 3 p.
Spiritual arranged. *Dn* 2'. *Pf* solo S, pno.

4949 PREOBRAJENSKA, Vera N. **Cycle of art songs, op. 1**
mm (facsimile of autograph at NNAMC, 1945-71) 38 p.
Song cycle. *Dn* 24'. *Da* 1945-71. *La* composer. *Pf* solo S, pno. *Ct* Parting (*At*
Cloyce Martin), In my garden (*At* T.N. Preobrajenska), 'Tis spring (*At* T.N.
Preobrajenska), Dreams (*At* T.N. Preobrajenska), Thoughts (*At* T.N. Preobra-
jenska), Face to face (*At* H.N. Spaulding), Two symbols (*At* H.N. Spaulding),
Sea shells (*At* H.N. Spaulding), Awakening (*At* T.N. Ostraumova), Unknown
destiny (*At* composer), Brief momentums (*At* composer), Moods (*At* composer),
Carefree life (*At* composer). *(Composer)*

4950 PREOBRAJENSKA, Vera N. **Undertones of frost** (facsimile
mm of autograph at NNAMC, 1960) 31 p.
Dn 20'. *Da* 1960. *At* Lillian V. Inke. *St* Time is a dream. *Pf* solo S, pno. Also for
solo S, flu, obo, bsn, tba, vln, vcl, cbs (*WIAM* 3685).

4951 RICHTER, Marga. **She at his funeral** (facsimile of MS on
mm rental; New York: C. Fischer, 1975) 2 p.
Dn 3'. *Da* 1954. *La* composer. *At* Thomas Hardy. *Pf* solo S, pno. *(Composer)*

4952 RICHTER, Marga. **Transmutation. Eight songs to Chinese
mm poems** (facsimile of MS on rental; New York: C. Fischer, 1975) 21
p.
Dn 9'. *Da* 1947. *La* composer. *Tr* Henry H. Hart. *Pf* solo S, pno. *Ct* Twilight
(*At* Ch'ên Yün), The orchid (*At* Liu Sung), Change (*At* Hsiao), Desolation (*At*
Chang Chi), On seeing a red cockatoo on the road to Mount Shang (*At* Po Chü
I), Sleeplessness, A song of Chäng An, Transmutation. *Rg* MGM, E3546.
(Composer)

4953 RICHTER, Marga. **Two Chinese songs** (facsimile of MS on
mm rental; New York: C. Fischer, 1975) 4 p.

Dn 3'. *Da* 1952. *La* composer. *Pf* solo S, pno. *Ct* The hermit (*At* Li Hai-ku),
Fishing picture (*At* Ta Chung-kuang). *Rg* MGM, E3546. *(Composer)*

4954 RICHTER, Marion Morrey. **Daffodils, The** (facsimile of MS at
mm NN, 1955) 5 p.
Dn 3'. *Da* 1955. *La* composer. *At* Wordsworth. *Pf* solo S, pno. Published under
the composer's maiden name, Morrey. *(Composer)*

4955 RICHTER, Marion Morrey. **Longing** (facsimile of MS at NN,
mm 1950) 4 p.
Dn 3'. *Da* 1950. *La* composer. *At* Matthew Arnold. *Pf* solo S, pno. Published
under the composer's maiden name, Morrey. *(Composer)*

4956 RICHTER, Marion Morrey. **Silence sings** (facsimile of MS at
mm NN, 1935) 4 p.
Dn 3'. *Da* 1935. *La* composer. *At* Thomas Sturge Moore. *Pf* solo S, pno.
Published under the composer's maiden name, Morrey. *(Composer)*

4957 ROSSER, Annetta Hamilton. **Meditations on the cross** (rev.
mm ed.; Madison, Wis.: Gilbert, 1977) 25 p.
Sacred song cycle. *Dn* 18'. *Da* 1977. *Pf* solo SM or SBar, org. *Ct* Father, forgive
them; Thou shalt be with me in Paradise; Behold thy mother; My God, why
hast thou forsaken me?; I thirst; It is finished; Father, into thy hands I
commend my spirit. *(Composer)*

4958 ROSSER, Annetta Hamilton. **Offering of song, An** (Madison,
mm Wis.: Gilbert, 1977) 124 p. $8.
Dn 98'. *Da* 1976. *Pf* solo S or M or T or Bar, pno. *Ct* Songs of love, The
appreciation of nature and beauty, Songs from the Chinese, Elizabethan and
Jacobean songs (*Pf* solo S or M or T or Bar, flu or rec), Songs of whimsy, Songs
for children, Winter songs, Songs for Christmas, Songs of faith. Optional flu
and vln parts are available from the publisher. *(Composer)*

4959 ROSSER, Annetta Hamilton. **Tears, idle tears** (Madison, Wis.:
mm Gilbert, 1977) 3 p.
Dn 3'. *Da* 1976. *At* Tennyson. *Pf* solo M or Bar, pno. *(Composer)*

4960 SINGER, Jeanne. **American Indian song suite** (West Babylon,
mm N.Y.: H. Branch, 1977) 9 p.
Dn 5'. *Da* 1976. *La* composer. *St* traditional Indian: Pawnee, Maliseet,
Laguna, Kiowa. *Pf* solo S or M, pno. *(Composer)*

4961 SINGER, Jeanne. **Arno is deep** (facsimile of autograph at
mm NNAMC, 1976) 3 p.
Dn 2'. *La* composer. *Pf* solo M or Bar, pno. *(Composer)*

4962 SINGER, Jeanne. **Cycle of love, A** (West Babylon, N.Y.: H.
mm Branch, 1976) 13 p. $4.
Dn 9'. *Da* 1975. *La* composer. *Pf* solo S, pno. *Ct* Discovered (*At* Anne Marx),
Fulfilled (*At* Amy Lowell), Lost (*At* composer), Transfigured (*At* Madeline
Mason). *(Composer)*

4963 SINGER, Jeanne. **Dirge** (facsimile of autograph at NNAMC,
mm 1972) 4 p.
Dn 4'. *La* composer. *At* Madeline Mason. *St* Sonnets in a new form. *Pf* solo M
or Bar, pno. *(Composer)*

4964 SINGER, Jeanne. **Downing the bell tower**, *Composers and
mp Authors Association of America Magazine XXX/3-4 (fall 1975) 8-10.*
Dn 2'. *Da* 1974. *La* composer. *At* Suzanne Dale. *Pf* solo M or Bar, pno.
(Composer)

4965 SINGER, Jeanne. **Gift**, *Composers and Authors Association of
mp America Magazine XXVIII/4 (spring 1973) 6-7.*
Dn 2'. *Da* 1972. *La* composer. *At* Patricia Benton. *Pf* solo S or T, pno.
(Composer)

4966 SINGER, Jeanne. **Hannah** (facsimile of autograph at NNAMC,
mm 1977) 6 p.
Dn 3'. *La* composer. *At* Lloyd Schwartz. *Pf* solo M or Bar, pno. *(Composer)*

4967 SINGER, Jeanne. **Memoria** (facsimile of autograph at NNAMC,
mm 1977) 5 p.
Dn 4'. *La* composer. *At* Frederika Blankner. *Pf* solo S or T, pno. *(Composer)*

4968 SINGER, Jeanne. **Sanguinaria** (facsimile of autograph at
mm NNAMC, 1973) 4 p.
Dn 4'. *La* composer. *At* Bernard Grebanier. *St* The angel in the rock. *Pf* solo M
or Bar, pno. *(Composer)*

4969 SINGER, Jeanne. **Summons** (West Babylon, N.Y.: H. Branch,
mm   1975) 4 p. $2.
Dn 4′. *Da* 1975. *La* composer. *At* Patricia Benton. *Pf* solo M or Bar, pno.
(Composer)

4970 SINGER, Jeanne. **Where do the wild birds fly?** (facsimile of
mm   autograph at NNAMC, 1971) 6 p.
Dn 4′. *La* composer. *At* composer. *Pf* solo M or Bar, pno.
(Composer)

4971 SINGER, Jeanne. **Winter identity. Duet for two sopranos**
mm   (facsimile of autograph at NNAMC, 1971) 5 p.
Dn 4′. *La* composer. *At* Patricia Benton. *Pf* solo SS, pno.
(Composer)

4972 SLEETH, Natalie. **Christmas is a feeling** (Chapel Hill, N.C.:
mm   Hinshaw Music, 1975) 7 p. $1.
Dn 2′. *At* composer. *Pf* solo S, pno, optional flu. Also for choral unison or duo,
pno, optional flu (*WIAM* 4157).
(Composer)

4973 SMITH, Julia. **Three love songs** (MM 104; New York: Mowbray
mm   Music, 1967) 8 p.
Song cycle. *Dn* 5′. *Da* 1953-55. *At* Karl Flaster. *Pf* solo S, pno. *Ct* I will sing the
song, The door that I would open, The love I hold.
(Composer)

4974 STEWART, Ora Pate. **Our glorious land** (Provo, Utah: Fern-
mm   wood, 1975) 2 p. $1.
Dn 2′. *At* composer. *Pf* solo S, pno. Also can be sung by solo SA, pno or choral
SA, pno.
(Composer)

4975 STEWART, Ora Pate. **Song of love** (Provo, Utah: Fernwood,
mm   1965) 3 p.
Dn 3′. *At* Nephi J. Bott. *Pf* solo S, pno. Also can be sung by solo SA, pno or
choral SA, pno. *Rg Many ways to say "I love you"*, Medallion Records, KM-
1418.
(Composer)

4976 STEWART, Ora Pate. **To a child** (Provo, Utah: Fernwood,
mm   1964) 5 p.
Dn 3′. *At* composer. *Pf* solo A, pno. Also for choral SSA, pno, optional vln and
vla (*WIAM* 4221).
(Composer)

4977 SUCHY, Gregoria Karides. **When I was but a foolish boy**
mm   (facsimile of MS at NNAMC, 1960) 4 p.
Dn 7′. *La* composer. *At* Donald Emerson. *Pf* solo S or T, pno.
(Composer)

4978 SWISHER, Gloria Wilson. **Love's shadow comes slow** (fac-
mm   simile of MS at NNAMC, 1977) 3 p.
Dn 3′. *Da* 1962. *La* composer. *At* Lee M. Mac Arthur, Jr. *Pf* solo S or M, pno.
(Composer)

4979 SWISHER, Gloria Wilson. **Rest, love** (facsimile of MS at
mm   NNAMC, 1977) 4 p.
Dn 3′. *Da* 1963. *La* composer. *At* Elizabeth Weise. *Pf* solo M, pno. *(Composer)*

4980 SWISHER, Gloria Wilson. **Sisters** (facsimile of MS at
mm   NNAMC, 1977) 11 p.
Song cycle. *Dn* 6′. *Da* 1977. *La* composer. *St The world split open. Pf* solo S or
M, pno. *Ct* Sit and sew (*At* Alice Dunbar Nelson), Tenebris (*At* Angelina Weld
Grimke), The cabal at Nickey Nackeys (*At* Aphra Behn).
(Composer)

4981 TALMA, Louise. **Carmina Mariana** (New York: composer,
mm   1943) 9 p.
Sacred duets. *Dn* 6′. *Pf* solo SS, pno. *Ct* Ave Maria, Regina caeli, Salve Regina.
Also for choral SS, org (*WIAM* 4230) and for choral SS, 2 tpt, 2 tbn, org, str.
(Composer)

4982 TALMA, Louise. **Have you heard? Do you know?** (New York:
mm   composer, 1976) 70 p.
Dn 45′. *At* composer. *Pf* solo SMT, pno. Full score in preparation. *(Composer)*

4983 TALMA, Louise. **Leap before you look** (New York: composer,
mm   1945) 10 p.
Dn 3′. *At* W.H. Auden. *Pf* solo S, pno. *(Composer)*

4984 TALMA, Louise. **Letter to St. Peter** (New York: composer,
mm   1945) 3 p.
Dn 3′. *At* Elma Dean. *Pf* solo S, pno. *(Composer)*

4985 TALMA, Louise. **One need not be a chamber to be haunted**
mm   (New York: composer, 1941) 3 p.

Dn 3′. *At* Emily Dickinson. *Pf* solo S, pno. *(Composer)*

4986 TALMA, Louise. **Rain song** (New York: composer, 1973) 5 p.
mm
Dn 2′. *At* Jean Garrigue. *Pf* solo S, pno. *(Composer)*

4987 TALMA, Louise. **Terre de France** (New York: composer, 1945)
mm   26 p.
Dn 8′. *Pf* solo S, pno. *Ct* Mère, voici vos fils (*At* Charles Péguy); Sonnet:
Heureux qui comme Ulysse (*At* Joachim Du Bellay); Ballade: En regardant
le païs de France (*At* Charles d'Orléans); Ode: Dieu te gard l'honneur du
printemps (*At* Pierre de Ronsard); Adieux à la Meuse (*At* Charles Péguy).
(Composer)

4988 TALMA, Louise. **Two songs** (New York: composer, 1946) 4 p.
mm
Dn 3′. *At* Gerard Manley Hopkins. *Pf* solo S, pno. *Ct* Pied beauty, Spring and
fall. *(Composer)*

4989 TALMA, Louise. **Two sonnets of despair** (New York: com-
mm   poser, 1946, 1950) 4, 4 p.
Dn 9′. *At* Gerard Manley Hopkins. *Pf* solo Bar, pno. *Ct* I wake to feel the fell
of dark, not day; No, I'll not, carrion comfort, despair. *(Composer)*

4990 THEMMEN, Ivana Marburger. **Ode to Akhmatova** (facsimile
mm   of MS at NNAMC, 1977) 21 p.
Dn 16′. *Da* 1977. *At* Anna Akhmatova. *St Requiem 1935-40. Pf* solo S, pno.
Also for solo S and orchestra (*WIAM* 4540). *(Composer)*

4991 VAN DE VATE, Nancy. **Cradlesong** (facsimile of MS at
mm   NNAMC, 1962) 4 p.
Dn 2′. *Da* 1962. *La* composer. *At* Clemens Brentano. *Tr* Herman Salinger. *Pf*
solo S, pno. *(Composer)*

4992 VAN DE VATE, Nancy. **Five somber songs** (facsimile of MS
mm   at NNAMC, 1977) 26 p. $3.
Song cycle. *Dn* 14′. *Da* 1970. *La* composer. *Pf* solo S, pno. *Ct* Eastern front (*At*
Georg Trakl, *Tr* C. Middleton); Alone (*At* Poe); A great, dark sleep (*At*
Verlaine, *Tr* Kate Flores); The earth is so lovely (*At* Heine, *Tr* Howard Hugo).
(Composer)

4993 VAN DE VATE, Nancy. **Two songs for medium voice**
mm   (Waterloo, Ontario: Waterloo Music, 1966) 7 p.
Dn 5′. *Da* 1960. *La* composer. *Pf* solo S, pno. *Ct* Death is the chilly night (*At*
Heine, *Tr* Kate Flores), Loneliness (*At* Rilke, *Tr* Kate Flores). *(Composer)*

4994 VAN DE VATE, Nancy. **Youthful age** (facsimile of MS at
mm   NNAMC, 1960) 2 p.
Dn 1′. *Da* 1960. *La* composer. *At* Greek, 6th c. B.C. *Pf* solo S, pno. *(Composer)*

4995 VAZQUEZ, Alida. **Acuarelas de Mexico (Watercolors of
mm   Mexico)** (facsimile of MS at NNAMC, 1968) 20 p.
Songs. *Dn* 12′. *Da* 1968. *La* composer. *At* composer. *Lt* Spanish, English. *Pf*
solo M, pno. *Ct* Despierta (Awake), Los ninos de Mexico (Children of Mexico),
La cuerda (Jumping rope), La basura (Garbage), El arco iris (The rainbow), La
hora del pan (Time for bread), Noches claras (Clear night), El velador (The
watchman). *(Composer)*

4996 WALKER, Gwyneth. **Songs for medium voice and guitar**
mm   (New Canaan, Conn.: Walker, 1976) 9 p. $2.
Dn 8′. *Da* 1976. *La* composer. *Ct* Tell me not here (*At* A.E. Housman), Back
and side go bare, Country girl (*At* G.M. Brown). *(Composer)*

4997 WARREN, Elinor Remick. **Christmas candle** (39125; New
mm   York: G. Schirmer, 1940) 5 p.
Dn 3′. *Da* 1940. *La* composer. *At* Kate Louise Brown. *Pf* solo voc, pno.
(Composer)

4998 WARREN, Elinor Remick. **For you with love** (46503; New
mm   York: G. Schirmer, 1969) 4 p.
Dn 3′. *Da* 1967. *La* composer. *At* Louis Untermeyer. *Pf* solo voc, pno.
(Composer)

4999 WARREN, Elinor Remick. **More things are wrought by
md   prayer** (GV 487; New York: H.W. Gray, 1968) 3 p.
Dn 3′. *La* composer. *At* Tennyson. *Pf* solo S or M, org or pno. *Tm The legend of
King Arthur* (*WIAM* 4247). Also for choral SATB (*WIAM* 4249). *(Composer)*

5000 WARREN, Elinor Remick. **Snow towards evening**, *Songs by*
mc   *22 Americans.* Ed. by Bernard TAYLOR (44538; New York: G.
Schirmer, 1960) 136-38.
Dn 2′. *Da* 1958. *La* publisher. *At* Melville Cane. *Pf* solo voc, pno.   *(Composer)*

5001 WARREN, Elinor Remick. **We two** (41534; New York: G.
mm   Schirmer, 1947) 6 p.
Dn 3′. *Da* 1946. *La* composer. *At* Whitman. *Pf* solo S or B, pno.   *(Composer)*

5002 WEAVER, Mary. **Cradlesong** (New York: G. Schirmer, 1940) 4
mm   p.
Dn 4′. *Da* 1924. *La* MoKU. *At* Padraic Colum. *Pf* solo S, pno.   *(Composer)*

5003 WEAVER, Mary. **Heart of heaven, The** (New York: Galaxy
mm   Music, 1952) 5 p.
Dn 3′. *Da* 1950. *La* MoKU. *At* composer. *Pf* solo S or A, pno.   *(Composer)*

5004 WEIGL, Vally. **Beyond time** (New York: Composers Facsimile
mm   Ed., 1956) 16 p. (score, part).
Song cycle. *Dn* 12′. *Pf* solo S or T, pno, optional vln or flu. *Ct* Desert is not;
Remainder; The hills have great hearts; Happy summer; Fill, fill the cup;
Treasure; Epilogue. *Rg* NNAMC.   *(Composer)*

5005 WEIGL, Vally. **Songs from** *No boundary* (New York: Com-
mm   posers Facsimile Ed., 1963) 19 p.
Dn 7′. *At* Leonore Marshall. *Pf* solo M, pno, optional vla or cla. *Ct* Cricket
song, Song from the meadow's end, Shell song, New born, April.   *(Composer)*

5006 YOUSE, Glad Robinson. **April is forever** (2422; New York:
mm   Bourne, 1953) 4 p.
Dn 3′. *At* Edythe Hope Genee. *Pf* solo S, pno. Also for choral SSA, pno
(*WIAM* 4280). *Rg* Golden Crest, CRS 4138.   *(Composer)*

5007 YOUSE, Glad Robinson. **As long as children pray** (New York:
mm   Bourne, 1941) 3 p.
Dn 3′. *At* Iris Jean Crawford. *Pf* solo S, pno. Also for choral SSA, pno (*WIAM*
4281).   *(Composer)*

5008 YOUSE, Glad Robinson. **Beatitudes, The** (New York: Breg-
mm   man, Vocco & Conn, 1946) 3 p.
Sacred song. *Dn* 3′. *Pf* solo S, pno.   *(Composer)*

5009 YOUSE, Glad Robinson. **Hear me Lord** (New York: Bourne,
mm   1942) 3 p.
Sacred song. *Dn* 3′. *At* composer. *Pf* solo S, pno. Also for choral SATB, pno
(*WIAM* 4286).   *(Composer)*

5010 YOUSE, Glad Robinson. **I knelt at thy altar** (New York:
mm   Chappell, 1953) 4 p.
Sacred song. *Dn* 3′. *At* composer. *Pf* solo S, pno.   *(Composer)*

5011 YOUSE, Glad Robinson. **Little lost boy, The** (New York:
mm   Southern Music, 1950) 3 p.
Dn 3′. *At* Grace Noll Crowell. *Pf* solo S, pno.   *(Composer)*

5012 YOUSE, Glad Robinson. **My dream of springtime** (3274; New
mm   York: C. Fischer, 1947) 3 p.
Dn 2′. *At* Grace Noll Crowell. *Pf* solo S, pno. *Rg* Golden Crest, CRS 4138.
(Composer)

5013 YOUSE, Glad Robinson. **Red bird** (40475; New York: G.
mm   Schirmer, 1943) 3 p.
Dn 3′. *At* Grace Noll Crowell. *Pf* solo S, pno.   *(Composer)*

5014 YOUSE, Glad Robinson. **Some lovely thing** (New York: C.
mm   Fischer, 1957) 4 p.
Dn 3′. *At* composer. *Pf* solo S, pno. *Rg* Golden Crest, CRS 4138.   *(Composer)*

5015 YOUSE, Glad Robinson. **This would I keep** (New York: Leeds,
mm   1943) 4 p.
Dn 3′. *At* Grace Noll Crowell. *Pf* solo S, pno.   *(Composer)*

5016 YOUSE, Glad Robinson. **Thou wilt light my candle** (40474;
mm   New York: G. Schirmer, 1943) 4 p.
Sacred song. *Dn* 4′. *At* Grace Noll Crowell. *Pf* solo S, pno. *Rg* Golden Crest,
CRS 4138.   *(Composer)*

5017 ZAIMONT, Judith Lang. **Ages of love, The. Song cycle for
mm   baritone and piano** (facsimile of autograph at NNACA, 1971) 31
p.
Dn 11′. *La* composer. *Ct* Chaste love (*At* Byron), Love's white heat (*At* Edna
St. Vincent Millay), Disdainful, fickle love (*At* Millay), An older love (*At*
Millay), Love's echo (*At* Christina Georgina Rossetti).   *(Composer)*

5018 ZAIMONT, Judith Lang. **Chansons nobles et sentimentales
mm   for high voice and piano** (facsimile of autograph at NNACA,
1974) 31 p. $8.
Dn 13′. *La* composer. *Lt* French. *Ct* Harmonie du soir (*At* Baudelaire),
Chansons d'automne (*At* Verlaine), Claire de lune (*At* Verlaine), Dans
l'interminable ennui de la plaine (*At* Verlaine), Départ (*At* Rimbaud). *Rg*
Sunny airs and sober. Music for voice by Judith Lang Zaimont, Golden Crest,
ATH 5051.   *(Composer)*

5019 ZAIMONT, Judith Lang. **Coronach for soprano and piano**
mm   (facsimile of autograph at NNAMC, 1970) 35 p.
Dn 9′. *La* composer. *Ct* By fire and ice (*At* Doris Ellen Kosloff and Adelaide
Cropsey), A death in summer (*At* composer), American primitive (*At* William
Jay Smith), War is kind (*At* Stephen Crane).   *(Composer)*

5020 ZAIMONT, Judith Lang. **Four songs for mezzo and soprano**
mm   (facsimile of autograph at NNAMC, 1965) 13 p.
Dn 7′. *La* composer. *At* E.E. Cummings. *St* 95 poems. *Ct* Any one lived in a
little how town, Three wealthy sisters, The sky was candy, Most (people simply
can't).   *(Composer)*

5021 ZAIMONT, Judith Lang. **Greyed sonnets** (rev. ed.; facsimile of
mm   MS at NNACA: 1975, 19).
Songs. *Dn* 14′. *Da* 1975. *La* composer. *Pf* solo S, pno. *Ct* Soliloquy (*At* Edna
St. Vincent Millay), Let it be forgotton (*At* Sara Teasdale), A season's song (*At*
Millay), Love's autumn (*At* Millay), Entreaty (*At* Christina Georgina Rossetti).
The original edition includes only Soliloquy, Love's autumn, and Entreaty. *Rg*
Sunny airs and sober. Music for voice by Judith Lang Zaimont, Golden Crest,
ATH 5051.   *(Composer)*

5022 ZWILICH, Ellen Taaffe. **Einsame Nacht [Night]** (facsimile of
mm   MS at NNAMC, 1977) 25 p.
Song cycle. *Dn* 15′. *Da* 1971. *La* composer. *At* Herman Hesse. *St* Die Gedichte.
Lt German. *Pf* solo Bar, pno. *Ct* Über die Felder, Wie sind die Tage schwer,
Schicksal, Elisabeth, Wohl lieb ich die finstre Nacht, Mückenschwarm. *(Compo-
ser)*

5023 ZWILICH, Ellen Taaffe. **Im Nebel [In the fog]** (facsimile of
mm   MS at NNAMC, 1977) 7 p.
Dn 4′. *Da* 1972. *La* composer. *At* Herman Hesse. *St* Die Gedichte. *Lt* German.
Pf solo A, pno.   *(Composer)*

5024 ZWILICH, Ellen Taaffe. **Trompeten [Trumpets]** (facsimile of
mm   MS at NNAMC, 1977) 7 p.
Dn 4′. *Da* 1974. *La* composer. *At* Georg Trakl. *St* Die Dichtungen. *Lt* German.
Pf solo S, pno. Also available in an English version by the composer (facsimile
of MS at NNAMC).   *(Composer)*

INDEXES

BURLEIGH, Cecil, 912ac[58]
Burleigh, Harry T.
  performances, by Folk Song Coterie, 776ap[57]
  works, songs, viewed by M. Jordan, 905ap[58]
Burlin, Natalie, *see* Curtis-Burlin, Natalie
Burnett, Frances Hodgson, literary works, *Editha's burglar,* set by A. Thomas, 1222bm[58]
BURNS, Don, 118ap[25]
BURR, Hobart H., 913ap[58]
Burrowes, Katharine, life and activities, Detroit, 564ap[55]
Bush, Grace, manuscripts, Delta Omicron Music Composers Library, 25bm[01]
Busoni, Ferruccio
  influence on M. Carreras, 2281an[68]
  life and activities, teacher of A. Cottlow, 887ap[58], 1032ap[58]
  ———teacher of C.D. Mannes, 798bm[57]
  ———teacher of Mana Zucca, 2004ap[66], 2040ap[66]
  ———teacher of R. Deyo, 1169ap[58]
Butz, Elizabeth Anne, manuscripts, 42bm[01]
Buzzi-Peccia, Arturo
  life and activities, teacher of A. Gluck, 872an[58]
  ———teacher of S. Braslau, 2360ap[68]
Byrne, Maria, manuscripts, collection of European secular songs, 193ap[35]
C., 2159ap[68]
C.A., 753ap[57]
C.R., 574ap[55]
C.S., 2004ap[66]
Caballé, Montserrat
  discographies, 172bm[25]
  life and activities, 3198ap[78], 3316an[78], 3336ap[78]
Cadman, Charles Wakefield
  influence on career of T. Redfeather, 436ap[50]
  performances, *Shanewis,* with A. Gentle, 866ap[58]
  relation to A.C. Beach, 657ap[56]
  relation to L. Nordica, 162bm[25]
  relation to N.R. Eberhart, 1954ap[64]
  works, N.R. Eberhart lyrics, 148bf[25], 162bm[25], 1955an[64]
Cady, Calvin Brainerd, life and activities, teacher of N.C. Cornish, 760bm[57]
Cahier, Sarah Jane
  correspondence, 47bm[01]
  relation to M. Anderson, 2383bf[68]
  tribute, 1173an[58]
  views about Anglo-Saxon habit of self-repression, 1144ap[58]
Caldwell, Anne
  life and works, songs, 454ap[50]
  tribute, 554an[54]
CALDWELL, Belle, 2076ap[67]
Caldwell, Sarah
  collections, 28bm[01]
  interviews, 3228ap[78]
  life and activities, 2975an[75], 3237an[78], 3264an[78], 3274ap[78]
  ———accomplishments, 3225an[78]
  ———Boston, 3212an[78]
  ———conducting first New York Philharmonic concert of women's works only, 3056ro[76]
  ———conducting New York Philharmonic, 3240an[78]
  relation to B. Sills, 3334bm[78]
California
  Los Angeles, musical life, influenced by Woman's Orchestra, 1248ap[58]
  musical life, 1830-40, 173bf[25]
  ———1849-1940, 563bm[55]
  ———1850s, 305bm[48], 312bm[48]
  San Francisco, history of opera, 1840-1900, 302bm[48]
  ———history of opera, 1900-38, 1017bm[58]
  ———musical life, 1848-1940, 293bm[48]
  ———musical life, 19th c., 898bm[58]
Callas, Maria
  discographies, 172bm[25], 3217an[78]
  life and activities, 3249bm[78], 3257an[78], 3302an[78]
  ———Chicago, 123bm[25]
  ———dropped from Metropolitan Opera, 3304an[78]
  tribute, 3236an[78]
  viewed by T. Votipka, 2221an[68]
Calloway-Byron, Mayme, life and activities, 121bf[25]
CAMERON, Allan Gordon, 914bm[58]
Campanini, Cleofonte, influence on R. Raisa, 2378ap[68]
Campbell, Georgia, *see* Irwin, May
Canning, Effie I.
  correspondence, 47bm[01]
  works, *Rock-a-bye baby,* 430bm[50], 439bm[50], 442an[50]
CAPPIANI, Luisa, 616ap[55]
Cappiani, Luisa
  life and activities, 66bm[05]
  ———Music Teachers National Assoc. convention, 1897, 853ap[57]
  ———teacher of J.E. Crane, 775ap[57]
  ———Woman's Musical Congress, 613ap[55]
  tribute, from Women's Philharmonic Soc., 771ap[57]
  views about A. Fay, 815ap[57]
  views about music in girls' trade school curriculum, 804ap[57]

CARACAPPA, Michael, 2160ap[68], 2970ap[75]
Carey, Clive, life and activities, teacher of J. Sutherland, 3254bm[78]
Caribbean, *see* Latin America
Carl, Catherine Carolyne, theoretical works, 3bm[01]
Carl, William Crane, views about social acceptance of women as organists, 1917, 953ap[58]
Carlsmith, Lillian, correspondence, 4bm[01]
CAROSSO, Vincent P., 119ap[25]
Carpenter, John Alden
  performances, sung by P. Frijsh, 2236ap[68]
  works, songs, viewed by M. Jordan, 905ap[58]
Carpenter, Mrs. George, views about status, 1893, 613ap[55]
Carr, Sarah Pratt, literary works, *Narcissa,* set by M.C. Moore, 723rm[56]
Carré, Albert, influence on M. Garden, 986bm[58]
Carreño, Teresa
  collections, scrapbook, 38bm[01]
  correspondence, 4bm[01], 33bm[01], 47bm[01]
  life, 56bc[05], 162bm[25], 1206ap[58]
  ———youth, 886ap[58]
  life and activities, 57bm[05], 59bm[05], 113md[25], 602bf[55], 793ac[57], 1096bf[58], 1226ap[58], 3266an[78]
  ———Boston, 274bm[45]
  ———Chicago, 1230bm[58]
  ———organizer of European opera company, 638ap[55]
  ———San Francisco, 293bm[48]
  ———social acceptance, 1136ap[58]
  ———student of E. Rudersdorff, 769ap[57]
  ———teacher of M. Wright, 30bm[01]
  ———teacher of R. Deyo, 1169ap[58]
  ———teacher of R.P. Burgess, 752ap[57]
  ———technique and teaching method, 752ap[57]
  performances, 6bm[01]
  ———with Mana Zucca, 2040ap[66]
  ———works by F.C. Dillon, 724ap[56]
  relation to C.K. Rogers, 623bm[55]
  tribute, 1219an[58]
  viewed by A. Cottlow, 1034ap[58]
  viewed by W. Pyle, 1061ap[58]
  views about F.C. Dillon, 671ap[56], 715ap[56]
  views about pleasing audiences, 1046ap[58]
  views about women's rights, 917ap[58]
  works, *Teresita. Kleine Waltzer,* 1046ap[58]
Carreras, Maria
  life and activities, 2231ap[68]
  tribute, 2281an[68]
Carrington, Abbie, life, 66bm[05]
CARROLL, Amy Keith, 2161ap[68]
Cartwright, Ellen M., life and activities, 53bm[05]
Caruso, Enrico
  influence on career of A. Fitziu, 1135ap[58]
  influence on career of R. Ponselle, 2320ap[68]
  relation to O. Fremstad, 938bm[58]
Carver, Catherine, life and activities, prodigy, 973bm[58]
Cary, Annie Louise
  life, 56bc[05], 66bm[05]
  ———Me., 134bm[25]
  life and activities, 57bm[05], 59bm[05], 585bm[55], 602bf[55], 913ap[58], 978ac[58], 1050bm[58], 1091ac[58]
  ———audience appeal, 1003ap[58]
  ———Boston, 274bm[45]
  ———San Francisco, 293bm[48]
  relation to C. Marco, 918an[58]
  views about A. Sawyer, 625bm[55]
Cary, Mary Flagler, collections, donated to Pierpont Morgan Library, 23bm[01]
Cary, Phoebe
  literary works, hymn texts, 557bd[54], 560ap[54]
  works, hymns, 150bm[25]
Casals, Pablo, influence on career of E. Hilger, 2162ap[68]
Casals, Susan Metcalfe, correspondence, 5bm[01]
Case, Anna
  life and activities, 3bm[01], 1129ap[58], 1194ap[58]
  ———illness, influence on career of D. Giannini, 2339an[68]
  performances, P. Curran songs, 720an[58]
  ———with M. Dilling, 2127ap[68]
Cassatt, Mrs. Alexander, life and activities, Philadelphia, 582bf[55]
Cassel, Flora H.
  literary works, gospel song and hymn texts, 555bf[54]
  works, hymn tunes, 150bm[25]
Castle, Florence, life and activities, American Conservatory, 842ap[57]
catalogues and indexes, *see also* **bibliographies; catalogue** subdivisions below; **checklists;** specific topics; individual names
  all-female orchestras active in 1938, 2327ap[68]
  American women composers, 1919, 695ap[56], 711ap[56]
  Branscombe, G., 2014dd[55]
  ———works, 2011ap[66]
  concert programs of women's works, 76bp[10]
  Dillon, F.C., list of works to op. 39, 658ap[56]
  female composers active in Europe, 17th-19th c., 177bm[25]
  National Orchestral Assoc. graduates and affiliation, 2357bm[68]
  notable musical women, 77bp[10]
  orchestral works by American women, to 1976, 14ap[01]
  popular songs, known in 1950, 430bm[50]

festivals *(continued)*

N.M., Santa Fe, opera festival, 122bm[25]
N.Y., Festival of American Music, 1925-71, 42bm[01]
——Lockport, 1919, performances by W. Pyle, 1260ap[58]
——Mostly Mozart Festival, appearances of A. de Larrocha, 3266an[78]
National Music Week, 1927, 2111ap[67]
National Women's Music Festival, 15bm[01]
Ohio, Cincinnati, May Festival, 269bm[45]
——Cincinnati, participation of C. Rider-Kelsey, 1157bm[58]
——Cincinnati, Saengerfest, 1873, 978ac[58]
Parade of American Music, 1969, 3183ap[77]
Peace Jubilees, activity of J.T. Kempton, 1239ap[58]
Penn., Bach festivals, participation of C. Rider-Kelsey, 1157bm[58]
rural festivals for families, 1932, 1994bm[65]
South, Negro songs and spirituals, organized by E.A. Hackley, 633ap[55]
Vt., Marlboro Music Festival, viewed by B. Valente, 3306an[78]
Washington, D.C., Festival of American Women Composers, 1925, 2064ap[66]
FFRENCH, Florence, 52bm[05]
Field, Mrs. H. Moylan, life and activities, patronage, 132bm[25]
Fierro, Nancy, performances, Calif. State U. at Los Angeles, 2987ap[75]
FILLMORE, J.C., 974ap[58]
film, *see also* **mass media**
Brico, A., documentary, 3326an[78]
Callas, M., 3257an[78]
Farrar, G., activity, 966bm[58], 967bf[58]
Howard, K., activity, 1930s-40s, 1102an[58]
influence on popular attitude toward music, 2969bm[75]
Jepson, H., activity of singer, 2293ap[68]
Moore, G., activity, 2303bf[68]
Stevens, R., *Going my way* with Bing Crosby, 3213bm[78]
Sylva, M., activity, 1049ap[58]
Finch, Margaret, life and activities, songster compiler, 22bm[01]
FINCK, Henry T., 579-80ap[55], 975ap[58]
FINE, Vivian, 3037ap[76]
Fine, Vivian
correspondence, 33bm[01]
interviews, 30-31bm[01]
life and works, 3083dm[76], 3098an[76], 3160bm[76]
——*Guide to the life expectancy of a rose* and *Four pieces for two flutes,* 3125ap[76]
——1940s, 63bf[05]
manuscripts, 32bm[01], 35bm[01], 2153ap[68], 3035ap[76]
performances, *Concerto for piano strings and percussion for one player,* 3054rm[76]
——*Meeting for equal rights 1866,* 3000rm[76]
——radio, 3095ap[76]
style, *Four songs,* 2022ap[66]
——*Opus 51,* 3068ap[76]
——*Race of life,* 3068ap[76]
views about women working within musical community, 3080ap[76]
works, 3134bd[76]
——early, 3133ap[76]
FINK, Ella Louise, 775ap[57]
Finley, Lorraine Noel, manuscripts, Delta Omicron Music Composers Library, 25bm[01]
Fischer, Emil, life and activities, teacher of R. Fornia, 1164an[58]
FISCHER, Mary Chappell, 976ap[58]
FISHER, Barbara E. Scott, 2017an[66], 3038an[76]
Fisher, Emma Roderick, life and activities, educator, 2071ap[67]
Fisher, Kate, life and activities, 585bm[55]
Fisher, Majory Markres, literary works, *Musical America,* critic, 563bm[55]
FISHER, Marjory Markres, 2207ap[68]
Fisher, Mrs. William Arms, *see* Fisher, Emma Roderick
FISHER, William Arms, 1967ac[65]
Fitzgerald, Ella, life and activities, 3bm[01]
FITZGERALD, Gerald, 3245-46ap[78]
Fitziu, Anna
life and activities, 1135ap[58]
——teacher of S. Verrett, 3353an[78]
tribute, 881an[58]
FLAGG, Marion, 2086ap[67]
Flagler, Anne Lamont, influence on musical life in New York, 23bm[01]
Flagstad, Kirsten, relation to H. Traubel, 2219ap[68], 2381bf[68]
Flanders, Helen Hartness, influence on musical life, 112ap[25]
FLANNAGAN, William, 3039rm[76]
FLEMING, Shirley, 67bp[10], 3040ap[76], 3175ap[77]
FLETCHER, Alice Cunningham, 429bf[50], 612ap[55]
Fletcher, Alice Cunningham
tribute, 640ap[55]
views about Omaha tribe, 590bm[55]
FLETCHER, Richard D., 977ap[58]
Fletcher-Copp, Evelyn
interviews, 770ap[57]
life and activities, teacher of N.C. Cornish, 760bm[57]
tribute, 764an[57]
Flick-Flood, Dora, manuscripts, 35bm[01]
FLINT, Mary H., 978ac[58]
flute playing, ideal instrument of women, 1891, 1198ap[58]
folk, *see* **folk** headings below
folk dance, *see also* other **folk** headings
taught at Cornish School of Music, 760bm[57]
folk music, *see also* other **folk** headings; **popular music**
black tradition, 146ap[25]
gathering and transcribing by R.C. Seeger, 2033ap[66]
Hungary, played by Helen Ware, 1014ap[58]

viewed by M. Jordan, 905ap[58]
folk song, *see also* other **folk** headings; **popular music**
black, collection of U.S. Moore, 3050ap[76]
——history in USA, to 1867, *Slave songs of the United States,* 183bm[30]
influence on progress of native composers, 1912, 599ap[55]
influence on R.C. Seeger, 2020dd[66]
Ky., gathered by J. McGill, 604ap[55]
promoted by Stephen Foster Soc., 2097ap[67]
folklorists, *see* ethnomusicologists
Follen, Eliza Lee, literary works, abolition song texts, 94bm[17]
Fonaroff, Verna
life and activities, Olive Mead Quartet, 957ap[58]
performances, 1210ro[58]
Fonda, Mary Alice, life and activities, 66bm[05]
Foote, Arthur
life and activities, teacher of A.L. David, 2139ap[68]
——teacher of F.M. Ralston, 2035ap[66]
performances, by K. Heyman, 1224ap[58]
works, songs, viewed by M. Jordan, 905ap[58]
FOOTE, Henry Wilder, 261bm[44]
Foote, Mrs. Charles B., life and activities, manager of Russian Symphony Orchestra, 594ap[55]
Ford, Anne, life and activities, Maud Powell Trio, 1151ap[58]
Ford, M. Estelle, life and activities, 602bf[55]
Ford, Miriam Chase, life, 66bm[05]
Ford, Mrs. Seabury, life and activities, Rubinstein Club in Ohio, 740ap[57]
Fornia, Rita
tribute, 1164an[58]
views about native and foreign performers, 950ap[58]
Forrester, Maureen
life and activities, 3bm[01], 3313bm[78]
performances, Town Hall, New York, 1976, 3271an[78]
Forsyth, Josephine, life and works, 61bm[05]
Forsythe, Mrs. George, influence on Oklahoma City Symphony Orchestra, 2203bm[68]
Forten, Charlotte L.
correspondence, 266ap[45]
life and activities, gathering of black folk songs, 183bm[30]
Foss, Lukas
life and activities, teacher of B. Kolb, 3057an[76]
performances, *Song of songs,* performed by E. Davis, 2197an[68]
FOSTER, Agnes Greene, 581bm[55]
Foster, Fay
correspondence, 42bm[01], 47bm[01]
life, judge of Girl Scouts marching song contest, 2039ap[66]
life and works, 144bm[25]
manuscripts, 46bm[01]
works, *Americans come,* 726ap[56]
Foster, Lorraine, life and activities, founding of Stephen Foster Soc., 2097ap[67]
Foster, Stephen
performances, by A. Nielsen, 1242ap[58]
——by S. Jones, 1121ro[58]
foundations
Bagby Music Lovers' Foundation, influence on E. Nevada and M. Hauk, 959ap[58]
Bok, award to M. Anderson, 1941, 2374an[68]
Eleanor Steber Foundation, aid to young singers, 3233an[78]
Elizabeth Sprague Coolidge Foundation, 2027bm[66], 2079an[67], 2084ap[67]
——relation to Library of Congress, 2029an[66]
——sponsor of chamber music on radio, 2078bm[67]
Fromm Music Foundation, commission of *Trobar clus* by B. Kolb, 3055rm[76]
Fulbright fellowship, B. Brown, 3279an[78]
Hans Kindler Foundation, tribute, 11th anniversary concert, 3051rm[76]
International Music Fund, music library rehabilitation, 145ap[25]
John Simon Guggenheim Memorial Foundation, 2983as[75]
Julius Rosenwald Fund, award to M. Anderson, 1930, 2383bf[68]
Martha Baird Rockefeller Fund for Music, Inc., 2983as[75], 3180an[77]
Musicians Emergency Fund, 2107ap[67]
National Endowment for the Humanities, 2983as[75]
Naumburg Foundation award, 1975 award to C. Dale, 3260an[78]
New Jersey State Council of the Arts, 27bm[01]
Parnell Defense Fund, benefit by S. Jones, 897an[58]
Rockefeller, grant to B. Brown, 3279an[78]
Steiner Foundation, 1201bm[58]
support for women, 2983as[75]
Fox, Carol
life and activities, 2975an[75]
——director Chicago Lyric Opera, 123bm[25]
Fox, Charlotte, manuscripts, 32bm[01]
Fox, Della
life and activities, 56bc[05]
——musical comedy, light opera, vaudeville, 1209bm[58]
performances, A. Thomas's *Editha's burglar,* 1222bm[58]
tribute, 947an[58]
FRAME, Florence K., 3247ap[78]
Franchetti, Arnold, life and activities, teacher of B. Kolb, 3057an[76]
Francis, Muriel, life and activities, New Orleans and New York, 1985bm[65]
FRANK, Leonie C., 269bm[45]
FRANKENSTEIN, Alfred, 987rb[58]
Frankl, Edna, manuscripts, Delta Omicron Music Composers Library, 25bm[01]

Franklin, Aretha, life and activities, 435bm[50]
Franklin, Gertrude, life, 66bm[05]
FREEMAN, John W., 140bm[25], 3248ap[78]
Freeman, Waldemar, life and activities, teacher of G. Bachauer, 3289an[78]
FREER, Eleanor Everest, 675ap[56], 676bm[56]
Freer, Eleanor Everest
   correspondence, 47bm[01]
   life, 139ac[25]
   ——Philadelphia, 582bf[55]
   life and works, 581bm[55], 673bm[56], 2026bm[66]
   ——opera, 685bf[56]
   manuscripts, 32bm[01], 46bm[01]
   performances, 699ap[56], 3348an[78]
   ——*Legend of the piper*, 678rm[56]
   style, *Brownings go to Italy, op. 43*, 656ap[56]
   ——*Frithiof, op. 40*, 677ap[56]
   views about vocal music performed in English, 581bm[55], 666ap[56]
   works, opera, 147bm[25]
   ——*Sonnets from the Portuguese, op. 22*, 656ap[56]
Fremstad, Olive
   collections, scrapbooks, 34bm[01]
   correspondence, 33bm[01], 47bm[01]
   life and activities, 893ap[58], 948ap[58], 3265an[78], 3327an[78]
   ——San Francisco, 293bm[48]
   ——1911-18, 938bm[58]
   performances, Wagner at Metropolitan Opera, 1162ap[58]
   relation to D. Becker, 952ap[58]
   tribute, realization of Wagnerian roles, 902an[58]
   views about singer's career choice — concert, church, or opera, 884ap[58]
French, Mrs., life and activities, Boston, 198bm[35]
Freund, John C., views about European study-life, 873ap[58]
Friedberg, Annie
   life and activities, management in New York, 1985bm[65]
   ——management of M. Hess, 2284bm[68]
   tribute, 1976an[65]
Friedberg, Carl, life and activities, teacher of J. Smith, 3038an[76]
Friedheim, Arthur, life and activities, teacher of G. Branscombe, 2021an[66]
Frijsh, Povla
   correspondence, 33bm[01]
   interviews, 2236ap[68]
   life and activities, teacher of H. Ohlin, 2291an[68]
   tribute, song recitalist, teacher, and coach, 2347ap[68]
   views about American audiences and performance conditions, 2175ap[68]
Friskin, Rebecca Clarke, *see* Clarke, Rebecca
FRY, Stephen M., 19bm[01]
Fryberger, Agnes Moore, influence on music education, 800ac[57]
Fuchs, Lillian, life and activities, 2313ro[68]
Fugère, Lucian, life and activities, teacher of M. Garden, 986bm[58]
FULD, James J., 430bm[50]
FULLER, Sarah, 105ap[20]
funding, *see* foundations; patronage
Fürtwangler, Wilhelm, influence on career of A. Kullmer, 2233ap[68]
Fuschi, Olegna, life and activities, student of R. Lhevinne, 2117an[67]
G.F., 2212ap[68]
G.M.S., 2088ap[67]
G.V., 2217ap[68]
Gabrilowitsch, Ossip
   influence on C. Clemens, 924-25bm[58]
   influence on O.S. Stokowski, 2314ap[68]
   life and activities, patronage of New York Women's Symphony Orchestra, 2397an[68]
Gadski, Johanna
   correspondence, 33bm[01], 47bm[01]
   discographies, 172bm[25]
   interviews, German Grand Opera tour, 1041ap[58]
   ——management of career and private life, 1001ap[58]
   life and activities, 585bm[55], 1162ap[58], 3265an[78]
   ——Chicago, 1110bf[58]
   ——San Francisco, 293bm[48]
   performances, Baltimore Symphony Orchestra, 2146bm[68]
   ——Miss. State Col. for Women, 1910, 850ap[57]
   relation to Chicago Opera, 1922 suit, 985an[58]
   relation to L.S. Proehl, 901bm[58]
   tribute, life and activities, 1105an[58]
Gadski-Busch, Charlotte, life and activities, teacher of P. Stoska, 3309ap[78]
Galajikian, Florence G.
   life and works, 1940s, 63bf[05]
   manuscripts, 2153ap[68]
   performances, *For freedom*, 2047an[66]
   ——*Girl with a Spanish shawl*, 2047an[66]
   ——*Song of joy*, 2047an[66]
   ——*Symphonic intermezzo*, 2008rm[66], 2024rm[66]
GALATOPOULOS, Stelios, 3249bm[78]
GALDBERT, Albert, 678rm[56]
GALKIN, Elliott, 3041rm[76]
Galli-Curci, Amelita
   collections, scrapbooks, 34bm[01]
   correspondence, 33bm[01], 47bm[01]
   discographies, 172bm[25]
   influenced by E. Liebling, 2085an[67]
   interviews, 2352ap[68]
   life and activities, 885bm[58], 2249bm[68]

   performances, 6bm[01]
   relation to C.L. Wagner, 1238bm[58]
GALT, Martha Caroline, 17bd[01]
Ganz, Rudolph
   life and activities, teacher of E. Mitchell, 2101bm[67]
   ——teacher of G. Branscombe, 2021an[66]
   ——teacher of I. Krehm, 3220ap[78]
   performances with Helen Ware, 1014ap[58]
Garcia, Manuel
   life and activities, teacher of A. Phillipps, 308ap[48], 318bm[48]
   ——teacher of A.E. Schoen-René, 1179bm[58]
   ——teacher of J. Lind, 303an[48]
   ——teacher of J.E. Crane, 775ap[57]
GARDEN, Mary, 986bm[58], *987-89rb[58]
Garden, Mary
   collections, scrapbook, 34bm[01]
   correspondence, 33bm[01], 47bm[01]
   discographies, 891ap[58], 977ap[58]
   life and activities, 132bm[25], 885bm[58], 977ap[58], 993ap[58], 1027bm[58], 2328ap[68], 2975an[75]
   ——Chicago, 123bm[25], 1110bf[58]
   ——debut at Opéra-Comique, 879ap[58]
   ——Manhattan Opera, 930bm[58]
   ——relation to Metropolitan Opera, 944ap[58]
   performances, Chicago, Washington, D.C., New York, and Boston, 1026an[58]
   relation to C.L. Wagner, 1238bm[58]
   relation to O. Fremstad, 938bm[58]
   tribute, 1188ap[58]
   viewed by T. Votipka, 2221an[68]
Gardner, Isabella Stewart
   correspondence, 47bm[01]
   life and activities, patronage, 795ap[57]
   views about Wagner, 796ap[57]
GARDNER, Kay, 69bp[10]
Gardner, Margaret A., life and activities, Providence, 125bm[25]
Garland, Judy, life and activities, student of C. Lazzari, 2077an[67]
Garnett, Louise Ayers, life and works, 665ap[56]
Garrett, Augusta Browne, *see* Browne, Augusta
Garrett, Elizabeth, life and activities, El Paso, Tex., 1986bm[65]
GARRISON, Lisa, 69bp[10]
Garrison, Lucy McKim
   life and activities, 267ap[45]
   ——gathering of black folk songs, 183bm[30]
   works, notated first spiritual, 266ap[45]
Garrison, Mabel
   life and activities, first American-trained coloratura at Metropolitan Opera, 2389ap[68]
   tribute, 2270an[68]
   views about first European trip and risks, 2223ap[68]
Garwood, Margaret
   performances, *Cliff's edge*, 3012rm[76]
   ——*Nightingale and the rose*, 3135rm[76]
Garza, Maryana Sue, manuscripts, 42bm[01]
Gates, Ellen M.H., literary works, hymn texts, 150bm[25]
Gates, Lucy
   life and activities, Germany, 2329ap[68]
   performances, *Serva padrona*, 2232ap[68]
   tribute, 2267ap[68]
GATES, W. Francis, 780ap[57], 990ap[58]
Gatti-Casazza, Giulio
   influence on career of M. Garrison, 2389ap[68]
   life and activities, Musical Union of Women Artists, 571ap[55]
   ——performance of *King's henchman*, 1953ap[64]
   relation to F. Alda, 862bm[58]
GAUL, Harvey, 139ac[58]
GAUME, Mary Matilda, 2020dd[66]
GAUTHIER, Eva, 2210ap[68]
Gauthier, Eva
   correspondence, 33bm[01], 33bm[01], 47bm[01]
   life and activities, 1091ac[58]
   ——Java, 2365ap[68]
   performances, 1959ap[65]
   ——1936, 2182an[68]
   tribute, 2201an[68]
Gaw, Esther Allen, life and activities, Salt Lake Women's Orchestra, 1262ap[58]
Gaynor, Jessie L.
   life, 568ap[55]
   life and works, 52bm[05], 144bm[25], 665ap[56], 686an[56], 698bf[56]
   ——children's music, 800ac[57]
   ——songs, 717ap[56]
   manuscripts, 46bm[01]
   ——sheet music, 24bm[01]
   works, 668bd[56]
Gay-Zenatello, Maria, life and activities, teacher of N. Martini, 2083ap[67]
Gebhardt, Heinrich, life and activities, teacher of A.L. David, 2139ap[68]
Gedalge, André, life and activities, teacher of M. Bauer, 2042an[66]
GEHRES, Eleanor M., 11bm[01]
GELATT, Roland, 2211bm[68]
Gelda, Claire, life and activities, teacher of R. Grist, 3308ap[78]
GELLER, James J., 431bd[50]
Genet, Marianne
   life, 139ac[25]

GREENFIELD, Edward, 3254bm[78]
Greenfield, Elizabeth Taylor
   life and activities, 56bc[05], 121bf[25], 161bm[25], 1227bf[58]
   ——England, 316bm[48]
   tribute, 315an[48]
Greenwalt, Mary Elizabeth Hallock, tribute, specialist in Chopin and
   Schumann piano works, 609an[55]
GREENWAY, John, 434bd[50]
Greenwood, Flora, life and activities, student of L. Lawrence, 2266ap[68]
GREENWOOD, Grace, 298ap[48], 1004bm[58]
Gregory, Euphemia, life and activities, teacher of J. Blegen, 3197ac[78]
Grever, Maria, life and works, 144bm[25]
GRIDER, Rufus A., 208bf[38]
Grieg, Edvard, editions, prepared by B.F. Tapper, 791ap[57]
Griffes, Charles, performances, sung by P. Frijsh, 2236ap[68]
GRIFFITH, M. Dinorben, 1005ap[58]
Griffith, Yeatman, life and activities, teacher of F. Macbeth, 1229ap[58]
Grist, Reri
   interviews, operatic experiences, 3202ap[78]
   life and activities, 3285bm[78], 3308ap[78]
Griswold, Anna, life and activities, Calif., 312bm[48]
Griswold, Mrs. Putnam, influence on husband's career, 641ap[55]
Gro, Josephine, collections, songs and piano music, 729bc[56]
Groom, Joan Charlene, manuscripts, 42bm[01], 42bm[01]
GRUEN, John, 3045rm[76], 3255-59an[78]
Guagni, Alessandro, life and activities, teacher of M. Craft, 860ap[58]
Gubert, Louise, tribute, 297an[48]
Guggenheimer, Minnie
   life and activities, New York Philharmonic Soc., 169bm[25]
   ——stadium concerts, 2124bm[67]
Guilbert, Yvonne, correspondence, 5bm[01]
Guilliams, Ruby Lois, theoretical works, 3bm[01]
guitar playing, conflict with responsibilities of marriage, 1850, 321ap[48]
Gunn, Anita, views about M. Hess, 2245bm[68]
Gurewich, Marinka, life and activities, teacher of M. Arroyo, 3287ac[78]
GUSSOW, Mel, 3046-47an[76], 3260an[78]
Guth, Otto, life and activities, teacher of J. Marsh, 3341an[78]
Gutheil-Schoeder, Marie, life and activities, teacher of R. Stevens,
   3213bm[78]
GUZZO, R. Louis, 3048rm[76]
Gyring, Elizabeth
   correspondence, 47bm[01]
   life and works, Adagio for clarinet, Fantasy for organ, and woodwind
     quintet, 3159ap[76]
   performances, radio, 3095ap[76]
H., 626rb[55]
H.A.S., 684ap[56], 2222ap[68]
H.B., 1013ap[58], 2225ap[68]
H.G.K., 2025ap[66]
H.S., 2230ap[68]
H.W.L., 1030ap[58]
HACKETT, Karleton, 2024rm[66]
Hackley, Emma Azalia
   life and activities, 12bm[01], 56bc[05], 575bm[55], 2264bf[68]
   ——promotion of black music, 633ap[55]
   views about black Americans in music, 575bm[55]
Hadley, Mrs. Henry, life and activities, board of directors of Boston
   Women's Symphony Orchestra, 2366ro[68]
HAENSEL, Fitzhugh W., 1007ap[58]
HAGEMAN, Richard, 2090ap[67]
Hageman, Richard, life and activities, teacher of H. Jepson, 2293ap[68]
Hagen, Elizabeth von, see Von Hagen, Elizabeth
Hagen, Helen E., life and activities, 2264bf[68]
Hahr, Emma, life, 66bm[05]
Haimsohn, Naomi Carroll
   life and works, 1958dm[65]
   manuscripts, 26bm[01]
Haines-Kuester, Edith, life and works, 665ap[56]
Hale, Mrs. Philip, life and activities, board of directors of Boston
   Women's Symphony Orchestra, 2366ro[68]
HALE, Philip, 299an[48], 682an[56]
Hale, Sarah Josepha, life and activities, editor of Godey's Lady's Book,
   259ap[44]
Hall, Betty S., manuscripts, 2153ap[68]
HALL, Constance Huntington, 588bm[55]
Hall, Edythe Pruyn, life and works, 665ap[56]
Hall, Elsie, life and activities, performances with Boston Symphony
   Orchestra, 1130ap[58]
Hall, Elvian Mabel, literary works, hymn texts, 150bm[25]
Hall, F. Jeannette
   influence on musical life, 112ap[25]
   life and activities, 602bf[55]
Hall, Geraldine, influence on creation of German Grand Opera, 1041ap[58]
HALL, J.H., 555bf[54]
Hall, Josephine, life and activities, musical comedy, light opera,
   vaudeville, 1209bm[58]
Hall, Lily May, works, Pretty pond lilies, 455bf[50]
Hall, Mrs. R.J., see Hall, Elsie
Hall, Pauline
   life and activities, 66bm[05]
   ——musical comedy, light opera, vaudeville, 1209bm[58]
Hall, Walter Henry, life and activities, conductor of ladies' chorus of
   New York Mozart Soc., 808ap[57]

HALLOCK, Mary, 781ap[57]
Halstead, Margaret, life and activities, Europe and USA, 2294ap[68]
Hamlin, Anna, life and activities, teacher of J. Raskin, 3195an[78],
   3291ap[78]
HANAFORD, Phebe A., 53bm[05]
HANCHETT, Dr. Henry G., 1008ap[58]
Hancock, Mrs. General, works, Te Deum laudamus, 713ap[56]
HANDY, D. Antoinette, 2977ap[75]
Hanifin, Ada, life and activities, critic, 563bm[55]
Hanks, Nancy, influenced by women's movement, 2973ap[75]
Hannas, Ruth, correspondence, 42bm[01]
HANSEN, Ruth, 2218an[68]
HANSL, E.E. von B., 148bf[25]
HANSLICK, Eduard, 1009ap[58]
Hardester, Jane Skinner, life and activities, 3252ap[78]
Harding, Bertita, literary works, Daisy libretto, 3163an[76]
Harding, Janet, manuscripts, 46bm[01]
HARDING, William G., 782ap[57]
HARK, J. Max, 185bd[30]
HARKINS, Elizabeth R., 29-30bm[01]
HARMAN, Carter, 3049rm[76]
Harmati, Sandor, life and activities, Women's Orchestral Club, 2220ap[68]
Harnden, Ethel, life and works, 2987ap[75]
Haroldson, Ruth, life and activities, California Women's Symphony
   Orchestra, 3247ap[78], 3276ap[78]
harp music, encouragd by C. Salzédo, 1172ap[58]
harp playing
   appropriateness for women, 1962, 3332ap[78]
   conflict with responsibilities of marriage, 1850, 321ap[48]
   livelihood, recommended 1899, 1010ap[58]
   viewed by J. Chatterton, 616ap[55]
   viewed by M. Dilling, 2238ap[68]
harpsichord playing, colonial times, 211ap[38]
Harrill, Mrs., manuscripts, sheet music, 283ap[46]
Harriman, Mrs. E.H., life and activities, New York Philharmonic Soc.,
   169bm[25]
HARRIS, Carl G., Jr., 3050ap[76]
HARRIS, Henry J., 586ap[55]
Harris, Hilda, performances, D.R. Moore's From the dark tower, 3017rm[76]
Harris, Margaret
   life and activities, 3274ap[78]
   ——Broadway, 3212an[78]
   ——conducted Hair, 3210an[78]
Harris, Mehitabel, life and activities, Salem, Mass., 209dd[38]
Harrison, Hazel
   life and activities, 170bm[25], 2967bm[75]
   relation to F. Douglass, 1970ap[65]
HARRISON, Jay S., 2221an[68]
Harrison, Miss, life and activities, Salem, Mass., 209dd[38]
Harschbanger, Dema, life and activities, management in New York,
   1985bm[65]
Harshaw, Margaret, life and activities, teacher of B. Valente, 3306an[78]
HASKINS, John, 3051rm[76]
Hassler, Avery, literary works, librettos for C.W. Cadman, 1954ap[64]
HAST, Lisette, 587bm[55]
Hastreiter, Helene, life and activities, 602bf[55], 913ap[58]
Haswin, Mrs. Francis R., life, 66bm[05]
Hatch, Edith, life, 2067ap[66]
Hatch, Mabel Lee, life, 2067ap[66]
Hatch, Mrs., life and activities, Salem, Mass., 209dd[38]
Hatton, Anne Julia, literary works, librettos, 212bm[38]
Haubiel, Charles, works, commission for V.B. Lawrence and H. Triggs,
   2230ap[68]
Hauck, Minnie, see Hauk, Minnie
HAUGHTON, John Alan, 1011ap[58], 2223ap[68]
Haughton, John Alan, life and activities, teacher of D. Maynor, 2185ap[68]
HAUK, Minnie, 1012bm[58]
Hauk, Minnie
   correspondence, 33bm[01], 47bm[01]
   influence on establishment of American national opera co., 119ap[25]
   interview, views about Liszt, Massenet, J. Lind, and H. Sontag,
     1184ap[58]
   life, 56bc[05], 66bm[05], 1143ap[58]
   ——assistance of Bagby Music Lovers' Foundation, 959ap[58]
   life and activities, 57bm[05], 602bf[55], 1012bm[58], 1050bm[58], 1078bf[58]
   ——Chicago, 1230bm[58]
   ——New Orleans, 1044ap[58]
   relation to J.H. Mapleson, 1167bm[58]
Hausenfluck, Frances Wright, manuscripts, Delta Omicron Music
   Composers Library, 25bm[01]
HAVENER, Helen, 2224ap[68]
Hawes, Charlotte W.
   life, 66bm[05]
   life and activities, Music Teachers National Assoc. convention, 1897,
     853ap[57]
Hawks, Annie, literary works, hymn texts, 150bm[25]
Hawley, Annie Audios, correspondence, 4bm[01]
HAYBURN, Robert F., 3261bd[78]
Hayes, Roland, relation to M. Anderson, 2341an[68]
Hays, Doris
   interviews, 31bm[01]
   life and activities, "Meet the woman composer" concert series, 1975,
     3076ap[76]
hearing, see physiology

manuscripts — individual author *(continued)*

Beach, P.A., 42bm[01]
Beecroft, N., 35bm[01]
Behrend, J., 35bm[01], 2153ap[68]
Berckman, E., 42bm[01]
Beyer, J., 35bm[01]
Birch, H.L., 2153ap[68]
Boyd, J., 35bm[01], 42bm[01], 46bm[01]
Bradley, R., 46bm[01]
Branscombe, G., 32-33bm[01], 46bm[01], 3035ap[76]
Braun, R., 32bm[01]
Brinsley, L., 32bm[01]
Britain, R., 46bm[01], 2153ap[68]
Brosius, V., 42bm[01]
Brown, G.M., 42bm[01]
Brown, M.H., 46bm[01]
Butz, E.A., 42bm[01]
Cevee, A. de, 2153ap[68]
Clark, E., 35bm[01], 42bm[01]
Clark, R., 42bm[01]
Clarke, R., 46bm[01]
Cole, U., 46bm[01]
Coolidge, E.S., 32bm[01], 46bm[01]
Cowdin, Mrs. V.G., 283ap[46]
Crane, H., 32bm[01]
Curtis-Burlin, N., 46bm[01]
Cushing, S.M., 33bm[01]
Daly, J., 283ap[46]
Daniels, M.W., 46bm[01], 3035ap[76]
Diemer, E.L., 42bm[01]
Dillon, F.C., 9bm[01], 19bm[01], 46bm[01]
Dirks, J.D., 42bm[01]
Drill, A., 42bm[01]
Du Page, F., 35bm[01]
Dutton, T., 46bm[01]
Dyer, S., 46bm[01]
Eakin, V., 2153ap[68]
Eggleston, A.E., 42bm[01]
Escot, P., 35bm[01]
Fenner, B., 2153ap[68]
Fenstock, B., 35bm[01]
Fergus, P., 46bm[01]
Fine, V., 32bm[01], 35bm[01], 2153ap[68], 3035ap[76]
Flick-Flood, D., 35bm[01]
Foster, F., 46bm[01]
Fox, C., 32bm[01]
Freer, E.E., 32bm[01], 46bm[01]
Galajikian, F.G., 2153ap[68]
Garza, M.S., 42bm[01]
Gaynor, J.L., 46bm[01]
Gideon, M., 38bm[01], 46bm[01], 3035ap[76]
Glanville-Hicks, P., 2153ap[68]
Goode, B., 46bm[01]
Gould, E., 3035ap[76]
Groom, J.C., 42bm[01]
Haimsohn, N.C., 26bm[01]
Hall, B.S., 2153ap[68]
Harding, J., 46bm[01]
Harrill, Mrs., 283ap[46]
Hensler, B., 42bm[01]
Heyman, L., 32bm[01]
Hier, E.G., 32bm[01]
Hodges, F.H., 46bm[01]
Holloway, E., 42bm[01]
Holmes, B.E., 42bm[01]
Hood, H., 46bm[01]
Hooker, A.F., 42bm[01]
Hopekirk, H., 46bm[01]
Housman, R., 32bm[01]
Howe, M., 35bm[01], 46bm[01], 2153ap[68], 3035ap[76]
Howell, J., 42bm[01]
Hytrek, M.T., 42bm[01]
Ivey, J.E., 42bm[01]
Jacobs-Bond, C., 32bm[01]
Jardon, D., 33bm[01]
Jones, M.E., 42bm[01]
Kalich, B., 32bm[01]
Kapp, M.E., 42bm[01]
Kessler, M., 35bm[01]
Kettering, E., 1bm[01]
Kinscella, H., 32bm[01]
Knight-Wood, M., 32bm[01], 46bm[01]
Knowlton, F.S., 32bm[01]
Kramer, T.B., 42bm[01]
Kremer, J., 32bm[01]
Lang, M.R., 32bm[01], 46bm[01]
Laufer, B., 35bm[01]
Leginska, E., 32bm[01]
Lehman, E., 46bm[01]
Lehmann, L., 43bm[01]
LeSeige, A., 42bm[01]
Lipscomb, H., 35bm[01]
Lissow, A., 42bm[01]
Liventhan, S., 32bm[01]
Manning, K.L., 19bm[01], 2153ap[68]
Marshall, E.C., 2153ap[68]

McCann, E., 42bm[01]
McCollin, F., 36bm[01], 46bm[01]
McFaul, A., 42bm[01]
McLean, J.G., 42bm[01]
Merington, M., 32bm[01]
Merriman, M.L., 42bm[01]
Midelfart, M., 42bm[01]
Miller, E.B., 42bm[01]
Moore, L.L., 46bm[01]
Moore, M.C., 19-20bm[01], 46bm[01]
Norton, Hon. Mrs., 283ap[46]
Oehme-Foerster, E., 33bm[01]
Orchard, L.C., 283ap[46]
Overmiller, J., 42bm[01]
Owen, B., 42bm[01]
Pagliughi, L., 33bm[01]
Palmer, R.M., 42bm[01]
Panetti, J., 35bm[01]
Penico, G.P., 42bm[01]
Price, F.B., 16bm[01]
Priesing, D., 35bm[01]
Proctor, A., 42bm[01]
Quartararo, F., 33bm[01]
Radcliffe, L., 32bm[01]
Ralston, F.M., 9bm[01], 19bm[01]
Rapoport, E., 35bm[01]
Reed, N.J., 42bm[01]
Restelle, J.L., 42bm[01]
Rhoden, N.C., 42bm[01]
Riesland, M.S., 42bm[01]
Roberts, S.P., 42bm[01]
Rogers, C.K., 46bm[01]
Saffran, P.J., 42bm[01]
Salter, M.T., 46bm[01]
Seeger, R.C., 46bm[01]
Selinger, N., 42bm[01]
Semegen, D., 42bm[01]
Servine, M., 32bm[01]
Shaffer, H.L., 19bm[01]
Sherman, E., 35bm[01]
Shrago, A., 42bm[01]
Simons, N., 3035ap[76]
Smith, J., 3035ap[76]
Spencer, F.M., 32bm[01]
Stair, P., 46bm[01]
Steiner, G., 35bm[01]
Stevens, B.F., 42bm[01]
Strickland, L., 32bm[01], 35bm[01], 46bm[01]
Talma, L., 3035ap[76]
Terhune, A., 46bm[01]
Terry, F., 46bm[01]
Tureck, R., 33bm[01]
Urner, C.M., 2036dd[66]
Van Vleck, A.A., 236ap[40]
Vanderlip, R.W., 2153ap[68]
Vardell, M., 42bm[01]
Vietor, A., 32bm[01]
Ware, Harriet, 32bm[01], 46bm[01]
Warren, E.R., 35bm[01], 46bm[01], 3035ap[76]
Webb, C., 32bm[01]
Wendelburg, N.R., 42bm[01]
Westbrook, H.S., 2153ap[68]
Wickham, F., 32bm[01]
Williams, G., 35bm[01]
Wilson, G.A., 42bm[01]
Windham, E., 42bm[01]
Wood-Hill, M., 32bm[01], 46bm[01]
Workman, M., 42bm[01]
Wren, E., 283ap[46]
Wright, L.D., 46bm[01]
Wylie, R.S., 42bm[01]
Zaremba, S., 33bm[01]

manuscripts — location or title
Boston Public Library, clippings on women in American music, 4bm[01]
Chicago, Newberry Library, Fairbank song collection, 2153ap[68]
N.M., U. of, Fine Arts Library, E. Kettering manuscripts, 1bm[01]
New England, Shakers, 46bm[01]
Northampton, Mass., Sophia Smith Collection, 28bm[01]
Philadelphia, Ephrata Cloister MSS, 46bm[01]
——Free Library of Philadelphia, Ephrata Cloister MSS, 182ap[30]
——Historical Soc. of Philadelphia, Ephrata Cloister MSS, 182ap[30]
Plainfield, N.J., Seventh Day Baptist Historical Soc., 182ap[30]
Washington, D.C., Library of Congress, Ephrata Cloister MSS, 182ap[30]
Winston-Salem, N.C., Moravian Music Foundation, Salem Band, Van Vleck military music, 236ap[40]

Mapleson, James Henry ("Colonel")
influence on career of E. Abbott, 1080bm[58]
life and activities, manager of M. Hauk, C.L. Kellogg, E. Nevada, and A. Patti, 1167bm[58]

Marchesi, Mathilde
life and activities, Abbott, E., student, 1004bm[58], 1080bm[58]
——Abott, B., student, 945ap[58]
——Alda, F., student, 862bm[58]
——Eames, E., student, 954bf[58], 1076ap[58]
——Freer, E.E., student, 581bm[55], 676bm[66]

Marchesi, Mathilde *(continued)*

——Liebling, E., student, 2092ap[67]
——Linne, R., student, 842ap[57]
——Marriner-Campbell, L., student, 766bm[57]
——Nevada, E., student, 1244ap[58]
——Renard, A.O., student, 1194ap[58]
——Sanderson, S., student, 1076ap[58]
——Yaw, E.B., student, 1216an[58]
relation to M. Garden, 986bm[58]
views about American students, 1076ap[58]
Marchisio, Barbara, life and activities, teacher of R. Raisa, 2217ap[68]
Marco, Caterina
life and activities, New Orleans, 1044ap[58]
tribute, 918an[58]
Marcus, Adabelle Gross, life and works, 8bm[01]
Marcus, Adele, life and activities, 3241an[78]
MARCUS, J. Anthony, 2273an[68]
MARGRAVE, Wendell, 3090rm[76]
Mario, Queena
life and activities, resignation from Metropolitan Opera, 2336an[68]
——teacher of H. Jepson, 2351an[68]
——teacher of L. Monroe, 2301ac[68]
——teacher of R. Bampton, 2343ac[68]
views about opportunities for young opera singers, 2335an[68]
MARION, John Francis, 2278bm[68]
Maris, Barbara English, 72ap[10]
Markham, Edwin, relation to Harriet Ware's *Undine*, collaborator, 2043ap[66]
MARKS, Edward B., 1078bf[58]
marriage, *see also* **sociology**
compatibility with career, viewed by A. Cottlow, 1034ap[58]
development of music in home and public life, 806ap[57]
family responsibilities, influence on composing, 1894, 654ap[56]
——influence on creation of large-scale works, 1970, 166bd[25]
influence on A.L. Cary's career, 978ac[58]
influence on ambition of pianists, 1877, 614an[55]
influence on career, 820ap[57], 951ap[58], 1205ap[58]
——Cravath, A.H., 1113an[58]
——Freer, E.E., 676bm[66]
——Giteck, J., 3138ap[76]
——1893, 785ap[57]
——1909, 869ap[58]
——1916, 1202ap[58]
——1947, 2052bd[66]
influenced by careers, 1916, 2200ap[68]
influenced by music study, 1065ac[58]
——influence on children's education, 1850, 321ap[48]
isolation, balanced by music clubs, 832ap[57]
leisure created by modern appliances, 77bp[10]
motherhood, influence on career, 1909, 1114ap[58]
——influence on career, 1916, 639ap[55]
music in home to ease daily life and influence children, 1994bm[65]
reduction of housework to expand rights and opportunities, 1858, 319ap[48]
relation to professional woman, responsibilities, 1900, 1259ap[58]
transmission of appreciation of music to children, 320ap[48]
viewed by A. Gluck, 1186an[58]
Marriner-Campbell, Louisa, life and activities, 766bm[57]
Marsh, Fanny, life and activities, theater manager, 585bm[55]
MARSH, J.B.T., 438bm[50]
Marsh, Jane, life and activities, Chaikovskii competition, 1966, 3341an[78]
Marsh, Lucile Crews, life and works, opera, 685bf[56]
MARSH, Robert C., 600bm[55]
Marshall, Charles, influenced by E.A. Hackley, 575bm[55]
Marshall, Elizabeth C., manuscripts, 2153ap[68]
Marshall, Frank, life and activities, teacher of A. de Larrocha, 3235an[78]
Marshall, Gertrude
life and activities, American Quartet, 878ap[58]
——trio with A.L. Tolman, 903ap[58]
Marshall, Gloria Cotton, interviews, views about value of music in home, 951ap[58]
Marshall, Grace, life and works, 688bm[56]
Marshall, Hattie, works, *Little Willie*, 455bf[50]
Marston, George W., life and activities, teacher of K. Vannah, 693ap[56]
MARTENS, Frederick Herman, 601ap[55], 1079bd[58], 2043ap[66], 2234bf[68]
MARTIN, Mylas, 2281an[68]
MARTIN, Sadie E., 1080bm[58]
Martineau, Harriet, views about musical life in Cincinnati, 1835, 269bm[45]
Martinez, Isidora
correspondence, 6bm[01]
life and works, 665ap[56]
Martini, Nino, life and activities, student of M. Gay-Zenatello, 2083ap[67]
Martinot, Sadie, life and activities, 585bm[55]
Marx, Harpo, life and activities, student of M. Dilling, 2238ap[68]
Maryland, Baltimore, musical life, to 1960, 149bm[25]
Mascagni, Pietro, influence on A. Galli-Curci, 2352ap[68]
Mason, Caroline A., life and works, 261bm[44]
MASON, Daniel Gregory, 1974bf[65]
Mason, Edith Barnes
life and activities, 2289ap[68]
——Chicago, 123bm[25]
tribute, repertory, 2193an[68]
Mason, Lowell, influence on music in Boston public schools, from 1833, 259ap[44]

Mason, Margaret C., correspondence, 4bm[01]
Mason, William
life and activities, teacher of E. Spencer, 2194ap[68]
——teacher of Harriet Ware, 2015ap[66]
——teacher of R. Deyo, 1169ap[58]
performances, by J. Rivé-King, 1231ap[58]
mass media, *see also* **film; radio; television**
job opportunities, 1937, 2092ap[67]
Massachusetts
Boston, musical life, 1795-1830, 198bm[35]
——musical life, 1850-54, 317ap[48]
——musical life, 1880-1930, 623bm[55]
——musical life, 1899, 274bm[45]
——musical life, 1909-25, 567ap[55]
——private schools, before 1776, 218bm[38]
——recommendation for expanded school music instruction, 1869, 288ap[47]
Brockton, musical life, influenced by community singing, 1918, 446ap[50]
Salem, musical life, 1783-1823, 209dd[38]
Massant, Lambert-Joseph, life and activities, teacher of C. Urso, 992ap[58]
Massenet, Jules, life and activities, teacher of S. Sanderson, 1191an[58]
MASSMANN, Richard Lee, 1975dd[65]
Masson, Elizabeth, correspondence, 4bm[01]
MATES, Julian, 212bm[38]
MATHEWS, William S.B., 602bf[55], 603ap[55], 705ap[56], 706bf[56], 1082-84bf[58]
MATTFELD, Julius, 439bm[50]
Matthay, Tobias
life and activities, teacher of M. Hess, 2171an[68]
——teacher of R. Lev, 2259ap[68]
Matthews, H.A., life and activities, teacher of F. McCollin, 1999ac[66]
Matthias, Georges, life and activities, teacher of T. Carreño, 1096bf[58]
Matzenauer, Margaret
life and activities, debut, 1146ap[58]
——Germany, 1007ap[58]
——Metropolitan Opera, 1085an[58]
performances, Baltimore Symphony Orchestra, 2146bm[68]
——with E. Ferrari-Fontana, 1202ap[58]
MAUDE, Jenny Maria Catherine Goldschmidt, 307bf[48]
Maxwell, Elsa
life and works, 665ap[56]
——songs, 454ap[50]
MAXWELL, Leon R., 1091ac[58]
Maxwell, Mary H., literary works, abolition song texts, 94bm[17]
May, Edna, life and activities, musical comedy, light opera, vaudeville, 1209bm[58]
May, Juliana, life and activities, early opera, 174bf[25]
Mayer, Alice, life and activities, prodigy, 973bm[58]
MAYER, Anne, 106as[20]
MAYER, Martin, 3288an[78]
Maynor, Dorothy
life and activities, 170bm[25], 2185ap[68]
——Harlem School of the Arts, 3185an[77]
——research on Negro songs and spirituals, 2307an[68]
Mazzucato, Elisa, works, 689ap[56]
MCARTHUR, Alexander, 707ap[56]
McCallup, Emily, life and activities, conducting Girls' Music Club, 831ap[57]
MCCANN, Anabel Parker, 3091rm[76]
McCann, Evelyn, manuscripts, 42bm[01]
MCCARRELL, Lamark, 2283an[68]
MCCARTHY, Mrs. John, 708ap[56]
MCCARTHY, Sr. Margaret W., 72ap[10]
MCCLURE, W. Frank, 1092ap[58]
McCollin, Frances
correspondence, 35bm[01], 47bm[01]
life and works, 139ac[25], 2026bm[66]
——church and choral music, 1999ac[66]
——1931 winner of choral prize in National Federation of Music Clubs competition, 2019ap[66]
manuscripts, 36bm[01], 46bm[01]
MCCONATHY, Osbourne, 800ac[57]
McConnell, Adelaide
interviews, activities of Mozart Soc., 2087ap[67]
life and activities, Mozart Soc., 809ap[57], 812ap[57]
MCCORKLE, Donald M., 72ap[10], 199bm[35], 236ap[40]
McCormick, Edith Rockefeller, life and activities, Chicago, 123bm[25]
McCoy, Rose, life and works, 665ap[56]
McDonald, Charlotte, life and activities, McDonald School of Music, 564ap[55]
McDonald, Emma, life and activities, McDonald School of Music, 564ap[55]
McDonald, Kate, life and activities, McDonald School of Music, 564ap[55]
MCELROY, Peter J., 801an[57]
McFarland, Ida Kruse, influence on restoration of Central City, Colo. opera house, 1985bm[65]
McFaul, Arthede, manuscripts, 42bm[01]
MCGILL, Anna Blanche, 604ap[55]
McGill, Josephine, life and activities, 604ap[55]
MCGRAW, Cameron, 3092rm[76]

premières *(continued)*

___ *War and peace, op. 91,* American première conducted by S. Caldwell, 3237an[78]

Puccini, G., *Manon Lescaut,* S. Kronold in American première, 920ap[58]

___ *Trittico,* performed by C. Muzio, 2147bm[68]

___ *Turandot,* performed by M. Attwood, 2279an[68]

Rameau, J.-P., *Hippolyte et Aricie,* American première conducted by S. Caldwell, 3237an[78]

Respighi, O., *Campana sommersa,* E. Rethberg in lead, 2174ap[68]

___ *Fiamma,* American première included H. Ohlin, 2291an[68]

Richter, M., *Blackberry vines and winter fruit,* 3073rm[76]

___ *Landscapes of the mind I,* 3007rm[76]

Schönberg, A., *Glückliche Hand, op. 18,* first American staged performance, 1983bm[65]

___ *Gurrelieder,* American première with R. Bampton, 2344ap[68]

___ *Moses und Aron,* American première conducted by S. Caldwell, 3264an[78]

___ *Pierrot lunaire,* American première, viewed by A. Lowell, 567ap[55]

Scriabin, A., sonata no. 8, op. 66, American première, K. Heyman, 1093ap[58]

Shostakovich, D., sonata for piano no. 2, op. 64, performed by V.B. Lawrence, 2980an[75]

Sibelius, J., violin concerto in D minor, op. 47, American première, performed by M. Powell, 1234an[58]

Smith, J., *Cynthia Parker,* 3091rm[76]

___ *Daisy,* 3163an[76]

___ piano concerto, 3127rm[76]

___ *Trio — Cornwall for violin, cello, and piano,* 3023rm[76]

Strauss, R., *Ägyptische Helene,* E. Rethberg in lead, 2174ap[68]

___ *Ariadne auf Naxos,* with M. Jeritza, 2234bf[68]

___ *Elektra,* K. Branzell in Metropolitan première, 2322ap[68]

___ *Frau ohne Schatten,* with L. Lehmann, 2257bm[68]

___ *Rosenkavalier,* American première, F. Hempel as Marschallin, 1015bm[58]

Stravinsky, I., *Oedipus Rex,* first American staged performance, 1983bm[65]

___ *Sacre du printemps,* first American staged performance, 1983bm[65]

Talma, L., *Alcestiad,* 3096rm[76]

___ *Summer sounds,* 3053rm[76]

___ *Tolling bell. Triptych for baritone and orchestra,* 3158ap[76]

Taylor, D., *Highwayman,* 808ap[57]

Thomson, V., *Mother of us all,* S.B. Anthony played by T. Stich-Randall, 3246ap[78]

Vecchi, O., *Amfiparnasso,* American première, 2376ap[68]

Verdi, G., *Aida,* American première, A.L. Cary in cast, 978ac[58]

___ *Falstaff,* American première with Z. De Lussan, 1263an[58]

Wagner, R., *Parsifal,* American première included F. Mulford, 981an[58]

___ *Walküre,* New York première with E. Pappenheim, 1124an[58]

Warren, E.R., *Abram in Egypt,* 1961, 3028ro[76]

Weill, K. and B. Brecht, *Dreigroschenoper,* 2263ac[68]

Wickham, F., *Rosalind,* 2032ap[66], 2061ap[66]

PRESLEY, Carl, 723rm[56]

Price, Florence B.
life and activities, teacher of M. Bonds, 161bm[25]
life and works, 121bf[25], 2031ap[66], 2967bm[75]
manuscripts, 16bm[01]
style, 165bm[25]
tribute, public school dedication, 2028an[66]
works, symphony in E minor, piano concerto, and violin concerto no. 2, 2028an[66]

PRICE, Isabel M., 619ap[55]

Price, Leontyne
discographies, 172bm[25]
influence on opportunities for blacks, 3204an[78]
life and activities, 170bm[25], 3245ap[78], 3285bm[78], 3318an[78], 3322bm[78]
___ opening of new Metropolitan Opera house, 3206an[78]
relation to Metropolitan Opera, 2371an[68]

PRIDGETT, Thomas, 447ap[50]

Priesing, Dorothy M., manuscripts, 35bm[01]

printers, *see* publishers and printers

printing, *see* publishing and printing

Proctor, Alice, manuscripts, 42bm[01]

Proctor, Edna Dean, works, new settings to *John Brown's body,* 197bm[35]

Proctor, George, life and activities, teacher of M.B. Rockefeller, 2144ap[68]

Proehl, Lena Sauter, life and activities, 901bm[58]

program notes, developed by M. Powell, 1148ap[58]

programming, pitfalls of mixing amateur and professional groups, 817ap[57]

protest song, *see* popular music

Protestant church music, *see* religious music — Protestant

psalm singing, *see also* singing
Mass., Salem, 209dd[38]

Ptaszynska, Marta, interviews, 3139ap[76]

publications, *see* periodicals

publishers and printers, *see also* catalogues — publishers'; dealers; individual names
Carl Fisher, Inc., M. Montgomery on staff, 2974ap[75]
Cowell, H., *New Music Edition,* 2022ap[66]
directory, 1970, 64bm[05]
H. Ware Publishers, Inc., 2013ap[66]
___ relocation in New York, 2048ap[66]
Jacobs-Bond, C., 692ap[56], 2013ap[66]
John C. Church Co., 715ap[56]
New York, 1786-1875, directory, 62bm[05]
Oxford U. Press, M. Montgomery on staff, 2974ap[75]
Schirmer, G., support of G. Branscombe, 1998ap[66], 2001ap[66]
Schmidt, A.P., relation to G. Branscombe, 2001ap[66]

Soc. for Publication of American Music, 2056ap[66]

Stern, J.W., interest in M. Nugent's *Sweet Rose O'Grady,* 433an[50]

Wa-Wan Press, support of G. Branscombe, 1998ap[66]

___ 1901-11, contributions of V.B. Lawrence, 2982an[75]

Witmarks, Isadore and Julius, history to 1929, 455bf[50]
1900, 632ap[55]
1977, 37bm[01]

publishers' catalogues, *see* catalogues — publishers'

publishing and printing
growth, influenced by reforms of music clubs, 745ap[57]
1920s, suggestive texts to plagiarized tunes, 1967ac[65]

Puccini, Giacomo, relation to L. Lehmann, 2112ap[67]

Pugh, Helen, performances, A.C. Beach's piano concerto in C-sharp minor, op. 45, 647ap[56]

Pulitzer, Mrs. Ralph, life and activities, patronage of New York String Quartet, 1988ac[65]

PUPIN, A., 824-26ap[57]

Purdy, Constance, views about repertory, 874ap[58]

PUTNAM, Alice, 612ap[55], 1156ap[58]

Putnam, Effie Douglas, collections, 28bm[01]

Pyle, Wynne
interviews, views about equal rights, 1061ap[58]
life and activities, 908ap[58]
___ American debut after European study, 1150ap[58]
performances, Berlin debut, 877ap[58]
___ MacDowell's *Keltic sonata, op. 59,* 1260ap[58]

Quaile, Elizabeth
correspondence, 47bm[01]
life and activities, Diller-Quaile School of Music, 2122ap[67]

Quaintance, *see* Eaton, Frances Quaintance

Quartararo, Florence, manuscripts, scrapbook, 33bm[01]

QUELER, Eve, 2971ap[75]

Queler, Eve
life and activities, 3209ap[78], 3234an[78], 3274ap[78]
___ Opera Orchestra, 3212an[78]

QUINN, Arthur Hobson, 214bf[38]

R., 2048ap[66]

R.M., 724ap[56]

R.P., 2346ro[68]

R.S., 3131rm[76]

Rabinof, Sylvia, life and activities, performances at 1967 salute to United Nations by National Federation of Music Clubs, 3184ap[77]

Rachmaninoff, Sergej, life and activities, teacher of R. Slenczynska, 2355bm[68]

Radcliffe, Letitia, manuscripts, 32bm[01]

radio, *see also* **mass media**
broadcasting of chamber music, influenced by E.S. Coolidge, 2078bm[67]
Columbia Broadcasting System, staff pianist, position held by V.B. Lawrence, 2980an[75]
educational possibilities, viewed by A. Cottlow, 888ap[58]
employment for women, 2233ap[68]
Ewer, M.S., first female announcer in Penn., 2305an[68]
first opera on radio, lyrics by N.R. Eberhart, 1955an[64]
influence on popular attitude toward music, 2969bm[75]
influence on taste, 1931, 1974bf[65]
Jepson, H., activity, 2351an[68]
"Musical Americana", produced by CBS, 2007ap[66], 2240ap[68]
program of American Women Composers, 1972, 3095ap[76]
program of P. Curran, 720an[58]
promotion of women's music, 3165ap[76]
Rappold, M., appearances, 933ap[58]
Scheff, F., activity, 1070an[58]
WNYC, National Federation of Music Clubs, 1967 salute to United Nations, 3184ap[77]
___ National Federation of Music Clubs, 1974 salute to United Nations, 3124ap[76]
___ National Federation of Music Clubs, 1975 salute to United Nations, 3150ap[76]

ragtime, *see also* **jazz**
Irwin, M., 425an[50], 437an[50]
performances by F. Bloomfield-Zeisler, 1092ap[58]
viewed by M.B. Rockefeller, 2400ap[68]
1900, 1073ap[58]

RAINES, Leonora, 620ap[55]

Rainey, Gertrude ("Ma")
discographies, blues, 21ap[01]
influence on B. Smith, 448bd[50]
influence on B. Smith, Armstrong, Davenport, Dodds, 450ap[50]
life and activities, 56bc[05], 435bm[50], 447ap[50]
___ blues recordings, 441ap[50]

Rainey, "Ma", *see* Rainey, Gertrude ("Ma")

Raisa, Rosa
life and activities, Chicago, 123bm[25], 2378ap[68]
___ repertory, 2217ap[68]

Ralston, Frances Marion
life and works, Mo., 698bf[56]
manuscripts, 9bm[01], 19bm[01]
___ Delta Omicron Music Composers Library, 25bm[01]
performances, 2025ap[66]
___ Festival of American Women Composers, 1925, 2064ap[66]
style, piano sonata, 2035ap[66]

RALSTON, Jack L., 39bm[01]

RAN, Shulamit, 2971ap[75]

Ran, Shulamit
performances, *Double vision for two quintets and piano,* 3094rm[76]

Ran, Shulamit *(continued)*

____*Ensembles for 17,* 3026rm[76]
____*Hatzvi Israel eulogy,* 3148rm[76]
____*Structures, Toccata for piano,* and *O the chimneys,* 3124ap[76]
RAND, Josephine, 612ap[55]
Randall-MacIver, Mabel Holden, life and activities, patronage, 2108an[67]
RANDOLPH, Harold, 1982ac[65]
Randolph, Harold, life and activities, teacher of M. Howe, 2074an[67]
RANDOLPH, Sarah N., 215bm[38]
Rankin, Nell, life and activities, student of K. Branzell, 2322ap[68]
Rapoport, Eda
  life and works, 1940s, 63bf[05]
  manuscripts, 35bm[01]
Rappold, Marie
  correspondence, 33bm[01]
  life and activities, 933ap[58]
  ____career goals, 943ap[58]
  ____Metropolitan Opera, 1094ap[58]
  views about opera in English translation, 1094ap[58]
Raskin, Judith
  life and activities, 3195an[78]
  ____started with Baroque music, 3291ap[78]
RASPONI, LanFranco, 2337an[68]
RAU, Albert G., 200bm[35]
Ravel, Maurice, relation to E. Gauthier, 2182an[68]
Ray, Lillian, works, *Sunshine of your smile,* 439bm[50]
Ray, Ruth, life and activities, 912ac[58]
RAYE-SMITH, Eugénie M., 96bc[17]
Raymond, Annie Louise Cary, *see* **Cary, Annie Louise**
Raymond, Emma Marcy, life, 66bm[05]
Raymond, Maud, life and activities, musical comedy, light opera, vaudeville, 1209bm[58]
Read, Sarah Ferris, life and works, 665ap[56]
REAMER, Lawrence, 2339an[68]
RECHEL, Michael W., 42bm[01]
recitals, *see* **performers; performing organizations**
Redfeather, Tsianine
  life and activities, C.W. Cadman concert tour, 162bm[25]
  ____New York tour, 436ap[50]
REDWAY, Virginia, 62bm[05]
Reed, Caroline Keating, life, 66bm[05]
Reed, Ida L.
  literary works, gospel song and hymn texts, 555bf[54]
  ____hymn texts, 150bm[25]
REED, Lynnel, 1157bm[58]
Reed, Nona Jean, manuscripts, 42bm[01]
REED, Peter Hugh, 40ap[01], 1158ap[58]
Reeves, Charlotte, theoretical works, 3bm[01]
Regal, Mary
  influence on introduction of music appreciation courses in high schools, 748bm[57]
  influence on music education, 800ac[57]
REHMANN, J.W., 1159ap[58]
REICH, Nancy B., 72ap[10]
Reid-Parsons, Susan, performances, S. Ran's *Hatzvi Israel eulogy,* 3148rm[76]
Reimers, Paul, life and activities, teacher of M. Lipton, 2205ap[68]
Reinecke, Carl, life and activities, teacher of B.F. Tapper, 791ap[57]
Reiner, Fritz
  influence on career of E. Rethberg, 2348an[68]
  relation to M. Hillis, 3238an[78]
REINHART, Carole Dawn, 2971ap[76]
REIS, Claire, 63bf[05], 1959ap[65], 1983bm[65], *1984rb[65]
Reis, Claire
  correspondence, 33bm[01]
  interviews, 30bm[01], 68ap[10]
  manuscripts, 47bm[01]
  tribute, life and activities, New York, 1963an[65]
Reisenberg, Nadia, correspondence, 47bm[01]
religion and music, *see also* **religious music** headings
  history, women barred from official participation, 126bf[25]
religious music
  American composers, 1876-1928, 1999ac[66]
  American Shakers, 232bf[40]
  congregational singing, N.H., 1623-1800, 213bm[38]
  Dickinson, H.A., 2104an[67]
  first American attempts, Ephrata Cloister, 182ap[30]
  hymn settings and texts, 1885, 91ma[15]
  involvement of upper-class women, 1809, 192bm[35]
  male dominance, influence on women's status, 1970, 166bd[25]
  New England, church choirs, 1829, 207bm[38]
  women as writers of hymn texts and music, 19th c., 451ap[50]
religious music — Moravian
  catalogue, 1742-1842, 200bm[35]
  1741-1871, 208bf[38]
religious music — Protestant, history of choral singing, 1600-1830, 222bm[38]
religious music — Roman Catholic
  encyclical letter of Pope Pius XII, 1955, 3261bd[78]
  history of choral singing, 1600-1830, 222bm[38]
  limitations on female singing, 1903, 922ap[58]
  restoration of authentic music, effort of G. Stevens, 2072ap[67]
Remick, Bertha
  life and works, 665ap[56]
  performances, 699ap[56]

reminiscences, *see* **correspondence, reminiscences, etc.**
Renard, Augusta O., life and activities, teacher of A. Case, 1194ap[58]
Renié, Henriette, life and activities, teacher of M. Dilling, 2149an[68], 2238ap[68]
Renzi, Dorothy, performances, M. Richter's *Transmutation. Eight songs to Chinese poems,* 3039rm[76]
repertory, *see also* **opera; performer** headings; **performing organizations; radio;** specific countries; **television**
  contemporary music, viewed by A. Cottlow, 910ap[58]
  Easton, F., 2190ap[68]
  Pessl, Y., early American composers, 2296ap[68]
  Powell, M., critic's plea for new concerto, 1907, 1057ap[58]
  Wagnerian roles, of J. Gadski, 1041ap[58], 1105an[58]
  ____of J. Gadski, L. Nordica, and O. Fremstad, 1162ap[58]
research, *see* **ethnomusicology; musicology**
Resnik, Regina
  life and activities, 3218an[78]
  ____preference for mezzo-soprano roles, 3292ap[78]
Restelle, Josephine Lorraine, manuscripts, 42bm[01]
Reszke, Jean de
  influence on B. Abott, 983ap[58]
  life and activities, teacher of D. Speare, 2177an[68]
  ____teacher of K. Howard, 1025bm[58]
  ____teacher of R. Fornia, 1164an[58]
  ____teacher of S.J. Cahier, 1173an[58]
  relation to A. Mitchell, 1120an[58]
Rethberg, Elisabeth
  discographies, 172bm[25]
  life and activities, 2174ap[68], 2328ap[68]
  ____Europe and USA, 2228bf[60]
  tribute, 2348an[68]
REVELLI, William D., 2114ap[67]
reviews, *see* **criticism**
Reynolds, Veda, collections, 11bm[01]
Rhetts, Edith, influence on music education, 800ac[57]
Rhode Island
  music and musicians, 1733-1850, 58bm[05]
  Providence, First Baptist Church, musical life, 125bm[25]
  ____musical life, 1636-1886, 175bm[25]
Rhoden, Natalie Claire, manuscripts, 42bm[01]
Rhodes, Laura Andrews, life, 66bm[05]
Rice, Alice May Bates, life, 66bm[05]
RICE, Curtis E., 3123rm[76]
RICE, Susan Andrews, 1160ap[58]
RICH, Alan, 2340-41an[68]
Rich, Thaddeus, life and activities, Philadelphia Women's Symphony Orchestra, 2387ap[68]
RICHARDS, J.B., 41ap[01]
Richings, Caroline
  life and activities, 57bm[05], 314an[48], 602bf[55]
  ____Chicago, 1230bm[58]
Richter, Ada, life, 139ac[25]
Richter, Hans
  influence on M. Van Dresser, 1054ap[58]
  life and activities, teacher of B.F. Tapper, 791ap[57]
Richter, Marga
  interviews, 30-31bm[01]
  performances, *Blackberry vines and winter fruit,* 3073rm[76]
  ____clarinet sonata, 3049rm[76]
  ____*Lament for string orchestra,* 2994rm[76]
  ____*Landscapes of the mind I,* 3007rm[76]
  ____*Landscapes of the mind II,* 3044rm[76]
  ____piano sonata, 3112rr[76]
  ____*Transmutation. Eight songs to Chinese poems,* 3039rm[76]
RICHTER, Marion Morrey, 3124ap[76], 3183-84ap[77]
Richter, Marion Morrey
  life and activities, National Federation of Music Clubs, 3172ap[76]
  manuscripts, Delta Omicron Music Composers Library, 25bm[01]
RIDER-KELSEY, Corinne, 1161ap[58]
Rider-Kelsey, Corinne
  collections, scrapbooks, 34bm[01]
  life, 56bc[05]
  life and activities, 1157bm[58], 1163ap[58]
  ____to 1908, 935ap[58]
RIDLEY, N.A., 1162ap[58]
RIEGGER, Wallingford, 3125ap[76]
Riesland, Mary Scott, manuscripts, 42bm[01]
RINGENWALD, Richard D., 3126dm[76]
Risher, Anna Priscilla
  life, 139ac[25], 2067ap[66]
  life and works, 146bm[25]
RITTENHOUSE, C. H., 2094ac[67]
RITTER, Fanny Raymond, 621bm[55], 827ap[57]
Ritter, Fanny Raymond
  correspondence, 4bm[01]
  influence on women in music, 618ap[55]
  life and activities, 164bm[25]
  ____Ohio Female Col., 290ap[47]
  views about women as composers, 727ap[56]
RITTER, Frédéric Louis, 164bm[25]
Rivé, Caroline, life and works, 57bm[05], 61bm[05]
Rivé-King, Julie
  correspondence, 33bm[01], 47bm[01]
  influence on musical life, 112ap[25]
  life, 56bc[05], 66bm[05]

status of women in music (*continued*)

___emotional force and imagination, 1894, 654ap[56]
___Europe and America, 1919, 695ap[56]
___faculty and students, 1975, 3171ap[76]
___failure to produce music of power and intensity, 1904, 679bd[56]
___influenced by male dominance in religious music, 1970, 166bd[25]
___influenced by male patron-employer, 3130ap[76]
___influenced by thorough music education, 1883, 737ap[56]
___orchestral music, 1907, 697ap[56]
___problems gaining performances, 1936, 2069ap[66]
___relation to work of men, 1900, 690bd[56]
___viewed by P. Oliveros, 1975, 3077ap[76]
___1890s, 659ap[56], 689ap[56], 706bf[56], 725ap[56]
___19th c., 71ap[10]
___1900, 649ap[56], 674ap[56]
___1902, 580ap[55]
___1914, 669ap[56]
___1917, 701ap[56]
___1940s, 116ap[25], 2009ap[66]
___1954, 3088ap[76]
___1975, 3164ap[76]
conductors, viewed by A. Brico, 3326an[78]
___1925-50, 71ap[10]
educators, applied music teachers, 1972-74, 106as[20]
___black college teachers, 1976, 108as[20]
___college, 1969-72, 97ap[20]
___college, 1975, 67bp[10], 73bs[10], 104as[20]
___public music teaching and supervision, 2086ap[67]
___success of women due to self-control and detail observation, 1899, 790ap[57]
___women in Music Teachers National Assoc., 1903, 774ap[57], 789ap[57]
___1951, 2094ac[67]
harp players, 1899, 1010ap[58]
hotel musicians, 1919, 1257ap[58]
influence on advance of women composers, 1917, 722ap[56]
influenced by education differences, 613ap[55]
married woman, 1858, 319ap[48]
music in school curriculum, Moravian settlement, 1787, 199bm[35]
music in women's college curriculum, 1904, 598ap[55]
musical participation in religion, history to 1948, 126bf[25]
musicologists, 1978, 105ap[20]
orchestral musicians, during World War II, 2152ap[68]
___since World War II, 3229ap[78]
___viewed by G. Yost, 1938, 2401ap[68]
___1881, 1251ap[58]
___1919, 1257ap[58]
___1925-50, 71ap[10]
___1947, 2361ap[68], 2364ap[68]
___1948, 2362ap[68]
organists, 1899, 1045ap[58]
___1912, 1142ap[58]
performers, accountable by physical and temperamental differences, 1937, 1991an[65]
___black musicians, viewed by E. Davis, 2170ap[68]
___college hiring and promotion patterns, 98as[20]
___mediocre talent, 571ap[55]
___profession creates independence, 1154ap[58]
___1833, 280ap[45]
piano study, 1880s, 1133ap[58], 1243ap[58]
piano teachers, 1954, 3088ap[76]
piano tuners, 1900, 631ap[55]
___1942, 1989ap[65]
professional women, employment possibilities, 1906, 566ap[55]
___influenced by F.E. Sutro, 836ap[57]
___to 1901, 630ap[55]
___viewed by College Music Soc., 103ap[20]
___1870-1910, 586ap[55]
___1900, 1259ap[58]
___1906, 990ap[58]
___1974, 100ap[20]
___1975, 3166ap[76]
students, graduates of Vassar Col., 1879, 827ap[57]
___1894, 635ap[55]
theorists, 1954, 3088ap[76]
violinists, in orchestras, 1893, 613ap[55]
___1912, 937ap[58]
women in culture, 1904, 579ap[55]
women in society, history, 37bm[01]
women's orchestras, 1871, 1233ro[58]
women's studies within musicology, 1977, 68ap[10]
Staub, Maria, life, 66bm[05]
STEANE, J.B., 172bm[25]
Steber, Eleanor
correspondence, 6bm[01]
life and activities, 3207ap[78], 3233an[78]
Steeb, Olga, life and activities, leading woman pianist, 882ac[58]
STEFAN, Paul, 2120ro[67]
Stein, Gertrude, literary works, librettos, 148bf[25]
STEINBERG, Michael, 3339ro[78]
Steiner, Emma Roberto
life and activities, 66bm[05], 1201bm[58]
___conducting, 2326ap[68]
___conducting Brooklyn Philharmonic, 929an[58]
life and works, 137bf[25], 686an[56], 1069bm[58]
performances, comic operas, 1201bm[58]

Steiner, Frances, life and activities, 3274ap[78]
Steiner, Gitta, manuscripts, 35bm[01]
Steiniger-Clark, Anna, life and activities, 57bm[05]
Steinway, Julia Cassebeer, tribute, 2107ap[67]
Stempel, Alice Margaret Menninger, theoretical works, 3bm[01]
Stengel, Wilhelm, life and activities, teacher of M. Sembrich, 1141bm[58]
Stenzel, Alma, life and activities, prodigy, 973bm[58]
Stepanov, Lev, life and activities, teacher of R. Deyo, 1169ap[58]
Sterling, Antoinette
correspondence, 33bm[01]
life and activities, 57bm[05], 66bm[05], 602bf[55]
views about opera as career choice, 1091ac[58]
STERLING, Elizabeth, 1206ap[58]
STERNBERG, Constantin, 635ap[55]
STEUERMANN, Clara, 2971ap[75]
Steuermann, Edward, life and activities, teacher of N. Hinderas, 3232an[78]
Stevens, Betsy Finck, manuscripts, 42bm[01]
Stevens, Georgia, life, 56bc[05], 135bf[25], 2072ap[67]
Stevens, Neally, life and activities, 602bf[55]
Stevens, Risë
correspondence, 28bm[01]
influence on R. Elias, 3248ap[78]
influenced by women's movement, 2973ap[75]
life and activities, 2975an[75], 3213bm[78]
___pupil of A.E. Schoen-René, 1179bm[58]
___teacher of J. Simon, 3273ap[78]
STEVENSON, Robert, 188bd[30], 1986bm[65]
Stich-Randall, Teresa, life and activities, 3246ap[78]
STILMAN, Julia, 3152dd[76]
Stock, Frederick, influence on E.S. Coolidge, 2078bm[67]
STODDARD, Eugene M., 840dd[57]
STODDARD, Hope, 2361-62ap[68], 3340ap[78]
Stoeckel, Carl, life and activities, organize Norfolk Music Festival, 1912, 1234an[58]
Stoeckel, Ellen Battell
influence on E.S. Coolidge, 2078bm[67]
life and activities, 56bc[05]
___organize Norfolk Music Festival, 1912, 1234an[58]
___patronage, 810an[57]
Stoeckel, Gustave J., influenced by I.B. Larned, 289bm[47]
Stoessel, Albert, life and activities, teacher of G. Branscombe, 2021an[66]
Stojowski, Sigismund
life and activities, executive board of New York Women's Symphony Orchestra, 2398ap[68]
___teacher of Harriet Ware, 2015ap[66]
Stokowski, Leopold
influence on career of E. Hilger, 2162ap[68]
influence on R. Deyo, 2051an[66]
life and activities, All-American Youth Orchestra, 2324an[68]
performances, duo-piano concerto with Sutro sisters, 1192ap[58]
relation to S. Verrett, 3353an[78]
views about talent of women in orchestras, 2327ap[68]
STOKOWSKI, Olga Samaroff, 76bp[10], 1987bm[65], 2363ap[68]
Stokowski, Olga Samaroff
correspondence, 33bm[01], 47bm[01]
influence on career of J. Madeira, 3286ac[78]
influence on musical life, 112bm[25]
life and activities, 56bc[05], 908ap[58]
___executive board of New York Women's Symphony Orchestra, 2398ap[68]
___leading woman pianist, 882ac[58]
___teacher, 1971ap[65]
___teacher of Baltimore's first music appreciation course, 132bm[25]
___teacher of N. Hinderas, 3232an[78]
___teacher of R. Tureck, 3347an[78]
performances, Beethoven sonatas, 2314ap[68]
___with L. Stokowski, 1202ap[58]
viewed by W. Pyle, 1061ap[58]
views about equal opportunity, 1937, 2081ap[67]
STOLBA, K. Marie, 561ap[54]
STOLFUS, Mary L., 2364ap[68]
Stone, Ellen, life and activities, New Friends of Music orchestra, 2180an[68]
Stone, Mary, influence on J. McGill, 604ap[55]
Stone, Mrs. Galen, influence on career of C. Brice, 2143an[68]
STORER, H.J., 1207ap[58]
Storer, Maria
life and activities, 184bm[30]
___opera before 1800, 220bf[38]
performances, 219bm[38]
Storer, Maria Longworth Nichols
life and activities, 56bc[05]
___initiator of Cincinnati May festival, 132bm[25]
Stoska, Polyna, life and activities, 3309ap[78]
STOUT, Rex, 2137rb[68]
STOUTAMIRE, Albert, 277bm[45]
STOWE, Harriet Beecher, 316bm[48]
Stowe, Harriet Beecher
life and activities, Hartford literary community, 1197ap[58]
literary works, hymn texts, 93bc[17], 560ap[54]
relation to C. Kummer, 432ap[50]
STRAKOSCH, Avery, 1208ap[58], 2365ap[68]
Strakosch, Harriet Avery, correspondence, 4bm[01]
Strakosch, Maurice
life and activities, teacher of A. Patti, 1047bf[58]

Terry, Frances
life and works, 2026bm[66]
manuscripts, 46bm[01]
testing, *see* **aptitude**
TETLOW, Helen Ingersoll, 588bm[55]
Tetrazzini, Eva, influence on R. Raisa, 2378ap[68]
Texas, El Paso, musical life, 1919-39, 1986bm[65]
Thayer, Eleanor W., correspondence, 28bm[01]
theaters (the buildings), *see also* **auditoriums and concert halls; performing organizations**
Annie Russel Theater at Rollins Col., donation of M.C.B. Zimbalist, 2105an[67]
N.Y., Aeolian Hall, 735bm[56]
——Aeolian Hall, office for A. Sawyer, 624ap[55]
——City Center of Music and Drama, patronage of M.B. Rockefeller, 3180an[77]
——Lincoln Center for the Performing Arts, patronage of M.B. Rockefeller, 3180an[77]
Penn., Pittsburgh, Carnegie Music Hall, 596ap[55]
Thebom, Blanche
life and activities, 3299ap[78]
——singer and manager, 2975an[75]
thematic catalogues, *see* **catalogues – thematic**
theorists, status, 1954, 3088ap[76]
theory, *see* **performance practice** headings; specific names and topics
therapy
contributions of women, 1956ap[65]
Lathom, W., therapist, 2971ap[75]
music can help sick people, 1899, 857ap[57]
music in home to ease daily life, 1994bm[65]
veteran's hospital programs, 145ap[25]
women mental patients, use of music, 1895, 583ap[55]
wounded and disabled soldiers, promoted by National Federation of Music Clubs, 1962ac[65]
Thiede, Alexander, relation to Boston Women's Symphony Orchestra, 2380an[68]
THIEDE, Henry A., 1221ap[58]
Thillon, Sophie Anna, life and activities, Boston Musical Fund Soc., 317ap[48]
Thiral, Roger, life and activities, teacher of G. Moore, 2303bf[68]
THOMAS, Augustus, 1222bm[58]
Thomas, Emma A.
life and activities, Detroit, 748bm[57]
——Thomas Normal Training School, 843ap[57]
THOMAS, Fannie Edgar, 1223ap[58]
Thomas, Jennie Louise, life and activities, Detroit, 564ap[55]
THOMAS, Jessie M., 2060ap[66]
THOMAS, Margaret F., 160bm[25]
THOMAS, Rose Fay, 613ap[55], 844ap[57]
Thomas, Rose Fay
correspondence, 47bm[01]
influence on increase of music clubs, 762ap[57]
influence on increased membership in music clubs, 777ap[57]
views about aims of women's amateur musical clubs, 823ap[57]
views about Rossini Club, 2070ap[67]
Thomas, Theodore
influence on career of M. Powell, 1200ap[58]
influence on D. Becker, 952ap[58]
influence on increase of music clubs, 762ap[57]
performances, works by M.R. Lang, 704ap[56]
relation to T. Carreño, 886ap[58]
THOME, Diane, 2971ap[75]
THOMPSON, Helen M., 3186bm[77]
Thompson, Helen M.
life and activities, manager New York Philharmonic Soc., 169bm[25]
tribute, 2978an[75], 2986ap[75]
THOMPSON, Oscar, 174bf[25], 2061ap[66]
THOMPSON, Ralph, 996rb[58]
Thompson, Randall
life and activities, judge for composition competition of Boston Women's Symphony Soc., 2088ap[67]
performances, songs, sung by P. Frijsh, 2347ap[68]
THOMSON, Virgil, 2379ap[68], 3160bm[76], 3161rm[76], 3187an[77]
Thomson, Virgil, influence on T. Stich-Randall, 3246ap[78]
Thorner, Dhyani, interviews, 31bm[01]
Thornton, Big Mama, interviews, 30bm[01]
THRASHER, Herbert Chandler, 175bm[25]
Thuile, Ludwig, life and activities, teacher of M.W. Daniels, 2005bm[66]
Thurber, Jeanette
life and activities, 56bc[05]
——American Opera and National Opera, 627bd[55]
——establishment of National Conservatory, 899ap[58]
tribute, 818ap[57]
Thursby, Emma Cecilia
correspondence, 33bm[01]
influence on D. Becker, 952ap[58]
life, 56bc[05], 66bm[05], 995bm[58]
——European tour, influence on career, 1101an[58]
life and activities, 585bm[55], 602bf[55], 935ap[58]
——contract with M. Strakosch, 1104ap[58]
——student of E. Rudersdorff, 769ap[57]
——teacher of G. Farrar, 892ap[58]
performances, with M. Morgan, 1103ap[58]
tribute, memorial in Brooklyn Museum of Art, appearance of M. Morgan, 1086an[58]

views about upgraded musical taste, 934ap[58]
Tibbett, Lawrence, life and activities, coached by F. Alda, 862bm[58]
TICK, Judith, 68ap[10], 71ap[10], 110as[20], 176ap[25], 285dd[46], 637ap[55]
Tick, Judith, views about status of women in music profession, 1974, 100ap[20]
Tidden, Paul, life and activities, teacher of C. Beebe, 1031ap[58]
Tippy, relation to T. Votipka, 2221an[68]
TIPTON, Albert, 3162rm[76]
Toedt, Mrs. Theodore, life and activities, teacher of C. Rider-Kelsey, 1157bm[58], 1163ap[58]
Tokatyan, Armand, life and activities, teacher of G. Bumbry, 3278an[78]
TOLL, Katherine, 2380an[68]
Tolman, A. Laura, life and activities, 903ap[58]
Tomlinson, Eliza Clayland, influence on her son Stephen Foster, 197bm[35]
Torpadie, Greta, performances, 1959ap[65]
Torrens, L.A., life and activities, teacher of C. Rider-Kelsey, 1163ap[58]
Torry, Jane Sloman, *see* **Sloman, Jane**
Toscanini, Arturo
influence on career of Z. Milanov, 3293ap[78]
relation to F. Alda, 862bm[58]
relation to L. Lehmann, 2112ap[67]
relation to O. Fremstad, 938bm[58]
Tosso, Joseph, life and activities, directed Female Academy of Music, 269bm[45]
Tosti, Francesco Paolo, relation to Mana Zucca, 2040ap[66]
Tourel, Jennie
life and activities, recordings, 3226an[78]
——teaching, 3175ap[77]
——views about audiences, 3199an[78]
tribute, 3270an[78]
Tower, Joan
life and works, 3083dm[76]
performances, *Black topaz,* 3020rm[76]
——*Breakfast rhythms I and II for clarinet and five instruments,* 3084rm[76]
TOWERS, John, 65bm[05]
Towne, Laura H., life and activities, gathering of black folk songs, 183bm[30]
TOWNSEND, C.A., 845ap[57]
Townsend, Mansfield, *see* **Allen, Marie Townsend**
TRACEY, James M., 1226ap[58]
Tracy, Cateau Stegeman, life and activities, Denver, 611bm[55]
transcription
Bach and Couperin, by M. Wood-Hill, 2045an[66]
ethnic music, 142ap[25]
translation, opera in English, viewed by M. Rappold, 1094ap[58]
TRAUBEL, Helen, 2381bf[68]
Traubel, Helen
discographies, 172bm[25]
life and activities, 3bm[01], 2312bm[68], 3265an[78]
——career influences, 2154an[68]
——first American to sing Wagner exclusively, 2219ap[68]
——resignation from Metropolitan Opera, 2300an[68]
tribute, 2350an[68]
Triggs, Harold, performances, with V.B. Lawrence, 2230ap[68]
trio, *see* **chamber music;** individual composers
Tripp, Emily, life and activities, instrument and sheet music dealer, 608ap[55]
trombone, *see* **wind instruments**
trombone playing, physical stamina, 2319ap[68]
TROTTER, James M., 1227bf[58]
troubadours, contribution of women, 116ap[25]
Troyanos, Tatiana, life and activities, 3269an[78]
TRUETTE, Everett Ellsworth, 136bm[25], 1228ap[58]
Truman, Margaret
life and activities, 119ap[25]
relation to H. Traubel, 2381bf[68]
trumpet, *see* **wind instruments**
trumpet playing, physical stamina, 2319ap[68]
TUBBS, Arthur L., 732ro[56], 1229ap[58]
Tucker, Tui St. George
life and works, 8bm[01]
performances, 3002rm[76]
Tureck, Rosalyn
correspondence, 47bm[01]
life and activities, conducted New York Philharmonic, 3264an[78]
——National Federation of Music Clubs, Young Artist Award, 3350ap[78]
——Town Hall Young Artist Award, 3347an[78]
manuscripts, scrapbook, 33bm[01]
performances, Bach, 3281an[78]
TURNER, Chittenden, 2123ap[67]
Turner, Claramae, life and activities, 3205ap[78]
Turner, H. Godfrey, relation to M. Powell, 1088an[58]
Turner, Miss, life and activities, Salem, Mass., 209dd[38]
Turner, Nancy Byrd, literary works, *In the beginning,* set by J. Barthelson, 2159ap[68]

voice *(continued)*

____replacement with mezzo-soprano in opera after 1920, 2134ap[68]
Volkman, Elizabeth, performances, J. Smith's *Daisy,* 3163an[76]
Von Elsner, Marie Eugenia, life and activities, 57bm[05], 602bf[55], 1185bm[58]
Von Hagen, Elizabeth
  life and activities, Boston, 198bm[35]
  ____N.H., 213bm[38]
  ____Salem, Mass., 209dd[38]
  performances, 219bm[38]
  views about advantages of female voice teacher for girls, 206bm[38]
Von Kunits, Luigi, life and activities, teacher of V. Barstow, 868ap[58]
Von Stade, Frederica, life and activities, 3296an[78]
Votipka, Thelma
  life and activities, 2221an[68]
  tribute, 3345an[78]
VOUGHT, Ruby S., 3167ap[76]
Vries, Rosa de, life and activities, opera presentation, 132bm[25]
W., 2063ap[66]
W.B.M., 2387ap[68]
W.F.G., 850ap[57], 1239ap[58]
W.H.H., 735bm[56]
W.J.Z., 1245ap[58], 2389ap[68]
WAGENKNECHT, Edward, 1235bm[58], 1236ap[58]
WAGNALLS, Mabel, 1237bm[58]
WAGNER, Charles L., 1238bm[58]
Wagner, Cosima, influence on O. Fremstad, 893ap[58]
Wagner, Richard, performances, by M. Lawrence, 2246bm[68]
Walker, Edyth
  life and activities, 56bc[05], 876ap[58]
  ____study in Europe, 1100an[58]
  ____teacher of B. Thebom, 3299ap[78]
  ____teacher of I. Dalis, 3192ap[78]
Walker, Eliza, life and activities, Jubilee Singers of Fisk U., 445bm[50]
Walker, Ida, collections, songs and piano music, 729bc[56]
Walker, Rachel, life and activities, 121bf[25]
Wallace, Lila Acheson, life and activities, grant for development of young American conductors, 3177an[77]
WALLACE, Robert Kimball, 2125bm[67]
Walter, Bruno
  influence on A. Brico's career, 3262an[78]
  life and activities, patronage of New York Women's Symphony Orchestra, 2397an[68]
  performances, with L. Lehmann, 2262an[68]
Walton, Minnie, life and activities, San Francisco, 293bm[48]
Wann, Lois, life and activities, New Friends of Music orchestra, 2180an[68]
Ward, Genevieve, life and activities, early opera, 174bf[25]
WARD, Justine Bayard, 922ap[58]
Ward, Justine Bayard, life, 135bf[25]
Ware, Charles Pickward, relation to L.M. Garrison, 267ap[45]
Ware, Harriet (composer)
  interviews, 2048ap[66]
  life, judge of Girl Scouts marching song contest, 2039ap[66]
  life and activities, publishing, 2013ap[66]
  ____teaching, 2058ap[66]
  life and works, 144bm[25], 665ap[56], 686an[56], 688bm[56], 2015ap[66]
  ____opera, 685bf[56]
  manuscripts, 32bm[01], 46bm[01]
  performances, 2007ap[66]
  ____Festival of American Women Composers, 1925, 2064ap[66]
  works, opera, 147bm[25]
  ____*Sir Oluf* cantata, 2050rm[66]
  ____song cycle for children and piano suite, 2048ap[66]
  ____*Undine,* 2043ap[66]
Ware, Harriet (ethnomusicologist), life and activities, gathering of black folk songs, 183bm[30]
WARE, Helen, 639ap[55]
Ware, Helen
  life and activities, move to New York, 1014ap[58]
  ____Philadelphia, 582bf[55]
  ____studies abroad, 880ap[58]
Warner, Anna, literary works, hymn texts, 150bm[25]
Warner, Mrs. Charles Dudley, *see* Warner, Susan Lee
Warner, Susan, literary works, hymn texts, 150bm[25]
Warner, Susan Lee
  influence on musical taste in Hartford, 926bm[58], 1197ap[58]
  life and activities, Hartford, 786bd[57]
WARNKE, Frank J., 3351ap[78]
WARREN, Dale, 3352ap[78]
Warren, Elinor Remick
  life and works, 3083dm[76], 3098an[76]
  manuscripts, 35bm[01], 46bm[01], 3035ap[76]
  performances, 3027ap[76], 3348an[78]
  ____*Abram in Egypt,* 3028ro[76]
  ____radio, 3095ap[76]
Warren, Mercy, works, *Liberty song,* 148bf[25]
Wartel, François, life and activities, teacher of E. Abbott, 1004bm[58]
Washington, D.C.
  musical life, 19th c., 217ac[38]
  White House, musical life, influenced by First Lady, 119ap[25]
  ____performances by M. Anderson, 2242an[68]
  ____performances of F. Hempel, 1015bm[58]
Washington, Rachel M., life and activities, 1227bf[58]
Wassells, Grace, life and works, 665ap[56]

WASSON, D. DeWitt, 3168-69rm[76]
Watanabe, Ruth, correspondence, 42bm[01]
Waterhouse-Wilson, Lelia, life and works, 665ap[56]
WATERSTON, Anna Cabot Lowell, 318bm[48]
Watson, Claire, life and activities, 3253ap[78]
WATSON, Dorothy DeMuth, 640ap[55], 2065ap[66], 2386ro[68]
Watson, Mabel Madison, life, 2067ap[66]
Watson, Regina, life and activities, influence on Chicago music club, 772ap[57]
Watts, Nellie, life and activities, 12bm[01]
Wear, Mrs. T.H., life and activities, management, 576ap[55]
Webb, Bertha, life, 66bm[05]
Webb, Caroline, manuscripts, 32bm[01]
Webb, Harriet, performances, with Brooklyn Philharmonic Orchestra, 929an[58]
Webb, Mary Isabella, life and activities, Boston Musical Fund Soc., 317ap[48]
Weber, Alice Little, collections, 11bm[01]
Weber, Hannah, life and activities, Moravian organist and copyist, 200bm[35]
Webster, Laura, life and activities, women's string quartet, 1256ap[58]
Webster, Margaret, life and activities, 1985bm[65]
Webster, Mary Cushing, life and activities, 287ap[47]
Webster-Powell, Alma
  life and activities, Berlin Royal Opera, 1199ap[58]
  views about women's fashion, 895an[58]
Weidig, Adolph, life and activities, teacher of F.M. Ralston, 2035ap[66]
Weigl, Vally
  interviews, 31bm[01]
  life and works, 8bm[01]
  performances, *Songs from Do not awake me,* 2989rm[76]
Weill, Kurt, relation to L. Lenya, 2263ac[68]
Weldon, Constance, life and activities, 3176ap[77]
Wellesz, Egon, life and activities, teacher of E.G. Hier, 2121ap[67]
Wells, Lois, life and activities, 3252ap[78]
Wendelburg, Norma Ruth, manuscripts, 42bm[01]
Wentworth, Laura A., life and activities, director of music department at Elmira Female Col., 1870, 767ap[57]
West, Julia E. Houston, life, 66bm[05]
WEST, Richard, 3170rm[76]
Westbrook, Helen Searles, manuscripts, 2153ap[68]
Weston, Mildred, life, 2067ap[66]
Wexburg, Lili, life and activities, teacher of J. Marsh, 3341an[78]
Wheatley, Julia, life and activities, early opera, 174bf[25]
Wheeler, Henry, life and activities, teacher of J.E. Crane, 775ap[57]
WHITCOMB, E.O., 851ap[57]
Whitcomb, Mrs., influence on economics of church musicians, 851ap[57]
WHITE, Barbara A., 13bm[01]
White, Lillian Spencer, collections, 11bm[01]
WHITE, William Braid, 1989bm[65]
WHITEHEAD, George C., 1242ap[58]
Whitney, William L., life and activities, teacher of E. Steber, 3207an[78], 3233an[78]
Whittall, Gertrude Clark, life and activities, patronage, 2075an[67]
Wickham, Florence
  life and activities, 139ac[25]
  manuscripts, 32bm[01]
  performances, *Rosalind,* 2061ap[66]
  ____*Rosalind,* European première, 2032ap[66]
  tribute, 2018an[66]
  works, *Rosalind, Legend of Hex Mountain,* and *Ancestor maker,* 2018an[66]
Wiener, Alma Morgenthau, relation to League of Composers, 1959ap[65]
WIJEYERATNE, James de S., 736bd[56]
Wilcox, Ella Wheeler, works, *Laugh and the world laughs with you,* 455bf[50]
Wilcox, John C., life and activities, teacher of T. Redfeather, 436ap[50]
Wilhorst, Cora de, life and activities, early opera, 174bf[25]
WILKINSON, Margaret, 1244ap[58]
WILLARD, Frances E., 66bm[05], 91ma[15]
Willard, Katherine, life, 66bm[05]
WILLETS, Gilson, 642ap[55]
WILLHARTITZ, Adolph, 178bm[25], 179ap[25]
Williams, Camilla, life and activities, first Negro to sing Madame Butterfly, 3298an[78]
Williams, Charlotte Demuth, life and activities, head of violin school in Chicago, 1256ap[58]
Williams, Emma J., life and activities, Providence, 125bm[25]
Williams, Grace, manuscripts, 35bm[01]
Williams, Louise Brewster, life, 66bm[05]
Williams, Mary Lou, style, 165bm[25]
WILLIAMS, Ora, 180bm[25]
WILLIAMSON, Alix, 2124bm[67]
Williamson, Esther, *see* Ballou, Esther Williamson
Willis, Love Marie Whitcomb, literary works, hymn texts, 262an[44]
WILLS, Garry, 3353an[78]
Wilson, Alma, life and activities, Philadelphia, 582bf[55]
Wilson, Gloria Agnes, manuscripts, 42bm[01]
Wilson, Jennie, literary works, gospel song and hymn texts, 555bf[54]
Wilson, Kate DeNormandie, life and activities, Pittsburgh, 596ap[55]
Wilson, Kate V., life and activities, manager and teacher, 636ap[55]
Wilson, Margaret, life and activities, 119ap[25]
Wilson, Ruth, life and activities, Committee for the Recognition of Women in the Musical Profession, 2244an[68]

OGDEN, Mary Alice, 2514mm[69]
OLIVEROS, Pauline
    chamber music, 3644-49mm[79]
    choral music, 4076-78mm[79]
    mixed media, 4349mm[79]
    orchestral and band music, 4483-85mm[79]
    solo instrumental music, 4693mm[79]
    stage works, 4827-28mm[79]
O'NEILL, Eugene, 4815-16mm[79]
O'NEILL, Moira, 1731mm[59], 1743ma[59]
ORGEL, Irene, 3821mm[79]
ORLEANS, Charles d', 4987mm[79]
ORLOVA, Gita, 1637md[59], 1687mm[59]
OSGOOD, Frances Sargent Locke, 1641md[59]
O'SHAUGNESSY, A., 2570mm[69]
OSLER, Edward, 3855mm[79]
OSTERLING, Eric
    orchestral and band music, 4514mm[79]
OSTRAUMOVA, T.N., 4949mm[79]
OURUSOFF, Lisenka, 2900mm[69]
OUSLEY, Clarence, 1743-44ma[59]
OWEN, Anita, 534-35mm[51], 537mm[51]
OWEN, Anita
    vocal music, 534-37mm[51]
OWEN, Blythe
    chamber music, 3650-53md[79]
    choral music, 4079-83md[79]
    solo instrumental music, 4694-96mm[79]
PARACELSUS, 1909md[59]
PARIS, Angela, 3425mm[79]
PARKER, Alice, 4093mm[79], 4096mm[79], 4829mm[79]
PARKER, Alice
    chamber music, 3654mm[79]
    choral music, 4084-4123mc[79]
    stage works, 4829-30mm[79]
PARKER, Gilbert, 1508ma[59]
PARKER, Mrs.
    solo instrumental music, 354mm[49]
PARKER, William Henry, 3846mm[79]
PARKHURST, Susan, 398mm[49]
PARKHURST, Susan
    solo instrumental music, 239mm[41]
    vocal music, 247-56mm[41], 398-405mm[49]
PARRY, Robert, 4940mm[79]
PARTRIDGE, William Ordway, 1741ma[59]
PATCHEN, Kenneth, 2486mm[69]
PATTERSON, Frances Taylor, 2538md[69]
PAULL, Barberi, 3655mm[79], 4124-27mm[79], 4351-52mm[79], 4831mm[79]
PAULL, Barberi
    chamber music, 3655-56mm[79]
    choral music, 4124-27mm[79]
    mixed media, 4350-53mm[79]
    stage works, 4831mm[79]
PAYNE, William Morton, 1654mm[59]
PEABODY, Josephine Preston, 1449mm[59], 4921mm[79]
PEATTIE, Elia W., 1348ma[59], 1451mm[59], 1659md[59]
PECK, Elizabeth, 4365mm[79], 4854mm[79]
PECK, Samuel Minturn, 1737ma[59], 2897mm[69]
PEELE, George, 4320mm[79]
PÉGUY, Charles, 4987mm[79]
PENDLETON, Charlotte, 1827mm[59]
PERCY, William Alexander, 2880mm[69]
PERRONET, Edward, 1287mm[59]
PERRY, Julia Amanda
    chamber music, 3657-60mm[79]
    choral music, 4128-32mm[79]
    orchestral and band music, 4486-88mm[79]
    stage works, 4832mm[79]
    vocal music, 4945-48mm[79]
PHILLEO, Estelle
    vocal music, 538mm[51]
PHILLIPS, Charles, 1850md[59]
PICKTHALL, Marjorie, 1834mm[59]
PICKUP, S.H., 1285mm[59]
PIERCE, Alexandra
    chamber music, 3661-66mm[79]
    orchestral and band music, 4489mm[79]
    solo instrumental music, 4697-703mm[79]
PINCHARD, Edith, 4892-93mm[79]
PINSKY, Robert, 3561mm[79]
PITMAN, Melrose, 4014mm[79], 4017mm[79], 4019mm[79]
PO, Chü I, 4952mm[79]
POE, Edgar Allen, 4832mm[79], 4992mm[79]
POLIN, Claire
    chamber music, 3667-77mm[79]
    mixed media, 4354-55mm[79]
    orchestral and band music, 4490-92mm[79]
    solo instrumental music, 4704-11mm[79]
    stage works, 4833mm[79]
POLLOCK, Muriel
    solo instrumental music, 491mm[51]
PORTER, Ellen Jane, see LORENZ, Ellen Jane
PORTER, Mrs. W.V., 405mm[49]

POWNALL, Mary Ann, 227-28mm[39]
POWNALL, Mary Ann
    vocal music, 227-30mc[39]
PRATT, James B., 2848md[69]
PREOBRAJENSKA, T.N., 4949mm[79]
PREOBRAJENSKA, Vera N., 4949mm[79]
PREOBRAJENSKA, Vera N.
    chamber music, 3678-85mm[79]
    choral music, 4133-39mm[79]
    orchestral and band music, 4493-95mm[79]
    vocal music, 4949-50mm[79]
PRICE, Florence B.
    choral music, 2587-92mm[69]
    solo instrumental music, 2714-18mm[69]
    vocal music, 2949-61mm[69]
PROCTER, Adelaide A., 387mm[49], 1302md[59], 1533md[59]
PRUDHOMME, Sully, 2965mm[69]
PYLE, Katharine, 4120mm[79]
PYLE, Molly, 4084mm[79]
QUARRY, Lucille, 3883mm[79]
QUENNELL, Peter, 2761mm[69]
QUINTERO, Joaquin Alvarez, 4798mm[79]
QUINTERO, Serafin, 4798mm[79]
R.A.T., 254mc[41]
RACINE, Jean, 3466mm[79]
RADCLYFFE-HALL, Marguerite, 1765md[59]
RALSTON, Frances Marion
    chamber music, 2473mm[69]
    orchestral and band music, 2648md[69]
    solo instrumental music, 2719-23mm[69]
RAN, Shulamit
    chamber music, 3686-89mm[79]
    mixed media, 4356mm[79]
    orchestral and band music, 4496mm[79]
    solo instrumental music, 4712mm[79]
RANDOLPH, Thomas, 1644md[59]
RANDS, William Brightly, 1299md[59]
RAY, Lillian
    vocal music, 539mm[51]
RAY, Maude Louise, 1285mm[59]
RAYMOND, Margaret, 4143mm[79], 4834mm[79]
READ, Andrew, 1600mm[59]
REED, Dave, Jr., 523mm[51]
REED, John S., 2736mm[69], 2744mm[69]
REED, Nan Terrell, 1743ma[59]
REESE, Lizette Woodworth, 1747md[59], 1752md[59], 1760md[59], 1783md[59], 1787md[59], 1795mm[59], 1815md[59], 1817md[59], 1825md[59], 1900mm[59], 2582mm[69], 4083md[79], 4248mm[79]
REID, Dorothy E., 2903ma[69]
RESSEQUIER, Jules de, 1591md[59]
REYNOLDS, Charles Lee, 3841mm[79]
RICE, Cale Young, 1472mm[59], 2493mm[69], 2643mm[69], 2735mm[69]
RICHARDS, Grace, 231mm[39]
RICHARDS, Grace
    vocal music, 231mm[39]
RICHMOND, Dolly
    solo instrumental music, 492mm[51]
RICHTER, Marga
    chamber music, 3690-98mm[79]
    choral music, 4140-42mm[79]
    orchestral and band music, 4497-506mm[79]
    solo instrumental music, 4713-17mm[79]
    vocal music, 4951-53mm[79]
RICHTER, Marion Morrey
    chamber music, 3699mm[79]
    choral music, 4143-44mm[79]
    orchestral and band music, 4507mm[79]
    solo instrumental music, 4718-19mm[79]
    stage works, 4834mm[79]
    vocal music, 4954-56mm[79]
RILEY, James Whitcomb, 1461mm[59]
RILKE, Rainer Maria, 2906ma[69], 3950mm[79], 4833mm[79], 4993mm[79]
RIMBAUD, Jean Arthur, 3464mm[79], 5018mm[79]
RINEHEART, Daisy, 1839mm[59]
RINGAI, 3719mm[79]
RITCHIE, Barclay, 1735mm[59]
RITTENHOUSE, Jessie B., 1466mm[59], 2892mm[69]
ROBERTS, Charles George Douglas, 1810md[59]
ROBERTS, Charles S.D., 1508ma[59]
ROBERTS, Gertrud
    orchestral and band music, 4508-09mm[79]
    solo instrumental music, 4720-23mm[79]
ROBERTSON, C.R.W., 3909mm[79]
ROBERTSON, C.R.W., see also DAVIS, Katherine K.
ROBINSON, Edward Arlington, 2551mm[69]
ROBINSON, Eloise, 2440mm[69]
ROBINSON, Paul, 4937mm[79]
ROGERS, Clara Kathleen
    chamber music, 1284mm[59]
    solo instrumental music, 1440-41mc[59]
    vocal music, 1864-96mm[59]
ROGERS, John William, 4843mm[79]
ROHDE, Q'Adrianne, 4042-43mm[79]

ROMA, Caro, 542mm[51], 546mm[51]
ROMA, Caro
  solo instrumental music, 493mm[51]
  vocal music, 540-46mm[51]
ROMAY, Paula, 4243mm[79]
RONSARD, Pierre de, 4987mm[79]
ROSS, Jeanette
  solo instrumental music, 4695md[79]
ROSSER, Annetta Hamilton
  chamber music, 3700-05mm[79]
  solo instrumental music, 4724-25mm[79]
  vocal music, 4957-59mm[79]
ROSSETTI, Christina Georgina, 1706md[59], 1746ma[59], 1801mm[59],
    3540mm[79], 4278mm[79], 5017mm[79], 5021mm[79]
ROSSETTI, Dante Gabriel, 1864md[59], 1891md[59]
ROYLE, Josephine Fetter, 4840mm[79]
RUELLE, Jules, 2905ma[69]
RUFINUS, 1658md[59]
RUKEYSER, Muriel, 3432mm[79]
RUNCIE, Constance Faunt Le Roy
  vocal music, 1897mm[59]
RUTH, John, 4830mm[79]
RUTLEDGE, Archibald, 3916mm[79]
SACHS, Nelly, 4356mm[79]
SALAMON, Nina, 1937mm[59]
SALTER, Mary Turner, 1366mm[59], 1899mm[59], 1906md[59], 1908mm[59],
    1911mm[59], 1914-15mm[59], 1918mm[59], 1921mm[59], 1923md[59],
    1928mm[59], 1930mm[59], 1934md[59], 1939mm[59]
SALTER, Mary Turner
  choral music, 1366mm[59]
  vocal music, 1898-1939mm[59]
SAMPLEY, Arthur M., 4200mm[79]
SAMSON, Frederic, 4821mm[79]
SANBORN, Carrie Phippen
  solo instrumental music, 494mm[51]
SANDBURG, Carl, 2480mm[69], 4244mm[79], 4270mm[79]
SANDFORD, Lucy A.
  vocal music, 406mm[49]
SANDIFUR, Ann, 4145mm[79]
SANDIFUR, Ann
  chamber music, 3706mm[79]
  choral music, 4145mm[79]
  electronic music, 4309mm[79]
  mixed media, 4357mm[79]
  solo instrumental music, 4726mm[79]
SANKEY, Ira A.
  choral music, 457-59mc[51]
SANSON, Ellen, 1846md[59]
SAPPHO, 1912mm[59]
SARETT, Lew, 2963mm[69]
SASSOON, Philip, 4036mm[79]
SAULS, R. Lynn, 4939mm[79]
SAUR, Frederick, 4016mm[79]
SCHAFFY, Mirza, 2906ma[69]
SCHEFFEL, Joseph Victor von, 1819mm[59]
SCHERENBERG, Christian Friedrich, 1578md[59]
SCHILLER, Friedrich von, 1317mm[59], 1530mm[59], 1543md[59]
SCHREYVOGL, Friedl, 4900mm[79]
SCHWARTZ, Lloyd, 4966mm[79]
SCOLLARD, Clinton, 1467mm[59], 1495mm[59], 1505mm[59]
SCOTT, Duncan Campbell, 1665-66md[59]
SCOTT, Lady John, 1861md[59]
SCOTT, M. B.
  vocal music, 407mm[49]
SCOTT, Sir Walter, 1781md[59], 1871md[59]
SEDULIUS, Coelius, 3913mm[79]
SEEGER, Alan, 2769mm[69]
SEEGER, Charles
  vocal music, 87ma[15]
SEEGER, Ruth Crawford
  chamber music, 2474-80mm[69]
  choral music, 2593mm[69]
  solo instrumental music, 2724-26mp[69]
  vocal music, 87-88ma[15], 90ma[15]
SEEGER, Winifred, 2730mm[69]
SEELEY, Blossom, 547mm[51]
SEELEY, Blossom
  vocal music, 547mm[51]
SEGAL, Edith, 3789mm[79]
SEGAR, Mary G., 3861mm[79]
SELNECKER, Nicolaus, 3849mm[79]
SEMEGEN, Daria
  chamber music, 3707-10mm[79]
  electronic music, 4310mm[79]
  orchestral and band music, 4510-11mm[79]
  solo instrumental music, 4727mm[79]
  stage works, 4835mm[79]
SEYMOUR, George Steele, 1639md[59]
SHAKESPEARE, William, 1297mm[59], 1303md[59], 1323md[59], 1341md[59],
    1535md[59], 1581md[59], 1605md[59], 1608mm[59], 1697md[59],
    1886md[59], 2424mm[69], 2902ma[69], 2915mm[69], 2966mm[69],
    3496mm[79], 3538mm[79], 3687mm[79], 3919mm[79], 3927mm[79],
    4073mm[79], 4229mm[79], 4268mm[79], 4301-02mm[79], 4334mm[79],
    4537mm[79], 4883mm[79], 4908mm[79]
SHARP, William, 1491mm[59], 1670md[59]

SHAW, Frances, 1636md[59], 2898ma[69]
SHAW, John, 1709md[59]
SHELLEY, Percy Bysshe, 1483mm[59], 1489mm[59], 1515md[59], 1664md[59],
    3489mm[79], 4301mm[79], 4863mm[79]
SHEPHERD, Adeline
  solo instrumental music, 495-97mm[51]
SHERMAN, Frank Dempster, 1771-72md[59], 1809md[59], 1905md[59],
    3489mm[79]
SHERRILL, Evelyn Norcross, 4033mm[79]
SHIKI, 3517mm[79], 3897mm[79]
SHINDLER, Mary Dana, 83-84ma[15], 368md[49]
SHINDLER, Mary Dana, see also DANA, Mary S.B.
SIDNEY, Philip, 4908mm[79]
SILL, Edward Rowland, 1596-97ma[59], 2745mm[69]
SILSBEE, Ann
  chamber music, 3711-21mm[79]
  choral music, 4146mm[79]
  solo instrumental music, 4728-29mm[79]
SILVERMAN, Faye-Ellen, 4512mm[79], 4836mm[79]
SILVERMAN, Faye-Ellen
  chamber music, 3722-27mm[79]
  choral music, 4147mm[79]
  mixed media, 4358mm[79]
  orchestral and band music, 4512-13mm[79]
  solo instrumental music, 4730-32mm[79]
  stage works, 4836mm[79]
SIMMS, William Gilmore, 1654mm[59]
SINGER, Jeanne, 4148mm[79], 4962mm[79], 4970mm[79]
SINGER, Jeanne
  chamber music, 3728-34mm[79]
  choral music, 4148-51mm[79]
  solo instrumental music, 4733-36mm[79]
  vocal music, 4960-71mm[79]
SLATER, Mary White, 1743ma[59]
SLEETH, Natalie, 4152-87mm[79], 4190-97mm[79]
SLEETH, Natalie
  choral music, 4152-97mm[79]
  orchestral and band music, 4514mm[79]
  vocal music, 4972mm[79]
SLOMAN, Jane
  choral music, 328ma[49]
  solo instrumental music, 355mm[49]
  vocal music, 408-11mm[49]
SMIRNOFF, U.O., 4134mm[79]
SMITH, Chard Powers, 2903ma[69]
SMITH, Dexter, 252mm[41]
SMITH, Edgar, 1458mm[59]
SMITH, Ethyl B.
  solo instrumental music, 498mm[51]
SMITH, Eva Munson
  vocal music, 91ma[15]
SMITH, Fred Jacobs, 1743ma[59]
SMITH, J. Denham, 458mc[51]
SMITH, Julia, 4199mm[79]
SMITH, Julia
  chamber music, 3735-38mm[79]
  choral music, 4198-200mm[79]
  orchestral and band music, 4515-23mm[79]
  solo instrumental music, 4737-39mm[79]
  stage works, 4837-43mm[79]
  vocal music, 4973mm[79]
SMITH, La Donna
  choral music, 4201-02mm[79]
  electronic music, 4311-13mm[79]
  orchestral and band music, 4524-25mm[79]
SMITH, Miss, 412mm[49]
SMITH, Miss
  vocal music, 412mm[49]
SMITH, Samuel F., 1309mm[59]
SMITH, Stevie, 4085mm[79]
SMITH, William Jay, 5019mm[79]
SORENSON, Virginia, 4853mm[79]
SPARROW, William A., 1550md[59]
SPAULDING, H.N., 4949mm[79]
SPAULDING, Millicent, 3995mm[79]
SPENCER, Frank, 246mm[41]
SPENCER, Williametta
  chamber music, 3739mm[79]
  choral music, 4203-10mm[79]
SPENSER, Edmund, 3752mm[79], 4103md[79]
SPEYER, Leonora, 1522mm[59], 1573mm[59], 1588mm[59], 2444mm[69],
    2891mm[69], 2916mm[69]
SPICER, A.H., 2851mm[69]
SPIVEY, Elvera, 2501mm[69]
SPOFFORD, Harriet Prescott, 1579md[59], 1595md[59], 1609md[59]
SPOKES, Gary, 3483mm[79]
SPRAGUE, Charles, 361mm[49]
SPRAGUE, Charles J., 1888mm[59]
ST. FRANCIS OF ASSISI, 1294mm[59], 4236mm[79]
ST. HENRI, Dom, 1943mm[59]
STAFFORD, Wendell Phillips, 1324mm[59]
STANTON, Frank, 1741ma[59], 1743ma[59], 1746ma[59]
STARR, Hattie, 548-49mm[51], 551mm[51]
STARR, Hattie
  solo instrumental music, 499mm[51]

INDEX TO RECORDINGS

About the Compilers

Adrienne Fried Block is Assistant Professor of Music and Music Education at the College of Staten Island of the City University of New York.

Carol Neuls-Bates is Assistant Professor of Music at Brooklyn College of the City University of New York.

Professors Block and Neuls-Bates cooperated in the preparation of *The Status of Women in College Music.*